"By examining child development and the impact of trauma exposure in detail in specific developmental epochs, the *Handbook of Trauma, Traumatic Loss, and Adversity in Children* provides both clinicians and researchers with a uniquely developmentally sensitive, resilience-based, and trauma-focused basis on which to develop and conduct psychotherapy with children who have severe self-regulatory and relational difficulties. It will be an invaluable resource in my practice and research for years to come."

Julian D. Ford, PhD, ABPP, professor of psychiatry and law, director of the Center for Trauma Recovery and Juvenile Justice

"In this handbook Dr. Nader brilliantly details the developmental impact of trauma during childhood. The structure of the book provides an easy way to learn how trauma affects child development and the potential long-term impact of trauma. The healing role of parents and teachers as well as the resilience of children are highlighted, and the often cascading adversities after trauma are discussed. Having treatment methods for each developmental period offers great hope for helping children who have experienced traumatic events."

Alison Salloum, PhD, LCSW, professor, School of Social Work, University of South Florida

"This comprehensive volume brings a welcome developmental approach to understanding trauma in children—from its far-reaching effects to individualized treatment. This is essential reading for practitioners and policy makers concerned about the effects of early adverse experiences on children."

Charles H. Zeanah, MD, Mary Peters Sellars Polchow Chair in Psychiatry, professor of psychiatry and pediatrics, and vice chair for child and adolescent psychiatry at the Tulane University Institute of Infant and Early Childhood Mental Health

"As an adoptive parent as well as a certified babysitter for foster children, I found the information Dr. Nader shares about the factors contributing to childhood trauma and approaches that may best serve these children to be insightful. The breadth of research that Dr. Nader covers over a broad range of ages and trauma conditions is truly staggering. This body of work will prove valuable for those working with children suffering from trauma."

Fiona McInally, transactional attorney

Handbook of Trauma, Traumatic Loss, and Adversity in Children

The *Handbook of Trauma, Traumatic Loss, and Adversity in Children* is a developmentally oriented book rich with findings related to child development, the impact of trauma on development and functioning, and interventions directed at treating reactions to trauma.

Aspects of attachment and parenting and the use of interrelationships toward therapeutic ends are included in each age-related section of the book, ranging from 0 to 18+. Consolidating research from a range of disciplines including neurobiology, psychopathology, and trauma studies, chapters offer guidance on the potentially cascading effects of trauma, and outline strategies for assisting parents and teachers as well as children. Readers will also find appendices with further resources for download on the book's website.

Grounded in interdisciplinary research, the *Handbook of Trauma, Traumatic Loss, and Adversity in Children* is an important resource for mental health researchers and professionals working with children, adolescents, and families during the ongoing process of healing from traumatic exposure.

Kathleen Nader, DSW, is the former codirector of the UCLA Trauma, Violence, and Sudden Bereavement Program and an internationally recognized expert, consultant, and clinician working with childhood trauma. Among her publications are *Understanding and Assessing Trauma in Children and Adolescents* and *Assessment of Trauma in Youths.*

Handbook of Trauma, Traumatic Loss, and Adversity in Children

Development, Adversity's Impacts, and Methods of Intervention

Kathleen Nader

Routledge
Taylor & Francis Group
NEW YORK AND LONDON

First published 2020
by Routledge
52 Vanderbilt Avenue, New York, NY 10017

and by Routledge
2 Park Square, Milton Park, Abingdon, Oxon, OX14 4RN

Routledge is an imprint of the Taylor & Francis Group, an informa business

Library of Congress Cataloging-in-Publication Data
A catalog record for this title has been requested

ISBN: 978-1-138-60519-0 (hbk)
ISBN: 978-1-138-60520-6 (pbk)
ISBN: 978-0-429-45636-7 (ebk)

Typeset in Bembo
by Wearset Ltd, Boldon, Tyne and Wear

Visit the eResources: https://www.routledge.com/9781138605206

Contents

Tables

Tables in the Appendix (available online)

Boxes

Preface

When I was flying to a school to consult after a catastrophic event, the young man who sat in the aisle seat in our row was quickly surrounded by women (including every female flight attendant on the large plane). They hovered around him and seemed to want to touch him. He was very polite. While looking to understand, I realized that he had no tension in his face. No one else on the plane showed such an absence of tension (some of whom I learned were his teammates). When I asked him about it after lunch, he said that it was true, he didn't feel stressed or tense. He attributed it to being an athlete and to clean-living—he ate right, exercised daily, and had caring parents. Since then, I've looked for faces that showed such a lack of tension and that communicated the same being at-peace with self. Even in younger age groups (ages 3 or 4), there have not been many such tension-free and at-peace faces. Although part of people's attraction to the young man on the plane may have been his athletic status (not one of the best publicized sports; I had not heard of him before), when I've found others who have had the same lack of tension and apparent peace with self, people inevitably seem attracted to them. The quality of connections (e.g., to parents, other adults, peers/team) seems to contribute to the tension-free, peaceful demeanor or state of mind. The quality of connections and parenting are important aspects of what is discussed in this book.

Even in a country where more frequent mass shootings and other catastrophic events occur, actions can be taken that reduce the likelihood that a child will be depressed and/or anxious, become violent or disruptive, or develop other maladaptation. After some events, such as school shootings, the ways we (as a nation or community) had failed to prevent escalation in the shooter are sometimes glaring (e.g., long mental health wait lists; failure to connect; lack of preventive or other interventions). Preventive actions include improving connection (e.g., caregiver–child attachments, teacher and peer connections to a youth), enhancing resilience (e.g., coping skills, self- and other-awareness skills, self-talk), and assisting repair after adversity, loss, traumatization, or other developmental disruption. Programs are available to accomplish each of these improvements or types of repair and are described in this book.

This book discusses important developmental domains (Chapters 1, 5, 8, 11, 14); the variables that affect them (Chapter 4 and age-related chapters); the influence of trauma or significant adversity on developmental skills, mental health, health, and functioning, initially and across time (Chapters 2, 3, 7, 9, 12, 15); and treatment or preventive methods to increase protection and to assist repair and recovery (Chapters 7, 10, 13, 16). Four different age groups are discussed—ages 0–3, 3–6, 6–12, and 13–17 or older (Chapters 5–16). For each age group, one chapter examines developmental skills or tasks, a second describes trauma's possible effects on development and some of the trauma symptoms relevant to the age group, and a third provides interventions. Sensitive periods of development relevant to an age group are included as well as general information about the kinds of developmental tasks that can be interrupted by exposure to traumatic events or loss. The final chapter includes issues related to goodness-of-fit, personality—rapport versus clash—and burn-out prevention. Relevant topics are discussed as they apply to each age group (in age-related chapters), and topics important to a specific age group are also discussed. The book is peer-reviewed and extensively researched. To save space, summary references, rather than individual references, are often used, indicated by *see* (see Author et al., 2019).

Kathleen Nader

Acknowledgments

The *Handbook of Trauma, Traumatic Loss, and Adversity in Children: Development, Adversity's Impacts, and Methods of Intervention* is a well-researched, peer-reviewed book. I am deeply grateful to all reviewers (anonymous and known) for their feedback and suggestions as well as to those of you who provided articles related to your methods. My deep thanks to those of you who took the time to read more than one chapter: Charles Zeanah, Nancy Boyd Webb, Alison Salloum, Gayle Rowland, Fiona McInally, Julian Ford, and the many anonymous reviewers. Thank you also to Mary Dozier, Paul Frewen, Robert McMahon, and Michelle Pearlman, who read individual chapters. I am sincerely grateful to the method authors who reviewed the descriptions of their methods: Rony Berger, Paul Boelen, Neil Boris, Heather Bryant, Judith Cohen, Mary Dozier, Sheila Eyberg, Peter Fonagy, Paul Frewen, Phillip Kendall, Sheila Kuhn, Luc LaFreniere, Alicia Lieberman, Sandee McClowry, Robert McMahon, Michelle Pearlman, Julie Poehlmann, Lois Sadler, Alison Salloum, Irwin Sandler, Michael Scheeringa, Kimberly Schonert-Reichl, Karen Thierry, Carolyn Webster-Stratton, Leo Wolmer, and Charles Zeanah. I have really enjoyed learning the details of your interventions. Thank you also to the colleagues who recommended or endorsed some of the methods included in the book: Michael Scheeringa, Judith Cohen, Julian Ford, Joseph Spinazzola, Alison Salloum, Lisa Amaya-Jackson, and Chandra Ghosh Ippen. Thank you, Sam, for helping with article gathering. I very much appreciated the help of Jim Nageotte and Nancy Boyd Webb in shaping the nature of the book. Thanks to those who reviewed the original proposal for confirming content that I believed important to the book. Last but certainly not least, my thanks to the Taylor and Francis staff for all of their assistance in bringing the book to final completion, including Ellie Duncan, Sally Evans-Darby, Pip Clubbs, and Abigail Stanley. Thank you, Anna Moore, for all of your help and patience.

Abbreviations

5-HTTPLR	a serotonin polymorphism (see Appendix Table A4.1—serotonin)
7r	7 repeat allele
a-f	attachment figure
AAI	adult attachment interview
ABC	Attachment and Biobehavioral Catch-Up
ABFT	Attachment-Based Family Therapy
ACC	anterior cingulate cortex
ACEs	Adverse Childhood Experiences
ACTH	adrenocorticotropic hormone
ADHD	attention deficit hyperactivity disorder
AEDP	Accelerated Experiential Dynamic Psychotherapy
AKA	also known as
AM	autobiographical memory
ANS	autonomic nervous system
APA	American Psychological Association
APD	antisocial personality disorder
ApoE	apolipoprotein E gene
AQS	Attachment Q-Set
ARC	Attachment, Self-Regulation, and Competency (treatment)
ASAD	adult separation anxiety disorder
ASD	acute stress disorder
ASPD	antisocial personality disorder
ATT	Attention Training Technique
AuSD	autistic spectrum disorder
AVP	vasopressin
AVPD	avoidant personality disorder
BAS	behavioral activation system (Gray, 1972, 1991)
BD	bipolar disorder
BDNF	brain-derived neurotrophic factor gene
BEIP	The Bucharest Early Intervention Program
BI	behavioral inhibition (see also NE)
Big 5	five well-studied personality traits (see Glossary)
BIS	behavioral inhibition system (Gray, 1972, 1991)
BMI	body mass index
BPD	borderline personality disorder
CAPSLE	Creating a Peaceful School Learning Environment
CBCL	Child Behavior Checklist (Auchenbach, updated for DSM-5)
CBT	cognitive behavior therapy

CD	conduct disorder
CDI	child-directed interaction (component of PCIT)
CDIP	Children of Divorce Intervention Program
CEN	the central executive network (a neural connectivity network)
CG	complex or complicated grief (see TG, PG)
CNS	central nervous system
COMT	catechol-O-methyltransferase (gene)
COplay	Child-Oriented Play
COS	Circle of Security (COSP: COS parent; COSI: COS intensive)
CPP	Child–Parent Psychotherapy
CPS	Child Protective Services
CPT	Cognitive Processing Therapy
cPTSD	complicated or complex PTSD or complicated trauma
CRH	corticotropin-releasing hormone
CRHR1	CRH receptor 1
CS	complex span
CSA	child/childhood sexual abuse
CSG	complicated spiritual grief
CT	cortisol
CU	callous-unemotional (traits)
CWMT	Cogmed Working Memory Training
D-amnesia	dissociative amnesia
DA	dopamine
DAT1	dopamine transporter 1 (see Table A4.1)
DBT	dialectical behavior therapy
DC 0–3R	*Diagnostic Classification of Mental Health and Developmental Disorders of Infancy and Early Childhood*, revised
DD	dissociative disorder
DES	Dissociative Experiences Scale
DHEA	dehydroepiandrosterone
DHEA-S	DHEA sulfatre
DID	dissociative identity disorder
DMN	default mode network (a neural connectivity network)
DNA_m	DNA methylation (see Glossary)
DoG	delay of gratification
DPD	dependent personality disorder
DQ	developmental quotient
DRD2	dopamine receptor D2
DRD4	dopamine receptor D4
DSED	disinhibited social engagement disorder
DSM-IV	*Diagnostic and Statistical Manual of Mental Disorders*, 4th edition
DSM-5	*Diagnostic and Statistical Manual of Mental Disorders*, 5th edition
DT	developmental trauma
DTD	developmental trauma disorder
DV	domestic violence (see also IPV)
DVD	digital versatile disk or digital video disk
EA	emotional abuse
EC	effortful control
EEG	electroencephalogram (measures brain electrical activity)
EFs	executive functions

EF-CBT	emotion-focused CBT
EFTT	emotion-focused therapy for trauma
EFTT-EE	EFTT with empathic exploration
EFTT-IC	EFTT with imaginal confrontation of the perpetrator(s)
EMT	Enhanced Milieu Teaching
ER	emotion regulation
ERASE-SPS	Enhancing Resiliency among Students Experiencing Stress and Promoting Prosocial Orientation (intervention method)
ERN	error-related negativity
ERP	event-related potential
ERS	excessive reassurance seeking
F-B	false belief
FBP	The Family Bereavement Program
FC	foster care
F-F	forward-focused
FKBP5	(genotype) FK506 binding protein 5
FL	Florida
fMRI	functional magnetic resonance imaging
F-P	foster parents
FnC	functional connectivity
G-H	Grief-Help
GABA	gamma-aminobutyric acid (see Glossary)
GAD	general anxiety disorder
GC	glucocorticoid
GDD	global developmental delay
GR	glucocorticoid receptor
GTI	Grief and Trauma Intervention
GTI-C	GTI with coping skills only
GTI-CN	GTI with narrative and coping skills
HA	harm avoidance
HAB	hostile attribution bias
H-D	high-decreasing (a separation anxiety group)
H-I	high-increasing (a separation anxiety group)
HPA	hypothalamic-pituitary-adrenal (axis)
HPD	histrionic personality disorder
HTR2A	see Appendix Table A4.1—serotonin
IC	institutional care
ICAM-1	intercellular adhesion molecule-1
ICD-10	*International Classification of Diseases and Related Health Problems* (10th edition)
ICD-11	ICD, 11th edition
ICN	intrinsic (neural) connectivity networks
IGTC	Integrated Grief Therapy for Children
INSIGHTS	Insights Into Children's Temperaments (a parent, teacher, student program)
IPP	Infant–Parent Psychotherapy
IPV	inter-parental violence (AKA domestic violence)
IQ	intelligence quotient
ITCT-A	Treatment for Complex Trauma-Adolescent
IWM	internal working model
IY	Incredible Years Series®

IYTCM	IY teacher classroom management program
K	kindergarten
KC	Kindness Curriculum
KIDNET	children's Narrative Exposure Therapy
LCA	latent class analysis
LD	language difficulties or language delay
LI	language impairment
MAO-A	monoamine oxidase A
MBT-A	Mentalization-Based Treatment for Adolescents
MBT-C	Mentalization-Based Treatment for Children
MBTI®	Myers–Briggs Type Indicator
MBTI-C	MBTI-child
MDD	major depressive disorder
Met	methionine (see Val)
MI	Motivational Interviewing
MindUp™	a mindfulness-based school program
MMTT	Mindfulness and Metta Trauma Therapy
mPFC	medial prefrontal cortex
MTB	Minding the Baby®
MTFC-P	Multidimensional Treatment Foster Care for Preschoolers
N	number (number of subjects/people in the study)
N2 amplitude	see Glossary
NA	negative affectivity (see NE)
NPD	narcissistic personality disorder
NE	negative emotionality or neuroticism
NE/BR	negative emotionality/behavioral dysregulation
NET	Narrative Exposure Therapy
NF	intuitive feeling (Jungian-based personality type)
NFS	negative feedback seeking
NI	never institutionalized
NICHD	National Institute of Child Health and Human Development
NPD	narcissistic personality disorder
NR3C1	nuclear receptor subfamily 3—a glucocorticoid receptor gene
NS	novelty seeking
NSSI	non-suicidal self-injury or self-injury
NT	intuitive thinking (Jungian-based personality type)
NWC-distress	normal waking conscious posttrauma distress
NYLS	New York Longitudinal Study
OCD	obsessive-compulsive disorder
ODD	oppositional defiance disorder
OGM	over-general memory (see Glossary)
OT	oxytocin
P	persistence
P3 amplitude	see Glossary
PaCT	Psychoanalytic Child Therapy
PanD	panic disorder
PanD-AGO	panic disorder with agoraphobia
PC	parent coach
PCBD	persistent complex bereavement disorder
PCC	posterior cingulate cortex

PCIT	Parent–Child Interaction therapy
PD	personality disorder
PE	psychotic episode
PEP	pre-ejection period reactivity
PFC	prefrontal cortex
PG	prolonged grief
PIP	Parent–Infant Psychotherapy (see IPP)
PNS	parasympathetic nervous system (has sometimes been called PSNS to distinguish it from peripheral nervous system)
PO-MDD	preschool onset major depression
PPD	paranoid personality disorder
PPT	Preschool PTSD Treatment
PT	posttraumatic
PTC	posttraumatic cognitions
PTE	potentially traumatic event
PTG	posttraumatic growth
PTS	posttraumatic stress
PTSD	posttraumatic stress disorder
PTSD<6	PTSD for children age 6 and under
PTSD-DS	PTSD-dissociative subtype
PTSS	posttraumatic stress symptoms
PUFA	polyunsaturated fatty acids (e.g., omega-3)
PV	poly-victimization
PVN	hypothalamic paraventricular nucleus
R&T	rough-and-tumble play
rACC	rostral anterior cingulate cortex
RAD	reactive attachment disorder
RD	reward dependence
REM	rapid eye movement (a sleep state)
RF	reflective functioning (see also metacognitive monitoring, mentalizing in Glossary and in Table 1.2)
RS	rejection sensitivity
RSA	respiratory sinus arrhythmia
rvlPFC	see vlPFC
sAA	salivary ∝-amylase
SAD	separation anxiety disorder
SD	subclinical depression
SE®	Somatic Experiencing® (an intervention)
self-reg	self-regulation
SES	socioeconomic status
Short-Term PaCT	Short-Term Psychoanalytic Child Therapy
SI	social inhibition
SJ	sensing judging (Jungian-based type)
SN	salience network (a neural connectivity network)
SNAP-25	synaptosomal nerve-associated protein 25
SNS	sympathetic nervous system
SoA	social anxiety
SoAD	social anxiety disorder
SP	sensing perceiving (Jungian-based type)
SPARCS	Adolescents Responding to Chronic Stress (a treatment)

SRP	School Resilience Program
SSP	Strange Situation Procedure (young attachment assessment)
ST	secondary traumatization
SU	substance use or abuse
SW	social worker
SYG	Settle Your Glitter (an intervention)
SZPD	schizoid personality disorder
T1	time 1
T2	time 2 …
TARGET	Trauma Affect Regulation (a treatment)
TF or T-F	trauma-focused
TF-CBT	trauma-focused CBT
TF-CBT-YC	trauma-focused CBT (British version for young children)
TG	traumatic grief
TG-CBT	traumatic grief-CBT
TGCT-A	Trauma and Grief Component Therapy for Adolescents
TMS	transcranial magnetic stimulation
TOM	theory of mind
TPH	tryptophan
TRASC	trauma-related altered states of consciousness
TSRD	trauma- and stressor-related disorders (see DSM-5)
UK	United Kingdom
US or U.S. or USA	United States
Val	valine (a BDNF variant includes Val66Met; a COMT variant includes Val158Met; see Appendix Table A4.1—BDNF, COMT)
vlPFC	ventrolateral PFC (rvlPFC: right vlPFC)
vmPFC	ventromedial PFC
vs	versus
VS	ventral striatum
WHO	World Health Organization
WM	working memory
WOJ	The Worry Outcome Journal
YPT	PPT adapted for older children

Part I
Introduction

1

Child Developmental Domains That May Be Influenced by Trauma or Other Adversity

This is an era when youth are aware of the many dangers in the world (e.g., via news, internet, friends, adult warning, or teaching protection). Everyday stressors—e.g., socioeconomic issues, family conflict, stressful community conditions, displacement, expectations of school violence, and media exposures to a variety of threats (Box 1.1)—may directly influence or add to adversity's impact or to a child's vulnerability to stressful or frightening events. Nonverbal young children may be affected by conflict levels and by news reports (Box 1.1). If youth hear or see news reports, in a single week they may learn, for example, that priests may sexually abuse children, adults may teach children to carry out school shootings, and children die when left in hot cars or buses. For weeks, the 2018 Parkland, Florida high school shootings were in the news. After a subsequent threat to his school, a youth in Alabama wrote a will, "Just in case" [he was killed]. A mother in Texas asked her adolescent daughter if she knew what to do if there was a school shooting. She answered, "There's nothing you can do, Mom." A Florida youth from the school where the shooting occurred cried in distress after learning that there was another shooting, even though no one was killed. She pleaded, "We're supposed to be healing ..." For traumatized youth, each similar or new event may increase distress. When 10 were killed in a school shooting in a Santa Fe, Texas school, later in 2018, a student said she wasn't surprised. She said, "We expect things like this to happen."

As will be discussed in the chapters that follow, stress and trauma can have deleterious effects on children, including effects on important developmental domains such as brain and skill development. Although this chapter periodically mentions some of the effects of trauma, its primary focus is the important developmental domains that may be affected by adversity. Chapter 2 focuses on trauma's impact on these domains. Chapter 3 looks at cascading and long-term effects of traumas. Chapter 4 examines variables that influence outcomes. Later chapters examine age-related developmental issues, trauma/adversity's potential impact on them, and proven treatment methods. This chapter provides a brief overview of the developmental skills/domains that may be affected by stress or trauma.

Child Development and Stress

Normal stress—tolerable, short-lived adverse experiences—may cause minor physiological changes—e.g., increased heart rate and hormone levels (e.g., cortisol). Such stress can be important to the developmental process and development of coping and resilience (Gunnar, Doom, & Esposito, 2015; Middlebrooks & Audage, 2008). Intense adverse experiences, in contrast, may

Box 1.1 Hurricane Harvey: Response to Media Coverage

Effects on Central Texas (away from the Gulf) *with* ***Televised Hurricane Harvey*** *and rain and wind damages*

Prediction: a week of heavy rain and high winds; possible flooding and wind damage.

TV: warning videos showing people trying to drive through what looked like a few inches of water and finding themselves with a flooding car; constant coverage of the hurricane.

History: a 12-year drought; numerous floods, severe storms, and tornadoes; devastating floods with loss of life after trying to drive through "a little water" or not heeding evacuation orders.

2015: a storm that resulted in flooding had washed away homes (e.g., 72 in San Marcos) or damaged homes (e.g., 1200–1300 in Hays County). In a badly flooded region, a couple with two young children inside their home when it washed away in the flood waters. The father was rescued and hospitalized. For weeks, people watched the news, first to see if the wife and children would be found, then to see if their bodies would be found. Houses had flooded before in the flood zone, but this was devastating. Trees were broken in multiple pieces; homes were ripped off foundations and washed away. People were washed away. Especially because children and families were involved, many people had felt the loss and now watched with worry as Hurricane Harvey unfolded.

Janie

Three-year-old Janie was left to play with toys while the family watched the hurricane on TV. When she started crying, they assumed it was play or sibling related, comforted her a bit, and interested her in coloring. For several nights after the hurricane, Janie would run down the hall to her parents' bedroom, screaming. On TV they talked of the eye of the hurricane, among other things. One night when she screamed and her mother went to check on her, she told her mother, "The eye was chasing me! The eye is going to get me!" In her play, she sent toys hurtling across the room making whooshing sounds. She chased her friends, saying she was the eye coming for them.

Sources: ABC news, CBS news, CNN, Foxnews.com, MSN.com, NBC News, *The Statesman* (Austin newspaper), friends and family; Texas Department of Public Safety.

Note:
Case examples are disguised, may be combined cases, and have had details changed to protect individuals.

produce traumatic/toxic stress and lead to permanent changes in brain and other aspects of development (Middlebrooks & Audage, 2008; Lanius et al., 2015; see Nader & Fletcher, 2014)—e.g., high levels of stress hormones (e.g., cortisol) can suppress the immune response, resulting in vulnerability to a variety of chronic health problems. Children's cortisol dysregulation can also affect their psychological development and mental health (over time; e.g., Koss & Gunnar, 2018; Suor et al., 2015). In addition to the effects of traumatic stressors, other stressors—especially high-level chronic stressors without sufficient protective factors, including risk in the parenting system (e.g., divorce, conflict, harsh parenting, parental distress; Box 1.2), related to resources (e.g., poverty), in

Box 1.2 Lilly and Jonah

Lilly was five and Jonah was three when Hurricane Harvey hit Houston. Lilly and Jonah stayed in a shelter with Granddad when Grammy and Mommy went to see the house. Grammy Bonnie's house still had six inches or more of standing water when they were allowed to return to check the damage. Particle board absorbs water, so some of the furniture Grammy had for when Lilly and Jonah stayed there was ruined. Grammy hoped the water would recede before any more damage was done. Next, they went to Mommy's house (Daddy was at work). The house had been completely submerged under water. The roof had collapsed on top of everything, destroying their home and belongings, including the children's toys, furniture, and clothes. Mommy couldn't stop crying. She couldn't think clearly enough to function (e.g., drive, take care of her children, work, cook). Grammy drove back to the shelter, and Mommy just sat crying. When the children came over, Mommy told them the house was destroyed. Young children often reflect their parents' emotions. Lilly and Jonah started crying, too. Knowing that a mother's lack of sensitive care for her children and ongoing upset could upset the children, possibly result in their symptoms, and disrupt the children's ongoing development (Chapters 3–7), Grammy tried to reassure the children. She told them it would all be okay. She told them that Mommy was really upset right now, because it was worse than she expected, but she would be better in a couple of days. Granddad came over and held and comforted their daughter (Mommy) like she was a small child. He told the children they would all stay at the shelter for now and would return to Grammy and Granddad's house when the water went down. While Granddad comforted their daughter, Grammy Bonnie tried to make the shelter experience more of an adventure for the children as well as to teach them kindness to others and to recognize when someone wanted to be left alone. They saw other families where the Mommy was upset and not taking good care of their children. Sometimes the children were screaming and throwing things. Sometimes, it was okay for Lilly to give them a hug. Then Grammy traded places with Granddad, and she comforted her daughter, while Granddad took the children on adventures. They spent another week in the shelter. Mommy improved steadily with her parents' and husband's help.

the attachment system (insecure or disorganized attachments), and in the community (e.g., low resources, ongoing threat)—have also related to negative outcomes for children. In addition to their disruption of normal development, reactions to stressors include a wide variety of disorders and difficulties. Among reactions are posttraumatic (PT) or other stress-related disorders (e.g., PTSD; persistent complex bereavement disorder; reactive attachment disorder [RAD], Chap 5), chronic distress, exacerbation or triggering of genetic vulnerabilities (e.g., anxiety, depression), increased reactivity to stress, changes in self and life (e.g., traits, inter-relating, life satisfaction, confidence, sense of safety), and many potentially long-term consequences (e.g., epigenetic changes [see Glossary], health; Table 3.1).

Normal Variation

An hour in a day care or classroom can make clear how important adult care and value are to children, that things may be different than they initially seem, and how children behave differently in different contexts (e.g., with different adults or children; Boxes 1.3, 10.1, 10.2). A youth's individuality is key to important aspects of intervention (Chapter 4). As will be seen, although most children respond to gentle, attentive care, the route to rapport can vary significantly for different children or child groups (Boxes 10.1, 13.2). As well, when assessing, diagnosing, and treating youth behavior and reactions, it is essential to recognize developmentally normal characteristics. Although symptoms like impulsivity, dissociation, or reticence or withdrawal can be normal following traumas, they must be distinguished from behaviors common at specific phases of development or for specific temperaments (Nader, 2008). For example, when evaluating sexual behaviors, thoughts or actions common to an adolescent male (e.g., thinking about sex, difficulty stopping sex thoughts, sexual feelings in the body) may be a sign of disturbance (e.g., sexual molestation; exposure to adult TV) in an eight-year-old or younger male (Friedrich, Jaworski, Huxsahl, & Bengtson 1997; see Box 10.2). Some behaviors/styles (e.g., fearful inhibition) occur normally at certain developmental phases and are commonplace for certain personality styles (e.g., slow-to-warm—see Glossary and Nader, 2008). By around eight months, hesitance in approaching novel or intense objects is normal for infants (Putnam, Ellis, & Rothbart, 2001). Additionally, particular reactions (e.g., fear) manifest differently at different ages—e.g., infants' crying, clinging, or increased activity; adolescents' internalizing (Putnam et al., 2001; Rothbart, Chew, & Gartstein, 2001b). When assessing dissociation, it is important to recognize that young children often exhibit forgetfulness, attention shifts, and a variable sense of identity; daydreaming may be common for youth, and feeling unreal and detached from experience common for adolescents (Putnam, 1997; Friedrich et al., 1997).

Box 1.3 University Day Care: 3-year-olds

Children behave at least somewhat differently in the presence of or in response to different individuals and in different contexts. For that reason, for a full understanding of a child—his/her skills, participation levels, temperament, and other qualities—it is important to observe a child in different contexts and among different people. In a university day care, one or both parents rotated in to assist for an hour or two once in a 3- or four-week rotation. When an observer walked into the three-year-old's room at the day care center in order to observe "normal" children's behaviors before studying disordered children, she was impressed at the different personalities so evident in each of the children. Very rapidly the children began to treat her like one of the teachers. For the first two weeks, one boy seemed to be playing *follow-the-leader* even though no one was playing the game. He picked the person who was doing the most notable behavior (e.g., running, jumping, spinning, block building) and followed along behind, mimicking the behavior, regardless of gender, status, or IQ level in the one he followed. Although otherwise verbal and assertive, he later described himself as sometimes shy (a teacher agreed with him), and may have felt unsure about how to join in socially. Ali was a bright, pretty, outgoing three-year-old girl, who interacted well with other children. Ali smiled at each adult who entered the room and waited. She relaxed if the adult delighted in seeing her and seemed slightly distressed if they gave a lukewarm hello. However, when her mother was there, she pouted most of the hour, e.g., when any other child sat on her mother's lap or her mother assisted another child—e.g., she said something like, "No, you're only supposed to let me sit on your lap." Joshua was a bright, active little boy whose activity escalated whenever other boys joined in with his play—that is, they all quickly became a bit rowdy. He was quick to figure out tasks for activity time and to answer questions during learning time. However, when his parents were co-teachers, he seemed to freeze or regress when his very bright, take-charge mother led activities. Unlike his usual behavior, he would scribble instead of color and seemed less able to do things or provide answers to lesson questions.

Note:
Case examples are disguised, may be combined cases, and have had details changed to protect individuals.

Developmental Skills/Domains: Part I

Many developmental domains evolve in skill and complexity over time and gain prominence during certain age periods (Chapters 5, 8, 11, 14). For children, a number of developing skills influence the ability to relate to others, the beliefs a youth holds about her/himself, and the nature and levels of her/his personal achievement and other functioning (Carrion, Weems, Ray, & Reiss, 2002; see Nader, 2008). Skills are used in combination and sometimes have interrelated components. For example, self-awareness, other-awareness, memory (Table 1.1), and executive functions

Table 1.1 Types of Memory

GENERAL

Encoding

- *Explicit memory* (Declarative or Conscious memory)—requires conscious focused attention for encoding
  - may suddenly emerge in consciousness or be intentional
  - evident between ages 6 and 12 months, but far from fully developed until subsequent development of hippocampus sub-regions and connections to and from associated neocortical areas
  - a conscious recollection (e.g., elephant at the zoo)
  - recollection of subjective awareness of information encountered in the past
    - auto-noetic or self-knowing—e.g., ability to think back and re-experience
    - noetic or knowing—e.g., a historical or personal fact
- *Implicit memory* (Non-declarative or Unconscious Memory)—does not require conscious attention for encoding
  - being able to recollect information without remembering the experience in which it was learned
  - present from birth
  - things learned from practice or exposure (e.g., cultural standards)
  - behavioral or procedural memories (e.g., riding a bike; skill learning)
  - priming (facilitated processing of a stimulus because of prior experience with it)
  - emotional memories (e.g., fear associated with injury or threatening experiences)
  - indirect memory (e.g., studying a list of words including elephant, then completing root ele…)

Direction

- *Prospective memory*—remembering to perform a planned action or intention (e.g., take med; Skype Sully)
- *Retrospective memory*—memory for the past or for the effects of past experience on current behavior

References: Bjorklund & Sellers, 2014; Damon & Lerner, 2008; De Bellis & Zisk, 2014; Einstein, 2008; Nelson, Thomas & de Haan, 2008; Reynolds & Richards, 2008; Roediger et al., 2008; Sapolsky, 1998; Siegel, 1996

SHORT-TERM MEMORY

- *Short-term memory*—information one is currently aware of or thinking about; recently stored memories; duration and capacity are much lower than long-term memory
  - brief maintenance of a few memory items (number of items increases with age and cognitive abilities; held up to 20–30 seconds), before long-term storage
  - can also have short-term influence of unconscious/implicit memories (e.g., taking the accent of a person you're speaking to)
- *Short-term Sensory Memories*—implicit sensory inputs/impressions held briefly in short-term memory before storage in long-term, implicit or explicit memory

References: Cowen, 2008; Fuhrmann et al., 2015

continued

Table 1.1 Continued

LONG-TERM MEMORY
• *Long-term memory*—vast store of knowledge and record of past events • *Long-term Sensory Memory*—encoded sensory impressions (e.g., visuo-spacial, olfactory, tactile impressions/experiences) – implicit, sensory impressions in infants or toddlers may later express in play, repetitious activities, or verbalizations without conscious awareness of their link to experience – includes non-verbal memories of possibly fragmented, sensory and emotional elements of a traumatic experience *References:* e.g., Nelson et al., 2008; Roediger et al., 2008; Talwar, 2007 • *Episodic Memory*—self-referent; placing self in a set of circumstances at a particular time (Bjorklund and Seller, 2014) • *Autobiographical memory (AM)*—memories about the self (e.g., Furhmann et al., 2015) • *Autobiographical Memory specificity*—AM can be represented at varying degrees of specificity (Williams and Broadbent, 1986) – semantic memories on periods of life (e.g., name of favorite football team) (see Eisma et al., 2015) – events that extended over a period of time (e.g., learning or teaching a team) – memories in a category of similar events (e.g., watching a season of football games) – occurrences in a specific time and place (e.g., at the stadium, in Los Angeles, Sunday) – in contrast to over-general memories (general and without specifics) • *Semantic Memory*—abstract factual knowledge (e.g., remembering 1st U.S. president) • *Procedural memories*—how to do something (e.g., make recipe, play piano [Bjorklund and Sellers, 2014])
WORKING MEMORY
• *Working Memory*—temporarily stored and manipulated information (e.g., Luciana et al., 2005) – improves with age—lower or less efficient use of dorsolateral PFC is involved in differences for middle childhood (Nelson et al., 2008); may be derailed by mood state (Luciana, 2016) – long-term memory contributes by organizing and grouping information in working memory into categories or smaller units (e.g., remembering IRSCIAFBI more easily because it represents government agencies, Cowen, 2008) – updating—i.e., constant monitoring and rapid addition/deletion of working memory contents (Bunge & Crone, 2009; Rose et al., 2012; e.g., not adding the same ingredient twice when baking, solving a math problem, Cowen, 2008) – cross-domain associations (e.g., retention of links between names and faces, Cowen, 2008)

(EFs) all contribute to interpersonal relating. Self-awareness is important to perspective-taking. The ability to take the perspective of another also is important to social skills, which include the ability to influence others, express and understand humor, and display empathy (Semrud-Clikeman & Glass, 2010; Table 1.2). On one end of a continuum, a well-liked child who can appropriately interpret and respond to others' behaviors and intentions is likely to laugh at their jokes and make jokes of his/her own. In contrast, at the other end of the continuum, a child with an autistic spectrum disorder (AuSD) who has low perspective-taking skills (Southall & Campbell, 2015) may be unable to grasp humor (Wu et al., 2014). The ability to communicate feelings to caregivers, regulate emotions, and actively explore the environment provides the groundwork for later social-emotional competence, readiness to enter school, and effective academic and social performance (Bowlby, 1969/1982).

Table 1.2 Definitions for Self- and Other-Relatedness

Empathy
- perspective-taking combined with emotional reaction usually engendering compassion or sympathy
- the ability to understand and share in the feelings of another person
- a combination of perspective-taking and empathic concern
- divided into *affective, cognitive,* and *somatic empathy*—e.g., theory of mind may be considered a cognitive aspect of empathy
- a part of temperamental affiliativeness

Affective empathy
- sharing of emotional states
- ability to feel emotions congruent with the other's emotions
- ability to infer the emotional states of others
- identifying emotions felt in response to a story that might elicit empathy

Cognitive empathy
- perspective-taking
- ability to understand another's mental and emotional states
- recognizing the "how" and "why" of another's affective states
- ability to infer the thoughts of others
- ability to understand why s/he responded to a story with the emotions felt

Somatic empathy
- reacting within the body empathetically—e.g., heart beating fast when a movie character or person is in danger

Behavioral empathy
- actions taken to help someone
- what s/he thinks s/he would do to help a person in a story that might elicit empathy

---

Mentalizing—seeing the self from the outside, and seeing others from the inside
- self-reflective functioning + perspective-taking
- the ability to think about and interpret self and others in terms of mental states
- ability to understand others' behavior in terms of mental states (e.g., beliefs, desires, feelings, and memories)
- ability to reflect on one's own mental states, and the ability to understand that one's own states of mind may influence others' behavior
- ability to engage with an infant mentally—i.e., to imagine the infant's psychological experience and interpret and respond to her/his behavior in terms of what it communicates about the infant's underlying subjective experience or mental states

Hyper-mentalizing
- presumptions are made about the mental states of others that go beyond available data
- hypersensitivity to the mental states of both self and other

---

Metacognitive monitoring
- ability to step back and consider one's own cognitive processes as objects of thought or reflection
- thoughts about thoughts, emotions, and behaviors
- suggests an ability to understand one's own and others' behaviors in terms of mental states or psychological experiences

---

Mind-Mindedness
- parents use of more mental state words toward and about the child
- is typically inferred through analysis of a mother's mind-related comments, which may be either attuned and accurately reflecting the infant's mental states or non-attuned and misunderstanding the infant's mental states

continued

Table 1.2 Continued

Perspective-taking • the ability to understand the perceptual, cognitive, emotional, or motivational reactions of other people, even when reactions are different from one's own • recognizing one's own perspective in relationship to that of others—as consistent and distinct from others • may be able to view a situation from a self-, other-, or 3rd-party vantage point
Reflective functioning or self-reflective functioning—like metacognitive monitoring or theory of mind • suggests an ability to perceive and understand one's own and others' behaviors in terms of mental states or psychological experiences • competence to envision self and others' thoughts, feelings, desires, and intentions • ability to interpret the meaning of others' behavior by considering underlying mental states and intentions • a continuum from denial of mental states, to a basic capacity to recognize simple thoughts and feelings, to emergence of true reflective awareness, i.e., the ability to understand behavior in relationship to mental states and to understand both the nature and dynamic interplay of such states
Theory of Mind • the ability to attribute mental states—e.g., beliefs, intentions, desires, pretending, knowledge—to oneself and others • ability to understand that others have beliefs, desires, and intentions different from one's own • linked to empathy

References: Bensalah et al., 2015; Boltz et al., 2015; Coplan et al., 2005; Ensink et al., 2017, 2018; Evans & Rothbart, 2007; Fonagy and colleagues: e.g., Fonagy et al., 1998, Fonagy & Bateman, 2016; Fosha, 2003; Hoffman, 2015; Longobardi, Spataro, & Colonnesi, 2018; Main, 1995; Moran et al., 2018; Muller & Midgely, 2015; Premack & Woodruff, 1978; Rochat, 2003; Steele et al., 2015; Waller et al., 2015; Chapters 4, 6, 8, 10.

As noted, child development is influenced by many factors—e.g., environments; child factors; relationships; exposures; audio and visual media (Box 1.1; Chap 4, 8). Even exposure to stress before conception or in utero (e.g., to family conflict) as well as exposure to early or ongoing stress, traumatic stress, and/or significant loss may impact the lives and development of children and adolescents. The impact of such stressors may have cascading and long-term effects (Chapter 3). A sampling of multiple risk and protective factors that may influence outcomes of exposure to stressors is presented below and in detail in Chapter 4 and the Appendix (Tables A1.1–A1.4):

- environmental factors—e.g., caregiving, stressors, resources, opportunities (e.g., to learn, explore)
- child factors—e.g., genetics, attributes, reaction style, coping capacity, history, resilience
- exposures factors—e.g., number and severity of exposures, nature of the event, personal meaning
- event aftermath—support systems, safety, media exposures, additional stressors

To follow are some important skills—executive functions, social skills, language, play, and humor. Although some skills (e.g., self-regulation) are a part of EFs, self-skills are addressed in the next section of this Chapter. Trauma and adversity's impact on skills is discussed in Chapter 2. Age-specific information about skills and general information about outcome-influencing variables are provided in other chapters (e.g., attachment, genetics, personality, Chapter 4). Early and ongoing caregiver–child attachments are the basis for a number of developing skills—e.g., provide a basis for coping and styles of inter-relating (Bauminger et al., 2008; Chapter 4). Caregivers are important to development and to posttrauma and developmental recovery.

Executive Functions (EFs)

EFs include higher-order cognitive abilities that are necessary for goal-directed behavior—e.g., memory, mental flexibility, inhibition, strategy development, abstraction, cognitive switching, and flexible thinking (Cassidy et al., 2017; Fatima, Sheikh, & Ardila, 2015; Jurado & Rosselli, 2007; Monette, Bigras, & Lafrenière, 2015; Glossary). EFs also include purposeful, goal-directed activity, such as self-regulation, planning, and problem-solving (Rose, Feldman, & Jankowski, 2012a). EFs are apparent in infancy and generally improve with age. Large-scale brain networks important to cognitive functions dynamically integrate with and segregate from one another to enable behavior (Chai et al., 2017). These networks, predominantly linking frontoparietal regions of the executive system, increase in both expression and flexibility from childhood to young adulthood (N = 200, ages 8–11 and 19–22; Chai et al., 2017; Glossary—e.g., default mode network). Nevertheless, aspects of EFs have significant continuities over time (Rose et al., 2012a). Although children vary in their processing speeds, attention, and memory, for a significant number of infants, their cognitive abilities are consistent through adulthood. Often studied EF abilities are *working memory*, *inhibition*, *planning*, and *cognitive shifting* as well as *self-regulation* and *generativity* (Glossary; Bunge & Crone, 2009; Del Giudice, 2014; Rose et al., 2012a).

Age-related increases in attention efficiency, evidenced by the ability to filter out irrelevant information, are associated with age-related improvements in working memory (Cowan, 2011). From middle childhood to late adolescence, brain regions involved in EFs increase in expression and in dynamic, flexible switching behavior. EFs used in cognitive flexibility (Glossary) improve and mature at different rates—e.g., switching in context of distracting information, ages 2–3; switching with conflicting information, ages 3–3.5 (Blakey, Visser, & Carroll, 2016); inhibition at ages 10–12; working memory in adolescence (Simlesa & Cepanec, 2015). Children with higher EFs are significantly more socially adept, have better academic skills, perform better in school, and appear to be at lower risk for behavioral and emotional problems than those with lower EF. Low EFs have been related to a number of problems. For example, obese youth have shown broad impairments on EFs, including on tasks primarily utilizing inhibition, cognitive flexibility, working memory, decision-making, verbal fluency, and planning, while overweight youth have had only inhibition and working memory problems (meta-analysis, Yang, Shields, Guo, & Liu, 2018).

Inhibition

Although inhibition commonly refers to an ability to suppress a dominant, automatic or pre-potent response, it also includes other forms of control—e.g., interference control, directed forgetting, emotional control, and motor control (Best, Miller, & Jones, 2009; Glossary). Inhibition may include attentional, behavioral, thought, and/or emotional control to override a strong internal predisposition or an external lure (Roskam, Stievenart, Meunier, & Noel, 2014). Inhibition improves significantly in preschool years (especially ages 5–8; e.g., better able to follow odd instructions such as to say, "Night," when seeing a sun picture), and continues to improve through middle childhood (e.g., motor tasks, looking tasks) and up to age 21 (e.g., cognitive inhibition; refinements in speed and accuracy; Best et al., 2009). In later childhood and adolescence (ages 7–17), improvements are reflected in brain changes (e.g., EEG: decreased frontal N2 amplitudes showing increased neural efficiency—e.g., after prefrontal cortex [PFC] pruning [see Glossary]; Best et al., 2009; Sanger & Dorjee, 2016). Development of inhibition throughout preschool years has been related to later social and academic development (Roskam et al., 2014). Controlling for age-related improvements and other relevant variables, for both parents (more for mothers), positive parenting style, and parenting behaviors that included higher monitoring and include lower levels of discipline, inconsistency, and negative controlling were linked to better development of inhibition capacities in children (ages 2–8, across two years; Roskam et al., 2014). Inconsistent discipline (e.g., threats of discipline without follow-through) and/or frequent punishment have had detrimental effects over time. Parenting improvements have been linked to improvements in children's inhibition. Inhibition has been improved by a number of interventions (Chapter 16; e.g., mindfulness for adolescents; Sanger & Dorjee, 2016).

Shifting

Shifting—consciously directing attention from one focus to another—includes the ability to switch between mental states or sets, operations, strategies, or tasks (Bunge & Crone, 2009; Glossary). Shifting includes activities such as the ability to redirect attention in or back to meditation or during complex tasks. Children ages 3–4 can generally *shift* reliably between two response sets, when rules are clear; improvements occur from ages 5–6 (Best et al., 2009). Shifting ability improves with age, typically until early adolescence, when, e.g., youth can shift between more complex task sets, with increases in number and rule complexity (Best et al., 2009), and show greater speed than younger youth (Bunge & Crone, 2009). Mature task shifting is reflected in brain development (e.g., youth: increased inferior frontal and parietal regions: adults: superior temporal regions).

Shifting is a part of cognitive flexibility (Glossary). In fact, cognitive flexibility has sometimes been called cognitive switching (Babb, Levine, & Arseneault, 2010). It enlists inhibition and working memory (Dajani & Uddin, 2015). Cognitive flexibility is the readiness/efficiency with which one can selectively switch between mental processes and adapt to the environment in order to generate appropriate behavioral responses (Dajani & Uddin, 2015; Darby, Castro, Wasserman, & Sloutsky, 2018). Cognitive flexibility can be critical to survival—e.g., quickly and efficiently changing from the task engaged to respond to danger. It also includes the ability to flexibly shift between multiple incompatible perspectives or descriptions of an object or an event (Farrant, Fletcher, & Maybery, 2014). In sorting tasks, evidence has shown that three-year-olds have substantial difficulty shifting to a second dimension (see Darby et al., 2018). They tend to perseverate by continuing to sort by the prior dimension. When pigeons, children, and adults were assessed for their cognitive flexibility related to the same stimuli in different circumstances—e.g., sorting cards by different dimensions (color, shape, number)—all three demonstrated memory for learned information (included 70 preschoolers; Darby et al., 2018). Although pigeons showed some adjustment, they also showed greater perseveration than humans (reflecting difficulty inhibiting the now irrelevant dimension and shift to another dimension). Children and adults showed some perseveration in the first but not the subsequent shift. Older children usually have higher cognitive flexibility and coping flexibility skills than younger children (Babb et al., 2010). Low flexibility has been found for disorders/problems such as ADHD, CD, incarceration, eating disorders, obesity, and autism (e.g., Olvera, Semrud-Clikeman, Pliszka, & O'Donnell, 2005). High cognitive flexibility has been linked to better reading ability, better academic performance, higher resilience in response to adverse life events, higher creativity, school readiness, job performance, social-emotional well-being, and better quality of life in old age (Dajani & Uddin, 2015; Suchodoletz, Slot, & Shroff, 2017).

Planning

Planning is a complex ability. It requires an ability to formulate actions in advance (e.g., goals; multiple steps to take), to approach a task with organization, strategy, and efficiency (e.g., evaluate actions and possibly change course; Best et al., 2009), and to evaluate and select a sequence of actions to achieve a desired goal (Kipping et al., 2018). Planning may include internal rehearsal and temporal sequencing (Kipping et al., 2018). Other EFs are used in planning (e.g., attention, WM, shifting, inhibition; Best et al., 2009). Abilities are related to complexity of a task and age (Best et al., 2009).

Planning ability during childhood appears to be partially achieved through specific brain networks—i.e., engagement of cerebello-cortical functional connectivity but not cortico-cortical association networks, which are less connected and more fragmented in childhood (age six; Kipping et al., 2018; Table A4.2—PFC, Cerebral Cortex). In adolescence, performance may be influenced by neural changes or injury (e.g., PFC pruning or damage). Early life maltreatment has been related to reduced lateral cerebellum volume, as well as poor performance in planning and memory in early adolescence (see Kipping et al., 2018). Adults with damage to the lateral regions of the cerebellum also have shown poor performance in planning skills. Parenting has influenced planning skills (encouraging planning; Lombardi et al. 2017; Chapter 5). Good planning skills in childhood have predicted later academic achievement and social maturity (Kipping et al., 2018; Lombardi et al., 2017). Children use skills differently at different ages. For example, in a cooperative task (child dyads), better planning skills related to more competitive behaviors for younger children (ages 5–8), whereas better planning and verbal abilities related to fewer competitive behaviors for older youth (ages 9–12; Huyder, Nilsen, & Bacso, 2017). Better theory of mind skills also related to lower levels of competitive behaviors in younger children. Partners' cooperative and competitive behaviors correlated, suggesting an influence on each other.

Attention

Attention is essential to safety, learning, interacting, doing, and accomplishing. For example, whereas attention to a popping sound may be automatic, volitional attention to whether the sound is a car backfiring or gunfire is essential to knowing whether or not to self-protect. Across life, attention-focusing activities assist the success of other activities such as learning—e.g., attention-drawing materials in academics (Karagözoğlu, 2017)—and exercise—e.g., focusing on pushing the floor away instead of tightening a region of the body while doing the exercise (Schoenfeld & Contreras, 2016). Attention can be thought of in terms of at least three functionally, neuroanatomically distinct networks—alerting, orienting, and executive attention (Federico, Marotta, Martella, & Casagrande, 2017; Posner, Rothbart, & Voelker, 2016; Glossary; Table A4.1). A small sample of children demonstrated that attentional networks are still developing from ages six to 10 years and underscored the importance of face information in modulating efficiency of executive control (ages 6–10; N = 66; Federico et al., 2017). Looking at faces is important for learning an array of social signals and visual communication cues. For example, gaze direction is an important social cue. We tend to follow the direction of others' gaze. Looking away from faces at key points can be crucial for reducing cognitive load in order to complete tasks (Federico et al., 2017).

Although attention improves with age until adolescence, it varies for different functions and is not necessarily linear. For example, although some aspects of visuospatial attention—ability to attend to and to process stimuli in one's surrounding space—improve until age 13 (e.g., related to movement planning and motor control), others remain stable with increasing age (e.g., spatial reference, N = 160, ages 4.87–19.1; Ickx, Bleyenheuft, & Hatem, 2018). The former may depend on self-body representation, which is developing through age 10. An ability for longer sustained attention to focal events supports linguistic development (low distractibility; Salley, Panneton, & Colombo, 2013; Chapter 5). For determining categorization, adults have used selective attention (Deng & Sloutsky, 2016). In an experimental setting, both 7-year-olds and adults relied on cued features for categorization and remembered cued features better than non-cued features (cued to attend; Deng & Sloutsky, 2016). Although attentional cueing assisted categorization, 4-year-olds showed equally good memory for both cued and non-cued features and remembered non-cued features better than adults.

It is impossible to attend to all incoming stimuli at the same time, therefore we must select (Wetzel, 2014). In an environment providing an influx of numerous stimuli to multiple senses, selective attention is essential to picking out information important to goals, needs, and interests, while ignoring irrelevant information—e.g., separating human speech from other sounds, regardless of accent and intonation; separating aspects of a visual array into coherent objects (Bahrick & Lickliter, 2012). *Selective attention* can be either involuntary or voluntary—e.g., something draws full focus such as inter-sensory redundancy (Glossary; Reynolds, Bahrick, Lickliter, & Guy, 2014) versus goal-driven attention (Deng & Sloutsky, 2016). Selective attention assists processing of goal-relevant events/stimuli and inhibits processing of goal-irrelevant events/stimuli (Wetzel, 2014). Attentional control develops until the second decade of life, closely related to brain development (especially PFC). Attentional control is also influenced by sleep, experience, bias, environmental distractors, preterm birth, emotions, and more. For example, using a go/no-go task requiring attention to neutral, happy, and fearful faces (ages 6–25), there was a linear increase in response-inhibition performance with increasing age for both task-relevant and irrelevant affective emotions (Schel & Crone, 2013). Particularly for young children, a task in which the emotions were relevant affected performance on response-inhibition more strongly than a task in which the emotions were irrelevant. Happy emotions were associated with better performance; fearful faces with reduced performance. Prematurely born children have shown poorer attentional performance in sustained and focused attention, distractibility, and lower processing speed in divided attention and flexibility tasks (assessed ages 5–6; Giordano et al., 2017). Preterm children also showed decreased volitional attention compared to automatic attention (no problems in alertness or inhibition).

Diagnosing an attention deficiency accurately may influence the success of treatment. Berger et al. suggest that attention abnormalities—e.g., decreased attention span, distractibility, hyperactivity, and impulsivity—should be viewed in terms of underlying developmental processes and not as components of discrete non-overlapping disorders (Berger, Remington, Leitner, & Leviton, 2015). They suggest focusing on, e.g., brain delay in otherwise healthy children compared to their age group; effects of age and task load on attentional success; nutritional issues (e.g., effects of alpha lipoic acid on ADHD); relationship between environmental distractors and performance; and differential diagnosis (e.g., ADHD vs sensory modulation disorder).

Memory

What is unique to human-related cognition is self-conscious and intentional, symbolic representation (Bjorklund & Sellers, 2014)—particularly the ability to form memory representations of objects, people, and events in the past and to generate imaginary and possible events in the future (Sellers & Bjorklund, 2014). More than one kind of memory has been conceptualized (Table 1.1) and can be affected by traumatic exposures. Memory is essential to all aspects of functioning—e.g., academic, other productive, and interpersonal functioning (Howe, 1997). Across middle childhood and adolescence, improvements in working memory and cognitive control (Glossary) correspond to increased recruitment of task-related brain regions (Brown et al., 2005; frontal, parietal, and striatal, Bunge & Crone, 2009; Casey, Jones, & Somerville, 2011; shift from diffuse to focal activation, Durston et al., 2006; Rubia, 2013). Normally, memory can be affected by age, stress, sleep, biological factors, parental support, and the nature of a stressful experience.

Working Memory (WM). WM is essentially the ability to briefly hold and manipulate information in short-term memory (e.g., using inhibition, shifting attention, updating information; Bunge & Wright, 2007; van Dooren & Inglis, 2015; Table 1.1; Glossary). Age-related differences in performance depend on the complexity of a task (Best et al., 2009). Problems such as aggression and hyperactivity (ADHD) have been linked to poor working memory (children followed from preschool to age 15; N = 303 males; Séguin, Nagin, Assaad, & Tremblay, 2004; Séguin & Zelazo, 2005)—e.g., a 12-year-old boy, Derek, exhibited ADHD, anger outbursts, arguing, throwing things, knocking over desks, and poor functioning (e.g., social; academic—memory, math, language). The link to poor working memory suggests that children who are better equipped to mentally represent and simultaneously consider multiple options for responding (and consequences)

Box 1.4 Memory

When Kate was in her 30s she was searching for children's books. She asked her mother about the book about the upside-down train. She periodically remembered her mother reading that book to her, but she couldn't find it. She remembered sitting across from her mother on the bed, when her mother read the story. She described to her mother the features of the house, and remembered that only she and her older brother lived there with Mom and Dad, at the time. She also remembered playing in the back yard alone and finding some very interesting snails there. This confirmed her as age two. Her mother told her that it was "The Little Train that Could" and that, although the book was not about an upside-down train, she may have had a view of the train being upside down when she sat across from her mother, while she was reading. The memory of an upside-down train remained until corrected in her 30s. Because the train was upside down to a two-year-old's sight and mind, it remained so in long-term memory, until corrected.

Note:
Case examples are disguised, may be combined cases, and have had details changed to protect individuals.

may engage in more adaptive methods of problem-solving when confronted with hostile or threatening circumstances (Cassidy et al., 2017).

Memory Processing and Long-Term Memory. Although some researchers suggest that our inability to recall very early memories (before age 3.5 or 4) is because infants and young children encode information differently than older children (Box 1.4), later memory deficits also are common (Bauer, 2009; Bjorklund & Sellers, 2014; Howe, Courage, & Rooksby, 2009; Chapter 5). Normally, at age 35 or later, individuals are more likely to recall autobiographical memories from ages 10 or 15 to 30 than memories prior or subsequent (the "reminiscence bump"; Fuhrmann, Knoll, & Blakemore, 2015; Koppel & Berntsen, 2014). Koppel and Berntsen (2014) found a reminiscence bump from ages 5 to 19 for both autobiographical and public event memories (e.g., fall of Berlin Wall). Although the reminiscence bump may reflect changes across the lifespan in memory encoding efficiency, which operates optimally during adolescence and early adulthood, to be remembered, events may require significance to one's life story (see Koppel & Berntsen, 2014); be very positive (e.g., exciting, very happy), very distressing (not neutral events; Lenore Terr, 1995, committee presentation), or one's most important experiences (high and low points on a timeline); or be personal events connected to self-concept (Janssen, 2015). Depending on other variables, traumas may enhance trauma memories and interfere with other memory processes (Chapter 5).

Language Development

Language influences other developmental skills and affects functioning throughout life (e.g., social, occupational). The quantity and quality of early language exposure (e.g., parent–child conversation) are associated with the quality and rate of young children's acquisition of skilled language use (Bauer, 2009; Reese, Haden, & Fivush, 1993; Salmon, O'Kearny, Reese, & Fortune, 2016; Chapter 5). Language development is a basis for emotional, behavioral, and academic functioning—e.g., through language children learn about emotions, communicate needs and wants, learn basic rules of conduct and engagement, learn aspects of self-regulation, create and express narratives (e.g., autobiographical), develop understanding of self and others, perform in schools, and engage in social exchanges (Salmon et al., 2016). Narrative skills are emerging in the preschool years and continue to develop through adolescence (Kelly & Bailey, 2012; Salmon et al., 2016).

Late language emergence has ranged from 10–20% in the general population (Zubrick, Taylor, Rice, & Slegers, 2007, N = 1766). Such delays have persisted in 50–80% at age two and resolved in most children by age three (40–60%) or four (70%; Reilly et al., 2007). However, not all children with later language difficulties have had late emergence of language. Around 6–7% of children show speech and language delays at school entry (Boyle, 2011; Pickles et al., 2016). For preschool children, delays have been associated with family history of speech and language problems, birth order, early neurobiological growth, male gender, non-English-speaking background, parental education, dysfunctional parenting practices, lower maternal vocabulary, and older maternal age (Nelson, Nygren, Walker, Panoscha, 2006; Reilly et al., 2007; Zubrick et al., 2007). Larger studies have produced smaller lists of factors (male gender, both parents' social status, and mother's concern about child's language, Korpilahti, Kaljonen, & Jansson-Verkasalo, 2016; not being first born or only child, suboptimal fetal growth, male gender, premature birth, Zubrick et al., 2007). Lower levels of motor, adaptive, and personal social performance have predicted or co-occurred with language delays (Zubrick et al., 2007). Like many other children, those with language impairments (LI) are sociable (in contrast to autism spectrum children; Pickles et al., 2016). When LI children exhibit higher prosocial behaviors, they have more positive peer relationships and better social outcomes (Pickles et al., 2016). Failure to achieve age-appropriate language proficiency has been related to increased risk of problems in language-related cognitive and socioemotional domains, and to escalating and enduring emotional and behavioral problems (e.g., externalizing; Masten & Cicchetti 2010; Pickles et al., 2016; Salmon et al., 2016). Children with language problems have had greater risk of reading problems as well (Pickles et al., 2016). Reading problems are also linked to conduct and antisocial behavior problems. Children with comorbid conduct and hyperactivity problems have had both language and reading problems.

Internal Dialogue—The Dialogical Self

Children learn dialogue exchanges from observation, interaction, and pretend play—taking on the role of different characters and articulating a theory of that character's mind. When internal dialogue develops, it includes tendencies that influence life quality. For example, self-criticism and self-compassion have been related to negative and positive outcomes/life quality, respectively (e.g., see Iancu, Bodner, & Ben-Zion, 2015; Table 1.3; Self-Evaluation, to follow). Observation and research suggest that each person contains a multiple self with different internal voices—each having a set of wishes, needs, and action tendencies as well as a unique perspective and an at least subtly different information processing style—that vary depending on the demands of interpersonal situations, the problems to be confronted, and mood (Dimaggio, Hermans, & Lysaker, 2010). Some evidence suggests that whether these internal voices—e.g., parent self, child self, self-criticizer, self-enhancer, intellectualizer, emoter, optimist, pessimist (e.g., Hermans, 2010)—represent an adaptive or a maladaptive self is related to the nature (e.g., positive or negative) and dominance of voices as well as to an individual's awareness of them, ability to coordinate or negotiate differences (e.g., via internal and external dialogue), and integration of the different aspects of self represented in these voices (Chapter 2). Like the importance of dialogue among individuals, dialogue between parts of self assist creation of a nuanced, integrated, and adapted self. Awareness and skills for coordination and integration permit a sense of coherence and enable conflict resolution, sometimes with more effective solutions (Dimaggio et al., 2010). Dialogue is used to organize or integrate a fragmented self, enrich an impoverished self, and as a central technique of treatment (e.g., Emotion-Focused Therapy, Hermans & Dimaggio, 2004).

Social Skills

Social skills are behaviors learned from infancy that enable effective interpersonal interactions (see Mello & Nader, 2012; attachment, Chapters 4, 5). Early mother–child joint attention includes a form of information processing that is necessary to an increasing aptitude with the processing of multiple streams of information (in real time) during social interactions. Consequently, it contributes to social cognition and skill. Social skills deficits are associated with problems in school adjustment (e.g., academic performance, failure), relationships (loneliness; victimization; difficulty maintaining relationships; peer rejection; social dissatisfaction), mental health (e.g., behavioral disorders; aggression, criminality), and work (e.g., difficulty maintaining employment; opportunities) in childhood, adolescence, and adulthood (Bakker et al., 2011; Cohen, 2006; Kramer, Caldarella, Christensen, & Shatzer, 2010; Maag, 2005).

Table 1.3a Self-Concept (S-C): Self-View

ASPECT OF S-C, DEFINITIONS, AND ASSOCIATIONS
Self-Efficacy or Self-Confidence • belief in one's skills/capabilities and resources to accomplish goal-oriented strivings in a variety of or in specific domains   – self-confidence may become real-world competence • self-efficacy is among resilience factors associated with positive outcomes • domains of self-efficacy: e.g., interpersonal (e.g., social self-efficacy), achievement (e.g., academic self-efficacy), physical (e.g., athletic self-efficacy), skills (competence) • perceived self-efficacy and emotional competence have proven important to children's ability to cope with traumas (e.g., CSA) • self-efficacy and social initiative have positively correlated with self-disclosure • securely attached individuals have been more likely to show high self-confidence and to express greater warmth interpersonally • in maltreated children, positive self-schemas have been associated with dissociation and may be a part of defensive self-processing (e.g., maltreated children ages 7–14 overestimated their self-efficacy in conflictual peer interactions; inflation of perceived skills may increase their sense of personal control and competence) • posttrauma treatment has sometimes increased self-efficacy (e.g., via increasing skills such as problem-solving or coping)

Self-Esteem or Self-Worth
• extent to which a person approves of, values, likes, or prizes her/himself
  – explicit self-esteem—conscious and reflective self-evaluation (higher cognitive processes)
  – implicit self-esteem—characterized by automatic and unconscious self-evaluation
  – self-esteem via mattering—an internalized feeling of being important or significant to other people ("I matter," "I'm valued")
• low self-esteem—focus is on unfavorable attributes of self
  – linked to poor mental health outcomes—e.g., adolescent anxiety disorder (e.g., SoAD), suicide attempts, exclusion; attentional biases toward social rejection (may be domain specific—e.g., weight, academics, approval)
• high self-esteem—focus is on strengths or favorable aspects of self
  – positive associations—e.g., resilience; lower risk of problems (e.g., SU); positive emotions; life satisfaction; adjustment and well-being in social relationships; school achievement; resilience to stressful life events; less likelihood of anxiety or depression

Sources: Barnard & Curry, 2011; Barnett & Sharp, 2016; Brake et al., 2017; Chang et al., 2018; Donnellan, Murray, & Harrison, 2013; Flett, Flett, & Wekerle, 2015; Fraley et al., 2013; Hunter et al., 2011; Iancu et al., 2015; Jiang et al., 2017; Kolubinski et al., 2017; Lee et al., 2018; see Moran et al., 2018; see Nader, 2008; Neff, 2003; Ravary & Baldwin, 2018; Sroufe, 2018; Valentino, Cicchetti, Rogosch, & Toth, 2013; Yu, Norton, & McCracken, 2017 (for Table 1.3b as well).

Table 1.3b Self-Concept (S-C): Self-Talk—Contempt vs Compassion

SELF-TALK AND S-C Self-dialogue (criticism or compassion) may both reflect and contribute to self-concept

Self-Criticism
- the inner negative voice that judges and attacks the self (e.g., related to actions, traits)
  - persistent, negative self-judgments, some level of which are involuntary
  - in contrast to introspection or self-analysis without negative judgment
  - internal dialogue that expresses intense hostility/contempt toward the self, often after failure to meet personal high standards; can also be related to personal traits (e.g., genetics, personality)
- may lead to a perseverative, specific form of rumination (distinct from depressive rumination and from posttrauma intrusions)
  - self-critical rumination involves focusing attention specifically on self-critical thoughts
  - rather than on emotions, focus is on aspects of self of which one is ashamed and on one's overall self-worth
- rumination mediates the relationship between self-criticism and both suicidal ideation and depression
- self-criticism has been related to feelings of being a failure; mood disorders (e.g., depression); despair; guilt; anxiety (e.g., SoAD); substance use (SU); reduced self-efficacy; poor adaptation; eating disorders; psychosomatics; lower levels of problem-solving; feelings of helplessness and/or hopelessness in stressful situations

Self-Disgust
- disgust directed internally—disgust with self (e.g., physical and/or personality traits) or with personal behavior
  - as an evolutionary adaptive reaction (toward self-preservation), disgust is a negatively valenced reaction characterized by revulsion and rejection, intended to protect oneself from contaminants
  - maladaptive when directed toward self—overlaps with but is distinct from and may be more extreme than self-criticism, shame, or self-contempt
- PTSD symptom severity has been associated with self-disgust, disgust with own behaviors, and suicide risk (beyond effects of depression or gender), e.g.,
  - after controlling for PTSD severity and other covariates, only increased self-disgust was linked to suicidal risk
  - all PTSD symptom clusters related to suicide risk via self-disgust, except arousal and reactivity (not disgust with behaviors)
  - theoretically, self-disgust may increase feelings of hopelessness, burdensomeness, and thwarted belonging

Self-Compassion
- Buddhist compassion—"compassion entails being moved by and desiring to alleviate both others' and one's own distress," pain, or suffering (see Barnard & Curry, 2011, p. 289)
  - ability to respond mindfully toward the self with kindness and self-acceptance after experiencing interpersonal adversities, after committing social blunders, and/or after failing to meet social expectations
- Western self-compassion (see Neff, 2003):
  - (a) self-kindness rather than self-judgment or self-criticism
    - extending to self: empathy, forgiveness, sensitivity, warmth, and patience
    - to all aspects of oneself—e.g., all of one's actions, feelings, thoughts, and impulses
    - may include self-soothing, warmth, and compassionate self-reassurance
  - (b) personal fallibility as part of a larger human condition rather than as isolating
    - recognizing our connection to others
    - especially in our confusion, sorrows, imperfections, and weaknesses
  - (c) mindfulness
    - nonjudgmental awareness of, attention to, and acceptance of the present moment
    - holding personal painful thoughts and feelings in mindful awareness rather than avoiding/repressing them, overidentifying with them (e.g., ruminating on personal limitations), or trying to change them

- higher levels of self-compassion have been associated with greater life satisfaction, happiness, social connectedness, and emotional intelligence as well as with lower levels of anxiety, depression, shame, fear of failure, self-injury, and burn-out
- maladaptive perfectionism has been related to lower self-compassion, which in turn is related to lower body image satisfaction; people with high self-compassion are more likely to have higher body image satisfaction, and may be less likely to compare themselves to others

Friendships are both a consequence of and a learning ground for social skills (Bowker, 2004). Closeness to another person and openness in sharing thoughts and feelings are among the characteristics of intimate school-age friendships (Bauminger et al., 2008). Friendship intimacy utilizes several skills—e.g., support seeking, support-providing, negotiating, and feeling comfortable as an autonomous self (Bauminger et al., 2008). Such skills are learned in early infant–caregiver relationships. A variety of relationship rules emerge across childhood—e.g., related to compromising to prevent conflict or standing firm; staying away from or staying by someone when s/he is grouchy; being and acting independent; letting others know when you're upset vs handling it in other ways; and inhibiting behavior when indicated (e.g., Bigelow et al., 1996). Positive and stable intimate friendships have had positive effects on children's psychological adjustment (e.g., higher self-esteem) and are associated with reduced risk of psychopathology (i.e., fewer emotional problems; reduced aggression; Bowker, 2004; see Nader, 2012c). Youth who possess certain social skills and traits (e.g., agreeableness and friendliness) tend to be less often victimized than those who lack such traits or skills (Christiansen & Evans, 2005).

Normal Play

Play helps children achieve cognitive, physical, and social milestones (Capurso & Pazzagli, 2016; Zosh, Fisher, Golinkoff, & Hirsh-Pasek, 2013). Its benefits may be immediate or deferred. In general, play is associated with a sense of mastery and of well-being in children (Pellegrini & Smith, 1998; Piaget, 1962) and may assist coping (Capurso & Pazzagli, 2016; Tessier, Normandin, Ensink, & Fonagy, 2016), flexibility, and innovation (Pellegrini, Dupuis, & Smith, 2007). Play is important to brain and skill development as well as to well-being (Lipton & Fosha, 2011; Chapter 5). Play permits ventilation, working through, and the creation of a reality where there can be autonomy, control, independence, and survival and thriving in the face of adversity (Capurso & Pazzagli, 2016; Sutton-Smith, 2009). Play is important for learning to recognize and interpret social signals and others' affective states (Brown, 2014b), to respond effectively interpersonally (Pellegrini & Smith, 2005), and to self-regulate—e.g., behavioral inhibition, executive control (underlying creativity, self-reflection, and empathy; Panksepp, 2007; Tessier et al., 2016; Chapter 5). Panksepp (1998) suggests that *Play* is one of six neural-based networks that influence personality (Davis, Panksepp, & Normansell, 2003; see Chapter 4). Some medications inhibit playfulness (e.g., psychostimulants for ADHD, Panksepp, 2007).

Although normal play varies somewhat by culture—e.g., African farm children play aggressively significantly more often than African forager children (Boyette, 2016)—research has demonstrated developmental purposes for different types of play (see Nader, 2008). For example, rhythmic play is associated with neuromuscular development (Pellegrini & Smith, 1998; Chapter 5). Exercise play appears to assist the development of physical strength, endurance, and economy of movement. A break in cognitive tasks (play or other break) maximizes cognitive performance (e.g., increased attention and learning; Hirsh-Pasek, Golinkoff, Berk, & Singer, 2009; Pellegrini & Smith, 2005). Vigorous play correlates with preschoolers' abilities to decode emotional expressions, and elementary school rough-and-tumble play (R&T) is linked to an ability for decoding play-engagement signals and establishing dominance (Pelligrini & Smith, 1998; Chapter 8). Skill sets used in careers (e.g., creativity, critical thinking, collaboration, communication, confidence) begin with playtime (Nader, 2008; Zosh et al., 2013). In play, children can take behaviors observed in adults and others and then recombine elements to use new strategies or routines (Pellegrini et al., 2007). Behavioral flexibility may emerge from encountering uncertain environments with the freedom to play. Play has predicted later performance on theory of mind tasks (Glossary; Chapter 8), mental state verbalizations during interactions, affect regulation, empathy, social competence, and affective understanding (Pellegrini & Smith, 2005; Tessier et al., 2016).

Dramatic or fantastical pretend play, specifically—involving physicalizing emotional states or traits, pretending to be human or animal characters, and/or enacting pretend scenarios—in a small group, has been related to improved emotional control (N = 97, low SES four-year-olds, Goldstein & Lerner, 2017). Some evidence suggests that children of lower SES engage in less pretend play and less sophisticated play overall than middle- and high-SES children. Studies have shown improvements in preschoolers' language, literacy skills, representation of emotional states, and self-inhibition after story-acting/dramatic play interventions (see Goldstein & Lerner, 2017).

Humor

Positive emotions, in general, are associated with better coping, improved well-being, protection from disease, and resilience in the face of loss and adversity (Papa & Bonanno, 2008). The study of humor begins with an infant's smiling and laughter and her/his reactions to the absurd or incongruent (see age-related chapters). Theories of humor include focus on developmental stages of humor (incongruity theory), some of the possible uses of humor (superiority theory), and types of incongruities (theory of the absurd, Loizou & Kyriakou, 2016; see Table 1.4; see also Tables A2.1 and 11.2). Most researchers agree that most humor includes a simultaneous manifestation of incompatible elements or a sudden contradiction of expectations (Semrud-Clikeman & Glass, 2010). Differences in the types of humor used emerge with age—e.g., related to cognitive and emotional development; creativity (Cameron, Fox, Anderson, & Cameron, 2010; Loizou & Kyriakou, 2016). Creativity influences humor and humor influences creativity. Although humor often is related to positive experiences—e.g., laughter, stress relief, and bonding—its use can be either benign or detrimental (see Table 11.2, A2.1—Adult Humor Styles).

When mature and/or skilled enough to do so, with the use of humor, a youth may relieve tension, reduce stress, regulate emotions, improve relationships, increase or maintain group unity, save face, laugh at him/herself, reduce social awkwardness, build confidence, attract or maintain attention, increase dominance or status, express otherwise difficult-to-communicate views, provide an alternative view of something, enhance memory, promote creativity, or express aggression in a socially acceptable way (Scott, Lavan, Chen, & McGettigan, 2014; Semrud-Clikeman & Glass, 2010). A sense of humor is one aspect of social competence and is, itself, an aspect of resilience (Semrud-Clikeman & Glass, 2010). A sense of humor is among traits considered attractive in self, friends, and members of the opposite sex (Del Giudice, Ellis, & Shirtcliff, 2011) and is associated with emotional well-being and personal development (Herzog & Strevey, 2008). Humor has been used for pain and anxiety management. Adaptive humor has correlated with parental warmth (Kazarian, Moghnie, & Martin, 2010); parental warmth is associated with a youth's later happiness and well-being. While under normal circumstances humor may help to relieve a child's tension or help her/him "get past" a problem, trauma can make it more difficult for children or adults to use, respond to, or have a sense of humor.

Table 1.4 Humor Theories and Observations

Theory	Aspects of the Theory
Incongruity	McGhee's (1979) Developmental Stages of Humor 1. incongruous actions toward objects 2. incongruous labeling of objects and events 3. conceptual incongruity 4. humor in multiple meanings
Superiority	Humor Produced and/or Appreciated as a Social Process (Gruner, 1978) • an attempt to feel superior to someone – to make fun of someone – to underestimate them • to ridicule someone
Of the Absurd	Mismatches from a Child's Existing Schemata (Loizou & Kyriakou, 2016) 1. funny gestures/positions/sounds/words 2. actions (e.g., violate expectations) or empowerment (e.g., violate rules, misbehave; resolve incongruities) 3. incongruous use of materials • included violation of expectation, feeling empowered when someone was in some kind of trouble
"A Day in the Life" of Toddlers	Video tracking of a day in an age group (Cameron et al., 2010; consistent with McGhee's list) 1. clowning—deliberately repeated acts/speech to re-elicit laughter; may or may not be motoric 2. teasing/playful mocking directed to, appealing to, or attempting to provoke a response 3. jokes: word play and playful language 4. Playful physical use of the body and other objects for amusement • used in primarily social-emotional functioning (affiliative) and used in exploring cognitive and linguistic functioning
"A Day in the Life" of Adolescents Ages 13–16	Video tracking of a day in an age group (Cameron et al., 2010; N=2) • like toddlers: joking, teasing, physical play • additional types: light tones (e.g., asking can I push you, when sitting on a fence), irony, sarcasm, mocking/parody • used to maintain a positive outlook, to elicit or deflect attention or laughter, to navigate sensitive areas (e.g., sexual), to protect others, for affiliation (e.g., solidarity), for fun, for affiliation, to reduce or avoid embarrassment or discomfort, to create distance • can be benign or detrimental humor (see Table 11.2)

Sources: Cameron, 2010; Loizou & Kyriakou, 2016; see age-related chapters and Tables 5.5, 11.2, A2.1.

Humor and Neurobiology

The brain uses multiple regions for humor (Feng, Ye, Mao, & Yue, 2014; Restak, 2013; Scott et al., 2014), and it releases "feel good" neurotransmitters (hormones) when a punch line or humorous event hits home (Shibata, Terasawa, & Umeda, 2014). Laughter triggers the brain's emotional and reward centers (e.g., contributes to the release of dopamine), which help the brain process emotions and enhance pleasure (Campbell et al., 2015). Humor triggers serotonin, to lift the mood, and releases endorphins that regulate pain and stress and can induce euphoria (Glossary; Dunbar et al., 2012). Right hemisphere brain damage may interfere with the ability to appreciate humor (Feng et al., 2014). Good, hearty laughter can relieve tension and stress, can boost the immune system—e.g., by reducing stress hormones and increasing activity among immune cells and antibodies—and help to reduce the risk of heart attack and stroke—e.g., by improving blood flow and blood vessel function (Morgan & Jorm, 2008). Thus, laughter, which usually follows appreciated humor, has demonstrated health benefits—e.g., muscle tone; cardio-respiratory; increased memory; reduced cortisol (Bains et al., 2015; Bennett & Lengacher, 2007).

Humor Styles

Adaptive humor styles (affiliative humor and self-enhancing humor)—in contrast to maladaptive humor styles (aggressive or self-defeating humor)—have predicted self-esteem and subjective happiness (Yue, Liu, Jiang, & Hiranandani, 2014; Fox, Hunter, & Jones, 2016). The kinds of humor children like and understand are influenced by age and social factors. Fox et al. confirmed that youth, like adults, exhibit distinct humor styles (Tables 11.2, A2.1). Additionally, they demonstrated that individuals use combinations of humor styles, and the combinations are differentially associated with psychosocial adjustment (see Chapters 11, 10). For example, Fox et al. found that the negative effects of using self-defeating humor could be offset to some extent when it was used in combination with other humor styles.

Neurobiological Development

Growth spurts in brain development are accompanied by disorganization in brain and behavior (e.g., approximately age three, middle childhood, puberty, and adolescence, Stein & Kendall, 2004). A pattern of overproduction, elimination, and reorganization characterizes early brain development—i.e., overproduction of synapses (e.g., in corpus collosum, anterior commissure, prefrontal associational circuitry) is followed by pruning of unused connections and emergence of new neural networks (Huang et al., 2015; Stein & Kendall, 2004). Many aspects of post-birth brain development depend greatly on experience (Bick et al., 2015). Interactions between children and caregivers shape the ultimate architecture of the brain (Schore, 2003; Siegel, 2003). From birth to age two, the human brain undergoes several dramatic changes including rapid volume increases corresponding to rapid development of a wide range of cognitive and motor functions (Huang et al., 2015). The brain has reached adult volume by two years, plateaued to three and four years, maintained until age nine, and begun to decline after adolescence. Formative periods of brain growth (e.g., early childhood, adolescence) seem to correspond to sensitive periods of development in particular brain regions. Research has found attenuated development within the medial prefrontal cortex, medial frontal gyrus, anterior cingulate gyrus, hippocampus, and corpus callosum in individuals who experienced traumas during childhood (Dackis, Rogosch, Oshri, & Cicchetti, 2012; Table A4.2). For example, Andersen et al. (2008) found the hippocampus has been maximally affected by abuse at ages 3–5 (second most strongly between ages 11–13), corpus callosum at 9–10, and frontal cortex at 14–16 (N = 26 abused; 17 non-abused, healthy comparisons). Normally, from birth to adolescence, the brain undergoes dramatic changes in connectivity and network configuration, and brain connectivity grows stronger and more efficient. For example, the default mode network (DMN) supports mental activities such as episodic memory, mentalizing, and self-projection (see Huang et al., 2015; Chapter 11). The DMN has been shown in neonate brains. In early school years (ages seven to nine), default regions are only sparsely functionally connected. Studies show that even highly connected regions of brain networks can withstand extensive damage; damage leads to reorganization of the network (Joyce, Hayasaka, & Laurienti, 2013). However, the younger the age, the more vulnerable are brain networks to targeted attacks or random failures (Glossary; Huang et al., 2015).

Although multiple systems mediate the impact of stress on development (e.g., sympathetic-adrenomedullary system, Glossary), from a developmental perspective, the key system is the hypothalamic-pituitary-adrenocortical (HPA) system (Gunnar, Doom, & Esposito, 2015). An HPA axis product, cortisol—a steroid hormone that acts in all parts of the body—is important to development, neural plasticity, and the fight-flight response. Coping with early life stress—when stress challenges but is not enough to overwhelm the child (stress inoculation)—may foster adaptation that enhances emotion regulation, cognitive control, and curiosity (and their interrelated facets) as well as diminish stress-induced HPA axis activation (Gunnar, Frenn, Wewerka, & Ryzin, 2009a; see Shonkoff et al., 2012). Accordingly, coping with early manageable stress increases prefrontal myelination (Glossary) and expands a cortical region that relates to arousal regulation and resilience (e.g., animal studies, Katz et al., 2009). Overwhelming stress seems to affect a wide range of neurobiological systems and brain structures (van der Kolk, 2003)—e.g., early interpersonal violence (e.g., extra- and intrafamilial) has led to changes in the structure and function of neural circuits that underlie emotional learning, some of which may not be measurable until adulthood (McLaughlin, Sheridan, & Lambert, 2014a; Chapter 5). Such changes have been related to a wide range of diseases and disorders (Alexander et al., 2018; Table A4.1—DNA$_{m}$; Chapter 4).

More recent studies have shown that, after puberty, cortisol reactivity is modulated by sex hormones (testosterone, estrogen, progesterone; mixed findings on the nature of the influence; Barel et al., 2018). For adults, controlling for sex hormones has diminished the stress-related differential pattern of cortisol reactivity, suggesting a need to control for sex hormones when examining cortisol and alpha-amylase reactivity to stress. Higher levels of progesterone have been related to higher levels of cortisol reactivity to stress in some studies. Barel et al. found that reactions were different for those whose cortisol became elevated from baseline after a stress task compared to those whose cortisol was already high and did not increase. For those with initially high cortisol (not for those with increases in cortisol), higher estrogen and progesterone were linked to lower cortisol change following stress (some N = 58; Barel et al., 2018).

Developmental Domains: Part II—The Self-Skills

Self-regulation, self- and other-awareness skills, and emotion awareness are important to all domains of functioning—e.g., interpersonal, academic, career, communication, behavioral, cognitive, emotional functioning. Trauma or adversity may influence alterations in self-skills.

Self-Regulation

At all ages, self-regulation is essential to successful functioning (Nader & Fletcher, 2014). It includes methods by which a person's mind exercises control over its functions, states, and inner processes—effortful control, delay of gratification (Del Giudice, 2014; Rueda, Posner & Rothbart, 2005; Glossary; Chapter 5). It is present, at a basic level, from early infancy—newborns can regulate affect by looking at mother or by sucking on fingers (e.g., Kopp, 1982). Self-regulation includes self-controlled and disciplined behaviors that influence inter-relating (e.g., by inhibiting undesirable behaviors) and achievement (e.g., by enhancing goal-directed behaviors; Del Giudice, 2014). It requires the ability to stop oneself from acting on an urge or from completing an automatic reaction. *Behavioral self-regulation* is the ability to adjust behaviors according to the demands of a situation—e.g., a toddler focuses on a toy and away from a cookie that's for later; an adolescent stops her/himself from saying mean things back to someone (Box 1.5; see Koenen, 2006). *Emotion regulation* combines awareness, understanding, and acceptance of personal emotions, as well as the capacity to control emotion-related impulsive behaviors and to modulate affective responses in order to achieve individual goals or adjust to situational circumstances—e.g., calming anger or sorrow to maintain bonds with others or to concentrate (Box 1.5; Goldsmith, Chesney, Heath, & Barlow,

Box 1.5 Self-Regulation after Death of a Mother

When he was nine, Jackson's mother was murdered. Everywhere he went in his house, he was reminded of her. He cried when no one could see him and longed for her. He felt he couldn't live without her. She had been his best advocate, his comforter, and his encourager. Anyone who looked at them could see how proud she was of him and how much she liked him. He had been a confident, bright, and happy boy. His dad was like he had always been. He was friendly to people, calm, and competent. He would ask, "How ya' doin', Buddy?" Jackson wondered if his dad missed his mother. One night after one of his nightmares (he had not seen the murder but imagined it), he went to the door of his father's room and saw him crying with his head in his hands. It was a comfort to Jackson to see he wasn't alone in his grief. They cried together.

After his mother died, it was a relief for Jackson to go to school every day. He was away from the constant reminders that, instead of treasured mementos, had become reminders of her absence and of her violent death. Although it was harder than before, he could force himself to concentrate on his studies. He would come home sometimes and want to rush in and tell her something, then feel deep pain again at her absence and at the thoughts of how she was murdered. At school, he could play soccer (football) and think of the murderer when he kicked the ball to someone or toward the goal. The first time he did it in practice, his friend jumped out of the way, because he kicked it so hard. He was "lucky" at school (he was well liked). People sometimes make fun of children with dead mothers. Jackson was a secure, friendly, kind, and popular boy. His friends rallied around him. They would make jokes or get him to join in games or activities to cheer him up. He stopped himself from telling them how angry he was, stopped himself from snapping at people because he was irritable and angry and felt like they didn't understand. He let their support temporarily lift him out of the constant, painful thinking about his mother. He liked it that they cared about him and wanted him to feel better. He felt a bit of what he'd lost (his mother's support) from their efforts to make him feel better. Aunt Kathryn and Uncle Mike also helped. They brought food and helped with chores. Aunt K would sit with Jackson's head in her lap (like mother used to) and stroke his head. She didn't mind if he cried, and he knew that she really loved him. She took him to a therapist, and he could tell the therapist about his angry, "mean" feelings.

Note:
Case examples are disguised, may be combined cases, and have had details changed to protect individuals.

2013; Gratz & Roemer, 2004). Inhibiting emotional distraction and/or negative affect are aspects of emotional self-regulation (Barry, Kochanska, & Philibert, 2008; Kochanska, Philibert, & Barry, 2009; see Nader & Fletcher, 2014). While emotion-regulatory goals and skills generally increase with age (Gross, 1998), an ability, at a young age, to delay gratification and to inhibit or delay responses is a good indicator of ability to self-regulate in adolescence (Eigsti et al., 2006). At least in part, because children have different coping repertoires, tendencies, or capacities, which may be influenced by attachment and social competence, self-regulation varies among children of the same age.

Conscious versus Automatic Regulation

Regulatory processes may be automatic or controlled, conscious or unconscious, and may occur at one or more points in the emotion-making or behavior-choosing process (Gross, 1998).

Self-regulation efforts include a number of types of conscious actions (see Nader, 2012c). For example, a child may regulate emotions or behaviors by approaching or avoiding specific people, places, or things—e.g., individuals who encourage certain behaviors or elicit certain emotions. After traumas, avoidance of reminders may be unconscious or conscious attempts to regulate emotions and reactions. Another conscious regulation method involves modifying a situation or one's reaction to it in order to alter its emotional or behavioral impact (e.g., problem-focused coping). An individual may adapt to a situation, for example, through self-talk or reappraisal of the situation—e.g., reframing, intellectualizing, isolating, or denying—or through attempting to regulate physiological and experiential aspects of emotion with calming techniques (e.g., deep breathing, meditation, or mellowing visualizations), exercise (e.g., running; gym visits), or other self-soothing methods—e.g., muscle massage; *walking it off*—involves taking oneself out of the setting, exercise, and change of focus. Additionally, youth may alter attention—e.g., by self-distracting; focusing elsewhere such as on a different goal or on specific aspects of a situation (Gross, 1998). Youth can change emotional responses by imagining something that elicits different emotions. When disrupted by distress or trauma, these skills may be regained in treatment interventions.

Self-Regulation and Outcomes

Childhood self-regulation skills predict later behavior problems in youth (Causadias, Salvatore, & Sroufe, 2012) and predict health, financial, and criminal activity outcomes in adulthood (Moffitt et al., 2011). High self-control has been related to intellectual achievement; low self-control has been related to conduct disturbances and criminality (Boisvert et al., 2013). Youth with higher levels of self-regulation have been less affected by the influence of deviant peers (Dishion & Patterson, 2006). Not all high self-control yields positive outcomes. Both *overcontrollers* and *undercontrollers* have difficulties (Block & Block, 1980; Caspi, 1998; see Nader, 2008). For example, chronic hostility and inhibition of anger both are associated with hypertension and coronary heart disease (Gross, 1998).

Because emotions often influence actions, emotional and behavioral self-regulation may both be necessary in a given situation. As well, individuals may experience dysregulation in both positive and negative emotional systems (Linehan, Bohus, & Lynch, 2007; Weiss, Gratz, & Lavender, 2015). For example, impulsive tendencies in response to intense positive emotions have been linked to clinically relevant maladaptive behaviors—e.g., drug and alcohol use, gambling, and risky sexual behavior (Cyders, Flory, Rainer, & Smith, 2009; Weiss et al., 2015). Under normal circumstances, ability to self-correct in response to the environment and/or to anticipate the future can assist self-regulation (Del Giudice, 2014). In moderately unpredictable environments (e.g., potentially dangerous), monitoring the environment with moment-to-moment self-correction (i.e., adaptation or adjustment) can be advantageous—e.g., for youth who live in neighborhoods with frequent violence.

Self-Awareness

Self-awareness can be defined as the degree to which a person comprehends her/his personal attributes, beginning with physical self-awareness, and later including strengths and weaknesses, emotions, values, interests, and impact on others (Denham, Ji, & Hamre, 2010; London, 2003; Table 5.4). Self-awareness assists social interactions as well as personal development and success (London, 2003; Mundy, Gwaltney, & Henderson, 2010). According to Avolio (2004), self-awareness is integrally entwined with social sensitivity and confidence in interpersonal relationships. Self-awareness, from an emotional growth perspective, requires the ability to self-reflect (London, 2003). Self-evaluation involves some form of self-representation (Bandura, 2012). Life experiences are processed through the self-referential system with some personal investment in what one is doing or accomplishing (e.g., Bandura, 2008). Some believe that self-awareness leads to self-regulation, which, in turn, increases self-development (London, 2003). Posner and Rothbart (2007a) have argued that an infant's intentional use of shifts of attention to manage arousal and conflict is a primary step in the development of self-awareness and self-regulation. Autistic children demonstrate early impairments in the capacity for rapid, integrated processing of self-referenced and other-referenced information, with cascading effects on the development of self-awareness (Mundy et al., 2010). For autistic and non-autistic children, early attention-sharing efforts—coordinating attention with a social partner (e.g., in infancy, with a parent)—assist ongoing social learning. Joint attention involves self-referent information (i.e., information about self), information about another (i.e., their attentional efforts), and information about an object or situation.

Self-Evaluation

Self-evaluation influences other traits such as self-esteem, self-confidence, and outlook. More than one conceptualization has been used to assess self-concept and its outcomes (see Table 1.3a–b). Contextual Behavioral Science delineates three aspects of self-concept: *self-as-content* (the narrative self; self-schemas); *self-as-process* (in-the-moment verbal and experiential self-awareness); and *self-as-context* (the transcendent self; third-party perspective, metacognitive monitoring; Moran, Almada, & McHugh, 2018). Rigidly believing that self-schemas are actual truth or over-conceptualization of self may lead to dysfunction (e.g., feeling inadequate, unlovable; greater distress). In contrast, the observing self (-as context) enables self- and other-skills and has been related to lower depression (see Moran et al., 2018).

Self-esteem and social confidence are influenced by many factors including attachment security; family, peer, and teacher evaluation; and performance (e.g., at school; see Nader, 2012c). Successful people generally outperform less successful people in forming accurate judgments of how well they performed (Bass & Yammarino, 1991). Qualities such as intelligence, internal locus of control, and an achievement orientation also have been associated with self-evaluation accuracy (Glossary; London, 2003). While for some, self-monitoring is a part of self-awareness processes, evidence suggests that perpetual self-monitors are greatly influenced by group rather than internal dispositions and values, and they may be high in apprehension about the evaluations of others (London, 2003; Pontari & Schlenker, 2000; see the Dialogical Self, Chapter 2). Severe self-reflection deficits are linked to poorer verbal memory, lower insight, and poor social functioning, and with increased emotional withdrawal and paranoia (Dimaggio et al., 2010).

Although poor self-esteem has been associated with high rates of poor mental health outcomes (e.g., high stress levels, anxiety, victimization) and suicide attempts (see Table 1.3a), attempts to build adolescent self-esteem to improve mental health have frequently failed or had negative outcomes (see Iancu et al., 2015; Moran, Almada, & McHugh, 2018)—e.g., aggression, narcissism, bullying, a self-serving bias, avoiding constructive feedback (see Moran et al., 2018). Some current treatments address self-talk/dialogue, including the tendency toward self-criticism versus self-compassion (see Table 1.3b). Self-compassion has been enhanced by methods like mindfulness (e.g., Chapters 10, 16) and other practices (e.g., Chapter 16—AEDP, yoga).

Shame and Guilt

Both shame and guilt are self-conscious emotions that may include intense feelings of regret, responsibility, and desire to make amends (Tangney, Miller, Flicker, & Barlow, 1996; see Nader, 2008). Although some researchers suggest that individuals either are shame-prone or guilt-prone (Tangney, 1990), Tangney and colleagues (1992) found a positive correlation between guilt- and shame-proneness in college students. Guilt focuses on behaviors—actions, inactions, survival, or omissions—that are inconsistent with internalized standards (Tangney, 1990). It often includes a nagging preoccupation with a specific transgression (Tangney et al., 1996). Young children are predisposed to see themselves as causes of events (ages 2–6, see Fletcher, 2014; Chapters 5, 8). Shame is a product of negative self-evaluation rather than of evaluation of specific behaviors (Tangney, 1990). The self observes and disapproves of personal shortcomings of the *defective self* (Tangney et al., 1996).

Emotion Awareness: Understanding and Labeling Emotions

The ability to identify emotions has a survival function—e.g., a child must recognize that fear in the face of danger means s/he must seek protection, comfort, and safety (Baldwin, 2013). Even when some skills decline (e.g., at puberty onset), survival-related skills remain intact (e.g., fear and disgust recognition, Blakemore & Choudhury, 2006). Children learn emotions from their caregivers and often reflect their caregivers' emotional expressiveness—e.g., fear, anger, happiness (see Berk, 2009; Box 1.6). Emotions influence cognitive processes (e.g., decision-making, assessments, attention, concentration), behavior (e.g., rapid motor responses; action choices), and social responses (e.g., accord vs discord; e.g., Gross, 1998). In addition, emotions inform expectations (e.g., of threat or reward; others' behavioral intentions) and evaluations (e.g., of the positive or negative value of something).

Box 1.6 Child Mirrors Parent's Distress

Alana, who wasn't used to being a speaker, gave a talk to a group of friends, acquaintances, and strangers. When she went to the front of the room, she welcomed everyone and began the social preliminaries before beginning her talk. Her two-year-old son started to cry. She explained that she wasn't used to public speaking and that young children often reflect their parents' emotions. "Now you know how I feel," she said.

Note:
Case examples are disguised, may be combined cases, and have had details changed to protect individuals.

Emotion Awareness Skills

Emotion awareness skills include those related to self, others, and groups (see Alonso-Alberca et al., 2012). They are linked to an ability to adapt. Emotion self-awareness skills consist of the abilities to recognize, express, and label personal emotions correctly. Other-related emotion skills include the ability to recognize and understand others' emotions in facial expressions, voice, and/or behaviors. Both skills include the ability to identify causes or triggers of emotions and to anticipate resulting emotions. As well, an individual must be able to make associations between social rules and emotions, to express emotions in culturally acceptable manners, to cope with negative emotions, and to understand how emotions influence human relationships. Girls tend to have greater emotional knowledge than boys (perhaps due to maturation and socialization differences; Alonso-Alberca et al., 2012).

Emotion awareness begins in infancy and is influenced by the caregiver–child relationship (Tables 5.4, A4.1—oxytocin). Perhaps because fearful facial expressions may convey important threat-related information, even in infancy, neurological responses to fearful faces are greater than to happy or neutral faces (Bick et al., 2017; Taylor-Colls & Fearon, 2015; Chapter 5). Recognition of sad faces continues to mature into late childhood and adolescence (Bick et al., 2017). As early as age six and generally by age 11, children are able to understand mixed or blended emotions, and diverse emotions arising in one person toward another person or situation (Steele & Steele, 2005). Children first recognize, reflect on, and make judgments about their own emotions; then they generalize to other people. Often, a child's social competence is assessed based on the type/nature, frequency, and duration of her/his expressed emotions.

Taking the Perspective of Others and Empathy

Perspective-taking—ability to understand the perceptual, cognitive, emotional, or motivational reactions of other people, even when they are different from one's own (Boltz et al., 2015; Table 1.2)—has been described as the ability to *walk in another's shoes* or as imagining the world from another's vantage point or frame of reference (see Boltz et al., 2015; Galinsky, Ku, & Wang, 2005). Cognitive empathy (perspective-taking), affective empathy (sharing of emotional states), and somatic empathy (bodily reactions) have been studied as distinct aspects of empathy (Liu et al., 2018; Glossary). Perspective-taking does not require identification with another; it involves simply recognizing another's emotions. Affective perspective-taking is believed to elicit stronger empathic concern and responding (more helping). Perspective-taking is critical to an ability to differentiate between personal and others' emotional reactions (e.g., distress; Schonert-Reichl, 2012). It has a survival value (Decety & Jackson, 2004)—e.g., it helps to recognize the intentions of others and helps courtship (important to perpetuating the species).

Perspective-taking requires cognitive as well as other skills (e.g., mirroring). Even though similar past experience may not influence emotions toward another person, similarity between one's own and another's past experience makes it subjectively easier to take that person's perspective—especially with greater similarity and more reflection on the experience (Gerace, Day, Casey, & Mohr, 2015; N = 164). Human offspring first learn about perspectives within the context of joint attentional engagement (sharing perceptions and experiences, Moll & Meltzoff, 2011; Tables 5.3–5.4). That is, the early ability and motivation to jointly attend to objects and events with caretakers/others lays the foundation for later perspective-taking. Perspective-taking is enhanced by social experiences (e.g., with siblings) and by good language skills. With increasing maturity, children take into account more information relevant to a situation. They realize that different people can react differently or view things from a different vantage point. They begin to be able to assess the perspectives of several people from a third-party, unbiased perspective, and they can imagine how culture, group, or social values influence perceptions (Selman & Byrne, 1974).

Currently, egocentric thinking is most people's default perspective (Knowles, 2014). As well, some evidence suggests a decline in empathy in the US between 1979 and 2009 (Konrath, O'Brien, & Hsing, 2011), along with an increase in narcissism and individuality (and a decrease in donations and volunteering; Boltz et al., 2015). Understanding instructions requires an ability to perceive what another is perceiving (from their vantage point) and may include recognition of the person's goals or beliefs. Studies show that around half the time, even adults fail to use information about another's perspective and instead use their own (egocentric) viewpoint when trying to follow another's instructions (Hillebrandt, Dumontheil, Blakemore, & Rosier, 2013).

Perspective-taking includes understanding how objects look to another person (e.g., concrete objects, circumstances) as well as how another feels and thinks. For adults, correlation was found between the ability to take the visuospatial perspective of another (Erle & Topolinski, 2015)—e.g., recognizing what they are viewing (Bukowski, Hietanen, & Samson, 2016)—and empathic perspective-taking. Individuals who use perspective transformations generally have performed better on visuospatial perspective-taking tasks than those who employ object rotation. Conson et al. (2015) found that individuals with AuSD mainly rely on mental object rotation, whereas typical youth adopt an imagining oneself in the other's position strategy. Youth with AuSD also had more difficulties inhibiting other-perspective when directed to keep one's own point of view.

Mirror Neurons

Emotions, actions, and sensations (e.g., physical touch) experienced by one individual are activated automatically—in the same neural network—in an observer of those emotions, actions, and sensations, via the brain's *mirror neuron system*. Hence, both experiencing and witnessing disgust on another person's face activate the same neural structure at the same overlapping location (Gallese, Eagle, & Migone, 2007). Observing a picture of a facial expression has resulted in spontaneous and rapid electromyographic responses in the observer's corresponding facial muscles. The mirroring response occurred even when a final critical part of the observed action was hidden and even when only associated sounds were produced (e.g., eating noises). The shared neural activation pattern and its results may constitute a fundamental biological basis for understanding another's mind and mental states (Gallese et al., 2007). Empathic response does not literally mirror another's behavior; rather empathic attunement enables empathic understanding, which can eventually lead to complementary or modulating responses to another. Children with AuSD and those with pervasive developmental disorder appear to have a deficit in the mirror neuron system, even though non-social intelligence may be preserved in AuSD (Brüne & Brüne-Cohrs, 2006; Dawson et al., 2002; Gallese et al., 2007; Kajiume et al., 2013). Reflective neural activation also has implications for the therapy process. Physical mirroring may occur when rapport or connection is established. A therapist is likely to experience feelings and emotions similar to the patient's, including the patient's unconscious attempts to induce certain emotions in the therapist.

The Need for Perspective-Taking

Perspective-taking skills are important to the ability to have empathy for others, to appropriately interpret and respond to others' behaviors, to influence others, to create narratives, to foster harmony, and to express and understand humor (Schonert-Reichl, 2012; Semrud-Clikeman & Glass, 2010). For adults, it is a part of leadership skills and can be protective—e.g., physicians perceived as empathetic have fewer malpractice suits, higher patient treatment-adherence, better clinical outcomes, and higher patient satisfaction (Boltz et al., 2015).

Narratives. Pragmatic skills—e.g., ability to initiate conversations, respond socially, and acknowledge turn-taking cues—and an appreciation of the role of mental states in predicting and explaining behavior are essential to the ability to narrate stories—e.g., autobiographical and storytelling (Fernandez, 2013). Narrative development is apparent in increasing ability to integrate, logically and cohesively, an individual's motivations and the role of mental states in predicting and explaining behavior as well as apparent in the ability to provide a sequence of events and themes that form a story (Fernandez, 2013; Peterson & McCabe, 1991). Young children's narratives tend to increase (ages three to five) with a mother's prompting and early elaborative speech (Chapter 5).

Overcoming Rejection. Social threat appears to motivate a shift to others' perspectives—i.e., rejection increases social perspective-taking (Knowles, 2014). Perspective-taking may be adaptive for the socially rejected, because it improves social coordination, fosters social bonding, and may permit better understanding of reasons for rejection (Galinsky et al., 2005; Knowles, 2014). Although cognitive busy-ness disrupts a shift in perspectives that normally occurs after rejection, rejected people have been motivated to exert extra effort to take others' perspectives (Knowles, 2014).

Fostering Harmony. Perspective-taking is important to increasing social bonds and social harmony (e.g., Galinsky et al., 2005) and to reducing conflict between groups. Both empathic concern and perspective-taking are common targets in prejudice reduction interventions (e.g., see Levin et al., 2015). Evidence suggests that perspective-taking leads people to see more of themselves in others, and it affects how they evaluate and describe others (Galinsky et al., 2005). When someone takes a person's perspective, they are more likely to see the person, their point of view, and their peer groups in a much more positive light (Goldstein, Vezich, & Shapiro, 2014). Both taking the perspective of another and perceiving another is taking one's own perspective have been associated with an increased liking for, greater sense of self–other overlap, compassion toward, and more help provided to that person (i.e., more prosocial behavior, Goldstein et al., 2014). Perspective-taking efforts must be perceived as successful to enhance self–other effects.

Fostering Empathy. Empathy has positively correlated with an ability to identify and describe personal emotions and to recognize others' perspectives (Grynberg et al., 2010; Table 1.2). These skills are believed to foster empathy and sympathy and, thus, foster more and higher-quality prosocial behaviors. For example, youth who engage in altruistic and other forms of helping behaviors generally have good perspective-taking skills, among other qualities—e.g., sympathy, a sense of responsibility (Eisenberg, Fabes, & Spinrad, 2007; Laible, Eye, & Carlo, 2008). Youth who perpetrate social cruelty (e.g., relational or physically aggressive bullying) tend to lack empathy, compassion, and, sometimes, lack perspective-taking skills (Cunningham, 2007; Nader, 2012c). However, children who bully or manipulate others may be good at understanding others and use it for gain or effect. Children who are well liked are less likely than poorly liked children to have negative outcomes—e.g., psychopathology, behavior problems (see Gerson, Bekkering, & Hunnius, 2017). Children who are good at understanding others' motives are often more popular.

Conclusions

Stress and trauma can have deleterious effects on children, including effects on important developmental domains. Stressors may negatively influence brain and skill development. Among the domains influenced by parenting, trauma, stress, and other variables are executive functions, language skills, social skills, normal ability to play, humor, and self-skills—e.g., self-regulation, self- and emotion awareness, and perspective-taking skills. Skills are interrelated and build on earlier stages of development. Interruptions in skill development may cause significant problems.

For optimal development, infants and children need sensitive, synchronous, and trustworthy care in an enriched environment. The absence of these, failure of protection, or exposure to trauma may waylay the progression or emergence of developmental skills. From a prevention perspective, it is essential to recognize the levels of adversity that may undermine life trajectories for specific age groups. Pre-natal and early environmental conflict, caregiver separations, and recognized traumas (e.g., violence, disasters, neglect) may handicap a child through life (e.g., in goal achievement, interpersonally, emotionally; Boxes 3.1, 3.2). As shown in deprivation studies (e.g., institutional or parental neglect), without timely repair, lack of sensitive care, synchrony, and appropriate, enriching stimulation for an infant or young child may have ongoing ill effects on development, mental health, and quality of life (e.g., Young et al., 2017). For children, treatment of faulty caregiver–child relationships is as important as other posttrauma interventions.

2 Effects of Trauma and Adversity on Developmental Domains

According to Sapolsky (1998), trauma is one of the means by which an individual is "no longer himself" but is a product of "the biology that is distorting him." Non-traumatic adversity—e.g., pre- or post-natal family conflict; faulty attachments; child chronic illness, homelessness—as well as traumatic adversity may disrupt or influence brain, personality, and skill development. Both can be significantly life changing—e.g., lead to an over-reactive stress response system (e.g., HPA axis). Adverse experiences that may traumatize happen daily, worldwide. Around 70–80% of adults and two thirds of children have been directly exposed to traumatic events (Breslau, 2009; see Nader & Fletcher, 2014)—e.g., severe accidents (e.g., vehicle, plane, ship; oil tanker; burns); disasters such as fires (e.g., wildfires, residence/building fires, arson), floods, hurricanes (e.g., Florence, Harvey, Irma, Katrina; Boxes 1.1, 1.2, 3.4, 13.2), earthquakes, tornadoes, mudslides, and avalanches; parental death; interpersonal violence such as child abuse or neglect, sexual crimes, inter-parental abuse, school shootings, other violent crimes (e.g., assault, murder, armed robbery, Boxes 2.1, 3.2), wars (Boxes 2.2b, 13.1, 16.3); and more. Children also have endured losses during or related to traumatic events and/or have endured the perpetual stress of displacement from home, deprivation, community violence, or having a parent away at war. Potentially traumatic events appear to have increased, e.g., since warming trends have combined with natural events (e.g., hurricanes, fires; Lindsey, 2017), and the internet has been used for bullying or to encourage terrorism. For example, vehicles plowing into crowds increased after a terrorist website advocated it.

Most children show resilience after traumatic events (up to 70%). Nevertheless, trauma may delay or interrupt a number of developmental skills (e.g., self-skills) and result in a wide variety of symptoms. Across 27 studies of neuropsychological functioning, compared to non-exposed comparisons, a significant number of trauma-exposed children ages 0–18 showed cognitive deficits, visuo-spatial deficits, poorer language skills, deficits in information processing, learning and memory problems, and poorer executive skills (Malarbi, Abu-Rayya, Muscara, & Stargatt, 2017). Those with posttraumatic stress disorder (PTSD) showed lower intelligence levels and visuospatial skills than without PTSD. Some traumas (e.g., deprivation) may alter the neural correlates underlying multiple cognitive domains, and may not be fully reversible (Stamoulis et al., 2017). Evidence suggests a more persistent course of PTSD for children compared to adults (Scheeringa, 2011; Scheeringa, Zeanah, Myers, & Putnam, 2005). As will be seen in age-related chapters, general stressors also may define a child's life trajectory—e.g., early family conflict may alter personality and functioning. Insecure attachments to caregivers may shape a child's need-driven behaviors and style of inter-relating with others across life (Chapter 4; Tables A3.1–A3.4).

Box 2.1 Trauma and Attentional Focus

- John, age 10, was walking home from school when he realized the popping sound was gunfire. A boy dropped, bleeding, and a teenage boy with a gun ran away carrying a satchel. The boy looked right at him and pointed his gun at him, but he didn't fire. He pulled out the phone his mother gave him for emergencies and called 911, but the whole time he was afraid the shooter would come back and kill him, because he saw the whole thing. He had nightmares. Every time he heard a "pop" or a "bang" in the classroom, he jumped and turned to see what it was. He couldn't pay attention in school, because he was looking for the next bad thing to happen, was distracted by sounds, felt anxious and antsy, and feared the shooter would find him and shoot him, because he called the police.
- Celia, age 11, was molested repeatedly by her live-in uncle until she was removed to a foster home. In school, the teacher said she would space out a lot or seem to be daydreaming and didn't pay attention in school (dissociation).

Note:
All case examples are disguised, may be combined cases, and have had details changed to protect individuals.

Box 2.2 Long-Term Memory and Trauma

a. When she was 2.5, JA was molested by a male, adolescent babysitter (Hewitt, 1994). She became aggressive, angry, had disturbed sleep, could not be soothed or calmed, and had expressive language and social skill lags. Her parents disciplined her for her infractions by spanking her. At age four, when her mother began to educate her about not letting anyone touch her bottom, she revealed that her cousin had done so. After disclosure, sleep and behavior problems diminished. Despite earlier speech and language problems and reduced language when the abuse occurred, JA clearly articulated the details of the abuse to a therapist (see Hewitt, 1994 for more detail).
b. When Luka was 10 and her little sister was three, they experienced the chronic stress of war. When Luka was 12, they moved to a northern European country. When she was an adolescent, she and her girlfriends would sit around talking. On any given topic, Luka gave more general memories rather than the elaborate descriptions of experiences given by other girls her age who had not been exposed to war. For example, when asked what she did for the holidays, she might say, "We went to Serbia. There really wasn't anything to do there" without telling that she stayed with her grandmother, saw relatives for the first time in years, and visited places where she had played as a child and had been afraid during the war. Her friends provided descriptions of multiple activities and experiences—e.g., movies, feasts, presents, people—with details such as their feelings and how things looked. When asked about what made her afraid or when she felt the happiest, Luka might say, "When I lived in Serbia" without elaborating.

Note:
All case examples are disguised, may be combined cases, and have had details changed to protect individuals.

For children with or without PTSD, trauma's effects may evolve over time—e.g., with age-related changes in understanding, in perceptions of what is most relevant, or in significance issues might have (Nader, 2008). Because growth is not always linear, it may not be easy to recognize such changes in youth (Casey, Jones, & Somerville, 2011)—e.g., a normal plateau or lag occurs in some skills following puberty onset (Blakemore & Choudhury, 2006). Additionally, secondary stressors after traumatic events—e.g., lost property, jobs/incomes, resources, status, locations, routines—add to a child's stress and sense of loss. For example, after Hurricane Katrina, although gender and exposure levels accounted for most of the variance in PTSD symptoms (62%), stressors such as loss of clothes and toys, damage to a home, parent's unemployment, moving to a new place, going to a new school, moving away from friends, and/or living away from parents strongly related to the degree of PTSD symptoms as well (35%; Osofsky et al., 2009).

After traumas, a number of symptoms are common to all age groups but may manifest differently and require different versions of an intervention (Nader, 2008). For example, while children below a certain age tend to take things literally and concretely, increased concreteness has been observed in trauma victims of all ages (Punamäki, Qouta, & El-Sarraj, 2001). All age groups may regress following traumatic events. Accordingly, the ways that supporting individuals assist for these problems are likely to vary somewhat by the youth's age, personality, and symptom set as well as by functioning age level. For moderately or severely traumatized children, after a few weeks or months, parents sometimes seem to forget what was normal for a child—e.g., related to initially reported new symptoms, a year later a parent may say, "S/he was always like that" (Nader, 2008). Such a parental or peer attitude may add to a youth's sense of loss and may affect what a clinician learns about a child. Some of the possible effects of stress and/or trauma on developmental domains (see Chapter 1) are presented briefly here and are discussed in age-specific chapters. After a discussion of general distress, life trajectories, and poly-victimization or cumulative trauma, this chapter discusses the stress response system and discusses trauma's impact on specific developmental domains, on self-skills, and on psychopathology.

General Distress

Although there are many studies on variables such as attachment or divorce, few studies were found that specifically assessed children's general distress rather than their traumatic stress exposure and reactions. In addition to the effects of chronic or severe stressors, distress that is considered non-traumatic, such as stress with parents, in school, and/or in communities, has been associated with problems similar to those found for traumas—e.g., misattributions of emotions, ADHD symptoms, and difficulties in problem-solving (Fishbein et al., 2009). Even light levels such as no relief from nighttime light exposure or low levels of winter light have been related to anxiety and depression (Fonken et al., 2009). Low socioeconomic status (SES) has been associated with cognitive delays and emotional problems (e.g., 6–13 IQ points lower than norm; Britto & Noble, 2014). Having a depressed mother has been related to increased chronic and episodic stress with peers, with mothers, and with family (Feurer, Hammen, & Gibb, 2016). Insecure attachments have been related to poorer social skills, and temperamental negative or inhibited children have also had social difficulties. Supervisory neglect (Glossary) or inconsistent care has been related to reduced emotional well-being, anxiety, and depression (Font & Berger, 2015). Parental divorce has been linked to the risk of mental health problems (Chapters 9, 10; Boring et al., 2015; blunted cortisol, Mahrer et al., 2014 [see Chapters 4, 6]). Lack of having a best friend has been related to a number of risks—e.g., increased loneliness, risk of victimization by peers, lack of social skills, increased timidity and sensitivity, internalizing, guilt, and anger (Rubin, Bukowski, Parker, & Bowker, 2008). Whereas popular children have been described by observers, teachers, and peers as friendly, cooperative, sociable, sensitive, and rarely interfering with the goals of others, rejected children were described as either withdrawn, timid, and wary or as aggressive and disruptiveness (see Rubin et al., 2008). Aggression and disruptiveness have led to rejection, unless children had other positive qualities or, in older child groups, were male.

General negative affect (e.g., anger, sadness, or anxiety) has interfered with the ability to attend to environmental stimuli and to persevere through difficult tasks, and undifferentiated negative affect (lack of discrete emotions) has significantly predicted lack of planning and impulsivity (Tomko et al., 2015; Chapter 3). Attachment issues, which may arise from and/or translate into distress in family relationships, are discussed in Chapter 4 and in age-related chapters. Insecure and disorganized attachments with caregivers and related styles of inter-relating have been associated with troubled interpersonal relationships, aspects of behavior (e.g., lower empathy and lower prosocial behavior), and mental health problems across the lifespan (e.g., Magai, Frias, & Shaver, 2018; Shaver et al., 2018). Personality and genetic factors that may relate to distress (e.g., negative emotionality; stress sensitivity) are also discussed in other chapters.

Parents' own distress and parenting have also influenced children's development. Parental distress is believed to interfere with sensitive parenting (De Vries et al., 2017; Giallo et al., 2015). As will be discussed in Chapter 11, fathers' persistent and increasing distress and hostility has been related to lower positive parenting than shown by low-distress fathers (Giallo et al., 2015). Fathers' self-reported pre-natal stress and hostility and harsh discipline in the child's preschool years as well as mother-reported family distress have been linked to child's early elementary school bullying behavior (peer nomination; De Vries et al., 2017; Chapter 12). Mothers' distress after divorce has been related to blunted cortisol in young adulthood for children, and, for adolescents, it marginally predicted blunted cortisol in young adulthood (if childhood stress was low; blunted cortisol is linked to psychopathology, Mahrer et al., 2014; Chapter 6). The separation of children from their parents became a topic of concern after the Trump administration separated illegal immigrant children from their parents. Evidence has shown that childhood separations from parents can have deleterious effects on life trajectories (e.g., psychopathology, Paksarian et al., 2015; Chapter 7). A robust body of evidence has shown that early institutionalization has been related to developmental damage across diverse domains—e.g., cognitive function, neurodevelopment, physical growth, behavior, and social-psychological health (see Berens & Nelson, 2015). Effects have been especially pronounced when individualized caregiving is low, and when deprivation coincides with sensitive periods of early development.

Some researchers have included emotional abuse among a list of stressors, while others recognize it as a form of traumatic stress. Emotional abuse includes such parental behaviors as thwarting of the child's emotional needs, persistently or extremely; insensitivity to a child's developmental level; communicating that the child is flawed, unlovable/unloved, worthless, unwanted, unsafe, or only there to meet another's needs; and/or exploiting or rejecting, spurning, or terrorizing (see Spinazzola et al., 2014). Emotional neglect includes parental lack of emotional attunement, nurturance, and responsiveness. The results for the child may include such problems as poor sense of psychological safety, a variety of maladaptive problems and behaviors, and/or disrupted normative development with such problems as poor emotion regulation, low self-acceptance and -esteem, low autonomy, and poor self-sufficiency. Even having a mother who does not find a child pleasing has been linked to problems in the child's development (e.g., language delays; Sylvestre & Merette, 2010). For a national sample of children with lifetime histories of maltreatment, although profiles were distinct from physical or sexual abuse, psychologically maltreated youth exhibited greater or equal baseline levels of behavior problems, symptoms (e.g., PTSD, internalizing), and disorders as physically or sexually abused youth (N = 5616; Spinazzola et al., 2014). Psychological maltreatment was the strongest predictor of internalizing and of substance abuse. It predicted externalizing as well as physical abuse and better than sexual abuse. When psychological maltreatment co-occurred with physical or sexual abuse, it exacerbated most outcomes, suggesting its importance as a focus of intervention for youth.

Both distress and traumas may interfere with body regulation. For example, both stress and trauma have negatively affected sleep regulation, which in turn can have negative repercussions across the lifespan (APA, 2013; Marks, 2018; Chapters 5, 7, 8, 9, 12, 15). Sleep influences functioning throughout the day—e.g., coping, cognitive ability, self-concept. Studies have shown an association between sleep deprivation and increased stress as well as a number of other poor-sleep-related negative outcomes such as obesity, depression, pain, low quality of life, and health problems (e.g., osteoarthritis, inflammatory diseases; adult studies, Marks, 2018). A history of childhood adversity (e.g., emotional neglect) has been related to poor sleep during stressful life transitions, such as entering university (John-Henderson, Williams, Brindle, & Ginty, 2018). Poor sleep may exacerbate problems that interfere with sleep. For example, pain or stress may interfere with sleep, and poor sleep may worsen pain or stress. Stress and trauma also have been related to dysregulation in eating habits—either in under- or overeating (e.g., eating disorders; Chapters 3, 4, 15).

Life Trajectories

Although traumas also may be followed by growth and other positive consequences (Box 6.3, Chapter 7—grief), negative effects of trauma may be persistent, cascading, or evolving (Boxes 3.1, 3.2, 3.5; Chapter 3). For children, life trajectories may be undermined greatly by stress that overwhelms or persists; by traumatic reactions and altered neurochemistry; by failure of the caregiver–child relationship to protect, soothe, teach, delight in, and provide sensitive care for a child; and by difficulties contributed by genes and temperaments. Feldman (2015) found that war-exposed children with chronic PTSD were much less competent in meeting the next developmental transition from early to middle childhood (ages 2–5, 7–8). They showed the worst stress-hormone-related outcomes (e.g., cortisol), affiliation-hormone-related outcomes (e.g., oxytocin), relationships with parents, and psychopathology. Personality and/or attachment styles may contribute to posttrauma outcomes, and/or become exaggerated or changed following traumas. Parenting and attachment issues cannot be ignored at any age. Combined symptoms or disorders have been even more foreboding. For example, youth with both anxiety and depressive problems have shown greater chronicity, higher recurrence and suicide rates, greater functional impairment, poorer treatment outcomes, and greater mental health service utilization (Moser et al., 2015a). All of these issues must be addressed in preventive or posttrauma interventions. As a society and as clinicians it is our responsibility to provide protections, preventive measures, treatments, and repairing experiences to permit and promote each child's normal life trajectory. For example, among preventive interventions, school programs are associated with increased resilience and reduced posttrauma symptoms (Chapters 13, 16).

Poly-Victimization or Cumulative Trauma

Cumulative trauma—multiple traumas, especially multiple types of trauma (Briere, Dietrich, & Semple, 2016; Cloitre et al., 2009)—or *poly-victimization* (Finkelhor, Ormrod, & Turner, 2007)—exposure to multiple types of trauma—is associated with increased symptomatology (Glossary; Ayer et al., 2018; Finkelhor, Shattuck, Turner, & Ormrod, 2014), with significant comorbidity (Hodges et al., 2013), with symptom complexity, and has explained a large proportion of associations between individual forms of victimization and symptom levels (Glossary; Hodges et al., 2013; Martin, Cromer, DePrince, & Freyd, 2013; Turner, Finkelhor, & Ormrod, 2010). A number of researchers include four or more traumas in poly-victimized groups; for others the cut-off has been seven. Finkelhor et al. (2014) found that while older children were likely to have more victimizations, children at higher levels of victimization in each age group were much more likely to have higher levels of other types of adversities (e.g., illnesses, family problems, accidents) and to be distressed (nationally representative sample, N = 4046 ages 0–17). They set thresholds for poly-victims at five or more for ages 2–5; at six or more for ages 6–9; seven or more for 10–13; and eight or more for ages 14–17 (Table 15.1). Some researchers suggest that certain traumas (e.g., sexual abuse) be weighted more heavily than others, whereas others suggest a more individualized approach to exposure and vulnerability (see Ford, Charak, Modrowski, & Kerig, 2018a). Multiple methods of identification have found poly-victims, each group with unique profiles (Ford & Delker, 2018; Table 15.1).

For adults with cumulative traumas before age 18, researchers have observed a significant linear relationship between number of childhood trauma types and number of symptom-cluster types (symptom complexity) reported simultaneously in adulthood (Briere, Kaltman, & Green, 2008; Briere et al., 2016; Cloitre et al., 2009). A history of more than one type of childhood trauma is related to increased likelihood of a number of disorders, including psychosis in adulthood (Alvarez et al., 2015; Shevlin, Dorahy, & Adamson, 2007). Additional victimizations are common for aggressive traumas (Finkelhor et al., 2007; see Nader & Fletcher, 2014). Pathways to revictimization may involve failure to recognize risky situations or betrayal or involve dissociation (see Nader & Fletcher, 2014). Strom et al. (2018) found that half of adults who had experienced other severe violence in childhood were also bullied as youth. Subsequent victimizations may not match the original form of victimization. For example, Hébert and colleagues (2016) found that many child sexual assault victims were also victimized by their peers at school—60% reported being picked on, 51% reported verbal victimization, and 35%, physical victimization. Peer victimization has increased the likelihood of dissociation and PTSD symptoms up to three-fold.

Cumulative traumatization has been related to pathological dissociation (N = 89; Chiu et al., 2015). While childhood (not adulthood) traumas were important to the development of non-taxon dissociation, adulthood trauma exacerbated the effects of childhood nonspecific dissociation on the emergence of pathological dissociation. De Bellis, Woolley, and Hooper (2013) found that maltreated youth with PTSD experienced more maltreatment types as well as greater physical abuse severity, PTSD and dissociative symptoms, and greater internalizing and total behavior problems. They had lower levels of functioning (general; lower academic achievement) compared with maltreated youth without PTSD. Finkelhor et al. (2007) suggest more than one possible mechanism by which poly-victimization leads to more severe and less reversible outcomes—e.g., multiple stressor exposures may lead to more people, places, and things that serve as traumatic reminders, interfering with coping; self-blame may be more likely after more than one exposure. Cumulative traumas have been related to the intensity of dissociative symptomatology—patients without multiple traumas had an average Dissociative Experiences Scale (DES) score of 6.64; healthy controls, DES average = 7.43; and poly-traumatized individuals (with four or more types of trauma), DES average = 27.27 (Alvarez et al., 2015).

Trauma's Effects on Neurobiology and Development

The body's stress response system mobilizes reactions to danger and may be affected by trauma or adversity (see Nader, 2008; Stein & Kendall, 2004). The Hypothalamic-Pituitary-Adrenal (HPA) and other brain regions may be altered by stress. Stressors also may affect the range of developmental domains.

The Stress Response System

Limbic and cortical regions relay information about threats that can activate or terminate stress response systems—e.g., detect, integrate, and/or respond to threat (e.g., amygdala, hippocampus, prefrontal cortex; Hostinar & Gunnar, 2013; Luyten & Fonagy, in press; Table A4.2). Early parental support corresponds to amygdala-dependent emotional circuitry that can appropriately differentiate threatening from nonthreatening stimuli (Hostinar & Gunnar, 2013). In contrast, when biological risk factors combine with trauma (e.g., child abuse), altered amygdala development may be perpetually primed for stress responsiveness. Excessive or age-inappropriate stress—possibly combined with stress sensitivity—may trigger a developmental cascade with increasing impairments in reward sensitivity, autonomy, agency, capacity for mentalizing (Glossary) and/or social cognition—all relevant to the emergence of internalizing disorders, which additionally interfere with development (Luyten & Fonagy, in press). Trauma combined with genetic factors (e.g., FKBP5 variants) can lead to long-term changes in skills, such as stress regulation (Kohrt et al., 2015).

Childhood traumas have affected multiple areas of brain and nervous system development (e.g., Botterill et al., 2014; hippocampus, Carrion et al., 2010a; may cause kindling, Glossary, Dackis et al., 2012; HPA axis, autonomic system), including areas critically involved in inhibiting the stress response (e.g., Carrion et al., 2007). Brain regions such as the HPA axis, the sympathetic nervous system (SNS), and the serotonin system are negatively affected by trauma (Kavanaugh & Holler, 2014; Chapter 14). Under normal circumstances, through several feedback control loops influencing regulatory centers in the brain, the HPA axis constantly attempts to maintain the day-to-day exposure of tissues to normal cortisol levels. Childhood trauma has altered stress reactivity by altering HPA axis functioning—e.g., has interfered with a feedback loop that inhibits activation (Gillespie, Phifer, Bradley, & Ressler, 2009; Roy et al., 2010). While the HPA axis also has positive effects on functioning—e.g., supports positive mood; prepares the body for coping with threat/stress—it is responsive to many stressors, and its products have widespread effects that influence neurodevelopment, behavior, and health (see Koss & Gunnar, 2018). For humans, the stress hormone, cortisol, is the predominant glucocorticoid of interest (Glossary). Long-term or severe exposure to cortisol can have damaging effects on the body. Insufficient serotonin, a hormone important to mood and emotion regulation, may result in over-activation of the HPA system and release of increased cortisol. Prolonged activation may lead to over-activation or under-activation (hyper- or hypo-cortisolism; McCleery & Harvey, 2004). Either hypo- or hyper-cortisolism may lead to altered brain function, to mental health problems, and/or to disease (Alexander et al., 2018; Carpenter et al., 2009; McEwen & Wingfield, 2010; Weems & Carrion, 2009). Individuals with traumatic or chronic stress may initially show frequent and prolonged cortisol elevations, then low or blunted cortisol levels that may co-occur with the hyper-responsivity of other stress systems (Koss & Gunnar, 2018). Blunted cortisol has been linked to a number of problems—e.g., suicidality, lower memory function (with lower income), mood disorders, conduct problems, and aggression (Bernard et al., 2015a; O'Connor et al., 2018; Raffington, Prindle, Keresztes, & Shing, 2018).

Chronic hyperactivity of HPA axis and consequent long-term exposure to stress hormones (e.g., cortisol) also can result in neuronal loss in a brain region that directs learning and memory (hippocampus; Cicchetti, 2003; see Nader, 2008; Sapolsky, 1998, 2000; Stein & Kendall, 2004), along with inhibited neuronal regrowth (neurogenesis), impairments to other brain processes, and cognitive and affective functional impairment. Suicide victims with a history of maltreatment have had greater decreases in the hippocampal mechanisms that inhibit HPA axis activity than individuals with sudden accidental death and no abuse (McGowan et al., 2009). Chronic stress early in development has led to long-term dysfunction in the mesolimbic dopaminergic pathway, contributing to depressive-like behavior—e.g., reductions in motivation to obtain rewards, social motivation, and acquisition and expression of Pavlovian appetitive conditioning (Auerbach, Admon, & Pizzagalli, 2014).

Other Brain Effects

During periods of brain maturation, stress and elevated levels of stress hormones and neurotransmitters may lead to adverse brain development through delays in myelination, apoptosis (programmed cell death), abnormalities in developmentally appropriate pruning, the inhibition of neurogenesis, or other stress-induced decreases in brain growth factors (see De Bellis & Zisk, 2014). Trauma may affect multiple brain regions and their connectivity. Brain changes have been evident with or without overt psychopathology. Such changes can predict future symptomatology (McCrory, Gerin, & Viding, 2017)—e.g., altered threat responsiveness, changed reward processing, increased effort to self-regulate. For example, across maltreatment studies, threat processing studies have shown heightened or depressed neural responsiveness in maltreated youth (especially in the amygdala), likely reflecting threat hypervigilance and avoidance respectively (McCrory et al., 2017). Reward processing influences goal-directed behavior. Studies of reward processing usually reported blunted neural response in anticipation and receipt of rewards (especially in striatum), which has been associated with depressive symptomatology. Emotion regulation studies have reported increased activation of the anterior cingulate cortex (ACC) during active emotion regulation, which may reflect greater effortful processing (Table A4.2). Atypical connectivity and focal activity in fronto-limbic neural circuits and in ventral ACC and amygdala may reflect increased allocation of cognitive resources in order to effortfully modulate emotional responses (McLaughlin et al., 2015c)—e.g., increased dorsal ACC activity during error monitoring and inhibition (related to attentional control; executive control; McCrory et al., 2017). Hence traumas may result in the necessity of having to expend more effort to process emotions and to self-regulate.

Language Development and Trauma

Language development may be undermined, e.g., by premature birth, poor hearing, neglect, low verbal interaction, punishment for attempts to speak, or other abuse (Becker-Weidman, 2009; Charollais, 2014; Manso, Garcia-Baamonde, & Alonso, 2011). Early traumas may delay or alter language development with ongoing repercussions (e.g., related to sensory modulation dysfunction, Glossary; Atchison, 2007). Loss of a parent also may interrupt language development, especially if the parent was the one who best understood what the child was trying to say (Atchison, 2007). Loss of one's best interpreter can be difficult at any age.

In 2000, for general disability, typically developing children had a maltreatment prevalence rate of 9%, whereas children with a range of disabilities had a maltreatment prevalence rate of 31% (3.4 times more likely to be maltreated; Sullivan & Knutson, 2000). Disabled children were more likely to be maltreated at younger ages. Children with speech and language impairments had essentially five times the risk for physical abuse or neglect, three times the risk for sexual abuse, and seven times for emotional maltreatment. Maltreated children have shown poorer skills in expressive language, receptive vocabulary, and language (see Byrne, Lyddiard, & Furniss, 2017). Exposure to violence—witnessed or experienced—or to neglect has been related to language delays. Children exposed to mothers' intimate partner violence have scored significantly lower on verbal ability than same-age children in a national sample (N = 1787 preschoolers, Graham-Bermann et al., 2010). Maltreated children placed in out-of-home care and severely neglected children have had language delays, even if the severe neglect began before nine months of age (Byrne et al., 2017; Sylvestre & Merette, 2010). Although an accumulation of biological and psychological risk factors appeared to have a "pile-up" effect on language development, the effects of neglect on cognitive development had a stronger influence on language delays than total risk factors (N = 68, ages 2–36 months, Sylvestre & Merette, 2010). Mothers' own abuse/neglect experience or mother not finding the child pleasing also were related to language delays (Sylvestre & Merette, 2010). By school age, abused youth have had more severe language delays (Atchison, 2007). For neglected children, exposure to early intervention programs that promote increased quantity and quality of language stimulation for the child have improved outcomes (Sylvestre & Merette, 2010)—e.g., engaging in social, play, and communication interactions with foster siblings (Byrne et al., 2017). Child Welfare supervised children placed in early care and education programs—e.g., Head Start, preschool—have shown better language skills than those not enrolled (N = 1652; Merritt & Klein, 2015). It is important to recognize the other effects of trauma on children when addressing language delays—e.g., effects on the child's individual identity formation, sensory systems—e.g., noise sensitivity, neurological development, executive functions such as memory and attention, socials skills, and ability to make and maintain relationships (Byrne et al., 2017).

The Dialogical Self and Trauma

Patterns of internal dialogue are influenced, from childhood onward, by caregiver–child and other relationships and by impactful experiences such as traumas or successes (Chapters 1, 4). From a multiple-self perspective, psychopathology has been associated with lower levels of self-complexity—i.e., use/awareness of fewer internal voices, low complexity and excessive rigidity (e.g., personality disorders, PD); dominance of negative internal voices (e.g., depression); inability to organize aspects of self or organization involves low complexity of self-aspects (e.g., schizophrenia); disorganization of internal voices or lack of an observer-self—e.g., express one unrelated self-facet after another, unpredictably and without reference to the other facets (narrative disorganization, e.g., can happen in schizophrenia, BPD, dissociative disorder); and/or difficulty recognizing personal thoughts and affects and the antecedents to affects (e.g., complicated trauma, personality disorders) (Bateman & Fonagy, 2004; Dimaggio et al., 2006, 2010). Reduced ability to use a range of internal voices has been observed in traumatized individuals. One defining impact of a trauma is that it can install a "traumatic self" as the nucleus around which a person's self-narrative develops, consequently elaborating subsequent life experiences that are emotionally congruent with that traumatic self-narrative (Neimeyer, Herrero, & Botella, 2006; see victim coping or mythology, Ford, 2002; Tinnen, Bills, & Gantt, 2002). Regardless of treatment method, individuals with psychopathology have improved—e.g., in emotional state, responses from others—when they were less dominated by a single voice/pattern; were able to generate representations of self and of others more flexibly—e.g., had better recognition of personal and others' wishes, feelings, and behavior; had increased access to formerly suppressed voices; had increased self-reflection (RF) or mentalizing skills—i.e., seeing self from the outside, seeing others from the inside (Fuggle et al., 2015); and had better ability to assimilate problematic internal voices into a broader self-narrative (Dimaggio et al., 2010).

Executive Functions

Both traumas (e.g., emotional and physical neglect) and stressors (e.g., with parents, in school) have been associated with poorer general intelligence and at least one impairment in cognitive functions—e.g., intelligence, problem-solving, cognitive flexibility, decision-making, emotion attributions (Fishbein et al., 2009). Poverty often includes chronic stressors such as noise, household chaos, and conflict among family members, and it has been related to brain changes and to stress sensitivity (Blair & Raver, 2016). Poverty has been linked to reduced brain gray matter in regions related to EFs, academic achievement, school readiness (e.g., frontal and temporal cortex), and elevated cortisol (infancy-age 22; see Blair & Raver, 2016). With or without PTSD, stressors are associated with decrements in general intelligence and problems with higher-order neurocognitive functions (see Fishbein et al., 2009). For children assessed from birth through age nine, early childhood maltreatment was associated with lower age three cognitive skills and more behavior problems and was modestly linked between ages three and nine with children's poorer cognitive skills and greater behavior problem trajectories (ages 3–9; Font & Berger, 2015). As will be noted in age-related chapters, caregivers, child-focused educational support, and high-quality early education have been important to recovery from EF deficits and to children's stress-related physiologic reactivity, cognitive control, and self-regulation (Blair, 2017).

Altered Attentional Focus and Information Processing

Attachment style/history, traits (e.g., genetic, personality), and experience (e.g., intense or traumatic) may change attention and processing by interrupting attention to some things, increasing attention to other things, and altering the way that incoming information is processed. Children with insecure-resistant attachments have shown preoccupations with caretaking relationships and sometimes have held attention away from mainstream peers or lessons (Tables A3.2–3.4; Box 10.2; Chapter 4). Attentional problems have been linked to cognitive problems and to developmental and psychological disorders—e.g., ODD, ADHD, depression, anxiety (Giordano et al., 2017). Attention problems have had problematic effects on other EFs. Selective attention can constrain working memory and inhibition processes (Kane & Engle, 2003; Rose et al., 2012a). In addition, posttrauma neurobiology can impair the brain's ability for flexible thinking (including the shifting of attention) and for learning and reasoning (Nader, 2008; Neimeyer et al., 2006; Siegel, 1999).

Information processing may be significantly and dynamically influenced by traumatic experiences (or by other intense experiences; see Nader, 2008—Chapter 14). Traumas may result in script-like behaviors (Chapter 3) and/or in changes in attentional focus such as selective attention to trauma-related stimuli and emotions, along with negative expectations, which influence behaviors (Box 2.1; Herman, 1997; Nader, 2008; Goodman, Harnett, & Knight, 2018; adults, Bardeen & Read, 2010). For example, youth with multiple exposures in violent communities may develop a "kill or be killed" attitude that increases focus on the potential for another to retaliate and results in anticipatory violent aggression (Garbarino, 1999). On the other hand, youth who show fear in violent communities may invite victimization (Bruyere & Garbarino, 2012; Garbarino, 1999). Children may exhibit rigidly controlled behavior patterns such as compulsive compliance, inflexible rituals, and/or rigidly controlled eating patterns (Finn, Warner, Price, & Spinazzola, 2017).

Some attention or attributional biases may increase both positive and negative behaviors. Bondü (2018) points out that individuals who are altruistically sensitive to injustices toward others or who have a hostile attribution bias have been shown to have selective attention to cues of untrustworthiness and may withdraw cooperation after only slight cues of untrustworthiness. Hostile attribution biases (HAB) have been associated with trauma and have been linked to aggressive behaviors (Helfritz-Sinville & Stanford, 2014; Chapters 3, 15). Across 27 studies, for both genders, HAB was more strongly and consistently related to reactive than to proactive aggression (age range: 7–18; perhaps more strongly for youth who have been victimized; Martinelli et al., 2018). While maltreatment (e.g., neglect) has been related to misattribution of emotions to others (Fishbein et al., 2009), grief has been related to altered attention to facial emotions. For adults with complicated grief, 1.5–3 years after the death, Bullock and Bonanno (2013) found an attention bias away from happy faces in neutral conditions and away from closed-mouth sad faces when primed with the deceased's name.

Memory and Trauma

Young children normally recall memories in general categories and increase in recalling specific memory episodes with age (Burnside et al., 2004). Multiple variables may affect memory—e.g., attachment issues; stress levels; sleep; trauma (e.g., Steenari et al., 2003). While moderate stress levels may assist memory—e.g., strengthen plasticity of the hippocampus (responsible for cold memory; Ruf & Schauer, 2012), traumatic experiences can disrupt many cognitive functions—e.g., memory, concentration, imagination, clarity of thinking, information processing, resulting in delayed or faulty processing of information, poor memory processes, and difficulty reading others' emotions or intent (see Nader, 2008 for a summary). Stress hormones such as adrenalin and glucocorticoids enhance memory, while opioids and GABA or benzodiazepine receptor agonists impair memory (Glossary; McCleery & Harvey, 2004). After traumas, memory may become enhanced for and repeatedly drawn to aspects of the traumatic experience and may be disrupted for other functions (Nader, 2008; Boxes 2.1, 2.2a). Enhanced memory of emotionally arousing stimuli has been well documented (e.g., McCleery & Harvey, 2004)—trauma details may become "etched-in" and long-lasting memories (Koss et al., 1996; Nader, 1997; Pynoos & Eth, 1985; Terr, 1979, 1991). Such memories may replay repeatedly or in response to trauma reminders.

On the other hand, severe or prolonged stress can interfere with memory mechanisms (Bremner, 2003, 2006; Gould et al., 2012; Sapolsky, 1998; Savitz et al., 2007). Severe or repeated traumas may injure or reduce volume in brain regions related to memory (e.g., hippocampus) or other cognitive functions (e.g., prefrontal cortex [PFC]; Bunge & Wright, 2007; Table A4.2). PTSD patients have reported problems with declarative memory (e.g., remembering facts or lists), memory fragmentation, dissociative amnesia (memory gaps), memory problems related to poor concentration (Bremner, 2011), and/or dissociative tendencies (linked to lapses of memory, compromised emotional memory, Oates & Ray, 2008). Greater degrees of brain atrophy (not minimal) have been linked to explicit memory deficits; severe atrophy has predicted severe dissociative symptoms (Bremner, 2003; Sapolsky, 2000; Tables 1.1, A4.2). Aspects of an event may be unavailable to conscious memory (e.g., amnesias).

In the general population, higher levels of children's perceived communication with mothers has been related to increased memory specificity (N = 80; ages 10–13; Bosmans, Dujardin, Raes, & Braet, 2012). Additionally, higher levels of trust in maternal support related to higher self-reported communication about experiences with mothers, which in turn was linked to enhanced retrieval of specific autobiographical memories. Hence, by talking about memories with children, mothers assist youth to have recollection of specific memories. Over-general memory (OGM; Glossary)—nonspecific, autobiographical memory—has been found in relationship to depression, PTSD, impaired problem-solving, and unhealthy repetitive thinking (Bosmans et al., 2012). For children exposed to significant stressors in early and middle childhood, OGM retrieval may initially serve as a protective mechanism that later becomes a risk factor for depression or anxiety (Brennen et al., 2010). Since specific memories may be used as a frame for problem-solving or decision-making, the lack of specific memory retrieval may interfere with those processes (van Daele et al., 2014). Although both depressive symptoms and abuse have been related to OGM, abuse has been related to OGM with low or high depressive symptoms (Valentino, Bridgett, Hayden, & Nuttall, 2012). Distancing coping used by individuals traumatized as children (e.g., sexual abuse) has predicted over-general memory in adolescence and adulthood (Harris et al., 2015a). Individuals with PTSD also have had more difficulty retrieving and disclosing positive events/memories than others (Bedard-Gilligan, Jaeger, Echiverri-Cohen, & Zoellner, 2012; Moore & Zoellner, 2007; Box 2.2b).

Trauma and Inhibition

Although inhibition is essentially the ability to suppress a dominant, automatic or pre-potent response, it also includes attentional, behavioral, thought, and/or emotional control to override a strong internal predisposition or an external lure (Best, Miller, & Jones, 2009; Roskam, Stievenart, Meunier, & Noel, 2014; Chapter 1; Glossary). Trauma has been related to poorer performance on EF skills, including on inhibition tasks, even after controlling for variables such as SES and anxiety (e.g., DePrince, Weinzierl, & Combs, 2009). Deficits in such skills influence other skill development.

Brain regions related to inhibitory control have been affected by traumas. Reduced activation in the rostral anterior cingulate cortex (rACC) has previously been associated with PTSD, anxiety disorders, and fear-inhibition deficits (Stevens et al., 2016). Childhood maltreatment was related to lower inhibition-related activity in rACC and long-lasting reduction in inhibitory PFC activation in individuals with PTSD (not for those without PTSD; Stevens et al., 2016). Decreased rACC activation was linked to more severe depressive symptoms as well. Increased activation in the rACC has been associated with treatment success and spontaneous recovery from PTSD. When individuals with PTSD demonstrate exaggerated fear responses to trauma-related stimuli with difficulties inhibiting fear even in safe environments, it has been described as reduced fear-inhibition and decreased contextual cue processing (e.g., do not recognize safe contexts). Although a similar study was not found for youth, combat PTSD patients have shown behavioral and neural deficits in inhibition and contextual cue processing (van Rooij et al., 2015). For example, they failed to deactivate the motor cortex during response-inhibition, and they showed decreased cue processing combined with decreased activation of brain regions important to regulating attention (right inferior frontal gyrus). Inhibition and cue processing deficits were unaffected by treatment and may represent either vulnerability factors or the scars of PTSD. In contrast, increased activation of regions important to contextual cue processing (left inferior parietal lobe [IPL]) at baseline and reduced activation of IPL posttreatment predicted percentage of symptom improvement. This suggests that contextual cue processing may facilitate the effects of psychotherapy.

Trauma and Humor

Of course, it isn't reasonable to try to force or cajole a child to use or respond positively to humor. "Getting a joke" requires flexible thinking and at least normal processing speed and attention (Campbell et al., 2015; Vaid et al., 2003), and trauma can interfere with both. In fact, for depressed individuals, the brain regions used in processing humor show decreased activity (Edwards, 2010). After traumas, some children will enjoy humor or use humor to relieve tension, and others will either miss the point of attempted humor or will find humor distressing or annoying. The return of a sense of humor may be a sign of progress in recovery, for some children. Others may be able to move between periods with an ability to respond to or use humor and periods of disability. Humor can become a part of treatment when a person is ready for it. Humor has been used as a part of therapy and for rapport building (Fox, 2016; Kerig & Alexander, 2012; Lanktree & Briere, 2008; Chapter 16). Specific types of humor therapy have been used to improve the well-being of adults with specific problems (e.g., depression, Proyer, Gander, Wellenzohn, & Ruch, 2014). Overuse of humor as a method of avoidance or avoidant coping may interfere with recovery or prolong posttrauma reactions (e.g., grief, Boelen, van den Hout, & van den Bout, 2006; PTSD, Cloitre et al., 2012; grief, Nader & Salloum, 2011; Chapter 13).

Trauma and Social Skills

Traumatic experiences can interfere with interpersonal functioning. For a variety of traumas, children may strain or lose their friendships and/or social status because of changes in temperament, behaviors, and deficient use of social skills (Nader, 2008; Box 3.1). For example, posttrauma irritability, fearfulness, impairments in emotional awareness, or other posttrauma distress can interfere with interpersonal relating and may affect reactions from others. Following traumas, for some severely traumatized children, symptoms such as noise intolerance or distress in the presence of other children or loss of self-confidence have contributed to reductions in popularity (Chapter 3—Cascading Effects).

Social competence has been reduced in children in out-of-home placement. Maltreated foster care (FC) children have performed lower than normal children on social and academic competence (Pears et al., 2010). Children raised in institutional care (IC) have exhibited unusual social behaviors (e.g., RAD, DSED, Zeanah, Smyke, Koga, & Carlson, 2005; Chapter 5) and have demonstrated greater speech reticence and lower social engagement—e.g., lower confidence in initiating and maintaining social interactions with unfamiliar peers—than FC children (in middle childhood, Almas et al., 2015; Chapter 5). IC children's greater reticence in a speech task (not FC intervention children's) elicited lower social engagement from other children. Although some intervention results for IC children have shown timing effects, social behaviors were not influenced by age of placement (in foster care). Children in the FC intervention program showed less social reticence.

PTSD has altered brain function in a way that alters social processing. A significant number of adult PTSD patients with childhood traumas have shown profound interpersonal dysfunction—e.g., within the family, with friends, with romantic partners (see Lanius et al., 2014). Empathy and perspective-taking are important to inter-relating. Some studies have found deficits in face-emotion recognition and in theory of mind processes for PTSD patients, including less accurate judgment of complex mental states (Lanius et al., 2014; Table 1.2). Increasing reflective functioning/theory of mind skills may be important for youth with PTSD and their parents.

For healthy individuals in *Western* countries (some Asian cultures consider direct eye contact to be rude/inappropriate), eye contact initially leads to activation of a fast, subcortical pathway that then modulates a cortical route eliciting social-cognitive processes (Steuwe et al., 2014). That is, they respond with a reflective, cognitive route of direct gaze processing that serves to mentalize (think about own and others' mental states; Table 1.2) and evaluate the ongoing social interaction. Direct rather than averted gaze evokes higher-level social cognition. In a study using angry, happy, and neutral virtual characters, healthy adult Canadians (N = 16) reacted to prolonged direct gaze exposure with cortical activation that enhances evaluative processes underlying social interactions. In contrast, PTSD patients (N = 16) with a history of prolonged child abuse did not respond with the typical rapid brain activation involved in social cognition. They reacted to prolonged direct gaze with sustained activation of a subcortical route of eye contact processing that is related to more general face processing that has sometimes been described as an innate alarm system (regardless of emotion content; Steuwe et al., 2014). This system may serve to detect potential threat. The region activated has been shown to elicit defensive behaviors—e.g., exaggerated startle, hypervigilance, cowering, and escape reactions. Steuwe and colleagues suggest that instead of higher-level social cognitions, the response in PTSD patients may be linked to a state of *primary process consciousness* or a *lower-level* state of consciousness, based on basic neural representations of pain, fear, anger, separation distress, sexual, and maternal behavior. Larger studies are needed.

Box 2.3 Play Room

Sixteen abandoned Romanian children were examined for their play behaviors in a therapeutic intervention (Brown, 2014b). The children (ages 1–10) were restrained to a cot, lacked normal social interactions, lacked attachments, did not play, and had suffered chronic abuse and neglect. There was an absence of crying, laughing, yelling, or other normal sounds. Children functioned below chronological ages (e.g., 4–7 years younger). The children generally had flat affect and exhibited seemingly irrational fears that resulted in frantic rocking and sometimes head-banging.

Children were introduced to a play room, and initially played or sat alone. Over time, their social interactions became more complex. They caught up to age-normal physical size and some developed meaningful engagement. The Playworkers followed the children's lead, honoring Axline's belief that, with enough time and space, children find a solution to problems in their play. All children made progress, and some made rapid progress (see Brown, 2014b for examples and details).

Trauma and Play

Trauma may interrupt the ability to play normally as well as the ability to use play for skill development or for stress reduction. Under-stimulating environments—e.g., institutionalization or other neglect—may not encourage communication, exploration, or use of imagination with toys (Byrne et al., 2017; Box 2.3). Neglected children have exhibited poor play skills—e.g., showed inability to manipulate age-appropriate toys (Byrne et al., 2017). Sexually abused children have had significantly more difficulties developing and concluding play narratives and have had significantly lower reflective functioning (RF, Glossary; Tessier et al., 2016; TOM deficits re: self and others, Ensink et al., 2014). A young child's ability to create meaningful and coherent play sequences after sexual abuse has been associated with the development of better RF (Tessier et al., 2016). Their capacities to elaborate and conclude play narratives predicted later TOM abilities regarding others (but not for themselves). Hence, restoring the ability to create and complete play narratives may be an important aspect of therapeutic play.

Traumatized youth may be compelled to enact traumatic experiences in play or activities (Gaensbauer, 2002; Nader & Pynoos, 1991; Chapter 7). As a form of reenactment or other re-experiencing, traumatic play may represent attempts to process aspects of the trauma (Nader, 2008). However, traumatized youth may be unable to process experiences through play without assistance or a therapeutic presence (Nader & Pynoos, 1991; Terr, 1981; Webb, 2015; Chapter 13). For children exposed to terrorism, PT play was associated with higher PTSD levels (Cohen, Chazan, Lerner, & Maimon, 2010; Chapter 8). When it included mainly negative affects, frequent morbid themes, a lowered developmental level, and reduced awareness of self as a player, it significantly predicted more PTSD symptoms. Play or other posttrauma methods in the presence of a therapist, with a benign interest in a child's internal world, may restore access to important inner resources (Box 2.3).

The Impact of Trauma on Self-Skills

Self-regulation and self- and other-awareness skills are essential to functioning. For young children, traumas may undermine the scaffolding of specific skills (the effectiveness of parental just-enough-assistance e.g., to self-awareness, perspective-taking, Glossary, Chapter 5). It may undermine developing skills. The symptom complexity of proposed Developmental Trauma Disorder (DTD) or complicated childhood trauma has been described as failures in self-regulation—behavioral, emotional, and interpersonal regulation (Ford, 2011; see Symptom Complexity, later in this chapter).

Disruption of Self-Regulation

Trauma and attachment insecurity each are among variables associated with emotion and behavioral regulation difficulties and maladaptive responses to stress (Mikulincer & Shaver, 2007, 2008). Both for resilient and for susceptible individuals, traumas may disrupt self-regulation in a number of ways (e.g., maltreatment, Teicher & Samson, 2016). Extreme stress may disrupt the functioning of brain regions (particularly prefrontal cortex) and thus undermine executive functions—e.g., self-regulation, attention, organization, planning, and inhibition of the stress response (Nader & Fletcher, 2014; Rothbart & Rueda, 2005; Stevens, Kiehl, Pearlson, & Calhoun, 2007; Teicher & Samson, 2016). Trauma may disturb regulation-related beliefs. For example, after a tornado (10 children died), some elementary school children were heard to ask why they should bother to be good, if you can die anyway (Nader, 2008). Posttrauma agitation, fear, or other arousal symptoms also may make it difficult to control reactions. Deficits or problems in self-regulation are associated with the development of many forms of maladaptation or psychopathology—e.g., conduct disorder, ADHD, OCD; depression; borderline PD; PTSD; deliberate self-harm;

substance use; risky sexual or overall risky behaviors (Koenen, 2006; see Nader, 2008; Weiss, Gratz, & Lavender, 2015).

Trauma and Self-Awareness

Trauma reactions may undermine self-awareness, e.g., by undermining self-view and confidence, judgment, and the ability to evaluate the actions and interactions of self, others, or situations (Nader, 2008). Through cognitive integration processes, higher-order self-concepts develop of self as a whole person with differing context-bound abilities (Harter, 1999). Dissociation may be a product of trauma exposure (especially multiple exposures). Harter has suggested that, until late adolescence, humans do not have the cognitive capacity to create a coherent self-structure. Hence, dissociation may disrupt self-concept and the developing sense of self. Traumatization may result in changes in identity and self-concept. Trauma may undermine emotional and social processing, and thus may interfere with the social and the personal self (Steuwe et al., 2014). Posttrauma shame may instigate a redefinition of self in negative terms (bad, despicable, helpless) (Lanius et al., 2014). A negative self-view may increase the risk for interpersonal violence victimization.

PTSD has been associated with profound disturbances in self-referential processing and has been linked to altered neural activation patterns in brain regions related to self-referential processing (see Lanius et al., 2014). Research has shown that healthy individuals demonstrate faster neural responses to the relevance of personal characteristics than to general facts, whereas PTSD patients have shown no difference in response times to the two types of information (e.g., with less activation of the medial PFC in contrasting information). Adults with childhood abuse have shown significantly reduced resting-state connectivity—i.e., reduced connectivity of regions within the brain's Default Mode Network, important to self-referential processing, autobiographical memory, and social cognition (Glossary).

Normally, the time it takes to switch between first- and third-person perspective-taking decreases with age (Sebastian, Burnett, & Blakemore, 2008). Trauma arousal may make it difficult to focus on the self from a direct or third-person (onlooker) perspective. The frontal, temporal, and parietal networks of the brain support the processing of self- and other-referenced information; the medial PFC has been observed to activate during self-referential emotional-processing tasks (Northoff et al., 2006). Reduced activation of the medial PFC in individuals with PTSD may be consistent with a more pronounced deviation from normal levels of reflective/self-referential processing (Frewen & Lanius, 2006).

Trauma and Shame and Guilt

Following traumas, guilt may be for real or imagined misdeeds—e.g., survivor guilt, guilt with an element of wishful thinking about one's ability to act, a young child's tendency to believe she/he is the cause of things (Danieli, 1984; see Nader, 2008). Herman (1997) described posttraumatic shame as a response to helplessness, violation, and indignity. Shame is often accompanied by a sense of exposure, shrinking, smallness, worthlessness, and powerlessness. Both guilt and shame are among emotions that have been associated with increased and prolonged posttrauma symptoms (Feiring, Taska, & Chen, 2002; Fletcher, 2014; Nader, 2008; Chapters 1, 9, 11, 14). For example, a multitude of negative effects have been documented for victimization by bullying—e.g., poor health, mental health difficulties (e.g., depression, anxiety, aggression; dissociation), impaired functioning (e.g., managing chores, work, school life, social life), impaired self-concept (e.g., self-blame; defective self, Chapter 1), poor social relationships (e.g., peer rejection, loneliness, social avoidance; Nader, 2012c; Strom et al., 2018). Both bullying victimization and severe violence have been significantly and independently related to psychological distress, impaired functioning, and greater barriers to social support in adults who were bullying-victimized in youth—e.g., trouble seeking support; feeling others do not understand them; feeling others would be overburdened or are tired of hearing about their problems (N = 681; ages 19–37; Strom et al., 2018). Although bullying has a direct and unique effect on outcomes, entering shame into the analysis rendered the effect insignificant. When childhood physical violence, sexual abuse, and sociodemographic factors were controlled, shame mediated 70% of the association between bully-victimization and distress, 55% between victimization and impaired functioning, and 40% of the association between bullying victimization and social support barriers (Strom et al., 2018). Shame has also been associated with aggression (e.g., Scott et al., 2015; Chapter 11).

Trauma and Emotion Awareness

Trauma and complex trauma reactions have been linked to reduced emotion awareness and/or to attentional biases for specific emotions (Frewen et al., 2008a, 2012; Pollak, 2008), which, in turn, may impede functioning (e.g., men, substance use frequency, Dell'Osso et al., 2012; impaired response to social signals, Pollak, Cicchetti, Hornung, & Reed, 2000; aggression, Tull, Jakupcak, Paulson, & Gratz, 2007). For example, maltreated children may become particularly attentive to abuse-related emotions (e.g., anger, fear; Masten et al., 2008; Pollak, 2008). While normal children attend to happy, fearful, sad, and angry faces equally (Pollak, 2008), neglected children have had more difficulty seeing the distinction between facial emotional expressions—e.g., saw greater similarity between happy and sad faces than physically abused or non-maltreated children (Pollak et al., 2000).

Alexithymia. Traumas (e.g., unpredictable and abusive parenting) may result in emotional lability and/or confusion and may interfere with the ability to identify, label, and communicate emotions (alexithymia, Glossary; e.g., Frewen et al., 2008b). In turn, alexithymia is related to higher levels of stress, depression, and anxiety and to lower happiness (Hesse, 2008). For chronically traumatized youth, difficulty identifying and labeling emotional feelings and a tendency toward externally oriented thinking (i.e., superficiality) is robustly associated with PTSD (Frewen et al., 2008a; Frewen, Dozois, Neufeld, & Lanius, 2012). *Difficulty identifying emotions* has been most strongly associated with psychopathology. *Difficulty describing emotions* may reflect a number of problems (see Frewen et al., 2012). Childhood physical and sexual abuse have predicted impairments in emotional awareness and expression (alexithymia; Paivio & McCulloch, 2004). Feeling unsafe in childhood and low family expressiveness have later been associated with alexithymia—e.g., in abusing or neglecting families; when emotional expression was punished, ignored, or out of control.

Trauma and alexithymia have been related to each other and to other outcomes. After childhood sexual abuse, alexithymia has been linked to adult depression (Thomas, DiLillo, Walsh, & Polusny, 2011). In contrast to other traumas, the number of high betrayal traumas—violence perpetrated by someone on whom a victim depends or is close to (e.g., spouse or parent)—has predicted levels of college students' alexithymia, anxiety, depression, dissociation, and physical health complaints (e.g., number of days sick during past month; Goldsmith et al., 2013). Traumatic stress symptoms and alexithymia have been associated with each other and each has mediated the role between high betrayal traumas and somatic complaints. Maltreatment severity and higher levels of alexithymia have been related to later self-injury (SI; Paivio & McCulloch, 2004). The link between SI and maltreatment has been partially mediated by dissociation, alexithymia, and self-blame for females and dissociation and self-blame for males (Swannell et al., 2012). Traumatic experiences have been associated with hostility, anger, and aggression. Above and beyond PTS symptom severity and trait anger, experiential avoidance and emotional inexpressivity each have accounted for a significant amount of unique variance in aggressive behavior (adults; Tull et al., 2007). Expressing and receiving affectionate communications has partially mediated the relationship between happiness (not stress) and alexithymia (Swannell et al., 2012).

Facial Emotion Recognition. Children raised in institutional care have shown differences from other children in their facial recognition skills. For children raised in ongoing institutionalized care (IC; deprivation), placed in trained foster care, or never institutionalized (average age eight and again at ages 11–14, Bick et al., 2017), at intense emotional levels, accuracy was higher for very intensely happy faces than for intensely fearful, sad, or angry faces for all three groups. For a range of emotional intensities, all groups more readily identified fearful than other emotional faces. Recognition of sad faces was more difficult than other emotions. At average ages eight and 12, IC children had a subtly more difficult time identifying happy faces. IC children also had small magnitude accuracy problems in identifying increasingly intense fearful faces, which was more strongly apparent at ages 11–14 (average age 12). Children in trained foster care were not different from normal comparison children, suggesting that specialized foster placement may normalize developmental trajectories of processing negative emotions (fear).

Psychopathology and Perspective-Taking

A number of psychological conditions include disturbances in perspective-taking—e.g., PTS, bipolar affective disorder, schizophrenia spectrum disorders, social anxiety, autism, some forms of dementia, psychopathy (Brüne & Brüne-Cohrs, 2006; Hendriks et al., 2016). Traumatic and depressive reactions may interfere with aspects of empathy—i.e., interfere with perspective-taking and accurate recognition of others' emotions (D'Andrea et al., 2012; Nader, 2012c). Trauma has been associated with diminished cognitive and emotional perspective-taking (Ensink et al., 2016a; Chapter 12). Burack et al. (2006) found that maltreated children and adolescents were more egocentric and delayed in their social perspective-taking development than non-maltreated peers and that maltreated children reported lower levels of global self-worth as well. Both problems may undermine social ties and inter-relating (Brüne & Brüne-Cohrs, 2006; Nader, 2012c; Chapter 15). As described earlier, traumas may be followed by attentional and attributional biases that interfere with perspective-taking (Chapter 9).

Trauma and Stressor-Related Disorders

As has been demonstrated, PTSD is associated with a number of problems, including disrupted development. The *Diagnostic and Statistical Manual of Mental Disorders*, 5th edition (DSM-5) Trauma and Stressor-Related Disorders (APA, 2013) include PTSD in children age six and under and other disorders most often studied in children under age six—Reactive Attachment Disorder and Disinhibited Social Engagement Disorder (described in Chapter 6)—as well as PTSD and PTSD-dissociative subtype (PTSD-DS) for individuals over age six, including adults (APA, 2013; Chapter 15). Many trauma symptoms overlap with symptoms of other disorders, possibly complicating diagnosis (see Nader, 2015). TSRD are appropriate when youth are exposed to traumatic events directly, through witnessing or learning that someone close has been directly exposed to a violent or accidental traumatic event, or has had repeated, non-media exposure to the details of an event. Vulnerability to traumatization in response to specific adversities may vary by age and other factors, sometimes not captured in DSM-5 TSRD (see age-related chapters; see Chapter 13 and Appendix—comparison of ICD and DSM PTSD). Persistent Complex Bereavement Disorder is listed with disorders for additional study and is discussed in age-related chapters (Chapters 7, 8—grief, 12, 15, 16—Complicated Grief). To follow is a discussion of complex posttrauma reactions or symptom complexity. Both PTSD and cPTSD have had substantial comorbidity (Ford, 2018; see Nader, 2008; Scheeringa, 2016). Evidence suggests that people with less than a full PTSD diagnosis also have significantly elevated scores—e.g., in distress-impairment, suicidality, comorbidity, and PTSD (McLaughlin et al., 2015a).

PTSD and PTSD-DS

Associations of DSM 5 PTSD and PTSD with dissociative symptoms (PTSD-DS) are described in age-related chapters. The DSM-5 PTSD exposure criterion does not describe some events that have been linked to trauma and/or other adverse reactions, including developmental disruptions—e.g., nonviolent and non-accidental death of a parent or sibling; adverse family environments (especially early family conflict, harsh parenting) that do not include diagnosable abuse or witnessing of physical violence. DSM-5 PTSD includes core symptoms of posttrauma reactions such as *intrusive symptoms* (re-experiencing; APA, 2013)—e.g., recurrent, distressing memories and/or dreams, repetitive play or activities reminiscent of the event, dissociative episodes (including flashbacks), and physiological and/or psychological reactions to reminders of the event or other trauma-related triggers (e.g., fast heart beat; prickly skin)—and *avoidance symptoms*—e.g., external reminders; thoughts/feelings related to the experience (Criterion C). It now includes trauma-associated *negative alterations in cognitions and mood* (Criterion D). The latter and some of the Criterion E symptoms (*arousal symptoms*) are among symptoms described for complex posttrauma reactions (to follow). Some debate continues about the need for a more developmentally appropriate set of disorders for children over age six. Some evidence suggests that PTSD for children under six is more applicable for children over age six (see age-related chapters).

PTSD with Dissociative Symptoms (PTSD-DS)

Dissociation has been linked to trauma, poly-victimization (cumulative traumas), insecure or disorganized attachments, inmate status (vs general population), and fantasy proneness (e.g., Briere, Dietrich, & Semple, 2016; Frewen, Brown, & Lanius, 2017; Gusic, Cardena, Bengtsson, & Sondergaard, 2016; Haltigan & Roisman, 2015; Hébert, Langevin, & Daigneault, 2016; Stein et al., 2013; Glossary; Chapter 11). Some evidence suggests that dissociative symptoms in addition to derealization and depersonalization are also associated with a PT dissociative profile (e.g., adults, Műllerová et al., 2016). For adults, Briere and colleagues have provided evidence for differences in dissociative complexity—i.e., numbers of dissociative types experienced (Glossary). Dissociative complexity was related to cumulative traumas and to comorbidity (e.g., substance abuse, suicidality; Briere et al., 2016). Evidence suggests that the link of PTS and depression to non-suicidal self-injury is mediated by their shared association with dissociation (Briere & Eadie, 2016; shame, dysregulated neurobiology in autism disorders, and attachment insecurity were not assessed; see Chapter 16).

PTSD may occur with or without dissociative symptoms (e.g., trauma-related altered states of consciousness, TRASC, adults, Frewen et al., 2017). Approximately 15–30% of PTSD patients have fit the dissociative PTSD subtype (PTSD-DS, APA, 2013; Brand, Loewenstein, & Lanius, 2014). PTSD-DS has been associated with greater symptom complexity (Glossary) and may relate to a more difficult course (e.g., Briere & Eadie, 2016). For adults, Frewen et al. (2017) found that voice hearing (thought-related TRASC) and depersonalization (body-related TRASC) were strong TRASC-factor items, while flashbacks and emotional numbing had moderately strong cross-loadings on a normal waking conscious posttrauma distress (NWC-distress) factor as well. TRASC occurs less frequently than NWC-distress, is strongly correlated with measures of dissociation, and is strongly linked to trauma severity (e.g., childhood emotional neglect, particularly in persons with both BPD and PTSD; Frewen, Kleindienst, Lanius, & Schmahl, 2014; Frewen, Brown, & Lanius, 2017). Lanius (2015) suggests without dissociation, PTSD patients exhibit exacerbated arousal and monitoring of internal bodily states, whereas PTSD-DS patients display attenuated or dampened arousal and interoception (Glossary). Each has independently predicted social and occupational impairment (e.g., 12-week self-reported levels; Frewen et al., 2015a). Without childhood trauma, adult TRASC are less likely than NWC-distress. The brain's insula and amygdala and their connectivity are strongly implicated both for PTSD and PTSD-DS (depersonalization, derealization; Lanius, 2015; Appendix—memory consolidation).

By enabling separation of reactions and sensations from conscious awareness, dissociation may serve to protect from facing overwhelming emotions and/or body sensations (Silberg, 2000; Wieland & Silberg, 2013; Chapter 11). As a consequence of the splitting-off process, youth may develop an unstable and unreliable sense of self, others, and the world, which may ultimately lead to identity fragmentation. It has been linked to immediate and long-term negative effects—e.g., high PTSD symptom levels, emotion dysregulation, poor attention, diminished memory and processing, suicidality, incarceration, functional impairment, lower likelihood of treatment seeking, and comorbid psychiatric disorders (e.g., Bennett, Modrowski, Kerig, & Chaplo, 2015, Bozkurt, Mutluer, Kose, & Zoroglu, 2015; De Bellis et al., 2013; Parlar et al., 2016; Stein et al., 2013). Over time and in treatment, dissociation may interfere with necessary cognitive and affective processing of traumatic experiences and lead to failure of integration of episodic and AM (Bozkurt et al. 2015; Cloitre et al., 2012; Resick et al., 2012b; Wieland & Silberg, 2013). Specific methods are essential to effectively treat PTSD with dissociative symptoms (e.g., self-regulation methods; Chapters 13, 16).

Symptom Complexity: Complex or Developmental Trauma (cPTSD or DTD)

Symptoms described in early conceptualizations of complicated posttrauma reactions have been linked to developmentally adverse interpersonal traumas, especially those occurring in periods of rapid brain development—i.e., rapid growth of neuronal connections, followed by pruning in adolescence and in early childhood (Schore, 2003)—or linked to poly-victimization (Finkelhor et al., 2007, 2014; Ford, 2017, 2018; Ford & Courtois, 2014). Like multiple trauma exposures (earlier in chapter), complicated posttrauma reactions have had a number of names (e.g., cPTSD, DTD, symptom complexity) and a number of conceptualizations. DTD, cPTSD, or complicated/complex trauma was not included as a separate disorder in DSM-5 (see Resick et al., 2012a). Instead, some cPTSD/DTD symptoms are now in DSM-5 PTSD—e.g., persistent or more frequent negative emotional states such as fear, guilt, sadness, shame or confusion (over age six: D4; under age six: C3); distorted blame of self or others (over six: D3); exaggerated negative expectations (over six: D2); reckless or self-destructive behavior (over six: E2); and anger and aggression symptoms (over six and under six: E1, D1 respectively) (APA, 2013; see Nader & Fletcher, 2014; see Ford, 2018).

As discussed earlier, cumulative traumas or poly-victimization have been linked to symptom complexity—number of different types of symptoms or symptom clusters simultaneously elevated into the clinical range for an individual (e.g., Briere et al., 2016; Ford, 2017; Hodges et al., 2013; Chapters 15, 16; Table 15.1). Complex traumatic reactions include symptoms and impairments that extend beyond PTSD to include a wide range of psychological disorders and behavior problems (Ford, 2018; Chapter 15). However, some traumas may not follow one specific disorder pattern. For example, childhood sexual abuse can have profound and debilitating outcomes in adolescence and adulthood. Some evidence suggests that some but not all features of both PTSD and DTD have been related to sexual abuse (Spinazzola, van der Kolk, & Ford, in press).

Childhood Complex Reactions: Developmental Trauma Disorder (DTD)

Proposed Developmental Trauma Disorder (DTD) recently has been assessed as (1) preceded by at least two interpersonal traumas and disruption of caregiver–child attachment relationships, which are followed by (2) *dysregulation of emotion and somatic functioning*—e.g., inability to recover from extreme emotional states, dissociation, alexithymia; (3) *dysregulation of attention, cognition, and behavior*—e.g., attentional biases away from or toward threat, self-harm, risky behavior, self-soothing behaviors, difficulties with goal-directed behaviors; (4) *dysregulation of identity and relationships*—e.g., attachment insecurity or disorganization, self-loathing, expectations of betrayal or abandonment, poor boundaries, reactive aggression, diminished or excessive empathy (Ford, 2018; see *DTD Semi-structured Interview* [DTD-SI], Ford et al., 2014). Although DTD as measured by the DTD-SI was associated with poly-victimization, this preliminary assessment showed that DTD was linked to psychosocial impairment independent of the effects of PTSD, poly-victimization, and demographics (Ford et al., 2018b). DTD was related to but distinct from PTSD and was distinguishable from other DSM-5 diagnoses with some symptoms that closely parallel some DTD symptoms. Some overlap exists between cPTSD/DTD and borderline personality disorder (see Chapter 15).

DTD has been associated with sexual trauma, emotional abuse, interpersonal violence, family or community violence, an impaired caregiver, and war as well as with traumatic loss (separation from caregiver, Ford, 2018; Murphy, Elklit, Dokkedahl & Shevlin, 2016; Stolbach et al., 2013). In a study of youth exposed to multiple trauma types, children with chronic exposure to violence, maltreatment, and disruptions in protective caregiving were much more likely to meet proposed DTD criteria (N=214, ages 3–17; Stolbach et al., 2013). For Ugandan child soldiers 10 years after the war (N=214, ages 19–25, Murphy et al., 2016), child soldier status predicted both cPTSD and PTSD. Researchers found three classes of reactions (Murphy et al., 2016): (1) the *cPTSD* group (40.2%) had the highest number of war experiences and were five times more likely to have been abducted; the group was likely to endorse all PTSD items and disturbances in self-organization items—i.e., affect regulation, negative self-concept, disturbed relationships; had significantly more anxiety, depression, somatic complaints, and conduct problems (higher comorbidity) than other groups; (2) the *PTSD* group (43.8%) had higher war experiences and comorbidity than the *low PTSD* group; reported high re-experiencing and arousal, moderate sense of threat, and hyper-activation with comparatively low deactivation of affect regulation; low disturbed relationships, and low-negative self-concept; and (3) the *low PTSD* group (16%) reported lower symptom levels than other groups. Female gender was not a risk factor in this highly war trauma-exposed group. Although high levels of emotional reactivity were apparent in all three groups, they were markedly elevated in the cPTSD group and moderately in the PTSD and low-symptom groups. Emotional reactivity was indicated in hyper-activation—e.g., episodes of uncontrollable anger, taking a long time to calm down when upset (needs replication). Both PTSD and DTD have been associated with several types of interpersonal trauma and attachment adversity (Spinazzola et al., in press). Childhood trauma and disrupted attachments are common in the histories of patients with PTSD-DS, cPTSD, and BPD (e.g., Ford, Spinazzola, van der Kolk, & Grasso, 2018b). When children show dysregulation, both trauma and disrupted attachments warrant assessment.

Adult Complex Reactions: cPTSD

A history of childhood and other trauma exposures that evoked complexity has been associated with adult difficulty recovering from extreme distress states, difficulty inhibiting reckless or self-harming behavior, somatic problems, dissociation, preoccupation with the instigator(s) of a trauma, seeing self as a victim, interpersonal difficulties, despair or loss of faith (Ford, 2017, 2018). In DSM-5, some symptoms included in conceptualizations of complex traumatization are now included in the PTSD diagnosis (APA, 2013; see Nader & Fletcher, 2014). In the International Classification of Diseases (ICD-10; World Health Organization, WHO, 1992/2004), complicated reactions are encompassed under *enduring personality change following catastrophic experience*, which is preceded by PTSD and lasts at least two years. This adult disorder includes symptoms described for complex trauma (cPTSD) or DTD—e.g., hostility or distrustful attitudes toward the world, hopeless or empty feelings (Ford, 2018). cPTSD is under consideration for ICD–11 (Ford, 2017).

cPTSD has been associated with a particular brain profile which is also consistent with findings for adults with abuse histories (with or without PTSD) and for individuals with BPD (Ford, 2018). Some studies have shown that, when compared to normal adults, childhood abuse-related adult cPTSD has been related to reduced hippocampal, anterior cingulate (ACC), and orbital prefrontal cortex (PFC) volumes, which has been linked to greater problems with anger, impulsivity, and hyperarousal; as well as to increased activation of the left hemisphere hippocampus, amygdala, ACC, ventromedial PFC, and insula (the latter, marginally), some of which has been reduced by treatments for cPTSD (Ford, 2017).

Traumas sometimes referred to as "complex traumas"—e.g., abuse—are not the exclusive precursors to cPTSD. Cloitre et al. (2013) found three classes of reactions in adults: *complex PTSD* (cPTSD)—i.e., high in PTSD symptoms and in affective, negative self-concept, and interpersonal problems (greatest functional impairment); *PTSD*—high in PTSD while low in other symptoms; and a *low-symptom class*: low in all symptoms. While, in this study, worst trauma identified as childhood abuse predicted cPTSD, and 9/11 exposure predicted PTSD, the low-symptom group had comparable numbers to both other classes of both worst-trauma types, suggesting resilience. There were individuals in the abuse group who had only PTSD and those in the 9/11 group who had cPTSD, demonstrating that the disorders are symptom-based rather than trauma-history-based.

Trauma or Adversity and General Psychopathology

In addition to trauma and other stressor-related disorders, childhood trauma has been associated with a number of different psychological difficulties and disorders—e.g., personality, mood, anxiety, somatic, and psychotic disorders; aggression, cognitive or physical disabilities; rigid behavioral patterns. Although resilient coping may lower rates of distress and buffer effects of adversity, childhood traumas have been associated with lower levels of resilience, social support, and adjustment as well as with increased distress and somatic complaints (Beutel et al., 2017). Although parenting may buffer the effects of trauma exposure in early life, with multiple exposures (e.g., war, maltreatment) psychopathology may nevertheless emerge later (e.g., school age; Chapter 7).

Trauma may trigger genetic vulnerabilities to disorders. The study of multiple neurobiological factors and their influence on childhood trauma/adversity outcomes is growing. For example, trauma increases the likelihood of gene-related dysfunction (Lau & Pine, 2008) and particular genes and their combinations influence long-term posttrauma outcomes—e.g., whether maltreated youth maltreat their children; poor long-term health outcomes (South, Schafer, & Ferraro, 2015). Retrospective studies have found that childhood adversities are significantly associated with adult psychiatric disorders (Kessler, Davis, & Kendler, 1997). The interaction of genotype and early stressors—especially multiple stressor types—has demonstrated a vulnerability model that surpasses symptom categories (Comasco et al., 2015)—i.e., effects of particular adverse events were not confined to any one class of disorder (Kessler et al., 1997). In contrast, youth with protective or less environmentally sensitive gene variants, without traumatic experiences, have shown a decreased likelihood for the development of psychiatric disorders.

A variety of childhood traumas and some stressors (e.g., maternal hostility, problematic attachments; parenting) have been associated with a range of disorders in children and adults—e.g., PTSD, PTSD-DS, personality disorders, psychopathy, self-injury, conduct disorders, mood disorders, anxiety disorders (Chapter 3). OCD patients have had higher levels of childhood adversities than their relatives and more than normal comparisons (N = 383; Bey et al., 2017). OCD patients also showed significantly higher levels of the trait *harm avoidance* (HA) than relatives who showed higher levels of HA than controls. In a study from birth to age nine (N = 4898), all forms of early maltreatment—physical neglect, supervisory neglect, emotional abuse, and physical abuse—were associated with increased initial and later social-emotional (e.g., behavior problems) and cognitive difficulties (e.g., vocabulary skills; Font & Berger, 2015). For example, supervisory neglect was linked to increased anxiety and depression, withdrawal, and aggressive behavior problems. Both emotional and physical abuse were strong predictors of initial and later aggression. Clinical samples sometimes differ from nonclinical samples. For example, in clinical samples, neglect and parental separation/divorce had a strong impact on depressive risk (Mandelli, Petrelli, & Serretti, 2015). For adults, studies and meta-analyses have shown that multiple forms of childhood abuse and other traumas have been linked to depression (especially neglect and emotional abuse; Mandelli et al., 2015), to hostility, and to narcissism (Dragioti et al., 2012; Chapters 15, 16). Higher hostility levels and all forms of childhood abuse and neglect were associated with aggression. Hostility has mediated the relationship between childhood emotional abuse, sexual abuse, and physical neglect and aggression (Dragioti et al., 2012). Many of the disorders subsequent to traumas will be discussed in age-related chapters.

Conclusions

Stressful experiences may either assist development or negatively influence personality, development, and well-being. Even with PTSD, traumas may aid personal growth. On the other hand, in addition to the marked increase in risk of psychopathology—e.g., PTSD, personality disorder, depression, schizophrenia—exposure to trauma may produce a cascade of neurobiological changes associated with a number of immediate and long-term outcomes (Chapter 3). As will be discussed in subsequent chapters, caregivers, families, and communities each influence outcomes and recovery. Genetics, environmental factors, support systems, and developmental issues all help to shape the immediate and long-term consequences of trauma exposure. For children's recovery from adversity, age-adapted treatments are needed. Single disorder treatments may fail when there are several presenting problems (e.g., complicated reactions).

In addition to traumas' influence on core developmental processes—e.g., attachment, self-regulation, self- and other-awareness, stress response/reactivity, EFs, arousal—and their link to risk of psychopathology, immediately and over time (Dunn et al., 2013), trauma exposure is identified as a potential trigger for the expression of genetic and temperamental vulnerabilities (Lau & Pine, 2008; see Nader & Fletcher, 2014). Traumatic exposure, especially when it is repeated (cumulative traumas or multiple types of exposure), severe, or in sensitive periods, can impact brain development and subsequent vulnerability to negative outcomes (Gillespie et al., 2009; Chapter 4). For example, such stress may increase the size of the right side of the amygdala, which is related to the processing of negative emotional stimuli (Pechtel et al., 2014; Chapters 5, 14). Trauma may interfere with the neurochemical feedback that signals that there is no real danger, resulting in increased release of stress hormones, which has potential long-term negative consequences (Gillespie et al., 2009; see Nader & Fletcher, 2014; Roy et al., 2010).

3

Cascading and Long-Term Effects of Childhood Trauma

Childhood traumas have had cascading and/or long-term effects on a child's life and functioning. Childhood is a period of rapid physical, cognitive, and emotional development (Osofsky, Kronenberg, Bocknek, & Hansel, 2015b; Stamoulis et al., 2015). Traumatic reactions may interrupt the developmental progression of any or all of these realms (Boxes 3.1, 3.2). While subsequent chapters (5, 8, 11, 14) discuss the developmental processes for specific age groups, and some chapters discuss the impact of trauma on them (6, 9, 12, 15), this chapter is devoted to trauma's long-term and cascading consequences and to how developmental processes are disrupted across time into adolescence and/or adulthood.

For some time, studies have examined the long-term consequences of a variety of traumas including numerous ongoing or emerging psychological, behavioral, interpersonal, and/or health consequences (Table 3.1). With a history of childhood adversity, individuals show higher rates of anxiety, depression, eating disorders, substance abuse, psychoses, suicidality, personality disorders, and poorer responses to treatment. Childhood adversity accounts for an estimated 26 to 32% of risk for all adolescent and adult psychiatric disorders (Cloitre & Beck, 2017). For example, Krammer et al. (2015) found that older adults with a history of childhood traumatic stress reported classic PTSD (anxious arousal, intrusive experiences, defensive avoidance) and related symptoms (depression and dissociation; impaired self-reference) later in life (ages 59–98; N = 116). Early traumatic experience also increases risk of psychotic symptoms in response to later life adversity (Lataster et al., 2012). Although psychotic disorders may occur without traumas, some studies show a high percentage of individuals with psychotic disorders have trauma histories (e.g., 75%; any form of trauma, Duhig et al., 2015), and trauma history was associated with increased symptoms. Across 20 studies, evidence suggests that childhood traumatic experiences are related to the persistence of psychotic experiences and clinically relevant psychotic symptoms—two-fold increased odds of persistence (Trotta, Murray, & Fisher, 2015).

Although some findings are inconsistent, even preconception, pre-natal, and early post-natal maternal stress have been linked to childhood psychopathology (Class et al., 2014). For example, mother's exposure to the death of a first-degree relative either six months before conception, during pregnancy, or in the first two months of the child's life corresponded to marginally increased, but not significant likelihood of bipolar disorder or schizophrenia (preconception exposure), increased risk of childhood autism (AuSD) and ADHD (highest in third-trimester exposure), and moderately increased risk of suicide attempt or completion (maternal bereavement, post-natal year 1; population study: child outcome—N = 738,144; adult outcome—N = 2.2 million; Class et al.,

Table 3.1 Possible Long-Term Consequences of Childhood Traumas (documented)

Realm	Increased Risk Of
General	poorer quality of life; poorer quality of health; poor quality of relationships
Behavioral	aggression (e.g., reactive; active violence); alcohol or other substance abuse; commission of ACEs; compulsive compliance; conduct disturbances (e.g., delinquency, gang involvement, violent crimes) and adult criminality; externalizing behavior problems; internalizing problems; gambling; inconsiderateness; isolation or withdrawal; passivity or hyperactivity; physical inactivity; promiscuity; regression; risk taking; re-victimization; smoking; truancy
Cognitive	academic problems (e.g., grade repetition; dropout); aggressive interpersonal negotiation strategies; cognitive delays; executive function difficulties (e.g., adaptive response inhibition, cognitive flexibility, memory deficits, and/or attention problems); language deficits; lower IQ; moral reasoning difficulties; problematic thought patterns (e.g., hostile or other attribution biases; attentional biases (e.g., negative self-talk; selective attention); cognitive distortions; exaggerated defensive responding; negative emotional processing
Interpersonal	attachment quality problems; dependence; inconsiderate behaviors; ongoing biases in attention and reaction; relationship difficulties (e.g., social incompetence; poor social sensitivity; trust problems); risk of intimate partner violence/rape; lower empathy; poor perspective-taking; undesirable patterns of interaction; negative view of self and/or others (see also Cognitive)
Neurobiological Systems	hypo-activity in brain regions (e.g., prefrontal cortex; limbic system; paralimbic system); increased ACTH and elevated cortisol response to stressors; specific increases or decreases in brain volumes; limbic impairment; shorter telomere length (may be gender specific)
Physical Problems	asthma; autoimmune disease; cardiovascular disease (e.g., ischemic heart disease); diabetes; digestive problems; fatigue or chronic fatigue syndrome; fetal death; general physical complaints (e.g., headaches, stomach aches); hypertension; liver disease; lung disease (e.g., asthma; cancer; poorer lung functioning; chronic obstructive pulmonary disease); neurochemical changes; obesity; pain; physical growth reductions; unintended pregnancy; inflammation (e.g., increased C-reactive protein and/or ICAM-1)
Psychiatric Disorders and Symptoms	ADHD; alexithymia; antisocial behavior; fear and/or anxiety symptoms and disorders; bipolar and related disorders; conduct disorders; depressive disorders and symptoms; dissociation; eating disorders; guilt, self-blame, and/or shame; mood and affect disturbances (depressive disorders; suicidal ideation and attempts; persistent anger); oppositional defiance disorder; personality disorders (e.g., antisocial; borderline; dependent; depressive; narcissistic; paranoid; passive aggressive); psychotic disorders; self-injury or self-mutilation; sexualized behavior; sleep problems; substance use/abuse; suicide attempts; trauma-related disorders (e.g., lifetime PTSD)
Self-Skills	coping difficulties (e.g., lack of flexibility; poor adaptation to non-controllable situations; failure of action in controllable situations); self-concept (e.g., low self-esteem; lack of confidence; low self-efficacy; lower body satisfaction); poor self-protection and/or poor danger detection; poor self-regulation (e.g., behavioral and/or emotional/affect); problematic reward processing; problems with locus of control (e.g., belief in external control; self-blame; failure to recognize controllable or non-controllable situations); stress reactivity and sensitivity

Sources: Anda & Feletti, 2003; Asok et al., 2014; Middlebrooks & Audage, 2008; APA, 2013; Briere et al., 2008; Briere et al., 2016; Bynum et al., 2010; Champagne & Meaney, 2007; Child Welfare, 2013; Dackis et al., 2012; De Bellis & Zisk, 2014; Hansel et al., 2013; Hensch & Bilimoria, 2012; Hodges et al., 2013; Lupien et al., 2009; Maikovich-Fong, Speltz; & Jaffee, 2015; Moss et al., 2012; Nader, 2008; Nader & Fletcher, 2014; Pechtel et al., 2014; Spann et al., 2012; Taylor et al., 2013b; Wekerle et al., 2014.

Box 3.1 Cascading Effects After a Death

Before the incident, Elizabeth (E) was happy, popular, and gregarious. Her mother describes her pre-"breakdown" persona as "a little ball of sunshine. So easy, feisty in a good way, full of energy." E felt safe and loved. Her older brother was more outgoing than she, and she relied on him for creating a social network. Until he started to pull away when she was in fifth grade, they "ran the neighborhood." Her grandfather died when she was age nine, and things changed. The family surrounded her grandfather, until he flat-lined. Then he suddenly looked up at his wife once more, and then was gone. E and everyone in the family were allowed alone time with him to say goodbye. Although her parents were spiritual, they were not church-goers (At the funeral, E asked, "Who's the guy on the 't'?"). She believes that this is why she didn't know where her grandfather had gone, or what had happened to him.

During her alone time with her grandfather, his lifeless eyes and mouth were open. E leaned in and hugged him, and the remaining air in his lungs expelled. She heard his breath and thought he was alive again. She "panicked" and thought that she should do something to help him. Although you could see into the room where the family was, no one was paying attention to her. She felt as though she had let him die again. She was terrified and ashamed. Some people came in and put him in a black bag—"It looked like a garbage bag." When she went back in with family, they seemed to be having a spiritual experience—all were happy that he had died so peacefully. She told no one. No one asked her about her experience.

She "never felt safe again." "The ground dropped out from under me, that someone could be there, then just be gone." It could happen to anyone—her parents, her brother, her. She began to sleep covered by stuffed animals, in case someone came in the night to stab her—they would stab them instead. She developed severe separation anxiety. Her parents were unaware of her distress and later planned a trip out of the country. She was to stay in her grandfather's house—where he had died—with her step-grandmother (with whom she was not close). During her stay, E fell and had a concussion. She says that she exaggerated her symptoms so that her parents would come home. She didn't ever want to be apart from them. She stayed home from school for three months. She felt unsafe everywhere—even the back seat of the car. Although loving and accepting, her parents became exasperated with her clinging. They didn't connect it to her grandfather's death. E's brother didn't have difficulty, and E never told them. After three months, her mother had her write a letter to her grandfather telling him all that bothered her. Then they burned the letter. She felt some relief after this. E does not remember therapy at that time. However, her mother reported that they took her to her first therapy at age 10, because after grandfather died, she had a "breakdown"—separation anxiety, didn't want to go to school, crying, depression. They had not known until six months after the death that E had seen them put her grandfather in a "black garbage bag"—they were horrified. She was never the same happy little girl after that. Then she went through bullying that they didn't learn about until her senior year in high school.

Loss of Status and Being Bullied. Formerly popular, when she returned to school, she was ostracized. She was now an outsider who had been out of school for random reasons. Again, she felt unsafe. Bullying started in fifth grade. In order to belong, her brother, who was more outgoing but less popular than she had been, made a glib remark about her that started a sexual rumor. Although it gained him some popularity points, she was labeled a slut (in fifth grade). She felt betrayed and afraid. In sixth grade, going to the school cafeteria was torturous because of the bullying, and she spent a great deal of time in the nurse's office. The bullying continued. In her sophomore year, she became a part of an out-group. Even in high school, she would hide when her brother's friends came over—feeling unsafe. She has never had a large friend group—she has two or three good friends. She remains, as an adult, uncomfortable in a crowd of strangers (describes herself as somewhat introverted).

At around 14 or 15, even though E felt damaged, had low self-esteem, and made poor boyfriend choices, she always did well in school. She describes her high school friends as also damaged (had broken lives) and often traumatized in some way. She no longer knew how to get along with mainstream, happy, popular kids. Although E doesn't remember it, her mother took her to therapy when she was 14 (graduating from eighth grade). Her dad worked a lot, and her mother became very ill during that year (with resulting low energy, intolerance of strong smells). It was not easy to have friends over because of her mother's illness. She was alone a great deal. Although they seemed unaware of the depth of her being bullied, her depression, and her fears, she felt completely accepted by her parents. Nevertheless, she worried that her mother was frustrated with her and that her father was disappointed in her. She never told them of her worries. She wanted to keep her home a place free of all of that. Also, the bullying began around a sexual rumor that was started by her brother. She didn't want her parents to think that way about her. She didn't want that conflict at home. She became seriously depressed. In truth, her mother had been relieved that, during her rebellious phase, she only stopped showering.

Turning the Bad into Something Good. At some point, E knew that she had to become a tougher version of herself. Punk rock provided an opportunity in the summer after her freshman year. Her parents didn't learn of her being bullied until a family session in her senior year of high school. E says that, although she always cared about how she looked, as a punk rocker, they showered infrequently, wore Good Will clothes, had a Vegan diet (she says being Vegan was a way of controlling something in her life), were politically active, and were into angry punk rock music that allowed her to express her anger. She gained a lot of weight. She became "against typical white America" and "a part of the underdogs." She removed herself from the mainstream, met friends out of the area, went into unsafe, poor areas of the nearby city. They protested, were activists, provided outreach (food drives), and were protective of animal rights as well. She looks back on this period as actually a good thing—it allowed her to figure things out, to see there was more to life than high school, and to express her anger (through punk rock and protest). She gained a sense of power from these activities. She and her friends (all broken in some way) were trying to turn the bad into something good. Her parents "remained unconditionally accepting of her and of her purple-haired and smelly, Vegan friends." When asked why she didn't tell her parents, she explained that being accepted and feeling safe are two different things. She never wanted them to know about the sexual rumors and always wanted home to be a safe place, free of all of that. Also, her mother was very ill, and her dad was not a talker.

Therapy. E remembers "a slew of therapists" between beginning college and age 20. Although she feels she did have a chance to grieve her grandfather in her different therapies, she cried and appeared deeply sad when she told the story of her grandfather's death. Her few minutes alone with him had re-defined her and her life. In those few minutes, she lost her sense of safety, her joy, her peace, and her social status. She developed a persistent fear and sense of deep aloneness and damage, unable to share her pain or subsequent painful experiences. The life path she was on took a sharp turn, and, as she put it, "My life spiraled" out of control.

She says that the exposure therapies helped—she could talk about things that had happened without getting emotional. At one point, she had a psychiatrist for meds and a therapist for talking. It felt good to discuss things. However, over time, she learned to do a good job of telling the story. In addition, she dreaded going because she might go in happy, but always left feeling depressed. Although narrative processing had helped her initially, in retrospect, she felt the therapies that helped her to move forward were more helpful than talking about the past. One therapist had her bring her parents and brother in. She had a chance to tell them what she had been through, and how they had played a role in it. She told them that she had forgiven them, and they had a chance to apologize to her. It was a very helpful session. Years later, she was given anti-depressants because of brain scan results. They seemed to worsen traits that she then learned were signs of ADD. Both she and her mother consider treating the ADD was a turning point in her recovery. Learning about her ADD and being able to put words to some of her behaviors helped a lot (she could tell people, "Don't think I don't like you, if I don't call you back right away. Sometimes I forget or avoid it because I get anxious." The ADD meds really helped. Her mother also feels that E's marriage was a part of improvement. She is now a well-liked young mother. She knows her limitations. She is very involved in her church and still helps those less fortunate than she, but without the anger, uncleanliness, or protest. She is considered by those who know her to be a very lovely person, inside and out—competent, caring, and faithful.

Note:
All case examples are disguised, may be combined cases, and have had details changed to protect individuals.

Box 3.2 Faulty Attachment and Negativity Translate into Sibling Abuse and Additional Victimization

Danya

Danya's parents were very much in love and spent as much time as possible with each other. After Danya's mother (Mom) became pregnant, her father (Dad) had to move to Europe for his work. When Danya was born, her mother sailed with her to join her father. Mom described Danya as always cranky and nasty, since she was a baby. She called the ship-ride to Europe "the trip from Hell." Although there was some stress related to the separation from her husband during her pregnancy, Mom stated that her own mother was like Danya—angry, grumpy, bitter, and held grudges. Dad seemed to feel that Danya had undermined his relationship with his wife. He resented and wanted nothing to do with his cranky first child. His coolness toward Danya never fully abated, and she never stopped trying to find her way into his good graces. Danya was described as "always difficult to love." She was mean and picked on her sister and neighborhood kids. As an adult, she was described as "like the 45th president" ("deflects everything off of herself"; "even if she's done horrible things, she makes the other guy wrong"; uses name-calling to diminish others ... boils everyone down to a specified negative name" ...). As a child, she called sister Tally a fat pig, stupid, and/or a loser. As an adult, Danya has called Tally a "fat f_ _k." She tried "all of her life" to gain her father's favor without success. Finally, she began to say that he was a child-beater (completely unfounded—he never hit her or any of his children according to Tally and Mom). She is described as having remained an angry, mean person, who periodically threatens and always disrupts. She has been banned from family gatherings because of her behaviors, which adds to her rage. As an adult, she has threatened to burn Tally's house down. Tally's husband describes Danya as being the most negative, unlucky person he has ever met—she has a great deal of bad luck; "bad things happen to her all the time." Tally describes Danya as very negative, fearful, mean, and angry.

Tally

Danya's sister, Tally, was born when Danya was four years old. When his second daughter was born, Dad fell very in love with her. She was his adorable baby, and they remained close throughout his life.

As a result, Danya resented Tally and grew more and more angry. She picked on Tally relentlessly. Tally's earliest memory was of being in a stroller (around age 18–24 months) and Danya taking her up to the top of a hill and pushing her. Tally went flying down the hill and rolled into the street. She was terrified.

When Tally was three or four, her grandfather molested her. On school vacations, she was left with her grandparents for a weekend or longer. The grandparents would take two children to alleviate stress in Mom and Dad's home. It was a treat to go, because there were pancakes and candy (Tally said, "No wonder food is my anesthesia"). She described how, on one occasion, her grandfather forced her to open her mouth and permit him to place his penis inside. She vividly described the choking sensation and being unable to breathe, the intense fear … she thought she was going to die. On occasion, Tally was left at her aunt and uncle's house. Her uncle was on disability and at home all of the time. Two or three times he took Tally on his lap and fondled her, while the wife was in another part of the house cleaning or cooking. Tally thought it was really creepy. When Tally was 4 or 4.5, Danya pushed her into some bushes that caused paper-like cuts all over her. When Tally was age 4.5 or 5, she was climbing up the ladder to the top bunk, when Danya pushed the ladder backward. She remembers being afraid she was going to die as she was falling backward. She hit her head. This time, her father saw what happened, took care of her, and put a stop to Danya's threatening behaviors. His protection lasted until he had to start traveling for his work again. When Tally was 12 (seventh grade), Danya, knife in hand, chased her down the alley yelling, "I'm going to kill you." During that year, Dad went to see a psychiatrist regularly "for help with his wild and unruly four children" (especially Danya and Tally who were in "regular drag-out fights"). Dad sent Tally to his psychiatrist when she was 12.

Refuge. In contrast to her own home that felt "dry, dark, scary, stressful, exhausting, and void of creativity," a childless neighbor had a beautiful home with many mosaics and other art projects. When Tally was 4–5 years old, she would go there to escape. She would water color and do other art projects with the woman who lived there. It was very peaceful. Tally says, "[Neighbor, N] moved slowly, spent a lot of time 'Seeing' me"—she "acknowledged my person." N loved her art, and regularly gave Tally tours of her work. She never ran out of ideas. Her house smelled like oil paints. There was a beautiful pond with turtles and a bamboo grove. Tally says, "It was peace." It "was creativity" and was "magic." It was "like heaven." Tally told people she wanted to be an artist when she grew up. As an adult, in treatment, she is learning to use these images as one method to restore a sense of peace.

Symptoms. Tally developed negative expectations ("someone's out to get me") and persistent nightmares and night terrors about a tiger chasing her. She would run down the hall in the night to get away from the tiger. Dad went to a psychiatrist for advice. Dad started sitting with Tally on his lap asking her about the tiger—what he was like and what he did. He began reframing the tiger into a kitten who was harmless. Tally stopped having the tiger dreams, but remained fearful. There were many children in the neighborhood. She couldn't watch cartoons with them, because cartoons were violent with threatening characters. Her parents forbade her to watch, because she became extremely distressed. When friends watched "Wiley Coyote" or "Little Mermaid" or "Chiller," she could not stand to watch. She couldn't watch *Wizard of Oz* because of the flying monkeys and the witch. In adulthood, *flying monkeys* became a metaphor to describe endangering persons (some of whom were not actually dangerous).

In kindergarten, Tally wanted to stay home sick with her mom. Her mom was very nurturing when she was sick, and being sick became a way out of danger. During school years, she became an isolationist. She never could participate fully. She would create reasons why being around other people was not worth her time—e.g., boys were too stupid. In the fifth grade, she had one close friend who was, like her, more mature than other children. One day the friend came to her and said she was moving away. Tally was very "upset and demoralized." That was another reason to be an isolationist—"you can't trust anyone." She's never had a good friend since then (has never felt she could fully trust them). After that she had only fleeting friends. "People hurt you." She became rageful. Her mother "never stepped up and protected me" and "my father was a rager—he would put up with it and put up with it, then blow, with a full six-months-worth of complaints, he exploded."

Tally's Adulthood. As an adult, Tally still fears that her sister will find a way to kill her. Adult Tally worked, and was less often ill. However, as an adult, she has developed an autoimmune disease (autoimmune ailments have been significantly linked to trauma). She is a successful executive businesswoman. One of Tally's adult coping practices has been great self-sufficiency. Taking charge and taking control are frequently used responses to feeling threat. Outwardly, the excuse is that people won't do things right. She says she is aware that she must be in control so that she won't get hurt. Her control issues sometimes alienate people, including family. Her social interactions (including with husband) are curtailed in a number of ways—e.g., no even mildly scary movies. Even as an adult, Tally cannot stand to watch cartoons or violence. She couldn't see Harry Potter movies or other movies with threat. She will only go to mild movies (usually romantic comedies or other harmless movies). She did okay with C.S. Lewis's tales of Narnia, however. She felt the characters were less threatening and more human. Because she could not go to most movies and doesn't trust anyone, she has missed opportunities in childhood and adulthood for building comraderies. She has missed some of the lessons that can be learned from tales—e.g., to say "Riddikulus" and change the mental image for some fears or to use the Patronus charm (or other self-talk or imagery method) to keep away the Dementors who drain away all of her happy memories (Harry Potter).

Avoidance. Tally still avoids doing things because they are risky. Her self-talk, days or weeks before an event (e.g., a wedding, a gathering of friends), may tie her in knots, make her feel really bad in her body, and cause such physiological distress that she feels "I don't feel well" becomes a truthful although self-made excuse to stay home. Being with others is "too risky"—"too many flying monkeys" ... "they come out of nowhere." She has learned from her mother to be pleasant and upbeat on the surface, and believes that she looks calm. Tally occasionally feels "in the zone." She has practiced yoga for years, and feels that without it she would have become agoraphobic, among other things.

Yoga. Tally functions well, despite her fears. She feels better if home and office are uncluttered and tidy, "free of mess." She feels she can replicate that internally. She also feels safe on her corner of the couch watching comedies and light or spiritual fare. Although she said she does not have faith in God or man, she feels unbalanced all day if she doesn't spend at least 10 min. in the morning reading spiritual books, praying, and meditating.

Family. Tally says, "Metaphorically, my children got a mother who is calling 911 all of the time and a father who doesn't recognize the need to call 911, when it's there." A pattern of frequent overreaction by Tally and minimization by her husband has been observed by others. Tally remains fearful of her sister. She spent the summer after Danya threatened to burn down her home, unable to sleep waiting to hear the gasoline pouring around the house. They went to a family cabin with the extended family, and she feared Danya would come and burn all of the family (who had shut her out) at once. As time has passed, Tally's brother has also become negative and grumpy and is trying to undermine or take Tally's business, with legal actions. Tally says she is living in terror and doesn't know what to do. She has discussed the type of attorney she needs to face her brother's multiple, "cut-throat" attorneys. Her attorney is mild mannered and kind.

Now. Tally has started to increase her support systems, to improve her coping repertoire, to change her self-talk, and has recently been inspired both by a book about how to be happy, written by a master Yogi (after visiting a retreat site with a group of very peaceful people), and by participation in Somatic Experiencing® Therapy—a body-focused treatment that has been used for PTSD (e.g., Brom et al., 2017). She is beginning to find that she can have a different attitude toward what is happening in her extended family. Danya, again recently, threatened to come to her house and kill her while her husband was away, and her brother continues litigation. For the first time, Tally now doubts that her sister will actually hurt her—recognizing how many times she has threatened, and she asks, "What can they take from me, really? I have other family, now. If I lose the business, we'll adjust."

Note:
All case examples are disguised, may be combined cases, and have had details changed to protect individuals.

2014). Preconception but not pre-natal stress has also increased the risk of premature birth and infant mortality (Class et al., 2013). Additionally, maternal anxiety and pre-natal stress have been linked to subsequent neurodevelopmental or behavioral problems and to difficult temperament in infants and children (Beydoun & Saftlas, 2008; Charil, Laplante, Vaillancourt, & King, 2010; Chapter 5). Difficult temperament may result in distress and interpersonal difficulties that in turn affect self-esteem and ongoing quality of life.

Attachment has proven to be a potent, long-term moderator of social and behavioral cascades from infancy (Boldt, Kochanska, & Jonas, 2017). For mother– and father–child relationships at infant age 15 months, externalizing in preadolescence was only significant for insecure attachments. Traumas also may have an indirect effect on children's trajectories and recovery through their impact on parenting—e.g., undermining parenting quality (Masten & Osofsky, 2010) and/or their impact on how others (e.g., peers, teachers) see or respond to a youth (Boxes 3.1, 3.2). As the Parkland, Florida school shooting demonstrated, victimization may lead to increased support and/or admiration for some youth. In contrast, victimization of a child or her/his posttrauma behaviors has sometimes elicited disdain from other youth and adults, with losses in well-being and opportunity.

In addition to the ongoing consequences of childhood trauma is the impact of such traumas or PT symptoms on treatment for specific disorders. For example, emotional abuse predicts longer treatment for depression (Maikovich-Fong, Speltz, & Jaffee, 2015; Walker et al., 2000) and has been a factor in non-completion or increased treatment resistance (Maikovich-Fong et al., 2015). Childhood traumas have been related to cPTSD and PTSD symptoms in later life (Krammer et al., 2015). The ability versus the inability or reluctance to talk about past traumatic experiences in spite of a need or urge to do so (dysfunctional disclosure) and social acknowledgment (e.g., whether people react with understanding and acknowledge the individual as a victim or survivor or are rejecting) are important social-interpersonal factors that each mediate PT adjustment across life (Krammer et al., 2015; Maercker & Horn, 2012). However, the two factors are not independent—a cascade has been found in more than one study: type of social acknowledgment influences level of dysfunctional disclosure, which in turn influences PTSS (Krammer et al., 2015; Müller, Forstmeier, Wagner, & Maercker, 2011).

Posttrauma Narratives that Influence Communities and Individuals

Traumas affect communities as well as individuals. The way a community defines an event and its aftermath as well as the community's working hypothesis and prevailing mindset influence ongoing reactions. This may be especially true when groups of trauma-exposed individuals remain in their less urban communities over time. For example, in a community where a natural disaster killed 10 elementary school children and injured many others, over time a working hypothesis emerged among community members suggesting that this was a community with bad luck or maybe even a jinx that attracted bad experiences to them. A couple of years after the initial disaster, every car accident, act of nature, or other negative event joined the list of proofs of the bad luck community. Ten years after the event, one youth described a lightning-strike (small property damage; no injuries) as a sign of the jinx. One reporter insisted that there were more suicides in this area than others in the 10 years since the disaster, even though his own research showed that the numbers were within the normal range for a community of that size. As a consequence of expectations, community members awaited the next bad thing.

In contrast to the preceding community, another community where a bomb went off in an elementary school in which children were held hostage (there were injuries but no children died), the community was heartened by the story that an angel or angels had assisted children to safety. Community members sought evidence for a miraculous preparation and protection before and during the event and found hope and upliftment. Many years later, the affected adults, sometimes tearfully, focused on the miracle of their survival and of the things that happened before and during the event. One mother—who had been a child in the room when the bomb went off—spoke of how her children are a miracle because of the miracle of her own survival.

In locations affected by mass violence or disaster, subgroups of individuals may progress with their own theories that engender either hope (e.g., beliefs in growth and protection), helplessness (e.g., conspiracy theories or evidence that suggest the threat endures), or other emotion-inducing beliefs. For example, in New Orleans after Hurricane Katrina, one group spoke of an explosion purposely set that caused massive destruction. The *explosion* was discussed as a conspiracy against poorer land owners or blacks and was described variously, e.g., as attempted genocide or to gain property (Myers, 2006). While the Army Corps of Engineers stated that Katrina was too massive for a protection system intended for a category 3 hurricane, the LSU Hurricane Center explained that the "explosion," in fact, was the loud structural failure of the "protective" barriers that should have handled Hurricane Katrina with relative ease (Grunwald & Glasser, 2005). As is true for other multifaceted traumas, after war and massive amounts of destruction, the intense and horrific exposures—e.g., repeated horrible events, prolonged fears, and many witnessing or injuring experiences—have been associated with traumatic and other reactions (e.g., Thabet, Tawahina, Punamäki, & Vostanis, 2015). Nevertheless, a group of less exposed adults in one war-torn region remained upbeat in the belief that renewed spirituality would serve to protect them. Clinicians and researchers do not always remain in an affected region long enough to hear the emergence of posttrauma community narratives. It is important to anticipate the possible development of such working theories in order to enhance the possibility of hopefulness and growth—e.g., a lightning-strike with little damage and no injuries can be defined in a positive way.

Cascading Effects of Trauma

Briere and Jordan (2009) have noted that maltreatment-related symptoms in adult women likely reflect "a complex, interdependent, sometimes interactive cascade of conditions and events, leading to a range of negative psychological outcomes that may vary significantly from woman to woman" (p. 383). Terms such as cumulative effects, cascading or snowball effects, progressive effects, transactional effects, chain reactions, or contagion effects refer to the effects of traumas that can spread or increase over time (over weeks, months, or years), from one level to another, from one area of functioning or domain to another, from one person to another, from persons to communities, and from one generation to the next, through multiple mediating processes (Caspi, 1998; Cicchetti, 2003; Masten & Cicchetti, 2010; Masten & Narayan, 2012; see Nader, 2008). A youth on a successful path among peers and toward a career may be derailed by the effects of traumatic experiences (Nader, 2008). Death or injuries of loved ones may have additional cumulative effects.

Because, from each phase of development, children take the biological, cognitive, social, and emotional knowledge, skills, and other resources they have gained into future situations and challenges (Geiger & Crick, 2001; Nader, 2008; Price & Lento, 2001), trauma's effects on the brain and developing skills can have such cascading and cumulative effects for youth (Caspi, 1998; Cicchetti, 2003; Lupien, McEwen, Gunnar, & Heim, 2009; Nader, 2008). Consequently, early traumas may have a greater capacity to impose significant and cascading dysfunction than experiences occurring later (e.g., in adolescence or adulthood) when skills such as self-regulation have already been established. Traumatized children may show developmental delays (Chapter 1—e.g., brain, language; Chapter 4)—e.g., adopted and foster children diagnosed with reactive attachment disorder have exhibited developmental delays in communication, daily living skills, and socialization (e.g., developmental-age equivalency of 4.4 years for average chronological age of 9.9 years; Becker-Weidman, 2009).

Traumas (e.g., maltreatment) that occur during early brain development "may potentiate a cascade of maturational and structural changes that eventuate in the neural system proceeding along a trajectory that deviates from ... normal neurobiological development" (Cicchetti, Handley, & Rogosch, 2015a, p. 563)—e.g., changes in volume (e.g., amygdala, hippocampus; Aas et al., 2012; Baker et al., 2013; Bremner, 2006), dendrite atrophy (i.e., impaired receptors of electrochemical signals), and suppression of brain cell growth (neurogenesis; Aas et al., 2014; Herpfer et al., 2012; Sapolsky, 1998; Wolf, 2003; Chapter 1). For example, limbic system impairments (e.g., related to motivation, emotion expression; Glossary) persist into adulthood, and relate to the risk of developing, e.g., depressive and/or PTS symptoms (Dackis, Rogosch, Oshri, & Cicchetti, 2012; Gibb et al., 2010). On the other hand, as noted, some effects are age period specific (Chapter 1, age-related chapters). For European males in a cohort study (France, England and Wales, Sweden), stressors experienced during ages 10–14 were more strongly associated with decreased life span than those experienced during infancy, ages 1–4, 5–9, and 15–19 (Falconi, Gimmel, Dahl, & Catalano, 2014). Some evidence suggests that youth consistently abused into adolescence and those abused at an older age (mean 10.6) are more likely to be incarcerated than maltreated younger children (see Danielson, Moreland, & Walsh, 2015).

Trauma-related disruptions to academic and interpersonal functioning as well as other disturbed processes—e.g., changes in neurobiology, personality, cognition, reactivity, friend choice—may drastically alter a youth's life course (see Nader, 2008; Perry, 2006). Childhood ill-temperedness (a personality trait and/or a result of trauma), for example, has been found to lead to cumulative consequences such as contentious relationships with caretakers and peers, difficulties with school authorities, negative school experiences, and lower occupational status (Caspi, 1998). Initially and over time, negative self-talk may result in such experiences as failures, avoidance of seeking desired goals, and unpleasant interactions. The consequences of failures, negativity, and lack of effort to attain desired goals may include missed opportunities, lost respect from others, disruption of relationships, and loss of status—e.g., a previously popular girl was described as a bully, because of increased irritability after a trauma in which she was shot.

Following trauma, normally viable coping methods may become faulty. Self-distraction, self-soothing—e.g., reasonable amounts of comfort food or drink; calming or "head-clearing" activities such as a warm bath, a run, a game, etc.—or arousal reduction (e.g., through meditation, activities) can be beneficial ways of coping with stress. However, for traumatized youth and later as adults, self-soothing or distraction to reduce or avoid trauma-related and subsequently other distress may include dissociation, substance abuse, or non-productive tension reducing behaviors such as promiscuity, overeating and/or purging, impulsive behaviors (e.g., aggression, suicidal behaviors, dangerous risk-taking), or self-mutilation (Briere & Jordan, 2009), each of which may undermine ongoing functioning. Spinazzola and colleagues (2014) point out that, following psychological maltreatment, substance abuse may become a coping mechanism and, itself, a cascading secondary outcome.

Cascades from Individual Symptoms

At any age/stage, strong challenges to self-concept and disruptions to the development of important life skills—e.g., trust, self-worth, sense of control, autonomy, and cognitive processing, among others—may have a major adverse impact on a person's life and course of development (Nader, 2008). For example, negative reactivity in school children (ages 6–7) has predicted poor social preference in later childhood and early adolescence. Poor social standing among peers, in turn, has predicted greater engagement in antisocial behavior in later adolescence (Buil et al., 2017). Negative life events may trigger a cascade of negative results starting from loss of resilience and/or protective factors and may lead to increased risk of developing mental health, interpersonal, and other problems. Specific individual symptoms (e.g., impulsivity, emotionality, dissociation, aggression, anxiety, reduced attention; poor sleep) that may themselves trigger cascades of outcomes following traumatic events influence ongoing environmental (e.g., reactions from others; academic climate), behavioral, and other effects (Nader, 2008; Tomko et al., 2015). For example, poor sleep may result in many other symptoms, such as poor attention, poor concentration, increased irritability, and clumsiness, which in turn may result in additional and prolonged other reactions. Evidence suggests that trauma plays an important role in the emergence of catatonia in children, which may lead to premature death (Benarous et al., 2017). The individual PT symptoms to follow include a sampling of the possible cascading results from an individual symptom.

Aggression

Aggression has many associations (e.g., shame, trauma; Chapters 1, 4, 8, 11; Nader, 2008), including traumatic exposure (Ford, 2002; Greenwald, 2002), which in turn may lead to peer rejection followed by evolving symptoms related to exclusion and/or aggression (Nader, 2008; Chapter 1). Youth who are aggressive may show more externalizing behaviors (e.g., impulsivity, oppositional behavior) in middle childhood, and, in adolescence, more conduct problems (e.g., delinquency, antisocial personality features) than peers (Crick et al., 1997). Following traumas, youth may develop negative attribution and expectation biases, changed morality, script-like patterns of interaction, and/or additional experiences that increase the likelihood of continued aggression (see Nader, 2008—Chapter 14). They may choose friends who are also aggressive and/or who have been through similar experiences. Laird et al. (2001) found that nearly two thirds of youth who continued to show externalizing behavior problems, from early childhood to adolescence, had endured peer rejection in childhood, and over one third were highly involved with antisocial peers. Aggression or other antisocial behaviors in childhood increase the risk of later exposure to significant negative life events and psychosocial adversities (Rutter, 2003). Additionally, traumas may translate into patterns of interpersonal aggression that become a part of later parenting or spousal behaviors as victim or perpetrator. For example, childhood sexual or physical abuse is a risk factor for adult domestic violence (Wekerle, Wolfe, Dunston, & Alldred, 2014).

Highly psychopathic inmates convicted of violent crimes—e.g., homicide, kidnapping, organized crime, torture—have significantly undergone higher levels of victimization and exposure to stressful events—e.g., physical and sexual abuse; compared to inmates with minor offenses (Borja & Ostrosky, 2013). To achieve personal goals, psychopaths show arrogance, callousness, and superficial charm, interpersonally. Although they may appear normal, they are manipulative, are unable to develop strong affective bonds, and lack empathy, guilt, or remorse. Irresponsibility and impulsivity are commonly related to psychopathy and to antisocial personality disorder (the latter may be a low- to mid-level of psychopathy). Borja and Ostrosky (2013) found that the sum of traumatic events experienced along with emotional abuse correlated with psychopathy scores. While a hostile environment may have favored development of an antisocial lifestyle (e.g., robbery, frauds, illegal acts) to obtain financial rewards, intended abuse aimed at hurting victims physically and emotionally favored the affective detriments observed in psychopaths, leading to extreme violence to achieve goals.

Impulsivity and Negative Emotions

Impulsivity and negative emotions may follow trauma. Both impulsivity and emotional lability at an early age can be amplified (e.g., by family and other environmental invalidation; by trauma) and lead to later emotional and behavioral dysregulation (Crowell, Beauchaine, & Linehan, 2009). Negative emotional states may result in an emotional cascade and consequently result in dysregulated or impulsive behavior (perhaps used to distract from the rumination) or result in other problematic outcomes (Selby, Anestis, & Joiner, 2007). For example, an individual may ruminate on negative emotions or the situation inducing such emotions—e.g., thinking about an argument and repeatedly, mentally fighting with the other person—thereby increasing negative states (e.g., anger), followed by impulsive actions to "get back at" the other or to harm the self. PTSD-associated alexithymia (difficulty identifying and labeling emotions) was discussed in Chapter 1. In a discussion of borderline personality disorder (BPD, a disorder linked to trauma and to other variables), Tomko and colleagues (2015) demonstrated that negative emotion-related impulsivity may result from poor differentiation of emotions. Undifferentiated affect has, in turn, been associated with reduced quality of interpersonal relationships, increased alcohol use, and non-suicidal self-injury. For individuals with borderline PD or depressive disorder (N = 131; Tomko et al., 2015), while general negative affect (e.g., anger, sadness, or anxiety) has interfered with the ability to attend to environmental stimuli and to persevere through difficult tasks, undifferentiated negative affect (lack of discrete emotions) significantly predicted negative urgency (being prone to respond impulsively, rather than adaptively to negative affect), lack of planning or premeditation, and motor impulsivity. Across time (28 days), lower differentiation of negative affect states related to an increased tendency to act rashly in response to extreme negative mood states and to a greater inability to plan or persist through tasks. Although the propensity to experience negative affect is also a strong predictor of impulsivity, the interaction of negative affect and undifferentiated negative affect was especially predictive of momentary impulsive feelings (Tomko et al., 2015). Impulsiveness may result in a multitude of problems (e.g., incarceration, relationship problems), which may have *snowballing* or devastating effects.

Attention Problems

Attention and its associated control systems are recognized as critical common processes underpinning important aspects of cognitive and emotional functioning (Fearon & Belsky, 2004). Good attention is needed to perform well in all realms of life—academic, professional, and relationship. Problems with attention and/or concentration following traumatization may lead to dysfunction in multiple realms simultaneously. When youth have difficulty maintaining attention needed for learning, congruent conversations, and task performance, then relationships, academic status, and job performance may suffer and continue to decline. Deficits in attentional control have been implicated in many psychological disorders (Fearon & Belsky, 2004). A strong link between PTSD and attention problems in childhood or adulthood has been documented (Kaplow et al., 2008). Garrido, Taussig, Culhane, and Raviv (2011) found that both minor and severe physical abuse were associated with greater levels of attention problems and with aggressive behavior. Attention has mediated the association between abuse severity and aggression, accounting for over three quarters of direct effects of severe abuse on aggression and about one quarter to one half between minor abuse and aggression. Higher degrees of attentional control have predicted higher levels of recovery from trauma-related negative moods following retelling of a trauma (Bardeen & Read, 2010).

Dissociation

Peri-traumatic and persistent dissociative symptoms have predicted the development and continuation of PTSD symptoms (Werner & Griffin, 2012) and reduced treatment success without inclusion of specific methods to reduce dissociation (Brand et al., 2014; Cloitre, Petkova, Wang, & Lu, 2012). Witnesses as well as direct victims of traumas have demonstrated dissociation (Hagan, Hulette, & Lieberman, 2015). Dissociation predicts later attention problems (Kaplow et al., 2008). Children sexually abused by a family member and/or who reported symptoms of dissociation upon disclosure of abuse have shown increased risk of developing attention problems eight to 36 months after disclosure. For children with more types and severity of forms of childhood maltreatment as well as higher levels of depressive, dissociative, and posttraumatic symptoms (than non-self-injuring children), Franzke, Wabnitz, and Catani (2015) found that dissociative symptoms (but not post-traumatic or depressive symptoms) mediated the relationship between childhood maltreatment and later non-suicidal self-injury (NSSI). Franzke and colleagues suggest that NSSI may be an attempt to interrupt dissociation or to counteract the feelings of numbness and emptiness associated with dissociation (Chapter 16). Wekerle et al. (2014) have suggested that the fragmentation of affect and experience may progress over time into borderline personality disorder, chronic pain, or dissociative identity disorder.

Anxiety or Irritability

Anxiety or irritability may impact youth in a cascade of results. For example, anxious individuals may be more sensitive to peer rejection (Chapter 11), which may make them more vulnerable to peer influence—e.g., to drink or use drugs, linked to its own cascade of life changes (Oshri, Sutton, Warner, & Miller, 2015; Purdie & Downey, 2000). Irritability is a common expression of distress for both traumatized and depressed youth (Hammen & Rudolph, 2003). Hypersensitivity to stimuli, such as sounds, may lend to irritability (Bloch, Silber & Perry, 1956; Carrion, Weems, Ray, & Reiss, 2002; Nader, 2008). Irritability may repel others, and consequently, adults as well as peers may avoid and/or see a youth as less worthy of receiving opportunities. In contrast, posttrauma withdrawal and/or quiet suffering may result in neglect and also interfere with social development, learning, and other important tasks.

Self-Concept

Diminished self-esteem may follow events that directly devalue a child, expose a child to stigma, or decrease opportunities to engage in esteem-enhancing activities (Haine et al., 2003; Boxes 3.1, 3.2, 2.3). Low self-concept is a risk factor for PTSD and can be a result of traumatization (e.g., a result of inter-parental violence; maltreatment; assault; peer victimization; e.g., Fosse, 2006; Levendosky & Graham-Bermann, 2001; Litman et al., 2015; Nader & Fletcher, 2014; Spinazzola et al., 2014). For example, adults bullied in childhood have had lower self-esteem, higher psychiatric symptoms, and external locus of control (Fosse, 2006). Trauma or loss may affect self-esteem, and lower self-esteem may affect competence, which in turn affects more than one area of ongoing functioning. Low self-esteem has been linked to psychopathology, vulnerability to criticism, self-destructive behaviors, negative feelings about self and others, interference with relationships, negative emotionality, and social withdrawal. In contrast, high self-esteem has been linked to positive emotions; life satisfaction; aggression under threat; adjustment and well-being in social relationships; school achievement; resilience to stressful life events; and the reduced likelihood of anxiety or depression (see Nader, 2008—Table 1.3). Poor self-image has been a factor in the perpetuation of anxiety and of depression (adults: Iancu, Bodner, & Ben-Zion, 2015; Wegener et al., 2015) as well as in other problems that influence ongoing quality of life (see Information Processing, to follow; Box 3.1).

Trauma also may interfere with the ability to achieve optimal creativity (e.g., "flow" Csikszentmihalyi, 1990, 1997a, 1997b; Glossary) or previously automatic and/or well-focused, skilled, esteem-enhancing activities (Nader, 2008). Such interference may greatly reduce success, future opportunities, and self-concept, especially if self-concept is highly linked to such activities. For example, when success and self-concept are tied to athletic skill or to a skill involving creative problem-solving, the loss of creativity and automatic excellence can devastate self-concept with ongoing repercussions.

Information Processing

Faulty or changed information processing may follow traumatic experiences and may combine with other symptoms creating a cascade of outcomes (Nader, 2008). Increased biochemical reactivity may combine with alterations in information processing—e.g., attributional biases; changed expectations; negativity or perceptual biases; negative self-talk in stressful or challenging situations—and/or combine with trauma-related automatic reactions—e.g., aggressive self-protection; failure to protect oneself; watchful freezing (Dalgleish et al., 2003; Dodge, Bates, & Pettit, 1990; Dodge et al., 1995). Combined, they may contribute to outbursts of anger or aggression or withdrawal and subsequent school and interpersonal difficulties.

Changes in information processing may include trauma-compelled script-like behavior patterns that greatly influence ongoing interactions and goal-directed behaviors—e.g., identification with a victim, perpetrator, rescuer, witness, etc.; preoccupation with thwarted, intense peri-traumatic desires to act (Nader, 2008—Chapter 14). In a television interview, an actor, well known in the mid-20th century, told of an incident when he was a baby: when his mother accidentally let go of it, his baby carriage went flying down a hill and into the street. He explained that this had become a metaphor for his life. He repeatedly flew into dangerous situations, feeling unable to control the outcome. Another example of posttrauma script-like behavior is one evoked from an intense peri-traumatic desire to assist a friend and/or other victims: a mass violence victim who desperately wanted to but was unable to help others—especially his best friend who died during the mass shooting in a public place—subsequently repeatedly tried to rescue friends, sometimes putting himself in life-threatening danger to do so (later, he was stabbed protecting others; Nader, 2008).

Individuals are selectively responsive to information that is consistent with their self-views and expectations, and they selectively interpret information based on personal biases (Caspi, 1998; Crick & Dodge, 1994; Dalgleish et al., 2003; Nader, 2008). For example, individuals with social anxiety disorder believe the world to be and experience the world as threatening and dangerous (Iancu et al., 2015). They fear and expect others to judge them and expect to be embarrassed by their own behaviors. They may interpret another's gaze as an indicator of criticism and/or rejection. Following trauma exposure, individuals may develop changed expectations such as expectations of hostility or harm from others. Such expectations may increase reactivity, thereby changing what youth evoke from others and influencing the environments youth create for themselves (Caspi, 1998; Nader, 2008; Nader & Fletcher, 2014). In a reactive world, expectation or interpretation biases may create corresponding facts (Caspi, 1998; Crick, 1995; Nader, 2008—Chapters 4 and 14). That is, expectations may lead to behaviors that in turn elicit reactions that perpetuate the expectations (Caspi, 1998; Boxes 3.3, 15.1; Chapter 12—ODD and Interpersonal Relating). For example, negative expectations (e.g., of hostility, rejection) may lead to anticipatory rudeness or retaliation that in turn elicits anger or hostility from others (confirming expectation). Similarly, a youth's fears of abandonment or rejection may lead to excessive reassurance seeking or to tantrums in response to perceived signs of rejection that in turn make people want to stay away from them (Box 15.1).

Box 3.3 In-Kind Response

For most people it's easier to be around people who are kind and/or seem to like them than to be around a person who is negative and/or seems to think ill of them. Social threat also may elicit fight, flight, or freeze reactions.

a. Diane was a friendly, outgoing, and securely attached teenager. When she called someone, there was a joyful, "Hi [name], this is Diane," and a pause as if waiting to hear welcome and delight in the other person's voice. Even slight acquaintances often responded with the expected welcome and delight—sometimes to their surprise. In person, Diane showed validation to others and seemed to expect the same from them. She expected the best from others. It was easy for people to be around her. People enjoyed her company and felt validated in her presence. They seemed to respond in kind.
b. Collin's father had committed suicide when he was a boy. Collin was a "good-looking" boy but was generally a pessimistic person. He expected things to go wrong, and he expected that people would be hostile, would not give him a chance, and/or would misinterpret him. He complained a lot about things. He was often irritable and seemed angry or contemptuous toward others. They responded to him by either finding a reason to stay away from him, returning the anger or contempt, or becoming immobilized in his presence. Startled or "dirty" looks, exclusion, or snapping back were frequent responses to him. He was so difficult to be around that no one thought about how lonely or depressed he was. Collin could frequently be heard saying, "I can never get a break." He was nice to another person who was being supportive of him, but, from an external perspective, he seemed to turn on them and often lost their support. He would say negative things about peers he thought had less power than he did. Occasionally, out of anger or frustration, he threatened others (although he never actually physically hurt anyone). People lost trust toward him and some feared him. He seemed to elicit all of his worst fears from others—e.g., hostility, rejection, things turning out poorly. He began to take or buy things to comfort himself.

Note:
All case examples are disguised, may be combined cases, and have had details changed to protect individuals.

Self-Reflection

Childhood traumatic experiences may result in poor metacognitive monitoring or reflective functioning—the ability to step back and consider one's own cognitive processes as objects of thought or reflection (Fonagy, 2006; Fonagy & Bateman, 2016). In turn, the absence of a self-reflective function may result in lack of a capacity to empathize with others and to place personal emotions in a meaningful context (Knox, 2003). Such conditions influence ongoing personal and interpersonal functioning (see Developmental Skills, Chapter 1—Perspective-Taking).

Attachment Style and Emotion Dysregulation

Chronic stress induced in caretaking environments can interfere with the successful achievement of developmental skills (e.g., secure attachments, emotion regulation strategies), which may potentiate a cascading effect of deficits resulting in maladaptation during young adulthood (Oshri et al., 2015;

Chapter 4). Adult attachment style and emotion dysregulation are among potential mechanisms through which maltreatment leads to risk behaviors (e.g., risky sex; substance abuse). In a study of undergraduate students (N = 361; Oshri et al., 2015), emotional and sexual maltreatment (but not verbal abuse) related to anxious and avoidant attachment styles, emotion dysregulation, and a variety of risk behaviors. Verbal abuse was directly related to alcohol use. Individuals with a history of childhood trauma and avoidant attachment styles may engage in risk behaviors through use of strategies that include emotional disengagement (e.g., when participating in antisocial behaviors; Mikulincer, Shaver, & Pereg, 2003).

Cascades from Neurobiological Changes

In addition to a marked increase in risk of psychopathology (e.g., PTSD, depression, bipolar disorder, schizophrenia), exposure to early life trauma can produce a cascade of neurobiological changes (e.g., associated with adult cognitive deficits; Gould et al., 2012; see Nader & Fletcher, 2014; Savitz et al., 2007) as well as a cascade of negative consequences related to stress sensitivity and responsiveness and to limbic system development and functioning (Dackis et al., 2012; Lupien et al., 2009). For example, child maltreatment is linked to lasting changes in neuroendocrine regulation, alterations in brain structure and function, and symptoms of "limbic irritability"—e.g., somatic and perceptual distortions, brief hallucinatory events, motor automatisms, and dissociative symptoms; like temporal lobe epilepsy—which may stem from increased excitatory neurotransmission following maltreatment (Dackis et al., 2012). Dackis et al. found significant indirect effects of maltreatment on depression and dissociation via limbic irritability (moderated by FKBP5 genetic polymorphism; Chapter 1; Table A4.1). Posttrauma changes in glucocorticoid sensitivity and posttrauma hypo- or hyper-cortisol production have been related to increased risk in the occurrence and maintenance of PTSD and other post-adversity psychopathology, sometimes influenced by diathesis-stress vulnerability or reactivity (see Alexander et al., 2018).

Box 3.4 Exposure to Hurricane Katrina

For hours after Hurricane Katrina, six-year-old Tanya was on the roof of a house with her sisters waiting for rescue. She saw bloated bodies float by and every time the water started to slap against the edges of the roof or spray on her, she feared that she would end up dead in the water, eaten by gators or killed by snakes. After rescue, they were relocated. In her new school, she became particularly distressed on rainy days, especially if the streets started to have water buildup. She screamed and cried when anyone splashed water on her. She screamed and pulled back when they tried to give her a bath, in the house where she, her mother, and her sisters were staying, since their relocation after the hurricane. By age 12, although she less frequently needed to use her meditative, breathing techniques when it rained, she began insisting that they live only on high ground and far away from the coast-line. At age 19, when another hurricane threatened to bring flooding rains to her area, she was anxious but had effective coping strategies to employ.

Note:
All case examples are disguised, may be combined cases, and have had details changed to protect individuals.

Long-Term Consequences of Childhood Trauma Exposure

In addition to potential and documented posttrauma cascades of symptoms, numerous long-term effects have been identified for multiple types of trauma—e.g., natural and man-made disasters, severe accidents, and interpersonal traumas such as maltreatment, bullying, or other violence. Types of trauma often co-occur—e.g., physical abuse with other interpersonal violence (e.g., witnessing domestic violence; psychological abuse; sexual abuse; Hodges et al., 2013). Although researchers have attempted to show differences in the results of different trauma types, a variety of traumas are linked to many of the same outcomes (Perez, Abrams, Lopez-Martinez, & Asmundson, 2012; Schafer & Ferraro, 2013). For example, female undergraduates with a variety of previous trauma exposures reported significantly more physical health symptoms, PTSD, and depressive symptoms—e.g., after life-threatening situations; armed robbery; traumatic death of a close person; abuse; witnessing violence (Perez et al., 2012, N = 516). Hyperarousal and depressive symptoms uniquely mediated the relationship between trauma exposure and physical health symptoms.

To follow are some of the long-term consequences found after specific types of traumas (see Table 3.1). In general, severe disasters (e.g., Katrina, Box 3.4; Kronenberg et al., 2010), war exposure (see Masten & Osofsky, 2010; Punamäki, Qouta, & El-Sarraj, 2001; Qouta et al., 2008), school violence (Pynoos et al., 1987; Nader et al., 1990; Turunen et al., 2014), and other traumas have shown that greater severity and number of experiences, adversity in the recovery environment, and lower social support are associated with more negative outcomes and fewer prosocial behaviors (Masten & Osofsky, 2010; Nader, 2008; Nader & Fletcher, 2014). Children with poly-victimization—multiple types of trauma exposure (e.g., maltreatment, accidents, disasters, robbery, and interpersonal losses)—fare worse than those with single trauma types and are significantly more likely to exhibit problems (e.g., delinquent behaviors with both juveniles and adult arrests; Danielson et al., 2015; Finkelhor, Shattuck, Turner, & Ormrod, 2014; Ford, Elhai, Connor, & Frueh, 2010; Ford, Chapman, Connor, & Cruise, 2012; Wekerle et al., 2014).

Maltreatment and Family Dysfunction

Many studies have examined *adverse childhood experiences* (ACEs—maltreatment and family dysfunction traumas) over time. ACEs include verbal, physical, or sexual abuse; family dysfunction such as a mentally ill, an incarcerated, or a substance-abusing family member; domestic violence; and/or parental absence because of divorce or separation (Felitti et al., 1998). ACEs have been linked to a range of adult adverse outcomes (e.g., SA; psychological distress—e.g., depression; physical maladies—see ACEs and Health; Bynum et al., 2010). For adults seen at San Diego's Kaiser Permanente (N = 17,000; Anda & Felitti, 2003), 33% reported no ACEs, 26% reported 1, 16% related 2, 10%–3, 6%–4, 5%–5, and 6%–6. For a larger sample of adults (N = 26,229; Bynum et al., 2010), although 41% reported no ACEs, more than half (59.4%) had at least one ACE; 8.7% reported more than five adverse experiences with a sharp decrease in reporting of ACEs for individuals over age 55 (e.g., reports of physical abuse were 16.9% for ages 18–24 & 9.6% for ≥55). The effects of ACEs were cumulative: e.g., in stepwise fashion, the higher the score, the greater the chance of being a user of street drugs, tobacco, or having problems with alcohol abuse (see poly-victimization, Chapter 1; Bynum et al., 2010; Naramore, Bright, Epps, & Hardt, 2017).

Many maltreated children are able to become well-functioning adults (Afifi & MacMillan, 2011; Wekerle et al., 2014). Nevertheless, as will be discussed in other chapters, maltreatment is related to a number of negative outcomes (e.g., physical and psychological difficulties) that persist or occur in adulthood (Wekerle et al., 2014; Box 3.5). For example, maltreatment at one time-point significantly has predicted future maltreatment (also predicted by not living with biological parent or primary caregiver substance abuse, SA; Harpur, Polek, & van Harmelen, 2015). Across 13 studies, a clear, independent link was found between childhood maltreatment and poor economic outcomes

Box 3.5 The Throw-Away Child

Because it was believed that her adolescent mother would be able to take her back after she stabilized her situation, Wendy was placed in temporary foster care. She moved from one foster home to another (up to two years per placement), until her mother finally could take her, years later. She was abused in one household, but her mother never believed her claim of abuse. Although the exact nature of some of the early attachments is unknown, at least after the first placement, she never formed a secure attachment to a caregiver. In Wendy's teens, her mother felt unable to deal with her numerous problems and asked that she be placed again in foster care. By age 20, Wendy was unable to function without assistance. She exhibited below-age-level functioning at multiple levels and exhibited hyperactive behaviors (e.g., inability to sit still; attention problems; constant speed-talking), personality and attachment disordered behaviors (e.g., inability to form secure attachment relationships; impulsivity; unstable self-image and self-care, goals, and relationships), depressive episodes, and suicidal ideation (and thoughts of self-injury). In some ways, she functioned at a preschool level (e.g., animistic thinking). She could not be easily comforted when distressed. She also exhibited young adolescent behaviors (e.g., rebellious defiance, risk-taking, demands for the privileges of independence without recognition of the consequences of her actions or understanding of how to attain resources). She frequently, angrily described herself as a throw-away child—her mother didn't want her and sent her away fairly quickly after each time she tried to return to her—and she expected to be thrown away, if she formed an attachment. She was finally placed with a caring family, who agreed to assist her transition to independent living. When the family went on a trip, they moved her to another placement for a week (she could not be left alone in the house without available assistance for food, emergencies, etc.). Feeling like she had again been thrown away, she withdrew, stopped eating, then ran away until it was too cold to stay on the street. Although this functionally young woman may have benefitted from an attachment-based treatment such as AEDP (Chapter 16), it would require finding resources not generally available to a state-sponsored young person.

Note:
All case examples are disguised, may be combined cases, and have had details changed to protect individuals.

in adulthood (Bunting et al., 2018). Eight studies showed relationships to maltreatment type (more study and larger samples are needed): Neglect was consistently related to a number of long-term economic outcomes, while physical abuse has a more consistent relationship with income and employment and had a similar magnitude effect as sexual abuse. Consistently witnessing violence/abuse also related to lower net worth and income. Although sexual abuse studies found less of an association with income and employment (a range of severity across studies), they found a relationship with other outcomes—e.g., absence due to sickness, fewer assets, welfare receipt, reduced adult SES, and financial insecurity (Bunting et al., 2018). Some evidence suggested reduced employment for physically abused males and reduced likelihood of employment for sexually abused females.

Although more study is needed, among protective factors against the adverse effects of ACEs are positive peer relationships, school engagement, and school attainment, each of which have mitigated some negative outcomes, while peer conflict has exacerbated outcomes (Moses & Villodas, 2017). For adults with histories of ACEs (N = 2486 German subjects ages 14–92), Beutel et al. (2017) found that high symptom scores were found in those with high ACEs and low resilience. The lowest symptom scores were found in those with high resilience and low adversity. Both distress (depression, anxiety, trauma symptoms) and somatic complaints were associated with low resilience, low social support, and low income.

Adverse Childhood Experiences (ACEs) and Health

Early studies of ACEs demonstrated that the number of categories of ACEs showed a graded relationship to the presence of adult diseases—ischemic heart disease, cancer, chronic lung disease, skeletal fractures, and liver disease (Felitti et al., 1998). Recent studies have shown an inverse relationship between ACEs and health-related quality of life (Maikovich-Fong et al., 2015; Schafer & Ferraro, 2013): with autoimmune, liver, cardiovascular, and lung (cancer) disease (Maikovich-Fong et al., 2015), alcohol or drug abuse, obesity, physical inactivity, promiscuity, smoking, suicide attempts, diabetes, cancer, and premature mortality (Bynum et al., 2010) that emerge or persist decades after the adversity has been documented. Categories of ACEs have been strongly interrelated; multiple kinds of childhood exposures have corresponded to multiple health risk factors later in life (Anda & Felitti, 2003). Faulty behaviors may be used as attempts to alleviate the emotional or social distress that result from ACEs. High-risk behaviors in turn may have adverse results. For example, high-risk sexual behaviors or drug usage may result in AIDS and other sexually transmitted disease, cancer, cardiovascular disease, chronic obstructive pulmonary disease, unwanted and/or high-risk pregnancies, and a cycle of child abuse.

Of course, there are a number of pathways to poor health outcomes—e.g., stress, no exercise, poor eating habits, smoking. As noted, maltreatment has been related to "limbic irritability," which in turn is linked to somatic, sensory, and behavioral symptoms (Dackis et al., 2012; Wekerle et al., 2014). Another trauma-related pathway includes childhood trauma's effects on C-reactive protein—a biomarker of inflammation and tissue necrosis; linked to autoimmune disease (Glossary; Danese et al., 2007; De Bellis & Zisk, 2014; Jones et al., 2011; Maikovich-Fong et al., 2015; Szalai, 2004). New Zealand adults (birth cohort N = 1037) with histories of poverty, social isolation, or maltreatment showed higher rates of depression and age-related metabolic disease risks in adulthood (e.g., greater body mass index, total cholesterol, and higher levels of C-reactive protein, Danese et al., 2009; De Bellis & Zisk, 2014). Platinga et al. (2013) studied inflammation (C-reactive protein and other markers—e.g., intercellular adhesion molecule-1 [ICAM-1], fibrinogen, white blood cells)—in adults with or without PTSD in response to past traumas—i.e., a major disaster, very serious accident, or fire; being physically assaulted or raped; seeing another person killed, badly hurt, or a dead body; or hearing about something horrible that has happened to someone you are close to (N = 562 twin males—238 pairs). Trauma-exposed individuals with PTSD had significantly higher levels of c-reactive protein and ICAM-1 compared to those without PTSD (Platinga et al., 2013).

Adverse Childhood Experience Type and Other Outcomes

Interpersonal violence has been a robust predictor of negative psychosocial outcomes (Hodges et al., 2013). ACEs have been linked to negative academic outcomes and school dropout as well as to mental health and health problems (Moses & Villodas, 2017). Up to two thirds of individuals who enter substance abuse treatment report a history of some form of maltreatment (Wekerle et al., 2014). Wekerle et al. note that a sexual abuse history is linked to impairments in self-regulation, self-concept, and psychological disturbances (e.g., depression, dissociation, PTSD). While neglect may be more likely to result in delayed physical development and dependence issues, physical abuse, neglect, and/or sexual abuse may result in social, emotional, and interpersonal problems, which may influence ongoing development.

Based on a nationally representative US survey, ACEs are among variables associated with chronic school absenteeism (ages 0–17; Stempel et al., 2017)—e.g., maltreatment, parental substance use, family conflict, and poverty; poor school climate and neighborhood violence. Odds were higher for absenteeism with two or more ACEs. In addition to missing critical learning opportunities, chronic absenteeism has predicted school dropout (better predictor than low grades or standardized test scores). School dropouts have been shown to experience higher levels of chronic diseases, substance abuse, mental health problems, and early death.

Although most maltreated children do not later commit crimes, the risk of doing so is higher than in the general population (Wekerle et al., 2014). Juvenile offenders (e.g., delinquency; trading sex) with histories of ACEs have been more difficult to rehabilitate and more likely to re-offend (N = 64,329; ages 11–22 adjudicated before age 18; Naramore et al., 2017). In addition to criminality, ACEs have been linked to risky sexual behaviors and to revictimization as well as to becoming sexual offenders. For males, any type of maltreatment is linked to alienation, inappropriate sexual behavior, and social incompetence in adolescence (Wekerle et al., 2014). Studies have found, for childhood maltreatment, that women report more self-capacity disturbance—i.e., in interpersonal relatedness, identity, and affect regulation—and more relationship difficulties than men (Bigras, Godbout, & Briere, 2015). For women, a sexual abuse history is associated with adult sexual adjustment difficulties—e.g., anxiety, low arousal, flashbacks, guilt, use of sex as an interpersonal strategy (Wekerle et al., 2014). Multiple ACEs (nearly all of 10 types) were more prevalent among girls engaged in trafficking sex (prostitution) compared to other offenders (Naramore et al., 2017). These behaviors put them particularly at risk of revictimization throughout adulthood. For such youth, it is important that interventions ensure consistent contact with caring adults in protective environments, ensure that belonging and self-esteem needs are met healthfully, and include appropriately monitored positive peer relationships and social media contacts screened for possible predators.

ACEs are risk factors for mental health problems—e.g., self-injury, bipolar disorder, catatonia, PTSD, depression, anxiety, personality disorders (Benarous et al., 2017; Beutel et al., 2017; Thomassin, Shaffer, Madden, & Londino, 2016; Welles, Patel, & Chilton, 2017; Chapter 15). Although bullying has been strongly linked to self-injury (SI), ACEs, especially emotional abuse and neglect, have been related to SI as well (Brown & Plener, 2017; Thomassin et al., 2016). For those with ACEs, symptoms such as anxiety and depression may make it difficult to deal with life's challenges (Beutel et al., 2017). Helplessness and low self-efficacy may interfere with adaptive coping such as help-seeking and functional internal beliefs and self-talk. In turn, these results may lead to more depression, anxiety, and somatic difficulties. For young adults, ACEs' link to depression has been increased with high levels of exposure to community violence (N = 103; Welles et al., 2017). Although self-efficacy—belief in one's own ability to draw on motivation, cognitive resources, and action plans to meet a situation's demands—did not influence ACEs' link to depression, both self-efficacy and the hope of employment mildly reduced the association between community violence and depression.

Domestic or Intimate Partner Violence (IPV)

Youth raised in households with family violence (intimate partner violence, IPV) are at risk of mental health difficulties (e.g., ongoing sadness), problematic health, and cognitive and social problems (Harris, York, & Giardino, 2015; for high-reactive infants at 7 months and 15 months, higher asthma, and higher cortisol 20 min. after task; Lamb, Humphreys, & Hegarty, 2018). Such youth may be unintentionally injured during IPV or become victims of maltreatment as well. They have often had lower levels of immunization and higher levels of risk-taking (Bair-Merritt, Blackstone, & Feudtner, 2006). Youth exposed both to maltreatment and domestic violence have had greater emotional and behavioral problems than youth exposed to one of the two types of trauma (Maikovich-Fong et al., 2015). Although less studied, very young as well as older children are affected by spousal abuse (Osofsky, 2018). During the first year of life, infants are able to recognize fearful facial expressions. Parental conflict has been linked to infants' negative personality traits (Chapter 5). Early relationships influence young children's abilities to trust and to develop positive relationships across life as well as influence ongoing mental health (Osofsky, 2018). Early intervention is recommended.

Domestic violence has been linked to both short- and long-term consequences such as behavioral, emotional, cognitive, physical, and social difficulties (Bowyer, Swanston, & Vetere, 2015). For example, children have described an ongoing sadness that interfered with their inter-relating at school and after (Lamb et al., 2018). For children exposed to interpersonal violence, shifting, discordant views of the father may develop—e.g., the kind father who does everything for his children vs the mean, violent father who hurts mother and should be punished (Staf & Almqvist, 2015). Conflicting or confused feelings also have included being so afraid of a father that a child never dared to be angry with him or feeling both angry with and missing an absent father. Children exposed to IPV may be confronted directly with violence or threats during which they learned to suppress their own feelings or desires, learned to avoid sharing information in order to avoid escalation or because it was ignored, felt in a constant state of unsafety and uncertainty, had a need to take control in a parenting way, and/or had an ongoing sense of powerlessness (U.K. youth ages 10–16, Bowyer et al., 2015; Swedish children ages 8–13; Staf & Almqvist, 2015). Memory confusion or forgetfulness, a compulsion to be compliant or to be controlling, self-protective strategies (dissociation, suppression, or aggression), and/or suppression of feelings and desires may become a continuing style.

Information was elicited from a small number of youth, ages 6–19, related to their views of their spousal abusing fathers (Lamb et al., 2018). This information prescribes targets of intervention. Even though a few youth wanted nothing to do with their fathers, all of them wanted their fathers to make some reparative action that would allow them to move on with their lives. Most youth wanted fathers to admit they had done something wrong, did not want excuses/reasons for the father's behavior, and wanted a *sincere* apology (including *owning up to his behavior*). Some youth had heard repeated apologies before, followed by repeated offenses. Some youth wanted a sincere apology followed by some form of penance—e.g., jail time; accepting that their children don't trust them and do feel weird around them; actions that prove contrition (not bribes); fathers getting help so they can be a father that youth are not scared of; to actually make them feel safe; not get angry and say mean things; positively co-parent with the mother; to stop diminishing the mother. Some youth wanted actual trust building, not reassurance. Others thought actual change was not possible for the father. Their fathers had "played the good-guy" and had not ceased the abuse. Cessation of abuse was/is essential.

Natural and Man-Made Disasters

Natural disasters may affect a child's personal, interpersonal, and community life. Routines, families, and communities may be in a state of disarray after disasters (Bernstein & Pfefferbaum, 2018). Natural (e.g., hurricanes, tornadoes, brush fires) and man-made disasters (e.g., oil spills, nuclear plant accidents) also have been linked to a number of mental health problems—e.g., PTSD, anxiety, depression, aggression. As noted, post-disaster reactions are often linked to severity of exposure, to number of trauma experiences (during and prior to the disaster), and/or to adverse life-environmental conditions as well as to child intrinsic issues such as genetics, personality, and resilience factors (Masten & Osofsky, 2010; Nader, 2008; Nader & Fletcher, 2014). Trauma also may affect personality and neurobiology. For example, a study of Hurricane Sandy showed that infants' in utero exposure alone had a considerable impact on both infant temperament and developmental trajectory of temperament from infancy to childhood (Zhang, Su, Li, & Chen, 2018a). Pre-natal maternal stress was a robust predictor of 6-month-old infants' dysregulated affective traits and both positive and negative emotional reactivity—i.e., higher pleasure seeking, greater approach tendencies;

higher perceptual sensitivity (to environmental stimuli); more vigilance/fearfulness; affiliation problems (low cuddliness); more attention problems (duration of orientation). This profile is considered adaptive in a threatening environment. In utero stress exposed infants showed improvements in fearfulness by age two. Cuddliness decreased from six to 18 months, then improved.

After a natural disaster, the prevalence of youth mental health problems tends to decrease over time (McLaughlin et al., 2010). However, the severity or complexity of some disasters has been linked to increased levels of serious emotional disturbance over time (i.e., considerably greater than predisaster prevalence, McLaughlin et al., 2010; Nader, 1997). Complex disasters with multiple types of and/or opportunities for exposures may have more complex and persistent outcomes. After complex events, symptoms may be prolonged and may include, for example, persistent PTSD, aggression, emotion dysregulation, depression, anxiety, and emotional distress (Hansel et al., 2013; Nader, 2008; Osofsky et al., 2015a). Ten years after a tornado that included multiple traumatic exposures—e.g., life threat, witnessing deaths and injuries, multiple losses of many well-known individuals, and futile attempts at rescue or resuscitation—when youth were in or graduating from high school, treated children showed improvements. Some youth exhibited a variety of continued or delayed onset reactions—e.g., personality changes; greater intensity of emotional reactions; no initial trauma reported but a panic attack after a tornado-related SAT test question. The community as a whole seemed to change—e.g., increased expectations of danger and of bad experiences (Nader, 1997, 2015).

Symptom Trajectories After Disasters

Some children have been followed across time after disasters. For children followed across time after Hurricane Andrew, also a high-impact disaster, La Greca and colleagues (2013) found three main trajectories of PTS reactions following disaster as well as a delayed trajectory (N = 568, third to fifth graders): resilient (37%), recovering (43%), and chronic distress (20%). Youth who exhibit chronic distress a year or more after an event have often been shown to have persistently high levels of PTS. Delayed trajectories did not differ from chronic distress trajectories for the youth exposed to Hurricane Andrew (La Greca et al., 2013). PTSD with delayed expression (DSM-5) is PTSD that is diagnosable after six months following an event (full criteria not met before then; APA, 2013). It can be persistent and debilitating (Hartman, 2014; see Nader & Fletcher, 2014).

Children in New Orleans (42% were still displaced) were assessed for levels of social support in separate domains and PTS at four time points from 3–7 months after Hurricane Katrina to 25–27 months after (N = 426; Lai et al., 2018). Greater PTSS were associated with avoidance of sources of social support, lower perceived levels of social support, or selected supportive relationships. Initial PTSS predicted perceived decreased parental, teacher, and peer social support (especially parent and peer support)—i.e., whether they felt understood, could talk to them, spent time with them. At time 4, children perceived greater support from parents and peers. Increased support may have been related to reductions in parent and peer distress, that prolonged distress may trigger greater response, and/or some return of normalcy made support easier to provide (or perceive). Low peer social support, rather than parent or teacher support, 13–17 months after Katrina was linked to higher PTSS at 19–24 months after.

After an earthquake in China, children were assessed four months after and more than two years, four years, and five years later (Cheng, Liang, Fu, & Liu, 2018). PTSD symptoms four months after predicted depressive symptoms more than two years later; depressive symptoms at four months after predicted PTSD symptoms more than two years later. Depressive symptoms more than two years later predicted PTSD symptoms more than three years later; depressive symptoms more than three years later predicted PTSD symptoms more than four years later.

Risk Factors After Disasters

Child risk factors and event factors contribute to reactions to natural disasters (Chapter 4). In the Hurricane Andrew study, children in the chronically distressed trajectory showed greater odds of reporting high anxiety, lower social support, more intervening stressful life events, and higher use of poor emotion regulation strategies (La Greca et al., 2013). After an earthquake in China, being female, poor parental relationships, and higher exposure levels were risk factors for PTSD or depressive symptoms (Cheng et al., 2018). Zuromski et al. (in press) found suicidal ideation in 5% of adolescents following tornado exposure (N = 2000). Even controlling for symptoms of PTSD and depression, prior interpersonal violence exposure was most robustly related to suicidal ideation. Emotional abuse and depression after an earthquake contributed to suicide risk, with emotional neglect and PTSD making somewhat smaller contributions (N = 6132 children and adolescents, Tang et al., 2018). Mediation analysis suggested that PTSD and depression symptoms partially mediated the link between suicidality and emotional neglect or abuse. Symptom scores were generally higher for females than for males—i.e., higher PTSD, depression and suicidality. Depression and suicidality were more common for older youth.

A number of factors have been related to persistence. Three years after Hurricane Katrina, children and adolescents with high stress exposure had the greatest likelihood of continued serious emotional distress (McLaughlin et al., 2010; Box 3.4). Hurricane Katrina overwhelmed the coping resources of many children, regardless of their pre-hurricane functioning (McLaughlin et al., 2010). For Hurricane Katrina, risk factors for persistence of reactions have included ongoing stress—e.g., from long-term family or community disruption following disaster; separation from a parent; parental unemployment; guests in the home; prior decrements in functioning (only among youth with low to moderate hurricane stress); highest levels of hurricane stress—e.g., severe threat to life, witnessing: injuries, bodies, deaths; lower levels of environmental and relational support; prior traumatic experience; and being female (Hansel et al., 2013; McLaughlin et al., 2010; Box 3.4). This is in agreement with other findings that cumulative stressors and exposure levels strongly influence child mental health outcomes. Highly exposed children were more likely to experience ongoing stressors—e.g., forced relocation after the storm, housing instability, ongoing disruption, lack of access to services, and dissolution of support networks (McLaughlin et al., 2010). Among adults, ongoing stress predicts persistence and delayed onset of PTSD; findings for youth have been mixed, which may be related to disaster severity or circumstances (sociodemographic factors were unrelated to findings, McLaughlin et al., 2010). In a follow-up study of Swedes exposed to the 2004 tsunami in Thailand, elevated risk of worsening mental health was related to prior life events as well as to exposure to life-threatening experiences and to loss of known individuals during the tsunami (Wahlström, Michelsen, Schulman, & Backheden, 2010).

War and Terrorism

In wartime, for young children, either separation or alterations in the parent–child relationship influence outcomes (Osofsky et al., 2015b). As early as World War II (WWII), young children have been observed during and after wartime experiences (Nader & Fletcher, 2014; Osofsky et al., 2015b). Freud and Burlingham (1943) observed that children who were separated from caregivers during WWII exhibited regression, aggression, depression, and withdrawal. War is among the traumas that often include multiple types of exposure—e.g., multiple instances and kinds of life threat, witnessing death or injury, separations, witnessing and/or experiencing torture, being used as or witnessing a human land mine, forced killing or injuring others, lack of life-necessary resources (e.g., food, water, medicine, clean air; e.g., Cook et al., 2015; Thabet et al., 2009; Boxes 13.1, 16.3)—which are associated with a number of adverse and sometimes complex mental health outcomes (Finkelhor et al., 2007). After concentration camp experiences, some latency age children did well until they had difficulties in preadolescence (delayed onset or DSM 5 *PTSD with delayed expression*; Freud, A, 1954 in Hartman, 2014). PTSD with delayed expression has been associated with persistence and severity (see Nader, 2008). Thabet et al. (2009) suggest that children in war-torn countries may be more likely to have their social development inhibited, which may influence ongoing inter-relating. In part, changes in social development may be attributed to greater sanctioning of violence in their environments and to greater fear of others.

War: Influencing Variables

In adverse living conditions, such as war, whether resiliency factors (e.g., intellectual competence, creativity) lead to outcomes such as optimal development or delinquency depends, in part, on mediators such as a youth's attentional style or emotion regulation and such as parental attitudes and behaviors toward the child (Punamäki et al., 2001). Qouta, Punamäki, and El-Sarraj (2008) found that loving and wise parenting, children's flexible information processing, high cognitive capacity, flexible and multiple coping strategies, and narrative and symbolic nocturnal dreaming—i.e., dreams with a beginning, intensification or turning point, and an end; with bizarre, vivid, and symbolic scenes and themes, but with joyful feelings and happy endings—as well as social support and good peer relations served as protective factors for youth exposed to war. For former Ugandan child soldiers, Klasen et al. (2010) found protective associations for posttrauma resilience and fewer guilty cognitions, less desire for revenge, better family socioeconomic situations, and greater perceived spiritual support. On the other hand, Klasen et al. found higher levels of trauma and other symptoms for older former child soldiers. For the Sierra Leone former child soldiers, Betancourt et al. (2010) found less family acceptance for older than for younger children—older children may evoke less sympathy or more fear. Betancourt and colleagues found that nearly a third of the child soldiers improved over time (assessed baseline 2002; again in 2004 and 2008; N = 529). Nevertheless, a few child soldiers experienced an increase in symptoms over time. Family environment was central in results. For example, while toxic war experiences such as surviving rape or perpetrating violence were strongly linked to initial symptom levels, post-conflict family abuse and neglect were associated with higher levels of symptoms as well. Risk factors for worsening symptoms over time included death of a parent and post-conflict stigma in the community (Betancourt, Newnham, McBain, & Brennan, 2013b). Increases in family acceptance were associated with decreases in PTSD symptoms. Youth also showed improvements in internalizing symptoms over time related to improvements in parental mental health over time (Betancourt, McBain, Newnham, & Brennan, 2015b). Intergenerational effects of war and other traumas on children have been demonstrated repeatedly (Betancourt et al., 2015b; Danieli, 1998; see Saile, Ertl, Neuner, & Catani, 2015). Evidence shows that trauma can be passed on and that parental mental health is an important factor in children's early and ongoing PTSD and other mental health problems (e.g., internalizing, externalizing) including after war (Betancourt et al., 2015b; Danieli, 1998; Saile et al., 2015).

Rape During War

Rape has been a part of war for thousands of years (Tanak, Bible). Kuwert and colleagues (2014) found that, compared to female long-term survivors of non-sexual WWII trauma, women exposed to war-related sexual violence (aged 12–26, during war; 1 to 71 events per person) reported greater severity of PTSD-related avoidance and hyperarousal symptoms, as well as anxiety more than six decades later (in 2009; total N = 129). Almost 81% of sexually violated women also reported severe sexual problems during their lifetimes (compared to 19% of women with non-sexual war trauma). Studies have also found increases in cortisol levels in long-term studies of war-rape survivors (Gola et al., 2011). In contrast, women with war-related sexual violence exposure also reported greater posttraumatic growth (Glossary, Chapter 4), despite less social acknowledgment as trauma survivors, compared to survivors of non-sexual war trauma (Kuwert et al., 2014). Both controls and rape victims were exposed to multiple wartime experiences—e.g., forced displacement, looting, witnessing extreme violence including the killing of relatives, air raid experiences.

Conclusions

For all types of potentially traumatic events, trauma exposure in childhood is associated with numerous cascading and long-term effects for a significant number of children. Both long-term positive growth and negative reactions may follow a variety of traumas and stressors. Outcomes may be complex, reduce the quality of life, and undermine functioning. The complexity of events—e.g., severity and/or multiple types of exposures—increase the likelihood of multiple and/or persisting symptoms. For many types of trauma, there is evidence of a possible remedy for posttrauma immediate and ongoing reactions when appropriately timed interventions are provided (Nader, 2012a). For example, an intervention that facilitated high-quality parent/child attachment relationships with foster care providers showed effects on foster-placed children's brain development (Zeanah et al., 2011b; Chapters 7 and 10). With the exception of the body of the corpus callosum and superior corona radiata, the foster care group did not significantly differ from the never-institutionalized group, suggesting a potential remediation of specific white matter pathways for children removed early in life from institutional care and placed in responsive families. As will be discussed in Chapter 4, the type, intensity, and persistence of reactions to traumatic events depends on a variety of factors, including the nature of the event, the risk and protective factors of the child, and her/his previous and ongoing environments.

4

Recognizing Risk and Protective Factors

Child-, Environment-, and Posttrauma Aftermath-Related Variables

Each child is unique, and his/her experience of a trauma or other stressor(s) is also unique. Failing to recognize individuality, unique reactions, risk and protective factors, and other factors that may influence reactions and a child's response to treatment may impede the ability to assist recovery. As will be discussed, treatments must be adapted for the individual child, parent–child dyad, family, or group members and their specific needs, symptomatic and recovery timetables, rates of progress, personalities, trust levels, and other characteristics. Although some studies follow individual children across time, many provide group results. Treatments often focus on unique individuals, dyads, or families. Studies give findings for a significant number of those studied. Treatment may serve individuals who were not in significant groups. Problems in functioning have occurred for children with symptoms that do not meet criteria and algorithms for clinical disorders as well as those with disorders (De Bellis, Woolley, & Hooper, 2013; Nader, 2008). Stress reactions and treatment outcomes are influenced by a number of variables (Tables A1.1–A1.4). The relationship between these variables and outcomes is not always direct.

Child-related variables such as neurobiology (e.g., genetics; stress sensitivity), personal traits (e.g., personality; developmental skills; confidence levels), and personal history (e.g., loneliness vs security; demographics; past experiences) may be protective or may increase vulnerability. For example, resilience factors, such as intellectual competence or creativity, in adverse living conditions may lead to outcomes such as optimal development or delinquency depending on mediators—e.g., the youth's attentional style or emotional regulation; parental attitudes and behaviors toward the child (Punamäki, Qouta, & El-Sarraj, 2001). The highly intelligent and creative child's capacities may not translate into emotional well-being, if the youth feels rejected and alienated. Among *environmental variables* are support systems, family conditions (e.g., resources, conflict levels), attachment relationships and parenting quality, and community factors. *Event-related variables* involve exposure levels (objective and subjective experiences), the way the traumatic experience unfolded, and its personal impact on a child (e.g., on self-esteem, neurobiology, life story). Some of these variables were discussed in Chapter 2. Immediate and ongoing *intervention variables* (e.g., the timing and nature of interventions) also influence status and recovery. *Cultural variables* may fully or partially define reactions and treatment needs; they require consideration as well (see Nader, 2008). Child, environmental, and event-aftermath variables follow (see also age-related chapters). Variables related to the clinician–patient/client relationship are discussed in Chapter 17.

Exposure levels have been robustly linked to posttrauma outcomes (e.g., Saile, Ertl, Neuner, & Catani, 2015; Udwin et al., 2000). In addition to objective exposure variables (physical proximity, life threat, witnessing threat), intense subjective experiences or peri-traumatic emotions (e.g., perceptions, fear, panic) are important predictors of reactions (see Perception, this chapter). A single-exposure, specific posttrauma symptom (e.g., reactivity, avoidance, aggression) and/or specific association (e.g., past traumatic experiences, grief or number of losses, guilt, poor sleep, dissociation) may have important effects on a child (Laor et al., 2002; see Nader, 2008; see Nader & Fletcher, 2014; Osofsky & Lieberman, 2011). Cumulative traumas or poly-victimization (Chapter 2) have been related to increased reactions and to symptom complexity. Many risk factors have been associated with a variety of disorders—e.g., risk factors such as trauma(s), poverty, parental psychopathology, non-secure attachments, forms of parenting, genetic polymorphisms, temperament, dissociation/avoidance, faulty information processing, and reactivity (see DeKlyen & Greenberg, 2018; Fearon et al., 2010; Nader, 2008). Protective and risk factors are discussed after a discussion of mixed findings.

Mixed Study Findings

We rely on research findings to shape out theories and interventions. In many fields of study, findings are mixed for a number of variable associations. The reasons for mixed findings are likely multiple (Nader, 2008). For example, studies are often small, focus on different populations exposed to a variety of circumstances (traumatic and other), and use differing methodologies. Variables studied may be limited, and important variables excluded—e.g., those related to child, event, environment, previous experiences, etc. Sometimes variables that should be included in assessments are not obvious—e.g., temperamental characteristics (e.g., behavioral inhibition [BI]) may affect cortisol levels (see Chapter 6). Variable combinations or combined types are not always recognized—e.g., gene combinations; behaviorally inhibited, behaviorally activated/disinhibited, and combined type (Chapter 10; see Nader, 2008). Groups are studied at specific points in time, which may yield different findings from groups of individual children compared to themselves across time. Surprising or contradictory findings suggest the need to examine multiple variables or variable types, to use multiple sources of information, and to observe large samples of children in different contexts (Nader, 2008; Scheeringa, Myers, Putnam, & Zeanah, 2015).

Genetics provide an example of the difficulties in making conclusions from contradictory or varied findings (see Chapter 12). Many studies of genetics are included in the findings reported in this book. However, our understanding of this and other realms is continually evolving. In addition, specific brain region activation may mediate the relationship between genes and outcomes (e.g., van Rooij et al., 2016). Some of the earlier findings on associations of genes and traits have been contradicted by a number of studies (Arias et al., 2012). For example, there is currently some uncertainty about the relationship of 5-HTTPLR to depression or to *neuroticism* (Munafo, 2012). Although 5-HTTPLR has been linked to neuroticism, a recent meta-analysis (Munafo et al., 2009; Munafo, Clark, & Flint, 2004) and recent studies (e.g., Arias et al., 2012) have shown a lack of association between the 5-HTTLPR polymorphism of the SLC6A4 gene and *harm avoidance* or *neuroticism*. A gene–gene interaction may underlie some inconsistencies in findings (Arias et al., 2012). Consistent findings for common disorders (e.g., depression) have only emerged when sample sizes exceeded 10,000 (Munafo, 2012). Meta-analyses are an imperfect solution to this problem given between-study heterogeneity. Hence, a study with 5,000 cases likely will be superior to a meta-analysis with 5,000 cases combined. When meta-analyses provide weak evidence of a link (e.g., 5-HTTLPR with depression and antidepressant response), it should be treated with some caution.

Some seemingly contradictory findings in treatment studies may be related to semantic issues. For example, a body of evidence has demonstrated that avoidance interferes with resolution. Accordingly, studies have shown that dissociation, which may be considered a form of avoidance, is linked to PTSD severity, suicidality, functional impairment, and to poorer treatment outcomes (see Briere & Eadie, 2016; Stein et al., 2013). Methods have been employed to reduce dissociation toward more successful treatment outcomes (Cloitre et al., 2012; Resick et al., 2012b). In seeming contrast, a body of evidence now suggests that *self-distancing* methods—e.g., viewing from the perspective of a distanced observer and/or reasoning about the experience in a psychologically removed manner, in contrast to a self-immersed perspective, may lead to an adaptive shift. It has been linked to reduced depressive thought and lower negative affect (compared to a comparison group; Kross et al., 2012). Rather than promoting avoidance, it appears to permit the pursuit of meaning-making (e.g., the meaning of negative events) and permits recounting negative events or experiences in a manner that buffers individuals from overwhelming, negative affects (Kross et al., 2012). In fact, after traumas, both countering and allowing some avoidance can be helpful.

General Risk and Protective Factors

Protective factors and posttraumatic growth, which occur with or without PTSD, are discussed here followed by a discussion of cumulative risk.

Protection and Growth Factors

Protective and resilience factors have been linked to reduced symptom levels. "What doesn't kill you makes you stronger" may refer to the growth that can occur for some following traumas.

Protective Factors

Many factors protect or buffer against negative outcomes from adversity (Table A1.4). Healthy and safe environments that permit a child to play, explore, and maximize personal capacities are among conditions that enhance protective factors (Sciaraffa, Zeanah, & Zeanah, 2018). Among protective factors are good support systems, effective coping skills, personal qualities (e.g., resilience), environmental factors (e.g., resources, positive parenting), and aspects of the adverse experience (e.g., successes in protective efforts; Table A1.4). Positive support systems have repeatedly proven to be protective (e.g., Ben-Zur & Almog, 2013; Nader & Fletcher, 2014). In addition to sensitive, supportive parents (good attachment relationships), early childhood educators also can provide secure relationships and can provide an additional layer of protection against adversity (Sciaraffa et al., 2018). Having adult school personnel make a connection with at-risk youth is among methods used in the prevention of school violence (e.g., school shootings; Daniels et al., 2010b; Nader, 2012c).

Resilience factors (Glossary), a subset of protective factors, are personal qualities that assist a person to do well in the face of adversity. They include higher levels of positive self-perception (e.g., self-esteem and -confidence), positive perceptions of the future, personal strength, academic competence, good self-regulation skills, flexibility/adaptability, good problem-solving skills, use of positive emotion and laughter, secure attachment style, trust, accurate locus of control, good coping skills as well as family cohesion, enriched environments, and social resources (Table A1.4; Bonanno, 2008; see Nader, 2008; Gundogar, Kesebir, Demirkan, & Yaylaci, 2014; Chapter 2). Skills such as self-regulation and flexibility are essential to all aspects of functioning (Chapter 1). Multiple pathways to resilience levels are likely (Bonanno, 2008). Resilience is fairly common after trauma or loss (up to 70%; Bonanno, 2008; Scheeringa, 2016), and has been inversely related to trauma (Simeon et al., 2007). After a loss or trauma, resilience suggests the ability to maintain relatively stable, healthy levels of psychological and physical functioning, despite periodic perturbations in functioning.

Posttraumatic Growth (PTG)

Positive results may also follow traumas. Posttraumatic or stress-related growth is the experience of positive change related to the struggle with stressful situations or traumas (Tedeschi & Calhoun, 1996, 2004). The expanded five dimensions of PTG include the *ability to relate with others*, *new possibilities*—e.g., new path, interests; do better things; opportunities; likely to try to change things; *personal strength*—e.g., self-reliance, confidence to handle difficulties; accept what can't change; *spiritual change*—e.g., stronger faith and understanding; and an *appreciation of life* (Jia et al., 2015; Tedeschi & Calhoun, 1996, 2004). PTG is different from resilience and can co-occur with PTSS or disorders (Duan, Guo, & Gan, 2015; Jia et al., 2015). Following exposure to traumatic events, by definition, posttraumatic growth is reflected in increased personal strength, renewed meaning of life, and improved personal relationships (Schuettler & Boals, 2011; Tedeschi & Calhoun, 1996).

PTG and PTSD have associations in common. Schuettler and Boals (2011) found that PTG was predicted by event centrality (Glossary), problem-focused coping, and positive trauma perspectives, while PTSD symptoms were best predicted by event centrality, visceral reactions to the event, avoidant coping, and a negative perspective of the event. Individuals with PTSD have scored higher in appreciation of life and spiritual change than those without PTSD (Kilmer & Gil-Rivas, 2010; Nishi, Matsuoka, & Kim, 2010). However, individuals without PTSD have scored higher in self-reported personal strength than those with PTSD.

Personality influences PTSD and PTG (Jia et al., 2015; Tedeschi & Calhoun, 1996). For example, neuroticism has been negatively related to PTG and positively to PTSD (Jia et al., 2015; Lauterbach & Vrana, 2001; Lawrence & Fauerbach, 2003; Shakespeare-Finch, Gow, & Smith, 2005). Extraversion has been positively related to PTG and negatively to PTSD (Jia et al., 2015). Social support mediates the relationship between *extraversion* and PTSD and partially mediates the relationship between extraversion and PTG (Jia et al., 2015). Social support has been negatively related to PTSD. Extraverts have shown higher levels of social support, hence lower PTSD. Big 5 personality traits of *conscientiousness*, *vitality*, and *relationship* contributed to PTG more than trait resilience in both non-PTSD and PTSD groups; however, trait *resilience* and *relationship* predicted lower levels of PTSD symptoms even when other traits were controlled (Duan et al., 2015).

While individuals who report more distress also report lower levels of deliberate rumination and higher levels of intrusive rumination, those who experience high levels of PTG report more deliberate rumination (Jia et al., 2015). Deliberate processing and/or reflection on ways of reconfiguring core beliefs may be occurring among persons who report more PTG.

Risk Factors

Risk factors may be single or multiple. Negative outcomes often relate to multiple risks.

Cumulative Risk Factors

Increased numbers of risk factors correspond to increased risk of negative outcomes (Lanza et al., 2010; predict more emotional and behavioral problems, Anda et al., 2006; Osofsky & Lieberman, 2011). Problematic outcomes have generally been linked to combinations of rather than to single risk factors, via multiple pathways (DeKlyen & Greenberg, 2018; Ghosh Ippen, Harris, Van Horn, & Lieberman, 2012; Nader & Fletcher, 2014). In addition to environmental risk factors (e.g., pre- and post-natal, economic, parental, school, traumatic), risk has been associated with traits such as those that put children at odds with others (e.g., neuroticism, aggression), indicate poor coping capacities (e.g., avoidance, substance use), suggest reduced skills (e.g., low problem-solving), or indicate an impaired sense of self (e.g., low self-esteem, Tables A1.1–A1.3). Children may differ by age, trait, or group membership in their vulnerability to risk factors (see Stress Sensitivity, this chapter)—e.g., urban white youth have shown fewer risk factors and a weaker link to negative outcomes (e.g., incarceration; unemployment; persistent violence) than urban African American youth, particularly poor urban youth (Dodge, Coie, & Lynam, 2008).

Early adverse experiences can impact multiple developmental processes, which can eventuate similar or different behavioral outcomes in groups of individuals (Cicchetti & Valentino, 2006; Oshri et al., 2015). Social and economic deprivation and ethnic discrimination are linked to negative effects on children and adults, and also may intensify the effects of and/or levels of exposure to trauma victimization (Breslau, 2009; Briere & Jordan, 2009). Such circumstances also may correspond to reduced internal and external resources for coping (Briere & Jordan, 2009). When children with social, emotional, and/or behavioral problems are not supported, risk factors can intertwine and cascade to increasingly negative outcomes (Chapter 2)—e.g., emotional and behavioral dysregulation, disrupted social skills, and other symptoms may initially influence developmental and academic delays, and conduct problems in elementary schools and may translate into academic failure, school dropout, delinquency, or substance use/abuse in middle or high school (Nader, 2012c; Webster-Stratton, 2008).

Critical and Sensitive Periods

Perry et al. (1995) suggest that either deprivation of experiences or over-activation of important neural systems during critical periods may be the most destructive result of early traumas (e.g., maltreatment). Plasticity is the nervous system's ability to adapt its structure and function in response to environmental demands, experiences, and physiological changes (Pascual-Leone et al., 2005). Windows of heightened plasticity during brain development are called critical or sensitive periods (Glossary; Hensch & Bilimoria, 2012). Heightened plasticity may result in both increased opportunities for development and in increased vulnerabilities (Fuhrmann, Knoll, & Blakemore, 2015). Sensitive or critical periods are considered times during which certain types of experience have a foundational effect on skill and competency development (Fox & Rutter, 2010).

During *critical periods*, if the brain circuit in question is left unstimulated, the brain function served by that circuit may be permanently compromised (Perry et al., 1995). It can be shaped by later life experiences, but to a lesser degree. Documented critical periods in children originally included, e.g., those for seeing, hearing, receptive language, speech production, and higher cognitive functions (Hensch & Bilimoria, 2012; Shonkoff & Phillips, 2000). A *sensitive period*—a time period when environmental experiences strongly affect brain circuitry (Hensch & Bilimoria, 2012; Zeanah et al., 2011b; see BEIP, Chapter 7)—is less stringent than a critical period (Hensch & Bilimoria, 2012). Nevertheless, during sensitive periods, environmental influences may have profound effects on physical, social, and emotional development (Goff & Tottenham, 2014).

Human complex or multifaceted brain functions are likely to reflect cumulative sensitive periods rather than one critical period (Hensch & Bilimoria, 2012). Many aspects of brain development depend greatly on experience (Bick et al., 2015). Exposure to stressors at different ages is likely to lead to differential neurobehavioral phenotypes (Glossary—phenotype; Goff & Tottenham, 2014; Marshall, 2016). For example, after early life deprivation of a caregiver, later but not early adoption has been related to increased risk of psychopathology (e.g., depression in adolescence), learning, and self-regulation problems (Goff & Tottenham, 2014). Without supportive parenting, preschool exposure to low SES conditions has been related to brain volume and other changes (e.g., stress regulation regions: hypo- or hyper-reactive HPA axis; hippocampus size, Montirosso & Provenzi, 2015).

Child Variables Influencing Outcomes

A youth's traits (e.g., neurobiology, individuality, perception) and circumstances may enhance or deter optimal development (Tables A1.1–A1.4). Children vary in their readiness to trust, understanding of events and death, reactions to experiences, and in their most vulnerable brain regions, depending on age or phase of development. For example, in laboratory tests of trust, older children (average age 11) were less initially trusting than mid-adolescents who were less initially trusting than adults; however, all age groups adjusted their subsequent behaviors based on experiences with trustworthy and untrustworthy people, during the test (van den Bos, van Dijk, & Crone, 2012).

Individual Style

A child's posttrauma reactions and recovery reflect her/his individuality. Children in the same location, during the same traumatic incident, will have varied personal experiences of the event and will process and remember the experiences in somewhat unique ways (Nader, 1999). They may display differences in (1) the nature or intensity of symptoms or reactions; (2) personal meaning of aspects of an event and of symptoms; (3) timetable and speed for processing aspects of an event—e.g., need to sit with it (to process it); to slow impulsive or shallow processing; to overcome dissociative tendencies; for time out from trauma-related memories and emotions; (4) the time it takes to recover from specific reactions; (5) the need for, level of, and length of regressions over time; (6) comfort levels with different types of support, (7) the way aspects of her/his reaction interact with and affect aspects of life, and (8) other issues. Reactions may be additionally complicated by previous stressful experiences or problems trusting others (e.g., prior trauma, attachment-related). Recognizing a child's unique style, past experiences, and her/his personal processing rhythms can be important for clinicians and other adults, who provide assistance after an event. After traumas, it will be important for adults to adapt their actions and reactions to a child so that they meet an individual child's evolving needs, timing, and processing of an event.

Personality/Temperament

Individual differences in temperament may be critical moderators of stress's effects on developmental trajectories (Gunnar, Doom, & Esposito, 2015). Personality is influenced by biology (genetics) and by life experiences (e.g., pre-natal stress, early attachments; Caspi, 1998; Cisler, Amstadter, & Nugent, 2011). Because of biological make-up, living circumstances, personal experiences, or combinations of factors, some children tend to expect things to go badly and to interpret things in a negative manner (e.g., negative emotionality/neuroticism; Pluess, Belsky, Way, & Taylor, 2010). Such children may be more sensitive to environments/experiences, and more prone to depression, anxiety, emotional reactivity, and sympathy for others' pain, among other traits. Another set of children, among those who are more sensitive to environmental influences, including traumas, may be more prone to increased impulsive behaviors and conduct problems (Bakermans-Kranenburg & van IJzendoorn, 2009; Drury, Theall, Keats, & Scheeringa, 2009; see Koenen, 2007; Table A4.1). Although, regardless of nature, some traits or symptoms may follow traumas (e.g., impulsiveness, anxiety), pre-trauma tendencies influence posttrauma needs and outcomes (e.g., Box 16.3; Chapters 10, 17—personality).

There are many ways to classify personality traits (see Nader, 2008—Chapter 9, for a summary; Tables A5.1–A5.2, 17.1). Even morningness versus eveningness (preferred time of day for being active) has influenced traits—e.g., morningness has been negatively related to novelty seeking, positively to persistence, and been independent of trait anxiety (Caci, Robert, & Boyer, 2004). Psychological type theory suggests a psychophysiological drive to act in accordance with one's natural personal style/type that, when thwarted, produces a stress response that may lead to fatigue, frustration, and other reactions (Berens, 2002/2013; Keirsey & Bates, 1978). Each type has its own set of stressors and typical reactions to stress (Chapter 17). Discussions of personality commonly include such traits as introverted versus extraverted, agreeableness or difficulty, and activity levels. In general, extraverted children enjoy and are revitalized by being around other people, while introverted children rebuild and restore energy when they are alone (Murphy, 2013; Table 17.1). However, after a traumatic event, a child's needs may be different from her/his normal style (Chapter 16). For example, if a parent leaves a child alone for periods of time—because of necessity, choice, the child's usual style, to allow them to process the event, or for some other reason—it may be important to let the child know the reason for allowing alone time. For example, a boy's parents were allowing him his normal amount of time alone. He felt the need to be with them more after the trauma but did not ask for more time. Instead, he interpreted their behavior to mean that they did not like being around him as much anymore.

Many aspects of life—e.g., skills (e.g., learning strategies), traits, psychopathology, stress reactivity—are influenced by emotional strengths and weaknesses, including by aspects of personality (Davis, Panksepp, & Normansell, 2003; Ginevra et al., 2015; see Nader, 2008; Chapter 14). Predominant traits vary by culture (Rothbart et al., 2001a). For example, for Chinese individuals, effortful control has been correlated negatively with extraversion but not with negative affectivity; for U.S. respondents, effortful control has been correlated negatively with negative affectivity, not with extraversion (Rothbart et al., 2001a). In societies that require controlled behaviors (e.g., Kenya, Thailand, Jamaica), children exhibit more *over-controlled* problem behaviors (e.g., fears, guilt, somatic concerns, depression, anxiety; Mash & Dozois, 2003). U.S. children, in contrast, have been rated particularly high on *under-controlled* problems (e.g., arguing, disobedience at home, cruelty; see Nader, 2008).

Combinations of traits have been found in groups of children—e.g., easy, difficult, slow-to-warm (Chess & Thomas, 1991; Glossary). Rettew and colleagues found three main groups emerged from four temperament dimensions—novelty seeking (NS), harm avoidance (HA), reward dependence (RD), and persistence (P; N = 447, ages 6–18, Rettew et al., 2008). The most prevalent group (*moderate*, 45%) had average scores across the four domains (similar to Chess & Thomas's *easy* group, perhaps with less approach). The second group (*steady*, 36%)—low NS and High P—were not impulsive and could persevere despite frustration or obstacles. Although in many studies NS and HA are inversely related, the final group (*disengaged*, 19%)—high NS and HA, low P and RD—were stimulus-seeking although somewhat fearful and fatigued, with low social connection (mostly boys; Chess & Thomas's *difficult* group). While the *disengaged* group showed higher psychopathology and lower wellness, the *steady* group related to lower psychopathology and higher wellness.

Neurobiology and Traits. Recent examinations have recognized neurobiological contributions to personality and traits (Davis et al., 2003). Genetic differences explain a significant amount of variance in temperamental traits (Bokhorst et al., 2003; Brumariu et al., 2016; Roisman & Fraley, 2008; Table A5.1). In turn, personality influences the ways that people interpret and respond to what they see and experience. Selective neural mechanisms are associated with *Extraversion* and with *Neuroticism*. Although culture may influence what is experienced as rewarding, an "internal sensitivity to rewards" is a basis for Extraversion and is unaffected by culture (Davis et al., 2003; Depue & Collins, 1999). Davis et al. conclude that neural-based systems are the basis of all personality traits including those described in the Big 5. The Five-Factor-Model (Big 5) examines five personality factors found for adults—*Extraversion, Agreeableness, Conscientiousness, Emotional Stability,* and *Openness to Experience* (Glossary—Big 5). Number of factors/traits vary by age. The Spielberger State-Trait Personality Inventory (STPI) elicits self-reported feedback concerning the putative influences of neural-based networks (Glossary—neural-based ...)—*Play* or *Playfulness, Seeking, Caring, Fear, Anger,* and *Sadness* systems. Davis and colleagues added *Spirituality*. The associations of each neurobiologically related trait are not surprising. Davis et al. found that *Playfulness* was robustly associated with *Extraversion*, and *Agreeableness* with *Care* (inversely with anger). *Emotional Stability* was inversely linked to all three negative emotions (fear, sadness, anger). *Conscientiousness* was weakly related to the three negative emotions. *Playfulness* (Extraversion) initially emerges as infant smiling, laughter, and sensitivity to tickling. Later it is present in happy childhood games and social interactions, and it appears in adult personalities through engagement in joke telling, ribbing/teasing, and general social fun. The *Seek* system may provide a basis for both the *openness to experience* as well as the *affinity for problem-solving* traits. Fear and sadness are linked and may be similar at a neurological level. Aspects of *negative emotionality*-related 5-HTTLPR demonstrate this link. *Anger* correlated negatively both with *Emotional Stability* and with *Agreeableness*. *Anger* and *Care* were independent of each other.

Genetics and Personality. Some aspects of personality have been associated with specific genetic properties (see Nader & Fletcher, 2014). A short allele serotonin polymorphism (5-HTTLPR) has corresponded to increased reactivity to the environment, to sympathetic reactivity to others' pain, and to information processing biases (e.g., negative bias, Caspi et al., 2010) as well as to PTSD, suicidality, and depression (Roy et al., 2007). Dopamine polymorphisms have been related to more than one aspect of behavior—e.g., novelty seeking, susceptibility to ADHD (see Dragan, Oniszczenko, Czerski, & Dmitrzak-Weglarz, 2012). Dopamine haplotypes in DAT1 and SNAP-25 have been related to sensory sensitivity (Glossary; N = 154, ages 3–12 and 283 adults; Dragan et al., 2012). Dopamine polymorphisms also may be related to a nonspecific vulnerability to a wide range of impulsive and reward-inducing behaviors as well as to increased sensitivity to environmental influences (preschool; Drury et al., 2009). Cortisol level has been associated with a behavioral inhibition phenotype (e.g., tendency to withdraw and avoid novel situations; Chapters 8, 9; Box 8.2; Table 5.2—infant BI), which has predicted anxiety and depressive disorders (Fox et al., 2005; see Nader & Weems, 2011).

Positive vs Negative Emotions. Generally, people who are happy-prone tend to have more trust (Kaliterna-Lipovčan & Prizmić-Larsen, 2016) and tend to focus on their successes, while children who are trait-unhappy tend to focus on their failures. Following the 9/11 attacks, links between personality-related resilience factors and adjustment were mediated by positive emotions (e.g., interest, gratitude, love; Fredrickson et al., 2003). For sex abuse survivors, positive emotional expression has predicted better adjustment and social relationships over time (Bonanno, 2008; Bonanno et al., 2007). Among reactions, trauma may induce an ongoing state of unhappiness that may change a child's predominant focus (e.g., DSM-5 PTSD negative emotional states). Childhood trauma is implicated in disorders such as major depression (MDD), with variations related to temperament. For MDD, depressive, irritable, and anxious temperament scores were higher in individuals with a history of childhood trauma (Gundogar et al., 2014). Gundogar et al. found an inverse relationship between psychological resilience and irritable and anxious temperament with or without childhood trauma, and found a positive link between resilience and hyperthymic temperament (exceptionally positive disposition) for cases without childhood trauma. Temperaments that have influenced outcomes (e.g., behavioral inhibition, impulsivity) are discussed in age-related chapters.

Internal Dialogue

As described in Chapters 1 and 2, how we talk to ourselves and our ability to recognize and utilize self-components influences symptoms and emotions—a factor that may be utilized in treatments. Dialogue between parts of self may assist creation of an integrated and adapted self as well as enable a sense of coherence and ability for conflict resolution (Dimaggio et al., 2010). Self-compassion and self-reassurance have proven to be protective factors (Flett, Flett, & Wekerle, 2015; Longe et al., 2010; Table 1.3b). In contrast, negative self-talk and failure to recognize and integrate internal voices may have negative results (Chapter 1). With some variation across cultures, a tendency toward self-criticism has served as a vulnerability factor. For example, self-criticism has been linked to depression, eating disorders, and anxiety, while self-reassurance has been inversely related to such outcomes (Longe et al., 2010). For Jewish study participants, self-criticism affected depression directly; for Bedouins, indirectly through avoidant coping (Abu-Kaf & Braun-Lewensohn, 2015; Zuroff, Sadikaj, Kelly, & Leybman, 2016).

Self-criticism has been associated with harsh personal standards, elevated striving for mastery and achievement, and a marked need for acknowledgment, resulting in vulnerability to depression (Abu-Kaf & Braun-Lewensohn, 2015). In addition to its associations with intense negative affect and poor affiliative relationships, self-criticism is associated with self-blame or a tendency to assume blame and hopelessness (see Abu-Kaf & Braun-Lewensohn, 2015). For example, for young adults sexually abused as children (CSA), CSA had a direct and an indirect negative effect on romantic relationship satisfaction—i.e., self-criticism mediated the relationship between CSA and relationship dissatisfaction over time (N = 135 women, ages 18–39; Lassri, Luyten, Fonagy, & Shahar, 2018; avoidant attachment also related to dissatisfaction). The relationship between adversity and eating disorders has been mediated by emotional and behavioral dysregulation as well as by such cognitive factors as self-criticism (review of studies; Trottier & MacDonald, 2017).

Comfort Style

Being able to be comforted when distressed is important to life in general as well as after stressful experiences. Not everyone can be comforted in the same way (e.g., by distraction, talk, soothing). Under normal conditions, an adequate caregiver–infant attachment relationship in which the infant can openly signal discomfort and receive a sensitive response helps to buffer the infant against extreme levels of fearful arousal (Lyons-Ruth, Dutra, Schuder, & Bianchi, 2006). From an early age, disturbed parental affective communications become a part of patterns of identity and behavior as well as a part of the biologic stress regulation system. Faulty early parenting or trauma can impair the ability to be comforted. As well, traumatized children have exhibited disruptions in the endogenous opiate system that also leads to difficulty being comforted (Siegel, 2013). In addition to the quality of relationships, the congruence of relationships—e.g., between parent and child, therapist and patient, and perhaps even treatment modality and help-seeker personality—can play an important role in reactions and in the effectiveness of treatment (Nader, 2008; Chapter 17). For example, goodness-of-fit between child temperament and parent responsiveness has had a major effect on a child's ability to be comforted before, during, and after frightening and painful medical procedures (Lee, Cohen, Stuber, & Nader, 1994). When parents of bone marrow transplant recipients applied a comforting style that matched their young child's preferred method of being comforted—e.g., distraction with activity, provision of information, or holding and verbally soothing—the child's distress was more likely to diminish visibly, whereas it clearly increased when the parent used a different style (Lee et al., 1994). Following trauma exposure, children in a classroom or a family are likely to exhibit differences from each other and from their own pre-trauma patterns of processing and of behavior. After trauma, it is important to discover when a child needs a silent presence or verbal reassurance or information, needs closeness or separateness, needs to be held or to have physical distance, and/or needs activity or inactivity. In other words, watchful attentiveness and/or patient observation and intuition are likely to be especially important after a trauma or other important stressor.

Grieving Style

Some evidence suggests that troubles arise when an individual employs a grieving style that does not fit his/her nature (Doughty, 2009). Grief trajectories vary, sometimes depending on the nature of the relationship and/or nature of the griever (Bonanno, Boerner, & Wortman, 2008; see Nader & Salloum, 2011). Individuals (especially children) may try to grieve in ways deemed socially, culturally, personally, or religiously acceptable or advisable and may be unaware that they are trying to meet others' expectations instead of grieving naturally. For example, although individuals may use varying degrees of both *intuitive* and *instrumental* grieving, usually one style is more dominant than the other (Martin & Doka, 2000). An *intuitive* grieving style is evident in the heightened experience and expression of emotions (Glossary). An *instrumental* grieving style is a more cognitive behavioral, problem-solving approach (Glossary). All types of grievers may seek social support. Differences in grieving or processing style may or may not help to explain why some children benefit and others feel worse after engaging in activities to help others or to memorialize the dead following a traumatic event (see Nader & Salloum, 2011). When a large enough group of symptoms are assessed (in addition to those delineated for adults), we may find more than two different grieving styles for children, influenced by age.

Coping Style

Although consensus has been that problem-focused or active coping is important to adaptation and that avoidant coping is problematic following traumas or loss, more recent research has shown that coping flexibility is more important than using a particular coping strategy (Burton et al., 2012; Nader, 2008; Table 14.1). For example, during war, information gathering—e.g., proximity of the enemy; location of resources—becomes especially important. Active coping methods (e.g., memorialization of the dead) may increase symptoms when such methods serve as traumatic reminders or are ill-timed (see Nader, 2008). Self-criticism and blaming as coping styles have increased symptoms (Table 14.1; Chapter 12).

Through interactively regulating an infant's positive and negative states and through ongoing inter-relating, a sensitive parent directly influences development of a child's brain and stress response system and manner of coping with distress (Schore, 2003; Siegel, 1999). Coping style is influenced by personality/traits, genetics, learning, and experience. Coping methods include behavioral responses (e.g., escape, fight, change environment) and cognitive responses (e.g., problem-solving, attributions/biases, denial, intellectualization) (Lazarus & Folkman, 1987; Mello & Nader, 2012; see Table 14.1—coping dimensions). Coping skills deficits have been associated with adjustment problems and behavioral disorders—e.g., delinquency; lower subjective well-being; reduced social functioning; depression; and poor physical and emotional health (Lazarus & Folkman, 1987; see Mello & Nader, 2012). Avoidant coping has been associated with both adaptive (Bonanno, 2005; Bonanno, Rennicke, & Dekel, 2005) and maladaptive (Holahan et al., 2005; Penley, Tomaka, & Wieve, 2002) posttrauma outcomes. Primary control beliefs include beliefs in one's ability to change a situation; secondary control beliefs include beliefs that one can adapt to uncontrollable situations (Deardorff, Gonzales, & Sandler, 2003). Secondary control may include, e.g., interpretive control (e.g., developing a healthy understanding of events) and vicarious control (trusting in powerful/authoritative others). Primary control beliefs have been less adaptive in truly uncontrollable situations—e.g., ongoing violence (Deardorff et al., 2003). In such situations, strategies like altering self, managing emotions, or controlling arousal may be more adaptive.

Coping Flexibility. The effectiveness of specific methods of coping varies in different contexts (Bonanno, Pat-Horenczyk, & Noll, 2011; Nader, 2008). For example, the effectiveness of expressing strong emotions depends in part on the receptivity and reactions of potential listeners. Advisability or inadvisability of avoidance depends on the nature of avoidance, circumstances, and the needs of the individual. The effectiveness of problem-solving or active coping versus inactive may depend on the controllability of the situation and the nature of activities.

Flexible coping has had a stress-buffering function (Atal & Cheng, 2016; Nader, 2008). For youth, both the ability to focus on and the ability to periodically avoid focus on aspects and reminders of a trauma have been important to recovery. Coping flexibility permits, e.g., the combined use of *forward-focused coping* (F-F coping—e.g., optimism, distraction, calm, avoidance; see Glossary) and *trauma-focus coping* (T-F coping—effortful focus on event; Glossary; Burton et al., 2012). Both types of coping have been found to independently contribute to overall adjustment, especially with high trauma exposure. For both American and Chinese samples, bereaved individuals who were asymptomatic or had complicated grief (CG) had higher levels of T-F coping than a comparison group, but only the CG group had lower levels of F-F coping (Burton et al., 2012). That is, the CG group was less flexible than either the normal comparison or the asymptomatic grieving group. Similarly, undergraduate groups with pathological levels of distress were significantly less likely to use F-F coping behaviors than a low-distress group (Galatzer-Levy, Burton, & Bonannno, 2012). While the *high-distress* group demonstrated equivalent degrees of T-F coping as the *stable-resilient* and *stable-moderate distress* groups, the *distressed-recovered* group displayed greater trauma focus. Coping flexibility greatly outweighed the use of specific coping types in adaptation to both traumas and general life stressors.

Atal and Cheng (2016) found that compared to a higher SES group, individuals with lower SES tended to be more flexible and varied the use of coping strategies consistent with the perceived controllability of stressful situations. Coping flexibility moderated the link between SES and health-related quality of life and between adverse effects of stress and health-related quality of life. Strategies such as positive reappraisal, focusing on a sense of purpose in life, and perceived control were associated with better health results (Atal & Cheng, 2016; Chen et al., 2011). Atal and Cheng suggest that flexible coping skills may be particularly useful in highly stressful situations, which often include varied and fluctuating demands.

Perception

Research has shown that perception may be more important than objective experience. Perception influences well-being and vice versa. Perception also influences reactions to stress (Nader & Fletcher, 2014). For example, even when an occupation is highly demanding, individuals who perceive that they have control experience less stress than those who perceive little control in low-demand occupations (Sapolsky, 2007; see Abshire et al., 2008). Adults with low health/well-being are more likely to report difficult childhoods with an upward recall bias (Sheikh, Abelson, & Olsen, 2016). Evidence has shown that peri-traumatic emotions (e.g., fear, panic, shame, guilt, anger, worry about others) or intense subjective experiences are important predictors of traumatic reactions (Ahern, Galea, Resnick, & Vlahov, 2004; Laufer & Solomon, 2009; see Nader, 2008; Pfefferbaum, Stuber, Galea, & Fairbrother, 2006). Even though exposure levels have been robust predictors of posttrauma symptoms, peri-traumatic emotions (e.g., subjective sense of fear) have often proven to be more strongly associated with posttraumatic symptoms than actual objective exposure (e.g., Dyregrov, Gupta, Gjestad, & Mukanoheli, 2000; Laufer & Solomon, 2009). Subjective assessments of injury rather than actual injury levels have influenced reactions and well-being. For youth exposed to war, subjective perception—i.e., subjective severity of earthquake-related experiences—explained more variance than the severity of objective earthquake-related experiences (11% of variance vs 2%; Israeli adolescents exposed to second Lebanese war; Ben-Zur & Almog, 2013). Predictors of the severity of war-related PTS reactions also included the level of depression (27% of total variance), difficulties at home (1%) and, combined, damage to home, age/school-grade, sex, and thoughts of revenge (1%).

Negative posttraumatic cognitions (e.g., appraisals of the trauma; perceptions of self, world) have been linked to psychological distress, symptoms (e.g., ADHD, ODD symptoms), internalizing and externalizing (Liu & Chen, 2015), and with persistence of PTS symptoms or disorder (Meiser-Stedman et al., 2009). After a potentially traumatic event (PTE), subjective perception rather than objective assessment of injury severity has been a more consistent predictor of acute and chronic PTSS. A child's accurate or inaccurate perception that a significant other was endangered during a PTE has been sufficient to result in PTS symptoms or traumatic grief (Cohen et al., 2002; Nader, 1997; Nader & Salloum, 2011). For example, youth who experienced the injury or death of a family member or friend in the 9/11 World Trade Center terrorist attacks were more likely than those who knew no one injured or killed to report PTSD symptoms (not more likely to meet criteria for a diagnosis of PTSD; Gould et al., 2004; Pfefferbaum et al., 2013).

Gender and Perception

Findings on PT gender differences have been mixed, and sometimes differences disappear when exposure or other variables are included in the assessment. Compared to men and boys, women and girls may experience comparable threats as more threatening (Laufer & Solomon, 2009). For example, overall, adolescent girls exposed to missile attacks reported feeling afraid significantly more than adolescent boys, and girls reported more intense fear than boys (Laufer & Solomon, 2009; N = 2999). Accordingly, girls reported more PTSS; however, boys reported twice the proportion of very severe symptoms. Gender was not a direct predictor—it predicted through fear, which was the best predictor of PTSD. Similarly, for children at the epicenter of an earthquake and those in a nearby city (ages 9–18), girls more often than boys endorsed subjective exposure items (i.e., four items on fear of death or injury to self or others; Roussos et al., 2005; N = 1937). In addition, perceptions influence other, age- and gender-related behaviors. For example, the dual perception that a stressful situation was threatening and frightening and was exhilarating and had potential benefit has been related to adolescent boys' increased risk-taking (two years after war exposure; Ben-Zur & Almog, 2013).

Stress Reactivity

Stress reactivity has been related to genes and to the effects of trauma (e.g., Castro-Vale et al., 2016). Stress reactivity has influenced reactions to both positive and negative experiences and environments.

Gene-Influenced Reactivity

Gene variations may influence reactivity and outcomes through their link to vulnerability (*diathesis-stress;* Glossary) and/or through their link to a person's increased susceptibility (*differential susceptibility)* to her/his environment (e.g., to adversity; Belsky & Pluess, 2009; Vaughn & Bost, 2018). Individuals who carry particular "vulnerability genes" (or "risk alleles") are more likely to develop a specific, gene-related problem (e.g., psychopathology or other maladaptation—e.g., poor health), when exposed to stressors of note (*diathesis-stress;* Belsky & Pluess, 2009; Del Giudice, Ellis, & Shirtcliff, 2011; Glossary). For example, breastfeeding has affected IQ (by 5–10 points) for infants with a particular gene variant (Bjorklund, 2013; Caspi et al., 2007). Nevertheless, breastfeeding has been robustly related to a number of positive outcomes—e.g., language development (Smith, 2015).

Some individuals are very reactive to their environments—i.e., far more affected than others both by negative and by positive conditions (*differential susceptibility;* Belsky & Pluess, 2009; Pluess et al., 2011). Among genes implicated in *susceptibility* are serotonin (e.g., 5-HTTLPR short allele), dopamine (e.g., DRD4), FKBP5, an MAO-A low activity variant, and others (Table A4.1; see Bakermans-Kranenburg & van IJzendoorn, 2018; Belsky & Pluess, 2009; Brüne, 2014; Dackis et al., 2012; Fox et al., 2005; Nader & Weems, 2011; Nikitopoulos et al., 2014; see Nader & Fletcher, 2014). Some evidence suggests that 5-HTTLPR short allele carriers have heightened amygdala reactions in response to emotional stimuli (Munafo, Brown, & Hariri, 2008; Table A4.1). Hence, they may require significantly more time than other variant carriers to disconnect from negative stimuli. Parents with the COMTval and DRD4 7-repeat alleles have shown the highest responsivity to their offspring's needs with low stress levels, whereas responsivity was lower than average with high stress levels (see Brüne, 2014). Attachment-related interventions have proven effective for high-reactive children and their parents (Klein et al., 2006; Vaughn & Bost, 2018).

Box 4.1 Increased Reactivity

Traumatic Ankle Injury. Nathan injured his ankle in football practice. When he stepped down on it, it felt like it was both numb and vibrating. The ankle was diagnosed as severely sprained, and he was prescribed rehabilitation. The physical therapist (PT) followed the protocol for a bad sprain, prescribed by the high school sports-medicine doctor. However, the PT became alarmed at the results and sent Nathan back to the doctor. It turned out that there were chipped bones in the ankle and the subtalar joint was tilted. Surgery removed some of the bone debris. Afterward, any time Nathan slightly twisted his ankle (e.g., to turn), walked on hard or uneven surfaces, or picked up something heavy with his right hand, his ankle muscles tightened "... like I was wearing that brace you gave me when I first hurt it, but I wasn't." Later in the day it was painful enough to prevent walking without a cane or crutches. His ankle seemed to overreact to the smallest jar. His body acted like he was about to re-injure it, and it over-responded with tightening and pain. The doctor called it a traumatic injury. Whenever Nathan saw a person fall or jump off a structure in a movie, he had a strange feeling in his legs: "Like my legs felt excited and scared at the same time."

Psychological Trauma with Increased Reactivity. Hassan was a secure, well-adapted, outgoing boy before he was exposed to multiple frightening conditions of war at age 13 (see Box 16.3 for a fuller description). After the war, his body would begin to shake when he remembered his experiences (especially the long ride through enemy soldiers pointing guns at him). His body would also shake uncontrollably at times when he didn't know why. It may have been because his heart was beating faster than usual, his muscles had tightened like they did during the ride when he feared death, or he saw something in a person's face or stance that unconsciously reminded him of the threatening soldiers. When it happened, he felt helpless and embarrassed. He didn't want anyone to see him.

Note:
All case examples are disguised, may be combined cases, and have had details changed to protect individuals.

Trauma-Induced Stress Reactivity

Research has shown that childhood trauma—particularly chronic, repeated, or severe stress, which may keep self-protection neurochemicals elevated (serotonin, dopamine, acetylcholine, norepinephrine; Hulme, 2011)—influences stress reactivity by altering HPA axis function upward or downward (Chapter 1; McCleery & Harvey, 2004; e.g., lower morning cortisol with chronic [not acute] stress, Fisher et al., 2006; Heim et al., 2008; see Nader & Fletcher, 2014; Roy et al., 2010; Yehuda et al., 2015). That is, trauma may trigger epigenetic changes resulting in greater stress sensitivity—a more reactive HPA system; reduced inhibition of the stress response (Alexander et al., 2018; Castro-Vale et al., 2016; Kohrt et al., 2015; Lupien, McEwen, Gunnar, & Heim, 2009; McGowan et al., 2009; Nader & Fletcher, 2014; Yehuda et al. 2015; Box 4.1; Chapter 1; Tables A4.1, A4.2—hypothalamus). A hyper-reactive cortisol system has been found in depressed patients as well. Adults with general anxiety disorder (GAD; no trauma history) have shown higher morning cortisol levels than normal comparisons, indicating hyperactivity of the HPA axis (may vary by onset age; Wang et al., 2017; Table A4.1—GR). Individuals with both childhood traumas and a mixed phenotype of psychopathology (depression + anxiety + psychotic symptoms) showed increased reactivity to daily stressors at baseline and more symptoms at follow-up (14 months later; regardless of trauma type; van Nierop et al., 2018). Those with a history of trauma and a mixed phenotype perceived some events as more stressful than individuals with a history of trauma and no mixed phenotype, suggesting that a less negative bias may be protective.

Trauma has also predicted blunted cortisol reactivity (O'Connor et al., 2018; Chapter 6—cortisol slope). Blunted baseline cortisol has been found, e.g., in suicide attempters. For example, for individuals with a suicidal history, childhood trauma was a significant predictor of blunted cortisol reactivity to stress and of lower resting cortisol levels, such that higher levels of trauma were associated with lower cortisol levels. The highest levels of childhood trauma—moderate and severe, cumulative traumas—were found in those who had attempted suicide (N = 160, ages 18–62 with childhood traumas; O'Connor et al., 2018). Whether hypo- or hyper-cortisol reactivity follows moderate to severe traumatization appears to be influenced by epigenetic changes in a glucocorticoid receptor region (Table A4.1—DNA_M; see also FKBP5; Alexander et al., 2018).

Adults and children with PTSD also have demonstrated increased autonomic nervous system reactivity as indicated in significantly higher RSA reactivity (Glossary). Adults and children with PTSD have shown higher levels of reactivity (Gray, Lipschutz, & Scheeringa, 2018). Dynamic parasympathetic control of arousal supports appropriate engagement in parent–child and other social interactions (see Gray et al., 2018). For three groups of children—non-exposed, exposed with PTSD, or exposed without PTSD—RSA was assessed during memory tasks. Heightened RSA reactivity related to recollection of a traumatic memory, but not to other memory tasks (N = 247 maternal caregivers and their 3–6-year-olds; Gray et al., 2018). Meta-analysis has shown that children with psychopathology are less likely to suppress RSA during social stressors than children without psychopathology (Shahrestani et al., 2014 in Gray et al., 2018).

Factors in a Child's History that Influence Outcomes

Among factors in a child's history that may influence posttrauma outcomes are prior adversities including traumatic stressors—especially multiple types of trauma or adversity—and loss. Heightened and sustained activation of neural and neuroendocrine circuits in response to stress may result in chronically dysregulated systems and in maladaptive psychological and physiological outcomes that persist across the lifespan (Cicchetti, Rogosch, & Oshri, 2011). Because biological systems are interconnected, changes in the functioning of one adaptive system may cascade or spread its effects across other systems (Cicchetti et al., 2011).

Traumatic Event(s) and Exposures

As noted, approximately two thirds of children are exposed to traumas (Copeland, Keeler, Angold, & Costello, 2007; see Nader & Fletcher, 2014). Meta-analysis suggests that, toward the end of the last century, PTSD prevalence rates varied somewhat by age group (Fletcher, 2003): 39% of preschool children, 33% of school-age children, 27% of adolescents, and 24% of adults. Recent studies have confirmed around a 70% resilience rate (Scheeringa, 2016). Although different types of traumas have symptoms in common (Nader, 2008), different types of trauma also may be more likely to show certain impacts (Hodges et al., 2013)—e.g., sexual traumas and later sexual fears or maladaptive sexual behaviors (e.g., Briere & Runtz, 1990); physical assaults (e.g., physically bullied or attacked) or abuse may produce subsequent anger or aggression (e.g., see Bigras, Godbout, & Briere, 2015), and psychological abuse may be especially associated with low self-esteem. However, findings related to the associations of specific events have been mixed. Variables not studied shape reactions and reactivity as well (e.g., poly-victimization, Chapter 2; genetics, above).

PTSD or Previous Trauma Exposure as a Risk Factor

PTSD is a risk factor for a number of symptoms, disorders, and lifelong difficulties—e.g., increased risk of suicidal ideation, internalizing, externalizing, brain and biological changes (Gould et al., 2012; Koenen et al., 2008; Nader & Fletcher, 2014; Yehuda et al., 2015). As discussed in Chapter 2, poly-victimization and/or cumulative trauma has served as a risk factor for symptoms and reactions and for symptom complexity. Exposure to aggressive traumas is a risk factor for revictimization (Chapter 2). In addition to youth with PTSD, children exposed to traumas who do not meet full criteria for PTSD (subclinical PTS) or who have specific trauma symptoms have had disturbances in functioning (Nader, 2008). For example, although maltreated youth with PTSD present clinically distinct profiles from maltreated youth without PTSD, in a study with comprehensive neuropsychological testing, both maltreated groups performed significantly lower than controls on IQ, academic achievement, and most of the neurocognitive domains tested (De Bellis, Woolley, & Hooper, 2013). Kimber et al. (2018) found that, although better quality studies are needed, all but three of 19 studies showed that exposure to intimate partner violence in childhood is significantly associated with children's commission of intimate partner violence in adulthood, among other negative psychosocial outcomes—e.g., persistent social, emotional, and behavioral problems. Prior trauma has been a risk factor for health and economic problems as well (Chapter 2).

Complicated Grief (CG)

Grief has been related to increased trauma symptoms and trauma has been related to more complicated forms of grief (Nader, 2008). Most individuals experiencing nonviolent death of a loved one are able to adapt within one to two years after the death (Bonanno & Mancini, 2008). The adjustment period can be much shorter for approximately 45–50% of highly resilient bereaved individuals (Bonanno & Kaltman, 2001). For 10–15% of bereaved, severely disabling CG symptoms (e.g., profound separation distress; an inability to accept the loss) are linked to long-term physical and mental health impairments—e.g., early mortality; increased PTSD; depression; worse mental health scores; reduced social functioning; lower energy levels; and/or increased suicidal ideation (Prigerson et al., 1997, 1999; for adults and children). Violently bereaved samples have shown much higher rates of CG (e.g., 31%–70%; see Burke & Neimeyer, 2014). During a school shooting at age 13, Shawna ran for her life and also watched helplessly while her friend and other students were shot and killed. She entered treatment three weeks after the shooting. She remained perpetually frightened, jumped at any unexpected noise, cried easily, and had a number of other trauma symptoms that made it difficult to function at school and in crowds. A good support system and positive reaction to therapy improved her ability to respond to crises. Months after her treatment, she did better than peers during an earthquake. She knew to move to a safe location and to protect herself from frightening sounds and sights until the earthquake stopped.

Spiritual beliefs, religious practices, and the spiritual community can be important resources for coping with grief (see Burke & Neimeyer, 2014). For spiritually inclined individuals, such beliefs generally have been linked to reduced distress and to good decision-making, healthy living, and altruistic behaviors. Poor adaptation to loss (CG) after homicide prospectively predicts the development of complicated spiritual grief (CSG; Shear et al., 2006)—a sense of discord, conflict, and distance from God, and sometimes from the survivor's spiritual community (Burke & Neimeyer, 2014; Neimeyer & Burke, 2017). Burke and Neimeyer (2014) found that, while all forms of bereavement distress have been correlated with spiritual crisis, only CG uniquely predicted the subsequent development of CSG, beyond the variance explained by PTSD and depression. For young and older traumatized children, CSG or CG can undermine attachment and support systems. For spiritually aware children, it can undermine the spiritual support system as well. While positive religious coping (e.g., "Focused on religion to stop worrying about my problems") may not blunt the pain of grieving; negative religious coping (e.g., "Felt punished by God for my lack of devotion") signals elevated/complicated grief (see Neimeyer & Burke, 2017). Mourners whose loved ones died violently (i.e., by suicide, murder, or fatal accident) reported the greatest difficulty adjusting to the loss emotionally and spiritually and had significantly more CG and CSG than did those bereaved by natural death. In part, this may be related to the suddenness, traumatic nature, or role of human intention or inattention that can undermine faith (e.g., because of unpredictable, uncontrollable randomness of life; Burke & Neimeyer, 2014).

Environmental Factors Influencing Outcomes

Among environmental influences on posttrauma outcomes are social support (e.g., community connectedness; parental; other), culture, resources (e.g., housing adequacy, enrichment opportunities, sustenance), levels of crime and violence, and emotional climate (e.g., marital quality; family conflict). Support systems have been protective against the ill effects of adversity/traumas (Kaufman et al., 2004). To follow are discussions of social support, isolation, societal issues (resources and communities), attachment, and parenting.

Social Support versus Isolation

Support can be multifaceted. It may include comfort, encouragement, praise, warmth, sensitivity, and support for a child's individuality (Hsieh & Yen, 2017; Williford, Carter, & Pianta, 2018). Following traumas, it includes emotional support and a child-desired form of comforting. These kinds of support may come from parents, other family members or trusted adults, peers, and teachers. As mentioned, social support is a robust protective factor against the severity of reactions to adversity or trauma (e.g., Jia et al., 2015) and has been linked to other positive outcomes (e.g., self-esteem, Harter, 1999). In contrast, loneliness can be a problem across age groups and has been linked to poor psychological and physical health (Rotenberg et al., 2010). In addition to its associations with better outcomes after adversity, social connection is linked to longevity and quality of life. For adults, health risks of social isolation and loneliness have exceeded risk from obesity or hypertension—e.g., isolation has been linked to cardiovascular health, immune function, and cognitive decline (Holt-Lunstad & Smith, 2016; Table A4.1—oxytocin).

Loneliness

From their beginnings, children need to belong. In infancy they need synchronous relationships with a caregiver (e.g., Beebe et al., 2016; Rotenberg et al., 2010). Social functioning usually develops within the context of a mother–child relationship. In early childhood, children need and expect friendships that include enjoyable activities (see Hsieh & Yen, 2017). In middle childhood, they need and expect to be liked by a close friend. In adolescence, they need and expect to be accepted by a peer group and, at some point, a romantic relationship. Loneliness is separate from being alone (Chipuer, 2004). It includes social deficits and distressing/aversive emotions and may include feeling alone when with others (Hsieh & Yen, 2017). It can be a transient or a persistent experience.

Social loneliness has been described as the lack of a desired relationship with a group of individuals and consequently the lack of social activities (Rotenberg et al., 2010). Emotional loneliness has been described as the loss or absence of a close/intense, relatively enduring relationship with another person—e.g., family, friend, romantic partner. Loneliness has been linked to negative outcomes such as suicidal behavior (Eskin, 2001), hopelessness (Page et al., 2006), increased sexual compulsion (loneliness combined with internet addiction, Lawal & Idemudia, 2017), severe cybervictimization (when combined with avoiding communication with mother, Larrañaga, Yubero,

Ovejero, & Navarro, 2016), low self-esteem, and depression (Hsieh & Yen, 2017). Feelings of loneliness, thwarted belongingness, or feelings of not belonging to a family or peer group and feeling like a burden (burdensomeness) have been among factors associated with suicidal ideation and attempts (see Holland et al., 2017). For Taiwanese children, the more parents were involved with their children (not harsh parenting), the lower the levels of loneliness and the greater the decrease in loneliness over time into adolescence (N = 4990 first and fourth graders; Hsieh & Yen, 2017).

In a four-study report (Rotenberg et al., 2010), individuals in varying age groups were assessed for their trust beliefs, social maturity, and loneliness. Trust and social maturity influenced loneliness. When trust beliefs were measured as beliefs in peer's keeping promises and secrets (N = 278 UK 5–7-year-olds), young children with low trust beliefs showed lower social maturity in school, which in part contributed to their increases in loneliness a year later (N = 211). For another group of children, assessed in middle childhood (ages 9–11; N = 505), boys' trust beliefs negatively, directly predicted loneliness a year later, while the effects of girls' trust beliefs on loneliness were mediated by their social maturity (like the 5–7-year-olds; N = 434). For undergraduates (N = 331, ages 16.5 to 22), self-reported attachment mediated, in part, the relationship between trust beliefs in peers and emotional loneliness the next semester; social maturity mediated, in part, trust beliefs relationship to social loneliness the next semester (N = 220; belief in promise-keeping; worried a person was laughing critically at them). In the fourth study, when 80 undergraduates were primed with either trust or distrust words, when youth were primed with distrust words, they reported more withdrawal affect, including loneliness, than when primed with trust words, suggesting that trust vs distrust related cognitions influence loneliness (Rotenberg et al., 2010).

Resources and Communities

At every age in a society, the harsher and poorer the environment (e.g., parenting, SES), the higher the rate of morbidity (e.g., disease, injury) and mortality (death; Simpson & Belsky, 2018). In addition to these outcomes, the lower the childhood SES, the poorer the mental health, general health, and well-being in adulthood (Sheikh et al., 2016). Minority and poverty-level children exposed to violence in homes and communities are at greater risk for multiple traumas and adversities (see Ghosh Ippen et al., 2011). Culture and acculturation also may influence stress levels and the frequency and outcomes of trauma exposure (Nader, 2008). For Latino adults, when their worst trauma was in childhood (not in adulthood), the lowest levels of acculturation were associated with the highest levels of PTSD symptoms (DiGangi et al., 2016). SES, psychological abuse, and physical abuse have independently predicted adulthood outcomes (adjusted for each other). Childhood SES has had both a direct and an indirect effect on adult mental health, general health, and well-being (Sheikh et al., 2016). Sheikh et al. (2016) showed that the negative effects of SES can be substantially reduced by interventions aimed at preventing childhood psychological and physical abuse.

In lab situations, stress hormones (e.g., cortisol) are evoked when unpredictability, uncontrollability (over a situation or outcome), and social-evaluative threat (potential negative appraisal by others) combine (Gunnar, Talge, & Herrera, 2009c; Chapter 9). Some evidence suggests that early (ages 0–5) real-life *unpredictability* has impacted later life (age 23) more than later childhood (ages 6–16) real-life *unpredictability* (e.g., job and/or marital status fluctuations, residential moves; lower resources)—e.g., more sexual partners, aggression, delinquency (Simpson et al., 2012). When adolescents were compared to each other, exposure to greater environmental *unpredictability* and *harshness* (e.g., resource scarcity, predator threats) in adolescence independently predicted problems as well (e.g., deviant social behavior; Brumbach, Figueredo, & Ellis, 2009; N = 20,745 adolescents; 15,197 re-interviewed as young adults).

Attachment

Attachment is a significant predictor of outcomes in general and in relationship to traumatic exposure (Tables A3.1–3.5). In most of evolutionary history, children likely were born approximately four years apart and raised with much assistance from extended family members and perhaps non-kin group members as well (see Simpson & Belsky, 2018), increasing the likelihood of attentive care. Extensive evidence has demonstrated the importance of sensitive caretaking—the caregiver's ability to synchronize with an infant's rhythms, personality, and/or temperamental and other needs and sensitivities as well as to adapt to a child as s/he grows and develops. Studies underscore the inadvisability of long separations of infants from mothers (e.g., Paksarian et al., 2015; for premature infants, Polan & Hofer, 2018, Chapters 5, 7), and have linked secure parent–child attachments to sociability, compliance, and effective emotion regulation, in contrast to insecure attachments, which are linked to poor peer relations, anger, and poor behavioral self-control (DeKlyen & Greenberg, 2018; Sroufe, Egeland, Carlson, & Collins, 2005). Research also supports the idea that greater levels of parental well-being, marital quality, and social support correspond to more sensitive, responsive, stimulating, and less detached (or hostile) parenting (Simpson & Belsky, 2018). Caffaro and Conn-Caffaro (2013) point out that youth learn from sibling relationships as well (a different kind of attachment, Ludolph & Bow, 2012; Shumaker, Miller, Ortiz, & Deutsch, 2011), and such relationships also influence future style and expectations in relationships (Box 3.2—Tally). Siblings have been found to be important to the development and well-being of children of divorce (Shumaker et al., 2011). Like parental abuse, sibling abuse has negative repercussions (Box 3.2—Tally).

Original attachment studies were somewhat small. Larger, recent studies suggest that maternal sensitivity accounts for only a portion of the variance in attachment status (Simpson & Belsky, 2018). Additionally, caregiver sensitivity is not as simple as often undivided, sensitive attention. In addition to sensitive caretaking, it is essential to know when to allow a child to struggle somewhat—e.g., to cry or struggle for a reasonable period; to explore or experiment—with new toys, with new ideas—vs when not to follow a child's lead (Chapters 5, 10, 17; Chapter 7—COSP, Child's Play). Early developmental research does not always fit Bowlby's concept of a unitary attachment system at work within the mother–infant interaction (Polan & Hofer, 2018). In animals and humans, relatively independent systems, organized to carry out functions—e.g., searching, following, orienting, early learning and memory, thermo-regulation (regulation of body temperature), vocalizing and other early expressions of affect—each have organizing principles. As a child develops, the neuro-biological, behavioral, and psychological processes at work seem very different (Polan & Hofer, 2018). In addition to attachment, parenting becomes important over time.

Numerous theorists and researchers have noted that an attachment style is formed in response to infant and primary caregiver relationships, and the resulting attachment style forms the basis of relationships throughout life (Cassidy & Shaver, 2018; Wynter, Rowe, Tran, & Fisher, 2016; see Tables A3.1–A3.4). From an evolutionary perspective, secure attachment patterns may best prepare offspring for reproductive fitness in a predictable, secure environment in which prolonged parental investment in offspring is possible, whereas insecure attachment patterns may be more adaptive in chaotic, dangerous, and depriving or overwhelmed environments where fearful responses maximize short-term survival and early sexual maturation maximizes offspring numbers (Simpson & Belsky, 2018). Paradoxically, a maternal cue associated with abuse (e.g., the mother's scent) in infancy still attracts offspring as adults, diminishes adult fear learning, and relieves depression, which may ultimately add to our knowledge of revictimization (e.g., Özdemir & Tüfekci, 2014; Zhang et al., 2018a).

Although a mother's attachment status influences her child's attachment status via her parenting style, children vary in their susceptibility to parenting and other influences (see Stress Reactivity, above; Belsky & Pluess, 2009, 2013). Although mother-sensitivity has been the focus of many attachment studies, children in the same family, with the same sensitive mother, may have different attachment classifications (even twins, Fearon et al., 2006). The personalities of infant and of caregiver, their reactions to each other, and other environmental conditions may affect caregiver–infant relationships initially and over time—e.g., shared and nonshared experiences; parental distractions such as number of children, outside involvements/duties. Family group behavior may differ from one-to-one mother–child relationships (e.g., response to male vs females; responses to specific personality traits). Attachment classification usually has been unrelated to genes (Brumariu et al., 2015; Fearon et al., 2006, 2014; exceptions: serotonin, cortisol, Table A4.1). Recent studies control for birth order when examining attachment. Theoretically, it would seem reasonable that, under normal circumstances in a family looking forward to having children, that a first, desired child would receive more undivided attention than a subsequent child, greater excitement and/or pleasure over the novelty of the infant's behaviors and developmental achievements, and other signs of welcoming and delight (exception, e.g., Box 3.2—Danya).

Internal Working Models (IWM)

Sroufe (2018) suggests that attachment variations may be seen as the foundation for personality formation, and *internal working models* (IWM, representations of a child's interactive history) are "the means by which lived experience is carried forward" (p. 1000). Whether using the term *IWM* or *patterns of thinking* or *scripts* or some other term, these mental processes translate into patterns of thought, expectations, and behaviors (see Nader, 2008—Chapter 14); they show in needs, fears, and biases versus a sense of safety and ease of living. These patterns elicit synchrony or discord from others. Associations of attachment-related IWMs/scripts are especially strong for self-management, dependency, and peer relationships (Sroufe, 2018). Although attachment history is not the only

Box 4.2 Context and Other Stressors

Madison (age three) and her infant brother (six months old, Connor) were placed in a children's institution by Child Protective Services (CPS), after her brother was found with bruises and burns on his arms and legs. Their mother and her boyfriend (not the father) denied responsibility for the injuries. According to normal procedure, the children remained in the facility until the case was adjudicated, which might (and did) take months. There were only two workers in the nursery, which at that time had nine babies, so Connor did not receive as much one-to-one care as he might in a foster home. Madison was very tall (looked age six instead of three), and workers expected her to act older than her age. They fussed at her frequently. She appeared confused and distressed at their admonitions. She wanted to see her little brother and her mother but was rarely allowed to see them. Madison and Connor endured separation from their primary attachment figure and from each other, without the ability to clearly understand why. While in the institution the children received less one-to-one care than at home and had no constant attachment figure nurturing their development. Madison received more frequent admonition and not enough assistance from workers who seemed not to keep in mind her age, even after her age was discussed with them by Madison's first Social Worker. Although the institutional placement was for the children's protection, it contributed additional stressors to the children's lives.

Note:
All case examples are disguised, may be combined cases, and have had details changed to protect individuals.

influence on outcomes and does not influence all outcomes, attachment influences expectations regarding self, others, and relationships; a person's basic sense of security; the capacity to draw support from as well as to offer support to others; emotion regulation; and functioning. IWMs are not the only things that elicit differences in responses from others. Child characteristics, circumstances, and those responding to the child also influence (Boxes 4.2, 8.2). Nevertheless, a large body of evidence has demonstrated the importance of attachment to children's resiliency, quality of life, and interpersonal styles (Cassidy & Shaver, 2018; Nader, 2008).

Synchrony

Synchrony—also known as reciprocity, coordination, co-regulation, or mutual responsiveness (Feldman, Bamberger, & Kanat-Maymon, 2013a; Chapter 5) or as interactive contingent communication (Beebe et al., 2016)—is an important aspect of attachment formation. Synchrony is seen, e.g., in emotion-matching/attunement, reciprocal and mutually rewarding interactions, and compatible or complementary states (Hutman & Dapretto, 2009). For example, typically mothers exaggerate facial expressions and maintain visual contact longer when interacting with infants than with others as well as use slower speech, accentuate certain syllables, and speak an octave above normal (Simpson & Belsky, 2018). Such patterns are preferred by most young infants and assist their developing visual and auditory as well as interactive capacities.

Synchrony is a health and relationship promoting factor and is important to development during infant–parent dyadic interactions and in inter-relating across life (e.g., see Beebe et al., 2016; Gray et al., 2018; Chapters 5, 17). Cortisol synchrony has been observed between toddlers and sensitive mothers. For children exposed to traumas, high synchrony in autonomic reactivity was shown between exposed-no-PTSD mothers and young children, but not in those with PTSD, during child or parent's recall of traumatic memories (measured by RSA, Glossary; Gray et al., 2018).

Attachment Stability

Some evidence suggests that the stability of the caregiving environment has been a better predictor of later child outcomes than infant attachment (see Levendosky et al., 2011). Also, some authors have found only weak stability of attachment classifications over time (Groh et al., 2014). Although some confirmation exists that infants classified as disorganized are more likely than their non-disorganized counterparts to be rated insecure in adulthood (high-risk adults; Weinfield, Whaley, & Egeland, 2004), individual differences in later adult attachment style have been linked to variations in the quality of caregiving environments (early and changes over time), father absence, early and ongoing social competence, quality of best friendships, ongoing experiences in interpersonal relationships, life events, other issues/endeavors, or other environmental changes (e.g., demands, safety issues) (e.g., Fraley et al., 2013; Levendosky et al., 2011). Additionally, individuals tend to increase in felt security on days when their interpersonal needs are met, and to decrease in security when such needs are not met (e.g., needs for competence, autonomy, and relatedness; La Guardia, Ryan, Couchman, & Deci, 2000). Social support during adulthood acts as a protective factor for those with histories of poor-quality early caregiving (see Raby, Steele, Carlson, & Sroufe, 2015). Higher-quality social support has been associated with shifts from attachment insecurity during the first generation to security during the next generation (Raby et al., 2015).

Booth-LaForce and colleagues (2014) found that, from early childhood (15, 24, and 36 months) to late adolescent attachment states of mind (N = 825), 40% remained secure, 17% insecure, 20% changed from insecure to secure, and 23% changed from secure to insecure. Youth who became insecure reported a greater decline in maternal sensitivity, lower likelihood of fathers living with them, and higher mother-reported increase in negative life events over time. Youth, who changed from insecure in infancy to secure in late adolescence (compared to stably insecure) reported higher levels of maternal sensitivity in the intervening years. Compared to stably secure youth, stably insecure youth experienced less maternal sensitivity from six to 36 months and from 54 months to age 15. Similarly, consistently secure youth (vs youth who changed from secure to insecure) and those who changed from insecure to secure (vs consistently insecure) had more sensitive mothers at 12 months of age, and a trend toward greater sensitivity at age 14 (see Raby et al., 2015). Both paternal depressive symptoms and the amount of father absence forecasted stable insecurity.

Attachment Classifications

Evidence suggests that attachment begins before birth—the strength of the attachment of either parent to an unborn child influences subsequent attachment and development (Alhusen, Hayat, & Gross, 2013). Unless altered, the attachment style established in early life influences an individual's characteristic reactions to distress and characteristic inter-relating. For example, in times of crisis or distress, the attachment system is activated (Bowlby, 1969/1982), and without conscious volition, individuals high in attachment anxiety may experience hyper-activation of the attachment system (Main, 1990) and/or of attachment behaviors (Beeney et al., 2015)—e.g., dependence, neediness. Although prevalence rates may differ within and among cultures, four main attachment patterns (assessed in Strange Situation Procedure, SSP) have emerged across cultures—secure, insecure avoidant, insecure resistant, and disorganized (also insecure/other; Zeanah et al., 2016; Tables A3.1–A3.4). Secure attachments are protective; insecure patterns have been linked to psychopathology; and disorganized or insecure/other patterns more strongly linked to pathology.

Threat-Related Reactions. Attachment insecurities may be less related to processing of neutral information than to processing of threat-related information (Ein-Dor et al., 2011). While relatively secure individuals react to threat with secure base scripts, insecure individuals may access rich alternative scripts (see Ein-Dor, Mikulincer, & Shaver, 2011; Mikulincer & Shaver, 2009; Shaver et al., 2018). When in trouble or in need of assistance or support, securely attached individuals expect others to be available and responsive and to help them cope with dangers or stressors, while less secure individuals do not rely confidently on such expectations (Ein-Dor et al., 2011). As demonstrated in a series of studies, while story-writing about threat, insecure-anxious-resistant individuals noticed external danger before others did and warned others about the danger (*sentinel schema*; see Nader, 2008, PT script-like protector/rescuer). The most anxious-resistant individual

Box 4.3 Traumatic Associations

Attachment classification is not the only thing that predicts a specific behavior. Ginger was securely attached to both parents and was always a child with a positive attitude. She was asleep when the smoke alarms sounded. She ran to her parents' room. Her parents had gone to rescue her two younger siblings. The smell of smoke was strong, coming from downstairs. Her mother went down the rope ladder first with the baby in a pouch. Ginger went down next, and father and two-year-old Andy last. Ginger's parents praised her for going down the ladder so bravely. Ginger had trouble sleeping for a few weeks. After her experience with the fire, she was always the first to notice the smell of smoke or something burning.

Note:
All case examples are disguised, may be combined cases, and have had details changed to protect individuals.

in a group was quickest to detect a threat (e.g., a smoking computer in the room; see also Box 4.3). Avoidant attachment, on the other hand, was linked to a rapid fight-flight schema—escaping a dangerous situation without assisting others; acting rapidly without depending on others or their actions; not cooperating or deliberating with others. The most avoidant group member was least likely to recognize and broadcast a laboratory threat. Both childhood sexual (CSA) and emotional abuse are linked to insecure attachment dimensions (resistance and avoidance; Cicchetti & Valentino, 2006).

Secure Attachments. Attachment security emerges when an infant or child experiences that attachment needs are routinely met, which promotes development of IWMs of the self as lovable and of others as dependable, helpful, and supportive (Beeney et al., 2015; Bowlby, 1982; Table A3.1). Secure attachments are characterized by "felt security" (Sroufe & Waters, 1977), which frees an individual to have cognitions that are unrelated to attachment needs. Instead of worries about threat or the ability to cope, *felt security* permits engaging in high-level thinking and social cognition (Mikulincer & Shaver, 2007). Securely attached children show greater social competence, fewer externalizing and internalizing behaviors, and greater adaptation overall (vs insecure, Barone & Lionetti, 2012). Secure adults have had lower PTSD scores following traumas (Escolas et al., 2012).

Preoccupied/Resistant/Anxious-Ambivalent Attachments. Resistant individuals tend to respond to distress using attachment *hyperactivating* strategies that include high levels of dependence on others for assistance and support (Shaffer, Vogel, Wei, 2006; Table A3.2). Such individuals may frequently worry about whether others will reject or tire of them, because they have negative IWM of self (e.g., doubting their self-worth and competence) and may perceive themselves as unworthy of support. Although resistant individuals show desire for and want to pursue long-term mating strategies, a strong desire to be attractive to and merge with romantic partners can result in unstable, short-term sexual relationships (Simpson & Belsky, 2018). Resistant attachment status has been linked to body dissatisfaction (Lev-Ari, Baumgarten-Katz, & Zohar, 2014); to childhood BI (Glossary); to adolescent social anxiety (particularly males; Lewis-Morrarty et al., 2015); and to anxiety disorders across age groups and cultures (Schimmenti & Bifulco, 2015)—e.g., higher levels of worry (Brown & Whiteside, 2008), more school phobia (Bar-Haim, Dan, Eshel, & Sagi-Schwartz, 2007; Schimmenti & Bifulco, 2015), more anxiety symptoms and interpersonal difficulties (adolescents; Brown & Wright, 2003), more generalized anxiety disorders, social phobia, or panic with or without agoraphobia (Schimmenti & Bifulco, 2015)—than secure youth. Across studies, a moderate link has been found between resistant attachment and negative temperament, compared to secure or avoidant children (Groh et al., 2016). Resistant-preoccupied adults have had disorders such as social anxiety and panic disorders, and higher addictive profiles (see Baise-Takir, Aydemir, Okay, & Goka, 2015).

Dismissing/Avoidant. Avoidant attachments are believed to result when caregivers reject, ignore, or fail to respond to an infant's distress (Borelli et al., 2013; Table A3.3). Although avoidant infants show physiological signs of distress during attachment stressors (e.g., separation from caregiver), they often avoid or do not express distress to the caregiver, when accessible. Dismissing children's cortisol levels decrease more slowly over the course of such an interview compared to secure children, and dismissing adolescents show greater cardiovascular reactivity during a conflict interaction task with their mothers (see Borelli et al., 2010). At least temporarily, dismissing attachments seem to be over-represented in adolescents (Bakermans-Kranenburg & van IJzendoorn, 2009). Avoidant individuals generally pursue short-term mating strategies and have less committed relationships (Simpson & Belsky, 2018). Relevant to treatment, research suggests that individuals with attachment avoidance engage in less self-disclosure to others and are less willing to acknowledge distress (Shaffer et al., 2006). They use attachment *deactivating* strategies to regulate distress—e.g., keeping distance from others; self-reliance. These youth, described as having a tendency to devalue the importance of others, have been less willing to seek counseling. Some evidence suggests that they use more indirect strategies for obtaining support when distressed. Shaffer and colleagues found that cognitive processes (i.e., anticipating risks and benefits) fully mediated their intentions to seek counseling.

Attachment Disorganization. Attachment disorganization is exemplified by an infant's either inconsistent or lack of a coordinated strategy for seeking comfort after distress (Clay et al., 2015; Main & Solomon, 1990; van IJzendoorn et al., 2009; Table A3.4). Infant disorganization is a measurable indicator of a risk trajectory that may lead to adult psychopathology (Ballen, Demers, & Bernier, 2006; van IJzendoorn, Schuengel, & Bakermans-Kranenburg, 1999) and health problems (e.g., more upper respiratory infection, diarrhea, Clay et al., 2015). Disorganized attachments have been subtyped for both children and adults (Table A3.4). For adults, in addition to *unresolved* adult classifications, Lyons-Ruth, Yellin, Melnick, and Atwood (2005) added *hostile helpless states of mind*. Hostile states of mind are indicated by narratives that combine devaluing a caregiver as hostile or threatening while also identifying positively with the caregiver, without recognizing the discrepancy (known as *splitting*). Splitting is characteristic of individuals diagnosed with BPD, which is often linked to childhood trauma (especially CSA; see Breidenstine et al., 2011). For a low-income sample (MacDonald et al., 2008), early disorganized attachment status (at 12 months of age) was associated with higher levels of PTSD symptoms, more symptoms of PTSD avoidance, and more PTSD re-experiencing symptoms at age 8.5, supporting a belief that early disorganized attachment status may relate to a greater difficulty coping with traumatic and stressful experiences in later childhood.

A body of research indicates that one of the best predictors of attachment disorganization is a parent's *unresolved* state of mind regarding a loss or a trauma in the parent's own attachment history (Ballen, Demers, & Bernier, 2006). Such parents often exhibit atypical parenting practices (Chapter 5). When parents' childhood traumatic or loss experiences are not successfully resolved—evidenced in unintegrated emotional reactions, disorientation, or dissociative-like responses—their children are more likely to be disorganized (Breidenstine et al., 2011; van IJzendoorn, 1995). Ballen and colleagues (2006) suggest a difference between the effects of unresolved trauma versus unresolved loss (may also differ for type of trauma). Maternal history of childhood loss is associated with decreased interactions with the infant and with increased risk of parental depression, which is also a risk factor in offspring's development. Maternal history of physical or sexual abuse is associated with increased risk for dissociation. Some evidence suggests that mothers with a history of CSA tend to be more withdrawn, uninvolved, and less sensitive in interactions with an infant, in contrast to those with a history of physical abuse, which is associated with increased hostility and intrusiveness (Ballen et al., 2006). Lyons-Ruth et al. (2005) found that problematic maternal behavior—related to maternal childhood trauma or loss—increased linearly with the progression from unresolved loss to unresolved abuse.

Attachments to Fathers or to Mothers and Fathers

Although most attachment studies examine mother–child relationships (Al-Yagon, 2012; Ford, Nalbone, Wetchler, & Sutton, 2008), some studies have examined the child's relationship to fathers or to both parents (Chapters 5, 9, 11, 14). Father–child attachment security influences numerous outcomes. Children securely attached to fathers or whose fathers show caring—e.g., through cognitively stimulating activities, caregiving activities, and paternal warmth—have fewer behavior problems, greater sociability, and more reciprocal friendships (Veríssimo et al., 2011), reduced risk of internalizing and externalizing problems (Phares, Rojas, Thurston, & Hankinson, 2010), and reduced likelihood of cognitive delay (see Wynter et al., 2016) than insecure children (Brown, Mangelsdorf, & Neff, 2012; Wynter et al., 2016). Although mother–child attachment has been associated with cognitive and language skill development and later academic performance, a study of both parents found only father attachment to be associated with academic self-concept and grade point performance (language but not reading, Bacro, 2012; Chapter 11).

Reciprocity or synchrony consists of different behavioral components for fathers and mothers that likely support distinct aspects of social functioning (Feldman et al., 2013a). Mothers engage in more face-to-face interactions that involve social gaze, co-vocalizations, and affectionate touch (Feldman, Weller, Zagoory-Sharon, & Levine, 2007), whereas fathers induce high positive arousal, exploratory focus, and rough-and-tumble play (see Anderson, Qiu, & Wheeler, 2017; Feldman et al., 2013a). Some evidence suggests that fathering particularly contributes to self-regulation and management of aggression (e.g., ability to negotiate conflict), while mothers appear to contribute to dialogical abilities (e.g., empathy and perspective-taking) during relaxed, positive social interactions (Feldman et al., 2013a). During father–child exchanges, children may practice "rougher" forms of inter-relating and learn to maintain reciprocity when others are intrusive and self-directed (behaving to get their own way)—affording a competitive advantage in social fitness. Simpson and Belsky (2018) suggest that paternal investment may influence male–male competition, multiple partners, and later paternal involvement as well as child competitiveness and risk-taking (especially boys) and adoption of avoidant versus anxious attachment patterns (particularly in girls). Mother reciprocity, on the other hand, may influence a sense of security affording collaboration in joint prosocial activities and supporting creativity and social initiation.

Parenting

Parenting involves more than attachment (more than a safe haven and secure base for exploration). For example, it involves limit-setting and providing boundaries; modeling the expression of emotions and values; promotion or inhibition of social interaction; teaching problem-solving; and exposing a child to a variety of environments and experiences (Sroufe, 2018). Attachment and rearing each have contributed uniquely and significantly to the variance in outcomes (e.g., Clay et al., 2015). For children, Polcari, Rabi, Bolger, and Teicher (2014) found that parenting practices of both mother and father influenced psychiatric symptom scores—verbal aggression was dominantly associated with symptoms scores, whereas verbal affection was principally associated with well-being scores. While verbal affection appears to be an important component of healthy development (rather than a protective factor; Polcari et al., 2014), an aggressively verbal parent's or the other parent's verbal affection did not protect against the effects of verbally aggressive parenting (e.g., depression, anger, and somatic symptoms). Although ADHD is not well related to attachment, it has been related to parenting (e.g., parent–child boundary problems at 24 and 42 months; overstimulating rather than supporting and providing calm for an overtaxed child; Sroufe, 2018). Externalizing behaviors are associated with a number of variables, including harsh and inconsistent parenting in response to misbehavior (Nikitopoulos et al., 2014), possibly mediated by the child's poor self-confidence and ineffective emotion regulation (Fearon et al., 2010). Hsieh and Yen (2017) found that harsh parenting related to aggression in Taiwanese school children. Qouta, Punamäki, and colleagues confirmed that if parents showed love, caring, and wise guidance, children had better psychological adjustment and fewer PTSD symptoms in spite of exposure to extreme war conditions (Punamäki, Qouta, & El-Sarraj, 2001; Qouta et al., 2008; Qouta et al., 2016).

Parents' histories have contributed to the occurrence of maltreatment. For example, multiple contributing factors were found in the assessment of risk for child neglect. Across 36 studies from the 1990s to 2016, the strongest risk factors for child neglect were parental characteristics including parent history of antisocial behavior or criminal offending, mental health/psychiatric problems, low educational level, and a history of child abuse or neglect (Mulder et al., 2018). Non-Caucasian children were more likely to be neglected. In Mulder's meta-analysis, social support, pre-natal problems, parental substance use, parental negative cognitions re: pregnancy, gender, and age were not significant predictors of neglect.

Timing and Nature of Early Interventions

For success, interventions must be appropriately timed, skillfully executed, and take into account the child's individuality, phase of response, and specific reactions (Cloitre et al., 2012; Nader, 1999; Scheeringa, 2016). Immediately and in the first days after an event, restoration of safe conditions and assisting a child to feel safe is important (Nader, 1999; Nader & Pynoos, 1993; Pynoos & Nader, 1988). Primary goals include providing safe environments (away from danger), shelter, sustenance, and welcomed forms of social support (e.g., warmth, kindness, respect for needs related to space or proximity; respect for individual needs and differences). Reducing arousal, increasing normalcy, providing a sense of hope, and enabling victims to have a sense of control are important as well (Hobfoll et al., 2007). In fact, the presence of or conversation with a supportive significant other (e.g., parent) can dampen cortisol production (stress hormone) and increase oxytocin (anxiety-reducing hormone that increases social bonding) (*social buffering*, Hostinar & Gunnar, 2013; Seltzer, Ziegler, & Pollak, 2010; Glossary), if the parent does not engage in anxiety-provoking behaviors—e.g., looks of fear; an unwelcomed method of support (Nader & Pynoos, 1993).

The Initial Aftermath of an Event

Public perception is that the sooner a counselor goes in, the better. Children do need immediate restoration of safety and social support. However, immediate in-depth counseling is ill-advised. In the first few weeks after an event, trauma survivors may not be ready cognitively or emotionally to engage in intensive emotional processing of their experiences (Hobfoll et al., 2007). In order to protect the child and to prevent long-term negative reactions, it is essential to wait for the reduction of arousal before providing therapeutic interventions that include psychological processing. Although psychological debriefings are still the norm in some settings, evidence suggests that harm can result when debriefings are poorly timed (too soon) or are offered by inexperienced individuals (see, e.g., Hobfoll et al., 2007; see Nader, 2008; Ørner, 2007). Even though some children may need to tell their story (even repeatedly) soon after an experience, probing for traumatic details, during this phase of response—i.e., first few weeks—has been associated with risk of poor long-term outcomes for children and adults. Instead, a supportive presence and attentive listening are recommended (Nader, 1999). Because some symptoms will subside and/or some youth are disconnected from their reactions in the first two or three weeks after an event, earlier assessment may result in false positives or false negatives.

Early Interventions

Although assessment and psychological processing may be inadvisable in the immediate aftermath of events, long delays between identification of children's mental health or developmental impairment and the initiation of appropriate interventions may derail the child's normal developmental trajectory and have other negative outcomes (Cicchetti, 2003; Nader, 2008; Osofsky & Lieberman, 2011). Early interventions may prevent long-term negative effects. Early dysfunction can trigger a cascade of maladaptive consequences; consequences may become progressively more entrenched and resistant to treatment (Duncan, Tildesley, Duncan, & Hops, 1995; Chapter 2). Additionally, evidence suggests an intergenerational transmission of stress dysregulation (e.g., as represented in stress hormone levels) (see Osofsky & Lieberman, 2011). Early preventive interventions tailored to the needs of specific age groups, such as those that arm youth with good social, coping, and other skills or improve parent competence, also provide a measure of protection for youth exposed to potentially traumatic events (e.g., Greenberg & Riggs, 2015; Reid, Littlefield, & Hammond, 2008; Nader, 2012a, 2012c; Webster-Stratton & Reid, 2010; Chapters 9, 16).

Reuniting Family Members

When family members are apart during traumas, it is important to have a pre-planned and appropriate location for children and parents to reunite (Nader & Pynoos, 1993). For example, safe alternative locations, methods of contact (e.g., between school staff members or administration and parents; between parents and youth), and plans for good record keeping about where children are sent (hospital or safe location) and to whom they are released must be established ahead of time. After a trauma, the first sight of a caregiver may cause relief or increase distress. Children have described increased fear or anxiety levels in response to seeing an extremely distressed look on a parent's face. To prevent symptom escalation, a brief transition period prior to reunion is recommended to provide information and to assist caregivers to regain personal composure before they join their children.

After the First Few Weeks

If a person's reactions cause significant disruption to personal, familial, social, or occupational functioning and persist for more than one month, short-term interventions are indicated (e.g., Ørner, 2007). For the prevention of long-term difficulties, it is important to address the needs of all youth and adults with risk factors, particular or intense experiences during an event, or who display subclinical signs or symptoms of a given disorder—even those without the full disorder (e.g., see Nader, 2012c). Children with symptoms of PTSD but not the full disorder (*subsyndromal* or *subclinical* PTSD) have been disabled functionally, in notable distress, or suffered developmental delays or disruptions (Abdeen et al., 2008; Nader & Fletcher, 2014; Scheeringa, Myers, Putnam, & Zeanah et al., 2012). Intense, repetitive and/or multiple traumas, especially during early or important phases of development, may suggest the need for long-term and multifaceted interventions (e.g., medical, personal, social; Byrnes, 2001; see Nader, 2008). Delayed traumatic reactions—with no or only a few early symptoms—have often been associated with severe and prolonged reactions (e.g., Hartman, 2014; Yule et al., 2000). This suggests the need for youth assessments at intervals for a few years after the event. Appropriately timed, sensitive assessments can help to facilitate recovery. After a school shooting, exposed children assessed three weeks to three months after the event had significantly fewer symptoms than exposed children first assessed a year later.

Regression

Regression to an earlier or younger state of functioning is not always easy to recognize. Following traumas, children and adolescents may be in a regressed state much of the time or may regress spontaneously, for example, in response to traumatic reminders. Children, adolescents, and adults may use more concrete and literal levels of processing information, become more easily distracted, or engage in activities characteristic of younger individuals (Nader, 1999).

Regressions are not always apparent. Because reminders can be internal—e.g., a fast heartbeat or a certain sensation—adults may not always be aware when and if a child has been reminded of a traumatic experience (Boxes 3.1, 3.2, 16.3). As well, childlike behaviors are common under some normal circumstances—e.g., during anger, playfulness, or endearment. Additionally, regression may be as subtle as desiring a person, place, or situation that previously represented good or safe feelings. Regressions such as loss of skills may indicate, be complicated by, or be exaggerated by trauma reminders or by specific trauma symptoms—e.g., changed biochemistry; increased reactivity to stress or reminders of the experience; lack of sleep; cognitive difficulties such as trouble concentrating, trouble thinking clearly or more concrete thinking; preoccupations with, e.g., aspects of the experience, guilt, symptoms/reactions. It may be tempting for adults to interpret regression as laziness, sloppiness, defiance, or attention-getting behavior.

Because each child is unique, it is important to learn to identify specific regressive tendencies (Nader, 1999). It may not be enough to approach a traumatized child with age-level language and expectations. It is important to recognize functioning and emotional age (which may change from contact to contact) following an event. Speaking to the child in age-appropriate language, with respect for chronological age, while adapting to her/his emotional functioning age, may be important. For example, for a traumatized eight-year-old, it may be necessary to use a tone or the patience appropriate for a two-year-old while speaking in the language of the eight-year-old child. Allowances must be made for more concrete and less imaginative thinking and functioning. It may be necessary to state instructions simply and be willing to repeat. When recognized, regression can be met with patience, understanding, and, when needed, the gentle firmness that would be used with a younger child (functioning age), while still respecting chronological age.

Conclusions

A number of variables influence posttrauma outcomes—e.g., family and community environments, parenting, child traits, nature of traumas, timing and quality of interventions. Awareness of risk and protective factors as well as of youth's individuality, regressions, and changed needs may assist prevention as well as posttrauma triage and treatment. We are still learning of the ways that the multiple individual qualities of youth interplay with each other and with symptoms and treatment needs. For example, recent studies of adult BPD have found a relationship to childhood precursors—e.g., greater emotionality, inattention, and relationship dysfunction; to temperament—e.g., adolescent high harm avoidance and novelty seeking, low reward dependence; to trait impulsivity and affect dysregulation; to affective dysfunction and disinhibition (mediated by self-regulation); to psychopathology—e.g., major depression by age 18; externalizing; non-suicidal self-injury; adolescent risk-taking and/or trauma (Courtney-Seidler, Klein, & Miller, 2013). Following traumas, timing and nature of interventions as well as skilled implementation are important to success.

In addition to the potential negative effects of traumas are the possible positive effects, the protective factors that may reduce negative reactions, and the hope for repair, in childhood or adulthood. Many factors (before, during, or after an event) may serve to protect against poor outcomes (Table A1.4). As well, correctly identifying a child's personal coping style, functioning age, grief style, and other aspects of individuality can help a parent, teacher, or clinician to assist a child's or children's recovery after exposure to traumatic events or other adversity. Personal growth may follow traumatic experiences. Growth can co-occur with traumatic reactions. Although insecure or disorganized attachments have had negative associations and have been linked to faulty interpersonal styles, social support after trauma and later during adulthood has served as a protective or a healing factor for those with histories of poor-quality early caregiving. Higher-quality social support has been linked to lower levels of PTSD and to shifts from attachment insecurity during one generation to security during the next.

Part II

Ages 0–3

5

Development of Infants and Toddlers

A young child's nature and development are strongly influenced by attachment relationships and environmental conditions. In infancy and toddlerhood, the foundations are set for many developmental skills, often through caregiver–child interactions. Early interactive experiences and levels of stimulation (or deprivation) have affected ongoing functioning. From infancy to age three, major developmental tasks include exploration of the environment, gaining self- and other-awareness (precursors to empathy), identification of basic emotions, a basic level of coping with normal stressors, and the beginnings of humor. This chapter examines important influencing variables and early development in infants and toddlers. Discussions address sensitive periods, brain development, traits, attachment, and developmental skills and domains. Chapter 6 discusses effects of adversity, and Chapter 7 will provide interventions for symptoms and problems in this age group. Similar to those for attachment disorders, trauma-related treatment methods for this age group usually focus primarily on the caregiver–child relationship (see Chapters 7, 10).

The first five years of life are an important period for growth of the brain and neurobiology (e.g., maturation of the stress response system), the beginnings of development of affect regulation strategies, and the formation of basic relationship schemas (see Ghosh Ippen et al., 2011). Environmental resources and conditions in early childhood impact growth and development and may have enduring consequences for a child's developmental trajectory (Lupien, McEwen, Gunnar, & Heim, 2009). For example, safety and sustenance levels, brain stimulation, stress levels, and trauma/stressor exposure, especially multiple exposures, affect infants' and toddlers' ongoing patterns of behavior and difficulties or ease. Even the nature of initial contact—i.e., skin-to-skin contact or breastfeeding beginning 30–120 min after birth vs delayed contact—is linked to later outcomes—e.g., mother–infant bonding; mother's level of interaction and interest in the infant (Klaus, 2009; maternal sensitivity, Bystrova et al., 2009). Across studies, compared to delayed contact infants—i.e., infants in the nursery for the first two hours after birth, then roomed in and breast fed—early contact infants have shown greater self-regulation, dyadic mutuality, and reciprocity; calmer natures; more time in quiet sleep, lower and more stable heart rate, less apnea, and maintained body temperature (Bystrova et al., 2009; Klaus, 2009; Rochat, 2011). With initial skin-to-skin contact, oxytocin is released (from the hypothalamus) creating calm, increasing affection, and reducing pain and anxiety (Klaus, 2009) and increasing bonding (Colonnello, Chen, Panksepp, & Heinrichs, 2013; Table A4.1). Subsequent, ongoing sensitive care, or its lack, shapes the infant's level of trust, coping, self-regulation, self-confidence, and inter-relating (e.g., Lyons & Parker, 2007). The way a child interacts with and responds to the world (e.g., people, experiences) is also influenced by genetic and personality traits (see Nader & Fletcher, 2014). In contrast, coping with normal levels of early life stress—when stress challenges but is not enough to overwhelm the child (stress inoculation)—may foster adaptation (Chapter 1; Shonkoff et al., 2012).

Infant Traits

Genetic differences explain a significant amount of variance in temperamental traits (Bokhorst et al., 2003; Roisman & Fraley, 2008). Temperament, a substrate of personality, refers to a person's characteristic emotional style or disposition—e.g., individual differences in reactivity and self-regulation (Rothbart, 2011; Table A5.1) or differences in a person's style of approach and response to the environment (Posner et al., 2014; Table A5.2). It has proven stable across infancy regardless of birth order, gender, or SES (2–13 months, but not for infants on ventilators, Bornstein et al., 2015; 18–36 months, Bouvette-Turcot et al., 2015a). For infants, Bornstein et al. (2015) found two infant temperament factors: *positive affectivity*—smiling and laughter, soothability, and duration of orienting; and *negative emotionality* (NE)—activity level, fear, and distress to limitations (total N = 408). In other research, for ages 3–12 months, three main temperament factors have emerged: *surgency*—approach, smiling and laughter, activity level, vocal activity; *NE*—sadness, frustration, vocal reactivity, and fear; and *orienting/regulation*—cuddliness, soothability, duration of orienting, low-intensity pleasure (Rothbart, 2011). Higher self-regulation has been related to higher *surgency* and lower NE (Rothbart, 2011). Higher *effortful control* and lower NE have predicted better self-regulation (outcomes mediated by parenting; N = 198, 27 then 33 months, Song et al., 2018).

Attachment is important to temperament-related outcomes. McElwain, Holland, Engle, and Wong (2012) showed that children with high *anger-proneness* (high reactives) were the least self-assertive and least compliant when they were less securely attached and were the most self-assertive and compliant when they were more securely attached. In contrast, children low in *anger-proneness* tended to be more self-assertive when insecure but less self-assertive when securely attached. Although temperament is generally believed stable and a basis for later personality (Bornstein et al., 2015), a fearful infant can learn to self-sooth and one who reacts with distress to limitations may be rated differently, when a mother learns to structure environments.

Persistence of Traits

Traits such as activity, approach, fear tendencies, and positive emotional disposition have been significantly persistent (Rothbart, 2011). Girls have shown somewhat greater stability of positive reactivity, perhaps due to girls' socialization or greater relatedness to mothers (Bornstein et al., 2015). Although generally desirable in Westerners, extraversion/surgency at 18 months has predicted increased maternal anxiety during infant's second year, likely due to changes in assertion, ambulation, and social engagement (Agrati et al., 2015; Putnam, Gartstein, & Rothbart, 2006). Infant smiling and laughter have predicted *surgency* at age seven (see Rothbart, 2011), and have been related to executive network performance at age seven (Posner et al., 2014, 2016; Attention-related networks, below). Temperament (e.g., approach, soothability) at seven months has correlated with the attention network at age seven—allows voluntary control of goal-directed behavior (Posner et al., 2014, 2016).

Temperament and Brain Networks

Connectivity plays an important role in brain networks that develop in infancy and childhood (Posner et al., 2016). Some evidence suggests subtypes of reactions or disorders (e.g., anxiety; autism) are related to temperamental traits and brain networks—e.g., compared to controls, subtypes of ADHD include *surgent* (higher impulsivity; lower shyness), *irritable* (high negative affect), and *mild* (less attentive and more impulsive than normals; better than other subtypes; Posner et al., 2016). Training designed to improve the attention network has sometimes related to improvements in the executive network and to other cognitive functions such as IQ and self-control.

Negative Emotionality/Negative Affectivity (NE)

In a number of studies, children with angry, difficult temperaments expressed high levels of negativity, showed little remorse for transgressions, and had more maladaptive outcomes, only if they were insecurely attached to parents (Kim & Kochanska, 2017). Some evidence suggests that infant right frontal brain asymmetry reflects a disposition toward NE and anxiety (Bernier, Calkins, & Bell, 2016). Although some evidence suggests a two-way relationship between parenting and infant-toddler NE, other studies show none, suggesting that other factors are at play. Not all studies make a distinction between trait NE and age-related negative emotional states (common for toddlers) and studies often assess children and parents separately. In general, children's NE has been linked to lower levels of parental sensitivity, responsiveness, and/or warmth and to higher levels of parental intrusiveness, rejection, and/or negativity (see Fields-Olivieri, Cole, & Maggi, 2017) as well as to pre- and post-natal conditions. Generally, children's positive emotional states are linked to more sensitive parenting. A few studies have found that NE related to increased parental sensitivity (see Fields-Olivieri et al., 2017). After controlling for family factors, Cha (2017) found that early NE significantly predicted lower responsive parenting at a later point and vice versa only for Korean girls during infancy but not in toddlerhood. It was not predictive of parenting for Korean boys.

In a study of young children and parents in their homes, Fields-Olivieri et al. (2017) found that toddlers' temperamental differences did not predict their emotional expression (N = 120). Expression of negative emotions is common at this age. Although parents expressed high negative affect to toddlers, they were not predominantly negative with them. Parents' were more likely to express negative emotions when children's negative emotional states interacted with either their NE or *surgency* traits (not related to frequency of child's negative states). NE and surgency were negatively related in these children (less likely to be combined). However, NE or surgency X emotional state (interaction) did not predict mother or father sensitivity. Only fathers expressed more negative emotion whether a child with NE expressed positive or negative emotions. Authors speculated that this may relate to NE children expressing emotions more intensely, in general. In contrast to their negative emotional expression, mothers expressed more positive affect if a toddler more frequently expressed positive emotions, and mothers expressed less positive affect if the toddler was more frequently negative, perhaps reflecting a kind of synchrony or matching behavior (Fields-Olivieri et al., 2017).

Caregivers and Children

Caregivers serve more than one function in children's lives. For example, they assist skill development (e.g., emotional, cognitive, social) and provide monitoring and protection (Polan & Hofer, 2018). Attachment and parenting are discussed here and in Chapter 4.

Attachment

Between six and nine months, infants show stranger wariness and develop one or more selective attachment relationships that develop over time and are well established by 12–18 months (Bowlby, 1969/1982; Lyons-Ruth, 2015; Zeanah et al., 2016). Selective attachment appears to be linked to significant amounts of interaction with a caregiver and the experience that the infant can count on the caregiver to provide comfort, support, nurturance, and protection, especially when stressed (Zeanah et al., 2016; Chapter 4). It is characterized by deep emotional bonds, evident in the depth of mourning and behavioral disruption that follows loss of an attachment figure as well as in a young child's selective referencing and modeling of attitudes and values of attachment figures (Lyons-Ruth, 2015). With more than one attachment, strength of the infant's preference appears to be hierarchical (Zeanah et al., 2016). Soon after birth, although they show no preference for a particular person to comfort when distressed, newborns recognize a mother's smell and sound (Simpson & Belsky, 2018; Zeanah et al., 2016). From 2–7 months, they interact socially with a variety of individuals (Zeanah et al., 2016) and begin to show greater discrimination—i.e., distinguish family from strangers and show preference for certain individuals (Simpson & Belsky, 2018). At four months, both too much or too little self- and interactive-contingency are associated with insecurity (Beebe et al., 2012, 2016; Glossary—contingency; see Synchrony, to follow). From seven months to three years, children more actively engage in proximity-seeking, initiate and maintain contact with caregivers, and turn to the caregiver for comfort (Simpson & Belsky, 2018). During this phase, prolonged separations from attachment figures engender the three stages of response to separation: protest, despair, and detachment (Bowlby, 1969, 1980). Beginning age three, theory of mind skills (Glossary; Chapter 8; Table 1.2) and increased language skills influence interactions with a caregiver—e.g., increased joint plans and activities. Sensitive and supportive parenting from both mothers and fathers has been related to positive outcomes (e.g., executive functions at age three; Towe-Goodman et al., 2014; Meuwissen & Carlson, 2015).

Infant security has served as a protective factor and appears to defuse some risks, whereas insecurity has been a risk factor and may amplify detrimental cascades (Boldt, Kochanska, & Jonas, 2017; Tables A3.1–A3.2). For example, for children who rejected rules and parental modeling attempts at ages 2, 3, 4+, and 5.5, externalizing problems and lower quality of parent–child relationships were only apparent at ages 10 and 12 for children who were insecurely attached at 15 months (mother–child and father–child attachments and relationships; Boldt et al., 2017).

Mothers

As discussed earlier, numerous studies have demonstrated the value of initial skin-to-skin contact between mothers and infants (Bystrova et al., 2009; Klaus, 2009; Rochat, 2011). It has stabilized neonates' blood-oxygen levels, body temperature, and breathing rate, has promoted bonding, enhanced parent–child attachment relationships, increased parent confidence, reduced infant crying, enhanced infant growth and development, stimulated early breastfeeding, and increased lactation (Chen, Gau, Liu, & Lee, 2017). Infant attachment classification and brain development are essentially shaped by the quality of infant–caregiver connection and interaction (Newman et al., 2016). When ecological variables were controlled (maternal education, depression, paternal support and infant maternal grandmother support), adolescent-mothers' sensitivity and not their own attachment classification were related to infant security (see Levendosky et al., 2011). However, evidence showed women reporting higher maternal–fetal attachment (i.e., connection to unborn infant) during pregnancy had more secure attachment styles (Chapter 4), and their children had more optimal early development than women reporting lower attachment to their unborn child and less secure attachment styles (Alhusen, Hayat, & Gross, 2013).

The nature of maternal interactions contributes to brain development in more than one way—e.g., through the richness and sensitivity of interactions. EEG power has served as a measure of brain development (Bernier et al., 2016). It reflects the excitability of groups of neurons. Greater frontal neural activity (greater EEG power in frontal regions) has consistently been related to better cognitive performance—e.g., working memory, inhibitory control. Mothers who interacted with their five-month-old infants with more positive affect and less physical stimulation had infants whose frontal resting alpha and theta EEG power was higher at 10 and 24 months than other infants', and their EEG power increased more rapidly between five and 10 months and between 10 and 24 months than other infants'.

Depression during pregnancy is a strong predictor of post-partum depression (Toohey, 2012). Maternal depressive symptoms adversely affect sensitive parenting and subsequent quality of caregiver–infant attachments (Alhusen et al., 2013; Overbeek et al., 2006), and may result in early childhood developmental delays (mothers with higher avoidant attachment styles and more depressive symptoms, Alhusen et al., 2013), child depressive symptoms, cognitive impairment (most severe in male infants), and anxious attachments (Newman et al., 2016). Maternal anxiety is also linked to infant insecure or disorganized attachments and is associated with children's stress, behavioral dysregulation, and long-term vulnerability to mental health disorders (Newman et al., 2016).

"Atypical" maternal behaviors include *communication* errors—e.g., mother positive when infant is distressed; *disorientation*—e.g., frightened expression, sudden complete loss of affect; and *negative-intrusive behaviors*—e.g., mocking; pulling infant's body (Lyons-Ruth, 2005). They correspond to the atypical behaviors of many disorganized infants—e.g., behaviors indicating fear, conflict (approaching and moving away), or disorientation. "Anomalous" maternal behaviors—e.g., *distressing* behaviors such as frightening, threatening, looming; *dissociative* behaviors such as haunted voice, deferential/timid; or *disrupted* behaviors like failure to repair (e.g., interactive repair; of negative emotional states); lack of response; insensitive/communication errors (Lyons-Ruth, 2005)—have been strongly associated with disorganized attachment at 12 to 18 months (caregiver unresolved trauma, Barlow et al., 2016).

Fathers

Five facets of early positive fathering have been identified: "... sensory stimulation, physical care, warmth, nurturing, and 'fathering' ..." (see Chen et al., 2017, p. 2). For adult males, greater levels of their own early environmental unpredictability have forecasted their reduced involvement and less supportive parenting behavior (ages 0–5; mediated by their quality of early maternal care; see Simpson & Belsky, 2018). Recent findings suggest that, like mother skin-to-skin contact, fathers' skin-to-skin contact, face-to-face contact, and hugging and touching newborns has enhanced the father–infant relationship (Chen et al., 2017). Father–neonate skin-to-skin contact has engendered a strong connection between fathers and neonates and enhanced positive fathering.

Brown, Mangelsdorf, and Neff (2012) found that father–child attachment security was relatively stable from 13 months to three years of age and was linked to both the quantity and quality of early fathering behavior (N = 115). Although father's sensitivity and self-reported responsibility were not linked to attachment at 13 months, sensitivity and involvement, independently and interactively, were strong predictors of more secure relationships at age three. Specifically, children were most securely attached when fathers were both highly involved and highly sensitive, and least securely attached when fathers were both less sensitive and less involved. When fathers engaged in sensitive interactions with children, infants were generally securely attached to fathers regardless of level of involvement. In contrast, for relatively less sensitive fathers, greater involvement was positively related to attachment security. Secure father–child relationships predicted increased paternal sensitivity over time (Brown et al., 2012).

Some evidence suggests that father–infant attachment is impeded by infant temperament—i.e., fussy or difficult temperament (Condon, Corkindale, Boyce, & Gamble 2013), paternal depression (see Wynter et al., 2016), father's personality traits (i.e., lack of assertiveness and oversensitivity to the opinion of others), father's increased anxiety symptoms, and father's perception of partner criticism on the way he cares for the infant (Wynter et al., 2016). Fewer paternal positive interactions with infants as well as lower paternal warmth and greater psychological control toward infants are associated with paternal depression, which in turn is associated with subsequent infant conduct and hyperactivity problems (Wynter et al., 2016). While maternal and paternal depressive symptoms at infant's age six months have been associated with more difficult temperament at 24 months, in one study, father depression was only significant for male children (Hanington, Ramchandani, & Stein, 2010). In a small sample (N = 94; 21 with history), Lucassen et al. (2017) found father's history of depression or anxiety did not significantly relate to father–infant attachment security with 14-month-olds. In fact, their daughters were more secure than daughters of fathers with no psychiatric history. The effects of depression or anxiety may depend on how much they affect other things (e.g., reflective functioning; emotion awareness and openness; sensitive care).

Father-to-infant attachment is enhanced by a better couple's relationship between parents (Carlson, Pilkauskas, McLanahan, & Brooks-Gunn, 2011). Although not found in African American samples, father absence predicts accelerated pubertal development for girls (see Simpson & Belsky, 2018). Even though father effects on puberty are from studies that do not include assessments of mother influence, research shows that the earlier a father's absence (especially within the first five years), the more strongly it predicts pubertal development, and puberty is delayed in association with the more time fathers spend caring for daughters (during the first five years) and the more fathers have positive/affectionate interactions with their daughters at age 5 (see Simpson & Belsky, 2018).

Rough-and-tumble play (R&T play) has been linked to children's social and emotional competencies (St. George & Freeman, 2017; see Normal Play, below). Father–child R&T play has been linked to lower aggressive behavior in 2–6-year-olds when fathers provided dominant control over play (see St. George & Freeman, 2017) or during competitive antagonistic play that challenged a child's abilities, the father provided opportunities for the child to *win* (N = 48 Chinese 2–3-year-olds; Anderson, Qiu, & Wheeler, 2017). Across 16 studies of father–child physical play including R&T play (N = 1521, ages 2–6; St. George & Freeman, 2017), such play was positively associated with important child behavior domains, most strongly with social competence. Although it was less robustly associated with emotional skills and self-regulation (e.g., weakly associated with aggression), children who engaged in regular physical play, with positive affect, playfulness, and physicality, showed higher emotion skills (emotion encoding & decoding). Self-regulation—i.e., cognitive control, sustained attention, and effortful control—has been positively associated with frequency and quality of physical play (assessed by observation; St. George & Freeman, 2017).

Synchrony

As Feldman points out (2015), songbirds must hear their species' song during a very narrow window of time in order to become members of the flock. Similarly, with some individual and cultural variation, infants must experience, within the *nursing dyad*, "synchronous coordination of their social behavior and affiliative biology" during a sensitive period, between birth and approximately 9–10 months (Feldman, 2015, p. 376). Evidence shows that mother–infant synchrony predicts attachment security (age one year; Jaffee et al., 2002; Table 5.1—inter-relating), self-regulation (age two; Feldman, Greenbaum, & Yirmiya, 1999), moral orientation, empathy (child and adolescent; Feldman, 2007), lower cortisol levels (Feldman, Vengrober, Eidelman-Rothman, & Zagoory-Sharon, 2013b), and, from infancy, predicts lower adolescent depression and better adjustment (Feldman, 2010). During maternal–infant reunions and maternal mirroring and responsivity episodes, endogenous opioids are released that the infant experiences as soothing and nurturing (see Bolen, Winter, & Hodges, 2013). By 3–4 months, mothers and infants coordinate their behaviors—mutual and other gaze (at and away from the other's face), facial expressions (affective mirroring), vocal rhythms, touch patterns, and approach or approach-avoidance patterns (Beebe et al., 2016). By four months, infants are adept at perceiving contingent relations (social partner's response to their behaviors), recognizing the strength of them, and predicting events and their time course based on them (see Beebe et al., 2016). This serves as one foundation for the infant's communication capacity, facilitating information processing, memory, and representation of interpersonal events—in facial affect, vocal affect, facial-visual engagement and orientation (Beebe et al., 2016).

Table 5.1 Learning and Inter-Relating

Learning

- early basis of executive *functions* is in place (e.g., attention, processing speed, short-term working memory)
- begin to learn cause and effect—actions lead to consequences
- learn contingent relationships
  - sensitive care teaches infants to cope with stress, self-soothe, regulate emotions, and begin to become self-aware
- toddlers discover the difference between reality and pretense (18–24 months)
  - can distinguish between the representation of a real event and of a hypothetical state, e.g., a thought
  - start to engage in "pretend play" as well as learn to recognize self in a mirror

Inter-relating—synchrony/contingency (interactive dyadic communication at 4 months; Beebe et al., 2016)

(a) characterized by significant moment-to-moment predictability
  - within each (self-contingent) and between both (interactive contingent) infant and caregiver partners
  - self-contingency—often out of awareness, anticipation of one's behavior in the next moment
    - personal behavioral rhythms are an organizing feature of the dyadic system
    - excess self-contingency may be a risk factor (e.g., being stuck in the no-touch phase)

(b) in communication modalities of attention, affect, facial-visual engagement, orientation, and touch, both self- and interactive contingency organize dyadic face-to-face communication, a bidirectional, asymmetrical process
  - maternal contingent coordination with infant is higher than infant contingent coordination with mother
  - self-contingency organizes communication more than interactive contingency

(c) in facial affect, facial-visual engagement, and orientation (not gaze, not touch), self- and interactive contingency processes each affect the other; each is either more *self-directed* or more *socially oriented*
  - partners follow the direction of affective change in each other
  - gaze is employed in monitoring the environment and in communication

Across 1st year (between 6 and 12 months)

- joint attention to an object becomes more salient than dyadic face-to-face interaction
- infants learn symbolic communications (gestures and words)
- infants initiate more

Additional sources: e.g., Beebe et al., 2016; Bjorklund, 2013; Brüne & Brüne-Cohr, 2006; Cassidy & Shaver, 2018; Kagan et al., 1988, 2007; Nader, 2008; Posner et al., 2014; SNS = sympathetic nervous system.

Beebe et al. found that when a mother's loom (movement toward the child) elicited an infant's dodge (move away or arch), then mothers moved back from looming to upright. When infants were more likely to touch, mothers touched more affectionately. When infants touched less, mothers likely used more arousing touch. Mothers coordinated and adjusted their behaviors to infants more than infants adjusted to mothers.

Studied individuals seemed either to be more socially oriented or more self-oriented. At age four months, both mother and infant were more self-contingent (S-C)—i.e., more "self-rooted" than coordinated with the other (Beebe et al., 2016). Too much S-C in the infant (e.g., staying stuck in "no-touch" state) predicted future-disorganized attachment. When mothers and infants remain more loosely self-organized (more flexible), they were more open to influence of the other. Those more tightly self-organized—i.e., more on their own program or behaving relatively independently of the other—were less open to the influence of the other. Particularly between six and 12 months, person–person–object relationships (joint attention on an object) take center stage (Beebe et al., 2016). Infants begin to comprehend symbolic gestures and to utter words. Infant initiation becomes more important in social interactions. Father– and mother–child reciprocity each have been stable, have interrelated at each stage, and have consisted of distinct behavioral components. Each uniquely predicted social competence and lower aggression in preschool, which shaped dialogical skills in adolescence (Feldman, Bamberger, & Kanat-Maymon, 2013a; Glossary—dialogical skills).

Neurobiology plays a part in parent–infant synchrony (Hane & Fox, 2018). Although affectionate contact was more characteristic of mothers, and stimulating contact more characteristic of fathers, regardless of gender, parents with high baseline oxytocin (OT) levels had more affectionate contact with infants, increased synchronous gaze, and increased behaviors with social salience than those with low OT (Apter-Levi, Zagoory-Sharon, & Feldman, 2014). Higher levels of vasopressin (AVP) were related to increased stimulatory behavior and joint attention to inanimate objects with the infant, with increased object salience. Additionally, affectionate warm contact and gaze duration, emphasizing the parent's ability to engage synchronously with the infant (directing attention to the social context) predicted high OT; higher stimulatory behavior and duration of joint attention with increased prominence of objects (directing attention to the environment) predicted higher AVP (Apter-Levi et al., 2014). When there are deficits in synchrony during an infant's sensitive period (age 9–10 months, synchrony is missing or altered; Feldman, 2015), children show social and regulatory deficits and disruptions in OT functionality, the stress response system, sympathetic and parasympathetic functioning, sleep–wake rhythmicity, and executive control. Dopamine-OT interactions appear to influence affiliative behaviors as well (Apter-Levi et al., 2014).

Synchrony has proven important to adults and children, has enabled social belonging, and may facilitate prosocial behaviors (Feldman, 2015; Box 5.1). Many studies have shown that adults spontaneously fall into synchrony with each other, increasing the perception of similarity, rapport, and cooperation (Tuncgenc, Cohen, & Fawcett, 2015). Early in life, infants show aspects of social coordination and synchrony in more than one realm—e.g., to faces, emotions, behaviors, human speech (not to nonsocial sounds like tapping). For example, neonates differentiate between different

Box 5.1 Lack of Reciprocal Interaction

Ronny was born with cocaine in his system. His mother had little education and low confidence. Her older child was raised by his father. Ronny's mother seemed distant and sometimes disinterested in him. She fed and clothed him but interacted with him little. Some evidence suggests that, although "cocaine babies" have been found to avoid eye contact and to seem aloof, they otherwise have not been significantly different from other children (with some effects in adolescence, Betancourt et al., 2011). Ronny would look haphazardly around, rarely holding eye contact with anyone or with objects. He had a lot of physical problems—reactions to his formula, allergies, asthma, adenoid removal. He otherwise has seemed to meet developmental milestones within normal range. He was trying to make sounds into words and was beginning to try to walk at 13 months. Nevertheless, the visiting volunteer had to work for some time to engage Ronny so that he would look at her and interact with her. She tried to model for Ronny's mother, but it was not instinctual for her. With prenatal exposure to cocaine, children raised in nurturing homes have done better than those in less nurturing homes. Poverty and caregiving have been important contributors to outcomes.

Note:
All case examples are disguised, may be combined cases, and have had details changed to protect individuals.

languages and coordinate body movements to human speech (see Tuncgenc et al., 2015). Although a preference for matched rhythms emerges before seven months—e.g., preference for rhythms a seven-month-old has been bounced to—rhythmic body-movement engagement is not precise even at age two. Nevertheless, movement synchrony has proven important in guiding 12-month-olds' social preferences—i.e., in a social condition (talking bear vs flower box), 12-month-olds (not nine-month-olds) preferred those who moved synchronously with bear over those who did not (rocking chair; two studies, total N = 81; Tuncgenc et al., 2015). Movement synchrony also influenced prosocial behaviors—e.g., 14-month-old infants were more likely to be helpful to an experimenter who bounced him/her in synchrony with music than if experimenter bounced out of synchrony with the music (see Cirelli, Wan, & Trainor, 2016). In another study, synchrony vs asynchrony to music translated into helpfulness toward another experimenter only if the other experimenter showed friendliness with the synchronously bouncing original experimenter (N = 48; Cirelli et al., 2016).

Attachment Classifications

Infants with different attachment styles react differently to stress (Chapter 4). Secure infants miss mothers, greet them happily after separation, and use mother-oriented self-regulation strategies (e.g., look at mother, seek proximity; Solomon & George, 2018). Adolescents and adults who had infant insecure attachment classifications (vs secure) have shown greater difficulty and greater cognitive effort, when actively attempting to increase positive emotions (Moutsiana et al., 2015; White et al., 2012b). Given the importance of positive emotions to ongoing health and well-being, these findings suggest the importance of repair of the attachment relationship in infancy (Chapter 7). Insecure resistant and disorganized infants and toddlers may exhibit exaggerated expressions of distress and signs of physiological distress—e.g., show elevated cortisol on separation (Table A3.2). On separations and in general, insecure-avoidant infants demonstrate greater sympathetic nervous system arousal (stress response) than secure infants and use self-oriented regulation—e.g., self-comforting, exploration (Table A3.3—self-regulation, RSA, and sAA; Hill-Soderlund et al., 2008). Infant avoidant attachment later has been linked to more uninhibited, less fearful, and sometimes aggressive behavior than for children with secure and especially insecure-resistant attachments (see Hill-Soderlund et al., 2008 for studies; Table A3.2). Genetics has explained lowered reactivity for avoidant infants who do not show the usual physiological signs of distress during separation (Borelli et al., 2010; Lewis-Morrarty et al., 2015). Although not optimal for development, the parenting style associated with insecure-avoidant attachments—a caregiving style that tends to ignore overly reactive behaviors, consequently preventing reinforcement of heightened reactivity in unfamiliar situations—may reduce reactivity characteristic of high *behavioral inhibition* (BI, Glossary; e.g., see Lewis-Morrarty et al., 2015; Table 5.2; Box 8.2; Chapters 8, 9).

Neural systems subserving emotion processing in early life appear to be influenced by parental care, attachment status, and neurobiology (e.g., genetics; Moutsiana et al., 2015; Taylor-Colls & Fearon, 2015). Infants of mothers with high positive affect, who also scored high on positive affect, showed greater reactions to negative (fearful) than to positive emotion expressions (de Haan et al., 2004). Although infants may respond more neurologically to fearful than to happy and neutral faces (seven-month-olds; N = 40), infants of more sensitive, responsive mothers respond more to happy faces than to neutral faces (Taylor-Colls & Fearon, 2015). Thus, warm, responsive, and contingent, thus predictable, caregiving may lead the developing brain to encode/evaluate positive emotional expressions as stronger cues to rewarding social interaction.

Table 5.2 Infant Behavioral Inhibition

Normal Behavioral Inhibition

- fear or behavioral inhibition appears naturally at 6–9 months (e.g., fear of strangers)
- for some infants, levels of fear may inhibit earlier rapid approach to novel objects

Behavioral Inhibition (BI)

- characterized by exaggerated tendency to automatically orient toward novel stimuli, respond as if they are threats
  - infant temperamental bias toward being highly reactive to unfamiliar stimulation (people, events)
- high levels of motor agitation and distress in response to complex unfamiliar sounds, sights, and smells (4-months-olds)
  - enhanced sensitivity to novelty at 9 months (e.g., exaggerated startle)
  - higher levels of BI at 14 months than less reactive infants
- may reflect restraining fearlessness and spontaneity rather than correspond to anxious or introverted type
- *Related to*
  - cortisol in breast milk may influence infant toward BI and is predictive of anxiety and depressive disorders
  - parental overprotection has been related to higher anxiety symptoms in children with BI (e.g., over 1 year)
  - parental anxiety has been related to lower-quality co-parenting, which in turn is linked to more child fearful temperament
    - undermining co-parenting (not supportive co-parenting; co-parenting may be a target for prevention/treatment)
    - parental anxiety disorder severity (ages 4, 12, and 30 months)
  - parental depression (3-year-olds) linked to higher negative emotionality (NE) or to BI for children with moderate to high positive emotionality (PE)
    - at lower levels of NE, child PE was inversely correlated with parental depression
  - right frontal EEG asymmetry (not left) more likely to exhibit BI later in childhood (9 months old)
  - more power in EEG higher frequency range
  - infants with a low threshold in amygdala
  - a sympathetically reactive cardiovascular system
  - not all infants with early reactivity to novel stimuli display social withdrawal at age 4 or later social anxiety

References: e.g., Coplan et al., 2009; Fox & Calkins, 2003; Fox et al., 2001, 2005; Glynn et al., 2007; Henderson et al., 2015; Howard et al., 2017; Kagan & Snidman, 1999; Metz, Majdandzic, & Bogels, 2016; Morris, Hudson, & Dodd, 2014; Olino et al., 2010; Putnam, Ellis, & Rothbart, 2001; Rothbart et al., 2001a, 2001b.

Stability of Attachment Classification

Some studies have shown a high correspondence between attachment styles found in infants and their later adult attachment styles, and secure adults are three to four times more likely to have securely attached children (Fonagy, Target, Gergely, 2000; van IJzendoorn, 1995). When stressful life experiences occur—e.g., those that affect parent's availability and sensitivity, result in changes in the child's perception or expectation of parent availability, and/or when the actual relationship quality changes—attachment security is less likely to be stable. Fraley (2002) provided meta-analytic evidence that attachment security was less stable in groups considered to be at higher risk (e.g., family instability, marital discord, abuse) than those at lower risk. Other disruptions to attachment security include trauma (e.g., death of a caregiver; Main, Hesse, & Kaplan, 2005), experiences that interfere with parenting (e.g., parent's depression, PTSD, stressful life experiences), and the physical availability of the father in the home (see Booth-LaForce et al., 2014).

Parenting

Parenting includes, e.g., providing a stable, enriching environment; monitoring; and limit-setting. Higher-quality parenting includes support, autonomy-promoting, stimulation, lack of hostility, and confidence in the child; lack of these qualities is seen in lower-quality parenting (Posner et al., 2014). Oxytocin has been implicated in increased bonding with infants and as a biomarker of awareness of social cues as well as linked to prosocial and affiliative behavior (see MacKinnon et al., 2018). Higher levels of oxytocin during late pregnancy also have been related to less intrusive maternal behaviors and more structuring via mother's theory of mind skills (N = 189 mother and 2–3-year-old dyads, MacKinnon et al., 2018). While in infancy, mother–infant positive relationship has proven more significant than father–infant (Kim & Kochanska, 2012), for toddlers (and infants), positive relationships with both parents have supported positive development (e.g., emerging regulation, Kochanska & Kim, 2014). Parental attitudes, styles, and discipline methods have influenced young children's trajectories. For example, higher levels of parental stress, parental hostility toward a child, and parent-perceived vulnerability in the child are among modifiable parenting characteristics that have predicted increased externalizing in children (N = 59, ages 2–5 years; Schappin, Wijnroks, Venema, & Jongmans, 2018). Young children's internalizing and externalizing behaviors are fairly common in toddlers and have been significantly stable from toddlerhood to preschool (see Sher-Censor, Shulman, & Cohen, 2018). Parenting stress has been associated with maternal criticism and fewer positive comments in a five-minute speech sample (N = 55 Israeli toddlers ages 19 to 47 months and mothers; Sher-Censor et al., 2018). Stress may influence the valence of parents' representations of their relationships with their children. Parenting stress, maternal criticism, and lower narrative coherence regarding the relationship with the child were linked to child externalizing, whereas only parenting stress and lower narrative coherence related to child internalizing. Positive comments were not related to internalizing and externalizing and parental stress was not related to coherence. Even after controlling for family factors and infant negative emotionality, supportive co-parenting has predicted toddler social-emotional adjustment.

Parenting Style

Parenting style has been linked to a number of outcomes (e.g., effortful control, EC; shame, guilt; Glossary—parenting style). Positive parenting is important to the development of toddlers' self-regulation. A pathway was identified from early parent–child positive relationship (e.g., reciprocal, close, and mutually receptive) to child EC and from EC to internalization of conduct standards, offsetting risks from parenting, child temperament, and genetics (see Kochanska & Kim, 2014). Toddlers' lower NE and higher EC (at 27 months) have predicted better self-regulation at 33 months, moderated by positive parenting—positive affect and sensitivity (at 27 and 33 months; N = 198; Song et al., 2018). Higher positive parenting with at-risk toddlers has had a buffering effect, while low positive parenting has had a deleterious effect even when toddlers showed temperamental strength (Song et al., 2018). For example, economically disadvantaged mother's and father's positive play with two-year-olds has been related to EFs at age three (Towe-Goodman et al., 2014). Comparatively, children have been less guilt-prone when mothers used more assertive parenting (Kochanska, Gross, Lin, & Nichols, 2002). Children whose fathers disciplined them usually had fewer difficulties than children with fathers who set fewer limits (Parisette-Sparks, Bufferd, & Klein, 2015).

Negative or disengaged parenting has had negative effects for toddlers. Shame and/or guilt has been linked to authoritarian parenting (e.g., Mills, 2003), marital dissatisfaction, fathers' (not mothers') history of depression and permissive parenting—i.e., warmth but low involvement, few demands, and inconsistent rules and consequences—and at age three predicted shame/guilt, age six (Parisette-Sparks et al., 2015). From permissive parenting, children may not learn when they are transgressing and may infer that they are unworthy of parent's attention. Paternal permissive parenting and depression may reflect fathers' withdrawal and disengagement, contributing to a child's shame and guilt-proneness. Mothers' negative parenting—negative affect, hostility, and negative control—has been associated with toddlers' poorer self-regulation (Song et al., 2018). Depressed mothers (no comorbidity) also have displayed more negative parenting—e.g., negative affect, open anger, hostility, anxiety, depressed mood during interactions; shifts between negative affect and withdrawal—and their offspring have shown more Axis-I psychopathology and social withdrawal (Apter-Levi et al., 2016).

The type of discipline used may model or suggest, for young children, ways of handling conflicts. Physical discipline (e.g., spanking) is widely used in the U.S. with young children (Thompson et al., 2017). A number of researchers have found that parents who reported using physical discipline were more likely to report aggressive child behaviors (e.g., hitting/kicking, throwing; e.g., Gershoff, 2002; 2.8 times more likely, Thompson et al., 2017). Spanking at age one has been related to higher levels of aggression at age three; spanking at age three predicted increased aggression at age five (Lee, Altschul, & Gershoff, 2013). Maternal warmth did not counteract the effects of spanking. However, the relationship between children's aggression and physical parenting may be bidirectional—i.e., spanking may increase child aggression, and, in turn, child aggression may increase spanking (Thompson et al., 2017).

For good outcomes, parenting involves knowing when to allow the child to explore, cry, or engage in other behaviors as well as when to intervene. A mother's "mind-mindedness"—ability to accurately reflect an infant or toddler's mental states (analysis of parent's mind-related comments; see also Reflective function)—has predicted attachment security and children's theory of mind, language, and symbolic play skills as well as their school readiness and levels of internalizing and externalizing (Longobardi, Spataro, & Colonnesi, 2018). Even though almost two thirds of a mothers' physical interventions are done with either highly positive or pleasant affect (Ispa, Cook, Harmeyer, & Rudy, 2015), researchers have linked maternal interrupting behavior—in a situation that invited toddler exploration of new objects—to later toddler vocabulary deficits. Language development appears to be facilitated when adults follow toddlers' leads, engaging with them in joint attention to objects of interest to the toddlers (see Ispa et al., 2015; see Chapter 7—COSP, Child's Game; Chapter 10—Helping the Noncompliant Child). Interrupting parents often do so to teach toddlers the conventionally proper use of toys, for protection (e.g., prevent mouthing a toy), or to engage in a joking manner (playful; see Ispa et al., 2015). Ispa et al. found that infants were not upset when mothers' gestures were protective. Their upset was primarily in response to taking toys away, grabbing the toddler, and offering alternative toys when a toddler was engaged in play with toys they had. Especially in response to grabbing the toddler, boys registered more negative affect than girls in this age group (Gunnar, Kryzer, Van Ryzin, & Phillips, 2011; Ispa et al., 2015).

Developmental Domains and Skills

A single developmental skill is influenced by and influences other skills and domains (e.g., Tables 5.3, 5.4) and can be disrupted by trauma. For example, developing language skills influence interpersonal relating and self-regulation. Aspects of development important to treatment (Chapter 7) and outcomes follow—e.g., language, general executive functions (memory, attention), self-regulation, humor, normal play, self- and other-awareness (e.g., perspective-taking), and social skills.

Table 5.3 Beginnings of Skills Used in Perspective-Taking (see also Table 5.4)

AWARENESS OF OTHERS' KNOWLEDGE

Infants
- imitation provides scaffolding for understanding others are "like me" (see imitation, below)
- imitation underlies theory of mind and empathy development

Toddlers
- 12 and 18 months: can tell, from experience, whether a parent has previous knowledge of an object, if the object was a part of shared joint experience
- 18 months—able to help others instrumentally in a number of contexts

References: Meltzoff & Decaty, 2003; Moll & Meltzoff, 2011; Tomasello et al., 2005; Tomasello & Carpenter, 2007.

EMPATHY (HAS PREDICTED LATER PROSOCIAL BEHAVIOR)

Infants
- responsive to others' emotional signals
- around age 1, begin to make helpful gestures toward a distressed person (i.e., patting, touching)
- caregiver responsiveness to distress and caregiver warmth are related to empathy development

Toddlers
- gender: boys' empathy was lower than girls' (at 18 months); improves with age
- influenced by:
  - children's ego-resiliency (flexible, adaptable behavior; 18 months)
  - mothers' expressive encouragement
- influenced by (each uniquely predicted child empathy; 24 months)

References: Davidov & Grusec, 2006; Eisenberg, 2000; Taylor et al., 2013; Zahn-Waxler & Radke-Yarrow, 1982; Zhou et al., 2002.

IMITATION (infants can use others' perceived acts to generate matching acts)
- through social interaction and imitation, children learn skills, object-use techniques, and cultural practices
  - imitation is the basis for theory of mind skills

Infants
- neonates (1st 4 weeks) spontaneously imitate basic facial emotional expressions—e.g., happy, sad, surprised faces
  - imitate mouth opening, tongue protruding, head shaking, finger movements
  - imitation at 2–3 days and 3 weeks has predicted visual attention span at 3 months
  - younger infants imitate a gesture but do not switch gestures for the other to imitate
  - facial imitation declines after 1st month, while sound and hand imitation increase
- 2–3 months—some imitation cannot occur until physical systems necessary to reaching and grasping mature
- human infants are more prolific imitators than young of other species
- infants can imitate from memory
  - mediated by expected emotional response of others to an action
- older infants (14 months) go beyond imitation of a gesture, and treat the interaction as a shared matching game
  - infants switch to a mismatched gesture for the adult/other to copy

Toddlers
- 16–18 months—can defer imitation; information can be retained up to 2 years
- 18 months—helped an adult more readily, if the adult had imitated the infant beforehand than if the adult had played with them without mimicking beforehand; will imitate an adult's intended but failed action

References: Bjorklund & Seller, 2014; Carpenter et al., 2013; Carver & Bauer, 1999; Coates, 2016; Field et al., 1982; Marshall & Meltzoff, 2014; Meltzoff & Decety, 2003; Meltzoff & Moore, 1977, 1995.

---

continued

Table 5.3 Continued

MENTAL STATE UNDERSTANDING

Infants

- *parent's use of mental state references* usually correlates with child's later emotion understanding
  - mothers adapt to children's characteristics

Toddlers

- close link between frequency and variety of mothers' mental state words and some semantic and conceptual skills
- *mothers' use of cognitive terms* may be more strongly related to children's theory of mind performance than mothers' references to other mental states (e.g., desires, emotions)
- *shared reading* is one vehicle to make mental state references and to facilitate child mental state understanding (ages 3–4 and 5–6)

References: Rollo & Buttiglieri, 2009; Rollo & Sulla, 2016; Taumoepeau & Ruffman, 2006.

MIRROR NEURONS (see glossary—Mu rhythm; some disagreement over finding interpretations)

Infants

- mapping the similarities and differences between self and others is considered an important task for infants
- 6 months and 8 months—*mirror neuron system* appears to be operational for goal-directed actions, but may require sensorimotor familiarity with the action

Toddlers

- 14–16 months—response to viewing walking versus crawling depended on crawling experience
- 18–30 months—mu wave suppression correlated with quality of imitation rather than with age or language skills
  - mu suppression (indicator of mirror neuron activity) during action observation and execution as well as for intransitive (not goal directed), mimicked hand movements
- 30 months—mu desynchronization for observation and execution of video emotional and non-emotional face-expressions

References: Marshall & Meltzoff, 2014; Nystrom, 2008; Nystrom et al., 2011; Rayson et al., 2016; Southgate et al., 2009; van Elk et al., 2008; Virji-Babul et al., 2012; Warreyn et al., 2013.

PERSPECTIVE-EGOCENTRISM

Infants

- *egocentricity* suggests a young child's inability to experience the world from any perspective other than own

Toddlers

- age 2½–a child can tell what they can see on one side of a card and what another person can see on the other side when the images are different
- under age 3 (and chimpanzees) are able to infer someone else's *false belief* about an object—i.e., can recognize that another person cannot see something they can see (e.g., blocked from their vision; *perceptual perspective-taking*)
- under age 4 usually responds according to her/his own mental state when asked about another's mental state

References: Dice & Dove, 2011; Moll & Meltzoff, 2011; Piaget, 1952; Piaget & Inhelder, 1969; Samson, Apperly, Braithwaite, Andrews, & Scott, 2010.

Table 5.3 Continued

UNDERSTANDING INTENTION

Infants

- 9 months—1st learn they and others are intentional agents in *joint attention* interactions

Toddlers

- 14–18 months—can copy and complete a behavior, recognizing the other's intention
  - can engage in *shared intentionality*
  - *copy* twice as many intentional adult actions as accidental actions
- around 25 to 36 months, differentiate between another person's intentional and accidental actions
- around age 3, children begin to understand that a person can *pretend* to accomplish a task

References: Carpentar, Akhtar, & Tomasello, 1998; Moll & Meltzoff, 2011; Semrud-Clikeman & Glass, 2010; Tomasello et al., 2005; Tomasello & Carpenter, 2007.

Language Skills

Although both adults and infants generally orient toward faces, from six months to 12 months (during speech learning), infants orient toward the mouth (Posner et al., 2014). Infants' visual attention distractibility—i.e., ability to volitionally maintain attention while inhibiting attention to competing events/objects—and infants' more frequent joint attention—i.e., more frequent response to a tester's bids for attention—have been related to larger vocabulary size (accounted for 48% of variance in vocabulary, after controlling for baseline status; across 11–18 months; N = 52, Salley, Panneton, & Colombo, 2013). Distractibility (not joint attention) directly affected level of multi-word production (45% of variance). That is, an infant's ability to sustain attention longer supports language development (Salley et al., 2013). The ability to speak at age one year has negatively associated with adulthood alexithymia (population sample; Kokkonen et al., 2003).

In general, about 23% of language-delayed children have later tested positive for autistic spectrum disorder, perhaps more if the sample includes delays in both receptive and expressive language (N = 91; ages 12 or 18 months and again 24 and 36 months; Henry et al., 2018). In a small sample, Henry et al. found that, in a best fitting model for language trajectories, 66% demonstrated age-appropriate verbal mental age, 23% delayed but catching up, and 11% consistently delayed. Among delayed children (not age appropriate; both receptive and expressive delays), by 36 months, 40% showed AuSD, 27% delays without AuSD, and 23% had reached age-appropriate language levels by age three (Henry et al., 2018). Toddlers who fall below the 10th percentile in language development at 24 months may catch-up before school entry, although they often remain below normative levels (Dale, Price, Bishop, & Plomin, 2003a). In a large study of UK twins (N = 8386 Dale et al., 2003a), toddlers with language delays at age two were significantly more likely to have delays at ages three and four, than those without early delays. That is, for toddlers who were language-delayed at age two, testing at age three showed 44.1% with persistent delays (vs 7.2% delayed in the not-early-delayed group) and at age four showed 40.2% still delayed (vs 8.5%). The persistently-delayed were not necessarily those with the most severe initial delays. When transient and persistent language-delayed children were compared to each other (N = 2800; Dale et al., 2003b), environmental factors were more substantial than genetics in accounting for early delays. For late-talking two-year-olds referred to professionals at age four, heritability of vocabulary was moderate and significant (not for those not referred at age four), although not significant for vocabulary, grammar, and abstract language when parental concerns and referral-status were left out of the equation (as reported by parents; Dale et al., 2003b).

A 2006 US task force found that male gender, perinatal factors (twin birth, preterm birth, birth weight), minority status, SES, birth order, family history of speech and language problems, parental education, and maternal age predicted speech and language delays in preschool-aged children

(Nelson, Nygren, Walker, & Panoscha, 2006). Risk factors more accurately predict language problems in older children than in those age two (Reilly et al., 2007). This may be a product of continuing in an environment that is not language rich. Evidence suggests that influences on language outcomes present at age two are still present at age four, with social disadvantage becoming increasingly important (Reilly et al., 2010). Toddlers with language delays have shown poorer self-regulation skills and poorer executive function (EF) skills in kindergarten (K) than those with typical or better language (broad or expressive delays; Aro et al., 2014). The lower EF and self-regulatory skills for toddlers with broad early language delays was evidenced in poorer social skills and lower attentional EF. Early expressive delays were associated with a broader range of generally lower K-age EF and self-regulation skills. Both earlier and current language skills had an effect on children, especially on attentional EFs (Aro et al., 2014).

General Executive Functions (EF)

EF are driven by basic information processing abilities (Rose, Feldman, & Jankowski, 2012a; Chapter 1; Table 5.4). From infancy (7 and 12 months) to toddlerhood (24 and 36 months) to age 11 there is significant continuity in information processing (e.g., attention, processing speed, and memory) suggesting that infant cognitive abilities provide the roots of later, more complex abilities (Rose et al., 2012a). EFs underpin the ability to set and work toward goals (Hendry, Jones, & Charman, 2016). Attentional control, self-regulation, processing speed, and cognitive flexibility are essential to these skills. By the end of age three, toddlers use impulse control and cognitive flexibility to achieve goal-directed responses in novel situations.

Processing speed, storage, and attentional allocation significantly have been correlated with the complex functions—e.g., planning, complex reasoning, problem-solving, and verbal fluency (Magimairaj, Montgomery, Marinellie, & McCarthy, 2009). Caregiving relationships provide the scaffolding and assist the development of many skills. For example, parental support of three-year-olds planning skills—e.g., identifying incremental steps in block building; encouraging child's planning—has been related to later math achievement (age 4.5) and reading skills (4.5 and first grade; Lombardi et al., 2017). Mothers' and fathers' parenting influence a child's EF development (Meuwissen & Carlson, 2015). In particular, parents' support of a child's autonomy—i.e., guidance that facilitates a child's success and sense of mastery in contrast to taking over and controlling a task or letting a child struggle alone—enhances their EFs. This includes when a parent takes the child's perspective, respects the child's pace, and ensures that the child plays an active role in completing a task as well as provides the child with choices, suggestions, and opportunities to use their own approaches, the parent helps to build the scaffolding on which children learn problem-solving and decision-making skills (Meuwissen & Carlson, 2015). It is essentially another method of following the child's lead, while facilitating the process and the child's learning. For example, for three-year-olds, fathers' controlling behaviors negatively predicted young children's EFs, while autonomy support marginally significantly, positively predicted EFs above income and child's verbal ability (N = 84 ages 2.5 to five; Meuwissen & Carlson, 2015).

Memory

Even newborns demonstrate memory—e.g., they can recognize a mother's voice (Coates, 2016) and can imitate after delay (Buttelmann et al., 2013, Meltzoff & Decety, 2003; Tables 5.1, 5.4). In an object preference task, infants imitated their cultural in-group more faithfully than a cultural out-group (66 14-month-olds; Buttelmann et al., 2013). Early memory ability corresponds to later memory—e.g., recall at 20 months to recall at ages six and 11 (Rose et al., 2012a). Between six and 18 months, infants can defer imitation (i.e., imitate after significant delay) suggesting mental representation in memory (Bjorklund & Sellers, 2014; Carver & Bauer, 1999; Coates, 2016), retained as

Table 5.4 Ages 0–3 EF, Awareness Skills, Humor

EXECUTIVE FUNCTION (EF)

- 5½ months—adult emotions influence infant recognition
  - after a video of a woman's emotional response to an object (e.g., happy vs fearful), a 5½-month-old selectively reaches for the actual object paired with the happy expression
- 9 and 19 months—when children were given photographs of objects
  - most of youngest treated photos as if they were real objects, sometimes trying to grasp them
  - most of older children pointed at depicted objects rather than trying to manipulate them, suggesting they recognized that they were representations
- near end of 1st year—attentional control emerges and develops slowly
- around 2.5 years—children recognize that a picture showed them where an object was hidden in a real room
- around age 3—could find the object in a scale model of the room

References: Bahrick & Lickliter, 2012; Bjorklund, 2013; Wass et al., 2011.

SELF-AWARENESS AND PERSPECTIVE-TAKING

Infant self-awareness

- learns that her/his personal body is distinct from surroundings
- initially no self-recognition in mirror
- respond differently to another's touch
- by 4 months, reach for objects
- 4 to 7-month-olds respond differently to self in videos than to others in videos
- 14 and 18 months, if displayed self-recognition of own mirror image, then demonstrated higher rates of initiating joint attention at 18 months compared to same-age infants who did not evidence mirror self-recognition

Perspective-taking

- age 2: can discuss their own and others' emotions; skill improves between 18 and 36 months
- age 3–4: able to distinguish between own and others' beliefs and knowledge of the world
  - young child generally believes it impossible that another person can hold a belief that the child knows to be false
- ages 5–6: until now, understanding another person may hold false beliefs about someone's beliefs is still unstable

References: Berk, 2007; London, 2003; Bretherton, Fritz, Zahn-Waxler, & Ridgeway, 1986; Brüne & Brüne-Cohrs, 2006; Kuhn, 2000; Nichols, Fox, & Mundy, 2005; Rochat, 2003.

EMOTION AWARENESS AND REGULATION

- 5 and 7 months—infants distinguish emotional expressions in faces
- end of 1st year –emotion awareness and control seem to increase
- by ages 1–2, evidence of affect-modulation through control of facial musculature
  - before age 3, in ambivalent/ambiguous situations, young children tend to examine the parent's facial expression and use the emotional information expressed to modulate their behavior (i.e., to influence choice of behavior)
- 12-month-olds can infer a person's next behavior based on his/her gaze direction and facial emotions and can recognize dispositional content of some basic emotion-states
- 14–18 months—increased joint attention initiation linked to reduced risk of self-regulatory problems
- beginning around age 2, children show insights into how emotions influence their own and others' behaviors
  - negative emotions (e.g., sadness, anger) can be intentionally changed by using regulation strategies
- ages 2–6: develop a growing understanding of the self-conscious emotions (e.g., pride, embarrassment, guilt), which suggests the ability for emotion perspective-taking

continued

Table 5.4 Continued

- by age 3, social partners influence emotions expressed
  - can change intensity and mode of expressiveness depending on the demands of a situation or on personal goals (e.g., crying loudly for attention)
  - learn cultural rules for the expression of emotions

References: e.g., Burnett & Blakemore, 2009; Dennis & Keleman, 2009; Sheinkopf et al., 2004; Vaughan Van Hecke et al., 2007.

HUMOR

- infants spontaneously laugh when they perceive unexpected stimuli in nonserious/nonthreatening contexts
- 5-months-olds—smile whether parent is smiling or neutral faced when acting absurdly toward infant
  - smile longer (at 5 months) and sooner (at 7 months) when parent smiles or laughs (gives humor cues)
  - 7-month-olds more likely to smile with humor cues than without (parental affect influences affect as early as 5 months)
- humor development (includes shared laughter and joint attention)—lower trait humor (low assessed smiling and laughing) at 6 months predicted higher attachment security at 12 months, suggesting less good-humored infants elicit greater parental engagement, which benefits attachment, or vice versa
- parents decrease gaze to objects and increase gaze toward and smiling at younger toddlers when joking (possibly so toddler won't generalize the false information to objects), and toddlers respond appropriately; no such distinguishing between joke and other contexts occurred for older toddlers (may rely on more subtle cues)
- ages 15–22 months—appreciate and express humor through actions, noises, and facial expressions, e.g.,
  - bending knees, bringing legs up, and looking through legs
  - wordplay or errors (e.g., mispronouncing chives as tchwives)
- infants laugh at
  - the absurd, incongruity (e.g., altering the way something is normally used or handled, e.g., banana on the head; shoes on hands instead of feet), feeling empowered over adults (violating expectations/rules)
  - general violation of expectations (sponge on head instead of cleaning as asked; sticker on head instead of paper)
- abused children ages 1–17 accompanied by a medical clown (a trained pediatric professional) expressed less fear, reported lower pain, and had fewer intrusive thoughts during ano-genital examinations
  - the child is a creative partner in the play experience during the examination
- 18-months to 2-year-olds use humor to connect to peers (e.g., with incongruity or violation of expectations; twirling around and falling, especially together)

References: Gervais & Wilson, 2005; Hoicka, 2016; Loizou, 2005; McGhee, 1979; Mireault et al., 2012, 2015; Sroufe, 2018; Sroufe & Waters, 1977; Tener et al., 2012; Wittmer, 2012.

much as 1–2 years (see Coates, 2016). From 2.5 to four years, young children's recall (i.e., verbal and memory capacities) increase with age. Between ages three and four, children have imitated a series of three adult actions, two of which were unnecessary for retrieving a gummy bear from inside a box (Horner & Whiten, 2005).

Autobiographical Memory (AM). AM—a person's recollection of experienced past events—requires the addition of self-referent and self-aware qualities to episodic memory, which happens late in the second year of life (Bjorklund & Sellers, 2014; Howe, 2011). Language and pragmatic skills are also essential to create a narrative. For most people, the earliest memory is between ages three and four years (Bauer, 2009; Miles, 1893). Females, first-born, and children without siblings tend to have earlier first memories (closer to three). Specific kinds of experiences (e.g., age two hospitalizations) are likely to be remembered (Bauer, 2009). However, the "amnesia of childhood" may extend substantially (e.g., age six or eight years; Bauer, Stennes, & Haight, 2003). Very young children with interest, readiness to participate in conversations about the past, and elicited and deferred imitation show better memory performance (Bauer, 2009; Bauer & Burch, 2004; Farrant & Reese, 2000). Kelly and Bailey (2012) showed that between ages three and five, mothers first prompt young children's narratives until they reliably provide them on their own. When mothers are more elaborative—e.g., provide rich descriptions of past events for the very young, even preverbally—children provide longer and more detailed reports about past events (Bauer, 2009; Reese, Haden, & Fivush, 1993). Securely attached four-year-olds provide longer and more elaborate narratives than insecure four-year-olds—i.e., provide more descriptive words, locations, emotions, and mental state evaluations. For example, a secure four-year-old might say,

> We saw a peacock with long feathers. We were supposed to get a feather but we didn't. She didn't have the key. We were so angry … so she couldn't open the cage so we couldn't get a feather. We were so angry.
>
> *(McCabe, Peterson, & Connors, 2006, p. 12)*

Attention

Attention can be spontaneous or volitional (Chapter 1). For infants, attention involves exploratory behavior—e.g., orienting, eye movements, and active interaction with the environment such as reaching, head turning. Attentional problems can cause difficulties in other cognitive skills (Giordano et al., 2017). Spontaneous gaze-following at 10 months has been related to language ability at 18 months and to theory of mind abilities in adulthood (Federico et al., 2017). For toddlers, problem-solving and memory tasks have proven more susceptible to distraction (vs categorization and free-play tasks; Wyss, Kannass, & Haden, 2013). In the distractor condition (four tasks, total eight minutes, administered twice)—turning on a DVD, toddlers increased attention to the task and reduced attention to the distractor in the second half of the session. By three years, children with Autism Spectrum Disorders (AuSD) show a variety of impairments in social and communicative functioning that include attentional problems—e.g., less eye contact, lower attention to social partners, and poor joint attention skills as well as poor facial recognition, altered emotional responsiveness, and little imitation (Bahrick & Lickliter, 2012). Focused/selective attention is essential to effective social interacting, later productivity, and achievement (Bahrick & Lickliter, 2012). Development of attentional selectivity is believed to be influenced by an infant's sensitivity to salient properties of stimulation (e.g., contrast, movement, intensity; see Bahrick & Lickliter, 2012), and to *inter-sensory redundancy* (overlapping information across the senses and/or proprioceptive stimulation; Bahrick, 2010; Glossary).

Focused attention is essential to functioning. For social and nonsocial events, attention and learning are less likely when only one sense is stimulated (Reynolds, Bahrick, Lickliter, & Guy, 2014). In early development, when attentional resources are most limited, redundancy across the senses promotes attention (Reynolds et al., 2014). Engaging multiple senses enhances learning—e.g., an infant learns an object best if the adult names and shows the object at the same time (temporal synchrony). Inter-sensory redundancy—involving experiencing with more than one sense organ (e.g., eyes, ears, fingers, nose)—assists in organizing aspects of early selective attention (Bahrick & Lickliter, 2012) and fosters earlier and enhanced perceptual processing (Reynolds et al., 2014). As well, four-month-old infants' attention can be "educated" to amodal properties of a stimulus (perception of a whole structure/item, when only parts are visible) by pre-exposing them with inter-sensory redundancy (Bahrick, 2010). Hence, *inter-sensory* perception is important to social, emotional, and cognitive development for very young children and continues to enhance attention across time.

Attentional Biases in Infants. Regardless of attachment status, infants and older persons (children and adults) show a preference for looking at attractive faces (Damon, Mottier, Meary, &

Pascalis, 2017). Nevertheless, early patterns of attention to facial expressions, which may be among cues that signal potential threat—e.g., fearful faces—have predicted later attachment security (Peltola et al., 2015). During the course of developing emotional perception, infants around 5–7 months show an attentional bias toward fearful facial expressions, evidenced by prolonged attention to fearful faces (vs happy or neutral), along with heart rate and electrocortical brain changes. Infants' normal attention bias to fearful faces at seven months predicted attachment security at 14 months (N = 126 at seven months, 73 at 14 months; Peltola et al., 2015). In contrast to securely attached infants, avoidant-insecurely attached infants exhibited a smaller attentional bias to fearful faces and a larger bias to neutral faces. Exploratory analysis suggested that smaller attention to fearful faces was associated with increasing signs of attachment disorganization. Evidence has linked disorganized attachments to externalizing (e.g., aggression, oppositional behavior). Such behaviors have been linked to lower sensitivity to fearfulness in others (see Peltola et al., 2015).

Fear or anxiety may create biases. Otte and colleagues (2015) found that the higher the pre-natal maternal anxiety experienced by a fetus, the more infants attended to fearful vocalizations, regardless of visual prime (fearful or happy faces). Maternal post-natal depression has shown detrimental effects on a child's cognitive and emotional development (see Barlow et al., 2016)—e.g., has been related to infants' decreased attentional disengagement from fearful facial expressions relative to happy or neutral expressions (Taylor-Colls & Fearon, 2015) and greater right frontal activation (alpha frequency range) than infants of non-depressed mothers (Jones, Field, & Almeida, 2009; Taylor-Colls & Fearon, 2015), which appears to be associated with differences in emotion in adults and children (particularly negative affect and withdrawal). Attention to fearful facial expressions in seven-month-old infants has been related to maternal stress and depressive symptoms (see Peltola et al., 2015). Attention to angry faces has been higher in school-age children with histories of parental maltreatment (see Peltola et al., 2015). For children assessed at ages 2–3 (N = 268), five (N = 207), and seven (N = 174), there was no direct association between an attention bias toward threat and anxiety (White et al., 2017). However, behavioral inhibition (BI) and a high attention bias to threat or no attention bias (0 score) predicted anxiety five years later. Higher attention bias to threat conferred greater vulnerability to anxiety for BI children. With a low attention bias to threat—attention away from threat—BI was not associated with anxiety. Positive attention biases were not directly related to anxiety or BI. However, BI children with a low attention bias to the positive (attention away from positive) or a 0 score positive bias had greater anxiety scores at age seven. BI children with high attention bias to the positive did not have later anxiety (White et al., 2017). Bias to positive was unrelated to bias to threat. In this study (not in some others), the moderating effect of attention bias to threat was not found at age five.

Self-Regulation

Behavioral and emotional self-regulation show substantial overlap in age-related development. Even pre-natal sleep states are relevant—e.g., the time a typically developing fetus takes to pass from quiet sleep in the last month before birth is linked to higher levels of self-regulation at ages 8–9 and in adolescence (non-synchronized transitions lasting >3 minutes, Van den Bergh & Mulder, 2012). Risk factors may be the targets of intervention for conduct problems. For a nationally representative child sample (born in UK 2000–2001; 6458 boys, 6340 girls), Gutman et al. (2018) identified four gender-specific trajectories in conduct problems from age three to age 11—a. *low* (more common in girls, 78% vs 54%), b. *early-onset, persistent* (more common in boys, 8% vs 5%), c. *early-onset, desisting* (34% male; 10% female), and d. *school-onset* (3% boys, 6% girls; Gutman, Joshi, Parsonage, & Schoon, 2018). Girls high in conduct problems (age three) showed a dip from ages 5–7, and a spurt at age 11; boys desisted earlier (soon after age three). Risk factors were sometimes gender-specific—e.g., maternal detachment was especially problematic for boys. Unlike early-onset conduct problems, school-onset problems were not related to socioeconomic disadvantage and were related to smoking in pregnancy and maternal detachment for boys and maternal depression for girls. Early-onset was related to low parent education, smoking in pregnancy, maternal depression, and difficult temperament for both genders and, for boys, to single parent, maternal detachment, and neglectful parental attitudes. Early-onset persisting was related to SES and to boys' delayed infant development. Language problems have also been related to conduct disturbances (Chapter 6).

Preterm birth is a known association of behavior problems in school-age children (Arpi & Ferrari, 2013). Very-preterm, very-low-birthweight, and moderately preterm infants have shown more behavior problems at ages 0–2 and 3–5 than term-born comparison children, even after controlling for perinatal and social risk factors and cognitive performance (across 14 cohort studies; Arpi & Ferrari, 2013). Additional risk factors have been associated with behavior problems for these children—e.g., hospitalization length; disadvantaged social conditions, mother–infant interactive patterns. The most common behavior problems included poor social/interactive skills, poor behavior and emotion self-regulation, emotional difficulties, and reduced attention. In addition, behavior problems tended to co-occur with difficulties in cognitive, motor, neurological, and language domains. Behavior problems in infancy have predicted later behavior problems.

Sleep Regulation

REM sleep, associated with vivid dreaming, has been linked to neuronal development, learning and memory (see Adams, Stoops, & Skomro, 2014; reviewed 30 studies of sleep and attachment). It has been associated with the release of attachment-promoting hormones (prolactin, oxytocin) and been found to increase in an infant when co-sleeping with the mother and to decrease following separation. Studies have shown that mother–infant co-sleeping leads to increased synchronicity between mother and baby's sleep, enhances a mother's sensitivity to a baby's awakenings, and enhances feeding. The three phases of non-REM sleep (gradations in depth of sleep) have been associated with immune function and regulation. Maturation of sleep regulation overlaps with the attachment system (see Adams et al., 2014). Studies of infants have shown that infants with insecure-anxious resistant attachments had the most sleep problems—e.g., woke the most at six months, difficulty settling, use of parent's bed, longer waking periods, persistent sleep problems (to 12, to 15 months, to two years)—while avoidant infants woke the least (10 studies; some mixed findings). Parents tended to underestimate night waking when measured otherwise as well.

Other factors influence the relationship between attachment and sleep (see Adams et al., 2014). Infants who slept in communal settings rather than in home-based settings were more likely to have insecure attachments. When mothers were more emotionally available and attentive at bedtime, infants showed less sleep disruption. Preterm infants who napped more and longer during the day were more likely to have secure attachments. In one study, all mothers of toddlers with sleep problems were insecurely attached (in contrast to 57% of controls). For infants rated high in negative emotionality, attachment and sleep were more strongly linked in toddlerhood and sleep problems were more strongly related to subsequent emotional and behavioral problems at 54 months (age four, see Adams et al., 2014).

Difficulty falling asleep and night waking are the most frequent sleep disturbances during infancy (20–30% of infants; Martin et al., 2007; Sadeh, Tikotzky, & Scher, 2010). The inability to soothe themselves back to sleep or to resume sleep with minimal parental help has been identified as a main problem (Sadeh Flint-Ofir, Tirosh, & Tikotzky, 2007). Sleep problems have been related to difficult temperament—e.g., fussiness, irritability, and increased crying (Mindell & Lee, 2015) and to maternal depression as well (Sadeh et al., 2010). Increased sleep duration has been linked to more positive temperament. Some evidence suggests that early sleep disturbance related to later anxiety symptoms or disorders, in later childhood or adulthood (may be explained by genetics or environments; Gregory & Sadeh, 2016).

Mindell and Lee (2015) found significant relationships between sleep (fragmentation and decreased duration) and mood outcomes (negative mood, especially morning; N = 1351 Brazilian infants, ages 3–13 months), but found no associations with developmental skill outcomes—communication, fine and gross motor skills, problem-solving, or personal social relationships. In general, worse mood was associated with longer and increased night waking, decreased night- and daytime sleep duration, later bedtime, earlier wake-time, and parents' increased perceptions of sleep problems (Mindell & Lee, 2015). Although sleep may have a direct, short-term impact on daily functioning, sleep disturbances in the first year have generally not been linked to ongoing poor development. Nevertheless, poor sleep in the first month of life has been linked to longer first gaze at four months and longer distraction episodes at 18 months. Alterations in orienting attention at four months predicted likelihood of distraction during the second year of life (Geva, Yaron, & Kuint, 2016). A few studies suggest a link between sleep and internalizing and externalizing problems mediated by mood (Mindell & Lee, 2015). Snoring at one month has been associated with poorer cognitive development at six months and at one year. Sleep duration has been related to later problems. For example, greater RSA suppression (Glossary) to fear-eliciting stimuli and to inhibitory control challenges in combination with longer sleep duration was associated with less internalizing (N = 123 toddlers; Cho, Philbrook, Davis, & Buss, 2017). Greater RSA augmentation to an inhibitory control task with shorter sleep duration predicted more externalizing a year later.

Caregivers and Regulation

Caregivers help infants and young children learn self-regulation (Fosha, 2003; Nader, 2008; Schore, 2003). When a caregiver provides sensitive care, a dyadic regulatory system evolves in which the infant learns that arousal will not lead to disorganization beyond his/her coping abilities when the caregiver is there to reestablish equilibrium. Schore (2003) has explained that, when the *good-enough* primary caregiver induces an infant's stress response through a mis-attunement, s/he quickly re-invokes a re-attunement, which is critical to enabling a shift from negative to positive affective states. Reestablished synchrony permits coping and recovery from stress. The dyadic attachment system psycho-biologically modulates positive states (e.g., joy and excitement) as well as negative states (e.g., aggression and fear). For uncontrollable arousal, the infant seeks proximity to the caregiver for soothing and recovery of homeostasis (Fonagy, Target, & Gergely, 2000).

Attention-Related Networks

Attention capacities—alerting responses, orienting, and executive monitoring of performance—are considered independent yet interrelated systems/networks that underlie observational learning, self-regulation, and adaptive behavior (Geva, Zivan, Warsha, & Olchik, 2013). *Alerting* responses include readiness to receive information, which precedes activation—readiness to respond. The brain's *orienting network* directs attention to a target stimulus and wields much of the control over other brain networks during infancy and early childhood (Posner et al., 2014). It interacts with sensory systems to prioritize information. The brain's *executive network* involves error monitoring, mental resource recruiting, and cognitive load management and is required for conflict resolution and acting contrary to habit/expectation. It is involved in resolving competing actions; when it enhances activity in networks related to goals and inhibits activity in conflicting networks, self-regulation occurs. Contemporary evidence suggests that the executive attention network can be conceived as two separable networks—a control system related to maintaining a task set and a network related to moment-to-moment performance feedback (Hendry et al., 2016). In a study of children from ages seven months to seven years, Posner et al. (2014) found that the earliest form of regulation seemed to come from the orienting rather than the executive network. That is, while orienting was maintained, infants showed a reduction in overt distress, but appeared distressed again if orienting was broken. Additionally, the time that infants examined a novel toy before reaching for it, and the total time they examined the toy were significantly related to the orienting network at both ages four and seven years. Both infants and adults orient toward the eyes of a picture of a face (except during speech learning). Although by four years, a child's executive network dominates (Posner et al., 2014), it is at least partially active by age one, and over the next 12 months, it takes dominance over the other attention networks in a range of domains—visual orienting, motor behavior, and self-regulation (Hendry et al., 2016). Aspects of the brain's orienting system show greater connectivity during infancy. Sleep–wake regulation patterns appear to be related to infants' emerging attention-regulation competence in complex environments (Geva et al., 2016).

Infant orienting has predicted soothability, effortful control, and interest at age four (Posner et al., 2014). Development of executive attention and effortful control permits observing one's own actions and selecting other actions (Rothbart, 2011). By six months, infants' abilities to shift attention in response to bids for joint attention has predicted the tendency at age two to utilize shifts of attention to self-regulate and resist temptation in a delay of gratification task (Morales et al., 2005). Measures of infant smiling and laughter, vocal reactivity, and cuddliness have been negatively related to the ability to resolve conflict at seven years (about things competing for attention, Posner et al., 2014).

Age and Effortful Control

From 12–40 months, regulatory problems (e.g., behavioral, emotional, eating, sleeping) are significant predictors of long-term difficulties—e.g., motor, language, and cognitive delays; attachment difficulties; difficult temperament, noncompliance, aggression. Caregiver–child relationship difficulties, adversity, and low parental reflective function are risk factors for such problems (Barlow et al., 2016). Toward age one, an association exists between structural changes in the prefrontal cortex (PFC) and emergence of simple forms of emotion regulation (Diamond, 1991). Individual differences in cognitive control are evident as early as 18 months of age—inhibition of task-irrelevant responses (Rothbart, Derryberry, & Posner, 1994). At 18 months, prospective motor control during reaching (the ability to control and plan actions) is related to infants' performance on a simple-inhibition task (ability to inhibit reaching for an attractive toy) and working memory tasks (hide a toy; Gottwald, et al., 2016). As early as 22 months, young children demonstrate effortful control (EC)—the ability to suppress a dominant response and perform a subdominant response (e.g., not grab the toy from the other child, wait your turn; Kochanska, Aksan, & Joy, 2007; Rothbart & Bates, 2006).

Studies have found positive associations between language skills and prosocial and self-regulatory skills in 3–5-year-olds ("Use your words"; e.g., see Longobardi et al., 2018). Both concurrent and prior vocabulary at 24 months have positively predicted children's levels of self-regulation over time (Vallotton & Ayoub, 2010). Girls generally use language to self-regulate before boys (Vallotton & Ayoub, 2010). The ability to slow oneself down because of a previous error emerges at around age three (Posner et al., 2014). Toddlers' levels of restraint (ages 14, 20, 24, 36 months) relate to EFs in adolescence (age 17; Friedman, Miyake, Robinson, & Hewitt, 2011). As early as 38 months, in situations designed to induce young children to violate clearly specified rules, when they believe they are not being monitored, young children exhibit *self-regulated, rule-compatible conduct* (Kochanska et al., 2007). Although cognitive control increases with development, it does not reach maturity before age 12 (Eigsti et al., 2006).

Emotion Regulation

From pre-natal 30 weeks and immediately after birth, fetuses/babies display highly organized facial expressions (pleasure—smiling; displeasure—scowling; fatigue—yawning; Rochat, 2011). Young infants make nearly all the muscle movements used by adults to express the primary emotions (e.g., joy, disgust, surprise, and distress). They communicate using body movement (reaching), sounds (e.g., crying, cooing), and facial expressions (e.g., smiling, distress). Children learn about emotions when caregivers and siblings model, label, and read stories about emotions for them (Aldao, Nolen-Hoeksema, & Schweizer, 2010; Oshri et al., 2015). Most young children learn that a smile elicits a smile, reaching (when smiling or crying) often precedes being picked up, and hugging a fuzzy bear can be comforting (e.g., Tanyel, 2009). They also learn from a trusted adult who can give reassuring looks, a pat on the back, a verbal explanation (e.g., about a scary noise), or reassurance (e.g., that s/he is safe).

Because of the potent influence of early attachments, factors that affect the infant–caregiver relationship exert a determining role in a young child's emotional functioning (Zeanah et al., 2000, 2005)—e.g., babies with avoidant attachment styles seem to suppress separation-induced negative affect, indicated by an increased heart rate and increased cortisol level. Cognitive and emotional skills emerge simultaneously (Tanyel, 2009). Infants vary in their abilities to focus on a visual stimulus (directly in front of them) in the presence of a second, (distracter) stimulus; such abilities relate to emotional control (and social behavior; Fox & Calkins, 2003).

Emotion Regulation Strategies. Emotion regulation includes strategies to achieve emotional control—e.g., awareness, understanding, and acceptance of emotion states, then use of effective strategies to modulate emotions or act in desired ways (Gratz & Roemer, 2004; Oshri et al., 2015; Chapter 1). Infants may use attentional focus (e.g., turning away from a noisy toy) or self-soothing behaviors to reduce/regulate negative affect (e.g., looking at mother; Fox & Calkins, 2003). Frustration-related distress at five months has been linked to use of fewer regulation behaviors at 10 months (e.g., less self-soothing, Fox & Calkins, 2003). With age, sensitive care, and encouragement, infants progress from self-soothing (e.g., infant finger sucking; young toddler rocking) to labeling and sharing feelings (Gaensbauer, 1995; Tanyel, 2009). Temperament influences emotion regulation and strategies (Table A5.1)—e.g., easily frustrated infants and toddlers (e.g., difficult temperament, NE) have difficulty with emotion regulation and are much less likely to use regulation strategies such as distraction or redirection of attention (Table A5.2—BIS).

Mature emotion awareness includes recognition that internal states can be intentionally modified (Dennis & Keleman, 2009). Toward the end of the first year, evidence seems to indicate a new level of emotional awareness and control (see Mireault et al., 2015; Tables 5.3, 5.4). Three and four-year-olds use language, cognitive and behavioral distraction, and repairing a situation as relatively effective self-regulation strategies—e.g., socially appropriate actions to make a negative situation better (N = 62, Dennis & Keleman, 2009; Tanyel, 2009). Children with resistant attachments, higher NE, more internalization, or mothers with depressive symptoms have shown higher cortisol (Khoury et al., 2015). Infants of more depressed mothers who employed more independent regulatory behaviors—e.g., withdrawal, wandering away, distraction, scanning, orienting to an object—have had greater cortisol secretion (vs those with higher parental and social engagement). Mother's negative emotional responses (e.g., anxiety) may induce avoidance of "aversive" emotions or actions (Gratz et al., 2007).

Humor

Smiling, laughter, and humor are forms of social behavior with positive associations (e.g., health; inter-relating; Chapter 1). Humor has been used to assist learning as well as inter-relating (Fagard et al., 2016). Most people have seen a baby laugh long and delightedly. For example, placing the mouth on an infant's belly and blowing with lips fluttering may elicit such laughter. A baby may laugh repeatedly each time a piece of paper is torn, during peek-a-boo play, or when lovingly lifted up over the head (perhaps combined with soothing baby-talk). A few studies have been conducted on young infants' laughter. Whether or not a parent is smiling/laughing or neutral faced, five-month-olds smiled when someone acted absurdly toward the infant—e.g., book on the head; ball on the nose and poking it repeatedly (N = 37; Mireault et al., 2015). Infants smiled longer at five months and smiled more often and sooner at seven months, when parents smiled or laughed (gave humor cues). Hence as early as five months, infants respond to parent's cues that something is humorous. In a separate study, using ambiguous-absurd situations, in response to the parent's smile and/or laughter, six-month-old infants smiled or laughed toward the parents rather than toward the event—affect sharing, which is part of the social experience of humor (N = 10, 6; Mireault et al., 2014). By 12 months, infants looked more at the experimenter and were more likely to smile at the event.

For toddlers, humor involves behaving contrary to expectation (or absurdly), mispronouncing words, nonsense rhyming, exaggeration of words or expressions, or making noises (Table 5.4—humor). Some young children are more physical in their expressions of humor and some are much more expressive than others (N = 6, ages 15–22 months; Loizou, 2005). For example, a child may bend his knees, raise his bottom, and look through his legs. A child might make exaggerated facial expressions and laugh. If an adult or child makes the expression back, they laugh even more. Normally, between ages 18 months and three years, children appreciate cartoons and enjoy slapstick and use of objects in an unusual manner—e.g., putting a banana on the head like a hat (age two, McGhee, 1979; Semrud-Clikeman & Glass, 2010). From 18 months to two years old, toddlers use humor to connect to peers—e.g., incongruity or violation of expectations; twirling and falling, especially together (Loizou, 2005; Semrud-Clikeman & Glass, 2010). Toddlers appreciate joking, teasing, and physical play (Cameron et al., 2010). By age three, a child begins to use word play—e.g., rhyming, nonsense words. From ages 2–7, children appreciate visual and physical humor—e.g., sudden visual surprises, incongruity in pictures, grimaces, funny faces; unusual sounds or voices (Loizou & Kyriakou, 2016); parent pretending not to know where they are.

Parents have been observed to give cues that they are joking to younger (16–20 months) but not to older toddlers (20–24; N = 25 and 43, respectively, Hoicka, 2016). For younger toddlers, they increased smiling and gaze toward toddlers when joking over pretend and literal contexts. Parents decreased gaze to objects, when joking, perhaps to avoid toddlers generalizing false information in jokes. Not distinguishing contexts for the older group may be because older toddlers rely on more sophisticated cues such as language.

Normal Play

Research has shown the importance of play to development (Nader, 2008; Chapter 1). Rhythmic play, predominant in infancy, includes sensorimotor exploration and gross motor movements—e.g., body rocking, arm waving, foot kicking, without apparent goal—and is associated with neuromuscular development (Pellegrini & Smith, 1998; see also Campbell et al., 2018). Specific rhythmic movements appear to increase just prior to achievement of voluntary control of a specific motor pattern and the associated neuromuscular systems, which may proliferate, eliminate, or modify corresponding brain neural growth or synapse formations (Pellegrini & Smith, 1998). Rhythmic play (e.g., drumming) has been used in treatments to repair the effects of trauma (e.g., neurobiological effects). Exercise play increases from toddlerhood to its peak in preschool. It includes physically vigorous gross motor locomotion—e.g., chasing a ball, running, jumping, climbing, lifting, fleeing, and pushing and pulling—and is associated, e.g., with preschool abilities to decode others' emotional expressions (see Fathers, above). Later play skills build on earlier skills (Campbell et al., 2018).

Temperament may influence play behaviors, and social play behaviors can be interdependent. That is, play behaviors of a social partner influence behaviors of a peer (Walker, Degnan, Henderson, & Fox, 2015). For example, although a two-year-old's social fear and wariness was unrelated to wariness in an unfamiliar play partner at age two (see Behavioral Inhibition, Glossary), at age three, the child's social fear was linked both to the child's and the peer's lower levels of social engagement with each other and to less peer-dysregulated behavior and negative affect (perhaps increased sympathy for the shy child; N = 296, Walker et al., 2015). Socially fearful children have exhibited assertive behaviors to directly and indirectly control a peer's behaviors (McElwain et al., 2014).

Pretend Play

By the end of the first year and early in the second year, play becomes more elaborated and functional—i.e., toddlers use toys in routine ways (e.g., block stacking, moving a toy car). Pretend play emerges, initially at a basic level with simple acts alone or with a doll or a social partner (see Campbell et al., 2018). Between 22 and 34 months of age, toddlers with AuSD, toddlers without AuSD but with a sibling with AuSD, and low-risk toddlers all went through developmental changes in their play with age, including showing more bouts of pretend play and higher scores on pretend and other play tasks (N = 168; Campbell et al., 2018). Children with AuSD lagged behind the other two groups on assessments. Although parents of all groups were highly engaged with their children, children with AuSD engaged less with parents or examiners and showed the least developmental change. Authors suggest that lower social engagement may be an important aspect of less advanced pretend skills. Temperament was not assessed.

Fonagy and Target (2000) suggest that between ages two and three, play enables a child, entering pretend mode, to discover representational aspects of thoughts, which contributes to mentalization skills (Glossary) and to autobiographical narratives. Symbolic functioning requires recognizing that one thing can stand for something other than itself (Bjorklund, 2013). Between 18 months and two years, children begin to use symbolic play and language to represent experience (Piaget, 1952) and may demonstrate perceptual memories of experiences in play (even those not consciously remembered, Gaensbauer, 2002). Thus, aspects of traumatic exposure often appear in very young and older children's play and activities (Nader, 2008, Chapter 6). As early as age two, children can show what did and did not happen to them. Play and therapeutic play have been important to recovery from traumas (e.g., deprivation, neurobiological effects, early traumas, e.g., see Chapters 1, 7, 10, Boxes 2.3, 13.5) and for restoration of a number of undeveloped or interrupted skills (Box 2.3; Chapter 8, 10).

Parents and Play

There are both similarities and differences between fathers and mothers' play with young children. Ability to follow the child's lead and how skillful a parent is as a playmate are among measures of the quality of play (Dozier, Meade, & Bernard, 2014; Chapter 7)—e.g., avoids violating a child's play concept; adjusts to the child's gender; provides felt security; enjoys the play; shows sensitivity (Ahnert et al., 2017). Some evidence suggests that paternal quality of play is higher with boys, independent of fathers' personality or parenting stress, while maternal quality of play is higher with girls and is linked to her perceived parenting competence, her felt pressure to accept the child (both related to improved quality), and her neuroticism (related to lower enjoyment and quality of play; N = 400, ages 12–68 months, Ahnert et al., 2017). Fathers with adverse childhoods or with preterm babies scored significantly lower on quality of play. They improved with increasing child age, birth weight, and cognitive (not motor or temperament) scores. Child internalizing behaviors were negatively related to paternal quality of play (see Negative Emotionality/Negative Affectivity, above). Contrary to expectation, mothers activated children as intensely as fathers. Although fathers with adverse childhood experiences activated children more moderately, most fathers activated children in the same manner regardless of gender or pre-/full-term status (Ahnert et al., 2017).

Toys

Evidence has suggested that an enriched environment relates to greater developmental gains (e.g., Box 2.3; Hensch & Bilimoria, 2012). The question becomes, "What enriches an environment for children of specific ages?" Animal studies have suggested that an enriched environment may be one in which the toys are periodically changed (Hensch & Bilimoria, 2012). One study showed that fewer toys (4 vs 16) resulted in toddlers engaging in longer periods of play with a single toy (twice as long), possibly permitting increased exploration of the toy and more creativity in play (1.5 times as many types of play with a toy; Dauch, Imwalle, Ocasio, & Metz, 2018). Although all toddlers explored the toys in their environments, toddlers with 16 toys more frequently moved from toy to toy. More toys may have served as a distraction for younger children who have less mature development of attention skills. Although larger studies that follow toddlers across time are needed, it is possible that, normally, four or so toys at a time may be more developmentally appropriate for toddlers.

Toys are best chosen for their age-appropriateness, a child's developmental level, and a child's interests, with consciousness of the possibility of teaching, e.g., inclusiveness (dolls dressed for different cultures; Guyton, 2011). Toys provide opportunities to use skills such as cognitive—e.g., problem-solving, cause and effect, imitation; social—e.g., helping, joint play/attention; and other skills (see Guyton, 2011). Toys have played a part in affiliation. In general, people tend to associate with like others (Caspi, 1998). In one study, toddlers preferred to affiliate with puppets who played with the same toys they did, and they copied these puppets when they played with new toys (Gerson, Bekkering, & Hunnius, 2017).

Self- and Other-Awareness

Distinction between self and other is essential for self-awareness and for awareness of others (Filippette, Farroni, & Johnson, 2016). Self-awareness begins with body awareness—the infant learns that her/his personal body is distinct from her/his surroundings (Berk, 2009; London, 2003; see Table 5.3, 5.4). Body-related cues (related to body position, self-produced movement) are believed fundamental to body perception (Filippette et al., 2013). Filippette et al. (2013) showed that newborns looked longer when seen and felt touch were matched—newborns were touched when a video face was touched (visual-tactile synchrony and inter-sensory redundancy; see Attention; Filippette et al., 2016). Infant brain responses (five months old) are similar to those of adults in response to multi-sensory, body-related stimuli (watching live video while moving body; Filippette et al., 2015). Also, infants respond differently to their own and another person's touch/stimuli (Rochat, 2003). Young babies correct their imitative behavior, suggesting both active comparison and lack of confusion between self and other (Meltzoff & Decety, 2003; Meltzoff & Moore, 1997). An individual can be self-aware about one facet of self (e.g., mirror appearance; aspect of own personality), while being completely ignorant about another facet (e.g., video self; personal weaknesses) (Suddendorf & Butler, 2013). In a study of self-recognition and self-regulation, more than half of toddlers (58% of 20-month-olds) pointed to themselves in a photo when asked, "Where's [toddler's name]?"; 78% at 27 months (Jennings et al., 2008).

Mirror Recognition

Although five- and eight-month-old infants look longer at a video of their own faces than to those of peers and dolls (only when the video is moving; Rochat, 2003), if placed in front of a mirror, initially, infants do not show recognition of self (Meltzoff & Moore 1997). Mother's scaffolding has appeared to enhance mirror self-recognition, for example, by asking, "Who's that?" or by looking at the mirror and at the infant and pointing to direct an infant's attention (Bard et al., 2006). Generally, by age two, children have recognized themselves as physically distinct from others (e.g.,

14–18-months) and displayed self-recognition of their own mirror image (Nichols, Fox, & Mundy, 2005). Toddlers with mirror self-recognition have demonstrated higher rates of initiating joint attention at 18 months compared to same-age infants without mirror self-recognition. More optimal joint attention in the first 18 months of life has been associated with reduced risk for self-regulatory problems at 30 and 36 months in at-risk, normally developing children (Sheinkopf et al., 2004; Vaughan Van Hecke et al., 2007). Self-referent and self-aware qualities occur in episodic memory late in the second year (I, me; Bjorklund & Sellers, 2014; Howe, 2011). Nevertheless, a 3-year-old may note that it is "Jennifer" (child's own name) in a video but ask, "Why is she wearing my shirt?" (see Rochat, 2003). After viewing a three-minute-old video in which a sticker was placed on them, four- but not three-year-olds retrieved the sticker (Suddendorf & Butler, 2013; a red dot has also been used for such experiments, see Bard et al., 2006).

Caregiver–Child Interaction and Self-Awareness

Caregiver–child interaction is important to infant self-awareness. Beebe et al. (2012) observed that, in response to lower mother-coordinated engagement with an infant (e.g., mother's unchanging or "still" face), four-month-old infants showed lowered engagement predictability—a less stable rhythm of facial-visual interactive behaviors; reduced ability to anticipate his/her own moment-to-moment action tendencies; developed disorganized attachments at 12 months. Beebe inferred that, over time, this corresponded to a decreased ("destabilized") sense of self-familiarity and coherence. One future-disorganized infant produced smiles that corresponded to his mother's smiles while continuing to whimper when his mother pushed his head back and roughly smacked his hands and feet together (Beebe et al., 2012)—perhaps reflecting a need for facial-affective contingency with the mother, despite distress in response to her rough handling. Such discrepant (mother) and contradictory (child) affect may make it difficult for future-disorganized infants ultimately to know what/how they feel, or to integrate conflicting feelings—i.e., leads to difficulty "knowing and feeling known" by their mother's mind and knowing their own minds (Beebe et al., 2012, p. 14). Discrepant affect at four months has predicted contradictory behavior (approach/withdrawal) at 12 months (Beebe et al., 2012). Fonagy (2001) suggests that a parent's "minding the mind of the baby"—understanding his/her mental states, desires, needs, emotions, and intentions (reflective function)—is a necessary precondition for development of the infant's own self-awareness, affect regulation, and interpersonal understanding (Söderstrom & Skårderud, 2009).

Language and Self-Awareness

Between 18 and 30 months, infants recognize a categorical self—e.g., based on age, sex, physical characteristics, and goodness or badness (Berk, 2009). Toward the end of the second year of life, children gain language that includes labels for emotions, which assists emotional self-awareness (Hollinger, 2012). From 12 to 36 months, children begin to know and refer to themselves by name, to use pronouns "I, me, mine," and to specify personal likes, dislikes, needs, and wishes (Hollinger, 2012). This period (e.g., mirror self-awareness and use of "mine") seems to mark recognition of the self situated in a world with rules and values (Rochat, 2011; necessary to self-conscious emotions—Chapter 1). Ages two to three are well known for a toddler's self-assertion—e.g., pushes to do it her/himself; refuses to do, "No!"—suggesting self-awareness and the early move to independence (Berk, 2009).

Taking the Perspective of Others

Although many observed infant/toddler behaviors can be considered precursors to the ability for mature perspective-taking (Table 5.3), they may also demonstrate efforts at exploration and awareness of the unique properties of individuals (e.g., that adults can assist in pursuit of goals; Dice &

Dove, 2011). Young children learn to understand themselves and others as *intentional agents*, whose behavior is based on what they want, and who act deliberately to achieve goals—i.e., they do things "on purpose" (Bjorklund, 2013; Tomasello & Carpenter, 2007). This first occurs in joint attention interactions, generally possible from around nine months (Bjorklund, 2013; Tomasello & Carpenter, 2007). Approximately age one (Moll & Meltzoff, 2011), children can share and can urge joint attention—gaze-following; alternating gaze between the object and other person; directing attention by holding up and showing or pointing to objects/events until the other shares attention. Imitation is a precursor to theory of mind skills (see Gaensbauer, 2016).

The exact same physical movement may be used for giving an object, sharing it, loaning it, moving it, getting rid of it, returning it, trading it, selling it, etc., depending on a person's goals and intentions (Tomasello et al., 2005). Social learning and teaching require the observer both copy significant aspects of another's behavior and understand that the other has in mind a specific goal or intention (Bjorklund, 2013). Unlike autistic children, gradually during the first 14 months, normal children develop skills for shared intentionality—the ability to participate with others in collaborative activities with shared goals and intentions (Tomasello et al., 2005). Between 14 and 18 months, toddlers can copy and complete a behavior (even if the behavior is not completed by another), recognizing the other's intention (Meltzoff, 1995). When parents or siblings frequently refer to mental states when talking to infants, infants acquire theory of mind abilities (TOM, Glossary) more rapidly than other children (Brüne & Brüne-Cohrs, 2006; Carpendale & Lewis, 2004). TOM abilities emerge similarly across cultures. Despite shyness and lower participation, social-emotional reactivity (shyness) at 18 months has predicted TOM skills at age three (better reasoning about others' mental states; Mink, Henning, & Aschersleben, 2014; Krause & Rohlfing, 2016). Young children are unable to fully understand another's perspective, emotions, or experience—e.g., preschoolers' comments following the challenger space ship explosion showed lack of full comprehension. For example, "Somebody should have moved the clouds" or "The people [in the spaceship] went to the ocean," or "… to visit their moms" (Monaco & Gaier, 1987, p. 87).

Empathy and Helping

Perspective-taking and empathy are evident in young children's interpersonal tendencies (Burnett & Blakemore, 2009). Infants are responsive to others' emotional signals and may use them to guide behavior in ambiguous situations (Eisenberg, 2000). Empathy becomes more sophisticated in toddlers (Vaish, Carpenter, & Tomasello, 2010). Soon after age one, infants begin to make helpful gestures toward a distressed person (i.e., patting, touching; Zahn-Waxler & Radke-Yarrow, 1982), begin to understand the mental states of desire and intention and the causal relation between emotions and goals (see Brüne & Brüne-Cohrs, 2006), and can discuss, simply, their own and others' emotions (Bretherton, Fritz, Zahn-Waxler, & Ridgeway, 1986). During year 2, self-distress responses decrease and prosocial responses increase (Hutman & Dapretto, 2009). Such changes co-occur with several important milestones in cognitive development—e.g., self-recognition, agency, and awareness of other perspectives. Children ages three or four understand that desires and expectations mediate happiness and surprise reactions (Pillow, 1995). However, when asked to infer someone else's desire or belief, a child under age four usually responds according to her/his own mental state (egocentrism, Piaget & Inhelder, 1969; see Samson et al., 2010).

In observational studies, children's care for others is influenced by contextual factors—e.g., relationship to the person in distress, presence of others, salience of emotional cues, and the setting/location—e.g., more help after friendly social interactions with an adult or after synchronous music making (see Shaver et al., 2018). Helping has also been related to the type of prosocial behavior—e.g., instrumental helping such as to clean up or sharing toys/supplies; helping in emotional circumstances such as in response to a person's distress; or helping victims—one harmed by others even with no display of distress (Shaver et al., 2018). Some evidence suggests that, depending on attachment security, young children are more likely to help when there are no others present who could help (see Shaver et al., 2018). Eighteen-month-olds may spontaneously engage in helping behaviors. Waugh and Brownell (2017) found that most young toddlers (18 months) do not help during the opportunity for helping—e.g., when an adult dropped things or showed emotional distress. Characteristic of young children, they were more likely to play with toys and other items, during an emotion-based task. By 30 months, most children helped (Waugh & Brownell, 2017). Evidence links attachment relationships, modeling, and other factors (e.g., temperament) to empathy and prosociality (Kim & Kochanska, 2017). At 18 months, children's ego-resiliency (flexible, adaptable behavior) and mothers' expressive encouragement each have uniquely predicted child empathy (at 24 months; N<th.=242; Taylor et al., 2013a). Young children's empathy has positively predicted later prosocial behavior (at 72/84 months). Toddlerhood may be an important age for fostering empathy (Taylor et al., 2013a).

Attachment security with mothers has been related to higher empathy to mother's distress (not father attachment; Study 1: N=101, ages 14–80 months; Kim & Kochanska, 2017). Some evidence suggests that, generally, fathers are more punitive to negative emotions, whereas mothers encourage expression as well as emotion- and problem-focused strategies. Insecurely attached, non-empathic children were significantly less prosocial than their equally non-empathic but secure peers (second and third study; N=108, ages 15 to 45 months; 186, age 30 months; Kim & Kochanska, 2017). When helping toddlers were compared to non-helping toddlers, on an action-based helping task (adult dropped her things) and an emotion-based helping task, in both age groups (18 months, 30 months), non-helpers were more likely than helpers to exhibit wariness and to seek parent security (Waugh & Brownell, 2017). Temperament or attachment security may have played a part in responses (not assessed). Some evidence suggests that three-year-olds' prosocial behavior is mediated by the intentions/behaviors of others (Vaish, Carpenter, & Tomasello, 2010; Vaish et al., 2011). Three-year-olds protest against a person doing or attempting harm to another or their possessions/creations and are less helpful to a harming (or attempting) person than to a neutral or helpful person (e.g., puppet or adult, Vaish et al., 2011). In fact, six- and 10-month-olds take into account an individual's actions toward others when evaluating whether they are appealing or aversive—infants choose (reach for and have increased looking time toward) those who help rather than those who hinder another (Hamlin, Wynn, & Bloom, 2007).

Mirror Neurons

Mirror neurons have been identified as a part of the mechanism of imitating others, of learning, and of the later ability to reflect on and experience others' emotional states (Gallese et al., 2007; Shoemaker, 2012; Glossary; Chapter 1). For infants, while some neonatal movements may be related to basic reflexes, others seem to involve more complex, coordinated intentional movements (Casile et al., 2011). Newborns (as early as 36 hours old) spontaneously imitate basic facial emotional expressions (e.g., happy, sad, and surprised faces; Field et al., 1982; Meltzoff & Moore, 1977). Some imitation is not possible until other aspects of development are accomplished. For example, Jones (2012) found that almost no children below age two imitated bending the arm to form an elbow and moving the bent elbow laterally. Almost all children who knew the word, elbow, imitated both behaviors, demonstrating the need for some cognitive and motor competencies in order to accomplish imitation. Neural mirroring is believed to play an important role in the processing of other's actions (Endedijk et al., 2017). It is therefore considered important for social interaction, which involves action coordination, synchrony, and cooperation. Mirror neurons are involved in the processing and imitation of facial expressions (Rayson, Bonaiuto, Ferrari, & Murray, 2016). For 2.5-year-olds, the sensorimotor system is involved in both the observation and execution of facial expressions (right hemisphere lateralized for emotional; bilateral for non-emotional expressions during observation), for positive, negative and neutral faces (N=28; Rayson et al., 2016). In a study of neural mirroring and social interaction with peers, young children who showed more motor system involvement when observing a peer's actions (e.g., drumming, building) exhibited better cooperation skills with peers (N = 29, EEG study of Dutch children ages 28 months and 44 months; Endedijk et al., 2017).

Social Skills

Information relevant to social behavior was discussed in the preceding section. Infants and toddlers develop styles of interacting based, in part, on their early attachment relationships. In addition, joint attention studies show that engagement with a responsive adult enhances social and communicative development (Dice & Dove, 2011; see Synchrony, above). From a few weeks old, infants direct smiles toward the caregiver and other humans more than to inanimate objects (Burnett & Blakemore, 2009). Imitation (discussed earlier) can be seen as a way of affiliating, aligning with, and identifying with others (both dyadic and group levels; Buttelmann et al., 2013; Carpenter, Uebel, & Tomasello, 2013). Infants engage and redirect the attention of a caregiver by vocalizing or pointing (around age one; Burnett & Blakemore, 2009). Observation of 12-month-olds across 4.5 months showed development in peer relationships was reflected in language development, decreases in quarrels, play with "absent entities," and increases in caring behaviors to peers. Laughter with others was already present before 12 months (Kawakami & Takai-Kawakami, 2015). Conflict is common for toddlers (ages 21 and 25 months; more often instigated by socially outgoing and initiating toddlers; see Rubin, Bukowski, Parker, & Bowker, 2008). Toddlers often reciprocate with individuals based on their previous positive or conflictual interactions with them. By age 2.5, children may exhibit complex social tactics—e.g., teasing; lying and saving face, bravado; younger children mainly use deception for self-serving purposes such as to avoid punishment. Between ages 2–6, children learn to use social tactics flexibly in different social situations.

Conclusions

For infants and toddlers, caregiver–child interactions provide the scaffolding for development of important skills—inter-relating, self-regulation. Sensitive care, secure attachments, and early synchrony as well as environmental enrichments that provide sufficient but not overwhelming stimuli to promote growth and exploration help to provide an environment for young children's positive development. Cognizance of when to permit exploration or learning and when to intervene for the child's protection is also essential. Although children ages 0–3 exhibit the precursors to and some of the qualities of skills such as perspective-taking, the qualities exist without the cognitive or emotional understanding of an older youth or adult. Skills inter-relate—e.g., imitation and self-awareness are among the precursors of reflective function.

For traumas, other stressors, and other developmental interruptions, the attachment relationship is key to emotional healing. A parent is needed to reestablish equilibrium and buffer against stressors during and after traumas. Trauma may interrupt or waylay developmental skills (Chapter 6). Reestablished synchrony between caregiver and child may permit coping and recovery from stress. Many of the skills discussed in this chapter are important to and/or are targets of treatment (Chapter 7). Repair may be needed in a caregiver's interactional skills and/or own interfering experiences, so that s/he can ease the child into recovery and healthful development. Practices, e.g., play and rhythmic activity, are a part of brain and behavioral development and may be a part of healing.

6

Trauma and Adversity's Influence on Infants and Toddlers

Early traumas or other adversities may impair normalcy (e.g., sleep, memory, inter-relating) in significant ways that directly or indirectly undermine development and functioning. Insecure or disorganized attachment relationships with caregivers have been related to ongoing styles of interacting and a variety of problems. Pre- and post-natal stressors (e.g., poverty; family conflict) have been associated with symptoms/behaviors and/or traits (e.g., negativity) that may influence a child's self-view, vulnerability, and life trajectory. Even stressors that would not be traumatic for older individuals can change infants' brain functioning, other functioning, and well-being (e.g., parent separations; Graham et al., 2015). Traumas or other significant adversity may disrupt development and propel a young child toward problem behaviors and psychopathology through life (see Box 6.1). Tally was terrorized by her sister beginning when she was a toddler, followed by additional traumas (Box 3.2). Her early experiences shaped her school years and her adulthood, interfering with interpersonal functioning, ability to participate, and sense of safety. Gaensbauer (2002) described a young boy who was repeatedly severely abused by his father at ages 3–10 weeks. In response to adult or adolescent males approaching him (not adult women, except occasional startle reactions), he would look fearful, cry inconsolably, startle, scream, freeze, and/or hyperventilate markedly. A number of symptoms in addition to PTSD and other trauma and stressor-related disorders may result from trauma exposure—e.g., specific phobias, selective mutism with depression (Egger & Angold, 2006; Nader & Fletcher, 2014). To follow are risk factors, manifestations of trauma in children, and stressor-related and other disorders related to ages 0–3.

Risk Factors

A number of risk factors influence very young children's reactions to adversity—e.g., environments, traits, support systems.

Environmental Unpredictability

Environmental unpredictability—fluctuations in the harshness of environmental conditions—e.g., including caregiver behaviors, a high level of marital discord, or poverty—has been related to children's maladjusted behaviors or developmental lag (Simpson & Belsky, 2018; Tearne et al., 2015). Frightened or frightening parenting, such as a parent who is grieving, has unresolved trauma(s), or is traumatizing (Simpson & Belsky, 2018; Chapter 4), has been associated with

Box 6.1 Sensory Memories of Traumas

Ingrained, automatically operating pathological patterns of social behavior and affective expression can take on a life of their own and strongly shape a child's subsequent socioemotional functioning (Gaensbauer, 2016).

Audrey

At ages 3–4 years old, a girl who, at 12 months, had witnessed her mother's death from a letter bomb explosion would fall on the floor writhing around as the mother's friend was still doing when help arrived. Adopted by relatives, she exhibited poor sleep, nightmares, reactions to traumatic reminders (e.g., noise, sirens; colors—burgundy-colored spots or smears; drew this color and commented on it). Although she could not yet describe what had happened to her mother, she would suddenly appear terrified and say she was having a bad dream about her dead mommy (see Gaensbauer, 1995 for a more elaborate description).

Rachel

At age 19 months, Rachel's father shot her mother, while the mother was holding Rachel. He had first broken through a window, then broken through the neighbor's door after the mother fled there. Rachel's symptoms included withdrawal, sadness, regression, frequent crying, poor sleep, refusal to eat, separation anxiety, and violent shaking when afraid. Although symptoms dissipated over time, she reacted to reminders (e.g., blood, her grandmother's red coat, fireworks). At age four, during July 4 fireworks, she shouted out, "Stop shooting my Mommy!!" and cried uncontrollably. After neighborhood teenagers threw a rock through her window when Rachel was 11, she again had uncontrollable bouts of crying while screaming that someone was going to get her. She refused to eat, had night terrors, violently trembled, and had separation anxiety. In treatment, she avoided speaking about either of her parents and appeared not to remember the trauma (see Kaplow et al., 2006 for a more detailed description).

Eliot

From birth to age three, Eliot was exposed to domestic violence, physical abuse (e.g., head and facial trauma), chronic neglect, and three removals from caregivers. He exhibited rage, tantrums, aggression, and/or screaming (e.g., when his head was touched; during bowel movements, if looked at). He showed lack of vitality and agency. After failed treatment methods, combined therapies were used (e.g., psychotherapy, ARC, SMART). SMART began with his having stuffed animals bounce and dance on a trampoline. The therapist joined in, then Eliot jumped as well. Other physical activity followed, leading to a sense of relief and release (see Finn et al., 2017 for more details).

Note:
All case examples are disguised, may be combined cases, and have had details changed to protect individuals.

disorganized attachments, which appear to place children at increased risk for both externalizing and internalizing problems (Fearon et al., 2010; Moss, Pascuzzo, & Simard, 2012). Strong associations have been found between inter-parental conflict and PTSD symptoms (PTSS), internalizing (anxiety, depression), externalizing (delinquency, impulsivity), higher infant negative emotionality (NE; 23 healthy 6–12-month-olds), and later, greater rumination on distress (El-Sheikh, Buckhalt, Keller, & Granger, 2008; Graham et al., 2015). Early unpredictable environments have been linked to negative outcomes such as comparatively more sexual partners by age 15—directly linked and mediated by maternal depressive symptoms and maternal sensitivity, during the first five years of life (Belsky, Schlomer, & Ellis, 2012), more aggressive and delinquent behaviors, and possible criminal activities (Simpson et al., 2012).

Infant Traits

Infant traits were discussed in Chapter 5. To follow is a discussion of trauma or adversity's influence on traits, including pre-natal and post-natal influences. Genes and temperament may influence a child's responding—e.g., reactivity, proneness to depression and/or anxiety versus proneness to impulsivity and/or conduct disturbances (Chapter 4).

Pre-Natal Influences on Infant Temperament

Influences on temperament begin before birth (e.g., genetics; parent status and behaviors). Mothers with childhood adversities—e.g., family separations; parental rejection; physical, psychological, or sexual abuse—are significantly more likely to have stressful pregnancies (Agrati et al., 2015; Buist, Gotman, & Yonkers, 2011; Gutteling, de Weerth, & Buitelaar, 2005; Lim et al. 2005). For example, mother's childhood maltreatment is a risk factor for generalized anxiety during gestation, pregnancy complications, increased excretion of glucocorticoids during birth, *negative emotionality* (NE) and behavioral dysregulation in offspring, and a number of disorders (see Agrati et al., 2015; Buist et al., 2011; Bouvette-Turcot et al., 2015b; Lim et al., 2005; van Veen et al., 2013; Chapter 3). Pre-natal maternal psychological states or trait anxiety are associated with infant brain changes and temperament (difficult temperament, NE, Agrati et al., 2015; Chan, 2014; Davis et al., 2007). Mother's pre-natal depression has been related to newborns' neurobehavioral regulation—e.g., more fussing and crying as well as more sleep problems and lower ability to attend to visual and auditory stimuli (Goodman & Rouse, 2017). Higher pre-natal maternal anxiety has predicted for infants: (1) greater temperament reactivity (at eight weeks); (2) greater negative behavioral reactivity (at four months); (3) more difficult temperament (at four and six months); and (4) decreased attention regulation (three and eight months; Pluess et al., 2011); and to modified neurodevelopment in functions normally related to smiling and laughter in seven-month-olds—e.g., complex variation in COMT and cortical thinning in right ventrolateral PFC (N = 189 infants; Qiu et al., 2015; Table A4.2). In contrast, mothers who meditated before a birth had infants with better temperaments than non-meditating controls (Chan, 2014; Chapter 7).

Trait Vulnerability and Parenting

A number of characteristics have been associated with problematic outcomes for young children. As will be discussed (The Pre-Natal Period), studies have shown that fearlessness at age two has been associated with higher conduct problems and callous-unemotional traits at age 13 (see Zhang et al., 2018b). Negative emotions (NE; e.g., anger) have been related to negative outcomes as well. Infants and toddlers with NE have been studied for their increased sensitivity to their environments (positive or negative) and for outcomes over time (Chapter 5; see Glossary—behavioral inhibition). Increased sensitivity to environments has meant increased vulnerability to environmental stressors.

For example, children with increased stress sensitivity have tended to have less secure attachments than comparisons when mothers were less sensitive/responsive and more secure attachments when they were more sensitive/responsive, whereas some evidence has shown that the association between security and sensitivity has been non-significant for children with low stress reactivity (Vaughn & Bost, 2018; some findings have been mixed). Reactive children have benefitted more from training their mothers (see Chapter 10—INSIGHTS). Evidence also has shown that sensitive maternal care has moderated the effects of infant fear reactivity—e.g., smaller increases in reactivity than fearful infants with less sensitive mothers (see Vaughn & Bost, 2018). Less sensitive care has been related to greater stress reactivity and emotionality. Some evidence has shown that, at age 24 months, maternal controlling behaviors related to negative emotional distress for boys but not girls, which may confirm that girls are socialized to suppress negative emotions (see Smith & Day, 2018). However, Smith and Day found, for both genders, higher levels of anger were associated with more externalizing for toddlers into the preschool years (N = 140, age 30–36 months and two years later; Smith & Day, 2018). Early high anger has been shown to persist and may interfere with use of emotion regulation strategies. Children at risk for externalizing have had difficulties dealing with negative emotions.

Supporting differential susceptibility to environments (Chapter 4), infants high in NE assessed at age nine months and 27 months showed lower levels of dysregulation when in a more supportive co-parenting context and higher levels of dysregulation (e.g., sleep, eating, behavior, emotions) within less supportive co-parenting contexts (Altenburger et al., 2017). Evidence suggests that dysregulation may persist. In this study, supportive co-parenting was not relevant to dysregulation for infants low in NE at nine months. For older children, studies have suggested vulnerability to greater trauma symptoms for children with NE (Weems et al., 2007). One study showed that positive parenting—i.e., specifically support for autonomy—may buffer against at least one of trauma's potential effects, on inhibitory control. For example, in both maltreated and non-maltreated groups, temperamentally negative children whose mothers provided higher levels of warm autonomy support exhibited greater inhibitory control, like low-negative children (other outcomes not assessed; Cipriano-Essel, Skowron, Stifter, & Teti, 2013; see Box 8.2).

Autonomy support has been important for children with behavioral inhibition (BI) as well (Box 8.2; shares traits with NE, Glossary; Table A5.1). Infants at age 4 months who show motor agitation and distress in response to unfamiliar smells, sounds, or sights have exhibited higher levels of BI by 14 months (Henderson, Pine, & Fox, 2015). Such infants have shown sensitivity to novelty in an exaggerated startle reaction at nine months—a brain-stem mediated defensive reflex. Toddlers who are *behaviorally inhibited* are slow to approach unfamiliar stimuli (e.g., objects, people) and instead remain in close proximity to caregivers (Henderson et al., 2015; Chapter 9). Children rated as consistently high in BI between age 14 months and age seven have had significantly higher risk of social or other anxiety disorder in adolescence.

Traumas and pre- or post-natal family conflict each have been associated with young children's difficult temperaments. For example, mother-rated difficult temperament was linked to intimate partner violence and to the mother's own history of childhood abuse and neglect (birth to 23 months; Casanueva et al., 2010). From a community sample, three-year-olds' chronic irritability predicted depression, ODD, and greater functional impairment at age six (over and above baseline psychopathology; see Dougherty et al., 2015). In the same group, age nine, difficult temperament predicted anxiety disorders (e.g., current and persistent GAD), current separation anxiety, disruptive behaviors symptoms or disorders, ADHD symptoms or disorders, depressive symptoms, functional impairment, and treatment use (N = 541 age three; then at age nine, N = 446; after controlling for baseline anxiety disorder; Dougherty et al., 2015). Childhood GAD has predicted the poorest long-term outcomes.

Trauma and Parenting

Attachment relationships influence outcomes and recovery from early stressors, including traumas, and shape how such experiences are incorporated into a developing autobiographical narrative (Coates, 2016; Kelly & Bailey, 2012). For infants, primary experiences of threat include the threat of caregiver separation or lack of response to infant distress signaling (Table 6.1). Infants have limited assessment and coping capacities on their own. The experience of threat is often closely related to a caregiver's affective signals and availability rather than to the actual degree of threat posed by potentially traumatic events (Lyons-Ruth, Dutra, Schuder, & Bianchi, 2006). Secure early attachments and/or sensitive parenting may reduce the likelihood or levels of negative outcomes from trauma or from problematic traits (e.g., negativity, Boldt, Kochanska, & Jonas, 2017).

Trauma Exposure and Parenting Signals

The severity of a child's exposure and parental stress in response to the exposure or injury each have been predictors of young children's reactions. Infants and young children rely on parents to interpret the valence and seriousness of experiences. While the severity of a young child's injury (e.g., burn; fall out of a car) influences severity of her/his stress reaction, it may do so, at least in part, indirectly via severity of the mother's reactions (not fathers; Haag & Landolt, 2017). That is, the more injured the child, the more distressed the mother. In turn, mother's reactions may increase a young child's distress. For example, Sam said he panicked when the car door flew open and his three-year-old daughter fell out of the moving car. She appeared to have enjoyed the roll down into the ditch, until she saw his face and started to cry. For young burned children (N = 138, ages 1–4; Haag & Landolt, 2017), mothers' but not fathers' acute stress reactions mediated between exposure severity and children's reactions.

As will be discussed (age-related chapters), both parents and children may be affected by children's exposures to traumas (Breidenstine et al., 2011). Both may be traumatized by the event, and there is evidence of a bidirectional influence of parents' and children's symptoms on each other. Children who have not been directly traumatized may be affected by parents' traumas (Sichari, Wakhungu, & Maragia, 2015; e.g., holocaust, Lyons-Ruth & Jacobvitz, 2018; parent PTSD, Brand et al., 2011). A child's ability to recover from the effects of traumatic events is greatly influenced by the quality of caregiver–child attachments and by a parent's ability to respond sensitively to a child's traumatic reactions (Breidenstine et al., 2011; Lieberman, 2004).

Parenting and Treatment

In addition to using the caregiver–infant dyad to assist recovery, treatment must address trauma's influence on caregiver and parenting. For example, new mothers generally show some soothing

Table 6.1 Manifestations of Distress in Infants

Manifestations of Distress (Bowlby, 1969/1982)

- contact-eliciting behaviors (smiling, reaching, gazing, friendly tones)
- protestation (unfriendly utterances or desperate crying)
- distress (persistent fretting, crying excessively, clinging, disturbed eating, and restless or fitful sleep)
- emotionless silence and withdrawal (resignation; detachment; resuming normal activities and learning self-reliance)

Sensorimotor disorganization and disruption to biological rhythms (Lieberman & Van Horn, 2005)

- prolonged crying; difficulty being comforted; muscular irregularity—e.g., flailing, rigidity; eating and/or sleep disturbances; restlessness; agitation skills initially and become better at handling crying, at recognizing differences in reasons for crying, and at using more successful soothing methods, by the time the child is three months old (studied at 6–8, then 12–14 weeks; N = 15; Kurth et al., 2014). Additionally, they learn to assess and mitigate their personal stress reactions with more realistic expectations and with self-soothing. Experienced mothers know that the infant will cry less over time (Kurth et al., 2014). Trauma can cause regressions and other changed behaviors in infants and young children, as well as disrupt maternal confidence in her ability to handle what may be normal behaviors for a younger infant. Hence, mother's self-soothing and infant soothing may become disturbed.

Bidirectional Impact of Trauma: Parent and Child

Parents are often, directly or indirectly, affected by children's traumas. Across trauma types, children with more maladaptive posttrauma outcomes—e.g., PTS, internalizing, externalizing problems—often have caregivers and families with greater problems—parental symptoms; dysfunctional family patterns (Scheeringa & Zeanah, 2001). This suggests a bidirectional impact of trauma on parent–child dyads (Scheeringa, Myers, Putnam, & Zeanah, 2015). Parents' and children's symptoms have correlated robustly in some studies (Feldman & Vengrober, 2011; Scheeringa et al., 2015). Some evidence suggests that parent and child symptoms correlate more over time but not proximal to traumas (Scheeringa et al., 2015). For example, studies have shown no correlations between child and parent symptoms/problems three or six months posttrauma, but significant correlations nine or 30 months after (Laor et al., 1997—for ages three and four but not 5). Correlating symptoms also may be influenced by shared genetics.

When young children and caregivers are exposed to the same event (e.g., war, natural disaster), evidence suggests parallel physiological stress markers (e.g., cortisol; salivary alpha-amylase, sAA, Glossary; Feldman, Vengrober, Eidelman-Rothman, & Zagoory-Sharon, 2013b; Ruttle et al., 2011). For children ages 1–5 near the Gaza border (N = 232), war-exposed children had different stress responses (cortisol and sAA) and more negative emotional reactions to fear elicitation than unexposed children (Feldman et al., 2013b). Mothers of war-exposed children reported more PTSD symptoms, were less reciprocal during interactions, and had higher cortisol and sAA. At each assessment (baseline, after challenge, and recovery), exposed-no-PTSD children had the highest levels of cortisol and consistently high sAA—generally associated with lower adaptation, and higher internalizing and externalizing symptoms (El-Sheikh et al., 2008). Exposed-no-PTSD children used more approach, comfort seeking strategies for emotion regulation and had more reciprocal mothers. Children with PTSD exhibited hypo-cortisolism and more withdrawal strategies (Feldman et al., 2013b; Gunnar & Vazquez, 2001; Pfeffer, Altemus, Heo, & Jiang, 2007; Chapter 4—trauma-related stress reactivity). Maternal cortisol, PTSS, low reciprocity (caregiver–child), and negative emotionality have predicted child cortisol levels during ongoing stress conditions (see Feldman et al., 2013b).

Studies have reported mixed results related to parenting's impact on the long-term outcomes of children's PTS symptoms (Scheeringa et al., 2015). Relatively small studies have sometimes suggested that parenting mediates the effects of trauma (e. g., war; domestic violence) on children's reactions—e.g., PTSD; problem behaviors; depression (Feldman & Vengrober, 2011; Levendosky & Graham-Bermann, 2001); other studies have not confirmed such a link (see Levendosky et al., 2003; Scheeringa et al., 2015). When observational methods were used, age 1–5 war-exposed children's PTSD was linked to low maternal sensitivity and increased caregiver symptoms (higher PTSD, depression, and anxiety symptoms, Feldman & Vengrober, 2011). For children and caregivers, both with marked levels of initial PTSD after trauma exposure (a variety of different types of trauma), some evidence suggests that parenting may be affected more strongly by children's symptoms than by mother's symptoms (prospective study; N = 62, T1; N = 35, T2; multiple methods—e.g., observation, Scheeringa et al., 2015; children traumatized between ages one and six).

Different parenting skills—e.g., being able to interact warmly with child in a structured lab task; to talk warmly about children; or to manage distressed child—may influence outcomes. Differences also exist for disengaged, authoritarian, authoritative, and permissive parenting (Glossary)—e.g., depressed mothers showed both more authoritarian and disengaged parenting (e.g., Pelaez, Field, Pickens, & Hart, 2008). Their toddlers less often followed their instructions, more often showed aggressive play behaviors, and had more time not-on-task and less on-task than other toddlers. In addition, for infants and young children, anomalous parenting (Glossary; e.g., frightening parenting; Chapter 5) is associated with a four times greater likelihood of disorganized attachment which in turn is linked to problems in cognitive, behavioral, and socioemotional development—e.g., dissociation, depression, anxiety, behavior problems (Becker-Weidman, 2009; see Beebe et al., 2012; Briere et al., 2017). Depressed mothers have also shown more negative parenting (Parenting, above), which has been related to increased psychopathology and more social withdrawal as well as to lower baseline cortisol levels and less decrease in cortisol over the course of a stressful experience (e.g., testing situation; Apter-Levi et al., 2016). In turn, social withdrawal in infants and preschool children has predicted more social-emotional problems and psychopathology. Low baseline cortisol also predicted low empathy.

Parents' Own Trauma Histories

Parents' own childhood adversity has diminished the quality of their interactions with offspring, which may result in young children's vulnerabilities (see Chapters 4, 5; e.g., Ahnert et al., 2017)—e.g., the lowest levels of maternal sensitivity were found in mothers with high levels of early adversity and a variant of vasopressin (AVPR1A gene; Apter-Levi et al., 2014). Some evidence suggests that fathers' histories of adversity have been related to hyper-excretion of AVP—related to differential activation of the amygdala, a marker for parental attunement to the infant's emotional state (see Chapter 5—synchrony). As noted (Chapter 5), fathers with adverse childhoods or with preterm babies have scored significantly lower on quality of play with infants and young toddlers (Ahnert et al., 2017).

Manifestations of Trauma in Young Children's Memory and Behavior

Traumatized young children can retain internal representations of traumatic experiences for months or years, demonstrated in trauma-specific behavioral reenactments, affective responses to traumatic triggers/reminders, sensory and somatic symptoms, expressive play, and verbal recall (Gaensbauer & Jordan, 2009; Nader, 2008; Peterson & Rideout, 1998; examples to follow in Trauma and Memory—e.g., man with heel pain when stressed was pricked in the heel as neonate; three-year-old stabbed in infancy; Coates, 2016). For example, young children treated in an emergency room for injuries were interviewed days and months after treatment (6, 12, and 18 or 24 months; N = 36; Peterson & Rideout, 1998). The youngest children (ages 12–18 months) showed little long-term verbal recall, while a few children in the middle group (20–25 months), who could not narrate about the event at time of injury, verbally recalled the event 18 months later. Most of the oldest children (26–34 months; able to provide a narrative at time of injury) demonstrated good verbal recall two years later—i.e., were fully able to recall important aspects of experience (e.g., what happened, treatment given). Nevertheless, preverbal children may retain somatic memories of events (next section). Also, among important issues for treating young children is a young child's vulnerability to suggestion (Gilstrap 2004; Peterson, Dowden, & Tobin, 1999; Siegel, 1996).

Infant Distress

Living in close association increases the likelihood of survival (evolutionary theory, see Simpson & Belsky, 2018). Infants use *signaling behaviors* (e.g., vocalizing, smiling), *aversive behaviors* (e.g., crying, screaming), and *active behaviors* (e.g., approaching, following) in order to maintain contact or proximity to a caregiver (Simpson & Belsky, 2018). Attachment theory focuses attention on the survival-oriented behaviors of infant and caregiver dyads. First, *protest* (e.g., crying, screaming, tantrums) to draw the caregiver's attention (Bowlby 1969/1982; Table 6.1). If protest does not bring the caregiver, it is followed by *despair* (e.g., decline in movement, silence) that might prevent accidental injury or attracting predators. When there is still no reuniting with a caregiver, *detachment* ensues—resumption of normal activities and learning to behave independently and self-reliantly (reorganization in adults; Bowlby 1969/1982; Simpson & Belsky, 2018). Even very young infants (e.g., 0–2 months) show responses to pain and the ability for both instrumental and classical conditioning (Gaensbauer & Jordan, 2009; see burned hand case in Trauma and Self-Regulation, to follow). Hence, they can experience stress reactions and can pair them with accompanying stimuli. Infants are unable to verbally express feelings; they respond with sensorimotor disorganization and disruption to biological rhythms—e.g., prolonged crying; difficulty being comforted; muscular irregularity–e.g., flailing, rigidity; eating and/or sleep disturbances; restlessness; agitation (Lieberman & Van Horn, 2005). Infants with trauma or stress histories may be easily over-aroused and difficult to soothe (Graham et al., 2015; Pluess et al., 2011; Ribaudo, 2016) or may withdraw and avoid interaction (Ribaudo, 2016). Infants who witness threats to caregivers may later become fearful or aggressive.

As demonstrated in behaviors of young children following the 9/11 terrorist attacks in 2001, very young children may either make their distress known or withdraw. During the attacks, young children were described as *cooperative and calm*—e.g., permitting a mask over the face; as *quieter than usual*—perhaps withdrawn; as *difficult*—e.g., screaming, kicking, noncompliant; or as *fearful*—e.g., separation anxiety; frozen or dazed; "white-as-a-sheet" (N = 67 parents; 104 children under age six; Nov. 2001 to May 2002; Klein, DeVoe, Miranda-Julian, & Linas, 2009). On the day of the attacks, they had sleep (excessive) and eating disturbances (poor eating), increased arousal and irritability (e.g., tantrums), and/or increased motor activity—e.g., running around uncontrollably (see Klein et al., 2009 for details). Over the next months, young children displayed sadness—e.g., over loss of objects/places, areas of activities, routines. They showed increased clinginess; separation anxiety; fearfulness; irritability/crankiness (sometimes, loss of even-temper); low frustration tolerance; crying; tantrums. They had persistent sleep disturbances; nightmares. They showed new fears—e.g., of noise; recurrence of falling buildings; TV show watched during event; the dark; being alone; dust or smoke—or showed renewal of old fears. Trait differences were evident in some symptom manifestations—e.g., while many children became anxious about not being constantly near a parent, one child became distressed even upon leaving a newly met friend. Media images might trigger fear that an event was happening again. One year later, for children ages 0–5 within a mile (or closer) of the 9/11 attacks, child PTSD symptoms significantly associated with in-person exposures, to parental reactions, and to previous traumas as well as with negative parenting changes and increased couple tension since the event (DeVoe, Klein, Bannon, & Miranda-Julian, 2011).

Somatic Memories

Traumatic memories from infancy may be held in nonconscious, nonverbal memory connected to body locations, rather than as accessible, episodic memories that can be verbalized. When they are later remembered, young children may describe indirectly or use non-literal descriptions. For example, for Laura, who had endured painful medical procedures at age three months (Bernstein & Blacher, 1967 in Coates, 2016), construction in the house next door triggered distress (like the construction in the hospital during her procedures; hammering was a traumatic reminder). Young children may regress or may be precocious after traumas—e.g., dream, play, or understand like an older child. In contrast to normal children, traumatized children may begin to have dreams more

Box 6.2 Precocious Dreaming

Young children may have nightmares (general scary dreams or dreams about the trauma) or night terrors after traumas (e.g., running for safety or enacting aspects of the trauma, without memory of the episode; Nader, 2008).

Following numerous hospital procedures, Lonnie, age three, described elaborate dreams of trying to get away from the "cutters"—people who were coming to cut her (see Nader, 2008 for more detail).

Five-year-old Dawnesha's older brother was on the playground when a shooter started shooting at children. Her brother ran off, thinking she was right behind him. She looked everywhere for him and couldn't find him, thinking he was shot. She finally ran home and found him there. She frequently checked on him to make sure he was safe and alive, including during the night. For a week, while still asleep, she ran through the house, screaming, as though to get away from something.

David, a five-year-old boy with relapsed leukemia, dreamed repeatedly of scary spacemen coming to take him to their planet. In his later dreams, he developed a comfortable relationship with them. He died a few months later [© Nader, 2008; Nader K (2008). *Understanding and Assessing Trauma in Children and Adolescents: Measures, Methods, and Youth in Context.* New York: Routledge. Reproduced/extracted by permission of Taylor and Francis Group, LLC, a division of Informa plc].

Note:
All case examples are disguised, may be combined cases, and have had details changed to protect individuals.

like those of older children (Nader, 2008; Box 6.2). Between ages three and seven, children normally report few dreams when awakened from REM sleep, and dreams contain few human characters (Foulkes, 1990; Foulkes, Hollifield, Sullivan, Bradley, & Terry, 1990). At age three, when Laura wakened screaming from sleep (as she had in hospital as an infant), she suggested that her dolly was not sleeping, because the man who was knocking might knock her head off. When her mother asked what had happened in the hospital, she said that the man stuck her in the "tushie" and knocked off her head—meaning that he gave her a headache (see Coates, 2016).

Gaensbauer has assessed, in play therapy sessions, the memories of children who had experienced different levels of trauma in the preverbal period (ages 3–15 months; e.g., Gaensbauer, 2002, N = 3). Even though they were not told any details of their experiences, the children were able to convey accurate sensory and somatic details of the trauma, behaviorally and verbally, when provided with the means to represent and reenact the trauma (Box 6.1). Hence, children who were traumatized as infants may not consciously remember their experiences but may reenact them or have body experiences related to them (Coates, 2016; Ribaudo, 2016). Thus, interventions include enhancing the efforts of an attuned, nurturing caregiver who can soothe the child's affective overload as well as assist in deriving meaning of a child's reactivity, pain, distress, and/or dissociation, until the child's understanding or sense of mastery emerges (Ribaudo, 2016). For the child described at the beginning of this chapter (Gaensbauer, 2002), after six months in foster care his symptoms reduced with foster family members but not with strangers.

Trauma in Toddlers

Toddlers or preschoolers may be able to flee or fight in response to traumas or may try—e.g., the five-year-old who ran to the kitchen for a knife and tried to stab the man who was strangling his

Box 6.3 Age and Relationship Differences in Reactions to Inter-Parental Violence

Trevor Noah, a well-known comedian, described growing up during and after apartheid in South Africa. His often-drunk stepfather's abuse started when he was nine and his half-brother, Andrew, was an infant (Noah, 2017). Andrew could only cry and scream. Trevor learned to recognize the warning signs and never to let his stepfather get between him and a door. He would run away to be safe. Until age 25, Trevor had nightmares about the look on his stepfather's face. Trevor's stepfather never beat his first-born son, Andrew. Andrew put himself between his father and mother sometimes, and once was nearly injured by a flying object. The police sided with the husband—a well-liked, "nice guy" when he wasn't drunk or angry. When he learned that his stepfather shot his mother, Trevor responded with rage and pain. Fourteen-year-old Andrew responded by feeling helpless—he loved his father. Likely without understanding the permanence of death, their 4-year-old younger brother asked his father why he killed mom, and told him that he shouldn't kill mom (see Noah, 2017 for details). A child that age might look for and ask where the mother was a little later, perhaps because he wanted her to make him something to eat.

mother (Nader, 2008). They can use symbolic play and often simple verbalizations about experiences (Lieberman & Van Horn, 2005; Nader, 2008; Nader & Pynoos, 1991; Terr, 1981; Webb, 2002). Toddlers or preschoolers may seek to understand causality and may be prone to self-blame. They may be torn between loving/needing and fearing a parent (Chapter 5—self-awareness; Box 6.3). Symptoms may include recklessness, which may reflect, e.g., posttrauma arousal, impulsivity, or reenactment; a secure base distortion subtype; accident proneness, which may reflect, e.g., poor sleep; body dissociation; precocious competence, withdrawal, and/or inhibition of exploration that may relate to PTS withdrawal or avoidance (Lieberman & Van Horn, 2005; Nader, 2008; Ribaudo, 2016). Coates (2016) described a boy she treated from ages 2–8 (saw again at age 22). At two years old, he had been repeatedly terrorized by his mother—shaking him hard with her hands around his neck. At age three, he was aggressive with his peers. At age four, he said that his neck became hot and cold when his guinea pigs fought; his parents said he turned white. At age 22, when a violent movie scene was impending, his neck would become very weak and he had to hold it up—he demonstrated the exact position of his mother's hands when she had scared him.

Young children (ages 3–4) are able to provide highly accurate, although sometimes sparse information in free recall of an event (see Nader, 2008; Nigro & Wolpow, 2004). After traumas, toys and toy-like replicas permit the child to demonstrate the traumatic experience or its episodic segments (see Nader, 2008). Physical props have consistently increased the volume of information provided by young children (Nigro & Wolpow, 2004). Such props may serve as both memory-retrieval cues and aids to communication for emotionally difficult information. Toys/replicas can provide an indirect method of communication for reluctant or guarded youth and even for older youth (Nader, 2008). As discussed, play may be a method of trauma reenactment. However, if toys signal that pretense is an acceptable mode, it may affect younger children's recall or enactment of events. In contrast to toys provided to aid young children's play, learning, and/or development, in treatment, if too few toys are provided, it may suggest that the child follow a specific theme rather than permitting the child to choose a theme (Pellegrini, 2001).

The Stress Response System—Pre- and Post-Natal Effects

Sensitive periods are developmental periods when environmental influences may have profound effects on development (Chapter 1; Goff & Tottenham, 2014). Periods of rapid growth of neuronal connections followed by selective elimination (pruning)—ages 0–3 (right hemisphere) and adolescence (PFC and its connections with other regions)—are sensitive periods of brain development (Blakemore & Choudhury, 2006; see Nader, 2008; Schore, 2003; Siegel, 2003). For example, compared to children with late childhood brain injuries, children injured in infancy and preschool have had lower nonverbal abilities and processing speeds (Crowe et al., 2012, Table 6.2). From the pre-natal stage through 24 months is believed to be a crucially important determinant in human trajectory, influencing later health, development, and learning (Britto, 2013). Of course, variables

Table 6.2 Infancy to Age 3: Brain Development

BRAIN—high rate of brain growth in 1st year of life

- **Activity**—subcortical regions predominate (continues, for the first 3 years)
  - no activity in prefrontal cortex (PFC)
  - minimal activity in sensorimotor areas of the cortex
  - lower centers are active—infants can use all senses to respond to stimuli with emotions
- **Growth**—experience-dependent growth and maintenance (*use it or lose it*)
  - repeated patterns of emotion, behavior, and interaction build neural connections in the brain
  - frequent use is related to persistence and strength of synaptic connections
  - connections selectively pruned as a result of inactivity
  - higher-quality parenting and an enriched environment contribute to brain development
- **Brain Regions**—all brain regions grow from 3–13 months
  - putamen—important to learning-anterior temporal lobe sharply increases to age 2 (e.g., semantic memory; includes amygdala)
  - cerebellar hemisphere/total cerebellum—important in motor activity, cognitive and emotional processing
    - may be particularly vulnerable in infancy due to rapid growth and decrease with pruning
    - shift from larger left cerebrum to larger right, after 1st year of life (spatial and motor learning processing)
  - rightward hippocampal asymmetry in infants (episodic and spatial memory)
  - slower growth in amygdala (emotion and memory) and hippocampus (memory consolidation; full volume age 7–11)
    - very early development may be a critical period for hippocampus development and its connectivity
    - in utero or at birth changes in hippocampus and its connectivity, e.g., to PFC, linked to schizophrenia
  - a few gender differences
    - Males: smaller caudate volumes (also for ADHD; may contribute to ADHD) (learning; memory processing)
    - smaller cerebellar vermis volumes (also in autism) (maintains equilibrium; coordinates speech and movement)
- **Trauma** (e.g., with chronic, unregulated affective and somatosensory-motor experiences)
  - linked to hippocampal volume reduction in adults
  - may lead to SNS hyperarousal and long-term symptoms—e.g., sleep disturbance, chronic pain, muscle tension, panic, chronic rage, weakness, exhaustion, concentration problems
  - simultaneous activation of PNS and SNS may result in dissociative freeze response
    - activation of dorsal vagal branch of PNS—hyperarousal symptoms (e.g., muscle weakness, depression, chronic fatigue, gastro-intestinal symptoms, analgesic effects in the face of mortal danger)
  - chronic states of alert to danger
    - compromised flow of information between hemispheres
    - activation of right brain areas—emotion related
    - deactivation of left brain regions—communication
    - compromise of corpus callosum—intercommunication

Reference examples: Bernier et al., 2016; Brotman et al., 2008; Choe et al., 2013; Gilmore et al., 2007, 2011; Lipton & Fosha, 2011; Schore, 2001, 2003; Table A4.2.

that influence any mental health or health outcome often combine with other risk factors and vary by age (Nader, 2008). Nevertheless, although depression—a disorder associated with trauma—has been linked to genetics as well as early life adversity (Goff & Tottenham, 2014; Heim et al., 2008), early adversity has had a substantial role in depression beyond genetic influences (Francis et al., 1999; Goff & Tottenham, 2014)—e.g., deprivation and separation from caregivers are linked to a three to four times greater chance of depression than for no experiences that exceed coping abilities (Gunnar & Quevedo, 2007; Goff & Tottenham, 2014; Heim et al., 2008). HPA axis altered function has been linked to increased vulnerability to depression.

The Stress System: 0–3

Early traumatic stress has been related to infant brain function (Daniels, Frewen, McKinnon, & Lanius, 2011; Table 6.2). Traumas may result in an overactive stress response system (HPA axis reactivity) and in underdeveloped brain regions (e.g., hippocampus—related to memory; frontal cortex—e.g., cognitive function; Bremner, 2003; Nader, 2008; Sapolsky, 2000; van der Kolk, 2003). For example, some evidence suggests that children sexually or physically maltreated in the first five years of life have been more likely than those maltreated after the first five years to experience internalizing symptoms and limbic HPA axis dysregulation (also neglected or emotionally abused; see De Bellis, Woolley, & Hooper, 2013). Severity and cumulative traumas have been associated with HPA dysregulation, externalizing, and/or EF deficits (see De Bellis et al., 2013; Ford & Delker, 2018).

Although glucocorticoids (see Glossary; cortisol) are important for normal fetal development, either suppressed or heightened glucocorticoid levels can impair brain development, before birth as well as after (Otte et al., 2015). The HPA axis is critical in regulating cognitive, immune, and behavioral responses to stress (Kuhlman, Vargas, Geiss, & Lopez-Duran, 2016). For example, data suggest a critical period during which brain exposure to corticosterone (triggered by HPA axis response) influences fear learning, modulated by the quality of maternal care (Gillespie et al., 2009; Nader & Fletcher, 2014). The stress response system may be disrupted before or after birth.

Stressors in the Pre-Natal Period

Although affected by multiple factors—e.g., timing of exposure; maternal–fetal endocrine milieu; regulation of endocrine exposures (Glynn & Sandman, 2011), the intra-uterine brain is affected by stress, chaos, trauma, conflict, and poor attachment relationships (e.g., Perry, 2009). Progressively as gestation advances, women become less sensitive to environmental perturbations; thus, exposure to adversity may be less likely to shape development as time passes. For example, anxiety during early but not later pregnancy influences gray matter volumes (Buss et al., 2010). Both more total trauma exposure and early exposure have been related to slower recovery from acute stress (Kuhlman et al., 2016). Followed prenatally to age 14 (ages 2, 5, 8, 10, 14; N = 2900; Tearne et al., 2015), children exposed to adverse pre-natal environments—e.g., poverty, gestational hypertension, stressful events during pregnancy, mother's non-completion of high school—showed higher overall, internalizing, and externalizing problem scores. Studies have shown that fearlessness at age two after exposure to mothers' pre-natal stress was associated with more conduct problems and callous-unemotional traits at age 13 (see Zhang et al., 2018b).

Maternal negative mood states in pregnancy are linked to various cognitive, behavioral, and emotional disturbances in offspring (Egliston, McMahon, & Austin, 2007). When pregnant mothers are stressed—e.g., due to anxiety, relationship discord or conflict, natural disasters—a portion of glucocorticoids pass through the placenta to the fetus (Lupien et al., 2009; Sekl, 2007). For mothers with high cortisol during pregnancy, babies were delivered earlier, had lower birthweight/size, and had greater reactivity to stress at ages six months (Lyons-Ruth, Wolfe, & Lyubchik, 2000), five years (Gutteling, de Weerth, & Buitelaar, 2005), and 10 years (O'Connor et al., 2005)—e.g., increased basal HPA axis activity (Lupien et al., 2009). The infants showed more crying, fussing, and negative facial expressions (de Weerth, van Hees, & Buitelaar, 2003); had more difficult temperaments (with more emotion and activity; de Weerth et al., 2003); and later had more affective problems (mediated by increased right amygdala volume in girls at age seven, Buss et al., 2010). Among changes associated with pre-natal stress are inconsiderate behaviors, ADHD, and sleep disturbances as well as poor adult health and some psychiatric disorders—e.g., depressive symptoms, drug abuse, and mood and anxiety disorders; criminality; schizophrenia; other severe emotional disturbances; and social withdrawal (Egliston et al., 2007). Effects may not emerge until adolescence or adulthood (Halligan et al., 2007; Lupien et al., 2009; Nader & Fletcher, 2014).

Stressors in Infancy

The developing central nervous system has proven highly sensitive to glucocorticoids (Glossary; see Andiarena et al., 2017). Repeated exposure to stress hormones during development has a negative effect on brain growth in affected regions (e.g., limbic regions) with potentially neurotoxic effects—on neuronal migration, myelination, and neurogenesis, with consequent reduced dendritic spines (Glossary; gray and white matter connectivity, Dackis et al., 2012; Table 6.2). At moderate levels, glucocorticoids may enhance hippocampal-dependent cognitive processes (e.g., declarative memory); high levels may damage the hippocampus (Bernard, Butzin-Dozier, Rittenhouse, & Dozier, 2010). Even cortisol in breast milk may influence infant development—e.g., toward inhibited personality (see Kuhlman et al., 2016; Table A5.3).

Early life stress may variably influence longer-term neurodevelopment by gender—e.g., greater hippocampal stress sensitivity and higher risk for depression in girls (see Andiarena et al., 2017). Recent research has shown that girls' cortisol levels at 14 months were negatively associated with age four cognitive development—long-term declarative memory; executive function and gross motor development—whereas boys' cortisol levels were negatively associated with age four socioemotional development (e.g., autistic-like behaviors; N = 186; Andiarena et al., 2017). Salivary alpha-amylase (sAA; Glossary) positively linked to aspects of socioemotional development in four-year-old boys only—i.e., hyperactivity symptoms, inattention, social competence and autistic-like behaviors. For CPS-involved 0–3-year-olds, foster placement has appeared to provide a regulating influence on cortisol levels—less perturbation of diurnal patterns than children remaining with parents (Bernard et al., 2010).

Stress Sensitivity. Stress exposure in infancy may be one pathway to increased stress sensitivity (Belsky & Pluess, 2009; Boyce & Ellis, 2005; Del Giudice et al., 2011). Increased reactivity has been linked to vulnerability to mood and anxiety disorders (see Nader & Fletcher, 2014)—e.g., stressors such as maternal separation or parental conflict in infancy may result in hypersensitivity to stress and a predisposition to internalizing (via dysregulation of HPA axis activation, Kuhlman et al., 2016). Early post-natal life is a critical period for immune maturation as well (Sui-Ling et al., 2013).

Long-Term Effects. During the third trimester of pregnancy and the first two years of life, the brain undergoes great growth and developmental changes, including marked neurogenesis, synaptogenesis, and neural circuit formation. Excessive exposure to glucocorticoids can interfere with growth (Lagercrantz, 2016). During this period, glucocorticoids have been shown to influence later cognitive ability (e.g., visual working memory) and behavior, to augment neuroendocrine responsiveness to stress, to stunt body growth, and to lead to development of adult diseases—e.g., visceral fat or metabolic syndrome X (Glossary), type II diabetes, and cardiovascular manifestations of atherosclerosis (Kaldy & Sigala, 2004; Perlman et al., 2007; Chapter 3).

Normally, by age one, the HPA axis has become socially regulated and hypo-responsive, protecting a developing infant from damaging effects of excess glucocorticoids (see Kuhlman et al.,

2016). Stressors in infancy may interfere with development of a normal cortisol hypo-responsive phase and result in excess exposure to glucocorticoids, with developmental and long-term consequences (poor health; psychopathology; Kuhlman et al., 2016; Shonkoff et al., 2012)—e.g., Kuhlman et al. found that trauma before age one leads to HPA axis dysregulation measurable in adolescence.

Cortisol Slope

Cortisol is normally high in the morning—it is energizing. Low morning cortisol may include fatigue. Childhood trauma is a significant risk factor for chronic fatigue syndrome—e.g., six-fold increased likelihood for child-abused adults with low salivary cortisol (Heim et al., 2009). Cortisol is normally low at bedtime. High bedtime cortisol may interfere with sleep (e.g., shorter and poorer-quality sleep, El-Sheikh et al., 2008). Compared to low-risk children, children exposed to adversity have shown significantly flatter slopes of cortisol production across the day rather than the normally steep slope (high morning, low bedtime; Dozier, Meade, & Bernard, 2014). Children living with high-risk parents (i.e., maltreating) have shown the flattest slopes with lowest morning cortisol values and highest bedtime levels (ages 2.9–31.4 months). Sensitive and supportive care of early fostered children has normalized basal glucocorticoid levels after only 10 weeks in foster care (Gunnar & Quevedo, 2007). Children in foster care have shown intermediate waking and daytime levels; and low-risk children have shown the steepest slopes and highest wake-up values (Bernard et al., 2010). Across studies, a significant link has been found between flatter diurnal cortisol slopes and poorer physical (e.g., inflammation) and mental health (e.g., stress sensitivity) outcomes, with effects cascading over time (Adam et al., 2017). For example, a blunted cortisol pattern has been linked to later psychiatric disorders and problem behaviors—e.g., psychopathy, conduct disorder, antisocial personality disorder, substance abuse, aggression (Bernard et al., 2010). Foster care and specialized services have been effective interventions for neglect and for HPA axis dysfunction in very young children (no significant difference from low-risk children in bedtime cortisol levels; see Chapter 7, BEIP, ABC ...). There may be a sensitive period for intervention effects (McLaughlin et al., 2015b; Chapter 7).

Stress and Brain Regions

As noted in Chapter 1, early interpersonal violence may lead to changes in the structure and function of neural circuits that underlie emotional learning (some not measurable until adulthood; McLaughlin et al., 2014a). In part because of sensitive periods in neural plasticity, early life appears to be a time of particular vulnerability that is critical in depressive outcomes and in fear and stress reactions (Goff & Tottenham, 2014; Pizzagalli, 2014).

Amygdala

The amygdala-dependent emotional circuitry that, with early parental support, appropriately differentiates threatening from nonthreatening stimuli may become perpetually primed for stress responsiveness when biological risk factors combine with traumas such as child abuse. Both left and right amygdala develop shortly after birth and increase in volume through preadolescence (Uematsu et al., 2012). The left amygdala develops more rapidly and has been shown to be particularly responsive to maternal stimuli in childhood (Lyons-Ruth, Pechtel, Yoon, Anderson, & Teicher, 2016; Tottenham, Shapiro, Telzer, & Humphreys, et al., 2012; Uematsu et al., 2012; Table A4.2). The right amygdala has increased in volume after traumas (Pechtel et al., 2014; Chapter 8).

White Matter and PFC

Early brain alterations have been related to a number of problems. For example, brain impairments in the first 18 months of life have been associated with abnormal social and moral development and a later syndrome resembling psychopathy (Schore, 2003). Maltreatment before age three has been linked to alterations in the brain's white matter networks, in areas involved in affect regulation, and could underlie functional deficits and symptom patterns often observed in maltreated children (Puetz et al., 2017). For children maltreated and placed permanently out-of-home before age three, alterations in neural architecture, shown at ages 8–12, included significant reductions in the brain's working memory networks including global connectivity strength—especially in vmPFC, also in areas next to regions involved in regulation of affect; reductions in local connectivity; and reduced path length (N = 25; Puetz et al., 2017). Such deviations have been associated with psychopathology. Lower global connectivity was associated with 0–4 out-of-home placements and with attenuated cortisol secretion and higher levels of internalizing and externalizing behaviors. Early life brain alterations have been found in adulthood as well. Adults with early life emotional abuse have shown differing brain patterns in the handling of negative emotions (Khawli et al., 2018). Use of reappraisal in response to negative emotions engaged differing neural patterns for high versus low/no abuse. Reappraisal reduced negative emotions for those with early emotional abuse, while it increased positive emotions for comparisons.

Deprivation vs Threat and the Brain

McLaughlin, Sheridan, and Lambert (2014a) suggest that there are differences in the effects of threat versus deprivation on the neural structure and function (over- vs under-activation).

Deprivation. Across most developmental domains, deprivation (e.g., institutional rearing) for the first 4–6 months of life is not associated with increases in long-term adverse effects except in the social-emotional domain (Zeanah et al., 2011b). If adoption occurs after specific age-cutoffs, specific kinds of deficiencies are reported (Zeanah et al., 2011b). For adoptions after six, 12, or 18 months, studies have found parent-rated behavior problems and attachment security issues; after 15 months, problems in expressive and receptive language; after 18 months, parent-reported executive functioning (EF) problems; and after 24 months, deficiencies in IQ, attachment security, and EEG coherence.

Lack of an early attachment figure corresponds to increased susceptibility to difficulties (e.g., anxiety) that is apparently mediated by brain changes (e.g., thickness and volume; amygdala structure and function; Marshall et al., 2008; McLaughlin et al., 2010, 2014a; Tottenham et al., 2012). Institutional rearing (IC) is associated with, for example, decreased social and cognitive inputs of numerous kinds—e.g., language, interactions with adults, variation in routines and experiences, novel and age-appropriate cognitive stimuli such as books, toys; peer interaction; and a wide range of environmental stimulation (Nelson, Furtado, Fox, & Zeanah, 2009; Smyke et al., 2007; Zeanah et al., 2003). Neglect (emotional or physical), severe poverty, or early IC are linked to greater cognitive deficits, language deficits, and/or poorer cognitive performance (McLaughlin et al., 2014a; Müeller et al., 2010) as well as poorer mental and physical health and atypical social development (e.g., markedly elevated rates of ADHD; see McLaughlin et al., 2015b; Zeanah et al., 2009). These deficits are in turn associated with other problems—e.g., increased risk of behavior problems later in development (NICHD, 2002; Lupien et al., 2009; Chapter 5).

Threat. War-exposed children (ages 1.5–5 years) have shown a different physiological stress response from controls, as indexed by both cortisol and sAA (Glossary), and they have tended to react with more negative emotions to the elicitation of fear (Feldman et al., 2013b). As discussed, mothers reported more PTSD symptoms, were less reciprocal during interactions with toddlers, and showed stress physiology (higher cortisol and sAA). Only some war-exposed young children were diagnosed with PTSD. Interestingly, exposed no-PTSD children were those with the highest levels of cortisol and consistently high sAA (at baseline, following challenge, and recovery; HPA hyperactivity, Feldman et al., 2013b), which have been linked to higher externalizing and internalizing (e.g., El-Sheikh et al., 2008). They exhibited more comfort seeking emotion regulation strategies and had mothers who were more reciprocal than other groups (Feldman et al., 2013b). It is possible that, in the context of ongoing threat (continuous missile attacks), constantly aroused physiology and vigilance may be more adaptive. Results also demonstrate the importance of help-seeking regulation strategies and reciprocal care in times of stress (Feldman et al., 2013b). PTSD children had blunted cortisol at baseline—a profile consistent with severe trauma (HPA hypoactivity; Gunnar & Vazquez, 2001; see Chapter 4). PTSD children also had higher negative emotionality and, during fear paradigms, used withdrawal tactics for emotion regulation (gaze aversion), self-soothing behavior, and terminated verbal dialogue. They had at least two PTSD arousal symptoms, contrasted with hypo-activation in stress physiology and regulation (withdrawal; Feldman et al., 2013b). Their mothers had the highest PTSD levels which may have prevented enlisting their aid. However, by ages 7–8, 60% of war-exposed children had a psychiatric disorder (Feldman, Vengrober, & Ebstein, 2014); maternal sensitive support again reduced risk for psychopathology.

Trauma's Effects on Young Children's Developmental Skills

As noted, stress, perturbed attachments, and traumas can undermine aspects of development. The interrelationship of developmental domains means that undermining one area may cause problems in others. Stressor-related outcomes generally are influenced by combined risk factors.

Executive Functions (EFs)

Children's EF levels have been linked to their adjustment versus maladjustment. Trauma's relationship to memory and to attention are discussed here. Self-skills are discussed separately.

Trauma and Memory

As discussed in other chapters, trauma may have long-term effects on memory. Infants exposed to an earthquake (ages 3–12 months) had markedly lower scores on visuospatial memory tests than non-exposed (Li et al., 2015). Although less affected than infants with post-birth exposure to the earthquake, infants with pre-natal exposure in the second and third trimesters had significantly lower scores than those exposed in the first trimester. Autobiographical memory (AM) permits us to share memories with others and is often used in the treatment of trauma with children who can provide such memories. Young children can recall six to 12 months later, an event that occurred between ages 2¼ and 3¼ years, some say only if they had the vocabulary to describe it at the time of the experience (Simcock & Hayne, 2002). Although two- and three-year-old children can recall specific events that suggest episodic memories, researchers suggest that they cannot produce true AM, because they do not remember events in a timeline backward and forward (Bjorklund & Sellers, 2014; Gopnik, 2009). However, children and adults have shown evidence of somatic memories, reenacted, or even recalled extremely distressing infancy events (Coates, 2016; Box 6.1; see Laura, Chapter 7). For example, a man who had pain in his heels when distressed was repeatedly pricked in his heels as a neonate. When distressed, a three-year-old girl, Betsy, complained that the line in her belly hurt, while making a stabbing motion. She had been stabbed at 10 months (Coates, 2016). Parental behaviors may prevent aspects of traumatic and physical reactions. For example, Betsy's hospitalization was three weeks instead of the expected three months. Her parents moderated her reactions by providing comfort and helping her to contain anxiety (Coates, 2016; Scheeringa & Zeanah, 2001). After a trauma, children often retell their experience repeatedly or repeat aspects of trauma in their play (Nader, 2008). Although Betsy engaged in repetitive hospital play, in treatment sessions (age 4.5), there was no sense of dread in her stories (see Play, Chapters 1, 7, 13). In her play, people were helpful and helped the patients to heal. After she was told the story of her stabbing, she wanted to hear it repeatedly. Her play and questions became a part of her processing. The repetitive hospital play stopped after hearing, then processing the story (see Coates, 2016 for details).

Trauma and Attention

While fear downregulates PFC activity (EFs) and interferes with attentional mechanisms, it increases subcortical activity—e.g., related to fear conditioning, memory consolidation, and habit formation (de Barbaro, Clackson, & Wass, 2016). This is believed to correspond to a more rapid assessment of potential risks and more rapid response to environmental uncertainties (through learned reactions). Infants who responded with higher heart rates to a video of an infant crying showed shorter look durations, more novelty preference, and an apparent faster, more vigilant stimulus-ready attention profile with rapid encoding of an object's features, akin to hypervigilance (de Barbaro et al., 2016; see example of infant with burned hand—Trauma and Self-Regulation, below). Importantly, various aspects of attentional control (e.g., sustained attention, reduced saccadic reaction times) can be improved in infancy through training (Wass, Porayska-Pomsta, & Johnson, 2012; Rose et al., 2012a; Chapter 7).

Self-Skills

Self-skills such as self-awareness, self-image, and self-regulation can be negatively affected by traumas. The treatment of complicated traumatic reactions specifically addresses self-regulation and self-reflective information processing as well as attachment or relational engagement, safety, traumatic experience integration, and positive affect enhancement (Kinniburgh, Blaustein, & Spinazzola, 2005). Self-regulation and self-awareness in infants and toddlers are discussed here.

Trauma and Self-Regulation: Effortful Control and Body Regulation

Early self-regulatory competence has predicted better adaptive skills and fewer problem behaviors in later childhood (Jennings et al., 2008). Infants and toddlers who learn to recognize and express emotions and who develop effective self-regulation skills have an easier time controlling their own behaviors as they get older (Sciaraffa, Zeanah, & Zeanah, 2018). Self-regulation is related to better resilience, coping, and management of stress when there is trauma or other adversity.

Between ages one and three, self-regulation skills generally improve significantly. Maternal warmth has been a predictor of self-regulation. Infants/toddlers exposed to serious adversity—e.g., violence, other trauma, multiple medical procedures—have been more likely to exhibit abnormal patterns in emotion expression, unusual behaviors—e.g., increased motor activity, distractibility, and inattention; disruptions in feeding and sleeping, and/or developmental delays such a delayed motor and language skills (Scheeringa & Gaensbauer, 2000; 18 months but not 12 months after a hurricane; Delamater & Applegate, 1999; Box 6.4). For example, trauma can interfere with reflexive functioning—e.g., an infant with a hand burned while grasping a hot object may avoid pain by avoiding grasping (the brain now associates grasping with pain), which may interfere with development of the grasp reflex and manual skills (Masgutova, 2016). For children under age five years, global developmental delay (GDD) is a delay in two or more developmental domains—gross/fine motor, speech/language, cognition, social/personal, and activities of daily living (see Mithyantha, Kneen, McCann, & Gladstone, 2017). Degree of GDD has been subclassified as mild when functional age is <33% below chronological age, moderate when functional age is 34%–66% of

Box 6.4 Thwarted Attachment

At two months, Reggie, positive for crack cocaine at birth, was placed in long-term foster care and formed a solid attachment to his foster mother (Lieberman, 1997). When the foster mother became ill, he was placed with another family at eight months. On arrival, he was grieving the loss of his first foster mother and showed prolonged crying, poor sleep and appetite, and disorganized behavior. The new mother appeared to be depressed and withdrawn (grieving the loss of an earlier foster child). She and Reggie had not formed a mutual attachment 13 months later. At 22 months, he was functioning below age level. When an adoptive family was sought, he readily attached to the interested family during their first visit to his foster home. After a five-week transition period with increasing visitation, he moved to his new home. Two months later, he exhibited a growth spurt and gained 12 points on his developmental index (see Lieberman, 1997 for more details; see Chapter 7—IPP; Chapter 10—CPP).

chronological age, and severe when functional age is <66% of chronological age. Infant regulatory problems, such as excessive crying, feeding or sleeping difficulties, bonding/attachment problems, have been significant predictors of longer-term difficulties—e.g., motor, language, and cognitive delays; continuing relational problems (e.g., see Barlow, Bennett, & Midgley, 2013).

Externalizing and internalizing are problems that may follow traumas. Parenting (warmth/sensitivity) and other variables (e.g., genetics; good attention skills) have been related to young children's *effortful control* (at ages 18, 32, and 40 months, Eisenberg et al., 2010b). Higher *effortful control* (self-regulation) has been related to lower levels of externalizing behaviors—e.g., lower hyperactivity, conduct problems (Eisenberg et al., 2010b; for boys ages 2–3 and two years later; Smith & Day, 2018). Maltreatment has been linked to later risk behaviors via insecure attachments and ineffective emotion regulation strategies—e.g., child difficulty inhibiting inappropriate or impulsive behaviors such as hitting, grabbing things from others; trouble waiting for a turn; impulsiveness risk into adulthood (Oshri et al., 2015). Young children who are traumatized may have difficulty with body state awareness and its connection to experiences and emotions (Kinniburgh et al., 2005). They may be prone to negative affective states (e.g., shame, isolation) and may misinterpret cues of potential danger. For example, after witnessing domestic violence, young children may interpret traumatic reminders as signs of impending danger—e.g., a touch, a tone of voice, proximity. They may have difficulty with emotion recognition, expression, and control. Such combinations of outcomes may be the precursors to attentional and attributional biases (e.g., hostile attribution bias; Chapters 2, 15), which have in turn been related to emotional and behavioral dysregulation. Some evidence suggests that self-awareness skills predict self-regulation. For example, toddlers' 20- and 27-month-old self-recognition (self-as-object; with agency) as well as maternal warmth predicted self-regulation at 34 months (N = 100, Jennings et al., 2008).

Trauma and Self-Awareness

Although studies were not found on trauma and infant self-awareness, children who have not had adequate physical care often have rudimentary or no skills in self-care and self-regulation and may be oblivious to danger or pain (Bach et al., 2000). When negative experiences occur in infancy (e.g., severe illness, physical neglect), children often develop very poor coordination and an impaired sense of their personal physical abilities and limitations. In turn, this may produce a cascade of effects. Children with motor difficulties (e.g., poor motor coordination; reduced skills) are less inclined to participate in physical activities (in child- and adulthood), thus limiting opportunities for practice and further development—e.g., limits activities that increase awareness of others' states of mind; motor skill development in preschool has been linked to social and emotional development and to later cognitive efficiency and academic achievement (Pesce et al., 2016).

Trauma and Stressor-Related Disorders (TSRD)

Young children are at risk of trauma-related and other symptoms from direct exposures—e.g., to maltreatment, disasters, war, or terrorism traumas. For example, in addition to TSRD, young children may exhibit internalizing, externalizing, total problem scores (ages 3–6; Wang et al., 2006); trauma symptoms, adaptive problems (Wolmer et al., 2016); and a variety of other reactions—e.g., anxiety and/or depression, affective problems, withdrawal (Wang et al., 2006). For children ages 0–6 years, DSM-5 disorders include reactive attachment disorder (RAD); disinhibited social engagement disorder (DSED); and PTSD for children age six years and under. Treatments for infants and toddlers necessarily include or focus on caregiver–child dyads.

PTSD in Infants and Toddlers (For Ages 0–6)

PTSD for children ages 0–6 recognizes that young children may experience life threat or extreme stress in situations that may be less overwhelming for an older child (e.g., shorter separations from parents). Although DSM-5 does not permit witnessing to include events only witnessed in electronic media (APA, 2013), young children have also had posttrauma reactions from indirect exposures such as TV exposures to traumas (Box 1.1)—e.g., externalizing, emotional reactivity, sleep disturbances, externalizing such as aggression, or oppositional defiance (Wang et al., 2006; Wolmer et al., 2016). Fewer symptoms are required for a DSM-5 diagnosis for children under age six—e.g., only one (or more) intrusion symptom; one either from negative alterations in moods or cognitions or from persistent avoidance symptoms; two or more arousal/reactivity symptoms; and functional impairment. This diagnosis relies on observable behaviors rather than on symptoms younger children may not be able to report (APA, 2013; see Nader & Fletcher, 2014; Scheeringa et al., 2012). Although developmental regressions, difficulties regulating emotions or maintaining stable interpersonal relationships, and dissociative symptoms can be significant in children's ongoing development and functioning, they are in the associated features of PTSD 0–6 (APA, 2013).

Attachment-Related TSRD

The quality of caregiver–infant interaction has been implicated in the development of these disorders (e.g., RAD, Rutter, Kreppner, & Sonuga-Barke, 2009; Lyons-Ruth, 2015). For example, DSED has been related to disorganized attachments (see Lyons-Ruth, 2015); at 12 months to institutional caregiver; at 18 months to primary caregiver (PC; Lyons-Ruth, Bureau, Riley, & Atlas-Corbett, 2009); at 24 months to PC (Gleason et al., 2014). Although outcomes are generally linked to multiple factors, both traumas and specific attachment classifications have been linked to a number of subsequent disorders (Chapter 4; Tables A3.1–A3.4; Lyons-Ruth & Jacobvitz, 2018). Because securely attached children are able to rely on caretakers to assist them when distressed, sensitive and responsive caretakers are believed to assist in biological regulation thus relieving the necessity of stress hormone (cortisol) assistance from the limbic HPA axis system (Gunnar & Donzella, 2002). Evidence suggests that insecure-avoidant infants may experience high levels of internal distress while minimizing behavioral displays of distress (see Hill-Soderlund et al., 2008).

Reactive Attachment Disorder (RAD)

Because attachment disorders can only exist after a child has formed selective attachments, a developmental age of at least 9–10 months is necessary for diagnosis (APA, 2013; Zeanah, Berlin, & Boris, 2011a). Some evidence suggests that Reactive Attachment Disorder (RAD in DSM5 and ICD-10), Disinhibited Social Engagement Disorder (DSED in DSM-5; disinhibited attachment disorder in ICD-10), and a combined type are possible (Gleason et al., 2011). Both RAD and DSED are linked to neglect or deprivation (APA, 2013) and may arise from conditions limiting the formation of selective attachments (Zeanah et al., 2016). While not all children raised in institutional care show signs of one of these disorders, both are found in children who have been institutionalized (Gleason et al., 2011) as well as in other groups (e.g., foster care, maltreated; DeKlyen & Greenberg, 2018). The two disorders are related to different phenomenology, correlates, and responses to intervention (Rutter et al., 2009; Zeanah et al., 2011a; Zeanah & Smyke, 2009). RAD, which may also follow repeated changes in primary caregiver, is characterized by higher levels of inhibition, unexplained mood changes, low social or emotional responsiveness, and low social initiation (Zeanah et al., 2011a), and poor ability to be comforted (APA, 2013; Box 3.5). RAD has been linked to attachment security problems, reduced cognitive abilities (e.g., attention impairments), and depressive symptoms (Gleason et al., 2011; Smyke et al., 2012). If movement to foster care is early enough, symptoms of RAD have improved (Smyke et al., 2012; Zeanah et al., 2011b).

Disinhibited Social Engagement Disorder (DSED)

In contrast, Disinhibited Social Engagement Disorder (DSED) is characterized by little or no reluctance to approach, interact with, or leave with unfamiliar adults, excessively familiar behavior, little to no checking back with caregiver and/or by socially disinhibited behavior (APA, 2013; Zeanah et al., 2011a). Little or no checking back with a caregiver has also been demonstrated by avoidantly attached children without deprivation. DSED has not shown improvement with foster placement (Smyke et al., 2012). Indicators of DSED (although distinct from ADHD) have been linked to signs of activity/impulsivity and of ADHD as well as to aggressive behavior (Lyons-Ruth et al., 2009), reduced cognitive abilities, and (modestly) inhibitory control difficulties (Gleason et al., 2011; Scheeringa & Weems, 2014).

In the International Classification of Diseases, Tenth Revision (ICD-10), DSED is included among attachment disorders (e.g., disinhibited attachment disorder; Lyons-Ruth, 2015; Rutter et al., 2009). Indiscriminately socially uninhibited attachment behavior has been associated with maternal psychopathology and history of maltreatment (Zeanah et al., 2004), disrupted affective communication and duration of institutional care (Rutter et al., 2007; O'Connor et al., 2003). Evidence has implicated the quality of caregiver–infant interaction (e.g., disorganized attachments) during the first two years of life as critical to the emergence of DSED. For example, highly disrupted interactions with a primary caregiver at 18 months are associated with increased DSED (Lyons-Ruth et al., 2009). Gleason et al. (2011) found the association of DSED to quality of care only occurred at 42 months and was modest; nearly half of children who met DSED criteria showed organized attachment classifications (N = 122; infants ages 21–54 months).

Conclusions

For very young children, environmental stressors such as conflict or poverty; attachment disturbances such as insensitive, atypical, or anomalous care or caregiver–child separations; and traumas may disrupt development, functioning, and life course. The stress response system may undergo epigenetic changes and be dysregulated by traumas. Genetic, environmental, and/or individual characteristics may increase risk of problem behaviors and psychopathology. Pre- and post-natal stressors may affect infants functioning and temperament. Traumas in infancy and toddlerhood have had long-term or cascading effects. Trauma-specific reminders may trigger increased symptoms. Children's traits influence the manner such reactions may take. For traumas in very young childhood, traumatic memories may be held in somatic memory and may manifest as somatic symptoms or behavioral reenactments or script-like behaviors.

Not all of the circumstances that may result in TSRD such as PTSD or the symptoms that may manifest for very young children have been recognized in DSM-5. Especially for young children exposed to deprivation or other circumstances interfering with an early attachment bond, attachment-related TSRD may emerge. Some of the symptoms of attachment-related TSRDs may persist into adolescence. RAD, but not DSED, has improved after early placement with trained foster parents.

7

Treatment Methods for Infants and Toddlers

Ages 0–3

After traumatic and significant non-traumatic stressors, it is essential to employ effective early treatments for young children in order to prevent enduring patterns of maladaptive functioning (Ghosh Ippen, Harris, Van Horn, & Lieberman, 2011). For young children, psychological interventions can promote social and emotional competence and relieve psychological suffering (e.g., Osofsky & Lieberman, 2011; St Petersburg—USA Orphanage Research Team, 2008). Because the most powerful potential change agent for young children's development is the caregiver–infant relationship, interventions for this age group focus on the quality of the parent–child relationship (Osofsky & Lieberman, 2011; Scheeringa, 2016; Scheeringa & Zeanah, 2001). Toddlers can engage in some verbal as well as nonverbal treatment methods. Treatments are likely to be multifaceted—e.g., attachment-focused; multiple methods—e.g., executive functions have shown greater improvement when treatments had both physical and cognitive components (see Pesce et al., 2016).

Infants are dependent upon attachment figures to protect them against threat (Lyons-Ruth, Dutra, Schuder, & Bianchi, 2006; Scheeringa & Zeanah, 2001). The attachment relationship itself provides the context and scaffolding for development and can be the source of healing. Trauma may render parents less able to function as "protective shields." As well, a caregiver's emotional well-being and life circumstances may profoundly affect the quality of the infant–caregiver relationship (Osofsky & Lieberman, 2011). Attending to caregiver symptomatology (e.g., trauma symptoms, stress, overwhelm, anxiety) before treating the child is likely to help the caregiver to be more sensitive to the child's needs (Scheeringa & Zeanah, 2001). Additionally, children who experience early adversity may fail to clearly signal their needs (Bernard et al., 2012; see Bernard, Meade, & Dozier, 2013), making it difficult for parents to respond sensitively (Scheeringa & Zeanah, 2001). Treatment methods that focus on the parent–child relationship emphasize the interconnectedness of the child and family members and actively seek ways to increase safety, intimacy, and comfortable reciprocity/synchrony (Beebe et al., 2016; Osofsky & Lieberman, 2011). A clinician must move flexibly between the needs of the parent and those of the child.

Early life adversity/stress is associated with increased likelihood of adulthood disorders, underscoring the importance of early intervention. Important differences in individual timetables for development and for trauma or loss-processing as well as differences in personalities/temperaments, cultures, and styles suggest treatment must be adapted to specific needs of a child and parent (Lieberman & Van Horn, 2005; Nader, 2008; Nader & Pynoos, 1993; Scheeringa, 2016; Chapter 4).

Play

Normal play has been shown to aid brain development—e.g., increase synaptic plasticity and neurotransmission (Pellegrini, Dupuis, & Smith, 2007; Box 2.3). Nondirective play therapy methods have resulted in physiological catch-up for neglected children (Chapter 10; Nader, 2004; Webb, 2015). Under normal circumstances, a youth's qualities (e.g., conscience, creativity, independence) and play behavior (e.g., for fun, learning, emotional release) evolve over time (Nader, 2008). As a normal part of development, play provides *a way of expressing*—e.g., emotions, developing beliefs, symptoms, curiosity; *of exploring and learning*—e.g., about things, ways of doing things, joint/social skills, self-regulation; *of having fun*—e.g., through imagination, happy interactions; *of processing information*, and *of demonstrating experiences* (e.g., Pellegrini et al., 2007; St. George & Freeman, 2017). Play promotes brain growth and functioning (e.g., Goldstein & Lerner, 2017; Gordon et al., 2003). In play, young children practice and exaggerate adult behaviors, can engage in behavioral and cognitive innovations, and can practice newly developed strategies (Pellegrini et al., 2007).

Play or *Playfulness*—i.e., having fun vs being serious; being generally happy and joyful; playing games with physical contact; humor; laughter—is among a neurologically based set of proposed, basic personality traits (Glossary; Davis, Panksepp, & Normansell, 2003; Chapter 4). Ultimately, play becomes a part of a well-rounded life and possibly part of a successful career (Nader, 2008). Play as a normal part of development and as a method of coping and processing can be disrupted by trauma (Chapter 1). For young Israeli children exposed to terrorism (ages 3.5–7.5; N = 54), although only nine met full criteria for PTSD, exposed children's play was significantly different from comparison children's (medium to very large effect sizes; Cohen, Chazan, Lerner, & Maimon, 2010). They engaged in more traumatic play, more play interruptions, higher levels of negative and trauma-related affects, and greater frequency of acting-out morbid themes. Non-exposed children exhibited significantly more adaptive coping/defensive strategies when they did engage in traumatic play. Parent injury, child's own injury, or loss of a family member had an even greater impact on play (Cohen et al., 2010).

Simple Soothing by Parents and Teachers

After traumas, young (and older) children may need soothing and calming from a trusted adult, e.g., young ones by holding, rocking, distracting, gently verbally reassuring, or providing a reassuring hug (Sciaraffa, Zeanah, & Zeanah, 2018). Although touch has been associated with the reduction of distress, for some children the type of trauma, other past experiences, or temperament may make touch or other interventions more stress-producing than soothing. Adult knowledge, assessment, and adaptation are essential. Parents and nursery or day care professionals may need to (re-)establish trust and to engage in watchful moment-to-moment assessing of the child's needs as well as in comforting behaviors. As noted, this includes anticipating situations and other things that may trigger stress (e.g., traumatic reminders; Box 6.1; Table A6.1). Providing warm, dependable, consistent, and nurturing connection to a child, enjoying or delighting in the child, believing in her/his abilities, and engaging in developmentally appropriate, positive interactions with a child may assist her/his recovery and resilience (Lipton & Fosha, 2011; Sciaraffa et al., 2018). Predictable and dependable routines may be important to assist the reduction of arousal in children (Lieberman et al., 2003; Sciaraffa et al., 2018). Taking the child's emotions and reactions seriously without judging, criticizing, or diminishing the child's feelings is essential (Nader, 1999/2000; Sciaraffa et al., 2018). Posttrauma parenting or teaching may involve learning to assist the child in the ways that s/he needs assistance, recognizing regressions (Chapter 4), and finding helpful solutions when the child engages in unacceptable behaviors (e.g., McMahon & Forehand, 2003; Scheeringa, 2016).

Difficulties with the ability to identify, express, and manage emotions has been a result of childhood traumas (Chapter 2). Children exposed to significant adversity may particularly need help to identify, express, cope with, and manage conflicting or intense emotions (e.g., Sciaraffa et al., 2018). Modeling emotion-regulation in stressful situations may include adults' monitoring and managing their own distress, avoiding impulsive reactions, and modeling pausing before acting (e.g., verbally stating the need to think about it or need to take a deep breath).

Trauma Treatment Methods

Methods used with mother–infant dyads generally focus on changing the quality of the mother–child relationship through a transforming relationship between clinician (or other helper) and mother and/or through training a mother with her child (Slade et al., 2005). The associations of troubled child–parent relationships (with or without trauma) underscore the need for repair (e.g., Box 6.3). For example, effortful control (EC) is an important component of self-regulation (Eisenberg, Smith, & Spinrad, 2011). Intrusive parenting at 18 and 30 months has negatively predicted EC a year later (Taylor et al., 2013b). Infant–parent Psychotherapy (IPP, Fraiberg, 1980; with variations, also called, e.g., mother–infant, parent–infant—PIP; see also ARC and CPP, Chapter 10) is precursor to many methods with infants, toddlers, and preschoolers (Chapter 10). It is based on the idea that in disrupted mother–baby relationships exist a basic distortion of a mother's capacity to mentally represent the baby in a coherent and positive way, often stemming from her own early and/or traumatic relationship experiences (Fraiberg, 1980; Slade et al., 2005). IPP aims to disentangle these effects from the relationship with the infant through the parent-clinician relationship. IPP has been used with identified or at-risk mothers (e.g., with BPD; Newman & Stevenson, 2008). Classical authors of PIP (Fraiberg, 1980; Fraiberg, Adelson, & Shapiro, 1975) consider the nonverbal infant as actively involved in therapy and in need of a spokesperson (the clinician; Salomonsson, 2016). For example, Salomonsson (2016) suggests that the clinician/analyst might essentially translate the baby's behaviors by labeling them—e.g., may tell a baby who is looking terrified at the mother, "I think you get afraid when [you see that Mommy] doesn't look at you. Right now, she doesn't want to look at you because she's so sad, but she hopes [to be able to look] at you again one day" (Salomonsson, 2013, reworded from p. 769). Thus, while soothing tones are used with the infant, the mother hears her behavior and its effects on the child.

According to Bakermans-Kranenburg, van IJzendoorn, and Juffer (2005), interventions conducted prenatally have been less effective than those conducted after birth of children with a child's presence for interactions. The methods to follow have been used successfully for infants and toddlers, with birth and foster parents (see also Chapter 10). Both their differences and their similarities are of interest. Manuals are available and are generally distillations of years of clinical experience with particular target groups (e.g., age; disorder; see Lieberman & Van Horn, 2008). Formulaic use of them may stifle creativity and successful intuitive functioning.

Attachment and Biobehavioral Catch-Up (ABC)

The ABC method (Dozier, 2003), primarily for children between six and 24 months (sometimes earlier), includes a 10-session in-home intervention for mothers at-risk of neglecting infants. Goals are to increase the mother's synchronous responding to her child's signals and to enhance the mother's sensitivity to her child's distress (Bernard, Dozier, Bick, & Gordon, 2015a). ABC aims to help parents behave in nurturing ways, enabling children to develop secure, organized attachments; helps them to behave in contingent, responsive ways to aid children's regulatory capabilities; and helps them avoid frightening behavior, which undermines organized attachments and a child's self-regulatory abilities (Dozier, Meade, & Bernard, 2014). To assist children's regulatory capacities, ABC helps caregivers learn to reinterpret children's alienating behaviors and to override their own personal issues that interfere with providing nurturing care and an environment that assists self-regulation (Dozier et al., 2006).

ABC has been used both with foster parents and with maltreating birth parents (Dozier, Zeanah, & Bernard, 2013; Dozier et al., 2014). "Parent coaches" (PCs) provide in-the-moment feedback or suggestions to parents regarding targeted behaviors, in order to draw attention to opportunities to provide nurturance and synchrony. They provide supportive comments and link parental behaviors to children's responses. When rapport is established, PCs make gentle corrections when needed and encourage reflection when appropriate. Short video clips are often used for demonstration and discussion. PCs reinforce appropriate behaviors in sessions with the child. Parents learn that some children, especially when they have experienced early adversity, behave in ways that do not elicit nurturing care (see Dozier et al., 2013). Parents view videos of unfamiliar children (e.g., some show distress directly and some do not) to learn that children need their parents whether or not they signal the need clearly. PC's in-the-moment support of parent's nurturing care and synchronous behaviors are very important to treatment—e.g., a PC might say, "The baby [did this] and you [did this]. That's such a good example of...."

Sessions. Session 1 includes the importance of nurturing, dealing with a difficult-to-soothe child, and assigns the parent's at-home observation of the child's behaviors when distressed (Dozier et al., 2014). The latter is discussed in session 2, and videotapes of children with different attachment styles are viewed and discussed. The third and fourth sessions emphasize the importance of synchronous (contingently responsive) parenting behaviors that follow the child's lead. In session 5, the focus is how parent's behaviors (e.g., intrusiveness, frightening behavior) can have a negative effect. Session 6 focuses on frightening behaviors. In sessions 7–8, parents reflect on their own experiences that might influence parental behaviors, and they learn to override "voices from the past"—emphasis is on behaviors rather than on the parents. Sessions 9–10 are for consolidating gains—e.g., following their children's lead with delight, and behaving in non-frightening ways. Assessment includes the strange situation procedure (SSP), observation during the session, and ongoing observational evaluation of parents' strengths and weaknesses in targeted behaviors. Inasmuch as the method aims to increase sensitivity to distress (providing a safe haven) and sensitivity to non-distress (ability to respond in synchronous ways), both synchrony and nurturance are assessed (Bernard, Meade, & Dozier, 2013).

Studies. ABC has been linked to children's increased rates of organized, secure attachments (lower disorganized rates), more normal cortisol (CT) regulation, and increased receptive vocabulary than controls (Bernard et al., 2012, 2015a; Bernard, Lee, & Dozier, 2017; Dozier et al., 2008). ABC mothers (vs controls) have shown enhanced processing of infant facial emotions—crying and laughing (correlated with greater maternal sensitivity) and enhanced psychophysiological responsiveness compared to controls (Bernard, Simons, & Dozier, 2016). ABC foster-mothers have shown increased synchronous behaviors as well (Bick & Dozier, 2013; Bernard et al., 2015a; Bernard et al., 2012; Bernard et al., 2016). Frequency and quality of clinicians' use of in-the-moment feedback to parents has predicted change and posttreatment retention of change in parental intrusiveness and sensitivity (Caron, Bernard, & Dozier, 2016). Low waking cortisol is a biomarker for clinical, social, and physical maladjustment (e.g., Bernard et al., 2015a). For mother–child dyads who received either ABC or Developmental Education for Families (DEF, proven successful for improving intelligence when provided over a long period; Ramey et al., 1982; Chapter 5), ABC children showed both more normal CT levels and fewer behavior problems than younger and DEF children (not significant for the latter; Dozier et al., 2006, 2008). That is, neglected ABC children had higher waking cortisol values and a steeper waking to bedtime decline in cortisol than neglected controls (ages 5–32 months; N = 100; Bernard et al., 2015b). ABC-treated foster preschoolers exhibited stronger cognitive flexibility and theory of mind skills than foster children treated with a control intervention (Lewis-Morrarty et al., 2012); they were not significantly different from a normal control group in these skills.

Circle of Security Parenting™ (COSP)

COS™ (Hoffman, Marvin, Cooper, & Powell, 2006; manualized protocol) is an early intervention program conducted by trained, expert clinicians. It is a brief, behavioral and insight-oriented group approach that combines psychoeducation, cognitive behavioral methods, and psychodynamic understanding and intervention techniques (Ramsauer et al., 2014). For facilitators, COSP™ includes a four-day course to which paraprofessionals are welcome, whereas COS™ Intensive (COSI™) is a 10-day training, plus exam, plus at least one year of supervision. For parents/children, COSI™ uses individualized video-based assessment and treatment to improve attachment relationships (Huber, Hawkins, & Cooper, 2018). COSP™ is a preventive intervention for caregivers of young children, with a manualized and DVD-based protocol for groups or individuals (stock videos). Either can be delivered individually or in groups and can be conducted in center, home, or other location (e.g., prison) (http://circleofsecurityinternational.com). Groups allow 2.5 hours of focus per group member (e.g., eight members = 20 hours; six members = 15; personal communication Neil Boris, 10-4-18). In group or individually, the relationship process between facilitator and parent is used to influence parallel change in the parent–child relationship (Huber et al., 2018). The facilitator or group serves as a secure base and safe haven for parent(s).

COSI™ employs individualized video-based assessment and treatment to improve caregiver–child attachment relationships. Individualized treatment planning has included identification of (a) caregiver–child interaction patterns (including child attachment classification); (b) taking caregiver developmental history and internal working models of self and child and setting individual goals; and (c) a key issue—the linchpin or single most problematic attachment issue—that would be the focus of therapeutic work and shapes choice of video segments (Hoffman et al., 2006). Graphics, videos, and nonjudgmental dialogue are used for education/training—e.g., children expressing basic attachment and exploration needs on video—and for feedback purposes (on caregiver–child interactions). Videos are tailored to the parent–child dyad.

COSP™ (Cooper, Hoffman, & Powell, 2009) was created for broader implementation—for a wide age range and uses available resources (e.g., Head Start or other clinicians receive four-day training—to reduce costs; Cassidy et al., 2017). COSP™ aims to assist caregivers in providing a secure base for children and to reduce insecure and disorganized attachments (Cassidy et al., 2017). The emphasis is on sensitive responsiveness to a child's distress, which fosters expectations of comfort and use of caregiver as a secure base for exploration. The co-regulation of distress with a responsive caregiver helps to shape adaptive psychobiological responses (e.g., HPA axis) and mental representations of a caregiver as helpful and of stress as manageable. COSP™ provides a foundation for skills of reflective dialogue, emotion regulation, parental empathy toward the child, and caregiving sensitivity to child distress needed for secure base provision (via video footage; Cassidy et al., 2017). Videos of parents and young children permit the facilitator to ask parents questions from the manual designed to spur reflective dialogue and to relate what they see to the "needs on the Circle" (personal communication Neil Boris, 10-4-18).

COS™ has been related to significantly reduced attachment insecurity and disorganization for jailed substance-abusing mothers and Head Start toddlers and preschoolers (COS peri-natal program, Cassidy et al., 2010; COS-20 week, Hoffman et al., 2006; Huber et al., 2015a). Huber et al. (2015b) found significantly improved child protective factors and reduced behavioral concerns as well as less internalizing and externalizing problems (regardless of age, gender—ages 1–7+). Young children moved from borderline clinical to normal range. Children and parents with greater problems (behavior; caregiving) showed more improvement. For COSP™, Cassidy et al. (2017) found a main effect for maternal response to child distress—mothers showed fewer unsupportive but not more supportive behaviors than waiting list mothers—and a main effect for one type of child executive functioning—inhibitory control (but not cognitive flexibility, after controlling for maternal age and marital status). COS™ (10 session) was used with two caregiver–child dyads with

Autistic Spectrum Disorder (under age 5; Fardoulys & Coyne, 2016). COS™ assisted shifting one dyad from avoidant to secure attachment and maintenance of secure attachment for the second with increased parental attunement and better following the child's lead in play. Parents became more aware of their mental states and personal memories that influenced interactions with the child. There was a period of reorganization for the initially secure parent—i.e., a period of loss of confidence during learning. Ultimately, both parents improved in their sense of parenting competence.

Minding the Baby® (MTB)

MTB® (Sadler, Slade, & Mayes, 2006; mentalization-based treatment) is a home visiting program focused on young first-time, at-risk new parents (maternal age under 26, poverty, trauma history) recruited from pre-natal care groups (Sadler et al., 2006, 2013; Slade et al., 2005; Ordway, Webb, Sadler, & Slade, 2015). The Nurse Family Partnership (Olds, Sadler, & Kitzman, 2007) nurse home visiting and Infant–Parent Psychotherapy model (Lieberman, 2004). It includes weekly visits by a nurse and a clinical social worker (SW; most often alternating visits), from the second to third pre-natal trimester to infant age two. Sessions are generally 45–90 minutes (longer if in crisis) and once per week until age one, then every other week (Slade et al., 2005; Sadler et al., 2013). The nurse and SW jointly apply parental reflective functioning (RF) (Slade et al., 2005)—e.g., recognizing and identifying different levels and types of RF (Fonagy, Target, Steele, & Steele, 1998), mental health treatment approaches, and attachment theory, a complete review of Fonagy's work, and, when relevant, development and characteristics of teen mothers (Slade et al., 2005). This includes learning the ability to understand/reflect on the mental/emotional states of self and child (RF; Table 1.2). A supervisory relationship parallels and models the therapeutic relationship between nurse/SW and parent. It assists management of levels of complexity in the home, goal setting, identifying barriers and finding alternative routes to goals, and helps nurses and SWs to be clinically focused and to be able to "layer" the health and mental health work in their home visits.

In contrast to mothers' history of abuse, mothers' RF before a birth has predicted subsequent sensitivity or negative behaviors—i.e., intrusive, aggressive, withdrawn (Ensink, Normandin, Godbout, & Fonagy, 2016b; Stacks et al., 2014) and has been related to infant attachment (Ensink et al., 2016b). Lower maternal RF at infant six months has been linked to increased infant aggression, ages 12 and 20 months (Smaling et al., 2016; Chapter 5). Goals of MTB® include improved RF in mothers, secure mother–child attachments, and decreased maltreatment and poor mental health outcomes (Fonagy, Gergely, & Target, 2007; Ordway et al., 2014). It is considered well suited for highly traumatized mothers—e.g., addresses relationship disruptions stemming from mothers' early trauma and derailed attachment history. Assessment is conducted at intervals (mothers and babies).

MTB® has been linked to lower levels of externalizing, somewhat lower levels of internalizing, and lower total behavior problems in MTB® children compared to controls, and it has shown improved RF in mothers (N = 38, at ages 3–5; parent report, Ordway et al., 2014). MTB® toddlers have shown healthy body mass index versus controls who showed significantly higher obesity levels, including in Hispanic families who have had nationally, significantly higher levels of overweight in young children (N = 158, ages 0–2; Ordway et al., 2018). For 60 intervention mothers (45 comparisons; Sadler et al., 2013), team visits focused on child health and development, maternal and infant health and mental health, parenting, social support, maternal life course, and environment and safety. For intervention mothers there were fewer disrupted interactions at four months (not significant), more secure attachments, fewer disorganized attachments (at 12 months), and a strong trend toward fewer CPS referrals (at 24 months), than for comparison mothers (Sadler et al., 2013). MTB® infants were significantly more likely to have up-to-date immunizations and well-baby visits (at 12 months). Mothers had lower rates of rapid subsequent child-bearing. Control and intervention mothers had significantly increased RF scores over the 24-month period.

Interventions for Specific Symptoms

A wide variety of treatments (e.g., administration of probiotics, Callaghan, Cowan, & Richardson, 2016; massage; meditation) have emerged for a number of symptoms (e.g., gastrointestinal, later life anxiety, stress, concentration problems). Some interventions require adaptations for different cultures, for different personality or attachment styles, and/or for different problems (see Chapters 13, 16, 17). Additionally, personality matters with regard to parenting and to child outcomes as well as to treatment. A program that assists parents to effectively parent young children with different temperaments can be found in Chapter 10 (INSIGHTS).

Brain-Related Changes

From birth, right-brain-to-right-brain, contingent processes—e.g., "holding, touch, gaze sharing, face-to-face contact, entrained vocal rhythms, and spontaneous moments of play and delight" (Lipton & Fosha, 2011, p. 255)—are essential for (a) autonomic nervous system (ANS) regulation, (b) optimal brain development, (c) the emergence of self-regulation, and (d) the creation of secure attachments (Lipton & Fosha, 2011; Porges, 2009; Schore, 1996, 2003). Our earliest perceptions (of safety or danger) are nonverbal, somatosensory, and carried throughout life (Lipton & Fosha, 2011). The hippocampus (e.g., organizes AM) is not fully functioning until ages 1.5–3 years; hence early organization of emotional experience remains *a felt experience*. For example, a more complex self-organization first includes contingent affect regulation—dyadic striving toward repair when the child is in a dysregulated, negative state—which requires an opposite reaction from the caregiver (i.e., amplification and intensification of positive emotion; Lipton & Fosha, 2011; Schore, 2001). Methods above and in Chapters 10 and 13 address these issues.

Deprivation-Related Disorders

Fetal and infant deprivation cause a variety of negative effects that often can be treated. Severe neglect such as that found in institutional care is related to a number of disorders and problems. Such early psychosocial deprivation has had profound adverse effects on children's brain and behavioral development, including abnormalities in physical growth as well as cognitive, social, and emotional development (Young et al., 2017). It has shown a profound effect on psychopathology as well. Reactive attachment disorder (Boxes 3.5, 6.4), DSM-5 Disinhibited Social Engagement Disorder (DSED), later callous-unemotional traits (CU; a precursor to psychopathy; Humphreys et al., 2015b), profound developmental compromises, and other psychopathology are among them (Tibu et al., 2014). Severe early life psychosocial deprivation is associated with a persistent, pervasive pattern of blunted or elevated ANS and HPA axis reactions to both social and nonsocial stressors, especially after prolonged institutional care—e.g., hypo-responsivity to social stressors, blunted vagal withdrawal to a nonsocial stressor, and blunted cortisol reactivity; hyper-responsivity to potential stressors (McLaughlin et al., 2015b). Cumulative time in institutionalized care has negatively predicted IQ at age 12 (Almas et al., 2016).

Evidence suggests that quality of institutional and/or foster care may affect development and pathology (Almas et al., 2016; Tibu et al., 2014; Humphreys, Fox, Nelson, & Zeanah, 2017a)—e.g., in institutions, having fewer caregivers per child in a week—rather than multiple caregivers in a week—has been related to reduced DSED (Smyke, Dumitrescu, & Zeanah, 2002). Some institutional programs (not included below) that provided infants increased non-interactive stimulation or low adult–infant interaction have lost gains after interventions terminated (St. Petersburg–USA Orphanage Research Team, 2008). In contrast, the St. Petersburg–USA Orphanage Research Team (2008) employed two social-emotional interventions in orphanages (birth to 48 months; in St. Petersburg, Russian Federation), where children were primarily deficient in social-emotional experiences and opportunities for adult–child relationships. They provided caregiving—e.g., greater sensitivity, encouraging independence and development—and structural changes such as number of children per room. Children showed substantial improvements in physical, mental, and social-emotional development (typical and disabled children), with a dose-response effect for many outcomes—i.e., the more positive social-emotional experiences children had and the longer they spent in interventions, the greater the developmental gains. Some treatments listed in "Trauma-Focused Methods" above address these issues. In addition are the following interventions.

The Bucharest Early Intervention Project (BEIP)

BEIP (Zeanah, Nelson, Fox, & Smyke, 2003) employs child-centered foster care as an intervention for children exposed to abuse and deprivation in institutional care (Smyke, Zeanah, Fox, & Nelson, 2009). BEIP includes training social workers (SWs) extensively in the basic principles of infant mental health—e.g., attachment, post-institutional adjustment, and managing common behavior problems. SWs then organize groups of foster parents, assisting them through the licensing process and gaining insights for a good-fit match between foster-parent and child. SWs establish a relationship with foster parents and children and provide foster parents with a better understanding of children's institutional experiences. They also offer counseling, support, and parent training to biological parents seeking to be re-united with their children.

Foster parents were encouraged to invest in the children as if they were their own. The first six weeks of placement are often the most challenging; foster parents were invited to call social workers, as needed. Children exhibit a number of problems, such as *regulatory*—e.g., sleeping, eating, toileting; *developmental*—e.g., cognitive, speech/language, and gross motor delays; *social interaction*—e.g., extreme withdrawal, indiscriminate behavior, aggression; and *other problems*—e.g., agitation, loudness. Because of institutional experiences—e.g., fear or anger related to toileting or bath time—some normal expectations were delayed or altered—e.g., toilet training delayed six months; bath-times made more enjoyable (Smyke et al., 2009). Foster-parent support and training groups assisted progress. U.S. professionals used video-conferencing and on-sight visitation to provide reflective, supportive supervision and training. Social workers were taught a number of skills—e.g., persistence and nonjudgmental interest to elicit information from foster parents reluctant to complain. The intervention ended when children reached 54 months (age 4.5). About half of institutional children were living in foster care by 54 months.

Studies have shown the importance of a shorter duration of institutionalization, of the attachment with the foster parent, and of the stability of placements. Early studies showed differences for children placed early and between the genders. Later studies showed the importance of stable, ongoing care (quality attachments) and of assessing the stability of care. Romanian children were assessed at baseline (N = 208; ages 5–30 months) and regular intervals in the following years. When foster care (FC; N = 68), continuing institutional care (IC; N = 68), and never institutionalized children (NI; N = 72) were assessed again at 30 and 42 months, results suggested that the quality of foster caregiving was superior to IC and was indistinguishable from the quality of care for NI children (e.g., Smyke et al., 2009). Developmental quotients (DQ; at 30 and 42 months), IQ (at 54 months), secure attachments (42 months), and emotional responsiveness (54 months) were significantly higher in the FC children than in IC children, though DQ and IQ were significantly lower than for NI children (at every age assessed to 4.5). While there was little intervention effect for children placed in foster care when older than 24 months, the younger the child when placed, the greater the cognitive and language gains. Length of time in IC correlated negatively with brain electrical activity and differentiation. In a study of these children at age 12 (Almas et al., 2016), BEIP children had higher full-scale IQ and verbal comprehension scores than IC children (N = 107), although both remained lower than NI children—linked only to working memory at age 12 for FC children. Timing of placement was not significant for IQ at age 12.

Both internalizing and externalizing disorders were associated with IC. At 54 months, FC children showed significantly lower internalizing (i.e., anxiety, depression) but not externalizing disorders compared to IC children (i.e., aggressive behavior disorders, ADHD; Zeanah et al., 2009). When compared to government foster care (where foster parents were discouraged from attaching to children) at 4.5, BEIP foster care girls (not boys) had fewer signs of internalizing disorders and of ADHD symptoms than government foster care children (Tibu et al., 2014). Reductions in internalizing were mediated by attachment security with foster parents (McLaughlin, Zeanah, Fox, & Nelson, 2012). At 54 months, boys in both foster groups (BEIP & Government) were similar in all domains (e.g., signs of Oppositional Defiant Disorder or conduct disorder) and were more symptomatic than girls, showing no significant reduction in total psychiatric symptoms following placement (Zeanah et al., 2009). This may suggest girls' differential ability to form secure attachments (Tibu et al., 2014), a need for additional interventions to reduce externalizing (e.g., PCIT, Chapter 10), and/or differential age-related gender development (e.g., Aber, Brown, & Jones, 2003). At age 12, BEIP boys were more responsive to intervention, showing reduced externalizing (not girls; Humphreys et al., 2015a).

For FC children, there was a reduction in RAD at 30, 42, and 54 months (Zeanah et al., 2009). DSED was lower in FC children placed before 24 months than in IC children (30 months; Smyke et al., 2012). At age eight, IC and FC children did not significantly differ from each other in anxiety, depression, or RAD symptoms and had higher levels than NI children (placement stability was not assessed; see Humphreys et al., 2017a). At age 12, FC children had significantly fewer signs of RAD and DSED than IC children (no effects of age of placement; Humphreys, Nelson, Fox, & Zeanah, 2017b). Number of caregiving disruptions and percentage of time spent in IC significantly predicted signs of attachment disorders (a BDNF genetic contribution as well, see Humphreys et al., 2017a).

Although etiology for ADHD may be primarily genetic (Faraone & Doyle, 2001), signs of ADHD are much higher in abused or neglected children (e.g., see Tibu et al., 2014) and for IC children (Stevens et al., 2008). By age 4.5, 21% of children raised in institutions met criteria for ADHD (IC & FC, Zeanah et al., 2009; vs 3–10% of NI children, see Tibu et al., 2016a, 2016b), possibly a response to deprivation-related brain alterations (see Humphreys et al., 2017a). When the children were age eight, they were assessed for ADHD and executive function (EF; N = 136 IC, N = 72 NI; Tibu et al., 2016b). History of institutional care was related to inattention and impulsivity as well as to poorer performance on working memory, response-inhibition, and planning tasks. Deficits in working memory (both inattention and impulsivity) and in response-inhibition (impulsivity only) partially explained the association between early IC and ADHD symptoms (planning ability did not explain the link).

Importantly at age 12, previously institutionalized children who remained in stable, high-quality foster care (BEIP) showed important differences in psychopathology (e.g., lower internalizing and externalizing, not ADHD) from children whose placements were disrupted (more for girls than boys at this age; Humphreys et al., 2015a). With secure attachment status at age 12, during social tasks (likely reflecting increased propensity for social engagement), earlier age of foster care placement was linked to normalization of cortisol reactivity (if placed before 18 months) and enhanced vagal engagement (before 24 months), suggesting a sensitive period for environmental influence on stress response system development (McLaughlin et al., 2015b). Genetics and environment (e.g., maltreatment) are significantly linked to psychopathy, while caregiver responsiveness is related to empathy development (see Humphreys et al., 2015b). At age 12 (N = 47 IC, 48 foster care, 50 NI children; Humphreys et al., 2015b), children with histories of IC showed higher levels of callous-unemotional traits (CU) than NI children. BEIP foster care conditions significantly mitigated CU traits in boys at age 12.

Dissociation

Trauma and attachment have been related to dissociation. In a high-risk, low-income, ethnically diverse sample of traumatized 3–6-year-olds (N = 140; Hagan, Hulette, & Lieberman, 2015), almost one fourth had subclinical or clinical levels of dissociation (mother-reported). Contrary to previous findings (disorganized attachment linked to dissociation), Haltigan and Roisman (2015) found a reliable (but small magnitude) association between early avoidant attachment style (but not disorganized attachment) and dissociation in childhood and adolescence (N = 1,149). In this young age group, attachment-based methods are used to address dissociation (Trauma Treatment, above).

Executive Functions (EF)

Infant and parent training methods have assisted problems in infants' EFs. Wass, Porayska-Pomsta, and Johnson (2012) used gaze-contingent computer tasks to train 11-month-old infants—e.g., a butterfly flew only when infant gazed at it, visual distracters were included (five visits over 15 days, total 77 minutes; N = 42). Infants improved in cognitive control, cognitive flexibility, and sustained attention; saccadic reaction times and visual attention disengagement latencies were reduced (after exclusion of outliers; no improvements in WM; Wass et al., 2012). After training, infants demonstrated a trend in increased spontaneous looking behavior during free-play. In addition, some studies have shown post-training improvements in ADHD (see Wass et al., 2012). Review of findings suggests that both engagement during training and length of training may be important to outcomes (Wass et al., 2012). More training was associated with greater improvement. Low performance in executive functions and ADHD symptoms are common after early deprivation (e.g., institutional care; Tibu et al., 2016b). Tibu et al. (2016a) found that EFs (response-inhibition, working memory, not planning) mediated the link between early deprivation (institutional care) and ADHD symptoms (impulsivity and inattention). Low EF and ADHD symptoms have remained high after placement in families (and in pre-pubertal age), underscoring the need for early training interventions (Tibu et al., 2016b). Peng and Miller (2016) examined studies of attention training related to alerting (re: readiness to react), orienting (to stimuli), or executive attention (conflict of attention-eliciting stimuli, resolution), and like Wass et al., concluded that training younger subjects and youth with ADHD showed greater gains than training older or normally developing ones. Genes may influence how much a person benefits from training (Posner et al., 2016). Caregiver responsiveness has been related to children's executive functions (Merz et al., 2015). For 2.5–5-year-olds whose caregivers received either an online development course alone or the course with weekly mentoring, the youngest children in the group improved in delay inhibition and attention problems if caregivers received both (N = 141; there was no no-treatment comparison group; Merz et al., 2015).

Grief

Because infants and toddlers rely on caregivers for their survival and well-being, loss of an important attachment figure in very early life can have devastating repercussions (Lieberman & Van Horn, 2008)—e.g., disrupted attachment disorders; prolonged bereavement/grief reactions; psychiatric disorders (DC:0–3R; Lieberman & Van Horn, 2008; Markese, 2011). Given the many adverse consequences of parent or sibling loss and the impact of complicated grief (CG) on children, it is essential to differentiate childhood CG (and possible subtypes of grief), from normal grief, to avoid imposing adult conceptualizations of CG onto children, and to recognize CG's developmental impact (Dyregrov, Dyregrov, & Johnsen, 2013; Dyregrov, Salloum, Kristensen, & Dyregrov, 2015; Nader, 2008; Pearlman et al., 2010). Children with parent loss have shown a wide range of disorders and problems in adulthood—e.g., suicidality, depression, and anxiety disorders such as agoraphobia, panic, and phobic disorders; increased incidence of substance abuse; greater incidence of BPD and PTSD; unresolved attachment status (e.g., Lyons-Ruth, 2003; see Markese, 2011). In the 1920s, a future Olympian's mother died when he was age three. His father left him with others after her death, so he lost both parents. As an adolescent, his father abandoned him again, leaving him to find a way to survive on his own. His university rowing career and relationships were hindered by his "sensitivity" and low levels of trust. Helping coaches and later placement with a crew he could learn to trust and bond with were healing for him (see Brown, 2014a). After disasters, grief has been a risk factor for depression and for PTSD (Dyregrov et al., 2015; Nader et al., 1990; Tang et al., 2014). While some studies have shown that maternal loss is more strongly associated with psychiatric outcomes, others have shown loss of the same-sex parent to be of significance (Otawa et al., 2014; see Otawa et al., 2014; see Separation Anxiety, to follow).

Attachment figures are not interchangeable for young children (Lieberman, Compton, Van Horn, & Ghosh Ippen, 2003). Even as neonates they recognize the smell, sound, touch, and routines of a caregiver (Chapter 5). Reactions to the loss of an attachment figure may vary depending on the nature of the death, the child's qualities (e.g., temperament, strengths, vulnerabilities), the level of ongoing support, and other factors (Lieberman et al., 2003; Nader, 1997). As noted, Bowlby (1969/1982) suggested, in response to distress, a sequence of infant *protest*, *despair*, and *detachment* (Table 6.1). Grief may express as excessive crying or persistent fretting (sadness, protest); lack of affect and withdrawn states; separation anxiety; irritability, anger, and/or increased tantrums; regression; and/or changes in feeding and sleeping patterns (e.g., poor sleep; fear of going to sleep; nightmares; Corr & Corr, 1996). Normal grief includes loneliness and preoccupation with thoughts/feelings about the deceased (Scheeringa, 2016). It may include bodily symptoms and sensations (e.g., fast heart beat; trembling; aches; perspiration); thinking about, missing, and/or longing for the person; and/or other signs of protest or sadness (e.g., withdrawal, tantrums). Grief is considered abnormal when it is prolonged (longer than six months; APA, 2013) or severe—e.g., intense levels of mentioned symptoms; persistent self-blame. DC:0–3R prolonged bereavement/grief reaction includes the following symptoms (any three): persistent distress; searching for the absent caregiver; refusal of comfort from others; emotional withdrawal, sadness, and lethargy; eating and sleep disruptions; developmental regressions; reduced range of affect; and strong reactions to reminders of the loss (Zero to Three, 2005). To some extent, very young children may mirror a surviving caregiver's reactions (Nader & Salloum, 2011). They may move in and out of grief (are prone to living in the moment). Some of the methods presented earlier and in Chapter 10 have been used with bereaved infants and young children (e.g., CPP; PPT; Chapter 10).

Understanding of Death

Very young children do not understand the permanence of death and generally expect the deceased to return (Nader & Salloum, 2011). Toddlers tend to think that death is reversible or that the person is just sleeping (Corr & Corr, 1996). Although very young children can grieve, they are not likely to link symptoms to grief (Nader & Salloum, 2011). Young children's questions tend to reflect a concrete and literal interpretation of the world. Scheeringa (2016) suggests that the concept of heaven is too abstract for very young children. When they ask where the deceased is, telling them, e.g., that s/he is in a box in the ground at the cemetery often is a more satisfying answer (although perhaps shocking for adults). Wording should balance the developmental age and needs of the child with the beliefs of adult caretakers. A child's imagination can be worse than the truth.

Grief Treatment

Treatments for infants' and young children's grief seek to enhance the skills needed to deal with the loss—e.g., capacities to tolerate and regulate strong emotions; if verbal, to express feelings in words and in play; to rely on interpersonal relationships for coping with negative emotions such as fear or anxiety; to memorialize or have a keepsake of the deceased—and to create an environment that promotes recovery (Lieberman et al., 2003; Scheeringa, 2016; Webb, 2010). For example, a clinician may help a caregiver to provide a safe environment with consistent routines; facilitate emotional connection to a new or remaining attachment figure; assist acceptance and understanding of the permanence of the loss; assist child and caregiver with the child's reactions to reminders; help a caregiver to soften the effects of changes and help a child to adjust to changes; aid emotion-regulation (e.g., sadness, anger, or aggression outbursts), promote toddlers' healthy reminiscing; and assist normal development (e.g., Lieberman et al., 2003; see, e.g., Child–Parent Psychotherapy, Preschool PTSD Treatment, Chapter 10).

Language Problems

Language is important to all aspects of human life. Compared to same-age children with typically developing language, toddlers and preschoolers with language delays frequently have exhibited elevated problem behaviors (Curtis, Kaiser, Estabrook, & Roberts, 2017). Methods have emerged to assist young children with language development (see Appendix—Enhanced Milieu Teaching). They have also assisted with problem behaviors. Interventions often modify parental behaviors—e.g., increase their linguistic input and responsiveness to child communication; learn to follow the child's lead during interactions. Methods presented earlier (e.g., BEIP) and in Chapter 10 (e.g., PCIT) have also assisted language development.

Separation Anxiety

Separation anxiety emerges in humans at around 6–12 months, lasts to age three years, then steadily abates (Battaglia, 2015). Evolutionary brain growth (e.g., mass, capacities, ratio to body) and related, augmented plasticity has extended infant dependence on parental care and has reinforced and expanded the regulatory element of separation anxiety as an element of reciprocal regulation of infant–mother bond and as a moderator between environmental exploration, learning, and safe return to the mother. Nursing, play, and the "separation call" (intended to maintain mother–offspring contact) were probably made possible by the emergence of distinctively mammalian brain structures (e.g., cingulate cortex and "thalamo-cingulate;" Battaglia, 2015). Separation anxiety disorder (SAD) is an exaggerated and/or age-inappropriate manifestation of normal physiological separation anxiety. It includes at least three of eight symptoms indicating overt separation-related distress/fear and worry about the attachment figure, reluctance to sleep without nearness of the attachment figure, nightmares, and somatic complaints related to separation (APA, 2013; Battaglia, 2015).

Even a fairly brief early separation may have negative outcomes. For example, controlling for family and maternal characteristics and indicators of family instability, mother–child separation for a week or longer within the first two years of life has been related to higher levels of child negativity (at age three) and aggression (ages three and five; N = 2080 assessed age 1, 2, 3, 5; separations were not linked to maternal warmth or sensitivity; Howard, Martin, Berlin, & Brooks-Gunn, 2011). Separation from parents in childhood has been linked to a variety of psychopathology. Paksarian et al. (2015) found that risk from maternal separation was consistent across ages, while risk from separation from both parents increased with age. Otawa and colleagues (2014) found that parental death was specifically associated with later phobia and alcohol dependence (weakly), while non-death maternal or paternal separation was linked to a wide range of adult pathology—assessed diagnoses: major depression, generalized anxiety disorder, phobia, panic disorder, alcohol dependence, and drug abuse and dependence; most strongly for depression and drug abuse/dependence (11% of total variance; N = 2605 adult male twins; separation before age 17). Like a number of other studies, they found that genetic factors were important in the etiology of externalizing disorders, while environmental factors were important to internalizing disorders. Separations from mothers, fathers, and both parents each have been associated with increased risk of psychotic disorders—e.g., schizophrenia and bipolar disorder; increased risk with greater number of years and earlier separations, especially father separations (N = 985,058; Paksarian et al., 2015). Anglin, Cohen, and Chen (2008) found that duration of maternal separation before age two was positively linked to later trajectory of schizotypal symptoms (between ages 9–39 years). Methods discussed earlier in this chapter treat separation anxiety through treating the caregiver–infant relationship.

SAD Trajectories

In the normal population, SAD is common among preschool children—four trajectories have been identified (Battaglia et al., 2016). All trajectories except the *high-increasing* group (H-I) showed symptom reduction by age six. H-I children showed a remarkably stable, elevated separation anxiety profile throughout preschool years, though no significant link to externalizing (linked to high-decreasing, H-D). H-I predicted teacher-assessed separation anxiety profiles and internalizing at age six and was distinctively associated with higher maternal depression, smoking during pregnancy, and parental unemployment (Battaglia, 2015), and suboptimal parenting (also in H-D; and early divorce: ages 1.5–2.5; Battaglia et al., 2016). Childhood SAD and adult panic disorder (PD) share specific genetic similarities and share exaggerated emotional and respiratory reactivity to CO_2. SAD and a family history of PD with agoraphobia predicts earlier onset of PD-Agoraphobia. SAD has been linked to childhood parental loss (separation, divorce, death) and to early stressful life events. For example, in a study of anxiety disorders in Ugandan children (N = 286 <age five; 416 age 6–9; 550 ages 10–13; 335 ages 14–19), war exposure as well as chronic stressors—e.g., caregiver unemployment, living without parents, and no parent education—predicted anxiety disorders, especially in females (29.7% vs 23%, males; Abbo et al., 2013). Children under age 5 were significantly more likely to have SAD and specific phobia, while older children (ages 14–19) were more likely to have PTSD (Abbo et al., 2013). Individuals with 2+ comorbid disorders often had anxiety disorders (62.1%). Adult SAD has sometimes linked to childhood SAD (Bucci et al., 2012).

Divorce

Young children may experience separation anxiety in response to divorce (see Ludolph & Bow, 2012). Although young children generally do not reject a parent if they are well treated, they may become uncomfortable if exposed to alienating messages about a parent (Ludolph & Bow, 2012). *Alienation*—a child's persistent and unreasonable rejection of a competent parent (e.g., resisting visit time; Kelly & Johnston, 2001)—can be distinguished from *estrangement*—a child's rejection of a parent who psychologically or physically abuses, neglects, is absent, or is otherwise incompetent in parenting (Ludolph & Bow, 2012). In contrast, *enmeshment* suggests chronic alignment between a parent and child in which psychological boundaries blur (e.g., between parent's and child's intentions and feelings). Alienation may be accompanied by estrangement or enmeshment. Young children usually are unable to maintain alienation (when treated well), unless emulating an older sibling.

As noted in the discussion of SAD, divorce during toddlerhood or infancy can have early and long-term negative associations (see Chapter 9, Cohen & Weitzman, 2016). For example, attachment status may be undermined—adult unresolved states of mind have been related to early divorce or separations (Lyons-Ruth & Jacobvitz, 2018; change to insecure, Markese, 2011). Zeanah et al. (2011a) recommend that for children younger than ages two or three years, it is advisable for the custodial parent to be present during extended visits with a noncustodial parent, if they can be together without conflict, to prevent harm to the primary attachment relationship and to enhance the likelihood of a healthy attachment to the noncustodial parent. High conflict can lead to personality disturbances and to attachment relationship disturbances (Chapter 5). A child's comfort is usually increased when routines are maintained (e.g., sleep, activity, and eating schedules; favorite stuffed animal; similar parenting strategies; Zeanah et al., 2011a).

Sleep Disturbances

In addition to quiet sleep's function as a restorative mechanism (Chapter 6), it may serve as a stimulus barrier in early infancy, protecting the newborn from overwhelming stimulation (Dahl, 2007; Hostinar & Gunnar, 2013; Chapter 5). Issues related to sleep and intervention follow.

Treatments for Non-Traumatic Sleep Disturbance

Interventions for infant sleep problems generally include modifying parents' behavior and their cognitions and expectations. While parental beliefs, personality, and psychopathology influence infant sleep, the links are bidirectional and dynamic—poor infant sleep may influence parental behaviors and may be a family stressor (Sadeh et al., 2010). Parental difficulties with limit-setting (especially both parents) and anger at the child's demands have been important in explaining the variance in sleep problems. Infant protest and crying related to relative withdrawal of parents and discontinuation of the infant's preferred routines (e.g., rocking, nursing, falling asleep while held) can be a challenge to parents—e.g., concerns about infant's distress and about possible psychological damage to the infant. While the benefits of breastfeeding may make it worth increased awakenings (i.e., breast milk digests faster), increased parental involvement (e.g., holding, feeding, rocking) is associated with more fragmented sleep—i.e., more and longer night wakings—suggesting the possibility that increased parental involvement—e.g., excessive physical comforting; delayed encouragement of infant self-soothing; reduced encouragement of autonomy—interferes with an infant's development of self-regulation and self-soothing.

Online, preventive parent training has shown some success with moderate sleep disturbances in infants and toddlers (Gregory & Sadeh, 2016). Interventions with parents that encourage independence and self-soothing have been associated with extended and more consolidated sleep in contrast to more active parent soothing. If mothers continuously provide physical presence for the reduction of tension and anxiety, infants learn to depend on them for emotion regulation, and they experience heightened distress when separation occurs (both during the day and at night, see Sadeh et al., 2010). Behavioral interventions have proven efficacious (Sadeh et al., 2010). During the intervention process, infants learn to resume sleep faster (often without parental assistance) and the number of night wakings decrease. Maternal cognitions emphasizing the importance of limiting parental nighttime involvement have predicted more consolidated sleep. Poor sleep has been associated with mothers' emphasis on infants' distress upon awakening, more active use of soothing, maternal depression, and separations from caregiver—the latter linked to increased clinginess/dependency and linked to poorer sleep. Infants have also had poorer sleep when parents referred to them as less likeable and less agreeable (France, 1992).

Posttrauma Sleep Disturbance

Although the attachment-based methods described earlier and in Chapter 10 address and have assisted with posttrauma sleep disturbances (Coates, 2016), after traumas, regression and/or the use of sleep as a protective mechanism must be considered. For young children, disturbed sleep as well as disturbed appetite and/or motor activity are common to a number of disorders—e.g., depression, PTS symptoms, anxiety (Egger & Angold, 2006; Coates, 2016; Kletter & Carrion, 2018; Scheeringa, 2016). After traumas, children may sleep more than normal, may have trouble going to or staying asleep, and may have nightmares or night terrors (Chapter 6). Night terrors have been treated using scheduled waking—fully waking a child for a short time (e.g., 10–15 minutes) before they are expected to have a night terror, then allowing them to resume sleep (Gregory & Sadeh, 2016).

Socioemotional Skills and Behavioral Cooperation

Play is often an aspect of intervention and assessment as well as a context for learning, inter-relating, and cooperating (Chapter 5; above methods; Scheeringa, 2016; Webb, 2015). Children under age 5 have been assessed using a combination of observation and questions during play, along with supplemental information from caretaking adults (e.g., Nader, 2008; Scheeringa et al., 2001, 2016). In some play treatment methods, verbalizing experiences is used to assist the young child—e.g., verbalizing a child's actions may help to create connection without being intrusive. Other methods are nonverbal and provide a supportive presence (e.g., Axline's sand-tray play, Chapter 1). *Helping the noncompliant child*, used with three-year-olds, is described in Chapter 10. Permitting children to demonstrate their trauma experiences with toys may be especially important for those who were preverbal during their experience. Some play methods, including those used to increase cooperation in this age group, are based on "Child's Game" (to follow; Chapter 10). Parents learn effective, growth-enhancing coplay and, in some methods, learn effective limit-setting.

Child's Game

Child's Game (McMahon & Forehand, 2003) includes 10–15-minute play sessions. Rules or procedures for the activity include (1) allowing the child to choose the activity—e.g., with no introduction of something new into her/his play and no adult changes in the activity; (2) watching attentively, and allowing the child's activity to be the center of attention; (3) following the child's lead—e.g., within the activity; if the child changes the activity; (4) describing the child's activity aloud ("play-by-play"); (5) without structuring the activity, participate by handing needed materials, taking a turn, or by imitating the play (continue describing); avoid asking questions, giving commands, or teaching during the play (such actions interrupt the structure of a child's play; see McMahon & Forehand, 2003 for elaboration of methods; Chapter 10—Helping the Noncompliant Child).

Child-Oriented Play (COplay)

Recognizing the mutual, reciprocal nature of the caregiver–child socialization process, Child-Oriented Play (COplay, Kochanska, Kim, Boldt, & Nordling, 2014) employs play techniques drawn from "Child's Game" (McMahon & Forehand, 2003; above). COplay aims to increase children's socioemotional competence and to increase their cooperation with mothers (Kochanska et al., 2014). While both a play-as-usual group and parent–child dyads given 10 weeks of COplay training both improved significantly, a modest effect favored child-oriented play. Only the COplay group increased cooperation over the next six months.

Conclusions

Attachment styles affect children's development and quality of life across life—e.g., in their functioning, interpersonal relationships, mental and physical well-being. The outcomes related to attachment as well as to trauma have demonstrated both the importance of sensitive and synchronous attachment relations from infancy and the importance of early interventions after traumas. Infants depend on adults for survival, and they develop a hierarchy of attachment figures. The infant's bond includes the caregiver's smell, touch, sound, and other familiar factors. For young children, separations, rejection, and/or failure of protection are significant stressors. Inhibiting exploration and learning can interfere with development as well. As the child develops, aspects of the child (e.g., stress sensitivity or reactivity, other temperament issues, developmental level) and environmental issues (e.g., attachment relationships, support, resources, enrichment) influence the depth and nature of posttrauma reactions, behaviors in treatment, and treatment needs. Treatments are available that address these aspects of a child (e.g., temperament, Chapters 10, 17; see above).

Young children are very aware of and responsive to genuine, sensitive care from adults in their environments (Box 1.3). Treatment of trauma-exposed young children requires cognizance of the importance of caregivers to the child and attention to the caregiver–child relationship. Studies of children in institutional care have shown the importance of shorter duration of children's institutionalization, the need for high-quality care and strong attachments with foster parents, and the need for stable placements in order to protect children from greater psychopathology.

Because children respond differently in different situations and in response to different adults, initial treatment and progress assessments appropriately include evaluation of the child in different settings/contexts, of multiple aspects of the child and her/his environment, and of the trauma(s) experienced. Although specific methods may address particular developmental problems, for very young children, the caregiver–infant relationship is a focus of and means to recovery. Additionally, regression is among normal responses to extreme distress (Chapters 1, 4). Recognizing regressed states and adjusting behavioral and verbal responses to the child are important. Sensitive caretaking and gradual restoration to normalcy are also important. Soothing (reduction of arousal) necessarily precedes other forms of repair.

Part III
Ages 3–6

8

Development in Preschool and Early School-Age Children

Preschool-aged children are just beginning to develop the ability for sustained attention and the capacity to inhibit impulses (Posner et al., 2007). At the same time, they are developing self-awareness, engaging in more goal-directed behavior and advanced planning, and showing a desire for increased independence (Gerson, Bekkering, & Hunnius, 2016; Posner et al., 2007). The resistance to following directions and rules is normative for preschoolers. Joint attention endeavors begin to include joint social actions that are also important to cognitive and other aspects of development (Gerson et al., 2016). Between ages four and six, many skills improve measurably—e.g., perspective-taking, cognitive flexibility, humor, and autobiographical memory. Secure attachments, other positive experiences, enriched environments, and adequate or good resources provide advantages for young children's development.

Variables that Influence Development

Some of the influencing variables for preschoolers were discussed in earlier chapters (Chapters 4, 5). Attachment with parents and teachers is discussed here. Other variables, such as temperament and parenting, are discussed in the specific developmental domains to which they relate.

Attachment Classifications

For children ages 3–6, attachment classifications influence reactions to stress, their modes of operating, and their representations of experiences in play. Toddlers' desires for physical proximity begin to be replaced gradually by a desire to maintain psychological proximity (Simpson & Belsky, 2018). Secure preschool and school-age children generally show relaxed, mutually enjoyable interactions with caregivers (in separation–reunion assessments) and continue to use adults (e.g., parents, teachers) as a secure base to facilitate exploration of the environment (Moss, Pascuzzo, & Simard, 2012). Children generally do better when liked by their parents and shown sensitive care. With increasing development of language and perspective-taking skills, securely attached children's increases in communication, joint planning, understanding of others, and negotiations to jointly achieve a common goal replace the aggressive exchanges normative in toddlerhood, while aggressive exchanges persist in insecure children (especially disorganized). Secure children create stories that depict sensitive parental figures who serve as a secure haven in times of distress (in doll-play). Secure infant attachments have been strongly linked to self-management, autonomy, and positive peer relationships in preschoolers (Sroufe, 2018).

Insecure-avoidant children show neutral coolness toward, minimize physical and verbal contact and displays of intimacy to, and display excessive self-reliance from parent, teachers, and peers—e.g., rarely seeking assistance even when facing difficult tasks (Table A3.3). Their conversations focus on play activities rather than on personal references. They are less likely than secure peers to represent themselves as submissive to parents or in need of guidance (doll-play, Bureau & Moss, 2010).

Resistant children place excessive emphasis on the relationship with the caregiver to the detriment of exploration. Their relationships are often characterized by immature and dependent behaviors with adults and peers and attention-seeking strategies, presumably linked to representations of caregiver as inconsistently available (Bureau & Moss, 2010). Insecure-resistant children are more likely to create stories with parents who are less efficient at soothing distress, and with a protagonist's exaggerated emotional expressions (doll-play).

Dramatically, by the end of the preschool period, disorganized children begin to take charge of the relationship with parents, either in a caregiving or a punitive fashion. Genetics may play some part in outcomes. Highly disorganized children who were homozygous for a catechol-O-methyltransferase (COMT) valine allele (Val) developed significantly greater increases in aggression and decreases in self-oriented social skills (e.g., self-regulation and assertiveness) between ages four and six than those with the methionine allele (Met), whereas disorganized children carrying the COMT Met allele were more likely to increase in social skills (e.g., cooperation and responsibility; see Appendix—COMT). Hence genotype may contribute to differences in controlling–punitive and controlling–caregiving behaviors of disorganized children (704 Norwegian children; Hygen et al., 2014).

Change over time appears not to erase effects of initial attachment classification (Sroufe, 2018). In comparing children secure in infancy to those insecure in infancy, Sroufe and colleagues found that, even if they had a period of behavior problems in preschool, securely attached children were less likely to have behavior problems in grade 3, while insecure children with a period of doing well were more vulnerable to later problems. Secure children were significantly less likely to show problems in the face of stress (the definition of resilience; Sroufe, 2018). While attachment alone does not determine outcomes, attachment security plays a part in producing a well-adapted preschool child who can flexibly adjust behavior to meet a context's requirements—e.g., boisterous and active on the playground; quiet and attentive during story time—who can be self-directing in activities; who can follow rules without constant adult supervision; and who effectively engages in and sustains interactions with peers despite challenges. Parenting and the child's nature are also important. While specific examination did not find ethnic differences for abuse, parental use of non-abuse physical discipline was related to a high risk of externalizing for European Americans, but less so for African American youth (Sroufe, 2018).

Attachments: Parents and Teachers

Depending on other factors, secure caregiver–child attachments have been related to more positive outcomes across age groups. For example, child attachment classification has been associated with a child's social adaptation (Bureau et al., 2017). Securely attached children have shown better school readiness (see School Readiness, this chapter; Williford, Carter, & Pianta, 2018). As indicated in earlier chapters, insecure or disorganized attachments have corresponded to more problems—e.g., poor school adjustment, anxious-withdrawn behaviors, externalizing. There has been significant concordance between mother– and father–child attachment classification (Psychogiou et al., 2018). Children insecurely attached to both parents have had more problems than those insecurely attached to only one parent.

The preschool to first-grade period includes increased verbal negotiation and planning between parent and child (Bureau et al., 2017). Many studies have assessed the child's use of the parents as a safe haven when distressed. Parental sensitivity is reflected in promoting autonomy and exploration (secure base) as well as in comforting/reassuring a distressed child (safe haven). In pre- and elementary school, teachers may become surrogate attachment figures and provide the warmth, support, and sensitivity that assists a child's ongoing development (Williford et al., 2018). Teachers, too, contribute to a child's internal working models or life scripts. Teacher–child secure attachment supports school adjustment and permits engaging more fully in activities of learning. Preschoolers' attachments to parents guide their attachments to teachers. Preschoolers' positive relationships with a teacher increase the likelihood that they will have better academic performance, lower externalizing behaviors, and better social skills (see Williford et al., 2018).

Research has shown that fathers become more directly involved with their offspring as toddlers and especially as preschoolers (Bureau et al., 2017). In studies of both parents as caregivers, some evidence has suggested that attachment security with fathers (not mothers) has been related to lower externalizing problems, less anxious-withdrawn behavior, greater social competence, more reciprocated friendships, fewer self-reported behavior problems (see Bureau et al., 2017). However, both father–child and mother–child attachments have contributed to young children's outcomes—e.g., their emotion understanding (N = 74, preschooler and each-parent dyads; Psychogiou et al., 2018).

One of the contexts in which parental sensitivity is assessed is in caregiver–child play. Such assessments include a parent's sensitivity, cooperation, and gentle challenging behaviors. Some researchers suggest that father's attachment with a child is more likely to be evident during joint exploration and play (Bureau et al., 2017). In the highly arousing context of play, both fathers' and mothers' sensitivity were associated with child attachment security (N = 107 Canadian dyads, children ages 3–5; Bureau et al., 2017). Fathers showed higher parenting distress when, e.g., a child was hyperactive, showed lower adaptation in novel situations, did not measure up to expectations, had a negative mood, or was less reinforcing of the father. Fathers with higher levels of parenting stress showed higher rates of insecure child–father attachments, in this study significantly stronger for child–father than for child–mother dyads. Child–father attachment insecurity was more strongly associated with child social adaptation than child–mother attachment. That is, child–father attachment linked to child conduct problems, regardless of child–mother attachment classification. Therefore, fathers' modeling of aggressive behaviors in play may need to be combined with sensitivity and appropriate limit-setting to prevent a young child from viewing aggression as acceptable.

For adults, sleep disturbances—e.g., difficulty falling or staying asleep; nightmares—have often been accompanied by depression, anxiety, and/or cognitive changes/difficulties—e.g., attention problems (e.g., across 30 studies, Adams, Stoops, & Skomro, 2014). Persistent sleep difficulties are a risk factor for subsequent mental health problems and substance use disorders. At preschool age, children move to a more social sleep schedule. Securely attached preschoolers have shown better quality sleep (see Adams et al., 2014). Evidence suggests that attachment quality in adulthood also influences sleep—anxiously attached individuals reported poorer sleep quality compared to individuals with avoidant and secure attachment styles (depression controlled for; couples).

Developmental Domains

Young children are more concrete in their thinking than older persons (Lewis, 1995), and are more prone to literal interpretations, animistic thinking—i.e., belief in consciousness or abilities in animals or objects—faulty hypotheses, and inaccurate associations—e.g., linking causation to proximity; overgeneralization (Murray & Son, 1998). Preschoolers are able to focus on more than one aspect of a situation simultaneously and are aware that some actions can be reversed by subsequent actions (see Nader, 2004). Major developmental tasks for this age group include acquiring strategies for emotion regulation and behavioral self-control (e.g., delay gratification, goal-directed behavior), increased emotion awareness, and interpersonal skills. With growth of language and perspective-taking skills, preschool and school-age children become better able to communicate intentions and plans to adults and peers, to understand plans and intentions of others, and to engage in negotiations aimed at jointly achieving a goal (Marvin, 1977). The inter-relatedness of developmental skills becomes very clear in this age group. Trauma may undermine skills and/or may be followed by regression in some or many aspects of development (see effects of trauma on developmental domains, Chapter 9).

Language Skills

As will be seen in the discussion of other developmental domains, language is a part of the development and expression of many other developmental skills. For example, through language, a child can relate his/her own and understand others' autobiographical memories, express with others their thoughts and emotions about things that have happened, and others can share with them (Fivush, 2011). Language is influenced by parenting (e.g., verbal interchanges) and by attachment quality as well as by adversity (Pickles et al., 2016). For example, maternal responsiveness has strongly predicted receptive, expressive, and total language scores for three- and four-year-olds who were slow to talk at age two (Hudson et al., 2015b). Language impairments have been linked to skill deficits and to emotional and behavioral problems (Salmon, O'Kearny, Reese, & Fortune, 2016). As discussed, children with early language delays may catch-up by age three (e.g., Henry et al., 2018; Chapter 5). Language delays persisting to school entry have demonstrated adverse effects on literacy, behavior, social development, and mental health into adulthood (see Boyle, 2011). In the preschool period, children are more malleable to intervention. Some suggest that language should be one of the targets of intervention for preschoolers with behavioral problems (Salmon et al., 2016).

General Executive Functioning (EF)

Simple executive functions include memory, shifting, and inhibition (Chapter 1). As discussed, skills are interrelated and simpler EFs may set the stage for more complex EFs (Mann et al., 2017). For example, in a study of school readiness, age, working memory, and inhibitory control directly predicted academic readiness and predicted delay of gratification for 3–5-year-olds (N = 104; Mann et al., 2017). Delay of gratification predicted social-emotional readiness. Social-emotional readiness predicted academic readiness. A child's ability to resist interference by their own perspective when perspective-taking has strongly correlated with general EF abilities (e.g., false belief tasks, Carlson & Moses, 2001). Although for adults, EFs are divided into at least three main components—working memory, inhibition, and flexibility—for kindergarteners, evidence suggests a two-factor model—an inhibition and a working memory–flexibility factor (Monette, Bigras, & Lafrenière, 2015). Although from ages 3–5 children learn how to flexibly shift attention between competing demands, and they acquire critical emotion regulation skills (to respond to negative affective challenges, Li et al., 2017b), cognitive flexibility does not increase sharply and distinctly until ages 7–9 (Dajani & Uddin, 2015). Evidence suggests preschoolers who are bilingual or have high monolingual verbal skills perform cognitive shifting tasks better than other children (Okanda, Moriguchi, & Itakura, 2010).

A number of factors have influenced EFs (e.g., genes, parenting, language, sleep). For example, both father and mother sensitive and supportive parenting has been related to better EFs in preschoolers (Towe-Goodman et al., 2014). Mother and father parenting behaviors that include higher monitoring and more positive parenting along with lower discipline, inconsistency, and negative controlling are associated with better development of children's inhibition capacities (ages 2–8, N = 421 families, Roskam, Stievenart, Meunier, & Noel, 2014). Although more helpful for younger children or when children are off-task, parental directive language to preschoolers has negatively related to cognitive and EF outcomes, whereas autonomy support and scaffolding have been robust predictors of EFs (Merz et al., 2015). For children with the DRD4 7+ genotype, fewer hours in non-maternal child care were associated with better attention skills and with better inhibitory control skills in pre-K (age 4.5; not for those without the DRDR 7+ genotype, Berry et al., 2014). This also supports the idea of differential susceptibility to environment (Chapter 4). Some ethnic differences have been shown for tasks normally used to assess self-regulation (e.g., middle-class white preschoolers completed the Shape Stroop better than minority children; Caughy, Mills, Owen, & Hurst, 2013). In a study of African American and Latino children (N = 407; more than half Spanish-speaking), 2.5- and 3.5-year-olds were significantly behind in inhibitory control and cognitive flexibility skill development (Caughy et al., 2013; see Fuhs, Farran, & Nesbitt, 2013, 4–5-year-olds). However, when tested in their most proficient language (Spanish vs English), similarities in inhibitory control and working memory were found (Lonigan et al., 2016). Sleep disturbance in preschoolers has been associated negatively with performance on specific EF tasks—i.e., working memory and interference-suppression inhibition tasks—in elementary school, even after controlling for general cognitive abilities (N = 215; Nelson et al., 2015). In this study, sleep problems were not related to flexible shifting or response-inhibition.

Although linked to problem behaviors in both genders, some evidence has shown that poor EF has been particularly strongly associated with elevated problem behavior scores in girls with little educated mothers (Hughes & Ensor, 2009). Emotion understanding and EF have each uniquely associated with behavior, independent of background factors (e.g., maternal education, age, gender, verbal ability; N = 235 preschoolers, Hughes & Ensor, 2009). Both have mediated the relationship between low maternal education and problem behaviors and between maternal depression and problem behaviors, suggesting that enhancing children's understanding of emotions and their EF (e.g., self-regulatory skills) may assist prevention of problem behaviors. Other EFs also play an important role in early development of flexibility—e.g., EF and working memory for drawing flexibility (N = 123, 36–73-months-olds; Panesi & Morra, 2016).

Working Memory

Working memory improves from ages 4–15, with notable variability in each age group (Alloway, 2006). Differences influence ability to gain knowledge and new skills. Children's prospective memory performance—remembering to do something in the future, involving anticipating the future and planning for it—improves over preschool and school years (see Sellers & Bjorklund, 2014).

Autobiographical Memory (AM). Some researchers believe that children's sense of self is not adequately developed to form true AM until about age 4 years (e.g., Howe et al., 2009). In early childhood and in adolescence, mothers help children, through everyday conversation, to reexamine, reinstate, and compile their memories of personal experiences (AM). Children learn to understand event-related emotions, which fosters the development of AM (Bosmans et al., 2012). In a study of typically developing young children's AM, Nuttall et al. (2014) confirmed that a basic ability to retrieve and report specific memories is in place by age three (N = 79, age four; 63, age five; 65, age six; see also Fivush & Nelson, 2004). A mother's style of elaborating highly, when reminiscing with their preschool children about past events, uniquely has predicted the development of AM skills in childhood and in adolescence (even controlling for concurrent maternal reminiscing style; sees Fivush, 2011).

Inhibition/Flexibility

Both inhibition and cognitive flexibility assist other skills (e.g., self-regulation; Li et al., 2017b). Across 75 studies (N = 14,424, ages 2.7–6.7; meta-analysis: Allan et al., 2014), there was a moderate, significant relationship between inhibitory control and academic performance (with some variation by task or subject). Low levels of these skills have been related to problems. For example, low inhibition has been associated with internalizing and externalizing (e.g., Eisenberg et al., 2009; ADHD, McClelland et al., 2007). Inhibition includes the ability to act in opposition to a prepotent response or to delay or postpone a dominant response (a simple EF; Rollins & Riggins, 2016; Glossary). Preschoolers who are able to delay gratification by directing attention away from a tempting item have had greater success in a delay of gratification task years later (one cookie if don't delay; two cookies if do—ages 4–5; go/no-go task: ages 11–22, Eigsti et al., 2006). Preschool-age girls have been better than preschool-age boys at inhibition (Roskam et al., 2014). Parenting has influenced the ability to inhibit (Merz et al., 2015; Roskam et al., 2014). For example, for 2–4-year-olds, initial parental directive language—language used to control and guide a child's behavior—was significantly negatively associated with preschoolers' delay-inhibition abilities three months later (a form of controlling parenting; N = 247; Merz et al., 2015; Glossary—inhibition). Such language may reflect low autonomy support. Initial parental responsiveness—e.g., being attuned to the child, accurately interpreting child cues, and flexibly adjusting to the child' s play interests—was significantly positively related to delay-inhibition three months later. Parental monitoring has been related to lower behavioral problems and higher EFs, including increased inhibition in preschoolers (Roskam et al., 2014).

Cognitive flexibility—the ability to simultaneously manage multiple aspects of a task and actively switch between them—also improves across the preschool years (Li et al., 2017b) and enables better functioning—e.g., self-control, reading comprehension, social and academic functioning (e.g., Cartwright et al., 2010; ages 3–6, Farrant, Fletcher, & Maybery, 2014; Guajardo & Cartwright, 2016). Children who are able to flexibly shift attention, thoughts, or gaze have been able to reduce negative or positive affect or to delay reward (Carlson & Wang, 2007; Li et al., 2017b). During preschool years, cognitive and emotional neurodevelopment appear to be entwined (e.g., activate similar brain regions; Li et al., 2017b). Although irritability is unrelated to cognitive flexibility, irritable children employ both hemispheres during cognitive flexibility tasks (vs left hemisphere only). Beginning around age four, inhibition and working memory contribute to successful cognitive flexibility driven by improvements in children's goal-representation abilities (Dajani & Uddin, 2015). Specific interventions have been related to preschool-aged foster children's stronger cognitive flexibility and theory of mind skills (e.g., ABC, Chapter 10; Lewis-Morrarty et al., 2012).

Advanced Planning

Planning ahead occurs in social and in nonsocial contexts. It may involve, e.g., choosing or preparing an item that will be used in a task, planning a first step in advance, or deciding the placement of items in advance (Gerson et al., 2016). In social contexts, planning requires adapting to another's actions. Even though five-year-olds were still variable in their accommodation of another, a study showed that 3.5-year-olds, not 2.5–3-year-olds, significantly often accommodated their actions to a partner's actions (Meyer, van der Wel, & Hunnius, 2016). Similarly, four-year-olds but not three-year-olds, significantly anticipated an item needed in a future context, and five-year-olds planned in advance which of two tools would be needed in a joint context, better than three-year-olds (see Gerson et al., 2016, summary of studies). Gerson et al. found that three-year-olds were better at planning ahead when playing alone than with a social partner. That is, they took into account the color of balls when planning where to place a mixed-colored ball (placing balls in matching cups), in contrast to seemingly random placement with a social partner. They were able to correct placement errors whether playing alone or with another. It's possible that a social partner adds complexity and may require cognitive resources adding to cognitive load, that having a partner triggers a shift in cognitive processing, or that the interruption (to attention, to play) by the presence of another made planning more difficult (Gerson et al., 2016). Effects may be particularly salient for younger children who are still developing their attentional capacities.

Self-Regulation: Effortful Control (EC)

Effortful control (EC) includes the inhibition of a response in consideration of long-term consequences (Rueda et al., 2005). High levels of effortful control appear to promote adaptive development (e.g., Kryski et al., 2013). Attentional control also assists regulation—e.g., of negative emotion—by permitting a child to focus away from distressing stimuli (Fox et al., 2005). Control of impulses develops slowly from age one through grade school (Putnam, Ellis, & Rothbart, 2001). Studies are mixed about gender differences (Fuhs et al., 2013). During childhood and adulthood, EC/self-regulation correlate with indices of life success—i.e., with school performance for children and with health, income, and successful human relationships for adults (Posner, Rothbart, Sheese, & Voelker, 2014). For example, children high in EC demonstrate greater empathy, better school performance, and higher performance on conflict-related cognitive tasks.

EC includes both cognitive and behavioral control. Cognitive control includes an ability to inhibit task-irrelevant responses that may occur at different stages of processing (Eigsti et al., 2006). Preschoolers' ability to delay gratification (e.g., ability to wait) via attentional control (e.g., direct attention away from temptation) is precursor to adolescent ability to inhibit attentional and behavioral responses—e.g., adaptive social responses such as greater self-control and frustration tolerance; cognitive responses such as better attention and concentration; and emotional functioning such as less likelihood of using drugs, in adolescence and adulthood (Eigsti et al., 2006). Authoritative parenting with nurturance and autonomy support has been related to higher self-regulation skills in children ages 2–8 (Piotrowski, Lapierre, & Linebarger, 2013). Authoritarian parenting, with excess parental control, has been related to poorer self-regulation skills for ages 2–8.

Children with low self-regulation skills have had greater difficulty connecting with peers, generating positive relationships with teachers, and succeeding academically as well as socially (Piotrowski et al., 2013). In children ages 2–8, the older children had fewer self-regulatory problems than younger children, and children from low-income families and boys had more self-regulation problems (N = 1141; Piotrowski et al., 2013). While high ability to reduce arousal is protective, low ability has been linked to under-controlled externalizing behavior and to depressive and anxiety symptoms (Putnam et al., 2001). In response to anger, sadness, and fear scenarios, even the youngest preschoolers viewed cognitive and behavioral distraction and repairing the situation as effective measures (N = 62; Dennis & Keleman, 2009). They also favored likely-ineffective strategies (e.g., venting, rumination). Young children have believed that effective strategies depend on the emotion being regulated. Adults and preschoolers both have favored repair of a negative situation to reduce anger and behavioral distraction to reduce sadness and fear. On average, the higher a mother's report of a child's social skills the lower the child's beliefs that venting would reduce negative emotions (Dennis & Keleman, 2009).

Emotion Awareness

Emotion awareness is linked to positive outcomes and is important to self and other-awareness. Young children use happy, sad, and mad to express a wide range of emotions (Monaco & Gaier, 1987). The dispositional content of emotions is first learned by observing expressive displays of others and associating them with their accompanying situations and outcomes (see Fonagy & Target, 2006). As parents' education level increases, children's emotion-related skills have significantly increased (Durmuşoğlu-Saltali & Arslan, 2011). Both mother– and father–child attachments have been related to 3–5.5-year-old children's emotional understanding, when parental depression and child's age were controlled (Psychogiou et al., 2018). Insecure attachment with even one parent was associated with children's reduced emotion understanding.

Preschool children learn from everyday experience why basic emotions (fear, joy, sadness, and anger) occur in specific contexts. They can assess emotions of others based on context and can recognize and regulate personal emotions (Ashiabi, 2000). For 3–6-year-olds, increased age and stronger verbal abilities have been linked to better emotion knowledge (see Alonso-Alberca et al., 2012). By age six, children can have one, then a different emotion right after. By age 10, they have simultaneous emotions (Harter, Waters, & Whitesell, 1998). For 6-year-olds, emotional skills vary depending on gender, educational level of mother and father, previous preschool education, and number of siblings (Durmuşoğlu-Saltali & Arslan, 2011). Recognizing, understanding, and expressing emotions as well as total emotional skills have been significantly higher in girls than boys. Expression matching (pictures to the same emotion) has positively predicted adaptive abilities (N = 110, ages 3–6; Alonso-Alberca et al., 2012). Receptive emotion knowledge—ability to identify a named emotion in a picture—negatively correlated with externalizing problems.

Self-Awareness

Evidence suggests that young children's sense of self develops gradually over the preschool years (Semrud-Clikeman & Glass, 2010). Ages 2–3 are usually marked by a child's self-assertion (e.g., wants to do it her/himself; refuses to do), which suggests self-awareness and a move to independence (Berk, 2009). Not until around age three years do children begin to grasp the temporal dimension of self—the same enduring self—i.e., self pertains to what is experienced before and now, and what can be seen in a mirror now or in a movie tomorrow. By age four, children refer to themselves by name, use personal pronouns, and specify personal likes, needs, and wishes (Hollinger, 2012; Rochat, 2003). Moral self-awareness generally emerges between ages three and five, when children first begin to take an ethical stance (Rochat, 2011).

Self-Conscious Emotions

Toddlers and preschool children exhibit self-conscious emotions such as shame, guilt, and pride suggesting an awareness of self as seen by others (Rochat, 2003; Box 8.1). Children begin to express embarrassment by 2–3 years (e.g., call on mothers after successes; avoid gaze after failures; Berti, Garattoni, & Venturini, 2000). Young children sometimes link shame to events that older children might link to sadness, anger, or shyness. By age five or six they begin to understand the impact of their behaviors on others, can identify antecedents of shame—e.g., failing in performance, being a victim of attack, being the object of refusal or scolding—as well as the antecedents of sadness and guilt (total N = 120 Italian children; Berti et al., 2000). In contrast to a guilt-induced desire to make repair or apologize, shame has elicited a sense of being incapable or blocked as well as a desire to hide, escape, or do nothing. Parents are of comfort in some embarrassing situations and in some negative social situations—e.g., when around an unfamiliar person or a person in whom a child is interested. For 3–5-year-olds, depression severity has explained a unique and significant proportion of the variance in use of shame themes (re: emotionally evocative story stems; Luby et al., 2009). Generally, young girls have shown more shame than boys (consistent with socialization; Fletcher,

Box 8.1 Shame

Mehran and his family were from Afghanistan. When he attended school in the US at age five, he told his friends about his trip to Mecca with his father. His friends called his experiences "weird." Their disinterest and making fun of him made Mehran feel ashamed and hurt. He was also angry and wanted to retaliate but felt frozen. He negatively evaluated himself in response to their rejection (see Mann, 2010 for more details).

2014; Luby et al., 2009). Higher shame levels also have been associated with disruptive disorders (Luby et al., 2009; Tangney et al., 1992). Repeated shame experiences, especially in childhood, may become internalized as part of a shame-based identity (Kaufman, 1992).

Very young children can experience guilt over physically hurting someone but not emotionally hurting someone. While shame is tied to perceived deficiencies in the self, guilt is linked to specific actions or inactions (Tangney et al., 1992, 1996). Young children (ages 2–6) are prone to see themselves as causes of events (Gray Deering, 2000; Fletcher, 2014). Although unable to define guilt, by age 5–6, children can differentiate between guilt and other emotions (e.g., sadness and shame; Berti et al., 2000). They can describe that guilt is related to rule infringements such as aggression to peers or disobedience to authority figures, and they recognize that they must make amends. Five- to 6-year-olds may be more likely to feel guilt in the presence of an adult. Highly guilt-prone young children automatically may inhibit behavior, while EC is important for medium to low guilt children (Study 1, N = 57, ages 25–38 months, Kochanska et al., 2009). For children who were not highly guilt-prone, EC negatively predicted disruptive outcomes over time (Study 2: N = 99; toddler to early school age). Additionally, preschool onset depression (PO-MDD) has predicted brain volume differences at school age (smaller left and right side anterior insula, AI), but not after controlling for guilt, suggesting that the association between PO-MDD and smaller AI volume may be partially explained by the presence of pathological guilt before age 6 (Belden et al., 2015).

Some self-conscious emotions differ between Eastern and Western cultures. Lewis et al. (2010) found that Japanese preschoolers expressed less shame, sadness (after failure), and pride, but more exposure (embarrassment during success) and evaluative embarrassment (e.g., during failure) than American preschoolers (N = 149 Japanese, Black and White American children). While exposure embarrassment is not linked to negative self-evaluation or increased cortisol, evaluative embarrassment (after failure) has been linked to shame, negative self-evaluation, and higher cortisol responses to stressful events (see Lewis et al., 2010).

Taking the Perspective of Others

During the preschool years, children improve in observational and mental/emotional perspective-taking (the latter to follow). Both emotion understanding and false belief (F-B) understanding have been related to parents' mind-mindedness—i.e., parent views the child as a psychological agent, with increased frequency of mind-related comments to and about the child (Devine & Hughes, 2018). Beginning at ages five or six (to eight or nine), children recognize that attention and interpretation can be biased and that different perspectives may result from people having access to different information (Diesendruck & Ben-Eliyahu, 2006; Selman & Byrne, 1974).

The language skills of children ages 3–6 influence their F-B understanding. Across 25 years and 94 studies, even when children's language skills were accounted for, modest association existed between F-B understanding and family SES, number of siblings, parental mental state talk (references to mental states), and parental mind-mindedness (Devine & Hughes, 2018). Parenting, attachment security, and sibling and peer relationship quality have also related to F-B understanding (Devine & Hughes, 2018). Some cultural differences exist—e.g., some studies have shown a delay in F-B understanding in Hong Kong preschoolers vs preschoolers in mainland China (Hughes, Devine, & Wang, 2017). For example, although in Asian cultures there is a high emphasis on filial piety and conformity to social norms, in both the U.K. and Hong Kong, an emphasis on filial piety was linked to authoritarian parenting, while an emphasis on socioemotional skills was linked to authoritative parenting (N = 120 UK and 121 Hong Kong 3–5-year-olds; Hughes et al., 2017). Parental mind-mindedness (lower in the Hong Kong sample) related to F-B understanding in both cultures and has been related to sensitive parenting (positively; see also MacKinnon et al., 2018). Some of the differences between groups depended on where children were educated (e.g., local vs international schools).

Children make noticeable improvements between ages three and five in performance on various false belief, appearance-reality, and visual perspective-taking tasks, such that older but not younger preschoolers are usually able to understand that another child who has not seen inside a box labeled "cookies" but containing crayons will falsely believe that the box contains cookies (false belief), that a fake rock looks like a rock but is really a sponge (appearance-reality), and that a picture book that is right side up for them will look upside down to a person seated opposite (visual perspective-taking) (Flavell, 2000; Box 1.4). Before age four, depending on task characteristics and processes such as EFs, it is difficult for a child to attribute a false belief to others (Bjorklund, 2013). For example, if a three-year-old knows that an object has been moved from its original hiding place in a cupboard to a jar, the child believes that another person, who did not observe the change in location, will also know the correct whereabouts of the object (e.g., see Flavell, 2000; Bjorklund, 2013). By 4–5, children begin to be able to hold multiple representations and perspectives of objects and people (Rochat, 2003). They can tell that another person will see the front of something while they see the back of it (perceptual perspective-taking; Brambring, 2005; Cox, 1978). Perceptual locations (in front of or behind another person) are usually mastered by age seven, but 10-year-olds still make errors about left-right orientation (Cox, 1978).

Mentalizing or Theory of Mind (Glossary)

Between ages three and six, children develop (1) understanding of embedded mental state concepts, e.g., beliefs about beliefs or about intentions, (2) awareness that knowledge of others' internal states is interpretative and may vary from person to person, and (3) comprehension of speech that is not to be taken literally (e.g., jokes; N = 115, ages 4.8–8.8, Fernandez, 2013). A body of evidence suggests that mother's use of mental state words has been related to children's theory of mind skills (TOM; see Rollo & Sulla, 2016). Mothers tend to adapt their use of language to a child's age and gender. In addition to children's development of visual perspective-taking and false belief awareness, mothers using psychological terms when reading picture-books to their 3–6-year-old children has been related to children's emotional understanding (N = 50, ages 3–6; Rollo & Sulla, 2016). More empathetic mothers used more *ability* terms—e.g., to be able, to attempt. Interventions for kindergarteners have included conversations with children about inner states (Rollo & Sulla, 2016).

By age three, children acquire some level of awareness of themselves and others as knowers—i.e., distinguish thinking about an object from actually perceiving it; use verbs such as *think* and *know* (Flavell, 2000; Kuhn, 2000). The recognition indicated in such words is necessary for distinguishing between one's own and another's mental states (Frith & Frith, 2003). Between ages 3 and 4 years, a child becomes able to distinguish between his/her own and others' beliefs and knowledge of the world and understands that someone can hold beliefs about another person's beliefs (see Brüne & Brüne-Cohrs, 2006). From 3–4, children rapidly develop awareness of the sources of knowledge—e.g., how they came to know a thing (Kuhn, 2000). By age four, they understand that others' behavior is guided by beliefs and desires; others' beliefs may not match their own; and others' beliefs may be incorrect (false belief; Kuhn, 2000). During continued development, metacognition (Glossary) becomes more powerful, explicit, and effective as its operation becomes increasingly under a child's conscious control. Although, by age four, children can complete false belief and perspective-taking tasks (Callaghan et al., 2005; Nielsen, Slade, Levy, & Holmes, 2015), considerable instability remains for five-year-olds in understanding false beliefs, especially when the scenario relates to a person's volitional action rather than a physical object (see Brüne & Brüne-Cohrs, 2006). Young children do not understand metaphor or irony or reliably distinguish jokes from lies before age six or seven (requires going beyond literal meaning; Brüne & Brüne-Cohrs, 2006). Higher exposure to children's books has been associated with better empathy and theory of mind skills (TOM—ability to attribute mental states to self or others; Glossary; Table 1.2; see Guarisco & Freeman 2015).

In play, at least by 3–4 years, children show some ability to simulate events and roles and to act and elaborate on others' perspectives (see Coplan, Rubin, & Findlay, 2005; Rochat, 2003). Sociodramatic play is associated with social perspective-taking skills and with skilled interpersonal behavior (Rubin et al., 2008). Children's play has predicted later performance on TOM, mental state talk during interactions, affect regulation, empathy, social competence, and affective understanding (Coplan et al., 2005; Rochat, 2003). By 3–6, children can label visible feelings, know that others can have different emotions from them, although they are unaware of the reasons for another's emotions, and generally expect others to think the way that they do (egocentric; Selman & Byrne, 1974).

Emotion Perspective-Taking: Empathy

Researchers have investigated *affective*—e.g., feelings about a narrative; *cognitive*—e.g., why the emotional response to the narrative; and *behavioral* empathy—e.g., what would you do for a person in the narrative (Bensalah, Anduze, & Caillies, 2015; Table 1.2). To show empathy toward others requires the ability to interpret their signals of distress or pleasure (see Glossary and Chapter 1; Rothbart & Rueda, 2005). Preschoolers are more likely than toddlers to respond to others' distress with empathy and prosocial behaviors (Schonert-Reichl, 2012). Toddler and preschool children's reactions to another's distress range from sympathy and prosocial/helping behaviors to egocentric and unsympathetic reactions—e.g., laughing, aggression, ignoring (Zahn-Waxler, Radke-Yarrow, Wagner, & Chapman, 1992). Children with low levels of empathy, self-worth, and positive-engagement skills, who also are easily frustrated and dysregulated or are chronically inhibited, withdrawn, or angry are at a notable disadvantage for engagement in preschool (Sroufe, 2018). Positive associations between effortful control (EC) and empathy-related responding have been found for preschool and school-age children (Eisenberg, Smith, & Spinrad, 2011). EC has predicted sympathy over 2, 4, and 6–8 years (e.g., Eisenberg, Fabes, & Spinrad, 2007).

Social Skills

A number of skills are important to inter-relating. From ages 2–6, children learn to use social tactics flexibly in different social situations. For example, five or six-year-olds protect other people's feelings with "white" lies (Burnett & Blakemore, 2009). By age three, children's group behavior includes the ability to engage in sociodramatic play. Children share symbolic meanings/activities through social pretense, which uses the capacity to take on complementary roles and to agree on adopting specific imaginary roles in a rule-governed context (Rubin et al., 2008). Such behaviors suggest social perspective-taking (see Rubin et al., 2008). Children's semantic and syntactic abilities have predicted their effectiveness in using language in social contexts, which requires, among other things, comprehension of embedded mental states (e.g., beliefs about beliefs and about intention; Fernandez, 2013; perspective-taking, Semrud-Clikeman & Glass, 2010). From ages 4–6, children who were better at understanding others' motives for actions were most liked by peers both in the present and over time (Diesendruck & Ben-Eliyahu, 2006). Children with a better understanding that others may hold false beliefs about reality and others may have different emotions than their own were believed by peers (and rated by teachers) to most frequently engage in positive behaviors (e.g., prosocial; identified as leaders) and to least frequently engage in negative behaviors (e.g., aggressive behaviors). Children with poor understanding of these differences were more likely to be fighters or disrupters (peer-rated) or aggressive (teacher-rated; Diesendruck & Ben-Eliyahu, 2006). Thus, popular children seem better able to "read" others and to make consistent attributions based on this ability. Nevertheless, preschoolers ages 4–5 may engage in "collective monologue." That is, rather than listening to responses of others in a group, they process information into their own belief system and add their comments to other comments (Monaco & Gaier, 1987).

Traits and Social Competence

Highly impulsive and disinhibited children have had more social problems and exhibited lower social competence than children with greater self-control and behavioral regulation skills (Baer et al., 2015). Anxious, shy, and emotionally reactive children with a tendency to withdraw in novel situations or among strangers tend to exhibit less social competence and to have higher rates of social problems. In contrast, children with good attention-regulation skills, who tend to stick with things despite setbacks (show persistence) exhibit fewer social problems and greater competence.

Children with *behavioral inhibition* (BI, Glossary) have exhibited social difficulty (see Temperament, Chapter 9, Table A5.3, Box 8.2). In lab situations, BI children show long latencies to interact with unfamiliar people or objects, and they cease playing and talking and try to remain close to a parent when a novel event occurs (Coplan et al., 2009; Kagan, 1997; Kagan, Snidman, & Arcus, 1998). In familiar settings (rather than labs), Coplan et al. found that, although they did not differ

Box 8.2 Effective Parenting for BI

Brie had a fearful/inhibited temperament (seen by this clinician at age four; periodically observed through age 15), characterized by extreme shyness, wariness of others, clinging to parent or aunt (ages 2–6), and negative expectations. Her father took serotonin reuptake inhibitors because of poor transcription of serotonin. She may have inherited or learned some qualities from him (he voiced his negative views very strongly and repeatedly; complained of depression; was sometimes verbally aggressive). Brie was more comfortable in one-to-one situations, but less troubled when other children joined an already begun activity in the safety of home or Aunt's house, especially when much focus was on the activity. Her mother tried to influence Brie's father to reduce his negativity with her. Rather than berating Brie, keeping her out of group activities, or putting her in social situations that would make failure more likely, Brie's mother helped to build her social skills. For example, she taught Brie to ask timely questions and to notice and compliment the things that people had in their homes and valued; rehearsed situations with her and modeled outgoing and kind behaviors; joined her in a church Sunday School class for young children until she became comfortable with the children and teachers; took her on group outings that she would enjoy because of the event (e.g., the bouncing house at the mall or the water-slide park), built on her strengths (e.g., enrolled her in sports—which emphasized focus on the activity rather than on social fears [see Taylor, 2002])—and took her for one-to-one lessons to improve her skills. Her mother made her birthday parties a production with fun activities that could be engaged in a group with parallel interactions (e.g., bouncing house), and, later, in which her tendency to judge things could be employed (e.g., the children judged several cakes submitted by relatives and friends—as they do on the Food Network). Her mother encouraged Brie's compassion and sympathy for others with group church-related activities that kept the focus on the individuals receiving care. Although, as an adolescent, she still loves her times of solitude and loves to read, she bonded well with her teammates, functions well in small groups (especially with goal-directed behaviors, but has done pretty well in general as a teenager). She is gracious and kind and appears more extraverted. Her confidence and gracious outgoing behaviors increased over time with her increasing sense of belonging (see Taylor, 2002 for a similar child whose mother helped her with positive, encouraging parenting as well).

Note:
Case examples are disguised, may be combined cases, and have had details changed to protect individuals.

in frequency of observed play, BI preschoolers had significantly more emotional and peer problems, more reticence—e.g., watching but not joining in; remaining unoccupied—and anxious behaviors during preschool free-play and outside of school, and participated less in structured social activities than non-inhibited peers—e.g., less sports leagues. At-home-activities with a single friend were more likely, and they were less likely to have parent-initiated and organized activities (N = 24, ages 3.5 to 5.5; Coplan et al., 2009). Young inhibited children have been prone to emotional problems (internalizing)—e.g., anxiety, loneliness, low self-esteem (e.g., Bohlin, Hagekull, & Andersson, 2005; Coplan et al., 2009; Morris, Hudson, & Dodd, 2014), which may explain in part risk for poor peer relationships—e.g., peer rejection, exclusion (Coplan, Prakash, O'Neil, & Armer, 2004; Gazelle & Ladd, 2003). Behavioral inhibition has been related to later anxiety symptoms in children ages 2–6 (N = 59 South African children; Howard, Muris, Loxton, & Wege, 2017). Overprotective parenting has been related to the higher levels of anxiety and persistence of problems across time (Chronis-Tuscano et al., 2015; Howard et al., 2017).

Friends vs Non-Friends

Prosocial sharing, caring, and helping behaviors become more common with increasing age (see Eisenberg et al., 2007; Rubin et al., 2008). Manifestations of aggression usually peak in early childhood (around age three), then decline (Rutter, 2003). Toddlers' conflicts usually center on toys and resources, while preschoolers' conflicts are increasingly about differences of opinion, again suggesting an increasing awareness of the attitudes, opinions, and ideas of others (Rubin et al., 2008). As is true for older children, preschoolers choose friends who are similar to them (Caspi, 1998; Laird et al., 2001; Nader, 2008; Rubin et al., 2008). As young as 3.5 years, youth direct more social overtures, have more social interactions, and play more cooperatively and prosocially with friends (than non-friends), while they engage in more quarreling and in more active and reactive hostility (assaults/threats vs refusals/resistance) with non-friends (Rubin et al., 2008). However, they have more conflicts, and use more negotiation and disengagement (standing firm) during conflict resolution with friends than with neutral others. They are also more likely to remain present and continue to engage with friends.

Normal Play

Theorists suggest that, in stable environments, play increases to displace exploration (for toddlers; see Pellegrini, Dupuis, & Smith, 2007). However, children explore objects before playing with them. Upon entering preschool, young children explore and/or assess the physical and social environments (Pellegrini & Goldsmith, 2003). Play occurs after they feel safe in an environment. Children use play to learn and develop new and innovative behaviors. Play helps young children develop adaptability, bonding, and resiliency (Pellegrini et al., 2007). Pretend, social, and locomotor/exercise play peak during preschool age. The amount of time spent in each type of play differs somewhat by culture. Exercise play (physically vigorous gross motor locomotion; Chapter 1, Glossary) burns calories and aids the development of strength, endurance, and economy of movement (Pellegrini & Smith, 1998). Evidence suggests that dramatic pretend play games and engaging in pretend scenarios in a small group may improve children's emotional control (Goldstein & Lerner, 2017; see Chapter 1).

A study of the use of unstructured play to assist hospitalized children showed that 7–11-year-olds but not 4–7-year-olds benefitted from the use of unstructured play as an intervention (N = 53; Potasz et al., 2013). It is possible that school-age children are better able to use play as a distraction during the stress of hospitalizations. In contrast, 4–7-year-olds may need better attention to their differing coping styles—e.g., some may benefit from play while others benefit more from being comforted or from being given verbal explanations of procedures (see Chapter 4; Lee, Cohen,

Stuber, & Nader, 1994). For example, a hospitalized young boy, who needs to understand what is wrong with him—e.g., the tumor is the size of a tennis ball and is near his stomach; it must be removed to stop his bad stomach aches; needs to know what will be happen next—e.g., first they will do some tests and the mother or doctor will explain each test before it happens; and needs other details, is unlikely to be comforted by play until he is given information. The child who just wants to be played with or otherwise distracted may be distressed when a parent tries to explain things instead of engaging in distracting play.

Humor

When children develop a stable ability to distinguish between fantasy and reality, they become able to experience something incongruous—e.g., the violation of expectation, a mismatch, or a surprise—which then leads to humor (Loizou & Kyriakou, 2016; Semrud-Clikeman & Glass 2010). By age 4, a child begins to understand the difference between a lie and a joke. Children begin to use wordplay (Semrud-Clikeman & Glass, 2010). A child notices when things are not as they should be. Young children respond to unusual use of words or incongruent labeling of things/events (Buijzen & Valkenburg, 2004). Silly rhyming is a form of humor used. Between ages four and five, children with normal or above average communication skills use more humor than other children. Personality traits of *activity*, *approachability*, and *responsivity* are linked to appropriate use of humor (Carson et al., 1986; Semrud-Clikeman & Glass, 2010). Around age six, children develop an appreciation of irony and sarcasm (Cameron, Fox, Anderson, & Cameron, 2010; Glossary). When asked to comment on whether or not a picture was funny, to tell a funny story, and to draw a funny drawing, 4–7-year-old children were able to produce humorous stories and use jab lines (humorous lines) throughout a story rather than a punch line at the end. They appreciated both visual and verbal humor and seemed to employ multiple incongruities and empowerment episodes in their humorous story (N = 102, Loizou & Kyriakou, 2016; see Table 1.4). Although they could see the incongruity in a picture of a child's bed in a tree, they did not find it funny that the child would climb the tree and fall trying to get to the bed.

In general, children do not blindly trust individuals; they consider past and current behaviors, including joking behaviors (Hoicka, Butcher, Malla, & Harris, 2017). For example, they have shown trust for individuals who have been accurate over those who were not, regardless of the informants age (trust an accurate child over an inaccurate adult). They have trusted consistently inaccurate persons over intermittently inaccurate ones. Hoicka and colleagues found that three- and four-year-olds based trust on intentions or intentional cues alone. They trusted a sincere informant over a joker, even though no prior accuracy or inaccuracy was shown (N = 61, ages 3–4). In another study, three- and four-year-olds flexibly based trust on an informants' current intentions or intentional cues rather than on the person's initial ones—i.e., preschoolers trusted a sincere informant, who originally joked, above a joker, who was originally sincere (N = 32). In a third study, 3–5-year-olds tracked individuals changing intentions, and not just their intentional cues, when determining whom to trust (N = 89). For example, preschoolers trusted an informant who joked during training but was sincere during testing over an informant who was ignorant during training and sincere during test trials. Nevertheless, if an ignorant informant became knowledgeable and the joker continued to joke, trust was given to the knowledgeable person (Hoicka et al., 2017).

School Readiness

School readiness is evident in a preschool child's language and literacy development; approaches to learning; cognition and general knowledge; physical health; and social and emotional development (Williford et al., 2018). To be ready for school, a child must show adequate levels of emotional competence, self-regulation, and executive functions. Secure attachments contribute to a child's school readiness. Compared to insecurely attached preschoolers, securely attached preschoolers have demonstrated better verbal, reading, pre-reading, and pre-mathematic skills as well as better attention, metacognitive skills, and specific cognitive abilities (e.g., Granot & Mayseless, 2001; see Williford et al., 2018). In contrast, insecure preschoolers have shown lower cognitive, verbal, and math skills. In preschool, they have shown lower levels of curiosity, empathy, self-esteem, compliance, and social competence; shorter attention spans; and more dependence and higher levels of externalizing and antisocial behaviors (see Williford et al., 2018). Secure children have done better over time in school than insecure children—academically, socially, emotionally, behaviorally.

Understanding of Grief: Ages 4–6

Grief in young children is discussed in Chapter 7 and is addressed, when needed, in trauma treatments. Although they are capable of deep sadness and grief, between ages four and six, some but not all children understand that death is irreversible, makes people nonfunctional, and is universal (Nader & Salloum, 2011). Their reactions are generally similar to those of toddlers—i.e., may mirror caregiver reactions, have concrete and literal thinking, show fear at bedtime, have SA and other symptoms, move in and out of grief. Regression is common, and they may blame themselves for a death. Young children often express their grief symbolically (e.g., in play).

Conclusions

By age 4, children are better at skills such as autobiographical memory, perspective-taking, cognitive flexibility, and humor. Development of language in this age group is important to other developing skills—e.g., EFs, emotion awareness, learning, social functioning. Language and functioning show that younger children are more concrete and literal in their thinking than older children. A number of variables or variable combinations are related to emotional and behavioral problems in this age group—e.g., parenting, disorganized attachment, genes, temperament, stressor or trauma exposures, emotion dysregulation. For example, parenting may worsen or help to overcome a young child's fearful temperament and social anxieties. Temperaments and skills influence young children's vulnerabilities to stress and to negative outcomes. During or after stressful experiences, children may vary in their coping styles, their current needs, their needs for regression, and their timetables for recovery. Attachment and parenting can assist a child's ongoing development and prepare young children for school entry.

9

The Impact of Trauma and Adversity

Ages 3–6

Because of trauma's potential impact on development, a brief disordered period may have important long-term effects for preschool children (Chapter 3; Nader, 2008). Problems may persist and become even more troublesome—e.g., disruptive behaviors have preceded delinquency; early-onset delinquents have been more likely to become chronic, serious, or violent offenders (Nader, 2012c). Hence, providing intervention as early as the preschool years may be critical in preventing problems like delinquency and violence (Loeber, Farrington, & Petechuk, 2003). For children under age seven, some interruptions to development may be more problematic than for older children—e.g., separation from caregivers. They are more vulnerable to certain kinds of events. For example, children aged six and under are at highest risk for burn injuries and are over-represented in the US child welfare system (De Young, Kenardy, Cobham, & Kindle 2012; Merritt & Klein, 2015). Although percentages of children with problematic posttrauma outcomes vary by group and type of trauma (e.g., war, 81%; Halevi, Djalovski, Vengrober, & Feldman 2016), De Young et al. found that, while most burned children were resilient (stress was normal the first month after a burn; some recovered over six months), 35% had at least one diagnosis (e.g., PTSD, ODD SAD, ADHD) within the first six months, comorbidity with PTSD was common, and distress did not reduce over six months. Children with PTSD at one month were 4.8 times more likely to have another disorder by six months (De Young et al., 2012).

The impact of stressful life events—e.g., chronic illness; homelessness; exposure to loud, long arguments; traumas—during this age span may affect health and well-being across the lifespan (Roberts, English, Thompson, & White, 2018). For example, in a study that followed children from ages 4–6 and at age 18, adolescents who had experienced early sexual abuse were more likely to report anxious arousal symptoms; those who had experienced early physical maltreatment (blows or injury) and emotional maltreatment—i.e., threats to psychological safety and security, lack of acceptance and threats to self-esteem, failure to allow age-appropriate autonomy—were more likely to drop out of school; and adolescents who had been neglected—failure to provide for physical well-being or lack of supervision—had increased likelihood of dropping out of school, having unprotected sex, and using cigarettes (N = 1307 at ages 4–6, N = 847 at age 18; Roberts et al., 2018). These adolescents' life-event trajectories included three classes: chronic, moderate but declining, and low levels of life events (maltreatment and other stressor events). For the chronically exposed group at age 18, cumulative exposures uniquely and significantly predicted increased likelihood of anger/irritability—e.g., angry thoughts and behaviors; depression—dysphoric moods and thoughts; intrusive experiences—e.g., intrusive thoughts/memories, flashbacks; and dissociation—e.g., unconscious avoidance of unpleasant thoughts and distress as well as a significantly greater likelihood of other outcomes—more dropouts, drugs, arrests, and sexual partners (Trauma Symptom Inventory).

For this age group, cognitive and verbal immaturity, self-oriented/egocentric perception, reduced understanding of cause-effect relationships, and processes such as magical thinking, fantasy, and lack of autonomy influence comprehension and processing of events/experiences (Slone & Mann, 2016). Trauma's impact on the lives of 3–6-year-olds is influenced by attachment relationships (both parents), parental reactions, brain development, genetic and personality traits, opportunities for exploration and learning, and other variables (see Chapters 5–7 re: age three). For example, for children with unintentional burn injuries not requiring more than a week in intensive care (11.7% of children, DSM-5 PTSD; 15.3% with PTSS; <3% of mothers and <1% of fathers, PTSD), the effects of burn severity on Acute Stress Disorder (ASD) was mediated by mother's ASD (not by father's ASD; N = 138, ages 1–4; Haag & Landolt, 2017). Outcomes are influenced by multiple variables. For example, clinic-referred preschoolers with risk factors in all of four domains (biological vulnerability, insecure attachment, poor parent management, and adverse family circumstances) have been far more likely to have a diagnosis of Oppositional Defiant Disorder (ODD) than normal children (Greenberg, Speltz, DeKlyen, & Jones, 2001). Clinic-referred children were 34 times more likely than comparisons to have all four risk factors and rarely had fewer than two.

This chapter examines a few risk factors and the effects of adversity on the development of 3–6-year-olds and, then, reviews trauma's possible effects, including internalizing and externalizing and Trauma and Stressor-Related Disorders.

Risk Variables

Findings on specific variables and outcomes have been mixed, suggesting the possible influence of other, untested variables. For example, it is essential to control for inhibitory and working memory demands when assessing cognitive flexibility or children appear to outperform adults (Dajani & Uddin, 2015). Although children with low self-esteem, dysregulation, low empathy and social skills, easy frustration, or chronic anger or withdrawal are more disadvantaged for engaging in preschool, supportive parenting can assist better self-regulation and more positive expectations (Sroufe, 2018). Factors, such as SES disadvantage, can affect parenting and child well-being and psychological well-being and reactions as well (see Levendosky et al., 2011). Timing of a trauma, relationship variables, divorce, and risk factors for ADHD are discussed here. Outcomes for young children often are assessed as internalizing and externalizing problems. Temperament as a risk factor for internalizing and externalizing is discussed in the next section.

Timing of Trauma

Timing of traumas may influence outcomes. For example, in addition to the long-term effects of early traumas (e.g., brain, self-skill development), compared to children with late childhood brain injuries, children injured in infancy and preschool have had lower nonverbal abilities (i.e., lower processing speeds; ages 3–6 years; Crowe et al., 2012) and reduced hippocampal volume (childhood sexual abuse [CSA], ages 3–5; secondarily at ages 11–13; Andersen et al., 2008). Although abuse exposure at any age has been related to higher odds of depression and suicidal ideation in young adulthood (compared to non-maltreated; particularly physical abuse), exposure during early childhood (ages 0–5, especially 3–5), was most strongly associated with depression. Preschool physical abuse has been linked to 77% increased odds of depression; early sexual abuse corresponded to 146% increased odds of suicidal ideation compared to youth maltreated as adolescents (Dunn et al., 2013). Clinically depressed children (early years) are at risk for heightened HPA axis activity as well (reactivity to stress; Halligan, Herbert, Goodyer, & Murray, 2007). For preschool children, quality of childcare has been shown to buffer the HPA axis response to stress (Chapter 5). Some research showed early maltreatment (age 0–4) predicts greater anxiety symptoms in adolescence, whereas late childhood to early adolescent maltreatment (age 10–12) predicts more adolescent depressive symptoms (Harpur, Polek, & van Harmelen, 2015). For early maltreatment (age 0–4), mid-childhood intelligence has mediated the negative effects on later anxiety (age 14), but not on depressive symptoms (age 14; Harpur et al., 2015). However, mid and late childhood (ages 6–8 and 10–12) maltreatment dampened protective effects of IQ against adolescent anxiety.

Attachment—Parents, Teachers

In the preschool years, attachment is influenced by a number of factors—e.g., parental stress, child temperament, SES, trauma. Stability of the caregiving environment has sometimes been a better predictor of attachment stability than early infant attachment (Levendosky et al., 2011). For mother–child dyads exposed to domestic violence (DV; N = 150), only about half of children's attachment classifications remained stable from ages one to age four. For the secure-insecure group, when low levels of DV during pregnancy, increased, decreased, and increased again, then high levels of DV at age four disrupted a high-quality mother–infant relationship observed at age one (Levendosky et al., 2011). The component causes of the negative change are unknown—e.g., whether the trauma disrupted caregiving, young children are more vulnerable to family conflict, witnessing affected the child's behavior and the caregiver–child relationship, and/or other factors contributed to the change. As noted in Chapter 8, attachment styles influence young children's reactions to stress, modes of operating interpersonally, responses to clinicians and other adults, and representations of experiences (e.g., in play).

Parental psychopathology has been related to poorer caregiver–child attachments. Parents' major psychiatric disorders have been linked to greater risk of psychopathology in their children (Apter et al., 2017). The presence of psychopathology at an early age is likely to have cascading effects for children (Chapter 3; Apter et al., 2017). For refugee families, when parents own attachment representations were less secure, PTSD increased the risk of insensitive parenting of preschoolers (N = 53 refugee parents relocated to Netherlands; van Ee, Jongmans, van der Aa, & Kleber, 2016).

Relationship with Mothers

Until recently, most attachment studies assessed mother–child relationships (Chapters 4 and 5). Early mother–child attachments are instrumental in child development (e.g., brain, EFs, social skills)—i.e., secure attachments support the positive development of children's skills (e.g., EFs, Meuwissen & Carlson, 2015). Across studies, early attachment (ages 1–5) has been more strongly linked to social competence and externalizing behaviors than to temperament or internalizing (Groh et al., 2016). In kindergarten (K), close relationships with mothers have been linked to good academic and social skills across the school years (Granot & Mayseless, 2001). Positive relationships with mothers and teachers generally assist positive achievements, even with adversity. Although attachment predicts school dropout, the parental foundation for problem-solving—e.g., how well a parent structures and assists a child with problems (at age 3.5 years)—has been a stronger predictor of later dropout and academic outcomes (Sroufe, 2018; Sroufe, Egeland, Carlson, & Collins, 2005). The effects of parent affectivity (positivity or negativity toward a child) have sometimes varied depending on child characteristics (e.g., level of effortful control, EC). When children were low in EC and parents high in negativity (mothers and fathers), preschoolers had higher cortisol levels in response to lab stressors (not children high in EC; Kryski et al., 2013). For children with high EC (not those with low EC), greater parental positivity was associated with lower baseline cortisol levels.

Relationships with Teachers

Both teachers and mothers who offer higher levels of autonomy support, positive emotional warmth, and sensitivity are more likely to promote better self-regulation in children at home and in classroom environments (Fuhs et al., 2013). For socially disadvantaged preschool children, a close relationship with a preschool teacher has predicted improvements in observed child self-regulation skills by mid-year (Cadima, Verschueren, Leal, & Guedes, 2016). Children with lower self-regulation skills at the beginning of preschool benefitted most from higher classroom quality. For a study with multiple ethnic groups (N = 803; using a battery of tests), children showed more gains in cognitive self-regulation (CSR, Glossary) when teachers were more approving of behaviors, more encouraging to continue desirable behaviors, did less re-directing, and set a more positive emotional tone (marginally more gains when teacher was less disapproving; ages 4–5, Fuhs et al., 2013). Across the preschool year, proportion of observed time teachers spent delivering instructions, the quality of teacher instruction, and amount of time children were involved with mathematics and literacy—reflecting good classroom management—also related to children's gains. For African American children (ages 4–6), mother-closeness during K has predicted children's academic and social skills, whereas K teacher-closeness has predicted social skills (mother- and teacher-rated) and low internalizing but higher externalizing problems (influenced by teacher ethnicity; teacher-rated; Iruka, Burchinal, & Cai, 2010). Positive K teacher–child relationships have been linked to children's higher frustration tolerance, strong work habits, and reading and math achievement (moderate to strong link; see Iruka et al., 2010), while poor K teacher–child relationships (conflict and negative affective exchange) have predicted preschool and school-age increased maladaptive learning and adjustment, poor social skills and peer relations, and increased problem behaviors.

Relationships with Fathers

Fathers' involvement with preschoolers may enhance development (EFs, Meuwissen & Englund, 2016). Grossman, Pollack, and Golding (1988) found that father's pre-birth healthy autonomy and affiliation (e.g., closeness) was related to these same qualities in the child at age five (N = 23). Children with both of these qualities demonstrated better adaptation (Pollack, 1982) and more positive affect in interactions with parents than children with only one (see Grossman et al., 1988). Fathers who were more encouraging of their five-year-olds' affiliation were also supportive of the child's autonomy. Additionally, fathers who enjoyed their work demonstrated sensitive and responsive interactions with their five-year-old children. Fathers with satisfying, demanding careers, with relatively little time for family interactions, spent less time with their children. Despite a trend toward such fathers being more supportive of the child's autonomy, the more the mother supported her child's affiliation at age five, the less time a father spent with the child. As noted (Chapter 4), father–child rough-and-tumble play (R&T) has been associated with lower aggressive behavior in 2–6-year-olds, when fathers provided dominant control over the play (see St. George & Freeman, 2017). R&T increases neurochemicals involved in executive functions (EFs) and in affective learning aspects of play, which may facilitate neuronal development (ages 3–5; Gordon et al., 2003; Huber, Tonini, & Cirelli, 2007; Table A4.1—BDNF). Affective touch (e.g., affectionate touch; tenderness) has also shown positive effects on neurobiology (e.g., lower heart rate, blood pressure and cortisol; higher oxytocin, Field, 2010; Feldman, 2015). Across 16 studies (N = 1521 total), father's positive vigorous physical play (including R&T) with preschool boys and girls was positively associated with social competence (most strongly) and with emotional skills and self-regulation (St. George & Freeman, 2017).

In contrast, intrusive or controlling father parenting has had negative associations. Fathers who use intrusive parenting—i.e., verbal or nonverbal behaviors that restrict or derail a child's activity;

attempts to force a child to engage in an activity despite the child's disinterest or negative reactions; and/or continuous presentation of toys or overbearing behaviors without giving the child time to respond—has served as a risk factor for lower self-regulation and social abilities in children with developmental delays (N = 97, tested ages three, five, and six; Stevenson & Crnic, 2013). When controlling for mother's intrusiveness and child's behavior problems, father intrusiveness uniquely led to child's dysregulated behavior, which in turn was related to later lower social skills. Father's controlling parenting has been inversely related to EF composite scores above and beyond child's verbal ability and family income. Father's positive parenting marginally positively related to EF composite score (Meuwissen & Carlson, 2015).

Attachment and Symptoms in Preschoolers

Attachment classification has influenced the manner of reactivity to stress (see Chapter 8). In contrast to secure preschoolers, who have stayed physiologically stable (RSA), avoidant preschoolers have appeared to either physiologically minimize stress response activation, (RSA increase; Hill-Soderlund et al., 2008) or to be attempting to self-sooth and emotionally regulate (RSA reduction; Smith, Woodhouse, Clark, & Skowron, 2016a). Insecure-resistant preschoolers, who generally are less easily soothed and show more distress, have exhibited elevated signs of employing internal resources to cope with distress (RSA suppression, hyperarousal, Smith et al., 2016; Glossary).

Although findings are mixed, studies suggest that, at age six, children who were *disorganized infants* exhibit more dissociation, internalizing behaviors, a tendency to dissociate throughout childhood and into adulthood (Carlson, 1998); greater overall behavioral problems—e.g., externalizing behavior, lower academic self-esteem (Moss et al., 1998); controlling (role-reversing) behaviors toward mothers; hostile/aggressive behavior toward peers (Lyons-Ruth, Alpern, & Repacholi, 1993); and social incompetence in play groups (Wartner, Grossman, Fremmer-Bombik, & Suess, 1994; Ballen, Demers, & Bernier, 2006). Some evidence suggests intergenerational transmission of attachment (Main, Hesse, & Kaplan, 2005; Raby, Steele, Carlson, & Sroufe, 2015; Sroufe, 2018). For example, disorganized attachment and dissociation predict lack of resolution of loss or trauma (AAI), which predicts frightening parental behavior. Frightening parental behavior has predicted, infant disorganized attachment (Lyons-Ruth & Jacobvitz, 2018; Sroufe, 2018).

Divorce

Divorce is among adverse childhood experiences (ACEs). Across countries, research has shown that, for a significant number of youth, the negative consequences of divorce have included poorer school achievement, more behavioral problems, lower self-esteem, more problems in social relationships, and poorer psychological and emotional well-being than children from intact families (Klein Velderman, Pannebakker, Vliet, & Reijneveld, 2018; Chapter 10). Childhood parental separation/divorce was significantly linked to poor self-rated psychological health for men with parental separation/divorce at ages 0–4, and for women with parental separation/divorce at ages 0–4, 10–14 and 15–18 (N = 29 Swedish adults; Lindstrom & Rosvall, 2017). Hence, parents' divorce at ages 0–4 may be a critical period for men, whereas there are multiple sensitive periods for women, including ages 0–4. In another study, from birth to age 30, after controlling for a wide range of family SES and psychosocial factors and child characteristics, children and adolescents' more frequent exposure to parental separations related to their own adult parenting behaviors 15 to 25 years later—i.e., lower levels of parental sensitivity and warmth, greater over-reactivity, and increased use of physical punishment as a parent (N = 1265; conduct problems at ages 7–9 also related to outcomes; Friesen, Horwood, Fergusson, & Woodward, 2017).

Preschool children do not understand the permanence of divorce and may repeatedly ask for the missing parent (Cohen & Weitzman, 2016). They may blame themselves for a separation and begin acting-out as well as test limit-setting. Preschoolers may also have nightmares, separation anxiety, eating and/or sleeping problems; show defiance, become demanding, and/or have fear of abandonment. For school-age children, fantasies of parental reunion are common. Young school-age children may also exhibit changes in mood and behavior—e.g., anger, withdrawal, feeling abandoned. School performance may decline (Cohen & Weitzman, 2016). Parental involvement, SES, and other environmental and child factors influence outcomes over time (see Chapter 10). Treatment interventions are available for children of divorce (Chapter 10). Problems have also been significantly higher in children whose parent(s) are incarcerated—e.g., sleep and eating problems, academic or socioemotional skills deficits; mental health problems; illicit drug use (Jackson & Vaughn, 2017).

Parents can buffer the effects of divorce. For example, in a study of post-divorce mothers and preschoolers (N = 71), the quality of mother–child interactions at home was reflected both in children's and mother's representations of self-worth (Bretherton et al., 2013). Mothers with lower depression scores engaged in more positive dinner and bedtime interactions with their young children, and their accounts reflected greater sensitivity and effectiveness engaging children's cooperation. Dissatisfaction with divorced father's support did not influence outcomes. Their children's self-worth scores predicted preschooler–peer interaction quality (teacher-rated). Young girls produced considerably more stories with constructive problem-resolutions involving one or both parents than did boys.

High-quality co-parenting following divorce has benefitted children—e.g., parents negotiate boundaries, have frequent communication, show mutual trust, have low conflict, and show moderate to high support in contrast to qualities such as anger/hostility and/or withdrawal (Hardesty, Crossman, Khaw, & Raffaeli, 2016). For divorced mothers exposed to either no intimate partner violence, situational couple violence, or coercive controlling violence, the mothers in the coercive violence condition—with higher levels of hostility and intrusion such as harassment, threat and higher maternal fear—showed the poorest co-parenting quality, reported the greatest levels of hostility at separation, and, not surprising, placed less importance on the father–child relationship (N = 154; Hardesty et al., 2016). Positive feelings toward the co-partner, alone, predicted good quality co-parenting.

Risk for Attention Deficit Hyperactivity Disorder (ADHD)

Among children ages 4–17, those with ADHD have a higher prevalence of adverse childhood experiences (ACEs) than children without ADHD (N = 76,227; Brown et al., 2017). Children with 2, 3, or ≥4 ACEs were more likely to have moderate to severe ADHD. Other risk factors for increased likelihood of ADHD included SES hardship, divorce, familial mental health problems, neighborhood violence, and incarceration or have had early institutional care (Chapter 7).

Internalizing and Externalizing Problems

Of course, internalizing and externalizing are related to a number of factors—e.g., poor reading and inattention have been related to internalizing (5–6-year-olds, Garwood, Varghese, & Vernon-Feagans, 2017). Temperament has been related to both internalizing and externalizing depending on other factors. Evidence suggests that two traits considered markers of self-regulation—*ego control* and *ego resilience* (Block & Block, 1980; Glossary)—are stable across time (Causadias et al., 2012). Rated in preschool and elementary school, Causadias et al. (2012) found that ego-resiliency, but not ego-control, was a powerful predictor of later adaptive functioning (at ages 19–26), and negative predictor of internalizing and externalizing problems (at ages 16, 23, 26, and 32 years). Traumatic experiences have been related to a number of disorders and to both internalizing and externalizing symptoms—e.g., depression, anxiety, PTSD, behavior problems; for sexual abuse, also more sexualized behaviors, self-destructive behaviors, and externalizing (Séguin-Lemire,

Hébert, Cossette, & Langevin, 2017). After a discussion of anxiety in this age group, temperament's influence on internalizing and externalizing is discussed.

Anxiety

Increased child anxiety has been linked to trauma exposures as well as to child factors (e.g., higher reactivity; genetics; temperament—e.g., behavioral inhibition, to follow), to parenting practices, to parental mental health (e.g., maternal anxiety), to other environmental factors—e.g., insecure attachments, sibling domination, conflict (Hiebert-Murphy et al., 2011; Boxes 3.1, 3.2), and/or to combinations of factors (Halevi et al., 2016; Milrod et al., 2014; ages 3–4, Shamir-Essakow, Ungerer, & Rapee, 2005). For example, child maltreatment has increased risk and chronicity of depression and anxiety disorders (Bouvette-Turcot et al., 2015a). Although separation anxiety may be normal before age 3, its persistence may be pathological—e.g., impairs normal development, comfort in exploration, and autonomy; may translate into adult disorders such as panic disorder. High levels of selective mutism have been related to social anxiety symptoms (not related to behavioral inhibition; Glossary; N = 57 ages 3–6; nonclinical children; Muris, Hendriks, & Bot, 2016a).

Contrary to study findings that focus on the relationship of parental over-control and negativity to children's anxiety, a number of middle and upper middle-class parents of five-year-olds with higher than normal anxiety reported use of reasonable parenting strategies compatible with those recommended by research and clinical literature (Hiebert-Murphy et al., 2011). Parents expressed a strong willingness to learn more effective strategies as well. Their children's symptoms included, e.g., SAD, social anxiety, specific phobia, GAD, school refusal (16 of 23 qualified for anxiety diagnoses; 11, for more than one diagnosis; Hiebert-Murphy et al., 2011). It is possible that anxious children elicit over-control or overprotection (Hiebert-Murphy et al., 2011; Rubin & Burgess, 2001). In turn, over-control or overprotection, as the child develops, may translate into interactions or transactions between anxious child and parent that increase the child's insecurity, higher anxiety levels, poor anxiety regulation, and social withdrawal—e.g., keeping the child out of sports or other potentially stressful social situations (Hiebert-Murphy et al., 2011; BI, above).

About a third of preschool children with ADHD symptoms have had concurrent anxiety symptoms (Overgaard, Aase, Torgersen, & Zeiner, 2012). Preschoolers with moderate to severe ADHD (hyperactive/impulsive or combined type) have had high levels of comorbidity (both genders)—e.g., ODD, anxiety disorders, communication disorders (N = 303; Posner et al., 2007). Preschoolers with ADHD and communication disorders were more anxious and depressed. ADHD severity correlated with increased internalizing and lower functioning. Overgaard et al. (2014) found that emotion dysregulation (at 18 months) predicted co-occurring symptoms of anxiety and ADHD at three years, and also predicted anxiety and ADHD when one symptom cluster (anxiety or ADHD) occurred without the other.

Child anxiety may become especially important when the transition to kindergarten introduces increasing demands and opportunities for children to engage in peer activities, social interactions, and formal education. Traits such as insecurity and social withdrawal can inhibit the growth of social and other skills (Overgaard et al., 2014). Whether or not they are over-controlling or overprotective, parents (and siblings) of anxious children are faced with dilemmas such as whether to be confronting or to be supportive and accepting. Parents can be helpful in addressing child anxiety (Box 8.2; see Chapter 7 for treatments). After traumas, recognizing regression and trauma-related anxieties is important to decision-making.

Temperament and Problems

Differences in temperament are reflected in tendencies to evoke different responses from others and to selectively attend and react to circumstances (Caspi, 1998; Dalgleish et al., 2003; Dodge, Bates,

Pettit, & Valente, 1995; Nader 2008; see Chapters 1, 4). In contrast to traits like effortful control, which are more volitional or voluntary, traits like emotional and behavioral reactivity are more automatic and less voluntary (Eisenberg et al., 2010b). Accordingly, while impulsive children appear to be pulled, unthinkingly, by desires and potential rewards (reactive under-control), behaviorally inhibited children tend to be constrained, rigid, and inflexible in novel or stressful situations (reactive over-control; Eisenberg et al., 2010b).

Temperamental traits combine with each other and with environmental factors in their links to outcomes (externalizing, social problems; Table A5.1; Box 10.2). For example, evidence suggests that shy children benefit more from sensitive parenting than less shy children (e.g., in foster care; consistent with differential susceptibility; De Schipper, Oosterman, & Schuengel, 2012). Aspects of temperament are understudied, in this age group, in relation to traumatic reactions. For example, for children with behavioral inhibition (BI), some of the symptoms of trauma are already present—e.g., startle reactivity; hypervigilance (see Henderson et al., 2015). Temperament's relationship to maladaptation (externalizing, internalizing, both) is discussed here.

Behavioral inhibition (BI) has been a risk factor for internalizing disorders (e.g., anxiety) whereas behavioral disinhibition has been a risk factor for externalizing disorders (e.g., ADHD; Morris, Hudson, & Dodd, 2014). A number of studies have shown a link between BI and internalizing and between traits like surgency or exuberance and externalizing (Glossary—Hawk & Dove). Some qualities relate to both externalizing and internalizing—e.g., high *negative emotionality* (NE), plus low effortful control (EC); high surgency plus low EC (Gartstein, Putnam, & Rothbart, 2012; preschool, Overgaard et al., 2014; Table A5.1). Negative emotionality/behavioral dysregulation (NE/BR; linked to 5 HTTLPR) has shown stability from 1.5 to three years and has been linked to psychosocial problems at age five—e.g., conduct, emotional, peer, hyperactivity (Bouvette-Turcot et al., 2015a; N = 154; Glossary). An association between maternal childhood adversity and increased NE/BR in three-year-olds suggests a transgenerational effect of maternal adversity moderated by offspring 5-HTTLPR (independent of previous or concurrent maternal depression; Table A4.1—serotonin).

Using the CBCL externalizing and internalizing scales, Basten et al. (2013) identified four classes of outcomes in children followed from birth to ages 5–7: (1) both high internalizing and externalizing, (2) intermediate levels of internalizing problems, (3) predominantly intermediate levels of externalizing problems and emotionally reactive behavior, and (4) no problems. In this age group, the highly problematic class (1) may be precursor to the CBCL Dysregulation Profile (Chapter 11, Glossary). It was associated with high maternal and paternal psychological symptoms.

Temperament and Externalizing

Externalizing behaviors have been associated with high levels of NE, *reactivity*, or *surgency* and with low levels of *effortful control* (EC), *attention regulation*, and *harm avoidance* (HA), as well as with a *difficult temperament* profile, with lower cortisol levels, with *exuberance*, with respiratory sinus arrhythmia reactivity (RSA—as a measure of self-regulation; see Glossary, Table A5.1), and with particular genes (Baer et al., 2015; Gartstein et al., 2012; Hulme, 2011; Morales et al., 2015; Nader & Weems, 2011; Young & Veldhuis, 2006). Studies have also shown that the blunted stress reactivity that may follow trauma exposure has been associated with fearlessness and callous-unemotional traits (see Zhang et al., 2018b). Callous-unemotional (CU) traits also have predicted externalizing and proactive aggression (ages 3–6; teacher report; N = 240; Waller et al., 2015). CU behavior was related to lower moral regulation, lower guilt, and lower empathy (robustly and uniquely; mother and father reports; Zhang et al., 2018b). Given that early-onset conduct problems are a risk factor for adolescent and adult antisocial behaviors (Shaw & Gross, 2008; Waller et al., 2015), preschool CU or other aggressive behavior puts children at risk for more severe and proactive antisocial behavior (Hyde et al., 2013: Waller et al., 2015).

Extraversion: Surgency or Exuberance. Whether extraversion is a protective or a risk factor depends on self-regulation levels—e.g., whether sufficient to manage their exuberance in appropriate ways (Gunnar, Doom, & Esposito, 2015). Morales et al. (2015) found that *exuberance* alone did not predict externalizing—RSA reactivity at 24 and 42 months related to behavior at ages 5–6 (Glossary; N = 152; Table A5.1). For preschool boys with high *exuberance*, early lack of a physiological response (RSA augmentation) predicted externalizing problems. For girls with high *exuberance*, high reactivity—baseline high RSA and greater RSA suppression but not RSA augmentation—predicted more externalizing at kindergarten entry. Hinnant and El-Sheikh (2013) also found gender differences related to reactivity—i.e., girls with RSA suppression were more likely to show high externalizing and high internalizing symptoms across three time points; more likely for boys who displayed low RSA reactivity/RSA augmentation (see Chapter 4—trauma-related stress reactivity). Differences may be related, e.g., to differential reporting for the genders or gender differences in stress coping. Of importance, variables not always studied—e.g., both permissive or authoritarian parenting in combination with specific temperament—are thought to contribute to greater behavior problems (Rankin Williams et al., 2009).

Activity. High *activity* has been related to high social competence as well as to high externalizing (Baer et al., 2015). For Croatian five-year-olds, temperamental *activity* and *emotionality* were the best predictors of preschoolers' conduct problems—e.g., fighting, aggression, selfishness, provoking negative reactions (Glossary; N = 258; Brajsa-Zganec & Hanzec, 2014). Preschoolers' younger age and mothers' punishment and low inductive reasoning were also predictive of problems (strict discipline and punishment). Mothers' inductive reasoning—e.g., explaining the rules; tendency to converse about appropriate behaviors and consequences; helping to understand consequences of behaviors; and warmth (a close and warm relationship) were better predictors of preschoolers' prosocial behaviors. Older preschool age and temperamental lack of inhibition/shyness also predicted prosocial behaviors.

Temperament and Internalizing

Preschoolers' high *shyness*, *inhibition*, and *fearful temperaments* and low *surgency* have been associated with internalizing behaviors (Baer et al., 2015; Gartstein et al., 2012; not related to RSA, Morales et al., 2015)—e.g., traits at ages 4 and 8–9, linked to low social competence in middle childhood (see Baer et al., 2015, Henderson et al., 2015). Harm avoidance (HA), characterized by shyness, fatigability, anticipatory worry, and behavioral inhibition (BI, e.g., wariness, reticence), and BI itself have been linked to the development of internalizing behavior problems (Kagan & Snidman, 1999; Baer et al., 2015).

Behavioral Inhibition (BI; wariness, reticence, vigilance). BI has been linked to vulnerability to HPA axis activity (stress response) in response to adverse life events (Hostinar & Gunnar, 2013; Glossary; Chapters 5, 8). Temperamental shyness has been linked to the affective neurobiology of fear and to social phobia, which, when activated (e.g., through facing/approaching a challenge), trigger HPA axis activity (Gunnar et al., 2015; Kagan & Snidman, 1999). Resulting cortisol elevations, in turn, may enhance fear memories and increase vigilance (Gunnar et al., 2015). BI has been observed in infants and has persisted through childhood and even into adulthood (e.g., 15–20% of children, see Chronis-Tuscano et al., 2015; see Table A5.1—SI, BI, NE). Stable temperamental BI has predicted later anxiety disorders (e.g., social anxiety disorder; Chronis-Tuscano et al., 2015). Both high BI and high inhibitory control or high BI and low attention shifting have been related to highest risk of social anxiety (see Henderson et al., 2015).

BI has been linked to parenting with inappropriate warmth, lack of responsive supportiveness, high levels of control, intrusiveness, and overprotection (e.g., see Chronis-Tuscano et al., 2015). For example, parental protectiveness may mean that children do not participate in activities (e.g., sport, group) that may assist them to develop social skills and to learn adaptive coping strategies for potentially stressful social situations (Coplan et al., 2008, 2009; Rubin, Cheah, & Fox, 2001; see Box 8.2; see Baer et al., 2015). In contrast, parental sensitivity can reduce emotional negativity and possibly BI by enhancing self-worth (Fox et al., 2005). Importantly, firm parenting from ages 2–3 has reduced inhibition at age three, possibly because it assisted coping or required resisted action. Rankin et al. (2009) found toddlers with higher BI had higher internalizing problems in preschool (age four) and maintained levels of internalizing problems across childhood and adolescence beyond effects of parenting style with no impact on externalizing in preschool but it declined across childhood and adolescence. Age four internalizing problems were greatest among BI children with permissive mothers. Over time, more authoritative parenting was associated with lower internalizing, while more authoritarian parenting was associated with a steeper decline in externalizing problems (authoritarian parenting has often been linked to more externalizing).

5-HTTLPR. A serotonin gene polymorphism (5-HTTLPR), which appears to be linked to increased susceptibility to environmental influences (Belsky & Pluess, 2009; Table A4.1), has moderated the link between childhood depression and negative emotionality (NE) with other variables (e.g., pre-natal maternal anxiety, Pluess et al., 2011; social support, Fox et al., 2005; attachment security, Kochanska et al., 2009). There is currently some uncertainty about the relationship of 5-HTTPLR to depression or to neuroticism (Munafo, 2012). Although 5-HTTPLR has been linked to neuroticism, a recent meta-analysis (Munafo et al., 2009; Munafo, Clark, & Flint, 2004) and recent studies (e.g., Arias et al., 2012) have shown a lack of association between the 5-HTTLPR polymorphism of the SLC6A4 gene and HA or Neuroticism. A gene–gene interaction may underlie some inconsistencies in findings (Arias et al., 2012). Cicchetti, Rogosch, and Oshri (2011) found that it was the interaction of two (not one) TAT haplotype CRHR1A genes and long allele 5-HTTLPR genes (in this study: l/l not s/l or s/s) that related to internalizing. A group of children who experienced physical and sexual abuse in the first 5 years of life (not later) and developed internalizing symptoms (e.g., depression) exhibited an attenuated diurnal increase in cortisol, linked to the 2 TAT haplotype CRHR1A, not 5-HTTLPR (Cicchetti et al., 2011; Table A4.1—CRHR).

Effects of Trauma on Developmental Skills

For this age group, the effects of trauma on many developmental domains are understudied. Trauma and attachment each influence young children's development. As well, trauma may affect attachment behaviors, which then influences developing skills and functioning. For example, in contrast to children of non-traumatized mothers, when mothers were traumatized—e.g., raped; physically injured—e.g., disabled or had removed body parts; mentally tortured; watched or heard spouse being killed—during armed conflict, Kenyan preschool children exhibited shyness, sadness, anger, low self-esteem, forgetfulness, and withdrawal. They rarely displayed happiness or friendliness (Sichari, Wakhungu, & Maragia, 2015). Teachers reported that these children displayed disturbed behaviors at school—e.g., hyperactivity, tantrums, anxiety, aggression, or withdrawal. Specific symptoms—e.g., shame, guilt, depression and other posttrauma symptoms—may dampen the spirit and affect functioning in a number of realms. Arousal symptoms may increase irritability, reduce frustration tolerance, and undermine related skills. Initially and over time, symptoms and problems in addition to PTSD may follow young children's trauma exposures (Nader & Fletcher, 2014; Chapter 3). For ages 3–6, posttrauma reactions have included, e.g., internalizing or externalizing behavior problems such as anxiety, depression, aggression; low social competence; and somatic complaints—especially if mothers report both PTSD and depression for themselves (see Chemtob et al., 2010).

Trauma and Language Skills

As noted (Chapter 8), language is important to many other developmental skills. Children under age six in the child welfare system have shown a number of developmental problems, including language delays (see Merritt & Klein, 2015). Compared to matched controls, maltreated children have been found to use fewer words and less complex sentence structure, have had more trouble coherently connecting ideas when communicating, have shown less syntactical competence, and have had a reduced spoken vocabulary. They have shown both poorer receptive and expressive language skills, with larger delays in expression than in comprehension. Some but not all evidence suggests that neglected/deprived children lagged behind children with other forms of abuse as well as behind normal children (see Merritt & Klein, 2015). Maltreated children enrolled in early education/care programs such as preschool or Head Start have shown better language development 18 months later than maltreated children not enrolled (N = 1652; Merritt & Klein, 2015).

Executive Functions (EFs)

Trauma and adversity influence EFs. Poor mother– or father–child relationships (e.g., intrusive, controlling) have been related to poorer EF development (Meuwissen & Carlson, 2015). Although resilience factors (e.g., preschoolers' good general cognitive ability) may buffer against traumatic effects (e.g., adverse family environments; Hughes & Ensor, 2009; Luthar, Cicchetti, & Becker, 2000), other variables may alter such effects—e.g., trauma may result in hyper or hypo-cortisolism (Chapters 1, 4; Stress Reactivity, this chapter). A consistent, positive relationship between family income and EF skills has emerged for children with high cortisol response (a marker of biological sensitivity to context) but not for those with low cortisol response (Obradovic, Portilla, & Ballard, 2016, see Chapter 6—The Stress System). Evidence has suggested that narrative coherence (Glossary) has been related to an increased likelihood that a memory is retained over time. For normal 4–13 year-olds, a narrative's emotion (described with emotion) and both thematic and chronological coherence added to the prediction of a memory's survivability over two years (N = 140; 27 age 4–5, 23 age 6–7, 29 age 8–9, 35 age 10–11, 26 age 12–13; Peterson, Morris, Baker-Ward, & Flynn, 2014). In contrast, a memory's content, uniqueness, and parent-reported reminders did not contribute to the likelihood of persistence. In this study, older children's stories were more likely than younger to contain emotion. The importance of peri-traumatic emotion to memory and reactions has been demonstrated across age groups.

Trauma and Reporting Memories

Preschool children are able to recall considerable information about their traumatic experiences, whether or not they had initial intrusive thoughts (Howe, Courage, & Peterson, 1995). They more easily identify familiar people and details relevant to their lives than unfamiliar individuals and details (Murray & Son, 1998). However, young children may be more likely to include time and space distortions in trauma memories (Pynoos & Nader, 1988), and, as discussed earlier, are more susceptible to intrusion of faulty pre- and post-event information (i.e., may be more easily misled) that may result in distortions in recall (Siegel, 1996). A few months after a hurricane, for preschoolers (ages 3–4), the number of hurricane-related memories increased for a low to moderate stress-level group and marginally significantly decreased for a high-stress group (Bahrick, Parker, Fivush, & Levitt, 1998). Reports of forgetting traumas (e.g., early CSA) over time have been likely after periods of sustained attempts to recall past experiences—e.g., as more details are retrieved, difficulty of accessing memories may become more apparent (Ghetti et al., 2006). For CSA originally adjudicated from ages 4–17 (Ghetti et al., 2006; age of abuse 3–16; N = 138), 13 years later 15% of individuals reported complete forgetting of the CSA. However, none underwent long-lasting loss of memory (sometimes recovered in therapy). For a variety of reasons, memory may be poorer in non-adjudicated cases. Although individuals with more severe abuse reported more forgetting (subjective assessments) and more active attempts to put memories out of mind, they also exhibited more accurate long-term memories of documented abuse episodes as did those in the legal system with more opportunities to discuss/recount events. Those with more intrusive trauma thoughts remembered abuse better and also tended to report the experience of forgetting. Thus, subjective forgetting does not necessarily correspond to objective forgetting. While age at time of abuse was not related to subjective or objective memory, young age of abuse, low maternal support, and being African American were associated with reduced tendency to disclose abuse.

Trauma and Autobiographical Memory (AM)

As noted (Chapters 5–6), children and adults have difficulty providing verbal narratives of general experiences that occurred before age three (or late age two), although earlier memory contents remain as elements of physical/emotional networks (e.g., perceptions, sensations, emotions). Core features of traumatic experience, however, are better remembered (Ruf & Schauer, 2012). Reports of early traumatic events often become more detailed as children develop (Laura, Chapter 6). Supportive family members or clinicians help young children to reminisce in elaborated and evaluative ways about events, which helps them to develop more detailed, coherent, and evaluative AMs (and may assist language and narrative skills; Fivush, 2011; Ruf & Schauer, 2012). Nevertheless, at this age range, young traumatized children still are vulnerable to suggestion. Insecurely attached children (avoidant) may demonstrate avoidant coping strategies and may minimize experiences.

Posttrauma and other psychopathology may affect memory and information processing both in identified patients and in their school-age siblings. In a small study of attachment and family narratives, siblings of referred children were more likely than other children to use at-risk self-protective strategies in family narratives, with altered memory and information processing and signs of unresolved trauma or loss (N = 26; Kozlowska & Elliott, 2017). Children using more at-risk self-protective strategies showed poorer memory and information processing in narratives such as less integration and more extreme degrees of affect inhibition, exaggeration, and/or distortion. In response to threat, they exhibited more errors in information processing and the discrepancies between memory systems became more extreme. They engaged in increased efforts to inhibit negative affect. In the comparison group, siblings of controls who used at-risk strategies had parent(s) or grandparents with histories of danger(s) (e.g., war, poverty) and loss experiences.

Trauma and Self-Regulation

Well-regulated young children respond to the demands of a situation in socially acceptable ways and sufficiently flexibly to permit both spontaneity and inhibition of pre-potent behaviors (Kim-Spoon, Haskett, Longo, & Nice, 2012). Traumatic experiences may undermine self-regulation capacities. For example, maltreated children have shown greater difficulty regulating and differentiating emotions than non-maltreated children (see Kim-Spoon et al., 2012). Problems with self-regulation have in turn been related to maladjustment—e.g., internalizing, externalizing. Children with dysregulated emotions may exhibit both emotional and behavioral reactivity and deficits such as emotional constriction, inappropriate affective displays, and difficulty inhibiting behaviors. For sexually abused children ages 3–7 (CSA, N = 47), parents reported greater emotional lability/negativity and lower emotion regulation competencies (especially boys) in CSA children compared to non-abused (N = 74; Canadian children; Séguin-Lemire et al., 2017). One year later, CSA children showed increased difficulties and a larger difference from controls. Although their lability/negativity tended to subside over time, CSA victims showed lower emotion regulation abilities in school, a year later.

Normally across time/age for this age group, externalizing decreases (Yoon, 2017). One study examined maltreated 4–5 year-olds over an eight-year period (N = 449) and found three distinctive trajectory patterns for externalizing behavior problems (likely shaped by multiple risk and protective factors): *high-decreasing* (10%)—gradual decrease, but remained in clinical range across the study; *moderate-increasing* (13%)—with rapidly worsening problems, reaching clinical range in school age; and *low-stable* (77%; Yoon, 2017). Physically and sexually abused children were more likely to be high-decreasing, whereas male and Black/non-Hispanic children were more likely to be moderate-increasing than females or Hispanics. A gradual decrease in externalizing may reflect placement or treatment. Higher prosocial behaviors and better caregiver well-being were associated with less likelihood of being in the high-decreasing group over time (more likely to become low-stable). Caregiver depression or substance use increased likelihood of externalizing.

Trauma, Reactions, and Self-Control

A number of factors contribute to the likelihood of symptoms in young children—e.g., genetics, experiences, environments (Table A4.1). After the 9/11 terrorist attacks, preschool children whose parents had more mental health symptoms had more problems including issues of self-control—e.g., emotional reactivity and aggression (Chemtob et al., 2010). Concurrent maternal depression and PTSD has been associated with dramatic increases in rates of aggressive behavior, emotionally reactive behavior, and somatic complaints (especially 3-year-old boys, Nomura & Chemtob, 2009). For Middle Eastern refugee children, traumatic experiences before arrival and stressful events after predicted internalizing behavior, while witnessing violence and frequent school changes in exile predicted externalizing behavior (ages 3–15, Montgomery, 2011). Most suffered from anxiety, sleep disturbance and/or depression at arrival (73%). School participation, friends, language proficiency, and mother's education predicted lower levels of long-term psychological problems. Substantial evidence suggests that trauma-exposed children (e.g., maltreated) are at greater risk of developing externalizing problems such as aggression, disruptive behaviors, conduct problems, and delinquent behaviors (Evans, Simons, & Simons, 2012; Haskett, Stelter, Proffit, & Nice, 2012; Yoon, 2017). Young children with conduct problems have shown greater risk for serious negative outcomes in school-age and adolescence—e.g., peer rejection, poor academic functioning, antisocial activity, incarceration, and substance abuse (Niec, Barnett, Prewett, & Shanley, 2016).

Parenting and Posttrauma Self-Regulation

Parenting assists self-regulation by modeling emotion expression and affective and behavioral regulation, by setting reasonable limits with sensitivity and without hostility, and by providing a home-setting and caregiving conducive to emotional understanding and regulation and to behavioral regulation. For physically abused young children ages 4–7, both parenting and self-regulation contributed to changes in externalizing over time (at time 1 [T1] N = 43 preschoolers, T2 N = 63 in K, and T3 N = 54 in first grade; Kim-Spoon et al., 2012). In preschool, low self-regulation levels predicted high levels of externalizing. Positive parenting attenuated the link between low self-regulation and psychopathology. In addition, abused children with stable low levels of self-regulation, were more susceptible to the positive effects of positive parenting and to the detrimental effects of insensitive parenting—higher externalizing over time—than physically abused children with high self-regulation. Positive parenting also protected against the effects of low self-regulation in K. In grade 1, positive parenting and self-regulation had independent and additive effects on externalizing outcomes (Kim-Spoon et al., 2012). Hence, low self-regulation skills are a risk factor for externalizing, especially when parenting is insensitive.

For 94 physically abused children, abusive parents' frequent expression of positive emotions was associated with higher academic-related behaviors and with better parent- and teacher-rated child self-regulation (Haskett et al., 2012). Abusive parents' more frequent negative-submissive expressiveness (e.g., sadness) was linked to children's aggression. Parents' less frequent negative-dominant expressiveness, such as anger and contempt, did not relate to aggression. Robustly, abused children's poor self-regulation was related to their more frequent aggression toward peers and to lower levels of initiative (i.e., self-directed behavior—e.g., accepting challenges) and to lower cooperation in the classroom.

Trauma and Awareness

If trauma reactions take center stage, individuals may be "out of sync" with others, less able to recognize the thought and emotional processes of others, and less self-aware. Hence, trauma may interrupt self- and other-awareness skills. Following the Sandy Hook Elementary School shootings (Newtown, CT in 2012), parents of young children reported a number of symptoms including reduced self-awareness as well as sensory-motor integration problems; poor self-regulation—e.g., increased crying and hysteria, panic, anger; poor health; reduced communication—e.g., about emotions, general; memory, attention and focus problems; and poor academic performance (Glossary; ages 2–14, Masgutova, 2016).

Emotion Awareness

For five-year-old Finnish boys in the child welfare system (not girls), developmental factors—i.e., receptive language skills such as the ability to comply with multipart instructions—were related to adolescent alexithymia (Glossary; Karukivi et al., 2012). Later ability to speak has been associated with adolescent externally oriented thinking. Children with impaired speech development often have difficulties in social situations and in achieving deep, gratifying peer relationships—related to lack of communication and poor emotion-regulation skills—as well as difficulties interpreting emotional vocal and facial cues (Karukivi et al., 2012). Attachment, too, has been linked to alexithymia (Lemche, Klann-Delius, Koch, & Joraschky, 2004). In contrast to securely attached young children who have rapidly acquired language skills—i.e., emotion, physiology, cognition, and emotion-regulatory language—insecure and disorganized children have shown delayed skills—e.g., reduced internal state language; delayed emotion and cognition vocabulary.

Self-Conscious Emotions

In stressful situations, for adults and for children over age 4, the stress hormone, cortisol, is evoked when circumstances combine unpredictability, uncontrollability (over a situation or outcome), and social-evaluative threat—e.g., shame or embarrassment for children (Gunnar, Talge, & Herrera, 2009c; for adults: potential negative evaluation by others, Dickerson & Kemeny, 2004). Shame also may follow victimization. In one study (N = 84; Alessandri & Lewis, 1996), maltreated girls showed more shame and less pride in tasks than non-maltreated girls. Some research suggests that higher shame in abused children has been associated with parental behaviors—e.g., hostility, rejection, negative affective displays and comments during learning of abuse, and minimal recognition for good behavior (see Feiring & Taska, 2005).

Guilt has been strongly associated with posttrauma outcomes and with attachment and dissociation (e.g., PTSD severity; Kletter, Weems, & Carrion, 2009; see Nader, 2008). Reduced anterior insula volume related to preschool-age guilt has predicted depression in later childhood and adolescence. Increased depression severity was linked to children's increased frequency of guilt feelings and less frequent attempts at guilt reparation (hence to maladaptive guilt; N = 305, ages 3–5, Luby et al., 2009). Making amends must be individually timed and tailored for its effectiveness (e.g., age appropriate; Nader, 2001).

Empathy/Other-Awareness

As demonstrated in earlier chapters, mother's empathy is relevant to child empathy and other developmental skills. Parental empathy capacity has played a key role in children's socialization, affect regulation, symbolic expression and competence, cognitive functioning, and the child's ongoing ability to internalize a moral code and to empathize with others (e.g., Abraham, Raz, Zagoory-Sharon, & Feldman, 2018; Feldman, 2007, 2015). Functional connectivity within a parent's embodied simulation brain network during a child's infancy—suggesting increased parental emotional empathy—predicted the child's lower preschool-age cortisol production (lower cortisol reactivity; N = 87 followed infancy to age six; Abraham et al., 2018). Inter-network connectivity among embodied simulation and mentalizing networks was linked to preschoolers' more advanced emotion-regulation skills and related to age six lower internalizing problems mediated by emotion-regulation skills (see Table 1.2—mentalizing). Although, in general, men and women may use different cognitive and emotional strategies when empathizing, studies have found no gender differences in the empathy-related networks for both gender primary caregivers.

When parental empathy-related brain networks were assessed, parents' network integrity within and between empathy-related networks increased when viewing their own infant versus an unfamiliar infant (Abraham et al., 2018). Depressed or substance using mothers do not show such increased activations. Trauma and dissociation-proneness have also related to reduced empathy (e.g., Chiu, Paesen, Dziobek, & Tollenaar, 2016).

Posttrauma reactions (e.g., PTS, depression) may interfere with aspects of empathy—e.g., accurate recognition of others' emotions. For example, children exposed to aggression may attribute malicious intent to others even in ambiguous situations (Crick & Dodge, 1996, Box 3.2). Preschoolers with depressed mothers (e.g., posttrauma) have exhibited alterations in frontal lobe brain activity linked to diminished empathy and behavioral problems (Jones, Field, & Davalos, 2000).

Trauma and Social Skills

Poor social skills alone or in combination with other disturbances may lead to problems (e.g., peer rejection; poor functioning). Trauma may interfere with young children's social relating in a number of ways—e.g., increased irritability, fear or other difficulty being around others, disrupted perspective-taking; disrupted attachments, reduced prosocial influence, cognitive constriction—and may increase the likelihood of antisocial behaviors and/or antisocial friends (Nader, 2008). Interpersonal traumas have been associated with difficulties with trust, low interpersonal effectiveness, diminished social skills, inability to understand social interactions, poor perspective-taking abilities, expectations of harm from others, poor boundaries, and social isolation in children (D'Andrea et al., 2012). University students with histories of childhood traumas have shown problems in deontic reasoning—i.e., reasoning about duty and obligation—and with cognitive empathy, each of which are needed for social interacting (Chiu et al., 2016). Students with high dissociation-proneness showed the lowest levels of understanding others' mental states. However, controlling for emotional awareness and perceptions of their own parents' parental styles demolished the association, suggesting the importance of parenting and awareness.

Trauma and Playfulness: Play and Humor

After traumatic events (e.g., loss of a parent, violence, disasters), children's play, humor, and imagination may be disrupted (e.g., PTSD<6, C4). As described in Chapter 2, traumatic play may replace normal play (Box 1.1, 9.1; e.g., may undermine R&T, see Attachment), and the social, emotional, and skill building benefits normally gained from play may be undermined. In contrast, young children may move between periods of distress and normal play after events.

Box 9.1 Posttrauma Play

Tia, age three or four, used to be very happy and outgoing. One day, she went upstairs with mother and uncle. They were fooling around with each other and with her. There was pain, but she doesn't remember actual penetration. Father divorced her "adulterously promiscuous mother" and gained custody (Tia age five), but Tia visited her mother in summer and on holidays. When she was five, she remembers her uncle on the couch kissing a girl ("not sex, just kissing"). Tia went into the bedroom and started "humping" her panda bear, then "pee'd on it." During this age, it became her response to witnessing affection. At Tia's age seven, her father threatened to keep her away from Mom, when Tia reported being afraid when the bed was bouncing (mother and boyfriend in bed with her—Mom had a series of boyfriends). Mom would make a restaurant successful, then become bored and move to another town and start a new one. Tia remembers one *sleezy* guy being seductive and scary, but grade school is a blur. Tia's mother was variously diagnosed (across Tia's life) as depressed (prescribed valium, ineffective), paranoid (melaril, helped some, but mom felt stupid and tongue-tied), and then bipolar (lithium). As an adult, Tia is introverted and intellectual, priding herself on her innovation and observation skills. She sought treatment because every time she feels powerless in her business, she regresses, feels helpless, and "jumps into victim mode," which interferes with effective business practice. Her perspective-taking diminishes, she becomes tearful and dependent, and sometimes becomes angry and lashes out.

Note:
All case examples are disguised, may be combined cases, and have had details changed to protect individuals.

Other Stressor-Related Reactions

As discussed in Chapter 6, studies have shown that trauma-exposed preschoolers may exhibit a variety of problems (e.g., Basu, Malone, Levendosky, & Dubay, 2009; Nader & Fletcher, 2014)—e.g., internalizing or externalizing behavior problems, low social competence, and trauma symptoms (see Basu et al., 2009; Levendosky, Huth Bocks, Semel, & Shapiro, 2002). Trauma and Stressor-Related Disorders (TSRD) include disorders found in children age 6 and under. Reactive Attachment Disorder (RAD in DSM-5 and ICD10), Disinhibited Social Engagement Disorder (DSED; disinhibited attachment disorder in ICD-10), and PTSD for children ages 0–6 were described in Chapter 6.

Stress reactivity has been linked to temperament or genetics and to early, repeated, or severe trauma or stress exposure (see Nader & Fletcher, 2014; Yehuda et al., 2015). PTSD < 6 includes at least one intrusion symptom, one or more symptoms of avoidance or negative cognitions, and two or more alterations in arousal or reactivity (APA, 2013). PTSD has been documented in preschool children with significant comorbidity (Egger & Angold, 2006; Levendosky et al., 2002; Scheeringa, 2011; Scheeringa et al., 2012). Other symptoms (e.g., internalizing, externalizing) and impaired developmental skills also have followed traumas, for this age group (e.g., low social competence). Studies have shown that time does not heal the impact of prolonged stress (Halevi et al., 2016). Multiple types of trauma exposures (poly-victimization or cumulative trauma) increase and shape reactions (Finkelhor et al., 2007, 2014; Nader, 2014). Maltreated and war-exposed children, for example, often have more than one trauma exposure (Nader, 2008; Box 13.1). Across 35 war studies for children ages 1–6, Slone and Mann (2016) found that young children had PTSD or PTSS, behavioral and emotional problems, sleep disturbances, disturbed play, and psychosomatic symptoms as well as new fears, clinginess and over-dependency, lower frustration tolerance, increased aggression, and changes in eating habits. War-exposed children followed from early childhood (ages 1.5 to 5) through age 11 have exhibited disorders (PTSD, ADHD, anxiety disorders, disruptive behavior disorders) at some point in childhood (81%; N = 232; Halevi et al., 2016). Early war-exposures were linked to comorbidity in middle and late childhood. Some studies suggest parenting mediates children's traumatic reactions (Feldman & Vengrober, 2011; Halevi et al., 2016; Levendosky & Graham-Bermann, 2001; Scheeringa, Myers, Putnam, & Zeanah, 2015; Slone & Mann, 2016); others do not confirm such a link (e.g., Levendosky et al., 2003). However, traumas may directly or indirectly affect quality of parenting—e.g., reduced reciprocal interactions with child; reduced sensitivity (Feldman et al., 2013b; Scheeringa et al., 2015; van Ee et al., 2016). Histories of childhood traumas are associated with borderline personality disorder (BPD). Traumas before age six have been found for BPD versus other types of PD (Herman, Perry, van der Kolk, 1989; Vermetten & Spiegel, 2014). Some other possible posttrauma symptoms follow.

Dreams and Sleep

Following traumas, young children may experience difficulty falling or staying asleep and have dreams with trauma-related content or affect (APA, 2013). Normally, children ages 2–6 sleep an average of 10–11 hours per night (Touchette et al., 2007). Normal sleep levels differ to some extent by variables such as country—e.g., predominantly Asian countries show significantly shorter sleep—one hour less over the 0–12-year range (Galland, Taylor, Elder, & Herbison, 2012); temperament (Schaefer, 1990); or genetics—e.g., reduced sleep for 5HTTPLR (Bouvette-Turcot et al., 2015b). Poor sleep has been linked to a number of problems such as behavioral—e.g., hyperactivity, aggression; mood—e.g., crankiness; emotional control—e.g., low frustration tolerance; academic performance—e.g., short attention span, inattention, poor performance; decreased reaction time; increased accidents or injuries (e.g., Dahl, 1996; see Nelson et al., 2015; Paavonen et al. 2009a, b; Zhang et al., 2013). Specifically, for 3–5-year-olds, less than normal sleep is associated with cognitive, behavioral, and emotional problems (e.g., injury/falls, Boto et al., 2012); hyperactivity/impulsivity, lower cognitive performance on neurodevelopmental tests at school entry (age six, Touchette et al., 2007); poorer EF performance—e.g., working memory and interference inhibition (inhibiting attention to distractions; Nelson et al., 2015); and emotionality/behavioral dysregulation (for 5-HTTPLR genotypes, Bouvette-Turcot et al., 2015b). Even with sleep improvement during ages 3–6, children who had poor sleep patterns during age 2.5 were especially high in hyperactivity and cognitive deficits (N = 1124; Touchette et al., 2007).

Dream Content

Although the content of night terrors is not remembered, young children have sometimes enacted aspects of a traumatic experience or event during night terrors—e.g., running for safety while screaming with eyes wide open (Nader, 2008). For preschool children, elaborate dreams are one of the ways that traumas are followed by precocious knowledge or behavior (Chapter 6). Traumatized preschool children may have dreams more like those described for older children (Box 6.2).

Dissociation and Imaginary Friends

For children ages 3–6, dissociative symptoms (DS) have been linked to parental behaviors, traumas, and symptoms as well as to child trauma exposures. Childhood traumas, especially multiple trauma types, have been associated with increased likelihood of dissociation (e.g., Bozkurt, Mutluer, Kose, & Zoroglu, 2015; Frewen et al., 2014, 2017; Hébert, Langevin, & Daigneault, 2016). Dissociation prevalence rates vary by culture (Pole, Best, Metzler, & Marmar, 2005). As noted (Chapter 7), avoidant and disorganized attachment styles have been linked to dissociation, as well. In a high-risk, low-income, ethnically diverse sample of traumatized 3–6-year-olds, almost one fourth had subclinical or clinical levels of dissociation (mother-reported; N = 140; Hagan, Hulette, & Lieberman, 2015). For treatment-seeking families (children were nonclinical, had PTSD only, or PTSD-DS), odds of children being in the PTSD-DS group were greater for girls (twice as likely as boys), for sexually abused children (nearly three times more likely), and with every unit increase in parent avoidance symptoms or number of traumatic exposures (N = 297 trauma-exposed, ethnically and SES diverse, ages 3–6; Hagan, Gentry, Ghosh Ippen, & Lieberman, 2018). Peri-traumatic dissociation may contribute to the continuation of dissociative symptoms as a generalized pattern (Bennett, Modrowski, Kerig, & Chaplo, 2015). Over time, dissociation is associated with increased severity of both PTSD and PTSD-DS subtype (Bennett et al., 2015), with poor memory and attention performance (De Bellis, Woolley, & Hooper, 2013, ages 6–17; Kaplow et al., 2008; Parlar et al., 2016), with non-suicidal self-injury (Lev-Wiesel & Zohar, 2014), suicidality, functional impairment, less treatment seeking, and comorbidity (Stein et al., 2013).

Imaginary Friends

Imaginary friends are found to be most common between ages four and seven, but in some children, last through age 10 (Silberg, 2013). In a self-selected British sample (N = 264), imaginary companions served five purposes: for problem-solving and emotion management, for exploration of ideals, for joint fantasy play, to explore behavior and roles, and/or to overcome loneliness (Majors & Baines, 2017). Parents reported that 60% of children had more than one imaginary companion, mostly human companions (67%) and some animal companions (19%).

Children tend to feel protective of their imaginary friends and do not like interference from adults (Klein, 1985). Imaginary friends assist children with a variety of developmental challenges—to practice social skills; to project difficult feelings or unacceptable impulses; for help with feelings of loneliness; or to embody traits the child wishes to have. Some evidence suggests that dissociative youth are more likely to have imaginary friends than normal children and more likely to impersonate them (literature review; see Silberg, 2013). Comparing the imaginary friends of school children with those of inpatient dissociative children, Trujillo, Lewis, Yeager, and Gidlow (1996) found that the dissociative children's imaginary friends were more likely to have malevolent characteristics attributed to them than those of normal children. With dissociative identity disorder (DID) or other disordered dissociation, imaginary friends may later become manifestations among separate identities (Silberg, 2013). In such cases, a young child may feel s/he is being compelled to do things and may hear the sounds of conversations and conflicts between imaginary friends in her/his mind. Severe dissociative disorders (e.g., DID) have been attributed to severe stressors (e.g., chronic physical and sexual abuse; in some cases, repeated surgical procedures; imitation of family dissociative disorders; Silberg, 1998b, 2004). Silberg (1998a) observed a number of DID cases in children without a history of trauma or related disorders. In these cases, youths experienced a series of events viewed as intolerable or threatening and learned a pattern of avoidance to cope with the perceived stresses. Mersky (1992) observed that children use imaginary friends and additional identities to deal with severe emotional conflict or to protect themselves from intolerable experiences. Both authors caution against reinforcing use of separate identities in this way.

Stress Reactivity

Trauma has been related to increased HPA axis and autonomic nervous system reactivity (see Chapter 4). For example, young children with PTSD, exposure but no PTSD, and no trauma exposure were assessed in memory recall tasks (N = 247 3–6-year-olds; Gray, Lipschutz, & Scheeringa, 2018). All children showed autonomic reactivity during recall of pleasant memories and during theirs or parents' recall of personal traumatic memories, suppressing RSA compared to baseline. However, compared to the other groups, children with PTSD exhibited greater RSA reactivity than children without PTSD during recollection of personal traumatic memories. Under normal circumstances, in early life, caregivers act as external regulators of the stress system. Negative caregiving experiences early in life may have deleterious effects on the HPA axis system with perturbations in cortisol release and related behavioral risk (Fisher et al., 2016). As discussed, a blunted cortisol slope was found for children raised in institutional care—not the usual high morning cortisol and low bedtime cortisol levels. Some evidence suggests that repair occurs for children placed in foster care or adopted before age two or three (Chapter 7). Other studies show an earlier cut-off age (see Fisher et al., 2016). For children adopted between ages 15 months and 36 months, between 2 and 25 months post-adoption (ages 1.5 up to 5), children showed less steep daily cortisol slopes than normal, and even less steep when they were from more socially depriving pre-adoption settings (N = 66 adopted, 50 internationally adopted, and 53 non-adopted comparisons; Koss, Hostinar, Donzella, & Gunnar, 2014). That is, blunted cortisol persisted into the preschool years or later, suggesting early programming of the HPA axis. For a significant number of the adopted children the slope became even flatter for the first two years after adoption.

Conclusions

Especially for young children, parents are important to development and to recovery from the deleterious effects of adversity. Parents' own traumas may influence parenting. Siblings may be a part of support and healing and/or may be themselves affected by a sibling's mental health problems. For ages 3–6, teachers also become important and may influence both developing skills and the recovery process. Children's pre- and posttrauma temperaments may influence reactions, support, and need following traumas. Preschool traumas have been linked to many immediate and long-term outcomes—e.g., developmental delays, internalizing, externalizing, changes in brain volume and activity, body regulation, effortful control. Trauma may result in regression and may disrupt, delay, and/or undermine developmental skills. Caregivers may need to adjust behaviors and expectations to a young child's functioning age or stage before or while either restoring safety and easing the child back to normalcy or seeking professional assistance to repair emotional, behavioral, cognitive, and/or attachment-related disturbances. This is an important period of brain development, and neurological repair may be needed.

10
Treatment Methods for Children Ages 3–6

Treatment for young children aims to reduce symptoms and dysfunction and to restore resilience—e.g., confidence, trust, secure attachments, and ability to flourish. The healing of trauma-affected neurobiology is also important. In the past, a complaint has been offered that some manualized treatments, when rigidly applied, are less successful. Treatments presented here recognize the importance of adapting methods to the needs of the child and family and recognize that children regress in response to trauma and in the course of treatment (e.g., see Ribaudo, 2016; Chapter 4). Repeated experiences with emotionally attuned individuals can help a child and a parent to regain a sense of emotional control. Parents generally participate in treatments for young children. For all methods, cultural sensitivity is essential.

Children under age six have been assessed using combinations of methods—e.g., observation—in play or of adult–child dyads; questions, often during play; information from caretaking adults (Nader, 2008; Scheeringa, 2016; Scheeringa, Peebles, Cook, & Zeanah, 2001). Between ages three and six, children are usually able to recognize and understand emotions and are developing the ability to recognize causes of emotions (see Durbin, 2010). Minor changes occur between ages three and six without gender differences (N = 206 age 3–6; Durbin, 2010). Children who are as young as ages three or four are able to report basic emotions—happy, sad, angry, mad, or scared. Gathering information requires being able to speak the language of the reporting person (e.g., cultural, developmental, regional), or sometimes requires an interpreter (Nader, 2008). Children under age 8 may have difficulties with the concept of time and may need an identifying time period, if questioned—e.g., a date that is meaningful to the specific child like a birthday, holiday (e.g., Thanksgiving), or other known day (e.g., Halloween). To follow are issues related to questioning young children and treatment methods with demonstrated effectiveness.

Questioning Preschool Children

A number of age-related issues are important in interviewing and assessing young children (e.g., sense of safety, memory, suggestibility). Of course, enabling the child to feel safe and in a supportive environment is essential. Although a caregiver's initial presence may comfort a young child, evidence suggests that having a known person present during assessment can inhibit the child's information giving (see Nader, 2008). Additionally, if a parent is interviewed in front of a young child, when questioned, the child may only repeat what s/he heard the parent say.

Older children demonstrate better memories and less suggestibility. Young children have more problems resisting suggestive questions than older children (Eisen et al., 2007). Although, by age six, children are generally better able to resist being misled on central issues than on peripheral aspects of experience, this is less true for very young children. However, what constitutes central issues may differ for young children. Some research has shown that, after yes–no questions, preschoolers are biased toward saying "No," especially for questions incomprehensible to them, and toddlers are biased toward saying yes (Fritzley & Lee, 2003). Mehrani and Peterson (2016) found that, when questions are negatively framed, young children are more likely to respond negatively, and when questions are more positively framed, young children are more likely to respond affirmatively—i.e., likely to respond to questions in the direction implied.

Under traumatic circumstances, memory is enhanced for aspects of the traumatic experience. Trauma-related psychopathology has led to heightened attention and memory for trauma-related cues but less attention and worse memory for non-trauma-related cues (Eisen et al., 2007; Nader, 2008; Terr, 1991). Even when prone to dissociation in response to traumas, maltreated children as young as age three (with high dissociation) have had more (not less) detailed memories of their abuse experiences (unrelated to cognitive ability; Eisen, Qin, Goodman, & Davis, 2002; preschoolers 93% accuracy; omission errors were higher). Although children with dissociative tendencies, PTSD, and/or lower psychological functioning exhibited more distress (cortisol levels) during an anogenital exam/venipuncture, PTSD diagnosis was unrelated to memory performance or to suggestibility (Eisen et al., 2007). Highly dissociative children with higher cortisol levels and high self-reported trauma symptoms (not highly distressed, low dissociative children) made more commission errors—i.e., more memory and suggestibility errors. Although maltreated children were more likely to have a diagnosis (e.g., PTSD, dissociation), they were not more likely than non-maltreated to rate themselves as having trauma symptoms (Eisen et al., 2007), underscoring the importance of gathering diagnostic information from more than one source, using more than one method—e.g., observation, interview, parent report.

Trauma-Focused Treatment Methods

A number of treatment methods have proven successful in work with children ages 3–6. Some well-recommended methods are provided here. Treatments for young and school-age children often include creative methods (e.g., play, storytelling, drawing; see Chapter 7). For example, play permits processing experiences in a slightly distanced manner (see Ribaudo, 2016). In normal play, children can take their play very seriously, expending large amounts of emotion and energy during play (Solnit, 1987). Traumatic play may take on an almost driven quality (Nader, 2008; Nader & Pynoos, 1991; Terr, 1981). When a child can progress to a next step in a needed progression in play, s/he appears to enjoy the play. Resolution is not always possible without therapeutic assistance (see Chapter 7). Children's needs vary; play may assist connection (Box 10.1). Other methods, such as exercise, yoga, rhythmic or enhanced play, and meditation, have been used following traumas and have sometimes been linked to positive neurobiological changes as well (Gaskill & Perry, 2014).

Posttrauma Methods Developed or Adapted for 3–6-Year-Olds

The methods presented here have sometimes been used with younger children as well. Some methods have been adapted for use in other countries (e.g., TF-CBT-YC—British version of TF-CBT; Dalgleish et al., 2015; Goodall et al., 2017).

Box 10.1 Triplets, Age 4—More than One Route to Rapport

Most children in a brief care group were boys (left while parents attended lectures). Three of the boys were identical triplets (age four). At first, they appeared to be oppositional in their behavior. They ignored any instructions, refused to participate with the group, seemed slightly aggressive, and played only with each other. Before entering each week, the second-born triplet clung to his mother at the door and told her that he was scared. He would resist entering or go in reluctantly. One day, he sat with his back against the entry door, pouting. The observer said, "I see you're guarding the door well." He looked surprised and, then, seeming defiant, went into the room to play. He often played alone, only periodically joining in with the other two triplets. The other two triplets played together throughout the hour. They joined hands and twirled around in a circle, would slap at each other, or chased each other around. When the second born joined them, the other two would sandwich him, placing their heads against his head briefly, make a kind of cooing sound, then they would disengage and go back to twirling or running around with each other. It was by accident that the observer discovered that one could be invited into this closed, exclusive system, with its own set of rules. One day, third-born triplet tripped and fell, hitting his head hard on the floor. The observer was nearby and went to see if he was okay. He batted at her and kicked at her while she touched the back of his head (no blood or bump) and tried to get him to let her look at his eyes (he squeezed them shut). She stayed there with her hand on the back of his head, saying, "You're okay," "You're going to be all right," while dodging his kicks or bats. Then the other teachers came over and decided whether to contact his mother. Meanwhile, first-born triplet took the hand of the observer and the hand of third-born triplet and began their usual spinning around. They included her in their running and other play (pulling her along, at first) until the end of the hour. Without attempting to, she had passed a test that permitted her to be a part of this closed group. They now expected her to play in the way that they played. It was only then that she realized that their rough-and-tumble play was part of their way of creating their own little world into which it was not so easy to gain admittance.

Note:
All case examples are disguised, may be combined cases, and have had details changed to protect individuals.

Child–Parent Psychotherapy (CPP)

With increases in autonomy, the child becomes an active partner and the focus of sessions; play becomes an important aspect of intervention. For 3–6-year-olds (and 0–3-year-olds) exposed to one or more traumas, CPP (Lieberman, 2004; Lieberman & Van Horn, 2005, 2011; Lieberman, Ghosh Ippen, & Van Horn, 2015) originates in Fraiberg's (1980) infant–parent psychotherapy (ages 0–3). CPP allows parent and child to learn together (in joint sessions; at home or in office) and encourages the therapist to see from the family's perspective (Williams et al., 2014). CPP aims to enhance the parent's capacity to provide safety and developmentally appropriate caregiving (Ghosh Ippen, Harris, Van Horn, & Lieberman, 2011). It seeks to strengthen the relationship between child and caregivers; restore secure attachments, sense of safety, and appropriate affect; improve parenting—e.g., correct faulty perceptions, help to foster autonomy, and assist to meet the child's needs; and improve a child's cognitive, behavioral, and social functioning (Harley, Williams, Zamora, & Lakatos, 2014; Toth et al., 2002; Van Horn, Gray, Pettinelli, & Estassi, 2013). CPP clinicians attend to the effects of trauma on the child–parent relationship and enhance that relationship to help the child with trauma-related fear and dysfunction (Lieberman et al., 2015). CPP also includes trauma-specific content—e.g., managing arousal, reestablishing trust in bodily sensations and emotional cues, restoring a realistic response to threat, coping with traumatic reminders and expectations (Van Horn et al., 2013). The average number of sessions is 30. Some children with severe or repeated traumas may require longer treatment (e.g., years, Ribaudo, 2016, CPP/IPP, affect regulation focus). Treatment begins with forming a strong alliance with the parent and includes assessing, e.g., the situation, parent and child trauma histories, parent concerns and capacities (Van Horn et al., 2013). The clinician's interactions with parent and child are based on empathy, sensitivity, transparency and respect for their real-life experiences, linking trauma to presenting problems and to treatment (Lieberman et al., 2015). Clinician and parent co-create a treatment plan. Beginning child sessions communicate the therapist's ability to understand what the child is feeling, offer a safe environment for strong emotions, restore a sense of safety and of calm, and offer any needed assistance in containing affect (Ribaudo, 2016). Stories, drawings, and other creative methods may assist treatment.

Rather than a session-by-session map for intervention, CPP manuals provide a theoretical framework, guiding principles, and case examples (Harley et al., 2014; Lieberman & Van Horn, 2005, 2008; Lieberman et al., 2015). Child development is supported through play, physical contact, and language; reflective guidance; modeling appropriate protective behaviors; interpretation of feelings and behaviors; support and empathy; crisis intervention; and concrete assistance with daily problems (Van Horn et al., 2013). CPP seeks the meaning behind behaviors (of child and parent) and seeks to translate so that parents and children gain better understanding. A therapist applies specific interventions in response to what a family brings into the treatment session (see e.g., Ribaudo, 2016; Weinreb & Groves, 2015), and treatment is guided by both caregiver's and child's emotional and developmental capacities and treatment rhythms (Ghosh Ippen, Noroña, & Lieberman, 2014). Enlisting community resources—e.g., medical and other service providers, support persons, material resources; supporting parents—e.g., help to process reactions to disabilities or problems, reinforcement of competence and connection, provision of new parenting and coping skills, help to see child's potential and accurately assess limitations; and providing psychoeducation may be included in treatment. For the clinician, collaborative, *reflective* supervision (enhanced by videotaped sessions) provides an opportunity to reflect on self and session content. CPP has been used with a variety of cultures and has been used with children with developmental delays or disabilities as well (e.g., autistic; Ghosh Ippen et al., 2014; Harley et al., 2014).

Children treated with CPP have shown greater resilience than comparison groups—e.g., more securely attached, better cognitive test scores; fewer symptoms of traumatic stress, behavioral problems, avoidance symptoms, and lower prevalence of PTSD (see Lieberman & Van Horn, 2008 for a review). The method has been used effectively with infants and preschoolers exposed to maltreatment (Toth et al., 2002; Cicchetti, Rogosch, & Toth, 2006), to domestic violence (Harley et al., 2014; Lieberman, Ghosh Ippen, & Van Horn, 2006; Lieberman, Van Horn, & Ghosh Ippen, 2005), to depressed mothers (see Toth, Rogosch, Manly, & Cicchetti, 2006), and to multiple traumas (more than four) and for infants with anxious attachments (Ghosh Ippen et al., 2011). For example, after treatment, preschoolers with multiple trauma types, have had fewer behavior problems, less depressive symptoms, fewer DC: 0–3 diagnoses, and were less likely than comparisons to have PTSD (with large effect sizes; Ghosh Ippen et al., 2011). Additionally, their mothers experienced a reduction in depression and PTSD and showed improved parenting. Six months later, the CPP 4+-traumas group showed significant reductions in children's behavior problems and in maternal depression. An adaptation of CPP (P-CPP) has also been used beginning prenatally with at risk mothers (e.g., history of complex trauma, IPV; see Waters, Hagan, Rivera, & Lieberman, 2015). For example, 64 pregnant women (from third trimester through baby's age six months) showed improvements in depression, PTSS, and child-rearing attitudes (Lavi et al., 2015). Mothers with low maternal–fetal attachment showed greatest progress. CPP has shown increased and sustained secure attachments between caregivers and maltreated infants over time (see Waters et al.,

2015). Additionally, compared to non-depressed controls, depressed mothers who showed significant improvement in mother–child attachment, also reported slight increases in marital satisfaction (across three years; Peltz et al., 2015).

Multidimensional Treatment Foster Care for Preschoolers (MTFC-P)

Much evidence has demonstrated poor outcomes for foster care children (Fisher, Chamberlain, & Leve, 2009). For 3–6-year-olds, MTFC-P (Chamberlain, 1994; Fisher & Chamberlain, 2000) provides up to 12 months of intensive training and ongoing support for foster parents (Fisher et al., 2009) and assists them to increase consistent, positive parenting, using behavior management strategies and stress reduction techniques (Fisher, Stoolmiller, Gunnar, & Burraston, 2007).

As discussed in earlier chapters, trauma is linked to increased HPA axis reactivity (Fisher et al., 2016; Nader & Fletcher, 2014; Yehuda et al., 2015). MTFC-P has been linked to improved HPA axis functioning (Fisher et al., 2006, 2007). Cortisol reactivity in response to a naturally occurring stressor (start of school) was significantly higher (five days after start date) in the regular foster care child group than in MTFC-P children, who more closely resembled community control children (Graham et al. 2012). Additionally, MTFC-P foster parents had reductions in stress, in contrast to regular foster care parent groups who showed increases in stress (Fisher & Stoolmiller 2008). Fisher, Burraston, and Pears (2005) demonstrated that children with four or more foster placements had a very poor likelihood of achieving a permanent placement, while children with only two prior placements had an excellent chance (more than 80% better chance). MTFC (for older and preschool children) is associated with increased likelihood of achieving permanency as well as increased likelihood of children's attachment to caregivers and of participation in school (Fisher et al., 2009; Leve, Fisher, & Chamberlain, 2009). It is also linked to reduced levels of foster-parent stress, of older children's delinquency and antisocial behavior, and of subsequent incarceration. Although MTFC-P has shown success over treatment as usual or normal foster care in the U.S., in a Dutch study of preschoolers and early school age, children in MTFC-P and in usual treatment foster care showed similar gains (N = 55 in MTFC-P, 23 treatment as usual, 30 in regular foster care, 3–7-year-olds; Jonkman et al., 2017). Although replication is needed in a larger sample, in the Netherlands, MTFC-P was not superior to treatment foster care as usual in reducing behavioral problems, attachment disorder symptoms, foster-parent stress, or child and foster-parent neurobiological functioning, which may suggest the quality of usual care or the need for cultural adaptations.

Preschool PTSD Treatment (PPT)

PPT (Scheeringa, 2016) is based on cognitive behavioral therapy (CBT) with modifications for young children (Scheeringa, Amaya-Jackson, & Cohen, 2010). It includes a 12-session protocol (45–90-minute sessions) for 3–6-year-olds (Scheeringa, 2016). PPT provides interventions for biological parents, foster parents, and child care providers as needed. Specific techniques include psychoeducation about PTSD, behavior management (e.g., identify measurable target behaviors), recognition of feelings, training in coping skills (e.g., relaxation methods); graduated exposures to trauma-related reminders using drawings, imaginal, and in vivo methods; and safety planning. Primary maternal caregivers are present with the children during all of sessions 1, 2, and 12 and observe all other sessions on TV (with child's knowledge; to increase parent knowledge and attunement; Scheeringa et al., 2010). Session 2 includes identifying behavioral targets and addressing discipline (and if needed, grief) issues (Scheeringa, 2016). In sessions with children (beginning in session 3), their symptoms or feelings are given a name and are given a story form, and fears are placed in the larger context of other feelings and situations, thus utilizing the cognitive tasks of self-reflection, autobiographical memory, and causal reasoning (Scheeringa et al., 2010). A pictorial rating for scary feelings is used. Children and parents, individually, are given relaxation methods to assist self-control, in session 4. Sessions 5–10 include exposure exercises—telling the story, easy narrative exposure, medium narrative exposure, worst moment exposure (Scheeringa, 2016). In session 11, children imagine themselves in future situations (relapse prevention) and are prepared for termination. In session 12, they review drawing and homework sheets and graduate. A small piece of candy is offered before and a snack is offered during each session—toys and snacks are not stored in the therapy room to prevent using them to avoid exposure methods. A folder ("roadway book"; left in the office after sessions) is one method used to develop a coherent narrative. In it are the chronologically collected projects and homework from each session, and sometimes the symbolically contained distressing memories (Scheeringa, 2016). When it is difficult to understand young children, Scheeringa suggests it is less irritating for them if you act as if you understand. A matter-of-fact attitude toward discussing the trauma is recommended (Scheeringa, 2016).

Cooperation is essential to effective treatment and can pose challenges with young children who have limited conceptualizations of how psychotherapy is supposed to work. The manual describes several methods to deal effectively with uncooperative children (Scheeringa, 2016). Addressing reluctance and preparation for the next session are included at the end of sessions. Clinicians can anticipate with parents, their likely reluctance to attend sessions and can later discuss how they relinquished their own discomfort in order to help their child. In young children who are already cooperative, a strong rapport may readily occur. Young children may not make eye contact, pay attention, and frequently indicate their compliance even with good rapport. Therapists generally do not need to go to extra lengths to establish rapport with already cooperative children (personal communication, M. Scheeringa, 9-2-18).

PPT has reduced symptoms of PTSD, major depressive disorder (MDD), separation anxiety disorder (SAD), and oppositional defiant disorder (ODD) (Puff & Renk, 2015; Scheeringa et al., 2011). For 36–83-month-olds exposed to a variety of traumatic events, 40 children were assigned to immediate treatment (n = 20, completed) and 24 children were assigned to a 12-week wait-list condition (N = 11 completed) (Scheeringa et al., 2011). The immediate treatment group showed significantly more improvement in PTSD symptoms, but not in MDD, SAD, ODD, or attention deficit/hyperactivity disorder (ADHD) compared to the wait-list group. Children who completed the wait-list period were offered PPT. A single-group analysis of all children who completed PPT showed that immediately post-intervention and six months later, PTSD symptoms decreased significantly (large effect size) as did MDD, SAD, and ODD symptoms, but not ADHD symptoms (ADHD may have a neurobiological basis, Chapter 7). Treated children also have shown improvements in coping, problem-solving skills, and functioning—e.g., academic, social, emotional, and behavioral (Puff & Renk, 2015). Long-term findings are influenced by SES (e.g., lack of resources).

Creative Methods

Techniques such as drawings, stories, board games, or specific rule-guided interactions are often included among creative therapies and may be used as components of trauma interventions (Nader, 2004). A number of creative therapies have been used for PTS and for Developmental Trauma (e.g., play, art, storytelling; YogaKids, Wenig, 2003). Stories can present an opportunity to discuss aspects of an experience not previously shared or to learn self-skills. For example, the book, *Do You Have a Secret* (Moore-Mallinos, 2005), permits a child to discuss the meaning of a secret, to learn the difference between a good and a bad secret, and possibly to share a secret. The book, *Draw on Your Emotions* (Sunderland, 2018), includes exercises to assist children to communicate and deal with their emotions more effectively. *The Story of Ferdinand* (Leaf, 1936/2011) is a story about being different from others (not trauma-related; unabridged recommended).

With persistent or repetitive threat, fear, chaos, stress, and/or trauma, neural networks change in their baseline activity and reactivity—e.g., act as if there is persistent threat (Perry, 2009). Some creative methods reflect the belief that incorporating sensorimotor aspects—i.e., patterned, repetitive somatosensory activation of neural systems (Perry, 2009); tactile sensorimotor stimulation (Elbrecht, 2015)—is healing for the brain/neurobiology (see Gaskill & Perry, 2014; Perry 2006, 2009). For example, Clay Field is a sensorimotor method for young children to work through traumatic experiences, in an atmosphere of safety. It uses a flat, rectangular wooden box (holds up to 33 lbs. of smooth clay). Children are provided warm water, a sponge, and tools (e.g., ice cream scoop; Elbrecht, 2015). Additionally, yoga or mindfulness, music, movement, drumming, and massage as well as caregiver–child play therapy methods may assist brain reorganization (Chapters 7, 13; Baer, 2003; Barfield, Dobson, Gaskill, & Perry, 2011; Field et al., 1996; Perry, 2009; Appendix—repair of brain regions). Mindfulness programs are available for parents, teachers, school administrators, and for children from ages 3–18 (e.g., see Schonert-Reichl & Roeser, 2016). Mindfulness has been associated with improved executive functions (e.g., working memory, attention), emotion-regulation, stress relief, calm, well-being, and health (Quach et al., 2015; see Schonert-Reichl & Roeser, 2016; Thierry et al., 2018). A mindfulness training program for teachers showed reduced psychological symptoms, attentional biases, and burn-out as well as improved classroom organization, mindfulness, and self-compassion (Table 1.3b; Mindfulness-Based Stress Reduction, Flook et al., 2013).

Play Therapy

Play therapy methods have been adapted for use with single-incident and repeated traumas and is often a component of treatment methods (Lieberman & Van Horn, 2005, 2008; Nader, 2004; Scheeringa, 2016). Play therapy methods vary in the levels and nature of their structure/guidelines; in their emphasis on play versus verbalization; and in the levels of direction from, interpretation by, and participation of the therapist. Approach, sequencing of interventions, and focus on reconstruction of a traumatic event or its episodes also vary for clinician, method, and age group (Nader, 2001, 2002). Especially when play therapy is the primary mode of treatment, the therapy room usually includes a variety of drawing materials, toys, and other materials that permit a child either to focus on or to deviate from focusing exclusively on traumatic themes (Webb, 2015; Chapter 13). Axline's (1969) nondirective play therapy method for a child to process unmanageable emotions in a natural, self-directed way is believed to provide a bridge between the conscious and nonconscious and to repair the link between traumatic experience and narrative (hence a cognitive framework for processing, Gray, 2011; see Gil, 1998; Box 2.3). For young children, nondirective play therapy—e.g., in a sand-tray or with toys that may replicate the trauma plus other toys—may permit or assist the child to express her/his internal experience, to process aspects of a trauma(s), and to develop competencies (Arvidson et al., 2011). Child-centered play therapy uses an environment characterized by empathic understanding—receptively entering and becoming completely at home in the child's personal perceptual world while judgment-free (Rogers, 1980), unconditional positive regard, and congruence, permitting the clinician to "be with" the child and to facilitate change (Stulmaker, Lertora, & Garza, 2015; Box 2.3; see also Short-Term PsyCT, this chapter).

Posttrauma deficits in the ability to play normally interfere with play's function in facilitating skill development, competency, innovation, and a positive sense of self as well as in play's function in coping with or processing distress (Chapters 1, 2). Play and other creative therapies may increase access to trauma materials held in nonverbal memory and, therefore, is used with complicated trauma (developmental trauma, DT) as well. Play therapy methods may enhance caregiver–child relationships, improve empathy or reflective functioning (RF), and assist neurological repair (Chapter 7; Appendix—repair of brain regions).

Drawings

Art or drawings have been used in a number of ways following traumas (Malchiodi, 2015; Nader & Pynoos, 1991; Nader & Mello, 2001; Scheeringa, 2016). They have been used after events that affect many individuals (e.g., disasters, mass violence) to soothe and to restore a sense of safety and connection for young children (Malchiodi, 2012, 2015). The psychomotor activity of drawings may trigger sensory memories, make a trauma experience more concrete and manageable (safer to relate; Steele & Raider, 2001), and activate multiple brain regions (e.g., brain stem, Perry, 2009). Young children have provided a variety of trauma-related and other drawings (e.g., self and family). For example, they may depict emotions (e.g., fears; rage), traumatic episodes, or trauma-related desires/urges—e.g., revenge or intervention fantasies. Older children in this age group can provide a narrative to go with drawings. Draw-a-picture and tell a story, scribble drawings, and clay sculpting have been used in treatments with young children (Abrams & Pearman, 2007; Nader & Mello, 2001; Pynoos & Eth, 1986; Talwar, 2007).

Treatment of Specific Symptoms and Problems

Specific reactions/problems have responded to age-appropriate treatment methods discussed here and above. Methods described above (PPT, CPP) address the treatment of bereavement in young children. Reactions discussed here include aggression and reactivity, EFs, separation and other anxiety, and developmental trauma (see also Appendix—additional methods).

Aggression and Reactivity

In a famous study that influenced theories and studies on child development, Suomi (1991, 2005) demonstrated that monkeys bred for high aggression and reactivity can be changed through exposure to enriched social play experiences (with peers or nurturing adults) during the juvenile period (summary in Pellegrini, Dupuis, & Smith, 2007). For example, high-reactive (H-R) monkeys fostered by a nurturing female exhibited more playfulness, cooperation, and social competence, compared to peer-reared monkeys. In play, young children learn appropriate social behaviors including how to establish close relationships, enabling other close relationships. Young children's enhanced social-emotional development and reductions in externalizing (e.g., ADHD) have followed the use of programs that enhance positive parent–child play, reading aloud, and daily routines (ages 0–3 then 3–5; Mendelsohn et al., 2018). In addition to the enriched attachments and social environments encouraged by earlier methods, the two following treatment methods have been used with child behavior problems. Mindfulness parenting (see Separation and other Anxiety) has also been used for behavioral disturbances (ADHD, ODD, CD).

Incredible Years Series® (IY)

The *Incredible Years Series*® includes programs for parents, teachers, and children (to age 12, Webster-Stratton, 1987, 2001, 2016; Webster-Stratton & Reid, 2010; Webster-Stratton & Bywater, in press; incredibleyears.com/programs). These programs have been used to promote improved parenting and teaching skills; to decrease risk factors—e.g., ineffective and/or harsh parenting, family conflict, child developmental risk, isolation; increase child protective factors—e.g., emotional, social, and academic competence; to reduce/prevent problem behaviors—e.g., conduct problems; and to increase well-being (Webster-Stratton & Bywater, in press; see Nader, 2012c). Parent, teacher, and child training curricula have been used in schools for a variety of cultures and *Western* nations. Video vignettes are used for modeling and to trigger discussions. Over 300 vignettes depict culturally diverse families and varied child temperaments (Webster-Stratton & Bywater, in press; Webster-Stratton, Reid, & Hammond, 2001; Webster-Stratton & Reid, 2010). Puppets are used by parents, teachers, and group therapists with young children to promote language, emotional literacy, and empathy and to model social skills and problem-solving. Social, emotional, persistence, and academic coaching methods have been used to assist parent and teacher success.

IY basic parent training includes curricula for parents of children ages 1–9 months and 1–3, 3–5, and 6–12 years old (Webster-Stratton & Bywater, in press). These recently updated programs emphasize developmentally appropriate parenting skills. Parenting programs run from 9–22 weeks, depending on child age and whether or not the prevention or treatment protocol is being used. Trained group leaders/clinicians use videos (1–3 min) with 8–12 parents to promote understanding of child development and developmentally appropriate parenting. A home-based coaching model is used for parents unable to attend groups, to supplement group for high-risk families, or for a missed group session. Parents learn to provide a positive relationship with the child, which precedes use of clear, predictable discipline; learn to provide predictable routines; and learn to use attention to positive behaviors, emotions, and cognitions more frequently than to give attention to negative ones. Adjunct parenting programs include an advanced parenting program for high-risk families (e.g., depressed parent, marital discord), an attentive parenting program (ages 2–6 without significant behavioral problems), a school readiness program for preschoolers, and a program for parents of autistic children (Webster-Stratton & Bywater, in press).

Child programs include a classroom version (universal prevention) with social-emotional lessons utilizing small group activities twice per week (teacher delivered) and a therapeutic treatment group version (4–6 children, ages 4–8; may be delivered in a mental health setting or in schools; Webster-Stratton & Bywater, in press). Videos (180+ vignettes), role-play, games, play, and activities are used to teach emotion- and behavior-regulation, problem-solving, communication skills, social skills, literacy, and rule-following. The Incredible Years® programs may be used in conjunction with trauma-focused treatments, as a preventive method (e.g., for high-risk groups, foster care), and/or to deal with specific problems (see also www.incredibleyears.com/wp-content/uploads/tailoring-the-incredible-years-parenting-program_9-19-07.pdf). For example, IY has been used for decades to treat children diagnosed with conduct problems, ODD, and ADHD as well as high-risk and child welfare-referred populations (Webster-Stratton & Reid, 2010).

The IY teacher classroom management program (IYTCM) is a six-day program spread across the school year (Webster-Stratton & Bywater, in press; Webster-Stratton, Gaspar, & Seabras-Santos, 2012; Webster-Stratton & Herman, 2010). Groups include 14–16 teachers and a trained group leader, who may provide support for teachers throughout the school year (e.g., classroom visits). IYTCM aims to improve classroom management skills (proactive teaching and effective discipline); to increase use of coaching with students in academic, persistence, social, and emotional realms; to strengthen teacher–student bonding; to increase the ability to teach social skills, anger management, and problem-solving skills in the classroom; to improve parent–teacher bonding, home–school collaboration, and behavior planning; and to build a teachers' support networks (Webster-Stratton & Bywater, in press). Teachers are assisted with age- or trait-relevant issues (e.g., separation anxiety in preschoolers; language and communication skills for autistic children).

Numerous studies have demonstrated positive results with culturally diverse populations (in the U.S. and Europe) across IY programs in improving parental attitudes, positive parenting, and parent–child interactions; in increasing children's prosocial behaviors; and in reducing harsh discipline, child conduct problems, and child mental health problems (e.g., ODD, CD; e.g., at one year follow-up, N = 149 Northern Irish children, McGilloway et al., 2014; see Webster-Stratton et al., 2012; Webster-Stratton & Bywater, in press; ADHD, Webster-Stratton, Reid, & Beauchaine, 2011). For example, after a relatively brief IY intervention for children with ADHD (N = 99, hyperactive/impulsive & combined types of ADHD), posttreatment improvements included both parasympathetic- and sympathetic nervous system-linked cardiac function (RSA, PEP reactivity) mediated by reductions in negative parenting (criticism, negative commands, physical intrusions;

small sample, non-significant for combined group; Bell et al., 2017). Long-term studies have demonstrated positive, lasting effects of IY—e.g., for children with early conduct problems, 8–12 years after IY intervention 75% of adolescents were typically adjusted (Webster-Stratton, Rinaldi, & Reid, 2011). For IY children originally ages 3–7, compared to a control group at children's ages 9–13, parents showed greater warmth and better supervision of adolescents, and youth showed improvements in antisocial behaviors and traits and in reading skills (Scott, Briskman, & O'Connor, 2014). In contrast, a separate group of children with particularly high-risk factors did not show sustained improvement from the parent training only. Evidence has suggested that combining child and parent programs is most effective (e.g., Webster-Stratton et al., 2012). As has been demonstrated with other methods, children with multiple risk factors (or multiple traumas) may need multiple types of assistance.

Preschoolers with adjudicated, antisocial adolescent siblings and other risk factors for antisocial behavior—e.g., maternal depression, family stress, low SES, pre-natal maternal smoking, low cognitive abilities (Brotman, Gouley, O'Neal, & Klein, 2004)—were administered modified IY family treatment to enhance social skills and reduce or prevent aggression (N = 92, ages 33–66 months; Brotman et al., 2008). IY was modified by adding home visits (90 min. coaching parenting skills) and 30 minutes of activities, followed by a three-month booster (up to 15 hr.) approximately 4–6 months after the intervention (Brotman et al., 2008). Group intervention was also offered to school-age siblings. Positive changes were demonstrated in preschooler conduct problems and in increased effectiveness of parenting and teachers (Brotman et al., 2003). Compared to children with the same risk factors, at two-year assessment, IY children (now average age six) exhibited five times fewer physically aggressive acts. The greater the program attendance the better the outcomes. Children's social competence (with unfamiliar peers) also improved (N = 99; Brotman et al., 2005b). Sustained improvements included reductions in harsh parenting, increased responsive parenting, and more stimulation for learning (Brotman et al., 2008)—e.g., parents learned to follow the child's lead and to have a more enriched environment (books, toys that teach). Modified IY also showed positive effects on child cortisol response to social challenge (Brotman et al., 2007) and on antisocial behaviors of older siblings (Brotman et al., 2005a).

Parent–Child Interaction Therapy (PCIT)

PCIT (Brinkmeyer & Eyberg, 2003; Eyberg & Robinson, 1983) is a manualized 14- to 20-week treatment used for children ages 2–7 (Allen, Timmer, & Urquiza, 2014). PCIT was originally designed to reduce children's disruptive behaviors. Treatment aims first to assist a warm and responsive caregiver–child relationship and then to aid the parent in learning to more effectively manage a child's disruptive behaviors (Pincus, Santucci, Ehrenreich, & Eyberg, 2008). It teaches parents to provide positive attention to desired behaviors, and to use nonviolent consequences as needed (Allen et al., 2014). Each phase of treatment is typically 7–10 sessions (Allen et al., 2014). Weekly sessions (1 hour) begin with parent skill training, followed by parent-coaching (through a one-way mirror with an earpiece microphone) while the parent plays with her/his child (Pincus et al., 2008). This continues until mastery of skills is achieved. Two treatment phases (a minimum of three sessions each) are Child-Directed Interaction (CDI)—used to improve parent–child relationship quality, social skills, and child self-esteem—and the Parent-Directed Interaction (PDI)—to teach parenting skills. During CDI, while interacting with their child, parents learn to apply specific skills—to decrease criticism, questions and commands; increase praise, reflection, imitation, behavioral description, and enthusiasm—and are coached to differentially reinforce child behaviors—to praise appropriate responses/behaviors, while ignoring undesirable ones. During PDI, the parent learns skills for managing and reducing problem behaviors through consistent and appropriate application of behavioral consequences—e. g., to use clear and age-appropriate commands before imposing consequences.

Numerous studies have demonstrated the effectiveness of PCIT for reducing child behavior problems (e.g., Foote, Eyberg, & Schuhmann, 1998) and for treating SAD (Choate, Pincus, Eyberg, & Barlow, 2005; Pincus et al., 2008). PCIT has proven successful with abusive parents, depressed mothers, foster parents, and for adopted children with behavior problems (N = 85 ages 2–7 with a history of maltreatment; Allen et al., 2014). In play situations, parents have shown improved interactions with offspring (e.g., increased praise, decreased criticism) and reduced distress as well as significant improvements in child compliance and reduced disruptive behaviors, at home and school (Boggs, Eyberg, & Reynolds, 1990). Parenting stress scores have significantly lowered, and the child's externalizing and internalizing problems have significantly reduced (Allen et al., 2014; large effects for parenting stress, Niec, Barnett, Prewett, & Shanley, 2016). Treatment gains have persisted—e.g., to assessments up to 6 years posttreatment for both children and parents (Hood & Eyberg, 2003). For both group and individual PCIT, parents have reported significant improvements at posttreatment and follow-up in children's conduct problems and adaptive skills (large effects; Niec et al., 2016). Parenting skills also improved—e.g., increased child-centered behaviors; reduced negative parenting. A challenge for the group format is to make certain that each parent receives sufficient coaching. Children with callous-unemotional (CU) traits—i.e., lack of empathy, guilt, and lack of caring behaviors—tend to glean less benefit from treatments than children with low CU traits (N = 63, ages 3–5; Kimonis et al., 2014).

Behavioral Inhibition (BI)

Early intervention is implicated when possible for most difficulties. Because of risks associated with BI (later social reticence, anxiety problems, possible externalizing), it is no exception (e.g., Rankin Williams et al., 2009). As noted (Chapters 6, 9), sensitive/supportive parenting, autonomy support, and encouraging socialization that does not overwhelm the child (e.g., easing them into it; teaching social coping skills) is important for children with BI. Overprotection, high control, intrusiveness, and lack of responsiveness in parents is contra-indicated. Programs that address parenting and teacher skills have assisted youth with BI. For example, the Turtle Program, designed to treat children high in BI, has been related to BI children's increased social initiations and reduced displays of fear/anxiety (parent & teacher report; e.g., 8 weeks of concurrent parent and child treatment, Barstead et al., in press; Chronis-Tuscano et al., 2015). In addition, INSIGHTS is a school-based program that assists parents and teachers to deal with children based on their temperaments (to follow).

Adapting Methods to Temperaments

Temperament has predicted outcomes such as socialization success, risk of psychopathology, and academic achievement (see Iverson & Gartstein, 2018). Parental and teacher ability to respond sensitively to a child while successfully adapting approaches based on the child' s temperament has served to promote positive adjustment. A number of studies have tested the efficacy of temperament-driven programs that included parent and/or teacher training, training plus treatment (e.g., PCIT), or other interventions. Providing temperament-related information alone has not proven to increase acceptance of children by adults (Iverson & Gartstein, 2018). However, caregiver-focused interventions or interventions including parents and teachers (some include children as well) have had positive effects. For example, PCIT (above) for difficult children combined with temperament training reduced the frequency (but not the number) of children's behavior problems (Pade et al., 2006). Some programs have demonstrated reductions in problem behaviors, overt aggression, attentional problems, and off-task disruptive behaviors as well as increases in classroom engagement and academic performance (see Iverson & Gartstein, 2018). To follow is a description of INSIGHTS, a social-emotional learning intervention program aimed also at assisting parents and teachers to deal with children based on their temperaments.

INSIGHTS into Children's Temperament

INSIGHTS includes teacher, parent, and classroom programs that work synergistically to support children's ability to self-regulate by enhancing their attentional and behavioral repertoire (McClowry, 2002, 2003; see O'Connor, Cappella, McCormick, & McClowry, 2014a). Better self-regulated behavior is expected to enhance academic skills. Early achievement influences later achievement and adjustment (Cappella et al., 2015). Although temperament generally remains consistent, adults can change their responses and consequently influence children's behavior (O'Connor et al., 2014a). Teachers and parents explore an ideal combination of warmth and effective discipline strategies. INSIGHTS aims to enhance goodness-of-fit between child and adult/ environment via increasing positive interactions between adults and a child and among children (see Chess & Thomas, 1977, 1991; e.g., align demands, expectations, and opportunities, Cappella et al. 2015). Through understanding a temperament, a caregiver/teacher can discern whether a situation is likely to overwhelm a child and should be avoided or reduced in magnitude (or otherwise modified, Box 8.2) (O'Connor et al., 2014a). If the child is likely to manage a situation with support, then a supportive teacher or parent uses strategies that gently stretch a child's relevant emotional, attentional, or behavioral repertoire.

In a study of school-age children (New Englanders, ages 4–12), four temperamental profiles were delineated via parental report (total N = 883; McClowry, 2002). Two challenging temperaments included *high maintenance* and *cautious/slow-to-warm-up*. Two easy temperaments included *industrious* and *social/eager-to-try*. The *industrious* child was task-persistent, low in negative reactivity, and low in activity (6% of the sample; McClowry, 2002). Such children can sit at length working on tasks (e.g., puzzle, homework, play) and take pleasure in accomplishments. S/he may be distressed if not allowed to finish a task to her/his satisfaction, and adults may feel s/he needs to be more assertive (McClowry, 2003). The *social/eager-to-try* profile was similar to the New York Longitudinal Study (NYLS) easy temperament (Chess & Thomas, 1977, 1991; excluding their adaptability and regularity classifications, see McClowry, 2002)—high in approach and low in negative reactivity (9%; McClowry, 2002). Such a child is driven by needs to be with people and to try new experiences, is usually pleasant, and has a zest for life that draws others to her/him (McClowry, 2003). Concerns may be about an eager-to-try child's judgment related to safety or potential for getting into trouble. The *high maintenance* profile (similar to NYLS *difficult* temperament) was characterized by high activity, high negative reactivity, and low task persistence (8%; McClowry, 2002). Such children react strongly negatively to stress or change, can be very moody, may have problems completing tasks, and may have difficulty sitting still (McClowry, 2003). The *cautious/slow-to-warm-up* temperament (the same as the NYLS *slow-to-warm*) was high in withdrawal and high in negative reactivity (8%; McClowry, 2002). Such children do not like change and withdraw from new situations and people. With time and the right support, this child may become more comfortable and can respond more pleasantly (McClowry, 2003). Parents and teachers learn to respond to each child's behaviors in ways that are acceptable or optimal, without labeling or judging. Counterproductive responses are discussed.

Some children qualified as both types of challenging or easy profiles (6% were both challenging types; 4% were both easy types; McClowry, 2002). Both challenging profiles are characterized by negative reactivity. Such children are often honest but may complain frequently (McClowry, 2003). Challenging profiles were disproportionately found in boys, in low SES children, and in Hispanic children (McClowry, 2002). Girls were over-represented in the easy temperaments. *Social/eager-to-try* children were more often from higher SES families (McClowry, 2002).

INSIGHTS includes 10 weekly, two-hour sessions in three parts. Part 1 is *Learning about Child Temperament* focusing on the 3-Rs of child management—recognize, reframe (perceptions), and respond (Cappella et al., 2015; McClowry, Snow, Tamis-LeMonda, & Rodriguez, 2010). Parents and teachers learn to recognize a child's consistent temperamental/behavioral style (across settings;

O'Connor et al., 2014a). They learn to appreciate that every temperament has strengths as well as issues of concern, and that a child may not be trying to misbehave but may be reacting according to temperament (McClowry et al., 2010; O'Connor et al., 2014a). They learn optimal, adequate, and counterproductive responses to child behaviors (McClowry et al., 2010). In Part 2, *Gaining Compliance*, behavioral management strategies that can be adapted to child temperament are introduced. Part 3, *Giving Control*, addresses additional strategies that support children to become more competent in situations that are temperamentally challenging. A child's more effective self-regulatory capacity can be expanded and become more automatic (O'Connor et al., 2014a). The child/classroom program, over the same 10-week period in 45-minute sessions is delivered in two parts (Cappella et al., 2015). In Part I, using education, videotapes, and puppets, children learn that, based on temperament, some situations are easy to handle and other situations are more difficult. In Part 2, children interact with puppets and peers to practice ways to approach and resolve daily dilemmas in the classroom and at home (Cappella et al., 2015).

INSIGHTS has enhanced academic development and improved child behaviors. Success has been even greater among children with diagnostic levels of ADHD, ODD, and CD (without use of medication; McClowry et al., 2010). Boys in the INSIGHTS program exhibited a significant decline in attentional difficulties and in overt aggression (N = 116; vs comparisons). INSIGHTS has positively affected teacher practices, experiences, and attitudes as well (e.g., emotional support, classroom organization; Cappella et al., 2015). For example, INSIGHTS teachers have reported fewer difficulties managing boys' emotional-oppositional behavior, attentional difficulties, and covert disruptive behaviors (McClowry et al., 2010). They also perceived the boys as more competent (cognitively and physically). Additionally, half of first grade showed improvements in math and reading achievement (partially mediated by reduced behavior problems; reading partially mediated by sustained attention improvements) as well as in sustained attention, faster than children enrolled in a supplemental reading program that served as a control group (N = 435 low-income, urban children [ages 4–7] and parents, 122 teachers; O'Connor et al., 2014a). In contrast to children enrolled in the supplemental reading program who exhibited increases in behavior problems, INSIGHTS children evidenced decreases in behavior problems over time. Compared to shy peers in a reading program, shy children in INSIGHTS have shown more rapid growth in critical thinking and math during kindergarten and transition to first grade, in part mediated by improved behavioral engagement (O'Connor et al., 2014b).

Developmental Trauma (DT)

Developmental Trauma Disorder is a name that has been used to describe and assess children's complex traumatic reactions. Children with DT may or may not meet DSM criteria for PTSD and often have additional diagnoses (Kisiel, Fehrenbach, Small, & Lyons, 2009). DT has been associated with exposure to multiple types of trauma (poly-victimization or cumulative trauma) especially in the formative periods (e.g., early childhood, adolescence; Ford, 2018; Chapter 2). It has been linked to chronic or repeated, typically early-onset exposure to two or more interpersonal traumas—e.g., sexual, physical, or emotional abuse; domestic violence; neglect; chronic school or community violence—as well as to severe caregiver impairment (Kisiel et al., 2009; Spinazzola et al., 2013). Many of the methods described above address problems related to early and multiple traumas—e.g., attachment, self-regulation, and other developmental skill competency. A few methods have been developed specifically for DT in this and older age groups. Music, play, and art therapy have been used with complexly traumatized children as well (e.g., Barfield et al., 2011).

Attachment, Self-Regulation, and Competency (ARC)

ARC (Blaustein & Kinniburgh, 2007, 2010; Kinniburgh & Blaustein, 2005) is an evidence-informed method used to treat complex trauma in children and adolescents. ARC can be used for individual treatment or integrated into whole systems interventions—e.g., shelter, foster care, juvenile justice, or treatment facility staff training and milieu structure (adapted for age and other considerations). It recognizes the need for flexibility and to adapt methods for particular symptoms, patients, and/or populations (Blaustein & Kinniburgh, 2010). Key targets of intervention are identified for traumatized youth. As the name suggests, core interventions include attachment, self-regulation, and competency (Blaustein & Kinniburgh, 2010), three domains affected by exposure to chronic, interpersonal trauma (Arvidson et al., 2011). Goals include nine building blocks within the three key domains (Blaustein & Kinniburgh, 2010)—(1) *Attachment*: a. caregiver management of affect—e.g., assists the ability to provide support in the face of stressors and to effectively manage and regulate the personal emotional experience; provides psychoeducation about trauma, self-monitoring and -management skills; enhances support; b. caregiver attunement—learning to read the emotion behind the behavior; recognizing trauma triggers; reflective listening skills; c. caregiver consistency—e.g., experimenting in use of limit-setting, positive reinforcement, and praise with a traumatized child; providing a predictable environment; d. routines and rituals—predictability—routines/rituals that increase a sense of safety, assist transitions, and aid ability for a child to relax at home and in therapy; (2) *Self-regulation*: a. child's affect identification, building a feelings vocabulary; psychoeducation about human alarm response and trauma triggers; learning to identify emotions in self and others; connecting emotions to body sensations, thoughts, and behaviors; understanding the link between emotions and internal/external factors; b. modulation—learning to maintain optimal arousal levels and expand comfort zone; c. affect expression (essential to relationships)—learning to share emotional experience safely, appropriately timed, and attending to nonverbal issues like space and boundaries; developing verbal communication skills and self-expression strategies; (3) *Competency*: a. executive functions—problem-solving, planning, anticipation, and decision-making skills; learning awareness of choice and acting vs reacting; b. self-development and identity—development of a unique and positive sense of self; building internal resources, creating a narrative, building ability to imagine. These methods are followed by integration of the trauma experience (Blaustein & Kinniburgh, 2010).

ARC has been used with young children of diverse ethno-cultural backgrounds (e.g., maltreated children, Child Protective Services; Arvidson et al., 2011). With this age group, it is important that the method be grounded in the caregiving system. Clinicians have included play, sand-tray, and other creative methods (Blaustein & Kinniburgh, 2010). Different games and activities are used to increase positive affect or to reduce emotions (Arvidson et al., 2011). Because young children learn from and rely on adults for self-regulation and soothing, caregiver skills (e.g., self-management) are particularly important with this age group. If the parent is perpetrator of the trauma, repair must be made within the attachment system (Arvidson et al., 2011). Learning to read a child's reactions and behaviors may be more complicated when the child has reduced verbal skills.

As discussed, experiences may be linked to terror and the physiological experience rather than to a specific event. Young children's trauma processing often occurs during a child's heightened, in-the-moment physiological reactions. Identifying, validating, and modulation by a caregiver helps to restore an internal sense of safety. Over time, this practice helps to build the child's capacity for effective self-regulation and creates a sense of mastery over a physiological experience that was previously linked to loss of control and extreme distress (Arvidson et al., 2011). With foster parents or school/institutional personnel, it is essential to provide cultural education as well—a child's customary responses to parenting communications. Addressing identity formation may include awareness of sociocultural characteristics. For young children, development of a positive self is assisted when a caregiver identifies and reflects attributes of the child while indicating that the child is effective and capable. Although routines and rituals at bedtime and other transition periods are important for all age groups, they differ developmentally and must include consideration of the child's traumatic experience—e.g., bathing a child earlier because of trauma perpetrated in a bathroom; recognizing the increased need to reduce arousal and hypervigilance. For example, in addition to bedtime stories, for a very young child (or a regressed latency aged child), the caregiver might look under the bed and in closets to be certain no danger is lurking and may provide reassurance and a teddy bear or other toy to sleep with. The child may feel better either with snug sheets or loosely tucked-in. To teach modulation principles, a clinician might have the child pretend to be a slow-moving animal (e.g., elephant) and a fast-moving animal (e.g., bunny) and each time to connect the experience with body sensations. Culturally rooted experiences may be used—e.g., being as still as a hunter; quiet and careful as a fisherman. It may take time for the young child to internalize being soothed and comforted. Arvidson and colleagues had positive results working with preschool children of different cultures in the CPS system (N = 93, 3–12-year-olds). Treatment completers had a higher success rate for permanent home placement.

Divorce

As noted (Chapter 9), divorce has been related to a number of adverse consequences—internalizing (e.g., anxiety, depression), externalizing, lower adjustment, psychological distress, academic problems, and lower well-being (Fuller-Thomson & Dalton, 2011; Klein Velderman et al., 2018). In adulthood, there are lower levels of marriage, higher divorce rates, lower academic achievement, lower incomes, negative health outcomes, elevated anxiety levels, mood disorders, and more substance use (e.g., smoking, alcohol; see Fuller-Thomson & Dalton, 2011). Especially when there are other adversities (e.g., parental unemployment, addiction, abusive behaviors), adults who experienced divorce of their parents in childhood are at increased risk of suicidal ideation and attempts (Fuller-Thomson & Dalton, 2011). After controlling for known suicide ideation risk factors—e.g., childhood stressors, SES, adult health behaviors and stressors, marital status, and prior mood and/or anxiety disorders—Fuller-Thomson and Dalton found that, for men, the divorce–suicidal ideation relationship remained statistically significant, whereas for women, the association between parental divorce in childhood and suicidal ideation was reduced to non-significance when other childhood adversity was controlled (N = 6744 Canadian adults). Treatments aimed at assisting children and families after divorce have reduced divorce-related problems (Klein Velderman et al., 2018).

Children of Divorce Intervention Program (CDIP)

CDIP focuses on post-divorce family factors—parental conflict, parental psychological well-being, parenting quality, social support, and family stability—and focuses on child factors—e.g., effective coping skills, emotion regulation, age-appropriate understanding of family changes, a realistic sense of control—in order to reduce divorce-related problems in children as well as to instill a positive outlook and hope for the future (Pedro-Carroll, 2005). CDIP includes modules for different age groups—K-1st grade; 2nd–3rd grade; older latency age; early adolescents. Programs for older youth have been offered in schools. CDIP has been used with 4–8-year-olds in Europe. For children ages 4–8 (N = 43 Dutch children), divorce-related problems were reduced—i.e., children showed higher adjustment and lower problem behaviors (mother, teacher, group leader reports; Klein Velderman et al., 2018).

Executive Functions (EF)

As described (Chapter 7), some training methods have assisted EF in young children. For example, children with ADHD, ages 3–7, have shown improvement in EFs (i.e., visual and auditory attention, working memory, and cognitive flexibility) after an executive training method was used (Tamm & Nakonezny, 2015). Parents are trained to be interventionists and coached to apply the strategies to alternative domains of functioning (see Chapter 7). Children improved in attention shifting, inhibition, emotion-regulation, memory, and planning (parent report) and in attention, hyperactivity/impulsivity, and overall (clinician report, N = 26, ages 3–7). Additionally, the Attention Training Technique (ATT, Wells, 1990), which involves playing an ATT recording on any three separate occasions during a four-day intervention period, has significantly increased delay of gratification (DoG)—2.64 times higher in intervention children over non-intervention. Verbal inhibition moderated ATTs effects on DoG—i.e., 3.43 times better DoG (after controlling for age, time in school, and verbal inhibition)—and improved mood (ages 5–6; Murray, Theakston, & Wells, 2015). The recording consists of approximately 11 minutes of sounds (e.g., bird song, traffic, clock ticking) and a voice, which instructs participants to direct attention in different ways, e.g., from one sound to another.

Although mindfulness parent interventions are presented in a later section, mindfulness methods have assisted young children as well—e.g., EFs, self-regulation, attention, perspective-taking (Flook, Goldberg, Pinger, & Davidson, 2015; Thierry et al., 2018; Zelazo & Lyons, 2011; see MindUp, Chapter 13, Settle Your Glitter, to follow). Even a single session of mindfulness training for preschoolers, who are still developing an ability to disengage habitual reactions and control impulses, has helped them to control attention and relinquish default responses, thereby assisting self-control (Lim & Qu, 2016; see also O'Toole, Furlong, McGilloway, & Bjorndal, 2017, Razza, Bergen-Cico, & Raymond, 2013).

Kindness Curriculum (KC)

The Kindness Curriculum is available from the Center for Healthy Minds at the University of Wisconsin-Madison (https://centerhealthyminds.org/join-the-movement/sign-up-to-receive-the-kindness-curriculum). The original Kindness Curriculum was an eight-week program with three sessions per week, developed for four-year-olds (Center for Investigating Health Minds, 2013; Poehlmann-Tynan et al., 2016). Teachers attended a modified Mindfulness-Based Stress Reduction training program in order to promote the goals of the curriculum in the classroom. Trained instructors, who had engaged in daily use of the methods for 5–10 years, present the method. Mindfulness-themed books, posters, and art projects are used during intervention sessions and in classrooms throughout the year to facilitate generalization of mindfulness. Methods include breath practices (belly breathing), music (also, an inviting/opening ringing of a bell), and reading (on kindness and caring), and they focus on kindness, exploration of emotions and body sensations, identifying body-emotions in others, gratitude, and caring for others. An adapted version of the curriculum includes 20–30-minute sessions twice a week for 12 weeks and has been used to assess the effectiveness of KC (Flook et al., 2015; Poehlmann-Tynan et al., 2016). Mindfulness-based KC has succeeded in increasing a number of skills, which may set children on a positive trajectory: EF skills—e.g., cognitive flexibility, delay of gratification; social competence and prosocial behaviors, especially for children with low baseline skills; school performance; and less selfishness than controls (N = 68 ages 4–5; 12-week program; Flook et al., 2015). KC program has been related to increased self-regulation and attentional control in economically disadvantaged preschoolers (N = 29, ages 3–5 low-income children in a dialogic reading program; Poehlmann-Tynan et al., 2016).

MindUp

MindUp, a mindfulness program described in Chapter 13, has shown improvements for this age group in executive functions as well as in other outcomes—e.g., more prosocial behavior, improved self-regulation, better social competence, and better grades (see Thierry et al., 2018). MindUP also has modules for grades K-2 and for older children (see Chapter 13).

Settle Your Glitter (SYG)

SYG (by M. Kinder and H. Bryant) is a method that was developed specifically for pre-K students, in consultation with both education and mental health experts, with a trauma-informed lens (for pre-K to second grade, personal communication, Heather Bryant, Momentous Institute, 9-14-18; momentousinstitute.org). It is not to be confused with the formerly available app, "Settle your Glitter," which employed graphics to help children name their feelings and assess the intensity of feelings, and, using a glitter ball and a puffer fish image, taught mindfulness breathing for calming emotions. The SYG curriculum includes some lessons from other mindfulness curricula (e.g., teaching students about their brains). Lessons follow a social-emotional health model covering safe relationships, self-regulation (brain, belly breathing, feelings, the brain-body connection, impulse control), awareness of self (gratitude, optimism, grit, resilience), understanding of others (perspective-taking, empathy), and changemaker (kindness, compassion, hope; see momentousinstitute.org/social-emotional-health). For example, a glitter ball is used to show children how the ball gets cloudy when it is shaken—like it can feel in their brains when they are scared or upset (dysregulated; see Thierry et al., 2018).

Thierry et al. (2018) taught the SYG curriculum to pre-K teachers from four schools within an urban school district, while pre-K teachers from an additional four schools continued their usual practices. Teachers were given six professional training courses prior to implementation. They were taught about how adversity, trauma, and stress could negatively impact young children's development. For students, each teaching unit contained two to four lessons for a total of 18, with activities to enhance self-awareness and self-regulation. SYG had a positive effect on executive functions (EFs)—e.g., holding rules in working memory, inhibiting distractors, and flexibly focusing attention. Deep breathing was one of the self-regulation practices used across the school year and was taught the children three times per day, or more if needed. SYG children had quicker, accurate responses to an EF task (Heart & Flowers). At the end of the school year, using a more difficult task (Flanker), SYG children increased accuracy and maintained their speed, whereas comparison school children were slower than their original performance in order to achieve accuracy. Response accuracy was related to prosocial behavior and academic skills (N = 296, four-year-olds, Thierry et al., 2018).

Self-Regulation

Children's levels of self-control, especially at the lowest and highest levels, have predicted their adult outcomes approximately as well as low intelligence and low social class (Moffitt et al., 2011). For example, low levels have been associated with multiple health problems, substance dependence, low income, single-parent households, and crime conviction rates. For children followed from birth to age 32, children's self-control between ages three and five years significantly predicted their health, wealth, and conviction status at age 32 (N = 1000; Moffitt et al., 2011). Given that early childhood self-regulation has predicted adolescent problem behaviors, early interventions are indicated (Moffitt et al., 2011). Some of the methods already described address self-regulation. The importance of parenting in the attenuation of poor self-regulation was discussed in Chapter 9. To follow is a parent-training treatment method that uses play and specific limit-setting training to assist children with behavior problems.

Helping the Noncompliant Child

As a treatment for oppositional behavior, the Helping the Noncompliant Child parent training program enlists one or both parents and a child to treat young children's noncompliance (for ages 3–8, McMahon & Forehand, 2003). Treatment focuses on a single family (may include extended family; has been adapted for group use) and ideally includes two weekly sessions (75–90 minutes). The room includes a chair for each person (child, parent, therapist) and a time-out chair. Toys—e.g., legos, blocks, colors and paper, furnished dollhouse, vehicles, people, and animals; no board games, weapons, or messy toys—are conducive to imaginative, joint play and are placed farthest away from the exit door. If possible, a one-way mirror and bug-in-ear method is used with the therapist advising from behind the mirror. Helping the Noncompliant Child teaches five core skills in two phases. In phase 1 (differential attention), a parent learns to *give attends*—attending to and describing the child's appropriate behavior; verbally following, not directing, a child's activity; without asking questions, giving commands, or teaching; *give rewards*—positive physical attention—such as hugs, nonspecific or specific verbal praise, labeling the desirable behavior; and use *active ignoring*—i.e., avoid eye contact and nonverbal cues, avoid verbal contact, avoid physical contact, and no criticism, questions, or commands. Phase 1 homework (also encouraged in phase 2) includes 10–15 minute Child's Game sessions at home (Chapter 7), in which the child chooses an activity, parent follows the child (watches intently and follows), attends (describes enthusiastically what child is doing), and participates and imitates (takes a turn or imitates child, while attending), without structuring the play, questioning, or giving commands. Homework also includes, e.g., identifying "not OK" behaviors (e.g., whining) to decrease them and identifying incompatible "OK" behaviors (incompatible with "not OK" behaviors; e.g., talking in a regular voice) to increase them (R. McMahon, personal communication, 9-6-18). In phase 2 (compliance training), the parent learns to issue clear instructions—i.e., reduces unclear instructions such as chain, vague, or questioning instructions and employs clear instructions. That is, the parent gains the child's attention, states an instruction clearly, and waits 5 seconds. Parents learn to employ consequences—i.e., for compliance to a clear instruction, the parent uses positive attention and for noncompliance, s/he uses warning, followed by rewards for compliance or time-out for noncompliance. Phase 2 has a number of additional homework assignments and exercises related to clear and unclear instructions and standing rules, described more thoroughly in Chapter 7 of the McMahon and Forehand manual (R. McMahon, personal communication, 9-6-18).

Mindfulness Parenting Interventions

Parenting influences child outcomes in a number of ways—e.g., highly active five-year-olds whose parents responded with impatience, hostility, and frequent power struggles were aggressive, manipulative, and noncompliant at age seven (teacher report, Buss, Block, & Block, 1980; Caspi, 1998). Evidence suggests that when parents are coping well and when they have high self-efficacy, are happy, and are caring and affectionate, it positively impacts child well-being, adjustment, behavior and socioemotional functioning (see Waters, 2016). In contrast, when parents are highly stressed, they may become more controlling, more rejecting, colder, and more reactive toward children, with negative effects on children (Corthorn & Milicic, 2015; Waters, 2016; Box 10.2). Many of the methods described in this chapter provide parent-coaching/training.

Mindfulness—the ability to direct attention *mindfully* (e.g., remaining nonjudgmentally in-the-moment)—can be developed through Eastern meditation practices—e.g., involving self-regulation of attention (Baer, 2003; 2500-year-old Buddhist practice, O'Toole et al., 2017; Waters, 2016). It includes attending more fully to the aspects of one's experience (Zelazo & Lyons, 2011). Mindfulness parenting—e.g., mindful listening, emotional awareness, compassion and nonjudgmental acceptance; moment-to-moment awareness in interactions; warm and nurturing affective tenor

Box 10.2 Boy, Age 3–4—Attachment, Temperament, and Escalating Behaviors

Boy-3's mother left him in the day care at the university once a week while she attended a lecture. Boy-3 cried loudly, protested being left, and clung to his mother and didn't want to let go. Often his mother would stay for up to 15 minutes—she would try to talk him into staying, would threaten loss of something if he didn't go in and stop crying, and/or would peek in from the door (mostly hidden) to see if he had stopped crying. Teachers repeatedly told her just to go; she was late for the lecture. Eventually she would just leave. When his father dropped him off while holding a snuggling young daughter, he exasperatedly told Boy-3, "This has to stop!" If Boy-3 was afraid of not being wanted, his father's look might have seemed to confirm it. His parents appeared to be caring but overwhelmed. Over time, they both became exasperated with him and his reluctance to enter. Boy-3's behavior with other children was negative and rejecting.

Boy-3's weekly pattern of behavior in the three-year-old day care room: After entry, Boy-3 moved to a corner or a table away from everyone else (away from teachers and children) and continued to cry or scowl. Often a teacher would try to cajole him into participating with the group. Boy-3 resisted, but eventually participated in activities; however, he sat away from other children (at a separate table, otherwise unoccupied) and only allowed the one, originally cajoling teacher to assist him (refusing other help, saying, "I only want her/him to help me"), when he needed help with a project. Projects usually required some adult assistance. At some point in the hour, he seemed to attach himself to the teacher who had been most kind or cajoling with him that day (often the one who had gone to the door to greet him upon arrival). For example, he would sit on the cajoling teacher's lap or next to her/him. His behavior became predictable. Observer tested this by being the first to the door one day and becoming the attachment figure for the day. If another child sat on the first-supportive teacher's lap, Boy-3 sat next to the teacher but kept looking over at the child on the teacher's lap with a somewhat puzzled look on his face. With teachers, his attachment behavior could be described as overactivated compared to other children during the hour. He always seemed less interested in the other children than in a selected adult. When a parent returned for him, he calmly left the room, projects in hand. He did not attend during the summer.

Weekly behavior in the four-year-old room: In the fall after moving to the fourth-grade group, Boy-now4 no longer clung to parents at the door. He would play in the area where other children were playing, joining in if they were running around and making noise or playing with blocks side by side but not allowing anyone to join him (knocked the blocks down to the distress of another child when the child asked to join him). The *four*-year-old-room teachers did not cajole him. He still seemed to attach to one (first hello) and sat next to the teacher when activities resulted in everyone's sitting. At some point, he would hide behind something (e.g., the DVD player) and wait—a modified version of his three-year-old pattern of waiting for cajoling. At first, the other children would come over and tell him it was dangerous for him to be there, and they tried to cajole him away. By the second week, the children and the teachers ignored this behavior but were pleasant to him. The teachers described him as a problem child to each other when the children were not nearby. He would try hiding, but after a couple of weeks no one came. Even when a teacher was reasonably attentive, while also attending to story time or other room activities, he escalated his attention-eliciting behaviors—he began to behave in sexually inappropriate ways. For example, he kept putting his hand down a teacher's blouse. After he had put his hand down the teacher's blouse, he laughed and said, "Ha ha, I touched your private parts." This behavior continued while the teacher tried to push his hands away, until the nearby Observer firmly told him, "Stop it! That's not nice." He then sat next to Observer, and behaved for the rest of the class. He occasionally asked her questions (e.g., "Is that ring a wedding ring?").

Although the nature of the behavior had changed somewhat, he seemed to have maintained a pattern of needing an adult to cling to, engaging in behavior apparently intended to elicit cajoling or total focus, essentially separating himself from everyone except one adult. He seemed to use sexualized behavior to elicit attention and possibly with a subtle component of anger.

The next week, he was touching the lead teacher's derriere and laughing, although the teacher did not seem to notice. He seemed to be playing a hiding game with no one paying attention. He crawled around and hid (still visible) behind a table for a while, then gave up. He then sat beside another teacher. After a minute, he kept trying to stick his tongue on her derriere. She held his head away and attended to the storytelling, then firmly told him to sit. He did. And behaved for the rest of class sitting next to that teacher. The third week, the pattern was the same. This time, when he arrived, he said he wanted to go back to the three-year-old class (where teachers were more attentive), but his mother refused. Observer asked him if he would like to walk through the three-year-old class to go into the four-year-old class (adjoining rooms). He said yes and had walked through before it was possible to catch up to him. Observer was walking out when his mother came for him that day. She asked Observer if he (her son) was a ____. Observer asked, "A ____?" She said, "Yes, you know, a ____. He's a pain in the butt." He was there when she said it. He walked away. The family was referred for attachment therapy with a therapist who understands parenting children with negative emotionality and with behavioral inhibition.

Note:
All case examples are disguised, may be combined cases, and have had details changed to protect individuals.

(Waters, 2016)—has proven beneficial under normal circumstances and, in particular, when children are stressed (Corthorn & Milicic, 2015; Waters, 2016). Parents higher in mindfulness have exhibited higher mindful parenting (N = 62 mothers of 2–5-year-olds; Corthorn & Milicic, 2015). Mindfulness has correlated negatively with mental health problems—e.g., depression but sometimes not anxiety—and with parental and general stress.

In preschool, when children naturally become somewhat oppositional, mindfulness is particularly relevant in preparing them for school entry (Corthorn & Milicic, 2015). Mindful parenting has helped to reduce children's behavior and other problems—e.g., reduced attention deficits, hyper-reactivity, externalizing, aggression, and rumination (Corthorn & Milicic, 2015; Van der Oord, Bogels, & Peijnenburg, 2012; Waters, 2016; Chapters 13, 16). It is positively related to children's prosocial behaviors, to quality of life, and to improved parent–child interactions as well as to reduced parental stress (Coatsworth, Duncan, Greenberg, & Nix, 2010; Corthorn & Milicic, 2015; Singh, Lancioni, Winton, & Singh, 2007; Waters, 2016).

Mindfulness is linked to changes in the brain—e.g., in areas involved in self-regulation of attention and emotions, memory, meta-awareness (Glossary), inter-hemispheric communication (Barnhofer et al., 2016; O'Toole et al., 2017). It enhances the ability to stand back from thought processes, permitting observation of thoughts and feelings as mental events that come and go, rather than as aspects of self or as truths that dictate behavior (Baer, 2003; O'Toole et al., 2017).

Mindfulness Stress Reduction

Mindfulness techniques are taught for the reduction of stress as well as for the enhancement of parenting (Baer, 2003; Duncan & Bardacke, 2010). For example, this stress reduction and relaxation program (Kabat-Zinn, 1990; see Baer, 2003) is an 8–10-week course for groups of 30, meeting weekly for 2–2.5 hours. Around the 6th week, participants attend an all-day intensive meditation session (7–8 hr.). Methods include, for example, mindfulness meditation—focus on the breath, an object, or ideal; notice but do not become absorbed in thoughts, return to the moment; a 45-min. body scan (like deep relaxation); Hatha yoga practices; and mindfulness during ordinary activities (e.g., standing, eating, walking) (Baer, 2003; Flook et al., 2015). Homework is 45 minutes daily practice of skills. For some, a teacher/trainer or virtual coach has proven more successful for establishing regular practice than self-training (written and audio materials; Hudlicka, 2013, 2017). Yoga-based treatments may provide methods similar to mindfulness training (Chapters 13 and 16).

Mindfulness has improved self-observation, increased nonjudgmental observation of problems or problematic thoughts (reducing the need to avoid), improved RF (e.g., insight), enhanced EF (e.g., shifting/cognitive flexibility; attention), and improved emotion regulation. It has cultivated kindness and self-compassion and has reduced stress, chronic pain, psychological symptoms (e.g., anxiety and depressive disorders; binge eating), and relapse (e.g., depression, substance abuse; see Baer, 2003; Corthorn & Milicic, 2015; Flook et al., 2015). While mindfulness practices may induce relaxation, their purpose is to employ nonjudgmental observation of current states including, e.g., autonomic arousal, racing thoughts, muscle tension, other states incompatible with relaxation (Baer, 2003).

Mindfulness CBT

While CBT may train one to evaluate thoughts as rational or distorted, and teach systematic methods to change thoughts judged irrational, mindfulness teaches them to observe thoughts, notice their impermanence, and refrain from evaluating. Nevertheless, mindfulness methods have become a part of methods like CBT (eight-week, manualized treatment, for depression, Teasdale, Segal, & Williams, 1995; O'Toole et al., 2017; Williams, Russell, & Russell, 2008) and Dialectical Behavior Therapy (Baer, 2003; Chapman, 2006; for BPD, Feliu-Soler et al., 2013; one-yr. group, for BPD, Linehan, 1993a, 1993b). Such treatments have been used, for example, for eating disorders, trauma, and substance abuse (Baer, 2003). CBT for depression includes ideas such as *thoughts are not facts* and *I am not my thoughts* (Baer, 2003, p. 127). CBT for relapse prevention of substance use has employed metaphors such as *urge surfing*, which encourages individuals to imagine that urges are ocean waves that gradually grow until they crest and subside. Some clinical patients have difficulty with the full length or set of mindfulness techniques. Timing of employing mindfulness may depend on the stage and nature of difficulties or stressors—e.g., levels of traumatization or traumatic arousal.

Separation or Other Anxiety

Some evidence suggests that 0.3 to 6.5% of young children experience impairing anxiety disorders (Carpenter et al., 2016; Chapter 7). As noted, untreated moderate to severe anxiety disorders often persist or recur and predate other disorders (e.g., mood and anxiety disorders; Carpenter et al., 2016), resulting in severe dysfunction (Shal, White, Klein, & von Klitzing, 2014; Otawa et al., 2014; Paksarian et al., 2015). Anxiety disorders have genetic (Arias et al., 2012), familial (Costello et al., 2003), and environmental (e.g., trauma exposure; Nader, 2008) links. For example, perfectionistic parents may use language that communicates to children that mistakes are distressing, a threat, and lead to disapproval—e.g., increased use of "You," decreased adverbs, increased negative emotion and anger words—thereby increasing a child's anxiety (N = 71; Affrunti, Geronimi, & Woodruff-Borden, 2015).

Child anxiety can follow feeling excluded. Exclusion or a disposition with a high need for inclusion have been linked to anthropomorphizing of ambiguous or inanimate agents, augmenting the perception of social connection (Epley, Akalis, Waytz, & Cacioppo, 2008; Powers, et al., 2014).

Although exclusion-prompted children may anthropomorphize story-characters more strongly in an attempt to cope with exclusion—e.g., seeking solace in imaginary relationships, White et al. (2016) point out that this tendency instead may reflect adjustment of information processing and may assist mentalizing (though not when anxious). A number of treatment methods have been used for separation, social, or other anxiety, including some of the methods described above and below (see also Appendix). CBT (e.g., PPT, above; Scheeringa, 2016; mindfulness) and psychodynamic methods (Göttken & von Klitzing, 2014; Halfon et al., 2016) have been used to treat anxiety in children.

Adapted PCIT

Pincus and colleagues (2008) have added a component to PCIT (above) for use with separation anxiety (SA). They added an anxiety-specific treatment phase, *Bravery Directed Interaction* (BDI), to address specific anxiety issues reported by parents and to help children enter formerly avoided situations (Pincus, Eyberg, & Choate, 2005). It utilizes psychoeducation about anxiety for parents and graduated exposure to feared separation situations for children (Pincus et al., 2008). Therapist–parent–child create a fear hierarchy (Chapter 13) and a reward list for after the child completes the exposure exercise. Some evidence suggests that anxious children are given less psychological autonomy. Toward increasing autonomy, the child selects one exposure issue from the "Bravery Ladder" each week. Clinicians observe parental behaviors and reactions in order to discover those that reinforce the child's SA. Parents are taught to conduct exposure sessions outside of the therapy room. Preliminary findings suggest that, compared to waiting list children, children treated with PCIT+BDI have shown improvement in SAD symptoms and reductions of SAD to nonclinical levels. Parents have also reported siblings' improved behavior, treatment child's better academic performance, and parent distress reduction along with the acquisition of new parenting skills—e.g., increased warmth-building, anxiety and behavior management skills.

Short-Term Psychoanalytic Child Therapy (Short-Term PaCT)

Manualized short-term PaCT (Göttken & von Klitzing, 2014; Göttken et al., 2014) is a 20–25-session method used with anxious children ages 4–10. During sessions, therapist, parents, and child work to identify and modify central conflict themes underlying symptoms through interpersonal relationship and internal representations. The child is assisted during free-play. Parent sessions are held every 4th session and examine possible underlying meanings of a child's symptoms. The therapist examines transference and countertransference issues in the parent–child–therapist triad. Treatment aims to support the caregiver–child relationship and to reduce rigidly held, maladaptive defense mechanisms that contribute to internalizing symptoms and interfere with healthy development (Göttken et al., 2014).

Children with anxiety disorder diagnoses and a high degree of comorbid depression and externalizing were assessed with standardized measures, puppet interviews, and teacher report pre- and post-PaCT treatment (18 initially, while 11 wait-listed; Göttken et al., 2014). Treatment children had significantly greater symptom and diagnosis reduction compared to wait-list children on all measures and across informants (parent, teacher, child, interviewer; moderate to strong effects). Diagnosis remission after PaCT was high (66.7% of children) and comparable to CBT rates. Improvement was also shown in externalizing and internalizing (e.g., depression) symptoms. Halfon and colleagues (2016) used a longer-term psychodynamic method (average 55 sessions) to treat three 6-year-olds. Children's play was assessed using the Children's Play Therapy Instrument (Kernberg, Chazan, & Normandin 1998)—*adaptive*, *inhibited*, *impulsive*, or *disorganized* play profiles. Children's *play engagement*, *play themes*, and *relational themes* were also assessed (Halfon et al., 2016). Children improved in abilities to move between different states and to work on different aspects of internal experience in play. Less adaptive strategies and play interruptions decreased.

Conclusions

As is true with younger children, parents are important to preschoolers' recovery from trauma and related symptoms. Methods often use a few or many conjoint parent–child sessions and employ parent-training, parent-coaching, or feedback/reflection. Although many of the treatment methods in this chapter address traumatization or specific other symptoms, they may assist multiple symptoms and developmental skills. As discussed in earlier chapters, developmental skills build on each other. For example, emotional awareness and theory of mind skills are important to perspective-taking, which is important to empathy and social skills. Self-regulation (e.g., effortful control) is also important to social skills and to goal-directed behaviors. Assisting self-regulation—e.g., through improving attachment relationships and parent training—often assists other skills and prevents long-term negative outcomes. Treatments are available to assist repair or catch-up in many developmental skills. Trauma-focused and other treatments have assisted developmental repair, reduced symptoms, and improved parenting skills, which in turn assist development and healing. Creative methods such as play, drawings, and/or music as well as mindfulness methods are often employed for both PTS and DT symptoms, and/or for the repair of the neurobiological effects of trauma in this age group.

Part IV
Ages 6–12

11

Development in Children Ages 6–12

In middle childhood, school introduces another dimension to children's lives. In early life, parents are young children's primary social figures—i.e., their attachment figures, playmates, and teachers (Kerns & Brumariu, 2018). Although children ages 6–12 are still influenced by ongoing caregiver-attachment relationships (Moss, Pascuzzo, & Simard, 2012), their social worlds expand to include increasing influence from peers and other adults (e.g., teachers). Peer relationships grow increasingly important during transition into adolescence (Rabinowitz et al., 2016). With increases in peer importance, traits such as inflexibility, inattention, and fearfulness, and conditions that reduce peer approval (e.g., status, economics) may contribute to a sense of isolation and/or to vulnerability to bullying. It may be easier to observe behaviors that correspond to problems or lead to rejection than to know the meaning of the behaviors to an individual child (Box 11.1).

Although children of this age can report their own symptoms and reactions, using other sources and observation has assisted assessment and treatment. Between ages five and seven, a striking increase occurs in motor control, perceptual abilities, memory, complex reasoning skills, self-regulation, mentalizing, and moral reasoning (see Del Giudice, 2015). Major developmental tasks during this phase of life include learning whom to trust—at this age, based on recent encounters

Box 11.1 Misinterpreted Behaviors

A six-year-old boy was described by teachers as having a behavioral problem. At first, one teacher described his behavior as attention getting. When observed in his first-grade group, he would periodically make a strange loud noise and be asked to stop or was taken aside for a "talking to." Although some peers were kind to him in the first grade, others kept their distance. After a second observation period, it appeared that he made the sound when he didn't know answers or felt unsure of his ability to remember a song or something else being taught. Rather than aggressive or intentionally disruptive behavior, it appeared to be an attempt to distract from his learning difficulties.

Note:
All case examples are disguised, may be combined cases, and have had details changed to protect individuals.

(van den Bos, van Dijk, & Crone, 2012); moral reasoning (improves with age); and increases in perspective-taking, awareness of self and body image, emotion and behavioral regulation, social skills, and logical thinking—e.g., considering several parts of a problem. They must also learn to deal with competition and with failures (Del Giudice, 2014).

Gender

Gender differences become more apparent in middle childhood. Around ages 6–8, adrenal androgens activate sexually differentiated brain pathways, organizing the brain on different trajectories (Del Giudice, 2015). Across cultures, boys appear to enjoy physical fighting with each other, find their enemies captivating, and find competition entertaining (Benenson, 2014). Hence the qualities that later appear in war, politics, and intergroup competition emerge here, and may be preparation for survival in times of war/conflict. Although gender behaviors are influenced by parenting, socialization, and media, Benenson observed that boys are much louder and less private than girls; girls practice caring for vulnerable individuals—e.g., depicting (in play) and talking about others such as discussing their weaknesses or providing support. Benenson suggests this too is a survival mechanism; later, it makes girls better able to assess whom they can depend on for assistance (e.g., with childcare, safety).

Attachment may influence competitive strategies for the genders in this age period. Del Giudice (2015) has suggested that anxious/ambivalent styles may bias children to the possibility that social partners will betray or exclude them, prompting a range of countermeasures—e.g., exaggerated displays of distress, increased efforts for emotional and physical closeness, and anticipatory relational aggression. Avoidant styles, in contrast, may reduce reliance on the likely undependable partners and project strength and independence (see Attachment-Related Interpersonal Style in Middle Childhood, to follow).

Risk Factors

A few important risk factors influencing this age group are discussed here—attachment, personality/traits, and peer victimization. Poly-victimization is discussed in Chapter 12.

Caregiver–Child Attachment

As noted, in middle childhood, a child's social world expands from parents to include other adults and peers (Kerns & Brumariu, 2018). Children become more self-reliant. Nevertheless, parent–child relationships remain important to children and influence different aspects of socioemotional development (see Boldt, Kochanska, Yoon, & Nordling, 2014; Bretherton, 2010). Studies have found that preadolescent children rarely identify peers as attachment figures. Parents remain primary attachment figures (Kerns & Brumariu, 2018). In middle childhood, thirrd to sixth graders seek parental proximity in attachment-related situations and seek peers in companionship or affiliative situations (Kobak, Rosenthal, Zajac, & Madsen, 2011). With increased autonomy, self-regulation, and periods of separation (e.g., for school; sports; social activities), the goal of attachment changes from caregiver-proximity to caregiver availability (Mayseless, 2005; Psouni, & Apetroaia, 2014).

Some studies suggest an increase in perception of caregiver availability and in security during middle childhood (Kerns, Tomich, & Kim, 2006). When a child is better able to understand and to take into consideration a parent's desires, communications, and decisions when developing plans and goals, a greater co-regulation and collaboration of secure base contact and problem-solving can occur (Bowlby, 1973; Kerns & Brumariu, 2018). Even in middle childhood, maternal inadequacy to assist children to regulate stress increases a child's risk for later psychopathology (Dujardin et al., 2016). Lack of support in middle childhood has been related to adolescent depression (Dujardin et al., 2016; Mezulis, Hyde, & Abramson, 2006). In contrast, repeated experiences of parental support during stressful times shape children's expectations of parental availability and support. Dujardin et al. (2016) found that, in stressful tasks, insecurely attached children (avoidant or resistant) waited longer than secure before seeking support from parents (N = 98, 8–12-year-olds). Delayed support seeking was linked to depression at follow-up (N = 48, ages 10–14).

Mother- and/or Father–Child Attachment/Relationships

Evidence suggests that, in middle childhood, children feel more secure with mothers than with fathers (Verschueren & Marcoen, 2005), although father–child relationships may gain importance with age (Boldt et al., 2014; Kochanska & Kim, 2013). Even though much recent evidence has suggested the importance of both parents to children's development, some evidence has suggested that mother–child attachments were robust, independent predictors of 8–11-year-old children's emotional symptoms, in contrast to father–child attachment's indirect effects (Demby, Riggs, & Kaminski, 2017). Attachment security and positive family functioning together related to better child outcomes (N = 86; Demby et al., 2017). Secure attachments to mothers directly predicted lower levels of emotional symptoms (accounting for 40% of variance). Positive family affect (family harmony) also predicted lower symptom levels. The effects of father–child attachment security on lower symptom levels was moderated by family cohesion and positive affect. In a longitudinal study, observer-reported security with fathers at age two (AQS) predicted children's higher competence, with peers and in school, six years later at age 8.5 (child interview self-reports and parent reports; N = 100; Boldt et al., 2014).

Insecurity. Insecurity with both parents has been linked to more overall problems, and to more externalizing problems than security with at least one parent (teacher-rated; Kochanska & Kim, 2013). Children who use highly resistant strategies with both parents appear to be at higher risk for externalizing problems (vs secure; e.g., age eight), perhaps because of the difficulty in emotion regulation that is characteristic of this attachment style (Fearon et al., 2010; Kochanska & Kim, 2013). In two studies (from infancy; N = 214; Kochanska & Kim, 2012), for insecure parent–child dyads (not secure), a pattern of coercion emerged between *anger-prone* toddlers and both parents, resulting in parents' increased power-assertive discipline. In turn, parent's power assertion predicted children's rule-breaking and compromised capacity to delay (lab tasks), as well as oppositional, disruptive, callous, and aggressive behavior in early school age (parent and teacher ratings). Even one secure relationship in infancy may support emotion regulation and buffer against developing later behavior problems (Boldt et al., 2014; Kochanska & Kim, 2013).

For 8–12-year-olds (N = 205; 107 learning disabled, LD; 98 non-LD), Al-Yagon (2012) found that youth secure with both parents or with father only showed lower loneliness and higher coping resources and personal strength than others—i.e., they had a higher enduring tendency to see the world as comprehensible, manageable, and meaningful. Children insecurely attached to both parents experienced more loneliness and lower indicators of hope and effort—i.e., they perceived selves as having lower strategies for attaining goals, lower capacity to initiate and sustain movement along chosen pathways, and lower levels of investment, intensity, and persistence in accomplishing tasks. Insecurely attached children experienced increased internalizing and externalizing than securely attached children—e.g., more hyperactivity, aggression, and antisocial behaviors. Language-delayed children reported a significantly lower incidence of attachment security toward fathers (more secure attachments to mothers than to fathers; Al-Yagon, 2012).

Parenting. In an interaction task, even after controlling for demographic variables and parents' internalizing symptoms, mothers' and fathers' verbal and nonverbal controlling and rejecting behaviors were associated with child anxiety and depression (N = 90, ages 9–12; Morris & Oosterfoff, 2016). Mothers' unsolicited physical assistance was associated with child's greater social anxiety, whereas fathers' unsolicited assistance related to general anxiety (may hinder autonomy and confidence). Mothers' denial of requests for reassurance were associated with child's greater general anxiety; and fathers' critical statements related to child-reported depression. Anxious children may seek reassurance more frequently, and refusal of reassurance may have been aimed at promoting independence in anxious children (Morris & Oosterfoff, 2016). However, refusal of reassurance may have been experienced as rejection and may have increased anxiety.

As fathers' distress worsens over time and becomes clinically significant, a father's capacity to engage, sensitively, warmly, and affectionately with children may be compromised. For fathers followed from children's infancy to ages 8–9, Giallo et al. (2015) found that, in general, fathers tended to report fewer warm, close, and enjoyable interactions and fewer displays of affection to their children over time (N = 2662 Australian Fathers). Fathers were found to have either minimal distress (92%) or persistent and increasing distress (8%) trajectories. Distressed father's hostility was higher than minimally distressed at every assessment point, which has been related to a hostile parenting style (see Giallo et al., 2015). During infancy, early childhood, and ages 8–9, persistent and increasingly distressed fathers demonstrated significantly lower parenting warmth, lower consistency, and higher hostility, with faster declines in warmth than minimally distressed fathers. The differences were greatest during middle childhood.

Gender differences were found in response to parental controlling behaviors (Morris & Oosterfoff, 2016). Although verbal instructions during task interactions may be beneficial for many anxious and depressed children, such instructions may promote anxiety or depression within mother–daughter and father–son dyads. For example, although mothers' verbal instructions were linked to lower social and general anxiety for all youth, they were related to lower depressive symptoms for boys, but to greater depressive symptoms for girls. Fathers' verbal instructions associated with lower social anxiety for girls, but to higher social and anxiety symptoms for boys. Parents' controlling and rejecting behaviors may be important targets for treatment.

Academics. In some studies, mother–child attachment has been linked to child cognitive and language skills, in infancy and preschool, and later to children's academic performance (Granot & Mayseless, 2001; van IJzendoorn, 1995). In one study (N = 122 Italian children, ages 8–12; both parents assessed; Bacro, 2012), only attachment to father was a significant predictor of both academic self-concept and children's grade point average in language mastery (not reading performance). For 10–14-year-olds (N = 107; Kerns et al., 2015), children reported more safe haven support (when distressed) from mothers and more secure base support (for exploration) from fathers. Both mother–child and father–child relationships related to children's school adjustment and coping.

Security versus Insecurity or Disorganization

Sensitive, warm care continues to be associated with secure attachments in middle childhood (Bosmans & Kerns, 2015). Parents continue to function as safe havens (e.g., when afraid, sad, or distressed) and as a secure base for exploration—e.g., promote confidence in challenges, show confidence in child's abilities (Kerns & Brumariu, 2018). Both parents encourage exploration and experimentation (Bosmans & Kerns, 2015). Securely attached children are better about checking in (related to their whereabouts) and about communicating with parents about their activities. They report greater perceived and observed levels of acceptance by parents, parent support of autonomy, parental monitoring, and report lower levels of punitiveness toward child distress—more coaching, less dismissing (see Kerns & Brumariu, 2018). Attachment security (and temperament characteristics) has predicted social competence and personality (Bohlin & Hagekull, 2009; Table A5.1—BI).

During school age, insecurely attached children's families can no longer provide a buffer from stresses and failures (Simpson & Belsky, 2018). Although insecure children have shown better general adaptation and competence than disorganized youth, insecure youth were less competent socially than securely attached (teacher report; Barone & Lionetti, 2012). Insecure children also presented more internalizing symptoms than secure. A significant number of children with lower trust in the availability of a mother have interpreted maternal behavior more negatively and remember more negative interactions, even if her behavior could be seen as supportive (see Bosmans & Kerns, 2015; Dujardin, Bosmans, Braet, & Goossens, 2014). Insecurely attached children appear to over-focus on mothers, at the expense of exploration (Bosmans & Kerns, 2015).

Findings have been mixed about the relationship between internalizing and attachment—e.g., whether related to insecure-avoidant or disorganized attachments (Breinholst, Tolstrup, & Esbjorn, 2018). Few studies have examined both attachment and parenting. Negative/controlling parental behaviors—overprotection, psychological control, rejection—have modestly related to child anxiety. Some evidence has suggested that mother and father attachment may relate differently to children's anxiety. Contrary to some findings, in the Breinholst et al. study, mother–child attachment and mother report of behavior did not explain child anxiety (small sample). Child-reported insecure attachments to fathers fully mediated between fathers' report of rejection and child-reported anxiety (N = 54; ages 8.5–10.5; Breinholst et al., 2018).

When caregivers are unreliable, nonresponsive, or overwhelmed and distracted, a child may fail to develop a consistent strategy with the caregiver or may take control. The disorganized controlling type may emerge before or in middle childhood (see Bureau & Moss, 2010). Consistent with other findings (Fearon et al., 2010; Groh et al., 2012), Barone and Lionetti (2012) showed that children with disorganized attachments exhibited more externalizing and, to a lesser extent, more internalizing behavioral problems, poorer social competence, and poorer overall adaptation than comparisons (N = 64; ages 4.4–6.1).

Attachment-Related Interpersonal Style in Middle Childhood

Del Giudice (2009) has observed that, in middle childhood, peer group intra-sexual competition emerges for status, attention, and resources. One reason gender differences may become more apparent early in middle childhood for insecurely attached children is because, in middle childhood, avoidant and anxious-resistant attachment patterns have different adaptive value for boys versus girls—e.g., regarding competition in same-sex peer groups. Cross-culturally, in middle childhood, a peak occurs in spontaneous sex segregation and in sexually differentiated play (Del Giudice, 2015). Some cross-cultural research has shown boys are more likely to be avoidant, and girls to be anxious-resistant (see Del Giudice, 2009 for review; Simpson & Belsky, 2018; see van IJzendoorn & Bakermans-Kranenburg, 2010 for alternative view; Chapter 12). Some suggest that, in middle childhood, avoidant patterns—characterized by increased aggression, excessive self-reliance, and inflated self-esteem—are more effectively used by males under stress and to attain higher status and popularity (see Benenson, 2014; Simpson & Belsky, 2018; fueled by testosterone, Taylor, 2002). This theory suggests that, for girls, anxious patterns are more effective (to prepare for *tend and befriend*—Glossary; Taylor, 2002).

Interpersonal Styles

During the school years, children's attachment styles established in early caregiver–child relationships, may be brought forward as relatively stable patterns of interpersonal interaction (Adams, Stoops, & Skomro, 2014). Although some children's styles change over time, attachment styles have been reflected in one of several tendencies: (1) *Secure*—expect close others to be accessible, available, and responsive when support is needed; have positive self-esteem (e.g., Ein-Dor, Mikulincer, & Shaver, 2011); (2) *Insecure resistant/ambivalent*—view others as untrustworthy and self as undeserving of love and affection; engage in inconsistent and conflicted attempts to derive comfort and support from caregivers/others, interchanging clinginess with outbursts of anger (Fearon & Belsky, 2018; Simpson & Belsky, 2018; Solomon & George, 2018); (3) *Insecure avoidant/*

dismissing—perceive others as unavailable; show decreased expressions of needs and minimize distress; distance themselves from attachment figures and from close relationships (Cassidy & Shaver, 2018); (4) *Disorganized*—lack a coherent strategy for interacting with caregivers/others during times of distress; may include highly affective and contradictory behaviors or low affective/disengaged states combined with inhibited behaviors or dissociation; show controlling or parenting behaviors (Lyons-Ruth, Yellin, Melnick, & Atwood, 2003; Solomon & George, 2018; Tables A3.1–A3.4). Children with insecure and disorganized attachment styles often receive less peer acceptance than secure youth; depending on other factors (e.g., personality) resistant children may receive more acceptance than avoidant and disorganized children (Granot & Mayseless, 2001).

According to Crittenden, insecure-avoidant children use cognitive information to regulate behavior, whereas insecure-resistant children more often rely on emotional/affective information (Crittenden, Robson, Tooby, & Fleming, 2017). Because these strategies/styles are also associated with differences in personality type (NT vs NF; Berens, 2015; Table 17.1), studies are needed that assess personality and attachment style. Nevertheless, these differences are important to treatment, because the treatment strategies that work for one style or personality may not be effective for others (Crittenden et al., 2017).

Personality/Temperament in Middle Childhood

Specific trait or trait composites influence life in middle childhood.

Trait Flexibility

Flexibility assists goal-directed behavior and coping (Glossary—flexibility; see also EFs—cognitive flexibility, to follow). During the transition to adolescence (ages 10–12, then 12–14), for children with higher levels of *flexibility*, flexibility negatively related to both internalizing and externalizing (Rabinowitz et al., 2016). For youth lower in *flexibility*, fathers' lower positive parenting and other variables (e.g., parent diagnostic status) contributed to elevated internalizing and externalizing behaviors (father-reported). Hence, child flexibility may be protective when paternal positive parenting is at low levels.

The effectiveness of specific methods of coping varies in different contexts (Chapter 4). Post-trauma adaptability includes *coping flexibility* (Nader & Fletcher, 2014). Accurately perceiving the controllability of a situation is a key cognitive predictor of *coping flexibility*—i.e., people report more strategies directed toward adjusting to, rather than changing situations as situations become uncontrollable (Babb, Levine, & Arseneault, 2010). Age and diagnostic status have influenced coping flexibility—e.g., 10–11-year-olds without ADHD showed greater coping flexibility than 7–8-year-olds without ADHD and greater flexibility than either age group with ADHD.

Perfectionism

Perfectionism may be adaptive or maladaptive. Variables such as parenting (e.g., controlling; focusing on mistakes), hyperactivity, inattention, and social stressors (e.g., peer relationships) have predicted *perfectionism* (small effects; Cook & Kearney, 2014; Herman, Trotter, Reinke, & Ialongo, 2011; Table 11.1; Chapter 13, 15—Narcissism). Maladaptive but not adaptive *perfectionism* has been linked to negative outcomes (Glossary; ages 7–13, Affrunti & Woodruff-Borden, 2017). Temperamental fear (BI) and executive functions (EFs) combine to influence outcomes. Childhood BI has been linked to increased error monitoring (McDermott et al., 2009). *Fearful* temperament, deficits in cognitive shift (an EF), and their interaction have explained 9% of variance in perceived, socially prescribed *perfectionism* and 4% of variance in self-critical *perfectionism-striving* (N = 56, ages 7–13; Affrunti, Gramszlo, & Woodruff-Borden, 2016, moderate effects). Maladaptive perfectionism is

Table 11.1 Perfectionism (Personal, Perhaps Excessively High Standards for Performance)

Types	Definition	Associations
Adaptive vs maladaptive perfectionism	• positive goal strivings • *perfectionistic strivings* include tendencies to strive for the best and intolerance of not meeting high standards vs • self-critical achievement coupled with distress and criticism • strive to be faultless; hold unrealistically high standards; experience overly negative reactions to perceived mistakes • may include excessive self-monitoring • *perfectionistic concerns* include excessive worries of making mistakes, and hypersensitivity to others' judgment	• perfectionistic strivings have been associated with positive characteristics, whereas perfectionistic concerns have been related to negative ones • maladaptive but not adaptive perfectionism is linked to negative outcomes • related to emotional control deficits • fearful temperament and cognitive shift deficits may result in perseveration on perceived threat in novel and challenging situations • linked to child OCD, depression, and anxiety disorders; related to treatment outcomes • components of perfectionism are mediated by a strong need for belongingness and by shame (e.g., from failure to live up to one's ideals) • parental psychological control linked to personal standard, concern over mistakes, and doubts about action (latter also linked to inter-parental conflict); support of autonomy linked to personal standard and organization
Self-oriented perfectionism	• requirements imposed by an individual on him/herself to be perfect • maladaptive form—e.g., self-critical, ruminative thoughts; excessive need for goal attainment; discrepancies between the actual and the ideal self	• self-critical perfectionism found in fearful temperament (e.g., BI) and in fearful temperament with low cognitive shift • may play a role in cognitive shift deficits • more frequent in some cultures (e.g., Asian) • when high at age 7, linked to later higher internalizing and externalizing (ages 8, 9, 11) • found in grandiose narcissists • predicted by child surgency (temperament)

continued

Table 11.1 Continued

Types	Definition	Associations
Socially prescribed perfectionism	• perceptions that others require perfection from one • adaptive—internalized high standards; striving for perfection • maladaptive—includes being overly critical of self-performance	• parental expectations linked to adaptive form which is linked to academic achievement • parental criticism has been linked to maladaptive form, which links to negative affect • high maladaptive predicted by parental intrusiveness and negative parenting • maladaptive form has been linked to need to belong, shame, and insecure preoccupied attachment—perfectionism may be sought in order to belong, but may create greater disconnection and isolation • combined with emotional control deficits has been related to internalizing and externalizing • when high at age 7, linked to later higher internalizing and externalizing (ages 8, 9, 11)
Other-oriented perfectionism	• expect others to be perfect • are highly critical of others who fail to meet such expectations	• found in grandiose narcissists
Perfectionistic self-promotion	• brashly promoting a perfect image to others	• found in vulnerable narcissists • found in grandiose narcissists
Concerns over revealing imperfections	• nondisclosure of imperfections • nondisplay of imperfections • concealing or not disclosing flaws	• related to the need to belong, shame, and insecure preoccupied attachments • found in vulnerable narcissists

Sources: Affrunti et al., 2015, 2016; Affrunti & Woodruff-Borden, 2014, 2017; Chen et al., 2015; Cook & Kearney, 2014; Gong et al., 2016; Harvey et al., 2017; Hong et al., 2016; Smith et al., 2016b; Stoeber et al., 2015; Sullivan et al., 2015.

related to greater emotional control deficits. Both maladaptive perfectionism (15% of variance) and emotional control (30% of variance) have explained child worry (Affrunti & Woodruff-Borden, 2017). Perfectionism and emotion dysregulation have been linked to internalizing and externalizing (depression, anxiety disorders, conduct problems; internalizing, Affrunti & Woodruff-Borden, 2014; see Sullivan, Keller, Paternostro, & Friedberg, 2015). While single disorder treatments may fail when there are several presenting problems, treatments that successfully ameliorate perfectionism have also assisted emotion dysregulation (e.g., Transdiagnostic CBT, Sullivan et al., 2015).

Positivity Bias

Although less present in Asian cultures, in Western cultures, a self-serving or positivity bias is consistent across diverse age, gender, and cultural groups (N = 266; Mezulis, Abramson, Hyde, & Hankin, 2004; Nader, 2008; Glossary). Accordingly, successes and good outcomes are attributed to self and negative or failure events to things that are changeable, suggesting that negative outcomes can be avoided in the future (Mezulis et al., 2004). In that sense, the *positivity* bias is self-protective. Lower levels of the positivity bias have been associated with increased levels of psychopathology (Korn et al., 2014; Mezulis et al., 2004). For example, for adults with Major Depressive Disorder (MDD; N = 37 Berlin adult patients; Korn et al., 2014), an absence of a positivity bias correlated with severity of MDD. In contrast to individuals who update their future expectations (e.g., the likelihood of exposure to adverse events) based on positive/desirable information, patients with severe MDD showed a negative bias—i.e., updated more from negative/undesirable information. Trauma symptoms (e.g., PTS, depression) may reduce positive and increase negative bias as well. On the other hand, for children who were in institutional care, a positivity bias has been protective against internalizing (see Humphreys, Fox, Nelson, & Zeanah, 2017a).

In middle childhood, more securely attached youth exhibit positive but balanced views of the self, a positive bias in interpreting others' actions, and more prosocial solutions for peer problems (Kerns & Brumariu, 2018). For secure children, as distress increases, subjective distress responses also increase (Borelli et al., 2013). A positive bias used by avoidant/dismissing children in middle childhood appears to serve as self-protective and masks distress (Brumariu, 2015; Mezulis et al., 2004; White et al., 2012b). Avoidant children rate their parents as warmer and more caring than securely attached children, and they tend to focus on positive aspects of their relationships with parents—i.e., perceive caregivers as loving, kind, typical (*idealization*, Borelli et al., 2013). They also tend to deny vulnerability—e.g., unsupported denial of negative emotion, distress, need (Borelli et al., 2013; Hesse, 2008). When avoidant youth (or adults) use a positive bias during attachment interviews, they experience more physiological arousal than secure individuals (e.g., greater startle response, Borelli et al., 2013; negative left frontal slow-wave, White et al., 2012b). Their cortisol levels decrease more slowly over the course of such an interview (compared to secure children; Borelli et al., 2010).

CBCL Dysregulation Profile

A CBCL dysregulation profile (Glossary) has been linked to self-regulatory problems (e.g., ADHD; bipolar disorder), suicidality, low functioning, and poor adult outcomes (e.g., self-regulation disorders, PD; see Althoff et al., 2012). Althoff et al. found the CBCL dysregulation profile was characterized by traits of relatively high *novelty seeking* (NS; *exuberance*), high *harm avoidance*, low *persistence* (P), and low *Reward Dependence* (RD; ages 5–18, N = 382; Glossary). Such children have been described as reluctant to engage (e.g., with peers), having rage attacks, and as destructive and explosive.

Behavioral Inhibition (BI)

BI (shyness, wariness) has been related to fear, anxiety, and social phobia (Chapter 9; Glossary—behavioral inhibition). Children with early shyness have shown social, emotional, and adjustment difficulties (see Tsui, Lahat, & Schmidt, 2017). They have had poor peer relationships (e.g., peer rejection, victimization), social competence deficits, and internalizing. For 10–12-year-olds and 14–16-year-olds, BI has been associated with social anxiety symptoms, especially among girls (N = 119; Tsui et al., 2017). Both BI and negative affectivity (NA) have been linked to anxiety disorders. For diverse children with anxiety disorders, higher BI and higher NA significantly and uniquely related to higher social anxiety and higher anxiety disorder symptoms (parent-reported BI only). Anxiety sensitivity has partially explained the significant link of both child self-reported BI and NA to anxiety disorder symptom severity (N = 44, ages 8–12; Viana et al., 2017).

Studies of adults and children (fMRI) have shown disturbed functioning in brain regions underlying cognitive control. For BI children, high cognitive control has been related to increased anxiety and with markedly increased N2 amplitude (EEG) during task performance (Thai, Taber-Thomas, & Perez-Edgar, 2016; Glossary–N2, P1, P2). EEG has assessed higher-order and more controlled attentional processes. P1 reflects attention allocation to stimuli, with sensitivity to novel and emotional faces. P2 amplitude has been associated with sustained perceptual processing, greater attentional resource mobilization (on salient stimuli), and initial processing of emotion evaluation (faces). N2 amplitudes are believed to be involved in top-down executive function—to signal the need to inhibit a pre-potent response in favor of executing a subdominant behavior, which also reflects attentional control and conflict monitoring (divert attention away from a threat). N2 amplitude is augmented following training attention away from threatening faces. For children ages 9–12, augmented P2 was related to decreased social anxiety symptoms, and it moderated the relation between BI and social anxiety—as P2 increased, social anxiety symptoms weakened. Thus, increasing attentional mobilization may be compensatory, for attenuating social anxiety in high BI individuals (N = 99; Thai et al., 2016). Children with dysregulated fear have shown a bias away from threat; dysregulation fear has been related to increased social anxiety symptoms/scores (see Thai et al., 2016). Smaller N2 was associated with a bias toward threat, and larger N2 with avoidance of threat (Thai et al., 2016). With higher BI, larger N2 was associated with threat avoidance (over-controlled socioemotional functioning). Children with a bias away from threat recruited greater neural activation, possibly using greater effort to divert attention away from threat. Lastly, children without BI used a different processing sequence and had augmented P1 in response for angry faces, suggesting maintenance of attentional resources under threat-related contexts. As discussed, children with BI do best with parenting that helps them to face social fears at a pace and in a way that is not overwhelming (Box 8.2).

Peer Rejection/Victimization

Children's concerns about acceptance by peers rise sharply during middle childhood (Kuttler, Parker, & La Greca, 2002). Peer rejection, exclusion, and aggression are among stressful or traumatic experiences for school-age youth (Nader, 2012c; Silberg et al., 2016, N = 1412, 8–17-year-olds). Youth may be rejected by peers for a number of reasons—e.g., their antagonism and/or aggression combined with poor social skills (Peeters, Cillessen, & Scholte, 2010); bully or victim status (Beran & Lupart, 2009, Crick, 1995); psychopathology (Silberg et al., 2016); personality (Caspi, 1998); poor social or academic skills (Putnam, Helmers, Horowitz, & Trickett, 1995). The traits associated with rejection vary by culture (e.g., shyness and sensitivity in Western but not in Chinese cultures; e.g., Chen, Rubin, & Li, 1995; see Nader, 2008). The demeanor and attitudes of guilt or shame may elicit rejection or punishment from others.

The perception of rejection has been associated with subsequent commission of aggression or other behavior problems (e.g., Virginia Tech school shooter, Langman, 2015; reactive aggression, Schippell, Vasey, Cravens-Brown, & Bretveld, 2003; externalizing, Laird et al., 2001; *humiliated rage*, Fletcher, 2014; Garbarino, 1999; see Nader, 2012c). Gilligan (2003) suggested that for shame (or humiliation) to elicit violence from the person shamed, it is likely that (1) the individual has reduced emotion-regulation capacity or the situation has diminished this capacity; (2) the intensity of the shame and humiliation experience is so overwhelming that it threatens a person's sense of viability and cohesion of self; (3) the person believes that s/he has insufficient nonviolent means to save or restore self-esteem; and (4) cultural conditioning suggests that to maintain masculinity (or to save face or right a perceived injustice), certain situations call for violence.

Preadolescent youth with both parental and peer rejection have shown higher levels of rejection sensitivity and greater loneliness than peers (ages 9–13; Fergusson & Zimmer-Gembeck, 2014). Rejection sensitivity has been associated with BPD (e.g., when combined with low EC, Ayduk et al., 2008); aggression and hostility; more troubled, less satisfying, quicker to end relationships; and expectations of rejection (Ayduk et al., 2000). White et al. (2012b) found that, during exclusion by unfamiliar peers (ages 11–15), both secure and dismissing (attachment) youth showed distress related to a main brain waveform found in negative appraisals and in less approach motivation. Dismissing (avoidant) attachment style was related to a more negative left anterior slow-wave as well during rejection. Dismissing youth under-reported distress relative to neural signs of distress. They also showed greater negative left frontal slow-wave, which may suggest a bias to expect more extensive or lasting exclusion (Table A3.1).

Victimization by peers (e.g., humiliation, rejection, aggression) has been linked to maladjustment such as PTSD (England, 40% grades 8–11; 33%, ages 6–11, see Litman et al., 2015); anxiety, depression (see Biggs et al., 2010); other internalizing—e.g., self-blaming attitudes, negative self-view, negative appraisal of others (Biggs et al., 2010); later inflammation (Copeland et al., 2014—N = 1420, ages 9–16 then 19–21). Bullied youth have had a wide range of difficulties that can persist into adulthood—e.g., social anxiety or withdrawal, SA, ADHD (Box 3.1), suicidal ideation, externalizing, internalizing, hostility bias, low self-esteem, negative self-attitudes, low social status, cautiousness, lower academic performance, absenteeism, impaired social skill development; increased inflammatory response (Beran & Lupart, 2009; Bruyere & Garbarino, 2012; Copeland et al., 2014; Cunningham, 2007; Graham, 2010; Nader, 2012c; Peeters et al., 2010; Silberg et al., 2016). Among those who have committed school shootings are boys who have been victims of relational or other aggression (many but not all shooters; Langman, 2015; Nader, 2008, 2012c; e.g., Parkland, Florida shooter, Columbine shooters).

For elementary school children (N = 358, ages 6–11), peer victimization has accounted for 14.1% of boys' and 10.1% of girls' PTSD symptom severity (Litman et al., 2015)—twice as likely than non-peer-victimized to show high levels of PTSD symptoms. For this group, emotional victimization by peers was most strongly linked to girls' PTSD, and attacks on property most strongly linked to boys' PTSD severity. Across studies, bullying or cyber-bullying has significantly linked to suicidality or suicide (Klomek, Sourander, & Gould, 2010). In a prospective population-based study (Finnish children followed ages 8–25; Klomek et al., 2009), frequent bullying victimization of females lead to suicidality (above and beyond other risk factors), while, for males, frequent bullying lead to suicidality when accompanied by psychopathology (i.e., conduct problems). Children victimized in elementary school have been twice as likely to be victimized when older, than children not victimized in elementary school (Biggs et al., 2010; Litman et al., 2015; Wolke, Woods, & Samara, 2009). Victimization appears to increase with transitions into and out of elementary school (Biggs et al., 2010). Biggs et al. (2010) identified five distinct victimization trajectories—Low, Moderate, Increasing, Decreasing, and Chronic (by self- not peer report; N = 1528 third to fifth graders). *Chronic* victimization was associated with the greatest affective distress, while a *decreasing* trajectory was associated with partial but not full affective recovery.

Developmental Domains

Some skills regress or plateau at puberty (ages 10–11 for girls; 11–12 for boys)—e.g., perspective-taking (e.g., facial emotion recognition), multitasking (Blakemore & Choudhury, 2006). Matching faces to emotions requires working memory and decision-making skills, which decline in performance at puberty onset, and begin to improve at 13 or 14 and to recover by 16 or 17 (see Blakemore & Choudhury, 2006). Recognition of sad and angry expressions may plateau at puberty, but linear improvement continues in recognition of fear and disgust (may be important to survival).

Reading and Language Skills

Language and reading skills affect many aspects of functioning throughout life. In school, language difficulties (LD) that relate to reading problems may make test-taking and other academic endeavors difficult. Although not all children with language difficulties have regulation problems, language impairments have been linked to emotional and behavioral problems. Across studies, children with language impairments were about two times more likely to exhibit disordered levels of internalizing, externalizing, and ADHD problems than children without LD (Yew & O'Kearney, 2013). From school entry to age 11, both children with language difficulties (LD) and their peers (typical language) have shown curvilinear decreases in conduct problems across time (ages 4–5, 6–7, 8–9, and 10–11). LD children (both genders) had significant elevations in intensity and persistence of conduct problems between ages 4 and 11 (Australian; Yew & O'Kearney, 2015). For boys, having LD appeared to increase vulnerability to conduct problems, when there was harsh parenting and low SES. For girls, vulnerability was increased when they showed low prosocial behaviors at age 4 (higher prosocial behaviors were protective for boys). Hence, without intervention, low SES and early LD boys and shy/socially inhibited and early LD girls are at increased risk of conduct disturbances across childhood.

Trajectories of conduct disorder (CD) and hyperactivity are influenced by reading proficiency. Five trajectories of children with comorbid CD and hyperactivity were identified in UK school-age children (N = 242 UK children, ages 6–7 then 7, 8, 11, 16; Pickles et al., 2016). Trajectories included a *Persistent* group (15%)—consistently high hyperactivity and conduct problems peaking in adolescence; *Childhood Limited* group (17%)—equally high problems in both, resolving by age 16; *Low/No problems* group (nearly 30% of children)—no problems in either domain across time; *Resolving Hyperactivity* group (16%)—elevated hyperactivity in childhood, resolved by age 16 and problems with distractibility and task completion rather than restless/fidgety; and an *Adolescent onset* group (24%). The Persistent Group had significant reading difficulties. The No-Problem and Resolving Hyperactivity groups (little to no conduct problems) showed higher prosocial behaviors than the other groups. No gender differences were found.

General Executive Functions (EF)

Childhood EF skills—e.g., working memory, attention shifting, and verbal fluency—can be conceptualized as interconnected, distinguishable cognitive self-regulatory skills and processes that assist goal-directed behaviors (N = 352; ages 7–18, Cassidy et al., 2017; Monette, Bigras, & Lafrenière, 2015). EFs have been related to varied outcomes. Ability, at age 7, to stay focused on a task and persistent in problem-solving has predicted physical health 30 years later (Mischel et al., 2011). Inhibition, another EF, begins in infancy and is essentially mature by ages 10–12 (Glossary; Dajani & Uddin, 2015; Table A4.1, DRD4). Inhibition has been related to social, academic, and self-regulatory outcomes (Roskam et al., 2014). Externalizing behaviors have negatively associated with *working memory* and with *verbal fluency*. *Working memory* has accounted for marginally significant variance in internalizing problems, as well. Cassidy suggests that *working memory* impairments may influence internalizing problems when, for example, a child who is less able to consider multiple interpretations of a situation is hampered in his/her ability to divert initial negative thoughts toward alternative neutral or positive appraisals. Accordingly, diminished working memory abilities may promote rumination and lessen the capacity to cognitively reframe experiences away from negative interpretation biases.

As discussed, earlier and to follow, a number of variables influence executive function development—e.g., parenting, stressors, diet (Sheppard & Cheatham, 2017). For example, children ages 6–8 who had been exposed to pre-natal, maternal anxiety have shown EF impairment, especially girls (see Andiarena et al., 2017). For children with ADHD vs typically developing children

(N = 150 Israeli children), ADHD children had more insecure attachments and clinical impairment in EFs—in behavioral regulation, metacognition (Glossary), and overall EFs (ages 11–12; Al-Yagon, 2018). Both secure mother–child attachment (not father–child) and parental attachment concordance significantly predicted variation in children's EF difficulties (acted as buffers). Insecure attachments to both parents were related to the highest EF deficits; secure attachments to both parents were related to the lowest deficits; and mixed attachments were somewhere in between (secure attachments to mother alone provided some buffering; Al-Yagon, 2018). Dietary and plasma omega 6(n-6):omega 3(n-3) ratio and n-3 have predicted children's working memory and planning task performance (ages 7–12 y; Sheppard & Cheatham, 2017). Effects were different for the two age groups. For 7–9-year-olds, lower plasma n-6 : n-3 ratios (balanced levels) predicted better planning and working memory performance—e.g., predicted number of moves needed in five-step problems requiring considerable working memory and cognitive flexibility; predicted time spent thinking through the problems. In contrast, youth ages 10–12 performed better with higher plasma n-3 on EF tasks—on a six-step maze (no difference on other multiple step tasks) and on simpler tasks requiring less flexibility such as simpler working memory and planning tasks. Age differences may reflect pubertal brain changes that may be supported by n-3 fatty acids.

Memory

Basic, working memory is in place by middle childhood (Bunge & Wright, 2007). Working memory improves from ages 4–15. Compared to five-year-olds, memory capacity increases for 7–8-year-olds and again from early to mid-adolescence (Pasupathi & Wainryb, 2010). Children's prospective memory performance (remembering to do something in the future) improves over the preschool and school years (Sellers & Bjorklund, 2014). Memory in infancy (e.g., recognition and recall memory) has been related to later memory skills (through age 11; 20 months to six years, Rose et al., 2012a). At age 11, processing speed has mediated differences in working memory, shifting, and inhibition between youth born preterm vs full-term (Rose et al., 2012b).

Individual differences in children's working memory are associated with IQ, reading comprehension, writing ability, math (speed of computations), and memory skills (see Bjorklund, 2013). Age-related increases in processing speed are believed to result in improvements in working memory, which in turn influence fluid reasoning. Evidence suggests absolute limits in how much information children of different ages can hold in working memory (Bjorklund, 2013). Average span (information amount a person can attend to at a single time) has increased with age: around 2.5 digits for first graders, around 3.0 for fourth graders, and around 3.5 digits for adults (Cowan et al., 1999). Adult span of apprehension is around four items; adult memory span, 7 (±2). Though storage, processing speed, and attentional allocation have correlated significantly with complex span (CS; e.g., working memory in a dual task context), short-term memory storage and general processing speed have played critical roles in children's CS performance (sentence meaning comprehension or counting dots) and information storage (remembering words or number values; ages 6–12; Magimairaj, Montgomery, Marinellie, & McCarthy, 2009). Kerns (2000) had 7–12-year-old children play CyberCruiser using a joystick to maneuver around obstacles, while occasionally checking the fuel gauge to avoid running out of gas. Younger children ran out of gas more often than older children.

Autobiographical Memory (AM)

Youth ages 8–11 use broadly the same brain regions for AM as adults use, although adults' show greater activation in specific PFC and other regions (Bauer et al., 2017). Emotional content is especially prominent in AM and is one presumed source of their longevity (Bauer, Stevens, Jackson, & Souci, 2012; N = 22, 7.5–9-year-olds, Leventon, Stevens, & Bauer, 2014). Autobiographical recall develops from a general to a more specific memory style—i.e., with age, older children produce more specific AM, and recall positive and negative memories (ages 7–11, Drummond et al., 2006). Younger children produce fewer memories in response to negative cues, while older youth produce equal memories for negative and positive cues. In electrophysiological studies (frontal electrodes), girls showed faster processing of positive than negative emotion, whereas boys had faster processing of negative than of positive (N = 24, 7–11-year-olds, Bauer et al., 2012). Across ages, dysphoric (depressed) children retrieve significantly fewer specific positive memories than non-dysphoric children (N = 70, 7–8 and 10–11, Drummond et al., 2006). Although over-general AM retrieval (Glossary), is part of a stable, dysfunctional cognitive style, independent of current mood, it has been strongly associated with depression (Drummond et al., 2006) and linked to PTSD (see Bosmans et al., 2012).

Patterns of memory among cultures and among the genders illustrate some of their differences. For example, Palestine is among collectivistic societies (the group over the individual)—i.e., emphasizing family affiliation, social cohesion, and harmony (Peltonen, Kangaslampi, Qouta, & Punamäki, 2017). About 55% of Palestinian children had individually oriented earliest memories in contrast to 84% of Canadian children living in an individualistic society—emphasizing individualism, independence, and self-reliance. Girls had more social earliest memories and boys more traumas or accidents for earliest memories. As noted (Chapter 2), a traumatic exposure can install a "traumatic self" as the nucleus around which a self-narrative develops (Ford, 2002; Neimeyer, Herrero, & Botella, 2006). Severity of PTSS has been linked to the likelihood that traumatic memories form a central component of identity (Berntsen & Rubin, 2006, 2007).

Linking past to present emerges gradually across childhood (Fivush, 2011). Eleven-year-olds are generally highly proficient at organizing information to be remembered by categorization and hierarchic relationships and are capable of telling a coherent and integrated narrative/story about their thoughts, feelings, and experiences related to self, parents, siblings, and friends (Steele & Steele, 2005). The ability to construct a personal timeline appears to emerge in middle childhood and increases across adolescence (Habermas & de Silveira, 2008). Around age 12, children begin to link single events together causally, with increasing complexity and coherence across adolescence (Bauer et al. 2007; Habermas & de Silveira, 2008). As per Chapter 5, children whose parents elaborate more with them about their experiences subsequently demonstrate more, richer, and detailed memories (Bauer, 2009; Pasupathi & Wainryb, 2010). Through middle childhood, elaborate autobiographical remembering is associated with better retention of memories over time, more sophisticated self-development, better understanding of others, greater socioemotional competence, and better self-esteem (see Pasupathi & Wainryb, 2010). Girls generally provide more elaborative AM than boys. Across child ages, factual information (observable or perceptible) predominates over interpretive (e.g., desires, emotions, beliefs, and thoughts), with a jump in interpretive information in early adolescence (age 11) and mid-adolescence (for harm events).

Personal narratives are one of the ways that individuals make sense of themselves and of experiences (Bohanek, Marin, Fivush, & Duke, 2006). Bohanek et al. suggest that families contribute to children's processing of shared and personal narrative information. Families narrated their shared pasts in three different styles (Glossary, narration style)—coordinated perspective, individual perspective, and imposed perspective (N = 40 families with children ages 9–12). The coordinated style related to girls' self-esteem (not boys), while the individual perspective style was related to boys' external locus of control (not girls). Bohanek et al. suggest that families with coordinated perspectives are more likely than the others to absorb normal stress and adversity.

Cognitive Flexibility

EFs used in cognitive flexibility (Glossary) mature at different ages—e.g., inhibition—ages 10–12, working memory—13–15 (Simlesa & Cepanec, 2015; Chapter 1). Depending on method, research shows cognitive flexibility skills have sharply increased between ages seven and nine, and essentially matured by age 10, continuing to improve and peak at ages 21–30 (Dajani & Uddin, 2015; item selection tests) or that skills have improved ages 6–10 and reached adult levels between 13–15 (sorting task, Simlesa & Cepanec, 2015). To implement flexibility, children use qualitatively different strategies than adults (who use associations). Around ages 8–9, children change cognitive control strategies from orienting attention toward relevant stimulus features to using associations (e.g., cue-stimulus-response associations; Dajani & Uddin, 2015). As periods of rapid growth, early and middle childhood are targets for intervention (e.g., task-switching paradigms, Buttelmann & Karbach, 2017).

In grade school, levels of flexibility and the ability to adapt predict differences in school functioning—i.e., reading difficulties were improved by a cognitive flexibility intervention (children sort four sets of 12 printed words, a set at a time, by phoneme and meaning into a 2 × 2 matrix, Cartwright et al., 2010, 2017)—and differences in internalizing and externalizing problems into adulthood—e.g., fewer problems, greater adaptive flexibility (Causadias et al., 2012). Children with advanced cognitive flexibility skills, which enables better self-control, have had less hyperactivity/inattention (Farrant et al., 2014).

Self-Regulation—Emotions and Behavior

Better self-regulation has corresponded with enhanced well-being—e.g., better mental and physical health, ability to maintain effective social relationships, and adaptive functioning at home and school (Kaunhoven & Dorjee, 2017). Children with emotion or behavior self-regulation deficits have difficulty with peer and teacher relationships, with academic success, and with risk of dysfunction (Piotrowski, Lapierre, & Linebarger, 2013).

Brain networks underlying self-regulation undergo substantial maturation during preadolescence—e.g., move from short-term and inflexible to more strategic and complex (Kaunhoven & Dorjee, 2017). Executive attention skills, such as conflict monitoring, resolution, and response-inhibition, are increasingly prominent in self-regulation. The ability to inhibit pre-potent reactions, to hold-in-mind goal-relevant information, and to use it to select appropriate actions is adequate by middle childhood (Bunge & Wright, 2007; Mischel et al., 2011). From ages eight months through seven years, self-regulation generally increases with age, although low-income children and males generally have more difficulties (Piotrowski et al., 2013). Children ages 7–12 have shown greater difficulty than adults—e.g., on cognitive control tasks; slower reaction time, twice as many errors overall on go/no-go task (see Eigsti et al., 2006). Whereas, in early childhood, children show intensive fundamental changes in ability for pre-potent response-inhibition, in middle childhood they show greater changes in response speed and accuracy (Simlesa & Cepanec, 2015).

High levels of positive parental reactions to children's emotions—problem-focused, emotion-focused, and expressive encouragement—and low levels of negative parental reactions to their emotions—minimization, punitive, and distress reactions—have been associated with higher levels of children's effortful control (7–12-years; child- and parent report, Valiente, Lemery-Chalfant, & Reiser, 2007). Nurturing parenting practices that reinforce a child's sense of autonomy while maintaining a consistent presence (authoritative parenting) have been associated with better child self-regulatory skills, in contrast to excess parental control (authoritarian parenting) or permissive parenting (notable absence of control), which have been linked to weaker self-regulatory skills (Piotrowski et al., 2013).

Some gender differences have been related to regulation and outcomes. Girls have had higher levels of *effortful control* than boys (Else-Quest, Hyde, Goldsmith, & Van Hulle, 2006). While many studies show that boys are more likely to have externalizing symptoms and girls more likely to have internalizing symptoms (Daughters et al., 2013), some evidence has shown more of both in boys during the transition into adolescence (mother- and father-reported; N = 775; assessed at 10–12 and

12–14; Rabinowitz et al., 2016). Aber, Brown, and Jones (2003) found that although girls were generally at lower risk for aggression between ages six and 12.5, by 12.5 risk levels were almost equivalent to those of boys for both aggressive and competent interpersonal negotiation strategies as well as for conduct problems.

Play

For ages 6–12, play also fosters aspects of development (Chapter 1)—e.g., play is important to development of social competence with peers (see Boldt et al., 2014). Although parents' statements directed toward a child (in pretend mode) have been linked to disruptions of play flow (underscoring the importance of following the child's lead, Chapter 7—child's game, coplay), mother's and children's (not father's) mental state or exploratory talk within play (e.g., "I know she's hungry," "Look ..."; "What is that?") has been related to children's role-play ability, to lower internalizing, and to play-related affect regulation (moderately; ages 4–10, Halfon, Bekar, Ababay, & Gorlach, 2017). Beginning in toddler years, fathers are important to children's play (Boldt et al., 2014)—e.g., may help school children to deal with unexpected situations and competitiveness (Halfon et al., 2017). In elementary school years, *exercise play* may be replaced by running, walking fast, games, sports, and cycling (ages 9–10, Pellegrini & Smith, 1998; see Nader, 2008; Glossary—play types). Verbal and relational aggression (gossip, derogation, insults, threats) gradually replace direct physical aggression (Rubin et al., 2008). Rough-and-tumble play (R&T) behavior peaks in middle childhood and is associated with the ability to decode play signals (e.g., signals that "this is play"; Pellegrini & Smith, 1998; Glossary). R&T and aggressive behavior are separate systems (i.e., different neural and endocrine controls). R&T, before adolescence, generally does not correlate with or tend to escalate to aggression.

Humor

By age seven, a child can play with words to make riddles and puns, can recognize incongruity (e.g., exaggeration or distortion), and begins to appreciate irreverent or malicious humor (Buijzen & Valkenburg, 2004). Between ages eight and 11, children begin to show preference for more complicated and abstract humor—e.g., word play, sarcasm, or sexual allusion, but still like slapstick (Buijzen & Valkenburg, 2004). As the ability to take another's perspective increases, teasing and insulting humor is less popular; other's misfortunes are only funny in accidental/unintended situations or if the person is considered unpleasant. Understanding of *faux pas* requires a developmentally advanced theory of mind ability—simultaneous representation of the perspective of the person committing the faux pas and of a second person who may feel hurt or irritated by the remark, blunder, or breach of etiquette (Brüne & Brüne-Cohrs, 2006). *Faux pas* is generally not reliably understood before ages nine to 11. Disgust, violence, and irreverence are increasingly appreciated. By age 11, humor reflects growing understanding of language and the integration of increasingly richer knowledge and more complex cognitive mechanisms (Semrud-Clikeman & Glass, 2010).

For adults, four main types of humor have been identified (Fox, Hunter, & Jones, 2016; Chapter 1, Glossary—humor types): *self-enhancing*, *aggressive*, *affiliative*, and *self-defeating humor*. Clusters of types of humor were different for youth ages 11–13 than for adults. Fox et al. (2016) found a cluster that combined use of aggressive and affiliative humor (*Interpersonal Humorists*) as well as a *Self-Defeater* cluster, a *Humor Endorser* group, and a group of *Adaptive Humorists* (Table 11.2). Of the four groups, *Self-Defeaters* scored highest in psychosocial maladjustment. The *Self-Defeaters* had higher increases in depressive symptoms than *Interpersonal* and *Adaptive* Humorists. *Adaptive Humorists* scored highest for self-esteem and were less lonely than the Self-Defeaters and Humor Endorsers who were lonelier than Interpersonal Humorists. Fox et al. suggest that the negative effects of using self-defeating humor sometimes, but not always, can be offset to some extent when it is used in

Table 11.2 Humor and Humor Styles (see Table A2.1, adult humor types)

USES FOR HUMOR

- **coping**
  - with and adapt to difficult circumstances
  - tension relief; stress reduction
- **improve well-being**
  - improve health
  - manage pain and/or anxiety
  - improve resilience (e.g., self-esteem)
  - release of feel-good neurotransmitters
- **improve relationships**
  - increase group unity
  - reduce social awkwardness
  - express aggression in a socially acceptable way
  - laugh at self
  - save face
  - increase dominance or status
  - build rapport
- **enhance skills**
  - improve memory
  - improve creativity
  - communicate difficult-to-communicate ideas or feelings
- **reduce stress**
  - reduce tension
  - reduce resistance or lack of involvement
- **regulate emotions**
  - manage anxiety

References: Chapter 1; Agaibi & Wilson, 2005; Bains et al., 2015; Başak & Cann, 2014; Bennett & Lengacher, 2007; Campbell et al., 2015; Fox et al., 2016; Herzog & Strevey, 2008; Lanktree & Briere, 2008; Martin et al., 2003; Papa & Bonanno, 2008; Scott, Lavan, Chen, & McGettigan, 2014; Morgan & Jorm, 2008; Nader, 2008; Semrud-Clikeman & Glass, 2010; Shibata, Terasawa, & Umeda, 2014; Yue et al., 2014; Yue & Hui, 2015.

SKILLS REQUIRED

- perspective-taking
- language
- social skills and understanding
- understanding, e.g., incongruity, use of language, motivations of others; see Chapter 1

YOUTH HUMOR CLUSTERS (AGES 11–13)

- *adaptive humorists* (high only on the 2 adaptive styles—affiliative and self-enhancing humor)
- *humor endorsers* (above average on all 4 adult types; Glossary)
- *interpersonal* humorists (combines aggressive and affiliative styles)
- *self-defeaters*

Associations

- adaptive humorists—highest in self-esteem; less lonely than self-defeaters and humor endorsers; less depressed over time than self-defeaters
- aggressive humor—can be adaptive when used with affiliative humor
- humor endorsers—lonelier than interpersonal humorists
- interpersonal humorists—less depressed over time than self-defeaters
- self-defeaters—scored highest in psychosocial maladjustment (i.e., highest in depressive symptoms, loneliness, and change in loneliness; low self-esteem); higher increases in depression over time; negative effects can be offset by using combined styles

combination with other humor styles. For these youth, aggressive humor was not generally used in isolation and could be adaptive when used with affiliative humor.

Emotion Awareness and Processing

As early as age six and generally by age 11, children have the capacity to understand mixed or blended emotions, and diverse emotions arising in one person toward another person or situation (Steele & Steele, 2005). In contrast to poor attachments, children whose parents provided safe haven and secure base support (positive attachments) have been less likely to be low in emotional awareness, emotional clarity, or acceptance of emotions than those low in such support (N = 111, ages 10–14, Kerns et al., 2015; Table A3.1; see Chapter 4). Children with disorganized controlling–caregiving attachment styles have seemed to use emotional constriction to deal with painful emotional states. Controlling–punitive children have used angry, contradictory patterns of hostility and avoidance to capture and maintain attention, and have used overt power assertion through attacking or humiliating a parent to increase parental involvement (Moss et al., 2012; Moss & Lecompte, 2015). For 8–12-year-olds, children with somatic complaints and children with social maladjustment also have had trouble differentiating emotions, verbally sharing emotions, and analyzing their own emotions—higher body awareness and negative emotions were positively related to somatic complaints (Villanueva et al., 2015). When emotion dysregulation is operationalized as poorer awareness, higher levels of nonacceptance of emotions, and greater difficulties with goal-directed behavior, higher levels of dysregulation (all three types) prospectively predicted higher levels of anxiety symptoms across a study period of up to three years (even after accounting for initial anxiety and depression; N = 312, ages 8–16; Schneider, Arch, Landy, & Hankin, 2016).

Self- and Other-Awareness

From ages 5–7, children tend to have unidimensional thinking—all or none, black and white (Harter, 2008). They are able to link/relate representational sets—tall vs short, fat vs thin—and apply these opposites to self or others. Hence, the belief that "I'm good so I can't be bad" and difficulty integrating nice and mean (or happy and sad) may result in self-descriptions that are all positive (the typical self-representations for that age; Harter, 2008). Although some all-or-none thinking and proneness to positive self-perception persists in middle childhood, children become able to combine competencies (e.g., good at dodge ball and schoolwork) and to compare past to current performance, but not to make social comparisons (Harter, 2008). That is, they lack the cognitive skills for a more realistic self-perception. From ages 8–11, children continue to describe themselves in terms of competencies; however, self-attributes become increasingly interpersonal. They become able to express having opposites—e.g., mostly nice, but mean when in a bad mood; smart but dumb in math. By age 11, children generally are able to recall past interactions that illustrate evaluations of themselves and their relationships to others (Steele & Steele, 2005). They are able to use others as a source of information for self-evaluation; have a growing awareness that different situations may require different behavior toward others; and have an ability to compare and contrast relationships (e.g., to their mothers and fathers; Steele & Steele, 2005). They are becoming able to comment upon features of relationships they would most like to preserve or to change. However, insecure attachments and childhood traumas may derail the self-system (Harter, 2008). For example, the child's self-image may include thoughts/feelings of being unlovable and unable to get needs met.

A number of skills necessary to perspective-taking develop during middle childhood. Between ages six and 10, children's recognition of emotions represented in facial expressions increases (Blakemore & Choudhury, 2006). Between ages seven and 12, children begin to see from another person's perspective and recognize that others can do the same (Selman, 1971, Selman & Byrne, 1974). Although at ages 7–8, children can differentiate what is said from what is meant, they have difficulty with more complex tasks (e.g., understanding inferences; Blakemore & Choudhury, 2006). At age eight, when exposed to ambiguous stimuli, children assume that others will have the same perspective as they do (Kuhn, 2000). It is well beyond early school years before children can assign appropriate interpretations to different kinds of non-literal language (e.g., irony; see Brüne & Brüne-Cohrs, 2006). From ages 10–15, children can imagine how a third, non-biased party might view them and another person—i.e., can imagine looking at both sides/perspectives of issues (third-party perspective; Selman, 1971; Selman & Byrne, 1974).

Guilt

The self-conscious emotions evolve across this period of development. While five- to six-year-olds may be more likely to feel guilt, in the presence of an adult, the younger children between ages six and 11 have expressed more guilt over uncontrollable or accidental events; and older children have been more likely to express guilt over intentional and controllable events (Graham, Doubleday, & Guarino, 1984; Fletcher, 2014). By 7–8 years, children usually have a greater understanding of others' emotions and are able to feel guilt over causing emotional harm or failing to help someone (see Kletter et al., 2009). Guilt shifts from being a risk for punishment to a reason for sorrow. By 9–10 years, aside from simple wrong-doings (mild aggression to a peer), complex antecedents may also lead to guilt—e.g., violation of adults' rules (see Kletter et al., 2009). Guilt-proneness can serve as a deterrent to problematic behaviors (Tangney, Stuewig, & Martinez, 2014).

Social Skills

During early school years, social interactions involving peers increase (Rubin et al., 2008). During preadolescence and adolescence, youth must use their social skills flexibly to meet the demands of a given situation. Failure to acquire the skills to perceive, process, and respond to nonverbal social cues results in risk of long-term social difficulties (Miller et al., 2006). Children learn to evaluate social situations and generate behavioral responses critical for successful interactions with peers (Miller et al., 2006). In middle childhood, children's intrinsic ability to understand the thoughts, beliefs, and desires of others (theory of mind skills, TOM) may facilitate their real-life behavior in social interactions (Table 1.2)—i.e., TOM has predicted their prosocial behavior (both genders; N = 114, ages 5–7; Kuhnert, Begeer, Fink, & de Rosnay, 2017).

Friendships, Gender, and Social Interacting

Friendships provide a training ground for development of more complex social skills. By middle childhood, fairness and justice are evidenced in an emerging tendency to share resources equally (Burnett & Blakemore, 2009). Research has shown that girls are more attuned to their peers' emotional experiences (see Kuhnert et al., 2017). By age seven, girls appear to use their emotional understanding abilities during practical prosocial behaviors toward peers in a way that boys do not (Kuhnert et al., 2017). Given that girls' relationships are generally more interpersonal, by nature, emotional understanding may be needed and nurtured to maintain social bonds. Traits deemed *gender incongruent* (i.e., poor assertion in boys and poor self-control in girls) have been associated with peer victimization for Dutch 11–12-year-olds (Bakker et al., 2011). Both non-aggressive and highly aggressive boys tended to perceive their friendship relationships more positively than boys with moderate levels of overt aggression, while for girls, there was a negative, linear association between aggression and friendship quality (Fanti, Brookmeyer, Henrich, & Kuperminc, 2009).

Self-Regulation and Inter-Relating

From early to middle childhood, children develop the skills to self-regulate behaviors in response to social cues (Miller et al., 2006). By age 11, with meta-representational awareness of the positive and negative elements of relationships with family and friends (enhanced by intelligence/maturity), youth generally have strategies for how to resolve interpersonal and intrapersonal conflicts (e.g., letting a friend go first; Steele & Steele, 2005). Youth with behavior problems may have difficulties interacting socially, and friendships may influence behavior problems. For 10–13-year-olds, having delinquent peers has been linked to increased problem behaviors (externalizing) over time, if friendships included low intimacy (Gaertner, Fite, & Colder, 2011). They were associated with decreased externalizing over time with more intimate exchanges with delinquent friends—i.e., highly bonded social relationships can be protective against exacerbation of problem behavior.

Neurobiology influences behavior and inter-relating. Some evidence suggests that, while cortisol has been associated with negative affect and withdrawal behaviors, basal sAA levels have been associated with approach behavior and positive affect (two-year-olds; see Andiarena et al., 2017). Some evidence suggests that moderate sAA levels have predicted fewer behavior problems (ages 8 then 10), whereas either low or very high sAA levels are positively associated with behavior problems. Training in acquiescence combined with reinforcement for handling difficult situations was used with a small group of 6–8-year-old youth with problem behaviors (ADHD; ODD; Ducharme, Folino, & DeRosie, 2008). The result was considerable reduction in the frequency of antisocial behaviors and improvements in prosocial behaviors.

Conclusions

Under normal circumstances, developmental skills improve with age, with a lag or pause in some skills at puberty onset. Skill enhancement may serve as both a preventive and a reparative measure. Youth ages 6–12 may benefit from methods that enhance flexibility, empathy, coping, and other skills as well as benefit from improved positive parenting. Even dietary changes may benefit this age group—e.g., benefits of specific omega fatty acids vary by age within this group. Temperaments, attachment styles, and skills influence characteristic interacting, reacting, reporting, and treatment needs (see also Chapters 16, 17).

Support systems consistently have proven important before and after adversity. As is true for all age groups, parental and social support are important to well-being. Parenting style also becomes a factor in child well-being and development. Across age groups, authoritative parenting (vs authoritarian, lax, or uninvolved) has been beneficial to youth, with some adaptation for inhibited temperaments. Both parents are important to children's development and recovery. Their participation in treatment is often of benefit. Peers become increasingly important to school-age children, and gender differences may become more apparent in this age group (e.g., in play, stress style, reporting). Some differences in the influence of maternal versus paternal parenting/attachment have been related to gender.

12

Trauma's Impact on Life and Developmental Domains

Ages 6–12

For school-age children, developmental tasks such as the transition from parents to peers as social partners, development of perspective-taking, and evolvement of self-control may be disrupted or impaired by trauma or other adversity. Traumatized youth have shown constricted thinking and emotions and decreased imagination, processing, and other skills needed for some tasks. For example, a traumatized child's lower patience and processing may interfere with social and academic skills and with understanding, appreciating, or tolerating humor or the perspectives of others. Traumas may influence a youth's inter-relating styles, coping styles, and attitudes—e.g., children exposed to a parent's victimization by intimate partner violence have described parenting and protecting their mothers, hiding their emotions from mothers and from themselves (avoiding emotions), not seeking support, feeling powerless and constantly overwhelmed, and an altered self-image (e.g., shame), among other problems (ages 10–16; Bowyer, Swanston, & Vetere, 2015).

In addition to adversity's effects on development, developing skills may shape reactions (e.g., EFs, mentalizing). Although problem-focused or active coping has proven important to adaptation, and avoidant coping has often proven problematic after traumas or traumatic loss, each method has its uses—e.g., recent research has shown that coping flexibility is more important than using a particular coping strategy (Burton et al., 2012; Park, Chang, & You, 2015; Chapter 4; Table 14.1). Even after adjusting for comorbid symptoms, age and time elapsed since a most distressing event, for adults exposed to traumatic events, coping flexibility served as a protective factor against psychological distress (PTSD or depressive symptoms; Park et al., 2015). Risk factors and trauma or adversity's influence on development and on psychopathology are discussed.

Risk Factors

A number of the variables that influence outcomes, including number of trauma types a youth is exposed to, attachment, personality, and neurobiological factors, will be discussed.

Poly-Victimization or Cumulative Trauma

Numerous studies have shown that poly-victimization is linked to increased psychopathology (Chapter 2). In a study of adverse childhood experiences (ACEs; Glossary; N = 318; ages 8–12; child and parent report; Hodges et al., 2013), the total number of different types of interpersonal traumas experienced by children was associated with the subsequent number of different symptom clusters elevated simultaneously into the clinical range (i.e., complexity of symptomatology). Poly-victimization seems to play a more important role in the juvenile commission of sexual offenses than sexual victimization plays (see Barra, Bessler, Landolt, & Aebi, 2018). For juvenile sex offenders, 66.5% had several ACE types; 10% were highly poly-victimized; and most were not themselves sexually abused (N = 322, ages 12–16; Barra et al., 2018; Table 15.1). Similarly, like other severe adversity (Gunnar & Vazquez, 2001; Tarullo & Gunnar, 2006), ongoing war, with its multiple types of exposures, increases the likelihood of psychopathology (ages 7–8 and 10; Feldman, 2015).

Multiple intrafamilial and/or extrafamilial trauma types can have profound effects. For example, in a study of 672 poly-victimized youth in residential care (ages 11–17), a direct association was found between (a) trauma by a caregiver—e.g., physical, sexual, or emotional abuse—and PTSS; (b) trauma by a non-caregiver—e.g., physical assault; community, school, and extreme interpersonal violence; war and/or terrorism—and externalizing problems; (c) gender and PTSS with externalizing problems and internalizing problems; and (d) age and externalizing problems (Hodgdon et al., 2018). Caregiver traumas often begin earlier than non-caregiver traumas, potentially interfering with the foundations of skill development. When Executive Functions (EFs) were assessed as the abilities to modulate emotions, to inhibit pre-potent responses, to shift attention, to utilize working memory, and to organize thinking and behavior in a goal-directed manner (planning), the total number of caregiver-perpetrated traumas was associated with EF deficits, which in turn were linked to PTSS and externalizing problems (Hodgdon et al., 2018). Accumulations of a single type of trauma also have deleterious effects. For example, higher levels of childhood emotional abuse measured in school age were associated with higher levels of anxiety at each annual assessment across five years (ages 10–12, T1; Banducci, Lejuez, Dougherty, & MacPherson, 2017).

Patterns of Exposure

In general, numbers of types of adverse experiences have increased with age (Finkelhor et al., 2014; see Table 15.1). In a study based on the retrospective reports of treatment-seeking adolescents, their early, middle childhood, and adolescent epochs were assessed for trauma exposures (Grasso et al., 2016). A latent class analysis showed increasingly complex patterns of adverse/traumatic experiences in middle childhood (ages 6–12) and adolescence, compared to early childhood (ages 0–5) (N = 3754, ages 13–18; Grasso et al., 2016). That is, youth reported increasing numbers of classes and varieties of ACE types with age/epoch. Within epochs studied, for early and middle childhood subgroups with high-varied exposure (poly-victimization), ACEs significantly included intrafamilial adversity types, whereas the adolescent high-varied exposure group included physical assault, community violence, and emotional abuse. Adolescents exposed to early domestic violence but rarely exposed to other ACEs (e.g., abuse, neglect, impaired caregiver) were less likely to have clinically significant PTSD or internalizing than youth with a broader range of exposures. In contrast, youth with multiple types of early exposures were most likely to have clinically significant PTSD or internalizing in adolescence.

Attachment and Trauma

As discussed in preceding chapters, positive attachments have served as protective factors for children. Insecure and disorganized attachments have been associated with risk. Parents can serve as buffers against repeated stress for children. For example, children exposed to war with and without PTSD exhibited higher negative emotionality in a fear paradigm (Feldman, 2015). Children with PTSD utilized withdrawal for emotion regulation, whereas more resilient exposed children (no PTSD) utilized parent proximity-seeking behavior to regulate fear. Children with impaired caregiving have been at risk for trauma exposure (in and outside of the family), PTSD, internalizing symptoms, and behavior problems at home and in school (e.g., parents with mental health problems or substance abuse; N = 3988, ages 7–18; Vivrette et al., 2018). Children with impaired caregivers had more overall trauma exposures and more of each type of exposure. Problems occurred at higher rates with mental health problems (than with substance abuse). Number of types of trauma exposures mediated the relationship between impaired caregiving and child PTSD and behavior problems.

Attachment Style and Psychopathology

Attachment styles influence interrelationships, expressions of distress, and outcomes. Resistant children over-activate attachment behaviors, seeking to maintain caregiver availability (likely exposed to inconsistent parental care; Bosmans & Kerns, 2015). They show exaggerated negative emotional displays, and in middle childhood may provoke caregivers and initiate conflict. Insecure-avoidant children (likely parent rejects child's bids for contact and care) may become overly self-reliant. Avoidant children may under-report trauma and other symptoms (see positivity bias, Chapter 11). Across five of seven studies, characteristic hyper-activating strategies have mediated the link between anxious attachment and depressive symptoms, whereas findings are mixed for the mediation by characteristic deactivating strategies between avoidant attachments and depressive symptoms (age range 8–19; Malik, Wells, & Wittkowski, 2015). Consistent with other findings (meta-analysis: Fearon et al., 2010; van IJzendoorn, Schuengel, & Bakermans-Kranenburg, 1999), both early avoidant and disorganized attachments have predicted greater externalizing problems in grades 1–6 (Belsky & Fearon, 2002; Fearon & Belsky, 2011). However, effects of disorganized attachment were moderated by cumulative family risk and by gender and age. Disorganized boys from risky social contexts—i.e., low SES, father absent, low parent education—manifested increased behavior problems over time. While at age three (parent report), such associations were only for avoidant attachments (Belsky & Fearon, 2002), by school age, disorganization related to externalizing problems as well (grade 1, teacher report; a minimal effect), with a steeper increase in problems thereafter. Disorganized boys (not girls) with multiple risk factors scored higher in externalizing (aggression, conduct problems) than all other children by grades 5–6 (Fearon & Belsky, 2011).

ODD and Interpersonal Relating. Early attachments may influence outcomes; outcomes may influence attachments/relationships. Community rates of oppositional defiant disorder (ODD) in children have ranged from 2.6% to 15.6% (see Li et al., 2017a). ODD symptoms reported by either parents or teachers have predicted impairments in children's interpersonal functioning (N = 256 Chinese children ages 6–13; three time points in two years; Li et al., 2017a). More severe ODD symptoms predicted children's poorer relationships with father, mother, peers, and teachers (parent report). A child's interpersonal dysfunction with peers and teachers predicted subsequent increases in ODD symptoms (teacher-reported). By damaging interpersonal harmony, ODD symptoms may interfere with social support, result in isolation, and create ongoing risk (Li et al., 2017a). Hence, early intervention with ODD may prevent future problems in interpersonal relationships that may create risk and have cascading effects.

Attachment/Parenting, Coping, and Trauma

Combinations of attachment, coping, and the nature of posttraumatic (PT) reactions have also related to outcomes. For adults with childhood sexual abuse experiences (CSA), when PT avoidance symptoms were low and intrusive re-experiencing was high, regardless of dissociative levels, there was greater likelihood of later non-suicidal self-injury (NSSI, see Bolen, Winter, & Hodges, 2013). This suggests that avoidant PTS may become increasingly necessary for self-protection as intrusive PTS increases. NSSI increased both with increasing dissociation and with increasing PTS re-experiencing symptoms. It decreased with increasing attachment security. For university students, father attachments had an indirect effect on outcomes—on self-worth, self-esteem—through coping (see Hébert, Daspe, & Cyr, 2018)—e.g., fathers may influence how children cope by encouraging active or approach coping: facing or confronting a situation (Table 14.1).

CSA. Attachment and/or parenting may be the difference between positive and other outcomes. Some research has shown that a positive and approaching quality of parenting was related to lower anger and fewer total symptoms for CSA children (see Hébert et al., 2018). Increased symptoms—e.g., greater anxiety, depression, externalizing, and dissociation symptoms—were related to insecure attachment styles. For CSA children ages 6–12, support from a nonoffending parent has been related to better outcomes—e.g., to higher levels of social, interpersonal, and academic functioning; less psychological distress over time; has promoted a child's recovery (see Hébert et al., 2018). However, findings have been mixed and associations weak.

Fathers and mothers may provide different aspects of support for CSA children. In some studies, perceptions of secure attachments to fathers have been associated with higher self-esteem and with lower behavior problems, over and above mother-attachment security (see Hébert et al., 2018). In a study of CSA by someone not living with the child (N = 505, ages 6–13), for both genders, Hébert et al. (2018) found that security to the same-sex parent was associated with self-esteem, whereas attachment to the opposite sex parent was associated with both PTSS and self-esteem. There was a relationship between attachment and type of coping. For girls, less avoidant coping was linked to security with both parents, while for boys, avoidant coping was linked to mother-attachment security (Hébert et al., 2018). Active/approach coping was uniquely related to girl's secure attachments to mothers and to boy's secure attachments to fathers. In general, avoidant coping was associated with more PTSS and lower self-esteem for both genders. Approach coping was related to more PTSS for both genders as well, although it was related to better self-esteem in girls. As discussed, the use of multiple forms of coping has been linked to higher symptoms, possibly reflecting the need for more attempts at coping with higher levels of distress.

Changes in Attachment-Related Styles After Trauma

Most studies assess Bowlby's well-discussed and researched attachment strategies/styles (Tables A3.1–A3.4). Using danger as a starting point, Crittenden, Robson, Tooby, and Fleming (2017) defined attachment in the school years as the *strategies* used for protecting the self. Danger-related strategies used at home may not be used in other contexts, and strategies employed effectively at home may not be effective at school. For usual attachment classifications, children who have experienced danger (e.g., abuse) may be difficult to read—e.g., they may use false positive affect and/or caregiving or compliant behavior to appease a distressed or angry parent (e.g., N = 49, ages 5.5–5.9, then 6.0–6.5, Crittenden et al., 2017; replication is needed). In contrast, children with unpredictable parents may use increased negative affect or behavior to increase parental predictability and supportiveness. School-age children may behave as if they do not need comfort or protection; in contrast, may appear aggressively invulnerable; or may appear seductively helpless (when intensely angry).

Personality/Temperament

Personality/temperament traits may influence the effects of trauma and treatment needs as well as influence mood and behaviors (Nader & Fletcher, 2014; Table A5.1; see Chapters 16 and 17 for treatment issues). For children followed from 6 weeks old to age 21, temperament characteristics predicted problem behaviors, personality, and social competence, whereas attachment security only predicted social competence and personality (N = 1985 infants, 123 middle schoolers, 112 age 21; Bohlin & Hagekull, 2009). BI (Chapter 11) has been associated with low extraversion and was only linked to low externalizing at age four (Bohlin & Hagekull, 2009). In contrast to NE and *inhibition/shyness* (BI), preschool *activity* and *sociability* inversely related to internalizing. *Sociability* and *activity* levels related positively to social competence at school age (Bohlin & Hagekull, 2009). Outcomes may depend on trait combinations. Good effects of higher levels of a trait for one group of children may cause problems for another group. Although low *inhibitory control* has been associated both with internalizing and externalizing for 8–10-year-olds, findings are mixed (see Morris, Hudson, & Dodd, 2014). Some evidence suggests that, for behaviorally *uninhibited* children, greater *inhibitory control* is associated with reduced externalizing, whereas high levels of inhibitory control have been related to greater internalizing for behaviorally *inhibited* children (see Morris et al., 2014).

Traits may buffer or increase vulnerability to outcomes. High *activity* has been associated with high externalizing; low internalizing; high social competence, *extraversion*, and *openness*; but to low *agreeableness* (Bohlin & Hagekull, 2009). *Distress tolerance* is the perceived or actual ability to tolerate negative states such as negative emotions, discomfort, and/or uncertainty (see Banducci et al., 2017). School-age children with both higher levels of emotional abuse (adult verbal assaults and humiliating/demeaning behaviors toward child) and lower levels of *distress tolerance*, had the highest levels of anxiety at each of five annual assessments, even though anxiety normally decreases with age and low *distress-tolerant* youth had steepest decreases in anxiety across time (between ages 10 and 14; N = 277, T1; 244, T2; Banducci et al., 2017).

Negative Emotionality (NE; Neuroticism)

NE has been related to vulnerability and may shape posttrauma reactions and general outcomes (Table A5.1). High NE has been linked to severity of PTSD and to both internalizing and externalizing (combined type; Eisenberg et al., 2009; PTSD, Lauterbach & Vrana, 2001). Child trauma studies have linked NE to risk of PTSD (Weems et al., 2007). Across time, infant/preschool low *manageability*/high NE predicted high levels of co-occurring externalizing and internalizing (at age four and ages 8–9; Bohlin & Hagekull, 2009). Preschool NE and BI each associated with internalizing problems and related negatively to social competence at age four and 8–9. Children with high levels of negative reactivity and those with high externalizing behaviors tend to respond to distressing or difficult situations with emotional and behavioral dysregulation (Eisenberg, Spinrad, & Eggum, 2010a). Adverse parenting has contributed to increased risk for internalizing and externalizing problems among children with difficult temperaments (Glossary; Kochanska, Kim, Barry, & Philibert, 2011; Yaman et al., 2010; Zarra-Nezhad et al., 2014). When children (ages 6–7) had lower thresholds for reacting negatively and intensely to sensory stimuli (neuroticism/NE), they received lower acceptance/preference by peers than those with lower negative reactivity (end of K [age six] to end of grade 10 [ages 14–15]—Canada; Buil et al., 2017), which may translate into lower levels of support following traumas (a risk factor). Age 6–7 negative reactivity predicted antisocial behavior in later childhood and early adolescence (but not substance use), which in turn was linked to overt and covert antisocial behavior and substance use in later adolescence (Buil et al., 2017). For another group of children (followed ages 6–10), NE (especially anger), low *effortful control* (EC; attentional and inhibitory), and high *impulsivity* were linked to externalizing problems (alone or co-occurring with internalizing problems; Eisenberg et al., 2009). Low *impulsivity* and *sadness* related to internalizing problems. Children with later no- or improved-externalizing had high EC. Change from no-externalizing to externalizing was predicted by low EC and somewhat high *impulsivity*, suggesting a need to improve EC by early school years. Improved internalizing was also predicted by high EC as well as by low *anger* and *sadness*.

Brain Regions and Trauma

Although findings are sometimes mixed, some researchers suggest specific sensitive periods in brain development during this age range. In the last 15 years, studies have demonstrated a peak in myelination (Glossary) in middle childhood cognitive development (assessed infant, preschool, middle childhood, and late childhood, Crowe et al., 2012; Dackis et al., 2012; Lebel et al., 2008), including rapid development of abilities such as selective attention, executive skills (particularly inhibition and self-monitoring), and language skills (Crowe et al., 2012; Klenberg, Korkman, & Lahti-Nuutila, 2001). Each of these skills are critical for subsequent abilities and traits—e.g., learning; reasoning ability; task planning, time management; and working memory. Brain-injury in middle childhood (7–9 years) has been related to poorer performance on verbal IQ, nonverbal IQ, processing speed, and overall IQ than injury in late childhood (Crowe et al., 2012). Andersen et al. (2008) found a maximal effect of abuse at ages 9–10 (on the corpus callosum) and second most strongly associated effect of abuse at ages 11–13 (hippocampus volume reduction; maximally, at ages 3–5; N = 43). Exposure of the immature hippocampus to corticotropin-releasing hormone has resulted in delayed and progressive negative effects on brain growth (cell survival, dendritic branching; Glossary; Andersen et al., 2008; Brunson et al., 2001; age 8–12; Snook et al., 2005). A few brain regions are discussed in more detail here.

Amygdala

The amygdala plays a central role in emotional memory and fear. Peak ages of amygdala and hippocampal volumes occur during preadolescence (Uematsu et al., 2012). They peak and begin to decrease about 1.5 years earlier for girls than boys (9–11 years old, pubertal age differences; Uematsu et al., 2012; Table A4.2). While the left amygdala appears to develop more rapidly in the first few years of life, the right amygdala increases in volume over a longer time period, likely leaving it more vulnerable to stress-related effects during later developmental periods (Pechtel, Lyons-Ruth, Anderson, & Teicher, 2014; Uematsu et al., 2012). Stress-induced changes in the amygdala (hypertrophy/enlargement) have resulted in elevated anxiety-like behaviors, which remain even after three weeks of stress-free recovery (Romeo & McEwen, 2006; likely, in part, related to corticosterone actions).

Aberrant amygdala volume and function have been reported in psychiatric disorders marked by affect dysregulation (Lange & Irle, 2004; Pechtel et al., 2014). Right amygdala enlargement has significantly related to severity of maltreatment in middle childhood, with peak effect from maltreatment between ages 10 and 11 (Lyons-Ruth et al., 2016; N = 51 adults with childhood maltreatment; Pechtel et al., 2014). While severity of abuse, across ages, accounted for 27% of the variance in right amygdala volume, exposure during this sensitive period resulted in a steep dose-response effect. During the sensitive period, the right amygdala appears to be vulnerable to even modest levels of adversity, and to be affected by varied types of abuse—e.g., peer verbal abuse, witnessing violence to siblings—not detected in earlier studies (Table A4.2).

Prefrontal Cortex (PFC)

The PFC (important to executive functions) and its connectivity to other brain regions may be particularly vulnerable to trauma in preadolescence and in adolescence (Blakemore & Choudhury, 2006; Nader & Fletcher, 2014; Table A4.2; Chapter 14). Youth with PTSD symptoms (PTSS) have shown significantly decreased total brain tissue and cerebral gray volumes, compared to healthy controls (ages 10–17; Carrion et al., 2010a, b). Accordingly, exposure to extreme stress may alter EFs such as inhibition of the stress response, self-regulation, attention, attention set shifting (Glossary), organization, and planning (Rothbart & Rueda, 2005; Romeo & McEwen, 2006; Stein & Kendall, 2004; Stevens, Kiehl, Pearlson, & Calhoun, 2007), all of which are important to effective functioning.

Neurobiology: Genetic Activity and Trauma

Neurobiological studies have often focused on a few specific genes or gene combinations, and findings sometimes have been mixed. For example, findings related to 5-HTTLPR have been somewhat mixed (see Chapter 4). Nevertheless, a number of studies have found a link to internalizing and to NE. Cicchetti, Rogosch, and Oshri (2011) found that the interaction of CRHR1, 5-HTTLPR, and child maltreatment identified a subgroup of maltreated children with internalizing symptoms (ages 7–13; Table A4.1). Large, future studies assessing multiple variables and genes may better illuminate variations in post-stressor reactions based on multiple gene/neurochemical propensities and age. Nevertheless, studies have shown genetic links to increased sensitivity to environmental conditions. Studies of children in institutional care (IC) versus those placed in high-quality foster care (FC) have demonstrated increased sensitivity to context for serotonin short allele carriers (s/s)—i.e., s/s IC children had higher levels of internalizing than s/s FC children and higher than long allele carriers (Humphreys, Fox, Nelson, & Zeanah, 2017a; Chapter 7). Genetic vulnerabilities may be activated by trauma and/or may influence reactions.

Cortisol

Because significantly more corticotrophin-releasing hormone cells (not vasopressin) are activated in the paraventricular nucleus (PVN) in response to both acute and chronic stress in pre-puberty, the pre-pubertal brain may be more sensitive to corticosterone (vs adult animals, see Romeo & McEwen, 2006). A natural period of cortisol hypo-responsivity appears in early stages of puberty (Gunnar, Frenn, Wewerka, & Ryzin, 2009a; ages 10–12, Gunnar et al., 2009b; Nader & Weems, 2011; in infancy, Chapters 2, 4).

Although much larger studies that include assessment of cumulative trauma/poly-victimization levels are needed, some evidence suggests that different types of trauma and different age at exposure correspond to distinct anomalies in HPA axis functioning. A study of 9–16-year-olds found high exposure to non-intentional traumas was linked to intact diurnal regulation but elevated cortisol at bedtime; physical abuse was associated with faster reactivity to acute stress; and emotional abuse was linked to delayed recovery of cortisol following acute stress (N = 138, Kuhlman, Geiss, Vargas, & Lopez-Duran, 2015). For children ages 9–12, mother's distress after divorce has been related to blunted cortisol in young adulthood, although, for adolescents, it marginally predicted blunted cortisol in young adulthood (Mahrer et al., 2014; Chapter 6—blunted cortisol).

Childhood trauma's effects on circadian cortisol regulation may vary depending on age of exposure and gender (Kuhlman, Vargas, Geiss, & Lopez-Duran, 2016). As discussed in Chapter 6, cortisol levels are generally high in a.m., decrease over the day, and are generally low at bedtime. For a small sample of 9–16-year-olds (N = 97), when first traumatic exposure was during infancy, exposure related to slower downregulation of cortisol following acute stress (vs later in childhood). That is, exposure to a first traumatic event during infancy may impair the negative feedback of the HPA axis, potentially contributing to sensitivity to context (reactivity, Chapter 4; Kuhlman et al., 2016). In contrast, when first trauma exposure was long after age one, males' cortisol was increasingly high upon waking, lower throughout the day, and elevated in the evening. For females, later childhood exposure to a first trauma was related to higher circulating cortisol throughout the day (compared to early exposure).

Catechol-O-methyltransferase (COMT)

COMT is involved in the inactivation of catecholamines (dopamine, epinephrine, and norepinephrine; Castro-Vale et al., 2016) and in the modulation of functional connectivity between brain regions during information processing and task performance (see Tunbridge, Farrell, Harrison, &

Mackay, 2013). It has been studied in relation to executive functions (cognitive functioning) and to emotional and reward processing. COMT has been related to positive affect, problem behaviors, and anxiety disorders in children (Niarchou et al., 2014; Posner et al., 2016; van Rooij et al., 2016; Table A4.1). COMT high activity has indirectly associated with higher risk of psychotic episodes (PEs) via impaired processing speed, IQ, and attention (ages 8–11, Niarchou et al., 2014; see psychotic-like symptoms, to follow). Childhood PEs have been related to adult psychosis.

Childhood trauma experiences have interacted with a COMT genotype to affect inhibition-related hippocampal activation (van Rooij et al., 2016). Hippocampal recruitment during inhibition may improve a person's ability to use contextual information to guide behavior, enhancing resilience. For women methionine (Met) allele carriers, higher levels of childhood trauma were associated with decreased hippocampal activation, whereas for Val/Val carriers, childhood trauma was related to increased hippocampal activation (inhibition-related activation; N = 73; van Rooij et al., 2016). Hippocampal activation correlated negatively with PTSD and depressive symptoms and positively with trait resilience.

Carriers of the Met allele have shown lower enzymatic activity in contrast to the high-activity valine allele (Val; see Niarchou et al., 2014). Both alleles appear to relate to positive and to negative outcomes, likely influenced by other variables. The Val allele has been linked to emotional resiliency (van Rooij et al., 2016), to higher dispositional anger and impulsive anger (with sexual abuse; Perroud et al., 2010), to increasing levels of dissociation associated with increasing levels of childhood trauma, and to increased dopamine in the PFC (Perroud et al., 2010). The latter has been related to EF deficits (see De Bellis & Zisk, 2014). COMT has been significantly associated with prefrontal neural activity, and Met allele carriers have had significantly better EFs (see Tunbridge et al., 2013). At age 7, IQ scores of children with the Met/Met genotype were, on average, four points higher than with Val/Val homozygotes (Thompson et al., 2011). For adults, the Met allele has been associated with better cognitive performance and, for children, with better attention as well as with increased risk of PTSD and of depression after stress or trauma, and with increased risk of conduct problems and ADHD (see De Bellis & Zisk, 2014; Palmason et al., 2010).

Oxytocin/Arginine Vasopressin (OT-AVP)

For children assessed in preschool and middle childhood, as a whole, findings suggested that growing up in a continuous war zone increased the likelihood of an Axis-I psychiatric disorder by middle childhood (Feldman, 2015). The interaction of OT-AVP and maternal sensitivity buffered against emergence of psychopathology (Feldman, 2015). With exposure to repeated missile attacks, preschoolers with or without PTSD had low, flat cortisol levels and sAA levels (very high, although nonresponsive cortisol and sAA; N = 232; Feldman, 2015), suggesting that chronic early stress reduces stress response variability and reactivity to momentary stressors. Mother's ability to provide sensitive containment of a child's fears (assessed during free-play and child reenactments) and greater support networks predicted no PTSD. Maternal psychopathology—e.g., anxiety, depression, and PTSD symptoms—predicted child PTSD (Feldman, 2015). In middle childhood, gene variations on the OT-AVP pathway appeared to act as stress buffers—i.e., better functionality on the OT-AVP neuropathway attenuated school-age children's avoidance symptomatology (a central predictor of PTSD chronicity).

Trauma and Developmental Skills/Domains

As will be discussed, trauma may disrupt development in this age group in a variety of ways. Although some gender differences have been discussed in this age group (Chapter 11) and some studies show that girls have more symptoms than boys, findings for trauma and gender have been mixed. Gender differences in reactions or outcomes have sometimes disappeared when important additional variables were included in the analyses—e.g., language skills and externalizing (Pickles et al., 2016); trauma and exposure levels (see Nader, 2008). However, as discussed in Chapter 4, girls may perceive experiences as more threatening than boys, and post-pubertal hormonal differences may relate to elevations as well (Young & Altemus, 2004; Chapter 15). Studies of adults have shown that sex hormones (testosterone, estrogen, and progesterone) have a modulatory role for HPA and SNS reactivity—i.e., controlling for sex hormones has diminished the differential pattern of cortisol reactivity suggesting a need to control for sex hormone fluctuations when examining cortisol and alpha-amylase reactivity to stress (for assessed groups: men, women in luteal phase, women on the pill, Barel et al., 2018). Trauma's effects on developing skills are discussed here. Although trauma's effects on social skills/issues are discussed throughout this chapter, it is not a separate topic. Maltreated youth with fewer internalizing or externalizing symptoms have exhibited better skills at negotiating novel relationships than those with more symptoms (Burack et al., 2006). Although they seem to overestimate their own social competence and self-worth (Kim & Cicchetti, 2003), child care workers and teachers have described maltreated primary school-children as lacking social competence and positive self-esteem (Burack et al., 2006).

Body Regulation

During middle childhood, stresses in the attachment system, traumas, and other factors may disrupt aspects of physical regulation (e.g., pain, sleep). For example, children ages 9–17 with at-risk attachment patterns/strategies, high levels of earlier illness and/or injury, and high rates of unresolved loss and trauma were more likely to have chronic pain than other children (N = 96, Ratnamohan & Kozlowska, 2017). Trauma may disturb sleep as well. Sleep is important to children's physical growth, behavior, cognitive functioning (e.g., attention and learning), and emotional development (Zhang et al., 2013). Sleep disturbances have been associated with a number of disorders—e.g., PTS, neurodevelopmental (e.g., autism), psychotic, depressive, anxiety disorders (see Gregory & Sadeh, 2016). Children with ADHD have shown sleep disturbances in some but not all studies. Some evidence suggests that sleep disturbance may increase the likelihood of ADHD. Sleep disturbances may be an important indicator of depression severity and suicidal thoughts. Nightmares have been an independent predictor of suicidality for children in some studies (see Gregory & Sadeh, 2016). In an assessment of contributing factors to nightmares in children ages 6–11, anxiety, trauma history, dissociation, and baseline vagal tone accounted for 39% of variance in nightmare distress (N = 60; little effect of parent processing of emotions; Secrist, Dalenberg, & Gevirtz, 2018). Prediction was not entirely related to overlap in the variables.

Executive Functions (EFs) and Trauma

Childhood trauma has been linked to EF deficits. For example, number of maltreatment types has been related to reduced cognitive flexibility (through adolescence; Spann et al., 2012). Peer rejection or victimization related to lower EFs at least to adolescence, whereas better EFs reduced likelihood of peer problems in middle childhood only (Holmes, Kim-Spoon, & Deater-Deckard, 2016). Children who had ever been institutionalized recruited more neural P2 activation (Glossary; go no-go task), showed worse performance accuracy, and had slower erroneous reaction times than never institutionalized (NI) children, suggesting inefficient attention orienting (the former: continuous institutional care [IC] or IC then foster care, Lamm et al., 2018). Children with early deprivation also had smaller N2 activation (less negative; Glossary), suggesting limited conflict processing for initiating a correct response (N = 68, ages 12–13; Lamm et al., 2018; see BEIP, Chapter 7). N2 moderated the link between IC and externalizing. For youth in residential care, EFs were assessed in the form of emotion-regulation, inhibition of pre-potent responses, attention shifting, working memory, and planning—i.e., organizing thinking and behavior in a goal-directed manner (Hodgdon et al., 2018). The number of types of caregiver and non-caregiver-perpetrated traumas was related to EF deficits, which in turn were related to PTSS.

Trauma may impair attention and result in anxiety (Sørensen, Plessen, & Lundervold, 2012). High levels of anxiousness seem to make a child repressed and less cognitively flexible (Holmes et al., 2016). In primary school children, inattention has explained youth performance on tests of *shifting* (flexibility in everyday life) and *working memory* (to some extent assesses attention). Emotional problems (excessively worried, unhappy, easily scared, and/or somatic symptoms) also have explained performance on *shifting* tasks (Sørensen et al., 2012).

Memory

While adolescents have less difficulty resisting suggestions that interfere with accurate memory than 6–10-year-olds, 6–10-year-olds have less trouble resisting than younger children (i.e., are less suggestible, Eisen et al., 2007). Eisen and colleagues (2007) found that physically and/or sexually abused children tended to have more accurate memories than neglected children (N = 328; three age groups: 3–5, 6–10, 11–16). In this study, the 6–11-year-old children with abuse histories gave more correct answers to open-ended questions than neglected children. When working memory is impaired (e.g., disrupted by trauma), common failures may include forgetting lengthy instructions, making place-keeping errors (e.g., miss letters or words in a sentence), and failing to cope with simultaneous processing and storage demands (Alloway, 2006). Although memory for aspects of trauma may be enhanced, trauma may interfere with autobiographical memory (AM). For example, maltreated children (ages 9–12) have had reduced gray matter in brain regions linked to AM, to reinforcement-based decision-making, and to emotion regulation (medial orbitofrontal cortex, middle temporal gyrus), which are processes impaired in a number of maltreatment linked disorders (e.g., PTSD, depression; N = 38, ages 9–14; De Brito et al., 2013).

Traumas may influence a youth's earliest memories. Peltonen, Kangaslampi, Qouta, and Punamäki (2017) assessed earliest memories in Palestinian children exposed to ongoing conditions of war. About one-third of children reported a traumatic event as an earliest memory (N = 240, ages 10–12 in Gaza), compared to studies showing that one-quarter of North American children have a traumatic memory as their earliest memory. For the Palestinian children, memories were equally often positive or negative, and almost half were emotionally neutral. Authors point out that Palestinian mothers exposed to severe war trauma have shown especially high attachment to their children and may have provided an atmosphere of safety and neutrality in the children's early lives. For this group of children, PTSD and other reactions (e.g., depression) were not associated with children's earliest memories nor was war trauma exposure related to over-general memory (OGM; Glossary). Across 21 studies of children ages 7–18, a relationship between over-general memory and trauma was found as well as between OGM and depression (Hitchcock, Nixon, & Weber, 2016; more study is needed). Depression has predicted OGM.

As discussed in other chapters, narrative coherence—e.g., logical timeline, clear details—has been related to better outcomes than lack of coherence (e.g., Chapter 5—parenting; 9—autobiographical memory; 16—writing tasks), and coherence has been used as a measure of pathology persistence. Treatment has often related to improvements in narrative coherence for traumatized adults and narrative treatment methods are frequently used for traumatized youth (see Carpenter, Angus, Paivio, & Bryntwick, 2016; Hambrick, Vernberg, Greenhoot, & Hendrickson, 2018). For children ages 8–12 exposed to an EF-5 tornado (the highest severity category), coherence was positively associated with positive emotion (N = 50; Hambrick et al., 2018). However, contrary to other findings (positive emotional expression has been related to lower symptoms), when discussing, a year later, "bad" things that happened during the tornado, children whose narratives were more coherent and contained more frequent positive emotion terms were more likely to show symptoms. This may suggest that, a year after a tornado, the event had high centrality, children were over-focused on the event, positivity may have been an indicator of avoidance, or they were still actively processing the event. Psychological benefits may not occur during meaning-making but only after it has been successful (Hambrick et al., 2018). In contrast, children who more often mentioned having resolved trauma-related problems/feelings were less likely to show symptoms. This may mean that meaning-making had been achieved (Hambrick et al., 2018).

Self-Regulation

During regulation of emotional conflict, traumatized youth have shown a trauma-related deficit in automatic regulation of emotional processing and have shown greater sensitivity to emotional conflict—i.e., failed to shift brain networks like normal children and showed greater conflict-related amygdala reactivity (ages 10–17; Marusak, Martin, Etkin, & Thomason, 2015). Distress as well as traumatic stress relates to self-regulation. For example, in a prospective study of family adversity—parental hostility, family distress, and harsh disciplinary practices (from before children's births)—father's self-reported pre-natal stress, hostility, and harsh discipline in a child's preschool-age related to early elementary school bullying behavior (peer nomination; N = 1298, Netherlands Generation R study; De Vries et al., 2017). While mother-reported family distress related to bullying, father-reported family adversity (distress, hostility, and harsh discipline) related to child's bullying over and above any effects of life stress, contextual factors, other background issues, and child's externalizing. The effects of father's pre-natal stress and hostility were partially mediated by father's harsh discipline, confirming the theory that family negativity undermines parents' ability to sensitively respond to children (De Vries et al., 2017; see also Giallo et al., 2015).

Non-Suicidal Self-Injury (NSSI)

Childhood traumas (e.g., maltreatment), biological emotional vulnerabilities (e.g., impulsivity, heightened emotional sensitivity), and deficits in emotion-related competencies needed to modulate such vulnerabilities have been linked to non-suicidal self-injury (NSSI), which, e.g., may be used to reduce intense, negative affect or to avoid unwanted emotions (Thomassin, Shaffer, Madden, & Londino, 2016; see Box 12.1; Chapter 15). Emotion dysregulation also has been linked to NSSI in community and clinic populations. Social support has served as a mediator between trauma and NSSI (N = 9704 Chinese middle school students; Liu, Wan, Tao, & Hao, 2017). Controlling for psychiatric symptoms, NSSI has been linked both to being a bully and with being a victim (both genders) and independently with perceived low school safety among females, underscoring the need for safe school environments (N = 1865 Japanese eighth graders; Hamada et al., 2018). In a study of contextual variables and NSSI, females reported higher levels of external shame, self-criticism (hated self), fear of self-compassion, daily peer hassles, depressive symptoms, and NSSI than males (N = 782 Portuguese ages 12–18; Xavier, Pinto-Gouveia, & Cunha, 2016). Specifically, youth who believed they were thought of negatively by others—e.g., unvalued, undesired, and/or inferior—and who resisted compassionate feelings toward self tended to engage in NSSI. Self-hatred had both a direct and an indirect effect on NSSI via daily peer hassles and depressive symptoms. The same variables (especially shame, depression, and NSSI) were related to major risk of psychopathology in adolescence.

Self- and Other-Awareness

When qualities such as self-esteem, trust, or sense of control are diminished, other aspects of life are affected—e.g., relationships; opportunities, resilience, and/or competence; well-being; likelihood of psychopathology (Fletcher, 2003; Nader, 2008). Traumatic and other negative events may lead to diminished self-esteem—e.g., by directly devaluing a child, exposing a child to stigma, or

Box 12.1 Self-Injury

a. While in an affluent middle school, for Louisa and her seventh-grade classmates (ages 11–12), cutting had become a fad. When her mother became distressed after discovering her cutting, Louisa shrugged and said things like, "It's no big deal," "Other girls do it," "It feels good." She was clear that she had no intention of killing herself. When her mom discussed it with other mothers, they observed that it appeared to be more about a sense of belonging than anything—a way of dealing with "a real experience" and of saying, "Life is hard," or "It's not easy being a girl in this school." Nevertheless, Louisa's mother contacted more than one therapist. She was told that it was faddish at this age and that she would probably grow out of it by high school. Louisa did outgrow it by high school. Now when her mother asks her about it, she says, dismissingly, "Oh, that was what we did then. Everybody did it in middle school."

b. Janelle had always been opinionated. She argued with her peers over beliefs and opinions—e.g., often was in favor of the underdog and the less popular person. She frequently reacted negatively to her experiences and to the comments of peers. Often, peers ignored her or left her out of activities. Her parents were frequently annoyed with her. She was the second child and her mother had been very busy when she was a baby. Janelle felt like no one liked her or valued her. She brooded over being left out and over her lack of status. She felt depressed. Her mind wandered frequently. Her fantasy life was more pleasant than actual life. In her fantasies, she could be well liked or able to do something that made everyone admire her. Cutting herself was both an expression of her self-loathing and gave her some temporary relief. She did not stop her self-injury in high school.

Note:
All case examples are disguised, may be combined cases, and have had details changed to protect individuals.

decreasing opportunities to engage in esteem-enhancing activities (e.g., Haine et al., 2003). Maltreated children have reported lower levels of global self-worth than non-maltreated youth (Burack et al., 2006). Maltreated elementary school children (and adolescents) were more egocentric and more delayed in social perspective-taking than non-maltreated youth.

Emotion Awareness and Trauma

Trauma-exposed children have exhibited poor emotional self-awareness, inappropriate displays of emotion, and lack of empathy (e.g., maltreated, see Muller, Vascotto, Konanur, & Rosenkranz, 2013). Trauma or complicated trauma reactions have interfered with emotional awareness, clarity, and acceptance (e.g., alexithymia, Glossary) and have resulted in increased numbing, avoidance, or under-control of emotions (Carpenter et al., 2016). Adults with a history of child maltreatment (ages 0–11) were less accurate in emotion processing overall and in processing positive and neutral emotion-pictures than matched controls (Young & Widom, 2014). Childhood physical abuse predicted lower accuracy in neutral pictures, while child sexual abuse and neglect predicted lower accuracy in recognizing positive pictures. While MDD, GAD, and IQ predicted overall accuracy, only IQ mediated the relationship between child maltreatment and emotion processing deficits.

Poor emotion recognition/differentiation, -understanding, -expression, and -regulation may interfere with help-seeking, with enlisting helpful regulation strategies, and with psychological health. Inability to signal emotional states may interfere with receiving assistance (Muller et al.,

2013). Alexithymia (Glossary) has mediated between childhood maltreatment and later self-harm (NSSI; Paivio & McCulloch, 2004). Although physical, sexual, and emotional abuse have been directly related to NSSI, poor emotion-expressivity (but not emotion coping) is one variable that has mediated the relationship between emotional abuse and NSSI (emotional expressivity = emotion awareness + expression; N = 95, ages 10–17, Thomassin et al., 2016). A child is less likely to enlist appropriate emotion-regulation strategies when unable to clarify personal emotions or when misinterpreting others' nonverbal emotional displays (Muller et al., 2013). For maltreated children (ages 7–12), both poor emotion understanding and emotion dysregulation have significantly related to overall PTS and internalizing problems; emotion dysregulation has significantly related to externalizing. While parental mental health mediated treatment factors and decreases in PTS symptoms, increased emotion differentiation and decreased parenting stress were linked to decreased PTS symptoms (interpersonal violence, ages 6–12; Overbeek et al., 2015).

Perspective-Taking and Trauma

Trauma may diminish cognitive and emotional aspects of perspective-taking. Sexually abused (CSA) girls have had reduced cognitive and emotional understanding abilities (Ensink et al., 2017). CSA children have had significantly lower reflective functioning than comparisons as well as more dissociation, depressive symptoms, externalizing, and sexualized behavior problems (see Ensink et al., 2017). Fonagy and colleagues suggest that CSA may lead to avoidance of thinking of the thoughts of others with potentially malevolent intent as well as lead to disruptions in trust, curiosity, and openness (Ensink et al., 2017). Even when compared to same SES level youth, CSA has been related to significantly lower abilities in reflective functioning (RF) in relation to self and to others (age 7–12; Ensink et al., 2015). For children ages 7–12, both CSA and maternal RF independently contributed to child self-RF. CSA explained variance in other-directed RF. Mentalizing skill partially mediated the relationship between CSA and depression, and mentalizing and dissociation sequentially mediated the relationship between CSA and externalizing, including sexualized behaviors (Ensink et al., 2017). That is, CSA related to reduced mentalizing, which in turn related to increased internalizing and externalizing.

Following repeated earthquakes, both *active coping* strategies (problem-solving, cognitive restructuring, emotional regulation, social support) and *avoidant coping* strategies (distraction, social withdrawal, wishful thinking, resignation) were associated with greater mentalizing abilities (Glossary; Table 1.2), which in turn related to better cognitive performance (Cadamuro et al., 2015). In contrast, negative coping strategies (self-criticism, blaming others) were associated with reduced mentalizing ability and, in turn, with less positive cognitive performance.

Trauma and Stressor-Related Disorders

Children in this age group are included in DSM-5 PTSD for those over age 6. For a treatment-seeking sample of children, Mikolajewski, Scheeringa, and Weems (2017) found that more children ages 7–12 met criteria for a DSM-5 PTSD diagnosis than criteria for DSM-IV (unlike adolescents, ages 13–18; see also Chapter 13—Assessment and Diagnosis). Using DSM-5 PTSD for ages 6 and under with this age group resulted in more children meeting diagnostic criteria than for either DSM-5 or DSM-IV. Although children diagnosed with the younger age group criteria were less impaired and had lower comorbidity than those who met DSM-5 for over six criteria for the diagnosis, they were more impaired than those who did not meet criteria for a diagnosis.

TSRD designated primarily for younger children may continue in revised form. Most studies of RAD and DSED assess children who were raised in institutionalized care (ongoing or before foster placement). A British study examined children in non-institutionalized out-of-home care (N = 153 age 10–16; Kay & Green, 2013). Compared to a low-risk sample (no out-of-home or adoptive care), many youth with environmental adversity exhibited four RAD factors—*Disinhibited Indiscriminate*, *Attention Seeking*, *Superficial Relationships*, and *Unpredictability* (Kay & Green, 2013; Glossary). With or without adjusting for placement type, RAD was linked to multiple maltreatment experiences, earlier entry to non-familial care, and increased rates of psychopathology (e.g., externalizing disorders; N = 219; Kay & Green, 2013). RAD behavior was associated with severe functional impairment across adaptive and self-care domains as well as in relationships. To follow is a discussion of TSRD-related issues in middle childhood.

Factors Influencing Trauma-Related Outcomes

Two of the issues relevant to reactions—parents and betrayal traumas—are discussed here.

Influence of Parents After Traumas

Parents can help children after traumas (e.g., help to make meaning of their traumas) or may contribute to their distress—e.g., by suggesting that a child is permanently changed or vulnerable; by focusing on negative aspects of the trauma (Hiller et al., 2017). Parents' negative appraisals such as perceptions of the child's damage or continued vulnerability and/or the parent's self-blame as well as encouragement of avoidant coping (especially of places, people, and activities) have robustly predicted higher PTSS 6 months after a trauma (ages 6–13; even after controlling for initial symptoms, Hiller et al., 2017). A clear link has been documented between parental functioning and children's PT symptoms (N = 81, 8–10-year-olds, five years after war, Laor, Wolmer, & Cohen, 2001). A correlation between parent and children's symptoms has been highest in the youngest age group (age three during missile attacks, age eight at five-year follow-up; lowest correlations for age 10). Laor et al. found that, when mothers functioned well, children reported fewer arousal symptoms and were more likely to improve instead of worsen over time, than if mothers had moderate or poor functioning. For displaced children who endured multiple traumas (e.g., missile attacks, destruction of and displacement from home), adequate family cohesion was linked to better outcomes.

Impact of Betrayal Traumas

Considerable research (generally nonclinical, adolescent+) has suggested poorer outcomes for youth traumatized by a trusted or depended-on perpetrator (e.g., parent; see Kiser et al., 2014). Some recent research has provided mixed findings (Kiser et al., 2014). For a large sample of children ages 6–18 participating in clinical services (N = 2,133 with sexual or physical trauma), both parent and child report suggest that CSA by a non-caregiver showed higher PTSS, internalizing and externalizing behavior problems, depression, and dissociation compared to children victimized by a caregiver (Kiser et al., 2014). In this same sample, children otherwise physically traumatized by a non-caregiver also had higher PTSS and internalizing behavior problems. For CSA, penetration (not relationship to abuser or chronicity) has predicted dissociative and PTSD symptoms (Collin-Vézina & Hébert, 2005). For clinic-referred girls, non-caregiver perpetration has predicted higher rates of MDD, SAD, and poor general functioning (Sadowski et al., 2003). Findings also may be related to other aspects of the child-caregiver relationship—e.g., nurturing behaviors; abuse "done out of love"; lower levels of violence or invasiveness; someone was concerned about their distress and took them for treatment; underreporting of symptoms. This suggests the need for close attention to the details of an experience and to a survivor's view of the meaning of a sexual or physical trauma and their feelings toward the perpetrator (both negative and positive).

Evidence suggests onset of depression may occur years after abuse, with a surge in onset between 12–15 years or older (Teicher, Samson, Polcari, & Andersen, 2009), perhaps because of the maturity needed to understand the *wrongness* of the act (Kiser et al., 2014). Help-seeking and treatment have significantly mitigated *betrayal trauma* issues. Some variations in findings may be related to non-tested variables (Cicchetti, Handley, & Rogosch, 2015a). For example, experiencing multiple types of maltreatment and genetic variations have influenced outcomes (e.g., cortisol variations, Cicchetti, Rogosch, & Oshri, 2011; genes and recent maltreatment related to variations in c-reactive protein and internalizing, Cicchetti et al., 2015a).

PTSD and Its Related Symptoms

Two PTSD-related symptom groups—posttraumatic cognitions and dissociative symptoms—are discussed to follow.

Posttraumatic Cognitions (PTC)

Changes in mood and cognitions is among DSM-5 PTSD symptoms (D2, D3; APA, 2013). Reduction of dysfunctional posttraumatic cognitions (PTC) may be a key target for treatment. Altered cognitions may impair coping skills, increase distress, and reduce sources of support (Liu & Chen, 2015). Negative appraisals of traumas have been linked to the persistence of PTSD as well (Liu & Chen, 2015; Chapter 4—Perception). PTC have been significantly related to both internalizing and externalizing psychopathology. Although in some studies both children on waitlists and in treatment have shown some reduction of dysfunctional PTC, treatment has been related to greater changes in dysfunctional cognitions (e.g., TF-CBT, ages 7–17, Pfeiffer et al., 2017). The reduction of dysfunctional PTC mediated the link between treatment and reduced PTSS at the end of treatment. In another study, after controlling for age, gender, and trauma types, both maladaptive appraisals of the trauma and perceptions of being a fragile person in a scary world contributed uniquely to depression and to generalized anxiety symptoms (N = 285 Taiwanese ages 9 = 17, Liu & Chen, 2015). Only maladaptive appraisals had a direct longitudinal impact on chronic PTSD severity and remained weakly associated with externalizing problems (Liu & Chen, 2015).

Dissociative Symptoms

The PTSD-dissociative subtype is described in Chapter 2. Dissociation has been linked both to trauma and to nightmares in adults and children (Secrist et al., 2018). For school-age girls, sexual abuse (CSA) has been associated with a four-fold increase in odds of showing clinical levels of PTSD and with an eight-fold increase in odds of clinical-level dissociation (see Hébert, Langevin, & Daigneault, 2016). Peer victimization combined with CSA (as is common: 60% of CSA group) has increased odds of clinical-level dissociation by three-fold (N = 158; Hébert et al., 2016). PTSD has been described as a failure of traumatic memory consolidation resulting in involuntary intrusions linked to fear (van Marle, 2015; Appendix). Hence, dissociation posing increased risk for PTS symptoms may be because it hinders proper integration of trauma-related memories into existing cognitive schemas (see Ross & Kearney, 2017; Chapter 2). Ross and Kearney found that above average dissociative symptoms (derealization/depersonalization) were related to avoidance and to hyperarousal (N = 400 maltreated ages 7–18). Dissociation may become a maladaptive long-term coping strategy.

Specific Posttrauma Symptoms

Posttrauma symptoms may disrupt development and psychological health in more than one way. Non-trauma adversity as well as traumas have been associated with negative outcomes. For example, by age 11, 21% of Danish children had experienced parental break-up (N = 44,509; Dissing et al., 2017; the percentage is likely greater in the US). Children with a parental break-up, whether with shared parenting, step-parents, or single parents, showed higher risk of distress than intact families, regardless of age at break-up. Those with single parents showed the highest distress. To follow are discussions of internalizing, bereavement, dreams, shame, and guilt for this age group.

Anxiety and Depression

In a study of girls, Marshall (2016) found that, compared to other developmental periods, trauma during puberty (a period of HPA maturation) was associated with significantly more risk for girls' anxiety disorders (primarily social phobia, past-year), whereas trauma during pre-puberty conferred significantly higher risk for past-year depressive disorder (predicted 50.47% of variance; N = 2899 girls). Recent disaster, witnessing violence at home, or death of a loved one conferred risk of PTSD. For 8–10-year-olds, anhedonia was a marker of depression severity (Glossary; Wesselhoeft et al., 2016). Children with subclinical depression (SD) and MDD had more stressful life events, functional impairment, and family difficulties than non-depressed (e.g., marital problems, poor parental mental health, unemployment, and financial problems). Anhedonia, irritability, and worthlessness/guilt were more frequent in MDD than SD. Anxiety disorders and oppositional/conduct disorders were equally frequent comorbid conditions.

Middle childhood traumas may increase risk and reduce protection. In a study of anxiety, depression, and IQ, early maltreatment (age 0–4) predicted IQ (age six), which in turn predicted adolescent (age 14) anxiety symptoms (IQ not related to depression symptoms; N = 1354; Harpur, Polek, & van Harmelen, 2015). Age 14 depression symptoms were directly predicted by late childhood and cumulative maltreatment experiences, while anxiety symptoms were predicted indirectly by low family SES and the presence or absence of a biological mother at age 0–4 (through IQ age six). The protective effects of IQ were weaker when maltreatment was during ages 6–8 or 10–12. Trauma during any developmental period (especially pre- or post-puberty grade school) significantly increased risk of PTSD. Studies have shown school-age maltreatment is linked to adult PTSD and social anxiety disorder (e.g., abuse beginning age six or seven thru 9.75–13; Bishop, Rosentein, Bakelaar, & Seedat, 2014). Adults with social anxiety disorder have had lower self-esteem and self-efficacy and have had higher self-criticism and dependency (Iancu, Bodner, & Ben-Zion, 2015). Adult PTSD studies have demonstrated that after traumas, adults have heightened fear reactions, low ability to control fear, and impaired ability to discriminate between danger and safety signals (see Gamwell et al., 2015).

Fear Conditioning

Anxiety disorders have been associated with larger amygdala volume (e.g., fear processing) in children and adolescents, especially with early adverse experiences (Gamwell et al., 2015). Fear responses appear to be different between the genders, which may be hormone-related. For 8–13-year-olds exposed to traumas, using skin conductance (changes in sweat activity), startle reactions, and self- and parent reports of symptoms, girls showed less discrimination between danger and safety signals during a conditioning study compared to age-matched males (N = 105; Gamwell et al., 2015). Based on physiological measures, child-reported symptoms (not parent) were related to symptom severity. For boys, intrusive symptoms predicted fear responses, even after controlling for trauma exposure. For girls, conditioned fear to a danger cue predicted self-blame/guilt and fear of repeated trauma (guilt, fear of repeat, and avoidance were related). Unlike adults, fear reactions were associated with intrusive and avoidance symptoms rather than arousal symptoms. Skin conductance (not startle response) was related to PTSD (Gamwell et al., 2015).

Bereavement

Grieving may be adaptive or maladaptive (Nader & Layne, 2009). Normal bereavement may include symptoms such as shock, sadness, anger, guilt, anxiety, regrets, intrusive thoughts or images of the deceased or of the death, yearning for the deceased, depersonalization, feeling overwhelmed, fear, and loneliness (Bonanno, Boerner, & Wortman, 2008; Nader, 2012b; Nader & Salloum, 2011). Intensity, course, and duration of grieving are highly variable (Pearlman et al., 2014). Symptoms may seem ever-present or may occur intermittently. Painful feelings and memories may intermingle with positive memories. Although progress may be uneven and difficult, for most people, symptoms gradually subside. Progress is often evident by 6 months after a loss. When grief has disrupted normal functioning, activities, and relationships after loss, adaptive grief is characterized by the increasingly restored capacity to engage in meaningful relationships and activities. Most people improve with the support of friends and family or the help of bereavement support groups. In Complicated Grief, symptoms persist beyond six months.

Although grieving is normal following the death of a loved one, youth vary greatly in their responses to a death (Pearlman, Schwalbe, & Cloitre, 2010). For example, they differ in the timing, intensity, and nature of aspects of grief (Nader, 2008) and/or in their styles of grieving (Doughty, 2009; Martin & Doka, 2000; Nader & Salloum, 2011). Bereaved children who achieve high competence levels and low problem levels are considered resilient (Sandler et al., 2008). While children ages 6–8 may engage in magical thinking about the causes of death (e.g., wishing someone would go away can kill them), in general, they recognize that death is final and irreversible and that the deceased is no longer functional (Nader & Salloum, 2011). Even though loss of pets, death of grandparents, media exposure, and children's games and stories expose children to death (e.g., *ring around the rosies*; Hansel & Gretel; Corr, 2008), in this age range, they often do not fully believe that death is universal or could happen to them. Children 6–8 may experience anger at someone they think could have saved the deceased and may have anxiety, depression, somatic complaints, fears about safety or deaths of other loved ones, fear of isolation, and may feel a loss of control.

In addition to understanding that death is final, irreversible, and a natural part of life, children ages 8–12 have increased understanding of the cause of death and of what life may be like without the deceased (see Nader & Salloum, 2011). This age group also may intellectualize death, have morbid curiosity or want to understand the details of the death, be interested in religious and cultural death-related traditions, feel guilty, have difficulty identifying and dealing with feelings, and/or fear dying. At this age, children may be aware that they are different from some or most other children. Whether grief is adaptive or maladaptive, children may revisit and need to reprocess aspects of grief and of trauma as they grow older, gain knowledge and understanding, and have additional experiences, bringing back aspects of the event/grief. Children may feel different or stigmatized by a loss (Worden, 2009; stigma for traumatic deaths, Feigelman, Gorman, & Jordan, 2009). For example, 20% of studied children were taunted about the deceased, were avoided, and/or were excluded by peers (N = 35, ages 6–15; Cain & LaFreniere, 2015).

Normal grieving may be complicated by a number of factors (complicated grief, CG; Table 12.1; see Nader & Fletcher, 2014; Pearlman et al., 2010). Consequently, grief may be disrupted, prolonged, and/or intensified. After traumas, grief symptoms may become intertwined with other symptoms or trauma symptoms may interfere with adaptive grieving—e.g., grief and trauma dreaming or grief and trauma play (Nader, 1997; Nader & Salloum, 2011); intrusive trauma thoughts or images may interfere with reminiscing (Nader, 1997; Cohen, Mannarino, & Deblinger, 2006a; Nader & Layne, 2009). While, with adequate parenting, normal grief is not linked to psychopathology, TG and CG have been linked to serious psychiatric conditions (Allen, Oseni, & Allen, 2012; Brown & Goodman, 2005; Nader, 2008; Chapters 4, 13)—e.g., higher PTSD/PTS, depression, and functional impairment (Boelen & Spuij, 2013; Cohen et al., 2006a; Cohen Mannarino,

Table 12.1 Some of the Issues that May Complicate Grieving for Children (Alone or in Combination)

Complicators	Risk Factor Examples
Avoidance and poor integration	• poor elaboration and integration of the loss into autobiographical knowledge, negative beliefs and misinterpretations of grief reactions, and/or anxious and depressive avoidance strategies (Boelen, van den Hout, & van den Bout, 2006; Gray et al., 2004; Prigerson et al., 2009) • behavioral or cognitive avoidance; dissociation (Boelen et al., 2006; Boelen, 2015; Nader, 2012b; Nader & Salloum, 2011)
Anxiety	• may complicate grieving and influence treatment needs (Pearlman et al., 2010) • history of mental health problems, such as anxiety, is related to difficulties (Bonanno, 2004; Bonanno et al., 2008; Feigelman et al., 2009)
Behavior problems	• may complicate grieving and influence treatment (e.g., Cohen et al., 2006a, 2006b; Pearlman et al., 2010)
Poor coping	• coping that increases avoidance • methods that exacerbate symptoms (e.g., serve as traumatic reminders) (Brown & Goodman, 2005) • negative coping (Brent et al., 2009; Melhem, Walker, Moritz, & Brent, 2008) • blaming others (Sandler et al., 2008)
Depression	• may complicate grieving and influence treatment needs (e.g., Bonanno et al., 2008; Pearlman et al., 2010; Zisook et al., 2010) • history of mental health problems, such as depression, is related to difficulties (Bonanno, 2004; Bonanno et al., 2008; Feigelman et al., 2009)
Discovery	• posthumous disillusionment—discovering something about deceased after death (Stalfa, 2010)
Loss of faith	• a crisis of faith following loss that includes erosion of mourner's relationship to God and/or the religious community (Neimeyer & Burke, 2017) • negative religious coping e.g., spiritual discontent; reappraisals of God as punishing or of God's power; reappraisals of demons/the devil) (Barlé, Wortman, & Latack, 2015; Burke & Neimeyer, 2014)
Relationship with deceased	• poor relationship with deceased and surviving parent unavailable (see Nader & Salloum, 2011) • argument or negative encounter with deceased before the death (Nader, 1997) • loss of a parent or sibling (Cerel et al., 2006; Howell et al., 2016) • interdependence (Bonanno et al., 2008) • ambivalence (Bonanno et al., 2008)
Faulty support system	• unavailable surviving parent(s) or a succession of caretakers (Sandler et al., 2008) • low positive or high negative social support (Burke et al., 2010; Kristensen et al., 2010)

Complicators	Risk Factor Examples
Nature of death	• traumatic (e.g., Cohen et al., 2002, 2006; Melhem, Moritz, Walker, Shear, & Brent, 2007; Nader, 1997; Nader & Salloum, 2011; Pearlman et al., 2010) • posttrauma stigmatization, strain, or negative thinking (Boelen, 2015; Dillen et al., 2009; Feigelman et al., 2009) • multiple losses (deaths, personal items, locations, aspects of self and/or self–image) • parent's prolonged illness before death (Kaplow et al., 2014)
Personal history	• previous loss and/or trauma (e.g., Cerel et al., 2006) • previous mood disorder (e.g., Shear et al., 2011) • insecure attachment style (adults, Cohen & Katz, 2015)
Self-related cognitions	• negative cognitions about life, self, or the future (e.g., sense of personal worthlessness, meaninglessness of life) (Boelen et al., 2006) • misconceptions about likely reactions (pain will be unbearable; will lose control) (Boelen et al. 2006) • trying to grieve in a socially acceptable way instead of a personally meaningful way (Doughty, 2009; Martin & Doka, 2000)
Stress	• peritraumatic stress (Boelen, 2015) • environmental stress following the death (Sandler et al., 2008; Shear et al., 2011) • faulty support system

& Staron, 2006b), anxiety and depression (Dillen et al., 2008, 2009; Nader & Salloum, 2011), prolonged grief (PG, Prigerson et al., 2009).

Although findings are sometimes mixed, a number of risk factors are associated with increased complicated grief reactions (Table 12.1; Chapter 13; Box 3.1). For example, evidence suggests that individuals exposed to violent loss experienced more severe PG and PTSD compared to individuals confronted with illness (subsample, ages 7–17 = 265, Boelen, 2015). The latter had greater reactions when death was sudden and unexpected. Intensity of peri-traumatic emotions (fear, helplessness, horror, and dissociative experiences, Boelen, 2015) has been significantly related to both PG and PTSD severity (all four, helplessness and dissociation independently, Boelen, 2015; Boelen et al., 2012). Parenting has influenced outcomes (Morris et al., 2016; Table 12.1).

Parental Death

Studies have shown links between loss of a parent in childhood and immediate and later psychopathology (e.g., depression, Cerel et al., 2006; anxiety, Howell et al., 2016; suicidality, self-inflicted injury or poisoning, Rostilla et al., 2016). Impairments were greater for complex bereavement (i.e., grief with additional stressors) and after parental suicides (Brent et al., 2009). For ages 7–18, PG symptoms in parentally bereaved children have correlated with suicidality and functional impairment (Melhem et al., 2007). Cerel et al. (2006) found parentally bereaved children were more impaired than controls, especially when a surviving parent was depressed and financially struggling. They were less impaired than clinically depressed children (N = 360, ages 6–17, followed at two-year intervals after a death).

Parentally bereaved youth have had more psychopathology than controls—e.g., 21 months after, more MDD after accidents, more alcohol or substance abuse after parental suicide (N = 211, offspring ages 7–25, Brent et al., 2009). For low-risk 7–13-year-olds (Howell et al., 2016; parent illness/cancer, N = 31, vs parental death, N = 32), youth contending with parental illness had lower subclinical PTSS levels than children whose parent had died. Both groups showed similar subclinical levels of anxiety and depression. For both groups, expressive coping (providing clear and accurate representations of their emotional states to others) was associated with lower levels of each assessed outcome (PTSS, anxiety, and depression). For bereaved children, a surviving parent's positive parental reinforcement of children's positive behaviors and provision of supportive communications were inversely related to PTSS.

After the loss of a parent, a number of risk and protective factors may influence response (Sandler et al., 2008; Tables 12.1, 12.2). For example, loss of a mother, complicated grief, blaming others, low self-esteem, the surviving parent's impairment, stressful life events, previous depression or other disorder, and negative coping have been associated with symptoms in the first two years after a death (e.g., Brent et al., 2009; Melhem, Walker, Moritz, & Brent, 2008). Studies have shown that a consistent routine and positive parent–children relationship (e.g., warmth, discipline, child-centered parenting) have promoted a surviving parent's ability to assist their children's grieving (i.e., is protective, Howell et al., 2016; Kaplow, Howell, & Layne, 2014; Sandler et al., 2008; Table 12.2). A child's ability to adapt to the environmental disruption and restructuring that follows a parental death influences how much a death influences functioning (Sandler et al., 2008). In addition, a child's higher coping efficacy, self-esteem, and adaptive locus of control serve as protective factors (see Nader, 2008; Sandler et al., 2008). Multiple risk factors—e.g., stressful environments after the death; a surviving parent with high stress levels or mental health problems; unavailable parent; family health problems; and/or traumatic deaths—often indicate the need for treatment. A combination of thwarted belongingness, conflict with parents, feeling unimportant, and the perception of being burdensome to family have been risk

Table 12.2 Grief Protective Factors

Relationship to Deceased

- good relationship with the deceased

Ongoing Parenting and Home Environment

- a consistent routine
- child-centered parenting
- positive parent–children relationship (e.g., warmth, discipline, child-centered parenting)
- presence of a sibling or a single ongoing caretaker (especially one known or introduced by deceased beforehand)
- good relationship with a surviving parent
- open communication about the deceased and the death

Other Environmental Factors

- good support system(s)
- absence of stigma

Child Factors

- ability to adapt to the disruption and restructuring of the environment
- higher coping efficacy
- resilience factors: e.g., high self-esteem, adaptive locus of control
- coping flexibility
- good mental health (absence of psychopathology)
- lower avoidance
- positive religious coping—e.g., secure relationship with God; belief that s/he can find meaning in life; spiritual connectedness to others

References: Boelen et al., 2006; Bonanno et al., 2011; Davies, 2011; Feigelman et al., 2009; Howell et al., 2016; Kaplow et al., 2014; Nader, 2008; see Nader & Salloum, 2011; Sandler et al., 2008.

factors for suicidal behaviors (N = 482, ages 11–15, Holland, Vivolo-Kantor, Logan, & Leemis, 2017). For bereaved families (N = 58, ages 7–13), thwarted belongingness was higher for children bereaved by suicide of a parent than those bereaved after accidents, sudden natural death, or anticipated illness-related death (Roley-Roberts et al., in press). Children's lower thwarted belongingness was predicted by a surviving parent's positive reinterpretation and growth (e.g., learning from experience) and by the parent's use of behavioral disengagement (reduced problem-solving efforts; "... can't deal with it, ... quit trying"). The latter seemingly counter-intuitive finding may indicate less time and attention focused on death—i.e., less self-absorbed grief—and more time on children (Roley-Roberts et al., in press).

DSM-5 Persistent Complex Bereavement Disorder (PCBD)

PCBD is among *Other Trauma- and Stressor-Related Disorders* in DSM-5 (*Conditions for Further Study*). Although it includes a few clarifications for children, PCBD appears to be based on adult reactions and may not fully capture childhood CG, PG, or TG. For example, children under age 6 generally do not fully recognize the permanence or universality of death or that a dead person is non-functional and cannot return (PCBD C-1—difficulty accepting the death). For young school-age children, self-blame may be common. It will be important to recognize when self-blame cannot be relinquished and becomes maladaptive (PCBD C-5). The *traumatic bereavement* specifier only includes homicide or suicide, which is likely to be too restrictive for children (e.g., loss of a parent has ongoing impact). For all ages, it is important to discover when avoidance is therapeutic or is interfering with recovery. Studies are needed. It is hoped that studies will include a broader range of symptoms and variables than those indicated in DSM-5 PCBD in order to discover the full, age-related range of persistent grief symptoms.

Dreams

Between ages 11 and 12, dreaming begins to approximate that of adulthood, and children are able to construct dream narratives (see Nader, 2008; Box 6.2). Following traumas, youth may have recurrent distressing dreams that have content related to the trauma or traumatic emotions (APA, 2013). Children may also have comforting or normal dreams following exposure. Qouta et al. (2016) examined the dreams of war-exposed Palestinian youth (ages 10–13) and found three kinds of dreams—Unpleasant, Fragmented, and Lonely Dreams (Unpleasant); Practical, Narrative, and Social Dreams (Practical); and Pleasant, Active, and Symbolic Dreams (Pleasant). Youth who had Practical Dreams had no loss of well-being following war, while children who had Unpleasant dream scenes showed a decrease in psychosocial well-being. Practical dreams were associated with good resources, beneficial emotions, good self-esteem, and social affiliation. Pleasant dreams were associated with decreased PTSS.

Psychotic-Like Symptoms

Childhood adversity has been associated with psychotic experiences (PEs) and with their persistence and/or clinical relevance (Trotta, Murray, & Fisher, 2015). Adults with psychoses report a high level of victimizing experiences in childhood (e.g., bullying; physical abuse; sexual abuse; see Nader & Fletcher, 2014). Children reporting psychotic-like symptoms or experiences are at increased risk of developing psychosis in adulthood. Cognitive deficits and anxiety disorders have often preceded psychotic disorders and are linked to higher risk of PEs (see Niarchou et al., 2014). However, as noted, Niarchou et al. (2014) found a specific COMT gene indirectly associated with PEs through impaired processing speed, IQ, and attention (N = 6784, 8–12-year-olds). A complex developmental pathway may exist between genes and psychotic experiences.

Guilt and Trauma

> If you look guilty or scared, it makes me feel angry and like I want to punish you.
>
> *(Anonymous Adolescent)*

Guilt has been among symptoms of depression (feelings of worthlessness or inappropriate guilt, APA, 2013). Posttraumatic guilt has been associated with increased posttrauma symptoms for some. In the first 3 months after a school shooting, guilt—for being unable to help others, for being safe when others were harmed, or for doing things that endangered others—was infrequently reported but was associated with increased severity of PTS reactions (elementary school, Pynoos et al., 1987). One year after the school shooting, children with lower levels of exposure to the shooting who reported guilt showed increased PTSD symptoms (Nader et al., 1990). Those who had been on the playground (where the shooter was firing at children) had higher levels of symptoms (somatic complaints, fear, avoidance) with or without guilt. Guilt was associated with increased grief scores both for children on the playground and those who were at home that day. Similarly, for children ages 5–16 exposed to interpersonal violence (e.g., war, sexual abuse), guilt was associated with increased severity of PTSD (as were changed attachment and derealization, Kletter, Weems, & Carrion, 2009).

Shame and Trauma

Childhood traumas, such as violence or abuse exposures and peer victimization, may lead to maladaptive self-attributional styles and to poor body image, and there can be a cyclical relationship between victimization, bodily shame, and internalizing problems (Irwin, Li, Craig, & Hollenstein, 2016). For older sexually abused children (adjudicated, ages 8–15), higher shame levels 1 year after abuse (but not a few weeks after disclosure) have persisted and were unrelated to abuse characteristics or emotional support (Feiring & Taska, 2005). Higher shame was also related to more PTSD symptoms (Feiring & Taska, 2005; Feiring, Taska, & Chen, 2002). Although bullying has had a direct and unique effect on multiple negative outcomes—e.g., barriers to social support even as adults, poor functioning, psychological distress—when shame was factored into the analysis for previously bullied adults, the effects became insignificant (N = 681; ages 19–37; Strom et al., 2018; Chapter 2). That is, when childhood physical violence, sexual abuse, and sociodemographic factors were controlled, shame mediated very large percentages of the associations between bullying victimization and distress, bully-victimization and impaired functioning, and bully-victimization and social support barriers. Similarly, for 10–13-year-olds (N = 396), shame played a mediating role between peer victimization and mental health difficulties (Irwin et al., 2016). Characterological shame—about one's personal habits, manner with others, the sort of person one is, or personal ability—was associated with depression and social anxiety. Greater bodily shame was related to greater social anxiety for girls (not boys). Behavioral shame (about failure or wrong behavior) may be more akin to guilt than shame. In this study's primary model (Irwin et al., 2016), behavioral shame mediated the relationship between peer victimization and higher levels of externalizing problems for boys (not girls)—externalizing preceded shame and predicted increased victimization. Shame is likely to impede emotional processing (Feiring & Taska, 2005).

Conclusions

Trauma and other stressors—e.g., divorce, troubled attachment, poverty—may significantly disrupt developmental skills for school-age children. In this age period, trauma may affect specific brain regions and related skills more profoundly than at other times—e.g., amygdala, PFC. In contrast to insecure or disorganized attachments and harsh parenting, positive parenting and secure caregiver–child attachments may buffer the impact of stressors and may assist posttrauma or post-loss stress recovery. Particular personality traits or combinations of traits shape reactions and responses to helping individuals, variably. For example, higher effortful control may reduce the likelihood of externalizing for uninhibited children and increase the likelihood of internalizing for inhibited children. Multiple factors or experiences may complicate the grieving process. Death of a parent and unexpected deaths are among losses that are related to complicated bereavement. Parenting is important to loss reactions and recovery. Feeling burdensome or a lack of belonging have been related to increased grief reactions and to posttrauma suicidal risk. A number of variables are related to levels of posttrauma or post-loss problems and symptoms. For example, protective genetics, other resilience factors, and positive parenting have been linked to reduced psychopathology, whereas altered HPA functioning, problematic attachments and/or parenting, and reduced levels of support have been linked to increased risk.

13 Interventions for Children Ages 6–12

Following trauma exposures or significant adversity, interventions may be needed even without a full diagnosis of PTSD or other disorder. Functioning may be impaired and development disrupted. A number of methods and adjunct methods have been used successfully to assist school-age children. Some interventions used in middle childhood are also used for older youth (Chapter 16). Effective methods are adaptable and flexible, honor cultural differences, include efforts toward a child's self-efficacy, and have caregiver involvement (Cohen et al., 2006a; Kerig et al., 2010; Nader, Dubrow, & Stamm, 1999). Modifications are sometimes necessary in common methods, when they are used for specific problems (e.g., types of anxiety, behavior problems). Children's responses to such methods are influenced by child temperament (see Chapter 16), functioning age, family functioning, social support, and coping efficacy as well as a program's ability to adapt to and address such issues (Pearlman, Schwalbe, & Cloitre, 2010; Nader, 2008; Box 13.1).

Intrinsic brain connectivity networks (central executive, salience, and default mode networks; Chapter 16) are crucial to higher cognitive functioning and can be affected by psychopathology such as PTSD (Lanius et al., 2015). Neuroscientifically informed treatment interventions will be important to ongoing treatment efforts. Some methods that aim to assist neurological repair are now available. Pharmaceutical interventions have been discussed for this age group (e.g., D-cycloserine, a partial N-methyl-d-aspartic acid agonist; see Chapter 9). Across 22 trauma studies, no pharmaceutical treatments demonstrated effectiveness for youth (Forman-Hoffman et al., 2013). Additionally, concerns persist related to possible long-term effects of medications in childhood.

Posttrauma Treatment Methods

Problems have occurred for traumatized individuals when interviews that review a traumatic experience have been ill-timed or conducted by an untrained and/or inexperienced interviewer (Hobfoll et al., 2007; Nader, 2012a; Chapter 4). Well-timed, effective interviews can assist the processing of trauma and grief-related thoughts and emotions, help provide a new view of an experience and its aspects, and contribute to repairing the self-concept (Nader, 1997; Ochberg, 2002; Boxes 13.1, 13.2). At the end of an evaluation or session, a child may need assistance to resolve distress or other issues that arose during the interview (see Nader, 2008), may feel better after talking to a trained, supportive person, and/or may need to reorient attention (e.g., to present, external world). As noted, youth may experience new symptoms and need to process aspects of grief as they grow older. After a brief discussion of assessment and diagnosis, to follow are a number

Box 13.1 War-Tortured Boy

Abdul, age 10 (appeared younger; slightly overweight), was captured by enemy soldiers and imprisoned in the soldiers' country. Before they were captured, his family endured the war inside their home. They were afraid of the bombs and gunfire they could hear; afraid soldiers would come and kill or mutilate them like they had done to others ...; were worried about what was in the water and were afraid of running out of food. The electricity was off.... Eventually, soldiers broke the door and entered. Abdul was adamant that he and his brother had killed an enemy soldier with a knife before they came for them, so it was his fault they were captured (his family said that this had not actually happened, but the tortures and imprisonment were real). On the way to enemy prison, he saw numerous dead, burned, and mutilated bodies. Some bodies had their eyes open. In the prison, soldiers burned Abdul and scratched his hand. Abdul pulled up his sleeves to show large round burns on his arms. Early in treatment, he said he couldn't talk about being burned, because it would scare him too much. While incarcerated, soldiers forced him, his brother, and his mother to watch while they tortured his father daily until he died. They were not always fed and were hungry and terrified. They weren't released until the Americans came. They had to walk all the way home. After he returned home, he saw a boy on TV whose leg had been blown off by a mine. At the beginning of treatment, when asked to draw an initial drawing of anything he wanted to, he drew the boy with the blown-off leg.

Abdul was both afraid of telling his story and needed to tell his story. He was assisted to increase his coping repertoire before the treatment phase of intervention. During the treatment phase, he was allowed to have a good friend outside of the door, which remained very slightly ajar. He was told that he could go to his friend, if he needed to. He became very agitated on several occasions while describing war-related upsetting experiences—there were many. Sometimes when upset, he would recite, "God is generous." It also seemed to help him to recite a list or a statement about what the enemy soldiers had done to his country and his people (e.g., he would stop to say how "they stole from us"; "they burned our land"; "they took all of our food and animals" ...). Sometimes, he would say he had done very bad things to many enemy soldiers with a knife (these seemed to be traumatically charged desires rather than actual occurrences). When he described his experiences during the incarceration, he became very agitated and upset. He would leave the room briefly to see his friend who waited in the hallway. He would touch the tops of his friend's hands with his own hands and look into his friend's eyes. He took deep breaths then returned to the therapy room to tell his story.

Note:
All case examples are disguised, may be combined cases, and have had details changed to protect individuals.

of proven trauma-focused methods (Emotion-Focused therapy is described under Separation and Other Anxiety; see Chapter 10).

Assessment and Diagnosis

DSM-5 PTSD (20 symptoms, five symptom criteria) differs from proposed ICD-11 PTSD (six symptoms, three symptom criteria; see La Greca, Danzi, & Chan, 2017), and both differ from DSM-IV PTSD (17 symptoms, three symptom criteria; APA, 2013). Criteria for both DSM-5 and proposed ICD-11 PTSD appear to fit elementary school-age children's post-disaster reactions (N = 327, ages 7–11, La Greca et al., 2017). With data from Hurricane Ike (e.g., life threat,

Box 13.2 Trauma and Grief

On the day of a natural disaster, Angie, age seven, was sitting next to her sister, Janie, age eight, in the school cafeteria near "the wall" that fell into the cafeteria. When the windows blew out and the wall started to fall, Angie yelled "Run!" and ran out of the cafeteria thinking that Janie was running out behind her. Janie was crushed to death under bricks. School staff who tried unsuccessfully at length to resuscitate her as well as children who saw the attempts had symptoms related to the unsuccessful resuscitation experience. Prior to the disaster, Janie had been a bit defiant and had required much of her mother's attention. Angie, the "good child," had been jealous of Janie and felt that her mother loved Janie more. She was grieving and despondent after her sister's death and also was contending with traumatic symptoms—extreme anxiety in response to wind, rattling windows, dark skies; intrusive imagery and bad dreams; attempts to avoid feelings; regression; problems with impulse control and somatic complaints. She exhibited some of the behavior problems her sister had shown when alive. In her treatment sessions, she had remained despondent and unresponsive (see Nader, 2002).

This was before manualized treatment methods, and the method used included, among others (e.g., body-emotion awareness), narrative exposure methods (e.g., sometimes beginning before an event or significant traumatic moment), directive and spontaneous play therapy, and coping assistance. In a consultation session, Angie again told her story beginning before the sudden event and wall collapse, using dolls and doll-sized cafeteria tables. She told of running out of the cafeteria to safety only to discover that her sister had not run behind her. The clinician recognized anger in the way that Angie had told of yelling, "Run!" and said, "You must have been really angry at your sister for not running when you told her to." Angie animatedly said "Yes!" Then returned to her original flat affect. Angie was directed to send the Angie doll back into the cafeteria to tell the Janie doll how angry she was that Janie did not run. She did this despondently, was told that the Janie doll was probably ignoring her because she wasn't being forceful enough. To model and permit greater intensity, she was asked (in a forceful tone) to say it like she meant it. The Angie doll grabbed the Janie doll by the arms, shook her, yelled "I told you to run!" She had the Angie doll shake the Janie doll some more, then slapped her and dragged her out of the cafeteria as she (the Angie doll) ran out.

Angie then became animated and remained so for the rest of the session. Her play no longer needed direction. She put Janie in a coffin but declined when asked if she wanted to say something about Janie in the way people sometimes do at funerals. She was asked if she wanted someone else to speak about Janie. Angie spontaneously made two lines of mourners, each line taking a turn walking up to the coffin to say something about Janie. Children (dolls) in the first line talked about what a mean, bad, and "yukky" girl Janie was. In the second line, they said loving and nice things and talked about how much Janie would be missed.

Before the lines finished, Angie turned her attention to elaborately building a tomb using blocks in the same shape as the cafeteria table but "too strong to fall down." Janie would be protected from being crushed while in this structure. She placed Janie inside to protect her, then let the lines finish their eulogies. In the end, she hugged the Janie doll to herself, and placed her back into the tomb. A week after this session, her mother reported symptom and behavior improvement, and Angie was less despondent in treatment sessions with her therapist. Her therapist reported Angie's movement between trauma and grief work (for detail see Nader, K [2002]. Treating children after violence in schools and communities. In NB Webb [ed.], *Helping Bereaved Children* [2nd ed., pp. 214–244]. New York: Guilford).

Note:
All case examples are disguised, may be combined cases, and have had details changed to protect individuals.

witnessing injury, extensive property damage), La Greca et al. compared the three sets of criteria. DSM-IV and 5 PTSD showed an acceptable fit, while ICD-11 demonstrated an excellent fit (better than DSM-IV or 5; La Greca et al., 2017; see Glossary—ICD-11 PTSD). Children meeting full criteria for either DSM-5 or ICD-11 PTSD had higher PTS symptom severity than those who did not meet full criteria (greater severity if meeting DSM-5 criteria). The ICD-11 latent structure of PTSD was simpler than that found in DSM-5, and researchers suggest that the ICD-11 model permits ease of diagnosis and treatment management (N = 388 treatment-seeking adults with childhood or adult traumas, Cloitre et al., 2013; children: La Greca et al., 2017). DSM-5 PTSD includes symptoms overlapping with depression (e.g., anhedonia, excessive guilt or blame, insomnia) and anxiety (e.g., negative emotional states, physiological reactions; La Greca et al., 2017). Children meeting DSM-5 criteria (not ICD-11) reported more co-occurring anxiety and depression than others.

In a study that enlisted children exposed to Hurricane Ike (N = 327) and children exposed to Hurricane Charley (N = 383, ages 7–11, Danzi & La Greca, 2016), those identified only by ICD-11 showed higher "core" symptom severity (linked to more established PTSD risk factors—e.g., life threat—than DSM-5) but had lower functional impairment, while DSM systems identified more noncore symptom severity and higher impairment. Although rates of PTSD were relatively similar for the three diagnostic systems, overlap was low. The new DSM-5 category (Cognitions/Mood) was the least endorsed by the two disaster exposed youth groups, which may suggest that the criteria for children under six are more appropriate for this age group as well (see also Mikolajewski, Scheeringa, & Weems, 2017). For each group of children, DSM-5 PTSD rates (required six symptoms) were slightly lower than DSM-IV (required six) or ICD-11 (required three). When impairment criterion was included, PTSD rates reduced for all three systems. This age group was often precluded from PTSD by the DSM-IV Avoidance Criterion and DSM-5 Cognitions/Mood criterion (both include such symptoms as anhedonia, amnesia, and detachment). The ability to report (and/or to experience) these symptoms may be more difficult or less likely prior to adolescence (Danzi & La Greca, 2016; Scheeringa, Zeanah, & Cohen, 2011). While ICD-11 demonstrated gender differences (girls four times more likely), DSM-5 showed no gender differences for this age group. Most interestingly, the three different systems identified different groups of children (only about one third of cases overlapped, N = 327 + N = 383, Danzi & La Greca, 2016).

Assessments usually precede and are intermittently used during and/or after treatment. Although assessments that include multiple sources and contexts are recommended, children ages 6–12 can provide self-reports of symptoms as well. Many questionnaires have been more effective for youth ages 8 and older. You and colleagues (2015) provided recent confirmation that youth are better informants about their own PTSD symptoms and about their own internalizing symptoms (than adult-reports for them; N = 458, 11–16-year-olds). However, youth do not always acknowledge traumatic events without a semi-structured interview specifically inquiring about such experiences. Youth reported symptoms even if they did not initially report an event. Interviews are recommended in addition to or instead of filling out checklists (see also Nader, 2008). Multiple sources provide a fuller picture of a youth's functioning, distress, and strengths.

Trauma Treatment Methods

To follow are three trauma-focused methods that have been used successfully—YPT, KIDNET, and TF-CBT. KIDNET has been used for multiple traumatic experiences and may need supplemental methods for work with institutionalized youth.

Adapted PPT (YPT)

Preschool PTSD Treatment (PPT; described in Chapter 10 for 3–5-year-olds), adapted for older youth (YPT), has effectively reduced trauma symptoms (for ages 7–17, Humphreys, Weems, & Scheeringa, 2015; Scheeringa & Weems, 2014; see also stepped care trauma-focused CBT based on PPT, Salloum et al., 2016). Using this method with a small group of youth (N = 47; ages 7–18; Scheeringa et al., 2017), four narrative styles were identified—*expressive*—provided details of event; emotionally expressive during telling; increased details with subsequent telling; *avoidant*—provided significantly fewer data elements about event than each of the other groups; *fabricated*—included distortions; may represent developmental differences; and *undemonstrative*. Both avoidant and undemonstrative groups tolerated structured, directive therapy techniques. When avoidant, undemonstrative, and fabricated groups were combined, the outcomes suggested that, with this method, both non-expressive and expressive styles were viable toward good outcomes. In use of this method, distortions did not need to be acknowledged for treatment to be successful.

Narrative Exposure Therapy (NET or KIDNET)

NET was developed to treat survivors of war and torture (Neuner et al., 2008). Instead of focusing on a single event as the treatment target, a patient constructs a whole life narrative (birth to the present), with detailed report/focus on each traumatic experience (or an identified worst moment). It permits, e.g., the documentation of multiple political/personal rights violations. KIDNET is an adaptation of NET for use with traumatized children and adolescents. The process begins with assessment and a list of traumatic events.

KIDNET, used for youth with a diagnosis of PTSD (substance abuse and psychosis are excluded; Neuner et al., 2008), is a short-term form of exposure therapy that usually takes 4–10 sessions (90–120 minutes). Child methods of NET may include role-play, drawings, use of toys or other items to recreate the trauma or to use symbolically (Cloitre, Petkova, Wang, & Lu, 2012; Hermenau et al., 2013; Neuner et al., 2008; see Boxes 13.2, 13.3). Treatment begins with psychoeducation of parent and child (topics: trauma, memory, treatment; preparation for activation of painful memories). Then the therapist presents a rope to the child that symbolizes her/his life; the child lays the rope out on the floor, leaving part of it unextended to represent the future (Neuner et al., 2008). Different sized and colored flowers (represent happy moments in life) and stones (represent bad experiences—e.g., sad, fearful, or painful) are given to the child to place along the rope to mark significant life events (therapist assists child to find the right chronology). The child gives only a very short description or headline of each event, makes a drawing of the lifeline (older child may take a photograph), and writes the headline next to each symbol. The picture is corrected if, during treatment, more events are revealed.

Box 13.3 Symbolic Representations

Eight-year-old John had lived with three different foster families (one year with current family). His natural mother was an adolescent. In MBT-C therapy, he used seashells to represent his two important families (current foster family and his mother) (the largest shell represented his very large foster father). John put the two families in separate chairs and placed a shell representing himself balanced between the arm-rests of the two chairs. He told the therapist that he sometimes didn't know which family he really belonged to. In assessment sessions, the therapist observed John's sensitivity to sound (e.g., others talking in the next room; slamming doors) as well as his difficulties in maintaining attention (see Muller & Midgley, 2015 for details).

After the first session, treatment is with the child alone (Neuner et al., 2008). KIDNET maintains a trauma narrative and habituates the patient to associated emotional responses. Each session revisits the lifeline. In session 2, the child begins her/his narration of life. The therapist may ask questions to facilitate. The child writes the narrative. Some events/traumas may be dramatic and require a break. At the beginning of subsequent sessions, therapist and child review how it has been since the last week (e.g., any intrusive or other symptoms). The child is asked if s/he wants to modify the lifeline in subsequent sessions. The therapist re-reads the narration from the previous session, instructing the child to be very attentive, to again imagine the events, and to make corrections to the story (the child usually adds some information or new events). The lifeline is again followed from the last location of the narrative (Neuner et al., 2008). The clinician demonstrates empathic understanding, active listening, congruency, and unconditional positive regard for the youth (Ruf et al., 2010). The child is asked for details related to emotions, cognitions, sensory experiences, and physiological reactions during the trauma. S/he records them meticulously, linking each aspect to autobiographic context (time and place). The narrative is driven forward in a supportive, directive guiding style (countering avoidance and aiming for full recovery of implicit information related to the experience). In the last session, the lifeline is laid down and extended, so that hopes and wishes for the future can be added (Neuner et al., 2008). At the end of treatment, the child is given the written documentation (Ruf et al., 2010).

Compared to controls, clinically significant improvements have been shown for refugee children from six countries (reduced PTSD; N = 26, ages 7–16, averaged four traumas, Ruf et al., 2010), Sri Lankan children exposed to war and tsunami (N = 31, ages 8–14, Catani et al., 2009; PTSD symptoms reduced with six sessions both for KIDNET & for meditation-relaxation treatment group; six months follow-up recovery rates: 81% KIDNET, 71% MED-RELAX), and African orphan children exposed to violence (reduced PTSD but not depressive symptoms, internalizing, externalizing; Hermenau et al., 2011).

Trauma-Focused Cognitive Behavioral Therapy (TF-CBT)

TF-CBT is a manualized, skill- and strengths-based intervention, often conducted in 12–16 sessions (Cohen, Mannarino, & Deblinger, 2006a, 2012, 2017; for ages 3–18). Treatment is modified for culture and specific symptom complexes (e.g., longer for more complex cases; Allen & Kronenberg, 2014; Allen, Oseni, & Allen, 2012; Cohen et al., 2012; Cohen & Mannarino, 2008; Cohen et al., 2006a; Deblinger, Stauffer, & Steer, 2001; Murray, Cohen, & Mannarino, 2013; Salloum et al., 2016; Scheeringa & Weems, 2014; Box 16.1). Treatment has included three distinct phases: (1) To improve a child's emotional stability and control—e.g., via psychoeducation, parenting skills (see Bloomquist, 2012), relaxation skills, affect modulation skills, cognitive coping methods; (2) To desensitize traumatic experiences—e.g., via cognitive processing; developing a trauma narrative; and (3) To consolidate treatment gains—e.g., via in vivo desensitization, conjoint child–parent sessions, and enhancing personal safety and development (Allen & Hoskowitz, 2017). Skills progressively build on previously consolidated skills (Cohen et al., 2006a). Review and closure follow treatment. Relaxation skills may include progressive relaxation, positive imagery, mindfulness meditation, and/or exercise (Allen & Hoskowitz, 2017; Cohen et al., 2006a, 2017). Affect expression and modulation skills involve identifying and expressing feelings and enhancing problem-solving and social skills. Conjoint child–parent sessions are numerous throughout treatment (other family members are encouraged to participate in treatment). TF-CBT emphasizes the therapeutic relationship—e.g., therapeutic rapport, genuine empathic responses, and reflective listening; flexibility and adaptability; respect for cultural values; a family focus; and self-efficacy (Cohen et al., 2006a; see also TG-CBT, to follow).

Culturally modified methods have been used—e.g., for Jordanian (Damra, Nassar, & Ghabri, 2014) and for Latino youth (e.g., De Arellano et al., 2014). CBT has been used in group format, e.g., including trauma-specific interventions, anger management, and social skills training (e.g., Deblinger, Pollio, & Dorsey, 2016; Hudson et al., 2015a), and it has a spiritually oriented modification (Haiti slave children ages 6–20, Wang et al., 2016). The basic method has been modified for children who need personalized assistance to fully engage and tolerate the process as well (e.g., listening with a child who liked to listen to her voice on tape and transcribing the narrative—permitting child, as director of this movie, to add the characters' additional thoughts, feelings, and emotions, Kerig et al., 2010). It has been modified for continuous traumas (e.g., domestic violence, abuse, ongoing community violence; Cohen et al., 2012; Murray et al., 2013; Appendix—Additional Treatment Methods).

In addition to reduction of PTSD and other symptoms (e.g., internalizing, externalizing, Webb et al., 2014), TF-CBT has shown improvements in *emotion regulation* (ER; ages 7–12; N = 58 post-treatment, 44 at six-month follow-up; Thornback & Muller, 2015). Statistically significant improvements (small effect size), following therapy, were found for maladaptive use of ER strategies (inhibition, dysregulation, lability/negativity) but not for ER skill scores—combines ability to express positive and negative emotions in adaptive and socially appropriate ways and empathy skills (does not measure maladaptive behaviors). Parent-reported improvements in inhibition best predicted improvements in post-TF-CBT child-reported (c-rep) PTS, while parent-reported change in dysregulation and lability/negativity best predicted improvement in c-rep PTS symptoms at six-month follow-up. Caregiver involvement in TF-CBT has resulted in better outcomes (Yasinski et al., 2016). In a study of in-session caregiver behavior (N = 71 caregiver–youth dyads, ages 7–17; low SES), Yasinski et al. found that caregiver cognitive-emotional processing (e.g., explores, tries to understand, challenges, and makes meaning of personal and child's trauma) during the trauma narrative phase was linked to reductions in youth internalizing and externalizing symptoms during treatment (not at follow-up). Caregiver support (e.g., concern, empathy, care) corresponded to maintenance of reduced internalizing. In contrast, caregiver blaming the child (for trauma and symptoms) and avoidance (e.g., pulling away from trauma-related problems, issues, emotions) predicted worsening of externalizing and internalizing at follow-up. Caregiver blame and avoidance during the narrative phase positively correlated with overgeneralization (Glossary; Yasinski et al., 2016), which has predicted worse outcomes (e.g., increased externalizing, Ready et al., 2015). Blame of the child for the trauma or for related issues was linked to less child accommodation (less balanced beliefs of self, other, world; Yasinski et al., 2016).

Adjunct Creative Methods

Creative methods (e.g., play, art, storytelling, music, directed writing, commemorative rituals or objects) have been used with traumatized and with grieving youth (e.g., Edgar-Baily & Kress, 2010; Webb, 2015; Boxes 13.2, 13.3; Chapter 16). Such methods have many potential benefits. They have assisted rapport, aided accessing and depicting trauma memories in a nonthreatening way, and provided an outlet for emotional expression. They have served as natural and/or comforting methods for a child to process experiences, and they have been related to improved functioning (Boxes 13.2, 13.4, 13.5).

Music and Art Training

Art and music have been used to assist recovery after exposure to adversity. Art is often used as an adjunct method or component part of treatments (Chapter 10—Drawing; Boxes 13.1, 13.5). Music has been used to increase social reciprocity and to reduce symptoms (e.g., children with cPTSD, Hussey, Reed, Laymen, & Pasiali, 2007; for veterans). Studies have shown that rhythm-centered music making (especially drumming and percussion music) has a positive impact on physical health, mental health, and social health (Yap, Kwan, & Ang, 2016). Music training has been associated

Box 13.4 Rapport Building with Edgar and the Wadded Kleenex

Ten-year-old Edgar was badly injured in a school shooting (Nader, 2002). Even after his physician approved his entry into therapy and return to school, he remained anxiously attached to his mother and refused to go to school or to therapy sessions. In therapy sessions, he clung to his mother's arm and screamed at her that he hated her and for her to take him home. Edgar did not respond to any question or comment from the therapist until a therapist began to calmly engage him regarding his anger. He loudly protested each time the therapist labeled his anger (e.g., over having the injury—to which he yelled "No!"; that no one protected him—he yelled, "Shut up!"). The therapist then lightly wadded a Kleenex and threw it at Edgar—it landed close to his foot. He kicked it back and resumed yelling at his mother. The therapist continued to throw the Kleenex, until Edgar spent 10 minutes focusing equal time between therapist and mother, and then a few minutes focusing more time interacting with the therapist. Lightly wadded, a Kleenex had little power and was harmless (a Nerf ball may have worked). Edgar was congratulated on a good session expressing his anger well without hurting anyone and was allowed to go home early. Subsequent sessions included more of the same until his mother was gradually moved outside of the therapy room (see Nader, K [2002]. Treating children after violence in schools and communities. In NB Webb [ed.], *Helping Bereaved Children* [2nd ed., pp. 214–244]. New York: Guilford for more detail).

Note:
All case examples are disguised, may be combined cases, and have had details changed to protect individuals.

Box 13.5 Directed and Spontaneous Traumatic Play and Regressed Play after a Mass Shooting

Mathew saw a number of therapists and was hospitalized by the time his mother found a trauma specialist. He had had a previous trauma and more than one stepfather (one who was a harsh but not abusive parent). At age 15, a few years after he was shot twice in the arm during a hostage taking and mass shooting, Mathew entered treatment with a trauma specialist (see Nader, 2008). He had witnessed multiple shootings, bodily mutilation, and deaths while enduring more than an hour of the gunman walking around the room shooting people. Every time he moved, his friend's father was shot. His best friend and best friend's mother were killed during the experience.

Mathew had learned to use drugs to deal with his distress while in the hospital, before meeting his new therapist. During trauma treatment, Mathew exhibited some self-contempt. He described many reasons to feel guilty—actions that endangered his friend's father; living when his friend died; taking drugs (admitted much later). During one session he seemed to depict himself. Mathew had inked in "Dead Kennedy's Society" above a skull-and-crossbones on his jacket sleeve. By his own design, his short hair was bleached blond with darker roots. He demonstrated his self-contempt by taking a Barbie doll, cutting her hair and coloring it to look just like his own, dressing her in boys' clothes that looked like his, and writing the same inked symbol on the arm of the doll's jacket. Mathew then began to beat the doll, break her arms, slam her against the table, and hang her. In addition to traumatic play, for a few weeks, he moved to the floor and regressed to the play and toys of a very young child.

Although Mathew began each session disavowing the need for therapy, he then readily described his experiences and depicted them in drawings and with toy replicas, as requested. He often engaged in spontaneous play that re-created his traumatic experience—e.g., he depicted multiple people endangered and injured, his feelings of helplessness, general danger with violence, his need to fight back without being shot, and his strong desire to protect his best friend who was killed in the event. Mathew often put himself in the position of rescuer, defeating the aggressors. Mathew's need to rescue his friend was repeated for years after, when he rescued or protected others from danger even when putting himself in danger (see Nader, 2008 for elaboration). Across life, he has had a few segments of treatment. He is now a good father, an administrative-level employee, a helper of others (without endangerment), and a very spiritual person who enjoys his family and his life (© Nader, 2008; Nader K [2008]. *Understanding and Assessing Trauma in Children and Adolescents: Measures, Methods, and Youth in Context.* New York: Routledge. Reproduced/extracted by permission of Taylor and Francis Group, LLC, a division of Informa plc).

Note:
All case examples are disguised, may be combined cases, and have had details changed to protect individuals.

with children's improved functioning (better verbal memory, second language pronunciation accuracy, reading ability and EFs, Miendlarzewska & Trost, 2014). Children in visual arts or music programs were compared to controls not in school music or art lessons (N = 176 Amsterdam children, age six, then 6.5, then seven, then 7.5; Jaschke, Honing, & Scherder, 2018). The school music program included 1–2-hour lessons weekly, with an opening song, followed by theoretical and historical music information related to the song, and ending with collective music making, singing, and improvising (Jaschke et al., 2018). There was also a music group with prior music knowledge (Music+; private lessons outside of school). The children in the visual arts program were given lessons in painting, sculpting, and art history. When EF skills were assessed, the visual arts group improved over the three other groups on visuospatial memory tasks. Scores on inhibition, planning, and verbal intelligence rose significantly for the two music groups over time, compared to visual art and controls. Academic performance scores improved with EF and verbal IQ improvements as mediators showing a possible transfer effect.

Play Therapy

Youth often reenact, in play and behaviors, aspects of traumatic and other experiences (Nader, 2008). Nader and Pynoos (1991) suggested that children's traumatic play either provoked anxiety or provided relief for a child, depending on the degree they achieved (1) perceived control over outcomes, (2) a satisfactory ending, (3) freedom to express prohibited affects, or (4) with therapeutic assistance, a cognitive reworking of aspects of the traumatic experience. Play may serve as a kind of gradual exposure to aspects of a trauma (Gil, 2006). In therapeutic interventions with a trusted clinician, directed or spontaneous play can facilitate a youth's facing emotional moments with associated affects (Nader & Mello, 2001). In play, a youth may reenter a traumatic moment or fantasy in order to reprocess, experience release, and/or redefine aspects of it (Levy, 1938; see Nader, 2008; Nader & Mello, 2001; Nader & Pynoos, 1991; Pynoos & Eth, 1986; Box 13.5). Methods may be directive or nondirective (nondirective: Box 2.3; Chapters 10 and 16—play therapy). Whether methods are directive or nondirective, progress may be evidenced, for example, in greater engagement in the play, less constricted affect, more physical movement and/or less physiological constriction, changed or elaborated themes, and/or some evident release (Gil, 2006; Nader, 2002). For a time, play may take on a driven quality.

Directive play therapy may focus a child on personally identified traumatic moments (e.g., worst or significant moments, event-related fantasies of action—e.g., revenge, rescue; Eth & Pynoos, 1985; Nader & Mello, 2001; Nader, 2002; Box 13.4). Depending on the type of treatment and age of the child, directive play therapy may include narrative processing of the experience or its episodes and may include abreactive reprocessing of traumatic impressions and emotions (Nader, 2002). Like nondirective play therapy (Chapter 10; Gil, 1998), directive play therapy permits a child to direct the action and/or assign characters, during re-processed event episodes. A therapist's directions may be detailed or as simple as a request to focus more intensely and/or in more detail on a scene or to tell or retell a specific episode of the traumatic experience using replicas to demonstrate. During treatment sessions, traumatized youth may engage in play at older ages (Box 13.5), may relapse into more juvenile play than would normally be expected, and may be willing to demonstrate the event with toy replicas (Nader, 2002). Episodes may be followed by interpretation or viewed as a silent witness in a safe and nurturing atmosphere (Nader, 2002).

Repetitive and/or Rhythmic Play or Activity

Using any variety of patterned, repetitive somatosensory activities, Perry (2009) suggests that the lowest brain region that is abnormally functioning is a first target of intervention. For example, a poorly organized brain-stem and diencephalon may have been thwarted by trauma, with related self-regulation, attention, arousal, and impulsivity problems. Yoga and mindfulness have been associated with positive brain changes. Repetitive, rhythmic, bilateral activity is believed to cause positive brain changes as well (Perry, 2006). Because brain regions develop in a sequential manner, Perry recommends that, after improvements in self-regulation, therapeutic work may then move to relation-related problems (limbic) using more traditional therapies. When basic dyadic relational skills have improved, therapy may be more verbal and insight-oriented (cortical; Perry, 2009). As adjunct methods, a number of repetitive activities (e.g., drumming, movement, music, yoga, grooming a horse, trampoline, swaying while reciting liturgical prayers, therapeutic massage) are believed to assist brain reorganization (MacKinnon, 2012; may be used in a group, Perry, 2009). Similarly, massage to both sides of neck/shoulders has reduced cortisol and other symptoms (Field, Seligman, Scafidi, & Schanberg, 1996; Hart et al., 2001).

Treatments for Specific Symptoms or Issues

Traumatization has been linked to a number of subsequent disorders and symptoms (e.g., TSRD, psychosis, personality disorder, bipolar symptoms; see Nader & Fletcher, 2014). For example, non-suicidal self-injury (SI) has been associated with PTS (e.g., PTSD, hopelessness) as well as with previous SI, personality disorders (i.e., antisocial, borderline, histrionic, narcissistic), exposure to peer SI, depression, eating disorder, externalizing, internalizing, general psychopathology, and affect dysregulation, some of which are also risk factors for suicidal ideation and completion (Fox, Hunter, & Jones, 2015). As discussed, combined risk factors are stronger than individual risk factors (Chapter 4). A number of methods (some trauma-focused, others skill focused and preventive) are available to assist children with developmental skills (e.g., coping, social skills, empathy, bullying prevention, disorganized attachments, Cassidy & Shaver, 2018; Nader, 2012c), with specific symptoms (e.g., behavior problems, also assisted by improved parenting), and/or to reinstate resilience. Mindfulness has had multiple benefits; it has reduced stress and anxiety, increased mindful parenting, and increased calmness, relaxation, attention, restful alertness, well-being, and emotional regulation in children and adolescents (Chapter 10; e.g., regulation via improved attentional focus, Kaunhoven & Dorjee, 2017; Schonert-Reichl & Roeser, 2016; Waters, 2016). Mindfulness may decrease anxiety at least in part by increasing emotion awareness, which is a key component of emotion-regulation (Schneider, Arch, Landy, & Hankin, 2016). In a study of school-age children and parents given stress management activities and mindfulness practices (N = 68; Waters, 2016), following training, children's stress levels were significantly, negatively related to their levels of mindfulness as well as to their parents self-rated levels of mindfulness. Child and parent mindfulness scores were significantly, positively related. Mindfulness practices are described in Chapter 10 and 16, and yoga methods in Chapter 16. Such methods are a part of a number of treatments. Additional methods for particular developmental skills and trauma or other symptoms are presented here.

Executive Functions (EF): Memory Training

Working memory (WM) shares neural circuitry with other EFs, and working memory training has shown improvements in WM and other EFs. Three weeks of visuospatial memory training (30 min./day) for 10–16-year-olds demonstrated significant performance increase in auditory working memory compared to passive controls (Pugin et al., 2015; N = 14, 2.5-fold immediate, and N = 15, 4.7-fold long-term increase in training group vs controls). For children with ADHD (ages 7–12; N = 66; Bigorra, Garolera, Guijarro, & Hervas, 2015), 1–2 weeks and six months after computerized working memory training, youth showed improved EFs (parent report: metacognition, working memory, and planning/organizing; teacher report: metacognition, working memory, initiating, monitoring, and shifting). At follow-up, youth also improved in performance-based EFs (e.g., academics), in ADHD symptoms (not significant in parent report of later treated controls), and in functioning (reduced impairment). In this study, children were rewarded by families after each training session and upon completion of the 25 sessions. The treatment did not work as well for youth with both learning disorders and ADHD. Additionally, a period of continuous or intermittent exercise (e.g., moderate-intensity treadmill) has been linked to improved EF in 8–10-year-olds (Lambrick, Stoner, Grigg, & Faulkner, 2016).

Dissociative PTSD

Dissociation has been linked to high PTSD symptom levels, suicidality, functional impairment, less treatment seeking, attention problems, and comorbid disorders (De Bellis, Woolley, & Hooper, 2013, ages 6–17; Stein et al., 2013; Chapter 12). Traumatized individuals often cycle between or are characterized by states of emotional undermodulation (Glossary, e.g., in PTSD) and emotional overmodulation (PTSD-dissociative subtype, PTSD-DS; Frewen & Lanius, 2006; Lanius, 2015, et al., 2012; Nicholson et al., 2016). History of childhood trauma/PTSD (e.g., abuse or neglect) or of poly-victimization has been associated with increased likelihood of dissociation or PTSD-DS (see Frewen, Brown, & Lanius, 2017; Stein et al., 2013). While Stein et al. found that dissociation was not related to trauma type (N = 20,018), it was related to early age trauma and repeated trauma exposures.

An association has been found between mentalizing and dissociation. One of the negative associations of traumas like child sexual abuse (CSA) is the impact on children's mentalization capacities, which in turn may influence self and affect regulation and interpersonal functioning (see Ensink et al., 2017; Table 1.2). Both depression and trauma have been related to lower reflective functioning (RF). As discussed (Chapter 12), CSA has led to lower RF/mentalization, which in turn related to higher dissociation leading to externalizing and sexualized behavior (ages 7–12; CSA: N = 265; Ensink et al., 2017; see Appendix—MBT-C for a mentalization-based treatment). Higher child and mother RF have been associated with less psychopathology. Ensink et al. (2017) suggest that dissociation may create a context in which the child initiates anomalous behaviors that would normally be inhibited through mental self-monitoring (Chapter 11). Mentalizing or RF (Table 1.2) has been among targets of treatment for disorders with dissociation.

For dissociative PTSD, complex PTSD, and Dissociative Identity disorder, treatment studies have demonstrated a lack of response or even clinical deterioration when standard, unmodified trauma-focused methods are used (e.g., progressive exposure or other CBT methods; Brand, Loewenstein, & Lanius 2014; Cloitre et al., 2010; D'Andrea & Pole, 2012). For DID treatment, Silberg (1998b) has recommended minimizing focus on traumatic memories and emphasizing the child's recognizing and taking responsibility for the emotions and actions of each part of the self (i.e., each alter). For adults with dissociative symptoms, methods that reduce in-session dissociation, that help to control emotions, and/or reduce the need for avoidance have been used with PTSD-DS (regulation skill training, Cloitre et al., 2012; lower state dissociation, Kleindienst et al., 2016; writing task, Resick et al., 2012b, see Chapter 16—Writing Tasks). Cloitre and colleagues suggest that the reduction of dissociation prior to use of trauma-focused methods (e.g., narrative/exposure therapy) may enable more effective cognitive and affective reappraisal and reorganization of trauma memories. Although these methods were not tested for children, Wieland and Silberg (2013) confirm the use of phased treatment (safety, stabilization, and strengthening—e.g., self-regulation; trauma processing; and reconnection or integration) for cPTSD in children and adolescents and underscore the need for identification and treatment of dissociation at every phase—i.e., reduction of dissociation and attention to its triggers (also for treatment of other trauma-related dissociation). Relaxation training methods (e.g., body scan methods of mindfulness; yoga savasana) have been used for both PTSD and PTSD-DS and may enhance interoceptive awareness and, consequently, may assist in overcoming posttrauma emotional detachment (Lanius et al., 2015). Self-distancing may reduce the need for avoidance as well (see Appendix—additional methods).

Somatic Dysregulation

Brain changes following traumas (e.g., HPA axis dysregulation) may be characterized by hypervigilance—a state of fear-related activation—and a tendency to respond to environmental stressors with a primitive, reflexive, and aggressive reaction that reflects less higher-level function and more of a persistent brain-stem-level CNS functioning rather than an effective, cortical-driven response (Atchison, 2007). Behaviors that are adaptive during threatening experiences (e.g., avoidance, dissociation) or deprivation (e.g., hoarding food) may become maladaptive after the threat has passed (Atchison, 2007). Traumatic experiences are often, in part, somatosensory (Finn, Warner, Price, & Spinazzola, 2017). Somatic dysregulation or somatic distress has also followed traumas or other stressors. Dissociation between body and mind may occur and manifest in somatic problems. Somatic dysregulation may prevent accessing cognitive skills needed to engage in verbal treatment (Warner, Koomar, Lary, & Cook, 2013). Somatic interventions have been used for sensory integration or modulation problems, for traumas occurring in the preverbal phase of development, for PTSD, and for complex PTSD (Finn et al., 2017; Kaiser, Gillette, & Spinazzola, 2010). For such experiences and for youth with insufficient language skills, somatic methods may be preferable to cognitive methods (Finn et al., 2017). A number of treatments address somatic dysregulation—e.g., Sensory-Motor Arousal Treatment (SMART; Warner et al., 2013); Sensorimotor Psychotherapy™ (Ogden, Minton, & Pain, 2006); Somatic Experiencing® (Levine, 2010; Chapter 17). Mindfulness and yoga methods have also been used to assist a more positive body-mind connection (Chapters 10, 16).

Emotional Awareness

Some evidence suggests increases in emotional awareness and self-regulation as well as reductions of stress, PTSD, and other symptoms through the use of yoga or mindfulness methods (ages 7–9, Kaunhoven & Dorjee, 2017; alexithymia, sometimes through better body awareness). Such methods are sometimes components of trauma-related methods (e.g., TF-CBT; SRP, ARC, this chapter and Chapters 10, 16). For UK 7–9-year-olds (N = 71, Vickery & Dorjee, 2016), trained teachers taught mindfulness to children—76% liked and wanted to continue practicing mindfulness. Mindfulness significantly decreased negative affect, improved emotion regulation, and improved emotional awareness and expression at follow-up.

Narcissism

Narcissism is defined and described in more detail in Chapters 15 and 16. Psychoanalytic methods have been used to treat narcissism (e.g., AEDP, Chapter 16). When children at risk of developing narcissistic personality disorder were offered a year of psychodynamic psychotherapy (N = 36, ages 9–13, Guilé, Mbékou, & Lageix, 2004), the more both parent and child showed narcissism, the less likely they were to utilize treatment services (12% of variance; Guilé et al., 2004). Parental narcissism correlated both with child's anhedonia and with denial of dependency and devaluation of others. Child narcissistic traits (e.g., self-blame and lack of empathy—40% of variance; vulnerability, avoidance) predicted less treatment utilization as well. Youth who expressed suicidality garnered school services. As shown in other studies, narcissistic preadolescents had reluctance to engage in pretend play, engaged in mirroring and sadistic play themes, and showed hypersensitivity to therapist's interventions (Guilé et al., 2004). Chapter 16 provides some guidelines for working with narcissism.

Traumatic Grief (TG)

Persistent Complex Bereavement Disorder (APA, 2013) is undergoing study for its applicability to children (Chapters 12, 15). Effective study will require examining more than the proposed symptoms (which were based primarily on adult conceptualizations of complicated grief). Grief affects different individuals differently (Pearlman et al., 2014). In contrast to a stage/phase-based focus on grief recovery, recent experts have focused on the individual nature of grieving—e.g., on meaning reconstruction in physical, psychological, behavioral, social, and spiritual dimensions (Neimeyer, 2001); resilience (Bonanno, 2008); grief style (Doka & Martin, 2010); developmental and cultural issues (see Corr, 2015, Nader & Salloum, 2011). Worden (2009) suggests a task-based method of dealing with grief (Tasks): (1) Accept the reality of the loss; (2) Process/work through the pain of grief; (3) Adjust to an environment without the deceased; (4) Find an enduring connection to the deceased while embarking on a new life. As discussed in Chapter 12, while grieving is often adaptive (see Bonanno, 2008), trauma or other factors may complicate the grieving process (e.g., memories of the deceased may trigger trauma memories; Nader, 1997; Nader & Salloum, 2011; Pearlman et al., 2010). With some mixed findings, compared to children of parents who die of sudden natural deaths (e.g., heart attack), children whose parents died after prolonged illness have shown higher levels of maladaptive grief and of PTS symptoms (Kaplow, Howell, & Layne, 2014; see Chapter 12). Some evidence suggests that, compared to other traumas, violence intensifies grieving, depression, PTS, and anxiety (adults: e.g., Boelen, 2015; children: e.g., Brown & Goodman, 2005; Dillen et al., 2009; Rynearson & Salloum, 2011). PTS symptoms are common in TG, as are depressive symptoms and survivor guilt (Cohen et al., 2006b). Some youth may have delayed grief reactions that may not be readily linked to the loss (Crenshaw, 2007). Children vary in their timetables for grieving (e.g., timing for processing aspects of grief; need to process aspects of trauma; amount covered in one session), in their movement between phases of grieving and/or between trauma and grief focus, and in their personal reactions to aspects of both trauma and grief. A number of clinicians have observed that, with TG, some trauma work may necessarily precede grief work for effective outcomes (Cohen et al., 2006a, 2006b; Nader, 1997).

Cultural adaptation of methods is also important (Box 16.1). For example, in Asian cultures, the dead continue to be an important focus and important participants in the lives of the living (e.g., ancestor worship; local/folk therapy methods; ideals of *one man per lifetime*, wholeness; Hsu et al., 2004). Restoration of harmony after loss of a husband/father in a Taiwanese home includes surviving parent and children's efforts toward reconnection—e.g., to preserve the deceased as a family member; preserve daily routines/normalcy; maintain a symbolic image of the deceased such as an altar, talking to the deceased, chastising in his name, awareness of him; communicating with the deceased—small talk to deeper talk (Hsu et al., 2004).

Mass Traumas and Multiple Deaths

Mass traumas (e.g., violence, disasters) may result in mass casualties, multiple traumatic exposures (e.g., witnessing, life threat, injury), and grieving that is complicated by the horrific or violent nature of deaths and the multiplicity of losses (including loss of family members; Nader, 2012a; Box 13.5). Some mass events (e.g., disasters) may result in secondary stressors such as displacement, loss of property/belongings, undermining of businesses and unemployment, loss of revenue, and raised prices (Box 1.2). Recovery efforts may be prolonged and outcomes may include significant short and long-term physical and emotional reactions. After such events, when chaos and a multitude of stressors accompany the event, it can be difficult to disentangle the associations of long- and short-term reactions (Dyregrov, Salloum, Kristensen, & Dyregrov, 2015). After mass events, it is important to make certain that people are safe and that immediate physical needs are met as well as to restore a sense of safety, calm, a sense of self- and community-efficacy, connectedness, and hope (Hobfoll et al., 2007; Nader, 2012a; Chapter 4). Multimodal interventions are indicated—e.g., that address both trauma and grief; assist positive caregiver capacities; secure life continuity (e.g., Dyregrov et al., 2015); address multiple losses: of life, property, aspects of life and self-image.

Grief Outcome Variables

Several variables may influence grief outcomes (Tables 12.3, 12.4). For example, depending on the child and the event, specific methods of coping may assist or impede grief resolution (Nader & Salloum, 2011). The efficacy of types of coping vary somewhat by event and child (Brown & Goodman, 2005; Nader, 2008). Coping flexibility is among identified protective factors (lower grief reactions; e.g., Cohen & Katz, 2015). Studies have found that coping that includes, e.g., acceptance and cognitive restructuring, has been linked to better functioning in contrast to avoidant coping or distraction, which have been linked to poorer psychological outcomes (e.g., increased PTSS and maladaptive grief, n = 38, 7–12-year-olds, Kaplow et al., 2013; Howell et al., 2016). Positive (vs negative) spiritual coping also may assist recovery (Chapter 3; Burke & Neimeyer, 2014). As noted earlier, some avoidance may be beneficial, if well-timed and not prolonged. Effective parenting (e.g., warmth, non-harsh discipline) has proven beneficial to outcomes (e.g., reduced mental health outcomes, Hagan et al., 2012). Some methods for treating CG, PG, or TG are presented here (see also School Interventions, below).

Treatment Issues for Posttrauma Grief

PTS may complicate grieving; grief has been associated with increased PTS symptoms (see Nader & Layne, 2009; Nader & Salloum, 2011). Guilt also may complicate or intensify both grief and traumatic reactions (Barlé, Wortman, & Latack, 2015; Nader, 2008). Clinicians may need to help the child manage PTS, grief, and the interplay of trauma and grief reactions (Cohen et al., 2002; Layne et al., 2017; Nader, 1997). A number of issues may be of import in the treatment of maladaptive grief. For example, in addition to a need to process the manner in which the death occurred (e.g., traumatic or other sudden, unexpected death, Boxes 13.2, 13.5; witnessing the death, Box 3.1; finding the body, Box 15.2c), a youth may need to contend with issues related to damage to the loved one's body, an intentional perpetrator, and/or whether the death was preventable. They may be grappling with whether the loved one suffered, the unfairness or unjustness of the death, and whether they feel they can live without the deceased. Youth may also be contending with the shattering of basic assumptions (e.g., beliefs about safety; spiritual beliefs). After a traumatic death, among other issues, it may be more difficult to accept the reality of the death and to process and make meaning of the death (e.g., related to the child, the death, or the environment) (e.g., Barlé et al., 2015). As always, support systems are important to recovery (Barlé et al., 2015; Pearlman et al., 2010; Salloum, 2015). It may be important to build youth skills (e.g., coping, self-skills), increase support, and/or to repair the neurological impact of trauma, during treatment. A number of methods are appropriate for youth ages 8–18 (see also Webb, 2002; Chapter 16). Four methods follow; others are in Chapter 16 or the Appendix.

Grief-Help (G-H)

G-H (Spuij, van Londen-Huiberts, & Boelen, 2013; adapted from methods effective with adults, Boelen, van den Hout, & van den Bout, 2006, 2012) is a manualized CBT treatment method for children, ages 8–18. It addresses insufficient integration of knowledge (e.g., irreversibility of the separation into AM; yearning), persistent negative thinking (e.g., about self, life, the future; misinterpretations—e.g., feelings of loss of control or of insanity), and anxious and depressive avoidance (e.g., of stimuli that remind of the loss; of adjustment-fostering activities; Spuij et al., 2013). CBT methods to promote integration of the loss include imagery exposure (telling the loss story, zooming in on painful aspects) and confrontational writing (a letter to the deceased, telling what is missed). Negative cognitions are addressed through cognitive restructuring (e.g., Socratic questioning re: maladaptive cognitions; behavioral experiments/homework to test cognitions). Maladaptive avoidance behaviors are replaced by more adaptive coping (e.g., exposure methods; behavioral activation). The method consists of nine sessions (45 minutes each at 1–2-week intervals) beginning with formulation of treatment goals, and ending with the youth's assessment of how s/he has profited from treatment. Five phases include *who died* (sessions 1–2, child: facts of the loss; things missed; wishes to share with the deceased; identifying maladaptive thinking; 1–4, parent: psychoeducation, improving parenting); *what is grief* (2–3, child: psychoeducation, homework); *cognitive restructuring* (4–5, child: learning to identify thoughts; questioning thoughts, behavioral change; 5, parent: summary of skills learned, plans for continued practice); *maladaptive behaviors* (6–8; targeting child's anxious avoidance—social sharing exposure; targeting poor problem-solving; addressing guilt; targeting depressive avoidance with behavioral activation); and *moving forward after loss* (e.g., summarizing skills learned, making plans for continuance, troubleshooting). Workbook activities and assignments (including three letters to a real or imaginary friend, to consolidate learning) correspond to each phase.

Evaluation of G-H has found reductions in PG/CG, PTSD, and depression symptoms (N = 6; Spuij et al., 2013; N = 10, ages 8–18; Spuij et al., 2015, large effect). Parents and children rated their experiences with the treatment favorably (e.g., felt understood, liked the workbook; Spuij et al., 2013). One child hesitated to confront the reality, consequences, and pain of his sister's death; he benefitted least from treatment. For such children, more than nine sessions will be needed. Supplemental treatments are needed for disorders other than grief (e.g., PTSD, depression). Treatment was less efficacious for deaths due to suicide or when it was years after the death (N = 16; Spuij et al., 2015).

Grief and Trauma Intervention (GTI)

GTI (Salloum, 2006, 2015) is an 11-session method (plus one parent meeting or as needed) used for children and adolescents with both loss and high levels of traumatic stress after exposure to disaster, violence, and/or death (Baggerly & Salloum, 2010). GTI combines CBT and narrative methods. It has been used in group or individual formats (Baggerly & Salloum, 2010; Salloum et al., 2009; Salloum & Overstreet, 2008). The themes of resilience (promoting coping skills), restorative retelling (narrative meaning-making and exposure methods), and reconnecting (to supportive people; reengaging in activities of interest; with positive images of the deceased) progress through three, overlapping treatment phases (Salloum, 2015). *Orientation* (five sessions) includes grief and trauma education; promoting coping skills—e.g., anger management, relaxation, guided imagery, focusing on supportive people, culturally relevant rituals, spirituality; focus on dreams, ways of ensuring safety, and relaxation (Salloum, 2015). The *Cohesion and Mutual Support* phase includes restorative retelling (3–4 sessions: telling the narrative); retelling—e.g., trauma, worst moment, correcting distortions, addressing guilt, reinforcing relaxation; use of coping skills; and reconnection. The child may choose first to tell about the person who died, to begin just before the death, or to tell about the death (individual needs are addressed; Baggerly & Salloum, 2010). The *Termination and Separation* phase also includes relaxation and retelling as well as memory meaning-making, positive focus, then celebration of progress and reconnection (Salloum, 2015).

Drawing (identified topic) and discussion (of images, thoughts, feelings about topic) are used with narrative methods such as exploring meaning and worst moments, seeking to enhance coherence, providing narrative exposure. With clinician-assistance, the child writes down her/his story. The book is shared at the end of intervention. The clinician and a person and/or group serve as empathetic, supportive witnesses to the child's story. Worksheets are provided for the child's use (Salloum, 2015). An adherence checklist is provided for clinicians. The manual discusses clinician self-care and monitoring methods as well as providing session-by-session outlines and a discussion of assessment (Salloum, 2015).

For children exposed to Hurricane Katrina (N = 50, 7–12-year-olds; Salloum & Overstreet, 2008), children in both group and individual GTI experienced reductions in PTS, depression, and traumatic grief (TG). Also, for children exposed to Hurricane Katrina (N = 70 African Americans, ages 6–12; Salloum & Overstreet, 2012), youth were assigned to GTI with narrative and coping skills (GTI-CN) or to GTI with coping skills only (GTI-C). Both groups experienced significant reductions in traumatic stress, depression, TG, and global distress and showed improvements in perceived social support. For all improvements except externalizing symptoms in the group without narrative methods, they maintained gains at evaluation one year later. GTI-CN youth showed considerable improvements in internalizing behaviors and more improvements in externalizing symptoms than the GTI-C group. GTI-CN youth experienced a slight increase in externalizing behaviors at 3 months, while they were still processing the traumatic experience. After processing the trauma, they exhibited lower externalizing behaviors at one-year follow-up.

The Family Bereavement Program (FBP)

FBP (Sandler et al., 2003, 2008, 2010a, 2010b) is a 12–14-week group grief treatment method using separate, concurrent sessions for caregiver and youth (plus two individual family sessions; for ages 8–12 and 12–16, Hagan et al., 2012). Half of the sessions include conjoint work for caregiver and youth. FBP targets family disruption, strengthens the caregiver–child relationship (e.g., assists more effective communication with caregiver, emotion expression, support seeking, Hagan et al., 2012), and promotes parenting skills (e.g., warmth, responsiveness, effective discipline, shielding children from negative experiences—e.g., financial worries, changes), as well as assists the child's coping skills and resilience (Sandler et al., 2008). To enhance parenting, groups include focus on family time, one-to-one time with each child, praise for positive behaviors, active listening, and clear, age-appropriate communication of expectations for behavior as well as consistent consequences (Ayers et al., 2010; Hagan et al., 2012). Parents also practice activities to improve their personal adjustment—e.g., goal setting; support seeking; cognitive reframing to reduce depression-related negative thinking (Sandler et al., 2016a). Modeling, role-play, and homework are used.

FBP has reduced immediate and long-term grief reactions (Sandler et al., 2008). Compared to controls, FBP youth have shown reductions in problematic grief (post FBP and six-year follow-up; N = 244, ages 8–16 initially; Sandler et al., 2010b). At 11-month follow-up, girls showed reductions in internalizing and externalizing, and FBP related to improvements in post-grief risk and protective factors (e.g., in the parenting/family system; Sandler et al., 2003). Baseline positive parenting, caregiver depression, and child externalizing problems predicted caregivers' use of program skills outside of group, and higher child internalizing problems predicted greater positive perceptions of the group environment (Schoenfelder et al., 2013). Higher levels of skill use during FBP predicted increased positive parenting, and positive perceptions of group environment predicted decreased caregiver depressive symptoms (N = 89 parents; Schoenfelder et al., 2013).

Positive parenting has been important after parental death or divorce (Chapters 2, 9). In a study of 114 girls, positive results three months after FBP—i.e., increased positive parenting, decreased negative events, lower inhibition of emotional expression—mediated positive effects of FBP on mental health outcomes at 11 months (Tein, Sandler, Ayers, & Wolchik, 2006). Comparing time 1 to 11 months later, for both children and parents, negative thoughts about *unknown control*-related beliefs (e.g., child doesn't know why the stressful event occurred) and about stressful events mediated mental health outcomes (especially for girls high in negative thoughts about stressor events). For children, girls' positive coping served as a mediator for positive outcomes.

Hagan et al. demonstrated increases in effective parenting persisting to six-year follow-up (N = 139 at follow-up; no booster sessions included, Hagan et al., 2012). Also six years after treatment (N = 218, now adolescents, Sandler et al., 2010a), FBP youth had significantly lower externalizing (teacher, caregiver, and youth report), lower internalizing, and higher self-esteem (teacher report). Bereaved FBP parents had lower levels of depressive symptoms, general psychiatric distress, prolonged grief symptoms, and alcohol problems immediately and at six-year follow-up (Sandler et al., 2010a, 2016a). FBP demonstrated positive effects on maternal warmth and on mothers' higher coping efficacy than controls. Evidence demonstrated multiple cascading effects of the program—e.g., changes in positive parenting influenced depression over six years (Sandler et al., 2016a). Six years after 12-week FBP (=139), youth randomized to treatment showed higher cortisol in response to conflict tasks compared to controls (in late afternoon and early evening; Luecken et al., 2010). Lower cortisol was significantly related to higher externalizing. Improvements in positive parenting partially mediated FBP effects on reduced depression and psychiatric distress (indirect effect on grief levels at 6-year follow-up; Sandler et al., 2016a). Parental bereavement poses a risk for suicide (among other psychopathology; see Sandler, Tein, Wolchik, & Ayers, 2016b; Chapter 12). At the six-year follow-up, FBP also was associated with reduced suicidal ideation and/or attempts (Sandler et al., 2016b).

At the 15-year follow-up, young adults who were in FBP showed significantly lower mental health problems, less use of mental health services, and lower use of psychiatric medication compared to controls (Sandler et al., in press). Key informants reported lower overall mental health problems for FBP young adults (parent- and teacher-, not self-report). Particularly those who were younger (11 or younger) during FBP had significantly lower internalizing and externalizing problems than controls. Bereaved parents reported significantly lower alcohol use problems and less use of support groups than controls (Sandler et al., in press).

Traumatic Grief-CBT (TG-CBT)

TG-CBT is a modified form of TF-CBT (described above) for youth with grief. It adds four sessions to the protocol (Cohen et al., 2006a, 2006b): *grief-focused psychoeducation* (e.g., child: reading, grief education game, picture drawing; parent: grief-focused issues in context of culture, religion, family; eliciting a child's understanding of death, addressing parent's personal and grief issues), *resolution of ambivalent and/or negative feelings toward the deceased* (e.g., what is missed and not missed), *consolidating and maintaining positive memories of deceased* (for parent and child, if applicable), and *placing the relationship to deceased in the appropriate context* (focuses on current relationships with others; Allen et al., 2012; Cohen et al., 2006a, 2006b). It is essential to recognize the impact of loss on the child and family and its impact on treatment. For example, formerly comforting things (e.g., a room, a song, a game, relaxing) may now serve as traumatic reminders (e.g., positive memories of a deceased parent may remind of the manner of death). Clinicians must then work closely with parent and child to find new comforting rituals that do not trigger trauma or loss reminders (see TF-CBT). Modifications have been made for children when needed (e.g., see Kerig et al., 2010). CBT for complicated grief has demonstrated improvements in TG, PTSD, depression, and anxiety (Cohen et al., 2006b). It has also been used in a group format (O'Donnel et al., 2014).

Separation and Other Anxiety

Untreated childhood anxiety may develop into chronic anxiety, depression, and/or substance abuse (Beidas, Mychailyszyn, Podell, & Kendall, 2013; Kendall, Safford, Flannery-Schroeder, & Webb, 2004). Some evidence suggests that SAD (separation anxiety disorder) is prevalent among diagnoses in preadolescents and occurs equally in male and female youth (Glossary; Costello, Egger, & Angold, 2005; Eisen & Schaefer, 2007). Anxiety management is among emotion regulation skills. Treatments for SAD may address regulation of anxiety and other emotions (Beidas et al., 2013).

Studies of anxious youth have found their family environments to be higher in control and conflict and lower in warmth and support than families of children without internalizing problems (Eisen, Raleigh, & Neuhoff, 2008). For example, for behaviorally inhibited (BI) children followed from age one, maternal over-control and child BI predicted higher separation anxiety symptoms at age seven and in adolescence (Glossary; Lewis-Morrarty et al., 2012). Family environments of separation-anxious youth have often included insecure-ambivalent parent–child attachments and/or overprotection. Because parental anxiety has been linked to poorer treatment outcomes, assessment and treatment of parental anxiety may be necessary before child treatments are started (see Eisen et al., 2008).

Use of CBT for Anxiety

Some evidence suggests that group CBT is less effective for social anxiety disorder (SoAD; slower rate of change and poorer diagnostic outcomes) and more effective for children with a primary pre-treatment diagnosis of GAD and possibly OCD (Hudson et al., 2015a; exception: see Brief CBT, below). In the treatment of anxiety, CBT focuses on modifying cognitive (e.g., maladaptive thinking patterns) and behavioral (e.g., avoidance) patterns (Afshari et al., 2014; Kendall & Treadwell, 2007; Silverman, Pina, & Viswesvaran, 2008). CBT assists children to cope with anxiety-provoking situations, to recognize the somatic aspects of anxiety, and to develop anticipatory plans (Afshari et al., 2014).

Findings have been somewhat modest for CBT trials with anxiety (Eisen et al., 2008). As a result, emotion-focused treatments, parent training, and adapted psychotherapeutic methods have emerged. Emotion-focused methods have been used for behavioral and emotional self-regulation problems (e.g., N = 320, 4–9-year-olds; parenting program, Duncombe et al., 2016), for trauma symptoms, and for complex trauma as well (e.g., for adolescents: Stavrianopoulos, Faller, & Furrow, 2014; for adults: Hirai et al., 2012; for childhood traumas, Ford et al., 2005; Paivio et al., 2010; Timulak & McElvaney, 2016). In Emotion-focused CBT (EF-CBT), the child focuses on the recognition of emotions (e.g., anxiety, anger, guilt, happiness, etc.) in oneself and others (Afshari et al., 2014; Suveg, Kendall, Comer, & Robin, 2006). In the second half of EF-CBT treatment (exposure treatment), the child is exposed to anxiety and other emotion-provoking scenarios, with which the child has difficulty, in order to learn to manage the experiences. Both CBT and EF-CBT may use relaxation methods to reduce stress.

In children referred for SAD, both CBT and EF-CBT have reduced separation anxiety and total anxiety symptoms (parent and child reports; N = 34, age 9–13; Afshari et al., 2014). Ashfari and colleagues found that EF-CBT effectively reduced sadness dysregulation and increased sadness coping (initially but not at three months), increased anger coping and decreased dysregulation of anger and negative cognitive strategies in children (initially and at follow-up). CBT reduced negative cognitive strategies at follow-up (3 months) and increased sadness coping initially. Neither treatment influenced anger and sadness inhibition and positive cognitive coping.

Brief CBT

To be effective with anxiety, CBT generally includes psychoeducation, skill training (e.g., affect recognition, cognitive restructuring, relaxation, and problem-solving), and exposure to fear stimuli (Crawley et al., 2013). Brief CBT (BCBT) modifies CBT for childhood anxiety to community settings by reducing the length of treatment (from 16 sessions to eight; reducing cost and increasing access; Beidas et al., 2013; Kendall, Beidas, & Mauro, 2012). The first session is 1.5 hours—including 60 minutes building rapport with the child, orienting her/him to BCBT, normalizing anxiety, setting three main goals, discussing how different emotions express differently physically, assigning an initial task (e.g., a simple writing task about a situation when s/he felt good); the next 30 minutes provide the parent information, elicit situations that evoke the child's anxiety, discuss ways the parent can be involved in the treatment, and provide a copy of *Parent Companion* (Beidas et al., 2013; Kendall, Podel, & Gosch, 2010). Session 2 introduces skills for coping with anxiety—increasing identification of body-reactions, normalizing the body's fear/stress response, identifying thoughts and learning coping self-talk (e.g., "Am I feeling frightened?"; learning to discover if s/he is expecting bad things to happen—differentiating anxious vs coping self-talk). A hierarchy of anxiety-provoking situations is created, and a task is assigned for completion during the week (Beidas et al., 2013; Box 13.6). Session 3 addresses continued aspects of learning to cope (focus on attitudes and actions that help) including coping self-talk, problem-solving skills, strategies to challenge mental catastrophization, brainstorming solutions, and results and rewards of facing fears (and review of homework). Session 4 is another 1.5-hour session to introduce the exposure half of treatment. The fear hierarchy (prioritized fear list) is finalized (although it can be altered). A low

Box 13.6 Brief CBT for Young Boy with GAD

Seven-year-old Mike was taken to treatment for excessive worry as well as difficulty sitting still, difficulty relaxing, stomachaches, and irritability (Beidas et al., 2013). In brief CBT, because Mike had trouble sitting still and attending, the clinician used games to impart psychoeducational materials. To describe what was happening inside his body when scared while his father was driving on the freeway, Mike said that his body gave him a "headache," an "upset tummy," and he was "red in the face." *Show that I can* (STIC) tasks were used beginning with a simple task—a trip to the zoo with his family. He received praise and a dinosaur sticker for doing well. To learn about self-talk, pictures with empty bubbles to fill in dialogue were used, beginning with neutral situations and then situations that might be fear-provoking. Mike was permitted to fill in two different bubbles—one with negative and one with positive self-talk. Mike learned to have coping thoughts (see Beidas et al., 2013 for more aspects of the method and more case details).

anxiety-producing situation is used for the first exposure task. The child works through the fear with coaching when needed. The half-hour with the parent includes information and ways s/he can assist the child. In sessions 5–7, after review of that week's task with possible assistance of the parent coach, the child ascends the anxiety hierarchy. In the final (eighth) session, tasks are reviewed and progress praised. A last task with modeling safe behavior is engaged. Child and therapist review and summarize treatment and then parent, therapist, and child celebrate the child's accomplishments (e.g., pizza party), followed by concluding remarks (closure).

The BCBT adaptation—with less psychoeducation and greater use of exposure tasks—was used with 26 youth with a principal diagnosis of SAD, GAD, or social phobia (SP; ages 6–13; mostly Caucasian, with moderate to high SES; Crawley et al., 2013). Eight weeks after treatment, 42.3% of youth no longer met criteria for an anxiety disorder, and 33.3% maintained gains 2 months later. With the chance to continue practicing skills over time, by 1-year follow-up, 65% of youth no longer met criteria for an anxiety disorder (55% sought additional treatment—possibly booster treatments; youth with SP did not show continued increased gains at one year). In a study of childhood anxiety (SAD and social anxiety disorder [SOC]) using individual CBT and modified group CBT, both with an emphasis on in-session exposures (in addition to homework exposures), youth ages 7–13 (N = 165) continued to show improvement between posttreatment and two-year follow-up assessment (Villabø et al., 2018). Although both methods were superior to wait-list conditions, youth with SOC responded better to a group treatment format. Effectiveness may vary for ethnic and national groups.

Psychoanalytic Child Therapy (PaCT)

Manualized short-term Psychoanalytic Child Therapy (PaCT; Göttken, White, Klein, & Klitzing, 2014) has been used with anxious children (ages 4–10) and is described in Chapter 10.

Preventive School Interventions

School interventions have been used to assist children following trauma exposures (e.g., war, Berger, Pat-Horenczyk, & Gelkopf, 2007; disaster, Nader, 2010; e.g., as locations for service-provision, Pynoos & Nader, 1988), after loss of a significant person (Lytje, 2016), and for preventive interventions (e.g., for bullying or other school violence, Cornell, Sheras, Gregory, & Fan, 2009; Fonagy et al., 2009; Nader, 2012c; Twemlow, Sacco, & Twemlow, 1999). Preventive programs may improve developmental skills and resilience (Nader, 2012c; Schonert-Reichl, 2012; Wolmer, Laor, & Yazgan, 2003). In addition to assisting children, some methods may improve parenting, teacher efficacy, and home and/or school support for children through training parents and/or teachers (e.g., after natural disasters, Wolmer et al., 2003, 2005; after war/terrorism, Berger et al., 2007, Wolmer et al., 2011a, 2011b, 2016; see also Nader, 2012c).

An early version of a teacher training program (Wolmer et al., 2003; N = 81, earthquake-exposed 8–10-year-olds) has shown that teacher interventions may assist but do not serve as substitutes for clinical interventions following traumas. Youth may need additional treatments for trauma reactions. For example, after a teacher intervention, 27.5% of children had increased PTSS (41% of those children had high-risk factors), 33.5% remained the same, and 39% had reduced symptoms. Years after an earthquake (ages 9–17; N = 67 intervention children, 220 comparisons, Wolmer et al., 2005), while PTSS, grief, and dissociation significantly decreased for control and intervention children, intervention children showed significantly better school functioning (academically, socially, general conduct) than comparison children (teacher report). However, 30–50% reported moderate PTSS and 17–18% severe PTSS, suggesting the need for additional specialized interventions for moderately and severely traumatized youth. Later versions of the teacher training program have focused on improving resilience (Wolmer et al., 2011a; to follow). Much like US school programs to improve resilience and/or reduce bullying (Nader, 2012c), it has improved developmental skills (e.g., stress management). Such programs have been related to reduced mental health and behavior problems. Preventing traumas and improving developmental skills is important for children's ongoing safety and sense of well-being (Chapter 10). Three methods are presented here (see also Virginia Threat Assessment Model: Allen et al., 2008; Cornell et al. 2009; Daniels et al., 2010a, 2010b; see Nader, 2012c).

MindUP™

Formerly called the *Mindfulness Education Program*, MindUP™ (modules for grades K-2, 3–5, 6–8) includes 15 lessons to cultivate well-being and emotional balance as well as to reduce aggression (includes mindfulness-based stress reduction and social-emotional learning, Schonert-Reichl, 2012; Schonert-Reichl et al., 2015; http://teacher.scholastic.com/products/mindup). Lessons are once/week and are 40–50 minute lessons that can be broken into 10- and 15-minute portions (Maloney, Lawlor, Schonert-Reichl, & Whitehead, 2016). Teaching scripts and manuals are available. MindUP™ aims to foster children's social and emotional competence, psychological well-being, and improved EFs, while decreasing acting-out behaviors and aggression (Schonert-Reichl, 2012). It was designed to enhance children's self- and social-awareness, focused attention, self-regulation, problem-solving, prosocial behaviors, and positive qualities (e.g., happiness, optimism, altruism). Each MindUP ™ component builds on previous skills learned, hence moving children from focusing on subjective sense-based experiences (e.g., mindful smelling, mindful tasting) to cognitive experiences (e.g., perspective-taking), to actions at home, in the classroom, and in the community (e.g., practice of gratitude, kindnesses to others; Schonert-Reichl et al., 2015). Mindfulness practices include 3 min./daily practice focusing on breathing and attending to a single, resonant sound. When six MindUP™ program classes were matched with six comparison classes (N = 246 seventh graders; Schonert-Reichl & Stewart Lawlor, 2010), both teachers and students reported satisfaction with the program.

MindUP™ children have exhibited significant improvements in attention and social competence as well as decreases in aggressive and dysregulated classroom behaviors (teacher-rated; Schonert-Reichl & Stewart Lawlor, 2010). Additionally, MindUP™ children reported greater optimism and mindful attention than comparison children. Teachers and children reported MindUp™-related improvements in empathy, prosocial behaviors, focused attention, self-concept, emotional regulation, and greater appreciation of learning. A British-Columbian (Canada) social responsibility program includes performance standards: contributing to the classroom and school community (e.g., sharing responsibility for social and physical environment); solving problems in peaceful ways; valuing diversity and defending human rights; and practicing democratic rights and responsibilities (see Schonert-Reichl et al., 2015). Compared to children in the usual social responsibility program (who significantly decreased in skills and became worse), MindUP™ children showed greater cognitive control and stress physiology improvements; reported greater empathy, emotional control, mindfulness, optimism, perspective-taking, and school self-concept; showed larger decreases in self-reported symptoms of depression and in peer-rated aggression; had greater increases in peer-rated prosocial behaviors and in peer acceptance (N = 99 fourth to fifth graders in the program; Schonert-Reichl et al., 2015). Other researchers have found an association between MindUP™ and children's increased prosocial behaviors, improved self-regulation, better social competence, and better grades for children (see Thierry et al., 2016).

Creating a Peaceful School Learning Environment (CAPSLE)

CAPSLE is a whole-school approach to bullying prevention (a systems and mentalization-focused program, Fonagy et al., 2009; Twemlow et al., 1999; www.backoffbully.com). It enlists all students (bystanders, bullies, victims), teachers, and counselor or social work staff as drivers of behavior and addresses the lack of regard for mental states associated with violent actions (personal communication, P Fonagy, 9-22-18). It also involves other school staff and parents (Twemlow et al., 2008). CAPSLE promotes peace by changing the entire social dynamic surrounding bullying—i.e., bully–victim interactions as well as behaviors of those who bully and are victimized and by improving school climate (e.g., use of posters to alter language and thinking; see Espelage & Low, 2012; see Twemlow et al., 2008). The program includes a teacher discipline program, a positive school climate program (usually headed by counselor or social worker), a *Gentle Warrior* program (e.g., martial arts; promotes self-esteem; teaches alternatives to using violence for self-protection), a peer mentoring program, adult role model program, and family power struggles workshop (Twemlow et al., 1999). Central tenets include respect for others, building a sense of responsibility among youth and adults to stop bullying when witnessed (see Twemlow et al., 2008).

Compared to non-intervention schools, CAPSLE reduced referrals for aggressiveness and improved achievement test scores (reduced suspension rates and related to fewer visits to the Principal's office; Twemlow et al., 2001). Benefits also included reductions in classroom off-task and disruptive behavior, fewer experiences of youth victimization, and reduced numbers of peers nominated as aggressive, victimized, or bystanders; helpful bystanding increased (Fonagy et al., 2009, 2005). Reduced aggression and victimization persisted to 3-year assessment. Preliminary evidence suggests the effectiveness of using a martial arts program (*Gentle Warrior*) with boys to address bullying in schools, by teaching self-control, empathy, and peaceful strategies to resolve conflicts (N = 254, grades 3, 4, and 5; Twemlow et al., 2008). Over time, boys who participated in more *Gentle Warrior* sessions reported lower aggression frequency and greater helpful bystanding frequency (vs boys with fewer sessions). Changes in empathy mediated the relationship between program participation and reduced aggression. Compared to traditional methods (i.e., psychiatry fellows consult with school student-intervention teams), CAPSLE schools have had more decreasing-bullying trajectories and fewer problematic trajectories (Biggs et al., 2010; see also Appendix—MBT-C and Chapter 16—MBT-A, Appendix—Come Sit with Us).

School Resilience Program (SRP)

The School Resilience Program (SRP, Wolmer, Hamiel, & Laor, 2011b) is a manualized protocol, including 12–14 sessions (weekly, 45-minute didactic modules), that aims to enhance coping and improve performance in conditions of ongoing threat (e.g., war threat). Implemented country-wide in Israel, the method is based on stress inoculation findings (Chapter 1). School counselors (20-hour training; biweekly supervision) and teachers (four-hour basic training + biweekly supervision [total about 30 hours]) are trained in SRP methods. The program includes the following: *psychoeducation*—accurate expectations of the stress-environment and stress reactions; *skill acquisition*—Sessions 1–5: e.g., identifying emotions and thoughts; working through experiences—positive or negative; replacing dysfunctional thoughts; identifying and reducing body tension—e.g., slowing breathing, muscle relaxation; Sessions 6–7: internal balancing and managing fears; 8: identifying and managing negative thoughts; 9: power of positive experiences; 10: effects of humor; *rehearsal*—to develop and practice a repertoire of anxiety-reducing coping skills, to enhance capacity to respond effectively to stress; and *application of coping skills across increasing levels of stressors*—sessions 11–13: e.g., imagery, behavioral rehearsal, modeling, role playing, and graded in vivo exposure; fostering positive emotions; 14: recognizing the power of the group (Wolmer et al., 2011a, 2011b). In a study of Israeli school children (N = 1488; Wolmer et al., 2011b), youth in schools with the SRP training program had significantly lower PTSS/PTSD and stress/mood difficulties (especially boys and children with moderate to high SES) than control youth (who had 57% more symptoms). The program now has been implemented in more than 2000 Israeli schools for preschool and older (> 700,000 children) with observed changes in school culture as well as reductions in anxiety (personal communication, Leo Wolmer, 3-30-17).

Conclusions

A number of methods and adjunct methods have been used to assist school-age children following trauma exposures or after discovery of exposures. Creative methods have been productive adjunct methods to trauma-focused methods. Methods may help to repair the neurobiological effects of trauma as well as reduce PTS and other symptoms. In addition, preventive methods have improved coping skills, mood and cognitions, and safety skills.

As discussed, parent involvement in treatment is important to children's recovery. For example, parent blame or avoidance has been linked to worsened child symptoms. Teachers have been of primary importance in the success of preventive efforts as well as in posttrauma efforts related to a traumatized child at school. Children with dissociative symptoms are likely to need the addition of methods that reduce in session dissociation, enhance emotional distancing without increasing avoidance, and/or increase emotion-regulation. A number of circumstances or symptoms may increase posttrauma or grief reactions and may need special attention (e.g., grief, shame, guilt, lowered reflective functioning, behavior problems, emotional awareness). Schools may serve as sites for both prevention (e.g., increase coping and other skills; increase resilience) and intervention.

Part V

Ages 13–18+

14

Development in Youth Ages 13–17

Normal development in youth ages 13–17 has many important features; it is complex and variable. If you add trauma or other adversity, the interrelationship and nature of its features may increase in complexity and impact. The onset of adolescence has been located somewhere between puberty and teenage (13) and its completion at legal adulthood (age 18) or later—e.g., some brain changes suggest age 24. Some researchers place "emerging adulthood"—the years between leaving secondary school and entry into adulthood—at ages 18–24 or 18–29 (Arnett, 2016). Adolescence may be considered a period of reorganization of biological, cognitive, emotional, and social functioning (Biro & Dorn, 2006). Increases in self-consciousness, mood variability, novelty seeking, risk-taking, and orientation toward peers are characteristic in adolescence (Blakemore & Mills, 2014; Spear, 2000). Accordingly, in addition to maturation of executive functions (PFC and connectivity to other brain regions), the adolescent brain consolidates neural pathways under the dominant influence of social cues, motivation for immediate rewards, avoidance of boredom/dysphoria, and proneness to react to stressors without fully considering consequences and with dysphoria (Ford, 2017). Adolescent growth and development are influenced by youth tendencies (e.g., genetics, traits) and environments.

Although some adolescents seem to navigate this period with relative ease, others find that the neurobiological and related changes make life more difficult or confusing. Adolescence can be a period of both vulnerability and opportunity (Guyer, Silk, & Nelson, 2016). From an evolutionary perspective, greater anxiety and emotional reactivity may have been adaptive for ancient adolescents by increasing vigilance to potential predators. Currently, increases in depression during adolescence may be related to increased stressors (Spear, 2000). The capacity for impulse control is not fully developed in adolescence, and proneness to sensation seeking may increase (Steinberg et al., 2008; Stevens, Kiehl, Pearlson, & Calhoun, 2007). Adolescents appear to attain lower reward value from a number of stimuli than other age groups, perhaps leading them to seek additional appetitive reinforcers (e.g., risk-taking or novelty seeking, Spear, 2000; Luyten & Fonagy, in press). From infancy through middle childhood, children use caregivers as a secure base for exploration (e.g., Kerns & Brumariu, 2018). Risk-taking and novelty seeking have been described as the adolescent version of exploration. Adolescents may both overestimate risks and expect potential rewards to be very high in situations. A sense of invulnerability (linked to increased risk-taking) combined with the onset of more adult-like behaviors (e.g., driving, dating, substance availability) may result in increased exposure to potentially dangerous situations (see Habib & Labruna, 2011). Discussions of adolescent risk factors and developmental skills follow. Disorders and trauma/adversity's effects on development are discussed in Chapter 15; treatment methods in Chapter 16.

Adolescent Risk Factors

A number of risk and protective factors influence life trajectories and posttrauma outcomes (Chapter 15: Tables A1.1–A1.4). Chapter 4 examined variables related to increased likelihood of trauma and stressor-related symptoms—e.g., personal and community environmental factors, genetics, poly-victimization. Social support—e.g., family, school, peer, religious community—has been a robust protective factor after traumas across ages. In addition to parental or peer support, teacher support has also been important—e.g., for prevention of aggression, hopelessness, sadness (Nader, 2012c; after parental incarceration especially for males, Thurman, Johnson, Gonzalez, & Sales, 2018). As discussed, multiple risk or protective factors exceed the impact of single factors (Glossary; see Evans et al., 2013, for a summary). Attachment/parenting, genetics, and personality are presented here.

Adolescent youth are faced with a number of challenges/stresses—e.g., puberty (e.g., hormonal and brain changes), socioenvironmental contexts, the need to explore and learn from novel stressors, the move to greater independence (Spear, 2000). For example, puberty brings changes in the mind and body—e.g., in hypothalamic-pituitary-gonadal axis—usually between ages 10 or 11 for girls, 11 or 12 for boys (Blakemore & Mills, 2014; Crone, van Duijvenvoorde, & Peper, 2016; Table A4.2, reward). Like risk or protective factors, normal adolescent challenges may influence developmental trajectories. For example, pubertal maturation earlier than that of peers seems to be advantageous for boys—e.g., they are significantly more often more poised, less anxious, more self-assured and successful into adulthood (Ellis et al., 2012). Late maturing boys are significantly more likely to experience problems—e.g., lower self-esteem and more smoking and substance use (Biro & Dorn, 2006). In contrast to boys, earlier puberty appears to be disadvantageous for girls—e.g., greater likelihood of body image concerns, earlier sexual activity, substance use, depression (Graber, Seeley, Brooks-Gunn, & Lewinsohn, 2004; Biro & Dorn, 2006).

Caregiver–Youth Attachment/Parenting

Even in older adolescence and young adulthood, caregiver–youth relationships influence well-being. Although adolescents more often may challenge parental authority, frequent, high-intensity fighting with parents is non-normative (Collins & Steinberg, 2008). Adolescents' increasing autonomy, increased connection in intimate relationships and to peers, better metacognitive abilities, and clearer self–other distinctions may offer an opportunity to reevaluate relationships with parents (see Allen & Tan, 2018; Steele et al., 2015). While time spent with adult caregivers reduces, the increased involvement with friends and romantic partners offers opportunities to develop skills and competencies—e.g., reciprocity, cooperation, reciprocal altruism, and conflict negotiation—that, in turn, assist peer attachment bonds, individuation, differentiation from parents, and autonomy. Exploration and mastery of new environments take a central role (Allen & Tan, 2018). The press for autonomy competes with that toward the attachment system.

Relationships between most youth and their parents seem not to change drastically after middle childhood (Bosmans & Kerns, 2015; van IJzendoorn & Bakermans-Kranenburg, 2010). Some evidence suggests youth ages 14–16 have higher mutual trust and communication quality and lower alienation with mothers than with fathers (N = 420 Indian boys and girls, Devi, Baruah, Pradhan, & Borah, 2017). Early adolescents begin to use peers for attachment functions; mid-adolescent teens may rely on a close friend or romantic partner as a safe haven or secure base in contexts with relatively low levels of danger or challenge. Outside of ongoing parental monitoring of youth, providing a secure base, and remaining "in reserve," parents are obvious as attachment figures only when situations elicit high levels of attachment system activity—e.g., dangerous or challenging situations, high distress, or threats to caregiver availability—as well as when parental expertise is needed—e.g., learning to drive, planning the future (Allen & Tan, 2018; Kobak, Rosenthal, Zajac, & Madsen, 2011). Some evidence suggests that securely attached teens are more likely to nominate parents as primary attachment figures, in contrast to insecurely attached teens who are more likely to nominate peers as primary figures (Freeman & Brown, 2001; Kobak et al., 2011).

During adolescence, the attachment hierarchy (preference for particular attachment figures; Chapter 5) becomes more flexible and multidimensional—peers, then romantic partners enter the hierarchy (Allen & Tan, 2018). Adolescents' mental representations of relationships that become evident with intimate partners resemble those with parents and peers (Allen & Tan, 2018). Quality of relationships with parents (e.g., availability, responsiveness) and peers may play an important protective role; their lack may predispose teens to premature autonomy (Chapters 4, 5; Dishion, Nelson, & Bullock, 2004; Kobak et al., 2011). In contrast, delayed reorganization of attachment hierarchies—i.e., continued reliance on parents as primary attachment figures—may result in tension and conflict in the parent–child system or may increase the likelihood of anxiety and/or depression, which in turn may increase dependence and delay reorganization (Kobak et al., 2011).

During late childhood and early adolescence, parental availability and responsiveness are indicated in caregivers' warmth; in their successful provision of monitoring of youth behaviors, peers, and school activities; and in their respect for adolescents' growing needs for autonomy and self-regulation (Kobak et al., 2011). Lower levels of parental monitoring and discipline have been linked to adolescent affiliation with deviant peers and to delinquent behaviors (Galambos, Barker, & Almeida, 2003; Kobak et al., 2011). Family environments have proven to be strong contributors to delinquency in adolescents (Beaver et al., 2012).

Influences on Parenting

Such variables as youth temperamental differences, the quality of bonds between youth and parent, genetics, and parent's own attachment style have been related to parenting styles (Glossary). For example, Lee et al. found that Chinese parents whose children were low on effortful control or high on anger/frustration became more authoritarian over time (studied ages 6–9 and 3.8 years later; no link for authoritative parenting; Lee, Zhou, Eisenberg, & Wang, 2013). The relationship appears to be bidirectional. Chinese children whose parents were highly authoritarian became less regulated and more prone to anger/frustration over time. Beaver et al. (2012) found that three dopaminergic genes influenced family environments—DRD2 showed significant effects on negative maternal parenting, negative paternal parenting (white fathers only), and childhood maltreatment; DAT1 significantly predicted negative maternal parenting (not paternal); DRD4 consistently was not significant on all parenting and maltreatment scales (N = >2500 genotyped of a larger sample).

Parent's own attachment insecurity has been associated with less sensitive, supportive, and responsive parental behavior (and partner relationship behavior; summary in Jones, Cassidy, & Shaver, 2015; Table A3.2, A3.3). Maternal insecurity has indirectly related to greater harsh, more distressed, and less supportive reactions to adolescents' negative emotions via maternal difficulties with emotion regulation (more study needed—adult attachment and parenting adolescents). Maternal attachment avoidance (not anxiety/preoccupation) has been related to less adolescent secure base use, directly and via greater mother-reported hostile behavior toward adolescents and via adolescents' negative perceptions of mothers—i.e., perception of less availability, warmth, and understanding and of greater hostility. Father anxiety/preoccupation (not avoidance) related to lower secure base use. Mothers' and fathers' attachment insecurity were associated with low knowledge of adolescents' whereabouts and activities (parent report). Maternal avoidance (not anxiety) and paternal anxiety (not avoidance) were linked to youths' perceptions that parents had lower knowledge of their whereabouts. The degree to which youth perceive their parents to be knowledgeable of their whereabouts has predicted lower levels of risk-taking and delinquency (see Jones et al., 2015).

Parenting Style

Although studies on parenting style and adolescents generally find positive associations for positive parenting and negative for negative parenting, studies of both parents have shown that some styles may compensate for others. Generally, for adolescents in Western cultures, authoritative parenting (warm, responsive, and demanding) has been related to greater competence, responsibility, and self-assurance (Steinberg & Silk, 2002; Glossary—parenting style). Authoritarian parenting (demanding and not responsive) has been linked to more dependence and passivity and to less social adeptness, self-assurance, and intellectual curiosity. Indulgent parenting has been related to lower maturity and less leadership ability and to higher irresponsibility and more peer conformity. Parental indifference has been related to impulsive and delinquent behavior, and early experimentation with sex, drugs, and alcohol (see *uninvolved* parenting in the following paragraphs).

Positive parenting has been associated with positive outcomes—e.g., increased adolescent self-disclosure (Hunter et al., 2011). Parental knowledge, which has been linked to monitoring and to youth self-disclosure, has proven consistently protective against adolescent negative outcomes—e.g., lower delinquency, behavior problems, manipulation of parents, mental health problems such as depression or expectations of failure (Hunter et al., 2011). Father–adolescent reciprocity has independently predicted youths' ability to handle conflict in dialogical ways—i.e., matters that play out in dialogues within and among the many aspects of self and the many aspects of others (Dimaggio, Hermans, & Lysaker, 2010), whereas mother–adolescent reciprocity has shaped youth's dialogical skills during positive interactions (Feldman et al., 2013a). Positive parenting has been linked to less relational aggression (meta-analysis; large effect sizes; Kawabata et al., 2011).

Negative parenting has been assessed variously as over-reactive (e.g., physical/corporal punishment); rigidly demanding and low warmth; inconsistent; harsh; or lax parenting (Egan et al., 2014; Steinberg & Silk, 2002). Parenting styles that include authoritarian parenting (high demandingness, low warmth)—e.g., mixtures of overt praise and coldness, low supervision, corporal punishment, and authoritarian parenting—have predicted future maladaptive behaviors (e.g., narcissism, Dimaggio, 2012; adaptive and maladaptive perfectionism, Gong, Paulson, & Wang, 2016). Parental conflict and parental psychological control each have been related to maladaptive perfectionism (Glossary; Gong et al., 2016). In addition to hyperactivity and poor emotional control, corporal punishment has accounted for significant variation in adolescent oppositional defiant behavior (Egan et al., 2014). A meta-analysis of studies on relational aggression and parenting style (N = 28,097) revealed that harsh and uninvolved parenting were related to higher levels of relational aggression in youth (Kawabata et al., 2011). Paternal (not maternal) psychologically controlling behavior was also related to higher relational aggression, especially for girls. Harsh fathering has been linked to child aggression and externalizing symptoms (Conger et al., 1994).

Reactions to parenting styles vary in some ways depending on a youth's temperament. Although findings are somewhat mixed on parenting and behavioral inhibition (BI), in a group of children followed from age four to age 15, greater authoritative parenting (warmth, support, firm control) was linked to a smaller increase in internalizing behavior problems in adolescents with BI, whereas greater authoritarian parenting (high control, low warmth, low autonomy support) related to a steeper decline in externalizing problems (Rankin Williams et al., 2009; see also Table A5.1). Overprotective parenting has been related to increased anxiety for BI children (Howard et al., 2017).

There are fewer studies of both parents' styles than of mother's style (see positive parenting, Conger et al., 1994, above). For European American adolescents (N = 451), having two authoritative parents was related to the lowest levels of depression and highest levels of school commitment (Simons & Conger, 2007). However, the lowest levels of delinquency were related to having an authoritative mother and an indulgent father (child report of parenting), or to an authoritative father with an indulgent mother (observer report). Having at least one authoritative parent fosters better outcomes than with none. Having an authoritative mother was most protective if the father was indulgent rather than authoritarian or uninvolved. Mothers have often remained primary caregivers for adolescent children. Combinations with an uninvolved mother were worse than with an uninvolved father. Authoritarian parents were usually married to an authoritative, indulgent, or uninvolved spouse (not all combinations were large enough to study; Simons & Conger, 2007).

The effects of parenting style persist into the college years. For example, in a study of 234 university students, low paternal care was predictive of general distress/negative affect (found in depression and anxiety; Rekart, Mineka, Zinbarg, & Grifficth 2007). Low maternal care was the best predictor of Anhedonic Depression (AD, Glossary). Higher paternal overprotection (for males; negligibly for females) and family conflict predicted higher somatic anxiety.

Youth Attachment Classifications

Adolescent attachment classification has been related to adjustment, aggression levels, self-worth, academic performance, perfectionism, procrastination, self-injury, and other outcomes (internalizing, externalizing), in expected directions (see Shame, this chapter; see Chapter 15). Adolescent attachment security has been related to higher levels of social and emotional adjustment, more positive relationships with both family and peers, better academic outcomes, and reduced likelihood of having emotional problems or engaging in problem behaviors with parents or peers (Innamorati et al., 2018; parent and peer attachment, Rashwan et al., 2017). For example, Italian adolescents' perceived attachment to mothers and fathers and their self-esteem were negatively related to depressive symptoms in both immigrant and non-immigrant youth (Miconi, Moscardino, Ronconi, & Altoe, 2017). Youth with high levels of parent–adolescent attachment were more likely to have high levels of self-worth, which in turn enhanced academic engagement and improved grades (Chen, 2017). Compared to insecure, secure adolescent attachments have been related to greater empathy (varies by culture, Laible, Carlo, & Raffaelli, 2000), more prosocial behavior, and better ability to regulate emotional arousal (see Allen & Tan, 2018; also for adults, Shaver et al., 2018) as well as to lower materialism and less defensive self-protection (Shaver et al., 2018). Attachment security has been negatively related to bullying, directly and through promoting prosocial values (N = 375 Italian adolescents, ages 11–12, 13–14, and 15–16; Innamorati et al., 2018).

Insecure attachments have been linked to more problems. Insecure attachments are more often characterized by ongoing problems with parents, increased hostility, poorer social skills, and more romantic but less qualitative relationships (Hesse et al., 2003). Both insecure styles have been linked to increased adolescent depression; directionality is unknown. For adolescent youth, engaging in bullying was linked to insecure attachment to mothers, while being victims of bullying was related to insecure attachments to fathers (Innamorati et al., 2018). Increased father emotional support of peer-victimized adolescents was associated with lower levels of emotional and behavioral problems concurrently and over time. For another group of bullying-victimized adolescents (N = 222, Portuguese adolescents ages 12–17), aggressive but not non-aggressive bullying victims perceived lower attachment security with both parents (Guedes et al., 2018).

Adolescents with infant ambivalent classifications have been more likely to have later anxiety diagnoses (both ambivalent and avoidant in some studies; DeKlyen & Greenberg, 2018). The normal adolescent shift away from the parental attachment system, at least temporarily, may show a rise in assessments finding dismissing attachments in adolescents (Allen & Tan, 2018). Avoidant/Dismissing adolescent classifications have been highly represented in an OCD population (DeKlyen & Greenberg, 2018). Youth with disorganized attachments may exhibit controlling or parenting behaviors to caregivers and show increased risk of psychopathology (Table A3.4). Disorganized attachments have been linked to aggression, dissociative-like behaviors, and psychopathology (Hesse et al., 2003).

Narrative Style

Steele et al. (2015) describe four or five narrative patterns of adolescents and adults in response to the Adult Attachment Interview that essentially reflected standard attachment classifications: (1) a typically healthy response of autonomy, marked by flexibility in the regulation of anxiety and guilt, and credible consistency in the narrative; (2) insecure-dismissing responses that usually deny anxiety and guilt, maintain that all is and was well despite evidence of childhood attachment difficulties that may be inferred from excessive defensiveness or other inconsistencies in the narrative; (3) insecure-preoccupying responses that show attachment difficulties governed by anger, passivity, and immaturity, or unremitting fearfulness, despite an urgent wish to connect meaningfully with others; it usually includes or ends with persisting disappointment; and (4) an autobiographical narrative that presents with dramatic shifts from dismissal—e.g., derogation or idealization toward one attachment figure—to preoccupation—e.g., anger and unsettled resentment toward another attachment figure at other points in the interview (unclassifiable; Steele, Bate, Nikitiades, & Buhl-Nielsen, 2015).

Prosocial Behaviors

Parenting and attachment have been related to prosocial behaviors (authoritative parenting to prosocial + social competence, Kawabata et al., 2011). Attachment, sometimes in combination with specific skills, has influenced prosocial behaviors—e.g., emotion-regulation has mediated the link between security and care for others (see Shaver et al., 2018). Similar to young children, some evidence suggests lower empathy and lower prosocial behavior in dismissing/avoidant youth but not in resistant/preoccupied youth. Although gratitude and forgiveness have had positive effects on well-being, they may be less positive for insecurely attached individuals (e.g., tainted with anxiety, see Shaver et al., 2018). Studies have found an inverse relationship between kind-heartedness—e.g., compassion, benevolence, concern for close others and/or humankind—and insecure attachments and have found a positive relationship between insecurity and personal distress—e.g., in response to story of another's loss. Insecure youth have been less involved in voluntary altruism (see Shaver et al., 2018). They may join such activities and choose a career with ulterior motives—e.g., *avoidant* for less altruistic reasons; *resistant* hoping for social acceptance and approval (Gillath et al., 2005; Shaver et al., 2018). Some evidence suggests that, when behaving generously, preoccupied youth may have greater feelings of emotional-cost/burden and guilt/self-criticism, whereas avoidant youth may feel emotional-cost/burden and have a reduced prosocial orientation (see Shaver et al., 2018). Resistant youth tend not to believe they deserve kindness, may worry they will be unable to reciprocate adequately or to meet a generous person's needs and expectations, and may fear that, "as usual," things begin well and end poorly (Mikulincer & Shaver, 2007).

Closeness

Although support seeking is not the same as attachment, adolescents increasingly use peers for support (Allen & Tan, 2018). A difference between insecure resistant (preoccupied) and avoidant (dismissive) youth is that in striving for intimacy and closeness, resistant adolescents worry a great deal about being valued, accepted, and cared for by others (strong and worried need for belonging), while avoidant adolescents worry about being hurt if they trust others completely or allow themselves to be too close (Feeney et al., 2008). A strong focus on their own attachment needs may explain resistant adolescents' acceptance of any type of peer behavior that centers on their needs and may explain impeded ability to respond to others' needs.

Although dismissing/avoidant adolescents have reported greater warmth and caring by parents than secure (Borelli et al., 2013), they show higher cardiovascular reactivity during a conflict interaction task with mothers (see Chapter 11). This positivity bias may or may not portend difficulties—e.g., in the short-term, highly avoidant adults cope well with relational stressors and other types of losses, although they may fare more poorly following divorce (Fraley & Bonanno, 2004). Avoidant youth have shown special ability to regulate their attention—e.g., away from negative attachment-related emotions; toward attentional tasks (Gillath, Giesbrecht, & Shaver, 2009). However, the ability can be hampered by reminders of a past insecure experience.

Feedback Seeking

Some evidence suggests that youth seek information that is consistent with their self-views (see Cassidy, Ziv, Mehta, & Feeney, 2003)—e.g., youth with better self-concepts, youth without depression, and youth with greater maternal acceptance sought significantly more positive feedback; youth with lower self-concepts or with depression sought significantly more negative feedback than comparisons (N = 293 11th graders; Cassidy et al., 2003). Global self-worth mediated the link between acceptance and feedback seeking.

Although seeking feedback is common to all attachment classifications and can be adaptive—e.g., self-enhancing; confirming or correcting self-perception—excessive reassurance seeking (ERS) and/or negative feedback seeking (NFS) can strain relationships (e.g., become annoying) and may increase negative moods and/or depressive symptoms (see Evraire et al., 2014). Insecure individuals appear to need others' approval to experience self-worth (e.g., Evraire et al., 2014). For college students (ages 17–48), higher levels of fear of abandonment as well as insecure attachments (anxious or avoidant) increased the risk for ERS (Evraire & Dozois, 2014). Attachment schemas and early maladaptive schemas (Glossary) have shown some parallels (see Evraire & Dozois, 2014). Beyond the effects of depression, showing an anxious or avoidant attachment classification or an abandonment/instability schema each added to the prediction of ERS. Avoidant attachment and abandonment/instability schema moderated the relationship between ERS and depression over time (N = 303). Evraire et al. (2014) found resistant students were more likely to exhibit ERS but distrusted the reassurance. These individuals were significantly unlikely to engage in NFS. Avoidant attachment was negatively but not significantly related to ERS (other researchers have found no or a significant negative correlation; see Evraire et al., 2014). Avoidant individuals were significantly more likely to engage in NFS. ERS may differ by disorder. For example, individuals with OCD reported reassurance seeking primarily about perceived general threats (e.g., theft, fire), whereas depressed individuals reported reassurance seeking primarily related to perceived social threats (e.g., abandonment, loss of support, N = 50, Parrish & Radomsky, 2010). For early adolescent girls (N = 126), rumination has been related to ERS, which in turn predicted increases in acute dependent and chronic interpersonal stress (Stroud, Sosoo, & Wilson, 2018).

Continuity of Attachment

Attachment styles are strongly influenced by ongoing experiences in interpersonal relationships, life events, and other issues—e.g., personal therapy, transition to parenthood, trauma (N = 551 twin pairs, age 15, Fearon et al., 2014). For a cohort of individuals followed from birth, differences in adult attachment (at age 18) were linked to variations in the quality of caregiving environments—early and changes in maternal sensitivity, father absence, maternal depression; emerging social competence; and the quality of best friendships (N = 707; Fraley et al., 2013). For a large sample of 15-year-olds originally assessed in infancy (at ages 15, 24, and 36 months, N = 857), Groh et al. (2014) found only weak stability in attachment security and disorganization—e.g., weak stability, age 15-month disorganization to preoccupied states of mind in adulthood; age 36-month disorganization to unresolved related to loss and/or trauma in late adolescence; stability in attachment security from 24 and 36 months to late adolescence. Temperaments and genetics (e.g., dopaminergic, serotonergic, and oxytonergic) were not correlated with adult attachments, with one exception—a serotonin receptor gene polymorphism predicted insecure attachment (Table A4.1—serotonin, HTR2A). The associations between early caregiving and adult attachment were relatively small. By age 18, decreases in social competence from childhood to adolescence were more robust predictors of attachment insecurity than were early levels of social competence (Fearon et al., 2014). Decreases in friendship quality across time were better predictors of avoidance than decreases in earlier family variables—i.e., maternal sensitivity, maternal depression, father absence.

The Power of Genetics

Although often tested and discussed individually, genes often work synergistically (Cerda et al., 2010; Chapter 4). Genes or gene combinations influence reactivity and reactions to stressors (Chapter 4). For example, genes have been linked to differential susceptibility to stress (e.g., serotonin, dopamine; Belsky & Pluess, 2009; Del Giudice et al., 2011; see Nader & Fletcher, 2014; Vaughn & Bost, 2018). Adolescents with protective or less environmentally sensitive genetics and no trauma exposure have displayed a decreased likelihood of psychiatric disorders. Those with sensitive genetics have had more problems in poor environmental conditions than non-sensitive youth.

Differential susceptibility suggests that youth fare better than others in positive environments and worse than others in negative environments. Youth with dopamine D4 receptor gene (DRD4 7r allele) who experienced less responsive and stimulating early maternal care (originally, age three months) have exhibited more symptoms of ADHD and CD/ODD—e.g., disinhibited, undercontrolled and hostile behaviors such as aggression, impulsiveness, violence, and delinquency—as well as higher levels of psychopathic behavior at age 15 (Nikitopoulos et al., 2014). However, DRD4 7r allele carriers had fewer ADHD symptoms and less psychopathic behavior when early caregiving was especially beneficial. Adolescents without the allele appeared insensitive to the effects of early maternal care. For 12 (N = 909) and 17 (N = 398) year-olds, an FKBP5 genotype (Glossary) has interacted with adverse events to influence poor mental health outcomes—e.g., depression, PTSD, psychosis, suicidality and attempts, aggression, differential cortisol recovery response after stress (consistent with adult findings; Comasco et al., 2015); threat-related right amygdala reactivity (emotional memory and fear) in adolescents (White et al., 2012a). A serotonin polymorphism (5-HTTLPR)—associated with greater emotionality and sensitivity to environmental stimuli has varied somewhat by attachment classification (Allen & Tan, 2018). Secure adolescents with 5-HTTLPR short allele have had greater agreeability in handling autonomy issues with parents, in contrast to insecure adolescents with the short allele, who have displayed more hostile autonomy in interactions with parents.

Genes have been related to specific symptoms as well as to developmental skills—e.g., slower disengagement from emotional stimuli (see Kretschmer, Sentse, Dijkstra, & Veenstra, 2014). For adolescents, serotonin has been implicated for a number of problems such as neuroticism (e.g., Kretschmer et al., 2014), callous-unemotional traits (HTR1b and HTR2a, ages 3–16, Moul et al., 2013), emotion-focused coping (vs problem-focused—5-HTTLPR, short allele; N = 18, Carkaxhiu Bulut, Rodopman Arman, Güney, & Gültepe, 2017), mood disorders—e.g., depression, anxiety (e.g., Kretschmer et al., 2014), suicidality (5-HTTLPR-s, e.g., suicidality and depression, Caspi et al., 2003a), and non-suicidal self-injury (5-HTTLPR, e.g., +high stress, Hankin et al., 2015). For children and adolescents, longer variants of DRD4 have been linked to poorer executive functioning (lower sustained attention and planning) and to poorer social/emotional development (prosocial behaviors, secure attachments; meta-analysis, N = 13,195; Pappa et al., 2015; see Table A4.1—DRD4).

Genes have also been linked to personality traits as well as to symptom types (e.g., Table A4.1—DRD2 and DRD4, Serotonin). Specific serotonin polymorphisms have been related to low levels of self-transcendence, self-directedness, and/or cooperatives and have been related to high levels of negative emotionality, worry- and distress-proneness, pessimism and harm avoidance (Table A4.1). The mesolimbic dopaminergic system has been shown to be central in motivated behaviors, reward, and cognitive processes (Alcaro, Huber, & Panksepp, 2007). For example, specific dopamine polymorphisms have been related to increased novelty seeking or to low self-directedness (see Delvecchio, Bellani, Altamura, & Brambilla, 2015; Table A4.1). When expressed at the motor level, DA transmission promotes neural activity patterns that induce active *seeking* behaviors (Alcaro et al., 2007). The seeking system may have evolved to promote seeking life-supporting stimuli and avoiding harm (Alcaro et al., 2007). The extended networks of seeking have influenced attention, incentive salience, associative learning, and anticipatory predictions. More study is needed.

Personality

Personality influences relationships, behaviors, reactions, needs, and treatment outcomes (Chapters 4, 11, 17). For example, personality differences may influence adult-youth rapport (Table 17.1, A5.1). Externalizing has been linked to traits such as *novelty seeking, impulsivity*, and *disinhibition* (and other variables—e.g., trauma, genetics; Table A5.1). Traits may influence, e.g., support seeking, support offered, and a discordant versus synchronous environment. Traits may also result in clashes, related to differences in style, with parents, teachers, clinicians, and other advisors (e.g., clergy). Areas of potential clash are discussed in Chapter 17. Traits in combination with each other may especially influence behaviors and outcomes. More than one personality system of combined traits has been applied to youth (see Nader, 2008; A5.1-A5.2)—e.g., the five-factor model (Glossary); Jungian-based types (Table 17.1). In addition to the five well-known factors found for adults, two additional factors were found for children and young adolescents (activity and irritability; Caspi, 1998). Personality traits may be interrelated, and their impact can be mediated by resilience factors—e.g., self-efficacy has mediated traits linked to increased risk-taking (adults, Merritt & Tharp, 2013; Risk-Taking, to follow). Some gender and genetic differences have been shown in personality traits (Table A5.1—Gender; see Trauma and Psychopathy, this chapter). Personality will be additionally discussed in relationship to other issues in sections to follow (e.g., risk-taking, externalizing).

Developmental Domains

Among major adolescent developmental tasks are separation and individuation; struggles with identity and self-perception (Habib & Labruna, 2011); and interdependence and relational issues (e.g., friendship, romantic intimacy), which may be magnified by struggles to find purpose and meaning in life (Bauminger et al., 2008; Collins & Steinberg, 2008). Family, peer, and other group and dyad contexts as well as a child's experiences influence these tasks. For example, the process of self-definition may vary in relationship to a youth's varied contexts (Box 14.1; see Self-Awareness).

Adolescence also includes prolonged development of the prefrontal cortex (PFC) and maturing cognitive and behavioral abilities–e.g., working memory (WM, e.g., mentally manipulating multiple items), processing speed, future planning, suppressing/inhibiting reflexive behavior, relational reasoning, and delay discounting (Glossary; see Blakemore & Mills, 2014, Chapter 15—Trauma's Effects on Development). Some aspects of development continue to progress and others are suppressed during adolescence. There are plateaus or regressions for some skills (Chapter 11)—e.g., contextual fear expression is intact in preadolescent age groups, is suppressed during adolescence, and re-emerges during adulthood (Glossary; Pattwell, Lee, & Casey, 2013). Cued fear learning is blunted but resistant to extinction during adolescence (essential to survival). Suppression of contextual fear (Glossary) may contribute to the characteristic adolescent fearlessness or sense of invulnerability that is needed for exploring new environments and new behaviors (Pattwell et al., 2013;

Box 14.1 Differences in Identity Formation: Conversations with Parents and Youth

a. Valerie and Jennifer both went to private school. Classrooms were small enough to permit teachers to incorporate each youth's personal likes and experiences, and aspects of their parents' values into the lessons. Although Valerie was more of a leader than Jennifer, both girls lived in loving families, had positive attachments to parents, and had a sense of their own beliefs and goals. Valerie had a solid self-image, often provided ideas for group goals, and volunteered to lead. When Jennifer's parents were transferred out-of-state, Jennifer went to a larger, secular private school. There, she was acculturated into a mainstream peer group that seemed to be struggling with identity issues that Jennifer had not encountered before (e.g., gay vs bisexual vs straight; rebel vs normal participant vs culture changer). She soon took on those struggles.

b. Topher attended an alternative school that focused on individual learning styles, teaching based on research findings, and group cohesion—every man for each other. School sports/games allowed everyone to play and included encouragement for each student from each other student and from all teachers. His mother worried when he entered regular high school that he would be bullied (more *Ferdinand the Bull* than *alpha male*). When he entered public high school, Topher was well liked because he was both intelligent and one of the kindest people around. He seemed to have a personal sense of peace. He had a very good relationship with his mother and an acceptable relationship with his sometimes more distant father (with whom he was very patient). His mother was a meditator and taught him to meditate. He had a clear sense of his own identity, and was unperturbed by other students who tried on one persona, then another. In fact, he was always friendly and encouraging to others. Not every youth from his original school was as easygoing and well defined as Topher. Some of them had busy, disengaged, or harsh parents, specific traits, or negative experiences that translated into increased struggles with identity issues.

c. Angela was very active in high school—on two sports teams at first, then specialized. She took AP classes and maintained an A average. When her mother suggested she take fewer AP classes, because they were very demanding and her schedule was also very demanding, Angela said, "No way! I'm not going back into regular classes. Those kids are struggling with things I don't need to fool with. I know who I am, and I know what I believe." Angela explained that there were a lot of kids at school with anxiety and not comfortable with themselves. "They try on a lot of things. One fad is to be bisexual. A lot of kids try it out—it's pretty popular and normalized. Some kids find their identities in grades—they're very competitive and become very anxious if they don't meet their parents' or their own standards. Some want to be liked for who their friends are or for sports ability. Not me. I'm comfortable with who I am."

Note:
All case examples are disguised, may be combined cases, and have had details changed to protect individuals.

Spear, 2000). Thus, suppression of some fear may assist autonomy. Increased novelty seeking and risk-taking also seem appropriate to the tasks of exploration and move toward independence.

Body Image and Regulation

Both sleep quality and body image are important to adolescent well-being.

Sleep Quality

A sense of interpersonal-security—affiliative connectedness—has been related to better sleep quality (see Gunn et al., 2017). Attachments to both parents, for toddlers and for adolescents, has moderated the relationship between sleep quality and both self-esteem and anxiety (Tu, Marks, & El-Sheikh, 2017). For a small sample of university students (N = 98), affiliation with a close-knit group and trust in others (not autonomy) were associated with better sleep during periods of stress (Gunn et al., 2017). Affiliation was linked to lower cognitive arousal and better sleep.

Sleep quality combined with attachment quality has influenced some outcomes (objective and subjective measures; Tu et al., 2017). Although less secure adolescent attachment to either parent tended to relate to higher levels of anxiety, independent of sleep quality (efficiency, long-wake episodes), more secure attachment alone did not buffer effects of poor-quality sleep. As toddlers and later as adolescents, good quality sleep combined with more secure attachment and was related to the lowest levels of anxiety (N = 106 US adolescents; Tu et al., 2017). Regardless of attachment quality, youth with less disturbed sleep had lower levels of externalizing and higher self-esteem. Adolescents with the highest levels of externalizing and lowest levels of self-esteem had less secure attachments and poorer sleep quality. Minutes of sleep and sleep efficiency were significantly directly related to depression but not to anxiety, externalizing symptoms, or self-esteem; depression was directly related to attachment. Best results were found for youth with good sleep patterns and good family contexts (secure attachments; non-aggression; more study is needed). Hence, good quality sleep is essential to functioning, and protective factors do not necessarily compensate for lack of good sleep.

Body Image

In more than the last decade, media has influenced body image. In 2008, across 77 studies, repeated media images depicting the thin ideal female body were associated with body image concerns or body dissatisfaction for girls and women (combined N = 15,047; Grabe, Ward, & Hyde, 2008). Findings were consistent with the idea that those exposed to such media significantly more often scored higher on indices of dieting, binging, purging, and/or anorexic attitudes. Though in 2018 women have strongly complained about the media-depicted thin ideal body, a number of girls and young women also have complained about or ostracized non-thin women and/or continued to strive for a thin body. For example, a political satirist pointed out that, numerous women criticized a non-thin actress for a movie depiction that they felt did not represent normal sized women well enough (e.g., her clothes, her style) at the same time they praised the thin model who played Wonder Woman without apparent reservation (Bill Maher, HBO, June 2018). Culture has played a role in body image—e.g., the average adult female dress size is higher in Texas than in California. In a comparison of African American, Asian American, and European American college students, African American women reported the greatest level of body satisfaction (Lupinski, 2003). For DSM-5 disorders, body image problems are common for individuals with psychopathology (Scheffers et al., 2017; Chapter 15).

Although poor body image is common among both genders, it is more prevalent among girls/women. Nevertheless, for boys, increased body mass index (overweight), more self-silencing behaviors (Glossary), and higher levels of internalization of a masculine body ideal (defined by age group cultural attitudes) have all contributed to poor body esteem in male youth (N = 1253, grades 7–12; Obeid et al., 2018). Self-esteem related to appearance and weight satisfaction were significantly related to externalized self-perception, self-silencing, internalization of male body ideals, awareness of media ideals, perceived importance of muscular looks, and caring for others before oneself. Male body dissatisfaction appears to be less tied to the thoughts and evaluations of others than to males' own esteem and self-perception. Media-driven ideals and self-silencing influenced all aspects of body esteem.

Executive Functions (EFs)

Early adolescence shows a major transformation in cognitive thought leading to abstract reasoning (Spear, 2000). However, adolescent decision-making capacity may be more easily disrupted by everyday stresses than adults' decision-making. This may be related to increased distractibility and poorer attention focusing. Across cultures, most EFs improve from early to later adolescence—e.g., Southeast Asian-Pakistani adolescents' age-related improvements in cognitive performance (EFs) have shown parallels with brain maturation—i.e., in processing speed, creativity, inhibition, and problem-solving ability (ages 13–19; Fatima, Sheikh, & Ardila, 2015). However, problem-solving scores on a card-sorting task were relatively low, suggesting that this skill is still maturing even in late adolescents. Assessments of psychomotor function, attention, WM, and visual learning have suggested reductions in reaction time and increases in accuracy across adolescent development (ages 10–18, N = 5788, Cromer, Schembri, Harel, & Maruff, 2015). Response-inhibition matures in late childhood, task-switching matures around early puberty, and WM in mid-adolescence (Crone et al., 2016; Huizinga, Dolan, & van der Molen, 2006).

A number of variables influence EF skill levels—e.g., gender, trauma, parenting, media use, personality, interventions (e.g., Fatima et al., 2015; Luu & Hall, 2015). Some evidence suggests that boys perform better on tests emphasizing visual-spatial abilities, and girls on tests emphasizing linguistic abilities (see Fatima et al., 2015). Baumgartner et al. (2014) found that youth's more frequent engaging in media multitasking was linked to more problems with EFs (WM, shifting, inhibition), although they were better at ignoring irrelevant distractions (lab; ages 11–15). Personality also has influenced aspects of EFs—e.g., had both a direct and an indirect effect on learning strategies and school attitude. For older Italian adolescents (ages 17–19), personality traits have been related directly to use of particular learning strategies and have been related to learning strategies via problem-solving skills (Ginevra et al., 2015; see Problem-Solving, to follow). Improvements in EFs have followed aerobic exercise, resistance training, meditation, breathing exercises (Luu & Hall, 2015; see Chapter 16).

Brain and EFs

Adolescent ongoing brain development (white and gray matter) has been linked to changes in cognitive function (e.g., IQ, WM, problem-solving improvements) and social cognition (Fuhrmann et al., 2015). Brain regions that integrate cognitive and affective information are later maturing regions (Biro & Dorn, 2006). While white brain matter volume and integrity normally increase with age in many cortical regions, gray matter volume increases from infancy through childhood, then declines throughout adolescence into the twenties (Fuhrmann et al., 2015), perhaps related to the normal overproduction of synapses followed by pruning during adolescence (and other periods; Huang et al., 2015).

Memory

Neural areas subserving memory and attention undergo significant maturation during adolescence (Putnam, Ellis, & Rothbart, 2001). Memory for even mundane events during adolescence and early adulthood appear to be over-represented in memory, suggesting heightened mnemonic capacity during this age range (Fuhrmann et al., 2015; Janssen & Murre, 2008). Emotionally arousing events usually elicit more attention and better memory (vs neutral events; Blakemore & Mills 2014). Changes in WM from middle childhood through adolescence are more dramatic when it is necessary to manipulate or work with information held in WM (Bunge & Wright, 2007). Complex EFs appear to build on simpler ones. For example, *inhibition* ability (Glossary; a simple EF) in middle childhood has predicted WM ability in adolescence (WM = a complex EF; to some extent, related to sustained attention; N = 47, T1: 8–12, T2: 12–15 years old, Tillman, Brocki, Sørensen, & Lundervold, 2013). For youth with externalizing behavior problems (ADHD), WM deficits in adolescence were accounted for by middle childhood problems with inhibitory control and sustained attention. For a small sample, deficits in WM proved salient throughout age groups (more for adolescents; effect size for mental set shifting deficits, larger in late childhood and adolescence), whereas deficits in simple EF (inhibition, sustained attention), more so in middle childhood (Tillman et al., 2013).

Autobiographical Memory (AM): Memory Narratives

Adolescents have better tools for creating narratives than younger children—e.g., more complex mental language; better ability to coordinate multiple perspectives into arguments/assessments; better ability to conceptualize self; appreciation of morality issues, autonomy, conventions, and their interplay; greater appreciation of context and complexity in advice-giving tasks; better grasp of the biographical structure of human lives; and better appreciation for mixed and complicated emotional experiences (see Pasupathi & Wainryb, 2010). Their recollections of the past are richer in interpretation, and their narratives may better serve the many functions of AM. With some variation by event type (e.g., harm events vs positive and negative peer experiences), adolescents had increased factual content (observable or perceptible information) than younger children (N = 30 each aged 8–9, 12–13, 16–17, Pasupathi & Wainryb, 2010). Interpretive content is low under age 12 and generally increases strongly from early to middle adolescence—e.g., interpretation of narrator's own and inferences about others' narratives. As has been true for younger children, according to reports of early adolescent youth, attachment-related AM specificity has been associated with greater mother-youth communication (N = 80, ages 10–13, Bosmans, Dujardin, Raes, & Braet, 2012). Greater trust in a mother's support related to early adolescents' greater communication about their experiences with their mothers, and so indirectly related to AM.

Problem-Solving

The ability to find solutions for difficult or complicated situations is important to goal achievement, career, academic, social and other functioning. Problem-solving is used in such skills as planning, self-regulation, and social interacting. Adolescents' self-appraised problem-solving skills have been related to their psychological health—inversely related to depression, anxiety, eating disorders, stress, and suicidal ideation levels—and have been related to physical health, learning, and vocational adjustment variables—i.e., to use of learning strategies, decidedness, career maturity, vocational identity (Ginevra et al., 2015). For example, youth with more effective problem-solving and coping skills have demonstrated more highly developed learning strategies (e.g., identifying what and how to study), better academic performance, and better vocational adjustment. Resilient individuals have used effective, active problem-solving patterns and adaptive appraisal styles for coping, enabling positive adaptation during extremely stressful circumstances (Beutel et al., 2017). Training has been used to improve problem-solving skills (Ginevra et al., 2015).

Although personality has been directly related to use of learning strategies, problem-solving has mediated the relationship between personality traits/types and learning style (N = 577; Ginevra et al., 2015; Table 17.1). *Extraversion* was related to self-appraised problem-solving ability which in turn linked to positive attitude toward school and the ability to identify important content to study. Myers-Briggs *intuition* related to self-appraised problem-solving ability which was then linked to positive attitude toward school (fully mediated) as well as to the abilities to memorize and monitor one's own learning and to identify important content to study (partially mediated). Myers-Briggs *thinking* also related to problem-solving ability which in turn linked to abilities to memorize and monitor one's own learning (fully mediated) as well as linked to positive attitude toward school and the ability to identify important content to study (partially mediated). Problem-solving ability also partially mediated between Myers-Briggs *judgment* and learning variables.

Self-Regulation

Self-restraint generally appears to be consistent across time. Toddler restraint has been related to EFs in adolescence—e.g., 17-year-old high self-restraint has been related to high self-restraint at infant ages 14, 20, 24, and 36 months old, while low restraint related to low inhibition and high shifting at those ages (Friedman, Miyake, Robinson, & Hewitt, 2011; Glossary). However, compared to adults, adolescents have had less mutual engagement of specific brain regions and/or engage less connectivity among regions that may be specialized for inhibitory control (Table A4.2; Stevens, Kiehl, Pearlson, & Calhoun, 2007). The increase in efficiency (speed and accuracy) of cognitive control (Glossary) from early childhood to adolescence is evidenced by a decrease in an individual's susceptibility to interference from competing information (Eigsti et al., 2006). Adolescents and adults have been better than children at ignoring irrelevant stimuli (Bunge & Wright, 2007). Across seven studies that assessed the relationship between attachment, emotion regulation, and depressive symptoms findings were mixed—e.g., some found that regulation mediated between attachment and depression; others did not (Malik, Wells, & Wittkowski, 2015). Variables such as secure attachments and high self-esteem have been protective (Rashwan et al., 2017), whereas male gender, sensation-seeking, and dynamic self-oriented values have significantly related to behavior problems such as bullying or other aggression (Innamorati et al., 2018).

Better self-control has predicted or mediated more positive outcomes. For example, religiousness has predicted decreased future criminality, partially mediated by increased self-control (N = 1354 adolescents, Pirutinsky, 2014). Poor self-control has been linked to a variety of negative outcomes. For young adolescents (both genders), poor self-control has been associated with conflict with authorities, lower executive functions (EF), and poorer relationships (Bakker et al., 2011; Crone et al., 2016; Oxford et al., 2000). Gender incongruence—e.g., low assertion in boys and low self-control in girls—has been associated with peer victimization (Bakker et al., 2011).

EF functions have been related to self-regulation (Crone et al., 2016). Working memory (WM) permits an individual to review past sequences of events and to anticipate a hypothetical future and, consequently, to inhibit an initial pre-potent response in order to delay or stop an action (often WM combined with prefrontal mechanisms of self-talk; Chapter 1). Self-control is more likely if an individual is able to perceive and value future over immediate outcomes. The ability to consider and think through future consequences of actions does not seem to emerge until later adolescence (ages 15–16; independent of inductive reasoning and WM capacity, Crone & van der Molen 2004).

Variable Associations and Self-Control

Variable relationships may influence lapses in self-control and related outcomes. For example, studies suggest that the earlier children initiate substance use (SU, e.g., drugs, alcohol), the more likely they are to engage in SU or misuse during adolescence and adulthood (Oxford, Harachi, Catalano, & Abbott, 2000). Oxford et al. (2000) found that antisocial peers were the strongest predictors of substance initiation for elementary school children and later. However, effective family management practices (e.g., parental monitoring and rules) and positive attachment contributed to both child peer-selection and lower likelihood of substance initiation. Successful emotion regulation in early adolescence (10–13 years) also has been influenced by adolescents' sensitivity to rejection and by emotion-related situational factors. Young adolescents find it more difficult than older adolescents (14–23 years) to regulate emotions when presented with social affective stimuli compared to nonsocial emotional stimuli.

Personality also has affected self-control and its related outcomes. For girls, *disinhibition*-related traits (*rash impulsivity*) have been directly linked to substance use (SU) and *reward drive* has indirectly associated with greater SU (Wood, Dawe, & Gullo, 2013). *Reward drive* conveyed indirect risk for boys. Successful emotion regulation in early adolescence (10–13 years) is also influenced by adolescents' sensitivity to rejection and by emotion-related situational factors. Young adolescents find it more difficult than older adolescents (14–23 years) to regulate emotions when presented with social affective stimuli compared to nonsocial emotional stimuli.

Risk-Taking

Risk-taking—choosing options with greater outcome variability—involves greater uncertainty and involves more than one trait—e.g., not just an *appetite for risk* (p. 211, Figner & Weber, 2011). Higher risks may correspond to higher returns as well as to greater losses than a safe choice. Risk-taking is influenced by the situation—e.g., whether it elicits emotion or deliberation; by the realm of risk—e.g., social, recreational, financial, health/safety, ethics; by the person—e.g., level of risk-taking accepted, personality, genetics; by the psychological processes triggered; and by the interaction of person and situation (Figner & Weber, 2011; Norbury, Manohar, Rogers, & Husain, 2013). Adolescents are more likely to make risky decisions in emotional contexts or among peers (Blakemore & Robbins, 2012). Although self-reported resistance to peer influence increases steadily between middle and late teenage (ages 14–18, Burnett & Blakemore, 2009), lab observation suggests that, in the presence of friends, adolescents take many more risks (e.g., during simulated driving).

Adolescence is a time of increased sensitivity to both stress and sexual hormones (Sinclair, Purves-Tyson, Allen, & Weickert, 2014). Trait sensation seeking—i.e., need for varied, complex, and intense sensations—has been related to increased risk of problems such as risky sexual practice, gambling, and substance use (Norbury et al., 2013). In adolescence, testosterone, estrogen, and glucocorticoids interact with each other and have particular, brain-region-specific impacts on dopamine neurotransmission (Sinclair et al., 2014). Aspects of cortical dopamine function do not mature until late adolescence or early adulthood. For young adult males, some evidence suggests a link between dopamine function and sensation-seeking (N = 20; Norbury et al., 2013).

Research suggests younger adolescents and girls report less frequent risk behaviors than older adolescents and boys (e.g., N = 459, groups ages 11–14 and 14–18, Gullone & Moore, 2000). Gender differences were more pronounced in older youth—i.e., disparity in judgments about risk. While some argue that real-life, reckless risk-taking (vs lab task) occurs only in a subset of adolescents, reflecting a lifelong trait (e.g., disinhibition) rather than a developmental stage (Bjork & Pardini, 2015; Chick, 2015), others have pointed to adolescent neurological changes related to aspects of risk-taking (Blakemore & Mills, 2014). Some argue that a propensity for risk-taking may already exist but go undetected until opportunities for risk-taking increase (Chick, 2015). Meta-analysis of risky decision-making (lab tasks) found that although adolescents take more risks than adults (with immediate rewards-loss feedback), adolescents take fewer risks than children on tasks with a sure/safe option (Defoe, Dubas, Figner, & van Aken, 2015). Nevertheless, the adolescent brain explains increased adolescent risk-taking.

Risk-Taking and Neurobiology. Even though there is much individual variability in risk-taking among adolescents, it may have a neurological basis (see Table A4.2). For example, studies have documented structural and functional asymmetry and under-connectivity between reward-sensitive and self-regulatory brain regions during adolescence (Baker et al., 2015; Chick, 2015; Hagmann et al., 2010; Mills et al., 2014). Longitudinal declines in specific brain region activation (e.g., vlPFC) or connectivity (e.g., mPFC to VS) have directly linked to declines in adolescent real-life risk-taking (ages 15–17, across 1.5 years; Qu et al., 2015; Table A4.2).

Dopamine has been linked to increased risk-taking decision-making and perhaps to novelty seeking (Table A4.1; Luyten & Fonagy, in press; Norbury, Manohar, Rogers, & Husain, 2013). Additionally, a longitudinal study has shown higher adolescent response in reward centers and in risk-taking behavior than child or adult response (performance, not self-report; continuous ages 8–27, Braams et al., 2015). Girls' earlier and faster pubertal development (until age 17), and boys' sharp increase in testosterone levels have been related to increased reward sensitivity (Braams et al., 2015). Laube et al. (2017) found that increased testosterone (not age) was related to increased sensitivity to immediate rewards (impatient decision-making), whereas increased age (not testosterone) was related to a reduction in general impatience (N = 72, ages 11–14).

Traits and Risk-Taking or Impulsivity. Although adolescence is characterized by increased neural risk-related sensitivity, adolescents may be risk-seeking or risk aversive (van Duijvenvoorde et al., 2015; Table A4.2), making individual assessments important. Even though risk-taking in one domain has been related to risk-taking in other domains, a person may not take risks in all domains. For adults, risk-taking has decreased with age (lower in females than males) and has appeared more frequently in some careers than others—e.g., where people strive for success, popularity, prominence, and gains. Findings are mixed in the study of Big Five personality traits—openness, extraversion, conscientiousness/constraint, agreeableness, and neuroticism—and risk-taking. Although being high or low in a particular trait does not guarantee the emergence of a particular type of pathology or risk, a number of researchers have found that *negative emotionality* (NE) is related to impulsivity but not to risk-taking, while trait *low-constraint* has been linked to risk-taking (see Glossary; Chapter 4; Finy, Bresin, Korol, & Verona, 2014). Adolescent *constraint* has been inversely correlated with externalizing, while *low-constraint* (more common in males) has predicted later substance abuse and antisocial behavior (N = 1048 17-year-old twins, Krueger et al., 2002). Although *low-constraint* has been a risk factor for risky behavior under no/low stress, some evidence suggests acute stress may keep *low-constraint* youth from engaging in risk-taking (Finy et al., 2014; Glossary; see BI, Chapters 8, 9). In high-stress lab situations, *low-constraint* (not NE) interacted with stress to predict greater cortisol reactivity (N = 88, ages 14–19, Finy et al., 2014). Findings have been mixed for cortisol's association with NE (e.g., Oswald et al., 2006; see Chapter 4). NE youth may be less worried in lab conditions, and mixed findings may reflect differential susceptibility to environmental stress (Chapter 4). Youth with high levels of temperamental NE have shown more harm directed to others with increasing family aggression (Zhang, Finy, Bresin, & Verona, 2015). At low levels of NE, family aggression was not related to other-directed-harm.

Variations in findings on traits and risk-taking may be a consequence of assessment methods and populations studied. Merritt and Tharp (2013) found that greater reckless risk-taking behaviors (in sports) were linked to high *neuroticism* and low *conscientiousness* (not *extraversion*), and *self-efficacy* exerted a significant indirect mediation (N = 277, ages 16–41). In contrast, Nicholson et al. (2005) found that overall risk propensity was related to high *extraversion* (especially sensation seeking) and *openness*, low *neuroticism* and *agreeableness*, and low *conscientiousness*. Both found low *conscientiousness/constraint* related to risk-taking. Personality factors relevant to risk-taking may depend on judgment of or type of risk—antisocial, thrill-seeking, or reckless risk-taking (Wood et al., 2013). High levels of *conscientiousness* (more often in girls), low levels of *agreeableness*, and younger age have predicted lower frequencies of rebellious risk-taking. In most cases, judgment of risk proved more important than personality. Youth most likely to judge behaviors as less risky included those with more antisocial behaviors (scored lower on *neuroticism* and were older), those with high reckless risk-taking (likely to be male and less *conscientious*), and adolescents who were more *extraverted* and more *agreeable*. Conscientious youth judged all types of risk-taking, except thrill-seeking, as riskier than ratings by less conscientious peers (Wood et al., 2013).

Attachment and Risk-Taking. When youth have attachment security, they can direct energy toward taking positive risks and engaging in autonomy-promoting activities (Mikulincer et al., 2003). Both insecure styles (anxious and avoidant) have significantly linked to negative risk behaviors. Oshri et al. (2015) found that anxious-ambivalent attachment-related to alcohol use, whereas avoidant attachment significantly related to drug use and antisocial behaviors. Anxious individuals may be more sensitive to peer rejection, thus, more vulnerable to peer influence. Avoidant individuals may engage in risk behaviors due to deactivation strategies—e.g., emotional disengagement when participating in antisocial behaviors (Mikulincer et al., 2003; Oshri et al., 2015).

Humor

Between 12 and 13, youth appreciate more sophisticated forms of humor such as puns, sarcasm, irony, mocking/parody, light tones (not taking things too seriously; using a humorous outlook), and sexual allusions (Buijzen & Valkenburg, 2004; Cameron, Fox, Anderson, & Cameron, 2010). They may enjoy grosser humor as well—e.g., slapstick, taboo topics, or disgust. Adolescents have preferred spontaneous humor over memorized jokes (Buijzen & Valkenburg, 2004). Those who used affiliative humor showed better global self-worth/esteem and self-reported social competence, and lower anxiety and depression symptoms (ages 11–16; Fox et al., 2016; Tucker, Finkelhor, Turner, & Shattuck, 2013a; Chapter 11; Table 11.2). Additionally, affiliative humor may be protective for socially anxious youth. In contrast, use of self-defeating humor has been linked to increasing depression and loneliness over time, and depression has been linked to an increase in self-defeating humor over time (Fox, Hunter, & Jones, 2015). In a study of Mexican American adolescents (N = 67; Aldridge & Roesch, 2008a), although youth most often used planning and least often used humor to cope, those who used positive thinking, acceptance, problem-solving, and humor coping strategies had more positive affect than adolescents who used religious coping, distancing, and acceptance (predicted negative affect). As discussed, trauma may undermine the ability for or appreciation of humor.

Self-Awareness

Significant physical, psychological, and social changes during adolescence encourage increased self-exploration and self-evaluation. Among primary adolescent tasks are identity development—i.e., discovering who one is and how one fits in (Erikson, 1963; Box 14.1)—and achieving self-evaluative competence (see Jankowski & Pfeifer, 2015). Adolescence may be described as a period of self-concept instability, catalyzing identity development subsequent to significant changes in self-awareness, perception of others, and social interactions (particularly ages 11–14, Jankowski & Pfeifer, 2015). They become more self-conscious and are more concerned about opinions of others. The social self becomes particularly important, and peers play an increasingly influential role in self-perceptions. Specific others' opinions (actual and perceived) become a part of self-evaluations, then incorporated into self-perceptions (Harter, 1999; Glossary—"looking-glass self," Cooley, 1902). Brain regions associated with self-processing (e.g., mPFC) change between early adolescence and adulthood (Sebastian, Burnett, & Blakemore, 2008). Hence, neurocognitive development may contribute to adolescent heightened self-consciousness and susceptibility to peer influence.

Adolescents identify more dimensions of self and employ multiple selves across different contexts and social roles—e.g., scholastic competence, athletic competence, peer acceptance, physical appearance, conduct/behavior, and self-worth (Harter & Pike, 1984; within family, Jankowski & Pfeifer, 2015; Box 14.2). Youth may consider themselves, e.g., a friend, a specific group member, a social self, and in individual contexts (Jankowski & Pfeifer, 2015)—e.g., with specific people, at school vs at home, or at church vs on the ball field/court. Adolescents employ more complex self-descriptions, with more mental state representations and more psychological and abstract terminologies than younger children—e.g., describe themselves with more social and interpersonal traits

Box 14.2 Self in Context

J. described himself in different contexts. With friends, he feels like he is extraverted, cheerful, talkative, rowdy, and funny. He is happy to be around them and to do things with them. However, with his parents, he described himself as more likely to be depressed, sad, angry, and/or hopeless. Their descriptions of him were negative—e.g., lazy, irresponsible—and he felt bad in response. At school, he was curious, creative in problem-solving, and smart. He had good grades and received positive feedback from the teachers. Around people he did not know, he felt shy, introverted, nervous, uncomfortable, and like a dork (feared non-friends think of him that way) (see Harter, 2008).

(e.g., helpful, fair, friendly). While both adolescents and adults recruit similar cortical structures during self-evaluations, they activate different neural patterns (e.g., in ventral mPFC and striatal regions). Early adolescents may be more fragmented and compartmentalized in their thinking—i.e., may lack ability to integrate single abstractions used to define the self in different relational contexts (Harter, 2008). By mid-adolescence, youth may be more concerned about seeming contradictions—e.g., introvert vs extravert, intelligent vs airhead, cheerful vs depressed (Box 14.2). The all-or-none thinking or overgeneralizations of early adolescence may contribute to faulty, vacillating self-representations—e.g., *awesome* one minute, and *a total dork* the next (Harter, 2008). Concerns with peer approval may add to this volatility. At a time of intensified self-consciousness, social and school comparison practices, such as posting grades or ability grouping, may negatively influence self-perceptions. Harter suggests that parenting practices toward the youth, such as lack of attunement to needs, lack of empathy, low validation, threats of harm, coercion, and/or enforced compliance may cause the youth's true self to go underground. Studies of reflective function or mentalizing and synchrony, reported earlier in this book confirm these suggestions. When caregivers make their approval contingent on a young adolescent's living up to unrealistic or unattainable standards of behavior, then unhealthy levels of false-self behaviors may emerge (Harter, 2008). Chronic and severe abuse pose even greater risk of suppressing the true self and presenting various forms of inauthentic or false-self behavior.

Self-Concept

Self-esteem can be related to two separate types of information processing. *Explicit self-esteem* employs conscious and reflective self-evaluation (higher cognitive processes), whereas *implicit self-esteem*[1] is characterized by automatic and unconscious self-evaluation (Wegener et al., 2015; Table 1.3). Cognitive restructuring addresses explicit self-esteem. Youth self-concept is shaped by such variables as attachment relationships, ongoing parent–youth interactions, peers, culture, birth cohort, and life events. Any life experience may alter self-view (Boxes 8.1–8.2, 9.1)—e.g., learning to play the violin might change the conception of one's hands, or becoming a basketball player may permit the image of oneself in relation to a midair jump while targeting a basket with a ball (Bach et al., 2000). In addition to feeling an action in our bodies, learning a new skill simultaneously revises body image, neurological-cortically and psychologically. Some evidence suggests that normally children's self-concepts become more negative in middle childhood and in early adolescence (see Nader & Fletcher, 2014). Some but not all assessment measures have shown a greater recovery for boys than for girls over time. For immigrant and non-immigrant Italian adolescents, Miconi et al. found gender difference in self-esteem only in a non-immigrant group (lower in females; Miconi, Moscardino, Ronconi, & Altoe, 2017).

High self-esteem has served as a protective/resilience factor for youth and low self-esteem as a risk factor (Lee et al., 2018; Nader, 2008; Yates, Egeland, & Sroufe, 2003). For example, individuals with high self-esteem have been rated as more attractive and as more desirable as partners (Zeigler-Hill, 2011). Low self-esteem and threats to self-esteem or status have been linked to aggression (Velotti, Elison, & Garofalo, 2014). Although, when combined with narcissism or antisocial PD, high self-esteem has been linked to aggression (see Shame, this chapter), Donnellan et al. (2005) found an effect of low self-esteem on aggression independent of narcissism. Although PTSD has been significantly related to suicidality, some evidence suggests that the link is mediated by self-disgust (N = 347 young adults with trauma histories, Brake et al., 2017; Table 1.3). In a U.S. population study from middle school and high school to young adulthood, the higher an adolescent's self-esteem, the lower the probability of substance use/abuse (marijuana, alcohol, cocaine; not at age 21 for marijuana or binge drinking; Lee et al., 2018). Boys used substances more than girls across age groups (Lee et al., 2018). Italian adolescents' self-esteem and their secure attachments to parents were negatively related to depressive symptoms in both immigrant youth and non-immigrant youth (N = 686 first-gen immigrant youth; N = 1295 non-immigrant Italian adolescents ages 14–20; Miconi et al., 2017). Additionally, adolescents who perceived their parents to be warm and caring were more likely to have high self-esteem, which was related to fewer depressive symptoms.

While achieving a sense of purpose during adolescence is an asset, searching for purpose may be a stressor—e.g., fear of isolation, disconnection from parents and peers (Blattner, Liang, Lund, & Spencer, 2013). Commitment to purpose has correlated positively with self-esteem. Searching for purpose has negatively predicted self-esteem (N = 207, economically privileged sixth to eighth graders; Blattner et al., 2013). However, youth's perceptions of parent–child alienation have significantly exacerbated the deleterious effects of search-for-purpose on girls' self-esteem (parental trust did not buffer effects). For privileged youth, search-for-purpose may be a first exposure to instability and uncertainty.

As noted (Chapter 1), treatments for self-esteem have proven ineffective or had negative results. Instead, enhancing self-compassion and reducing maladaptive self-criticism have had better associations and have resulted from some treatments (e.g., mindfulness, AEDP, Chapter 16; Table 1.3). Although the human capacity for social cognition or mentalizing brings also the capacities for self-awareness, self-consciousness, and striving to transcend (Luyten & Fonagy, in press), these abilities also bring the possibility of embarrassment, regret, shame, and guilt, which may be a part of depressive symptoms. Discussions of shame and guilt follow.

Shame

While guilt focuses on behaviors, shame is related to negative self-evaluation (e.g., defectiveness; see Chapter 1). Unlike guilt, the antecedents of shame do not appear to differ by age, between ages nine and 15 (Gavazzi, Ornaghi, & Antoniotti, 2009). Shame may be adaptive or maladaptive—i.e., benign (e.g., engendered by actual or potential embarrassment) or painful feeling states (e.g., engendered by disgrace or humiliation; see Velotti et al., 2014). On the one hand, shame may play a role in self-regulation and socially appropriate behavior and may motivate to work harder. Conversely, shame may confer greater likelihood of negative outcomes such as aggression, depression, or dissociation (Fletcher, 2014). Both socially prescribed perfectionism and perfectionistic self-presentation have positively linked to shame as well as to need to belong and to insecure attachment styles (Chen, Hewitt, & Flett, 2015; Table 11.1). The associations between preoccupied/resistant attachment and interpersonal aspects of perfectionism were mediated by a characteristic, strong need-for-belongingness and shame. Hence treatments for perfectionism may need to address both attachment relationships and shame (Chen et al., 2015).

Shame-proneness has been linked to parental neglect, harsh parenting, severe illness or injury, and higher use of maladaptive emotion-regulation (ER) strategies—e.g., self-blaming, catastrophizing—and lower use of adaptive strategies—e.g., refocus on planning, positive reappraisal (e.g., ages 13–17; ER explained 20% of variance in guilt- and shame-proneness; Szentágotai-Tătar & Miu, 2016). Both state and trait shame may confer higher vulnerability to angry reactivity and aggression than guilt (Fletcher, 2014; Gilligan, 2003; Scott et al., 2015; Velotti et al., 2014; Chapters 1, 8, 11). Trait shame (shame-proneness) in adolescents has slightly positively related to antisocial behaviors (see Velotti et al., 2014) and has been related to decreases in prosocial behavior over a 6-month period (Roos, Hodges, & Salmivalli, 2014).

Elison et al. (2014) reviewed multiple pathways through which social pain may lead to anger and aggression. Personal devaluation or social exclusion leads to social pain—e.g., shame, humiliation, embarrassment, hurt feelings. Social threat (e.g., shame or humiliation) may trigger threat-reactions (fight-flight-freeze …) and subsequent defensive/reactive aggression or self-destructive behaviors (Larkin, 2009; Nader, 2006, 2012c; Velotti et al., 2014). Adolescent girls, with high rates of actual shame experiences (not lab induced), have been four times more likely to commit physical aggression (Åslund, Starrin, Leppert, & Nilsson, 2009). Social status may influence risk of aggression when shamed (medium status was protective; N = 5396 ages 15–18, Åslund et al., 2009). High levels of shame have been found in extreme aggression—e.g., multiple within-family killings, violent offenders, inmate recidivism, school shootings (see Nader, 2012c; Velotti et al., 2014). For antisocial and narcissistic PD, aggression has been a maladaptive manner of regulating shame.

Guilt

In adolescence, youth are able to grasp more abstract concepts and can experience guilt over inequity and injustice as well as over transgression (Kletter, Weems, & Carrion, 2009). Adolescents also can experience anticipatory guilt or guilt over inaction. Guilt over inactions has increased with age (Gavazzi et al., 2009). Under non-traumatic circumstances, adolescents and young adults reporting higher levels of guilt tend to be less aggressive and less likely to engage in acting-out or externalizing behavior (see Fletcher, 2014). Children have reported guilt more frequently over external actions like damaging something or breaking rules or described being blamed for something they did not do, whereas adolescents more often framed guilt as a subjective, internal experience. In a study of Italian children (ages 9–10 and 14–15, Gavazzi et al., 2009), children most frequently reported guilt for actions—e.g., hurting someone, treating them badly. Adolescents focused on the consequences of their actions for other people—e.g., after breaking a promise not to betray a secret. In adolescence, gender differences become more apparent—girls' guilt more often reflected concern for others; boys guilt was more often rule or code-breaking related (Gavazzi et al., 2009). In contrast to shame-proneness, guilt-proneness has been linked to lower use of maladaptive emotion-regulation strategies (e.g., refocus vs catastrophizing) and has been a consequence of trauma exposure (Szentágotai-Tătar & Miu, 2016). Guilt-proneness has been related to prosocial behaviors and consistently low levels of aggression (across 6-month period; Roos et al., 2014).

Coping

Coping style tends to be consistent across time (may relate to temperament, Valiente et al., 2014), with some exceptions across development (N = 155, assessed at ages 9, 11, 13, 15; Table 14.1). Both avoidance (likely used as emotion regulation) and positive cognitive restructuring (e.g., as behavioral and environmental regulation) have increased with age, while emotional coping (especially for girls) and support seeking have decreased. Thus, socially sanctioned methods (e.g., active coping, e.g., problem-solving, distraction, avoidance) replace such methods as crying and emotional venting with age. Well-developed coping skills can reduce the likelihood of aggressive and other problem behaviors and can increase subjective well-being, social functioning, and physical and emotional health (Lazarus & Folkman, 1987; see Mello & Nader, 2012).

Table 14.1 Coping Methods

Divisions	Types
Coping dimensions	**(1) active or approach coping** • efforts to change the situation, its effects, or how one thinks about it • behavioral, cognitive, or emotional activities aimed at altering the stressful situation. • uplifting efforts (e.g., service to others) (can worsen symptoms in some situations) • accepting responsibility—facing culpability or assigning responsibility to self; may include, e.g., criticizing or lecturing self • problem-solving—e.g., developing and carrying out a plan of action – avoidance or distraction, e.g., when used as emotion-regulation or to prevent escalation of a situation **(2) avoidant coping** • efforts to avoid thinking about or experiencing the negative feelings or distress (e.g., by substance use, mental withdrawal/dissociation); distancing—e.g., acting as if nothing happened; confusion; placing cause for the worst outcomes external to self • wishing it would be over • distracting self (can be effective in the right circumstances) • avoiding facing the reality
Coping strategies	• adaptive: active, planning, instrumental support, positive reframe, humor, acceptance, religion, and emotional support • maladaptive: denial, self-distraction, venting, SU, behavioral disengagement, self-blame
Primary vs secondary coping	**(1) primary control coping**—trying to change the situation • efforts to change the situation • efforts to change the effects of the situation • confrontation—e.g., standing one's ground, fighting • efforts toward self-protection **(2) secondary control coping** • avoiding exacerbating a situation – e.g., self-control – e.g., stopping self from expressing feelings; managing feelings • cognitive reappraisal—e.g., finding useful meaning in the experience; recognizing one's actual culpability level; reassessing the situation – e.g., positive appraisal—e.g., renewed faith, other PTG – e.g., reframing—e.g., developing a new way of looking at things or of viewing some aspect of what happened – e.g., refocus on planning • support-seeking—e.g., talking to someone; accepting comfort and/or sympathy
Coping flexibility	• flexible use of coping methods • adaptability to the needs of the situation

continued

Table 14.1 Continued

Divisions	Types
Coping method factors (Tolan et al., 2002)	• seeking support—go along with, communicate with, do things with parent, family • venting emotion—blame others, let off steam complaining, get angry/yell, be mean • avoidance—substance use; smoking • distraction—play video games, physical activity, hobby, school activities, work • positive thinking—self-improvement efforts, focus on good things, see the good side • seeking guidance—talk to teacher, religious leader, parent; pray • humor—make light or try to be funny; joke and keep a sense of humor
Coping clusters (youth; Tolan et al., 2002)	1. Support and guidance seekers—high support-seeking, low venting 2. Minimal copers—low coping, avoidance by substance use (SU) 3. Emotional substance users—high avoidance-SU and venting 4. Emotion-focused copers—frequent use of low emotion expression 5. Complex copers—high use of coping across methods except avoidance-SU
Coping styles (adult; Aldridge & Roesch, 2008a, 2008b)	• *low generic copers* (multiple coping strategies at a low level) • *active copers* (emphasize active/approach strategies—e.g., planning) • *avoidant copers* (emphasize avoidant/passive strategies—e.g., substance abuse)

Other Sources: Folkman & Lazarus, 1987; Hébert et al., 2018; Mello & Nader, 2012; Valiente et al., 2014; PTG=posttraumatic growth (Glossary).

Poor coping skills are linked to increased likelihood of aggression, depression, and other problems. Effective coping can increase the possibility of safe schools and well-functioning youth—e.g., among other issues, the Parkland Florida school shooter demonstrated difficulties coping with rejection and loss (e.g., Fausset & Kovaleski, 2018; Murphy & Perez, 2018). Szentágotai-Tătar and Miu (2016) found that habitual use of rumination increased with age from 9–15. Maladaptive emotion-regulation/ coping strategies—e.g., rumination, self-blaming, catastrophizing, and blaming others—positively associated with depression and anxiety symptoms, while positive refocusing, refocus on planning, and positive reappraisal negatively associated with depression. Major depressive disorder (characterized by NE) has been associated with brain changes linked to increased rumination (adults, Berman et al., 2011; children, Graham et al., 2015). Some evidence suggests that depressed individuals use more confrontational, self-control, and avoidance coping (Lazarus & Folkman, 1987).

Although not well studied, different personalities and situations may suggest the need for different types of coping (Chapter 4). Evidence suggests that primary coping/control beliefs are less adaptive when a situation is truly uncontrollable (e.g., ongoing inter-city violence; Deardorff, Gonzales, & Sandler, 2003; Table 14.1). In such situations, strategies for altering the self—e.g., managing emotions, controlling autonomic arousal, learning ways to be safe—rather than trying to change the situation may be more adaptive. Flexible coping repertoires are associated with adolescents' improved adjustment to stress and increased positive thinking (Aldridge & Roesch, 2008a). While coping flexibility may be most important to adjustment, studies have often found that avoidant coping was associated with poor psychosocial adjustment (e.g., distress, depression, & PTSD; see Mello & Nader, 2012) and with complicated grief (e.g., Boelen, van den Hout, & van den Bout, 2006). Improvements in coping have shown positive results—e.g., reduced externalizing and internalizing; increased self-esteem (e.g., bereavement, Sandler et al., 2010a; Melhem et al., 2016). Avoidance methods have been included in both active and avoidant coping classifications and can be adaptive or maladaptive (see Table 14.1).

Types of Coping

Studies of coping have examined approach, active, or problem-oriented versus emotion-focused or avoidant coping styles or have generated a larger group of coping methods (Aldridge & Roesch, 2008b; Mello & Nader, 2012; Table 14.1). Aldridge and Roesch (2008b) found that adolescents from multiple American ethnic groups used three coping styles—*Low Generic Copers*, *Active Copers*, and *Avoidant Copers*. Active Copers showed significantly less depression and more stress-related growth than Low Generic Copers (N = 354, low income, ages 14–18). Low Generic Copers reported significantly less depression than Avoidant Copers although significantly less stress-related growth than Active Copers. Tolan et al. (2002) examined 12 identified coping responses in inner-city youth that organized into seven factors and ultimately into five clusters (Table 14.1—coping factors, coping clusters; N = 372, African American, Hispanic, and non-Hispanic Whites, ages 12–16). In this study, girls reported more *support seeking* and less *substance use (SU)-avoidance* than boys. Non-Hispanic Whites employed more *SU-avoidance*, while African Americans used more *support and guidance seeking*, and had lower symptom scores. Stress levels related to symptomatology—e.g., violence exposure to externalizing, a year later. *SU* and *emotion-focused* copers had higher levels of symptomatology (higher externalizing) than *support and guidance seekers* and *Minimal* copers (lower internalizing). After controlling for other variables, *minimal* Copers had greater increases in internalizing than *support and guidance seekers* a year later. *Emotion-focused* Copers and *Minimal* Copers had higher externalizing scores than *support and guidance seekers* or *complex* copers. Using more coping methods may be a response to greater distress.

Coping Method Selection

Coping methods that work in one situation may not work in others (Mello & Nader, 2012; Tolan et al., 2002; Table 14.1). For example, distraction (not ongoing avoidance) has had positive associations over time (Tolan et al., 2002), but may not be adaptive under threat (depending on age). Different youth—depending on emotional states and the circumstances—and different populations use different methods of coping (Gilbert & Morawski, 2005; Mello & Nader, 2012; Tolan et al., 2002). Some evidence suggests increased usage of *Reappraisal* with age, and older adolescents are more likely to use *Positive Thinking* (Tolan et al., 2002). A positive outlook can attenuate, substantially, the adverse effects of maltreatment on development (Oshri et al., in press; Chapter 15). Youth likely use combinations of methods rather than single methods to cope with specific evoked emotions (Gilbert & Morawski, 2005; see Mello & Nader, 2012).

Taking the Perspective of Others and Empathy

Perspective-taking proficiency improves from childhood to adolescence to adulthood (Jankowski & Pfeifer, 2015; Sebastian et al., 2008). Adolescents activate different brain regions from adults for facial emotion recognition. Matching faces to emotions requires working memory and decision-making skills—a decline in performance at puberty onset in these skills begins to improve at age 13 or 14 and to recover by 16 or 17 (see Blakemore & Choudhury, 2006). Recognition of sad and angry expressions may plateau at puberty, but linear improvement continues in recognition of fear and disgust (see Blakemore & Choudhury, 2006).

Multiple perspective proficiency increases with age. Youth (ages 10–15) can imagine looking at both sides/perspectives of an issue (Chapter 11; Selman, 1971; Selman & Byrne, 1974). From age

14 to adulthood, youth can understand that third-party perspectives (Glossary) can be influenced by societal values. Self-perspective inhibition—e.g., resisting interference from one's own perspective—relies on effortful processes (EF abilities, e.g., Carlson & Moses, 2001; Samson et al., 2010). More egocentric errors in perspective-taking occur under cognitive load (Glossary; Epley et al., 2004; Samson et al., 2010). Experiential avoidance in those with disorganized attachments has inhibited development of adolescent theory of mind skills (see Tessier et al., 2016). Youth may contend with issues of prejudice (Nader, 2012c). Although prejudice—e.g., toward specific gender, ethnic, gay, obese individuals—is related to multiple factors, lower empathy and lower perspective-taking significantly, independently predicted generalized prejudice (Chapter 1; Levin et al., 2015). Both empathic concern and perspective-taking are common foci in prejudice reduction interventions.

In trust games and online perspective-taking tasks, adolescents with higher perspective-taking tendencies have demonstrated greater trust toward others and higher levels of trust during cooperative interactions than low perspective takers (N = 50, ages 13–18; Fett et al., 2014). Although both groups adapted levels of trust in response to unfair behaviors by another, high perspective takers reduced trust more, showed a stronger reaction to less social behavior from another, and demonstrated less benevolent tit-for-tat behaviors when treated unfairly by another. Thus, at least on computer, high perspective-taking adolescents may be more trusting until crossed/thwarted.

Empathy

Empathy is a social skill that promotes prosocial behavior (Cohen & Strayer, 1996; Gambin & Sharp, 2016). As discussed, cognitive empathy (perspective-taking) and affective empathy (sharing of emotional states) have been studied separately (Lui, Barry, & Sacco, 2015; Chapter 1; Glossary). Ability to distinguish between self and others—*whose thoughts and feelings belong to whom*—when empathizing is an important self-regulatory component of empathy (Decety & Jackson, 2004, p. 71). The relationship between more than one type of psychopathology and empathy has been stronger for affective empathy (Gambin & Sharp, 2016)—e.g., lower levels of affective empathy in conduct-disordered youth (stronger for adolescents, Lovett & Sheffield, 2007; Miller & Eisenberg, 1998; Sterzer, Stadler, Poustka, & Kleinschmidt, 2007), and in DTD (Stolbach et al., 2013).

Outcomes have been related to both types of empathy as well. For 12–17-year-old inpatients, affective and cognitive empathy were negatively associated with girls' conduct problems (not with boys'; N = 507; Gambin & Sharp, 2016). Hence, empathy may be considered protective against conduct disturbance in girls. Empathy may help to deter harming others. However, in both parent and youth reports, affective empathy has positively related to internalizing problems and to self-reported ADHD symptoms in both genders. Accordingly, treatment must take into account differences in types of empathy with different psychopathology (Gambin & Sharp, 2016).

Callous-Unemotional Traits

Callous-unemotional traits (CU; Glossary) have negatively associated with cognitive and affective empathy (N = 103; ages 16–18; Lui et al., 2015). CU is linked to behavioral disturbances, e.g., more severe, chronic and earlier onset of delinquency, aggression, and conduct problems (Frick, Ray, Thornton, & Kahn, 2014), difficulties processing emotional stimuli (Kimonis, Frick, Fazekas, & Loney, 2006), and problems with empathy (Dadds et al., 2009; Lui et al., 2015). For males in the juvenile justice system followed from age 14 to age 24, compared to the moderate and low CU trait groups, youth with a high and stable CU trajectory had higher risk factor scores in individual characteristics (higher anxiety, more substance use), parenting (greater harshness, lower monitoring and knowledge), and broader contextual risk (more violence exposure; Waller, Baskin-Sommers,

& Hyde, 2016). Some evidence of malleability in adolescence suggests this is an important time for intervention.

Social Skills

Early adolescence is a sensitive period for social processing (Blakemore & Mills, 2014). During adolescence, youth generally spend more time with friends and less with family (Burnett & Blakemore, 2009). A more fully integrated social identity emerges. Different types of friendships are engaged—e.g., acquaintances, intimate friendships, romantic attachments, group relationships. For young adolescents (12–14), intimacy with friends (closeness and sharing) was predicted by their attachment characteristics, sense of coherence—the general belief/orientation toward the world as comprehensible, manageable, and a meaningful place—and the tendency to disclose private thoughts and feelings (Bauminger et al., 2008). Self-disclosure and a strong sense of coherence have interacted to influence intimacy. Self-disclosure contributes to intimacy to a greater extent when coherence is low. Girls self-disclose more than boys, and the tendency toward self-disclosure increases with grade level (Bauminger et al., 2008). As noted for 10–13-year-olds (Chapter 11), having delinquent peers has been linked to increased externalizing over time for low-intimacy friendships, but associated with decreased externalizing over time with higher levels of intimate exchange with delinquent friends (Gaertner, Fite, & Colder, 2011). This finding highlights the importance of closeness and belonging for youth.

Normally, from childhood to adolescence, peer-directed sympathy and prosocial tendencies appear to increase (Eisenberg, Fabes, & Spinrad, 2007). Although overtly aggressive adolescents (e.g., who hit or threaten) often are more vulnerable to poor-quality friendships and peer rejection, some aggressive adolescents are skilled socially and are popular with peers (see Fanti, Brookmeyer, Henrich, & Kuperminc, 2009). Personality characteristics such as NE have been related to poorer social functioning (Murphy et al., 2004). Gender influences the behaviors that enhance friendships. To maintain friendships, seventh- to eighth-grade girls, who use minimization strategies—e.g., thinking a conflict was no big deal, in contrast to being more assertive/confrontive, especially when one person is more dominant and the other more passive in the conflict—have had lower friendship stability, whereas for boys, minimization was positively related to friendship stability (Bowker, 2004; see Humor; Rejection). Discussions of social anxiety, social pain, and exclusion follow.

Social Anxiety

In Western cultures (e.g., U.S., New Zealand), approximately 8.4% meet criteria for social anxiety disorder with high rates of comorbidity (Australians ages 16–85; Crome et al., 2015). Rates have been higher for females and younger individuals (adolescents) and lower in countries like China, Mexico, and Korea. The rate doubled between 1997 and 2007. Individuals with social anxiety disorder expect to experience more negative reactions to positive social events than non-anxious youth (see Morrison & Heimberg, 2013). A youth's social anxiety has been related to increased distress and impairment and to reduced positive affect, lower positive, healthy functioning, and lower friendship quality (Biggs, Vernberg, & Wu, 2012; Morrison & Heimberg, 2013).

Attentional control—the capacity to effortfully regulate attention (Glossary)—is one mechanism that mediates the relationship between social anxiety and emotions. In a study of undergraduates, even after controlling for the effects of depression, social anxiety inversely related to attentional control; attentional control positively predicted positive affect (N = 112; Morrison & Heimberg, 2013). The ability to control one's attentional focus can reduce negative emotions. Trait social anxiety has uniquely, directly related to increased rumination (attention to anxiety-provoking thoughts) and has been related to increased rumination via perception of performance and via self-evaluation and inappropriate attentional focus (N = 314; Chen, Rapee, & Abbott, 2013). For young adults with increasing social anxiety, individuals show greater negative interpretation biases, especially with ambiguous cues (e.g., verbal & facial cues; Ritter et al., 2015). For example, they tend to interpret laughter as socially exclusive. Fear of being laughed at was an important part of findings. Socially anxious individuals showed an attention bias away from joyful laughter (not tickling laughter) and away from positive social cues, even after controlling for general anxiety and depressive symptoms (see Ritter et al., 2015). Attentional biases away from positive cues appear to help maintain social anxiety and may be an important target of treatment.

Socially anxious feelings and thoughts, which also may follow trauma, have been related to a tendency to withdraw and to adolescents spending less time with friends (Biggs et al., 2012; Box 3.1). For seventh and eighth graders, social anxiety was associated with social withdrawal, which in turn was related to lower companionship and intimacy in friendships. Social isolation during adolescence has increased likelihood of depressive-like behaviors and of alterations in PFC structure (reduced gray matter; see Blakemore & Mills, 2014; Table A4.2). Social exclusion and rejection are especially difficult for those with social anxiety (Zimmer-Gembeck & Skinner, 2015; see Rejection or Exclusion).

Social Pain

Among responses to harm or threat are pain, distress, and/or alarm. For some people, physical pain is preferable to social pain (Chen, Williams, Fitness, & Newton, 2008). Physical pain may be short-lived, may bring attention rather than exclusion or ostracism, and may provide evidence of suffering. Social pain can be relived (Meyer, Williams, & Eisenberger, 2015). Across studies (46; total N = 940; often using cyberball task), social pain resulting from social threat, exclusion, rejection, loss, or negative evaluation has activated specific brain regions (e.g., ventral & dorsal ACC; Rotge et al., 2015; Table A4.2). Some evidence suggests that some of the same brain regions that process physical pain also process the pain of social exclusion (Bungert et al., 2015a; Eisenberger, 2012). Social pain appears to accentuate the experience of physical pain for some (with engagement of related brain regions; Table A4.2). Chen et al. found that people reported higher levels of pain and performed worse on cognitively demanding tasks after reliving past socially painful events than after reliving physical pain events (N = 61 university students). Studies of BPD have found hypo vs hypersensitivity to physical pain, moderated by rejection sensitivity. Social rejection and social pain have both been related to social anxiety in subsequent situations (Fung & Alden, 2016).

Rejection or Exclusion

Although it is unlikely that social exclusion is enjoyed at any age, evidence suggests that adolescents are hypersensitive to the negative consequences of social exclusion (Blakemore & Mills, 2014). Adolescents often interpret peer rejection as a measure of their social and personal worth. In a study of young adolescents (11–14 years), mid-adolescents (14–16 years), and adults (22–47 years), mood was lowered from baseline by a social exclusion condition particularly strongly in the two adolescent groups (see Blakemore & Mills, 2014). While, in a lab test (see Velotti et al., 2014), exclusion appeared to dampen endorsing *attack other* in low self-esteem youth, it increased it in high self-esteem youth. Genes may influence reactions to rejection. For example, peer-rejected pre-adolescents (not early adolescents) with the 5-HTTLPR short allele genotype were more likely to exhibit antisocial behavior in late adolescence (especially with short-short variant; Kretschmer et al., 2014; Dutch cohort N = peer nominations—over 1700, ages 11 and 13; over 1650, age 19; genotype over 600 ages 11 and 13, over 1100 age 19; see Table A4.1). For a group of Flemish adolescents, peer rejection was linked to externalizing problems (peer acceptance was unrelated; N = 563; Janssens et al., 2015). Regarding the relationship of dopaminergic genes and peer rejection, in one of eight models tested, in line with differential susceptibility to context, DAT1 10R carriers engaged in more rule-breaking behavior when experiencing high peer rejection (parent report) but showed less rule-breaking than others when experiencing low peer rejection. Hence, adolescents with the DAT1 10R allele may be more susceptible to adverse environments—e.g., with high peer rejection. Contrary to other research, DRD4 non-long carriers showed higher aggression.

Chronic peer rejection compromises attitudes toward self and healthy peer relationships (Bruyere & Garbarino, 2012). It has predicted negative self-competence, depression, anxiety, and juvenile delinquency (see Biggs et al., 2010; lethal violence, Bruyere & Garbarino, 2012). Youth with higher levels of social anxiety have shown the most maladaptive responses to rejection threat—e.g., more emotional reactions, self-blame, and coping that includes more social isolation, rumination, and opposition (669 ages 10–14, Zimmer-Gembeck & Skinner, 2015). For socially anxious adolescents, a history of aggression predicted angry and oppositional responses to rejection. Depressed youth felt less in control and anticipated using less adaptive coping methods. Adolescents with higher relational victimization have reported more loneliness and depressive symptoms, partially mediated by rejection sensitivity (self- and peer reports, Zimmer-Gembeck, Trevaskis, Nesdale, & Downey, 2014). In socially unpredictable environments, socially isolated adolescents have experienced poorer physical and mental health (in the short term) and also adopted more problematic life strategies in young adulthood resulting in, e.g., poorer health, lower sexual restrictedness, and lower resource-accruing (Blakemore & Mills, 2014; Brumbach et al. 2009).

Rejection Sensitivity. As noted (Chapter 11), *rejection sensitivity* (Glossary) has been linked to BPD, aggression and hostility, more troubled relationships, poorer coping, and expectations of rejection (e.g., Ayduk et al., 2008). For example, in a sample of adults (ages 20–33), both acute and remitted BPD patients had higher scores on rejection sensitivity than healthy controls (N = 167; Bungert et al., 2015b). Lower self-esteem was positively correlated with increased BPD symptom severity and with higher rejection sensitivity, and it mediated the relationship between them. Individuals who expect rejection have more troubled, dissatisfying, quicker-to-end relationships as well as increased susceptibility to social anxiety, loneliness, and depression in response to rejection (Ayduk et al., 2000; Chapter 11). Early ability to delay gratification may moderate negative outcomes in rejection-sensitive youth (Nader, 2012c). Adults high on rejection sensitivity, who as children scored low in ability to delay gratification, have had lower education levels and lower self-esteem, self-worth, and coping ability (Ayduk et al., 2000). Being bullied or otherwise traumatized may increase the likelihood of expecting rejection.

Although broad insecurities may engender an attentional bias toward rejection, reinforcing social insecurity and negative expectations, some evidence suggests that people with specific insecurities demonstrate an attentional bias toward rejection under specific circumstances or in response to self-relevant cues or reminders (Ravary & Baldwin, 2018). Across four studies (Ravary & Baldwin, 2018): (1) highly socially anxious individuals significantly exhibited vigilance toward rejection when cued with social competence, flaw-related words (*foolish*) and show attentional avoidance of rejection when reminded of feared contexts (*date, conversation*; N = 24, ages 19–27); (2) individuals with low self-esteem oriented toward rejection when *failure* was brought to mind (N = 141 students, adults; compared to w/high self-esteem); (3) individuals with specific academic-related self-worth contingencies showed a bias toward rejection when cued with the word *stupid* (N = 52 undergraduates); and (4) people concerned with issues of maintaining their shape and weight demonstrated a rejection bias when cued with the word *obese* (N = 64 undergraduates).

Zimmer-Gembeck et al. suggested at least two types of rejection-sensitive youth. While rejection-sensitive adolescents with more depressive symptoms reported feeling less control and expected to use less adaptive coping—e.g., less support seeking, distraction, and negotiation—aggressive rejection-sensitive youth responded with more anger and coped using opposition. Over time (Zimmer-Gembeck et al., 2016), youth with more self-blame for rejection were likelier to withdraw in response to rejection threat, which was associated with more depressive symptoms over time, whereas angry adolescents reporting more peer-blame for rejection were more likely to seek retribution, associated with more overt/relational aggressive behavior over time. Unlike outcomes related to rejection sensitivity, friendship conflict was linked to emotional maladjustment more strongly for adolescents low, rather than high, in rejection sensitivity.

Conclusions

Some of the behaviors that may perturb adolescents and those around them are normal. It is important to distinguish posttrauma symptoms from normal increases in self-consciousness and self-absorption, mood variability, novelty seeking, and risk-taking. Although there are neurobiological changes that increase likelihood of risk-taking, there is more than one kind of risk-taking and more than one variable that influences its occurrence. Effective coping skills and good developmental skills (e.g., empathy) each have been associated with reduced problems. Some of these skills can be increased through school programs, preferably early (e.g., preschool, elementary school; Chapters 10, 13, 16). During the adolescent period of reorganization of biological, cognitive, emotional, and social functioning, adolescent youth are very attuned to their place among peers and are engaged in the move toward independence. Body image concerns, social anxiety, social pain, stigma, and rejection or exclusion may be particularly stressful for adolescents. Cognizance of adolescents' needs for autonomy and participation in decision-making as well as understanding their views of adults is important to interacting with and treating them. Personality and other traits, such as rejection sensitivity, may influence interactions with and trust of adults.

Note

1. Implicit self-esteem is measured by the Implicit Association Test and the Name-Letter Test (Wegener et al., 2015).

15

Adolescent Disorders and Adversity's Impact on Outcomes

Although some of the developmental issues of importance are different for adolescents, exposure to significant distress (e.g., poverty, family conflict, divorce, insecure or disorganized attachments), to traumatic stress, or to multiple stressors has been linked to stress-related disorders and to developmental disruptions. Reactions may be shaped by adolescent-typical increases and brain changes (e.g., increased self-consciousness, novelty seeking; PFC development). Some disorders are more prevalent in adolescence than in childhood. Significant stressors may increase the likelihood of a range of age-related or genetically linked disorders as well. To follow is a discussion of adolescent disorders, risk factors, adversity's influence on development, and trauma/adversity-related reactions and disorders—TSRD, personality disorders, and specific problems. Although treatment issues are occasionally mentioned, they are primarily addressed in Chapter 16. Many risk and protective factors have been discussed in other chapters (e.g., 4, 14, Tables A1.1–A1.4). A few risk factors follow the discussion of adolescent disorders.

Adolescent Disorders

Costello, Copeland, and Angold (2011) found that, across adolescent studies (ages 12–19), on average, around 21.8% of adolescents had a psychiatric disorder (14.8–22.8%). In order of frequency, disorders included substance abuse or dependence (SUD), anxiety, depressive, and behavioral disorders—e.g., ADHD, conduct disorder (CD), oppositional defiant disorder (ODD, Costello et al., 2011), any of which may occur co-morbidly or in association with trauma (Nader & Fletcher, 2014). Studies show that, after moving into adolescence, youth show increased rates of depression, bipolar, or personality disorders (PD; more girls), SUD and psychosis (more boys), as well as eating disorders (to age 30), CD and/or ODD (maintenance or increase), and agoraphobia. Rates of ADHD and separation anxiety disorders have decreased in adolescence (e.g., Costello et al., 2011; Kessler et al., 2012). Anhedonia, depressed mood, and worthlessness/guilt are the depressive symptoms most predictive of conversion of adolescent subclinical depression into MDD (Glossary; Wesselhoeft et al., 2016). Earlier depression has predicted anxiety disorders, and past anxiety has predicted SUD. Studies of youth exposed to specific traumas yield up to a 30–36% prevalence of disordered reactions (up to 70% resilience; Chapters 2, 4). Among less common disorders (5% or less of larger samples; 0.5% of British adolescents, N = 10,000; Ford, Goodman, & Meltzer, 2003), one or more childhood psychotic symptoms (e.g., hallucinations, delusions) increase the likelihood of adult onset psychosis (rare before late adolescence, see Costello et al., 2011; Nader & Fletcher, 2014). A few rare disorders (tic, autism spectrum) have diminished or become less impairing in adolescence.

Risk and Protective Factors

A number of factors have been linked to increased adolescent reactions—e.g., number of types of exposures, parenting, parent response, specific symptoms, skills. For example, higher emotion regulation difficulties were associated with greater PTSD and depressive symptom severity for sexually abused girls (Chang, Kaczkurkin, McLean, & Foa, 2018; Chapter 14). PTSD has also predicted other disorders—e.g., later depression in adolescents, three years after an earthquake, partially mediated by subsequent negative life events (N = 4137, Jin et al., 2018). For youth exposed to an 8.0 Richter scale earthquake in China, there were high rates of PTSD in adolescents and parents, with a significant decline in symptoms between 12 and 18 months after the earthquake—perhaps due to high levels of support and timely interventions (Shi et al., 2018). Shi et al. found a causal relationship between parents' PTSS and adolescent PTSS. In addition, adolescent PTSS prospectively predicted maternal PTSS at 18 months. Poly-victimization, attachment, coping, and posttraumatic growth are discussed here.

Poly-Victimization (PV) or Cumulative Trauma

Problems have occurred for youth after individual types of exposure (e.g., after caregiver loss, separations) and especially after poly-victimization (e.g., seven or more types; Ford, Grasso, Hawke, & Chapman, 2013; Chapter 2). Rates of adolescent PV appear to have increased in recent decades, and PV has been related to more severe mental and physical problems than single trauma exposures (Finkelhor, Ormrod, & Turner, 2009; Green & Myrick, 2014; Table 15.1). Among numerous possible outcomes, symptoms have included delinquent peer associations, poor self-regulation (e.g., reactive aggression), cognitive difficulties, and interpersonal problems (Ford et al., 2013; Kira et al., 2012). Among other associations, poly-victimization has been related to hypervigilance toward or away from cues of threat (e.g., places, situations; see Ford & Delker, 2018). Number of types of traumas has proven to be a more important predictor of worse outcomes than chronicity (Adams et al., 2016; Turner, Finkelhor, & Ormrod, 2010). For example, for multiply traumatized minority and refugee adolescents with a wide variety of trauma types (Kira et al., 2012), cumulative trauma exposure was linked to negative effects on all types of cognitive functions measured—perceptual reasoning, verbal comprehension, working memory, and processing speed.

Victim Profiles

In most studies of poly-victimization/cumulative trauma, increased numbers of types of trauma exposure have been related to increased negative outcomes. Although latent class analyses (LCA) often have found three main victimization profiles, the profiles have varied definitions of high, medium, and low based on population studied and/or author conceptualization (Table 15.1; Ayer et al., 2018; Finkelhor, Shattuck, Turner, & Ormrod, 2014; incarcerated youth, Ford et al., 2013, 2018a; exposure type, Roberts et al., 2018; Turner et al., 2010). For example, for youth in treatment at 10 sites, the three victimization profiles included poly-victimized, high witnessing of violence, and low victimization groups (N = 2776, ages 3–16; Ayer et al., 2018; see Chapter 9), whereas in another, multi-ethnic clinical sample followed across time, Adams et al. found high-, moderate-, and low-exposure groups with three subgroups for the moderate group—emotional abuse, loss/violence exposure, and multi-epoch emotional abuse (across multiple age groups; Adams et al., 2016; N = 3485, ages 13–18). Finkelhor et al. (2014) found that types of exposures increased with age and that poly-victimization (vs fewer trauma types) was associated with greater distress for each of four age groups (Table 15.1).

Adolescent girls and boys in the juvenile justice system often have had multiple traumatic exposures. Youth in the system are 3–8 times more likely than others to have psychological trauma or

Table 15.1 Adolescent Profiles/Trajectories with Multiple Exposures to Potentially Traumatic Life Events

Nationally Representative Sample (3 Profiles; Turner et al., 2010; N=4053, ages 2–17)
- 11 or more different types of victimization (10% of sample)—more highly related to trauma symptoms than experiencing repeated victimizations of a single type and explained a large portion of the associations between individual forms of victimization and symptom levels
- 5 or more types (30%)
- 1 type of victimization (close to 66%)

4 age group cohorts of poly-victimization (PV; N=3056; ages 2–17; Finkelhor et al., 2014)
Poly-victimization rates were examined as follows:
- ages 2–5—PV=5 or more types of victimization
- ages 6–9—PV=6 or more types
- ages 10–13—PV=7 or more types
- ages 14–17—PV=8 or more types

For 36 possible types of victimization:
- victimization types generally increased with age
- highly victimized children in each age group were considerably more likely to be distressed as well as to have higher levels of other adversities

Incarcerated youth (3 poly-victimization profiles; Ford et al., 2013; N=1959, ages 10–16)
- *high* (5% of sample)—12 types of victimization and 7 different types of other trauma exposures; had the most severe PTSD, affect dysregulation, substance use, suicide risk, and somatic complaints
- *medium* (36%)—3 types of other trauma exposures and 8 types of victimization; moderate symptom levels and behavioral problems
- *low* (59%)—usually no other trauma exposures and 6 types of victimizations; the lowest levels of symptoms and behavior problems, comparatively

Hurricanes and Gulf Oil Spill (4 profiles; Osofsky et al., 2015c; N=4619)
- *resistance*—stable-low symptoms (52%); half with high exposures
- *recovery*—steep declines following initial symptoms (21%)
- *delayed distress*—increasing symptoms (18%)
- *chronic*—stable-high symptoms (9%)

Both hurricane exposure and oil spill-related stress predicted trajectories and overall PTSD symptom levels
Older youth, girls, individuals with more exposures to hurricanes and with more oil spill distress showed more symptoms
Symptoms remitted more slowly (or may have increased) for those with both high hurricane exposure and high oil spill distress

Multi-ethnic, clinical sample (3 profiles, 5 total; Adams et al., 2016; N=3485, ages 13–18)
Across development:
- *high-exposure subgroup* (averaged 10 trauma types) (more Whites)
  - (a) high exposure rates to: physical abuse; emotional abuse; domestic violence; traumatic loss/separation/bereavement; impaired caregiver, community violence
  - (b) several trauma types occurred in multiple developmental epochs: physical abuse; emotional abuse; domestic violence; impaired caregiver
  - (c) the more trauma types, the more distress; more placement in residential treatment or correctional facility; more internalizing and externalizing; PTSD scores in the clinical range; more substance use; more suicidal behaviors
- *moderate-exposure groups*
  - (a) *emotional abuse subgroup* (average 6.1 types)—high exposures to physical abuse, neglect, domestic violence, impaired caregiver in one developmental period (more girls; more Whites)
  - (b) *loss/violence exposure subgroup* (average 5.4 types)—high rates of traumatic loss/separation and

continued

Table 15.1 Continued

community violence (community and school violence) (more boys; more Latinos; in nationally representative samples—more African Americans)

(c) *multi-epoch emotional abuse subgroup* (average 5 trauma types)—high exposure to maltreatment types; high rates of emotional abuse/psychological maltreatment in multiple developmental epochs; high, multi-epoch physical abuse, neglect, domestic violence, impaired caregiver; higher symptom levels than the low-exposure group; avoidance and suicidality were more likely than for 1 epoch emotional abuse (more girls; more Whites)

- *low-exposure group* (average 2.2 trauma types)—not poly-victimized; traumatic loss/separation/ bereavement was most common; 25% with clinically relevant PTSD scores

---

Sexual offenders (5 subtypes; N=322, ages 12–16; Barra et al., 2018)
general findings:
the majority of sexual offenders were not sexually victimized themselves; 66% with several ACE types (moderate to high); cumulative ACE score (not cumulative types) was related to penetration; no differences were found for use of physical violence; no differences for the choice of male, stranger, or multiple victims; younger age related to penetration and to choosing a child victim; older age and previous non-sexual delinquency were associated with elevated odds for current non-sexual convictions

SUBTYPES

- *low levels of ACEs*—1/3 of offenders
- *moderate ACE* subtypes
  (a) abuse and neglect in the family context
  (b) family-neglect only—had elevated odds of having a child victim (not an adolescent victim)—elevated offense severity (penetration); related to current non-sexual delinquency as well
  (c) elevated scores on peer bullying—related both to child victims and penetration (the latter regardless of age of victim)
- *high poly-victims* (almost 10%)—intra- and extra-familial contexts of victimization—related to the choice of child victims but not to penetration

---

Youth in the juvenile justice system (3 subgroups; lifetime exposure; see Ford et al., 2018a; N=809)
26 possible types of potentially traumatic events (PTEs):

- *mixed adversity class* (41% of sample)—less frequent PTEs reported; 40% of them reported a variety of adversities—e.g., severe injury or illness, physical abuse, parent arrested, someone they knew attempted suicide
- *violent environment class* (41%)—characterized by frequent reports (61–94%) of physical abuse or assault, severe injury or illness, witnessing physical assaults, parent using drugs, someone close attempting or committing suicide, someone close being violently injured or killed
- *PV class* (18%)—(80–90%) reported each of 10 types of victimization
  (a) sexual abuse, physical abuse or assault, emotional abuse, parent threatening to leave them, witnessing assaults, and unexpected death or attempted suicide of someone they knew
  (b) more than half also reported witnessing inter-parental or family violence, parental arrest, removal from or abandoned by parents, and a loved one violently injured or killed.
  (c) PTSD symptoms mediated the relationship between PV and problems with anger, depression/ anxiety, and somatic complaints (glossary-mediating).
  (d) alcohol/drug use was directly related to PV
  (e) for detained youth, dissociation symptoms mediated between PV and internalizing—i.e., depression, anxiety; suicidal ideation—but not externalizing (i.e., anger/irritability; alcohol/drug)
  (f) health problems were both directly related to PV and indirectly related via PTSD

Community-based sample (3 profiles, Ayer et al., 2018; N=2776, ages 3–16)

- *poly-victimized*—high endorsement of multiple types of trauma
  (a) higher baseline levels of PTSD and externalizing (caregiver and self-report); clinical symptom levels
  (b) still had the highest symptom levels after a year, although faster treatment gains

(c) steepest decreases in symptoms over a year (on average moved from possible PTSD to nonclinical levels; significantly steeper reduction in PTSD and externalizing than low group; improved more rapidly in PTSD than high witnessing group)
- *high witnessing of violence*—high endorsement of witnessing violence
  (a) had next highest mean baseline symptom levels
  (b) symptoms improved over the year of study (PTSD moved to nonclinical levels)
- *low victimization*—low victimization across types
  (a) symptoms improved over the year of study

Adolescents maltreated from preschool age (3 trajectories; Roberts et al., 2018; N=1307 ages 4–6, N=847 at age 18; longitudinal study)
- *chronic*—chronic exposure to adverse life events
  (a) multiple types of trauma symptoms—e.g., increased likelihood of internalizing and externalizing in late adolescence
  (b) more anger/irritability, depression, intrusive experiences, and dissociation
  (c) more likely to have school dropout, more sexual partners, more arrests, and more substance use (marijuana or other illicit drugs) than the other 2 groups
- *moderate/declining*—moderate exposure to stressful life events, declining across childhood into adolescence
  (a) significantly associated with dropping out of school
- *low levels*—exposure to few stressful life events

Some differences by type of trauma, e.g.,
- sexual abuse linked to greater likelihood of anxious arousal symptoms
- physical or emotional maltreatment linked to greater likelihood of school dropout
- neglect linked to likelihood of dropout, unprotected sex, and cigarette use

---

PTSD and are at high risk of revictimization (vs community youth; N=809, Ford et al., 2018a; into adulthood, Ford, 2018). For youth in juvenile detention facilities (N=1959, 10–16; Ford et al., 2013), LCA have demonstrated high levels of poly-victimization. Both high (12 types of victimization and seven other types of traumas) and moderate groups (eight victimization and three other trauma types) showed severe trauma symptoms and problems, especially the poly-victimized group (the high group). Both would be considered highly poly-victimized by normal standards. In another study of youth in the juvenile justice system, the PV class was exposed to 10 of 26 possible types of victimization, often with other potentially traumatic event exposures (Ford et al., 2018a; Table 15.1).

Youth who engage in animal cruelty have been at increased risk of perpetrating violence on other people—e.g., peers, loved ones, elder family members. Such youth often have been exposed to family violence, which may include animal cruelty perpetrated by violent adults on loved pets. In a study of 81,000 juvenile offenders with adverse childhood experiences, 466 youth self-reported engaging in animal cruelty (Bright, Huq, Spencer, & Applebaum, 2018). Compared to other juvenile offenders, youth who engaged in animal cruelty were younger at first arrest, more often male, and more often White. They were more likely than other juvenile offenders to have four or more ACEs and a range of other adverse experiences beyond family violence. Their early contact with law enforcement provides an opportunity for early intervention (Bright et al., 2018).

Revictimization

Revictimization is common after traumas and has increased the consequences of exposure (Finkelhor et al., 2007, 2014). Poly-victimization tends to persist for children (Finkelhor et al., 2014), suggesting that adolescent reports of poly-victimization in one year may link to earlier poly-victimizations. A decreased responsiveness to negative social behavior observed in assaulted adolescents, greater histories of assault exposure, and PTSD symptoms prospectively have predicted increased rates of revictimization for adolescents and adults (Cisler, Amstadter, & Nugent, 2011; Cougle, Resnick, & Kilpatrick, 2009). For women first sexually victimized (CSA) as adolescents and revictimized in college (assessed 743, ages 19–25), revictimized young adults significantly consumed more alcohol, with greater frequency, and engaged in greater peak drinking (large quantities in a single day), than those with no CSA. Revictimized youth used more illicit substances with more serious consequences than those victimized in high school only or with no CSA (study of CSA, alcohol and substance use; Angelone, Marcantino, & Melillo, 2018).

Consistent with other findings that one form of stress increases risk of subsequent forms, Turner et al. (2017) found that youth experiencing war-related parental absence or deployment were at elevated risk of cumulative victimization exposure and a variety of potentially traumatic exposure types—e.g., maltreatment, witnessing intimate partner violence, sibling assault, peer assault, property crime, sexual victimization, accidents, illnesses, deaths of close family and friends, disasters, chronic parental arguing, and parental imprisonment (studied to age 18; N = 13,052; Turner, Finkelhor, Hadley, & Henly). Parental war-related absence influenced increased delinquency and trauma symptoms through its link to past-year multiple victimizations and total number of adversities. Poly-victimization in childhood has been linked to multiple victimizations in adulthood (see Nader & Fletcher, 2014).

Symptom Complexity

Symptom complexity (Glossary, Chapter 2)—the number of different types of symptoms or symptom clusters that are simultaneously elevated in the clinical range for a person (e.g., Briere, Dietrich, & Semple, 2016; Hodges et al., 2013; see also dissociative complexity, to follow)—has been linked to poly-victimization or cumulative trauma exposure. Reactions have included combinations of anxiety and depressive symptoms; dissociation; relational, identity, and affect regulation disturbances; cognitive distortions; somatization; externalizing (e.g., self-mutilation), dysfunctional sexual behaviors; violence; substance abuse; eating disorders; revictimization; and/or complicated bereavement (with loss of family members or other significant attachment figures; Briere & Lanktree, 2013).

Insecure and Disorganized Attachments

Compared to secure, insecure attachments have been related to more problems and psychopathology—e.g., anxiety, depression (DeKlyen & Greenberg, 2018). Disorganized attachments have been linked to increased skill deficits and psychopathology as well—e.g., chronic affect regulation problems, stress management, dissociation, internalizing, externalizing—and a variety of disorders including Stressor-Related Disorders (Lewis-Morrarty et al., 2015; combined internalizing & externalizing, Lyons-Ruth & Jacobvitz, 2018; Schore, 2003; Table A3.4). Traumas have been linked to troubled attachments and to other disruptions in development. For example, Roazzi, Attili, Di Pentima, & Toni (2016) found that maltreated adolescents had significantly more disorganized and avoidant attachments and showed mainly external locus of control (feeling little control over events), in addition to increased likelihood of internalizing problems (N = 160, ages 5–14).

Attachment has mediated the link between adverse childhood experience (ACEs) and outcomes. For example, for Irish undergraduate university students exposed to at least one ACE, insecure attachments to mothers (not fathers or peers) mediated the relationship between adversity and psychological distress and lower subjective well-being (N = 190, Corcoran & McNulty, 2018). Childhood adversity was associated with greater likelihood of anxious or avoidant attachments. The degree to which youth distrusted how available people would be when needed (aspect of attachment anxiety) mediated the link between ACEs and adult depression, anxiety, stress, and well-being—the greater the distrust, the greater the problem levels. ACEs were associated with anxious attachment with a best friend and/or with mother; attachment anxiety was linked to adult depression. Avoidant attachment with mother also mediated between ACEs and adult well-being.

Among problems associated with attachment quality are, e.g., procrastination, problematic social media use (e.g., Facebook, Snapchat), and sibling bullying (see Sibling Aggression, this chapter). When aspects of parent–adolescent attachment—i.e., trust, communication, and alienation—along with general self-worth and procrastination were assessed, higher trust with both fathers and mothers and more communication with fathers was associated with lower levels of procrastination, whereas both paternal and maternal alienation positively associated with procrastination (mediated by self-worth; N = 384, ages 14–16, Chen, 2017). Although social media may encourage skills such as self-revelation and self-presentation, problematic social media use has been linked to difficulties such as preference for online rather than face-to-face social interactions, mood alterations, cognitive preoccupations, and/or compulsive internet use (see Assuncao, Costa, Tagliabue, & Matos, 2017). In a study of Portuguese adolescents, secure parent–adolescent relationships were associated with less alienation with peers and with less problematic social media use (explained 25% of variance in Facebook use; Assuncao et al., 2017). Insecure attachments were related to peer-alienation, separation anxiety, inhibition of exploration, and individuation problems. More information about the relationship of attachment to trauma or adversity is provided in sections to follow. Attachment-related treatments may be advised.

Coping

Resilient coping has been characterized as coping that includes tenacity, optimism, active problem-solving, and active extraction of positive growth (Beutel et al., 2017). Individuals without ACEs have reported higher resilience and better social support. Resilient copers with ACEs have reported much lower levels of depression, anxiety, and somatic symptoms than exposed youth low in resilient coping. For youth with ACEs—emotional, physical, or sexual abuse; emotional and physical neglect—traumas were linked to greater vulnerability such as low resilient coping ability, higher helplessness, and low self-efficacy, as well as to perceived lower social support over the lifespan, lower social status and social integration, fewer partnerships, less education, lower income, and more unemployment across time (N = 2508, ages 14–92, Beutel et al., 2017).

Better developed EFs are a resilience factor, clearly linked to more adaptive coping (Luciana, 2016). For youth (ages 9–15), better EFs—working memory (WM); cognitive flexibility (CF)—have been related to greater use of primary and secondary control coping (Glossary), which is related to lower levels of depressive symptoms (Evans, Kouros, Samanez-Larkin, & Garber, 2016). In contrast, WM deficits have predicted more depressive symptoms. WM—e.g., planning, implementing multistep solutions, holding several perspectives while evaluating their accuracy—has predicted use of both types of coping (primary and secondary). CF predicted use of secondary coping.

Positive Outlook Toward the Future

Among resilience factors, a positive outlook toward the future has significantly attenuated the negative effects of maltreatment (see Oshri et al., in press). A nationally representative sample of children ages 10 and older, followed for 3–5 years, showed that a large majority of maltreated children had high scores on positive future orientation (N = 1461; Oshri et al., in press). Oshri et al. found three trajectories of positive future orientation: *high-persistent* (76%)—into young adulthood; *low-start/increasing* (10%)—low in early adolescence, increasing over time to match high-persistents; *high-start/decreasing* (14%)—high in childhood, diminishing over time, low expectations entering young adulthood. High-persistent youth had higher resource and lower risk factor levels than other groups. In early adolescence, low-increasing youth experienced more physically abusive discipline and more disorganized community environments, and they showed lower self-esteem, peer relationship dissatisfaction, and less engagement in school, compared to high-persistent youth. Youth with high-persistent and low-start/increasing positive expectations were more likely to attain their young adulthood developmental milestones—e.g., independent living skills, social capital, employment, and higher weekly income (Oshri et al., in press).

Loneliness and feeling disconnected from others are important predictors of suicide risk (Chang et al., 2017). Chang and colleagues also found the protective effects of positive future orientation. Lonely college students—young emerging adults—with high positive future orientation—e.g., believing things would change for the better—reported significantly lower levels of depressive symptoms and of suicidal ideation, than lonely students with low positive future orientation. Context matters in the expression of positive emotions. Childhood sexual abuse (CSA) survivors who expressed positive emotion while describing a past sexual abuse experience had poorer long-term social adjustment, vs survivors who expressed positive emotion when describing a non-abuse experience (had improved social adjustment, Bonanno et al., 2007).

Coping and Adversity

Adolescents use a variety of coping strategies to face difficulties (e.g., relational difficulties with parents, Gagné & Melancon, 2013; maltreatment, Jackson et al., 2017). Dishion (2016) suggests that, under conditions of chronic marginalization (stressful social environments), children become adept at early detection and avoidance of punitive and/or rejecting relationships and environments. From a deficit framework, this could be seen as a negative attribution bias, while from an evolutionary perspective, it can be seen as adaptive (quick detection of potential threat or reward).

Coping has influenced posttrauma symptom levels. However, trauma may undermine coping skills. Children, who at ages 3–5 lived in homes with parental violence and/or parental alcohol abuse, were more likely to develop ineffective coping strategies (e.g., using alcohol) to decrease negative affect (assessed again at ages 12–14 and 18–20; no gender differences, this study, N = 1064; Jester, Steinberg, Heitzeg, & Zucker, 2015; see Asberg & Renk, 2012). PTSD has mediated the relationship between coping styles and quality of life—e.g., avoidant coping has been related to increased PTSD symptoms, which related to reduced quality of life (e.g., for refugees; path analysis; N = 335; ages 18+; Huijts et al., 2012). For Palestinian youth living in the Gaza strip (ongoing war/unrest conditions), adolescent resilience was predicted by stronger ethnic identity, stronger family sense of coherence (Glossary), higher self-regulation, more optimism, and more effective coping strategies and was related to lower depressive and anxiety symptoms (Aitcheson et al., 2017).

The Effectiveness of Coping Methods

The effectiveness of specific coping methods may vary after trauma or loss—i.e., is situation and/or person-related. Some active coping methods (e.g., memorializing) may serve as traumatic reminders or tax already overtaxed resources (Table 14.1). The relationship between coping (especially avoidant coping) and PTSD can be unclear, perhaps because the effectiveness of coping strategies is influenced by a variety of factors. Contrary to many findings, in one study, emotion-focused coping was positively related to quality of life, and support seeking did not influence PTSD symptoms, perhaps related to a significantly traumatized support system (Huijts et al., 2012). Similarly, avoidant coping has had mixed results. Avoidant coping has been linked to negative posttrauma outcomes (see Mello & Nader, 2012). However, avoidance can be a desirable option in uncontrollable situations or to relieve the burden of constant focus on a trauma (Brooks, Graham-Kevan, Robinson, & Lowe, 2018; Gagné & Melancon, 2013). Nevertheless, avoidance and loss of trust may interfere with support seeking or other more effective coping and may interfere with processing and resolution of trauma or loss. Gender may influence effectiveness. For a group of girls exposed to parental psychological violence, avoidant coping strategies partially mediated the link between psychological violence and girls' behavior problems (not for boys; Gagné & Melancon, 2013). Instead, approach coping strategies partially mediated the link between psychological violence and boys' behavior problems (not for girls; other mediators not tested).

For decades, social support (support seeking; receiving support) has proven protective against negative mental health outcomes (see Nader, 2008; Thabet et al., 2009). Forms of social support desirable to exposed individuals—e.g., warmth, kindness, respect for needs related to space or proximity, providing needed resources—including family, school, and peer support, have been linked to lower trauma symptoms (Jaycox et al., 2010; La Greca, Silverman, Lai, & Jaccard, 2010; Nader, 2008, 2012c; Udwin et al., 2000). Close individual friendships can be an important potential protective mechanism for adolescents. For British adolescents ages 11–19, perceived close friendship quality was positively related to resilience, and was facilitated by development of a constructive coping style (support seeking & active coping), effort, a supportive friendship network, and reduced disengaged and externalizing coping (Graber, Turner, & Madill, 2016). Boys were more vulnerable than girls to the deleterious effects of disengaged and externalizing coping.

Posttraumatic Growth (PTG)

When negative or traumatic events are severe enough to challenge core beliefs and trigger cognitive processing, they may result in both positive and negative effects on well-being (Brooks, Graham-Kevan, Robinson, & Lowe, 2018; Chapters 3, 4). For example, posttrauma growth has been evidenced in the increased ability to relate to others; new interests, opportunities, or pursuits; personal strength—e.g., increased self-reliance and confidence; spiritual growth—e.g., stronger faith and understanding; and/or an increased appreciation of life (Tedeschi & Calhoun, 2004). Degree of exposure may alter the likelihood of PTG. Although PTSD and PTG significantly positively correlated in a generally affected earthquake area, PTSD negatively correlated with PTG in most of the severely affected areas (N = 41,189 adolescents; Du et al., 2018). Recent findings suggest that intrusive thoughts and social support mediate the link between trauma and PTG (Brooks et al., 2018). Intrusive thoughts may instigate reassessment of the experience, leading to growth. Brooks et al. found that avoidance coping also mediated the relationship between multiple trauma types and PTG and between childhood trauma and PTG, suggesting that avoidance may be adaptive when there is inability to control exposures to significant stressors.

Trauma and Stressor-Related Disorders (TSRD)

Trauma or prolonged adversity has been associated with a number of disorders. As mentioned, youth with protective or less environmentally sensitive genetic variants and without traumatic experiences have displayed a decreased likelihood for the development of psychiatric disorders, in contrast to sensitive youth (Comasco et al., 2015). Increasing numbers of traumas have been related to increased symptoms and/or complexity. Youth who reported being both victims of and witnesses to family aggression have reported higher levels of aggression (i.e., self- and other-directed harm) compared to youth who only witnessed or were from low-aggression families (Zhang, Finy, Bresin, & Verona, 2015). A number of factors may increase the likelihood of being traumatized—e.g., SES, personality (e.g., levels of extraversion, neuroticism), earlier victimization. For example, 14-year-olds who displayed *neuroticism* were significantly more likely to be exposed to stressful life events as well as to have depression, suicidality, and/or anxiety disorders than others by age 30, whereas *extraversion* had no such link (Newton-Howes, Horwood, & Mulder, 2015). Genes have been implicated in a number of reactions. For example, Szentágotai-Tătar et al. (2015) found that trauma intensity positively related to guilt-proneness only in carriers of low-expressing Met allele of BDNF Val66Met (also assessed 5-HTTLPR, N = 271, ages 14–17). Trauma has been linked to a number of difficulties in addition to TSRD-related symptoms (later in this chapter)—e.g., violent, incarcerated adolescents have significantly shown histories of violent traumas (Ford, 2002; Ford et al., 2018a).

Attachment-related posttrauma disorders in school-age youth were discussed in Chapter 11. PTSD with and without dissociative symptoms and complicated grief are discussed here.

Posttraumatic Exposures and Disorders

For adolescents, too, traumas have been linked to a wide variety of problems—e.g., reduced skills, PTSD, or other psychopathology (e.g., mood disorders, 475 high school students, Italian earthquake, Dell'Osso et al., 2014)—and with comorbidity (Butler et al., 2018). Each type of trauma has shown a variety of negative outcomes as well as the possibility of positive outcomes (e.g., PTG, above). For example, among the significant negative effects of exposure to violence are lower IQ, brain alterations, physical problems, and psychopathology (Butler et al., 2018). Sexual abuse has been linked to psychiatric disorders including PTSD, depression, and emotion-regulation difficulties (Chang, Kaczkurkin, McLean, & Foa, 2018). Although cumulative traumas have affected all aspects of cognitive functioning measured, Kira et al. (2012) found some differences in effects on aspects of IQ based on type of trauma exposure—e.g., abandonment showed a negative effect on perceptual reasoning; sexual abuse, a negative effect on perceptual reasoning and working memory (N = 390, ages 11–18). Larger studies are needed for the study of trauma types and outcomes.

PTSD-DS

As discussed in Chapter 2, PTSD may occur with or without dissociative symptoms and has been related significantly to cumulative traumas (Chiu et al., 2015). For adolescents, PTSD with dissociative symptoms (derealization, depersonalization), has been related to attachment as well as to trauma exposures. Insecure attachment styles have predicted adolescent dissociation after traumas—e.g., at least in one study, more strongly than trauma exposure (N = 240 Swedish school youth, ages 13–15, 16–20; Gusic, Cardena, Bengtsson, & Sondergaard, 2016); after a school shooting (Turunen et al., 2014). For a group of Swedish adolescents, higher insecure attachments were associated with dissociation and PTS for variety of types of trauma exposure. Number of potentially traumatic exposures correlated with symptoms of PTS and dissociation as well.

Dissociation and Its Other Relationships

During a childhood traumatic experience, dissociation can be protective or even adaptive for attenuating distress in situations where there are no other options for escape (Choi et al., 2017). However, persistent dissociation can interfere with learning and development (e.g., identity formation, memory) and can become maladaptive—e.g., linked to NSSI, comorbidity (Chapter 2). For at-risk Israeli adolescent girls living in out-of-home placements (N = 93, ages 12–18, Lev-Wiesel & Zohar, 2014), although CSA increased, more than three-fold, the risk of self-injury, only persistent dissociation predicted NSSI (even with low DES scores, accounted for 11% of the variance). For adolescents, dissociation may disrupt self-concept and the developing sense of self (Harter, 1999). A small sample of adolescents with dissociative disorders (e.g., Dissociative Identity Disorder, DD not otherwise specified) significantly had histories of traumatization, especially poly-traumatization and had high rates of comorbidity and multiple symptoms—e.g., PTSD, depression, anxiety, suicidality, self-mutilation, learning difficulties, auditory hallucinations, ADHD, aggression, and sexual promiscuity (N = 25, ages 12–18; Bozkurt et al., 2015). Dissociation occurs in up to two thirds of patients with BPD as well (to follow). Combined risk factors are stronger than individual risk factors.

Dissociative complexity (Glossary) has been related to cumulative traumas and to comorbidity (Briere et al., 2016). Some evidence suggests that increasing the types of dissociative symptoms assessed is more appropriate for trauma-exposed adolescents (Choi et al., 2017). Latent class analysis of two models of dissociation—depersonalization and derealization only or 10 types of dissociation—identified distinct subgroups of adolescents seeking treatment (national sample, N = 3081, ages 12–16; Choi et al., 2017). A depersonalization/derealization model (DSM-5 PTSD-DS) had five classes/profiles: dissociative subtype/high PTSD; high PTSD; anxious arousal; dysphoric arousal; and a low-symptom/reference class. It did not fully capture the symptom profile for a subset of youth—e.g., dysphoric adolescents presenting without nightmares, flashbacks, avoidance, guilt, or fear. The expanded dissociation model, identified additional classes: a dissociative amnesia/ detached arousal class (D-amnesia/detached; e.g., more dissociative amnesia) and a dissociative subtype/high PTSD class (DS/high PTSD) with a minor role for depersonalization and derealization among other dissociation symptoms. DS/high PTSD had more overall trauma exposures and more PTSD symptoms. Both high PTSD classes had more other traumas and more maltreatment exposures and lower odds of neglect than the D-amnesia/detached class.

Complicated Grief (CG)

Complicated grief—e.g., posttraumatic grief (TG), prolonged grief (PGD), grief with comorbidity or other complicating factors (Table 12.1)—is a condition for further study in DSM-5 (*Persistent Complex Bereavement Disorder*, PCBD), and Prolonged Grief Disorder is included in WHO's ICD-11. For adolescents and adults, PCBD may persist for at least six months and may include persistent longing/yearning for the deceased, sorrow/emotional pain, or preoccupation with deceased or the circumstances of death as well as symptoms of reactive distress—e.g., difficulty accepting, disbelief/ emotional numbness, bitterness/anger, maladaptive appraisals of self related to deceased—social identity disruption, and interference with functioning (APA, 2013; Box 3.1). In an assessment of youth ages 8–18 (N = 367), youth who met either full PCBD disorder, PCBD Criterion B (preoccupation with deceased and/or circumstances of death), or Criterion C (reactive distress and/or social identity disruptions) reported higher PTS and depressive symptoms than other youth (Kaplow et al., 2018). Meeting the traumatic bereavement specifier (death due to homicide or suicide) was also associated with more frequent PTSS. Unresolved maladaptive grief may persist for years and may interfere both with children's and adolescents' psychosocial functioning and with their developmental progression (Melhem, Moritz, Walker, Shear, & Brent, 2007; Nader, 2008; Nader & Layne, 2009). Recognition of CG as an important risk factor for serious outcomes is important to countries with high rates of deaths by violence, war, terrorism, or other tragic circumstances (Layne et al., 2017).

CG in adolescence requires cognizance of factors such as increased autonomy, impulsivity, sensation seeking, peer pressure, risk-taking, and immature development skills (e.g., EFs; self-control) and of changing brain regions (e.g., PFC; Chapter 4; Baker et al., 2015; Blakemore & Mills, 2014; Layne et al., 2017). Suicide and homicide are the second and third leading causes of death (after unintentional injuries) for adolescents (Canada; Hewitt, Caelian, Chen, & Flett, 2014; U.S. ages 20–24, Layne et al., 2017; worldwide, World Health Organization [WHO], 2014). Adolescents may experience traumatic or other forms of CG after death of a peer as well as death of a loved one (e.g., suicidal death of friends or acquaintances, ages 11–23 years old, Melhem et al., 2004). For youth, loss of a parent or sibling may generate complicated grief reactions (Betancourt, Newnham, McBain, & Brennan, 2013b). The impact of sibling loss on primary caregivers may also provide relational challenges for the developing child (Charles & Charles, 2006). To some extent, post-loss behavior may depend on the type of loss and/or the combination of influencing variables. For example, Charles and Charles (2006) found that sibling loss stimulated greater support seeking than withdrawal, regardless of attachment style (age at sibling death, 0–19; needs larger studies). In their exploratory study, although, contrary to style, avoidant youth did not use more distancing coping strategies, youth with secure and preoccupied attachment styles were more likely to be support seeking. Positive coping methods—support seeking and problem-solving—were related to grief-related personal growth. There were no effects of negative coping, in contrast to studies that link negative coping to negative outcomes. Youth may appear to have adapted and still have difficulties—e.g., fears of close relationships (Charles & Charles, 2006).

Unexpectedness of a death and violent losses have been associated with increased reactions (e.g., see Barlé, Wortman, & Latack, 2015). For example, sudden loss has been associated with lower ability to concentrate and learn, lower academic achievement, less enjoyment of school, less school belongingness, and fewer beliefs that teachers treat youth fairly (Oosterhoff, Kaplow, & Layne, in press). Some evidence suggests that peri-traumatic dissociation and peri-traumatic helplessness may mediate the relationship between unexpectedness and reactions to loss (Barlé et al., 2015). People over age 17, who experienced violent losses (homicide, suicide, accident), reported more PGD and PTSD symptoms than when deaths were after illness (Boelen, 2015). Peri-traumatic helplessness and peri-traumatic dissociation each independently mediated the severity of PGD and PTSD (not peri-traumatic fear and horror). That is, violent and unexpected losses each exacerbated post-loss psychopathology, at least partially because such losses included a greater sense of helplessness and dissociative responses. Similarly, in another study both dissociative tendencies and level of integration of the loss into a personal narrative were related to PGD and psychological distress (adults; 66% disease-related losses; Hasson-Ohayon, Peri, Rotschild, & Tuval-Mashiach, 2017).

Personality Disorders (PDs)

Adolescents with the symptoms of PDs have had persisting problems into adulthood (e.g., 20 years later, Crawford et al., 2008; Rossouw, 2015). Trauma, genetics, and other factors have been associated with personality disorders. For example, young adults (ages 18–22) who carry the short 5-HTTLPR gene allele may be vulnerable to having traits of borderline and antisocial personality disorder (N = 96, low SES; Lyons-Ruth et al., 2007). Although more study is needed and not all insecure attachments result in disorders, some evidence links insecure attachment to personality disorders—e.g., preoccupied attachments to HPD (histrionic PD), dependent (DPD), borderline (BPD), and avoidant PD (AVPD, contrary to expectation); dismissing attachments to antisocial (ASPD), narcissistic (NPD), paranoid (PPD), and schizoid PD (SZPD); fearful attachments (high on preoccupation and avoidance) to AVPD, BPD, NPD, obsessive-compulsive PD, PPD, and schizotypal PD; unresolved attachment with BPD (see Levy et al., 2015). Some have suggested that attachment difficulties are at the heart of many personality disorders (Levy et al., 2015). For example, impoverished relationships are found in ASPD, AVPD, NPD, and SZPD, while intense aloneness and fears of abandonment are characteristic of BPD and DPD. BPD and NPD follow. It is important to remember that personality disorders share some traits with personality styles, temperamental styles, and attachment styles. Training and experience are recommended for accurate diagnosing.

Adolescent Borderline Personality Disorder (BPD)

Borderline Personality Disorder (BPD) is now a legitimate diagnosis for adolescents in ICD-11 (Sharp & Fonagy, 2015). DSM-5 BPD criteria must be met and have lasted a year for a diagnosis below age 18 (APA, 2013). BPD traits in adolescents often persist (Glossary; APA, 2013; Box 15.1). BPD has been significantly linked to traumas—e.g., ACEs, abuse, neglect, emotional neglect (Fonagy, Luyten, & Strathearn, 2011; Ford & Courtois, 2014; linked to genetics, to suicidality and NSSI, Courtney-Seidler, Klein, & Miller, 2013)—and its symptoms linked to early childhood relationship variables, e.g., attachment disorganization, maladaptive parenting (e.g., maternal inconsistency, maternal hostility), boundary dissolution (a form of over-stimulation), family disruption (father absence), and family

Box 15.1 Borderline Personality Symptoms

When Briana was born, her parents were having difficulties in their relationship, and her mother was depressed and distracted. Briana witnessed her father abusing her older brother when she was ages three and four, and then her parents divorced. Her father moved away, taking her beloved big brother with him. Abuse is often claimed in divorce cases, and there was no documented proof of injury. Briana was anxiously attached to her mother and protested loudly at any separation. She was always highly emotional and reactive as a child. Nevertheless, by the time she was an adolescent, she had a well-developed façade in order to belong among friends—she appeared extraverted, competent, and friendly. However, after a time in a relationship, she felt easily slighted and often engaged in reassurance seeking—looking for reassurance that she was doing okay in endeavors and in relationships. Friends were completely surprised at her hostility after minor slights or perceived insults and even more surprised when she periodically erupted with aggressive behaviors at any hint of being left out or abandoned. She could shift from needy to rageful in an instant. She yelled and threw things. Her boyfriend relationships were fairly short-lived. They described her as clingy, distrusting, moody, and sometimes aggressive. Other youth seemed, at first, confused by her behaviors, then unwilling to put up with them.

After graduation from high school, her boyfriend relationships seemed to last for weeks or for a few months at most. She went from job to job. She seemed to do well as a secretary or receptionist, but frequently decided she wanted a career like someone she admired. She did her best to take on the persona or prestige of the other person but was not as well suited or trained for the job. She had a poorly developed self-image and seemed unable to find her own best talent or to choose a career that suited her. She complained that her friend would not let her do well. Briana borrowed money to invest in something that a wealthier friend invested in. The market dipped and she was unable to hang on until its rise. Unlike her friend, she lost her investment and her collateral. She impulsively quit a job thinking she wanted another job she'd heard about. Quitting also permitted her to spend time taking friends places and doing other things with people. She didn't like being alone. After a different friend reduced the amount of part-time work she hired her for, she engaged in much reassurance seeking. She often sought reassurance. The friend avoided giving feedback because of past experiences—i.e., she didn't want her to throw something at her. The friend also knew that Briana sometimes became depressed and dysfunctional ("immobilized"), and she didn't want to be the cause of "one of her funks or tantrums." She sought guidance because she loved Briana as her friend but didn't want to have to mother her or to put up with her aggression. She had to redo the work that Briana was assigned, because Briana decided to do it differently than directed. Her friend felt like Briana was regularly sabotaging herself.

At one point, at the suggestion of a friend, Briana went for therapy. Without input from another, it was not clear that she had difficulty with both self- and other-understanding or that she moved out of depression into other states sometimes quickly. She gave selective information to the therapist. It was the first time she had admitted that she frequently had the desire to throw herself off of a high place (stairs, mountain tops) or to hurt herself in some other way. However, she said she never did and never would do that. She described hopelessness, feelings of emptiness, pessimism toward the future, and feelings of worthlessness. She said that she sometimes just didn't or couldn't do anything. Initial diagnosis: major depressive disorder.

When her roommate decided to move in with her boyfriend, Briana became extremely agitated, yelled at her, and punched her in the face. Friends helping with the move, who witnessed the encounter, were angry with Briana and no longer wanted to have anything to do with her. The cycle of fear of abandonment and behaviors that elicit abandonment continued.

Note:
Case examples are disguised, may be combined cases, and have had details changed to protect individuals.

stress (12–18 months to ages 12, 13, and 26, Carlson, Egeland, & Sroufe, 2009; Chanen & Thompson, 2014). Some evidence suggests high heritability as well as a risk from low SES and from early maternal separation (before age five years; Chanen & Thompson, 2014; see also Sharp & Fonagy, 2015)—e.g., involvement of genetics (5-HTTLPR; 5HT2a; TPH); link to hypo- and hyper-responsiveness of cortisol secretion (Sharp & Fonagy, 2015). Individuals with BPD symptomatology may have greater sensitivity to environments (Chapter 4). Childhood or adolescent disturbances in attention, emotion regulation, and disruptive behaviors (e.g., CD, ODD, SI, ADHD) as well as anxiety and depression have been among precursors to BPD.

It may be difficult to distinguish BPD from common adolescent behaviors—e.g., risk-taking and impulsivity—or from other disorders—e.g., self-harm, substance abuse, suicidality. BPD is highly comorbid with both internalizing and externalizing (Sharp & Fonagy, 2015). Although characterized by a superficially intact social façade (Sansone & Sansone, 2006), BPD often includes a disturbed sense of identity, affect dysregulation (e.g., anger regulation problems), poor cognitive empathy, impulsivity, and intense inner pain (especially relational) as well as feelings and fears of rejection, abandonment, and/or isolation and an intense sense of shame, which may prompt dissociation (Fonagy & Bateman, 2016; Fonagy et al., 2011; Rossouw, 2015). BPD patients may resort to maladaptive self-regulation strategies—e.g., SU, hyper-sexuality, being controlling vs avoidant, and/or NSSI (see Non-suicidal Self-Injury, to follow). For adults and sometimes for adolescents, self-regulation difficulties have also included poor money management, eating pathology (e.g., anorexia, bulimia, obesity), and/or chronic pain (Sansone & Sansone, 2006). Body image disturbances in BPD may play a role in self-harm and/or somatic complaints. Sansone and Sansone suggest that body image disturbances are part of the sequalae of childhood traumas (see Body Image Problems).

BPD and Attachment

Steele et al. (2015) suggest that BPD be seen as an adaptive response to traumatic or other stressors by a *temperamentally hypersensitive person* who has not had the benefits of a secure attachment relationship with an attentive and sensitive caregiver (p. 29). BPD symptomatology combines a biologically predisposed child with proximity-seeking behavior that triggers caregiver withdrawal, resulting in an ambivalent or disorganized attachment that "influences the sense of self, affect regulation, and social-emotional strategies found in BPD" (p. 29). BPD patients AAI interviews are often characterized by shifts between dismissal and preoccupation, preoccupied states of mind, or unresolved (disorganized) patterns (Steele et al., 2015). They may show lack of monitoring of speech or reason (poor RF) and/or unusually detailed attention to the specifics of a loss/trauma, suggesting lack of resolution (also common for PTSD). Lyons-Ruth et al. (2013) also followed infants from 18 months. Age eight disorganized attachment behavior (e.g., related to abuse) contributed independently to the prediction of BPD symptoms in late adolescence. Maternal withdrawal in infancy (in response to infant attachment cues) was a robust significant predictor of both borderline symptoms and suicidality/self-injury in late adolescence. The effects of maternal withdrawal were both independent of, and additive to, the variability explained by the severity of childhood abuse. In contrast to Carlson et al. (2009), they did not find that maternal hostile behavior (or intrusiveness) was related to BPD symptoms.

BPD and Perspective-Taking

Empathy requires responding in resonance with another (Fonagy & Bateman, 2016). Hypermentalizing—including faulty assumptions about others' mental states and hypersensitivity to their mental states—is uniquely related to BPD symptoms, including to low cognitive empathy (in adolescents; Fonagy & Bateman, 2016; Chapter 14). Both adversity and insecure attachments have been related to poor mentalizing (see Table 1.2, Glossary). With adversity and BPD, Fonagy and Bateman suggest that arousal may undermine perspective-taking in those who already have a tendency to make faulty presumptions about others' mental states (Fonagy & Bateman, 2016). For self-protection, individuals with increased sensitivity to environments may disengage the capacity to attend to and to respond appropriately to social cues (see Sharp & Fonagy, 2015). *Epistemic hypervigilance* (cognitive hypervigilance) has been used to describe this condition, in which such individuals are no longer able to update mental representations and coping strategies in response to experience. Such individuals may become impervious to positive experiences that would normally lead to increased resilience (Luyten & Fonagy, 2015).

BPD and Aggression

A number of personality disorders—e.g., BPD, NPD, APD—have been associated with aggression—e.g., physical, verbal, and/or relational aggression (e.g., cyber-bullying; Stockdale, Coyne, Nelson, & Erickson, 2015). Individuals with BPD (who show anger in response to minor slights), exhibit shame as a prominent emotion and show shame-specific reactivity (Gratz et al., 2010; Velotti et al., 2014). After controlling for guilt, adolescent girls at risk for BPD, with average SES, who reported high shame also tended to report higher levels of hostile irritability, even with only two or three of the nine BPD symptoms (N = 114, age 16, across one week, Scott et al., 2015). Low SES may confer greater irritability and aggression independent of shame. Hostile irritability occurred during shame but not during experiencing guilt. For adolescent youth in the juvenile justice system, poly-victimization (PV) was associated with dissociation and/or BP, which, in turn, were linked to offending and juvenile justice involvement (N = 782; Kerig & Modrowski, 2018). Callous-unemotional traits were linked to PV for both genders via emotional numbing (needs replication). Girls reported the highest rates of BP, dissociation, and PV (especially sexual abuse; maltreatment, dating partner victimization). Boys reported more community violence exposures.

Individuals with BPD have exhibited higher levels of jealousy in relationships and significant fears of abandonment (romantic and friendship; Stockdale et al., 2015). Stockdale et al. found that over half of all adolescents studied had engaged in cyber-bullying (e.g., rude comments on social media, spreading rumors online; with or without BPD; N = 106, ages 15–17). Adolescents with BPD features were significantly more likely to engage in cyber-bullying, and jealousy fully and significantly mediated the relationship between BPD features and cyber-bullying. For adolescents with BPD symptoms, high levels of jealousy, combined with already existing cognitive schemas and scripts that include pro-aggression beliefs, may contribute to aggressive behavior.

BPD and cPTSD (Complicated PTSD)

Although some evidence suggests a distinction between BPD and cPTSD (Cloitre et al., 2014), BPD mirrors aspects of cPTSD—e.g., perceived betrayal and victimization, fragmented sense of self, dissociation, somatization, desire to self-harm, and perceived inability to control extreme affects and impulses (Cattane, Rossi, Lanfredi, & Cattaneo, 2017; Ford & Courtois, 2014). BPD is often comorbid with PTSD. Both cPTSD and BPD require treatments that address multiple self-regulation domains (Bryant, 2010; Ford & Courtois, 2014; Chapter 16). Dissociative symptoms have been strongly linked to severity of interpersonal traumas in individuals with BPD and cPTSD (Ford & Courtois, 2014; Frewen, Kleindienst, Lanius, & Schmahl, 2014; Frewen, Brown, & Lanius, 2017). Both cPTSD and BPD present a unique neurobiological profile that is consistent with that found in adults with childhood trauma histories, with or without PTSD (altered HPA axis and endogenous opioid system for BPD, Cattane et al., 2017; reduced hippocampus, ACC, PFC for cPTSD; increased left hippocampus, amygdala, ACC, vmPFC for both except in adults with comorbid PTSD & BPD; see Ford, 2018).

Adolescent Pathological Narcissism

Adaptive narcissism is common in adolescence and is employed in engaging successfully in adolescent developmental challenges (Ensink et al., 2018). Non-pathological narcissism—characterized as a need to be the center of attention, feeling superior, vanity, and exploitativeness—has been considered relatively healthy in that it includes exuding authority in social situations and adaptive use of self-enhancement strategies (Lee-Rowland, Barry, Gillen, & Hansen, 2016). Trait narcissism can be seen as a continuum along which anyone can be located (Li et al., 2016). Trait narcissism can be triggered by manipulating a person's self-consciousness, and when followed by unexpected provocation may lead to aggression (mediated by anger; Li et al., 2016). Pathological narcissism, discussed below, has been shown to increase significantly among youth ages 14–18, decrease from 18–23, and decline then plateau. Ensink et al. (2018) found that both vulnerable and grandiose narcissism declined in girls and increased in boys ages 14–21. Maltreatment is a known risk factor for development of pathological narcissism (Lee-Rowland et al., 2016).

Precursors to Narcissism

Narcissism is often attributed to early life dyadic relationships and has been related to excessive parental admiration or to problematic parenting (Ensink et al., 2018). Individuals with NPD have shown problems in brain regions related to empathy (Levy et al., 2015). Fonagy and Target (2006) suggest that grandiose narcissism stems from parental failure to provide marked mirroring of the infant's emotions in dyadic interchanges. Such mirroring is required for the infant to learn mentalizing skills and to move away from the egocentric view that all share their reality. Narcissistic vulnerability also is seen as rooted in failure of mirroring, in which the parent is unavailable or does not assist the child to discover self in the parent's eyes/mind. Some evidence suggests that parents of narcissists have failed to provide a secure base while threatening separation and offering harsh discipline. Cater, Zeigler-Hill and Vonk (2011) found that the Entitlement/Exploitativeness feature of narcissism was associated with high parental discipline, high threats of separation, and low security (N = 330, undergraduates). Narcissistic Grandiosity was associated positively with peer affectional support and parental harsh discipline. Narcissistic Vulnerability was not uniquely associated with early life experiences, in the study.

Types of Narcissism Compared

Two main pathological forms of narcissism are grandiose and vulnerable narcissism. Grandiose narcissism—characterized by arrogance, self-focused agency, and self-aggrandizing behavior, hubris, dominance, devaluation of others, insensitivity to others' concerns and social constraints, and willingness to exploit for personal gain (see Ensink et al., 2018)—has been associated with psychological difficulties and personality disorders (Barry & Kauten, 2014). Vulnerable narcissism is characterized by low self-confidence, contingent self-worth, reactivity to threats from others, proneness to shame and envy, grandiose fantasies, and a lack of dominance (Besser & Priel, 2010; Ensink et al., 2018; Erkoreka & Navarro, 2017). Like grandiose narcissists, vulnerable narcissists share an underlying concern for fulfilling personal needs rather than needs of others. Both types need but devalue others (Barry & Kauten, 2014). There is a tendency to blame others for personal flaws or behavioral errors (Dimaggio, 2012). Depression or rage may follow if shortcomings are impossible to deny. Both have displayed a sense of entitlement. Some evidence suggests that for grandiose narcissism, aggression is directed at others, while for vulnerable narcissism, aggression is directed at the self (Barry & Kauten, 2014; Ensink et al., 2018). Both pathological and non-pathological forms of narcissism have been related to adolescent aggression, although some evidence suggests that the magnitude was large for pathological and small for non-pathological narcissism (Lee-Rowland et al., 2016). Higher levels of exploitativeness have been associated with reactive aggression and delinquency (Barry & Kauten, 2014). Aggression also has been high, particularly when there were callous-unemotional traits (CU; especially callousness). Although adolescent psychopathy-linked narcissism (narcissism + CU) presents as highly self-assured, it has been linked to internalizing (Lee-Rowland et al., 2016). Its link to aggression was mediated by CU traits.

Besser and Priel (2010) found that individuals with high grandiose narcissism were vulnerable to threatened failure in achievement-competition, while vulnerable narcissists were especially vulnerable to interpersonal threat of being humiliated and betrayed by a significant other (N = 448 adults). Expecting others to attain perfectionism has been found predominantly for narcissistic grandiosity, whereas thinking others expect perfectionism, predominantly related to narcissistic vulnerability (Stoeber, Sherry, & Nealis, 2015; Table 11.1). An examination of 25 years of research on perfectionism and narcissism showed that self-oriented perfectionism, other-oriented perfectionism, and perfectionistic self-promotion were all related to narcissistic grandiosity, whereas socially prescribed perfectionism, perfectionistic self-promotion, and non-disclosure of imperfections were linked to narcissistic vulnerability (meta-analysis; Smith et al., 2016b; Table 11.1). This suggests that grandiose narcissists strive for lofty goals, impose unrealistic demands on others, and promote an image of perfection, whereas vulnerable narcissists promote an image of infallibility while defensively concealing imperfections, and perceive others as demanding.

Some clinicians and researchers believe that narcissism includes both vulnerability and grandiosity (Li et al., 2016). Others consider the combination a separate type. Few studies have examined the combined type. For 16–18-year-olds with combined grandiose and vulnerable elements, pathological narcissism was linked to the greatest maladjustment (vs non-pathological adolescent narcissism; Glossary—adaptive narcissism). Youth with the combined type showed both reactive and proactive aggression, low self-esteem (assesses attitudes toward self), high contingent self-worth (self-perception tied to external feedback), internalizing, and social stress (Barry & Kauten, 2014).

Grandiose Narcissism

In children and adolescents, grandiose narcissism has been related to emotional and cognitive reactivity; physical, verbal, and relational aggression (e.g., cyber-bullying); proactive and reactive aggression; conduct problems; and low peer preference (Ensink et al., 2018). Grandiose narcissism may not be obvious in those who receive praise and affirmation. It manifests as rage when criticized or socially excluded. It also expresses in negative reactions when others have positive experiences. Researchers have found deficits in self-observation, reduced empathy, and lower gray matter in the insula (generates cortical representations of others' experiences; see Ensink et al., 2018). Grandiose narcissists are believed to divide people into those who have what they want and those who are not worthy of consideration. Those they idealize may invoke fear of being exploited.

Vulnerable Narcissism

For young and older adults, vulnerable narcissism has been linked to depression (e.g., dysthymic disorder; depressive personality disorder) and to depressive tendencies (e.g., self-criticism; Erkoreka & Navarro, 2017). Traits including a deep sense of dissatisfaction, of holding unattainable grandiose fantasies, of experiencing frequent shame, envy, or emptiness may explain the depressive symptoms in these individuals. For adolescents, vulnerable narcissism—especially the dimensions of hiding the self, contingent self-esteem, devaluation and entitlement rage—was linked to both internalizing and externalizing (Ensink et al., 2018). Adolescents with vulnerable narcissism have demonstrated reactive aggression and depression (Ensink et al., 2018).

Specific Trauma-Related and Other Reactions

Additional adversity experiences or problems are important to adolescents. Some gender differences have been found after traumas (e.g., see Trauma's Effects on Adolescent Development, this chapter). For example, some evidence suggests that maltreated girls are more likely to report trauma symptoms and maltreated boys are more likely to report risk and externalizing behaviors (Roberts et al., 2018). Not all issues can be discussed in this limited space. Discussions of important and well-studied issues—sibling aggression, psychopathy, self-injury, and suicidality—follow.

Sibling Aggression

Siblings, too, may be important objects of attachment (Charles & Charles, 2006). Like parents, they influence what a youth learns about relationships and self (Caffaro & Conn-Caffaro, 2013; predicted by less severe maternal aggression; N = 346, ages 7–18, Tompsett, Mahoney, & Lackey, 2016; Box 3.2). Youth exposed to sibling bullying have been at greater risk of depression, self-harm, and suicidal ideation than peers (see Bar-Zomer & Klomek, 2018). For Israeli students ages 10–17 (N = 279), although youth exposed to sibling bullying showed greater depression and suicidal ideation, positive father–adolescent (not mother–adolescent) attachment served as a protective factor.

When both sibling and peer physical and psychological aggression were assessed in a nationally representative U.S. sample, each uniquely predicted worsened mental health (N = 3599 through age 17; Tucker, Finkelhor, Turner, & Shattuck, 2013a). Both mild and severe forms of sibling aggression and either one or multiple types of sibling aggression were linked to poorer mental health outcomes. Mild forms of sibling assault (not other forms) were related to greater distress in younger children than in adolescents. While low frequency of sibling hostility—e.g., physical abuse, threats of violence, heated verbal conflicts—were of concern to outcomes, high levels of sibling hostility related to significantly higher risk of problems—e.g., CD symptoms, reactive aggression, lifetime acts of physical aggression, aggression subscale scores (20+% experienced recurrent hostility; King et al., 2017). This suggests that even low-frequency sibling aggression may have deleterious effects on affect control and behavior (temper management; retrospective reports of ages 5–16). Attachment-based interventions may be warranted for sibling bullying or abuse.

Aggressive vs Non-Aggressive Victims of Bullying

Bullying has involved bullies, victims, and bully-victims, who bully and are victimized (and sometimes bystanders; see Nader, 2008, 2012c). Some victimized adolescents manage peer victimization and rejection non-aggressively, through anxious withdrawal—e.g., by removing themselves from interactions with aggressors (see Guedes et al., 2018). Such behaviors, in turn, may label them as easy targets of bullying. Among bullied youth, both aggressive and non-aggressive youth victims were excluded by peers more than non-victims, although less so for aggressive victims (peer report; N = 222, Portuguese adolescents ages 12–17: Guedes et al., 2018). Aggressive victims may use hostile and punitive behaviors to attract attention or respect and/or induce fear in peers. Non-aggressive victims exhibited more anxiously withdrawn classroom behaviors than aggressive victims and non-victims. Victims were seen as less prosocial than others by their peers (especially non-aggressive victims). Victimized adolescents may lack the reciprocity and equality in peer relationships that promotes prosocial behavior. Only the aggressive victims perceived lower attachment security to both parents than non-victimized peers (Guedes et al., 2018). Hence, treatment may address issues such as school climate, attachment, social, and/or communication skills.

Trauma and Psychopathy

There may be more than one type of psychopathic-like youth. In a study of *callous-unemotional* traits (CU, ages 11–18), Kahn et al. (2013) found three youth groups: a low CU and two high CU groups—one with high and one with low anxiety. Both high groups had histories of abuse and exhibited impulsivity, externalizing behaviors, and aggression, but the low anxiety group under-reported theirs (contradicted by parent; behavioral activation, BAS, in high anxiety group; Table A5.2). In another study of CU traits and anxiety, youth with CU traits with or without high anxiety exhibited comparable levels of antisocial behavior, whereas those with high anxiety reported greater levels of severe childhood maltreatment and attachment insecurity as well as increased levels of psychological distress, ADHD symptomatology, and other emotional and behavioral risk—e.g., substance use, suicidal ideation, unsafe sex, affective dysregulation (irritability), and alexithymia (Cecil et al., 2018).

Clinically referred samples of psychopathic-like adolescents showed higher impulsive and irresponsible behavioral styles, more problem behaviors, more childhood victimizations (abuse by parent; adverse events), and perceived lower parent–adolescent attachment quality than non-referred psychopathic-like youth (Rucevic & Ajdukovic, 2016; N = 1346; Chapter 3). In both groups, the genders were similar in grandiose-manipulative and CU traits. Males were higher on an impulsive-irresponsible dimension. Both groups exhibited a lack of guilt, remorse, and empathy. Referred adolescents had more difficulties refraining from aggressive or disruptive behaviors (more violent and nonviolent offenses), despite punishment or non-reward experiences.

Body Image Problems

Body image includes a person's mental picture of her/his physical body and related perceptions and feelings about her/his personal appearance (Tirlea, Truby, & Haines, 2013)—e.g., negative image may include body dissatisfaction, negative body image, body dysphoria (feelings about one's body), sense of inadequacy or defectiveness (Sansone & Sansone, 2006). Youth in nonclinical samples with body image disturbances have shown poorer psychological adjustment (Scheffers et al., 2017). Poor body image has been related to poorer quality of life, to lower self-esteem/self-efficacy, to eating disorders, to dysmorphic disorder (e.g., preoccupation with imagined defect), depression, and other mental disorders (Mohr & Messina, 2015; Scheffers et al., 2017). For eating disorders, attention to body image issues has been important to improvement (Tirlea et al., 2013). Disordered adults have had poorer body image scores than healthy comparisons (N = 214, ages 18 and older, Scheffers et al., 2017). Among them, PTSD patients had the poorest overall body image scores and scored lowest on sexual fulfillment (largest effect sizes; event unknown). Individuals with eating disorders scored significantly lower than patients with mood, anxiety, and adjustment disorders on body image scores and had the lowest body-acceptance scores followed by PTSD patients.

Although they recognized the link between exposure to thin body ideals and girl/women's body dissatisfaction, body image disturbances, and eating pathologies, Mohr and Messina (2015) have suggested that eating disorders, obsessive-compulsive disorder, impulse control disorder, and addiction all may be related to a common brain network (right frontal lobe), hence belong to a common phenotype. In all instances of comorbid OCD, addiction, and disordered impulse control, individuals were preoccupied with a particular topic/substance/behavior, and were unable to detach from the preoccupation, acting upon it with inappropriate behavior. With a vulnerable right frontal lobe, different contexts led to different disorders—e.g., an adolescent girl bombarded with images of thin women may engage in social comparisons (including her body). With right frontal lobe dysfunction, she may struggle with suppression of negative thoughts that lead to clinical levels of body dissatisfaction and an eating disorder. In contrast, a person with similar vulnerability may be anxious about becoming ill, after illness has been a constant and worrisome topic in the family, and may develop OCD (Mohr & Messina, 2015).

Non-Suicidal Self-Injury (NSSI)

NSSI and higher levels of suicidal ideation can be difficult to treat, and adolescents can be treatment resistant (Ewing, Diamond, & Levy, 2015; Whitlock, Eells, Cummings, & Purington, 2009). NSSI has been linked to trauma (e.g., bullying, maltreatment), PTSD, previous NSSI, dissociation, exposure to peer NSSI, personality disorders (ASPD, BPD, HPD, NPD), hopelessness, depression, eating disorder, externalizing, internalizing, general psychopathology, and affect dysregulation (N = 107,518, Björkenstam, Kosidou, & Björkenstam, 2016; meta-analysis, Brown & Plener, 2017; Fox, Hunter, & Jones, 2015; Lev-Wiesel & Zohar, 2014; Box 12.1) as well as to *impulsivity* and to NE (N = 3453 Chinese females ages 12–18, assessed at three times, You, Deng, Lin, & Leung, 2016a). Of the Big 5 personality dimensions, NSSI has negatively related to extraversion and agreeableness, while NE was a risk factor for NSSI (N = 2874 Chinese high school students; You, Lin, Xu, & Hu, 2016b). Changes in impulsivity and NE were linked to changes in NSSI.

Although NSSI occurs in middle school youth (ages 11–12; Xavier, Pinto-Gouveia, & Cunha, 2016; Chapter 12), adolescence appears to be a vulnerable period for NSSI (Brown & Plener, 2017). NSSI is more prominent among girls than boys. Boys were more likely to hit a wall. For youth who engage in NSSI, neurobiological studies suggest abnormalities in the HPA axis, the endogenous opioid system, and in the neural processing of emotionally, socially, or physically adverse stimuli (Brown & Plener, 2017). Adolescents have reported a decrease in negative affect after self-injuring (for self-injurers and non-injurers, more for the former, Brown & Plener, 2017; Hamza & Willoughby, 2015).

Internet search terms related to NSSI have been sought 42 million times per year (Brown & Plener, 2017). Youth often seek reinforcement for NSSI behaviors, and urges to self-injure may be triggered online. Conversely, online activity may decrease social isolation, offer encouragement for recovery, and/or potentially help to reduce urges to self-injure. Although studies suggest a decrease in NSSI in late adolescence and young adulthood (Brown & Plener, 2017), adults with adversities between birth and age 14, with increasing indicators of family dysfunction, showed a graded positive association with later risk of NSSI (Björkenstam et al., 2016). Even those who discontinue NSSI in later adolescence are at continuing high risk of using dysfunctional emotion-regulation strategies (e.g., substance use; Brown & Plener, 2017). The association between maltreatment severity and NSSI frequency has been significantly mediated by emotion dysregulation. Emotion dysregulation and depressive symptoms have been associated with higher NSSI frequency (N = 108 adolescents; Peh et al., 2017). Girls who engage in NSSI behavior have had lower self-esteem, sense of control over life, commitment to society, and perception of society as just and orderly as well as higher depression levels, regardless of CSA history (Lev-Wiesel & Zohar, 2014). NSSI is a risk factor for suicide attempts (Brown & Plener, 2017). The combination of NSSI and depression has been linked to subsequent suicide attempts (e.g., Rossouw & Fonagy, 2012).

In addition to high levels of both depression and anxiety, youth who engage in NSSI have reported lower levels of support from friends, family, and significant others and lower levels of ethnic belonging (young adult college students; N = 282, Trepal, Wester, & Merchant, 2015). They have reported greater external shame, greater self-criticism in the form of self-hatred, resistance to self-compassion, more daily peer hassles (exclusion, conflicts), and more depressive symptoms (ages 12–18; Xavier et al., 2016). Current and past NSSI engagers have reported equal levels of anxiety and have reported less support from peers. Although attempting both more adaptive and maladaptive coping strategies than either past or no NSSI groups (Trepal et al., 2015; Table 14.1), some evidence suggests the use of more avoidant emotion-regulation strategies. Youth who engaged in brooding/rumination, used avoidance-focused emotion-regulation strategies, and dissociated in response to daily peer hassles had more depression, which in turn was linked to NSSI (Box 12.1; Xavier, Cunha, & Pinto-Gouveia, 2018; see Chapter 16 for treatment issues).

Compared to youth with NSSI, youth who do not self-injure have had better attachment qualities with parents, including better trust, communication, and closeness, and they have reported better self-compassion (N = 658 ages 11–16; 12-month period of NSSI; Jiang et al., 2017). Self-compassion can be protective during negative emotional states. Youth without NSSI have had higher levels of social support (family, peer), high ethnic belonging, and comparatively the lowest levels of depression and anxiety (Trepal et al., 2015). In a study of diverse university students in two locations (N = 1096), Wester and Trepal (2015) found that African and Asian Americans had lower levels of NSSI than other ethnic groups (Caucasian, Hispanic, and multi-ethnic). After controlling for anxiety and depression, lower NSSI was significantly related to a sense of belonging to one's racial/ethnic group. This also has important implications for international adoptions. Some evidence suggests higher rates of suicide (and other problems) for international adoptees (lower for sibling adoptions; Hjern, Lindblad, & Vinnerljung, 2002).

Suicidal Ideation

As noted, suicide is the second leading cause of death for youth ages 11–15 (Holland, Vivolo-Kantor, Logan, & Leemis, 2017; worldwide, WHO, 2014). For this age group, suicide is associated with risk factors such as mental health problems (Holland et al., 2017), stress or overwhelming stress (e.g., trauma, Brake et al., 2017; peer victimization and bullying are forms of trauma), peer victimization and bullying (e.g., Campbell-Sills, Kessler, Ursano, & Stein, 2017), biological factors, family history of suicidal behavior, PTSD and self-directed-disgust (e.g., toward one's enduring characteristics, linked to PTSD severity and suicide risk, Brake et al., 2017; see Box 13.5), and family problems—e.g., stress, conflict between parents or parent vs child; divorce, then move (N = 482, Holland et al., 2017). Adolescents who have completed suicide have had more than one risk factor (most frequently, relationship problems and parent–child conflict), shown a consistent progression toward suicidal behavior, and have felt lonely and like a burden to family. Subsequent experiences for these youth may have resulted in an acquired capacity to self-harm, which eventually lead to suicide—e.g., continued exposure to negative experiences such as conflict with parents, feeling unimportant, thwarted belongingness, feeling unconnected to peers; thoughts and/or plans about suicide, and/or self-injurious acts (Holland et al., 2017). Protective factors (against suicidal behaviors and against depression) include family cohesion—e.g., mutual involvement, sharing interests, supporting, warmth, emotional support, and parent availability and monitoring (Ewing et al., 2015). The efficacy of treatments used effectively for trauma or depression have had mixed results for treating suicidal ideation. Treatment engagement with adolescents has proven difficult, and medication has sometimes exacerbated suicidal thinking.

Loneliness and Lack of Connection versus Belonging

Loneliness reflects a discrepancy between actual and desired levels of quantity and quality of relationships (Maes, van den Noortgate, & Goossens, 2015), often includes sadness, and may include feelings of aloneness whether or not people are around. For youth, loneliness may include a perceived sense of thwarted belonging, of lack of depth of desired or needed connection to others, or lack of unconditional acceptance. It may include a sense of being alone in general or alone with some aspect of one's personal life or self. Loneliness may apply to any of several contexts—e.g., friends, parents, other family, teachers, specific groups, and/or community.

As has been discussed, loneliness has been related to a number of problems for youth (Chapters 2, 4, 14). For example, lonely youth have reported a reduced sense of well-being (see Maes et al., 2015). Loneliness and feeling disconnected from others has been strongly linked to suicidal risk and depression in youth and emerging adults (e.g., college students, Chang et al., 2017; see also Page et al., 2006). For Asian high school students, suicide attempters scored higher on a hopeless or pessimistic outlook toward the future and on loneliness than non-attempters (total N = 8450, from Taiwan, Thailand, Philippines; Page et al., 2006). When combined with internet addiction, loneliness has been related to sexual compulsion for youth ages 13–21 (Lawal & Idemudia, 2017).

Although theoretically, thwarted belongingness (a sense of isolation) combined with burdensomeness (feeling a burden to family/friends) are important to the emergence of suicidal desires, the importance of thwarted belongingness may vary for ethnicities. For undergraduates (N = 336, ages 18–23), even though Hispanic/Latinos reported lower suicidal desire and lower perceived burdensomeness compared to non-Hispanic Whites, they did not differ in levels of thwarted belongingness (Acosta, Hagan, & Joiner, 2017). Non-Hispanic Whites with higher levels of thwarted belongingness and perceived burdensomeness (not Hispanic/Latinos) reported higher levels of suicidal desire. Hispanic/Latinos have primarily adhered to a collectivistic orientation with strong connections to family and culture (generally serve as protective factors).

Youth who are lacking peer and/or family emotional and social support are at risk for loneliness (Page et al., 2006). Attachment security and positive outlook toward the future have been among protective factors for lonely youth (Resilience above; Chapter 11). Attachment insecurity and self-defeating humor have been among variables associated with increased loneliness (Chapters 11, 14). Trauma can increase loneliness. For example, increased exposures to being bullied, fighting, and injury have significantly related to increased odds of loneliness, insomnia, suicidal ideation, and suicide attempts for Pacific Island adolescent youth (4122 students total, from Kiribati, Solomon Islands, and Vanuatu; Sharma, Lee, & Nam, 2017). The highest odds of insomnia and suicide attempts were for students who were excluded from activities (vs non-bullied youth). Injury from physical attack was the most likely injury to relate to loneliness, insomnia, and suicidal ideation. Parental suicide has been related to a thwarted sense of belonging in bereaved youth (Roley-Roberts et al., in press).

Trauma's Effects on Adolescent Development

Adolescent traumas may engender positive or negative changes. For example, a posttraumatic sense of increased self-reliance or the determination to change things (see PTG, Chapter 4) may assist autonomy and/or create positive change. In 2018, after the Parkland, FL school shooting killed 17 youth, adolescent students engaged in impassioned and unrelenting efforts to effect change and prevent another shooting, with success in changing gun laws in more than one state. On the other hand, trauma may trigger genetic vulnerabilities, PTSD, or undermine the natural progression of predominantly adolescent qualities. For example, cognitive, self-reflective, behavioral, and/or emotional constriction may follow trauma (Chapters 11, 13; Bureau & Moss, 2010; Ensink et al., 2017) and may interfere with the progression of developmental skills, with functioning, and with treatment (Cloitre, Petkova, Wang, & Lu, 2012; Spinazzola et al., 2011). Constriction may interfere, e.g., with imagination and creativity; perspective-taking; emotion awareness, clarity, and acceptance; self-regulation; self-esteem; and with other essentials of inter-relating, productivity, and well-being. Increased risk-taking and novelty seeking are normal in adolescence (Chapter 14). Trauma may induce inhibition related to a heightened sense of vulnerability or result in dangerous risk-taking (Nader, 2008; Box 15.2).

Gender differences seem to be less evident with younger children, who rely on adults for protection and sometimes to define a situation as threatening or safe. Post-pubertal gender differences may be related to socialization, to brain and hormonal differences, and to other variables. For example, testosterone is a potent inhibitor of HPA axis responsiveness, whereas its inhibitory response is blunted in women (Young & Altemus, 2004). Estradiol and progesterone may enhance stress responsiveness and reduce resistance to feedback effects of glucocorticoids (may vary by basal cortisol levels, Chapter 1). This may explain why pre-pubertal depression is more common in boys, whereas by mid-puberty, rates for girls are twice as high. Girls are also more susceptible to anxiety

Box 15.2 Posttrauma Heightened Vulnerability or Increased Risk-Taking

a. Although she wasn't raped in her home, Ginger became very fearful and hypervigilant after the rape. She wouldn't leave the house unless she was with her mother or her older brother. She had insisted repeatedly that her father add a better lock to the entry doors. He told her she was being silly, like her mother. Ginger's father had often talked about how silly and incompetent his wife was. Ginger had believed him. After the rape, he started talking about Ginger that way. He often didn't bother to lock the doors at night. Ginger went around and checked every door and window before going to bed. It was still difficult to sleep. Ginger's mother finally found someone to install additional locks. She found a therapist for Ginger. It was the first time she stood up to her husband.

   Ginger had been a good student—AP classes, good grades. A home teacher was assigned to her, but Ginger's ability to pay attention was impaired by her perpetual arousal. She went to check both the front and back door locks each time she heard noises outside. From Ginger's therapist, her home teacher learned to go with her to make sure the locks were secure and soon anticipated the need when Ginger looked frightened in response to sounds. The home teacher might say, "Let's look out to see what it is on the way to check the locks." Then they checked the locks. Later she began to say, "Let's see if it's something to be worried about, before we check the locks," until Ginger became better at determining whether or not she should feel alarmed. Her therapy with a trauma specialist also helped.

b. After the war, Jamal repeatedly sped in the family car, increasing his speed even more when he approached the locations where enemy soldiers had set up check points and had made him and his family and friends stop for inspection. He said that it made him feel better to drive fast, especially to run straight through checkpoints.

c. Sandy returned home from a family gathering to find her younger sister, Rita, in the bathtub, bleeding from her head and nose. Rita began convulsing and drooled blood and mucous—she had shot herself in the head. Sandy did her best to stop the bleeding, called paramedics, and talked soothingly to her sister. At a party, Rita had said that she wanted to kill herself, and, two or three days before she shot herself, she had called Sandy at 2 a.m. needing to talk. Sandy was "too tired to really talk." Sandy felt guilty and repeatedly replayed thoughts of the call and how she might have prevented the suicide. She began taking risks—e.g., she would drive fast down mountains, made dangerous jumps over cliffs during hiking, "slashed her wrist" accidentally (Sandy's words) when she dropped the plastic wrap at work. During the work incident, while others were "hysterically rushing around," Sandy remained calm and took control of the situation, preventing a tragedy. She gave her coworkers instructions on how to stop the bleeding and instructed them to take her to the hospital for stitches. With the help of her therapist, Sandy recognized her competence in both situations—at work and with Rita. She had done her best to help. After Sandy attended a play about suicide, it exacerbated her intrusive re-experiencing—images of her sister bleeding, memories of the sticky blood on her sweating hands. She had flashback experiences of finding her sister and experienced a racing heart, quickened respiration, and feelings of anxiety and revulsion. It wasn't until after she had processed her traumatic memories that Sandy began to grieve. (Case described by a supervisee, for details see Nader, K [1994]. Countertransference in treating trauma and victimization in childhood. In J Wilson & J Lindy [eds] *Countertransference in the Treatment of Posttraumatic Stress Disorder* [pp. 179–205]. New York: Guilford.)

Note:
Case examples are disguised, may be combined cases, and have had details changed to protect individuals.

(Young & Altemus, 2004). Puberty amplifies social sensitivity, and processes that impact social sensitivity may be particularly vulnerable to stress/trauma (N = 2899, Marshall, 2016).

Trauma or Adversity and the Brain

Across many species, the adolescent brain is in transition—i.e., differs anatomically and neurochemically from the adult brain (Spear, 2000). Adolescence includes a significant period of developmental vulnerability—e.g., increase in morbidity and susceptibility to specific disorders (Andersen, 2003; Andersen et al., 2008; Dahl, 2004; Marshall, 2016, N = 2899; Spear, 2000; Romeo & McEwen, 2006; with subsequent onset of anxiety and/or depressive disorders in adulthood, Turner & Lloyd, 2004; Romeo & McEwen, 2006). Brain regions that continue to mature during adolescence—e.g., PFC and amygdala—are very sensitive to corticosterone (Gogtay et al., 2004; Romeo, 2003; Romeo & McEwen, 2006). Although maltreatment is associated with increased right amygdala volume (processes aversive emotions; Chapter 11), shame-proneness has been linked to reduced right amygdala (mixed results, Table A4.2; to reduced posterior cingulate cortex, Whittle et al., 2016; see Guilt and Shame, to follow). Current evidence suggests that a neural network that includes the PFC, hippocampus, and amygdala underlies learning, expression, and regulation processes that modulate emotional responses to threat (predictable threat; Goodman, Harnett, & Knight, 2018). Researchers suggest that dysfunction of this network may result in maladaptive anticipatory processes and consequently in the disruption of emotion-regulation in the face of threat (see Goodman et al., 2018; see Emotion Dysregulation, the Brain, and Trauma).

Chronic or overwhelming stress affects the developing nervous system with lifelong mental and physical health consequences (Shonkoff et al., 2012). For example, even after controlling for SES, adolescents exposed to violence had reduced gray volume in areas related to cognitive control, language production, and response-inhibition—left inferior frontal gyrus and anterior cingulate cortex (ACC; not in hippocampal or amygdala volumes; Table A4.2; Butler et al., 2018). Structural deficits in the ACC have also been found in youth with aggressive or antisocial behavior.

Prefrontal Cortex (PFC)

The PFC and related brain regions (e.g., ACC) do not fully mature until late adolescence (Decety & Meyer, 2008; Shaver et al., 2018). During periods of rapid growth of neuronal connections followed by selective elimination (*pruning*), children have shown particular sensitivity (e.g., ages 0–3; adolescence—PFC and its connections to other brain regions; Andersen et al., 2008; Blakemore & Choudhury, 2006; Nader, 2008; Schore, 2003). Since *pruning* occurs in a "use it or lose it" fashion (Glossary; Shors et al., 2012), experiences that withdraw or command attention (e.g., substance use, trauma) may affect brain development. Adolescent stress has exerted greater effects on the PFC than on the hippocampus (Teicher & Samson, 2016)—e.g., age-specific alterations occur in the balance between stressor-sensitive brain regions (dopamine in PFC and in ACC and amygdala), which influence motivationally relevant information (e.g., social, novel, drug-related). Pubertal youth (ages 10–17) with PTSS have had significantly decreased total brain tissue and cerebral gray volumes (e.g., left ventral and left inferior prefrontal gray; Carrion et al., 2010b; reduced volume and/or thickness of ventromedial PFC [vmPFC]; accelerated pruning; De Brito et al., 2013; see Hanson et al., 2010; Kelly et al., 2013; McLaughlin, Sheridan, & Lambert, 2014a). The intricate reciprocal balance between development in one brain region (e.g., PFC) may lead to alterations in another neural region (e.g., both hippocampus and amygdala—related to fear extinction, Fanselow, 2000; Pattwell, Lee, & Casey, 2013). In adolescence, fear extinction is impaired, and long-term fear maintenance is exacerbated by stress (Baker, Bisby, & Richardson, 2016; Pattwell et al., 2013).

The PFC is a key brain region involved in executive functions (EFs, e.g., abstract information processing), the regulation of emotional behaviors, and fear extinction (Romeo & McEwen, 2006; Sotres-Bayon, Cain, & LeDoux, 2006). Stress chemicals impair the PFC and EFs (De Bellis, Woolley, & Hooper, 2013)—e.g., high levels of stress-related catecholamine release may rapidly impair PFC cognitive functions, while strengthening emotional and habitual responses (of amygdala and basal ganglia; Arnsten, Raskind, Taylor, & Connor, 2015; Herringa et al., 2013; Table A4.2; Glossary). Children and early adolescents, like adults with injury to the vmPFC (important to decision-making, but not to WM), show preference for immediate gains and have more difficulty considering future consequences (Crone & van der Molen, 2004).

During adolescence, neural systems important for social media use—e.g., social reward processing, emotion-based processing, regulation, and mentalizing about other(s)—continue to be underdeveloped and undergoing change (Crone & Konijn, 2018). Such changes and the interrelationship of neural systems may contribute to sensitivity to online rejection or acceptance, to the importance of peer influence, and to emotion-loaded interactions in media environments. Brain cells using the neurochemical dopamine increase the density of connections with the PFC, and dopamine inputs in PFC grow dramatically during adolescence (may increase mature judgment and impulse control; e.g., Luyten & Fonagy, in press; Glossary, Table A4.1). Acute and chronic stress negatively affect reward processes (e.g., appetitive behaviors; reduced dopamine release, Glossary), and stress-induced dopaminergic output reduction has been linked to coping failures and maintenance of depression-like behaviors (e.g., helplessness; Auerbach, Admon, & Pizzagalli, 2014; McCrory, Gerin, & Viding, 2017). Blunted reward processing has been related to stress for children and adolescents—e.g., with histories of institutional care or maltreatment—and to risk of depression/anhedonia (McCrory et al., 2017). McCrory et al. suggest that blunting of the anticipatory response may hamper exploratory behavior in novel environments, a task important to adolescent development.

Executive Functions (EFs) After Traumas

High-level stress can harm EFs (see also Trauma and the Brain). For example, poor sleep (e.g., trauma-related) has been linked to reduced cognitive functioning (e.g., Deliens et al., 2018). Evidence suggests increased concerns about safety interfere with initiation and maintenance of sleep, which in turn may affect cognitive, emotional, and behavioral functioning (e.g., Bagley, Tu, Buckhalt, & El-Sheikh, 2016; Chapter 14). Exposure to community violence has predicted less efficient sleep, more long-wake episodes, more sleep/wake problems, and increased sleepiness, especially for girls, even after controlling for demographic variables and general anxiety (N = 252 adolescents; actigraphs worn on non-dominant wrist and self-report; Bagley et al., 2016). Boys had lower sleep quality, in general.

Trauma exposure may disrupt memory, attention, and self-control. Intrusive memories are believed to reduce WM capacity. Compared to maltreated adolescents without PTSD, those with PTSD have displayed lower EFs (e.g., overall and problem-solving/planning skills) and lower expressive language as well as increased anxiety and depressive symptoms (e.g., anhedonia and social anxiety; N = 53, Kavanaugh & Holler, 2014). Although parent education and SES have positively related to adolescents' EF scores, adolescent perception of parental neglect has negatively associated with EF scores—e.g., cognitive flexibility, verbal inhibition, problem-solving ability—with outcomes driven by multiple parent–youth relationship dimensions—protection, rejection, punishment, indifferent behavior, loving, neglecting (most robustly, neglect, Fatima et al., 2015). A variety of posttrauma disorders have been related to EF deficits—e.g., PTS, anxiety, depression, ADHD, disruptive behavior disorders (Han et al., 2016). Controlling for IQ, ADHD, and disruptive disorders, Han et al. (2016) found internalizing (depression, anxiety) was related to global and nonspecific EF difficulties but not robustly to cognitive flexibility. Strategies to reduce real and perceived stress have been recommended to improve context specific EF dysfunction in depressed adolescents (Luciana, 2016).

Autobiographical Memory (AM)

As noted in Chapter 12, across 21 articles, researchers have consistently confirmed the link between trauma and over-general memory (OGM; ages 7–18; Hitchcock et al., 2016)—a lack of specific AM. For example, adolescents with CSA histories have demonstrated reduced memory specificity relative to controls (more OGM, Ogle et al., 2013; N = 49 ages 14–17, not for N = 36 ages 18–37). Study adults with CSA histories produced more specific memories than the adolescents. Given the recency of CSA for adolescents, Ogle et al. suggest that avoidance may be a strategy to prevent overwhelming negative emotions still linked to the memories. Higher levels of trauma, number and severity, have been associated with reduced AM (de Decker, Hermans, Raes, & Eelen, 2003). Both trauma and depression have been related to OGM (Glossary; Eisma et al., 2015; Hitchcock, Nixon, & Weber, 2016). Adults with childhood traumas, have had greater difficulty retrieving specific memories in adulthood, even for non-trauma-related events (depressed women—CSA history, Burnside et al., 2004; Drummond et al., 2006). Children experiencing a severe trauma in middle childhood have shown reduced memory specificity in adolescence (N = 5792 age 13; Crane et al., 2014). Bosnian adolescents traumatized by war (at ages 3–7) demonstrated OGM in response to all types of cue words (vs non-traumatized; Brennen et al., 2010; Box 2.2b). OGM has also been found for complicated grief (CG). Compared to other mourners, adults with higher depressive and CG symptoms and more grief rumination showed significantly reduced AM specificity of non-loss-related memories but not for specificity of loss-related memories (Eisma et al., 2015).

Trauma and Self-Regulation

Emotion-regulation has been discussed in this chapter in relationship to poly-victimization, attachment, symptom complexity, reward processing, PTSD, BPD and other problems. To follow are brief additional discussions of emotion dysregulation and of risk-taking.

Emotion Dysregulation, the Brain, and Trauma

Difficulties in interpreting and regulating emotions is common to many disorders, including PTSD (McCrory et al., 2017). Traumas are associated with changes in neural regions associated with emotion-regulation (amygdala, McCrory et al., 2017; vACC, lPFC, and connectivity, McLaughlin et al., 2015c). The amygdala has a central role in emotion processing (Lyons-Ruth et al., 2016; Pechtel et al., 2014). It may be affected by trauma—e.g., increased right amygdala volume has been associated with negative emotions (Bunge & Crone, 2009; Pechtel et al., 2014; Table A4.2). Amygdala dysfunction is linked to emotion dysregulation. For example, childhood maltreatment has been related, e.g., to anxiety, conduct, depressive, and substance use disorders. It appears to heighten the salience of emotional stimuli and to require greater effort to modulate emotions—i.e., stimuli activate brain areas related to effortful control, unlike controls (e.g., adults with early emotional abuse, Khawli et al., 2018; neglect, verbal abuse, adolescents, McLaughlin et al., 2015c). Affect labeling, specifically, has diminished reactions to negative emotional images in the amygdala and other limbic regions, and has increased activity in regions related to symbolic processing of emotional information and top-down inhibitory processes (right ventrolateral prefrontal cortex, rvlPFC; Lieberman et al., 2007). During affect labeling rvlPFC and amygdala activity inversely correlated, mediated by activity in medial prefrontal cortex (mPFC; Lieberman et al., 2007). The mPFC has been linked to complex cognitive (e.g., decision-making, memory-integration) and emotional states (Teves, Videen, Cryer, & Powers, 2004; Thielen et al., 2018). Hence, affect labeling may diminish emotional reactivity.

Risk-Taking

Increased reckless behavior is included among DSM-5 PTSD symptoms (APA, 2013). Trauma-exposed individuals, with and without PTSD, have engaged in reckless or self-destructive behavior—e.g., unsafe sexual practices, drug and alcohol use, unsafe driving (e.g., Blevins et al., 2016; Box 15.2). Total number of traumas has been a greater predictor of risk behaviors than type of trauma (e.g., self-harm and suicide attempts, Harr et al., 2013). Some evidence suggests variation by trauma type. Oshri et al. (2015) found a direct path from verbal abuse to alcohol use, from emotional abuse to impulsivity and difficulties engaging in goal-directed behaviors when experiencing negative emotions, and from CSA to compromised impulse control (N = 361; ages 19–32). Posttrauma reckless behaviors may also exacerbate PTSD symptoms and increase risk of re-traumatization (Blevins et al., 2016). After mass trauma (Virginia Tech shootings; N = 1145), Blevins et al. found that low and high PTS symptom levels predicted recklessness, high PTSS predicted significantly higher recklessness, and negative changes in worldview mediated the relationship between PTSS and recklessness for youth with high PTS (only partially mediated in low PTSS).

Trauma and Self- and Other-Awareness

Trauma, depressive reactions, poor sleep, or insecure/disorganized attachments may interfere with self- and other-related information processing (Nader, 2008). For example, youth who experience violence or exclusion may attribute malicious intent to others more often than peers, even in ambiguous situations (Crick & Dodge, 1996). For example, college youth with less than 6 hours of sleep for three days have shown poorer perspective-taking and impaired executive functions that relate to perspective-taking (Deliens et al., 2018). Overall perspective-taking ability in traumatized adolescents has been comparable to that of elementary school-aged children (Burack et al., 2006)—e.g., maltreated adolescents (vs non-traumatized) have shown more age-inappropriate egocentric thinking, more impulsive, unilateral perspective-taking (unable to consider both views simultaneously), and delays in differentiating and coordinating conflicting needs and points of view. Roazzi et al. (2016) suggest that maltreatment-related external locus of control may interfere with autonomy and competence (ages 5–14). As noted (Chapter 11), maltreated youth with fewer symptoms have exhibited better skills at negotiating novel relationships than those with more symptoms. Lower-level perspective-taking skills in maltreated youth that persist across time into adolescence serve as a disadvantage in negotiating age-appropriate social-cognitive developmental tasks and suggest risk for social maladjustment and persistent difficulties in maintaining satisfying interpersonal relationships (Burack et al., 2006).

Mentalizing and Empathy

Trauma also has been associated with reduced mentalizing skills, which puts individuals at risk of symptoms of a number of disorders (see BPD, earlier; Fonagy & Bateman, 2016; Table 1.2). Mentalizing ability has mediated the relationship between abuse and externalizing problems in adolescents (Ensink et al., 2016a). Repeated or intense exposure to aversive interpersonal contexts has been linked to dissociative-proneness (Chiu, Paesen, Dziobek, & Tollenaar, 2016). High dissociation-proneness has significantly associated with lower accuracy of cognitive empathy (not emotional empathy), partly explained by difficulties in emotional awareness and perceived poor parenting styles (not explained by negative affect; average age 19, Chiu et al., 2016). For adolescents with and without BPD (controls), emotion dysregulation was associated with increased affective empathy—i.e., the feeling or conviction of knowing what others feel (Kalpakci, Vanwoerden, Elhai, & Sharp, 2016). However, for the BPD group only (not controls), hyper-mentalizing was associated with reduced cognitive empathy.

Studies have shown that emotional face processing is distinct in maltreated children compared to non-abused (van Hoof et al., 2017). Some studies have found attention biases away from threat with slower reaction times in maltreated groups (hypo-activation of relevant brain circuitry); other studies have shown attention biases toward threat, with faster reaction times for maltreated groups (hyper-activation). In both cases, there was hyper-activation of the amygdala (emotion memory and fear) and deactivation of brain regions associated with the processing and integration of emotions (rACC, insula, and superior temporal gyrus; Table A4.2; see van Hoof et al., 2017; Peng et al., 2017).

Guilt and Shame

Shame and guilt can be either state (experience-related) or trait (-proneness) emotions. As described in other chapters, parenting and stressful experiences have each related to the presence of shame, guilt, or proneness to either of the self-conscious emotions. Both guilt and shame have been related to increased psychopathology including to increased posttrauma reactions (see Nader, 2008). Following an earthquake (N = 869 Italians, ages 12–37), individuals with PTSD had higher rates of guilt, shame, or self-blame than those without PTSD, and guilt, shame, or self-blame were related to greater PTSD severity (Carmassi et al., 2017). In youth, Muris et al. (2016b) found that lack of guilt was predominantly associated with externalizing disorders—e.g., oppositional defiant and conduct problems—while guilt and shame were primarily linked with internalizing—e.g., affective and anxiety problems (N = 1000, ages 4–18). Dysregulation of self-conscious emotions has been more common in clinical populations. Some results are discussed in other sections of this chapter.

Guilt. Guilt and shame (e.g., peri-traumatic, posttraumatic) have been linked to a number of trauma types, and each has correlated with PTSD symptom severity (Carmassi et al., 2017; N = 29 male refugees, ages 11–20, Stotz, Elbert, Muller, & Schauer, 2015). Kletter et al. (2009) found guilt over acts of omission or commission (especially commission) each were highly associated with PTSD severity as were changes in attachment and derealization (N = 87, ages 5–16, abused). Guilt has been linked to increased Acute Stress Disorder severity (N = 101, 7–16-year-olds, Haag, Zehnder, & Landolt, 2015)—severity was also predicted by female gender, outpatient medical treatment, and maternal PTSS—and to behavior problems as well (teacher-reported, Maxwell, Zepeda, & Rzotkiewicz, 2018). Some evidence suggests that adolescent girls are more likely than boys to report guilt after traumas (Kar & Bastia, 2006; Fletcher, 2014; Stuewig & McCloskey, 2005).

Shame. As discussed, shame has been associated with a wide range of psychological problems, including PTSD, externalizing, anxiety disorders, depression, eating disorders, personality disorders, and alcohol and drug abuse (e.g., Chapter 4). For older adolescents (N = 347), PTSD is related to suicide risk via increased self-disgust (overlaps with shame, self-criticism, contempt and may be a more extreme form; controlling for depression; Brake et al., 2017). In a study of anxiety disorder symptoms, using more than one measure of guilt and shame, shame uniquely and positively associated with a wide range of anxiety disorder symptoms, and it correlated with personality traits—i.e., positively with neuroticism and negatively with extraversion (N = 118, 12–15-year-olds; Muris, Meesters, & van Asseldonk, 2018). The link of shame to anxiety remained after controlling for personality.

Proneness. Parenting, emotion regulation, and childhood trauma each have been associated with shame-proneness. Childhood trauma and emotion-regulation have been linked to guilt-proneness. Although trauma has also predicted them, differences in emotion-regulation (ER) have explained shame- and guilt-proneness, independent of sex, age, and history of childhood trauma (Szentágotai-Tătar & Miu, 2016). Shame-proneness was positively linked to depression and anxiety symptoms, while guilt-proneness was negatively associated with depressive symptoms (Szentágotai-Tătar & Miu, 2016; Stuewig & McCloskey, 2005). Harsh parenting in childhood has been related to shame-proneness in adolescence, mediated by parental rejection of adolescents (Stuewig & McCloskey, 2005). The rejected adolescents were more shame- and less guilt-prone than other youth and were likely to show higher depression two years later. Guilt-proneness was linked to less delinquent behavior.

Self-Concept

Greater self-worth has been protective after traumas (see Hong, Lim, Adams, & Lilly, 2012; Nader, 2008). High self-esteem may buffer some of the effects of negative life events (Haine et al., 2003; see Nader, 2008). On the other hand, trauma may undermine self-esteem with ongoing repercussions (Chapters 2, 14). Low self-esteem has been related to depression and to anxiety as well. Across 77 studies (Sowislo & Orth, 2013), low self-esteem had a significantly greater effect on depression than depression had on self-esteem. Nevertheless, for depressed adults (ages 20–65), improvements in both implicit and explicit self-esteem have followed successful inpatient treatment for depression (psychodynamic group and individual + movement + role-play therapy; Wegener et al., 2015). Across 18 studies of anxiety (Zeigler-Hill, 2011), self-esteem predicted anxiety, and anxiety predicted self-esteem.

For adults with childhood ACEs, the more ACEs experienced, the lower adult self-confidence and self-certainty tended to be (Wong, Dirghangi, & Hart, 2018). By type of ACE, emotional and sexual abuse, emotional neglect, domestic violence, and mental illness in the family were most strongly associated with self-concept clarity (an important adolescent task). Self-concept clarity mediated the link between ACEs and each tested mental health outcome: suicidal behavior, depression, loneliness, perceived stress, and life distress. After controlling for self-esteem as a mediator (similar and stronger indirect effects on outcomes), the indirect effects of self-concept clarity remained significant except on suicidal behavior.

Trauma and Social Skills

A number of factors influence social skills—e.g., insecure attachments, trauma. In contrast to insecure adolescents, securely attached youth have consistently had higher-quality friendships and lower stress in peer relationships (Allen & Tan, 2018). Such social competence may be related to better comfort in handling the emotional reactions of challenging situations. Securely attached youth have been more likely to seek peer support. Support has proven a robust protective factor after trauma. For 142 inpatient adolescents, there was not a direct association between attachment insecurity and PTSD (Venta et al., 2017; contrary to some findings). Instead, attachment insecurity was related to impaired social cognitions, which were related to PTSD.

Traumas have been associated with impairments in adolescent social skills (Coker et al., 2014; Ometto et al., 2016; across age groups and studies, Romano, Babchishin, Marquis, & Frechette, 2015)—e.g., with faulty information processing, low empathy, low social confidence, poor social problem-solving, distress or hypersensitivity in groups of people, or moral disengagement. Interpersonal childhood trauma (not adulthood interpersonal trauma) has significantly predicted dissatisfaction with adulthood social functioning. Compared to controls, adult women with assault-related PTSD have had slower learning rates during a trust game and smaller relationships between prediction errors and later behavior (Cisler et al., 2015a). This may reflect reduced flexibility in updating social expectations and lower use of social experiences to guide social decision-making, respectively. Some evidence suggests that as levels of trauma exposure increase, deficits in social problem-solving skills also increase (45 African American high school students; Coker et al., 2014). For inner-city African American youth exposed to multiple stressors, as social problem-solving decreased, moral disengagement increased (Glossary; disengaging normal self-censuring and judgment). Moral disengagement may become solidified with increasing exposures and when youth associate with other morally disengaged peers.

Specific traits and symptoms have been related to social skill difficulties (e.g., *behavioral inhibition*, Table A5.1, see Chapter 14). Adolescents with childhood traumas have presented with more psychopathic traits, independent of IQ or psychiatric disorders (N = 107 Brazilian adolescents; Ometto et al., 2016). In this small study, Ometto et al. found specific social skills deficits (empathy, self-control, and social confidence) were associated with psychopathic features. For individuals with childhood trauma and a first episode of psychosis (between ages 15 and 65), any type of childhood trauma was associated with poorer pre-morbid functioning, including poorer social functioning from childhood to adolescence to adulthood (Stain et al., 2014). By late adolescence, there was also evidence of poor academic functioning.

Biased Information Processing

Biased information processing has interfered with inter-relating (Nader, 2008). Posttraumatic hyperarousal may contribute to deficits in social-cognitive functioning, e.g., when there is misinterpretation of environmental cues, such as a biased perception of the world as hostile and dangerous (Coker et al., 2014; Dodge et al., 1997; Nader, 2008—attributional bias). In contrast to Martinelli et al. (2018; across 27 studies hostile attribution bias was more consistently related to reactive aggression), Bondü (2018) found that hostile attribution bias predicted physical and proactive aggression, whereas injustice sensitivity (Glossary) predicted physical, relational, verbal, reactive, and proactive aggression (N = 279 German adolescents). Victim injustice sensitivity and hostile attribution bias each added independently, directly to the prediction of aggression. Victimization has been related to impaired social cognition (Guy, Lee, & Wolke, 2017). For British students ages 11–16 (N = 754), Guy et al. found no link between bullies and hostile attributional biases. However, victims were biased toward endorsing characterological self-blame attributions, whereas bully-victims showed a greater hostile attribution bias. A link has been found between aggression—e.g., both impulsive and premeditated aggression (Helfritz-Sinville & Stanford, 2014, Chapter 2)—and hostile attribution bias.

Other trauma-related or general biases are relevant to inter-relating—e.g., a tendency to perceive rejection (see BPD, above; rejection sensitivity, Chapter 14). When another person's interpersonal behavior has an uncertain intent (is ambiguous), youth with prior experiences of verbal rejection (e.g., peer teasing and negativity) may infer rejection and react negatively—e.g., avoid, complain (N = 201, ages 18–46; Jones, Barnett, Wadian, & Sonnentag, 2016). Rejection experiences, hostile attribution bias, and rejection sensitivity related to negative emotional reactions have correlated with each other. When individual differences were accounted for, rejection experiences uniquely predicted a significant proportion of variance associated with negative emotional response.

Conclusions

Adolescents are vulnerable to a variety of disorders that are influenced by, e.g., life events, attachments, support levels, genetics, brain functions, reactivity levels, and personality traits. Adolescent TSRD vary from other age groups because of brain and cognitive maturity levels that are often higher and more complex than those of younger children, yet still different from adults' brain and cognitive functioning. As is true for all age levels, higher levels of exposure to stressors, traumas, and/or trauma types have been linked to greater psychopathology. The relationship between coping and outcomes is not straightforward. Although avoidant coping has been related to negative consequences, it has also been related to positive consequences. Coping flexibility that permits adjusting to circumstances is more important than using a specific type of coping.

Trauma or adversity may disrupt adolescent developmental domains—e.g., related to separation, individuation, identity, self-perception, interdependence, and relational issues as well as struggles to find purpose and meaning in life. Trauma may disrupt an adolescent's emerging identity, self-perception, and place among peers (Boxes 3.1, 3.2). Loneliness, which may result, has predicted many problems including suicidality. Because of increases in self-consciousness, posttrauma alterations in personality and functioning or any attached stigma may be particularly poignant in adolescence. Increases in risk-taking may become dangerous following traumas. Outcomes are often associated with multiple contributing factors. For example, although relational aggression has been linked to hostile attribution biases, which may follow victimization, relational aggression has also been associated with personality (callous-unemotional traits, negative emotionality), self-regulation processes (e.g., moral disengagement), BAS, and poor friendship quality (e.g., Kokkinos, Voulgaridou, & Markos, 2016). For all age groups, including adolescents, attachment security and support levels influence outcomes and recovery. Attachment influences life quality and the likelihood of negative outcomes across life. Adolescents, too, need support, cognizance of regressions, and respect for developing autonomy. A sense of belonging (e.g., ethnic, among peers, in family) is essential for youth (and all social beings) and, when absent, has been related to suicidal ideation and attempts.

16

Interventions for Youth Ages 13–17 or Older

As noted in Chapter 14, the age range of adolescence is considered to span somewhere between ages 10 and 24, depending on one's view of development. For treatment, pinpointing the age range of adolescence becomes more complicated when considering a youth's functioning age—i.e., youth who were traumatized in earlier, formative ages may be functioning below age level (or at combined levels, Box 3.5), while expecting to be treated like emerging adults. Even for chronological-age-functioning adolescents, adult treatment methods may require some alterations for success. Treatments proven successful with adults are not always associated with the same outcomes for adolescents—e.g., treatment for nightmares reduced other PTSD symptoms for adults, but not for adolescents (Krakow et al., 2001). Methods appropriate for adolescents are described in this chapter and in Chapter 13.

Progress in treatment may be influenced by factors such as the level and nature of traumatization, personality, genetics, available support, and goodness-of-fit between clinician, method, and youth (Chapter 17). In general, traumatized youth benefit from good support systems, increased coping and self-regulation skills, and a chance to narrate or otherwise process their experiences, in a timely fashion, with a benign, trusted other(s) (e.g., Fosha, 2006; Nader, 2008; Trivedi, Tripathi, Dhanasekaran, & Moussaoui, 2014). For all age groups, during treatment, symptoms (e.g., distress, internalizing, externalizing) may temporarily increase before reducing (e.g., Hirai, Skidmore, Clum, & Dolma, 2012; Salloum & Overstreet, 2012). Additionally, adolescent developmental changes may result in reactivation of earlier trauma symptoms, activation of new symptoms, and/or the need to reprocess traumas with knowledge gained and newly developed understanding.

It is important to distinguish normal adolescent traits from maladaptive ones, and to distinguish between subtypes of a disorder (e.g., adaptive, grandiose, or vulnerable narcissism; combined types—internalizing + externalizing; Chapter 15). For example, adaptive perfectionism has been related to academic achievement, whereas maladaptive perfectionism has been related to problems and disorders (Glossary, Table 11.1)—e.g., sensitivity to mistakes; need for admiration, organization, and order. Socially prescribed perfectionism has been related to anxiety (ages 13–15, Čerkez & Efendić-Spahić, 2016) and to suicidality even after controlling for depression, hopelessness, and prior attempts (Hewitt, Caelian, Chen, & Flett, 2014).

The Influence of Personality on Treatment and Other Outcomes

Youth with certain personality traits or types do not exhibit them all of the time, nor do traits account for all of the variance in outcomes (Rothbart & Bates, 2008; Shiner & Caspi, 2008).

Box 16.1 Culture, History, and Personality Matter

Personality: A mother's spiritual beliefs included the idea that each person essentially creates her/his own universe—i.e., as we think, so our world reflects that thinking; we attract things that happen to us based on our thinking. She was excited to tell her children, when they were adolescents, about this idea. One of her children felt a greater sense of control over life in response to her statements. The other began to cry. When asked why, the youth said, "You just told me that everything is all my fault."

Culture: "Cen Spirit Possession" is a common phenomenon in war-exposed Northern Ugandan youth (e.g., child soldiers, abducted children and adults), with extreme levels or multiple types of trauma. A youth may experience an altered state of consciousness akin to dissociative states/disorders, in which they feel their personal identity is replaced by a spirit such as a ghost of a dead person whom they killed (Neuner et al., 2012). Spirit possessions have been related to war trauma and dysfunction. Possessions predicted difficulties in daily functioning, suicidal ideation, and a high risk of suicide (see Neuner et al., 2012 for more information).

Note:
All case examples are disguised, may be combined cases, and have had details changed to protect individuals.

Situations and individuals affect each other's behaviors. Even when adolescents share characteristics and environments, each is unique (Box 16.1). Personality traits may influence outcomes and influence behaviors in treatment (Chapter 17). Additionally, traumas may alter personality. Treatment may need to address both parent's and youth's responses to changes in a youth. As a consequence of neurobiological and personality changes, a youth may be grieving the loss of aspects of self as well as loss of any persons killed or belongings lost during a traumatic event.

Personality Systems

As discussed in earlier chapters (e.g., 4, 5, 11, 14), several systems of personality and/or temperamental traits have been studied (e.g., Glossary—5-factor model; Jungian-based, Table 17.1; Chess & Thomas types [Chapter 17]; see Nader, 2008; Tables A5.1–A5.2)—e.g., neurologically based traits (Chapters 4, 7). Two or more problematic traits may increase risk of psychopathology. For example, negative emotionality (NE) and low impulse control have predicted externalizing behavior problems (Eisenberg et al., 1996, 2005; e.g., violence, Miller, Vachon, & Aalsma, 2012). NE and fearfulness have predicted internalizing (Gilliom & Shaw, 2004; Rothbart & Bates, 2008). Evidence suggests that maladaptive traits are similar for children, adolescents, and adults and include disagreeableness, emotional instability, introversion, compulsivity, and oddity (oversensitivity to feelings, extreme fantasy, daydreaming, and odd thoughts and behavior) (N = 1456, ages 7–19; Verbeke, De Caluwé, & De Clercq, 2017). Such traits represent the extreme (maladaptive) ends of the childhood 5-factor model domains (Big 5)—agreeableness, neuroticism, extraversion, and conscientiousness, respectively, plus an oddity domain that cross-loaded on the emotional stability domain. This is in line with findings that have shown a connection between neuroticism and cognitive-perceptual distortions in adults and youth, especially in samples with severe psychopathology (see Verbeke et al., 2017). Using multiple informants was important. A method to assist children with particular temperamental types (preferably early in childhood) can be found in Chapter 10—INSIGHTS.

Like other areas of research, some theory-based findings on identified traits do not hold over time, which may be related to failure to take into account additional influencing factors. For example, Kagan and colleagues examined high and low reactive children over time (Glossary). Contrary to expectations, only a small portion of high-reactive infants became consistently fearful, anxious children (Kagan, 2009; Kagan & Snidman, 1999). This suggests an important role for environmental or other factors. As adolescents, five of 26 girls, who were high-reactive at four months, suffered from depression rather than anxiety (ages 11–15, Kagan, Snidman, Kahn, & Towsley, 2007 in Kagan, 2009). A higher-reactive amygdala combined with high-reactive status (but not either status alone) corresponded to greatest risk for depression (Table A4.2).

Traits In-Session and at School

Whether influenced by genetics, by attachment, or by other variables, youth traits, including characteristic ways of relating to others and the world, are likely to influence in-session behaviors as well as behaviors in school or at home. Although youth will not always stay true to personality type, and type preferences may not predict behaviors, type may help to explain how a youth processes information, prefers to learn and communicate, interacts or clashes with others, and makes decisions (e.g., Jungian-based, Murphy, 2013; see Appendix—Personality/Temperament; Table 17.1). Clashes or strain may occur when a clinician, teacher, or parent has an opposing style to a youth. For example, extraverts are likely to enjoy active environments, need people time, prefer minimal time between questions and answers, be emotionally expressive, value outward behaviors in making assessments (e.g., a teacher may grade based on speaking up and outward behaviors), and tend to ask questions and offer suggestions (Murphy, 2013). For extraverts, doing is energizing, talking may help thinking, and quiet is needed for difficult tasks. In contrast, introverts are more likely to value quiet environments in general, need alone time, prefer to work alone or with one other person, need time between questions and answers, and may not feel like socializing at the end of the day. Introverts may prefer to think first, then share; may be energized by alone time; find it more difficult to express emotions when hurt, angry, or upset; but can focus and concentrate in noisy situations, if necessary (see Murphy, 2013 or Berens, 2013 for other aspects of personality).

Youth in treatment may demonstrate a variety of characteristics that influence reactions to teachers, to parents, to events, to clinicians, and to treatment as well as influence needs in treatment (Nader, 2008). For example, youth may be particularly attuned to injustice or to negative possibilities or be prone to positivity (minimize the negative), may be sensitive to the emotions of others or callous and indifferent, and/or may be prone to focus on the future or to focus on the past. Introverts or members of Asian cultures may be reluctant to give detailed or accurate descriptions of symptoms over the phone or in person. Introverts (see Berens, 2013), slow-to-warm or difficult temperaments (Chess & Thomas, 1991), BIS youth (Gray, 1991), youth with NE or specific genetic polymorphisms, and/or youth whose trust has been injured may need additional time to develop trust, to process aspects of treatment, and/or to think about things before speaking (Glossary). Silence or temporary "shutdown" may indicate symptoms (e.g., dissociation); an introverted or inhibited youth's need to reflect on thoughts, feelings, and ideas before sharing them; a need for more alone time or a break; or a tendency to share thoughts and feelings in bits and pieces (see Nader, 2008).

For MBTI® types (Myers–Briggs Type Indicator; MBTI-Child [C]), Berens (2013) has explained that *idealists/catalysts* (NF—emphasis: intuition and feeling) are especially stressed by betrayal, loss of meaning, insincerity, and lack of integrity. They seem to dissociate and/or become phony/fake in response to stressors. *Rationals/theorists* (NT—emphasis: intuition and thinking/knowledge) are particularly stressed by powerlessness, incompetence, and lack of knowledge and seem to become mindless and obsessive under stress (see also Keirsey & Bates, 1978; Table 17.1). *Stabilizers* (SJ—emphasis: membership, belonging; responsibility) are especially stressed by irresponsibility, instability, and being unable to make a contribution, and they may complain, become ill, tired, guilty, or worried. *Improvisers*

(SP—emphasis: freedom to act on needs of the moment; making an impact) are particularly stressed by constraint, boredom, and lack of having an impact. They may strike back or become reckless. Studies are needed that assess the relationship between type and traumatic stress and that include variables such as age, attachment, genetics, and diagnoses.

Interview and Treatment Issues for Adolescents

Adolescents are likely to prefer authenticity, truth, short waiting times, respectful treatment, individual time, cleanliness, skill, evening availability, and open discussions (e.g., pertinent issues, sex, drug use, nutrition; Cottrell, Nield, & Perkins, 2006; Hodgman & Jack, 1992). Interview methods, discussed first, are general rather than trauma-specific.

Interviewing Adolescents

Multiple factors influence the adolescent-clinician relationship and whether the adolescent facilitates or impedes successful treatment (Cottrell et al., 2006). Developmental stage or functioning age is as important as chronological age in treating and interviewing youth (Cottrell et al., 2006; Nader, 2008). Some have suggested that chronological age is equal to functioning age less than half the time in the general population, and even less frequently for foster children (Witkin, 2005). Harter and Pike (1984) say that mental age is more highly related to self-structure than chronological age. Nevertheless, adolescents generally need a greater role in their treatment process than younger children (Cottrell et al., 2006). With some exceptions, communication has improved when patients are similar to clinicians in gender and race (Cottrell et al., 2006; see Boxes 16.2, 16.3). Youth are also influenced by previous experience and the expectation of confidentiality.

Box 16.2 Mathew: Patient–Therapist Match

Although a body of evidence suggests that communication and progress are facilitated by having a same-sex, same-race therapist or physician, circumstances may alter its influence. For example, Mathew—exposed to a massacre in a fast food restaurant—made his best progress with female therapists. Perhaps it was because, in his life, fathers abandon you and/or use harsh discipline (not abuse, but high demands and angry, negative consequences, low warmth). His mother was always his energetic advocate and searched until she found him qualified assistance. She was always loving and supportive (see Nader, 2008, case of Mathew, for more detail) (see also Boxes 13.4, 16.3).

Mathew protested almost each time he entered a session that he did not belong in therapy. He was very conscious of his peers' beliefs about therapy. After his initial protest, he would cooperatively participate in treatment. Periodically, he would spontaneously engage in play. In one early session, he acted out a rescue scenario reminiscent of how much he wanted to intervene when the man with the gun walked around shooting people hiding under tables, including his friends. In a later session, he moved to the floor and seemed to be moving from playing with legos for a younger child up through those for preadolescents (also creating attack and rescue scenarios). (© Nader, 2008; Nader K [2008]. *Understanding and Assessing Trauma in Children and Adolescents: Measures, Methods, and Youth in Context.* New York: Routledge. Reproduced/included by permission of Taylor and Francis Group, LLC, a division of Informa plc.)

Note:
All case examples are disguised, may be combined cases, and have had details changed to protect individuals.

Box 16.3 Excerpts from Case of Hassan, Age 13: War-Related Trauma

Assessment Phase: Hassan and his mother individually answered questionnaires related to before, during, and after war-time, including his trauma exposures, symptoms, grief, attachment, and personality. He came to therapy because he periodically started to shake, and he couldn't control it. He was very embarrassed and bothered that he couldn't find a way to make it stop. His mother provided a loving, supportive presence, and Hassan related well to a female therapist, even though his culture may have caused one to guess otherwise.

Before the War: Privately and again in front of him, his mother described Hassan as a very intelligent and happy boy before the war. Everyone liked him. She described him as the youngest and the valuable star of the family. Hassan talked of being proud of how he could always figure out problems. His friends came to him for help. Both his and his mother's descriptions of Hassan and his life before the war depicted a well-liked, intelligent, competent, empathetic, confident, and happy young man who was a good friend and had many friends. Hassan described a good and supportive household, a very supportive mother, and an older father whose ill health only really worried him after the war started....

Psychoeducation: During the psychoeducation phase and periodically throughout treatment, Hassan's reactions were normalized. For example, one of the ways the body responds to being really afraid is the shaking he had described. Some youth describe itchy skin, prickling, feeling frozen, or other sensations in the body....

War Starts: When the war started, Hassan was by a lake with his relatives. They used to have fun water-skiing and riding recreational vehicles there. They were unaware of war until the water and electricity were cut off. A family member went to investigate and found out about the invasion. They heard bombs at midnight. Hasan was afraid to go outside. They later learned that the nearby military base had emptied all of its ammunition until it was completely gone. There were lots of enemy soldiers on the shore. Hassan worried about his own family. He and his relatives were too scared to sleep and decided to go home.

Worst Moment: Hassan's identified worst moment was a long period of time with many component parts—the long ride toward home. On the way home, a soldier pointed his gun at Hassan, while talking to him. Hassan's body started to shake and twitch as he told the story. The shaking happens now whenever he remembers, and sometimes, it just happens (perhaps in response to increased heart rate). As they drove toward home they were surrounded by invading soldiers, who were looking at them and pointing their tanks and guns at them. During the ride home, he couldn't move (his hands were crushing his fingers; his legs were trembling, his knees were knocking, and his whole body shaking). His mouth was dry. He was frozen but trembling. At one point, he tried to change the subject (distract everyone), because his cousin looked so distressed. They had to drive slowly along the soldier- and tank-lined road. All tanks, as they kept driving by, had their guns pointed at him. The soldiers had guns, and they moved them from their sides and pointed them at him. He could see in the soldiers' eyes that they wanted to kill him. He remained frozen and trembling....

At home, they heard horrible stories—about men and boys being given shots that made them sterile; about chemicals and germs; about people having their fingers or other body parts chopped off; about girls being raped. He was afraid for his sister and was worried about his mother, who had already left. His uncle decided they had to leave the country. They headed for a nearby neutral country. They divided the family so that only one adult male was in a car, so that they wouldn't be stopped.

Components of Sessions: As sessions progressed, aspects of the trauma and some of Hassan's individual symptoms were highlighted (i.e., shaking, being frozen, eyes closing ...). Hassan had a chance to talk to his body and to talk back to a described and depicted soldier....

The Single Worst Moment: When Hassan was ready to face his worst moment, he drew a picture of his uncle driving with Hassan and his younger cousin (close to Hassan's age) in the car. The story that goes with the picture: "I want to close my eyes." The gun was very close to him. He closed his eyes. He wondered about what will happen to his mother and family if he died.

As requested, Hassan drew a picture of the soldier who spoke to him and had pointed the gun at him, while they were talking. He said he thought that his body died when he saw those soldiers. He left the soldier's face blank and was asked to draw it. He said that he couldn't make his mouth and eyes. He drew the eyes outside of the man's face. Therapist commented: very frightening eyes. They would be even more so if they were inside his face. Hassan said, "Yes!". He said that he wasn't able to draw the mouth "mean enough." He drew a gun pointing to the side even though it had been pointed at him. When he re-drew it as it happened, the barrel was pointed at him, and he saw down the barrel and saw "the black thing inside." His body began to shake. He focused on the feelings inside his body ... He said that when he tells the story, his body feels like electric shock is going through it. "My cousins' and my faces became yellow"—he colored his face yellow. He remembered his hair was standing up....

Confronting the Soldier. At one point, Hassan was asked what he wished he could do or say to the soldier. First, he said he wanted to be everyone's friend (including the soldiers'). He was asked how he would make this soldier his friend. He looked at the face of the soldier and decided that this man would not be his friend. Hassan's mind only was enlisted, for the resistance; to make a plan for the military resistance. Hassan had always liked British spy movies, so his mind was given a code name (based on one of his mother's positive labels for him). His desire changed: He said he would need many many weapons and lots of ammo for the resistance (with so much he couldn't run out).... With his army of friends and family, he confronted the soldier, and then confronted the other soldiers.

Other Components e.g., Exposure, Punctuation, Reappraisal: Hassan had been proud of his mind and ability to figure things out. One early homework task was to observe the shaking. He was to let it happen and observe. A second assignment, after he had observed the shaking a few times, was to discover if he could make it more pronounced. He could have someone in the room or be alone to do the tasks. He decided to ask his mother to join him as a silent witness. He later reported that first he noticed that the shaking was not as visible as it felt to him. After a few days of observing, he tried but couldn't make himself shake harder, but he felt a little more in control afterward and less embarrassed.

... At one point, we talked about how, even though he was really intensely scared during the ride in the car with guns pointed at him, and his body became frozen ("like it was dead"), they could not paralyze his mind. His mind kept working. He was able to observe his cousin's distress and try to help. He was able to notice details of his and his cousin's response. He was able to notice the details of the soldiers and of the one soldier's face....

... "I had to be very still with the guns pointing at me." Additionally, he felt totally paralyzed for a period of time. He was praised for how very wise it was to be extremely still, when guns were pointed at him. Even though feeling paralyzed/frozen was out of the control of his mind, his body did the very best thing to keep him safe. It kept him perfectly still while guns were pointed at him. Realizing that his mind and body had continued to perform well even in the terrible moments relieved some of his fears and self-doubts.

Note:
All case examples are disguised, may be combined cases, and have had details changed to protect individuals.

With clinicians and other adults, adolescents may be exquisitely sensitive to falsehood or lack of candor (including half-truths). Unless a lie is congruent with what an adolescent wants to believe, falsehood or half-truth will confirm expectations that adults are liars. Hodgman and Jack (1992) have pointed out that an adult's abnormal candor shows that s/he is different from usual adults—i.e., from those who may dissimulate, rely on appearances, or assert authority to hide their discomforts. In general, age-appropriate, accurate information can prevent later confusion. Parent endorsement or support of treatment has predicted adolescent decisions about care as well (Cottrell et al., 2006).

Kuhn and Franklin (2008) suggest that, with adolescents, it is important to know ways to adjust information gathering in order to elicit authentic responses. For example, adolescent (and young adult) ability to generate a cogent argument (verbal or written; e.g., to support a claim) shows weaknesses when compared to mature adults. Few go beyond expressing a personal side of an argument. Without an interlocutor, adolescents tend to string together a sequence of true statements, while avoiding saying anything that might not be true. Having the youth include an imaginary *naysayer* or opponent into the argument has produced greater authenticity (see Kuhn & Franklin, 2008). Adolescents may need a reason for participating (Kuhn & Franklin, 2008).

Self-Disclosure

For adolescents, relational difficulties associated with trust are common and may be magnified by struggles to find purpose and meaning in life as well as by posttrauma symptoms (Habib & Labruna, 2011). Trust issues may complicate or prolong rapport building and subsequent treatment. Positive parenting has been linked to higher self-disclosure; nondisclosure has been linked to behavior problems (Hunter et al., 2011). With parents, youth nondisclosure has generally depended on the type of activity to conceal or disclose. In a study of multinational cultures (N = 2100 adolescents; Hunter et al., 2011), key reasons for disclosure included awareness of and adaptation to parental desires and expectations, for preventing parental worry, for parental protection, for feeling good about self, for strategic advantage of disclosing, and with selectivity about what to disclose and what to withhold (both genders, across cultures). Self-efficacy and social initiative have consistently positively correlated; social initiative was uniquely positively linked to self-disclosure. Although higher rates of disclosure have been found for females (to mothers, not necessarily fathers), adolescent males disclose more to both parents about risk-taking. The two following interview methods are generally problem-specific. In situations when trauma-exposed youth or caregivers are not open to reporting symptoms, Pat-Horenczyk, Kenan, Achituv, & Bachar (2014) suggest distress can be identified by screening for protective factors—e.g., self-efficacy, flexibility, and cognitive emotion regulation (84% of youth with PTSD were identified; needs replication).

Cognitive Interviewing

Cognitive interviewing is a technique used to enhance accuracy in research or other interviews (Norris, Torres-Thomas, & Williams, 2014). It assumes individuals use a four-stage process to answer questions—question comprehension, relevant information memory retrieval, decision-making, and response processes. Cognitive interviewing enhances accuracy of response by having respondents think aloud and using verbal probes to understand cognitive bias related to the response. It has been adapted for Hispanic adolescents by using peer focus groups.

Motivational Interviewing (MI)

For adults and adolescents who may feel coerced into treatment or feel ambivalent about change, MI (Miller & Rollnick, 2002) was developed to explore ambivalence and increase therapeutic alliance (MI; Manuel & Moyers, 2016). MI is a nonjudgmental, empathic, and collaborative method that includes warmth, respect, and compassion (Gruhl & Van Leuven, 2014). The stages of MI are (1) rapport building—engaging, asking permission to explore the issue; creating a circle chart with some blanks to fill in; (2) exploring pros and cons of problem behavior—using open-ended questions, affirmation, reflective listening; listening for change-talk; and summarizing when change-talk is heard (e.g., problems making the change); (3) delivery of computer-generated personalized assessment feedback; (4) imagining the future with and without the problem—e.g., asking questions that evoke plans for change such as "How would it look ..."; (5) reviewing a menu of change options and developing a change plan; and (6) enhancing self-efficacy for change (Berg-Smith, 2013; Gruhl & Van Leuven, 2014; Manuel & Moyers, 2016). MI is patient-centered. It aims to elicit and strengthen patient-motivation for change (Gruhl & Van Leuven, 2014). Trying to make an adolescent accept "the right way" is likely to meet with resistance. MI permits the youth to discover the right way through nonjudgmental, patient-led discussions about the behavior needing modification along with empathic listening that seeks to understand the youth's perspective (Gruhl & Van Leuven, 2014; Miller & Rollnick, 2002). MI empowers the patient, with belief in the youth's ability to change, by allowing her/him to take responsibility for actions and to control the decision-making process (Berg-Smith, 2013). Feeling accepted permits a youth freedom to consider rather than defend against change. MI is associated, e.g., with reductions in drinking (both MI and relaxation therapy, RT), marijuana use (N = 147 Hispanic 14–19-year-olds, Clair et al., 2013), smoking (N = 409 adolescents, with a booster session and a parent intervention, Manuel & Moyers, 2016), and predatory aggression (N = 189 incarcerated adolescents, if depression was low, MI was better than RT at 3 months post release, Clair-Michaud et al., 2016). A family therapy method that incorporates MI has reduced ADHD symptom severity; improvements persisted at six-month follow-up (N = 128 adolescents with ADHD, Sibley et al., 2016).

Treating Adolescents

Adolescents may be more reluctant to be in therapy (e.g., worry about peer judgment) or to share personal information (Nader, 2008). Once treatment begins, an adolescent may freely participate or require trust building. When drawings are requested, which may assist rapport, youth have sometimes become creative or have added humorous touches when asked for a second drawing, even while complaining that they already did that or that they don't need therapy (see Nader, 2008). Specifically, for working with adolescents, having objects available to handle during the interview may increase ease (e.g., blank paper and pencil, an inviting hand-sized object, Hodgman & Jack, 1992). After asking him if he wanted to be more relaxed, Hendel (2015) tossed a small cushion to a depressed adolescent and asked him to toss it back (see Box 13.4). The youth laughed and relaxed. Tossing continued in subsequent sessions, serving to get the youth moving, assisting connection, and increasing relaxation. Because direct eye contact is more comfortable for some adolescents and awkward for others (Hodgman & Jack, 1992), some clinicians recommend (e.g., with sexually abused youth) the interviewer refrain from either staring or avoiding the eyes (see Nader, 2008). Some cultures consider direct eye contact to be inappropriate (e.g., India, Southeast Asia). Tolerance of differences in motives or values—e.g., rejection of adult values; may not want to make good grades or do chores; may feel ambivalent—as well as providing honesty and respect toward the adolescent and respect for any limitations are essential to rapport. Accepting adolescents' ambivalence, exploring what they think, and helping to articulate a common cause between youth and adult family members may be of assistance.

Adolescent Support Systems

Attachments between parent and youth and between clinician and youth may assist recovery. Most methods include parents or families in the trauma treatment process. Caregiving relationships provide a context in which adolescents develop understanding of self, others, and self in relation to others (Green & Myrick, 2014). Positive relationships are conducive to developing trust, autonomy, and curiosity important to ongoing development and functioning as well as important to treatment and recovery after trauma exposure. When the caregiver–youth attachment relationship is and has been secure, under normal circumstances, adolescents are more likely to view themselves as lovable and the world as positive and predictable (Bowlby, 1969/1982; Green & Myrick, 2014). In times of distress, securely attached adolescents have been able to turn to parents for comfort, protection, and support. Insecurely attached adolescents may heighten expressions of anxiety and demand reassurance or may disengage and avoid expressions of distress, heightening difficulties for parents and youth (Stavrianopoulos, Faller, & Furrow, 2014).

Findings for adolescent suicide and depression suggest the importance of interpersonal, transactional issues, including broader environmental (e.g., community poverty, Deardorff, Gonzales, & Sandler, 2003) and family factors (e.g., belongingness, Ewing, Diamond, & Levy, 2015; thwarted/no belongingness—loneliness and feeling burdensome, Holland et al., 2017; see Chapter 15—belonging). The effectiveness of support seeking as a coping strategy may depend on the availability and nature of available support (Chapter 15—effectiveness of coping methods). Although less predictive of global self-worth, *validation support*—e.g., valuing, interest in, and respect for an adolescent's thoughts, verbalizations, and feelings—perceived within a specific context (e.g., with parent, teacher/trainer, classmate, therapist) has predicted self-worth in that context. A youth's global self-worth generally is more highly linked to one of her/his contexts. Although increasing support from more than one context is advisable following trauma exposure, in some cases, treatment may be more effective when support is especially enhanced from a particular group or when attention is refocused to other contexts.

For relationship stress, attachment-focused methods may be appropriate. For example, Stavrianopoulos et al. (2014) recommend Emotion-Focused family therapy (EFFT) to assist an adolescent's transition into adulthood (see also AEDP to follow). They suggest that, in families with high levels of distress, anxiety, and emotional conflict, the transition is often challenged. Both trauma and non-trauma-focused methods have addressed attachment issues for adolescents.

Trauma-Focused Methods

For adults and adolescents, trauma-focused methods have proven more efficacious than non-trauma-focused methods for the treatment of PTSD (adult meta-analysis; Ehring et al., 2014; N = 458, 11–18-year-olds, You et al., 2015). Additionally, although group and individual methods have shown success (Salloum & Overstreet, 2008), treatments with individual sessions have produced larger effect sizes than group treatments alone (Ehring et al., 2014; You et al., 2015). Although exposure therapies and cognitive processing have proven effective for the treatment of PTSD and of some complicated trauma symptoms (e.g., arousal regulation, dissociation), Gleiser, Ford, and Fosha (2008) suggest that they have been less effective for symptoms such as impaired self-reference—e.g., seeing oneself as permanently damaged or worthless (see AEDP, to follow). Traumatized youth may have lower threat–safety discrimination. They may respond with distress to a broad range of potential triggers versus only a few specific reminders of an event—e.g., to neutral or ambiguous images/faces; all people in brown clothes when the attacker wore brown; any increase in heart rate (Box 16.3).

TF-CBT

TF-CBT (described in Chapter 13) has been used effectively with adolescents. Variables like brain functioning, skills, behaviors, and environmental factors may be linked to symptom persistence or reduction of symptoms/reactions (Chapter 13). Treatment outcomes for TF-CBT for adolescent girls have significantly related to pre-treatment levels of brain activation (bilateral amygdala) when viewing fearful versus neutral images. Lower symptom reduction has corresponded to greater activation to both threat and neutral images (i.e., lower threat–safety discrimination), whereas greater symptom reduction corresponded to amygdala activation only for threat images (fMRI; Cisler et al., 2015b). In an additional study, lower posttreatment PTSD symptoms were associated with greater suppression of amygdala–insula functional connectivity (FnC) during reappraisal of negative images, whereas less improvement corresponded to failure to decrease FnC (N = 20, Cisler et al., 2016). Pre- to posttreatment improvements in emotion regulation ability have also positively related to improvements in PTSD symptoms (self-reported).

Cisler et al. (2016) suggest that training in specific affect regulation skills and traumatic memory cognitive reprocessing may stimulate functional reorganization of emotion regulation neural circuitry to suppress interoceptive representations of negative affective states. Other researchers have described methods that address PTS reactions as issues of memory consolidation (Appendix; see Glossary—reconsolidation). Adaptations or other therapies (e.g., PCIT, Chapter 10; dialectical behavior therapy, DBT, Linehan, 1993a, 1993b) may be needed when youth exhibit externalizing—e.g., SI, suicidality, substance abuse, inappropriate sexual behaviors, running away from home, severe aggression, criminality (Kliethermes, Nanney, Cohen, & Mannarino, 2013).

Emotion-Focused-CBT (EF-CBT)

EF-CBT, described in Chapter 13 and 9, addressed trauma and attachment-related issues. Especially for women and girls, childhood maltreatment has been significantly associated with additional exposures to interpersonal trauma (e.g., adolescents and adults, betrayal trauma, Owen, Quirk, & Manthos, 2012; partner violence, partially mediated by anxious-resistant attachment, N = 601 undergrads, Hocking, Simons, & Surette, 2016). Betrayal traumas have a high risk of PTSD and other problems (Hocking et al., 2016; Chapter 12). Childhood betrayal traumas have negatively related to well-being and to perceived partner respect (mediated by well-being and resistant attachment; separate from positive relationship perceptions), and positively related to anxious-resistant and avoidant attachments (N = 86, young adults, Owen et al., 2012). For insecure-resistant individuals or couples, reducing relationship-specific attachment avoidance and positively affecting attachment-related behaviors have improved relationship satisfaction (e.g., EF-CBT, N = 32, Moser et al., 2015b). Hocking et al. suggest that treatments focus on emotion-regulation and distress tolerance for individuals with insecure-resistant attachment styles—to temper characteristic intense emotional reactions in response to perceived rejection or abandonment—as well as focus on maladaptive behaviors—e.g., excessive reassurance seeking.

Emotion-Focused Therapy for Trauma (EFTT)

Methods that include confronting a perpetrator of a trauma have been used effectively with children and adolescents (Eth & Pynoos, 1985; Nader & Mello, 2001). In EFTT, the focus is on exploring trauma-related feelings and meanings through exploration of subjective, internal experience, constructing more adaptive meaning, and resolving issues with particular perpetrators. Greater depth of experiencing has been related to better outcomes (Mundorf & Paivio, 2011). For adults with histories of various forms of childhood maltreatment, Paivio et al. (2010) compared use of EFTT combined with imaginal confrontation (IC) of perpetrators (N = 20; see Box 16.3) to EFTT with empathic exploration (EE) of trauma material (N = 25). Although there was a lower attrition rate for EFTT-EE, the EFTT-IC group had greater clinically significant change—reduced distress symptoms, personal and interpersonal difficulties; abuse resolution.

Complex and Other Conditions Linked to Trauma

Although descriptions of and names for complicated trauma-related disorders are still evolving, a few treatment methods specifically address cPTSD/DTD in youth (see Chapter 2). As discussed, cultural adaptations of treatments and understanding of culture-specific differences in syndromes is essential (Danieli & Nader, 2006; Kirmayer, Young, & Hayton, 1995; Schnyder et al., 2016; Westermeyer & Uecker, 1997; Box 16.1). For example, a persistent condition found for adult immigrants and refugees also has been found in adolescent refugees—e.g., depressive and PTSD symptoms, mistrust or suspiciousness, anxiety, physiological symptoms, social withdrawal or isolation, and hostility that includes annoyance and irritation, temper outbursts, urges to harm someone or break things, and arguments (e.g., Kinzie, Boehnlein, & Sack, 1998).

Treatment Issues for Complicated Trauma

Although treatment issues may vary, some of the same methods—e.g., that address mentalizing, attachment, and self-regulation—have been used for cPTSD/DTD, PDs, and SI (see mindfulness, MBT-A, DBT to follow). Methods used for problems found in cPTSD, PDs, and SI are presented here and in the next section (see also ARC, Chapter 10), including specific treatment issues.

cPTSD/DTD Treatment Issues and Methods

Methods to assist youth with cPTSD/DTD have targeted attachment, self-regulation, and skill competency (e.g., ARC, Chapter 10) as well as safety (e.g., posttrauma self-endangerment), identity issues, and comorbidity (Briere & Lanktree, 2013). Expert cPTSD and trauma clinicians often endorse phased or sequenced treatment. Overlapping phases may include, e.g., a. stabilization and safety—therapeutic alliance, psychoeducation, symptom control (e.g., reducing self-destructive behaviors, affect and impulse control and/or coping skill building); b. trauma processing—exploring trauma memories, identifying cognitive distortions, developing a coherent narrative; and c. reconnection or integration—with aspects of self and life goals (e.g., Green & Myrick, 2014; Herman, 1997). As described, multiple types of treatment have been recommended for complex trauma (symptom complexity, Briere, Dietrich, & Semple, 2016; Cloitre et al., 2011; Ford, 2018; PTSD-DS, Chapter 13).

Adolescent complex trauma interventions include, e.g., CBT (Chapter 13), Integrative Treatment for Complex Trauma-Adolescent (ITCT-A, Lanktree & Briere, 2013; reductions in anxiety, depression, PTS, anger, dissociation, & sexual concerns, Lanktree et al., 2012), Trauma Affect Regulation (TARGET; e.g., reduction of dangerous behavioral incidents for incarcerated youth; improved PTSD, depression, anxiety, substance use risk, and features of cPTSD, see Ford, 2018 for a summary), and Adolescents Responding to Chronic Stress (SPARCS, DeRosa & Rathus, 2013). Individualized adaptations (e.g., cultural, social, personality), advocacy (interdisciplinary, resources), and relationship and support building are important as well (Briere & Lanktree, 2013).

Trauma-sensitive adjunctive methods have assisted success—e.g., Hatha yoga has improved self-regulation in institutionalized youth with chronic affective and somatic dysregulation and associated behavioral, functioning, and health complaints (Spinazzola et al., 2011). Among methods is a combination of integrative, Jungian-based play therapy with CBT phased intervention for complex trauma used for adolescents (insight-based, age-appropriate methods may be incorporated, Green, 2012; Green & Myrick, 2014). Play therapy has assisted affect regulation, self-efficacy, problem-solving, and trust formation (an empathic therapeutic relationship; Green & Myrick, 2014). For somatic dysregulation, several methods have been used with adolescents (see Chapter 13).

For dissociation, methods such as distress reduction, affect regulation training, emotional processing, and training to identify and respond to reaction-triggers may assist. For cPTSD or other trauma reactions that include a youth's dissociative feelings, cognitions, experiences, or self-states, Wieland and Silberg (2013) recommend dissociation-focused treatment (regardless of treatment approach) in order to assist the youth to reconnect with all aspects of self (see also Silberg, 2013). During in-session dissociative episodes, a clinician may assist processing and reintegration, while preventing reinforcing dissociative avoidance.

Accelerated Experiential Dynamic Psychotherapy (AEDP)

ADEP aims to promote recovery from PTSD and from cPTSD by translating diffuse distress, fear, and anxiety into more fully articulated, better regulated emotions, memories, and adaptive actions (Fosha, 2006). "The aim is to counteract the patient's unbearable aloneness in the face of feelings that necessitated reliance on strategies against experiencing" (Fosha, 2001, p. 230). AEDP integrates experiential and relational elements within a psychodynamic framework: for a "deep authentic affective experience" (and its regulation) through coordinated emotional, patient–therapist interchanges, with an empathic, affirming, open, and emotionally engaged clinician who does not back away. Treatment is grounded in the attachment-based therapeutic relationship (central focus on dyadic affect regulation (Fosha, 2001, 2009). Although the attachment relationship alone is not sufficient, the attachment relationship, including the therapeutic dyad, has the capacity to shift a person from fear-activating shrinking and constriction (avoidance) to curiosity-activating openness and expansiveness (moving toward; Fosha, 2006). It permits the individual to take more risks (i.e., feel more intense feelings) in the safety of the dyad, during emotion-focused interventions, with moment-to-moment assessment and gradually inviting fuller core affect experience—e.g., through somatic focusing, affective mirroring, and evocative portrayals (Fosha, 2001, 2009). AEDP provides a secure base from which to explore. Even with an understanding guide, survivors, who often are plagued by powerful, unmet needs for security and comfort, may continue to feel isolated and terrified (e.g., with dysregulated and dissociated feelings; Fosha, 2001, 2002; Gleiser et al., 2008; Box 3.2). AEDP seeks to co-create new emotional and relational experiences within the therapeutic dyad, thereby catalyzing a patients' natural resilience, and by providing alternate internal working models (Box 16.4). Dyadic painful emotion-regulation naturally culminates in emergence of positive emotional states. In turn, these states/affects help to access the emotional resources associated with resilience and emotional flourishing, which are a foundation to well-being throughout life—e.g., enable flexibility, generativity, playfulness, exploration, better coping and adaptation

Box 16.4 A Psychotic Mother

Fosha (2006) describes a patient who experienced terror while growing up with a psychotic mother who displayed unpredictable rages, and with a father who threatened to abandon the family. From a very young age she developed a *split self* and assumed a *caretaker identity*. With caution in response to both parents, those defenses helped her to maintain a happy façade. In the process of sharing frightening experiences and sharing the related emotions, she realized with surprise that she had revealed her secret—i.e., she had been deeply unhappy. The first meta-therapeutic intervention—asking how the patient felt sharing her secret—was liberating for the patient (see Fosha, 2006 for details).

(Russell & Fosha, 2008, see Glossary—flourishing). Clinicians have adapted AEDP for use with adolescents.

The *compromised self* is a survival-based self-organization that emerges in conditions of threat and stress (Fosha, 2013). The *resilient self* is a transformance-dominated self-organization. Transformational processes are an important aim of treatment. Methods, such as empathy and validation, are used to help promote coherent articulation (Fosha, 2006). Moment-by-moment tracking of fluctuations in bodily-based emotional experience (reading body language) is essential to relatively rapid and effective emotion-focused treatments. The process includes (1) Collaboration through making the implicit explicit; gaining permission to proceed promotes a sense of being in control of experiences that may feel out of control; (2) Connecting experience with its bodily correlates; verbalizations highlight that the essence of the experience has a positive effect; and (3) With each new unsettling focus of attention, the clinician helps to employ alternating waves of experience, somatic localization, and reflection (e.g., feelings about the feelings and sensations); after experience settles and then transforms, it leads to a new experience that becomes the next focus of attention (i.e., exploration and articulation of a sensation, begets another sensation), with the potential for cascading transformations (Fosha, 2006). The culmination of the transformational process is a deeply integrated state characterized by flow, ease, clarity, compassion, self-compassion, generosity, and creativity (Fosha, 2013).

Treatment Issues for PDs

Using the Mirror Interview (Kernberg, Buhl-Nielsen, & Normandin, 2007; Glossary), researchers have been able to distinguish between healthy adolescents and those with PD—healthy adolescents scored higher on organized affect and cognition, whereas adolescents with PD scored higher on alienation, wandering gaze, and fixed gaze scores. Aspects of BPD and NPD were described in Chapter 15. To follow, treatment issues are discussed for narcissism and BPD, followed by methods used for PDs—DBT and MBT-A. Adolescent BPD has been highly comorbid with other personality disorders—e.g., antisocial, dependent, obsessive-compulsive, avoidant, and/or paranoid personality disorders (Laos et al., 2013)—which may require consideration.

Treatment Issues for Narcissism

Deficits in mentalizing and poor attachment relationships suggest that mentalizing and attachment treatments may be appropriate for narcissism as well as for cPTSD (see above). For adults, a number of schemas relevant to treatment have been identified for narcissistic personalities—e.g., the "self" who desires to be recognized as being special and admired and the "other" who is dominant and critical; the self that reacts with overt antagonism or resorts to an *ivory tower*; the self that needs attention while the other rejects and criticizes, followed by compulsive self-soothing and denial of attachment needs (Dimaggio, 2012). Dimaggio suggests that clinicians avoid the following: challenging self-serving grandiosity, hastily promoting awareness of vulnerability, or (at least initially) trying to promote empathy. Instead, he recommends promoting agency with motives other than struggling for grandiosity, promoting self-awareness with accurate self-appraisal, and tactful confrontation of dysfunctional patterns. When youth have been referred for treatment for antisocial behavior problems, treatment was less successful for those with high levels of narcissistic or callous-unemotional traits (e.g., Multisystemic Therapy, Manders et al., 2013). Some school interventions have addressed increasing empathy (Nader, 2012c; Schonert-Reichl et al., 2015; to follow). Such early preventive interventions are recommended for a number of problems that include lack of empathy or other perspective-taking skills (e.g., CU, PD).

Treatment for BPD

BPD traits must be distinguished from normal adolescent traits. For example, trait affective lability, impulsivity, and hyper-aggression must be distinguished from normal adolescent developmental qualities (Chanen & Thompson, 2014). Normally impulsivity, attention seeking, and dependency decline from mid- to late adolescence, while social competence and self-control increase across time. In contrast, for personality disordered youth, BPD traits tend to persist across time (Chapter 15). Attachment issues and traumas have been prominent for personality disorders, including BPD (Steele, Bate, Nikitiades, & Buhl-Nielsen, 2015; Chapter 15), suggesting the need to address both issues in treatment. BPD patients have scored low on reflective functioning (Fonagy et al., 2000; Table 1.2). As described for narcissism (Chapter 15), caregiver's exaggeratedly reflecting back to the infant his/her emotions—a form of affective labeling (Steele et al., 2015)—followed by soothing, helps the child to learn, identify, and regulate emotions (see Fonagy & Target, 2006; see Beebe et al., 2016 on synchrony; Chapter 5). Sharp et al. (2013) observed that BPD was linked to hyper-mentalizing rather than lack of mentalizing (Glossary; N = 164, ages 12–17; independent of internalizing and externalizing). Additionally, in BPD, mental state awareness appears to be focused on external features of self and others (face, behavior), rather than on internal features (mental interiors, putative feelings, and thoughts). Fonagy suggests treatment emphasize the attachment system, while assisting mentalization skills. Such treatments include Adolescent Mentalization-Based Integrative Treatment (Allen & Fonagy, 2006; Bateman & Fonagy, 2012; Fuggle et al., 2015); Regulation Focused Psychotherapy—targets emotion-regulation (Hoffman, 2015); Mentalization-Based Treatment (MBT) for children—targets sense of self, emotion regulation, and ownership of behavior (Zevalkink, Verheugt-Pleiter, & Fonagy, 2012); and MBT group (Beck et al., 2016; Courtney-Seidler et al., 2013).

Some clinicians have used combined methods. For example, after DBT addressed BPD-common issues such as self-harm, additional treatments that address what Pos and Greenberg called "secondary treatment targets" such as self-invalidation, self-reflective processes, emotional reactivity, crisis generating behavior, inhibited grieving, and/or passivity have been used (Pos & Greenberg, 2012). Pos and Greenberg have used a combination of emotion-focused therapies (including trauma-focused), a two-chair method (e.g., a critic-chair and an experience/receiver-of-criticism-chair), and increased sensitive use of the therapy relationship, identification of maladaptive cycles (between self-organizations), dialectical empathic reflection, and genuine humor. The methods help to scaffold the individual's capacity to reflect on and regulate emotion.

Clinician reluctance to diagnose BPD in adolescents may be due to concerns about stigma. However, early identification of BPD traits permits prevention or early intervention. In Australia and the Netherlands, preventive interventions have been provided for youth with two to nine BPD symptoms (Chanen & Thompson, 2014). Cognitive Analytic Therapy (CAT) has improved BPD symptoms more rapidly than general manualized good care (N = 78, ages 15–18; N = 16, first-episode psychosis and BPD pathology; see Chanen & Thompson, 2014, for summary). MBT-A has also proven effective for adolescents with BPD symptoms (e.g., N = 83, better at reducing SI and depression than treatment as usual or CAT). One study examined the use of long-chain omega-3 polyunsaturated fatty acids (PUFAs; "fish oil") for adolescents who met ultra-high-risk criteria for psychosis or who presented with BPD symptoms (N = 15; Amminger et al., 2013). Baseline, erythrocyte omega-3 PUFA levels related positively to psychosocial functioning and negatively to psychopathology. At the end of intervention, omega-3 PUFAs associated with significantly improved functioning and reduced psychiatric symptoms, including BPD symptoms.

Non-Suicidal Self-Injury (NSSI)

BP has been associated with non-suicidal self-injury (NSSI). Evidence suggests that youth who engage in NSSI would benefit from better emotion-regulation strategies (reduction of avoidance, dissociation), changes in cognitive styles (reduced rumination/brooding increasing self-compassion), increased social support, a sense of safety, and a better sense of belonging (e.g., ethnic, group; see Chapters 12, 15). Using different treatment methods for a very small sample of NSSI patients (N = 8 patients, four different counselors), two extinguished NSSI (they increased problem-focused coping and decreased avoidant coping), four improved (decreased avoidant coping), and two increased frequency of NSSI (no decrease in avoidant coping) (Wester, Downs, & Trepal, 2016). This finding and the results presented in Chapters 12 and 15 suggest that regardless of the intervention method used, individuals who engage in self-injury require inquiry about emotive symptoms and about social support, sense of belonging, and coping strategies. Hence, in addition to assisting attachment and mentalizing, also teaching effective coping strategies and self-regulation methods as well as increasing ethnic belonging and other support systems are indicated for NSSI.

Dialectical Behavior Therapy (DBT)

DBT has been used for adolescents with BPD, cPTSD, and externalizing problems (e.g., 16–32 sessions, includes caregivers; DeRosa & Rathus, 2013). DBT was originally developed for the treatment of BPD (Feliu-Soler et al., 2013). Its approach to enhance mindfulness, distress tolerance, and emotion regulation may serve as prevention for adolescents with BPD features. For general psychiatric management (GPM) alone or with DBT combined with mindfulness (DBT-M) (N = 35, ages 18–46, Feliu-Soler et al., 2013), the DBT-M group showed greater clinical symptom improvement (observed) and self-reported reduced emotional reactivity. When DBT was combined with Native American cultural and spiritual practices (N = 229, Native American adolescents with SUD), DBT showed clinically significant reductions or recovery in substance use (Beckstead, Lambert, DuBose, & Linehan, 2015). As discussed (Chapter 13), dissociation and emotion dysregulation must be addressed for the effectiveness of cPTSD and PTSD-DS treatment. For individuals (with or without BPD) treated with DBT-PTSD (N = 24; ages 19–52), lower state dissociation during treatment has increased the likelihood of substantial improvement (Kleindienst et al., 2016).

Mentalization-Based Treatment for Adolescents (MBT-A)

MBT-A is an attachment-based, psychodynamic psychotherapy for adolescents that combines individual and family sessions. Duration is variable, depending on the program—e.g., outpatient: 1/week youth sessions, 1/month family sessions, MBT-F; inpatient: 2/week individual, 1/week MBT-F (Rossouw, 2015; Rossouw & Fonagy, 2012). Used for adolescent BPD, MBT-A focuses on impulsivity and affect regulation. Treatment includes four phases: a. assessment; b. written formulation of a crisis plan for youth and family; c. enhancement of patients' capacity to represent their and others' feelings accurately in emotionally challenging situations—e.g., rejection, interpersonal conflict; d. addressing separation issues and managing anticipated challenges in a mentalizing manner. Sessions are usually unstructured and focus on the youth's current and recent interpersonal experiences and the mental states evoked by them. Family sessions seek to improve the family's ability to mentalize, especially in the context of family conflict. MBT-A therapists exhibit a keen interest and curiosity in the patient throughout treatment—e.g., prioritize learning about the youth's feelings; look for the mental state underneath any described behaviors; and maintain a therapeutic stance—e.g., take responsibility for their own actions and words that may impact the patient (Bateman & Fonagy, 2004; Rossouw, 2015). Building a strong therapeutic alliance, while making authentic emotional contact, and providing a supportive atmosphere are essential (Rossouw, 2015). The focus is on the here and now, with detailed attention to the patient's affective states—e.g., through affect elaboration, exploration, and clarification—and for helping her/him to slow down and make sense of what happened—e.g., by reflecting on her/his own internal states and encouraging her/his curiosity about others' internal states. As a consequence, the youth is likely to be less prone to abandonment anxiety, self-esteem collapse, or affective storms. The clinician provides the youth concrete, practical assistance with the life tasks (e.g., school) that they fear and avoid. A one-year mindfulness-based MBT-A treatment for adolescents (44% recovery rate) was more effective than usual treatment (17% recovery) for reducing adolescent self-injury and depression (N = 80, Rossouw & Fonagy, 2012).

Treatments for Specific Problems

Suicidal ideation, complicated grief reactions, and victim-offenders are among conditions that have required specific treatment adjustments. A few methods appropriate for adolescents are presented. Not all proven treatments and issues can be presented in the space allowed—e.g., an online interactive program (Children of Divorce–Coping With Divorce) has been shown to improve coping efficacy and mental health problems in children of divorced parents (N = 147, ages 11–16; Boring et al., 2015). Some of the preceding treatments and *Seeking Safety* (see Other Adjunct ... to follow) have been used effectively for substance abuse. For enhancing interrupted developmental skills, practice assists learning. Bias modification programs, based on introducing new attributional explanations for occurrences when a child would automatically attribute hostility, has been used for attributional biases (Martinelli et al., 2018).

Suicidal Ideation

Treatments used effectively for trauma or depression have had mixed results for treating suicidal ideation (Ewing, Diamond, & Levy, 2015). Treatment engagement with adolescents has proven difficult, and medication has sometimes exacerbated suicidal thinking. An attachment-based treatment that has shown success follows.

Attachment-Based Family Therapy (ABFT)

ABFT is a manualized (Diamond, Diamond, & Levy, 2013), 12–16-week (approximately) family therapy method based on attachment, family therapy, and emotion-focused methods (may be multiple sessions per week; Ewing et al., 2015). It includes separate youth and parent sessions as well as family sessions (e.g., to help structure corrective attachment experiences; work through past hurts). Treatment is organized around five flexible treatment tasks: (1) The *Relational Reframe* (initial 60–90 minutes)—e.g., understand the problem; move from assessing depression to assessing attachment—"When you are feeling so hopeless and down that you are thinking of taking your own life or harming your own body, what gets in the way of going to your mom/dad for help?"; set treatment goals); (2) *Adolescent Alliance*—e.g., bond with adolescent; increase youth's understanding of core hurts; bring up expectations of being hurt with sensitivity and support; prepare youth to speak to parents respectfully and assertively; (3) *Parent Alliance*—e.g., get to know parents, highlight their strengths; explore stressors; educate and improve parenting strategies; increase caregiving motivation and attunement; (4) *Repairing Attachment*—e.g., use of parent–child interaction; adolescent discloses; clinician guides and coaches parents; parent responds supportively and non-defensively; and (5) *Promoting Autonomy* (usually 4–8 sessions)—e.g., focus on promoting adolescent's competence and autonomy in various contexts—peer, school, home; problem-solving training (Diamond et al., 2013; Ewing et al., 2015). The clinician is directive and must anticipate barriers to progress. Attachment-promoting parenting is attuned and responsive as well as developmentally flexible (Ewing et al., 2015). Adolescent attachment needs include verbal reassurance, open discussion, and guidance. Increased parental NE (rather than adaptation) in response to the youth may result in increased difficulty, defiance, and/or withdrawal by the youth. A repaired attachment environment is likely to improve the youth's security, self-efficacy, and self-perception. Studies on the use of

ABFT have found clinically significant reductions in depression (MDD, Diamond et al., 2010, Israel & Diamond, 2012; LGB youth, Diamond et al., 2012), in suicidal ideation (persisted at six-month follow-up, Diamond et al., 2010, 2012), and in anxiety and avoidance in relationships (Ewing et al., 2015).

Complicated Grief

A number of issues are important in treating traumatic or other forms of complicated grief (e.g., attention biases, Bullock & Bonanno, 2013; age, Chapters 7, 10; Tables 12.1–12.2)—e.g., adolescents have stated that it is important to be told when death of a loved one is imminent (e.g., N = 12, ages 13–16, parent died of cancer; Bylund-Grenklo et al., 2015). Although less frequently when means of death was a family member, feelings of revenge (e.g., after homicide, war) have been associated with CG (most strongly), with PTSD, and with reduced positive functioning (unrelated to time since loss or punishment given perpetrator; undergraduates and families; van Denderen et al., 2014). Individual, group, and school-based interventions have addressed grief in adolescents (e.g., Dyregrov, Salloum, Kristensen, & Dyregrov, 2015; Layne et al., 2008; IGTC, Pearlman, Schwalbe, & Cloitre, 2010; Chapter 13—GTI, Salloum, 2015; Appendix—Trauma and Grief Component Therapy for Adolescents, Saltzman et al., 2018)

In the treatment of CG, the importance of clinician training and of taking into consideration the needs of specific adolescent(s) have been established (e.g., Dyregrov, Dyregrov, & Johnsen, 2013). In addition to methods presented here and in Chapter 13, creative methods such as a writing technique (Dyregrov et al., 2013; more emotionally expressive writing linked to reduced young adult anxiety, Niles, et al., 2014) and music therapy techniques (e.g., PTS, soldiers, Bensimon, Amir, & Wolf, 2008; sexually abused, Robarts, 2006) have shown some promise for working with trauma and grief (Dyregrov et al., 2015; Rosner, Kruse, & Hagl, 2010; Spinazzola et al., 2011).

Integrated Grief Therapy for Children (IGTC)

After a death, when a child's symptoms persist and interfere with daily functioning, treatment is indicated. IGTC (Pearlman et al., 2010; ages 5–18) emphasizes the need to tailor treatment for individual children (e.g., for age, circumstances, presenting problems). Treatment increases strengths and addresses factors that may disrupt normal grieving—e.g., PTSD, anxiety, behavior problems, depression. IGTC includes assessment, psychoeducation, and assisting parents—e.g., restoring limit-setting, routines, and consistency. Assessment of both parent and child precedes treatment (e.g., for risk and protective factors; behavioral and emotional strengths and difficulties; age-appropriate functioning; suicidal ideation). Grief is the main focus. IGTC includes CBT techniques—e.g., cognitive strategies such as challenging negative thoughts and identifying alternative thinking; anxiety reduction such as relaxation techniques and creative methods; family systems work and interpersonal methods such as enhancing social skills and support. Specific treatments for grief are combined with those for depression—e.g., activity scheduling; counteracting growing up too quickly; strengthening family and peer relationships; for PTSD—e.g., enhancing coping and managing symptoms, improving/restoring competencies, creating a trauma narrative, enhancing emotional expression; for anxiety—e.g., psychoeducation, cognitive and behavioral coping, parent assisting the child to manage anxiety, addressing self-talk; and/or for behavior problems—e.g., placing the behavior in context (e.g., a response to change, loss of relationship with and support from deceased), increasing positive interactions (e.g., parental warmth, engagement in playful activities), restoring structure and routine (e.g., clear commands, positive reinforcement) (Pearlman et al., 2010). Building coping skills generally precedes creating a trauma narrative.

Assisting caregiver grief and other symptoms may be needed (Pearlman et al., 2010). For example, after the death of a parent, a child's positive outcomes have been linked to the availability of a supportive and consistent caregiver. After a sudden, unexpected death, the surviving parent may be struggling with depression, PTSD, anxiety, suicidal ideation, and/or impaired functioning. When a parent is not struggling with acute trauma symptoms or other psychopathology, sessions may focus on coping skill building, psychoeducation (e.g., building social support), and providing access to resources. Parents may learn to follow the child's lead when discussing the death, to facilitate her/his expression of feelings, and to support the child's experiences. When the parent is struggling with depression or other symptoms, separate individual therapy may be indicated (Pearlman et al., 2010).

Victim-Offenders

Victim-offenders (e.g., bully-victims; child soldiers) have been both victims and perpetrators and have had numerous problems (Glossary—bully-victims; Hermenau et al., 2013; Nader, 2012c). Although some of these children show resiliency, others experience difficulties such as TSRD (e.g., PTSD, traumatic grief), internalizing (e.g., depression, withdrawal, social isolation), externalizing (e.g., aggression, hostility), poor health, low school completion, and poor self-sufficiency (Betancourt et al., 2013a, 2013b, 2014). In addition to these problems, former child soldiers (e.g., Sierra Leone, Rwanda), are at risk of delinquency and appetitive aggression (aggression seen as fascinating, rewarding, and compelling), which hinders reintegration (Betancourt et al., 2014; Hermenau et al., 2013; see also Complex or Developmental Trauma, above). Former child soldiers (often abducted for two or more years), like other war-exposed youth, generally experience or witness multiple forms of violence, raids, killings, and rape; they are forced to commit atrocities as well (Betancourt et al., 2014; Turner, Finkelhor, & Ormrod, 2010, 2007; Box 13.1). Some treatments have enlisted communities (Betancourt et al., 2014) and/or have used trauma-focused methods (e.g., NET, Ertl et al., 2011; Hermenau et al., 2013; Chapter 13). For example, recognizing that child soldiers are both victims and perpetrators, a reintegration program—employs, e.g., vocational training, education, social support—has been combined with Narrative Exposure Therapy (NET) for Forensic Offender Rehabilitation (FORNET)—recalling experiences with narrative exposure methods (Hermenau et al., 2013). The program has reduced both PTSD symptoms and appetitive aggression (Hermenau et al., 2013; N = 58 ages 16–25; soldiering from age 12). While addressing PTS requires skilled interventions, reducing internalizing (depression and anxiety) has improved other life outcomes for these youth as well (Betancourt et al., 2015a).

Adjunct Methods: Body-Mind Treatments

Creative methods (e.g., drawings, play) have often been used to assist rapport and for neurological repair as well as symptom processing and reduction (Chapters 10, 13). Such methods may permit self-distancing and reduce resistance. Adolescents may benefit from many of the adjunct methods described in earlier chapters (e.g., creative methods; meditation; rhythmic stimulation, exercise). Body-mind methods for youth may include meditation, progressive muscle relaxation, deep breathing, sensorimotor therapy, eye movement desensitization, art or music therapy, and dance or rhythmic movement therapy (Spinazzola et al., 2011; van der Kolk et al., 2014). Yoga and mindfulness methods have been used for neurological repair and to reduce symptoms. Such practices also have enhanced self-compassion. Higher levels of self-compassion have been related to lower levels of symptoms (e.g., NSSI, depression, anxiety; Table 1.3). For Sudanese adolescents (ages 15–18, Harris, 2007), a dancing and drumming program related to improvements in group cohesion. When combined with psychotherapy, these methods were linked to former Sierra Leone boy soldiers reports of reductions in anxiety, depression, intrusive recollections, arousal, and aggression.

Brain Networks

fMRI studies suggest that psychopathology alters functioning in specific brain connectivity networks, corresponding to specific clinical symptoms—*Central Executive Network*, CEN: cognitive dysfunction; *Salience N*, SN: increased and decreased arousal/interoception; and *Default Mode N*, DMN: an altered sense of self (Glossary; Lanius et al., 2015; Patel, Spreng, Shin, & Girard, 2012; Yang et al., 2016). There is a dynamic interplay between externally- and internally-focused attention and cognitive-affective processing, related to the interplay of these networks (Lanius et al., 2015; Glossary). In addition to pharmacological treatments, neurofeedback, and repetitive trans-magnetic stimulation as neural treatments for adults, Lanius et al. have recommended, for DMN, psychotherapy to increase reflective functions; for SN, mindfulness methods; and for CEN, cognitive remediation.

Play Methods

Adolescents may regress to or engage in the play of a younger child after traumas (Chapter 13; Box 16.2; Nader, 2008). As well, adolescents may use toy replicas (people, scenes) to demonstrate aspects of an event and/or to work through, symbolically, emotional aspects of the event in play (Boxes 13.3, 16.2–16.3, Nader, 2008). Game play (e.g., board games) also has been used for adolescents (Homeyer & Morrison, 2008). Under normal circumstances, such games afford an opportunity to learn social skills—e.g., conversation skills; to play by the rules, take turns, and be a gracious winner or loser (Dimaggio, Hermans, & Lysaker, 2010; Homeyer & Morrison, 2008). In fact, play methods (e.g., sand-tray, doll-play, psychodrama, group play) are currently used therapeutically with adults, families, and adolescents, for a variety of problems (Schaefer, 2003). For example, sand-tray play therapy has been used with preadolescents with behavior problems (N = 56, ages 9–12, reduced internalizing, externalizing and total scores, Flahive & Ray, 2007) and has improved self-esteem in adolescent girls of varied ethnicity (African American, Hispanic, White) as well as improved academic competence, physical appearance, social acceptance, behavioral conduct, and global self-worth (N = 37, ages 11–13, Shen & Armstrong, 2008). Sand-tray therapy has been used for grief and to improve adolescent attachments (Green & Connolly, 2009; Green, Myrick, & Crenshaw, 2013).

Meditation

Meditation has become an important adjunct treatment for a number of different types of psychopathology, including PTSD. It has been associated with improvements in the symptoms of disorders like ADHD, depression, obsessive-compulsive disorder, autism, thoughts of SI, suicidal ideation, and other internalizing and externalizing (e.g., aggression; disruptive behavior) (Cheng, 2016; Semple, Lee, Rosa, & Miller, 2010; Singh et al., 2010; Yang et al., 2016). Specific developmental skills and tasks have shown improvement after meditation training—e.g., EF (e.g., attention), self-regulation, self-awareness, resilience factors (e.g., self-esteem, confidence), and social skills (Cheng, 2016; Coholic, 2011; Kochanska & Kim, 2012). For example, improvements in EFs have followed mindfulness and yoga meditations (attention, concentration) and also have been related to breathing exercises (attention, processing speed) (Luu & Hall, 2015). Short-term interventions have assisted children and adolescents. Length and type of meditation have varied among studies. Mindfulness and yoga meditations sometimes overlap. They are presented separately.

Mindfulness Interventions

Mindfulness interventions include guided training for present moment awareness with a kind and accepting attitude (Sanger & Dorjee, 2016). A review of numerous studies suggests, overall, that meditation training is associated with important improvements for children and adolescents (Cheng, 2016). At least one study has found differences in the benefits gained from mindfulness related to temperament/personality (neuroticism, conscientiousness and extroversion, de Vibe et al., 2015). Mindfulness was especially beneficial for stress-sensitive older adolescents—i.e., for those with *neuroticism*, intervention effects on well-being were higher than for other youth; and effects on reducing study stress were higher for youth with high *conscientiousness*. Mindfulness has been associated with reduced hyper-critical self-beliefs in adolescents (ages 16–18; training by school teachers; Sanger & Dorjee, 2016). It has enhanced older adolescents' task-relevant inhibitory control of attention (e.g., ability to disengage from task-irrelevant stimuli) and perceived mental competency. Enjoyment of the training has been associated with target response accuracy.

Problems like poor sleep have been linked to a number of problems—e.g., poor sleep was linked to reduced treatment success, even if treatment improved baseline sleep problems (e.g., CBT for OCD, ages 7–17, Ivarsson & Skarphedinsson, 2015). Meditation is associated with improvements in sleep quality, calmness or relaxation, and positive thinking, as well as with reductions in impulsivity, anger, anxiety, and behavior problems (Cheng, 2016). Parents with mindfulness training also have reported reduced stress and anxiety. Both amelioration of depressive symptoms and changes in whole brain networks have occurred with meditation—e.g., returned to connectivity states usually found in healthy controls (for MDD patients; N = 13 university students, 40-day training, Yang et al., 2016). Cheng pointed out that children have attained better quality of life, better academic performance, better mental well-being, and better parent–child relationships. EFs also have improvement after meditation—e.g., for a community sample (N = 198, ages 12–18, Quach, Jastrowski Mano, & Alexander, 2015), mindfulness meditation was linked to adolescents' improved working memory capacity (not for Hatha yoga without meditation or wait-listers with no practices). Practices included breathing techniques, formal meditation with focusing of attention, and discussion for a total of 45 min., twice per week for 4 weeks—participants were encouraged to meditate daily for 15–30 minutes. In Quach's study, all three groups showed some reduced stress (waitlist, Hatha yoga, and mindfulness groups; using a stress test designed for adolescents was important).

Mindfulness and Metta-Based Trauma Therapy (MMTT)

The six therapeutic principals of mindfulness and metta include remaining in the present, increased experiential awareness (e.g., sensory, emotion states), letting go of distress (letting distresses pass by; greater detachment from harmful impulses and desires), metta (increased loving kindness and compassion), re-centering and de-centering (greater safety in own body; increased ability for joy and pleasure, increased ability to tolerate bodily distress), and acceptance and change (recognizing what can and cannot be changed; acting on what can be changed, https://mmtt.ca, Paul Frewen). The MMTT website provides access to several guided meditation practices—e.g., Candlelight—concentration; Mindfulness breathing practices; breathing combined with imagery and affirmations—e.g., safety, freedom from suffering, less pain, peace, strength—and a journaling technique. Body scan techniques (e.g., focusing on and labeling physical sensations in different parts of the body) are used toward greater safety, awareness, and comfort in the bodily self. For older youth, MMTT will be adding a number of new, guided meditation videos—recorded using 360-degree video. They can be viewed in 2D or viewed in 3D with a VR headset (personal communication, Paul Frewen, 10-19-18).

Mindfulness and metta-based approaches have been shown to improve self-regulation and to assist recovery from TSRD. Independent of self-reported past psychiatric history and current PTSD and other symptoms, website users endorsed the credibility of interventions for improving self-regulation and well-being and for reducing PTSD symptoms, anxiety, depressive, and dissociative experiences (N = 177, Frewen, Rogers, Flodrowski, & Lanius, 2015b). Users also reported the ease, helpfulness, and informational value of the methods provided online. Participants found the guided and non-guided meditation practices more helpful than a journaling exercise. Those with higher PTSD symptoms less often endorsed metta (loving kindness) meditations than others.

Optional questionnaires related to the individual's website experience, an "automatic thought record" (then re-evaluation and replacement of thoughts; patterned after CBT), and a questionnaire related to trauma symptoms are available on the site (optional). For researchers who may want to use the site for youth studies, non-copyrighted questionnaires with standard format Likert-scales that are appropriate to a study-population can be administered within the MMTT site at specified timings (e.g., daily, weekly, monthly). Usernames can be administered such that a specific group of individuals can be identified with individual-level and group-level results downloadable from the site in a secure way (personal communication, Paul Frewen, 10-19-18).

Yoga Interventions

Yoga has been used effectively for the treatment of a number of clinical conditions—e.g., TSRD; comorbid conditions—e.g., insomnia, anxiety, and depression (Salmon, Lush, Jablonski, & Sephton, 2009; Spinazzola et al., 2011). It has reduced stress and improved quality of life and emotional well-being. To reduce trauma symptoms, yoga methods include breath-work, postures, meditation, and/or rhythmic movement (e.g., Spinazzola et al., 2011). Spinazzola et al. (2011) suggest that, for chronically trauma-exposed youth, yoga practices permit reconnection to and eventually feeling safe in their bodies. Meditation has sometimes been used with other techniques or activities (e.g., art, CBT, DBT, dance, play, physical education, music). Yoga treatments have been used effectively for traumatized adults (e.g., 20-week program reduced PTSD and dissociation, Price et al., 2017)—e.g., Trauma-Sensitive Yoga includes postures and movement, mindful in-the-moment attention, and breathing exercises. It has reduced extreme states of intrusive imagery or of constriction, and it has increased calmness, self-care, self-acceptance, positive expectations, and well-being for adults (Rhodes, 2015). Women reported improved connection with and a better sense of ownership and control over their bodies, emotions, and thoughts. For youth (e.g., for ages 12–21, Spinazzola et al., 2011), yoga has improved emotion regulation (Arch & Craske, 2006), has modulated sympathetic nervous system function and improved heart rate variability (Brown & Gerbarg, 2009), and has reduced PTSD (Descilo et al., 2010). Yoga practices have been linked to brain changes, e.g., in distinct cortical networks (Thomas, Jamieson, & Cohen, 2014), reduced cortisol levels (Evans, Sternlieb, Tsao, & Zeltzer, 2009), improved immune function (Infante et al., 2014), improved skill functioning (e.g., EF, Luu & Hall, 2015), reduced PTSS, and reduced depression, while increasing behavioral activation and mindfulness (Price et al., 2017). For example, meditation has been shown to increase brain gray matter concentration involved in learning, memory, emotion regulation, self-referential processing, and perspective-taking (Hölzel et al., 2011). Hatha yoga (physical postures—asanas) has shown benefit for EF in healthy adults (including older adults), children, and adolescents as well as in incarcerated, impulsive individuals and medical populations (not multiple sclerosis; Luu & Hall, 2015). It has increased brain GABA levels, which has been shown to be low in individuals with PTSD (Glossary—GABA).

Peaceful Play Yoga

Peaceful Play Yoga is administered by a trained/registered yoga teacher (Thygeson et al., 2010). Yoga practice was conducted in a dimly lit, empty room with relaxing instrumental music playing in the background. The 45-minute class included standardized, noncompetitive yoga practices—i.e., an opening seated meditation; warm-up and centering postures, including standing poses, balance poses, cool down/spinal twists, and final resting pose—and was modified as needed (e.g., for those with poor leg strength). The developmentally appropriate yoga curriculum included safe and easily executed yoga poses, and it stressed inner peace. In addition to meditation, the class was a blend of active and restorative (restful) Hatha (physical) yoga poses. For cancer patients, although children's anxiety was normal pre- and post-intervention, adolescents' and parents' anxiety was reduced (ages 6–18; Thygeson et al., 2010).

Exercise

Even for non-traumatized adolescents, exercise training has been linked to happier mood (e.g., Rocheleau, Webster, Bryan, & Frazier, 2004; Rusby, Westling, Crowley, & Light, 2014). For example, Qigong exercise has been linked to reduced depression, anger, anxiety, and fatigue scores (Johansson, Hassmen, & Jouper, 2008). Some exercise forms have been related to improved EFs—e.g., aerobic exercise was linked to improved inhibitory control, WM, planning, and to brain growth; resistance training was associated with inhibitory control and planning (not WM; Luu & Hall, 2015).

Increases in either duration or exertion of exercise has increased improvements—i.e., in negative mood and exhaustion (N = 135, adults and adolescents ages 16–58, weight training or cardiovascular exercise; Rocheleau et al., 2004). Females showed greater improvement in exhaustion. Adult and child studies also have shown that exercise is associated with the reduction of specific PTS and depressive symptoms and improvements in quality of life (see Chapter 13). For example, controlling for gender and lifetime number of trauma exposures, Harte, Vuajnovic, and Potter (2015) found that vigorous-intensity exercise (but not light- or moderate-intensity exercise) was significantly, inversely related to severity of hyperarousal symptoms (N = 108, ages 18–65). Vigorous-intensity activities also have negatively related to alcohol use coping for trauma-exposed adults (N = 58, ages 18–51; Medina et al., 2011). In the second week of adjunct exercise, Schuch et al. (2015) found reductions in depression and improvements in quality of life for inpatient depressed patients (N = 50). Individuals with an extensive child abuse history have had more emotion regulation difficulties and less emotion-self-awareness, which in turn has been related to lower self-esteem, more depression symptoms, somatization, PTSD, and physical illness (N = 89, Carroll, 2012). Although domains of emotion regulation were most significant in predicting physical and psychological well-being, beyond child abuse or exercise, undergraduates who exercised more frequently reported less difficulty engaging in goal-directed behaviors, when experiencing negative emotions.

Other Adjunct and Preventive Methods

A number of treatments have been used to reduce symptoms that interfere with treatment or for prevention. For example, *Seeking Safety* (Litt, 2013) teaches safe coping skills and has been used effectively with adults and adolescents for comorbid PTSD and substance use (see Ford, 2018). To follow are discussions of writing tasks and school-based interventions (see also Chapter 13). Writing tasks have been used for a number of problems—e.g., writing trauma narratives is among trauma-related writing tasks used for assessment, to record in-session work, and for dissociation reduction. School-based interventions have been used for skill improvement, for prevention of symptoms, and as intervention sites following traumas.

Writing Tasks

Writing tasks have been used to assist a number of treatment issues—e.g., dissociation reduction, improved self-esteem, processing or assessing traumas (e.g., narrative coherence), depression, anxiety, worry (see WOJ to follow). For example, individuals with low self-esteem have reported lower closeness to and perceived less regard from close partners than comparisons (Peterson,

Bellows, & Peterson, 2015). A perspective-taking writing task has improved closeness and perceptions for individuals with low self-esteem (Peterson et al., 2015). Subjects were directed to "adopt the perspective of this person and imagine a day in the life of this individual as if you were that person, looking at the world through [your partner's] eyes and walking through the world in his/ her shoes" (Peterson et al., 2015, p. 161).

Problems may occur when trauma survivors do not develop a clear understanding of the trauma—e.g., psychological problems; dissociation; incoherent or fragmented trauma narratives; inner confusion, distress (Mundorf & Paivio, 2011). Narratives tend to improve for individuals whose trauma symptoms have improved. Hence, narrative quality has provided an index of trauma disturbance. As discussed (Chapter 13), methods that reduce in-session dissociation have helped to improve treatment success. Both emotion-focused (facts + related emotions) and fact-focused writing tasks (about a specific trauma/stressful experience) have produced statistically significant symptom reductions in trauma avoidance, intrusion, and hyperarousal symptoms and in associated emotional distress (Hirai et al., 2012; Sloan et al., 2007). Compared to an online writing task emphasizing the facts of a traumatic experience, an online expressive writing task emphasizing expression of emotions associated with a traumatic or stressful experience was most effective for decreasing psychological symptoms for participants 5 weeks later (N = 183 Hispanic undergraduate students with trauma histories, Hirai et al., 2012). Emotion-focused posttrauma work may temporarily increase distress. In both cases, the task increased negative affect after writing.

The Worry Outcome Journal (WOJ)

Worry has been related to temperament, genetics, environmental stressors or threats, and/or traumas. Higher levels of anxiety and worry have been linked to higher estimations of negative outcomes (e.g., found in GAD; LaFreniere & Newman, 2016). Some evidence suggests that tracking worries and their costs, estimated outcomes, and actual outcomes (an adjunct method) demonstrates that most outcomes are not negative and that individuals cope better in most instances than anticipated. The Worry Outcome Journal (WOJ; LaFreniere & Newman, 2016) provides a method of tracking worries. The aim of WOJ is to help individuals to (1) mindfully attend to experiences (more comprehensively and objectively), (2) create more realistic predictions, (3) recognize the problems worry may cause (e.g., distress and interference), and (4) alter beliefs that excessive worrying is in some way worthwhile. The process includes keeping a record of worry-related predictions—i.e., what they are worried about; expectations of future negative outcomes—and noting the actual outcomes when they occur. Youth recorded (paper log; then online entry) (1) cost estimates: a. the degree of distress caused by each worry (scale of 1 = no distress to 7 = severe distress) and b. a best estimate of "How much time did the worry take, since I first had the worry?"; (2) probability estimates: two estimates of the worry's probable outcome—a. rates of how likely they felt it was that the feared outcome would occur (gut feelings or intuition), and b. how likely "a person would logically conclude the worried outcome would occur, if they were thinking as realistically as possible" (imagining the most logical person in the world was estimating, p. 832); (3) Actual outcome: youth marked whether or not the feared outcome came true (recording all outcomes). Probability estimates aim to train youth in realistic prediction formation, to draw attention to any discrepancy between subjective predictions and effortful objective forecasting, and to teach a way to gain distance from worries by taking the perspective of "the most rational person."

In a study of undergraduates, WOJ youth recorded worries and tracked outcomes, rated worry distress, interference, and expected outcome probabilities (LaFreniere & Newman, 2016). Control group youth completed a thought log record of their everyday thoughts and rated the associated distress. All youth were prompted four times daily via text message to record their data related to the preceding 2 hours, and they were also encouraged to record as worries occurred. Although Both methods had positive results, more WOJ than thought log control youth no longer met criteria for GAD, suggesting it is an effective adjunct method for GAD. WOJ users experienced a significant reduction in worry (maintained at 20-day follow-up) compared to controls, with decreases in beliefs about uncontrollability of thoughts compared to those using a thought log (10-day practice; clinically, generally used for 8–16 weeks; simple slopes analysis of beliefs; N = 51 undergraduates, not seeking treatment for GAD symptoms). WOJ did not reduce positive worry beliefs (LaFreniere & Newman, 2016).

> A participant may find that worry "isn't worth it" because its in-the-moment costs are high and it's inaccurate, yet still believe worry serves some positive functions (i.e., is motivating, shows caring and conscientiousness, lessens the impact of negative emotional shifts). Individuals without GAD hold similar levels of positive worry beliefs.
>
> *(Lucas LaFreniere, personal communication, 10-15-18)*

A secondary analysis has found that 91.4% of participants' worries did not come true, on average. Each individual's unique percentage of untrue worries mediated treatment effects (LaFreniere & Newman, submitted).

School-Based Interventions

Both youth without direct trauma exposures and those directly exposed and/or under continued or potential threat, with ongoing fears of trauma—e.g., terrorism, war-related conflict, school shootings—may show PTS or other symptoms that reduce resilience and functioning (see Chapter 13; Gelkopf & Berger, 2009). Following traumas, schools are an ideal setting for reaching large numbers of children in an environment that is familiar to and normal for them (Gelkopf & Berger, 2009; Nader, 2008). School-based programs also have aided prevention or reduction of negative effects after subsequent traumas. Teachers, peers, and administrators may be a part of evaluation and treatment efforts (Nader & Pynoos, 1993; Pynoos & Nader, 1988).

Teachers have often played an important role in school-based interventions. Although a number of factors contribute to school climate and a youth's experience at school (see Nader, 2012c), teachers are important to a youth's functioning and can play an important role in recovery. Ginott (1972) has purported that the teacher is the "decisive element in the classroom" (pp. 15–16)—his/her personal approach creates the climate and his/her daily mood determines the weather. He stated,

> As a teacher, I possess tremendous power to make a child's life miserable or joyous. I can be a tool of torture or an instrument of inspiration. I can humiliate or humor, hurt or heal. In all situations it is my response that decides whether a crisis will be escalated or de-escalated, and a child humanized or de-humanized.
>
> *(pp. 15–16)*

School-based preventive intervention programs have reduced behavior problems, increased resilience, improved developmental skills, and provided the skills to reduce or prevent PTS symptoms after exposure (see methods in Chapter 13). For example, students in Spain in a school-based emotional intelligence training program had lower levels of anger, physical and verbal aggression, hostility, personal distress, and fantasy (tendency to transport self imaginatively into fictitious characters' actions and emotions) compared to controls (N = 590, 11–17-year-olds, Castillo et al., 2013). Fantasy levels have been previously linked to social dysfunction—e.g., shyness, loneliness, social anxiety, and certain violent behaviors. By providing strategies to manage thoughts and physical changes that may arouse hostility and anger, training assisted youth to solve challenging situations more peacefully and improved empathic skills (particularly for boys; no differences found in perspective-taking). Similarly, some evidence suggests the greater effectiveness of threat assessment methods, which encourage teacher connection to students in order to reduce the likelihood of school aggression or shootings (in contrast to zero tolerance policies; DeMitchell & Hambacher, 2016; Daniels et al., 2010a, b; Nader, 2012c). A number of school-based preventive interventions have raised resilience and reduced the likelihood of posttraumatic symptoms or injuries (e.g., through bullying, school shootings, violence threat; see Nader, 2012c; see Chapters 9, 13). An additional program that has been used with high school youth is presented here.

Enhancing Resiliency Among Students Experiencing Stress and Promoting Prosocial Orientation (ERASE-SPS)

ERASE-SPS (Berger & Manasra, 2005) is a school-based, teacher delivered intervention that seeks to build resiliency, strengthen resources, and prevent and reduce trauma symptoms in students currently without direct exposure to terrorism or war events (Gelkopf & Berger, 2009). For school-age youth (grades 1–3 and 3–7, secondary school), it is a skill-oriented program aimed at increasing students' and teachers' coping skills, empathy, compassion, and prosocial orientation (e.g., valuing a shared/common humanity, tolerance toward others; personal communication, Rony Berger, 10-12-18). ERASE-SPS utilizes cognitive behavioral, narrative, and somatic interventions combined with a mindfulness approach. Teacher training lasts between 24 and 30 hours total and can be provided in a two- or three-day workshop. Weekly or bi-monthly supervision sessions (two hour) are provided for a minimum of six sessions, depending on the teacher's needs. Parents are required to attend two sessions—one before ERASE-SPS begins for their children and one in the middle of implementation. Additionally, teachers meet with parents for feedback during the program. Another feature of the program is that students take the program methods home via their workbooks. They are asked to teach and practice with family members (including parents) the skills and practices learned in the program (personal communication, Rony Berger, 10-15-18). Consequently, many utilize the methods in the home environment.

The short version of ERASE-SPS for students is 12 weekly 90 min. segments delivered by homeroom teachers during the school year, across three months. The long version is 16 classroom sessions (90 min). The structure of each session is as follows: homework review, a warm-up introduction, an experiential exercise, psychoeducational material, skill building, and a closure exercise followed by a new homework assignment. The program includes personal resource identification, developing sensory-motor strategies to control body-responses during stressful situations, promotion of emotional self-awareness, emotional self-regulation (e.g., cognitive coping skills; controlling anger/rage), increasing coping (e.g., with grief, fear), strengthening the support system, boosting self-esteem, dealing with negative thoughts, and future planning. Student sessions are designed as follows: Session 1. psychoeducation, 2. strengthening personal coping style, 3. body empowerment, 4. emotion awareness, 5. developing empathy (toward self [self-compassion] and others), 6. cognitively controlling emotions, 7. promoting independent/critical thinking, 8. recognizing group/personal biases/prejudices, 9. overcoming fears (e.g., of the other), 10. dealing with collective and personal anger and hate, 11. coping with grief and loss, 12. boosting self-esteem, 13. building a social shield, 14. learning to accept the other (shared humanity), 15. developing a prosocial attitude and active bystander behaviors, and 16. seeking a better future.

ERASE-S has been used successfully in multiple countries (e.g., Israel, Africa, Sri Lanka) and for a number of symptoms/reactions (14 as of 10-15-18, personal communication, Rony Berger). For Israeli seventh to eighth graders (N = 114, ages 12–14.5 males, Gelkopf & Berger, 2009), although exposure levels were lower than for some regions, the youth reported being present just prior to, during, or just after a terrorist attack or had planned to be in the location of the attack; had a close friend in the attack; knew someone who was hurt or who died in an attack (none were personally injured). They had much higher pre-treatment symptoms than another sample of youth without exposure to terrorism in Israel (n = 312, Pat-Horenczyk et al., 2007). Compared to the control group, ERASE-S youth had lower PTSD symptoms, depression, somatic complaints, and functional problems (Gelkopf & Berger, 2009). For adolescents with significant exposure to ongoing war conditions (e.g., constant mortar shelling, missile attacks; Israel, Gaza region), students showed significant reductions in symptoms after the ERASE-S school intervention—e.g., PTSD symptoms, functional impairment, somatic complaints, and generalized anxiety (N = 154, ages 11–13, Berger, Gelkopf, & Heineberg, 2012). A small group of students showed increases in symptoms (Berger et al., 2012), suggesting the need for additional interventions (see Chapter 13).

The training program has also shown positive effects for teachers or other helpers. After the Sri Lankan tsunami, ERASE-S was culturally adapted in cooperation with Sri Lankan professionals (e.g., emphasis on body processes, local names for normal reactions and gender differences, local systems of coping; Gelkopf, Ryan, Cotton, & Berger, 2008). Some of the CBT methods had to be modified as well—e.g., challenging negative thoughts and flexing rigid positions were ineffective and were replaced by the Buddhist concept of accepting and making peace with experiences or with accusing spirits of dead relatives; narrative techniques included identifying family sources of pride and inspiration (enforcing the cultural value of elders). Because of loss of social support networks, increased emphasis was given to improving children's social skills, social networks, and coping with loss. Of 62 education and mental health volunteers enlisted, 25 were in ERASE-S training and 37 controls participated in a befriending seminar. ERASE-S was associated with significantly improved perceived professional self-efficacy and sense of mastery, optimism toward the future, increased coping ability.

The current program version (described above) includes prosocial aspects. It has shown promise in reducing attitudes of prejudice and discrimination toward minority students as well as in increasing resilience and improving reactions. For third to sixth graders exposed to the 2008 Gaza War with high PTSS and significant stereotyping and discriminatory tendencies (e.g., toward Arab & Ethiopian children; N = 99 intervention, 101 controls; 15% higher probability of PTSD than 2012 study group), ERASE-SPS was strongly linked to reductions in reactions—PTS, anxiety, somatic complaints, and functional impairment (two months after intervention; Berger, Gelkopf, Heineberg, & Zimbardo, 2016). There was a strong link between PTS symptom reduction and changes in attitudes toward Arabs, suggesting that psychological distress and threat contribute to exclusionist attitudes and discriminatory behaviors. For youth in Sub-Saharan Africa, who live in conditions of daily chronic adversity—poverty, serious health issues, physical and sexual abuse, armed conflicts—with little access to mental health care, an ERASE-SPS school intervention was associated with significant improvements in somatic complaints, hyperactivity, anxiety, prosocial behavior, social difficulties, academic achievement, disciplinary problems, and functional impairment (compared to controls; N = 183, fourth to sixth graders; medium to large effects; Berger et al., in press). Improvements had persisted at the 8-month follow-up. Although the program was effective across adversities—e.g., children living at home or in orphanages; with or without parental loss—there were some differences. ERASE-SPS proved more effective for children in orphanages in improvements in academic achievement; more effective in reducing behavioral problems for children with parental loss; and more effective for boys in reducing hyperactivity and increasing prosocial behavior (Berger et al., in press). As has been demonstrated in other sections of this book, children with greater deficits or problems often benefit the most from interventions.

Conclusions

Specific issues are important to interviewing adolescent youth, for particular personality styles, and for the treatment of trauma or specific symptoms (e.g., dissociation, suicidality), personality disorders, and complicated reactions. Treatments often address aspects of attachment, reflective function, and self-regulation. Adjunct methods (e.g., meditation, writing tasks) have helped with a number of problems and with the neurobiological effects of traumas.

Caregivers remain important to youth and can be an important part of the therapeutic process. Although attachments to caregivers and to the clinician providing treatment are important, adolescents require respect, tolerance for ambivalence, and the ability to give input in the treatment process. Personality or temperamental traits and interactional style are important in treating adolescents. Some will need time before connecting and/or will need to take time to ponder before giving information. Some will answer superficially unless assisted to give more detail. Nevertheless, adolescents sometimes resist and complain about participation, even when continuing to participate. Neurobiological changes in adolescence make some issues particularly important to address. For example, self-image and identity formation, risk-taking and/or impulse control, and coping efficacy will likely need attention. Methods in this and earlier chapters have been used effectively with adolescents. Adult methods generally need adaptation for adolescents.

Part VI

Issues for Working with, Teaching, or Living with Youth Exposed to Adversity

17

Assisting Youth Recovery After Trauma or Adversity

The findings presented in this book have shown some important influences on child development. Some things are very clear. Others need additional study with larger, broad study populations and multiple variables assessed. Here are some clear findings presented in the book.

1. Traumatic and non-traumatic adversity (e.g., family conflict, divorce, illness) can undermine a child's development, functioning (e.g., inter-relating, perspective-taking, academics), and life trajectory.
2. Caregiver–child attachment relationships and parenting also have long-term, dynamic effects on a child's life, functioning, health, and mental health, providing buffering or risk.
3. Combined variables and numbers of trauma/adversity exposures influence life course and posttrauma outcomes. For example, child variables (e.g., genetics, personality, skills), environmental variables (e.g., caregiving, family, community, SES), trauma-related variables (e.g., nature, intensity; elements of the event; peri-traumatic emotions), support systems (e.g., ethnic, family, peer, spiritual), and child and family history (e.g., mental health, traumas, experiences) combine as risk or protective factors for a child. Age and personality matter.
4. Adversity has had important impacts on brain and neurobiological development and on levels of reactivity (e.g., cortisol/HPA axis reactivity; to environment).
5. Humans are social beings. A sense of belonging and effective support as well as safety and an enriched, interactive environment are essential to development and thriving.
6. A number of interventions, and often combined interventions, can help to repair the effects of trauma and adversity. Methods have aided developmental difficulties (e.g., improved EFs) and/or have restored positive emotions and flow or flourishing as well.
7. It is essential to help children to feel safe and to reduce arousal before trying to process traumas.
8. Preventive interventions (e.g., school programs; meditation) can assist the development of resilience factors that reduce the likelihood or severity of negative outcomes.
9. Specific programs assist the repair of trauma or adversity's impact on the developing brain and neurobiology.

The Nature of Efforts Toward Repair

Attention to the adults in a child's life, to the timing and nature of interventions, and to the whole child and her/his individuality has been important to outcomes (Chapter 4). Worsening of symptoms has occurred when interventions have been ill-timed or offered by untrained individuals (see, e.g., Hobfoll et al., 2007; Nader, 2008). Children's reactions, symptom levels, treatment needs, and recovery also are influenced by their personalities, genes, styles (e.g., preferred grieving or comforting style), coping skills/choices, perceptions, and previous experiences (e.g., traumas, family, community). These areas need greater study and may require modification of assessments and interventions.

Parents, Teachers, and Clinicians

In order to assist children's optimal development, parents must do more than provide sensitive care, teachers more than provide a learning environment, and clinicians more than offer learned interventions. For young children, evidence has shown the importance of warmth, of synchrony, and of following a child's lead. Jackson and Decety (2004) have pointed out, "the way our nervous system is organized and tailored by evolution provides the basic mechanism for resonating with others ..." (in Decety & Jackson, 2004, p. 92). Mother–infant synchrony predicts attachment security, moral orientation, empathy, and, from infancy, predicts later adjustment (Feldman, 2010; Chapter 5). For clinicians, teachers, and parents, establishing an age-appropriate synchrony and following a child's lead, when it can be done without endangering the child, is important across child age groups (see McMahon & Forehand, 2003; Chapter 7—ABC method, Child's Game). Cognizance of when to teach, when to permit exploration or learning, when to intervene or set limits, and when to reduce arousal helps to provide a safe environment after traumas and for children's positive development and recovery. Recognizing individual differences is also essential (Box 17.1). Although, as a field, we have much more to learn about how individual traits and conditions influence treatment needs and outcomes, recognizing individuality and variations in needs is a must (Chapters 4, 10—INSIGHTS).

Box 17.1 Clash of Personality Types

A mother divorced her husband after discovering that he had molested their adopted daughter for years. She clearly loved her daughter, and her complaints often seemed to be part of her worry about her daughter. Nevertheless, this extraverted mother complained repeatedly about her Southeast Asian daughter's introverted traits and her taking too long to answer as well as her lack of trust and negativity (likely trauma-related). The daughter's negativity seemed to increase with her perceptions of her mother's dislike of her and her mother's apparent annoyance with her. The mother also complained about a few other cautious or introverted people she knew. She said, "People like that just want to be negative. They don't want things to be better." She was asked, "Who would really want such a life?" The pause after the question was important for her. It seemed to mark a turning point. During the course of her daughter's treatment, she learned about what was normal after traumas and discovered, with better understanding, some of the traits and preferences normal for someone raised until school age in Southeast Asia. An avid reader, among the mother's homework tasks were reading parts of a book or articles about introversion (e.g., Cain, 2013) and about Southeast Asian culture. She also learned more about trait-related preferences and behaviors. Although the differences in personalities continued to influence some of her attitudes, the mother became more patient and accepting of her daughter (with some fatigue-related relapses). Several years later, after her daughter had a child, she was very proud (and pleasantly surprised) about what a good and conscientious mother her daughter was and how well she handled her life.

Note:
All case examples are disguised, may be combined cases, and have had details changed to protect individuals.

In addition, after traumas, in order to have the capacity to consistently assist children toward recovery, good self-care is important for caregivers, teachers, and clinicians. It is likely that goodness-of-fit of method, therapist/clinician, and child influence a child's recovery (see Box 17.1; Table 17.1). This aspect of method selection may also be important to a clinician's proneness to or safety from burn-out.

Table 17.1 Jungian-Based Trait Preferences—Clashes May Occur If a Youth Is the Opposite Style of an Adult

TENDENCIES THAT MAY INFLUENCE ADULT–YOUTH INTERACTIONS
Interaction style: Introversion (I) vs Extraversion (E) (inward versus outward orientation) *Extraverted adults* (e.g., teachers, parents, clinicians) (Murphy, 2008)—like active, energetic classrooms/homes; like quick answers in discussions or to questions; like people to speak out and to act; may like to ask questions or offer suggestions to engage youth *Introverted adults* (e.g., teachers, parents, clinicians) (Murphy, 2008)—like quiet classrooms/homes; may assign more independent tasks; may wait longer between questions and answers; may not feel like socializing at the end of the day ***Youth*** *Introverted youth*—need to think or process before sharing; need time before responding; may need extra time to trust; may have difficulty or need to process before expressing emotions; likes quiet; needs alone time; not as readily sociable *Extraverted youth*—may want to talk in order to process an idea or feeling; may gain energy from being around others or from doing; respond quickly; express emotions more readily; for difficult tasks, may require quiet
Perceptual style: Sensing (S) versus Intuition (N) (preferred manner of gathering or perceiving information: focus on concrete versus abstract; facts/details vs symbolic/theoretical) *Sensing adults:* may use multiple examples to demonstrate a point; may require a number of assignments to demonstrate knowledge of previously introduced concepts; may assess or look for recall of detailed, specific information; use directions and specific details for assigning tasks; provide information in small units, permit processing before moving to a new topic *Intuitive adults:* teach or work with stories and themes, symbolic connections, metaphors; use intuition to expand on ideas; may use themed units from month to month; rely on narrative tests or creative projects to assess learning or progress; may prefer to inspire by brainstorming all possibilities and/or providing open-ended options ***Youth*** *Sensing youth:* notice details and may become bogged down in them; prefer using skills already learned; like things definite and measurable; prefer precise directions; rely on experience to understand concepts; often memorize well; recall facts and specific information; like to study the practical and real *Intuitive youth:* greater focus on the whole or the theme than on parts, on possibilities rather than on what is concrete; future-focused; prefer to study new skills than to repeat or rehearse learned ones; learn best when presentation includes variety; enjoy designing more than doing projects; may skip over facts or get them wrong because of focusing on making connections among things
Decision-making style: Thinking vs Feeling (T vs F) (use objective, logical decision making vs subjective, personal judgment criteria; evaluate and make judgments based on objective criteria or logic vs evaluating based on personal, interpersonal, or universal values as guideposts) *Thinking adults*—value mastery; may use critical feedback more than supportive feedback; maintain a standard of learning or processing; value fairness *Feeling adults*—value effort; use supportive more than critical feedback; like cooperative groups; praise frequently; address multiple needs of the youth

continued

Table 17.1 Continued

Youth
Thinking youth: ask "Why?", value independence, enjoy competition, like problem-solving, use logic to problem-solve; need recognition for accomplishments; self-evaluate then seek feedback
Feeling youth: need to feel connected; try to please others; enjoy helping others; make decisions in accordance with own values; may ignore personal needs while caring for others; need appreciation for their work or service; like feedback from others before evaluating self

Orientation: Judging vs Perceiving (J vs P) (wanting things settled [closure] vs keeping options open [flexibility or need to continue])
Judging adults—plan ahead and want to follow the plan; prefer to decide and resolve questions quickly; value and use preparation; tendency to separate work and play (play follows completion of tasks)
Perceiving adults—value flexibility and may not fully plan a session/day; may not finish projects started—may never feel finished gathering enough information; like to incorporate fun into the learning or doing process; may become absorbed in a task and lose track of time

Youth
Judging youth—prefer completing one project before starting another; don't want to reconsider an issue once a decision is made; enjoy structure and predictability; like having a schedule to follow; like having a plan that can be followed; prefer to plan for possibilities (manner of controlling their world); natural ability to manage time
Perceiving youth—enjoy projects (the experience, the doing) and may not need to or enjoy the finishing of them (or may enjoy the finalizing but never feel finished gathering enough information); handle unexpected changes well; act spontaneously; try to incorporate fun into work; adapt as events occur (manner of controlling their world); like to keep options open until a decision must be made

Notes:
Assessed personality or temperamental types have generally been divided into the 16 subcategories—INTP, INTJ, INFP, INFJ, ISTP, ISTJ, ISFP, ISFJ, ENTP, ENTJ, ENFP, ENFJ, ESTP, ESTJ, ESFP, ESFJ (see Murphy, 2008 for elaboration)—or into 4 main subcategories—_NT_, _NF_, _S_J, _S_P (see Berens, 2013 for elaboration); References: Alcock & Murphy, 1998; Berens, 2010, 2013, 2015; Berens & Nardi, 2004; Jung, 1971; Kiersey & Bates, 1978; Murphy, 2008; Oakland, Glutting, & Horton, 1996; much is theoretical, although some testing has occurred (and numerous individuals have taken the Myers-Briggs test). Theoretically, we all have each of the qualities but are often more strongly prone to 1 of the 2 qualities in each of the 4 sets of qualities (questionnaires: Myers-Briggs Type Indicator for adults; Murphy-Meisgeier Type Indicator for children).

Adaptability/Flexibility

From both child and clinician, flexibility can be important to outcomes and to a child's recovery. Adaptability is no longer seen as a single trait or skill (McClowry, 2002). Block and Block (1980) have suggested that ego-resilient individuals are "resourceful in adapting to change, flexible in deploying their resources to solve problems, and are good at analyzing the goodness-of-fit between situational demands and behavioral possibilities" (in Causadias et al., 2012). For example, a child's coping flexibility/adaptability and accurate assessment of situations are important when situations are actually uncontrollable (not an internal locus of control for all situations). Child-tailored support giving and methods are more important than assuming that a single coping style, support method, or intervention "fits all." Avoidance has been linked to higher levels of complicated grief symptoms, non-suicidal self-injury, and other negative outcomes. While overuse of avoidance has interfered with recovery, avoidance has also been linked to better outcomes (e.g., Chapter 4; Appendix—self-distancing). Failure to sometimes avoid trauma focus can reduce energy needed for facing or for assisting others to face traumatic material. Those providing services/care and traumatized children are likely to need periodic breaks from trauma focus.

The Clinician–Patient Relationship

Clinicians have a variety of views on the nature of the patient/client-clinician relationship. Some emphasize relationship and/or alliance, while others emphasize dignity and cooperation. Clinicians who believe that the relationship (e.g., transference; attachment; alliance) is key to recovery must demonstrate good self-monitoring skills (e.g., mindfulness of countertransference; recognition of attachment issues) and respect for boundaries, in order to prevent hindering treatment outcomes. Those who believe that alliance is over-rated still must be respected by the client and have the communication skills to make treatment desirable for caretakers and children. When clinicians work to establish rapport or alliance, among other things, it is important to be cognizant of trauma's impact on trust, be aware of differences in processing, be understanding of timing issues, and be open to a child or parent's personal road to connection. In any case, a positive connection of some type must be made in order for treatment to be complied with and/or effective. Clinicians' needs for skill in employing their chosen method has been demonstrated. Additionally, no matter what type of treatment is used, support systems (especially family; peer) are important to well-being and to recovery. For all child age groups, some level of caregiver participation is essential. Siblings and sometimes peers can assist as well. Pollack (2001) has suggested that the "potency of connection" of family relationships is what protects youth from emotional harm and protects others from being harmed by them. For example, thwarted belonging (e.g., relational or physical bullying) and traumas each are among frequent precursors to school shootings (see Nader, 2012c). For youth to thrive, for positive youth development, and for successful youth functioning, a combination of successes, the feeling of connection or belonging, feeling valued, and an ongoing sense of safety are essential.

Prevention

Trauma and other outcomes are influenced by many variables, and usually by multiple variables. Some solutions can be reasonably simple and preemptive (e.g., school interventions; early attachment interventions). Resilience and other protective factors, including secure attachment relationships and positive parenting, can be improved early in a child's life.

Resilience

Resilience (e.g., confidence, self-esteem, self-compassion, creativity) or other protective factors may reduce the likelihood or levels of posttrauma reactions, increase the likelihood of posttraumatic growth (Glossary), or shorten recovery (Chapter 4). Some children have shown resilience because of the way they perceive experiences. For example, some youth view adversity and traumatic experiences as challenges (Thabet, Tawahina, Punamäki, & Vostanis, 2015) or perceive themselves to have been successful in some way during an event (e.g., helping others, protecting self). Other factors (e.g., rejection) can undermine the effects of resilience. Time-limited school interventions have improved resilience and other skills and have been associated with later reduced levels of trauma (Chapters 10, 13, 16; Nader, 2012c). Risk or low resilience factors have had negative posttrauma and/or other problematic long-term associations (Chapter 4).

Attachment

For infants, insecure or disorganized attachments have had dynamic, ongoing consequences—e.g., in a child's interpersonal functioning and later psychological and behavioral outcomes (e.g., poorer social competence, externalizing; Chapters 4, 5). For example, insecure and disorganized attachments have been related to long-term posttraumatic reactions as well as to view of others, to expectations, and to behaviors (Chapters 9, 14). Something as simple as skin-to-skin contact with newborns can increase bonding. Even parents' attachment to a child before birth increases positive connection later (Chapter 5, e.g., Alhusen, Hayat, & Gross, 2013). Especially for high-risk parents and likely for all new parents, it is important to implement the programs that provide teaching and coaching beginning before or right after a birth and continue for a reasonable period of time to effect positive change. Findings for parenting style suggest that parent training is important as well.

Repair of Neurobiology and Restoration of Positive Emotions

In contrast to the potentially cascading negative effects of trauma, treatment can result in cascading transformations, and flourishing may follow treatment (Fosha, 2009; Boxes 3.1, 13.5). Mindfulness or yoga practices, rhythmic interventions, and other creative or adjunct methods have corresponded to positive posttrauma (PT) neurobiological changes and have assisted the return of positive emotions (e.g., more self-compassion, happiness). For trauma-exposed and non-exposed individuals, positive emotions, which sometimes have been enhanced by treatment, are linked to positive traits—e.g., high self-esteem, playfulness—as well as to better PT outcomes—e.g., better health; resilience; broadened attention and behavioral repertoires; normalized diurnal cortisol; better adjustment and relationships (Chapters 1, 3, 4; e.g., Colak et al., 2003; Fosha, 2009; Nader, 2008; Papa & Bonanno, 2008).

Flow/Flourishing

PTSD is among the identified leading causes of disability worldwide (see Brake et al., 2017; Kessler et al., 2012). Trauma may undermine many skills—e.g., cognitive, behavioral, coping; imagination, creativity, flexibility, and ease (e.g., in functioning, inter-relating, performing a talent). Posttrauma treatments aim to reduce the symptoms of trauma, improve functioning, repair disrupted relationships/support systems, and return a child to as normal a life trajectory as is possible. In addition to repair of the often-measured effects of trauma (e.g., symptoms and functioning), restoring the more positive aspects of self also is very important to life. Creativity, imagination, humor, and other aspects of self-skills, sometimes treated as non-essentials in mental health interventions, are important to functioning well. Trauma can disrupt the capacity for "flow" (Glossary)—automatic excelling or undistracted engagement that permits skill in performing a task/action. *Flourishing* has been defined as "deeply positive experiences of aliveness, hope, faith, clarity, agency, simplicity, compassion, joy, and truth" (Fosha, 2009, p. 252). Focus on a traumatic experience along with experiential processing can be a key to flourishing. Although more than one method has resulted in the return of positive emotions (e.g., Webb, 2002, 2004), for some methods positive emotions are not a matter of focus or assessment.

Narratives and Well-Being

A coherent narrative has been one sign of health or recovery (Chapters 1, 3, 9, 13, 16). Narrative coherence tends to improve for individuals whose trauma symptoms have improved. Restoring the ability for or the creation of a coherent narrative is a part of many treatment methods. Creating narratives, first from a distanced perspective (e.g., writing methods; re-wording) and/or increasing self-regulation skills, has helped avoidance-prone individuals to engage in treatment more effectively (e.g., those who are dissociation-prone or overuse physical, cognitive, or emotional self-distraction; Chapters 11, 13, 16). For children, restoring the ability to create and complete play narratives/stories or to engage in the other development-promoting aspects of play is similarly important (Chapter 1). Knowing when to follow a child's lead or, after traumas, when to facilitate or permit the child's own processing is a part of enhancing the growth promoting aspects of play. Community narratives are also important to ongoing recovery of individuals and communities, and our anticipation of them is needed (Chapter 3).

Although most interventions use combinations of methods, most treatments include some narrative processing. The coherence of narratives and questionnaires/scales on symptoms and functioning have been used to assess progress. It may be that, as we expand our views of recovery to include the return of flourishing or flow or other lost positive emotions and skills, narrative and other assessments will expand their scope as well. For children, full recovery, including the capacity for joy, has been observed by clinicians (e.g., Fosha, 2006; personally). It is important that assessments and treatments routinely include developmental and child-related long-term issues, including positive emotions and the ability to engage in a talent or effort with flow (Glossary).

The Need to Belong

Fears and doubts about whether others will meet the needs for belonging and acceptance can cause people "to behave in ways that erode relationships and their sense of well-being..." (Ayduk et al., 2000, p. 776). From birth, humans exhibit a need for belonging, for consistently sensitive response, and for synchronous interaction. As Powers, Somerville, Kelley, and Heatherton (2016) note, from an evolutionary perspective, the members of one' s social in-group provide the best potential for affiliation and fulfillment of belongingness needs (p. 1). At any age, the things that isolate a child from others—e.g., traits, low acculturation, exclusion—have been related to emotional and behavioral problems. Infants and children seem to thrive when delighted in, including in their individuality. Social isolation is a recognized stressor that negatively impacts the well-being of social species, including humans (Gilles & Polston, 2017). Sense of belonging to family, community, and group (e.g., strong cultural identity) has served as protective across development and following traumas (Chapters 14, 16). Social support is linked to better mental health outcomes (e.g., trauma levels), to increased productivity, and to better health (Gilles & Polston, 2017). A low sense of belonging and feeling a burden to others have been related to suicidality (see Chapters 4, 12, 15, 16).

Feeling Accepted

Although we are all similar in some ways, we are each unique in other ways (Box 17.2; Tables 17.1, A5.1–A5.2). Recognizing, accepting, and validating (often without words) those differences can assist children to feel a sense of belonging and of being valued. Many adult behaviors influence the well-being of youth. Sincere acceptance of a child's individuality is communicated, often subliminally. A mother asked if it affected her child that she just did not like him; she could not help liking his sibling better than she liked him. The answer is, "Yes." Even when a young child feels loved and/or cared about, it can be confusing (or worse) to feel in some ways unacceptable, unlikeable, or not valued (Boxes 3.2—Danya; 10.2, 12.1b; Chapter 4).

Incongruence between caregiver, teacher, or clinician and youth traits can result in the communication (in or out of awareness) that a child is not acceptable, not likeable, or not valued (Tables A5.1–A5.2; Boxes 10.2, 17.1). Such communication may result in a child's over-focus on the attitudes of others and on how to belong (e.g., first with adults; then with peers) at the expense of exploration and of skill development, of positive identity formation, and of personal talent development. In and out of treatment (no matter how much or how little *connection* a method requires), youth need acceptance and to be valued (e.g., see Chapter 16—Motivational Interviewing; Chapter 10—child-centered play therapy). Especially for children, thriving and enjoying life and relationships is assisted by feeling "delighted in" by at least one other person. When there has never been or is no longer the experience of delighting in and/or being delighted in, relationships reach transition points and likely need repair. Even though certain temperaments may make it difficult for others to delight in someone, such delight or peaceful good will can be healing. For a four-year-old boy (Box 10.2), after nonjudgmental, firm limit-setting, he became a very congenial, likeable, adorable child. It was easy to delight in his presence.

Box 17.2 The Tendency for Like to Vibrate in Synchrony with Like

a. In a concert, a Swami visiting from India played his sitar for a welcoming university audience. After stopping to tune the strings, he began to place small, folded pieces of paper over each string. He explained that there was more than one F note and that he would pluck one of the F notes. When he did, although the surrounding papers shook a little, only the paper on the other F note vibrated intensely enough to leap off of the string. The Swami explained that things that are similar vibrate in response to one another (see Nader, 1999).

After the concert, people were discussing his demonstration (see Table 17.1 for acronyms).

- An extraverted nurse (ENFJ) was heard to say that it made her think of how we all inter-relate and how groups of us are in tune with one another.
- An introverted teacher (INFP) said that he agrees that like people and things vibrate in synchrony with one another. People connect with like-minded people. "Even with teaching, not everyone resonates with what I'm teaching. Some seem to 'get it' almost like osmosis; others don't." He also said that because of "tuning in" with each other it helps us to better attune with and understand each other—we vibrate in synch with them. It's a choice. We can choose to become more attuned to other people.
- An introverted academician (INTP) wondered what implications it had for the response of DNA to DNA. He mentioned mirror neurons and theorized that our reactions to each other may include vibratory issues at the cellular level. Jokingly, "We got vibes, Man." He didn't know whether the connection between twins had been proven (not his field of study), but he did know that certain animal species chose mates based on particular vibrations (e.g., Red Mason Bees—thoracic vibrations of the male, Conrad & Ayasse, 2015; Amarillo fish—vibrate related to aggression avoidance or courtship, Medina et al., 2013), and that ailments can be diagnosed through sound vibrations (e.g., ultrasound of vibrated breast tissue, Alizad, Fatemi, Wold, & Greenleaf, 2004; broken or fractured bones, File, Wood, & Kreplick, 1998; soft tissues surrounding vascular injuries vibrate at audible and palpable frequencies, Sikdar et al., 2006). At home, he looked up DNA and vibration. Protein-protein association is critical for all cellular processes. He found that protein binding (e.g., oxygen to hemoglobin; medications to protein) and protein folding (the process by which a protein chain gains four-dimensional structure) have been observed to vibrate with high frequencies (e.g., Haliloglu, Keskin, Ma, & Nussinov, 2005)....
- An ESTJ accountant said that she wanted to find a sitar and try it and experiment with it to see if she could get a different result. She might tune her violin so that it had two A notes. She said, "It is a physical thing, although you could look at it symbolically—people are drawn together because there's something in the two of them that harmonizes. If you thought of them as notes, they'd sound nice and resonate with one another. One person is responding to what another puts out."

Attachment Style and Belonging

Attachment styles and posttrauma symptoms have influenced the need for or thwarted the ability to belong. Securely attached youth generally feel like they belong among others (Table A3.1). In contrast, insecurely attached youth may have chronically unmet needs for acceptance and belongingness, in addition to negative affective reactions to actual or imagined social exclusion or ostracism

(Chen, Hewitt, & Flett, 2015; Mikulincer & Shaver, 2007; Tables A3.2, A3.3). Bartholomew and Horowitz (1991) suggested that adults internal working models toward self and others are based on attachment classification as follows: *secure*—positive self and positive others; *preoccupied*—negative self and positive others; *dismissing/avoidant*—positive self and negative others; *fearful*—negative self and negative others. Preoccupied individuals have shown a particularly strong need to belong, feel accepted, and fit in, and a hypervigilance to rejection (and proneness to shame; see Chen et al., 2015; see also BPD, Chapters 11, 14, 16). Their consequent behaviors may challenge the ability to form and maintain mutually supportive close relationships. The thwarting of a capacity to interrelate (including the avoidance of relationships), whether by faulty attachments, exposure to potentially traumatic events, or other cause, can have long-term consequences across the lifespan. It must be addressed early to prevent long-term difficulties.

Information Needed

Among issues that need more study and need much larger study samples are the combinations of genes that influence outcomes and personalities; the ways traits (singly and in combination) relate to rapport, compatibility, and recovery; and the ways that many variables (and subcategories of variables) combine to influence reactions, treatment, and outcomes. For example, assessing the continuity of foster placement versus placement-interruption(s) when evaluating the consequences of child institutionalization has added important information to our knowledge base (e.g., BEIP, Chapter 7). Although we have learned a great deal from a large body of research, often only the data related to specific child behaviors or symptoms are analyzed. Something is lost in the exclusion of examples of some non-significant behaviors or symptoms. Examining detailed descriptions or at least some examples of many children (even outliers and those not in the significant group) may assist a better understanding of the nature and function of referential behaviors (Dice & Dove, 2011).

Children's Individuality

Although we examine groups of children for their common reactions, children are unique individuals with genetic make-ups, personalities, and past experiences. They experience differences in ongoing parenting and other environment-related factors; levels of resources and opportunities; past traumas; past successes or failures; and unique, personal experiences. The marked variability in reactions among individuals exposed to the same trauma or environmental risk suggests that genetic, environmental, and other variables play an important role in reactions (Caspi et al., 2010; Cisler, Amstadter, & Nugent, 2011; Nader & Fletcher, 2014; Table A4.1). For example, in the assessment and treatment of youth, personality matters (Boxes 16.1, 17.1; Tables 17.1, A5.1–A5.2)—e.g., as discussed, increasing inhibitory control for uninhibited children can be protective; increasing inhibitory control for inhibited children may have adverse effects (Chapter 12).

Genetics

As suggested earlier, stressors (e.g., traumatic; family or community stressors) interact with genetic vulnerabilities to increase the likelihood of their expression (Lau & Pine, 2008; Taylor, 2002). Hence, traumas are related to more than one type of disorder. Directly and through intergenerational transmission, genes influence traits, behaviors, psychopathology, and recovery (Champagne & Mashoodh, 2009; see Nader & Fletcher, 2014). Even though individual gene variations have been linked to a number of traits and outcomes, it is likely that multiple genes in synergistic combination relate to reactions and disorders (Cerda, Sagdeo, Johnson, & Galea, 2010; Munafo, 2012). Very large studies that examine gene combinations are needed in relation to trauma (Munafo, 2012; Chapter 4).

Personality

Assessments of personality and temperament vary. As well, traits have varied implications, because they often occur somewhere on a continuum—e.g., between extravert and introvert, between negative and positive emotionality, between the need for fixed guidelines and for flexible rules. Opposite traits may both exist to some degree (e.g., extraverted in some circumstances); and traits often vary with time and circumstances (e.g., stress level, mood, how well needs are met that day). Individuals with the same personality type differ in their life experiences, maturity levels, well-being, physical and psychological health, and, as Berens put it, in the levels of their spiritual development or evolvement (Linda Berens, personal communication, 2018).

Personality variables may influence PTS reactions and recovery as well as may suggest different posttrauma needs. For example, children with behavioral inhibition (Chapters 5, 8, 9; linked to an overly active amygdala and/or 5HTT short allele, Caspi et al., 2010, Taylor, 2002; linked to a gene combinations, Munafo, 2012), who generally react to new situations with wariness that fails to give way to curiosity and/or interest (as it does in other children, Taylor, 2002), have shown increased reactivity to their environments (Belsky & Pluess, 2009; Caspi et al., 2010) and increased vulnerability for posttraumatic reactions (see Nader & Fletcher, 2014; Weems et al., 2007). Such children respond best to a particular kind of parenting and soothing (see Taylor, 2002; Box 8.2). Although such children are unlikely to be turned into extraverts, parenting (and/or parent training) can assist such a child to learn social skills, to enhance strengths and talents, and ultimately to have a normal adulthood with a partner, friends, and interests that are rewarding (Nader, 2012c; Taylor, 2002; see Goodness-of-Fit: Clinician–Client/Patient, to follow; Table 17.1). Although personality types are discussed to some extent in earlier chapters (10, 16) and to follow (Table 17.1; Box 17.2; Goodness-of-Fit: Clinician–Client/Patient), more study is need on personality's relationship to outcomes and to treatment.

Preventing Burn-Out

Working with traumatized children can be rewarding, enriching, and demanding. Watching children recover from horrific experiences and the process of aiding them can be greatly rewarding experiences. After mass traumatic events, it can be a joyful experience assisting people and communities to regain a sense of safety and normalcy, seeing hope return, and seeing important physical, emotional, and psychological needs met. For some who intervene, trauma work is when they achieve "flow" and skilled action. Additionally, there is always something to learn from those who have endured traumas, and often opportunity to be inspired. Nevertheless, sometimes under stressful and demanding circumstances, trauma clinicians have been inundated with potentially distressing stories and/or images and the suffering of children and adults. Compassion fatigue, secondary or vicarious traumatization, empathic distress, and burn-out are among terms used to describe, for clinicians and rescue workers, a possible negative impact of working in the field of traumatic stress. Sometimes, the emotional contagion of trauma can be used as a therapeutic tool (e.g., provides insights for therapeutic use; Boulanger, 2018), and sometimes it must be otherwise addressed (Rothschild, 2006; see Glossary—emotional contagion).

Compassion fatigue can impact one personally and professionally by adversely affecting timing, synchrony, empathic communication, relationships, and the ability to provide effective clinical interventions (e.g., Kemper, 2016; Osofsky, 2009, 2011; Rothschild, 2006). Some indicators of compassion fatigue are increasing irritability and/or rejection of others, fatigue, over-identification, blaming the patient (projective identification), avoidance, premature shutdown of cases, emotional shutdown, confusion, feeling shaken by stories (e.g., things that could have happened to your own children), and/or helplessness (Osofsky, 2009, 2011: Rothschild, 2006). For prevention or recovery from burn-out, clinicians have employed a number of methods. Some of the methods that may assist therapists (e.g., mindfulness, Frewen, Dozois, Neufeld, & Lanius, 2012; Kemper, 2016) are also appropriate for parents and teachers (e.g., Coatsworth et al., 2010; Singh et al., 2010). Others are specific to the field (e.g., increased reflective supervision, Osofsky, 2009).

Clinicians with secondary traumatization (ST) may have symptoms similar to PTSD (e.g., intrusive memories, nightmares, emotional blunting or numbness, hyperarousal, hypervigilance, insomnia; e.g., Thomsen, Püttker, & Weberling, 2017). ST has been related to high levels and extreme exposure to others' trauma details, to a personal history of trauma, and to a high capacity for empathy (Thomsen et al., 2017). Trait emotional intelligence (mediated by problem-focused coping), adaptive coping, and emotion management ability, in contrast, have inversely related to compassion fatigue (Zeidner, Hadar, Matthews, & Roberts, 2013). Evidence suggests that emotional empathy (sensing the feelings of others), rather than cognitive empathy (perspective-taking), was associated with ST (N = 312, Püttker, Thomsen, & Bockmann, 2015 in Thomsen et al., 2017; N = 91, Thomsen et al., 2017). Thomsen and colleagues found that behavioral strategies such as planning to solve the stressor or refocusing on resources buffered the relationship between emotional empathy and ST. Emotionally empathic therapists had higher ST at time 2 only if they were unable to employ specific coping resources (e.g., refocus on planning; accommodative coping, see Glossary). Other strategies were directly and indirectly protective (e.g., longitudinal: social support, accommodative coping; cross-sectional: leisure time activities, supervision sessions).

Goodness-of-Fit

The term "goodness-of-fit" has been used in a number of ways (e.g., to describe temperament and child development; statistical analysis). In their "Goodness-of-Fit Model," Chess and Thomas (1977) proposed that a child's temperament interacts with the environment to influence outcomes—i.e., with some cultural variations, when a child's temperament is consonant with his/her environment (e.g., in preschool, home), the child is likely to gain adaptive benefits (see also: Causadias, Salvatore, & Sroufe, 2012; depending on attachment quality, De Schipper et al., 2004; Hipson & Séguin, 2015). For example, a good fit between teacher–child relationship and temperament has predicted increased prosocial behavior (N = 60 preschoolers; Hipson & Séguin, 2015). With poorness of fit, maladaptive behavior is more likely (McClowry et al., 2010). Little study was found for goodness-of-fit related to treatment method issues. Nevertheless, comfort and skill in work with traumatized youth may require (in addition to training) a good fit between clinician and method, a reasonable fit for clinician and youth, and possible method modifications. Clinicians may be compatible with more than one method, and one method (or combination of methods) may particularly resonate. Few studies were found that relate personality to method. As discussed in Chapter 10 (INSIGHTS), treatment and/or training has assisted parents and teachers to understand individual differences (e.g., temperament, personality) and to improve their strategies with varying children in order to enhance children's emotional experiences, regulatory capacities, and other developmental outcomes (Iverson & Gertstein, 2018). Of course, earlier intervention is better (e.g., toddler, preschool). Chapter 16 and to follow (*Clash vs Accord*) discusses adult–child personality issues that may affect treatment.

Symptom increase during treatment does not indicate a poor fit. As discussed in Chapter 16, during treatment, children's symptoms or distress may temporarily increase before reducing (e.g., internalizing, or externalizing; Hirai et al., 2012; Salloum & Overstreet, 2012). For three treatment methods used with adults—Cognitive Processing Therapy (CPT) with a written narrative, CPT without a written narrative, or Prolonged Exposure—Larsen and colleagues found that, regardless of treatment type, a minority of patients exhibited PTSD exacerbations during treatment, although they experienced improvement by the end of treatment (Larsen, Stirman, Smith, & Resick, 2016). Variables studied (diagnostic, trauma-related) did not predict symptom exacerbations.

Goodness-of-Fit: Method and Clinician

Posttrauma work is a field that includes at least indirect exposure to horrific experiences and stories. It is important that the methods learned permit a clinician positive experience and skill rather than choosing a method because it is well regarded. Among other possible clinician attitudes (e.g., a distanced perspective; focus on how narrative content may lead to recovery), effectively doing work that gives one joy appears to be an important protective or burn-out prevention mechanism. In addition to training, both joy and skill may require goodness-of-fit between method and clinician. Methods are often similar in many ways, and they can vary greatly, in other ways. Some methods use the attachment relationship (with parent, e.g., Lieberman & Van Horn, 2005; with clinician, e.g., Fosha, 2009), some build alliance (Van Horn, Gray, Pettinelli, & Estassi, 2011), and others primarily require cooperation (Scheeringa, 2016). Each type of method may employ many techniques, including some of the same techniques. Some methods adhere to specific phases of intervention with implementation of specific methods in each phase (usually with adaptation to or modification for patient/client needs), while others more strongly follow the patient/client's lead. Goals also vary—e.g., symptom reduction and improved functioning; those plus recovery of positive emotions (and perhaps, recovery of flexibility, creativity, and/or capacity for flow); and/or the restoration of attachment relationships toward assisting repair. All of the methods presented in this book have gained respect and/or been proven to be successful for a significant number of clients/patients.

Goodness-of-Fit: Clinician–Client/Patient

Some youth have not benefitted from specific methods. It is likely that success is easiest, when clinician and method as well as patient/client and clinician are well suited (study is needed). The fit between client/patient and therapist may include aspects of personality, issues of trust, and other trauma and non-trauma-related factors (e.g., Tables A5.1, A5.2, 17.1). Little research was found on personality and fit. However, it is believed that adults (parents, teachers, and likely clinicians) who are effective with children adjust the environment to achieve *goodness-of-fit* with the child (between child temperament and practices, expectations, etc.; McClowry, 2003). Some differences have been found for clinician personality and medical outcomes. For example, with Australian pediatric diabetes patients, medical clinicians, who had no lower limit in their goals for patient glycated hemoglobin (HbA1c) and who were self-reportedly less agreeable (demanding and dogmatic), had patients with lower HbA1c (Cameron et al., 2017). Issues for medical compliance are not equivalent to those for therapeutic practice, however. Whether a method includes an ideal of alliance, cooperation, or connection, treatment requires a measure of synchrony. The ability for two people to develop an effective synchrony may not be easily discernable. The ease with which clinicians and patients develop ease with each other and an effective interpersonal and treatment rhythm has not been fully studied (related to personality and other factors). Even when such compatibilities are considered less important, clinicians will need to be prepared for and/or to adapt to youth differences.

Clash vs Accord. A number of theories suggest individual differences that may affect treatment and rapport. Because it includes ways that individuals may clash or connect, a brief discussion follows of traits originally based on Jungian observations (1971; Table 17.1, see also Box 17.2). In her extensive work with students and teachers, Murphy (2008) observed some of the ways that adults (i.e., teachers) and youth (students) related synchronously or clashed. When a youth and adult have opposite inter-relating, perceptual, decision-making, and orienting styles, they may have difficulties (Berens, 2015; Murphy, 2008; more study is needed). For example, an extravert may want to talk in order to process an idea or feeling, may gain energy from being around others (except when completing some difficult tasks) or from doing, may prefer giving and receiving quick responses to questions, and may express emotions more readily. An introvert (or behaviorally inhibited person) may need to think things out or process them before sharing or expressing emotions, may need time before responding (except in some areas of focus), may need extra time to trust, may need alone time to restore energy (with adjustments for any increased need for support), may not be as readily sociable, and may feel less comfortable writing private things down in a journal or workbook, especially before a strong trusting relationship has been established.

Some individuals relate more to the concrete and factual, while others engage more in and are engaged more by the intuitive and symbolic. Whether or not these are factors that influence grief or comfort style or treatment response is unstudied. Some people relate more to having a plan to follow; others prefer flexibility and/or enjoy the process more than completion of a task. Problems may occur when styles clash or when a person's style is not well known before engaging or intervening. Personalities may change after traumas. For example, a child with a strong intuitive sense before a trauma may be dealing with more than concrete losses (e.g., loss of parts of self such as intuitive skills). After a trauma, the child may find intuitive understanding and symbolism more difficult.

Goodness-of-Fit: Child and Method

Methods are usually chosen based on a child's needs and presenting problems—e.g., grief, trauma, depression, anxiety, or combinations; the need for parent or teacher education to assist with particular personalities (e.g., Boxes 8.2, 10.2). Attachment-related interventions have proven effective for high-reactive children and their parents (Klein Velderman, Bakermans-Kranenburg, Juffer, & van IJzendoorn, 2006; Vaughn & Bost, 2018), for very young children, and when attachment is a central issue of psychopathology (Box 3.5). Methods for personality disorders have sometimes addressed reflective functioning (cognitive perspective-taking) and attachment. Parent training, involvement, and/or attachment issues are included in most methods for children. Sometimes finances influence choices (Box 3.5).

As has been discussed in the treatment chapters of this book, proven methods are generally modified to address specific needs. For example, CBT methods have proven effective for many problems, and have required modifications for work with trauma, with multiple traumas, with anxiety, and for low SES conditions. CBT after traumatic experiences contains trauma-focused elements (e.g., coping methods; exposure methods to increasingly difficult aspects of an experience); CBT for anxiety contains anxiety focused content within session and in homework (e.g., fear hierarchy and exposure methods). Treatments suited for a specific problem (e.g., PTS, depression) are not always effective without modification—e.g., when a child has more than one problem (e.g., trauma or loss and conduct problems) or has a particular coping style (e.g., dissociative, maladaptively avoidant) (e.g., see Pearlman et al., 2010).

Few studies have specifically assessed goodness-of-fit between children and methods. However, some methods proven effective in one country have not proven so in another country (see Greenberg & Riggs, 2015; Chapter 10), suggesting that culture and/or community issues make a difference in the methodology or modifications indicated. Although beneficial to many, some evidence suggests that mindfulness is most beneficial for stress-sensitive older youth and for those with high conscientiousness (de Vibe et al., 2015). Large studies are needed that assess issues such as personality (clinician and patient/client), method, ethnicity/culture, and specific mental health issues (e.g., needed modifications).

Recovery for Adults

Adult recovery and self-care are important to children's recovery.

Resolution of Personal Reactions to a Trauma or to a Victim(s)

Especially if posttrauma reactions are ongoing in an environment, adults (and children) may employ a number of methods (i.e., things not normally chosen when level headed or calm) to escape the distress of the trauma's aftermath. Caregivers, teachers, and clinicians will need to find adaptive ways to cope and need to use available support systems for personal support as well as need to take time for relief from duties or from traumatized others, time for recovery from posttrauma demands, and time to renew energy and stress tolerance. Adults who are traumatized by an experience may need to seek professional assistance. Some traumatized clinicians will need to wait to participate as therapists until recovered. Having had a previous trauma is not necessarily an asset for clinicians, particularly if the trauma is not resolved. Understanding and working toward resolution of personal reactions to the event/experience(s) and to victims is likely to help adults (parents, teachers, and clinicians) to better assist children and adolescents. It will be important for clinicians and caregivers to resolve any personal emotions or reactions that prevent optimal listening (non-reactive; nonjudgmental; without probing; Chapter 4; e.g., KIDNET, Chapter 13). Youth may need to tell of the experience and/or to express trauma-related emotions repeatedly.

The Basics of Self-Care

Self-care is important to parents, teachers, and clinicians. Self-care involves caring for and nurturing the body, mind, and spirit as well as reducing the frequency of potentially harmful activities (e.g., overuse of alcohol or other drugs, Pearlman et al., 2014). It includes activities that restore energy and equilibrium. Good physical and emotional care of self can enhance the ability to work or be productive and can help the ability to assist others through their posttrauma reactions. Lack of self-care or resolution by adults may inadvertently contribute to symptoms or difficulties in youth, following events. Becoming tired of the trauma and its results or becoming depleted personally may impede assisting the recovery of others.

The basics of self-care include, e.g., healthy regular meals, reasonable exercise, rest and relaxation as needed, reasonable and appropriate actions to reduce stress, and reasonable recreation with sensitivity to personal and others' posttraumatic reactions (e.g., blowing off steam with loud music or other noise may be very distressing for traumatized individuals). Although the ability to take needed breaks from preoccupation with the traumatic event and its results will be important for everyone, different individuals may be on different timetables for focusing on or needing relief from event-focus.

Clinicians

Understanding empathy and mirror neurons and having a number of methods to reduce arousal also may help a clinician's self-protection (Rothschild, 2006; Glossary—mirror neurons). A number of behaviors and practices may aid the journey through helping children recover from traumatic reactions. For example, mindfulness is a form of meditation. It has been applied to a type of parenting (Chapter 10) that correlates with the kind of mindfulness learned in the meditation. In general, mindfulness and yoga have reduced stress; have increased nonjudgmental, in-the-moment caregiving/interacting; have increased self-compassion and kindness; and have reduced levels of mental health problems in adults and children (Chapters 1, 10, 13, 15, 16; Winblad et al., 2018; Glossary—mindfulness). They also have been linked to positive changes in the brain, which is desirable following traumatic exposure that may impact brain function.

Caregivers/Teachers

Whether personally traumatized or assisting the recovery of a traumatized child, adolescent, or adult, it is important for caregivers and support persons to engage in at least adequate or better-than-normal self-care. Caregivers are important to all child age groups. Children will need parental and teacher warmth, comfort, and support as well as attentive listening, patient observation, and adaptability, after a traumatic event. Without good self-care, it may be more difficult to provide these responses to children whose traumatic reactions may increase demands on a caregiver's and teacher's energy and patience. It will be essential to attend to parents' and teachers' self-care as well as to a clinician's own self-care. Some parents are naturally mindful. Nevertheless, parents and teachers may benefit from training or coaching in meditation and/or other stress reduction, in posttrauma parenting/teaching, and in other coping methods. Many treatments include such practices; some methods include both teachers and parents.

Methods to Prevent Burn-Out

A number of methods have been used to prevent burn-out, including those already discussed (Rothschild, 2006; Winblad, Changaris, & Stein, 2018). A flexible coping repertoire is essential. To follow is a brief description of *Somatic Experiencing*®, which has proven effective for professionals and for individuals with PTSD.

Somatic Experiencing® (SE)

Somatic Experiencing® (Levine & Frederick, 1997) is a resiliency-focused trauma method designed to address autonomic nervous system dysregulation as well as any resulting impact on physical health and mental health symptoms (Winblad et al., 2018). It has been used for the treatment of PTSD (Brom et al., 2017), to increase clinician resilience, and to address vicarious traumatization or burn-out in clinicians (Winblad et al., 2018). SE training has been used to support development of clinical skills that reduce physical and mental health symptoms such as those related to anxiety, depression, PTSD, chronic fatigue, fibromyalgia, and migraines. SE aims to restore both regulation of the autonomic nervous system and physical and emotional regulation (Briggs, Hayes, & Changaris, 2018). For the treatment of trauma, SE attempts to access involuntary posttrauma reactions, to build awareness of bodily reactions, and to process reactions toward adaptive resolution. It supports innate resilience and works to reduce stress (Winblad et al., 2018). Like Sensorimotor Psychotherapy™, SE has increased resilience and somatic mindfulness (Box 3.2).

Winblad et al. (2018) found that after SE treatment, mental health professionals showed reduced anxiety and somatic symptoms and increased physical and interpersonal well-being (N = 18). With SE treatment shortly after a tsunami, trauma-related symptoms improved or were eliminated up to the 8-month follow-up assessment (N = 150; Parker, Doctor, & Selvam, 2008; see Briggs et al., 2018). Using a brief SE treatment, Anderson, Qiu, and Wheeler (2017) reported reductions in the number of PTSD symptoms and in fear of movement in patients with PTSD and chronic back pain.

Conclusions

As we have learned more about children's posttrauma reactions and responses to treatment, our methods and studies have evolved. Successful interventions and burn-out prevention may be more likely when method and clinician, clinician and patient, and patient and method are well suited. A clinician's and youth's individuality will shape interactions and rapport as well as shape needs. It is essential that we understand individual differences, including developmental, temperamental, genetic, and other differences that influence reactions and treatment outcomes. Good self-care is important for adults (e.g., parents, clinicians, teachers) who work with or parent traumatized children. Restoring belonging and support as well as hope and the capacity for positive emotions and skilled actions, in addition to the reduction of symptoms and the restoration of functioning, is important to a child's ongoing life, well-being, and development.

Glossary

Accommodative coping e.g., reframing the problematic, seeing positive in negative

Activity (trait) the tendency to engage in behavior that is highly stimulating or that is a source of external or environmental stimulation (i.e., more active than peers; Oniszczenko & Dragan, 2012); full of energy and vivacious (Brajsa-Zganec & Hanzec, 2014)

Adaptive Humorists (youth humor type) scored high on the two adaptive styles of humor, and low on aggressive and self-defeating humor (see Humor styles)

Adaptive Narcissism beliefs of own superiority and in own capability to be a leader, to make decisions, or to take charge of a task; perceived positive relationships (see Chapters 15–16, adaptive and maladaptive forms of narcissism)

Adrenocorticotropic hormone (ACTH) corticotropin-releasing factor (CRF), released by the hypothalamus, causes the pituitary to release adrenal-corticotropic hormone (ACTH) (Stein & Kendall, 2004); via the adrenal glands, ACTH instigates the release of cortisol

Adverse Childhood Experiences (ACEs) used to refer to the following maltreatment and family dysfunction traumas: verbal, physical, or sexual abuse; family dysfunction such as an incarcerated, mentally ill, or substance-abusing family member; domestic violence; or parental absence because of divorce or separation (see Chapter 2)

Adversity difficulties, misfortunes; ongoing stress, significant stress, or traumatic stress

Affective empathy ability to feel emotions congruent with the other's emotions—to infer the emotional states of others (Evans & Rothbart, 2007; see also cognitive empathy and empathy)

Affective mirroring shared direction of affective change

Affiliation the act and/or desire for closeness with others; has been related to Agreeableness (a temperament trait)

Affiliative humor enhances relationships with others and reduces interpersonal tensions

Aggressive humor humor to enhance self at expense of other; sarcasm, teasing; use of humor to criticize or manipulate others; compulsive humor without care of effects on others (Martin et al., 2003)

AKA also known as

Alerting network brain network concerned with one's ability to achieve and maintain a state of increased sensitivity to incoming information (Federico et al., 2017; Posner et al., 2016; see also orienting network and executive control network)

Alexithymia constraints in the ability to label and identify emotions (Atkinson et al., 2015); difficulty identifying and labeling emotional experience (Carpenter et al., 2016; Frewen et al., 2008a) and a tendency to externally oriented thinking (Frewen et al., 2008a)

Allele a variant of a given gene that may influence traits and/or neurochemical functioning

Anhedonia inability to find pleasure in usually enjoyable activities (e.g., hobbies, social activities, sexual activities); appears to be a marker of depression severity for children, adolescents, and adults (anhedonia, irritability and worthlessness/guilt more common in MDD than in subclinical depression; Wesselhoeft et al., 2016); linked to stressors and PTSD (Kavanaugh & Holler, 2014; Wesselhoeft et al., 2016)

Anomalous parenting frightening, threatening—e.g., looming or abusive, dissociative—e.g., haunted voice; deferential/timid, disrupted—e.g., failure to repair, lack of response, insensitive/communication error (Beebe et al., 2010; Briere et al., 2017)

Anxious-ambivalent attachment AKA resistant or as preoccupied in adolescents or adults—insecure attachment (see Table A3.2)

Attentional control an executive function, executive attention includes the assorted mechanisms involved in monitoring and resolving conflict among cognitions, emotions, and behaviors (Morrison & Heimberg, 2013); one of the mechanisms used is attentional control—the general ability to effortfully regulate attention—i.e., voluntarily focus or shift attention (contrasts to reactive or less voluntary dimensions of attention)

Attention set shifting ability to strategically focus and to disengage attention while resisting interference and distractions (e.g., minor distractions; emotionally frustrating distractions) (see *shifting*)

Autobiographical memory (AM) memories about the self (Fuhrmann et al., 2015)

Autonomic nervous system a control system that regulates bodily functions (e.g., respiratory, heart rate, digestion, sexual arousal, pupillary response) and reflexive behaviors (e.g., swallowing, sneezing, vomiting), primarily unconsciously; regulated by hypothalamus with input from limbic system; two main branches include sympathetic nervous system and parasympathetic nervous system; during stress reactions, the sympathetic and parasympathetic branches of the autonomic nervous system generally produce coordinated and opposite physiologic reactions (see Nader, 2008; with some exceptions; see Koss & Gunnar, 2018)

Avoidant attachment AKA anxious avoidant or dismissing—insecure attachment (Table A3.3)

Behavioral Inhibition a temperament construct characterized by wariness, reticence, and decreased exploration in unfamiliar contexts and with unfamiliar people; show fear and withdrawal in response to unfamiliar objects, places, and people; may later show social anxiety or social phobia symptoms/disorders (e.g., Kagan, Snidman, Kahn, & Towsley, 2007); anxiety proneness (Howard et al., 2017); includes relatively moderate levels of negative emotions; appear unable to disengage attention from other children (carefully watch; do not reduce wariness) but make few attempts to join group activities; appear unable to use attentional control to regulate emotions—e.g., attention shifting, attention focusing, and cognitively manipulating thoughts about a situation (Fox et al., 2005); they tend to interact with others ineffectively and may receive rejection or have poor peer relationships as a result—over time, social failure may add to the sense of threat in social situations; BI is not the same as volitional inhibition of behaviors (see inhibition) (see Chapters 5, 8, 9; Box 8.2; Table A5.1)

Belongingness see thwarted belongingness

Benzodiazepine anti-anxiety, anti-convulsant, sedative/hypnotic, muscle relaxant agents used for anxiety, depression, insomnia, or life stress (Ashton, 2005)

Big 5 personality factors—intellect/openness to experience, extraversion/surgency/positive emotionality, conscientiousness/constraint, agreeableness, neuroticism/negative emotionality (e.g., Eysenck, 1967; Caspi, 1998; McCrae & John, 1992; Nader, 2008; Zhang et al., 2002; adult-based with variations in factors for children and for adolescents):

- *Extraversion* sociability, dominance, activity and/or sociability, positive emotionality
- *Agreeableness* helpfulness, manageability, honesty, sincerity and/or continuum from warmth and compassion to antagonism
- *Conscientiousness* degree of impulse control and ability to delay gratification and/or carefulness, faithfulness, diligence (less heritable than neuroticism and extraversion)

- *Emotional Stability* emotional reactivity, self-confidence, anxiety, fearfulness and/or the extent to which the world is experienced as distressing or threatening [neuroticism or negative emotionality = low emotional stability]
- *Openness to Experience* openness, interest, intelligence

Borderline Personality Disorder 5 or more symptoms: frantic avoidance of abandonment; unstable, intense relationships; disturbed identity; impulsivity; NSSI or suicidality; lability; chronically feeling empty; problems with anger—intense, difficult to control; transient, stress-related dissociation or paranoid ideation (APA, 2013; see Chapter 11)

Brain-derived neurotrophic factor (BDNF) gene expression and activation of its high-affinity TrkB receptor are essential in the amygdala, hippocampus, and PFC for the formation of emotional memories, including fear memories (Andero & Ressler, 2012); BDNF appears to enhance fear extinction

Briskness (BR) the tendency to react swiftly, to maintain a high-activity tempo (e.g., walk fast, even during a stroll), and to switch easily from one behavior to another, respond to changes in the environment (a personality trait)

Bully-victims may both bully (e.g., weaker individuals) and be victimized by others (by those more powerful than they; see Nader & Nader, 2012); are more like bullies in their attributional biases (Georgiou & Stavrinides, 2008); may be more aggressive than bullies (Salmivalli & Nieminen, 2002)

Callous-Unemotional trait related to lower moral regulation, lower guilt, lower emotionality, and lower empathy (e.g., Waller et al., 2015; Lui et al., 2015); callous use of others for personal gain, shallow affect, and lack of empathy and remorse (Lee-Rowland et al., 2016); callousness (no empathy, disregard for others), uncaring (lack of concern for rules or own performance), and unemotionality (lack of affective response to distressing stimuli, lack of emotional expression)

Cathexis investing mental or emotional energy in a person, idea, or object; a related positive or negative emotional charge linked to person, idea, or object (see decathexis)

CBCL Dysregulation profile high on attention problems, aggressive behavior, and anxious-depression scales; sometimes described as explosive or having rage attacks; a disengaged pattern; characterized by relatively high novelty seeking, harm avoidance, low persistence, low reward dependence (Althoff et al., 2012)

Central executive network (CEN) a neural network involved in verbal learning and executive functioning; during cognitive and emotional-processing tasks, the CEN generally increases and decreases proportionally and antagonistically (Lanius et al., 2015); the salience network (SN) mediates the interplay of CEN and DMN—e.g., engagement of CEN and disengagement of DMN

Cognitive control basis of ability to guide and control behavior; ability to control and monitor thoughts and actions in order to achieve goals; inhibition of task-irrelevant responses; operates through three partially separate EFs: inhibition, cognitive flexibility, and information updating in working memory (Lucenet et al., 2014); although generally considered non-automatic (consciously controlled), it can include automaticity (neural pathways are strengthened by practice and become automatic—e.g., learning such as bike riding, word recognition, or buttoning a button, Abshire et al., 2008; Blais et al., 2010; disattending to threatening thoughts/feelings, Gillath et al., 2009); neurocognitive processes permitting individuals to monitor and flexibly adapt behavior in an effort to achieve a goal (see Buzzell et al., 2018)

Cognitive empathy ability to understand and identify with another's emotional states; recognizing the "how" and "why" of another's affective states—to infer the thoughts of others (see also affective empathy and empathy)

Cognitive flexibility an important aspect of executive function; may be defined as the ability to efficiently adapt to changing task demands (Darby et al., 2018); coping flexibility, which employs cognitive switching, uses more strategies to adjust to rather than to change a situation (Babb et al., 2010); an executive function that enlists inhibition and working memory (Dajani & Uddin, 2015); the readiness with which a person can selectively switch between mental processes in order to generate appropriate behavioral responses (Dajani & Uddin, 2015); ability to flexibly shift between multiple incompatible perspectives or descriptions of an object or an event (Farrant et al., 2014); ability to adjust behavior to a changing environment—permits disengaging from a previous task, reconfiguring a new response set, and implementing the new response set for the task at hand (Dajani & Uddin, 2015); some suggest that there may be more than one kind of cognitive flexibility—i.e., response shifts, dimension shifts, and task shifts (see Darby et al., 2018); linked to better reading ability, higher resilience in response to adverse life events, higher creativity, better quality of life in old age

Cognitive inhibition stopping or over-riding a mental process (with or without intention; van Dooren & Inglis, 2015); may be seen as mental withholding; assumed to occur when mental interference can be elicited (e.g., Stroop tasks; see Inhibition, below); important to mathematic skills, working memory, and self-regulation

Cognitive load the effort needed in working memory; high load may have negative effects on performance

Cognitive self-regulation includes use of Executive Functions—inhibitory control, working memory, attentional flexibility; less affectively driven skills (Fuhs et al., 2013)

Coherence (family coherence) e.g., a family that sees the world as comprehensible, manageable, and meaningful (see also narrative coherence)

Complex span adds a processing demand to simple memory span or cognitive tasks; tasks that assess complex span may engage many subprocesses (e.g., attentional control, goal maintenance, and memory search); for example, tasks may include tests of memory for a word along with brief mathematical equations

Conscientiousness see constraint

Constraint (also called conscientiousness or inhibition) a personality trait; e.g., inhibits behavioral impulses; choose safe activities over exciting, dangerous ones (Finy et al., 2014); genetics contribute to this trait (Krueger et al., 2002; see BI, Chapters 8, 9; extreme inhibition is linked to anxiety; Finy et al., 2014)

Contextual fear fear acquired to contexts or places linked to aversive events (Pattwell et al., 2013); in the Pavlovian manner, a context and/or conditioned stimulus (e.g., auditory cue—ringing bell) is paired with an aversive stimulus (e.g., foot-shock); may include hippocampal activity (Fisher et al., 2016)

Contingency (Beebe et al., 2016) synchrony; interactive communication characterized by significant moment-to-moment predictability within each partner (self-contingent; within mother or child) and between partners (interactive contingent; between mother and child)

Control instantiation behaviors to increase the likelihood of achieving a goal; two common types/methods are inhibiting responses (inhibitory control) and switching between tasks (task-switching) (Buzzell et al., 2018; see Cognitive Control; see Monitoring—is complementary to monitoring)

Coping Styles see Table 14.1

Corticotropin-releasing harmone (CRH) see ACTH; a key limbic stress modulator

Cortisol a stress hormone; a steroid (Koss & Gunnar, 2018); a glucocorticoid hormone produced by HPA axis that, e.g., increases conversion of proteins and lipid into carbohydrates for needed energy during situations of environmental challenge or threat (or perceived threat; Rodrigues, LeDoux, & Sapolsky, 2009); the predominant glucocorticoid hormone in humans (Koss & Gunnar, 2018); helps prepare the organism for optimal functioning under conditions of stress (Belsky & Pluess, 2009); trauma is associated with either blunted or increased cortisol reactivity (e.g., may be influenced by trauma type, chronicity, and/or behavior problems, England-Mason et al., 2017)

C-reactive protein (CRP) CRP blood levels are a biomarker of inflammation and tissue necrosis; associated with autoimmune disease (Danese et al., 2007; De Bellis & Zisk, 2014; Jones et al., 2011; Maikovich-Fong et al., 2015; Szalai, 2004); studies of mice suggest that CRP blood concentration is disease-limiting during the emergence of arthritis and is disease-promoting (i.e., worsening) once arthritis is established (Jones et al., 2011); predicts poor outcomes for rheumatoid arthritis (Jones et al., 2011); children in a recent-onset-only maltreatment group with a minor allele of the CRP genetic variation (minor allele AA or AT) showed significantly higher levels of salivary CRP compared to recently maltreated children with the TT genotype, suggesting that CRP genotype variation may affect inflammation in context of recent onset trauma only (e.g., Cicchetti et al., 2015a)—CRP was not related to higher internalizing symptoms in non-traumatized youth or in maltreated youth with other than recent onset

Cumulative traumas multiple childhood traumas; experience of multiple types of trauma (e.g., assorted forms of abuse) and adversity (Cloitre et al., 2009); cumulative childhood traumas (not adult) have been related to both child and adult symptom complexity (Cloitre et al., 2009; Hodges et al., 2013)

Decathexis withdrawal of energy or investment [or invested connection] in a person or object

Declarative memories Table 1.1; conscious memory—e.g., recall of everyday facts and events (episodic memory)

Default mode network (DMN) neural network involving the anterior and posterior medial cortices and lateral parietal lobes (Lanius et al., 2015); involve pgACC (internal monitoring and mood states), ACC, dACC (focused attention; recruited in mindfulness meditation) (Yang et al., 2016); important in self-referential processing, autobiographical memory, and social cognition; although DMN (a task-negative network) is often considered distinctly separate from task-positive networks, it involves connections with the ventral attention systems (Chai et al., 2017); SN's anterior cingulate mediates engagement of CEN and disengagement of DMN

Delay of gratification foregoing short-term goals for long-term outcomes (Del Giudice, 2014)

Dendrite a branched extension from a nerve cell that conducts impulses from other nerve cells into the cell body; receptors of electrochemical signals

DHEA (dehydroepiandrosterone; an adrenal androgen) DHEA and cortisol have opposing functions on the nervous system and metabolism; DHEA and cortisol have been studied in relation to psychopathology (Koss & Gunnar, 2018)

Diathesis-stress risk tendency or vulnerability to develop or suffer from a malady—e.g., psychological or physical condition—which may be related to genetic vulnerability or risk alleles

Differential susceptibility differential susceptibility to context (i.e., to positive or negative environmental factors)—i.e., some individuals are far more affected than others both by negative and by positive contextual/environmental conditions (Belsky & Pluess, 2009)

Difficult temperament the difficult (challenging) child is characterized by low rhythmicity, high withdrawal, slow adaptation to change, intense reactions, and high frequency of negative mood (Chess & Thomas, 1977, 1991); may be vulnerable to stress reactions (see differential susceptibility); timid in initial reactions (withdraw in novel situations), low adaptability, high intensity, predominantly negative mood, and low regularity (Chess & Thomas, 1991; Rothbart, 2011)

Disengaged parenting e.g., inattention, distraction, or lack of awareness of child's needs (Briere et al., 2017); may be related to a parent's dissociation, distraction or interference by anxiety, depression, psychosis, substance abuse, or adverse social environments, and/or effects of unprocessed or unresolved prior trauma and/or neglect (Briere et al., 2017; Khoury et al., 2015)

Dismissing/Dismissive attachment avoidant attachment—an insecure attachment classification (Table A3.3)

Dissociation "… a disruption in normal integration of consciousness, memory, identity, emotion, perception, body representation, motor control, and behavior" (APA, 2013, p. 291); dissociative symptoms (e.g., amnesia, depersonalization/derealization, dissociative identity disturbance) can disrupt all areas of psychological and sometimes behavioral functioning; often believed to reflect an adaptive emotional-avoidance response to overwhelming distress (e.g., PT stress; Briere et al., 2016); can include, e.g., detachment from self and environment, segregation of psychological structures, separation of neurobiological systems (e.g., that integrate cognition, memory, affect), mental escape from overwhelming emotional or physical pain (see Ensink et al., 2017)

Dissociation Complexity a tendency to simultaneously endorse multiple dissociation symptom dimensions (Briere et al., 2016); is predicted by cumulative trauma (e.g., multiple childhood traumas); has been linked to suicidality and substance abuse—suggesting a need to avoid the psychological effects of multiple adverse events, whether through a range of dissociative responses, through anesthetizing or euphoric effects of drugs or alcohol, or, ultimately, through suicidality and attempts to end life (higher among inmates and women; Briere et al., 2016).

Distancing Coping a form of avoidant coping; avoiding or ignoring memories as a form of emotional coping (Harris et al., 2015a); see also self-distancing

DNA methylation a process by which methyl groups are added to a DNA molecule—can change the activity of a DNA segment without changing the sequence; when located in a gene promoter, typically acts to repress gene transcription (Schubeler, 2015)

Dopamine a neurotransmitter that has been related to inhibitory response (Albrecht et al., 2014), impulsivity, and reward seeking (Propper et al., 2008), and positive affect; increases the capacity to learn in response to reward; has been related to differences in parenting's influence on a measure of temperamental sensation-seeking in young children; findings have been consistent with DRD4 7-repeat allele's association with children's increased sensitivity to environmental factors (Sheese et al., 2012); see Table A4.1—dopamine; see endorphins to follow

Early maladaptive schemas a set of early core beliefs originating from repetitious, aversive childhood experiences such as insecure attachments (see Dozois et al., 2014; Evraire & Dozois, 2014); they include broad, pervasive themes or patterns (schemas) composed of memories, cognitions, emotions, and bodily sensations regarding self and relationships; they influence information processing and actions, thinking, feelings, and relating through life (15 schemas assessed by Evraire & Dozois, 2014—emotional inhibition, emotional deprivation, mistrust/abuse, social isolation/alienation, defectiveness/shame, abandonment/instability, failure, dependence/incompetence, vulnerability to harm or illness, enmeshment/undeveloped self, subjugation, entitlement/grandiosity, insufficient self-control/self-discipline, self-sacrifice, and unrelenting standards/hypercriticalness):

- Self-schemas include both core beliefs and organization properties (Dozois et al., 2014); maladaptive self-schemas often reflect themes of interpersonal loss or rejection, or failure to achieve a goal; has been treated with cognitive therapy and pharmaceuticals for depression

Effortful control young child's abilities to willfully or voluntarily focus and shift attention and/or inhibit or initiate responses, to plan, and to detect errors (Rothbart & Bates, 2006) (called self-regulation in older youth); inhibition of a response in consideration of long-term consequences (Rueda et al., 2005); ability to regulate attention and behavior; positively related to *Conscientiousness* and negatively related to *Impulsiveness* (a temperament trait)

Ego-control the capacity to regulate and express emotions and feelings

Ego-resilience well-functioning cognitively, emotionally, and interpersonally

Emotionality temperamentally sensitive; responds intensely to environmental stimuli

Emotional contagion a tendency to "catch" or take on (i.e., experience or express) another's or others' emotions, including action tendencies, emotional appraisals, physiological processes/patterns, subjective feelings, and instrumental behaviors (Hatfield et al., 1992, 1994); one or more person's condition elicits corresponding or complementary condition in one or more others (e.g., vocal, facial, postural, neuro-physical, autonomic, emotions, movement, micro-expressions) (Hatfield et al., 1992); attentional, emotional, and behavioral synchrony; may involve mirror neurons

Emotional reactivity (ER) the tendency to react intensely to emotion-provoking stimuli; high emotional sensitivity and low emotional resistance—e.g., stage-fright if to speak in public (personality trait)

Empathic guilt distress in response to negatively affecting other people (e.g., belief that one has hurt someone's feelings; Evans & Rothbart, 2007)

Empathy perspective-taking combined with emotional reaction usually engendering compassion or sympathy; the ability to understand and share in the feelings of another person (see also cognitive empathy and affective empathy); a combination of perspective-taking and empathic concern; theory of mind may be considered a cognitive aspect of empathy

Endorphins endogenous (within the body) opioid neuropeptides and peptide hormones (morphine-like) produced by the central nervous system and the pituitary gland; inhibit the transmission of pain signals (analgesic); produce a feeling of euphoria; beta-endorphin has a critical role in buffering stress (physical and psychological); play a role in social bonding; can be triggered by pain, vigorous exercise, laughter, certain drugs (Dunbar et al., 2012)

Endurance the capacity to respond adequately in conditions of intense external stimulation and/or in situations that demand prolonged or highly stimulating activity (e.g., work when it is noisy) (personality trait)

Epigenetics the genome is ever-changing as it adapts to the environment and epigenetics is the study of modifications to the genome that influence transcription of DNA without altering the gene's nucleotide sequence itself (see Fisher et al., 2016); chemical modifications leading to changes in gene expression without changing DNA structure (Montirosso & Provenzi, 2015)

Episodic memory memory for events or episodes (Bjorklund & Sellers, 2014); it is autonetic (self-knowing) (Bjorklund & Sellers, 2014; Tulving, 2002); placing self in a set of circumstances at a particular time (self-referent, Bjorklund & Sellers, 2014)

Error-Related Negativity (ERN) an EEG marker thought to reflect changes in dopamine after errors on a cognitive task (Frank, Woroch, & Curran, 2005); believed to be related to the monitoring system (Buzzell et al., 2018); can assess whether a person is biased to learn from mistakes or from positive experiences—e.g., larger ERN when choosing between two good options or two bad options has been found for positive learners (Frank et al., 2005)

Estradiol a major estrogen hormone produced in the female ovaries

Event centrality the extent to which an event has been incorporated into an individual's identity; the extent to which an event is tied to core aspects of identity (Berntsen & Rubin, 2007)

Event-Related Potential (ERP) an EEG pattern that helps to capture neural activity related to sensory and/or cognitive processes (Sur & Sinha, 2009)

Executive Control Network brain network that manages the ability to control our own behavior in order to achieve intended goals and resolve conflict among alternative responses (Federico et al., 2017; Posner et al., 2016; see also orienting and alerting networks)

Executive Functions the higher-level cognitive and self-regulatory skills needed for social and behavioral competence and academic achievement (Cassidy et al., 2017; Jurado & Rosselli, 2007); includes e.g., working memory, inhibition of response, shifting of attention, self-regulation, generativity; driven by basic information processing abilities (Rose, Feldman, & Jankowski, 2012a); has also been called executive control or cognitive control—mental processes believed to allow conscious control of thought and action toward goal-directed behavior (Monette et al., 2015); processing speed, storage, and attentional allocation significantly have correlated with the complex functions (e.g., planning, complex reasoning, problem-solving, and verbal fluency; Magimairaj, Montgomery, Marinellie, & McCarthy, 2009)

Explicit memory see Table 1.1

Externalizing externalized, conduct/behavior problems such as antisocial, defiant, rule-breaking, aggressive, destructive behaviors; attention problems (ADHD), substance abuse

Exuberant(ce) high approach, activity level, impulsivity, displays of high-intensity positive affect, and sociable behavior (a temperament trait)

Faux pas making a social blunder or a tactless or embarrassing remark, without or prior to grasping the mistake

FKBP5 genotype FK506 binding protein 5; involved in immuno-regulation; interact with childhood trauma to predict adult PTSD; also linked to higher rates of depression; a regulator of glucocorticoid receptor function and is regulated by the glucocorticoid receptor (GR; so is a modulator of GR-mediated regulatory feedback on HPA axis, in response to stress)

Flexibility willingness or ability to adjust to environmental demands; e.g., may have cognitive, behavioral, and/or coping flexibility; greater ability to adapt (see also cognitive flexibility)

Flourishing "deeply positive experiences of aliveness, hope, faith, clarity, agency, simplicity, compassion, joy, and truth" (Fosha, 2009, p. 252)

Flow (AKA the zone, the groove, a Zen experience) spontaneous self-hypnotic state (senses are gathered on a particular focus and conscious awareness of outer world fades, Rossi, 1993), characterized by involvement so deeply in something (e.g., meditating, resting, playing, interacting socially, working when the mind is stretched to its limits in order to accomplish something challenging and worthwhile) that nothing else seems to matter; action and awareness merge (Csikszentmihalyi, 1997a, b; see Nader, 2008); concentration is intensely focused in the moment so that time, fears, depression, worries about self or failure, and anxiety are out of consciousness (Csikszentmihalyi, 1997b; Stein & Kendall 2004)

Forward-Focused Coping optimism, distraction, and emotional avoidance, which may include positive thinking, attending to the needs of others, maintaining plans and goals, remaining calm, reducing painful emotions, and being able to laugh

Gamma-aminobutyric acid (GABA) the major inhibitory neurotransmitter in the central nervous system (CNS; Köhnke, 2008); GABA decreases excitability of individual neurons and limits excessive neuronal activity (Grigorenko, 2002; King et al., 2013); has a quieting effect (however, levels produced during stress may impair memory, McCleery & Harvey, 2004); child abuse's impact on the brain may interfere with GABA's soothing function on the limbic system (Siegel, 2003); functional impairment or aberrant development of GABAergic system has been linked to anxiety and depression (King et al., 2013); plays a role in EFs (working memory, learning, emotion regulation; Grigorenko, 2002); $GABA_A$ receptors are sensitive to ethanol (alcohol) in distinct brain regions and is relevant to alcohol tolerance and dependence; Alcohol results in an inhibition of excitatory glutamatergic neurotransmission and increases GABAergic inhibition; downregulation of GABAergic system and up-regulation of the glutamatergic system results in increased tolerance of alchohol; GABRA2, which encodes the $GABA_A$ $\alpha 2$ receptor subunit, may have a role in drug dependence (Johnson & North, 1992); GABA has been implicated in the aggression heightening effects of alcohol, stress, anxiety, and epilepsy (Grigorenko, 2002)

Generativity the ability to mentally generate new combinations of behavioral units (Barkley, 2001); concern for the next generation (Erik Erikson)

Glucocorticoids HPA axis activation involves a hormonal cascade: corticotrophin-releasing hormone (CRH; secreted in the paraventricular nucleus, PVN, of the hypothalamus) stimulates release of adrenocorticotropic hormone (ACTH) in the anterior pituitary; ACTH enters the bloodstream and ultimately stimulates release of glucocorticoids (cortisol in human and nonhuman primates; corticosterone in rodents) in the adrenal cortex, which, in turn exerts negative feedback, slowing the release of ACTH and CRH (Fisher et al., 2006); glucocorticoids also stimulate the immune system and metabolism of stored energy

Grieving style see *intuitive grieving style* and *instrumental grieving style*

Hardiness commitment to finding meaningful purpose in life; beliefs in one's personal ability to influence his/her surroundings and outcomes and that one can learn and grow from experiences; and ability to use active coping and social support

Harm avoidance (temperamental trait) shyness, fatigability, anticipatory worry, and behavioral inhibition, reluctance to engage with peers or in new situations; has been linked to the development of internalizing behavior problems (Althoff et al., 2012; Baer et al., 2015)

Hawk and Dove phenotypic dimensions *bold* and *inhibited* temperaments believed to correspond to evolutionary types—strategies for coping with stress are either Hawk-like strategies (characterized by approach, dominant-negative affect, and activity) or Dove-like strategies (evidenced by avoidance, inhibition, and vulnerable affect; show reticence, cautiousness, and vigilance—see behavioral inhibition) (Sturge-Apple et al., 2012); observed in toddlers responses to novelty and threat—for Hawks, a stressful rearing environment was primarily linked to elevated indicators of SNS activity; for Doves, harsh parenting was primarily linked to elevated parasympathetic and cortisol activity, as well as to dampened SNS activity

High-reactive infant/toddlers biased to become fearful to unfamiliar events under particular conditions (Kagan, 1997)

Hippocampus brain region involved in transferring new explicit memory information from short to long-term storage (Bjorklund & Sellers, 2014; Table A4.2)

Hostile Attribution bias attributing malicious intent to peers more often than other youth do (Crick & Dodge, 1996); tendency to interpret situations or the intentions and behavior of others as hostile even when there is conflicting, missing, or ambiguous information (Coker et al., 2014; Crick & Dodge, 1996; Dodge et al., 1997; Guy et al., 2017)

Humor endorsers (youth humor style) scored above average on all four humor styles (see Humor styles; Table 11.2)

Humor styles (see also Tables 1.3, 5.5, 11.2, A2.1; see irony); see the individual types of humor listed:

- Adult—self-enhancing, aggressive, affiliative, self-defeating
- Child (ages 11–13)—Self-defeater, Humor Endorser, Adaptive (see Chapter 11)

Hyper-mentalizing presumptions are made about the mental states of others that go beyond available data (Ensink et al., 2017); hypersensitivity to the mental states of both self and other (Fonagy & Bateman, 2016)

Hypothalamic-pituitary-adrenal (HPA) axis produces physiological mediators (glucocorticoid hormones—cortisol in humans) that increase the conversion of proteins and lipids into carbohydrates needed for restoring energy, increasing blood pressure and blood sugar, mobilizing amino acids, and reducing immune responses (Rodrigues, LeDoux, & Sapolsky, 2009); they remain elevated or lowered in response to chronic, repeated, or severe stress (Hulme, 2011; see Nader & Fletcher, 2014); HPA axis and sympathetic nervous system constitute the body's basic stress response (Yehuda et al., 2015); elevated stress hormones in PTSD are related to an unusual pattern of low basal (unstimulated) cortisol levels and raised catecholamine levels, have influenced daily cortisol patterns in trauma survivors (see Chapter 1); may produce negative health states from pathological harm related to prolonged cellular exposure to altered levels of the physiological mediators (McEwen & Wingfield, 2010)

Hypothalamic-pituitary-gonadal axis promotes secondary sexual characteristics, increased growth velocity, body changes, and fertility; usually begins ages 10 or 11 for girls, ages 11 or 12 for boys

ICD-11 PTSD (proposed) three criteria, six symptoms; Re-experiencing—nightmares, flashbacks; Avoidance—internal cues, external cues; and Arousal—hypervigilance, startle (World Health Organization, 2015)

If-then plans "If situation X is encountered, then I will perform Y" (Gawrilow et al., 2011); used to enhance performance; more successful than setting goal intentions; involves psychological processes related to both an anticipated situation (if-) and a goal-directed response (then-) using highly activated mental representations; have improved EF task performance; has been used with ADHD

Implicit memory see Table 1.1

Information processing *cognitive information processing*—e.g., (1) acquisition, classification, processing, and integration of information, (2) information storing and recall, (3) organization and reorganization of information, and (4) communication and enactment of information (see Nader, 2008—Chapter 14). *Social information processing* includes the ways that youth process information about social situations and others' behaviors. Skills, such as attention (keep focus on an object or idea while its information is processed, Reynolds & Richards, 2008) and perspective-taking (ability to examine from more than one perspective) influence information processing. Information processing may include or be influenced by biases (e.g., attributional biases; biased expectations, Crick & Dodge, 1994; see Nader, 2008—Chapter 14)

Inhibition deliberate suppression of pre-potent, dominant, or automatic reactions (a simple EF); *response-inhibition* (the intentional inhibition of a dominant response, Rollins & Riggins, 2016) has been divided into *conflict inhibition* and *delay inhibition*—*conflict inhibition* is the ability to act in opposition to a pre-potent response (e.g., saying thank you even though you don't like the gift); *delay* inhibition is the ability to delay or postpone a dominant response (e.g., waiting until the assigned time to open gifts; Rollins & Riggins, 2016); *delay inhibition* has also been defined as ability to suppress automatic responses or to control impulses in context of an appealing reward (Merz et al., 2015, 2016); *conflict inhibition* generally improves across middle childhood (Rollins & Riggins, 2016); inhibition also includes interference control, directed forgetting, emotional control, and motor control (Best et al., 2009); [see also constraint (personality trait), behavioral inhibition (temperament style), negative priming, cognitive inhibition]

Inhibitory control ability to inhibit a dominant response or activate a subdominant response; ability to plan; ability to detect errors (Zentner & Shiner, 2012)

Injustice sensitivity injustice is more aversive to some individuals than others; people with high injustice sensitivity often perceive injustice (observer injustice sensitivity) and/or intensely, negatively respond toward perceived causing of injustice (perpetrator injustice sensitivity) (Bondü, 2018); individuals high in victim injustice sensitivity feel unfairly treated frequently and tend to respond with anger and retaliation; victim injustice sensitivity has been linked to aggressive and antisocial behavior (see Bondü, 2018). Injustice sensitivity may also result in advocacy for others (see Box 3.1)

Internalizing internalized maladaptations/problems such as depression, anxiety, withdrawal, whining; some include low self-esteem, loneliness

Internal locus of control belief that control over events, outcomes, behaviors, or emotions is internal (within the person) versus external to or outside of the person (Bolger & Patterson, 2003); although early studies found that an internal locus of control was linked to more positive outcomes, later studies found that an accurate assessment of locus of control may be more beneficial—e.g., knowing when one can control and when one must adapt to situations

Interoceptive awareness monitoring of internal bodily states (may include exacerbated arousal, Lanius et al., 2015); awareness of internal (within the body) stimuli; awareness of feelings from the body that influence mood, sense of well-being, and emotions (yoga may increase this, Rhodes, 2015)

Interpersonal humorists (youth category) scored above average on aggressive and affiliative humor, and below average on the other two humor styles (Table 11.2)

Inter-sensory redundancy when the same information occurs synchronously across the senses; overlapping information across auditory, visual, and tactile senses, and/or proprioceptive stimulation for properties of objects and events (Bahrick, 2010); when amodal (rather than modality specific) information (rhythm, tempo, duration, intensity) is simultaneously available and temporally synchronous across at least two senses—e.g., hearing and seeing at the same time (Bahrick, 2010)

Intolerance of uncertainty an individual's dispositional incapacity to endure the perceived absence of key or sufficient, salient information, hence the perception of uncertainty (see Carleton, 2016)

Instrumental grieving style a more cognitive behavioral, problem-solving approach—e.g., keeping emotions under control, having a desire to manage emotions rather than express them openly, focusing on problem-solving or other activities rather than on the pain of a loss

Intuitive grieving style evident in the heightened experience and expression of emotions—e.g., sadness, anguish, and tears—that may persist long after the death

Irony language used to signify the opposite of what is stated or a condition that seems deliberately contrary to what is expected; has been used as a form of humor; may include, e.g., situational, verbal, hyperbole, understatement (Cameron et al., 2010; see Table 1.3)

Kindling evidenced by seizure-like neuronal activity and changes in affected neurons' excitability and behavior

Limbic system facilitates motivation and the expression and interpretation of emotion; has direct connecting fibers to and from all the cerebral lobes; functions for learning and memory, aggression, sexual behavior, and eating and drinking behavior (Atchison, 2007; Child Welfare Information Gateway, 2015); includes amygdala, thalamus, hypothalamus, and hippocampus

Long-term memory see Table 1.1

Looking-glass self significant others serve as "mirrors" to create reflected self-evaluations (i.e., inferred self-evaluations from another person's perceived perspective); perceived other-perspectives are incorporated into one's own self-perceptions (Cooley in Jankowski & Pfeifer, 2015; Mead, 1934 (in Jankowski & Pfeifer, 2015) extended the theory to include self-perceptions influenced both by the evaluations of close others and also by generalized evaluations of one's social group and the larger society

Low reactive infants/toddlers biased to become relatively fearless (Kagan, 1997....)

Mediation or mediating variable a variable that accounts for the relationship between the predictor variable and the outcome variable (Lindley & Walker, 1993; see Nader, 2008). For example, poly-victimization (predictor variable) is associated with dissociation (mediating variable) which in turn is related to internalizing symptoms (outcome variable). For another example, poly-victimization (predictor variable) is associated with PTSD (mediating variable) which influences anger and irritability (outcome variable) and may later lead to externalizing (downstream outcome variable) (see Ford et al., 2018a)

Memory see autobiographical memory, declarative and procedural memory, episodic and semantic memory, explicit and implicit memory, long-term memory, retrospective and prospective memory, semantic memory, sensory memory, or short-term memory (see Table 1.1)

Mentalizing (see also metacognitive monitoring, reflective functioning, theory of mind, and perspective-taking) seeing the self from the outside, and seeing others from the inside (i.e., self-reflective functioning +perspective-taking); the ability to think about and interpret self and others in terms of mental states (Fonagy & Colleagues); the ability to understand others' behavior in terms of mental states (e.g., beliefs, desires, feelings, and memories), ability to reflect on one's own mental states, and the ability to understand that one's own states of mind may influence the others' behavior (see Hoffman, 2015)

Metabolic Syndrome at least three of five risk factors that increase likelihood of developing heart disease, diabetes, and stroke; risk factors: high blood pressure (over 130/85); high blood sugar levels (insulin resistant); excess waist fat; high triglyceride levels; low good cholesterol levels (HDL)

Metacognitive index ability to initiate, plan, organize, and sustain future-oriented problem-solving in working memory (Bigorra et al., 2015)

Metacognitive monitoring (see also reflective function, perspective-taking, theory of mind) ability to step back and consider one's own cognitive processes as objects of thought or reflection; thoughts about thoughts, emotions, and behaviors (e.g., Fosha, 2003; Knox, 2003; Main, 1995); suggests an ability to understand one's own and others' behaviors in terms of mental states or psychological experiences

Metta loving kindness (Frewen et al., 2015b); compassion (Lang et al., 2012)

Mindfulness a present-focused, open, and nonjudgmental state of attention and awareness (Waters, 2016); a type of meditation practice that includes nonjudgmental, present-focused attention; has been combined with other methods—e.g., with CBT toward synthesizing acceptance and change: mindfulness *what* skills—observe, describe, participate; mindfulness *how* skills—nonjudgmentally, one-mindfully, effectively

Mindfulness parenting e.g., mindful listening, emotional awareness, compassion and nonjudgmental acceptance; moment-to-moment awareness in interactions; warm and nurturing affective tenor (Waters, 2016)

Mirror Interview inspired by Winnicot (1971), includes a set of questions posed to individuals while standing in front of a full-length mirror; individual is provided an experience of taking in the visual image of his/her own physical body while responding to questions posed regarding their thoughts and feelings about their bodies (Kernberg et al., 2007)

Mirror neurons the neural network involved in production of a given action is also activated during the perception of others engaging in that action (Gallese et al., 2007; Gervais & Wilson, 2005; visuomotor, Rizzolatti et al., 2002; Rizzolatti & Craighero 2004); neurons that are active during action, mental rehearsal of that action, observation of a similar action by others, and imitation of that action, or during perception of intransitive action (Gervais & Wilson, 2005); perception of others' emotional expressions leads to mirroring—i.e., behavioral synchrony and congruent emotion (emotional contagion; Hatfield et al. 1994; empathy, Gervais & Wilson, 2005); the difference between monkey and human mirror neurons is that human mirror neurons fire even while observing meaningless (intransitive) movements and that human mirror neuron systems code movements forming an action as well as those for action (goal—e.g., grasping a piece of wood or food; Mehta & Bhandari, 2016); assessed by EEG changes in Mu rhythms

Moderating variable a variable that may change the magnitude or direction of the relationship between a prdicotr variable and outcome variable (Lindley & Walker, 1993; see Nader, 2008). For example, the greater the level of social support, the greater the relationship between resilience and mental health—e.g., the lower the level of PTSD

Monitoring defined in relation to Behavioral Inhibition: "neurocognitive processes associated with detecting when something goes wrong or noticing when changes occur that will impair the ability to achieve a goal" (Buzzell et al., 2018, p. 216; parental monitoring is also discussed in the book)

Moral disengagement cognitive distortion that allows the doer of negative conduct to construe it as a justifiable and worthy endeavor (Bandura's descriptions in Coker et al., 2014); its components may include moral justification (giving behavior a moral or worthy purpose); sanitizing language (removing aggressive connotations); advantageous comparison (compared to something worse); diffusion of responsibility (everyone's fault); disregarding or distorting consequences (minimizing or ignoring results); dehumanizing victims (labeling, depersonalizing); and blaming the victim (Coker et al., 2014); otherwise moral children may perform aggressive acts by disengaging usual reactions such as self-censuring or evaluating aggression as something that will be punished (Bandura, 2008, 2012)

Mu rhythm (EEG) studies of sensorimotor mu rhythm suppression (or desynchronization) in the EEG, occurring in alpha frequency range, suggest infant neural systems map how an act is accomplished as well as map behavior and that infants can *imitate/mirror behavior based on this mapping and the recognition of like parts* (e.g., both have hands, Marshall & Meltzoff, 2014); e.g., greater Mu desynchronization for infants observing crawling compared to walking, when infants had already crawled but not walked (van Elk et al., 2008; mu response not found at 4 mo (Virji-Babul et al., 2012); seen as an indicator of mirror neuron functioning (Rayson et al., 2016)

Myelination development and formation of a myelin sheath around nerve fibers; protects and insulates nerve cells; myelin aids quick and accurate transmission of the electrical current carrying data from one nerve to the next

N2 amplitude (EEG) a medio-frontal event-related potential (ERP) component that is a negative going wave that peaks at 200–350 ms; has been related to cognitive control—e.g., response monitoring or response conflict (Lamm et al., 2018); believed to be involved in top-down EFs to signal the need to inhibit a pre-potent response in favor of executing a subdominant behavior, which also reflects attentional control and conflict monitoring (ages 9–12; Thai et al., 2016); may represent increasing neural efficiency after successful inhibition during tasks (ages 7–17, Best et al., 2009); larger N2 interacting with BI (shyness/wariness) has been related to threat avoidance with increasing BI (Thai et al., 2016); smaller in children who were ever institutionalized (Lamm et al., 2018)

Narration style (families) 1. coordinated perspective—parents structure and integrate several perspectives for a more complex understanding of one's own, of others', and integration of the two; incorporate child's perspective; safe and comfortable environment; 2. individual perspective—use of questioning to elicit children's perspectives; turn taking in telling stories; no integration—children's stories are one among many; 3. imposed perspective—a dominant parent ignores others' perspectives in controlling and unsupportive families; the latter was rare in this sample

Narrative coherence how well a particular memory is structured, organized, and elaborated (see Morris, Baker-Ward, & Bauer, 2010); it increases how well a memory is retained over time (Peterson et al., 2014); includes thematic coherence (extent to which there is a clear focus to the narrative) and chronological coherence; some studies have examined the breadth of the narrative—who, what, when, where, why

Negative affectivity mainly frustration, related to Neuroticism (see temperament trait)

Negative emotionality (AKA negative affectivity, neuroticism; see also behavioral inhibition phenotype) a temperamental trait characterized by, e.g., emotional reactivity, inhibition, tendency to withdraw and/or avoid novel situations, fear, anxiety, sadness, inhibition, anger (linked to 5HTTLPR gene polymorphisms) (a temperament trait)

Negative emotionality/behavioral dysregulation (the combination) positive ratings for discomfort, fear, frustration, activity level, motor activation, and sadness (Bouvette-Turcot et al., 2015b); negative ratings for attentional focusing, cuddliness, inhibitory control, and soothability; found in young children

Negative priming in order to achieve cognitive tasks, a subset of the available information in a situation must be attended, and other information must be ignored; shortly afterwards, processing of the ignored stimulus may be impaired—e.g., direction: pick out all words containing the letter A; the subsequent direction to pick out all with the letter D from those same words will result in slower performance (van Dooren & Inglis, 2015)

Neural-based personality traits (e.g., Spielberger State-trait Personality Inventory; Davis et al., 2003):

- *Play* or *Playfulness* having fun vs being serious, being generally happy and joyful, playing games with physical contact, humor, and laughter (associated with *Extraversion*)
- *Seeking* curiosity, desire for exploration, striving for solutions to problems and puzzles, positive anticipation of new experiences, confidence in ability to accomplish almost anything
- *Caring* nurturing, drawn to young children and pets, softhearted toward animals and people in need, empathetic, affection for and liking to care for others including the sick, liking to be needed (linked to agreeableness; negatively associated with anger)
- *Fear* anxiety, tenseness, worry, struggles with decisions, rumination about past decisions and statements, poor sleep, and not typically courageous (inversely related to emotional stability)
- *Anger* hotheaded, easily irritated and frustrated, frustration leads to anger, verbal or physical expression of anger, persistence of anger for long periods (inversely related to emotional stability)
- *Sadness* (formerly Panic) loneliness, frequent crying, rumination about loved ones and past relationships, and distress when not with loved ones (inversely related to emotional stability)
- *Spirituality* (added by Davis et al., 2003) feeling "connected" to humanity and creation as a whole, sense of "oneness" with creation, striving for inner peace and harmony, relying on spiritual principles, and searching life meaning

Neurogenesis process by which neural stem cells and progenitor cells generate neurons (Gilbert, 2013)

Neuron a nerve cell that plays a part in information processing (Byrnes, 2001)

Neuroticism see negative emotionality (a personality trait; see Table A5.1)

Novelty seeking tendency to seek out stimulation; characterized by impulsivity, extravagance, and disorderliness

Opioids all substances (endogenous or synthetic) that produce morphine-like effects (Colasanti et al., 2011)

Orienting network brain network that manages the ability to select and focus on a to-be-attended stimulus (Federico et al., 2017; Posner et al., 2016; see also alerting and executive control network)

Over-general memory (AKA over-general autobiographical memory) inability to retrieve specific memories or specific episodes from autobiographical memory; general memories are recalled instead (e.g., when on vacation rather than a specific aspect or incident from when on vacation); has been linked to high or increases in depression (van Daele et al., 2014; Harris et al., 2015a; Sutherland & Bryant, 2007) and to PTSD (Valentino et al., 2012); young children generally have more general memory recall; the ability to recall specific memories increases with age (Burnside et al., 2004; Harris et al., 2015a); after traumas, children may begin by having over-general trauma memories (a form of avoidance to distance self from negative affects) and then may become over-general in retrieving positive, negative, and neutral memories

Overgeneralization e.g., global, exaggerated, and/or overly abstract beliefs about self, others, the world

Overmodulation associated with profound emotional detachment or numbing—no positive or negative emotional experience; significant compartmentalization; affective shutdown dissociation (depersonalization, derealization); alexithymia; underactivity in the insula (e.g., in PTSD-DS; Dorahy & Van Der Hart, 2014; Frewen & Lanius, 2006; Lanius, 2015; Lanius et al., 2012; Nicholson et al., 2016)

Oxytocin (OT) a peptide hormone and neuropeptide that increases bonding between caregiver and newborn, increases social bonding, and can reduce fear and anxiety (Seltzer et al., 2010); along with vasopressin has been linked to altruism, trust, and perspective-taking as well as found to be a stress attenuator (some variation in brain activity between genders—under threat, more affiliative behavior in women; Hostinar et al., 2014); the OT system is an ancient, integrative system that cross-talks with stress, reward, immune, and brain-stem mediated homeostatic systems (Feldman et al., 2014); it supports mammalian sociality, plays a unique role in experience-dependent plasticity that buttresses sensitive period effects; synchrony—coordination of biology and behavior during social contact—may be a mechanism for these effects

P2 amplitude (EEG) a medio-frontal event-related potential (ERP) component reflecting post-synaptic neural activity that is a positive going wave that peaks at 200–300ms (Lamm et al., 2018); associated with sustained perceptual processing, greater attentional resource mobilization (on salient stimuli), and initial processing of emotion evaluation (faces; e.g., see Lamm et al., 2018); augmented P2 has been related to reduced social anxiety for those with BI (shyness/wariness; Thai et al., 2016); children who were ever institutionalized have shown larger P2 activation (Lamm et al., 2018)

P3 amplitude an ERP component that peaks around 300 ms in adults after stimulus onset; has been associated with context updating in working memory (Lamm et al., 2018); deficient activation in previously institutionalized children (see Lamm et al., 2018)

Parasympathetic Nervous System (PNS) PNS is calming; stimulates "rest and digest"—is activated when the body is at rest (e.g., after eating; preparation for sexual activity). The sympathetic nervous system (SNS) and PNS usually do not function simultaneously; one shuts off the other (as one increases the other decreases) (Sapolsky, 1998); helps shift physiological resources toward restorative, homeostatic functioning and reduce physiological arousal (Sturge-Apple et al., 2012); helps restore conditions under which the body can rest and repair (Gunnar et al., 2015)

Parenting style (Kawabata et al., 2011; Pelaez et al., 2008 primarily describes D. Baumrind's parenting styles):

- *authoritative parenting* firm control; provides limits or rules in a warm, respectful style; provides support, assistance, or modeling; gives clear instructions and positive encouragement
- *authoritarian parenting* verbal or physical rejection or control; lacks positive encouragement; high control and low responsiveness; low warmth and high demandingness; often use punitive discipline tactics, maintain an absolute standard, restrict autonomy, are low in warmth, and do not use induction as a means of explaining demands; has been related to children's negative social adjustment—e.g., moodiness, hostility toward others, and low self-esteem
- *punitive or coercive parenting* may be a part of authoritarian parenting; has been associated with aggression and hostility
- *permissive parenting* positive verbal communication; sets no limits; gives no specific instructions; high responsiveness and low control (no clear limits or boundaries); make

few demands, allow children to self-regulate, react in an accepting, non-punitive manner to children's impulses and demands; permissive or inconsistent parenting has been related to increased aggression in children (may not develop ability to control impulses or negative emotions); relational aggression was found in all age groups (preschool, school age, adolescent)

- *disengaged parenting* uninvolved; unresponsive or avoidant; rarely vocalizes; displays flat affect
- *psychologically controlling* covert, verbal or nonverbal, psychological intrusive skills used to manipulate children's emotions and behavior; interferes with children's behavioral autonomy; use tactics like love-withdrawal, guilt-induction, or negative affect-laden expressions (e.g., disappointment, shame), relational aggression; has been related to increased relational aggression across age groups and cultures
- *positive parenting* mutually contingent, warm, sensitive, responsive interactions with the child; linked to increased social competence, e.g., prosocial behavior and positive interactions with peers, and to less aggression and delinquency
- *negative parenting* has been assessed as over-reactive (e.g., physical/corporal punishment), rigid demanding and low warmth (authoritarian), inconsistent, harsh, or lax parenting (Egan et al., 2014; Steinberg & Silk, 2002)

Perfectionism pursuit of personal, excessively high standards for performance with value for attaining all goals set (Affrunti & Woodruff-Borden, 2017); see Table 11.1

Perseveration (PE) tendency to continue and repeat behavior after the evoking stimulus (situation) is discontinued (e.g., person remembers, for a long time, problems that the person could not solve) (a personality trait); when participants learn to attend to or sort by a particular aspect of stimuli—e.g., shape, color—perseveration happens when the contingencies/rules change and the individual/animal struggles to inhibit the now-irrelevant dimension and shift attention to the now-relevant dimension (Darby et al., 2018); perseveration occurs because of competition between latent (or long-term) memory and active (or working) memory

Persistence (P) ability to persevere despite frustration (personality trait)

Personality individual tendencies to think, feel, and behave in certain consistent ways (Caspi, 1998; see Nader, 2008)—the combined physical, mental, emotional, and social qualities, reflected in a person's thoughts, feelings, attitudes, beliefs, behaviors, and reaction patterns; temperament is a subcategory of personality (see also personality traits)

Personality traits see *Big 5*; see *briskness, perseveration, sensory sensitivity, emotional reactivity, endurance, activity, exuberance* (novelty seeking), *surgency* (Tables A5.1–5.2); see *neural-based personality traits*; see *temperament* and *integrated temperament dimensions*

Perspective-taking the ability and act of taking the perspective of another or others (Chapters 4, 6, 8, 10; Table 1.2)

Phenotype the composite of an organism's observable traits that result from the combination of her/his genetic code (genotype) and environmental influences (e.g., same moth species with color variant that may be related to evolutionary camouflage)

Play types (additional types of play are discussed in the book: dramatic or fantastical pretend play, free play, traumatic play):

- **rhythmic play** gross motor movements such as body rocking, arm waving, and foot kicking without an apparent goal; associated with neuromuscular development
- **exercise play** e.g., physically vigorous gross motor locomotion—ball chasing, running, jumping, climbing, fleeing, pushing, pulling; may be called vigorous play
- **rough-and-tumble play** e.g., "soft" or open-hand hitting, pushing, or teasing; positive affect: smiling or laughing and staying together after *rough* play; playful tumbling, hitting, grappling, wrestling, and kicking, and sometimes chasing

Poly-victimization (see also cumulative traumas) exposure to more than one (especially multiple) types of trauma; 4 or more traumas have been studied as poly-victimization; modified operational definition: multiple types of exposures to potentially traumatic events, with childhood maltreatment and sexual assault weighted 4 and 3 times greater, respectively, than other forms of victimization (Finkelhor, Ormrod, & Turner, 2009; Ford et al., 2018a); Ford et al. (2018a) recommend a "person-centered method of empirically identifying distinct profiles of types of victimization, without assuming a priori the relative contribution of each type to the individual's risk of impairment" (p. 327)—e.g., youth involved in the juvenile justice system

Positive affect/emotionality (trait) characterized by positive affect, reward sensitivity, and sociability (sociability may be less central than affective and motivational components, Olino et al., 2010)

Positive reactivity orientation to and exploration of novelty; related to Extraversion/Sensation-Seeking (a temperament trait)

Positivity bias inclination to view things such that a positive self-image is maintained

Posttraumatic growth (PTG) positive posttrauma changes such as an increased appreciation of life, setting new goals/priorities, a sense of increased personal strength, identifying new possibilities, increased closeness of intimate relationships, or positive spiritual change (see Chapter 4)

Pre-ejection period (PEP) reactivity the time between left ventricular depolarization and ejection of blood into the aorta (see Bell et al., 2017); a marker of SNS reactivity via β-adrenergic mechanisms

Primary control coping attempts to directly change a situation or one's emotional reactions to the situation (Evans et al., 2016); includes problem-solving, emotional expression, and emotion regulation

Progesterone a female steroid hormone released by the corpus luteum; stimulates the uterus to prepare for pregnancy

Proprioceptive stimulation/awareness overall sense of body position, movement/motion, and acceleration; infants experience continual proprioceptive feedback from joints, muscles, and the vestibular system (Bahrick, 2010); unconscious perception of the body related to self-propelled movement (stimuli arising from the body itself; Filippette et al., 2013)

Prospective memory memory for intention(s) to be performed in the future (involves recollection of a past intention); subjects may use environmental cue(s) to know when to retrieve the intention (Roediger et al., 2008)

Protective factors factors that reduce the likelihood of poor outcomes (DeKlyen & Greenberg, 2018; Greenberg & Riggs, 2015; Nader, 2008; Nader & Fletcher, 2014; Tables 3.2; see also resilience)

Pruning after periods of rapid growth of neural/synaptic connections, selective elimination (*pruning*) occurs in a "use it or lose it" fashion (Andersen et al., 2008; Blakemore & Choudhury, 2006; Nader, 2008; Schore, 2003)

Random failure (brain related) see targeted attacks

Reactive Attachment Disorder (ages 9 months to school age) see DSM-5 and ICD-10/11 (see Chapter 6)

Reactive Attachment Disorder (school age) categories: *Disinhibited Indiscriminate* (e.g., overfriendly behavior, asking strangers personal questions, seeking comfort from strangers, wandering away from caregivers); *Attention Seeking* (e.g., demanding and possessive behavior; wary and watchful behavior); *Superficial Relationships* (difficulty forming meaningful, reciprocal relationships with caregivers; superficiality in relationships with familiar or unfamiliar adults); *Unpredictability* (endorsed by comparison and out-of-home youth; may be developmentally normal) (Kay & Green, 2013)

Reconsolidation process by which a retrieved memory is stabilized again (e.g., social reward-related memory, Achterberg et al., 2013); successful transfer of memories to pre-existent, autobiographical cortical memory circuits (e.g., traumatic memory; van Marle, 2015); after retrieval or reactivation of a memory, a memory is believed to be labile and modifiable; if PTSD is viewed as a failure of traumatic memory consolidation (memories remain linked to fear and unconsolidated), reduction of PTSD symptoms requires reconsolidation (van Marle, 2015); while newly acquired memory is initially unstable and prone to facilitation and impairment, memory consolidation progressively stabilizes a memory, making it resistant to interference (Achterberg et al., 2013) (see Appendix—Additional Methods)

Reflective functioning or **Self-reflective functioning** like metacognitive monitoring or theory of mind, this suggests an ability to perceive and understand one's own and others' behaviors in terms of mental states or psychological experiences; ability to interpret the meaning of others' behavior by considering underlying mental states and intentions; a continuum from denial of mental states, to a basic capacity to recognize simple thoughts and feelings, to emergence of true reflective awareness, i.e., the ability to understand behavior in relationship to mental states and to understand both the nature and dynamic interplay of such states (e.g., Fonagy et al., 1998; Fonagy & Bateman, 2016)

Rejection sensitivity a tendency to anxiously or angrily expect rejection, to readily perceive rejection, and to overreact to rejection (e.g., Zimmer-Gembeck et al., 2014)

Relational aggression derogation, insults, gossip, threats; harms others through threat or actual damage to their relationships (see Nader, 2008)

Repressive coping a tendency to avoid unpleasant thoughts, emotions, and memories (see also over-general memory)

Resilience (subset of protective factors) qualities that assist a person to fare better in the face of adversity—e.g., accurate locus of control, higher self-esteem, increased self-regulatory skills, and ability to maintain friendships; reflects an ability to maintain a stable equilibrium in adverse circumstances (Bonanno, 2008; Gundogar et al., 2014); associated with reduced vulnerability and the presence of protective factors—e.g., enabling personal qualities and positive environmental conditions (Table A1.4; Fergusson & Horwood, 2003; Masten & Powell, 2003; see Nader, 2008)

Resistant attachment AKA *anxious-ambivalent*; *preoccupied* in adolescents or adults (Table A3.2)

Respiratory sinus arrhythmia (RSA) the cyclical variability in heart rate that occurs at the frequency of breathing—i.e., normal increase in heart rate upon breathing in and normally diminished heart rate during breathing out; is more pronounced in childhood (tends to persist for those who remain on a good exercise program; e.g., Morales et al., 2015); used as a cardiac index of parasympathetic (PNS) regulation; PNS stimulation downregulates heart rate, and higher RSA suggests greater PNS stimulation (Smith et al., 2016a); has been used as a cardiac-vagal index; likely serves in coordinating and maintaining the interplay between respiratory and cardiovascular systems and, for humans, is related to levels of alertness, types of emotions, mental activity, and arousal (Grossman & Taylor, 2007); under steady-state conditions, RSA is inversely related to respiration rate and directly related to tidal volume—i.e., rapid shallow breathing greatly attenuates RSA, and slow deep breathing produces maximal RSA levels (Grossman & Taylor, 2007)

- *Measurement* may be *measured* at the peak, on the breathing turning point before exhalation, and at its valley at end of exhalation, and then calculating the peak-valley difference (Leventon et al., 2014; Mortola et al., 2016); has been measured as the difference between peak and valley/trough heartbeat measure over the person's mean heart rate (difference in heart rate divided by mean heart rate, Mortola et al., 2016); is believed to be influenced by respiration rate, depth of breathing, activity level, and other factors (Grossman & Taylor, 2007)

- *Associations:* a key indicator of self-regulation in preschoolers (Smith et al., 2016a); higher baseline RSA (believed by many to indicate greater vagal influence on the heart) may reflect a greater ability to engage with the environment and to cope with environmental challenges (Porges, 2007); RSA has been associated with enhanced learning and sustained attention (de Barbaro et al., 2016)

RSA augmentation increase in RSA from baseline; inhibits the SNS and supports social engagement behaviors (Morales et al., 2015); augmentation to challenge has been associated with internalizing problems

RSA reactivity high RSA during baseline and RSA suppression during experimental challenge is positively related to children's emotion-regulation and socioemotional competence, while low baseline RSA and/or lack of RSA suppression have been linked to poor emotional regulation or extreme emotional responses (Morales et al., 2015; may differ by gender); low baseline RSA has been related to externalizing for boys or both genders and some evidence suggests it relates to internalizing (see Morales et al. for summary); higher RSA suppression has most consistently related to low externalizing and low internalizing; temperament may be a factor in inconsistent findings

RSA suppression (also called RSA withdrawal) is a decrease in RSA relative to baseline (Cho et al., 2017; Morales et al., 2015); permits more engagement of the sympathetic nervous system (SNS), mobilizing resources for a flight–flight response; in response to challenge may allow a child to shift focus from internal homeostatic demands to generation of coping strategies in order to control affective or behavioral arousal (Fox & Calkins, 2003; also permits sustained attention and behaviors indicative of active coping, and mediated by the PNS; may demonstrate greater effort (e.g., insecure-avoidant children who are engaged in minimizing distress and self-oriented regulation; Hill-Soderlund et al., 2008); indicates a defensive response suggesting the recruiting of internal resources to effortfully and actively cope with an external challenge (like sAA elevations)

- *Associations* has been associated with better emotion regulation and lower levels of behavior problems, negativity, aggression, and social withdrawal as well as with better social skills in young children (e.g., ages 1–2, Cho et al., 2017); across studies, Graziano & Derefinko (2013) found that it is only the interaction of RSA baseline and RSA withdrawal that predicts outcomes and found that RSA withdrawal contributed to children's adaptive functioning for externalizing, internalizing, and cognitive/academic domains but was not linked to social problems except for clinical populations (at-risk/clinical group levels of baseline RSA and RSA withdrawal were lower than for children from community/healthy samples)

Retrospective memory memory for the past or for the effects of past experience on current behavior (Roediger et al., 2008; Table 1.1)

Reward Dependence (trait) tendency to respond markedly to signals of reward (e.g., social reward; degree of sentimental response; attachment-related); has overlapped with extraversion and agreeableness (see Rettew et al., 2008); is among combined traits related to low social competence (with high novelty seeking and harm avoidance, low persistence; Baer et al., 2015; Brüne, 2014)

Risk factors variables empirically associated with a disorder that predict the increased probability of its occurrence (Ingram & Price, 2001; Nader, 2015; see Nader & Fletcher, 2014; Tables 3.1a–c); any environmental or personal factor associated with increased likelihood of negative or undesirable outcomes (Kraemer, Lowe, & Kupfer, 2005 in Evans et al., 2013); *Vulnerabilities* are a subset of risk factors—physiological (e.g., genes, health), cognitive (e.g., low IQ, attentional biases), affective (e.g., regulation, reactivity), behavioral (e.g., low sociable; withdrawn; aggressive, low proactive), or social systems

Rumination perseveratively thinking about one's own emotions or problems without actively changing the circumstances for the better or problem-solving (Kolubinski et al., 2017); it enhances the effects of mood on cognitive processes—to draw on negative thoughts/memories when conceptualizing the present; intensifies the emotion that is a basis of the rumination (e.g., anger, depression, anxiety, self-criticism)

Salience detection an attention mechanism that involves detection of what is most pertinent or of what stands out (e.g., may be guided by visual contrast, survival, incentive; see McCrory et al., 2017); directing the attention-to-behavior to the most pertinent actions requires emotions (hence posttrauma numbing may interfere with salience detection; Lanius et al., 2015); body scan meditations plus helping a person to identify which bodily sensations are associated with which emotions assists overcoming emotional detachment and reinstating salience detection

Salience network a neural connectivity network involved in salience detection; dorsal anterior cingulate cortex and the fronto-insular cortex have a key role in salience detection; SN's anterior cingulate mediates engagement of CEN and disengagement of DMN (Lanius et al., 2015)

Salivary Alpha-Amylase (sAA) an enzyme which breaks down starches and has shown increases, for adults and adolescents, in response to social and academic stressors (Hill-Soderlund et al., 2008); used as a measure of SNS activity (stress response; Barel et al., 2018; Hill-Soderlund et al., 2008); elevations indicate a defensive response in which an individual is recruiting internal resources to effortfully and actively cope with an external challenge (like RSA withdrawal; Hill-Soderlund et al., 2008); sAA but not cortisol raised following a mental arithmetic task (see Barel et al., 2018)

Scaffolding assisting a child just enough so that s/he can use her/his own skills toward successful completion of a task (Meuwissen & Carlson, 2015); providing support to a child during learning of a new skill; lessening support as a child learns the skill until the child can do the skill on her/his own; support may include, e.g., making suggestions while encouraging problem-solving, by asking probing questions, by modeling (see Stevenson & Crnic, 2013)

Secondary control coping involves efforts to adapt to a situation by regulating attention and cognitions, e.g., acceptance, cognitive restructuring, positive thinking, or distraction (Evans et al., 2016)

Self-defeaters (youth humor style) scored high on self-defeating humor, and low on the other three adult types (see Humor styles)

Self-defeating humor self-disparaging and ingratiating humor; humor to enhance relationships at one's own expense (Martin et al., 2003); may use humorous behavior as a means of hiding negative feelings or to avoid coping with problems constructively

Self-enhancement a more than average positive bias in favor of self

Self-enhancing humor used to enhance the self through activities such as maintaining a humorous perspective in the face of stress and adversity (Besser et al., 2015); may approach life, in general with an amusing point of view and find the amusing side even in negative situations (Başak & Can, 2014); relates to cheerfulness, optimistic coping, and well-being and to fewer PT symptoms (Başak & Can, 2014; Besser et al., 2015)

Self-esteem satisfaction with oneself as a person (Harter, Waters, & Whitesell, 1998)

Self-silencing behaviors process of silencing personal thoughts and feelings in order to make and maintain relationships (Obeid et al., 2018)

Semantic memories abstract factual knowledge (e.g., remembering 1st U.S. president; Bjorklund & Sellers, 2014)

Sensory memories Table 1.1

Sensory-motor integration problems e.g., hypersensitivity to sounds, tactile sensitivity, poor motor coordination; see sensory modulation dysfunction

Sensory modulation occurs within the central nervous system (CNS) by balancing both excitatory and inhibitory sensory inputs arising within one's sensory mechanisms and occurring external to the body (the balancing of these inputs are seen in adaptive behavior—e.g., screening out an interrupting noise while watching a pleasant scene with pleasant sounds; Atchison, 2007); based on the process of neuromodulation—changing the electrical properties of a neuron through chemical means via neurotransmitters or hormones; individuals modulate sensory input in different ways (e.g., infants—pacifier; cuddling; cuddling and rocking or gentle massage; Atchison, 2007)

Sensory modulation dysfunction (also referred to as sensory integration dysfunction) problems modulating or integrating internal and/or external stimuli; under-response (hyper-modulated) or over-response (hypo-modulated) to stimuli (Atchison, 2007); a child may shift between over (e.g., scream, cry, and cover ears) and under-response (e.g., covering eyes, crouching under table; fetal-like position; or less excitable than others in response to stimuli—requiring much more stimulation to be *charged up*); when sleep-deprived or exposed to significant stressors, the ability to modulate or integrate incoming stimuli may be compromised (Atchison, 2007); may be easily distracted by competing stimuli—e.g., a slightly buzzing noise in an overhead light or the temperature (Atchison, 2007); may include extreme sensitivity to sensory stimuli—e.g., noise or specific sounds, smells, textures/touch; sensory modulation dysfunction or disorders have been noted for a variety of diagnostic conditions—posttrauma conditions (e.g., HPA dysregulation e.g., after abuse or neglect), fetal alcohol syndrome, autistic spectrum disorder, learning disabilities, ADD, mental retardation, and central auditory processing disorder (Atchison, 2007)

Sensory sensitivity (SS) the capacity to respond to low level sensory stimuli (e.g., smell even subtle fragrances) (personality trait); the capacity to respond to sensory stimuli when stimulating value is low; more sensitive with specific aspects in dopamine DAT1 and SNAP-25 polymorphisms (see Table A4.1; Oniszczenko & Dragan, 2012; Dragan et al., 2012); low level of stimulation needed to evoke a sensory response (Zentner & Shiner, 2012)

Sensitivity to environment (sensitivity to context) fare worse than comparisons in negative environments, profit more than comparisons from positive environments

Separation Anxiety Disorder "developmentally inappropriate and excessive fear or anxiety concerning separation from those to whom the individual is attached" (APA, 2013, p. 190)

Shame trait shame includes, e.g., sense of self-directed disgust, anger, and/or global badness (Fletcher, 2014; Tangney, Wagner, Fletcher, & Gramzow, 1992)

Shifting flexible switching of attention, e.g., between tasks, mental sets, and strategies (Bunge & Crone, 2009; Rose et al., 2012a) (see attention set shifting) (see cognitive flexibility—AKA cognitive switching)

Short-term memory see Table 1.1

Slow-to-warm (temperament category) slow initial response (withdrawal), low initial adaptability but tendency to adapt with increased exposure, lower energy levels of response (low intensity), low activity, and a more negative mood (low intensity); a temperamental category in the New York Longitudinal Study, along with easy and difficult temperaments (Chess & Thomas, 1991)

Social buffering buffering of reactions by efforts of a trusted other; following conditions of stress/threat, the presence of or vocalizations with a supportive significant other (e.g., parent) can dampen cortisol production (stress hormone) and increase oxytocin (see above) (Hostinar & Gunnar, 2013; Seltzer, Ziegler & Pollack, 2010); the social buffering effect (cortisol dampening) has been found as early as 13 months in human infants (e.g., for securely attached children: accompanying toddlers to 1st few days of day care—although cortisol elevates 60 min. after mother's departure—for securely attached children with fearful temperaments (Hostinar et al., 2014); for infants, touch (tactile stimulation) also can dampen cortisol reactivity (e.g., by six-month-olds' mother; massage to facilitate calm states; for premature infants; see Hostinar et al., 2014)

Stress inoculation when stress challenges a person but is not enough to overwhelm them; may foster adaptation, resiliency, and better developmental skills; may decrease the reactivity of stress responsive neurobiological and neuroendocrine systems to stressors experienced later in life (Gunnar, Herrera, & Hostinar, 2009d; see Nader & Fletcher, 2014). For adults, some evidence suggests that stress inoculation (e.g., refuting/confronting six potentially stress-producing thoughts/ideas) may be more beneficial for men, and ventilation (e.g., two phone sessions talking to a counselor about safety and coping issues; connection) more beneficial for women in reducing *helplessness* under conditions of continuous war threat (Farchi & Gidron, 2010; neither reduced mental health outcomes)

Supervisory neglect caregiver is unable to adequately care for a child (e.g., because of intoxication), leaves child without an appropriate caregiver, and/or allows the child to be exposed to adverse events (e.g., criminal activity, domestic violence)

Sympathetic-Adrenomedullary system (SAM) the hormonal component of the sympathetic nervous system (SNS) producing epinephrine and norepinephrine (SNS is an arm of the autonomic nervous system, ANS, which serves many functions beyond fight-or-flight; Gunnar et al., 2015); SAM influences fight-flight and assists coping with threat; supports arousal and attention in the central nervous system—with increases in activity mediated by the ANS (i.e., heart rate, blood pressure) during effortful tasks (even without threat to social or physical selves—e.g., Stroop, mirror drawing) and usually does not increase activity of the HPA axis, nor increase production of epinephrine from the adrenal medulla (typically released after perception of threat; Gunnar et al., 2015)

Sympathetic nervous system (SNS) activated as a part of the stress response system; releases epinephrine and norepinephrine to enhance cardiovascular performance, inhibit digestion, increase alertness, and make energy available for the muscles; SNS responds to emergency and arousal (fear, flight, fight, and sex), while PNS is calming (above)

Symptom complexity the number of different types of symptoms or symptom clusters that are simultaneously elevated in the clinical range for a person (e.g., Briere et al., 2016; Hodges et al., 2013); multiple simultaneously presenting, although phenomenologically discrete psychological difficulties (Briere & Scott, 2015)—e.g., for Major Depressive Disorder, a given episode may simultaneously include high depressive, anxiety, cognitive, and vegetative symptoms (Briere et al., 2016); is predicted by cumulative trauma and may represent a complicated traumatic reaction (see Briere et al., 2016); for children, symptom complexity (e.g., symptoms of depression, anger, and posttraumatic stress) also has been predicted by poly-victimization or cumulative trauma exposure (i.e., exposure to multiple types of trauma; Hodges et al., 2013)

Synchrony reciprocity, coordination, co-regulation, or mutual responsiveness (Feldman, Bamberger, & Kanat-Maymon, 2013a); an interactive contingent communication (Beebe et al., 2016); an important aspect of attachment formation; consists of different behavioral components for fathers and mothers (Chapters 4, 5, 7, 10); patterns of behavior may elicit synchrony or discord; reestablished synchrony may restore coping and help recovery from stress (Schore, 2003); see also mirror neurons

Targeted attacks (brain related) in the assessment of brain networks, based on degree and number of links to which each brain region is functionally connected, a type of systematic removal of nodes from those that have the highest degree of connectivity (then the next highest and so on); after each removal, associated changes on network topology are evaluated; often random failures are also studied (Joyce, Hayasaka, & Laurienti, 2013)

Temperament a subset of personality traits reflecting early dispositions and emotional styles; early dispositions (e.g., affective, attentional, arousal) upon which personality is based (Caspi,

1998); 4 adolescent factors—negative affectivity, positive affectivity, effortful control, affiliation (see Baetens et al., 2011; see below)

- **Integrated Temperament dimensions**
  Zentner and Shiner, 2012 (combined from across studies):

1. Negative emotionality (neuroticism)
   - BI (inhibition from novel, unfamiliar people and situations)—fearfulness, harm avoidance, anxiety
   - Anger (aggressive or irritated behavior in response to pain or frustration)—irritability, frustration
2. Positive emotionality (extraversion)
   - high-intensity pleasure (propensity to positive emotions—e.g., pleasure, positive anticipation, excitement in social interaction)—exuberance, hyperthymia, sensation-seeking, high-intensity pleasure
   - low-intensity pleasure (ability for delight in response to sensuous gratification and comfort)—consummatory hedonia, low-intensity pleasure
   - activity level (frequency, briskness, vigor of motor movement, intolerance of enforced idleness)—briskness, tempo
3. Effortful control—constraint, willpower, inhibitory control, persistence; regulatory aspects of temperament; inversely correlated with impulsivity
   - attention/persistence—capacity for attentional focus; control as a basis for persistence; self-control willpower, low impulsivity, low under-control
   - inhibitory control—ability to inhibit a dominant response and/or activate a subdominant response, to plan, to detect error; delay of gratification
4. Sensory sensitivity—level of stimulation needed to evoke sensory response; perceptual sensitivity, threshold, high sensitivity, sensory defensiveness
5. Empathy/affiliativeness—disposition to recognize and value salient social cues as basis of affiliative reward; cuddliness, kindness, reward dependence.

- **Preschoolers:** De Pauw, Mervielde, and Leeuwen (2009) examined 28 temperament scales and 18 personality-scales for preschoolers (ages 4–5): Sociability, Activity, Conscientiousness, Disagreeableness, Emotionality, and Sensitivity

Tend and Befriend protecting offspring, blending into environment, and turning to others in the social group—e.g., for help, "talk it out" (Taylor, 2002)

Testosterone a steroid hormone that stimulates development of male secondary sexual characteristics, produced mainly in the testes; also in the ovaries and adrenal cortex

Theory of Mind the ability to attribute mental states—e.g., beliefs, intentions, desires, pretending, knowledge—to oneself and others as well as to understand that others have beliefs, desires and intentions different from one's own (Premack & Woodruff, 1978); linked to empathy (Coplan et al., 2005; Rochat, 2003); see also, perspective-taking, reflective function, metacognitive functioning; see Table 1.2

Third-party/person perspective observation of others interacting with each other; an outside perspective; a narrators' perspective, if the narrator is not "you" or "I," but is an observer or a person telling the story of others; may include seeing self from a distanced perspective

Thwarted belongingness the perception of social isolation—i.e., feeling a lack of social connectedness, feeling alone, feeling no one is/will be available in times of need (Joiner, 2005; Acosta et al., 2017)

Trauma-focused coping effortful focus on the thoughts, images, and memories associated with a traumatic event

Traumatic play play that includes traumatic themes (e.g., trauma-related script-like actions, fears, intense wishes or fantasies—e.g., revenge), reenactments, and/or emotions related to aspects of a traumatic event(s) (Nader, 2008; Nader & Pynoos, 1991; Terr, 1981); play activity with predominantly negative affects, frequent acting-out/morbid themes, lowered developmental level (lower than actual age), and reduced awareness by the child of him- or herself as a player significantly has predicted more PTSD symptoms (Cohen et al., 2010); also coping strategies classified as "overwhelmed re-experiencing" (e.g., mental states lack coherent structure; child may be overwhelmed by emotions or seem frozen, disconnected, tense or hypervigilant; narrative may be missing or contain catastrophic themes) rather than "reenactment with soothing" (e.g., reenactment of trauma themes; affect expressed freely; satisfactory ending achieved), which is characteristic of posttrauma play and PTSD (Cohen et al., 2010; Nader & Pynoos, 1991); other assessed form of content was "reenactment without soothing" (e.g., expression of disturbing—i.e., frightening, aggressive—affects or constriction of affect; activity fails to provide relief and does not end in satiation)

Undermodulation emotional dysregulation in which the individual experiences painful emotional states—e.g., fear, shame, anger, guilt; associated with hyperarousal, hypervigilance, increased interoceptive awareness, salience detection, and heightened insula activation; characteristic of PTSD (e.g., Lanius, 2015; Lanius et al., 2012)

Vagal tone the vagal nerve (an important component of the PNS, above) is responsible for the body at rest (e.g., heart rate, glandular activity)—"rest and digest"; assessed by measuring the variability in heart rate that occurs at the frequency of breathing (RSA, above); suppression of vagal tone is believed to be a physiological strategy that allows sustained attention and behaviors indicative of active coping that are mediated by the parasympathetic nervous system (Fox & Calkins, 2003; Morales et al., 2015)

Vulnerabilities see risk factors

Working memory holding and manipulating information in short-term memory; updating—i.e., constant monitoring and rapid addition/deletion of working memory contents (Bunge & Crone, 2009; Rose et al., 2012a); employs EFs such as inhibition (ignoring previous incoming information), shifting (from different mental models or to new or relevant information), and updating (based on incoming information; van Dooren & Inglis, 2015); in lab tests, complexity of tasks influences performance)—e.g., nonverbal face tasks (least complex) showed no performance increases after age 20; self-ordered search tasks (most complex) showed steady improvement until age 16—e.g., for three search locations, performance leveled age 6; for four, leveled age 17; for six to eight locations, performance varied for all groups (see Best et al., 2009)

References

Aas M, Djurovic S, Athanasiu L, Steen N, Agartz I, Lorentzen S et al. (2012). Serotonin transporter gene polymorphism, childhood trauma, and cognition in patients with psychotic disorders. *Schizophrenia Bull, 38*(1), 15–22.

Aas M, Haukvik U, Djurovic S, Tesli M, Athanasiu L, Bjella T et al. (2014). Interplay between childhood trauma and BDNF val66met variants on blood BDNF mRNA levels and on hippocampus subfields volumes in schizophrenia spectrum and bipolar disorders. *J Psychiatr Res, 59*, 14–21.

Abbo C, Kinyanda E, Kizza R, Levin J, Ndyanabangi S, & Stein D (2013). Prevalence, comorbidity and predictors of anxiety disorders in children and adolescents in rural north-eastern Uganda. *Child Adol Psych Men*, 7, 21. doi: 10.1186/1753-2000-7-21.

Abdeen Z, Qasrawi R, Nabil S, & Shaheen M (2008). Psychological reactions to Israeli occupation: Findings from the national study of school-based screening in Palestine. *Int J Behav Dev, 32*, 290–297.

Aber J, Brown J, & Jones S (2003). Developmental trajectories toward violence in middle childhood: Course, demographic differences, and response to school-based intervention. *Devel Psychol, 39*(2), 324–348.

Abraham E, Raz G, Zagoory-Sharon O, & Feldman R (2018). Empathy networks in the parental brain and their long-term effects on children's stress reactivity and behavior adaptation. *Neuropsychologia*, 116, Part A, 75–85.

Abrams H, & Pearman H (2007). *Art therapy for children of all ages: A cookbook for therapists*. Denver, CO: Outskirts Press.

Abshire C, Hagues R, Hermann M, Scherr A, & Walters L (2008). *The child's capacity to participate in deprivation proceedings*. Athens, GA: The Carl Vincent School of Government, U of Georgia. (unpublished research).

Abu-Kaf, S, & Braun-Lewensohn, O (2015). Paths to depression among two different cultural contexts: Comparing Bedouin Arab and Jewish students. *J Cross Cult Psychol, 46*(4), 612–630.

Achterberg E, Trezza V, & Vanderschuren L (2013). ß-Adrenoreceptor stimulation mediates reconsolidation of social reward-related memories. *PLoS ONE*, 7(6), e39639. doi: 10.1371/journal.pone.0039639.

Acosta L, Hagan C, & Joiner T (2017). Burdensomeness, belongingness, and suicidal desire among Hispanic/Latino individuals: Examining the effect of ethnicity in the interpersonal theory of suicide. *Psi Chi Journal of Psychological Research, 22*(1), 54–63.

Adam E, Gunnar M, & Tanaka A (2004). Adult attachment, parent emotion, and observed parenting behavior: Mediator and moderator models. *Child Dev, 75*, 110–122.

Adam E, Quinn M, Tavernier R, McQuillan M, Dahlke K, & Gilbert K (2017). Diurnal cortisol slopes and mental and physical health outcomes: A systematic review and meta-analysis. *Psychoneuroendocrino, 83*, 25–41.

Adams G, Stoops M, & Skomro R (2014). Sleep tight: Exploring the relationship between sleep and attachment style across the life span. *Sleep Med Rev, 18*, 495–507.

Adams R, Bukowski W, & Bagwell C (2005). Stability of aggression during early adolescence as moderated by reciprocated friendship status and friend's aggression. *Int J Behav Dev, 29*(2), 139–145.

Adams Z, Moreland A, Cohen J, Lee R, Hanson R, Danielson C et al. (2016). Polyvictimization: Latent profiles and mental health outcomes in a clinical sample of adolescents. *Psychol Violence, 6*(1), 145–155.

Afifi T, & MacMillan H (2011). Resilience following child maltreatment: A review of protective factors. *CJP, 56*, 266–272.

Affrunti N, Geronimi E, & Woodruff-Borden J (2015). Language of perfectionistic parents predicting child anxiety diagnostic status. *J Anxiety Disord, 30*, 94–102.

Affrunti N, Gramszlo C, & Woodruff-Borden J (2016). Executive function moderates the association between fearful temperament and dimensions of perfectionism. *Pers Indiv Differ, 89*, 117–122.

Affrunti N, & Woodruff-Borden J (2017). Emotional control mediates the association between dimensions of perfectionism and worry in children. *Child Psychiat Hum D, 48*(1), 73–81.

Affrunti N, & Woodruff-Borden J (2014). Perfectionism in pediatric anxiety and depressive disorders. *Clin Child Fam Psychol Rev*, *17*(3), 299–317.

Afshari A, Neshat-Doost H, Maracy M, Ahmady M, & Amiri S (2014). The effective comparison between emotion-focused cognitive behavioral group therapy and cognitive behavioral group therapy in children with separation anxiety disorder. *J Res Med Sci*, *19*, 221–227.

Agrati D, Browne D, Jonas W, Meaney M, Atkinson L, Steiner M, & Fleming A (2015). Maternal anxiety from pregnancy to 2 years postpartum: Transactional patterns of maternal early adversity and child temperament. *Arch Women's Ment Health*, *18*, 693–705.

Ahern J, Galea S, Resnick H, & Vlahov D (2004). Television images and probable Posttraumatic Stress Disorder after September 11: The role of background characteristics, event exposures, and perievent panic. *J Nerv Ment Dis*, *192*, 217–226.

Ahnert L, Teufl L, Ruiz N, Piskernik B, Supper B, Remiorz S et al. (2017). Father–child play during the preschool years and child internalizing behaviors: Between robustness and vulnerability. *Inf Mental Hlth J*, *38*(6), 743–756.

Ainsworth M (1973). The development of infant–mother attachment. In B Caldwell, H Ricciuti (Eds), *Review of child development research* (Vol. 3, pp. 1–94). Chicago, IL: University of Chicago Press.

Ainsworth MD (1989). Attachments beyond infancy. *American Psychologist*, *44*, 709–716.

Ainsworth M, Blehar M, Waters E, & Wall S (1978). *Patterns of attachment: A psychological study of the Strange Situation*. Hillsdale, NJ: Erlbaum.

Aitcheson R, Abu-Bader S, Howell M, Khalil D, & Elbedour S (2017). Resilience in Palestinian adolescents living in Gaza. *Psychol Trauma-US*, *9*(1), 36–43.

Albrecht B, Brandels D, Uebell-von Sandersleben H, Valko L et al. (2014). Genetics of preparation and response control in ADHD: The role of DRD4 and DAT1. *J Child Psychol Psyc*, *55*(8), 914–923.

Alcaro A, Huber R, & Panksepp J (2007). Behavioral functions of the mesolimbic dopaminergic system: An affective neuroethological perspective. *Brain Res Rev*, *56*, 283–321. abstract.

Alcock, M., & Murphy, E. (1998, March). Type development: From unconscious perfection through conscious imperfection to conscious completion. Paper presented at Counter attack: Rising to the challenges of education. The Role of Psychological Type Conference, Orlando, FL.

Aldao A, Nolen-Hoeksema S, & Schweizer S (2010). Emotion-regulation strategies across psychopathology: A meta-analytic review. *Clin Psychol Rev*, *30*(2), 217–237.

Aldridge A, & Roesch S (2008a). Coping with daily stressors. *Hispanic J Behav Sci*, *30*(3), 340–356.

Aldridge A, & Roesch S (2008b). Developing coping typologies of minority adolescents: A latent profile analysis. *J Adolescence*, *31*(4), 499–517.

Alessandri S, & Lewis M (1996). Differences in pride and shame in maltreated and nonmaltreated preschoolers. *Child Dev*, *67*, 1857–1869.

Alexander N, Kirschbaum C, Wankerl M, Stauch B, Stalder T, Steudte-Schmiedgen S et al. (2018). Glucocorticoid receptor gene methylation moderates the association of childhood trauma and cortisol stress reactivity. *Psychoneuroendocrino*, *90*, 68–75.

Alhusen J, Hayat M, & Gross D (2013). A longitudinal study of maternal attachment and infant developmental outcomes. *Arch Women's Ment Health*, *16*, 521–529.

Alizad A, Fatemi M, Wold L, & Greenleaf J (2004). Performance of vibro-acoustography in detecting microcalcifications in excised human breast tissue: A study of 74 tissue samples. *IEEE Trans Med Imaging*, *23*(3), 307–312. abstract.

Allan N, Hume L, Allan D, Farrington A, & Lonigan C (2014). Relations between inhibitory control and the development of academic skills in preschool and kindergarten: A meta-analysis. *Dev Psychol*, *50*(10), 2368–2379. abstract.

Allen B, & Hoskowitz N (2017). Structured trauma-focused CBT and unstructured play/experiential techniques in treatment of sexually abused children: A field study with practicing clinicians. *Child Maltreat*, *22*(2), 112–120.

Allen B, & Kronenberg M (2014). *Treating traumatized children: A casebook of evidence-based therapies*. New York: Guilford.

Allen B, Oseni A, & Allen K (2012). The evidence-based treatment of chronic posttraumatic stress disorder and traumatic grief in an adolescent: A case study. *Psychol Trauma-US*, *4*(6), 631–639.

Allen B, Timmer S, & Urquiza A (2014). Parent–child interaction therapy as an attachment-based intervention: Theoretical rationale and pilot data with adopted children. *Child Youth Serv Rev*, *47*, 334–341.

Allen J, & Fonagy P (2006). *The handbook of mentalization-based treatment*. Chichester, UK: Wiley and Sons.

Allen J, Porter M, McFarland F, Marsh P, & McElhaney K (2005). The two faces of adolescents' success with peers: Adolescent popularity, social adaptation, and deviant behavior. *Child Dev*, *76*, 747–760.

Allen J, & Tan J (2018). The multiple facets of attachment in adolescence. In J Cassidy, P Shaver (Eds), *Handbook of attachment* (3rd ed., pp. 399–415). New York: Guilford.

Allen K, Cornell D, Lorek E, & Sheras P (2008). Response of school personnel to student threat assessment training. *Sch Eff Sch Improv*, *19*(3), 319–332.

Alloway TP (2006). How does working memory work in the classroom? *Educ Res Rev-Neth*, *1*(4), 134–139.

Almas A, Degnan K, Nelson C, Zeanah C, & Fox N (2016). IQ at Age 12 following a history of institutional care: Findings from the Bucharest Early Intervention Project. *Dev Psychol*, *52*(11), 1858–1866.

Almas A, Degnan K, Walker O, Radulescu A, Nelson C, Zeanah C, & Fox N (2015). The effects of early institutionalization and foster care intervention on children's social behaviors at the age of eight. *Soc Dev*, *24*(2), 225–239.

Alonso-Alberca N, Vergara A, Fernandez-Berrocal P, Johnson S, & Izard C (2012). The adaptation and validation of the Emotion Matching Task for preschool children in Spain. *Int J Behav Dev*, *36*(6), 489–494.

Altenburger L, Lang S, Schoppe-Sullivan S, Dush C, & Johnson S (2017). Toddlers' differential susceptibility to the effects of coparenting on social–emotional adjustment. *Int J Behav Dev*, *41*(2) 228–237.

Althoff R, Ayer L, Crehan E, Rettew D, Baer J, & Hudziak J (2012). Temperamental profiles of dysregulated children. *Child Psychiat Hum D*, *43*, 511–522.

Alvarez M-J, Masramon H, Peña C, Pont M, Gourdier C, Roura-Poch P, & Arrufat F (2015). Cumulative effects of childhood traumas: Polytraumatization, dissociation, and schizophrenia. *Community Ment Hlt J*, *51*, 54–62.

Al-Yagon M (2018). Models of child–parent attachment in attention deficit hyperactivity disorder: Links to executive functions. *Personal Relationships*, *25*, 280–298.

Al-Yagon M (2012). Subtypes of attachment security in school-age children with learning disabilities. *Learn Disability Q*, *35*(3), 170–183.

American Psychiatric Association (APA) (2013). *Diagnostic and statistical manual of mental disorders*, 5th ed (DSM-5). Washington, DC: APA.

Amico F, Meisenzahl E, Koutsouleris N, Reiser M, Moller H, Frodl T (2011). Structural MRI correlates for vulnerability and resilience to major depressive disorder. *J Psychiat Neurosci*, *36*, 15–22.

Amminger G, Chanen A, Ohmann S, Klier C, Mossaheb N, Bechdolf A et al. (2013). Ω-3 fatty acid supplementation in adolescents with borderline personality disorder and ultra-high risk criteria for psychosis: A post-hoc subgroup analysis of a double-blind randomised controlled trial. *Can J Psychiatr*, *58*, 402–408.

Anda R, & Felitti V (2003). Origins and essence of the study. *ACE Reporter*, *1*(1), 1–4.

Anda R, Felitti V, Bremner J, Walker J, Whitfield C, Perry B et al. (2006). The enduring effects of abuse and related adverse experiences in childhood: A convergence of evidence from neurobiology and epidemiology. *Eur Arch Psychiatry Clin Neurosci*, *256*, 174–186.

Andero R, & Ressler K (2012). Fear extinction and BDNF: Translating animal models of PTSD to the clinic. *Genes Brain Behav*, *11*(5), 503–512. abstract.

Andersen S (2003). Trajectories of brain development: Point of vulnerability or window of opportunity. *Neurosci Biobehav Rev*, *27*, 3–18.

Andersen S, Tomada A, Vincow E, Valente M, Polcari A, & Teicher M (2008). Preliminary evidence for sensitive periods in the effect of childhood sexual abuse on regional brain development. *J Neuropsych Clin N*, *20*(3), 292–301.

Anderson S, Qiu W, & Wheeler S (2017). The quality of father–child rough-and-tumble play and toddlers' aggressive behavior in China. *Inf Mental Hlth J*, *38*(6), 726–742.

Andiarena A, Balluerka N, Murcia M, Ibarluzea J, Glover V, & Vegas O (2017). Evening salivary cortisol and alpha-amylase at 14 months and neurodevelopment at 4 years: Sex differences. *Hormo & Behav*, *94*, 135–144.

Andre K, Kampman O, Viikki M, Illi A, Setala-Soikkeli E, Poutanen O et al. (2013). TPH1 A218C polymorphism and temperament in major depression. *BMC Psychiatry*, *13*, 118. www.biomedcentral.com/1471-244X/13/118.

Angelone D, Marcantino T, & Melillo J (2018). An evaluation of adolescent and young adult (re) victimization experiences: Problematic substance use and negative consequences. *Violence Against Wom*, *24*(5), 586–602.

Anglin D, Cohen P, & Chen H (2008). Duration of early maternal separation and prediction of schizotypal symptoms from early adolescence to midlife. *Schizophr Res*, *103*, 143–150.

Apter G, Bobin A, Genet M, Gratier M, & Devouche E (2017). Update on mental health of infants and children of parents affected with mental health issues. *Curr Psychiatry Rep*, *19*, 72. abstract.

Apter-Levi Y, Pratt M, Vakart A, Feldman M, Zagoory-Sharon O, & Feldman R (2016). Maternal depression across the first years of life compromises child psychosocial adjustment; relations to child HPA-axis functioning. *Psychoneuroendocrino*, *64*, 47–56.

Apter-Levi Y, Zagoory-Sharon O, & Feldman R (2014). Oxytocin and vasopressin support distinct configurations of social synchrony. *Brain Res*, *1580*, 124–132.

Arch J, & Craske M (2006). Mechanisms of mindfulness: Emotion regulation following a focused breathing induction. *Behav Res Ther*, *44*, 1849–1858.

Arias B, Aguilera M, Moya J, Saiz P, Villa H, Ibáñez M et al. (2012). The role of genetic variability in the SLC6A4, BDNF and GABRA6 genes in anxiety-related traits. *Acta Psychiatr Scand, 125*, 194–202.

Arnett J (2016). Does emerging adulthood theory apply across social classes? National data on a persistent question. *EA, 4*(4), 227–235.

Arnsten A, Raskind M, Taylor F, & Connor D (2015). The effects of stress exposure on prefrontal cortex: Translating basic research into successful treatments for post-traumatic stress disorder. *Neurobiology of Stress, 1*, 89–99. abstract.

Aro T, Laakso M-L, Maatta S, Tolvano A, & Poikkeus A-M (2014). Associations between toddler-age communication and kindergarten-age self-regulatory skills. *J Speech Lang Hear R, 57*, 1405–1417.

Arpi E, & Ferrari F (2013). Preterm birth and behaviour problems in infants and preschool-age children: A review of the recent literature. *Dev Med Child Neurol, 55*, 788–796.

Arvidson J, Kinniburgh K, Howard K, Spinazzola J, Strothers H, Evans M et al. (2011). Treatment of complex trauma in young children: Developmental and cultural considerations in application of the ARC intervention model. *J Child Adolesc Trauma, 4*, 34–51.

Asberg K, & Renk K (2012). Substance use coping as a mediator of the relationship between trauma symptoms and substance use consequences among incarcerated females with childhood sexual abuse histories. *Substance Use & Misuse, 47*(7), 799–808.

Ashiabi G (2000). Promoting the emotional development of preschoolers. *Ear Child Ed J, 28*(2), 79–84.

Ashton H (2005). The diagnosis and management of benzodiazepine dependence. *Curr Opin in Psychia, 18*(3), 249–255.

Åslund C, Starrin B, Leppert J, & Nilsson K (2009). Social status and shaming experiences related to adolescent overt aggression at school. *Aggressive Behav, 35*(1), 1–13.

Asok A, Bernard K, Rosen J, Dozier M, & Roth T (2014). Infant–caregiver experiences alter telomere length in the brain. *PLoS ONE, 9*(7), 3101437.

Assuncao R, Costa P, Tagliabue S, Matos P (2017). Problematic Facebook use in adolescents: Associations with parental attachment and alienation to peers. *J Child Fam Stud, 26*, 2990–2998.

Atal S, & Cheng C (2016). Socioeconomic health disparities revisited: Coping flexibility enhances health-related quality of life for individuals low in socioeconomic status. *Health Qual Life Out, 14*, 1–7. doi: 10.1186/s12955-016-0410-1.

Atchison BJ (2007). Sensory modulation disorders among children with a history of trauma: A frame of reference for speech-language pathologists. *Lang Speech Hear Ser, 38*, 109–116.

Atkinson B, Lipton D, Baughman H, Schermer J, Harris J, & Vernon P (2015). How do emotional restrictions affect the use of humor? A behavior genetic analysis of alexithymia and humor styles. *Twin Res & Hum Genetics, 18*(2), 138–141.

Auerbach J, Faroy M, Ebstein R, Kahan M, & Levine J (2001). The association of the dopamine D4 receptor gene (DRD4) and the serotonin transporter promoter gene (5-HTTLPR) with temperament in 12-month-old Infants. *J Child Psychol Psychiat, 42*(6), 777–783.

Auerbach R, Admon R, & Pizzagalli D (2014). Adolescent depression: Stress and reward dysfunction. *Harvard Rev Psychiat, 22*(3), 139–148.

Avolio B (2004). Examining the full range model of leadership: Looking back to transform forward. In D Day, S Zaccaro, S Halpin (Eds), *Leadership development for transforming organizations* (pp. 71–98). Mahwah, NJ: Lawrence Erlbaum.

Axline VM (1969). *Play therapy*. New York: Ballantine Books.

Ayduk O, & Kross E (2010). From a distance: Implications of spontaneous self-distancing for adaptive self-reflection. *J Personal and Soc Psychol, 98*(5), 809–829.

Ayduk O, & Kross E (2009). Asking "why" from a distance facilitates emotional processing: A reanalysis of Wimalaweera and Moulds (2008). *Behav Res & Ther, 47*, 88–92.

Ayduk O, Mendoza-Denton R, Mischel W, Downey G, Peake P, & Rodriguez M (2000). Regulating the interpersonal self: Strategic self-regulation for coping with rejection sensitivity. *J Pers Soc Psychol, 79*(5), 776–792.

Ayduk O, Zayas V, Downey G, Cole A, Shoda Y, & Mischel W (2008). Rejection sensitivity and executive control: Joint predictors of borderline personality features. *J Res in Personal, 42*, 151–168. abstract.

Ayer L, Jaycox L, Setodji C, Schultz D, Malsberger R, & Kofner A (2018). Youth victimization profiles and change in mental health symptoms over one year. *Psychol Trauma-US*. Advance online publication. doi.org/10.1037/tra0000359.

Ayers T, Wolchik S, Sandler I, Towhey J, Lutzke Weyer J, Jones S et al. (2010). The Family Bereavement Program: Description of a theory-based prevention program for parentally-bereaved children and adolescent. *Omega-J Death Dying, 78*, 131–143.

Babb K, Levine L, & Arseneault J (2010). Shifting gears: Coping flexibility in children with and without ADHD. *Int J Behav Dev, 34*(1), 10–23.

Babkirk S, Saunders L, Solomon B, Kessel E, Crossman A, Gokhan N, & Dennis T (2015). Executive function and temperamental fear concurrently predict deception in school-aged children. *J Moral Educ.* doi: 10.1080/03057240.2015.1087393.

Bach S, Mayes L, Alvarez A & Fonagy P (2000). Panel 1: Definition of the self. *JICAP, 1*, 5–24.

Bacro F (2012). Perceived attachment security to father, academic self-concept and school performance in language mastery. *J Child Fam Stud, 21*, 992–1002.

Badcock P, Moore E, Williamson E, Berk M et al. (2011). Modeling gene-environment interaction in longitudinal data: Risk for neuroticism due to interaction between maternal care and the Dopamine 4 Receptor gene (DRD4). *Australian J Psychol, 63*, 18–25.

Baer J, Schreck M, Althoff R, Rettew D, Harder V, Ayer L et al. (2015). Child temperament, maternal parenting behavior, and child social functioning. *J Child Fam Stud, 24*, 1152–1162.

Baer RA (2003). Mindfulness training as a clinical intervention: A conceptual and empirical review. *Clin Psychol-Sci Pr, 10*, 125–143.

Baetens I, Claes L, Willem L, Muehlenkamp J, & Bijttebier P (2011). The relationship between non-suicidal self-injury and temperament in male and female adolescents based on child- and parent-report. *Pers Indiv Differ, 50*, 527–530.

Baggerly J, & Salloum A (2010). Deaths connected to natural disasters: Helping children and families cope. In N Boyd-Webb's (Ed.) *Helping bereaved children* (3rd ed., pp. 24–262). New York: Guilford.

Bagley E, Tu K, Buckhalt J, & El-Sheikh M (2016). Community violence concerns and adolescent sleep. *Sleep Health, 2*, 57–62.

Bahrick L (2010). Intermodal perception and selective attention to intersensory redundancy: Implications for typical social development and autism. In G Bremner, T Wachs (Eds), *Blackwell handbook of infant development: Vol. 1. Basic research* (2nd ed., pp. 120–165). Hoboken, NJ: Wiley-Blackwell.

Bahrick L, & Lickliter R (2012). The role of intersensory redundancy in early perceptual, cognitive, and social development. In A Bremner, D Lewkowicz, C Spence (Eds), *Multisensory development* (pp. 183–205). Oxford: Oxford University Press.

Bahrick L, Parker J, Fivush R, & Levitt M (1998). The effects of stress on young children's memory for a natural disaster. *J Exper Psychol: Applied, 4*(4), 308–331.

Baikie K, Geerligs L, & Wilhem K (2012). Expressive writing and positive writing for participants with mood disorders: An online randomized controlled trial. *J Affect Dis, 136*, 310–319.

Bains G, Berk L, Lohman E, Daher N, Petrofsky J, Schwab E, & Deshpande P (2015). Humor's effect on short-term memory in healthy and diabetic older adults. *Altern Ther, 21*(3), 16–25.

Bair-Merritt M, Blackstone M, & Feudtner C (2006). Physical health outcomes of childhood exposure to intimate partner violence: A systematic review. *Pediatrics, 117*(2), e278–290.

Baise-Takir A, Aydemir M, Okay I, & Goka E (2015). Relations between attachment to people, attachment to god, perception of God and addiction severity in an Islamic population in Turkey. *Bull of Clin Psychopharm, 25* (Suppl. 1), S67–S69. abstract.

Baker C, Arnold D, & Meagher S (2011). Enrollment and attendance in a parent training prevention program for conduct problems. *Prev Sci, 12*, 126–138.

Baker K, Bisby M, Richardson R (2016). Impaired fear extinction in adolescent rodents: behavioural and neural analyses. *Neurosci Biobehav Rev, 70*, 59–73.

Baker L, Williams L, Korgaonkar M, Cohen R, Heaps J, & Paul R (2013). Impact of early vs late childhood early life stress on brain morphometrics. *Brain Imaging Behav, 7*, 196–203.

Baker S, Lubman D, Yucel M, Allen N, Whittle S, Fulcher B et al. (2015). Developmental changes in brain network hub connectivity in late adolescence. *J Neurosci, 35*, 9078–9087.

Bakermans-Kranenburg M, & van IJzendoorn M (2018). Attachment, parenting, and genetics. In J Cassidy, P Shaver (Eds), *Handbook of attachment* (3rd ed., pp. 155–179). New York: Guilford.

Bakermans-Kranenburg M, & van IJzendoorn M (2009). The first 10,000 adult attachment interviews: Distributions of adult attachment representations in clinical and non-clinical groups. *Attach Hum Dev, 11*(3), 223–263.

Bakermans-Kranenburg M, & van Ijzendoorn M (2006). Gene–environment interaction of the dopamine D4 receptor (DRD4) and observed maternal insensitivity predicting externalizing behavior in preschoolers. *Dev Psychobiol, 48*, 406–409.

Bakermans-Kranenburg M, & van Ijzendoorn M, Juffer F (2005). Disorganized infant attachment and preventive interventions: A review and meta-analysis. *Inf Mental Hlth J, 26*(3), 191–216.

Bakker M, Ormel J, Lindenberg S, Verhulst F, & Oldehinkel A (2011). Generation of interpersonal stressful events: The role of poor social skills and early physical maturation in young adolescents—The TRAILS Study. *J Early Adolescence, 31*(5), 633–655.

Baldwin DV (2013). Primitive mechanisms of trauma response: An evolutionary perspective on trauma-related disorders. *Neurosci Biobehav Rs, 37*, 1549–1566.

Ballen N, Demers I, Bernier A (2006). A differential analysis of the subtypes of unresolved states of mind in the adult attachment interview. *J Trauma Prac, 5*(4), 69–92.

Banducci A, Lejuez C, Doughtery L, & MacPherson L (2017). A prospective examination of the relations between emotional abuse and anxiety: Moderation by distress tolerance. *Prev Sci, 18*, 20–30.

Bandura A (2012). On the functional properties of perceived self-efficacy revisited. *J Management, 38*(1), 9–44.

Bandura A (2008). Toward an agentic theory of the self. In H Marsh, R Craven, D McInerey (Eds), *Self-processes, learning, and enabling human potential* (pp. 15–49). Greenwich, CT: Information Age.

Bard K, Todd B, Bernier C, Love J, & Leavens D (2006). Self-awareness in human and chimpanzee infants: What is measured and what is meant by the mark and mirror test? *Infancy, 9*(2), 191–219.

Bardeen J, & Read J (2010). Attentional control, trauma, and affect regulation: A preliminary investigation. *Traumatology, 16*(3), 11–18.

Barel E, Abu-Shkara R, Colodner R, Masalha R, Mahagna L, Zemel O, & Cohen A (2018). Gonadal hormones modulate the HPA-axis and the SNS in response to psychosocial stress. *J Neuro Res, 96*, 1388–1397.

Barfield S, Dobson C, Gaskill R, & Perry B (2011). Neurosequential model of Therapeutics in a therapeutic preschool: Implications for work with children with complex neuropsychiatric problems. *Internat J Play Therapy, 21*(1), 30–44.

Bar-Haim Y, Dan O, Eshel Y, & Sagi-Schwartz A (2007). Predicting children's anxiety from early attachment relationships. *J Anxiety Disord, 21*, 1061–1068.

Barkley RA (2001). The executive functions and self-regulation: An evolutionary neuropsychological perspective. *Neuropsychol Rev, 11*, 1–29.

Barlé N, Wortman C, & Latack J (2015, August 3). Traumatic bereavement: Basic research and clinical implications. *J Psychother Integra, 27*(2), 127–139.

Barlow J, Bennett C, & Midgley N (2013). Parent-infant psychotherapy for improving parental and infant mental health. *Cochrane Db Syst Rev*, 5, CD010534. doi: 10.1002/14651858.CD010534.

Barlow J, Bennett C, Midgley N, Larkin S, & Wei Y (2016). Parent–infant psychotherapy for improving parental and infant mental health: A systematic review. *Campbell Syst Rev, 34*(5), 464–482.

Barnard L, & Curry J (2011). Self-compassion: Conceptualizations, correlates, and interventions. *Rev Gen Psychol, 15*(4), 289–303.

Barnett M, & Sharp K (2016). Maladaptive perfectionism, body image satisfaction, and disordered eating behaviors among US college women: The mediating role of self-compassion. *Pers Indiv Differ, 99*, 225–234.

Barnhofer T, Huntenburg J, Lifshitz M, Wild J, Antonova E, & Margulies D (2016). How mindfulness training may help to reduce vulnerability for recurrent depression: A neuroscientific perspective. *Clinical Psychol Sci, 4*(2), 328–343.

Barone L, & Lionetti F (2012). Attachment and social competence: A study using MCAST in low-risk Italian preschoolers. *Attachm & Human Devel, 14*(4), 391–403.

Barra S, Bessler C, Landolt M, & Aebi M (2018). Patterns of adverse childhood experiences in juveniles who sexually offended. *Sex Abuse-J Res Tr, 30*(7), 803–827.

Barry C, & Kauten R (2014). Nonpathological and pathological narcissism: Which self-reported characteristics are most problematic in adolescents? *J Pers Assessment, 96*(2), 212–219. abstract.

Barry R, Kochanska G, & Philibert R (2008). G X E interaction in the organization of attachment: Mothers' responsiveness as a moderator of children's genotypes. *J Child Psychol Psyc, 49*, 1313–1320.

Barstead M, Danko C, Chronis-Tuscano A, O'Brien K, Coplan R, & Rubin K (in press). Generalization of an early intervention for inhibited preschoolers to the classroom setting. *J Child Fam Stud.*

Bartholomew K, & Horowitz L (1991). Attachment styles among young adults: A test of a four-category model. *J Pers Soc Psychol, 61*, 226–244.

Bar-Zomer J, & Klomek A (2018). Attachment to parents as a moderator in the association between sibling bullying and depression or suicidal ideation among children and adolescents. *Front Psychiatry, 9*, 72. doi: 10.3389/fpsyt.2018.00072. abstract.

Başak B, & Can G (2014). The relationships between humor styles, shyness and automatic thoughts among university students. *Educa & Sci, 39*(174), 365–376.

Bass B, & Yammarino F (1991). Congruence of self- and others' leadership ratings of naval officers for understanding successful performance. *Appl Psychol-Int Rev, 40*, 437–454.

Basten M, Althoff R, Tiemeier H, Jaddoe V, Hofman A, Hudziak J et al. (2013). The dysregulation profile in young children: Empirically-defined classes in the Generation R Study. *J Am Acad Child Psy, 52*(8), 841–850.

Basu A, Malone J, Levendosky A, & Dubay S (2009). Longitudinal treatment effectiveness outcomes of a group intervention for women and children exposed to domestic violence. *J Child Adolesc Trauma, 2*(2), 90–105.

Bateman A, & Fonagy P (2012). *The handbook of mentalizing in mental health practice*. Arlington, VA: The American Psychiatric Association.

Bateman A, & Fonagy P (2004). *Psychotherapy for borderline personality disorder: Mentalization based treatment*. Oxford: Oxford University Press.

Battaglia M (2015). Separation anxiety: At the neurobiological crossroads of adaptation and illness. *Dialogues Clin Neurosci*, *17*(3), 277–285.

Battaglia M, Touchette E, Garon-Carrier E, Gionne D, Cote S et al. (2016). Distinct trajectories of separation anxiety in the preschool years: Persistence at school entry and early-life associated factors. *J Child Psychol Psyc*, *57*(1), 39–46.

Bauer P (2009). The life I once remembered: The waxing and waning of early memories. *Zero to Three*, *30*(2), 14–21.

Bauer P, & Burch M (2004). Developments in early memory: Multiple mediators of foundational processes. In J Lucariello, J Hudson, R Fivush, P Bauer (Eds), *Development of the mediated mind: Culture and cognitive development essays in honor of Katherine Nelson* (pp. 101–125). Mahwah, NJ: Erlbaum.

Bauer P, Burch M, Scholin S, Güler O (2007). Using cue words to inform the distribution of autobiographical memories in childhood. *Psychol Sci*, *18*, 910–916.

Bauer P, Pathman T, Inman C, Campanella C, & Hamann S (2017). Neural correlates of autobiographical memory retrieval in children and adults. *Memory*, *25*(4), 450–466.

Bauer P, Stennes L, & Haight J (2003). Representation of the inner self in autobiography: Women and men's use of internal states language in personal narratives. *Memory*, *11*, 27–42.

Bauer P, Stevens J, Jackson F, & Souci P (2012). Electrophysiological indices of emotion processing during retrieval of autobiographical memories by school-age children. *Cogn Affect Behav Neurosci*, *12*, 99–114.

Baumgartner S, Weeda W, van der Heijden L, & Huizinga M (2014). The relationship between media multitasking and executive function in early adolescents. *J Early Adolesc*, *34*(8), 1120–1144.

Bauminger N, Finzi-Dottan R, Chason S, & Har-Even D (2008). Intimacy in adolescent friendship: The roles of attachment, coherence, and self-disclosure. *J Soc Pers Relat*, *25*(3), 409–428.

Beaver K, Shutt J, Vaughn M, DeLisi M, & Wright J (2012). Genetic influences on measures of parental negativity and childhood maltreatment: An exploratory study testing for gene X environment correlations. *J Contemp Crim Just*, *28*(3), 273–292.

Beck E, Bo S, Gondan M, Poulsen S, Pedersen L, Pedersen J et al. (2016). Mentalization-based treatment in groups for adolescents with borderline personality disorder (BPD) or subthreshold BPD versus treatment as usual (M-GAB): Study protocol for a randomized controlled trial. *Biomed Central*, *17*, 314. doi: 10.1186/s13063-016-1431-0.

Becker-Weidman A (2009). Effects of early maltreatment on development: A descriptive study using the Vineland Adaptive Behavior Scales-II. *Child Welfare*, *88*(2), 137–161.

Beckstead D, Lambert M, DuBose A, & Linehan M (2015). Dialectical behavior therapy with American Indian/Alaska Native adolescents diagnosed with substance use disorders: Combining an evidence based treatment with cultural, traditional, and spiritual beliefs. *Addict Behav*, *51*, 84–87. abstract.

Bedard-Gilligan M, Jaeger J, Echiverri-Cohen A, & Zoellner L (2012). Individual differences in trauma disclosure. *J Behav Ther Exp Psychiatry*, *43*(2), 716–723.

Beebe B, Jaffe J, Markese S, Buck K, Chen H, Cohen P et al. (2010). The origins of 12-month attachment: A microanalysis of mother–infant interaction. *Attach Hum Dev*, *12*(1–2), 3–141.

Beebe B, Lachmann F, Markese S, Buck K, Bahrick L, Chen H et al. (2012). On the origins of disorganized attachment and internal working models: Paper II. An empirical microanalysis of 4-month mother–infant interaction. *Psychoanal Dialogues*, *22*(3), 352–374.

Beebe B, Messinger D, Bahrick L, Margolis A, & Buck K (2016). A systems view of mother–infant face-to-face communication. *Dev Psychol*, *52*(4), 556–571.

Beeney J, Stepp S, Hallquist M, Scott L, Wright A, Ellison W, Nolf K, & Pilkonis P (2015). Attachment and social cognition in Borderline Personality Disorder: Specificity in relation to Antisocial and Avoidant Personality Disorders. *Personal Disord*, *6*(3), 207–215.

Beeney J, Wright A, Stepp S, Hallquist M, Lazarus S, & Beeney JR (2016). Disorganized attachment and personality functioning in adults: A latent class analysis. *Personal Disord*, *8*(3), 206–216.

Beidas R, Mychailyszyn M, Podell J, & Kendall P (2013). Brief Cognitive-Behavioral Therapy for anxious youth: The inner workings. *Cog and Behavl Prac*, *20*, 134–146.

Belden A, Barch D, Oakberg T, April L, Harms M, Botteron K, & Luby J (2015). Anterior Insula volume and guilt: Neurobehavioral markers of recurrence after early childhood major depressive disorder. *JAMA Psychiatry*, *72*(1), 40–48.

Bell Z, Shader T, Webster-Stratton, Reid M, & Beauchaine T (2017). Improvements in negative parenting mediate changes in children's autonomic responding following a preschool intervention for ADHD. *Clinical Psychol Sci*, *6*(1), 134–144.

Belsky J, & Fearon R (2002). Infant–mother attachment security, contextual risk, and early development: A moderational analysis. *Dev Psychopathol, 14,* 293–310.

Belsky J, & Pluess M (2013). Beyond risk, resilience and dysregulation: Phenotypic plasticity and Hum Dev. *Dev Psychopathol, 25,* 1243–1261.

Belsky J, & Pluess M (2009). Beyond diathesis stress: Differential susceptibility to environmental influences. *Psychol Bull, 135,* 885–908.

Belsky J, Schlomer G, & Ellis B (2012). Beyond cumulative risk: Distinguishing harshness and unpredictability as determinants of parenting and early life history strategy. *Dev Psychol, 48,* 662–673.

Benarous X, Raffin M, Bodeau N, Dhossche D, Cohen D, & Consoli A (2017). Adverse childhood experiences among inpatient youths with severe and early-onset psychiatric Disorders: Prevalence and clinical correlates. *Child Psychiat Hum D, 48,* 248–259.

Benenson J (2014). *Warriors and worriers.* New York: Oxford University Press.

Bensimon M, Amir D, & Wolf Y (2008). Drumming through trauma: Music therapy with post-traumatic soldiers. *Art Psychother, 35*(1), 34–48.

Bennett D, Modrowski C, Kerig P, & Chaplo S (2015). Investigating the dissociative subtype of Posttraumatic Stress Disorder in a sample of traumatized detained youth. *Psychol Trauma-US,* 7(5), 465–472.

Bennett M, & Lengacher C (2007). Humor and laughter may influence health: [Part] III. Laughter and health outcomes. *eCAM, 5*(1), 37–40.

Bensalah L, Anduze M, & Caillies S (2015). Links among cognitive empathy, theory of mind and affective perspective taking by young children. *Res and Theory on Human Devel, 177*(1), 17–31.

Ben-Zur H, & Almog N (2013). Effects of community violence and adverse childhood experiences. *J Child Adolesc Trauma, 6,* 187–200.

Beran T, & Lupart J (2009). The relationship between school achievement and peer harassment in Canadian adolescents: The importance of mediating factors. *School Psychol Int, 30,* 75–91.

Berens L, & Nardi D (2004). *The sixteen personality types: Descriptions for self discovery.* Huntington Beach, CA: Telos Publications.

Berens A, & Nelson C (2015). Review: The science of early adversity: Is there a role for large institutions in the care of vulnerable children? *The Lancet, 386,* 388–398. abstract.

Berens L (2015). *Interaction Essentials.* Los Angeles, CA: Radiance House.

Berens L (2013). Perspectives: An integral approach to personality type. *J Integral Theory & Practice, 8*(3&4), 19–32.

Berens L (2002/2013). Multiple models of personality type: An historical, thematic perspective. *Australian Psychological Type Review, 4*(1 & 2). Revised 2013. Downloaded 11–19–16 from www.LindaBerens.com/the-leading-edge-of-psychological-type.

Berger I, Remington A, Leitner Y, & Leviton A (2015). Brain development and the attention spectrum. *Front Hum Neurosci, 9*(23), 1–2. doi.org/10.3389/fnhum.2015.00023.

Berger R, Benatov J, Cuadros R, VanNattan J, & Gelkopf M (in press). Enhancing resiliency and promoting prosocial behavior among Tanzanian primary-school students: A school-based intervention. *Transcultural Psychiatry.* doi.org/10.1177/1363461518793749.

Berger R, & Gelkopf M (2009). School-based intervention for the treatment of tsunami-related distress in children: A quasi-randomized controlled trial. *Psychother Psychosom, 78*(6), 364–371.

Berger R, Gelkopf M, Heineberg Y (2012). A school-based intervention for reducing traumatic stress related symptomatology in students exposed to ongoing and intense war-related stress: A quasi-randomized controlled study. *Adolescent Health, 51,* 453–461.

Berger R, Gelkopf M, Heineberg Y & Zimbardo P (2016). A school-based intervention for reducing post-traumatic symptomatology and intolerance during political violence. *J Educ Psychol, 108,* 761–771.

Berger R, & Manasra N (2005). *Enhancing resiliency among students experiencing stress (ERASE-STRESS CHERISH): A manual for teachers.* Tel Aviv, Israel: Natal, Trauma Center for Victims of terror and War (in Hebrew).

Berger R, Pat-Horenczyk R, & Gelkopf M (2007). School-based intervention for prevention and treatment of elementary-students' terror-related distress in Israel: A quasi-randomized controlled trial. *J Traum Stress, 20*(4), 541–551. abstract.

Berg-Smith S (2013). Motivational interviewing: Continuing the journey. *Advanced Motivational Interviewing Training Workbook.* Larkspur, CA: Berg-Smith Training and Consultations.

Berk LE (2009). Emotional and social development in infancy and toddlerhood. In L Berk, *Development through the lifespan* (5th ed., pp. 3–31 sample Chapter). New York: Pearson.

Berman M, Peltier S, Nee D, Kross E, Deldin P, & Jonides J (2011). Depression, rumination and the default network. *Soc Cognit and Affective Neurosci, 6,* 548–555.

Bernard K, Butzin-Dozier Z, Rittenhouse J, & Dozier M (2010). Cortisol production patterns in young children living with birth parents vs children placed in foster care following involvement of Child Protective Services. *Arch Pediatr Adolesc Med, 164*(5), 438–443.

Bernard K, Dozier M, Bick J, & Gordon M (2015a). Intervening to enhance cortisol regulation among children at risk for neglect: Results of a randomized clinical trial. *Dev Psychopathol, 27*, 829–841.

Bernard K, Dozier M, Bick J, & Gordon M (2015b). Normalizing blunted diurnal cortisol rhythms among children at risk for neglect: The effects of an early intervention. *Dev Psychopathol, 27*, 829–841.

Bernard K, Dozier M, Bick J, Lewis-Morrarty E, Lindhiem O, & Carlson E (2012). Enhancing attachment organization among maltreated children: Results of a randomized clinical trial. *Child Dev, 83*, 623–636.

Bernard K, Lee A, & Dozier M (2017). Effects of the ABC intervention on foster children's receptive vocabulary: Follow-up results from a randomized clinical trial. *Child Maltreat, 22*(2), 174–179. abstract.

Bernard K, Meade E, & Dozier M (2013). Parental synchrony and nurturance as targets in an attachment based intervention: Building upon Mary Ainsworth's insights about mother–infant interaction. *Attach Hum Dev, 15*(5–6), 507–523.

Bernard K, Simons R, & Dozier M (2016). Effects of an attachment-based intervention on Child Protective Services-referred mothers' event-related potentials to children's emotions. *Child Dev, 86*(6), 1673–1684.

Bernier A, Calkins S, & Bell M (2016). Longitudinal associations between the quality of mother–infant interactions and brain development across infancy. *Child Dev, 87*(4), 1159–1174.

Bernstein A, & Blacher R (1967). The recovery of a memory from three months of age. *Psychoanal Stud Chil, 22*, 156–161.

Bernstein M, & Pfefferbaum B (2018). Posttraumatic growth as a response to natural disasters in children and adolescents. *Curr Psychiat Rep, 20*, 37. https://doi.org/10.1007/s11920-018-0900-4.

Berntsen D, & Rubin D (2007). When trauma becomes a key to identity: Enhanced integration of trauma memories predicts posttraumatic stress disorder symptoms. *Appl Cognitive Psych, 21*, 417–431.

Berntsen D, & Rubin D (2006). The centrality of event scale: A measure of integrating a trauma into one's identity and its relation to posttraumatic. *Behav Research and Ther, 44*, 219–231.

Berry D, McCartney K, Petrill S, Deater-Deckard K, & Blair C (2014). Gene–environment interaction between DRD4 7-Repeat VNTR and early child-care experiences predicts self-regulation abilities in prekindergarten. *Dev Psychobiol, 56*, 373–391.

Berti A, Garattoni B, & Venturini B (2000). The understanding of sadness, guilt, and shame in 5, 7-, and 9-year-old children. *Soc & Genl Psychol Monogr, 126*, 293–319.

Besser A, & Priel B (2010). Grandiose narcissism versus vulnerable narcissism in threatening situations: Emotional reactions to achievement failure and interpersonal rejection. *J Soc Clin Psychol, 29*(8), 874.

Besser A, Weinberg M, Zeigler-Hill V, Ataria Y, & Neria Y (2015). Humor and trauma-related psychopathology among survivors of terror attacks and their spouses. *Psychiatry, 78*(4), 341–353.

Best J, Miller P, & Jones L (2009). Executive functions after age 5: Changes and correlates. *Dev Rev, 29*, 180–200.

Betancourt L, Yang W, Brodsky N, Gallagher P, Malmud E, Giannetta J et al. (2011). Adolescents with and without gestational cocaine exposure: Longitudinal analysis of inhibitory control, memory, and receptive language. *Neurotoxicol Teratol, 33*(1), 36–46.

Betancourt T, Brennan R, Rubin-Smith J, Fitzmaurice G, & Gilman S (2010). Sierra Leone's former child soldiers: A longitudinal study of risk, protective factors, and mental health. *J Am Acad Child Psy, 49*, 606–615.

Betancourt T, Gilman S, Brennan R, & VanderWeele T (2015a). Identifying priorities for mental health interventions in war-affected youth: A longitudinal study. *Pediatrics, 136*(2), e344–350.

Betancourt T, McBain R, Newnham E, & Brennan R (2015b). The intergenerational impact of war: Longitudinal relationships between caregiver and child mental health in postconflict Sierra Leone. *J Child Psychol Psych, 56*(10), 1101–1107.

Betancourt T, McBain R, Newnham E, & Brennan R (2013a). Trajectories of internalizing problems in war-affected Sierra Leonean youth: Examining conflict and post-conflict factors. *Child Dev, 84*(2), 455–470.

Betancourt T, Newnham E, McBain R, & Brennan R (2013b). Post-traumatic stress symptoms among former child soldiers in Sierra Leone: Follow-up study. *Brit J Psychiat, 203*(3), 196–202.

Betancourt T, Newnham E, Hann K, McBain R, Akinsulure-Smith A, Weisz J et al. (2014). Addressing the consequences of violence and adversity: The development of a group mental health intervention for war-affected youth in Sierra Leone. In J-P Raynaud, S Gau, M Hodes (Eds), *From research to practice in child and adolescent mental health-UK*. New York: Rowman & Littlefield.

Beutel M, Tibubos A, Klein E, Schmutzer G, Reiner I, Kocalevent R, & Brahler E (2017). Childhood adversities and distress: The role of resilience in a representative sample. *PLoS ONE, 12*(3), e0173826. doi.org/10.1371/journal.pone.0173826.

Bey K, Lennertz L, Riesel A, Klawohn J, Kaufmann C, Heinzel S, et al. (2017). Harm avoidance and childhood adversities in patients with obsessive-compulsive disorder and their unaffected first-degree relatives. *Acta Psychiatr Scand, 135*, 328–338. abstract.

Beydoun H, & Saftlas A (2008). Physical and mental health outcomes of prenatal maternal stress in human and animal studies: A review of recent evidence. *Paediatr Perinat Epidemiol, 22*, 438–466.

Bick J, & Dozier M (2013). The effectiveness of an attachment-based intervention in promoting foster mothers' sensitivity toward foster infants. *Inf Mental Hlth J, 34*(2), 95–103. abstract.

Bick J, Luyster R, Fox N, Zeanah C, & Nelson C (2017). Effects of early institutionalization on emotion processing in 12-year-old youth. *Dev Psychopathol, 29*, 1749–1761.

Bick J, Zhu T, Stamoulis C, Fox N, Zeanah C, & Nelson C (2015). Effect of early institutionalization and foster care on longterm white matter development: A randomized clinical trial. *JAMA Pediatrics, 169*(3), 211–219.

Bigelow B, Tesson G, & Lewko J (1996). *Learning the rules: Anatomy of children's relationships.* New York: Guilford.

Biggs B, Vernberg E, Little T, Dill E, Fonagy P, & Twemlow S (2010). Peer victimization trajectories and their association with children's affect in late elementary school. *Int J Behav Dev, 34*(2), 136–146.

Biggs B, Vernberg E, & Wu Y (2012). Social anxiety and adolescents' friendships: The role of social withdrawal. *J Early Adolescence, 32*(6), 802–823.

Bigorra A, Garolera M, Guijarro S, & Hervas A (2015). Long-term far-transfer effects of working memory training in children with ADHD: A randomized controlled trial. *Eur Child Adolesc Psychiatry, 25*(8), 853–867.

Bigras N, Godbout N, & Briere J (2015). Child sexual abuse, sexual anxiety, and sexual satisfaction: The role of self-capacities. *J Child Sex Abus, 24*, 464–483.

Biro F, & Dorn L (2006). Puberty and adolescent sexuality. *Psychiatr Ann, 36*(10), 685–690.

Bishop M, Rosentein D, Bakelaar S, & Seedat S (2014). An analysis of early developmental trauma in social anxiety disorder and posttraumatic stress disorder. *Ann Gen Psychiatr, 13*, 16.

Bjork J, & Pardini D (2015). Who are those "risk-taking adolescents"? Individual differences in developmental neuroimaging research. *Dev Cogn Neurosci, 11*, 56–64.

Björkenstam E, Kosidou K, & Björkenstam C (2016). Childhood household dysfunction and risk of self-harm: A cohort study of 107 518 young adults in Stockholm County. *Int J Epidemiol, 45*(2), 501–511.

Bjorklund D (2013). Cognitive development: An overview. In P Zelazo (Ed.), *Oxford handbook of developmental psychology.* Oxford, UK: Oxford University Press.

Bjorklund D, & Sellers P (2014). Memory development in evolutionary perspective. In P Bauer, R Fivush (Eds), *The Wiley-Blackwell-handbook on the development of children's memory.* New York: Wiley-Blackwell.

Blair C (2017). Educating executive functions. *WIREs Cogn Sci, 8*, e1403. doi: 10.1002/wcs.1403.

Blair C, & Raver C (2016). Poverty, stress, and brain development: New directions for prevention and intervention. *Acad Pediatr, 16*, S30–S36.

Blais C, Harris M, Guerrero J, & Bunge S (2010). Rethinking the role of automaticity in cognitive control. *Q J Exp Psychol, 65*(2), 268–276.

Blakemore S, & Choudhury S (2006). Development of the adolescent brain: Implications for executive function and social cognition. *J Child Psychol Psyc, 47*(3/4), 296–312.

Blakemore S, & Mills K (2014). Is adolescence a sensitive period for sociocultural processing? *Annu Rev Psychol, 65*, 187–207.

Blakemore S, & Robbins T (2012). Decision-making in the adolescent brain. *Nature Neurosci, 15*(9), 1184–1191.

Blakey E, Visser I, & Carroll D (2016). Different executive functions support different kinds of cognitive flexibility: Evidence from 2-, 3-, and 4-year-olds. *Child Dev, 87*(2), 513–526. abstract.

Blattner M, Liang B, Lund T, & Spencer R (2013). Searching for a sense of purpose: The role of parents and effects on self-esteem among female adolescents. *J Adolescence, 36*, 839–848.

Blaustein M, & Kinniburgh K (2010). *Treating traumatic stress in children and adolescents: How to foster resilience through attachment, self-regulation, and competency.* New York: Guilford.

Blaustein M, & Kinniburgh K (2007). Intervening beyond the child: The intertwining nature of attachment and trauma. *BPS, Briefing Paper, 26*, 48–53.

Blevins C, Wusik M, Sullivan C, Jones R, & Hughes M (2016). Do negative changes in worldview mediate links between mass trauma and reckless behavior? A longitudinal exploratory study. *Community Ment Health J, 52*, 10–17.

Bloch D, Silber E, & Perry S (1956). Some factors in the emotional reaction of children to disaster. *Am J Psychiat, 113*, 416–422.

Block, JH, & Block J (2006). Venturing a 30-year longitudinal study. *American Psychologist, 61*, 315–327.

Block JH, & Block J (1980). The role of ego-control and ego-resiliency in the organization of behavior. In WA Collins (Ed.), *Minnesota symposia on child psychology* (Vol. 13, pp. 39–101). Hillsdale, NJ: Erlbaum.

Bloomquist ML (2012). *A practitioner guide to skills training for struggling kids.* New York: Guilford.

Bluhm R, Williamson P, Osuch E, Frewen P, Stevens T, Boksman K et al. (2009). Alterations in default network connectivity in posttraumatic stress disorder related to early-life trauma. *JPN, 34*, 187–194.

Boelen P (2015). Peritraumatic distress and dissociation in prolonged grief and posttraumatic stress following violent and unexpected deaths. *J Trauma Dissociation, 16*, 541–550.

Boelen P & Spuij M (2013). Symptoms of post-traumatic stress disorder in bereaved children and adolescents: Factor structure and correlates. *J Abnorm Child Psych, 41*, 1097–1108.

Boelen P, van den Hout M, & van den Bout J (2012). Prolonged grief disorder: Cognitive behavioral theory and therapy. In M Stroebe, H Schut, J van den Bout (Eds), *Complicated grief*. New York: Routledge.

Boelen P, van den Hout M, & van den Bout J (2006). A cognitive-behavioral conceptualization of complicated grief. *Clin Psychol-Sci Pr, 13*, 109–128.

Boggs S, Eyberg S, & Reynolds L (1990). Concurrent validity of the Eyberg Child Behavior Inventory. *J Clin Child Psychol, 19*, 75–78.

Bohanek J, Marin K, Fivush R, & Duke M (2006). Family narrative interaction and children's sense of self. *Fam Process, 45*(1), 39–54.

Bohlin G, & Hagekull B (2009). Socio-emotional development: From infancy to young adulthood. *Scandinav J Psychology, 50*, 592–601.

Bohlin G, Hagekull B, & Andersson K (2005). Behavioral inhibition as a precursor of peer social competence in early school age: The interplay with attachment and non-parental care. *Merrill-Palmer Q, 51*, 1–19.

Boisvert D, Stadler W, Vaske J, Wright J, & Nelson M (2013). The interconnection between intellectual achievement and self-control. *Crim Justice Behav, 40*(1), 80–94.

Bokhorst C, Bakermans-Kranenburg M, Fearon R, van IJzendoorn M, Fonagy P, & Schuengel C (2003). The importance of shared environment in mother–infant attachment security: A behavioral genetic study. *Child Dev, 74*, 1769–1782.

Boldt L, Kochanska G, & Jonas K (2017). Infant attachment moderates paths from early negativity to preadolescent outcomes for children and parents. *Child Dev, 88*(2), 584–596.

Boldt L, Kochanska G, Yoon J, & Nordling J (2014). Children's attachment to both parents from toddler age to middle childhood: Links to adaptive and maladaptive outcomes. *Attach Hum Dev, 16*(3), 211–229.

Bolen R, Winter V, & Hodges L (2013). Affect and state dysregulation as moderators of the relationship between childhood sexual abuse and nonsuicidal self-injury. *J Interpers Violence, 28*(1), 201–228.

Bolger K, & Patterson C (2003). Sequelae of child maltreatment: Vulnerability and resilience. In S Luthar (Ed), *Resilience and vulnerability: Adaptation in the context of childhood adversities* (pp. 156–181). New York: Cambridge University Press.

Boltz L, Henriksen D, Mishra P, & the Deep Play Research Group (2015). Rethinking technology and creativity in the 21st century: Empathy through gaming—Perspective taking in a complex world. *Tech Trends, 59*(6), 3–8.

Bonanno G (2008). Loss, trauma, and human resilience: Have we underestimated the human capacity to thrive after extremely aversive events? *Psychol Trauma-US, S*(1), 101–113.

Bonanno G (2005). Resilience in the face of potential trauma. *Curr Dir Psychol Sci, 14*, 135–138.

Bonanno G (2004). Loss, trauma, and human resilience: Have we underestimated the human capacity to thrive after extremely aversive events? *Am Psychol, 59, 20–28.*

Bonanno G, Boerner K, & Wortman C (2008). Trajectories of grieving. In M Stroebe, R Hansson, H Schut, W Stroebe (Eds), *Handbook of bereavement research and practice: Advances in theory and intervention* (pp. 287–308). Washington, DC: APA.

Bonanno G, Colak D, Keltner D, Shiota M, Papa A, Noll J et al. (2007). Context matters: The benefits and costs of expressing positive emotion among survivors of childhood sexual abuse. *Emotion*, 7(4), 824–837. abstract.

Bonanno G, Field N, Kovacevic A, & Kaltman S (2002). Self-enhancement as a buffer against extreme adversity: Civil war in Bosnia and traumatic loss in the United States. *Pers Soc Psychol B, 28*, 184–196.

Bonanno G, & Kaltman S (2001). The varieties of grief experience. *Clin Psychol Rev, 21*, 705–734.

Bonanno G, & Mancini A (2008). The human capacity to thrive in the face of extreme adversity. *Pediatrics, 121*, 369–375.

Bonanno G, Noll J, Putnam F, O'Neill M, & Trickett P (2003). Predicting the willingness to disclose childhood sexual abuse from measures of repressive coping and dissociative experiences. *Child Maltreatment, 8*, 1–17.

Bonanno G, Pat-Horenczyk R, & Noll J (2011). Coping flexibility and trauma: The Perceived Ability to Cope with Trauma (PACT) scale. *Psychol Trauma-US, 3*(2), 117–129.

Bonanno G, Rennicke C, & Dekel S (2005). Self-enhancement among high-exposure survivors of the September 11th terrorist attack: resilience or social maladjustment? *J Pers Soc Psychol, 88*, 984–998.

Bondü R (2018). Is bad intent negligible? Linking victim justice sensitivity, hostile attribution bias, and aggression. *Aggressive Behav, 44*(5), 442–450.

Booth-LaForce C, Groh A, Burchinal M, Roisman G, Owen M, & Cox M (2014). Caregiving and contextual sources of continuity and change in attachment security from infancy to late adolescence. *Monogr Soc Res Child, 79*, 67–84.

Borelli J, Crowley M, David D, Sbarra D, Anderson G, & Mayes L (2010). Attachment and emotion in school-aged children. *Emotion, 10*, 475–485.

Borelli J, David D, Crowley M, Snavely J, & Mayes L (2013). Dismissing children's perceptions of their emotional experience and parental care: Preliminary evidence of positive bias. *Child Psychiat Hum D, 44*, 70–88.

Boring J, Sandler I, Tein JY, Horan J, & Vélez C (2015). Children of divorce coping with divorce: A randomized control trial of an online prevention program for Youth experiencing parental divorce. *J Consult Clin Psych, 83*(5), 999–1005.

Boris N, Zeanah C, Larrieu J, Scheeringa M, & Heller S (1998). Attachment disorders in infancy and early childhood: A preliminary investigation of diagnostic criteria. *Am J Psychiatry, 155*, 295–297.

Borja K, & Ostrosky F (2013). Early traumatic events in psychopaths. *J Forensic Sci, 58*(4), 928–931.

Bornstein M, Putnick D, Gartstein M, Hahn C-S, Auestad N, & O'Connor D (2015). Infant temperament: Stability by age, gender, birth order, term status, and socioeconomic status. *Child Dev, 86*(3), 844–863.

Bosmans G, Dujardin A, Raes F, & Braet C (2012). The specificity of autobiographical memories in early adolescence: The role of mother–child communication and attachment-related beliefs. *J Early Adolescence, 33*(5), 710–731.

Bosmans G, & Kerns K (2015). Attachment in middle childhood: Progress and prospects. In special issue: G Bosmans, K Kerns (Eds), Attachment in middle childhood: Theoretical advances and new directions in an emerging field. *New Dir Child Adoles*, 148, 1–14.

Boto L, Crispim J, de Melo I, Juvandes C, Rodriguez T et al. (2012). Sleep deprivation and accidental fall risk in children. *Sleep Med, 13*, 88–95. abstract.

Botterill J, Fournier N, Guskjolen A, Lussier A, Marks W, & Kalynchuk L (2014). Amygdala kindling disrupts trace and delay fear conditioning with parallel changes in FOS protein expression throughout the limbic brain. *Neuroscience, 265*, 158–171.

Boulanger G (2018). When is vicarious trauma a necessary therapeutic tool? *Psychoanal Psychol, 35*(1), 60–69.

Bouvette-Turcot A, Fleming A, Wazana A, Sokolowski M, Gaudreau H, et al. (2015a). Maternal childhood adversity and child temperament: An association moderated by child 5-HTTLPR genotype. *Genes Brain Behav, 14*, 229–237.

Bouvette-Turcot A, Pluess M, Benier A, Pennestri M, Levitan R et al. (2015b). Effects of genotype and sleep on temperament. *Pediatrics, 136*(4), e914-e921. abstract.

Bowker A (2004). Predicting friendship stability during early adolescence. *J Early Adolescence, 24*(2), 85–112.

Bowlby, J (1980). *Attachment and loss: Sadness and depression*. New York: Basic Books.

Bowlby J (1973). *Attachment and loss: Anxiety and anger.* Vol. 2. New York: Basic Books.

Bowlby J (1969/1982). *Attachment and loss*: Vol. 1. New York: Basic Books.

Bowyer L, Swanston J, & Vetere A (2015). "Eventually you just get used to it": An interpretative phenomenological analysis of 10–16-year-old girls' experiences of the transition into temporary accommodation after exposure to domestic violence perpetrated by men against their mothers. *Clin Child Psychol P, 20*(2), 304–323.

Boyce W, & Ellis B (2005). Biological sensitivity to context: I. An evolutionary-developmental theory of the origins and functions of stress reactivity. *Dev Psychopathol, 17*, 271–301.

Boyette A (2016). Children's play and culture learning in an egalitarian foraging society. *Child Dev, 87*(3), 759–769.

Boyle J (2011). Speech and language delays in preschool children. *BMJ*, 343. doi: 10.1136/bmj.d5181.

Bozkurt H, Mutluer T, Kose C, & Zoroglu S (2015). High psychiatric comorbidity in adolescents with dissociative disorders. *Psychia and Clin Neurosci, 69*, 369–374.

Braams B, van Duijvenvoorde A, Peper J, & Crone E (2015). Longitudinal changes in adolescent risk-taking: A comprehensive study of neural responses to rewards, pubertal development, and risk-taking behavior. *J Neurosci, 35*, 7226–7238.

Brajsa-Zganec A, & Hanzec, I (2014). Social development of preschool children in Croatia: Contributions of child temperament, maternal life satisfaction and rearing practices. *J Child Fam Stud, 23*, 105–117.

Brake C, Rojas S, Badour C, Dutton C, & Feldner M (2017). Self-disgust as a potential mechanism underlying the association between PTSD and suicide risk. *J Anxiety Disord, 47*, 1–9.

Brambring M (2005). Perceptual perspective taking in children who are blind: The state of research and a single-case study. *Br J Vis Impair, 23*(3), 122–127.

Brand B, Loewenstein R, & Lanius R (2014). Dissociative identity disorder. In Gabbard's treatments of psychiatric disorders. In G Gabbard (Ed.), *Treatments of psychiatric disorders* (5th ed., pp. 495–516). Washington, DC: APA.

Brand S, Schechter J, Hammen C, Le Brocque R, & Brennan P (2011). Do adolescent offspring of women with PTSD experience higher levels of chronic and episodic stress? *J Traum Stress, 24*(4), 399–404.

Breidenstine A, Bailey L, Zeanah C, & Larrieu J (2011). Attachment and trauma in early childhood: A review. *J Child Adolesc Trauma, 4*(4), 274–290.

Breinholst S, Tolstrup M, & Esbjorn B (2018). The direct and indirect effect of attachment insecurity and negative parental behavior on anxiety in clinically anxious children: It's down to dad. *Chld Adol Ment H-UK*, doi.org/10.1111/camh.12269.

Bremner JD (2011). The invisible epidemic: Post-Traumatic Stress Disorder, memory and the brain. Downloaded 2–1–16 from www.thedoctorwillseeyounow.com/content/stress/art1964.html.

Bremner JD (2006). Traumatic stress: Effects on the brain. *Dialogues Clin Neurosci*, *8*, 445–461.

Bremner JD (2003). The effects of stress on the brain. *Psychiatric Times*, *20*(7), 18–22.

Brennen T, Hasanovic M, Zotovic M, Blix I, Skar A-M, Prelic N et al. (2010). Trauma exposure in childhood impairs the ability to recall specific autobiographical memories in late adolescence. *J Traum Stress*, *23*(2), 240–247.

Brent D, Melhem N, Donohoe M, & Walker M (2009). The incidence and course of depression in bereaved youth 21 months after the loss of a parent to suicide, accident, or sudden natural death. *Am J Psychiatry*, *166*, 786–794.

Breslau N (2009). The epidemiology of trauma, PTSD, & other posttrauma disorders. *Trauma Violence Abus*, *10*, 198–210.

Bretherton I (2010). Fathers in attachment theory and research: A review. *Early Child Dev Care*, *180*(1–2), 9–23.

Bretherton I, Fritz J, Zahn-Waxler C, & Ridgeway D (1986). Learning to talk about emotions: A functionalist perspective. *Child Dev*, *57*, 529–548.

Bretherton I, Gullón-Rivera A, Page T, Oettel B, Corey J, & Golby B (2013). Children's attachment-related self-worth: a multi-method investigation of postdivorce preschoolers' relationships with their mothers and peers. *Attach Hum Devop*, *15*(1), 25–49.

Briere J, Dietrich A, & Semple R (2016). Dissociative complexity: Antecedents and clinical correlates of a new construct. *Psychol Trauma-US*, *8*(5), 577–584.

Briere J, & Eadie E (2016). Compensatory self-injury: Posttraumatic stress, depression, and the role of dissociation. *Psychol Trauma-US*, 8(5), 618–625.

Briere J, & Jordan, C (2009). Childhood maltreatment, intervening variables, and adult psychological difficulties in women: An overview. *Trauma Violence Abus*, *10*, 375–388.

Briere J, Kaltman S, & Green BL (2008). Accumulated childhood trauma and symptom complexity. *J Traum Stress*, *21*, 223–226.

Briere J, & Lanktree C (2013). *Integrative treatment of complex trauma for adolescents (ITCT-A): A guide for the treatment of multiply-traumatized youth, 2nd ed.* Los Angeles, CA: USC.

Briere J, & Runtz M (1990). Differential adult symptomatology associated with three types of child abuse histories. *Child Abuse Neglect*, *14*(3), 357–364.

Briere J, Runtz M, Eadie E, Bigras N, & Godbout N (2017). Disengaged parenting: Structural equation modeling with child abuse, insecure attachment, and adult symptomatology. *Child Abuse Neglect*, *67*, 260–270.

Briere J, & Scott C (2015). Complex trauma in adolescents and adults: Effects and treatment. *Psychiatr Clin N Am*, *38*, 515–527.

Briggs P, Hayes S, & Changaris M (2018). Somatic Experiencing® informed therapeutic group for the care and treatment of biopsychosocial effects upon a gender diverse identity. *Front Psychiatry*, *9*, 53. doi: 10.3389/fpsyt.2018.00053.

Bright M, Huq M, Spencer T, & Applebaum J (2018). Animal cruelty as an indicator of family trauma: Using adverse childhood experiences to look beyond child abuse and domestic violence. *Child Abuse Neglect*, *76*, 287–296.

Brinkmeyer M, & Eyberg, S (2003). Parent–child interaction therapy for oppositional children. In AE Kazdin (Ed.), *Evidence based psychotherapies for children and adolescents* (pp. 204–223). New York: Guilford.

Britto N, & Noble K (2014). Socioeconomic status and structural brain development. *Front Neurosci-Switz*, *8*, 276. doi.org/10.3389/fnins.2014.00276.

Britto P (2013). No second chances? Early critical periods in human development. *Soc Sci Med*, *97*, 238–240.

Brooks M, Graham-Kevan N, Robinson S, & Lowe M (2018, May 3). Trauma characteristics and posttraumatic growth: The mediating role of avoidance coping, intrusive thoughts, and social support. *Psychol Trauma-US*. http://dx.doi.org/10.1037/tra0000372.

Brom D, Stokar Y, Lawi C, Nuriel-Porat V, Ziv Y, Lerner K et al. (2017). Somatic experiencing for posttraumatic stress disorder: A randomized controlled outcome study. *J Traum Stress*, *30*(3), 304–312.

Brotman L, Dawson-McClure S, Gouley K, McGuire K, Burraston B, & Bank L (2005a). Older siblings benefit from a family-based preventive intervention for preschoolers at risk for conduct problems. *J Fam Psychol*, *19*(4), 581–591.

Brotman L, Gouley K, Chesir-Teran D, Dennis T, Klein R, & Shrout P (2005b). Prevention for preschoolers at high risk for conduct problems: Immediate outcomes on parenting practices and child social competence. *J Clin Child Adolesc*, *34*(4), 724–734.

Brotman L, Gouley K, Huang K-Y, Kamboukos D, Fratto C, & Pine D (2007). Effects of a psychosocial family based preventive intervention on cortisol response to a social challenge in preschoolers at high risk for antisocial behavior. *Arch Gen Psychiat, 64*, 1172–1179.

Brotman L, Gouley K, Huang K-Y, Rosenfelt A, O'Neil C, & Klein R (2008). Preventive intervention for preschoolers at high risk for antisocial behavior: Long-term effects on child physical aggression and parenting practices. *J Clin Child Adolesc, 37*(2), 386–396.

Brotman L, Gouley K, O'Neal C, & Klein R (2004). Preschool-aged siblings of adjudicated youths: Multiple risk factors for conduct problems. *Early Educ Dev, 15*(4), 387–406.

Brotman L, Klein R, Kambouko D, Brown E, Coard S, & Sosinsky L (2003). Preventive intervention for urban, low-income preschoolers at familial risk for conduct problems: A randomized pilot study. *J Clin Child Adolesc, 32*(2), 246–257.

Brown A, & Whiteside S (2008). Relations among perceived parental rearing behaviors, attachment style, and worry in anxious children. *J Anxiety Disord, 22*, 263–272.

Brown DJ (2014a). *The boys in the boat: Nine Americans and their epic quest for gold at the 1936 Berlin Olympics.* London: Penguin Books.

Brown E, & Goodman R (2005). Childhood traumatic grief: An exploration of the construct in children bereaved on September 11. *J Clin Child Adolesc, 34*(2), 248–259.

Brown F (2014b). The healing power of play: Therapeutic work with chronically neglected and abused children. *Children, 1*, 474–488.

Brown G, Mangelsdorf S, & Neff C (2012). Father involvement, paternal sensitivity, and father–child attachment security in the first 3 years. *J Fam Psychol, 26*(3), 421–430.

Brown L, & Wright J (2003). The relationship between attachment strategies and psychopathology in adolescence. *Psychol Psychother, 76*, 351–367.

Brown N, Brown S, Briggs R, German M, Belamarich P, & Oyeku S (2017). Associations between adverse childhood experiences and ADHD diagnosis and severity. *Acad Pediatr, 17*(4), 349–355.

Brown R, & Gerbarg P (2009). Yoga breathing, meditation, and longevity. *Ann NY Acad Sci, 1172*, 54–62.

Brown R, & Plener P (2017). Non-suicidal self-injury in adolescence. *Curr Psychiatry Rep, 19*(3), 20. doi: 10.1007/s11920-017-0767-9.

Brown T, Lugar H, Coalson R, Miezin F, Petersen S, & Schlagger B (2005). Developmental changes in human cerebral functional organization for word generation. *Cereb Cortex, 15*(3), 275–290.

Brumariu LE (2015). Parent–child attachment and emotion regulation. In G Bosmans & K Kerns (Eds), Attachment in middle childhood: Theoretical advances and new directions in an emerging field. *New Dir Child Adoles, 148*, 31–45.

Brumariu LE, Bureau J-F, Nemoda Z, Sasvari-Szekely M, & Lyons-Ruth K (2016). Attachment and temperament revisited: infant distress, attachment disorganisation and the serotonin transporter polymorphism, *J Reprod Infant Psyc, 34*(1), 77–89.

Brumbach B, Figueredo A, & Ellis B (2009). Effects of harsh and unpredictable environments in adolescence on development of life history strategies: A longitudinal test of an evolutionary model. *Hum Nature, 20*, 25–51.

Brüne M (2014). Life History Theory as organizing principle of psychiatric disorders: Implications and prospects exemplified by Borderline Personality Disorder. *Psychol Inq, 25*, 311–321.

Brüne M, & Brüne-Cohrs U (2006). Theory of mind: Evolution, ontogeny, brain mechanisms and psychopathology. *Neurosci Biobehav Rs, 30*, 437–455.

Brunet A, Saumier D, Liu A, Streiner D, Tremblay J, & Pitman R (2018). Reduction of PTSD symptoms with pre-reactivation Propranolol therapy: A randomized controlled trial. *AJP.* doi: 10.1176/appi.ajp.2017.17050481. abstract.

Brunson K, Eghbal-Ahmadi M, Bender R, Chen Y, & Baram T (2001). Long-term, progressive hippocampal cell loss and dysfunction induced by early-life administration of corticotropin-releasing hormone reproduce the effects of early-life stress. *Proc Natl Acad Sci USA, 98*(15), 8856–8861.

Bruyere E & Garbarino J (2012). A continuum of youth violence. In K Nader (Ed.) *School rampage shootings and other youth disturbances: Early preventive interventions* (pp. 83–100). New York: Routledge.

Bryant, R. (2010). The complexity of complex PTSD. *American Journal of Psychiatry, 167*(8), 879–881.

Bucci P, Plaitano E, De Riso F, Giugliano R, Mucci A, Galderisi S, Maj M (2012). Adult separation anxiety disorder: Clinical characteristics and attachment styles. *Eur Psychiat, 27*(1), 1. doi.org/10.1016/S0924-9338(12)74287-6. abstract.

Buckley P, Pillai A, Evans D, Stirewalt E, & Mahadik S (2007). Brain derived neurotropic factor in first-episode psychosis. *Schizophr Res, 91*(1–3), 1–5.

Buijzen M, & Valkenburg P (2004). Developing a typology of humor in audiovisual media. *Media Psychol, 6*(2), 147–167.

Buil J, van Lier P, Brendgen M, Koot H, & Vitaro F (2017). Developmental pathways linking childhood temperament with antisocial behavior and substance use in adolescence: Explanatory mechanisms in the peer environment. *J Pers Soc Psychol*, *112*(6), 948–966.

Buist A, Gotman N, & Yonkers K (2011). Generalized anxiety disorder: course and risk factors in pregnancy. *J Affect Disord*, *131*, 277–283.

Bukowski H, Hietanen J, & Samson D (2016). From gaze cueing to perspective taking: Revisiting the claim that we automatically compute where or what other people are looking at. *Vis Cogn*, *23*(8), 1020–1042.

Bullock A, & Bonanno G (2013). Attentional bias and complicated grief: A primed dot-probe task with emotional faces. *JEP*, *4*(2), 194–207. abstract.

Bunge S, & Crone E (2009). Neural correlates of the development of cognitive control. In JM Rumsey, M Ernst (Eds), *Neuroimaging in developmental clinical neuroscience* (pp. 22–37). Cambridge: Cambridge University Press.

Bunge S, & Wright S (2007). Neurodevelopmental changes in working memory and cognitive control. *Curr Opin Neurobiol*, *17*, 243–250.

Bungert M, Koppe G, Niedtfeld I, Vollstädt-Klein S, Schmahl C, Lis S et al. (2015a). Pain processing after social exclusion and its relation to rejection sensitivity in Borderline Personality Disorder. *PLoS ONE*, *10*(8), e0133693. doi: 10.1371/journal.pone.0133693.

Bungert M, Liebke L, Thome J, Haeussler K, Bohus M, & Lis S (2015b). Rejection sensitivity and symptom severity in patients with borderline personality disorder: Effects of childhood maltreatment and self-esteem. *BPDED*, *2*, 4. doi: 10.1186/s40479-015-0025-x.

Bunting L, Davidson G, McCartan C, Hanratty J, Bywaters P, Mason W, & Steils N (2018). The association between child maltreatment and adult poverty: A systematic review of longitudinal research. *Child Abuse Neglect*, *77*, 121–133.

Burack J, Flanagan T, Peled T, Sutton H, Zygmuntowicz C, & Manly J (2006). Social perspective-taking skills in maltreated children and adolescents. *Dev Psychol*, *42*(2), 207–217.

Bureau J-F, Martin J, Yurkowski K, Schmiedel S, Quan J, Moss E, Deneault A, & Pallanca D (2017). Correlates of child–father and child–mother attachment in the preschool years. *Attach Hum Dev*, *19*(2), 130–150.

Bureau J-F, & Moss E (2010). Behavioural precursors of attachment representations in middle childhood and links with child social adaptation. *British J Devel Psychol*, *28*, 657–677.

Burke L & Neimeyer R (2014). Complicated spiritual grief I: Relation to complicated grief symptomatology following violent death bereavement. *Death Stud*, *38*, 259–267.

Burke L, Neimeyer R, & McDevitt-Murphy M (2010). African American homicide bereavement: Aspects of social support that predict complicated grief, PTSD, and depression. *Omega-J Death Dying*, *61*(1), 1–24.

Burnett S, & Blakemore S-J (2009). Functional connectivity during a social emotion task in adolescents and in adults. *Eur J Neurosci*, *29*(6), 1294–301.

Burnside E, Startup M, Byatt M, Rollinson L, & Hill J (2004). The role of overgeneral autobiographical memory in the development of adult depression following childhood trauma. *Brit J Clin Psychol*, *43*, 365–376.

Burton C, Yan O, Pat-Horenczyk R, Chan I, Ho S, & Bonanno G (2012). Coping flexibility and complicated grief: A comparison of American and Chinese samples. *Depress Anxiety*, *29*, 16–22.

Buss C, Davis E, Muftuler L, Head K, Sandman C (2010). High pregnancy anxiety during mid-gestation is associated with decreased gray matter density in 6–9-year-old children. *Psychoneuroendocrino*, *35*(1), 141–153.

Buss D, Block J, & Block J (1980). Preschool activity level: Personality correlates and developmental implications. *Child Dev*, *51*, 401–408.

Butler O, Yang X, Laube C, Kuhn S, & Immordino-Yang M (2018). Community violence exposure correlates with smaller gray matter volume and lower IQ in urban adolescents. *Hum Brain Mapp*, *39*, 2088–2097.

Buttelmann D, Zmyj N, Daum M, & Carpenter M (2013). Selective imitation of in-group over out-group members in 14-month-old infants. *Child Dev*, *84*(2), 422–428.

Buttelmann F, & Karbach J (2017). Development and plasticity of cognitive flexibility in early and middle childhood. *Front Psychol*, *8*, 1040. doi: 10.3389/fpsyg.2017.01040.

Buzzell G, Troller-Renfree S, Morales S, & Fox N (2018). Relations between behavioral inhibition, cognitive control, and anxiety: Novel insights provided by parsing subdomains of cognitive control. In K Pérez-Edgar, N Fox (Eds), *Behavioral inhibition*. New York: Springer, Cham.

Bylund-Grenklo T, Kreicbergs U, Uggla C, Valdimarsdottir U, Nyberg T, Steineck G, & Furst C (2015). Teenagers want to be told when a parent's death is near: A nationwide study of cancer-bereaved youths' opinions and experiences. *Acta Oncologica*, *54*, 944–950.

Bynum L, Griffin T, Ridings D, Wynkoop K, Anda R, Edwards V et al. (2010). Adverse childhood experiences reported by adults–five states, 2009. *Center for Disease Control (CDC) and Prevention: The Morbidity and Mortality Weekly Report*, *59*(49), 1609–1635.

Byrne N, Lyddiard T, & Furniss R (2017). Considering the impact of maltreatment on children in out of home care when providing Speech Language Pathology intervention: Case examples. *Speech Lang Hear, 21*(3), 152–161.

Byrnes JP (2001). *Minds, brains, and learning*. New York: Guilford.

Bystrova K, Ivanova V, Edhborg M, Matthiesen A, Ransjo-Arvidson A, Mukhamedrakhimov R et al. (2009). Early contact versus separation: Effects on mother–infant interaction one year later. *Birth, 36*(2), 97–109.

Caci H, Robert P, & Boyer P (2004). Novelty seekers and impulsive subjects are low in morningness. *Eur Psychiat, 19*, 79–84.

Cadamuro A, Versari A, Vezzali L, Giovannini D, & Trifiletti E (2015). Cognitive performance in the aftermath of a natural disaster: The role of coping strategies, Theory of Mind and peer social support. *Child Youth Care For, 44*, 93–113.

Cadima J, Verschueren K, Leal T, & Guedes C (2016). Classroom interactions, dyadic teacher–child relationships, and self-regulation in socially disadvantaged young children. *J Abnorm Child Psychol, 44*, 7–17. abstract.

Caffaro J, & Conn-Caffaro A (2013). *Sibling abuse trauma* (2nd ed.). New York: Routledge.

Cain S (2013). *Quiet: The power of introverts in a world that can't stop talking*. New York: Broadway Books.

Cain A, & LaFreniere L (2015). The taunting of parentally bereaved children: An exploratory study. *Death Stud, 39*(1–5), 219–225.

Cairncross M, Veselka L, Schermer J, & Vernon P (2013). A behavioral genetic analysis of alexithymia and the dark triad traits of personality. *Twin Res & Hum Genetics, 16*, 690–697.

Callaghan B, Cowan C, & Richardson R (2016). Treating generational stress: Effect of paternal stress on development of memory and extinction in offspring is reversed by probiotic treatment. *Psychol Sci, 27*(9), 1171–1180.

Callaghan T, Rochat P, Lillard A, Claux M, Odden H, Itakura S et al. (2005). Synchrony in the onset of mental-state reasoning: Evidence from five cultures. *Psycholog Sci, 16*, 378–384.

Cameron E, Fox J, Anderson M, & Cameron C (2010). Resilient youths use humor to enhance socio-emotional functioning during a *Day in the Life*. *J Adolescent Res, 25*(5), 716–742.

Cameron F, Russell E, McCombe J, O'Connell M, & Skinner T (2017). The clinician factor: Personality characteristics of clinicians and their impact upon clinical outcomes in the management of children and adolescents with type 1 diabetes. *Pediatric Diabetes, 19*(4), 832–839.

Campbell D, Wallace M, Modirrousta M, Polimeni J, McKeen N, & Reiss J (2015). The neural basis of humour comprehension and humour appreciation: The roles of the temporoparietal junction and superior frontal gyrus. *Neuropsychologia, 79*, 10–20.

Campbell S, Mahoney A, Northrup J, Moore E, Leezenbaum N, & Brownell C (2018). Developmental changes in pretend play from 22- to 34-months in younger siblings of children with Autism Spectrum Disorder. *J Abnorm Child Psychol, 46*, 639–654.

Campbell-Sills L, Kessler R, Ursano R, & Stein M (2017). Associations of childhood bullying victimization with lifetime suicidal behaviors among new U.S. army soldiers. *Depress & Anx, 34*(8), 701–710.

Cappella E, O'Connor E, McCormick M, Turbeville A, Collins A, & McClowry S (2015). Classwide efficacy of INSIGHTS: Observed teacher practices and student behaviors in kindergarten and first grade. *Elem School J, 116*(2), 217–241.

Capurso M, & Pazzagli C (2016). Play as a coping strategy?: A review of the relevant literature, *Child Health Care, 45*(1), 39–66.

Carkaxhiu Bulut G, Rodopman Arman A, Güney İ, & Gültepe P (2017). Evaluation of 5-HTTLPR gene polymorphism and resilience: Components on the development of psychopathology in adolescent sexual abuse cases. *Arch Neuropsychiatry, 54*, 234–238. abstract.

Carleton, RN (2016). Into the unknown: A review and synthesis of contemporary models involving uncertainty. *J Anxiety Disord, 39*, 30–43.

Carlson E (1998). A prospective longitudinal study of attachment disorganization/disorientation. *Child Dev, 69*, 1107–1128.

Carlson E, Egeland B, & Sroufe L (2009). A prospective investigation of the development of borderline personality symptoms. *Dev Psychopathol, 21*(4), 1311–1334.

Carlson M, Pilkauskas N, McLanahan S, & Brooks-Gunn J (2011). Couples as partners and parents over children's early years. *J Marriage Fam, 73*, 317–334.

Carlson S, & Moses L (2001). Individual differences in inhibitory control and children's theory of mind. *Child Dev, 72*, 1032–1053.

Carlson S, & Wang T (2007). Inhibitory control and emotion regulation in preschool children. *Cognitive Dev, 22*, 489–510.

Carmassi C, Bertelloni C, Gesi C, Conversano C, Stratta P, Massimetti G et al. (2017). New DSM-5 PTSD guilt and shame symptoms among Italian earthquake survivors: Impact on maladaptive behaviors. *Psychiat Res, 251*, 142–147.

Caron E, Bernard K, & Dozier M (2016). In vivo feedback predicts parent behavior change in the Attachment and Biobehavioral Catch-up intervention. *J Clin Child Adolesc*, *4*, 1–12. doi 10.1080/15374416.2016.1141359. abstract.

Carpendale J, & Lewis, C (2004). Constructing an understanding of mind: The development of children's social understanding within social interaction. *Behav Brain Sci*, *27*, 79–96.

Carpenter K, Sprechmann P, Calderbank R, Sapiro G, & Egger H (2016). Quantifying risk for anxiety disorders in preschool children: A machine learning approach. *PLoS ONE*, *11*(11), e0165524. doi: 10.1371/journal. doi: 10.7910/DVN/N42LWG, Harvard Dataverse.

Carpenter L, Ross N, Tyrka A, Anderson G, Kelly M, & Price L (2009). Dex/CRH test cortisol response in outpatients with major depression and matched healthy controls. *Psychoneuroendocrinology*, *34*, 1208–1213.

Carpenter M, Uebel J, & Tomasello M (2013). Being mimicked increases prosocial behavior in 18-month-old infants. *Child Dev*, *84*(5), 1511–1518.

Carpenter N, Angus L, Paivio S, & Bryntwick E (2016). Narrative and emotion integration processes in emotion-focused therapy for complex trauma: An exploratory process-outcome analysis. *PCEP*, *15*(2), 1–28. doi: 10.1080/14779757.2015.1132756.

Carrion V, Garrett A, Menon V, Weems C, & Reiss A (2007). Posttraumatic stress symptoms and brain function during a response-inhibition task: An fMRI study in youth. *Depress Anxiety*, *25*, 514–526.

Carrion V, Haas B, Garrett A, Song S, & Reiss A (2010a). Reduced hippocampal activity in youth with post-traumatic stress symptoms: an fMRI study. *J Pediatr Psychol*, *35*, 559–569.

Carrion V, Weems C, Ray R, & Reiss A (2002). Toward an empirical definition of pediatric PTSD: The phenomenology of PTSD symptoms in youth. *J Am Acad Chld Psy*, *41*(2), 166–173.

Carrion V, Weems C, Richert K, Hoffman B, & Reiss A (2010b). Decreased prefrontal cortical volume associated with increased bedtime cortisol in traumatized youth. *Biol Psychiat*, *68*(5), 491–493.

Carroll L (2012). Can physical exercise buffer the negative sequelae of experienced child abuse? PsyD dissertation presented to the University of Hartford.

Carson D, Skarpness L, Schultz N, & McGhee P (1986). Temperament and communicative competence as predictors of young children's humor. *Merrill Palmer Q*, *32*, 415–426.

Cartwright K, Coppage E, Lane A, Singleton T, Marshall T, & Bentivegna C (2017). Cognitive flexibility deficits in children with specific reading comprehension difficulties. *Contemp Educ Psychol*, *50*, 33–44.

Cartwright K, Marshall T, Dandy K, & Isaac M (2010). The development of graphophonological-semantic cognitive flexibility and its contribution to reading comprehension in beginning readers. *J Cogn Dev*, *11*, 61–85.

Carver L, & Bauer P (1999). When the event is more than the sum of its parts: Individual differences in 9-month-olds long-term ordered recall. *Memory*, *2*, 147–174.

Casanueva C, Goldman-Fraser J, Rngeisen H, Lederman C, Katz L, & Osofsky J (2010). Maternal perceptions of temperament among infants and toddlers investigated for maltreatment: Implications for services need and referral. *J Fam Viol*, *25*, 557–574. abstract.

Casey B, Jones R, & Somerville L (2011). Braking and accelerating of the adolescent brain. *J Res on Adolesc*, *21*(1), 21–33.

Casile A, Caggiano V, & Ferrari P (2011). The mirror neuron system: A fresh view. *Neuroscientist*, *17*(5) 524–538.

Caspi A (1998). Personality development across the life course. In: Damon W, Eisenberg N, (Eds), *Handbook of child psychology, Volume 3. Social, emotional, and personality development* (5th ed.; pp. 311–388). New York: Wiley.

Caspi A, Hariri A, Holmes A, Uher R, & Moffitt T (2010). Genetic sensitivity to the environment: The case of the serotonin transporter gene and its implications for studying complex diseases and traits. *Am J Psychiat*, *167*(5), 509–527.

Caspi A, Harrington H, Milne B, Amell J, Theodore R, & Moffitt T (2003b). Children's behavioral styles at age 3 are linked to their adult personality traits at age 26. *J Personality*, *71*, 495–513.

Caspi A, Sugden K, Moffitt T, Taylor A, Craig I, & Harrington H (2003a). Influence of life stress on depression: Moderation by a polymorphism in the 5-HTT gene. *Science*, *301*, 386–389.

Caspi A, Williams B, Kim-Cohen J, Craig I, Milne B, Poulton R et al. (2007). Moderation of breastfeeding effects on the IQ by genetic variation in fatty acid metabolism. *Proceedings of the National Academy of Science USA*, *104*, 18860–18865.

Cassidy J, Brett B, Gross J, Stern J, Martin D, Mohr J, & Woodhouse S (2017). Circle of Security–Parenting: A randomized controlled trial in Head Start. *Dev Psychopathol*, *29*, 651–673.

Cassidy J, & Shaver P (Eds) (2018). *Handbook of attachment: Theory, research, and clinical applications* (3rd ed.). New York: Guilford.

Cassidy J, Ziv Y, Mehta T, & Feeney B (2003). Feedback seeking in children and adolescents: Associations with self-perceptions, attachment representations, and depression. *Child Dev*, *74*(2), 612–628.

Cassidy J, Ziv Y, Stupica B, Sherman L, Butler H, Karfgin A et al. (2010). Enhancing maternal sensitivity and attachment security in the infants of women in a jail-diversion program. *Attach & Hum Devel, 12*, 333–353.

Castillo R, Salguero J, Fernandez-Berrocal P, & Balluerka N (2013). Effects of an emotional intelligence intervention on aggression and empathy among adolescents. *J Adolescence, 36*, 883–892.

Castro-Vale I, van Rossum E, Machado J, Mota-Cardoso R, & Carvalho D (2016). Genetics of glucocorticoid regulation and posttraumatic stress disorder—What do we know? *Neurosci & Biobehav Rev, 63*, 143–157. abstract.

Catani C, Kohiladevy M, Ruf M, Schauer E, Elbert T, & Neuner F (2009). Treating children traumatized by war and Tsunami: A comparison between exposure therapy and meditation-relaxation in North-East Sri Lanka. *BMC Psychiatry, 9*, 22. doi: 10.1186/1471-244X-9-22. abstract.

Cater T, Zeigler-Hill V, & Vonk J (2011). Narcissism and recollections of early life experiences. *Pers Indiv Differ, 51*, 935–939.

Cattane N, Rossi R, Lanfredi M, & Cattaneo A (2017). Borderline personality disorder and childhood trauma: exploring the affected biological systems and mechanisms. *BMC Psychiatry, 17*, 221. doi: 10.1186/s12888-017-1383-2.

Caughy M, Mills B, Owen M, & Hurst J (2013). Emergent self-regulation skills among very young ethnic minority children: A confirmatory factor model. *J Exp Child Psychol, 116*, 839–855.

Causadias J, Salvatore J, & Sroufe L (2012). Early patterns of self-regulation as risk and promotive factors in development: A longitudinal study from childhood to adulthood in a high-risk sample. *Int J Behav Dev, 36*(4), 293–302.

Cecil C, McCrory E, Barker E, Guiney J, & Viding E (2018). Characterising youth with callous–unemotional traits and concurrent anxiety: Evidence for a high-risk clinical group. *Eur Child Adoles Psy, 27*, 885–898. abstract.

Center for Investigating Health Minds (2013). *Kindness Curriculum*. Unpublished manual. Waisman Center, University of Wisconsin-Madison.

Cerda M, Sagdeo A, Johnson J, & Galea S. (2010). Genetic and environmental influences on psychiatric comorbidity: a systematic review. *J Affective Dis, 126*, 14–38.

Cerel J, Fristad M, Verducci J, Weller R, & Weller E (2006). Childhood bereavement: Psychopathology 2 years postparental death. *CAP, 46*(6), 681–690.

Čerkez V, & Efendić-Spahić T (2016). Perfectionism in younger adolescents: Associations with different aspects of anxiety. *Human Res in Rehab, 6*(1), 70–80.

Cha K (2017). Relationships among negative emotionality, responsive parenting and Early socio-cognitive development in Korean children. *Inf Child Dev, 26*(3), e1990. abstract. doi: 10.1002/icd.1990.

Chai L, Khambhati A, Ciric R, Moore T, Gur RC, Gur RE et al. (2017). Evolution of brain network dynamics in neurodevelopment. *Network Neuroscience, 1*(1), 14–30.

Chamberlain P (1994). *Family connections: Treatment foster care for adolescents with delinquency*. Eugene, OR: Castalia Publishing.

Champagne F, & Mashoodh R (2009). Genes in context. *Curr Dir Psychol Sci, 18*(3), 127–131.

Champagne F, & Meaney M (2007). Transgenerational effects of social environment on variations in maternal care and behavioral response to novelty. *Behav Neurosci, 121*, 1353–1363.

Chan KP (2014). Prenatal meditation influences infant behaviors. *Infant Behav Dev, 37*, 556–561.

Chanen A & Thompson K (2014). Preventive strategies for Borderline Personality Disorder in adolescents. *Curr Treat Options Psychiatry, 1*, 358–368.

Chang C, Kaczkurkin A, McLean C, & Foa E (2018). Emotion regulation is associated with PTSD and depression among female adolescent survivors of childhood sexual abuse. *Psychol Trauma-US, 10*(3), 319–326.

Chang E, Wan L, Li P, Guo Y, He J, Gu Y et al. (2017). Loneliness and suicidal risk in young adults: Does believing in a changeable future help minimize suicidal risk among the lonely? *The Journal of Psychology, 151*(5), 453–463.

Chapman A (2006). Dialectical behavior therapy. *Psychiatry, 3*(9), 62–68.

Charil A, Laplante D, Vaillancourt C, & King S (2010). Prenatal stress and brain development. *Brain Res Rev, 65*, 56–79.

Charles D, & Charles M (2006). Sibling loss and attachment style. *Psychoanal Psychol, 23*(1), 72–90.

Charollais A (2014). Delayed language development at two years of age in very preterm infants in the Perinatal Network of Haute-Normandie. *Early Human Devel, 90*, 891–892.

Chemtob C, Nomura Y, Rajendran K, Yehuda R, Schwartz D, & Abramovitz R (2010). Impact of maternal Posttraumatic Stress Disorder and depression following exposure to the September 11 attacks on preschool children's behavior. *Child Dev, 81*, 1129–1141.

Chen B-B (2017). Parent–adolescent attachment and procrastination: The mediating role of self-worth. *J Genet Psychol, 178*(4), 238–245. abstract.

Chen C, Hewitt P, & Flett G (2015). Preoccupied attachment, need to belong, shame, and interpersonal perfectionism: An investigation of the Perfectionism Social Disconnection Model. *Pers Indiv Differ, 76*, 177–182.

Chen E, Gau M, Liu C, Lee T (2017). Effects of father-neonate skin-to-skin contact on attachment: A randomized controlled trial. *Nurs Res Pract*, Article ID 8612024. doi.org/10.1155/2017/8612024.

Chen E, Strunk R, Trethewey A, Schreier H, Maharaj N, & Miller G (2011). Resilience in low-socioeconomic-status children with asthma: adaptations to stress. *J Allergy Clin Immunol, 128*, 970–976.

Chen J, Rapee R, & Abbott M (2013). Mediators of the relationship between social anxiety and post-event rumination. *J Anxiety Disord 27*(1), 1–8.

Chen X, Rubin K, & Li Z (1995). Social functioning and adjustment in Chinese children: A longitudinal study. *Dev Psychol, 31*, 531–539.

Chen Z, Williams K, Fitness J, & Newton N (2008). When hurt will not heal: Exploring the capacity to relive social and physical pain. *Psychol Sci, 19*, 789–795.

Cheng FK (2016). Is meditation conducive to mental well-being for adolescents? An integrative review for mental health nursing. *IJANS, 4*, 7–19.

Cheng J, Liang Y, Fu L, & Liu Z (2018). Posttraumatic stress and depressive symptoms in children after the Wenchuan earthquake. *Eur J Psychotraumato, 9*(1), 1472992, doi: 10.1080/20008198.2018.1472992.

Chess S, & Thomas A (1991). Temperament. In M Lewis (ed.), *Child and adolescent psychiatry: A comprehensive textbook* (pp. 145–159). Baltimore, MD: Williams & Wilkins.

Chess S, & Thomas A (1977). Temperamental individuality from childhood to adolescence. *J Amer Acad Child Ps, 16*(2), 218–226.

Chick C (2015). Reward processing in the adolescent brain: Individual differences and relation to risk taking. *J Neurosci, 35*(40), 13539–13541.

Child Welfare (2013). *Long-term consequences of child abuse neglect*. Washington, DC: US Dept of Health and Human Services, Children's Bureau.

Child Welfare Information Gateway (2015). *Understanding the effects of maltreatment on brain development*. Washington, DC: US Dept of Health and Human Services, Children's Bureau.

Chipuer HM (2004). Australian children's understanding of loneliness. *Australian Journal of Psychology, 56*(3), 147–153.

Chiu C-D, Paesen L, Dziobek I, & Tollenaar M (2016). Weakened cognitive empathy in individuals with dissociation proneness. *J Soc Clin Psychol, 35*(5), 425–436.

Chiu C-D, Tseng M-C, Chien Y-L, Liao S-C, Liu C-M, Yeh Y-Y, & Hwu H-G (2015). Cumulative traumatization associated with pathological dissociation in acute psychiatric inpatients. *Psychiat Res, 230*, 406–412. abstract.

Cho S, Philbrook L, Davis E, & Buss K (2017). Sleep duration and RSA suppression as predictors of internalizing and externalizing behaviors. *Dev Psychobiol, 59*, 60–69.

Choate M, Pincus D, Eyberg S, & Barlow D (2005). Parent–child Interaction Therapy for treatment of Separation Anxiety Disorder in young children: A pilot study. *Cogn Behav Pract, 12*, 126–135.

Choe M-s, Ortiz-Mantilla S, Makris N, Gregas M, Bacic J, Haehn D et al. (2013). Regional infant brain development: An MRI-based morphometric analysis in 3 to 13 month olds. *Cereb Cortex, 23*, 2100–2117.

Choi K, Seng J, Briggs E, Munro-Kramer M, Graham S, Lee R, & Ford J (2017). The dissociative subtype of Posttraumatic Stress Disorder (PTSD) among adolescents: Co-occurring PTSD, depersonalization/derealization, and other dissociation symptoms. *J Am Acad Child Psy, 56*(12), 1062–1072.

Christiansen E & Evans W (2005). Adolescent victimization testing models of resiliency by gender. *J Early Adolescence, 25*(3), 298–316.

Chronis-Tuscano A, Rubin K, O'Brien K, Coplan R, Thomas S, Dougherty L et al. (2015). Preliminary evaluation of a multimodal early intervention program for behaviorally inhibited preschoolers. *J Consult Clin Psych, 83*(3), 534–540.

Cicchetti D (2003). Neuroendocrine functioning in maltreated children. In E Cicchetti, E Walker (Eds) *Neurodevelopmental mechanisms in psychopathology* (pp. 345–365). Cambridge, UK: Cambridge University Press.

Cicchetti D, Handley E, & Rogosch F (2015a). Child maltreatment, inflammation, and internalizing symptoms: Investigating the roles of C-reactive protein, gene variation, and neuroendocrine regulation. *Dev Psychopathol 27*, 553–566.

Cicchetti D, Rogosch F, & Oshri A (2011). Interactive effects of corticotropin releasing hormone receptor 1, serotonin transporter linked polymorphic region, and child maltreatment on diurnal cortisol regulation and internalizing symptomatology. *Dev Psychopathol, 23*, 1125–1138.

Cicchetti D, Rogosch F, & Toth S (2006). Fostering secure attachment in infants in maltreating families through preventive interventions. *Dev Psychopathol, 18*, 623–650.

Cicchetti D, & Valentino K (2006). An ecological-transactional perspective on child maltreatment: Failure of the average expectable environment and its influence on child development. In D Cicchetti, D Cohen

(Eds), *Developmental psychology: Risk, disorder, and adaptation* (2nd ed., Vol. 3, pp. 129–201). New York: Wiley.

Cipriano-Essel E, Skowron E, Stifter C, & Teti D (2013). Heterogeneity in maltreated and non-maltreated preschool children's inhibitory control: The interplay between parenting quality and child temperament. *Inf Child Dev*, *22*, 501–522.

Cirelli L, Wan S, & Trainor L (2016). Social effects of movement synchrony: Increased infant helpfulness only transfers to affiliates of synchronously moving partners. *Infancy*, *21*(6), 807–821.

Cisler J, Amstadter A, & Nugent N (2011). Genetic and environmental influences on posttrauma adjustment in children and adolescents: the role of personality constructs. *J Child Adolesc Trauma*. *4*(4), 301–317.

Cisler J, Bush K, Steele J, Lenow J, Smitherman S et al. (2015a). Brain and behavioral evidence for altered social learning mechanisms among women with assault-related posttraumatic stress disorder. *J Psychiatr Res*, *63*, 75–83.

Cisler J, Sigel B, Kramer T, Smitherman S, Vanderzee K, Pemberton J, & Clinton D (2015b). Amygdala response predicts trajectory of symptom reduction during Trauma-Focused Cognitive-Behavioral Therapy among adolescent girls with PTSD. *J Psychia Res*, *71*, 33–40.

Cisler J, Sigel B, Steele J, Smitherman S, Vanderzee K, & Pemberton J (2016). Changes in functional connectivity of the amygdala during cognitive reappraisal predict symptom reduction during trauma-focused cognitive–behavioral therapy among adolescent girls with post-traumatic stress disorder. *Psychol Med*, *46*, 3013–3023.

Clair M, Stein L, Soenksenn S, Martin R, Lebeau R, & Golembeske C (2013). Ethnicity as a moderator of motivational interviewing for incarcerated adolescents after release. *J Subst Abuse Treat*, *45*, 370–375.

Clair-Michaud M, Martin R, Stein L, Bassett S, Lebeau R, & Golembeske C (2016). The impact of Motivational Interviewing on delinquent behaviors in incarcerated adolescents. *J Subst Abuse Treat*, *65*, 13–19. abstract.

Class Q, Abel K, Khashan A, Rickert M, Dalman C, Larsson H et al. (2014). Offspring psychopathology following preconception, prenatal and postnatal maternal bereavement stress. *Psychol Med*, *44*, 71–84.

Class Q, Khashan A, Lichtenstein P, Langstrom N, & D'Onofrio B (2013). Maternal stress and infant mortality: The importance of the preconception period. *Psychol Sci*, *24*(7), 1309–1316. abstract.

Clay A, Bloomsmith M, Bard K, Maple T, & Marr M (2015). Long-term effects of infant attachment organization on adult behavior and health in nursery-reared, captive chimpanzees (Pan troglodytes). *J Comp Psycho*, *129*(2), 145–159.

Cloitre M, & Beck J (2017). Introduction to the special issue: The long-term effects of childhood adversity and trauma. *Clin Psychol Sci Prac*, *24*, 107–110.

Cloitre M, Courtois C, Charuvastra A, Carapezza R, Stolbach B, & Green B (2011). Treatment of complex PTSD: Results of the ISTSS expert clinician survey on best practices. *J Traum Stress*, *24*, 615–627.

Cloitre M, Garvert D, Brewin C, Bryant R, Maercker A (2013). Evidence for proposed ICD-11 PTSD and complex PTSD: a latent profile analysis. *Eur Psychotraumatol*, 4, 20706. doi.org/10.3402/ejpt.v4i0.20706.

Cloitre M, Garvert D, Weiss B, Carlson E, & Bryant R (2014). Distinguishing PTSD, Complex PTSD, and Borderline Personality Disorder: A latent class analysis. *Eur Psychotraumatol*, *5*, 25097.

Cloitre M, Petkova E, Wang J, & Lu F (2012). An examination of the influence of a sequential treatment on the course and impact of dissociation among women with PTSD related to childhood abuse. *Depress Anxiety*, *29*, 709–717.

Cloitre M, Stolbach B, Herman J, Pynoos R, Wang J, & Petkova E (2009). A developmental approach to cumulative PTSD: childhood and adult cumulative trauma as predictors of symptom complexity. *J Traum Stress*, *22*(5), 399–408.

Cloitre M, Stovall-McClough K, Nooner K, Zorbas P, Cherry S, Jackson C et al. (2010). Treatment for PTSD related to childhood abuse: a randomized controlled trial. *Am J Psychiat*, *167*(8), 915–924.

Coates SW (2016). Can babies remember trauma? Symbolic forms of representation in traumatized infants. *J Am Psychoanal Ass*, *64*(4), 751–776.

Coatsworth J, Duncan L, Greenberg M, & Nix R (2010). Changing parent's mindfulness, child management skills and relationship quality with their youth: Results from a randomized pilot intervention trial. *J Child Fam Stud*, *19*, 203–217.

Cohen D, & Strayer J (1996). Empathy in conduct disordered and comparison youth. *Dev Psychol*, *32*, 988–998.

Cohen E, Chazan S, Lerner M, & Maimon E (2010). Posttraumatic play in young children exposed to terrorism: An empirical study. *Inf Mental Hlth J*, *31*(2), 159–181.

Cohen G, & Weitzman C (2016). Helping children and families deal with divorce and separation. *Pediatrics*, *138*(6), e20163020.

Cohen J (2006). Social, emotional ethical, and academic education: Creating a climate for learning, participation in democracy, and well-being. *Harvard Educa Rev*, *76*(2), 201–237.

Cohen J, & Mannarino A (2008). Trauma-Focused Cognitive Behavioural Therapy for children and parents. *Chld Adol Ment H-UK, 13*(4), 158–162.

Cohen J, Mannarino A, & Deblinger E (2017). *Treating trauma and traumatic grief in children and adolescents* (2nd ed.). New York: Guilford.

Cohen J, Mannarino A, & Deblinger E (2012). *Trauma-Focused CBT for children and adolescents: Treatment applications*. New York: Guilford.

Cohen J, Mannarino A, & Deblinger E (2006a). *Treating trauma and traumatic grief in children and adolescents*. New York: Guilford.

Cohen J, Mannarino A, Greenberg T, Padlo S, & Shipley C (2002). Childhood traumatic grief: Concepts and controversies. *Trauma Violence Abus, 3*(4), 307–327.

Cohen J, Mannarino A, Kliethermes M, & Murray L (2012). Trauma-focused CBT for youth with complex trauma. *Child Abuse Neglect, 36*, 528–541.

Cohen J, Mannarino A, & Staron V (2006b). A pilot study of modified Cognitive-Behavioral Therapy for Childhood Traumatic Grief (CBT-CTG). *J Am Acad Child Ps, 45*(12), 1465–1473.

Cohen O, & Katz M (2015). Grief and growth of bereaved siblings as related to attachment style and flexibility. *Death Stud, 39*, 158–164.

Coholic D (2011). Exploring the feasibility and benefits of arts-based mindfulness-based practices with young people in need: Aiming to improve aspects of self-awareness and resilience. *Child Youth Care For, 40*, 303–317.

Coker K, Ikpe U, Brooks J, Page B, & Sobell M (2014). The effect of social problem solving skills in the relationship between traumatic stress and moral disengagement among inner-city African American high school students. *J Child Adol Trauma, 7*, 87–95.

Colasanti A, Rabiner E, Lingford-Hughes A, & Nutt D (2011). Opioids and anxiety. *J Psychopharmacol, 25*(11) 1415–1433. Page 1.

Collin W, & Steinberg L (2008). Adolescent development in interpersonal context. In W Damon, R Lerner (Eds), *Child and adolescent development: An advanced course (*pp. 551–590). New York: Wiley.

Collin-Vézina D, & Hébert M (2005). Comparing dissociation and PTSD in sexually abused school-aged girls. *J Nerv Ment Dis, 193*(1), 47–52.

Collins W, Steinberg L (2008). Adolescent development in interpersonal context. In W Damon, R Lerner (Eds), *Child and adolescent development: An advanced course* (pp. 551–592). New York: Wiley.

Colonnello V, Chen F, Panksepp J, & Heinrichs M (2013). Oxytocin sharpens self-other perceptual boundary. *Psychoneuroendocrino. 38*, 2996—3002. abstract.

Comasco E, Gustafsson P, Sydsjo G, Agnafors S, Aho N, & Svedin C (2015). Psychiatric symptoms in adolescents: FKBP5 genotype—early life adversity interactions effects. *Eur Child Adoles Psy, 24*, 1473–1483.

Condon J, Corkindale C, Boyce P, & Gamble E (2013). A longitudinal study of father-to-infant attachment: Antecedents and correlates. *J Reprod Infant Psyc, 31*(1), 15–30.

Conger R, Ge X, Elder G, Lorenz F, & Simons R (1994). Economic stress, coercive family process, and developmental problems of adolescents. *Child Dev, 65*, 541–561.

Conrad T, & Ayasse M (2015). The role of vibrations in population divergence in the Red Mason Bee, *Osmia bicornis*. *Curr Biol, 25*, 2819–2822. abstract.

Conson M, Mazzarella E, Esposito D, Grossi D, Marino N, Massagli A, & Frolli A (2015). "Put myself into your place": Embodied simulation and perspective taking in Autism Spectrum Disorders. *Autism Res, 8*(4), 454–466.

Cook L, & Kearney C (2014). Parent perfectionism and psychopathology symptoms and child perfectionism. *Pers Indiv Differ, 70*, 1–6.

Cook T, Shannon P, Vinson G, Letts J, & Dwee E (2015). War trauma and torture experiences reported during public health screening of newly resettled Karen refugees: A qualitative study. *BMC Int Health Hum R, 15*(8), 1–13. doi.org/10.1186/s12914-015-0046-y.

Cooley CH (1902). *Human nature and the social order*. New York: Charles Scribner & Sons.

Cooper G, Hoffman K, & Powell B (2009). *Circle of Security Parenting: A relationship based parenting program. Facilitator DVD Manual* 5.0. Spokane, WA: Circle of Security International.

Copeland W, Keeler G, Angold A, & Costello J (2007). Traumatic events and posttraumatic stress in childhood. *Arch Gen Psychiatry, 64*, 577–584.

Copeland W, Wolke D, Lereya S, Shanahan L, Worthman C, & Costello E (2014). Childhood bullying involvement predicts low-grade systemic inflammation into adulthood. *P Natl A Sci USA* USA 111, 7570–7575. abstract.

Coplan R, Arbeau K, & Armer M (2008). Don't fret, be supportive! Maternal characteristics linking child shyness to psychosocial and school adjustment in kindergarten. *J Abnorm Child Psych, 36*, 359–371.

Coplan R, DeBow A, Schneider B, & Graham A (2009). The social behaviours of inhibited children in and out of preschool. *Brit J Dev Psychol, 27*, 891–905.

Coplan R, Prakash K, O'Neil K, & Armer M (2004). Do you "want" to play? Distinguishing between conflicted-shyness and social disinterest in early childhood. *Dev Psychol, 40*, 244–258.

Coplan R, Rubin K, & Findlay L (2005). Social and nonsocial play. In D Fromberg, D Bergen (Eds), *Play from birth to twelve* (2nd edition). New York: Garland.

Corcoran M, & McNulty M (2018). Examining the role of attachment in the relationship between childhood adversity, psychological distress and subjective well-being. *Child Abuse Neglect, 76*, 297–309.

Cornell D, Sheras P, Gregory A, & Fan X (2009). A retrospective study of school safety conditions in high schools using the Virginia threat assessment guidelines versus alternative approaches. *School Psychol Quart, 24*, 119–129.

Corr C (2015). Let's stop "staging" persons who are coping with loss. *Illness, Crises, & Loss, 23*(3), 226–241.

Corr C (2008). Children's emerging awareness of death. In K Doka, A Tucci (Eds), *Living with grief: Children and adolescents* (pp. 5–17). Washington, DC: Hospice Foundation of America.

Corr C, & Corr D (1996). *Handbook of childhood death and bereavement.* New York: Springer.

Corthorn C, & Milicic, N (2015). Mindfulness and parenting: A correlational study of nonmeditating mothers of preschool children. *J Child Fam Stud*, 25(5), 1672–1683.

Costello E, Copeland W, & Angold A (2011). Trends in psychopathology across the adolescent years: What changes when children become adolescents, and when adolescents become adults? *J Child Psychol Psyc, 52*, 1015–1025.

Costello E, Egger H, & Angold A (2005). The developmental epidemiology of anxiety disorders: Phenomenology, prevalence, and comorbidity. *Child Adolesc Psychiatr Clin North Am, 14*, 631–648.

Costello E, Mustillo S, Erkanli A, Keeler G, & Angold A (2003). Prevalence and development of psychiatric disorders in childhood and adolescence. *Arch Gen Psychiat, 60*, 837–844.

Cottrell L, Nield L, Perkins K (2006). Effective interviewing and counseling of adolescent patients. *Psychiatr Ann, 36*(10), 674–681.

Cougle J, Resnick H, & Kilpatrick D (2009). A prospective examination of PTSD symptoms as risk factors for subsequent exposure to potentially traumatic events among women. *J Abnorm Psychol, 118*(2), 405–11.

Courtney-Seidler E, Klein D, & Miller A (2013). Borderline Personality Disorder in adolescents. *Clin Psychol Sci Prac, 20*, 425–444.

Cowan N (2008). What are the differences between long-term and short-term, and working memory. *Prog Brain Res, 169*, 323–338.

Cowan N (2011). The focus of attention as observed in visual working memory tasks: Making sense of competing claims. *Neuropsychologia, 49*(6), 1401–1406.

Cowan N, Nugent L, Elliott E, Ponomarev I, & Saults J (1999). The role of attention in the development of short-term memory: Age differences in the verbal span of apprehension. *Child Dev, 70*, 1082–1097.

Cox MV (1978). The development of perspective-taking ability in children. *Int J Behav Dev, 1*, 247–254.

Craig, AD (2011). Significance of the insula for the evolution of human awareness of feelings from the body. *Ann NY Acad Sci, 1225*, 72–82.

Crane C, Heron J, Gunnell D, Lewis G, Evans J, & Williams J (2014). Childhood traumatic events and adolescent overgeneral autobiographical memory: Findings in a UK cohort. *J Behav Ther & Exp Psychiat, 45*, 330–338.

Crawford T, Cohen P, First M, Skodol A, Johnson J, & Kasen S (2008). Comorbid Axis I and Axis II disorders in early adolescence. *Arch Gen Psychiat, 65*, 641–648.

Crawley S, Kendall P, Benjamin C, Brodman D, Wei C, Beidas R, Podell J, & Mauro C (2013). Brief cognitive-behavioral therapy for anxious youth: Feasibility and initial outcomes. *Cogn Behav Pract, 20*, 123–133.

Crenshaw D (2007). An interpersonal neurobiological-informed treatment model for childhood traumatic grief. *Omega, 54*, 319–335.

Crick N (1995). Relational aggression: The role of intent attributions, feelings of distress, and provocation type. *Dev Psychopathol, 7*, 313–322.

Crick N, & Dodge K (1994). A review and reformulation of social information processing mechanisms in children's social adjustment. *Psychol Bull, 115*(1), 74–101.

Crick N, & Dodge K (1996). Social information-processing mechanisms in reactive and proactive aggression. *Child Dev, 67*(3), 993–1002.

Crick N, Werner N, Casas J, O'Brien K, Nelson D, Grotpeter J, & Markon K (1997). Childhood aggression and gender: A new look at an old problem. In D Bernstein (ed.), *Gender and motivation: Nebraska symposium on motivation* (Vol. 45, pp. 75–141). Lincoln, NE: University of Nebraska Press.

Crittenden P, Robson K, Tooby A, & Fleming C (2017). Are mothers' protective attachment strategies related to their children's strategies? *Clin Child Psychol P, 22*(3) 358–377.

Crome E, Grove R, Baille A, Sunderland M, Teesson M, & Slade T (2015). DSM-IV and DSM-5 social anxiety disorder in the Australian community. *Aust NZ J Psychiat, 49*(3) 227–235.

Cromer J, Schembri A, Harel B, & Maruff P (2015). The nature and rate of cognitive maturation from late childhood to adulthood. *Front Psychol, 6*, 704. abstract. doi: 10.3389/fpsyg.2015.00704.
Crone E, & Konijn E (2018). Media use and brain development during adolescence. *Nat Commun, 110*(25), 425–431.
Crone E, van Duijvenvoorde A, & Peper J (2016). Annual Research Review: Neural contributions to risk-taking in adolescence—developmental changes and individual differences. *J Child Psychol Psyc, 57*(3), 353–368.
Crone E, & van der Molen M (2004). Developmental changes in real life decision making: performance on a gambling task previously shown to depend on the ventromedial prefrontal cortex. *Dev Neuropsychol, 25*, 251–279.
Crowe L, Catroppa C, Babl F, Rosenfeld J, & Anderson V (2012). Timing of traumatic brain injury in childhood and intellectual outcome. *J Pediatric Psychology 37*(7), 745–754.
Crowell S, Beauchaine T, & Linehan M (2009). A biosocial developmental model of Borderline Personality Disorder: Elaborating and extending Linehan's theory. *Psychol Bull, 135*, 495–510.
Csikszentmihalyi M (1997a). Finding flow. *Psychology Today, 30*(4), 46–48, 70–71.
Csikszentmihalyi M (1997b). Happiness and creativity: Going with the flow. *Futurist, 31*(5), 8–12.
Csikszentmihalyi M (1990). *Flow: The psychology of optimal experience*. New York: HarperCollins.
Cuevas C, Finkelhor D, Turner H, & Ormrod R (2007). Juvenile delinquency and victimization. *J Interpers Violence, 22*, 1581–1602.
Cunningham N (2007). Level of bonding to school and perception of the school environment by bullies, victims, and bully victims. *The J Early Adolescence, 27*(4), 457–478.
Curtis P, Kaiser A, Estabrook R, & Roberts M (2017). The longitudinal effects of early language intervention on children's problem behaviors. *Child Dev*, doi: 10.1111/cdev.12942.
Cyders M, Flory K, Rainer S, & Smith G (2009). The role of personality dispositions to risky behavior in predicting first year college drinking. *Addiction, 104*, 193–202.
Dackis M, Rogosch F, Oshri A, & Cicchetti D (2012). The role of limbic system irritability in linking history of childhood maltreatment and psychiatric outcome in low-income, high-risk women: Moderation by FK506 binding protein 5 haplotype. *Dev Psychopathol, 24*,1237–1252.
Dadds M, Hawes D, Frost A, Vassallo S, Bunn P, Hunter K, & Merz S (2009). Learning to "talk the talk": The relationship of psychopathic traits to deficits in empathy across childhood. *J Child Psychol Psyc, 50*, 599–606.
Dahl R (2007). Sleep and the developing brain. *Sleep, 30*(9), 1079–1080.
Dahl R (2004). Adolescent brain development: A period of vulnerabilities and opportunities. *Ann NY Acad Sci, 1021*, 1–22.
Dahl R (1996). The impact of inadequate sleep on children's daytime cognitive function. *Semin Pediatr Neurol, 3*, 44–50.
Dajani D, & Uddin L (2015). Demystifying cognitive flexibility: Implications for clinical and developmental neuroscience. *Trends Neurosci, 38*(9), 571–578.
Dale P, Price T, Bishop D, & Plomin R (2003a). Outcomes of early language delay: I. Predicting persistent and transient language difficulties at 3 and 4 years. *J Speech Lang & Hear Res, 46*, 544–560. abstract.
Dale P, Price T, Bishop D, & Plomin R (2003b). Outcomes of early language delay: II. Etiology of transient and persistent language difficulties. *J Speech Lang & Hear Res, 46*, 561–575.
Dalgard O, Thapa S, Hauff E, McCubbin M, & Syed H (2006). Immigration, lack of control and psychological distress: Findings from the Oslo Health Study. *Scand J Psychol, 47*, 551–558.
Dalgleish T, Goodall B, Chadwick I, Werner-Seidler A, McKinnon A, Morant N et al. (2015). Study Protocol: Trauma-focused cognitive behaviour therapy versus treatment as usual for post traumatic stress disorder (PTSD) in young children aged 3 to 8 years: study protocol for a randomized controlled trial. Dalgleish et al. Trials, 16, 116. doi 10.1186/s13063-015-0632-2.
Dalgleish T, Taghavi R, Neshat-Doost H, Moradi A, Canterbury R, & Yule W (2003). Patterns of processing bias for emotional information across clinical disorders: A comparison of attention, memory, and prospective cognition in children and adolescents with depression, generalized anxiety, and posttraumatic stress disorder. *J Clin Child Adolesc, 32*(1), 10–21.
Damon F, Mottier H, Meary D, & Pascalis O (2017). A review of attractiveness preferences in infancy: From faces to objects. *Adaptive Human Behavior and Physiology, 3*, 321–336.
Damra J, Nassar Y, & Ghabri T (2014). Trauma-focused cognitive behavioral therapy: Cultural adaptations for application in Jordanian culture. *Couns Psychol Q, 27*(3), 308–323.
D'Andrea W, Ford J, Stolbach B, Spinazzola J, & van der Kolk B (2012). Understanding interpersonal trauma in children: Why we need a developmentally appropriate trauma diagnosis. *Am J Orthopsychiat, 82*(2), 187–200.
D'Andrea W, & Pole N (2012). A naturalistic study of the relation of psychotherapy process to changes in symptoms, information processing and physiological activity in complex trauma. *Psychol Trauma-US, 4*(4), 438–446.

Danese A, Moffitt T, Harrington H, Milne B, Polanczyk G, Pariante C, Poulton R, Caspi A (2009). Adverse childhood experiences and adult risk factors for age-related disease: Depression, inflammation, and clustering of metabolic risk markers. *Arch Pediatr Adolesc Med, 163*(12), 1135–1143.

Danese A, Pariante C, Caspi A, Taylor A, & Poulton R (2007). Childhood maltreatment predicts adult inflammation in the life-course study. *P Natl A Sci USA of the United States of America, 104*(4), 1319–1324.

Danieli Y (1998). *International handbook of multigenerational legacies of trauma.* New York: Plenum Press.

Danieli Y (1984). Psychotherapist's participation in the conspiracy of silence about the Holocaust. *Psychoanal Psychol, 1*(1), 23–42.

Danieli Y, & Nader K (2006). Respecting cultural, religious and ethnic differences in the prevention and treatment of psychological sequelae. In Schein L, Spitz G, Burlingame H, Muskin P (Eds), *Psychological effects of catastrophic disasters: Group approaches to treatment* (pp. 203–234). New York: Haworth Press.

Daniels J, Frewen P, McKinnon M, & Lanius R (2011). Default mode alterations in posttraumatic stress disorder related to early life trauma: A developmental perspective. *J Psychiatry Neurosci, 36*(1), 56–59.

Daniels J, Royster T, Vecchi G, & Pshenishy E (2010a). Barricaded captive situations in schools: Mitigation and response. *J Fam Violence, 25*, 587–594.

Daniels J, Volungis A, Pshenishy E, Gandhi P, Winkler A, Cramer D, & Bradley M (2010b). A qualitative investigation of averted school shooting rampages. *Couns Psychol, 38*(1), 69–95.

Danielson C, Moreland A & Walsh K (2015). Clinical manifestations of trauma. In P Clements, S Seedat, E Gibbings (Eds) (pp. 87–102). *Mental health issues of child maltreatment.* St. Louis: STM Learning, Inc.

Danzi B, & La Greca A (2016). DSM-IV, DSM-5, and ICD-11: Identifying children with posttraumatic stress disorder after disasters. *J Child Psychol Psyc, 57*, 1444–1452.

Darby K, Castro L, Wasserman E, & Sloutsky V (2018). Cognitive flexibility and memory in pigeons, human children, and adults. *Cognition, 177*, 30–40.

Dauch C, Imwalle M, Ocasio B, & Metz A (2018). The influence of the number of toys in the environment on toddlers' play. *Infant Behav Dev, 50*, 78–87.

Daughters S, Gorka S, Magidso J, MacPherson L, & Seitz-Brown C (2013). The role of gender and race in the relation between adolescent distress tolerance and externalizing and internalizing psychopathology. *J Adolescence, 36*, 1053–1065.

Davidov M, & Grusec J (2006). Untangling the links of parental responsiveness to distress and warmth to child outcomes. *Child Dev*, 77, 44–58.

Davis E, Glynn L, Schetter C, Hobel C, Chicz-Demet A, & Sandman C (2007). Prenatal exposure to maternal depression and infant temperament. *J Am Acad Child Psy, 46*, (6), 737–746.

Davis K, Panksepp J, & Normansell L (2003). The affective neuroscience personality scales: Normative data and implications. *Neuro-Psychoanalysis, 5*(1), 57–69.

Dawson G, Webb S, Schellenberg G, Dager S, Friedman S, Aylard E, & Richards T (2002). Defining the broader phenotype of autism: Genetic, brain, and behavioral perspectives. *Dev Psychopathol, 14*, 581–611.

Deardorff J, Gonzales N, & Sandler I (2003). Control beliefs as a mediator of the relation between stress and depressive symptoms among inner-city adolescents. *J Abnorm Child Psychol, 31*(2), 205–217.

De Arellano M, Daniels A, Lyman D, Ghose S, Jobe-Shields L, Huang L et al. (2014). Trauma-Focused Cognitive-Behavioral Therapy for children and adolescents: Assessing the evidence. *Psychiat Serv, 65*(5), 591–602.

de Barbaro K, Clackson K, & Wass S (2016). Stress reactivity speeds basic encoding processes in infants. *Dev Psychobiol, 58*, 546–555.

De Bellis M, Keshavan M, Spencer S, & Hall J (2000). N-acetylaspartate concentration in the anterior cingulate in maltreated children and adolescents with PTSD. *Am J Psychiat, 157*, 1175–1177.

De Bellis M, Woolley D, & Hooper S (2013). Neuropsychological findings in pediatric maltreatment: Relationship of PTSD, dissociative symptoms, and abuse/neglect indices to neurocognitive outcomes. *Child Maltreatment, 18*(3), 171–183.

De Bellis M, & Zisk A (2014). The biological effects of childhood trauma. *Child and Adolescent Psychiatr Clin N Am., 23*(2), 185–222.

Deblinger E, Pollio E, & Dorsey S (2016). Applying Trauma-Focused CBT in group format. *Child Maltreatment, 21*, 59–73.

Deblinger E, & Runyon M (2005). Understanding and treating feelings of shame in children who have experienced maltreatment. *Child Maltreatment, 10*(4), 364–376.

Deblinger E, Stauffer L, Steer R (2001). Comparative efficacies of supportive and cognitive behavioral group therapies for children who were sexually abused and their nonoffending mothers. *Child Maltreat, 6*, 332–343.

De Brito S, Viding E, Sebastian C, Kelly P, Mechelli A, Maris H, & McCrory E (2013). Reduced orbitofrontal and temporal grey matter in a community sample of maltreated children. *J Child Psychol Psyc, 54*, 105–112.

Decety J, & Jackson P (2004). The functional architecture of human empathy. *Behavioral and Cognitive Neuroscience Reviews*, *3*(2), 71–100.

Decety J, & Meyer M (2008). From emotion resonance to empathic understanding: A social developmental neuroscience account. *Dev Psychopathol*, *20*(4), 1053–1080.

de Decker A, Hermans D, Raes F, & Eelen P (2003). Autobiographical memory specificity and trauma in inpatient adolescents. *J Clinical Child and Adolescent Psychology*, *32*(1), 22–31.

Defoe I, Dubas J, Figner B, & van Aken M (2015). A meta-analysis on age differences in risky decision making: Adolescents versus children and adults. *Psychol Bull*, *141*(1), 48–84.

de Haan A, De Pauw S, van den Akker A, Deković M, & Prinzie P (2017). Long-term developmental changes in children's lower-order Big Five personality facets. *J Personality*, *85*(5), 616–631.

de Haan M, Belsky J, Reid V, Volein A, & Johnson M (2004). Maternal personality and infants' neural and visual responsivity to facial expressions of emotion. *J Child Psychol Psyc*, *45*(7), 1209–1218.

DeKlyen M, & Greenberg M (2018). Attachment and psychopathology in childhood. In J Cassidy, P Shaver (Eds), *Handbook of attachment* (3rd ed., pp. 639–666). New York: Guilford.

Delamater A, & Applegate E (1999). Child development and post-traumatic stress disorder after hurricane exposure. *Traumatology*, *5*, 20–27.

Del Giudice M (2009). Sex, attachment, and the development of reproductive strategies. *Behav Brain Sci*, *32*, 1–21.

Del Giudice M (2014). Middle childhood: An evolutionary-developmental synthesis. *Child Development Perspectives*, *8*, 193–200.

Del Giudice M (2015). Attachment in middle childhood: An evolutionary–developmental perspective. In special series: G Bosmans, K Kerns (Eds), Attachment in middle childhood: Theoretical advances and new directions in an emerging field. *New Dir Child Adoles*, *148*, 15–30.

Del Giudice M, Ellis B, Shirtcliff E (2011). The Adaptive Calibration Model of stress responsivity. *Neuroscience & Biobehavioural Reviews 2011*, *35*(7), 1562–1592.

Deliens G, Bukowski H, Slama H, Surtees A, Cleeremans A, Samson D et al. (2018). The impact of sleep deprivation on visual perspective taking. *J Sleep Res*, *27*(2), 175–183.

Dell'Osso L, Carmassi C, Massimetti G, Conversano C, Emidio G, Stratta P, & Rossi A (2012). Posttraumatic stress spectrum in young versus middle-aged L'Aquila 2009 earthquake survivors. *Journal of Psychopathology*, *18*, 281–289.

Dell'Osso L, Stratta P, Conversano C, Massimetti E, Akiskal K, Akiskal H et al. (2014). Lifetime mania is related to posttraumatic stress symptoms in high school students exposed to the 2009 L'Aquila earthquake. *Compr Psychiat*, *55*, 357–362. abstract.

Deng W, & Sloutsky V (2016). Selective attention, diffused attention, and the development of categorization. *Cog Psych*, *91*, 24–62.

Denham S, Ji P, & Hamre B (2010). Compendium of preschool through elementary school Social-Emotional Learning and Associated Assessment Measures. An unpublished document. Chicago, IL: University of Illinois.

Delvecchio G, Bellani M, Altamura A, & Brambilla P (2015). The association between the serotonin and dopamine neurotransmitters and personality traits. *Epidemiology and Psychiatric Sciences*, *25*(2), 109–112.

Demby K, Riggs S, & Kaminski P (2017). Attachment and family processes in children's psychological adjustment in middle childhood. *Fam Proc*, *56*, 234–249.

DeMitchell T, & Hambacher E (2016). Zero tolerance, threats of harm, and the imaginary gun: "Good intentions run amuck." *BYU Education & Law Journal*, *1*(2), 1–23.

Dennis T, Hong M, & Solomon B (2010). Do the associations between exuberance and emotion regulation depend on effortful control? *Int J Behav Dev*, *34*(5) 462–472.

Dennis T, & Keleman D (2009). Preschool children's views on emotion regulation: Functional associations and implications for social-emotional adjustment. *Int J Behav Dev*, *33*(3), 243–252.

De Pauw S, Mervielde I, & Van Leeuwen K (2009). How are traits related to problem behavior in preschoolers? Similarities and contrasts between temperament and personality. *J Abnorm Child Psych*, *37*, 309–325.

DePrince A, Weinzierl K, & Combs M (2009). Executive function performance and trauma exposure in a community sample of children. *Child Abuse Neglect*, *33*, 353–361.

Depue R, & Collins P (1999). Neurobiology of the structure of personality: Dopamine facilitation of incentive motivation and extraversion. *Behav and Brain Sci*, *22*, 491–569.

DeRosa R, & Rathus J (2013). Dialectical Behavior Therapy with adolescents. In J Ford, C Courtois (Eds), *Treating Complex Traumatic Stress Disorders in children and adolescents* (pp. 225–245). New York: Guilford.

Derryberry D, & Rothbart M (1997). Reactive and effortful processes in the organization of temperament. *Dev Psychopathol*, *9*, 633–652.

Descilo T, Vedamurtachar A, Gerbarg P, Nagaraja D, Gangadhar B, Damodaran B, et al. (2010). Effects of a yoga breath intervention alone and in combination with an exposure therapy for PTSD and depression in survivors of the 2004 South-East Asia tsunami. *Acta Psychiat Scand*, *121*, 289–300.

De Schipper J, Oosterman M, & Schuengel C (2012). Temperament, disordered attachment, and parental sensitivity in foster care: Differential findings on attachment security for shy children. *Attachment & Human Devel, 14*(4), 349–365. abstract.

De Schipper J, Tavecchio L, van IJzendoorn M, & Zeijl J (2004). Goodness-of-fit in center day care: Relations of temperament, stability, and quality of care with the child's adjustment. *Early Child Res Q, 19*, 257–272. abstract.

Devi A, Baruah J, Pradhan N, & Borah T (2017). Parent–adolescent attachment as perceived by adolescents. *Indian Journal of Positive Psychology, 8*(2), 117–119.

de Vibe M, Solhaug I, Tyssen R, Friborg O, Rosenvinge J, Sørlie et al. (2015). Does personality moderate the effects of mindfulness training for medical and psychology students? *Mindfulness, 6*(2), 281–289.

Devine R, & Hughes C (2018). Family correlates of false belief understanding in early childhood: A meta-analysis. *Child Dev, 89*(3), 971–987.

DeVoe E, Klein T, Bannon W Jr, & Miranda-Julian C (2011). Young children in the aftermath of the World Trade Center attacks. *Psychological Trauma: Theory, Research, Practice, & Policy, 3*(1), 1–7.

de Vries E, Verlinden M, Rijlaarsdam J, Jaddoe V, Verhulst F, Arseneault L, & Tiemeier H (2017). Like father, like child: Early life family adversity and children's bullying behaviors in elementary school. *J Abnorm Child Psychol*, https://doi.org/10.1007/s10802-017-0380-8.

De Weerth C, van Hees Y, & Buitelaar K (2003). Prenatal maternal cortisol levels and infant behavior during the first 5 months. *Early Hum Dev 74*, 139–151. Abstract.

De Young A, Kenardy J, Cobham V, & Kindle R (2012). Prevalence, comorbidity and course of trauma reactions in young burn-injured children. *J Child Psychol Psyc, 53*(1), 56–63.

Diamond A (1991). Neuropsychological insights into the meaning of object concept development. In S Carey, R Gelman (Eds), *The epigenesis of mind: Essays on biology and cognition* (pp. 67–110). Hillsdale, NJ: Erlbaum.

Diamond GM, Diamond GS, & Levy S (2013). *Attachment-based family therapy for depressed adolescents*. Washington, DC: American Psychological Association.

Diamond GS, Diamond GM, Levy S, Closs C, Ladipo T, & Siqueland L (2012). Attachment-based family therapy for suicidal lesbian, gay, and bisexual adolescents: A treatment development study and open trial with preliminary findings. *Psychotherapy, 49*(1), 62–71.

Diamond GS, Wintersteen M, Brown G, Diamond GM, Gallop R, Shelef K, & Levy S (2010). Attachment-based family therapy for suicidal adolescents: A randomized controlled trial. *J Am Acad Chld Psy, 49*(2), 122–131.

Dice J, & Dove M (2011). A Piagetian approach to infant referential behaviors. *Infant Behav Dev, 34*, 481–486.

Dick D, Aliev F, Latendresse S, Porjesz B, Schuckit M, Rangaswamy M et al. (2013). How phenotype and developmental stage affect the genes we find: GABRA2 and impulsivity. *Twin Res & Human Genetics, 16*(3), 661–669.

Dickerson S, & Kemeny M (2004). Acute stressors and cortisol responses: A theoretical integration and synthesis of laboratory research. *Psychol Bull, 130*, 355–391.

Diesendruck G, & Ben-Eliyahu A (2006). The relationships among social cognition, peer acceptance, and social behavior in Israeli kindergarteners. *Int J Behav Dev, 30*(2), 137–147.

DiGangi J, Goddard A, Miller S, Leon G, & Jason L (2016). Differences in PTSD symptomatology among Latinos with childhood and adult trauma: The moderating effect of acculturation. *HSOA J Addict Neuropharmacol*, PMID: 27227166.

Dillen L, Fontaine J, & Verhofstadt-Denève, L (2008). Are normal and complicated grief different constructs? A confirmatory factor analytic test. *Clinical Psychol & Psychother, 15*, 386–395.

Dillen L, Fontaine J, & Verhofstadt-Denève L (2009). Confirming the distinctiveness of complicated grief from depressive anxiety among adolescents. *Death Stud, 33*, 437–461.

Dimaggio G (2012). Narcissistic Personality Disorder: Rethinking what we know. *Psychiatric Times*, 29(7), 17–25.

Dimaggio G, Hermans H, & Lysaker L (2010). Health and adaptation in a multiple self: The role of absence of dialogue and poor *metacognition* in clinical populations. *Theory & Psychology, 20*(3), 379–399.

Dimaggio G, Semerari A, Carcione A, Proccaci M, & Nicolo G (2006). Toward a model of self pathology underlying personality disorders: Narratives, metacognition, interpersonal cycles and decision-making processes. *J Pers Disorders, 20*(6), 597–617.

Dishion T (2016). Social influences on executive functions development in children and adolescents: Steps toward a social neuroscience of predictive adaptive responses. *J Abnorm Child Psychol, 44*, 57–61.

Dishion T, Nelson S, & Bullock B (2004). Premature adolescent autonomy: Parent disengagement and deviant peer process in the amplification of problem behaviour. *J Adolescence, 27*(5), 515–530. *The European Journal of Public Health, 27*(5), 829–834.

Dishion T, & Patterson G (2006). The development and ecology of antisocial behavior. In D Cicchetti, D Cohen (Eds), *Dev Psychopathol: Vol 3. Risk, disorder, and adaptation* (2nd ed., pp. 503–541). Hoboken, NJ: Wiley.

Dissing A, Dich N, Andersen A-M, Lund R, & Rod N (2017). Parental break-ups and stress: Roles of age and family structure in 44 509 pre-adolescent children. *Eur J Public Health, 27*(5), 829–834. abstract.

Dmitrieva J, Chen C, Greenberger E, Ogunseitan O, Ding Y (2011). Gender-specific expression of the DRD4 gene on adolescent delinquency, anger and thrill seeking. *Soc Cogn Affect Neur, 6*, 90–97.

Dodge K, Bates J, & Pettit G (1990). Mechanisms in the cycle of violence. *Science, 250*, 1678–1683.

Dodge K, Coie J, & Lynam D (2008). Aggression and antisocial behavior in youth. In Damon W, Eisenberg N (Eds), *Handbook of child psychology, Volume 3. Social, emotional, and personality development* (5th ed.; pp. 437–472). New York: Wiley.

Dodge K, Lochman J, Harnish J, Bates J, & Pettit G (1997). Reactive and proactive aggression in school children and psychiatrically impaired chronically assaultive youth. *J Abnorm Psychol, 106*, 37–51.

Dodge K, Bates J, Pettit G, & Valente E (1995). Social information-processing patterns partially mediate the effect of early physical abuse on later conduct problems. *J Abnorm Psychol, 104*(4), 632–643.

Doka K, & Martin T (2010). *Grieving beyond gender: Understanding the ways men and women mourn* (2nd ed.). New York: Routledge.

Donnellan D, Murray C, & Harrison J (2013). An investigation into adolescents' experience of cognitive behavioural therapy within a child and adolescent mental health service. *Clin Child Psychol P, 18*(2) 199–213.

Donnellan M, Trzensniewski K, Robins R, Moffitt T, & Caspi A (2005). Aggression, antisocial behavior, and delinquency. *Psychol Sci, 16*(4), 328–335. abstract.

Dorahy M, & Van Der Hart O (2014). DSM-5's posttraumatic stress disorder with dissociative symptoms: Challenges and future directions. *J Trauma Dissoc, 16*, 7–28.

Dorn L, & Biro F (2011). Puberty and its measurement: A decade in review. *J Res Adolesc 21*, 180–195.

Dougherty L, Smith V, Bufferd S, Kessel E, Carlson G, & Klein D (2015). Preschool irritability predicts child psychopathology, functional impairment, and service use at age nine. *J Child Psychol Psyc, 56*(9), 999–1007.

Doughty E (2009). Investigating adaptive grieving styles. *Death Stud, 33*, 462–480.

Dozier M (2003). Attachment-based treatment for vulnerable children. *Attach Hum Dev, 5*(3), 253–257.

Dozier M, Meade E, & Bernard K (2014). Attachment and biobehavioral catch-up: An intervention for parents at risk of maltreating their infants and toddlers. In S Timmer, A Urquiza (Eds), *Evidence-based approaches for the treatment of maltreated children* (pp. 43–59). New York: Springer.

Dozier M, Peloso E, Lewis E, Laurenceau J, & Levine S (2008). Effects of an attachment-based intervention on the cortisol production of infants and toddlers in foster care. *Dev Psychopathol, 20*(3), 845–849.

Dozier M, Peloso E, Lindhiem O, Gordon M, Manni M, Sepulveda S, Ackerman J, Bernier A, & Levine S (2006). Developing evidence-based interventions for foster children: An example of a randomized clinical trial with infants and toddlers. *Journal of Social Issues, 62*(4), 765–783.

Dozier M, Zeanah C, & Bernard K (2013). Infants and toddlers in foster care. *Child Development Perspectives*, 7, 166–171.

Dozois D, Bieling P, Evraire L, Patelis-Siotis I, Hoar L, Chudzik S et al. (2014). Changes in core beliefs (Early Maladaptive Schemas) and self-representation in cognitive therapy and pharmacotherapy for Depression. *Int J Cogn Ther*, 7(3), 217–234.

Dragioti E, Damigos D, Mavreas V, & Gouva M (2012). Effects of childhood trauma on hostility, family environment and narcissism of adult individuals. *Int J Caring Sciences, 5*(2), 137–146.

Dragan W, Oniszczenko W, Czerski P, & Dmitrzak-Weglarz M (2012). Dopamine genes and sensory sensitivity as a temperamental trait. *J Indiv Dif, 33*(4), 205–211.

Drummond L, Dritschel B, Atsell A, O'Carroll R, & Dalgleish T (2006). Effects of age, dysphoria, and emotion-focusing on autobiographical memory specificity in children. *Cognition & Emotion, 20*(3/4), 488–505.

Drury S, Brett Z, Henry C, & Scheeringa M (2013). The association of a novel haplotype in the dopamine transporter with preschool age Posttraumatic Stress Disorder. *JCAP, 23*(4), 236–243.

Drury S, Theall K, Keats B, & Scheeringa M (2009). The role of the dopamine transporter (DAT) in the development of PTSD in preschool children. *J Traum Stress, 22*, 534–539.

Du B, Ma X, Ou X, Jen Y, Ren P, & Li J (2018). The prevalence of posttraumatic stress in adolescents eight years after the Wenchuan earthquake. *Psychiat Res 262*, 262–269.

Duan W, Guo P, Gan P (2015). Relationships among trait resilience, virtues, posttraumatic stress disorder, and posttraumatic growth. *PLoS ONE 10*(5), e0125707.

Ducharme J, Folino A, & DeRosie J (2008). Errorless acquiescence training: A potential "keystone" approach to building peer interaction skills in children with severe problem behavior. *Behav Modif*, 32(1), 39–60.

Duhig M, Patterson S, Connell M, Foley S, Capra C, Dark F, Gordon A, Singh S, Hides L, McGrath J, & Scott J (2015). The prevalence and correlates of childhood trauma in patients with early psychosis. *Aust NZ J Psychiat, 49*(7), 651–659.

Dujardin A, Bosmans G, Braet C, & Goossens L (2014). Attachment-related expectations and mother-referent memory bias in middle childhood. *Scand J Psychol, 55*(4), 296–302.

Dujardin A, Santens T, Braet C, De Raedt R, Vos P, & Maes B (2016). Middle childhood support seeking behavior during stress: Links with self-reported attachment and future depressive symptoms. *Child Dev, 87*(1), 326–340.

Dunbar R, Baron R, Frangou A, Pearce E., van Leeuwen E, Stow J et al. (2012). Social laughter is correlated with an elevated pain threshold. *Proc R Soc B, 279*, 1161–1167.

Duncan L, & Bardacke N (2010). Mindfulness-based childbirth and parenting education: Promoting family mindfulness during the perinatal period. *J Child Fam Stud, 19*, 190–202.

Duncan T, Tildesley E, Duncan S & Hops H (1995). The consistency of family and peer influences on the development of substance use in adolescence. *Addiction, 90*, 1647–1660.

Duncombe M, Havighurst S, Kehoe C, Holland K, Frankling E, & Stargatt R (2016). Comparing an emotion- and a behavior-focused parenting program as part of a multisystemic intervention for child conduct problems. *J Clin Child & Adolescent Psychol, 45*(3), 320–334. abstract.

Dunn E, McLaughlin K, Slopen N, Rosand J, & Smoller J (2013). Developmental timing of child maltreatment and symptoms of depression and suicidal ideation in young adulthood: Results from the National Longitudinal Study of adolescent health. *Depress & Anx, 30*, 955–964.

Durany N, Michel T, Zochling R, Boissl K, Cruz-Sanchez F, Riederer P, et al. (2001). Brain-derived neurotrophic factor and neurotrophin 3 in schizophrenic psychoses. *Schizophr Res, 52*(1–2), 79–86.

Durbin CE (2010). Validity of young children's self-reports of their emotion in response to structured laboratory tasks. *Emotion, 10*(4). 519–535.

Durmuşoğlu-Saltali N, & Arslan E (2011). An investigation of emotional skills of six-year-old children attending nursery school according to some variables. *Educ Res Rev, 6*(7), 536–541.

Durston S, Davidson M, Tottenham N, Galvan A, Spicer J, Fossella J et al. (2006). A shift from diffuse to focal cortical activity with development. *Developmental Sci, 9*(1), 1–8.

Dyregrov K, Dyregrov A, & Johnsen I (2013). Positive and negative experiences from grief group participation: A qualitative study. *OMEGA, 68*(1) 45–62. abstract.

Dyregrov A, Gupta L, Gjestad R, & Mukanoheli E (2000). Trauma exposure and psychological reactions to genocide among Rwandan children. *J Traum Stress, 13*, 3–21.

Dyregrov A, Salloum A, Kristensen P, & Dyregrov K (2015). Grief and traumatic grief in the context of mass trauma. *Curr Psychiatry Rep., 17*(48), 1–8. doi: 10.1007/s11920-015-0577-x.

Edgar-Bailey M, & Kress V (2010). Resolving child and adolescent traumatic grief: Creative techniques and interventions. *Journal of Creativity in Mental Health, 5*, 158–176.

Edwards S (2010). Humor, laughter, and those aha moments. *On the Brain, the Harvard Mahoney Neuroscience Institute Letter*, 16(2), 1–3. Cambridge, MA: Harvard Medical School.

Egger H, & Angold A (2006). Common emotional and behavioral disorders in preschool children: Presentation, nosology, and epidemiology. *J Child Psychol Psyc, 47*(3–4), 313–337.

Egliston K, McMahon C, & Austin M (2007). Stress in pregnancy and infant HPA axis function: Conceptual and methodological issues relating to the use of salivary cortisol as an outcome measure. *Psychoneuroendocrinology, 32*(1), 1–13.

Ehlers A, & Clark D. (2000). A cognitive model of posttraumatic stress disorder. *Behav Res Ther., 8*, 319–345.

Ehring T, Welboren R, Morina N, Wicherts J, Freitag J, & Emmelkamp P (2014). Meta-analysis of psychological treatments for posttraumatic stress disorder in adult survivors of childhood abuse. *Clin Psychol Rev 34*, 645–657.

Eigsti I, Zayas V, Mischel W, Shoda Y, Ayduk O, Dadlani M et al. (2006). Predicting cognitive control from preschool to late adolescence and young adulthood. *Psychol Sci, 17*, 478–484.

Ein-Dor T, Mikulincer M, & Shaver P (2011). Attachment insecurities and the processing of threat-related information: Studying schemas involved in insecure people's coping strategies. *J Pers Soc Psychol, 101*, 78–93.

Einstein GO (2008). Prospective memory: Processes, lifespan changes, neuroscience. In J Byrne (Ed.), *Learning and memory: A comprehensive reference* (pp. 867–892). Oxford: Elsevier.

Eisen A, Raleigh H, & Neuhoff C (2008). The unique impact of parent training for Separation Anxiety Disorder in children. *Behav Ther, 39*, 195–206.

Eisen A, & Schaefer C (2007). *Separation anxiety in children and adolescents: An individualized approach to assessment and treatment.* New York: Guilford.

Eisen M, Qin J, Goodman G, & Davis S (2002). Memory and suggestibility in maltreated children: Age, stress arousal, dissociation and psychopathology. *J Exp Child Psychol, 83*, 167–212.

Eisen M, Goodman G, Qin J, Davis S, & Crayton J (2007). Maltreated children's memory: Accuracy, suggestibility, and psychopathology. *Dev Psychol, 43*(6), 1275–1294.

Eisenberg N (2000). Emotion, regulation, and moral development. *Annu Rev Psychol, 51*, 665–697.

Eisenberg N, Fabes R, Guthrie I, Murphy B, Poulin R, & Shepard S (1996). The relations of regulation and emotionality to problem behavior in elementary school children. *Dev Psychopathol, 8*, 141–162.

Eisenberg N, Fabes R, & Spinrad T (2007). ProSoc Dev. In R Lerner (Ed.), *Handbook of child psychology* (6th ed., pp. 646–718). New York: Wiley.

Eisenberg N, Guthrie I, Fabes R, Shepard S, Losoya S, Murphy B, et al. (2000). Prediction of elementary school children's externalizing problem behaviors from attentional and behavioral regulation and negative emotionality. *Child Dev, 71*, 1367–1382.

Eisenberg N, Sadovsky A, Spinrad T, Fabes R., Losoya S, Valiente C et al. (2005). The relations of problem behavior status to children's negative emotionality, effortful control, and impulsivity: Concurrent relations and prediction of change. *Dev Psychol, 41*(1), 193–211. abstract.

Eisenberg N, Smith C, & Spinrad T (2011). Effortful control: Relations with emotion regulation, adjustment, and socialization in childhood. In K Bohs, R Baumeister (Eds), *Handbook of self-regulation: Research, theory, and application* (2nd ed., pp. 263–283). New York: Guilford.

Eisenberg N, Spinrad T, & Eggum N (2010a). Emotion-related self-regulation and its relation to children's maladjustment. *Annual Review of Clinical Psychology, 6*, 495–525.

Eisenberg N, Valiente C, Spinrad T, Cumberland A, Liew J, Reiser M et al. (2009). Longitudinal relations of children's effortful control, impulsivity, and negative emotionality to their externalizing, internalizing, and co-occurring behavior problems. *Devel Psychol, 45*(4), 988–1008. abstract.

Eisenberg N, Vidmar M, Spinrad T, Eggum N, Edwards A, Gaertner B, & Kupfer A (2010b). Mothers' teaching strategies and children's effortful control: A longitudinal study. *Devel Psychol, 46*(5), 1294–1308.

Eisenberger N (2012). The neural bases of social pain: Evidence for shared representations with physical pain. *Psychosomatic Medicine, 74*(2), 126.

Eisma M, Schut H, Stroeb M, Voerman K, van den Bout J, Stroebe W, & Boelin P (2015). Psychopathology symptoms, rumination and autobiographical memory specificity: Do associations hold after bereavement? *Appl Cognit Psychol*, doi: 10.1002/acp. 3120.

Elison J, Garofalo C, & Velotti P (2014). Shame and aggression: Theoretical considerations. *Aggress Violent Beh, 19*(4), 447–453.

Elbrecht C (2015). The clay field and developmental trauma in children. In C Malchiodi (ed.). *Creative arts and play therapy for attachment problems* (pp. 191–210). New York: Guilford.

Ellis B, Del Giudice M, Dishion T, Figueredo A, Gray T, Griskevicius V et al. (2012). The evolutionary basis of risky adolescent behavior: Implications for science, policy, and practice. *Dev Psychol, 48*(3), 598–623.

Else-Quest N, Hyde J, Goldsmith H, Van Hulle C (2006). Gender differences in temperament: A metaanalysis. *Psychol Bull, 132*, 33–72.

El-Sheikh M, Buckhalt J, Keller P, & Granger (2008). Children's objective and subjective sleep disruptions: Links with afternoon cortisol levels. *Health Psychology, 27*(1), 26–33. abstract.

Egan K, Gondoli D, Gibson B, Morrissey R, Steeger C, & Miller R (2014). Poor emotional control, and negative parenting. *Adolescent Development Lab*, Poster.

Endedijk H, Meyer M, Bekkering H, Cillessen A, & Hunnius S (2017). Neural mirroring and social interaction: Motor system involvement during action observation relates to early peer cooperation. *Developmental Cognitive Neuroscienc, 24*, 33–41.

England-Mason G, Kimber M, Khoury J, Atkinson L., MacMillan H, & Gonzalez A (2017). Difficulties with emotion regulation moderate the association between childhood history of maltreatment and cortisol reactivity to psychosocial challenge in postpartum women. *Horm Behav 95*, 44–56. abstract.

Ensink K, Bégin M, Normandin L, Godbout N & Fonagy P (2017). Mentalization and dissociation in the context of trauma: Implications for child psychopathology, *J Trauma Dissociation, 18*(1), 11–30.

Ensink K, Bégin M, Normandin L, Godbout N & Fonagy P (2016a). Maternal and child reflective functioning in the context of child sexual abuse: pathways to depression and externalising difficulties. *Eur J Psychotraumato*, 7:1, 30611, doi: 10.3402/ejpt.v7.30611.

Ensink K, Berthelot N, Bernazzani O, Normandin L, & Fonagy P (2014). Another step closer to measuring the ghosts in the nursery: Preliminary validation of the Trauma Reflective Functioning Scale. *Frontiers in Psychology, 5*. doi: 10.3389/fpsyg.2014.01471.

Ensink K, Chretien S, Normandin L, Bégin M, Daigle D, & Fonagy P (2018). Pathological narcissism in adolescents: Relationships with childhood maltreatment and internalizing and externalizing difficulties. *Adolescent Psychiat, 8*, doi: 10.2174/2210676608666180119165731.

Ensink K, Normandin L, Godbout N, & Fonagy P (2016b). Intergenerational pathways from reflective functioning to infant attachment through parenting. *Canadian Journal of Behavioural Science, 48*(1), 9–18.

Ensink K, Normandin L, Target M, Fonagy P, Sabourin S, & Berthelot N (2015). Mentalization in children and mothers in the context of trauma: An initial study of the validity of the Child Reflective Functioning Scale. *Brit J Dev Psychol, 33*, 203–217.

Epley N, Akalis S, Waytz A, & Cacioppo J (2008). Creating social connection through inferential reproduction loneliness and perceived agency in gadgets, gods, and grayhounds. *Psychological Sci, 19*(2), 114–120.

Epley N, Keysar B, Van Boven L, & Gilovich T (2004). Perspective-taking as egocentric anchoring and adjustment. *J Personal and Soc Psychol, 87*, 327–339.

Erikson EH (1963). *Childhood and society* (2nd ed.). New York: Norton.

Erkoreka L, & Navarro B (2017). Vulnerable narcissism is associated with severity of depressive symptoms in dysthymic patients. *Psychiat Res, 257*, 265–269.

Erle T, & Topolinski S (2015). Spatial and empathic perspective-taking Correlate on a dispositional level. *Social Cognition, 33*(3), 187–210.

Ertl V, Pfeiffer A, Schauer E, Elbert T, & Neuner F (2011). Community-Implemented Trauma Therapy for former child soldiers in Northern Uganda: A randomized controlled trial. *JAMA, 306*(5), 503–512.

Ertl V, Pfeiffer A, Schauer E, Elbert T, & Neuner F (2011). Community-Implemented Trauma Therapy for former child soldiers in Northern Uganda: A randomized controlled trial. *JAMA, 306*(5), 503–512.

Escolas S, Arata-Maiers R, Hildebrandt E, Maiers A, Mason S, & Baker M (2012). The impact of attachment style on Posttraumatic Stress Disorder Symptoms in postdeployed military members. *U.S. Army Medical Department Journal*, Jul-Sep, 54–61. www.cs.amedd.army.mil/armeddjournal.aspx.

Eskin M (2001). Adolescent loneliness, coping methods and the relationship of loneliness to suicidal behavior. *Klinik Psikiyatri, 4*, 5–11. abstract.

Espelage D, & Low S (2012). Bullying among children and adolescents: Social-Emotional Learning approaches to prevention. In K Nader (ed.) *School rampage shootings and other youth disturbances: Early preventive interventions* (pp. 205–219). New York: Routledge.

Eth S, & Pynoos R (1985). Developmental perspectives on psychic trauma in children. In C Figley (ed.), *Trauma and its wake, Vol. I: The study and treatment of posttraumatic stress disorder* (pp. 36–52). New York: Bruner/Mazel.

Evans D, & Rothbart M (2007). Developing a model for adult temperament. *J Res Pers, 41*, 868–888.

Evans G, Li D, & Whipple S (2013). Cumulative risk and child development. *Psychol Bull, 139*(6), 1342–1396.

Evans L, Kouros C, Samanez-Larkin S, & Garber J (2016). Concurrent and short-term prospective relations among neurocognitive functioning, coping, and depressive symptoms in youth. *J Clin Child Adolesc, 45*(1), 6–20.

Evans S, Simons L, & Simons R (2012). The effect of corporal punishment and verbal abuse on delinquency: Mediating mechanisms. *J Youth & Adolescence, 41*(8), 1095–1110. In Yoon.

Evans S, Sternlieb B, Tsao J, & Zeltzer L (2009). Using the bio-psychosocial model to understand the health benefits of yoga. *J Complementary and Integrative Medicine, 6*, 1–22.

Evraire L, & Dozois D (2014). If it be love indeed tell me how much: Early core beliefs associated with excessive reassurance seeking in depression. *Canadian Journal of Behavioural Science, 46*(1), 1–8. doi: 10.1037/a0033486.

Evraire L, Ludmer J, & Dozois D (2014). The influence of priming attachment styles on excessive reassurance seeking and negative feedback seeking in depression. *J Soc Clin Psychol, 33*(4), 295–318.

Ewing E, Diamond G, & Levy S (2015). Attachment-based family therapy for depressed and suicidal adolescents: theory, clinical model and empirical support. *Attach Hum Dev, 17*(2), 136–156.

Eyberg S, & Robinson E (1983). Conduct problem behavior: Standardization of a behavioral rating scale with adolescents. *J Clin Child Psychol, 12*, 347–354.

Eysenck HJ (1967). *The biological basis of personality*. Springfield, IL: Charles C. Thomas.

Fagard J, Rat-Fishcer L, Esseily R, Somogyi E, & O'Regan J (2016). What does it take for an infant to learn how to use a tool by observation? *Front Psychol*, 7, 267. Abstract.

Falconi A, Gimmel A, Dahl R, & Catalano R (2014). Adolescent experience predicts longevity: Evidence from historical epidemiology. *Journal of Developmental Origins of Health and Disease, 5*(3), 171–177.

Fanselow MS (2000). Contextual fear, gestalt memories, and the hippocampus. *Behav Brain Res, 110*(1–2), 73–81.

Fanti K, Brookmeyer K, Henrich C, & Kuperminc G (2009). Aggressive behaviour and quality of friendships. *J Early Adolescence, 29*(6), 826–838.

Faraone S, & Doyle A (2001). The nature and heritability of attention deficit/hyperactivity disorder. *Child Adol Psych Cl, 10*, 299–316.

Farchi M, Gidron Y (2010). The effects of "psychological inoculation" versus ventilation on the mental resilience of Israeli citizens under continuous war stress. *J Nerv Ment Dis, 198*, 382–384.

Fardoulys C, & Coyne J (2016). Circle of Security Intervention for parents of children with Autism Spectrum Disorder. *Australian and New Zealand Journal of Family Therapy*, *37*, 572–584.

Farrant B, Fletcher J, & Maybery M (2014). Cognitive flexibility, theory of mind, and hyperactivity/inattention. *Child Devel Res*, *Article ID 741543*, dx.doi.org/10.1155/2014/741543.

Farrant K, & Reese E (2000). Maternal style and children's participation in reminiscing: Stepping stones in children's autobiographical memory development. *J Cogn Dev*, *1*, 193–22.

Fatima S, Sheikh H, & Ardila A (2015, June 8). Association of parent–child relationships and executive functioning in South Asian adolescents. *Neuropsychology*, *30*(1), 65–74.

Fausset R & Kovaleski S (2018, Feb 15). Nikolas Cruz, Florida shooting suspect, showed "every red flag." Retrieved 6-14-18, www.nytimes.com/2018/02/15/us/nikolas-cruz-florida-shooting.html.

Fearon P, Shmueli-Goetz Y, Viding E, Fonagy P, & Plomin R (2014). Genetic and environmental influences on adolescent attachment. *J Child Psychol Psyc*, *55*(9), 1033–1041.

Fearon R, Bakermans-Kranenburg M, van IJzendoorn M, Lapsley A-M, & Roisman G (2010). The significance of insecure attachment and disorganization in the development of children's externalizing behavior: A meta analytic study. *Child Dev*, *81*, 435–456.

Fearon R, & Belsky J (2018). Precursors of attachment security. In J Cassidy, P Shaver (Eds), *The handbook of attachment: Theory, research, and clinical applications* (3rd ed.; pp. 291–313). New York: Guilford.

Fearon R, & Belsky J (2011). Infant–mother attachment and the growth of externalizing problems across the primary-school years. *J Child Psychol Psyc*, *52*(7), 782–791.

Fearon R, & Belsky J (2004). Attachment and attention: Protection in relation to gender and cumulative social-contextual adversity. *Child Dev*, 7(6), 1677–1693.

Fearon R, van IJzendoorn M, Fonagy P, Bakermans-Kranenburg M, Schuengel C, & Bokhorst C (2006). In search of shared and nonshared environmental factors in security of attachment: A behavior–genetic study of the association between sensitivity and attachment security. *Dev Psychol*, *42*(6), 10–26–1040.

Federico F, Marotta A, Martella D, & Casagrande M (2017). Development in attention functions and social processing: Evidence from the Attention Network Test. *Brit J Dev Psychol*, *35*(2), 169–185.

Feeney B, Cassidy J, & Ramos-Marcuse F (2008). The generalization of attachment representations to new social situations: Predicting behavior during initial interactions with strangers. *J Pers Soc Psychol*, *95*(6), 1481–1498.

Feigelman W, Gorman B, & Jordan J (2009). Stigmatization and suicide bereavement. *Death Stud*, *33*, 591–608.

Feiring C, & Taska L (2005). The persistence of shame following sexual abuse: A longitudinal look at risk and recovery. *Child Maltreatment*, *10*(4), 337–349.

Feiring C, Taska L, & Chen K (2002). Trying to understand why horrible things happen: Attribution, shame and symptom development following sexual abuse. *Child Maltreatment*, 7(1), 25–39.

Feldman R (2007). On the origins of background emotions: From affect synchrony to symbolic expression. *Emotion*, 7(3), 601–611. abstract.

Feldman R (2010). The relational basis of adolescent adjustment: Trajectories of mother–child interactive behaviors from infancy to adolescence shape adolescents' adaptation. *Attachment and Hum Dev*, *12*, 173–192.

Feldman R (2015). Sensitive periods in human social development: New insights from research on oxytocin, synchrony, and high-risk parenting. *Dev Psychopathol*, *27*, 369–395.

Feldman R, Bamberger E, & Kanat-Maymon Y (2013a). Parent-specific reciprocity from infancy to adolescence shapes children's social competence and dialogical skills. *Attach Hum Dev*, *15*(4), 407–423.

Feldman R, Greenbaum C, & Yirmiya N (1999). Mother–infant affect synchrony as an antecedent of the emergence of self-control. *Dev Psychol*, *35*, 223–231.

Feldman R, & Vengrober A (2011). Posttraumatic stress disorder in infants and young children exposed to war-related trauma. *J Am Acad Child Psy*, *50*, 645–658.

Feldman R, Vengrober A, & Ebstein R (2014). Affiliation buffers stress: cumulative genetic risk in oxytocin–vasopressin genes combines with early caregiving to predict PTSD in war-exposed young children. *Transl Psychiatry*, *4(3)*, e370; doi: 10.1038/tp.2014.6.

Feldman R, Vengrober A, Eidelman-Rothman M, & Zagoory-Sharon O (2013b). Stress reactivity in war-exposed young children with and without posttraumatic stress disorder: Relations to maternal stress hormones, parenting, and child emotionality and regulation. *Devel & Psychopath*, *25*, 943–955.

Feldman R, Weller A, Zagoory-Sharon O, & Levine A (2007). Evidence for a neuroendocrinological foundation of human affiliation: Plasma oxytocin levels across pregnancy and the postpartum period predict mother–infant bonding. *Psychol Sci*, *18*, 965–970.

Felitti V, Anda R, Nordenberg D, Williamson D, Spitz A, Edwards V, Koss M, & Marks J (1998). Relationship of childhood abuse and household dysfunction to many of the leading causes of death in adults. The Adverse Childhood Experiences (ACE) Study. *Am J Prev Med*, *14*(4), 245–258.

Feliu-Soler A, Pascual J, Borras X, Portella M, Martin-Blanco A, Armario A et al. (2013). Effects of Dialectical Behaviour Therapy – Mindfulness Training on emotional reactivity in borderline personality disorder: Preliminary results. *Clin. Psychol. Psychother.* doi: 10.1002/cpp.1837.

Feng F, Ye X, Mao L, & Yue X (2014). The activation of theory of mind network differentiates between point-to-self and point-to-other verbal jokes: An fMRI study. *Neruosci Lett, 564*, 32–36.

Fergusson D, & Horwood L (2003). Resilience to childhood adversity: Results of a 21-year study. In SS Luthar (Ed.), *Resilience and vulnerability: Adaptation in the context of childhood adversities* (pp. 130–155). New York: Cambridge University Press.

Fergusson S, & Zimmer-Gembeck M (2014). Associations of parental and peer rejection with preadolescents' loneliness: Emotional sensitivities as mediators. *Journal of Relationships Research, 5*(e9), 1–11. doi 10.1017/jrr.2014.9.

Fernandez C (2013). Mindful storytellers: Emerging pragmatics and theory of mind development. *First Language, 33*(1), 20–46.

Fett A, Shergill S, Gromann P, Dumontheil I, Blakemore S-J, & Yakub F (2014). Trust and social reciprocity in adolescence: A matter of perspective-taking. *J Adolescence, 37*, 175–184.

Feurer C, Hammen C, & Gibb B (2016). Chronic and episodic stress in children of depressed mothers. *J Clin Child Adolesc, 45*(3), 270–278.

Field T (2010). Touch for socioemotional and physical well-being: A review. *Dev Rev, 30*(4), 367–383.

Field T, Seligman S, Scafidi F, & Schanberg S (1996). Alleviating posttraumatic stress in children following Hurricane Andrew. *Journal of Applied Dev Psychol, 17*, 37–50.

Field T, Woodson R, Greenberg R, & Cohen D (1982). Discrimination and imitation of facial expression by neonates. *Science, 218*, 179–181.

Fields-Olivieri M, Cole P, & Maggi M (2017). Toddler emotional states, temperamental traits, and their interaction: Associations with mothers' and fathers' parenting. *J Res Pers 67*, 106–119.

Figner B, & Weber E (2011). Who takes risks when and why? Determinants of risk-taking. *Curr Direct in Psychol Sci, 20*, 211–216.

File P, Wood J, & Kreplick L (1998). Diagnosis of hip fracture by the auscultatory percussion technique. *American J Emergency Med, 16*(2), 173–176.

Filippette M, Johnson M, Lloyd-Fox S, Dragovic D, & Farroni T (2013). Body perception in newborns. *Curr Biol 23*, 2413–2416.

Filippette M, Lloyd-Fox S, Longo M, Farroni T, & Johnson M (2015). Neural mechanisms of body awareness in infants. *Cereb Cortex, 25*, 3779–3787. Abstract.

Filippette M, Farroni T, & Johnson M (2016). Five-month-old infants' discrimination of visual-tactile synchronous facial stimulation. *Inf. Child. Dev. 25*, 317–322.

Finkelhor D, Ormrod R, & Turner H (2007). Revictimization patterns in a national longitudinal sample of children and youth. *Child Abuse Neglect, 31*, 479–502.

Finkelhor D, Ormrod R, & Turner H (2009). Lifetime assessment of poly-victimization in a national sample of children and youth. *Child Abuse Neglect, 33*, 403–411.

Finkelhor D, Shattuck A, Turner H, & Ormrod R (2014). Poly-victimization in developmental context. In K Nader (ed.), *Assessment of trauma in youths: Understanding issues of age, complexity, and associated variables* (pp. 132–141). New York: Routledge.

Finn H, Warner E, Price M, & Spinazzola J (2017). The boy who was hit in the face: Somatic regulation and processing of preverbal complex trauma. *J Child Adol Trauma*, doi: 10.1007/s40653-017-0165-9.

Finy M, Bresin K, Korol D, & Verona E (2014). Impulsivity, risk-taking, and cortisol reactivity as a function of psychosocial stress and personality in adolescents. *Dev Psychopathol, 26*, 1093–1111.

Fishbein D, Warner T, Krebs C, Trevarthen N, Flannery B, & Hammond J (2009). Differential relationships between personal and community stressors and children's neurocognitive functioning. *Child Maltreatment, 14*(4), 299–315.

Fisher P, Beauchamp K, Roos L, Noll L, Flannery J, & Delker B (2016). The neurobiology of intervention and prevention in early adversity. *Rev Cli. Psycho., 12*, 331–57.

Fisher P, Burraston B, & Pears K (2005). The Early Intervention Foster Care Program: Permanent placement outcomes from a randomized trial. *Child Maltreat, 10*, 61–71.

Fisher P, & Chamberlain P (2000). Multidimensional treatment foster care: A program for intensive parenting, family support, and skill building. *J Emot Behav Disord, 8*, 155–164.

Fisher P, Chamberlain P, & Leve L (2009). Improving the lives of foster children through evidenced-based interventions. *Vulner Childr and Youth Stud, 4*(2), 122–127.

Fisher P, Gunnar M, Dozier M, Bruce J, & Pears K (2006). Effects of therapeutic interventions for foster children on behavioral problems, caregiver attachment, and stress regulatory neural systems. *Ann NY Aca Sci, 1094*, 215–225.

Fisher P, & Stoolmiller M (2008). Intervention effects on foster parent stress: associations with child cortisol levels. *Dev Psychopathol, 20*, 1003–1021.

Fisher P, Stoolmiller M, Gunnar M, & Burraston B (2007). Effects of a therapeutic intervention for foster preschoolers on diurnal cortisol activity. *Psychoneuroendocrinology 32*, 892–905.

Fivush (2011). The development of autobiographical memory. *Annu Rev Psychol*, *62*, 559–582.

Fivush R, & Nelson K (2004). Culture and language in the emergence of autobiographical memory. *Psychol Sci*, *15*, 573–577.

Fjell A, Walhovd K, Brown T, Kuperman J, Chung Y, Hagler, DJ et al. (2012). Multi modal imaging of the self-regulating brain. *P Natl A Sci USA of the United States of America*, *109*(48), 19620–19625.

Flahive M, & Ray D (2007). Effect of group sand-tray therapy with preadolescents. *The J for Special in Group Work*, *32*(4), 362–382.

Flavell JH (2000). Development of children's knowledge about the mental world. *Int J Behav Dev*, *24*(1), 15–23.

Fletcher K (2014). Understanding and assessing traumatic responses of guilt, shame, and anger among children, adolescents, and young adults. In K Nader (ed.), *Assessment of trauma in youths: Understanding issues of age, complexity, and associated variables* (pp. 339–359). New York: Routledge.

Fletcher K (2003). Childhood posttraumatic stress disorder. In E Mash, R Barkley (Eds), *Child psychopathology* (2nd ed., pp. 330–371). New York: Guilford.

Flett G, Flett A, & Wekerle C (2015). A conceptual analysis of interpersonal resilience as a key resilience domain: Understanding the ability to overcome child sexual abuse and other adverse interpersonal contexts. *Int J Child Adolesc Resilience*, *3*(1), 4–33.

Flook L, Goldberg S, Pinger L, Bonus K, & Davidson R (2013). Mindfulness for teachers: A pilot study to assess effects on stress, burn-out, and teaching efficacy. *Mind, Brain, and Education*, 7(3), 182–195.

Flook L, Goldberg S, Pinger L, & Davidson R (2015). Promoting prosocial behavior and self-regulatory skills in preschool children through a mindfulness-based Kindness Curriculum. *Development Psychol*, *51*(1), 44–51.

Fonagy P (2001). Early Intervention and the Development of Self-Regulation. Paper presented at the Keynote address at the meeting of the Australian Association for Infant Mental Health, Perth, Australia, August 30, 2001.

Fonagy P (2006). The mentalization-focused approach to social development. In J Allen & P Fonagy (Eds), *Handbook of mentalization-based treatment*. New York: Wiley.

Fonagy P, & Bateman A (2016). Adversity, attachment, and mentalizing. *Compr Psychiat*, *64*, 59–66.

Fonagy P, Gergely G, & Target M (2007). The parent–infant dyad and the construction of the subjective self. *J Child Psychol Psyc*, *48*(3/4), 288–328.

Fonagy P, Gergely G, Jurist E, & Target M (2002). *Affect regulation, mentalization, and the development of self*. New York: Other Press.

Fonagy P, Luyten P, & Strathearn L (2011). Borderline Personality Disorder, mentalization, and the neurobiology of attachment. *Inf Mental Hlth J*, *32*(1), 47–69.

Fonagy P, & Target M (2000). Playing with reality: III. The persistence of dual psychic reality in borderline patients. *Int J Psychoanal*, *81*, 853–873.

Fonagy P, & Target M (2006). The mentalization-focused approach to self-pathology. *Journal of Personality Disorders*, *20*(6), 544–576.

Fonagy P, Target M, & Gergely G (2000). Attachment and borderline personality disorder. *The Psychiatric Clinics of North America*, *23*(1), 103–122.

Fonagy P, Target M, Steele H, & Steele M (1998). *Reflective Functioning Manual*. Unpublished manuscript. University College London.

Fonagy P, Twemlow S, Vernberg E, Nelson J, Dill E, Little T, & Sargent J (2009). A cluster randomized controlled trial of child-focused psychiatric consultation and a school systems focused intervention to reduce aggression. *J Child Psychol Psy*, *50*, 607–61.

Fonagy P, Twemlow S, Vernberg E, Sacco F, & Little T (2005). Creating a peaceful school learning environment: The impact of an antibullying program on educational attainment in elementary schools. *Medical Science Monitor*, *11*, CR317–325.

Fonken L, Finy M, Walton J, Weil Z, Workman J, Ross J, & Nelson R (2009). Influence of light at night on murine anxiety- and depressive-like responses. *Behav Brain Res*, *205*, 349–354.

Font S, & Berger L (2015). Child maltreatment and children's developmental trajectories in early- to middle-childhood. *Child Dev*, *86(2)*, 536–556.

Fonzo G, Goodkind M, Oathes D, Zaiko Y, Harvey M, Peng K et al. (2017). PTSD psychotherapy outcome predicted by brain activation during emotional reactivity and regulation. *AJP*, *174*(12), 1163–1174.

Foote R, Eyberg S, & Schuhmann E (1998). Parent–child interaction approaches to the treatment of child behavior problems. In T Ollendick, & R Prinz (Eds), *Advances in clinical child psychology* (pp. 125–151). New York: Plenum Press.

Ford JD (2018). Complex trauma and complex posttraumatic stress disorder. In S Gold (ed.), *Handbook of trauma psychology: Vol. 1. Foundations in knowledge*. New York: APA.

Ford JD (2017). Complex trauma and developmental trauma disorder in adolescence. *Adolescent Psychiat, 7*, 220–235.

Ford JD (2011). Assessing child and adolescent complex traumatic reactions. *J Child Adolesc Trauma, 4*(3), 217–232.

Ford JD (2002). Traumatic victimization in childhood and persistent problems with oppositional-defiance. *J Agress Maltreat T, 6*(1), 25–58.

Ford JD, Chapman J, Connor D, & Cruise K (2012). Complex trauma and aggression in secure juvenile justice settings. *Crim Justice Behav, 39*(6), 694–724.

Ford JD, Charak R, Modrowski C, & Kerig P (2018a). PTSD and dissociation symptoms as mediators of the relationship between poly-victimization and psychosocial and behavioral problems among justice-involved adolescents. *J Trauma Dissociation, 19*(3), 325–346.

Ford JD, & Courtois C (2014). Complex PTSD, affect dysregulation, and borderline personality disorder. *Borderline Personality Disorder and Emotion Dysregulation, 1*(9), open access.

Ford JD, Courtois C, Steele K, Van der Hart O, & Nijenhuis E (2005). Treatment of complex posttraumatic self-dysregulation. *J Traum Stress, 18*, 437–447.

Ford JD, & Delker B (2018). Poly-victimization in childhood and its adverse impacts across the lifespan: Introduction to the special issue, *J Trauma Dissociation, 19*(3), 275–288.

Ford JD, & DTD Field Trial Study Group (2014). Developmental trauma disorder semi-structured interview. Unpublished manuscript.

Ford JD, Elhai J, Connor D, & Frueh B (2010). Poly-victimization and risk of posttraumatic, depressive, and substance use disorders and involvement in delinquency in a national sample of adolescents. *J Adolescent Health, 46*, 545–552.

Ford JD, Grasso D, Hawke J, & Chapman J (2013). Poly-victimization among juvenile justice-involved youths. *Child Abuse Neglect, 37*, 788–800.

Ford JD, Spinazzola J, van der Kolk B, & Grasso D (2018b). Toward an empirically based developmental trauma disorder diagnosis for children: Factor structure, item characteristics, reliability and validity of the Developmental Trauma Disorder Semi-Structured *Interview. J Clin Psychiatry, 79*, 17m11675.

Ford JJ, Nalbone D, Wetchler J, & Sutton P (2008). Fatherhood: How differentiation and identity status affect attachment to children. *The Amer J Fam Therapy, 36*, 284–299.

Ford T, Goodman R, & Meltzer H (2003). The British Childhood and Adolescent Mental Health UK survey 1999: The prevalence of DSM-IV disorders. *J Am Acad Child Psy, 42*, 1203–1211.

Forman-Hoffman V, Knauer S, McKeeman J, Zolotor A, Blanco R, Lloyd S, Tant E, Viswanathan M (2013). Child and adolescent exposure to trauma: Comparative effectiveness of interventions addressing trauma other than maltreatment or family violence. Comparative Effectiveness Review No 107. (Prepared by the RTI International-University of North Carolina at Chapel Hill Evidence-based Practice Center under Contract No. 290–2007–10056-I.) AHRQ Publication No. 13-EHC054-EF. Rockville, MD: Agency for Healthcare Research and Quality. www.effectivehealthcare.ahrq.gov/reports/final.cfm.

Fortunato C, Dribin A, Granger D, & Buss K (2008). Salivary alpha-amylase and cortisol in toddlers: Differential relations to affective behavior. *Develop Psychobio, 50*, 807–818.

Fosha D (2013). A heaven in a wild flower: Self, dissociation, and treatment in the context of the neurobiological core self. *Psychoanalytic Inquiry, 33*, 496–523.

Fosha D (2009). Positive Affects and the transformation of suffering into flourishing. *Ann NY Acad Sci, 1172*, 252–262.

Fosha D (2006). Quantum transformation in trauma and treatment: Traversing the crisis of healing change. *J Clin Psychol: In Session*, 62(5), 569–583.

Fosse GK (2006). Mental health of psychiatric outpatients bullied in childhood. Thesis for the degree of doctor medicinae, Norwegian University of Science and Technology. ISBN 82-471-8182-7 synopsis.

Fosha D (2003). Dyadic regulation and experiential work with emotion and relatedness in trauma and disorganized attachment. In M Solomon & DJ Siegel (Eds), *Healing trauma* (pp. 228–281). New York: WW Norton.

Fosha D (2002). The activation of affective change processes in AEDP (Accelerated Experiential-Dynamic Psychotherapy). In JJ Magnavita (Ed.), *Comprehensive handbook of psychotherapy. Vol. 1: Psychodynamic and object relations psychotherapies* (pp. 309–344). New York: John Wiley & Sons.

Fosha D (2001). The dyadic regulation of affect. *J Clin Psychol/In Session, 57*, 227–242.

Foulkes D (1990). Dreaming and consciousness. *Eur J Cogn Psychol, 2*(1), 39–55.

Foulkes D, Hollifield M, Sullivan B, Bradley L, & Terry R (1990). REM dreaming and cognitive skills at ages 5–8: A cross-sectional study. *Int J Behav Dev, 13*(4), 447–465.

Fox C, Hunter S, & Jones S (2016). Children's humor types and psychosocial adjustment. *Pers Indiv Differ, 89*, 86–91.

Fox C, Hunter S, & Jones S (2015). Reciprocity between humor styles and psychosocial adjustment in children. Unpublished manuscript.

Fox L (2016). The use of humor in family therapy: Rationale and applications. *J Family Psychother, 27*(1), 67–78.

Fox N, & Calkins S (2003). The development of self-control of emotion: Intrinsic and extrinsic influences. *Motiv Emotion, 27*, 7–26.

Fox N, Henderson H, Marshall P, Nichols K, & Ghera M (2005). Behavioral inhibition: Linking biology and behavior within a developmental framework. *Ann Rev of Psychol, 56*, 235–262.

Fox N, Henderson H, Rubin K, Calkins S, & Schmidt L (2001). Continuity and discontinuity of behavioral inhibition and exuberance: Psychophysiological and behavioral influences across the first four years of life. *Child Dev, 72*, 1–21.

Fox N, & Rutter M (2010). Introduction to the special section on the effects of early experience on development. *Child Dev, 81*(1) 23–27.

Fraiberg S (1980). *Clinical studies in infant mental health: The first year of life.* New York: Basic Books.

Fraiberg S, Adelson E, & Shapiro V (1975). Ghosts in the nursery: A psychoanalytic approach to the problem of impaired infant–mother relationships. *J Am Acad Child Psy, 14*, 387–421.

Fraley R (2002). Attachment stability from infancy to adulthood: Meta-analysis and dynamic modeling of developmental mechanisms. *Pers Soc Psychol Rev, 6*, 123–151.

Fraley R, & Bonanno G (2004). Attachment and loss: A test of three competing models on the association between attachment-related avoidance and adaptation to bereavement. *Pers Soc Psychol Bull, 30*, 878.

Fraley R, Roisman G, Booth-LaForce C, Owen M, & Holland A (2013). Interpersonal and genetic origins of adult attachment styles: A longitudinal study from infancy to early adulthood. *J Pers Soc Psychol, 104*(5), 817–838.

France KG (1992). Behavior characteristics and security in sleep-disturbed infants treated with extinction. *J Pediatr Psychol, 17*, 467–475.

Francis D, Caldji C, Champagne F, Plotsky P, & Meaney M (1999). The role of corticotropin-releasing factor–norepinephrine systems in mediating the effects of early experience on the development of behavioral and endocrine responses to stress. *Biol Psychiat, 46*(9), 1153–1166.

Frank M, Woroch B, & Curran T (2005). Error-related negativity predicts reinforcement learning and conflict biases. *Neuron, 47*, 495–501.

Franzke I, Wabnitz P, & Catani C (2015). Dissociation as a mediator of the relationship between childhood trauma and non-suicidal self-injury in females: A path analytic approach. *J Trauma & Dissociation, 16*, 286–302.

Fredrickson B, Tugade M, Waugh C, & Larkin G (2003). What good are positive emotions in crisis? A prospective study of resilience and emotion following the terrorist attacks on the United States on September 11th, 2001. *J Pers Soc Psychol, 84*, 365–376.

Freeman H, & Brown B (2001). Primary attachment to parents and peers during adolescence: Differences by attachment style. *J Youth Adolescence, 30*, 653–674.

Freud A (1954). The widening scope of indications for psychoanalysis: discussion. In H Hartman, *The writings of Anna Freud* (vol. IV, pp. 356–376). New York: International UP, 1968.

Freud A, & Burlingham D (1943). *War and children.* New York: Medical War Books.

Frewen P, Brown M, & Lanius R (2017). Trauma-related altered states of consciousness (TRASC) in an online community sample: Further support for the 4-D model of trauma-related dissociation. *Psychol of Consciousness: Theory, Res, and Prac, 4*(1), 92–114.

Frewen P, Brown M, Steuwe C, & Lanius R (2015). Latent profile analysis and principal axis factoring of the DSM-5 dissociative subtype. *Eur J Psychotraumato, 6*(1), doi.org/10.3402/ejpt.v6.26406.

Frewen P, Dozois D, Neufeld R, & Lanius R (2008a). Meta-analysis of alexithymia in posttraumatic stress disorder. *J Traum Stress, 21*, 243–246.

Frewen P, Dozois D, Neufeld R, & Lanius R (2012). Disturbances of emotional awareness and expression in posttraumatic stress disorder: Meta-mood, emotion regulation, mindfulness, and interference of emotional expressiveness. *Psychol Trauma-US, 4*, 152–161.

Frewen P, Hegadoren K, Coupland J, Rowe B, Neufeld R, & Lanius R (2015a). Trauma-related altered states of consciousness (TRASC) and functional impairment I: Prospective study in acutely traumatized persons. *J Trauma Dissociation, 16*(5), 500–519.

Frewen P, Kleindienst N, Lanius R, & Schmahl C (2014). Trauma-related altered states of consciousness in women with BPD with or without PTSD. *Eur J Psychotraumato, 5*, 24863 dx.doi.org/10.3402/ejpt.v5.24863.

Frewen P, & Lanius R (2006). Toward a psychobiology of posttraumatic self-dysregulation: Re-experiencing, hyperarousal, dissociation, and emotional numbing. *Ann NY Acad Sci, 1071*, 110–124.

Frewen P, Lanius R, Pain C, Hopper J, Densmore M, & Stevens T (2008b). Clinical and neural correlates of alexithymia in Posttraumatic Stress Disorder. *J Abnorm Psychol, 117*(1), 171–181.

Frewen P, Rogers N, Flodrowski L, & Lanius R (2015b). Mindfulness and Metta-based Trauma Therapy (MMTT): Initial development and proof-of-concept of an internet resource. *Mindfulness, 6*(6), 1322–1334.

Frick P, Ray J, Thornton L, & Kahn R (2014). Can callous-unemotional traits enhance the understanding, diagnosis, and treatment of serious conduct problems in children and adolescents? A comprehensive review. *Psychol Bull, 140*, 1–57.

Friedman N, Miyake A, Robinson J, & Hewitt J (2011). Developmental trajectories in toddlers' self-restraint predict individual differences in executive functions 14 years later: A behavioral genetic analysis. *Develop Psychol, 47*, 1410–1430.

Friedrich W, Jaworski T, Huxsahl J, & Bengtson B (1997). Dissociative and sexual behaviors in children and adolescents with sexual abuse and psychiatric histories. *J Interpers Viol, 12*(2), 155–171.

Friesen M, Horwood J, Fergusson D, & Woodward L (2017). Exposure to parental separation in childhood and later parenting quality as an adult: Evidence from a 30-year longitudinal study. *J Child Psychol Psyc, 58*(1), 30–37.

Frigerio A, Ceppi E, Rusconi M, Giorda R, Raggi M, & Fearon P (2009). The role played by the interaction between genetic factors and attachment in the stress response in infancy. *J Child Psychol Psyc, 50*, 1513–1522.

Frith U, & Frith C (2003). Development and neurophysiology of mentalizing. *Philos Trans R Soc Lond. Series B Biol Sci*, 358, 459–73.

Fritzley H, & Lee K (2003). Do young children always say yes to yes–no questions? A metadevelopmental study of the affirmation bias. *Child Dev, 74*, 1297–1313.

Fuggle P, Bevington D, Cracknell L, Hanley J, Hare S, Lincoln J et al. (2015). The Adolescent Mentalization-based Integrative Treatment (AMBIT) approach to outcome evaluation and manualization: adopting a learning organization approach. *Clin Child Psychol P, 20*(3) 419–435.

Fuhrmann D, Knoll L, & Blakemore S-J (2015). Adolescence as a sensitive period of brain development. *Trends Cogn Sci, 19*(10), 558–566.

Fuhs M, Farran D, & Nesbitt K (2013). Preschool classroom processes as predictors of children's cognitive self-regulation skills development. *School Psychol Quart, 28*(4), 347–359.

Fuller-Thomson E, & Dalton A (2011). Suicidal ideation among individuals whose parents have divorced: Findings from a representative Canadian community survey. *Psychiat Res 187*, 150–155.

Fung K, & Alden L (2016). Once hurt, twice shy: Social pain contributes to social anxiety. *Emotion, 17*(2), 231–239. abstract.

Gaensbauer TJ (1995). Trauma in the preverbal period: Symptoms, memories, and developmental impact. *Psychoanalytic Study of the Child, 50*, 122–149.

Gaensbauer TJ (2002). Representations of trauma in infancy: Clinical and theoretical implications for the understanding of early memory. *Inf Mental Hlth J, 23*, 259–277.

Gaensbauer TJ (2016). Moments of meeting: The relevance of Lou Sander's and Dan Stern's conceptual framework for understanding the development of pathological social relatedness. *Inf Mental Hlth J, 37*(2), 172–188.

Gaensbauer TJ, & Jordan L (2009). Psychoanalytic perspective on early trauma: Interviews with thirty analysts who treated an adult victim of a circumscribed trauma in early childhood. *J Amer Psychoanalytic Assoc, 57*(4), 947–977.

Gaertner A, Fite P, & Colder C (2011). Moderating effect of intimate exchange on delinquent socialization processes. *J Early Adolescence, 31*(2), 258–270.

Gagné M-H, & Melancon C (2013). Parental psychological violence and adolescent behavioral adjustment: The role of coping and social support. *J Interpersonal Violence, 28*(1), 176–200.

Galambos N, Barker E, & Almeida D (2003). Parents do matter: Trajectories of change in externalizing and internalizing problems in early adolescence. *Child Dev, 74*(2), 578–594.

Galatzer-Levy I, Burton C, & Bonannno G (2012). Coping flexibility, potentially traumatic life events, and resilience: A prospective study of college student adjustment. *J Soc Clin Psychol, 31*(6), 542–567.

Galinsky A, Ku G, &Wang C (2005). Perspective-taking and self–other overlap: Fostering social bonds and facilitating social coordination. *Group Process InterG, 8*(2), 109–124.

Galland B, Taylor B, Elder D, & Herbison P (2012). Normal sleep patterns in infants and children: A systematic review of observational studies. *Sleep Med Rev, 16*, 213–222.

Gallese V, Eagle M, & Migone P (2007). Intentional attunement: Mirror neurons and the neural underpinnings of interpersonal relations. *JAPA, 55*(1), 131–175.

Galloway G (2010). Individual differences in personal humor styles: Identification of prominent patterns and their associates. *Pers Indiv Differ, 48*, 563–567.

Gambin M, & Sharp C (2016). The differential relations between empathy and internalizing and externalizing symptoms in inpatient adolescents. *Child Psychiat Hum D, 47*(6), 966–974.

Gamwell K, Nylocks M, Cross D, Bradley B, Norrholm S, & Jovanovic T (2015). Fear conditioned responses and PTSD symptoms in children: Sex differences in fear responses in children. *Dev Psychobiol, 57*(7), 799–808.

Garbarino J (1999). *Lost boys: Why our sons turn violent and how we can save them.* New York: The Free Press.

Garland E, & Howard M (2009). Neuroplasticity, psychosocial genomics, and the biopsychosocial paradigm in the 21st century. *Health Soc Work, 34*(3), 191–199.

Garrido E, Taussig H, Culhane S, & Raviv T (2011). Attention problems mediate the association between physical abuse severity and aggressive behaviour in a sample of maltreated children. *J Early Adolescence, 31*, 714–734.

Gartstein M, Putnam S, & Rothbart M (2012). Etiology of preschool behavior problems: Contributions of temperament attributes in early childhood. *Inf Mental Hlth J, 33*(2), 197–211.

Garwood J, Varghese C, & Vernon-Feagans L (2017). Internalizing behaviors and hyperactivity/inattention: Consequences for young struggling readers, and especially boys. *J Early Intervention, 39*(3), 218–235.

Gaskill R, & Perry B (2014). The neurobiological power of play using the Neurosequential Model of Therapeutics to guide play in the healing process. In C Malchiodi (Ed.), *Creative arts and play therapy for attachment problems* (pp. 178–194). New York: Guilford.

Gavazzi I, Ornaghi V, & Antoniotti C (2009). Narratives of guilt and shame: A study of situational antecedents in children and adolescents. In MA Pinto (Ed.), *Rivista di psicolinguistica applicate* (pp. 39–52). Rome: Fabrizio Serra. (English version).

Gawrilow C, Gollwitzer P, Oettingen G (2011). If-Then Plans benefit delay of gratification performance in children with and without ADHD. *Cognitive Ther Res, 35*(5), 442–455.

Gazelle H, & Ladd G (2003). Anxious solitude and peer exclusion: A diathesis-stress model of internalizing trajectories in childhood. *Child Dev, 74*, 257–278.

Geiger T, & Crick N (2001). A developmental psychopathology perspective on vulnerability to personality disorders. In R Ingram & J Price (Eds), *Vulnerability to psychopathology: Risk across the lifespan* (pp. 57–102). New York: Guilford Press.

Geiger T, & Crick N (2001). A developmental psychopathology perspective on vulnerability to personality disorders. In R Ingram & J Price (Eds), *Vulnerability to psychopathology: Risk across the lifespan* (pp. 57–102). New York: Guilford Press.

Gelkopf M & Berger R (2009). A school-based, teacher-mediated prevention program (ERASE-Stress) for reducing terror-related traumatic reactions in Israeli youth: a quasi-randomized controlled trial. *J Child Psychol Psyc, 50*(8), 962–971.

Gelkopf M, Ryan P, Cotton S, & Berger R (2008). The impact of a "training of the trainers" course for helping Tsunami-Survivor children on Sri Lankan disaster volunteer workers. *Int J Stress Manage, 15*, 117–135.

Georgiou S, & Stavrinides P (2008). Bullies, victims and bully-victims: Psychosocial profiles and attribution styles. *School Psychol Int, 29*(5), 574–589.

Gerace A, Day A, Casey S, & Mohr P (2015). Perspective-taking and empathy: Does having similar past experience to another person make it easier to take their perspective? *Journal of Relationships Research, 6*(e10), 1–14. doi: 10.1017/jrr.2015.6.

Gerretsen P, Graff-Guerrero A, Menon M, Pollock B, Kapur S, Vasdev N, et al. (2010). Is desire for social relationships mediated by the serotonergic system in the prefrontal cortex? An [18F]setoperone PET study. *Soc Neurosci, 5*, 375–383.

Gershoff ET (2002). Corporal punishment by parents and associated child behaviors and experiences: a meta-analytic and theoretical review. *Psychol Bull, 128*, 539–579.

Gerson S, Bekkering H, & Hunnius S (2017). Do you do as I do?: Young toddlers prefer and copy toy choices of similarly acting others. *Infancy, 22*(1), 5–22.

Gerson S, Bekkering H, & Hunnius S (2016). Social context influences planning ahead in three-year-olds. *Cognitive Dev, 40*, 120–131.

Gervais M, & Wilson D (2005). The evolution and functions of laughter and humor. *Q Rev Biol, 80*(4), 395–429.

Geva R, Yaron H, & Kuint J (2016). Neonatal sleep predicts attention orienting and distractibility. *J of Att Dis, 20*(2) 138–150.

Geva R, Zivan M, Warsha A, & Olchik D (2013). Alerting, orienting or executive attention networks: Differential patters of pupil dilations. *Front Behav Neurosci*, 7(145), 1–11.

Ghetti S, Edelstein R, Goodman G, Cordon I, Quas J, Alexander K, Redlich A, & Jones D (2006). What can subjective forgetting tell us about memory for childhood trauma? *Mem Cognit, 34*(5), 1011–1025.

Ghosh Ippen C, Noroña C, & Lieberman A (2014). Clinical considerations for conducting Child–Parent Psychotherapy with young children with developmental disabilities who have experienced trauma. *PCSP, 10*(M3, Article 2), 196–211.

Ghosh Ippen C, Harris W, Van Horn P, & Lieberman A (2011). Traumatic and stressful events in early childhood: Can treatment help those at highest risk? *Child Abuse Neglect, 35*, 504–513.

Giallo R, Cooklin A, Brown S, Christensen D, Kingston D, Liu C, Wade C, & Nicholson J (2015). Trajectories of fathers' psychological distress across the early parenting period: Implications for parenting. *J Fam Psychol, 29*(5), 766–776.

Gibb B, Uhrlass D, Grassia M, Benas J, & McGeary J (2010). Children's inferential styles, 5-HTTLPR genotype, and maternal expressed emotion-criticism: an integrated model for the intergenerational transmission of depression. *J Abnorm Psychol, 118*(4), 734–745.

Gil E (2006). *Helping abused and traumatized children: Integrating directive and nondirective approaches.* New York: Guilford.

Gil E (1998). *Play therapy for severe psychological trauma* [Videotape]. New York: Guilford.

Gilbert S (2013). *Developmental biology* (10th ed.). Oxford, UK: Sinauer Associates, Inc.

Gilbert S, & Morawski C (2005). Stress coping for elementary school children: A case for including lifestyle. *J Indiv Psychol, 61*(4), 314–328.

Gillath O, Bunge S, Shaver P, Wendelken C, & Mikulincer M (2005). Attachment-style differences and ability to suppress negative thoughts: Exploring the neural correlates. *NeuroImage, 28*, 835–847.

Gillath O, Giesbrecht B, & Shaver P (2009). Attachment, attention, and cognitive control: Attachment style and performance on general attention tasks. *J Exp Soc Psychol, 45*, 647–654.

Gilles Y, & Polston E (2017). Effects of social deprivation on social and depressive-like behaviors and numbers of oxytocin expressing neurons in rats. *Behav Brain Res, 328*, 28–38.

Gillespie C, Phifer J, Bradley B, & Ressler K (2009). Risk and resilience: Genetic and environmental influences on development of the stress response. *Depress Anxiety, 26*(11): 984–992.

Gilligan J (2003). Shame, guilt, and violence. *Soc Res, 70*(4), 1149–1180.

Gilliom M, & Shaw D (2004). Codevelopment of externalizing and internalizing problems in early childhood. *Dev Psychopathol, 16*, 313–333.

Gilmore J, Lin W, Prastawa M, Looney C, Vetsa Y, Knickmeyer R, et al. (2007). Regional gray matter growth, sexual dimorphism, and cerebral asymmetry in the neonatal brain. *J Neurosci 27*(6), 1255–1260.

Gilmore J, Shi F, Woolson S, Knickmeyer R, Short S, Lin W et al. (2011). Longitudinal development of cortical and subcortical gray matter from birth to 2 years. *Cereb Cortex, 22*(11), 2478–2485.

Gilstrap LL (2004). A missing link in suggestibility research: What is known about the behavior of field interviewers in unstructured interviews with young children? *J Exp Psychol, 10*(1), 13–24.

Ginevra M, Nota L, Heppner P, Heppner M, & Soresi S (2015). The relationship of personality type, problem-solving appraisal, and learning strategies. *J Career Assessment, 23*(4) 545–558.

Ginott HG (1972). *Teacher and child.* New York: Macmillan.

Giordano V, Fuiko R, Leiss U, Brandstetter S, Hayde M, Bartha-Doering E et al. (2017). Differences in attentional functioning between preterm and full-term children underline the importance of new neuropsychological detection techniques. *Acta Pædiatrica, 106*, 601–611.

Gleason M, Fox N, Drury S, Smyke A, Egger H, Nelson C et al. (2011). Validity of evidence-derived criteria for Reactive Attachment Disorder: Indiscriminately social/disinhibited and emotionally withdrawn/inhibited types. *J Am Acad Child Psy, 50*(3), 216–231.

Gleason M, Fox N, Drury S, Smyke A, Nelson C, & Zeanah C (2014). Indiscriminate behaviors in previously institutionalized young children. *Pediatrics, 133*(3), 657–665.

Gleiser K, Ford J, & Fosha D (2008). Contrasting exposure and experiential therapies for complex Posttraumatic Stress Disorder. *Psychother: Train Res Theory Prac, 45*(3), 340–360.

Glynn L, & Sandman C (2011). Pre-natal origins of neurological development: A critical period for fetus and mother. *Curr dir Psychol Sci, 20*(6), 384–389.

Goff B, & Tottenham N (2014). Early life adversity and adolescent depression: mechanisms involving the ventral striatum. *CNS Spectrums, 20*(4), 337–345.

Gogtay N, Giedd J, Hayashi K, Greenstein D, Vaituzis C, Nugent T et al. (2004). Dynamic mapping of human cortical development during childhood through early adulthood. *Proc Natl Acad Sci USA, 101*, 8174–8179.

Gola H, Engler H, Schauer M, Adenauer H, Riether C, Kolassa S et al. (2011). Victims of rape show increased cortisol responses to trauma reminders: A study in individuals with war- and torture-related PTSD. *Psychoneuroendocrino, 37*, 213–220.

Goldsmith R, Chesney S, Heath N, & Barlow M (2013). Emotion regulation difficulties mediate associations between betrayal trauma and symptoms of Posttraumatic Stress, depression, and anxiety. *J Traum Stress, 26*, 376–384.

Goldstein N, Vezich S, & Shapiro J (2014). Perceived perspective-taking: When others walk in our shoes. *J Pers Soc Psychol, 106*(6), 941–960.

Goldstein T, & Lerner M (2017). Dramatic pretend play games uniquely improve emotional control in young children. *Developmental Sci, 21*(4), e12603 doi.org/10.1111/desc.12603.

Gong X, Paulson S, & Wang C (2016). Exploring family origins of perfectionism: The impact of inter-parental conflict and parenting behaviors. *Pers Indiv Differ, 100*, 43–48.

Goodall B, Chadwick I, McKinnon A, Werner-Seidler A, Meiser-Stedman R, Smith P, & Dalgleish T (2017). Translating the cognitive model of PTSD to the treatment of very young children: A single case study of an 8-year-old motor vehicle accident survivor. *J clin Psychol: In Session*, *73*(5), 511–523.

Goodman A, Harnett N, & Knight D (2018). Pavlovian conditioned diminution of the neurobehavioral response to threat. *Neurosci Biobehav Rs*, *84*, 218–224.

Goodman S, & Rouse M (2017). Perinatal depression and children: A developmental perspective. In R Tremblay, M Bolvin, R Peters (Eds), *Encyclopedia of early childhood development*, www.child-encyclopedia.com/maternal-depression/according-experts/perinatal-depression-and-children-developmental-perspective [updated 2010–2017].

Gopnik A (2009). *The philosophical baby: What children's minds tell us about truth, love and the meaning of life*. New York: Farrar, Straus, & Giroux.

Gordon N, Burke S, Akil H, Watson S, & Panksepp J (2003). Socially-induced brain "fertilization": Play promotes brain derived neurotrophic factor transcription in the amygdala and dorsolateral frontal cortex in juvenile rats. *Neruosci Lett*, *341*, 17–20.

Gordon-Hollingsworth A, Yao N, Chen H, Qian M, & Chen S (2018). Understanding the Impact of natural disasters on psychological outcomes in youth from mainland China: A meta-analysis of risk and protective factors for Posttraumatic Stress Disorder symptoms. *J Child Adol Trauma*, *11*(2), 205–226.

Göttken T, & von Klitzing K (2014). *Manual for short-term psychoanalytic child therapy (PaCT)*. London: Karnac.

Göttken T, White L, Klein A, & von Klitzing K (2014). Short-term psychoanalytic child therapy for anxious children: A pilot study. *Psychotherapy*, *51*(1), 148–158.

Gottwald J, Achermann S, Marciszko C, Lindskog M, & Gredebäck G (2016). An embodied account of early executive-function development: Prospective motor control in infancy is related to inhibition and working memory. *Psychol Sci*, *27*(12), 1600–1610.

Gould F, Clarke J, Heim C, Harvey P, Majer M, & Nemeroff C (2012). The effects of Child Abuse Neglect on cognitive functioning in adulthood. *J Psychiatr Res*, *46*, 500–506.

Gould M, Munfakh J, Kleinman M, Lubell K, & Provenzano D (2004). Impact of September 11th terrorist attacks on teenagers' mental health. *Applied Developmental Science*, *8*(3), 158–169.

Grabe S, Ward L, & Hyde J (2008). The role of the media in body image concerns among Women: A meta-analysis of experimental and correlational studies. *Psychol Bull*, *134*(3), 460–476.

Graber J, Seeley J, Brooks-Gunn J, & Lewinsohn P (2004). Is pubertal timing associated with psychopathology in young adulthood? *J Am Acad Child Psy*, *43*(6), 718–726.

Graber R, Turner R, & Madill A (2016). Best friends and better coping: Facilitating psychological resilience through boys' and girls' closest friendships. *Brit J Psychol*, *107*, 338–358.

Graham A, Pfeifer J, Fisher P, Carpenter S, & Fair D (2015). Early life stress is associated with default system integrity and emotionality during infancy. *J Child Psychol Psyc*, *56*(11), 1212–1222.

Graham A, Yockelson M, Kim H, Bruce J, Pears K, & Fisher P (2012). Effects of maltreatment and early intervention on diurnal cortisol slope across the start of school: A pilot study. *Child Abuse Neglect*, *36*, 666–670.

Graham S (2010). What educators need to know about bullying behaviors. *Kappan*, *92*(1), 66–69.

Graham S, Doubleday C, & Guarino P (1984). The development of relations between perceived controllability and the emotions of pity, anger, and guilt. *Child Dev*, *55*, 561–565.

Graham-Bermann S, Howell K, Miller L, Kwek J, & Lilly M (2010). Traumatic events and maternal education as predictors of verbal ability for preschool children exposed to intimate partner violence (IPV). *J Fam Viol*, *25*, 383–392. abstract.

Granot D, & Mayseless O (2001). Attachment security and adjustment to school in middle childhood. *Int J Behav Dev*, *25*, 530–541.

Grassetti S, Herres J, Williamson A, Yarger H, Layne C, & Kobak R (2014). Narrative focus moderates symptom change trajectories in group treatment for traumatized and bereaved adolescents. *J Clin Child Adolesc*, *44*, 933–941.

Grassetti S, Williamson A, Herres J, Kobak R, Layne C, Kaplow J, & Pynoos R (2018). Evaluating referral, screening, and assessment procedures for middle school Trauma/Grief-Focused Treatment Groups. *School Psychol Quart*, *33*(1), 10–20.

Grasso D, Dierkhising C, Branson C, Ford J, & Lee R (2016). Developmental patterns of adverse childhood experiences and current symptoms and impairment in youth referred for trauma-specific services. *J Abnorm Child Psychol*, *44*, 871–886.

Gratz K, Bornovalova M, Delany-Brumse A, Nick B, & Lejue C (2007). A laboratory-based study of the relationship between childhood abuse and experiential avoidance among inner-city substance users: The role of emotional nonacceptance. *Behav Ther*, *38*, 256–268.

Gratz K, & Roemer L (2004). Multidimensional assessment of emotion regulation and dysregulation: Development, factor structure, and initial validation of the Difficulties in Emotion Regulation Scale. *J Psychopathol Behav*, *26*, 41–54.

Gratz K, Rosenthal M, Tull M, Lejuez C, & Gunderson J (2010). An experimental investigation of emotional reactivity and delayed emotional recovery in borderline personality disorder: The role of shame. *Compr Psychiat, 51*, 275–285.

Gray J (1972). The psychophysiological nature of introversion-extraversion: A modification of Eysenck's theory. In V Nebylisyn & J Gray (Eds), *Biological bases of individual behavior* (pp. 182–206). New York: Academic Press.

Gray J (1991). The neuropsychology of temperament. In J Strelau & A Angleitner (Eds), *Explorations in temperament: International perspectives on theory and measurement* (pp. 105–128). New York: Plenum Press.

Gray M, Bolton E, & Litz B (2004). A longitudinal analysis of PTSD symptom course: Delayed-onset PTSD in Somalia Peacekeepers. *J Consult Clin Psychol, 72*, 909–913.

Gray S (2011). Epigenetic treatment of neurological disease. *Epigenomics 3*, 431–450.

Gray S, Lipschutz R, & Scheeringa M (2018). Young children's physiological reactivity during memory recall: Associations with posttraumatic stress and parent physiological synchrony. *J Abnorm Child Psychol, 46*, 871–880.

Gray Deering C (2000). A Cognitive Deval approach to understanding how children cope with disasters. *JCAPN, 13*, 7–15.

Graziano P, & Derefinko K (2013). Cardiac vagal control and children's adaptive functioning: A meta-analysis. *Biol Psychol, 94*(1), 22–37.

Green C, Long D, Green D, Iosif A-M, Dixon J, Miller M et al. (2012). Will working memory training generalize to improve off-task behavior in children with attention-deficit/hyperactivity disorder? *Neurotherapeutics, 9*, 639–648.

Green E (2012). Facilitating resiliency in traumatized adolescents: Integrating play therapy with evidence-based interventions. *Play Therapy, 6*, 10–15.

Green E, & Connolly M (2009). Jungian family sandplay with bereaved children: Implications for play therapists. *Internat J Play Therapy, 18*, 84–98.

Green E, & Myrick A (2014). Treating complex trauma in adolescents: A phase-based, integrative approach for play therapists. *Internat J Play Therapy, 23*(3), 131–145.

Green E, Myrick A, & Crenshaw D (2013). Toward secure attachment in adolescent relational development: Advancements from sandplay and expressive play-based interventions. *Internat J Play Therapy 22*, 90–102.

Greenberg M, & Riggs N (2015). Prevention of mental disorders and promotion of competence. In M Rutter (Ed.), *Child and adolescent psychiatry* (6th ed., pp., 215–226). New York: Wiley-Blackwell.

Greenberg M, Speltz M, DeKlyen M, & Jones K (2001). Correlates of clinic referral for early conduct problems: Variable- and person-oriented approaches. *Dev Psychopathol, 13*, 255–276.

Greenwald R (2002). The role of trauma in conduct disorder. In R Greenwald (ed.), Trauma and juvenile delinquency: Theory, research, and interventions (pp. 5–23). New York: Haworth.

Gregory A, & Sadeh A (2016). Annual research review: Sleep problems in childhood psychiatric disorders – a review of the latest science. *J Child Psychol Psyc, 57(3*), 296–317.

Grigorenko E, DeYoung C, Eastman M, Getchell M, Haeffel G, Klinteberg B et al (2010). Aggressive behavior, related conduct problems, and variation in genes affecting dopamine turnover. *Aggressive Behavior, 36*, 158–176.

Groh A, Narayan A, Bakermans-Kranenburg M, Roisman G, Vaughn B, & Fearon R (2016). Attachment and temperament in the early life course: A meta-analytic review. *Child Dev, 88*(3), 770–795.

Groh A, & Roisman G (2009). Adults' autonomic and subjective emotional responses to infant vocalizations: The role of secure base script knowledge. *Dev Psychol, 45(3*), 889–893.

Groh A, Roisman G, Booth-LaForce C, Fraley R, Owen M, Cox M et al. (2014). IV. Stability of attachment security from infancy to late adolescence. *Mono Soc Res Child, 79*(3), 51–66.

Groh A, Roisman G, van IJzendoorn M, Bakermans-Kranenburg M, & Fearon R (2012). The significance of insecure and disorganized attachment for children's internalizing symptoms: A meta-analytic study. *Child Dev, 83*, 591–610.

Gross JJ (1998). The emerging field of emotion regulation: An integrative review. *Rev Gen Psychol, 2*, 271–299.

Grossman F, Pollack W, & Golding E (1988). Fathers and children: Predicting the quality and quantity of fathering. *Dev Psychol, 24*(1), 82–91.

Grossman P, & Taylor E (2007). Toward understanding respiratory sinus arrhythmia: Relations to cardiac vagal tone, evolution and biobehavioral functions. *Biol Psychol, 74*, 263–285.

Gruhl E, & Van Leuven K (2014). Motivational Interviewing for adolescents: Behavior counseling for diet and exercise. *JNP, 10*(7), 493–499.

Gruner CR (1978). *Understanding laughter: The working of wit and humor.* Chicago, IL: Nelson-Hall.

Grunwald M, & Glasser S (2005, September 21). Experts say faulty levees caused much of the flooding. *The Washington Post.* Downloaded 1-30-16.

Grynberg D, Luminet O, Corneille O, Grézes J, & Berthoz S (2010). Alexithymia in the interpersonal domain: A general deficit of empathy? *Pers Indiv Differ*, *49*, 845–850.

Guajardo N, & Cartwright K (2016). The contribution of theory of mind, counterfactual reasoning, and executive function to pre-readers' language comprehension and later reading awareness and comprehension in elementary school. *J Exp Child Psychol 144*, 27–45.

Guarisco M, & Freeman M (2015). The wonder of empathy: Using Palacio's novel to teach perspective-taking. *The ALAN Rev*, *43*(1), 56–68.

Guedes M, Santos A, Ribeiro O, Freitas M, Rubin K, & Verissimo M (2018). Perceived attachment security to parents and peer victimization: Does adolescent's aggressive behaviour make a difference? *J Adolescence 65*, 196–206.

Guerin D, Gottfried A, Oliver P, & Thomas C (2003). *Temperament: Infancy through adolescence*. New York: Kluwer.

Guilé J-M, Mbékou V, & Lageix P (2004). Child and parent variables associated with treatment response in narcissistic youths: The role of self-blame and shame. *Canad Child & Adolescent Psychia Rev*, *13*(3), 81–85.

Gullone E, & Moore S (2000). Adolescent risk-taking and the five-factor model of personality. *J Adolescence*, *23*, 393–407.

Gundogar D, Kesebir S, Demirkan A, & Yaylaci E (2014). Is the relationship between affective temperament and resilience different in depression cases with and without childhood trauma? *Compr Psychiat 55*, 870–875.

Gunn H, Critchfield K, Mackaronis J, Cribbet M, Troxel W, & Williams P (2017). Affiliative interpersonal behaviors during stress are associated with sleep quality and presleep arousal in young, healthy adults. *Sleep Health 3*, 98–101.

Gunnar M, & Donzella B (2002). Social regulation of the cortisol levels in early human development. *Psychoneuroendocrino*, *27*, 199–220.

Gunnar M, Doom J, & Esposito E (2015). Psychoneuroendocrinology of stress normative development and individual differences. In RM Lerner (ed.). *Handbook of child psychology and developmental sci, volume 3* (7th edition, pp. 106–151). New York: Wiley.

Gunnar M, Frenn K, Wewerka S, & Ryzin M (2009a). Moderate versus severe early life stress: Associations with stress reactivity and regulation in 10–12-year-old children. *Psychoneuroendocrino*, *34*(1), 62–75.

Gunnar M, Herrera A, & Hostinar C (2009d). Stress and early brain development. *Encyclopedia of early childhood development*, downloaded 6-14-17 from www.child-encyclopedia.com/brain/according-experts/stress-and-early-brain-development.

Gunnar M, Kryzer E, Van Ryzin M, & Phillips D (2011). The import of the cortisol rise in child care differs as a function of behavioral inhibition. *Dev Psychol*, *47*, 792–803.

Gunnar M, & Quevedo K (2007). The neurobiology of stress and development. *Annu Rev Psychol*, *58*, 145–173.

Gunnar M, Talge N, & Herrera A (2009c). Stressor paradigms in developmental studies: What does and does not work to produce mean increases in salivary cortisol *Psychoneuroendocrino*, *34*, 953–967.

Gunnar M, & Vazquez D (2001). Low cortisol and a flattening of expected daytime rhythm: Potential indices of risk in human development. *Dev Psychopathol*, *13*, 515–538.

Gunnar M, Wewerka S, Frenn K, Long J, & Griggs C (2009b). Developmental changes in HPA activity over the transition to adolescence: Normative changes and associations with puberty. *Dev Psychopathol*, *21*, 69–85.

Gusic S, Cardena E, Bengtsson H, & Sondergaard H (2016). Adolescents' dissociative experiences: the moderating role of type of trauma and attachment style. *J Child Adol Trauma*, *9*(4), 341–351.

Gutman L, Joshi H, Parsonage M, & Schoon I (2018). Gender-specific trajectories of conduct problems from ages 3 to 11. *J Abnorm Child Psych*, https://doi.org/10.1007/s10802-017-0379-1.

Gutteling B, de Weerth C, & Buitelaar J (2005). Pre-natal stress and children's cortisol reaction to the first day of school. *Psychoneuroendocrino*, *30*, 541–549.

Guy A, Lee K, & Wolke D (2017). Differences in the early stages of social information processing for adolescents involved in bullying. *Agressive Behav*, I: 10.1002/ab.21716.

Guyer A, Silk J, & Nelson E (2016). The neurobiology of the emotional adolescent: From the inside out. *Neurosci Biobehav Rs*, *70*, 74–85.

Guyton G (2011). Using toys to support infant-toddler learning and development. *Young Children*, 50–56.

Haag A, & Landolt M (2017). Young children's acute stress after a burn injury: Disentangling the role of injury severity and parental acute stress. *J Pediatr Psychol*, *22*(4), 294–302.

Haag A, Zehnder D, & Landolt M (2015). Guilt is associated with acute stress symptoms in children after road traffic accidents, *Europe J Psychotraumatol*, *6*:1, 29074, abstract. doi: 10.3402/ejpt.v6.29074.

Habermas T, & de Silveira C (2008). The development of global coherence in life narratives across adolescence: Temporal, causal and thematic aspects. *Dev Psychol*, *44*, 707–721.

Haberstick B, Smolen A, & Hewitt J (2006). Family-based association test of the 5HTTLPR and aggressive behavior in a general population sample of children. *Biol Psychiat*, *59*, 836–843.

Habib M, & Labruna V (2011). Clinical considerations in assessing trauma and PTSD in adolescents. *J Child Adolesc Trauma, 4*, 198–216.

Hagan M, Gentry M, Ghosh Ippen C, & Lieberman A (2018). PTSD with and without dissociation in young children exposed to interpersonal trauma. *J Affect Disorders, 227*, 536–541. abstract.

Hagan M, Hulette A, & Lieberman A (2015). Brief report: Symptoms of dissociation in a high-risk sample of young children exposed to interpersonal trauma: Prevalence, correlates, and contributors. *J Traum Stress, 28*, 258–261.

Hagan M, Tein J-Y, Sandler I, Wolchik S, Ayers T, & Luecken L (2012). Strengthening effective parenting practices over the long term: Effects of a preventive intervention for parentally bereaved families. *J Clin Child Adolesc, 41*(2), 177–188.

Hagekull B, & Bohlin G (2003). Early temperament and attachment as predictors of the Five Factor Model of Personality. *Attach Hum Dev, 5*, 2–18.

Hagmann P, Sporns O, Madan N, Cammoun L, Pienaar R, Wedeen V et al. (2010). White matter maturation reshapes structural connectivity in the late developing human brain. *Proc Nat Acad Sci, 107*, 19067–19072.

Haine R, Ayers T, Sandler I, Wolchik S, & Weyer J (2003). Locus of control and self-esteem as stress-moderators or stress-mediators in parentally bereaved children. *Death Stud, 27*(7), 619–640.

Halevi G, Djalovski A, Vengrober A, & Feldman R (2016). Risk and resilience trajectories in war-exposed children across the first decade of life. *J Child Psychol Psyc, 57*(10), 1183–1193.

Halfon S, Bekar O, Ababay S, & Gorlach G (2017). Dyadic mental state talk and sophistication of symbolic play between parents and children with behavioral problems. *J Infant Child Adolesc Psychother, 16*(4), 291–307.

Halfon S, Cavdar A, Orsucci F, Schlepek G, Andreassi S, Giuliani A, & de Felice G (2016). The non-linear trajectory of change in play profiles of three children in Psychodynamic Play Therapy. *Front Psychol, 7*, 1494. doi: 10.3389/fpsyg.2016.01494.

Haliloglu T, Keskin O, Ma B, & Nussinov R (2005). How similar are protein folding and protein binding nuclei? Examination of vibrational motions of energy hot spots and conserved residues. *Biophys J, 88*, 1552–1559. abstract.

Halligan S, Herbert J, Goodyer I, & Murray L (2007). Disturbances in morning cortisol secretion in association with maternal post-natal depression predict subsequent depressive symptomatology in adolescents. *Biol Psychiat, 62*, 40–46.

Haltigan J, & Roisman G (2015). Infant attachment insecurity and dissociative symptomatology: Findings from the NICHD study of early child care and youth development. *Inf Mental Hlth J, 36*(1), 30–41.

Hamada S, Kaneko H, Ogura M, Yamawaki A, Maezono J, Sillanmäki L et al. (2018). Association between bullying behavior, perceived school safety, and self-cutting: A Japanese population-based school survey. *Child Adol Ment H-UK, 23*(3), 141–147. abstract.

Hambrick E, Vernberg E, Greenhoot A, & Hendrickson M (2018). Recalling a devastating tornado: Qualities of children recollections and associations with mental health symptoms. *J Child Adolesc Trauma, 11*, 227–239.

Hamlin J, Wynn K, & Bloom P (2007). Social evaluation by preverbal infants. *Nature, 450*(22), 557–560.

Hammen C, & Rudolph K (2003). Childhood mood disorders. In E Mash, R Barkley (Eds), *Child psychopathology* (2nd ed., pp. 233–278). New York: Guilford.

Hampes W (2010). The relation between humor styles and empathy. *Europe J Psychol, 6*, 34–45.

Hamza C, & Willoughby T (2015). Non-suicidal self-injury and affect regulation: Recent findings from experimental and ecological momentary assessment studies and future directions. *J Clin Psychol, 71(6)*, 561–574. abstract.

Han G, Helm J, Iucha C, Zahn-Waxler C, Hastings P, & Klimes-Dougan B (2016). Are executive functioning deficits concurrently and predictively associated with depressive and anxiety symptoms in adolescents? *J Clin Child Adolesc, 45*(1), 44–58.

Han P, Holbrook T, Sise M, Sack D, Sise C, Hoyt D et al. (2011). Postinjury depression is a serious complication in adolescents after major trauma: Injury severity and injury-event factors predict depression and long-term quality of life deficits. *J Traum, 70*, 923–930.

Hane A, & Fox N (2018). Studying the biology of human attachment. In J Cassidy, P Shaver (Eds), *The handbook of attachment: Theory, research, and clinical applications* (3rd ed., pp. 223–241). New York: Guilford.

Hanington L, Ramchandani P, & Stein A (2010). Parental depression and child temperament: Assessing child to parent effect in a longitudinal study. *Infant Behav Dev, 33*(1), 88–95.

Hankin B, Barrocas A, Young J, Haberstick B, & Smolen A (2015). 5-HTTLPR X interpersonal stress interaction and non-suicidal self-injury in general community sample of youth. *Psychiat Res, 225*, 609–612. abstract.

Hansel T, Osofsky J, Osofsky H, & Friedrich P (2013). The effect of long-term relocation on child and adolescent survivors of Hurricane Katrina. *J Traum Stress, 26*, 613–620.

Hansen M, Hyland P, Armour C, Shevlin M, & Elklit A (2015). Less is more? Assessing the validity of the ICD-11 model of PTSD across multiple trauma samples. *Europ J Psychotraumatol*, *6*, 28766.

Hanson J, Chung M, Avants B, Shirtcliff E, Gee J, Davidson J, & Pollak S (2010). Early stress is associated with alterations in the orbitofrontal cortex: A tensor-based morphometry investigation of brain structure and behavioral risk. *J Neurosci*. *30*, 7466–7472.

Hardesty J, Crossman K, Khaw L, & Raffaeli M (2016). Marital violence and coparenting quality after separation. *J Fam Psychol*, *30*(3), 320–330.

Harley E, Williams M, Zamora I, & Lakatos P (2014). Trauma treatment in young children with developmental disabilities: Applications of the Child–Parent Psychotherapy (CPP) model to the cases of "James" and "Juan." *Prag Case Studies in Psychother*, *10*(3–1), 156–195.

Harpur L, Polek E, & van Harmelen A-L (2015). The role of timing of maltreatment and child intelligence in pathways to low symptoms of depressive anxiety in adolescence. *Child Abuse Neglect*, *47*, 24–37. abstract.

Harr C, Horn-Johnson T, Williams N, Jones M, & Riley K (2013). Personal trauma and risk behaviors among youth entering residential treatment. *Child Adolesc Soc Work J*, *30*, 383–398. abstract.

Harris DA (2007). Dance/movement therapy approaches fostering resilience recovery among African adolescent torture survivors. *Torture: J on Rehab of Torture Vic & Prevention of Torture*, *17*, 135–155.

Harris L, Block S, Ogle C, Goodman G, Augusti E-M, Larson R et al. (2015a). Coping style and memory specificity in adolescents and adults with histories of child sexual abuse. *Memory*, *24*(8), 1078–1090.

Harris T, York S, & Giardino A (2015b). Intrafamilial violence. In P Clements, S Seedat, E Gibbings (Eds) (pp. 103–121). *Mental health issues of child maltreatment*. St. Louis, MO: STM Learning, Inc.

Hart S, Field T, Hernandez-Reif M, Nearing G, Shaw S, Schanberg S, & Kuhn C (2001). Anorexia symptom are reduced by massage therapy. *Eating Disorders*, *9*, 289–299. abstract.

Harte C, Vuajnovic A, & Potter C (2015). Association between exercise and posttraumatic stress symptoms among trauma-exposed adults. *Eval & the Health Profess*, *38*(1), 42–52. abstract.

Harter S (2008). The developing self. In W Damon, R Lerner (Eds), *Child and adolescent development: An advanced course* (pp. 216–260). New York: Wiley.

Harter S (1999). *The construction of the self: A developmental perspective*. New York: Guilford.

Harter S, & Pike R (1984). The pictorial scale of perceived competence and social acceptance for young children. *Child Dev*, *55*(6), 1969–1982.

Harter S, Waters P, & Whitesell N (1998). Relational self-worth: Differences in perceived worth as a person across interpersonal contexts among adolescents. *Child Dev*, *69*(3), 756–766.

Hartman J (2014). Anna Freud and the Holocaust: Mourning and survival guilt. *Int J Psychoanal*, *95*, 1183–1210.

Harvey B, Moore A, & Koestner R (2017). Distinguishing self-oriented perfectionism-striving and self-oriented perfectionism-critical in school-aged children: Divergent patterns of perceived parenting, personal affect and school performance. *Pers Indiv Differ*, *113*, 136–141. abstract.

Haskett M, Stelter R, Proffit K, & Nice R (2012). Parent emotional expressiveness and children's self-regulation: Associations with abused children's school functioning. *Child Abuse Neglect*, *36*, 296–307.

Hasson-Ohayon I, Peri T, Rotschild I, & Tuval-Mashiach R (2017). The mediating role of integration of loss in the relationship between dissociation and prolonged grief disorder. *J Clin Psychol*, *73*, 1717–1728.

Hatfield E, Cacioppo J, Rapson R (1994). *Emotional contagion*. New York: Cambridge University Press.

Hatfield E, Cacioppo J, Rapson R (1992). Primitive emotional contagion. In MS Clark (Ed.), *Emotion and social behavior: Review of personality and social psychology*, *14*, 151–177.

Hébert M, Daspe M, & Cyr M (2018). An analysis of avoidant and approach coping as mediators of the relationship between paternal and maternal attachment security and outcomes in child victims of sexual abuse. *Psychol Trauma-US*, *10*(4), 402–410.

Hébert M, Langevin R, & Daigneault I (2016). The association between peer victimization, PTSD, and dissociation in child victims of sexual abuse. *J Affect Disorders*, *193*, 227–232.

Heim C, Nader U, Maloney E, Boneva R, Jones J, & Reeves W (2009). Childhood trauma and risk for chronic fatigue syndrome: Association with neuroendocrine dysfunction. *Arch Gen Psychiatry*, *66*(1), 72–80. abstract.

Heim C, Newport D, Mletzko T, Miller A, & Nemeroff C (2008). The link between childhood trauma and depression: insights from HPA axis studies in humans. *Psychoneuroendocrino*, *33*(6), 693–710.

Helfritz-Sinville L, & Stanford M (2014). Hostile attribution bias in impulsive and premeditated aggression. *Pers Indiv Differ*, *56*, 45–50. abstract.

Hendel HJ (2015, March 10). It's not always depression. *New York Times*.

Henderson H, Pine D, & Fox N (2015). Behavioral inhibition and developmental risk: A dual-processing perspective. *Neuropsychopharmacol*, *40*(1), 207–224.

Hendriks A, Barnes-Holmes Y, McEnteggart C, De Mey H, Janssen G, & Egger J (2016). Understanding and remediating social-cognitive dysfunctions in patients with serious mental illness using Relational Frame Theory. *Front Psychol*, 7(143), 1–7. doi: 10.3389/fpsyg.2016.00143.

Hendry A, Jones E, & Charman T (2016). Executive function in the first three years of life: Precursors, predictors and patterns. *Dev Rev*, *42*, 1–33.

Henry L, Farmer C, Manwaring S, Swineford L, & Thurm A (2018). Trajectories of Cognitive development in toddlers with language delays. *Res Dev Disabil*, *81*, 65–72.

Hensch T, & Bilimoria P (2012). Re-opening windows: Manipulating critical periods for brain development. *Cerebrum: The Dana Forum on Brain Science*, 11. PMID 23447797.

Herres J, Williamson A, Kobak R, Layne C, Kaplow J, Saltzman W et al. (2017). Internalizing and externalizing symptoms moderate treatment response to school-based Trauma and Grief Component Therapy for adolescents. *Sch Ment Health*, *9*(2), 184–193.

Herman JL (1997). *Trauma and recovery*. New York: Basic Books.

Herman J, Perry J, & van der Kolk B (1989). Childhood trauma in borderline personality disorder. *The Am J Psychiat*, *146*(4), 490–495.

Herman K, Trotter R, Reinke W, & Ialongo N (2011). Developmental origins of perfectionism among African American youth. *J Couns Psychol*, *58*, 321–334.

Hermenau K, Hecker T, Ruf M, Schauer E, Elbert T, & Schauer M (2011). Childhood adversity, mental ill-health and aggressive behavior in an African orphanage: Changes in response to trauma-focused therapy and the implementation of a new instructional system. *Child Adol Psych Men*, *5*, 29. doi: 10.1186/1753-2000-5-29.

Hermenau K, Hecker T, Schaal S, Maedl A, & Elbert T (2013). Addressing posttraumatic stress and aggression by means of narrative exposure: a randomized controlled trial with ex-combatants in the eastern DRC. *J Agress Maltreat T*, *22*, 916–934.

Hermans HJM (2010). The Dialogical Self Theory: Introduction. Viewed on 5-30-16 from huberthermans.com, www.youtube.com/wath?v=TKEKWzZOC31.

Hermans HJM, & Dimaggio G (2004). The dialogical self in psychotherapy: An introduction. In HJM Hermans, G Dimaggio (Eds), *The dialogical self in psychotherapy* (pp. 1–10). London, UK: Brunner-Routledge.

Herpfer I, Hezel H, Reichardt W, Clark K, Geiger J, Gross C et al. (2012). Early life stress differentially modulates distinct forms of brain plasticity in young and adult mice. *PLoS One*, *7*, e46004.

Herringa R, Birn R, Ruttle P, Stodola D, Davidson R, & Essex M (2013). Childhood maltreatment is associated with altered fear circuitry and increased internalizing symptoms by late adolescence. *Proc Natl Acad Sci*, *110*, 19119–19124.

Herzog T, & Strevey S (2008). Contact with nature, sense of humor, and psychological well-being. *Environment and Behavior*, *40*(6), 747–776.

Hesse E (2008). The adult attachment interview: protocol, method of analysis, and empirical studies. In J Cassidy, P Shaver (Eds) *Handbook of attachment: theory, research, and clinical applications* (pp. 552–598). New York: Guilford.

Hesse E (1999). The Adult Attachment Interview: Historical and current perspectives. In J Cassidy, P Shaver (Eds), *The handbook of attachment: Theory, research, and clinical applications* (pp. 395–433). New York: Guilford.

Hesse E, Main M, Abrams K, & Rifkin, A (2003). Unresolved states regarding loss or abuse can have "second-generation" effects: Disorganization, role inversion, and frightening ideation in the offspring of traumatized, nonmaltreating parents. In M Solomon, D Siegel (Eds), *Healing trauma* (pp. 57–106). New York: Norton.

Hewitt P, Caelian C, Chen C, & Flett G (2014). Perfectionism, stress, daily hassles, hopelessness, and suicide potential in depressed psychiatric adolescents. *J Psychopathol Behav Assess*, *36*(4), 663–674. abstract.

Hewitt S (1994). Preverbal sexual abuse: What two children report in later years. *Child Abuse & Neglect*, *18*(10), 821–826.

Hiebert-Murphy D, Williams E, Mills R, Walker J, Feldgaier S et al. (2011). Listening to parents: The challenges of parenting kindergarten-aged children who are anxious. *Clin Child Psychol P*, *17*(3) 384–399.

Hill-Soderlund A, Mills-Koonce W, Propper C, Calkins S, Granger D, Moore G, Gariepy J-L, & Cox M (2008). Parasympathetic and sympathetic responses to the strange situation in infants and mothers from avoidant and securely attached dyads. *Dev Psychobiol*, *50*(4), 361–376.

Hillebrandt H, Dumontheil I, Blakemore S-J, & Rosier J (2013). Dynamic causal modelling of effective connectivity during perspective-taking in a communicative task. *NeuroImage*, *76*, 116–124.

Hiller R, Meiser-Stedman R, Lobo S, Creswell S, Fearon P, Ehlers A et al. (2017). A longitudinal investigation of the role of parental responses in predicting children's posttraumatic distress. *J Child Psychol Psyc*, *59*(7), 781–789.

Hinnant J, & El-Sheikh M (2013). Codevelopment of externalizing and internalizing symptoms in middle to late childhood: Sex, baseline respiratory sinus arrhythmia, and respiratory sinus arrhythmia reactivity as predictors. *Dev Psychopathol*, *25*(2), 419–436.

Hipson W, & Séguin D (2015). Is good fit related to good behaviour? Goodness-of-fit between daycare teacher–child relationships, temperament, and prosocial behavior. *Early Child Dev Care, 186*(5), 785–798.

Hirai M, Skidmore S, Clum G, & Dolma S (2012). An investigation of the efficacy of online expressive writing for trauma-related psychological distress in Hispanic individuals. *Behav Ther, 43*, 812–824.

Hirshfeld-Becker D, & Biederman J (2002). Rationale and principles for early intervention with young children at risk for anxiety disorders. *Clin Child & Fam Psychol Rev, 5*, 161–172.

Hirshfeld-Becker D, Masek B, Henin A, Blakely L, Rettew D, Dufton L, & Biederman J (2008). Cognitive behavioral intervention with young anxious children. *Harvard Rev Psychiat, 16*, 113–125.

Hirshfeld-Becker D, Masek B, Henin A, Pollock-Wurman R, McQuade J, DePetrillo L et al. (2010). Cognitive Behavioral Therapy for 4- to 7-year-old children with anxiety disorders: A randomized clinical trial. *J Consult Clin Psych, 78*(4), 498–510.

Hirsh-Pasek K, Golinkoff R, Berk L, & Singer D (2009). *A mandate for playful learning in school: Presenting the evidence*. New York: Oxford University Press.

Hitchcock C, Nixon R, & Weber N (2016). A review of overgeneral memory in child psychopathology. *Brit J Clin Psychol, 53*, 170–193.

Hjern A, Lindblad F, & Vinnerljung B (2002). Suicide, psychiatric illness, and social maladjustment in intercountry adoptees in Sweden: A cohort study. *Lancet, 360*, 443–448.

Hobfoll S, Watson P, Bell C, Bryant R, Brymer M, Friedman M et al. (2007). Five essential elements of immediate and mid–term mass trauma intervention: Empirical evidence. *Psychiatry, 70*, 283–315.

Hocking E, Simons R, & Surette R (2016). Attachment style as a mediator between childhood maltreatment and the experience of betrayal trauma as an adult. *Child Abuse Neglect, 52*, 94–101.

Hodges M, Godbout N, Briere J, Lanktree C, Gilbert A, & Kletzka N (2013). Neglect Cumulative trauma and symptom complexity in children: A path analysis. *Child Abuse Neglect, 37*, 891–898.

Hodgdon H, Liebman R, Martin L, Suvak M, Besarra K, Rosenblaum W et al. (2018). The effects of trauma type and executive dysfunction on symptom expression of polyvictimized youth in residential care. *J Traum Stress, 31*, 255–264.

Hodgman C, & Jack M (1992). Interviewing. In E McAnarney, R Kreipe, D Orr, G Comerci (Eds), *The textbook of adolescent medicine* (pp. 180–185). Philadelphia, PA: WB Saunders.

Hoffman K, Marvin R, Cooper G, & Powell B (2006). Changing toddlers' and preschoolers' attachment classifications: The Circle of Security Intervention. *J Consulting & Clin Psychol, 74*, 1017–1026.

Hoffman L (2015). Mentalization, emotion regulation, countertransference. *J Infant, Child, and Adoles Psychother, 14*(3), 258–271.

Hoicka E (2016). Parents and toddlers distinguish joke, pretend and literal intentional contexts through communicative and referential cues. *J Pragmatics, 95*, 137–155. abstract.

Hoicka E, Butcher J, Malla F, & Harris P (2017). Humor and preschoolers' trust: Sensitivity to changing intentions. *J Exp Child Psychol, 154*, 113–130. abstract.

Holahan C, Moos R, Holahan C, Brennan P, Schutte K (2005). Stress generation, avoidance coping and depressive symptoms: A 10-year model. *J Consult Clin Psychol, 74*, 658–666.

Holland K, Vivolo-Kantor A, Logan J, & Leemis, R (2017). Antecedents of suicide among youth aged 11–15: A multistate mixed methods analysis. *J Youth Adolescence, 46*(7), 1598–1610.

Hollifield M, Warner T, Lian N, Krakow B, Jenkins J, Kesler J et al. (2002). Measuring trauma and health status in refugees. *JAMA, 288*(5), 611–621.

Hollinger P (2012, November 19). Great kids, great parents. *Psychology Today*, downloaded 2-6-13 from www.psychologytoday.com/blog/great-kids-great-parents/201211/self-awareness.

Holmes C, Kim-Spoon J, & Deater-Deckard K (2016). Linking executive function and peer problems from early childhood through middle adolescence. *J Abnorm Child Psychol, 44*(1), 31–42. abstract.

Holt-Lunstad J, Birmingham W, & Light K (2015). Relationship quality and oxytocin: Influence of stable and modifiable aspects of relationships. *J Soc Pers Relat, 32*(4), 472–490.

Holt-Lunstad J, & Smith T (2016). Loneliness and social isolation as risk factors for CVD: implications for evidence-based patient care and scientific inquiry. *BMJ, 102(13)*, 987–989.

Hölzel B, Lazar S, Gard T, Schuman-Olivier Z, Vago D, & Ott U (2011). How does mindfulness meditation work? Proposing mechanisms of action from a conceptual and neural perspective. *Perspect Psychol Sci, 6*(6), 537–559. abstract.

Homeyer L, & Morrison M (2008). Play therapy: Practice, issues, and trends. *Amer J Play, 1*(2), 210–228.

Hong B, Lim B, Adams L, & Lilly M (2012). Self-worth as a mediator between attachment and, posttraumatic stress in interpersonal trauma. *J Interpers Violence, 27*(10) 2039–2061.

Hong R, Lee S, Chng R, Zhou Y, Tsai F-F, & Tan H (2016). Developmental trajectories of maladaptive perfectionism in middle childhood. *J Pers, 85*(3), 409–422.

Hood K, & Eyberg S (2003). Outcomes of parent–child interaction therapy: Mothers' reports on maintenance three to six years after treatment. *J Clin Child Adolesc, 32*, 419–429.

Horner V, & Whiten A (2005). Causal knowledge and imitation/emulations switching in chimpanzees (*Pan troglodytes*) and children (*homo sapiens*). *Animal Cognition, 8*, 164–181.

Hostinar C, & Gunnar M (2013). The developmental psychobiology of stress and emotion in childhood. In IB Weiner, D Freedheim, R Lerner (Eds), *Handbook of psychology* (2nd ed., pp. 121–141). Hoboken, NJ: Wiley.

Hostinar C, Sullivan R, & Gunnar M (2014). Psychobiological mechanisms underlying the social buffering of the hypothalamic-pituitary-adrenocortical axis: A review of animal models and human studies across development. *Psychol Bull, 140*(1), 256–282.

Howard K, Martin A, Berlin L, & Brooks-Gunn J (2011). Early mother–child separation, parenting, and child well-being in Early Head Start families. *Attach Hum Dev, 13*(1), 5–26.

Howard M, Muris P, Loxton H, & Wege A (2017). Anxiety-proneness, anxiety symptoms, and the role of parental overprotection in young South African children. *J Child Fam Stud, 26*, 262–270.

Howe ML (2011). *The nature of early memory*. Oxford, UK: Oxford University Press.

Howe ML (1997). Children's memory for traumatic experiences. *Learn Individ Differ, 9*, 153–174.

Howe ML, Courage M, & Peterson C (1995). Intrusions in preschoolers' recall of traumatic childhood events. *Psychon B Rev, 2*(1), 130–134.

Howe ML, Courage M, & Rooksby M (2009). The genesis and development of autobiographical memory. In M Courage, N Cowan (Eds), *The development of memory in infancy and childhood* (2nd ed., pp. 177–196). Hove: Psychology Press.

Howell K, Barrett-Becker E, Burnside A, Wamser-Nanney R, Layne C, & Kaplow J (2016). Children facing parental cancer versus parental death: The buffering effects of positive parenting and emotional expression. *J Child Fam Stud, 25*, 152–164.

Hoyt L, Zeiders K, Ehrlich K, & Adam E (2016). Positive upshots of cortisol in everyday life. *Emotion, 16*, 431–435.

Hsieh Y, & Yen L (2017). Trajectories of loneliness and aggression from childhood to early adolescence in Taiwan: The roles of parenting and demographic predictors. *J Early Adolescence, 39*(3), 313-339.

Hsu M-T, Kahn D, Yee D-H, & Lee W-L (2004). Recovery through reconnection: A cultural design for family bereavement in Taiwin. *Death Stud, 28*, 761–786.

Huang H, Shu N, Mishra V, Jeon T, Chalak L, Wang Z et al. (2015). Development of human brain structural networks through infancy and childhood. *Cereb Cortex, 25*, 1389–1404.

Huber A, Hawkins E, & Cooper E (2018). Circle of Security. In J Lebow, A Chambers, D Breunlin (Eds), *Encyclopedia of couple and family therapy*. Cham: Springer.

Huber A, McMahon C, & Sweller N (2015a). Efficacy of the 20-week circle of security intervention: Changes in caregiver reflective functioning, representations, and child attachment in an Australian clinical sample. *Inf Mental Hlth J, 36*, 556–574.

Huber A, McMahon C, & Sweller N (2015b). Improved child behavioural and emotional functioning after Circle of Security 20-week intervention. *Attach Hum Dev, 17*(6), 547–569.

Huber R, Tonini G, & Cirelli C (2007). Exploratory behavior, cortical BDNF expression, and sleep homeostasis. *Sleep, 30*(2), 129–139.

Hudlicka E (2017). Enhancing Mindfulness-Based Cognitive Therapy with a virtual mindfulness coach. In MM Maheu, K Drude, S Wright (Eds), *Career Paths in Telemental Health* (pp. 171–182). New York: Springer, Cham.

Hudlicka E (2013). Virtual training and coaching of health behavior: Example from mindfulness meditation training. *Patient Educ and Couns, 92*(2), 160–166.

Hudson J, Rapee R, Lyneham H, McLellan L, Wuthrich V, & Schniering C (2015a). Comparing outcomes for children with different anxiety disorders following cognitive behavioural therapy. *Behav Res Ther, 72*, 30–37.

Hudson S, Levickis P, Down K, Nicholls R, & Wake M (2015b). Maternal responsiveness predicts child language at ages 3 and 4 in a community-based sample of slow-to-talk toddlers. *Int J Lang Commun disord, 50*(1), 136–142. abstract.

Hughes C, Devine R, & Wang Z (2017). Does parental mind-mindedness account for cross-cultural differences in preschoolers' theory of mind? *Child Dev, 89*(4), 1296–1310.

Hughes C, & Ensor R (2009). Independence and interplay between maternal and child risk factors for preschool problem behaviors? *Int J Behav Devel, 33*(4), 312–322.

Huijts I, Kleijn W, van Emmerik A, Noordhof A, & Smith A (2012). Dealing with man-made trauma: The relationship between coping style, posttraumatic stress, and quality of life in resettled, traumatized refugees in the Netherlands. *J Traum Stress, 25*, 71–78.

Huizinga M, Dolan C, & van der Molen M (2006). Age-related change in executive function: Developmental trends and a latent variable analysis. *Neuropsychologia, 44*, 2017–2036.

Hulme P (2011). Childhood sexual abuse, HPA axis regulation, and mental health: An integrative review. *West J Nurs Res, 33*, 1069–1097.

Humphreys K, Fox N, Nelson C, & Zeanah C (2017a). Psychopathology following severe deprivation:

History, research, and implications of the Bucharest Early Intervention Project. In A Rus, S Parris, E Stativa (Eds), *Child maltreatment in residential care* (pp. 129–148). New York: Springer.

Humphreys K, Gleason M, Drury S, Miron D, Nelson C, Fox N, & Zeanah C (2015a). Effects of institutional rearing and foster care on psychopathology at age 12 years in Romania: Follow-up of an open, randomised controlled trial. *Lancet Psychiat, 2*, 625–634.

Humphreys K, McGoron L, Sheridan M, McLaughlin K, Fox N et al. (2015b). High-quality foster care mitigates callous-unemotional traits following early deprivation in boys: A randomized controlled trial. *J Am Acad Child Psy, 54*(12), 977–983.

Humphreys K, Nelson C, Fox N, & Zeanah C (2017b). Signs of reactive attachment disorder and disinhibited social engagement disorder at age 12 years: Effects of institutional care history and high-quality foster care. *Dev Psychopathol, 29*, 675–684.

Humphreys K, Weems C, & Scheeringa M (2015). The role of anxiety control and treatment implications of informant agreement on child PTSD symptoms. *J Clin Child Adolesc, 46*(6), 903–914.

Hunter S, Barber B, Olsen J, McNeely C, & Bose K (2011). Adolescents' self-disclosure to parents across cultures: Who discloses and why. *J Adolescent Res, 26*(4), 447–478.

Hussey D, Reed A, Laymen D, & Pasiali V (2007). Music therapy and complex trauma: A protocol for developing social reciprocity. *Resid Treat Child Youth, 24*(1–2), 111–129.

Hutman T, & Dapretto M (2009). The emergence of empathy during infancy. *Cognition, Brain, & Behavior, XIII*(4), 367–390.

Huyder V, Nilsen E, & Bacso S (2017). The relationship between children's executive functioning, theory of mind, and verbal skills with their own and others' behaviour in a cooperative context: Changes in relations from early to middle school-age. *Inf Child Dev, 36*(2), 161–174.

Hyde J, Mezulis A, & Abrahamson L (2008). The ABCs of depression: Integrating affective, biological, and cognitive models to explain the emergence of the gender difference in depression. *Psychol Rev, 115*, 291–313.

Hyde L, Shaw D, Gardner F, Cheong J, Dishion T, & Wilson M (2013). Dimensions of callousness in early childhood: Links to problem behavior and family intervention effectiveness. *Dev Psychopathol, 25*, 347–363.

Hygen B, Guzey I, Belsky J, Berg-Nielson T, & Wichstrøm L (2014). Catechol-O-methyltransferase Val-158Met genotype moderates the effect of disorganized attachment on social development in young children. *Dev Psychopathol*, 26(4pt1), 947–961.

Hyland P, Shevlin M, McNally S, Murphy J, Hansen M, & Elklit A (2016). Exploring differences between the ICD-11 and DSM-5 models of PTSD: Does it matter which model is used? *J Anxiety Disord, 37*, 48–53. abstract.

Iancu I, Bodner E, & Ben-Zion I (2015). Self esteem, dependency, self-efficacy and self-criticism in social anxiety disorder. *Compr Psychiat, 58*, 165–171.

Ickx G, Bleyenheuft Y, & Hatem S (2018). Development of visuospatial attention in typically developing children. *Front. Psychol.* 8, 2064. abstract. doi: 10.3389/fpsyg.2017.02064.

Ikeda Y, Yahata N, Ito I, Nagano M, Toyota T, Yoshikawa T, et al. (2008). Low serum levels of brain-derived neurotrophic factor and epidermal growth factor in patients with chronic schizophrenia. *Schizophr Res, 101*(1–3), 58–66.

Infante J, Peran F, Rayo J, Serrano J, Dominguez M et al. (2014). Levels of immune cells in transcendental meditation practitioners. *Internat J Yoga*, 7, 147–151.

Ingram R, & Price J (2001). The role of vulnerability in understanding psychopathology. In R Ingram, J Price (Eds), *Vulnerability to psychopathology: Risk across the lifespan* (pp. 3–19). New York: Guilford Press.

Innamorati M, Parolin L, Tagini A, Santona A, Basco A, de Carli P et al. (2018). Attachment, social value orientation, sensation seeking, and bullying in early adolescence. *Front Psychol, 9*, 239. doi: 10.3389/fpsyg.2018.00239.

Iruka I, Burchinal M, & Cai K (2010). Long-term effect of early relationships for African American children's academic and Soc Dev: An examination from kindergarten to fifth grade. *J Black Psychol, 36*(2), 144–171.

Irwin A, Li J, Craig W, & Hollenstein T (2016). The role of shame in the relation between peer victimization and mental health outcomes. *J Interpers Violence*. doi: 10.1177/0886260516672937.

Ispa J, Cook J, Harmeyer E, & Rudy D (2015). Mothers' physical interventions in toddler play in a low-income, African American sample. *Infant Behav Dev, 41*, 88–101.

Israel P, & Diamond G (2012). Feasibility of attachment-based family therapy for depressed clinic-referred Norwegian adolescents. *Clin Child Psychol and Psychia, 18*(3), 334–350.

Ivarsson T, & Skarphedinsson G (2015). Sleep problems and cognitive behavior therapy in pediatric obsessive-compulsive disorder have bidirectional effects. *J Anxiety Disord, 30*, 28–33.

Iverson S, & Gartstein M (2018). Applications of temperament: A review of caregiver-focused temperament-driven interventions. *Early Educ Dev, 29*(1), 31–52.

Jackson D, & Vaughn M (2017). Parental incarceration and child sleep and eating behaviors. *J Pediatr, 185*, 211–217.

Jackson P, & Decety J (2004). Motor cognition: A new paradigm to study self–other interactions. *Curr Opin Neurobiol*, *14*, 259–263.

Jackson Y, Huffhines L, Stone K, Flemming K, & Gabrielli J (2017). Coping styles in youth exposed to maltreatment: Longitudinal patterns reported by youth in foster care. *Child Abuse Neglect*, *70*, 65–74.

Jankowski K, & Pfeifer, J (2015). Puberty, peers, and perspective-taking: Examining adolescent self-concept development through the lens of social-cognitive neuroscience. In Arthur W Toga (Ed.), *Brain mapping: An encyclopedic reference* (vol. 3, pp. 45–51). New York: Elsevier.

Janssen S (2015). The cognitive abilities account for the reminiscence bump in the temporal distribution of autobiographical memory. Presentation, *Society for Applied Research in Mem Cognit*, April 29, 2015.

Janssen S, & Murre J (2008). Reminiscence bump in autobiographical memory: unexplained by novelty, emotionality, valence, or importance of personal events. *Q J Exp Psychol*, *60*, 1847–1860.

Janssens A, van den Noortgate W, Goossens L, Verschueren K, Colpin H, de Laet S et al. (2015). Externalizing problem behavior in adolescence: Dopaminergic genes in interaction with peer acceptance and rejection. *J Youth Adolescence*, *44*, 1441–1456.

Jaschke A, Honing H, & Scherder E (2018). Longitudinal analysis of music education on executive functions in primary school children. *Front Neurosci*, *12*, 103. doi: 10.3389/fnins.2018.00103.

Jaycox L, Cohen J, Mannarino A, Walker D, Langley A, Gegenheimer K et al. (2010). Children's mental health care following hurricane Katrina: A field trial of trauma-focused. *J Traum Stress*, *23*, 223–231.

Jennings K, Sandberg I, Kelley S, Valdes L, Yaggi K, Abrew A, Macey-Kalcevic M (2008). Understanding of self and maternal warmth predict later self-regulation in toddlers. *Int J Behav Dev*, *32*(2), 108–118.

Jester J, Steinberg D, Heitzeg M, & Zucker R (2015). Coping expectancies, not enhancement expectancies, mediate trauma experience effects on problem alcohol use: A prospective study from early childhood to adolescence. *J Stud Alcohol Drugs*, *76*, 781–789.

Jia X, Ying L, Zhou X, Wu X, & Lin C (2015). The effects of extraversion, social support on the Posttraumatic Stress Disorder and Posttraumatic Growth of adolescent survivors of the Wenchuan earthquake. *PLoS ONE*, *10*(3), e0121480.

Jiang Y, You J, Lin M, Zheng X (2017). The qualities of attachment with significant others and self-compassion protect adolescents from non-suicidal self-injury. *School Psychol Quart*, *32*(2), 143–155.

Jin Y, Sun C, Wang F, An J, & Xu J (2018). The relationship between PTSD, depression and negative life events: Ya'an earthquake three years later. *Psychiat Res*, *259*, 358–363.

Johansson M, Hassmen P, & Jouper J (2008). Acute effects of Qigong exercise on mood and anxiety. *Internat J Stress Management*, *15*(2), 199–207. abstract.

John-Henderson N, Williams S, Brindle R, & Ginty A (2018). Changes in sleep quality and levels of psychological distress during the adaptation to university: The role of childhood adversity. *Brit J Psychol*, doi: 10.1111/bjop.12314.

Johnson D, & Casey B (2015). Extinction during memory reconsolidation blocks recovery of fear in adolescents. *Scientific Reports*, *5*, 8863. doi: 10.1038/srep08863.

Johnson S, & North R (1992). Opioids excite dopamine neurons by hyperpolarization of local interneurons. *J Neurosci*, *12*, 483–488.

Joiner, T. (2005). *Why people die by suicide*. Cambridge, MA: Harvard University Press.

Jones J, Cassidy J, & Shaver P (2015). Adult attachment style and parenting. *Pers Soc Psychol Rev*, 234–260.

Jones N, Field T, & Almeida A (2009). Right frontal EEG asymmetry and behavioral inhibition in infants of depressed mothers. *Infant Behav Dev*, *32*(3), 298–304.

Jones N, Field T, & Davalos M (2000). Right frontal EEG asymmetry and lack of empathy in preschool children of depressed mothers. *Child Psychiat Hum D*, *30*, 189–204.

Jones N, Pegues M, McCrory M, Kerr S, Jiang H, Sellati R et al. (2011). Collagen-induced arthritis is exacerbated in C-Reactive Protein–deficient mice. *Arthritis Rheum*, *63*(9), 2641–2650.

Jones S (2012). Human toddlers' attempts to match two simple behaviors provide no evidence for an inherited, dedicated imitation mechanism. *PLoS ONE*, 7(12), e51326.

Jones T, Barnett M, Wadian T, & Sonnentag T (2016). Individual differences associated with emotional and behavioral responses to ambiguous social situations in which rejection might be inferred. *J Gen Psychol*, *143*(4), 298–310.

Jonkman C, Schuengel C, Oosterman M, Lindeboom R, Boer F, & Lindauer R (2017). Effects of multidimensional treatment foster care for preschoolers (MTFC-P) for young foster children with severe behavioral disturbances. *J Child Fam Stud*, *26*, 1491–1503.

Joyce K, Hayasaka S, & Laurienti P (2013). The human functional brain network demonstrates structural and dynamical resilience to targeted attack. *PLoS Comput Biol*, *9*(1), e1002885.

Jung CG (1971). *Psychological types: The collected works of C Jung* (Vol. 6). Princeton, NJ: Princeton University Press.

Jurado M, & Rosselli M (2007). The elusive nature of executive functions: A review of our current understanding. *Neuropsychol Rev*, *17*, 213–233.

Kabat-Zinn J (1990). *Full catastrophe living: Using the wisdom of your body and mind to face stress, pain, and illness.* New York: Delacorte.

Kafaki H, Akerdi E, & Rezaei A (2014, September 8–10). The effectiveness of Gestalt Group Play therapy on improvement of behavioral problems in preschool children. *Proceedings of SOCIOINT14 – International Conference on Social Sciences and Humanities. ISBN: 978-605-64453-1-6.*

Kagan J (2009). Two is better than one. *Perspectives on Psychol Sci*, *4*(1), 22–23.

Kagan J (1997). Temperament and the reactions to the unfamiliarity. *Child Dev*, *68*, 139–143.

Kagan J, Reznick J, & Snidman N (1988). Biological bases of childhood shyness. *Science*, *240*, 167–171.

Kagan J, & Snidman N (1999). Early childhood predictors of adult anxiety disorders. *Biol Psychiat*, *46*, 1536–1541.

Kagan J, Snidman N, & Arcus D (1998). Childhood derivatives of high and low reactivity in infancy. *Child Dev*, *69*, 1483–1493.

Kagan J, Snidman N, Kahn V, & Towsley S (2007). The preservation of two infant temperaments into adolescence. *Monogr Soci Res in Child Devel*, Serial No. 287, 72.

Kahn R, Frick P, Youngstrom E, Youngstrom J, Feeny N, & Findling R (2013). Distinguishing primary and secondary variants of callous-unemotional traits among adolescents in a clinic-referred sample. *Psychol Assessment*, *25*(3), 966–978. abstract.

Kaiser AP (1993). Parent-implemented language intervention: An environmental system perspective. In AP Kaiser, D Gray (Eds), *Enhancing children's communication: Research foundations for intervention* (Vol. 2, pp. 63–84). Baltimore, MD: Brookes.

Kaiser AP, & Roberts M (2011). Parent-implemented Enhanced Milieu Teaching with preschool children who have intellectual disabilities. *JSLHR*, *56*, 295–309. abstract.

Kaiser E, Gillette C, & Spinazzola J (2010). A controlled pilot-outcome study of sensory integration (SI) in the treatment of complex adaptation to traumatic stress. *J Aggress Maltreat T*, 19, 699–720.

Kajiume A, Aoyama-Setoyama S, Saito-Hori Y, Ishikawa N, & Kobayashi M (2013). Reduced brain activation during imitation and observation of others in children with pervasive developmental disorder: A pilot study. *Behav Brain Funct*, *9(21*), 1–5. doi: 10.1186/1744-9081-9-21.

Kaldy Z, & Sigala N (2004). The neural mechanisms of object working memory: What is where in the infant brain? *Neurosci Biobehav Rev*, *28*(2), 113–121.

Kalk N, Nutt D, & Lingford-Hughes A (2011). The role of central noradrenergic dysregulation in anxiety disorders: evidence from clinical studies. *J Psychopharmacol*, *25*(1), 3–16.

Kaliterna-Lipovčan L, & Prizmić-Larsen Z (2016). What differs between happy and unhappy people? *SpringerPlus*. doi.org/10.1186/s40064-016-1929-7.

Kalpakci A, Vanwoerden S, Elhai J, & Sharp C (2016). The independent contributions of emotion dysregulation and hypermentalization to the "double dissociation" of affective and cognitive empathy in female adolescent inpatients with BPD. *J Pers Disorders*, *30*(2), 242–260.

Kane M, & Engle R (2003). Working memory capacity and the control of attention: The contributions of goal neglect, response competition, and task set to Stroop interference. *J Exp Psychol: General*, *312*, 47–70.

Kaplow J, Hall E, Koenen K, Dodge K, & Amaya-Jackson L (2008). Dissociation predicts later attention problems in sexually abused children. *Child Abuse Neglect*, *32*(2), 261–275.

Kaplow J, Howell K, & Layne C (2014). Do circumstances of the death matter? Identifying socioenvironmental risks for grief-related psychopathology in bereaved youth. *J Traum Stress*, *27*, 42–49.

Kaplow J, Layne C, Oosterhoss B, Goldenthal H, Howell K, Wamser-Nanney R et al. (2018). Validation of the Persistent Complex Bereavement Disorder (PCBD) checklist: A developmentally informed assessment tool for bereaved youth. *J Traum Stress*, *31*, 244–254.

Kaplow J, Saxe G, Putnam F, Pynoos R, & Lieberman A (2006). The long-term consequences of early childhood trauma: A case study and discussion. *Psychiatry*, *69*(4), 362–375.

Kaplow J, Shapiro D, Wardecker B, Howell K, Abelson J, Worthman C, & Prossin A (2013). Psychological and environmental correlates of HPA axis functioning in parentally bereaved children: Preliminary findings. *J Traum Stress*, *26*(2), 233–240.

Kar N, & Bastia B (2006). Posttraumatic stress disorder, depression and generalized anxiety disorder in adolescents after a natural disaster: A study of comorbidity. *CP&EMH*, *2*, 17. doi: 10.1186/1745-0179-2-17.

Karagözoğlu N (2017). Attention development activities for social sciences learning products. *Int J Adv Res*, *5*(10), 465–477.

Karukivi M, Joukamaa M, Hautala L, Kaleva O, Haapasalo-Pesu K-M, Liuksila P-R, & Saarijarvi S (2012). Deficit in speech development at the age of 5 years predicts alexithymia in late-adolescent males. *Comprehen Psychia*, *53*, 54–62.

Katz M, Liu C, Schaer M, Parker K, Ottet M, Epps A et al. (2009). Prefrontal plasticity and 665 stress inoculation-induced resilience. *Dev Neurosci*, *31*(4), 293–299.

Kaufman G (1992). *Shame: The power of caring* (3rd ed.). Rochester, VT: Shenkman Books.

Kaufman J, Yang B-Z, Douglas-Palumberi H, Houshyar S, Lipschitz D, Krystal J, & Gelernter J (2004). Social support and serotonin transporter gene moderate depression in maltreated children. *P Natl A Sci USA of the USA*, *101*, 17316–17321.

Kaunhoven R, & Dorjee D (2017). How does mindfulness modulate self-regulation in preadolescent children? An integrative neurocognitive review. *Neurosci Biobehav Rs*, *74*, 163–184.

Kavanaugh B & Holler K (2014). Executive, emotional, and language functioning following childhood maltreatment and the influence of pediatric PTSD. *J Child Adolesc Trauma*, 7, 121–130.

Kawabata Y, Alink L, Tseng W-L, van IJzendoorn M, & Crick N (2011). Maternal and paternal parenting styles associated with relational aggression in children and adolescents: A conceptual analysis and meta-analytic review. *Dev Rev*, *31*, 240–278.

Kawakami K, & Takai-Kawakami K (2015). Teaching, caring, and altruistic behaviors in toddlers. *Infant Behav Dev*, *41*, 108–112.

Kay C, & Green J (2013). Reactive Attachment Disorder following early maltreatment: Systematic Evidence beyond the institution. *J Abnorm Child Psych*, *41*, 571–581.

Kazarian S, Moghnie L, & Martin R (2010). Perceived parental warmth and rejection in childhood as predictors of humor styles and subjective happiness. *Europe's Journal of Psychology*, *6*(3), 71–93.

Keirsey D, & Bates M (1978). *Please understand me*. Del Mar, CA: Prometheus Nemesis.

Kelly J, & Johnston R (2001). The alienated child: A reformulation of parental alienation syndrome. *Fam Court Rev*, *39*(3), 249–267.

Kelly K, & Bailey A (2012). Becoming independent storytellers: Modeling children's development of narrative macrostructure. *First Language*, *33*(1) 68–88.

Kelly P, Viding E, Wallace G, Schaer M, De Brito S, Robustelli B, McCrory E (2013). Cortical thickness, surface area, and gyrification abnormalities in children exposed to maltreatment: neural markers of vulnerability? *Biol Psychiat*, *74*, 845–852.

Kemper K (2016). Brief online mindfulness training: Immediate impact. *CAM*, *22*(1), 75–80.

Kendall P, Beidas R, & Mauro C (2012). *Brief coping cat: The 8-session coping cat workbook*. Ardmore, PA: Workbook Publishing.

Kendall P, Podell J, & Gosch E (2010). *The coping cat parent companion*. Ardmore, PA: Workbook Publishing.

Kendall P, Safford S, Flannery-Schroeder E, & Webb A (2004). Child anxiety treatment: Outcomes in adolescence and impact on substance use and depression at 7.4 year follow-up. *J Consult Clin Psych*, *72*(2), 276–287.

Kendall P, & Treadwell K (2007). The role of self-statements as a mediator in treatment for youth with anxiety disorders. *J Consult Clin Psychol*, *75*, 380–389.

Kerig P & Alexander J (2012). Family matters: Integrating trauma treatment into Functional Family Therapy for traumatized delinquent youth. *J Child Adoles Trauma*, *5*, 205–223.

Kerig P, & Modrowski C (2018). Testing gender-differentiated models of the mechanisms linking polyvictimization and youth offending: Numbing and callousness versus dissociation and borderline traits. *J Trauma Dissociation*, *19*(3), 347–361.

Kerig P, Sink H, Cuellar R, Vanderzee K, & Elfstrom J (2010). Implementing Trauma-Focused CBT with fidelity and flexibility: A family case study. *J Clin Child & Adoles Psychol*, *39*(5), 713–722.

Kerla M (2015). Humor styles as predictors of school success and self-esteem. *Global International Scientific Analytical Project-an international research project: Section Innovational Summaries*. UK, London, March 1, 2015.

Kernberg P, Buhl-Nielsen B, & Normandin L (2007). *Beyond the reflection: The role of the mirror paradigm in clinical practice*. New York: Other Press.

Kernberg P, Chazan S, & Normandin L (1998). The children's play therapy instrument (CPTI): description, development, and reliability studies. *J Psychother Pract Res*, 7, 196–207.

Kerns KA (2000). The CyberCruiser: An investigation of development of prospective memory in children. *J Int Neuropsych Soc*, *6*, 62–70.

Kerns KA, & Brumariu L (2018). Attachment in middle childhood. In J Cassidy, P Shaver (Eds), *Handbook of attachment: Theory, research, and clinical applications* (2nd ed., pp. 349–365). New York: Guilford.

Kerns KA, Mathews B, Koehn A, Williams C, & Siener-Ciesla S (2015). Assessing both safe haven and secure base support in parent–child relationships. *Attach Hum Dev*, *17*(4), 337–353. abstract.

Kerns KA, Tomich P, & Kim P (2006). Normative trends in children's perceptions of availability and utilization of attachment figures in middle childhood. *Soc Dev*, *15*, 1–22.

Kessler R, Avenevoli S, Costello E, Georgiades K, Green J, Gruber M et al. (2012). Prevalence, persistence, and sociodemographic correlates of DSM-IV disorders in the National Comorbidity Survey Replication Adolescent Supplement. *Arch Gen Psychiat*, *29*, 372–380.

Kessler R, Davis C, & Kendler K (1997). Childhood adversity and adult psychiatric disorder in the US National Comorbidity Survey. *Psychol Med*, *27*, 1101–1119.

Khawli E, Fan Y, Aust S, Wirth K, Bonke L, Stevense A et al. (2018). Early life stress modulates neural networks associated with habitual use of reappraisal. *Behav Brain Res*, *337*, 210–217.

Khoury J, Gonzalez A, Levitan R, Masellis M, Basile V, & Atkinson L (2015). Infant emotion regulation strategy moderates relations between self-reported maternal depressive symptoms and infant HPA activity. *Inf Child Dev, 25*(1), 64–83.

Kilmer R, & Gil-Rivas V (2010). Exploring posttraumatic growth in children impacted by Hurricane Katrina: Correlates of the phenomenon and developmental considerations. *Child Dev, 81*, 1211–1227.

Kim J, & Cicchetti D (2003). Social self-efficacy and behavior problems in maltreated children. *J Clin Child Adolesc, 32*, 106–117.

Kim S, & Kochanska G (2017). Relational antecedents and social implications of the emotion of empathy: Evidence from three studies. *Emotion, 17*(6), 981–992.

Kim S, & Kochanska G (2012). Child temperament moderates effects of parent–child mutuality on self-regulation: A relationship-based path for emotionally negative infants. *Child Dev, 83*, 1275–1289.

Kim-Spoon J, Haskett M, Longo G, & Nice R (2012). Longitudinal study of self-regulation, positive parenting, and adjustment problems among physically abused children. *Child Abuse Neglect, 36*, 95–107.

Kimber M, Adham S, Gill S, McTavish J, & MacMillan H (2018). The association between child exposure to intimate partner violence (IPV) and perpetration of IPV in adulthood—A systematic review. *Child Abuse Neglect 76*, 273–286. abstract.

Kim-Cohen J, Caspi A, Taylor A, Williams B, Newcombe R, Craig I et al. (2006). MAOA, maltreatment, and gene-environment interaction predicting children's mental health: New evidence and a meta-analysis. *Mol Psychiatr, 11*, 903–913.

Kimonis E, Bagner D, Linares D, Blake C, & Rodriguez G (2014). Parent Training outcomes among young children with callous-unemotional conduct problems with or at risk for developmental delay. *J Child Fam Stud, 23*, 437–448.

Kimonis E, Frick P, Fazekas H, & Loney B (2006). Psychopathy, aggression, and the processing of emotional stimuli in non-referred girls and boys. *Behav Sci Law, 24*, 21–37.

King A, Ballantyne S, Ratzak A, Knutson S, Russell T, Polalz C, & Breen C (2017). Sibling hostility and externalized symptoms of psychological distress. *J Aggress Maltreat T, 27*(5), 523–540.

King E, Pattwell S, Glatt C, & Lee F (2013). Sensitive periods in fear learning and memory. *Stress, 17*(1), 13–21.

Kinniburgh K, & Blaustein M (2005). Attachment, self-regulation, and competency: A comprehensive framework for intervention with complexly traumatized youth. An unpublished treatment manual.

Kinniburgh K, Blaustein M, & Spinazzola J (2005). Attachment, self-regulation, and competency: A comprehensive intervention framework for children with complex trauma. *Psychiatr Ann, 35*(5), 424–430.

Kinzie J, Boehnlein J, & Sack W (1998). The effects of massive trauma on Cambodian parents and children. In Y Danieli (Ed.), *International handbook of multigenerational legacies of trauma* (pp. 211–221). New York: Plenum Press.

Kipping J, Margulies D, Eickhoff S, Lee A, & Qiu A (2018). Trade-off of cerebello-cortical and cortico-cortical functional networks for planning in 6-year-old children. *NeuroImage, 176*, 510–517.

Kira I, Lewandowski L, Yoon J, Somers C, & Chiodo L (2012). The linear and nonlinear associations between multiple types of trauma and IQ discrepancy indexes in African American and Iraqi refugee adolescents. *J Child Adolesc Trauma, 5*, 47–62.

Kirmayer L, Young A, & Hayton B (1995). The cultural context of anxiety disorders. The *Psychiatric Clinics of North America, 18*(3), 503–521.

Kiser L, Stover C, Navalta C, Dorado J, Vogel J, Abdul-Adil J et al. (2014). Effects of the child–perpetrator relationship on mental health outcomes of child abuse: It's (not) all relative. *Child Abuse Neglect, 38*, 1083–1093.

Kisiel C, Fehrenbach T, Small L, & Lyons J (2009). Assessment of complex trauma exposure, responses and service needs among children and adolescents in child welfare. *J Child Adolesc Trauma, 2*, 143–160.

Klasen F, Oettingen G, Daniels J, Post M, Hoyer C, & Adam H (2010). Posttraumatic resilience in former Ugandan child soldiers. *Child Dev, 81*, 1096–1113.

Klaus M (2009). Commentary: An early, short, and useful sensitive period in the human infant. *Birth, 36*(2), 110–112.

Klein A (1985). Humor comprehension and humor appreciation of cognitively oriented humor: A study of kindergarten children. *Child Study J, 15*, 223–234.

Klein T, DeVoe E, Miranda-Julian C, & Linas K (2009). Young children's responses to September 11th: The New York City experience. *Inf Mental Hlth J, 30*(1), 1–22.

Klein Velderman M, Bakermans-Kranenburg M, Juffer F, & van IJzendoorn M (2006). Effects of attachment-based interventions on maternal sensitivity and infant attachment: Differential susceptibility of highly reactivity infants. *J Fam Psychol, 20*, 266–274.

Klein Velderman M, Pannebakker F, Vliet W, & Reijneveld S (2018). Prevention of divorce-related problems in Dutch 4 to 8-year-olds: Cultural adaptation and pilot study of the Children of Divorce Intervention Program. *Res Social Work Prac, 28*(4), 415–427.

Kleindienst N, Priebe K, Gorg N, Dyer A, Steil R, Lyssenko L et al. (2016). State dissociation moderates response to Dialectical Behavior Therapy for posttraumatic stress disorder in women with and without borderline personality disorder. *Eur J Psychotraumato*, 7(1), 30375. dx.doi.org/10.3402/ejpt.v7.30375.

Klenberg L, Korkman M, & Lahti-Nuutila P (2001). Differential development of attention and executive functions in 3- to 12-year-old Finnish children. *Dev Neuropsychol*, *20*, 407–428.

Kletter H, & Carrion V (2018). Posttraumatic Stress Disorder in youth exposed to war and terror. In E Vermetten, A Germain, T Neylan (Eds), *Sleep and combat-related Post Traumatic Stress Disorder* (pp. 363–372). New York: Springer.

Kletter H, Weems C, & Carrion V (2009). Guilt and posttraumatic stress symptoms in child victims of interpersonal violence. *Clin Child Psychol P*, *14*(1), 71–83.

Kliethermes M, Nanney R, Cohen J, & Mannarino A (2013). Trauma-focused cognitive behavioral therapy. In J Ford, C Courtois (Eds), *Treating Complex Traumatic Stress Disorders in children and adolescents* (pp. 184–202). New York: Guilford.

Klomek B, Sourander A, & Gould M (2010). The association of suicide and bullying in childhood to young adulthood: A review of cross-sectional and longitudinal research findings. *Can J Psychiatry*, *55*(5), 282–288.

Klomek B, Sourander A, Niemelä S, Kumpulainen K, Piha J, Tamminen T et al. (2009). Childhood bullying behaviors as a risk for severe suicide attempts and completed suicides. *J Am Acad Child Psy*, *48*(3), 254–261.

Knox J (2003). *Archetype, attachment, analysis: Jungian psychology and the emergent mind.* New York: Brunner-Routledge.

Knowles M (2014). Social rejection increases perspective-taking. *J Exp Soc Psychol*, *55*, 126–132.

Kobak R, Rosenthal N, Zajac K, & Madsen S (2011). Adolescent attachment hierarchies and the search for an adult pair-bond. In M Scharf, O Mayseless (Eds), *Attachment in adolescence: New directions in child and adolescent development* (No. 117, 57–72). New York: Wiley.

Kochanska G, Aksan N, & Joy M (2007). Children's fearfulness as a moderator of parenting in early socialization: Two longitudinal studies. *Dev Psychol*, *43*, 222–237.

Kochanska G, Barry R, Jimenez N, Hollatz A, & Woodard J (2009). Guilt and effortful control: Two mechanisms that prevent disruptive developmental trajectories. *J Pers Soc Psychol*, *97*(2), 322–333.

Kochanska G, Gross J, Lin M, & Nichols K (2002). Guilt in young children: Development, determinants, and relations with a broader system of standards. *Child Dev*, *73*, 461–482.

Kochanska G, & Kim S (2014). A complex interplay among the parent–child relationship, effortful control, and internalized, rule-compatible conduct in young children: Evidence from two studies. *Dev Psychol*, *50*(1), 8–21.

Kochanska G, & Kim S (2013). Early attachment organization with both parents and future behavior problems: From infancy to middle childhood. *Child Dev*, *84*, 283–296.

Kochanska G, & Kim S (2012). Toward a new understanding of legacy of early attachments for future antisocial trajectories: Evidence from two longitudinal studies. *Dev Psychopathol*, *24*, 783–806.

Kochanska G, Kim S, Barry R, Philibert R (2011). Children's genotypes interact with maternal responsive care in predicting children's competence: Diathesis-stress or differential susceptibility? *Dev Psychopathol*, *23*, 605–611.

Kochanska G, Kim S, Boldt L, & Nordling J (2014). Promoting toddlers' positive social-emotional outcomes in low-income families: A play-based experimental study. *J Clin Child Adolesc Psychol*, *42*(5), 700–712.

Kochanska G, Philibert R, & Barry R (2009). Interplay of genes and early mother and child relationship in the development of self-regulation from toddler to preschool age. *J Child Psychol Psyc*, *50*, 1331–1338.

Koenen K (2007). Genetics of posttraumatic stress disorder: Review and recommendations for future studies. *J Traum Stress*, *20*, 737–750.

Koenen K (2006). Developmental epidemiology of PTSD: Self-regulation as a central mechanism. *Ann NY Acad Sci*, *1071*, 255–266.

Koenen K, Moffitt T, Caspi A, Gregory A, Harrington H, & Poulton R (2008). The developmental mental disorder histories of adults with posttraumatic stress disorder: A prospective longitudinal birth cohort study. *J Abnorm Psychol*, *117*, 460–466.

Köhnke MD (2008). Approach to the genetics of alcoholism: A review based on pathophysiology. *Biomed Pharmacology*, *75*, 160–177.

Kohrt B, Worthman C, Ressler K, Mercer K, Upadhaya N, Koirala S et al. (2015). Cross-cultural gene—environment interactions in depression, posttraumatic stress disorder, and the cortisol awakening response: FKBP5 polymorphisms and childhood trauma in South Asia. *Int Rev Psychiatr*, *27*(3), 180–196.

Kokkinos C, Voulgaridou I, & Markos A (2016). Personality and relational aggression: Moral disengagement and friendship quality as mediators. *Pers Indiv Differ*, *95*, 74–79.

Kokkonen P, Veijola J, Karvonen J, Läksy K, Jokelainen J, Järvelin M et al. (2003). Ability to speak at the age of 1 year and alexithymia 30 years later. *J Psychosom Res*, *54*, 491–495. abstract.

Kolubinski D, Nikčević A, Lawrence J, & Spada M (2017). The metacognitions about self-critical rumination questionnaire. *J Affect Disorders, 220*, 129–138.

Konrath S, O'Brien E, & Hsing C (2011). Changes in dispositional empathy in American college students over time: A meta-analysis. *Pers Soc Psychol Rev, 15(2)*, 180–198.

Kopp CB (1982). Antecedents of self-regulation: A developmental perspective. *Devel Psych, 18*(2), 199–214.

Koppel J & Berntsen D (2014). The reminiscence bump in autobiographical memory and for public events: A comparison across different cueing methods. *Memory, 24*(1), 44–62.

Korn C, Sharot T, Walter H, Heekeren H, & Dolan R (2014). Depression is related to an absence of optimistically biased belief updating about future life events. *Psychol Med, 44*, 579–592.

Korpilahti P, Kaljonen A, & Jansson-Verkasalo E (2016). Identification of biological and environmental risk factors for language delay: The Let's Talk STEPS study. *Infant Behav Dev 42*, 27–35. abstract.

Koss K & Gunnar M (2018). Annual Research Review: Early adversity, the hypothalamic-pituitary-adrenocortical axis, and child psychopathology. *J Child Psychol Psyc*, 59(4), 327–346.

Koss K, Hostinar C, Donzella B, & Gunnar M (2014). Social deprivation and the HPA axis in early development. *Psychoneuroendocrin, 50*, 1–13.

Koss M, Figueredo A, Bell I, Tharan M, & Tromp S (1996). Traumatic memory characteristics: A cross-validated mediational model of response to rape among employed women. *J Abnorm Psychol, 53*(3), 422–423.

Kozlowska K, & Elliott B (2017). Don't forget the siblings: School-aged siblings of children presenting to mental health services show at-risk patterns of attachment. *Clin Child Psychol P, 22*(2) 245–259.

Krakow B, Sandoval D, Schrader R, Keuhne B, McBride L, Yau C, & Tandberg D (2001). Treatment of chronic nightmares in adjudicated adolescent girls in a residential facility. *J Adolescent Health, 29*(2), 94–100.

Kraemer H, Lowe K, & Kupfer D (2005). *To your health*. New York, NY: Oxford University Press.

Kramer T, Caldarella P, Christensen L, & Shatzer R (2010). Social-emotional learning in kindergarten classrooms: Evaluation of the Strong Start curriculum. *ECEJ, 37*(4), 303–398.

Krammer S, Kleim B, Simmen-Janevska K, & Maercker A (2015). Childhood trauma and Complex Posttraumatic Stress Disorder Symptoms in older adults: A study of direct effects and social-interpersonal factors as potential mediators. *J Trauma Dissociation, 17*(5), 593–607.

Krause F, & Rohlfing K (2016). Poster: Shy 19-month-olds exhibit their perspective-taking abilities earlier by using pragmatically different means than their peers. downloaded 2-27-16, www.researchgate.net/publication/289745705.

Kretschmer T, Sentse M, Dijkstra J, & Veenstra R (2014). The interplay between peer rejection and acceptance in preadolescence and early adolescence, serotonin transporter gene, and antisocial behavior: the TRAILS study. *Merrill-Palmer Q, 60*(2), 193–216.

Kristensen P, Weisaeth L, & Heir T (2010). Predictors of complicated grief after a natural disaster: A population study two years after the 2004 South-East Asian tsunami. *Death Stud, 34*, 137–150.

Krueger R, Hicks B, Patrick C, Carlson S, Iacono W, & McGue M (2002). Etiologic connections among substance dependence, antisocial behavior and personality: Modeling the externalizing spectrum. *J Abnorm Psychol, 111*, 411–424.

Kronenberg M, Hansel T, Brennan A, Lawrason B, Osofsky H, & Osofsky J (2010). Children of Katrina: Lessons learned about post-disaster symptoms and recovery patterns. *Child Dev, 81*, 1241–1259.

Kross E, Gard D, Deldin P, Clifton J, & Ayduk O (2012). "Asking why" from a distance: Its cognitive and emotional consequences for people with Major Depressive Disorder. *J Abnorm Psychol, 121*(3), 559–569.

Kryski K, Dougherty L, Dyson M, Olino T, Laptook R, Klein D, & Hayden E (2013). Effortful control and parenting: Associations with HPA axis reactivity in early childhood. *Developm Sci, 16*(4) 531–541.

Kuhlman K, Geiss E, Vargas I, & Lopez-Duran N (2015). Differential associations between childhood trauma subtypes and adolescent HPA axis functioning. *Psychoneuroendocrino, 54*, 103–114. abstract.

Kuhlman K, Vargas I, Geiss E, & Lopez-Duran N (2016). Age of trauma onset and HPA axis dysregulation among trauma-exposed youth. *J Traum Stress, 29*, 1–8.

Kuhn D (2000). Adolescent thought processes. In A Kazdin (Ed-in-Chief), *Encyclopedia of psychology* (pp. 52–59). Washington, DC/New York: APA/Oxford University Press.

Kuhn D, & Franklin S (2008). The second decade: What develops (and how)? In W Damon, R Lerner (Eds), *Child and adolescent development: An advanced course (pp.* 517–550). New York: Wiley.

Kuhnert R, Begeer S, Fink E, & de Rosnay M (2017). Gender-differentiated effects of theory of mind, emotion understanding, and social preference on prosocial behavior development: A longitudinal study. *J Exp Child Psychol 154*, 13–27.

Kurth E, Kennedy H, Stutz E, Kesselring A, Fornaro I, & Spichiger E (2014). Responding to a crying infant: You do not learn it overnight—A phenomenological study. *Midwifery, 30*, 742–749. abstract.

Kuttler F, Parker J, & La Greca A (2002). Developmental and gender differences in preadolescents' judgments of the veracity of gossip. *Merrill-Palmer Q, 48*, 105–132.

Kuwert P, Glaesmer H, Eichhorn S, Grundke E, Pietrzak R, Freyberger H, & Klauer T (2014). Long-term effects of conflict-related sexual violence compared with non-sexual war trauma in female World War II survivors: A matched pairs study. *Arch Sex Behav, 43*(6), 1059–1064.

LaFreniere L, & Newman M (submitted). Exposing worry's deceit: Percentage of untrue worries in generalized anxiety disorder treatment. Manuscript submitted for publication.

LaFreniere L, & Newman M (2016). A brief ecological momentary intervention for generalized anxiety disorder: A randomized controlled trial of The Worry Outcome Journal. *Depress Anxiety*, 33, 829–839.

Lagace-Seguin D, & d' Entremont, M (2006). The role of child negative affect in the relations between parenting styles and play. *Early Child Dev & Care, 176*, 461–477.

Lagercrantz H (2016). Connecting the brain of the child form synapses to screen-based activity. *Acta Paediatrica, 105*(4), 352–357.

La Greca A, Danzi B, & Chan S (2017). DSM-5 and ICD-11 as competing models of PTSD in preadolescent children exposed to a natural disaster: Assessing validity and co-occurring symptomatology, *Europ J Psychotraumatol, 8*, 1, 1310591, doi: 10.1080/20008198.2017.1310591.

La Greca A, Lai B, Llabre M, Silverman W, Vernberg E, & Prinstein M (2013). Children's post disaster trajectories of PTS symptoms: Predicting chronic distress. *Child Youth Care For, 42*, 351–369.

La Greca A, Silverman W, Lai B, & Jaccard J (2010). Hurricane-related exposure experiences and stressors, other life events, and social support: Concurrent and prospective impact on children's persistent posttraumatic stress symptoms. *J Consult Clin Psych, 78*, 794–805.

La Guardia J, Ryan R, Couchman C, & Deci E (2000). Within-person variation in security of attachment: A self-determination theory perspective on attachment, need fulfillment, and wellbeing. *J Pers Soc Psychol, 79*(3), 367.

Lai B, Osborne M, Piscitello J, Self-Brown S, & Kelley M (2018). The relationship between social support and posttraumatic stress symptoms among youth exposed to a natural disaster, *Eur J Psychotraumatol, 9*, sup2, doi: 10.1080/20008198.2018.1450042.

Laible D, Carlo G, & Raffaelli M (2000). The differential relations of parent and peer attachment to adolescent adjustment. *Journal of Youth and Adolescence, 29*, 45–59.

Laible D, Eye J, & Carlo G (2008). Dimensions of conscience in mid-adolescence: Links with social behavior, parenting, and temperament. *J Youth Adolescence, 37*, 875–887.

Laird R, Jordan K, Dodge K, Pettit G, & Bates J (2001). Peer rejection in childhood, involvement with antisocial peers in early adolescence, and the development of externalizing behavior problems. *Dev Psychopathol, 13*, 337–354.

Lamb K, Humphreys C, & Hegarty K (2018). "Your behaviour has consequences": Children and young people's perspectives on reparation with their fathers after domestic violence. *Child Youth Serv Rev, 88*, 164–169.

Lambrick D, Stoner L, Grigg R, & Faulkner J (2016). Effects of continuous and intermittent exercise on executive function in children aged 8–10 years. *Psychophysiology, 53*(9), 1335–1342.

Lamm C, Troller-Renfree S, Zeanah C, Nelson C, & Fox N (2018). Impact of early institutionalization on attention mechanisms underlying the inhibition of a planned action. *Neuropsychologia, 117*, 339–346.

Lang A, Strauss J, Bomyea J, Bormann J, Hickman S, Good R, & Essex M (2012). The theoretical and empirical basis for meditation as an intervention for PTSD. *Behav Modif, 36*(6), 759–786.

Lange C, & Irle E (2004). Enlarged amygdala volume and reduced hippocampal volume in young women with major depression. *Psychol Med, 34*, 1059–1064.

Langman P (2015). *School shooters*. New York: Rowman & Littlefield.

Lanius R (2015). Trauma-related dissociation and altered states of consciousness: a call for clinical, treatment, and neuroscience research. *Eur J Psychotraumato, 6*, 27905 doi.org/10.3402/ejpt.v6.27905.

Lanius R, Bluhm R, Coupland N, Hegadoren K, Rowe B et al. (2010). Default mode network connectivity as a predictor of posttraumatic stress disorder symptom severity in acutely traumatized subjects. *Acta Psychiat Scand, 121*, 33–40.

Lanius R, Brand B, Vermetten E, Frewen P, & Spiegel D (2012). The dissociative subtype of posttraumatic stress disorder: Rationale, clinical and neurobiological evidence, and implications. *Depress Anxiety, 29*(8), 701–709.

Lanius R, Frewen P, Nazarov A, & McKinnon M (2014). A social-cognitive-neuroscience approach to PTSD: Clinical and research perspectives. In U Lanius, S Paulsen, F Corrigan (Eds), *Neurobiology and treatment of traumatic dissociation: Toward an embodied self* (pp. 69–80). New York: Springer.

Lanius R, Frewen P, Tursich M, Jetly R, & McKinnon M (2015). Restoring large-scale brain networks in PTSD and related disorders: a proposal for neuroscientifically-informed treatment interventions, *Eur J Psychotraumato, 6:1*, 27313. doi: 10.3402/ejpt.v6.27313.

Lanktree C, & Briere J (2013). Integrative Treatment of Complex Trauma (ITCT) for children and adolescents. In JD Ford and CA Courtois, *Treating complex traumatic stress disorders with children and adolescents: An evidence-based guide* (pp. 143–161). New York: Guilford.

Lanktree C, & Briere J (2008). Integrative treatment of complex trauma for children (ITCT-C): A guide for the treatment of multiply-traumatized children aged eight to twelve years. Unpublished manual (© Lanktree & Briere, 2008).

Lanktree C, Briere J, Godbout N, Hodges M, Chen K, Trimm L et al. (2012). Treating multi-traumatized, socially-marginalized children: Results of a naturalistic treatment outcome study. *J Aggress Maltreat T, 21*, 813–828. abstract.

Lanza S, Rhoades B, Nix R, Greenberg M, & the Conduct Problems Prevention Research Group (2010). Modeling the interplay of multilevel risk factors for future academic and behavior problems: A person-centered approach. *Dev Psychopathol, 22*(2), 313–335.

Laor N, Wolmer L, & Cohen D (2001). Mothers' functioning and children's symptoms 5 years after a SCUD missile attack. *Am J Psychiatry, 158*, 1020–1026.

Laor N, Wolmer L, Kora M, Yucel D, Spirman S, & Yazgan Y (2002). Posttraumatic, dissociative and grief symptoms in Turkish children exposed to the 1999 earthquakes. *J Nerv and Ment Disease, 190*(12), 824–832.

Laor N, Wolmer L, Mayes L, Gershon A, Weizman R, & Cohen D (1997). Israeli preschool children under Scuds: A 30-month follow-up. *J Am Acad Chld Psy, 36*, 349–356.

Laos G, Pham-Scottez A, Cailhol L, Perez-Diaz F, Corcos M, & Speranze M (2013). Axis II comorbidity of borderline personality disorder in adolescents. *Psychopathology, 46*, 172–175.

Larkin R (2009). The Columbine legacy: Rampage shootings as political acts. *American Behavioral Scientist, 52*(9), 1309–1326.

Larrañaga E, Yubero S, Ovejero A, & Navarro R (2016). Loneliness, parent–child communication and cyberbullying victimization among Spanish youths. *Comput Hum Behav, 65*, 1–8. abstract doi.org/10.1016/j.chb.2016.08.015.

Larsen S, Stirman S, Smith B, & Resick P (2016). Symptom exacerbations in trauma-focused treatments: Associations with treatment outcome and non-completion. *Behav Res Ther*, 77, 68–77.

Lassri D, Luyten P, Fonagy P, & Shahar G (2018). Undetected scars? Self-criticism, attachment, and romantic relationships among otherwise well-functioning childhood sexual abuse survivors. *Psychol Trauma-US, 10*(1), 121–129.

Lataster J, Myin-Germeys I, Lieb R, Wittchen H, Van Os J et al. (2012). Evidence for the behavioral sensitization hypothesis of psychosis: An 8-year longitudinal cohort study investigating the effects of cascading psychological stressors on psychosis outcome. *Acta Psychiat Scand, 125*(5), 388–399.

Lau J, & Pine D (2008). Elucidating risk mechanisms of gene-environment interactions on pediatric anxiety: Integrating findings from neuroscience. *Eur Arch Psy clin N, 258*, 97–106.

Laube C, Suleiman A, Johnson M, Dahl R, & van den Bos W (2017). Dissociable effects of age and testosterone on adolescent impatience. *Psychoneuroendocrino, 80*, 162–169. abstract.

Laufer A, & Solomon Z (2009). Gender differences in PTSD in Israeli youth exposed to terror attacks. *J Interpers Violence, 24*, 959–976.

Lauterbach D, & Vrana S (2001). The relationship among personality variables, exposure to traumatic events, and severity of posttraumatic stress symptoms. *J Traum Stress. 14*, 29–45.

Lavi I, Gard A, Hagan M, van Horn P, & Lieberman A (2015). Child–Parent Psychotherapy examined in a pernatal sample: Depression, posttrauamtic stress symptoms and child-rearing attitudes. *J Soc Clin Psychol, 34*(1), 64–82.

Lawal A, & Idemudia E (2017). Gender difference, class level and the role of internet addiction and loneliness on sexual compulsivity among secondary school students. *Int J Adolesc Youth*, doi.org/10.1080/02673843.2017.1406380.

Lawrence J, & Fauerbach J (2003). Personality, coping, chronic stress, social support and PTSD symptoms among adult burn survivors: A path analysis. *J Burn Care Rehabil, 24*, 63–72.

Layne C, Kaplow J, Oosterhoff B, Hill R, & Pynoos R (2017). The interplay between posttraumatic stress and grief reactions in traumatically bereaved adolescents: When trauma, bereavement, and adolescence converge. *Adolescent Psychiat*, 7, 220–239.

Layne C, Saltzman W, Poppleton L, Burlingame G, Pašalić A, Duraković E et al. (2008). Effectiveness of a school-based group psychotherapy program for war-exposed adolescents: A randomized controlled trial. *JAACAP, 47*(9), 1048–62.

Lazarus R, & Folkman S (1987). Transactional theory and research on emotions and coping. *European J Pers, 1*, 141–169.

Leaf M (2011). *The story of Ferdinand*. London: Penguin Books. (original 1936, New York: Viking Press).

Lebel C, Walker L, Leemans A, Phillips L, & Beaulieu C (2008). Microstructural maturation of the human brain from childhood to adulthood. *NeuroImage, 40*, 1044–1055.

LeDoux, LE (2003). The emotional brain, fear, and the amygdala. *Cell Mol Neurobiol, 23*, 727–737.

Lee C, Seo D, Torabi M, Lohrmann D, & Song T (2018). Longitudinal trajectory of the relationship between self-esteem and substance use from adolescence to young adulthood. *J School Health, 88*(1), 9–14.

Lee E, Zhou Q, Eisenberg N, & Wang Y (2013). Bidirectional relations between temperament and parenting styles in Chinese children. *Int J Behav Dev*, *37*(1) 57–67.

Lee M, Cohen S, Stuber M, & Nader K (1994). Parent–child interactions with pediatric bone marrow transplant patients. *J Psychosoc Oncol*, *12*(4), 43–60.

Lee S, Altschul I, & Gershoff E (2013). Does warmth moderate longitudinal associations between maternal spanking and child aggression in early childhood? *Dev Psychol*, *49*, 2017–2028. abstract.

Lee-Rowland L, Barry C, Gillen C, & Hansen L (2016). How do different dimensions of adolescent narcissism impact the relation between callous-unemotional traits and self-reported aggression? *Agressive Behav*, *43*(1), 14–25.

Lemche E, Klann-Delius G, Koch R, & Joraschky P (2004). Mentalizing language development in a longitudinal attachment sample: Implications for alexithymia. *Psychother Psychosom*, *73*, 366–374. abstract.

Leung C, Miller A, Kaciroti N, Chen Y, Rosenblum K, & Lumeng K (2015). Low-income pre-schoolers with higher temperamental surgency enjoy and respond more to food, mediating the path to higher body mass index. *Pediatric Obesity*, *11*(3), 181–186. abstract.

Lev-Ari L, Baumgarten-Katz I, & Zohar A (2014). Mirror Mirror on the wall: How women learn body dissatisfaction. *Eat Behav*, *15*(3), 397–402.

Leve L, Fisher P, & Chamberlain P (2009). Multidimensional treatment foster care as a preventive intervention to promote resiliency among youth in the child welfare system. *J Pers*, 77(6), 1869–1902.

Levendosky A, Bogat G, Huth-Bocks A, Rosenblum K, & von Eye A (2011). The effects of domestic violence on the stability of attachment from infancy to preschool. *J Clin Child Adolesc*, *40*(3), 398–410.

Levendosky A, & Graham-Bermann S (2001). Parenting in battered women: The effects of domestic violence on women and their children. *J Fam Violence*, *16*(2), 171–192.

Levendosky A, Huth-Bocks A, Semel M, & Shapiro D (2002). Trauma symptoms in preschool-age children exposed to domestic violence. *J Interpers Violence*, *17*(2), 150–164.

Levendosky A, Huth-Bocks A, Shapiro D, & Semel M (2003). The impact of domestic violence on the maternal–child relationship and preschool-age children's functioning. *J Fam Psychol*, *17*, 275–287.

Leventon J, Stevens J, & Bauer P (2014). Development in the neurophysiology of emotion processing and memory in school-age children. *Develop Cognit Neurosci*, *10*, 21–33.

Levin M, Luoma J, Vilardaga R, Lillis J, Nobles R, & Hayes S (2015). Examining the role of psychological inflexibility, perspective-taking, and empathic concern in generalized prejudice. *J Appl Soc Psychol*, *46*(3), 180–191.

Levine P (2010). *In an unspoken voice: How the body releases trauma and restores goodness*. Berkeley, CA: North Atlantic Books.

Levine P, & Frederick A (1997). *Waking the tiger: Healing trauma through the innate capacity to transform overwhelming experiences*. Berkeley, CA: North Atlantic Books.

Lev-Wiesel R, & Zohar G (2014). The role of dissociation in self-Injurious behavior among female adolescents who were sexually abused. *J Child Sex Abus*, *23*, 824–839.

Levy B, & Wagner A (2011). Cognitive control and right ventrolateral prefrontal cortex: reflexive reorienting, motor inhibition, and action updating. *Ann NY Acad Sci*, *1224*, 40–62.

Levy DM (1938). Release therapy in young children. *Psychiatry*, *1*, 387–390.

Levy K, Johnson B, Clouthier T, Scala J, & Temes C (2015). An attachment theoretical framework for personality disorders. *Can Psychol*, *56*(2), 197–207.

Lewis M (1995). Embarrassment: The emotion of self-exposure and evaluation. In J Tangney, K Fischer (Eds), *Self-conscious emotions: The psychology of shame, guilt, embarrassment, and pride* (pp. 198–218). New York: Guilford.

Lewis M, Takai-Kawakami K, Kawakami K, & Sullivan M (2010). Cultural difference in emotional responses to success and failure. *Int J Behav Dev*, *34*(1), 53–61.

Lewis-Morrarty E, Degnan K, Chronis-Tuscano A, Pine D, Henderson H, & Fox N (2015). Infant attachment security and early childhood behavioral inhibition interact to predict adolescent social anxiety symptoms. *Child Dev*, *86*(2), 598–613.

Lewis-Morrarty E, Dozier M, Bernard K, Terracciano S, & Moore S (2012). Cognitive flexibility and theory of mind outcomes among foster children: Preschool follow-up results of a randomized clinical trial. *J Adolesc Health*, *51*(2 Suppl), S17–S22. abstract. doi: 10.1016/j.jadohealth.2012.05.005.

Li C, Sun Y, Ho M, You J, Shaver P, & Wang Z (2016). State narcissism and aggression: The mediating roles of anger and hostile attributional bias. *Agressive Behav*, *42*, 333–345.

Li L, Lin X, Hinshaw S, Du H, Qin S, & Fang X (2017a). Longitudinal associations between oppositional defiant symptoms and interpersonal relationships among Chinese children. *J Abnorm Child Psychol*, *46*(6), 1267–1281.

Li N, Wang Y, Zhao X, Gao Y, Song M, Yu L et al. (2015). Long-term effect of early life stress from earthquake exposure on working memory in adulthood. *Neuropsych Dis Treat*, *11*, 2959–2965.

Li Y, Grabell A, Wakschlag L, Huppert T, & Perlman S (2017b). The neural substrates of cognitive flexibility are related to individual differences in preschool irritability: A fNIRS investigation. *Dev Cogn Neuros-Neth, 25*, 138–144.

Lieberman A (2004). Child-parent psychotherapy: A relationship based approach to the treatment of mental health disorders in infancy and early childhood. In A Sameroff, S McDonough, K Rosenblum (Eds), *Treating parent–infant relationship problems: Strategies for intervention* (pp. 97–122). New York: Guilford.

Lieberman A (1997). Reactive Attachment Deprivation/Maltreatment Disorder of Infancy and Early Childhood. In A Lieberman, S Wieder, E Fenichel (Eds), *The DC:0–3 Casebook*. Washington, DC: Zero to Three: National Center for Infants, Toddlers, and Families.

Lieberman A, Compton N, Van Horn P, & Ghosh Ippen C (2003). Losing a parent to death in the early years: Guidelines for the treatment of traumatic bereavement in infancy. Washington, DC: Zero to Three Press.

Lieberman A, Ghosh Ippen C, & Van Horn P (2015). *Don't hit my mommy!: A manual for child-parent psychotherapy with young witnesses of family violence* (2nd ed.). Washington, DC: Zero to Three Press.

Lieberman A, Ghosh Ippen C, & Van Horn P (2006). Child–parent psychotherapy: 6-month follow-up of a randomized control trial. *J Am Acad Chld Psy, 45*, 913–918.

Lieberman A, & Van Horn P (2011). *Psychotherapy with infants and young children: Repairing the effects of stress and trauma on early attachment*. New York: Guilford.

Lieberman A, & Van Horn P (2008). *Psychotherapy with infants and young children*. New York: Guilford.

Lieberman A, & Van Horn P (2005). *"Don't hit my mommy!": A manual for child-parent psychotherapy with young witnesses of family violence*. Washington, DC: Zero to Three Press.

Lieberman A, Van Horn P, & Ghosh Ippen C (2006). Child–Parent Psychotherapy: 6-Month follow-up of a randomized control trial. *J Am Acad Chld Psy, 45*(8), 913–918.

Lieberman A, Van Horn P, & Ghosh Ippen C (2005). Toward evidence-based treatment: Child-parent psychotherapy with preschoolers exposed to marital violence. *J Am Acad Chld Psy, 44*, 1241–1248.

Lieberman M (2010). Social-cognitive neuroscience. In S Fiske, D Gilbert, G Lindzey (Eds), *Handbook of social psychology* (5th ed., pp. 143–193). New York: McGraw-Hill.

Lieberman M, Eisenberger N, Crockett M, Tom S, Pfeifer J, & Way B (2007). Putting feelings into words: Affect labeling disrupts amygdala activity in response to affective stimuli. *Psychol Sci, 18*(5), 421–428.

Lim L, Ng T, Chua H, Chiam P, Won V, Lee T et al. (2005). Generalized anxiety disorder in Singapore: prevalence, comorbidity and risk factors in a multi-ethnic population. *Soc Psychiatry Epidemiol, 40*, 972–979.

Lim X, & Qu, L (2016). The effect of single-session mindfulness training on preschool children's attentional control. *Mindfulness, 8*(2), 300–310.

Lindley P, & Walker S (1993). Theoretical and methodological differentiation of moderation and mediation. *Nursing Research, 42*(5), 276–279.

Lindsey R (October 11, 2017). Climate conditions behind deadly October 2017 wildfires in California. www.climate.gov/news-features/event-tracker/climate-conditions-behind-deadly-october-2017-wildfires-california. Downloaded 10-23-17.

Lindstrom M, & Rosvall M (2017). Parental separation in childhood and self-reported psychological health: A population-based study. *Psychiat Res, 246*, 783–788.

Linehan M (1993a). *Cognitive behavioral treatment of borderline personality disorder*. New York: Guilford.

Linehan M (1993b). *Skills training manual for treating borderline personality disorder*. New York: Guilford.

Linehan M, Bohus M, & Lynch T (2007). Dialectical behavior therapy for pervasive emotion dysregulation: Theoretical and practical underpinnings. In JJ Gross (Ed.), *Handbook of emotion regulation* (pp. 581–606). New York: Guilford.

Lipton B, & Fosha D (2011). Attachment as a transformative process in AEDP: Operationalizing the intersection of attachment theory and affective neuroscience. *J Psychother Integra, 21*(3), 253–279.

Litman L, Costantino G, Waxman R, Sanabria-Velez C, Rodriguez-Guzman V, Lampon-Velez A et al. (2015). Relationship between peer victimization and Posttraumatic Stress among primary school children. *J Traum Stress, 28*, 348–354.

Litt L (2013). Clinical decision-making in the treatment of complex PTSD and substance misuse. *J Clin Psychol, 69*, 534–542.

Liu J, Qiao X, Dong F, & Raine A (2018). The Chinese version of the cognitive, affective, and somatic empathy scale for children: Validation, gender invariance and associated factors. *PLoS ONE 13*(5): e0195268.

Liu P, Wang L, Cao C, Wang R, Zhang J, Zhang B et al. (2014). The underlying dimensions of DSM-5 posttraumatic stress disorder symptoms in an epidemiological sample of Chinese earthquake survivors. *J Anxiety Disord, 28*, 345–351.

Liu S-T, & Chen S-H (2015). Community study on the relationship of posttraumatic cognitions to internalizing and externalizing psychopathology in Taiwanese children and adolescents. *J Abnorm Child Psychol, 43*, 1475–1484.

Liu W, Wan Y-H, Tao F-B, & Hao J-H (2017). Mediating effect of social support on relationship between childhood abuses and non-suicidal self-injuries in adolescents. *Chin Ment Health J*, *31*(3), 230–234. abstract.

Loeber R, Farrington D, & Petechuk D (2003). Child delinquency: Early intervention and prevention. Child Delinquency Bulletin Series. Washington, DC: US Department of Justice.

Loizou E (2005). Infant humor: The theory of the absurd and the empowerment theory. *Int J Early Years Educ*, *13*(1), 43–53.

Loizou E, & Kyriakou M (2016). Young children's appreciation and production of verbal and visual humor. *Humor*, *29*(1), 99–124.

Lombardi C, Casey B, Thomson D, Nguyen H, & Dearing E (2017). Maternal support of young children's planning and spatial concept learning as predictors of later math (and reading) achievement. *Early Child Res Q*, *41*, 114–125.

London M (2003). Antecedents and consequences of self-verification: Implications for individual and group development. *Hum Resour Dev Rev*, *2*(3), 273–293.

Longe O, Maratos F, Gilbert P, Evans G, Volker F, Rockliff H, & Rippon G (2010). Having a word with yourself: Neural correlates of self-criticism and self-reassurance. *NeuroImage*, *49*, 1849–1856. abstract.

Longobardi E, Spataro P, & Colonnesi C (2018). Maternal communicative functions and mind-mindedness at 16 months as predictors of children's internal and non-internal language at 20 months. *Infant Behav Dev 50*, 52–63.

Lonigan C, Lerner M, Goodrich J, Farrington A, & Allan D (2016). Executive function of Spanish-speaking language-minority preschoolers: Structure and relations with early literacy skills and behavioral outcomes. *J Exp Child Psychol*, *144*, 46–65.

Lovett B, & Sheffield R (2007). Affective empathy deficits in aggressive children and adolescents: A critical review. *Clin Psychol Rev*, *27*, 1–13.

Luby J, Belden A, Sullivan J, Hayen R, McCadney A, & Spitznagel E (2009). Shame and guilt in preschool depression: Evidence for elevations in self-conscious emotions in depression as early as age 3. *J Child Psychol Psyc*, *50*(9), 1156–1166.

Lucassen N, Tharner A, Prinzie P, Verhulst F, Jongerling J, Bakermans-Kranenburg M et al. (2017). Paternal history of depression or anxiety disorder and infant–father attachment. *Inf Child Dev*, *27*(2), e2070. doi.org/10.1002/icd.2070.

Lucenet J, Blaye A, Chevalier N, & Kray J (2014). Cognitive control and language across the life span: Does labeling improve reactive control? *Dev Psychol*, *50*(5), 1620–1627.

Luciana M (2016). Executive function in adolescence: A commentary on regulatory control and depression in Adolescents: Findings from neuroimaging and neuropsychological research. *J Clin Child Adolesc*, *45*(1), 84–89.

Luciana M, Conklin H, Hooper C, & Yarger R (2005). The development of nonverbal working memory and executive control processes in adolescents. *Child Dev*, *76*, 697–712.

Ludolph P, & Bow J (2012). Complex Alienation Dynamics and Very Young Children. *J Child Cust*, *9*, 153–178.

Luecken L, Hagan M, Sandler I, Tein, J-Y, Ayers T et al. (2010). Cortisol level six-year after participation in the Family Bereavement Program. *Psychoneuroendocrino*, *35*, 785–789.

Lui J, Barry C, & Sacco D (2015). Callous-unemotional traits and empathy deficits: Mediating effects of affective perspective-taking and facial emotion recognition. *Cognition Emotion*, *30*(6), 1049–1062.

Luijk M, Velders F, Tharner A, Bakermans-Kranenburg M, van IJzendoorn M, Jaddoe V et al. (2010). FKBP5 and resistant attachment predict cortisol reactivity in infants: Gene–environment interaction. *Psychoneuroendocrino*, *35*(10), 1454–1461.

Lupien S, McEwen B, Gunnar M, & Heim C (2009). Effects of stress throughout the lifespan on the brain, behaviour and cognition. *Neuroscience*, *10*(6), 434–445.

Lupinski K (2003). Cultural differences in body image: The perspectives of European American, African American and Asian American college women. Doctoral Dissertation Abstract. Cincinnati, OH: Division of Research and Advanced Studies of the U Cincinnati.

Luthar S, Cicchetti D, & Becker B (2000). The construct of resilience: A critical evaluation and guidelines for future work. *Child Dev*, *71*, 543–556.

Luu K & Hall P (2015). Hatha yoga and executive function: A systematic review. *J Altern & Complemen Med*, *22*(2), 125–133.

Luyten P, & Fonagy P (in press). The stress-reward-mentalizing model of depression: An integrative developmental cascade approach to child and adolescent depressive disorder based on the research domain criteria (RDoC) approach. *Clin Psychol Rev*, dio.org/10.1016/j.cpr.2017.09.008.

Luyten P, & Fonagy P (2015). The neurobiology of mentalizing. *Personality Disorders: Theory, Research, and Treatment*, *6*(4), 366–379.

Lyons D, & Parker K (2007). Stress inoculation-induced indications of resilience in monkeys. *J Trauma Stress, 20*, 423–433.

Lyons-Ruth K (2015). Commentary: Should we move away from an attachment framework for understanding disinhibited social engagement disorder (DSED)? A commentary on Zeanah and Gleason (2015). *J Child Psychol Psyc, 56*(3), 223–227.

Lyons-Ruth K (2005). Expanding the concept of unresolved mental states: Hostile/Helpless states of mind on the Adult Attachment Interview are associated with disrupted mother–infant communication and infant disorganization. *Dev Psychopathol, 17*(1), 1–23.

Lyons-Ruth K (2003). The two-person construction of defenses: Disorganized attachment strategies, unintegrated mental states, and hostile/helpless relational processes. *J Infant Child Adolesc Psychother, 2*, 105–114.

Lyons-Ruth K, Alpern L, & Repacholi B (1993). Disorganized infant attachment classification and maternal psychosocial problems as predictors of hostile-aggressive behaviour in the preschool classroom. *Child Dev, 64*, 527–585.

Lyons-Ruth K, Bureau J, Holmes B, Easterbrooks A, & Brooks N (2013). Borderline symptoms and suicidality/self-injury in late adolescence: Prospectively observed relationship correlates in infancy and childhood. *Psychiat Res, 206*(2–3), 273–281.

Lyons-Ruth K, Bureau J, Riley C, & Atlas-Corbett A (2009). Socially indiscriminate attachment behavior in the strange situation: convergent and discriminant validity in relation to caregiving risk, later behavior problems, and attachment insecurity. *Dev Psychopathol, 21*, 355–372.

Lyons-Ruth K, Dutra L, Schuder M, & Bianchi I (2006). From infant attachment disorganization to adult dissociation: relational adaptations or traumatic experiences? *Psychiatric Clinics of North America, 29*, 63–86.

Lyons-Ruth K, Holmes B, Sasvari-Szekely M, Ronai Z, Nemoda Z, & Pauls D (2007). Serotonin transporter polymorphism and borderline or antisocial traits among low-income young adults. *Psychiat Genet,17*, 339–343.

Lyons-Ruth K, & Jacobvitz D (2018). Attachment disorganization from infancy to adulthood: Neurobiological correlates, parenting contexts, and pathways to disorder. In J Cassidy, P Shaver (Eds), *Handbook of attachment* (3rd ed., pp. 667–695). New York: Guilford.

Lyons-Ruth K, Pechtel P, Yoon S, Anderson C, & Teicher M (2016). Disorganized attachment in infancy predicts greater amygdala volume in adulthood. *Behav Brain Res, 308*, 83–93.

Lyons-Ruth K, Wolfe R, & Lyubchik A (2000). Depression and the parenting of young children: making the case for early preventive mental health services. *Harvard Rev Psychiat, 8*, 148–153.

Lyons-Ruth K, Yellin C, Melnick S, & Atwood G (2005). Expanding the concept of unresolved mental states: Hostile/helpless states of mind on the Adult Attachment Interview are associated with atypical maternal behaviour and infant disorganization. *Dev Psychopathol, 17*, 1–23.

Lyons-Ruth K, Yellin C, Melnick S, & Atwood G (2003). Childhood experiences of trauma and loss have different relations to maternal unresolved and hostile-helpless states of mind on the AAI. *Attach Hum Dev, 5*(4), 330–352.

Lytje M (2016). The success of a planned bereavement response – a survey on teacher use of bereavement response plans when supporting grieving children in Danish schools. *Pastor Care Educ, 35*(1), 28–38.

Maag J (2005). Social skills training for youth with emotional and behavioral disorders and learning disabilities: Problems, conclusions, and suggestions. *Exceptionality, 13*(3), 155–172.

McCabe A, Peterson C, & Connors D (2006). Attachment security and narrative elaboration. *Int J Behav Devel, 30*(5), 8–19.

McCleery J, & Harvey A (2004). Integration of psychological and biological approaches to trauma memory: Implications for pharmacological prevention of PTSD. *J Traum Stress, 17*(6), 485–496.

McClelland M, Cameron C, Connor C, Farris C, Jewkes A, & Morrison F (2007). Links between behavioral regulation and preschoolers' literacy, vocabulary, and math skills. *Dev Psychol, 43*(4), 947–959.

McClowry SG (2003). *Your child's unique temperament: Insights and strategies for responsive parenting.* Champaign, IL: Research Press.

McClowry SG (2002). The temperament profiles of school-age children. *J Pediatr Nurs, 17*(1), 3–10.

McClowry SG, Snow D, Tamis-LeMonda C, & Rodriguez E (2010). Testing the efficacy of INSIGHTS on student disruptive behavior, classroom management, and student competence in inner-city primary grades. *Sch Ment Health, 2*(1), 23–35.

McCrae R, & John O (1992). An introduction to the Five-Factor model and its applications. *J Pers, 60,* 175–215.

McCrory E, Gerin M, Viding E (2017). Annual Research Review: Childhood maltreatment, latent vulnerability and the shift to preventative psychiatry – the contribution of functional brain imaging. *J Child Psychol Psyc, 58*(4), 338–357.

McDermott J, Perez E, Henderson H, Chronis-Tuscano A, Pine D, & Fox N (2009). A history of childhood behavioral inhibition and enhanced response monitoring in adolescence are linked to clinical anxiety. *Biol Psychiat, 65*, 445–448.

MacDonald H, Beeghly M, Grant-Knight W, Augustyn M, Woods R, Carbral H, et al. (2008). Longitudinal association between infant attachment and childhood posttraumatic stress symptoms. *Dev Psychopathol, 20*, 493–508.

McElwain N, Holland A, Engle J, & Ogolsky B (2014). Getting acquainted: Actor and partner effects of attachment and temperament on young children's peer behavior. *Dev Psychol, 50*, 1757–1770.

McElwain N, Holland A, Engle J, & Wong M (2012). Child anger-proneness moderates associations between child–mother attachment security and child behavior with mothers at 33 months. *J Fam Psychol, 26*, 76–86.

McEwen B, & Wingfield J (2010). What is in a name?: Integrating homeostasis, allostasis and stress. *Horm Behav, 57*(2), 105–111.

McGhee PE (1979). *Humor: Its origin and development.* San Francisco, CA: Freeman.

McGilloway S, NiMhaille G, Bywater T, Leckey Y, Kelly P, Furlong M et al. (2014). Reducing child conduct disordered behaviour and improving parent mental health in disadvantaged families: A 12-month follow-up and cost analysis of a parenting intervention. *Eur Child Adolesc Psychiatry, 23*, 783–794.

McGowan P, Sasaki A, D'Alessio A, Dymov S, Labonte B et al. (2009). Epigenetic regulation of the glucocorticoid receptor in human brain associates with childhood abuse. *Nature Neurosci, 12*, 342–348.

MacKinnon A, Carter S, Feeley N, Gold I, Hayton B, Santhakumaran S, & Zelkowitz P (2018). Theory of mind as a link between oxytocin and maternal behavior. *Psychoneuroendocrino, 92*, 87–94.

MacKinnon L (2012). The Neurosequential Model of Therapeutics: An interview with Bruce Perry. *Aust NZ Fam Ther, 33*(3), 210–218.

McLaughlin K, Fairbank J, Gruber M, Jones R, Osofsky J, Pfefferbaum B, Sampson N, & Kessler R (2010). Trends in serious emotional disturbance among youths exposed to Hurricane Katrina. *J Am Acad Chld Psy, 49(*10), 990–1000.

McLaughlin K, Koenen K, Friedman M, Ruscio A, Karam E, Shahly V et al. (2015a). Subthreshold Posttraumatic Stress Disorder in the World Health Organization World Mental Health Surveys. *Biol Psychiat, 77*, 375–384.

McLaughlin K, Peverill M, Gold A, Alves S, & Sheridan M (2015c). Child maltreatment and neural systems underlying emotion regulation. *J Am Acad Chld Psy, 54*, 753–762.

McLaughlin K, Sheridan M, & Lambert H (2014a). Childhood adversity and neural development: Deprivation and threat as distinct dimensions of early experience. *Neurosci Biobehav Rs, 47*, 578–591.

McLaughlin K, Sheridan M, Tibu F, Fox N, Zeanah C, & Nelson C (2015b). Causal effects of the early caregiving environment on development of stress response systems in children. *P Natl A Sci USA, 112*(8), 5637–5642.

McLaughlin K, Sheridan M, Winter W, Fox N, Zeanah C, & Nelson C (2014b). Widespread reductions in cortical thickness following severe early life deprivation: a neurodevelopmental pathway to ADHD. *Biol Psychiatry 76*, 629–638.

McLaughlin K, Zeanah C, Fox N, & Nelson C (2012). Attachment security as a mechanism linking foster care placement to improved mental health outcomes in previously institutionalized children. *J Child Psychol Psyc, 53*(1), 46–55.

McMahon R, & Forehand R (2003). *Helping the noncompliant child: Family-based treatment for oppositional behavior.* New York: Guilford.

McNeil C, & Hembree-Kigin T (2010). *Parent–Child Interaction Therapy* (2nd ed). New York: Springer.

Maercker A, & Horn A (2012). A socio-interpersonal perspective on PTSD: The case for environments and interpersonal processes. *Clin Psychol Psychot, 20*, 465–481.

Maes M, van den Noortgate W, & Goossens L (2015). A reliability generalization study for a multidimensional loneliness scale: The Loneliness and Aloneness Scale for Children and Adolescents. *Eur J Psychol Assess, 31*, 294–301.

Magai C, Frias M, & Shaver P (2018). Attachment in middle and later life. In J Cassidy, P Shaver (Eds), *Handbook of attachment* (3rd ed., pp. 534–552). New York: Guilford.

Magimairaj B, Montgomery J, Marinellie S, & McCarthy J (2009). Relation of three mechanisms of working memory to children's complex span performance. *Int J Behav Dev, 33*(5), 460–469.

Mahrer N, Luecken L, Wolchik S, Tein J, & Sandler I (2014). Exposure to maternal distress in childhood and cortisol activity in young adulthood. *Int J Behav Dev, 38*(6), 570–576.

Maikovich-Fong A, Speltz M, & Jaffee S (2015). Adverse childhood experiences and developmental sequelae. In P Clements, S Seedat, E Gibbings (Eds) (pp. 225–262). *Mental health issues of child maltreatment.* St. Louis, MO: STM Learning.

Main M (1995). Recent studies in attachment: Overview, with selected implications for clinical work. In S Goldberg, R Muir, J Kerr (Eds), *Attachment theory: Social, developmental, and clinical perspectives* (pp. 407–474). Hillsdale, NJ: Analytic Press.

Main M (1990). Cross-cultural studies of attachment organization: Recent studies, changing methodologies, and the concept of conditional strategies. *Hum Dev, 33*, 48–61.

Main M (1981). Avoidance in the service of attachment: A working paper. In K Immelmann, G Barlow, M Main, L Petrinovich (Eds), *Behavioral development: The Bielefeld Interdisciplinary Project* (pp. 651–693). New York: Cambridge University Press.
Main M, Hesse E, & Kaplan N (2005). Predictability of attachment behavior and representational processes at 1, 6, and 19 years of age. In KE Grossmann, K Grossmann, E Waters (Eds), *The power of longitudinal attachment research: From infancy and childhood to adulthood* (pp. 245–304). New York: Guilford.
Main M, & Solomon J (1990). Procedures for identifying infants as disorganized/disoriented during the Ainsworth strange situation. In M Greenberg, D Cicchetti, E Cummings (Eds), *Attachment in the preschool years: Theory, research, and intervention* (pp. 121–160). Chicago, IL: University of Chicago Press.
Majors K, & Baines E (2017). Children's play with their imaginary companions: Parent experiences and perceptions of the characteristics of the imaginary companions and purposes served, *Education & Child Psychology, 34* (3).
Malarbi S, Abu-Rayya H, Muscara F, & Stargatt R (2017). Neuropsychological functioning of childhood trauma and posttraumatic stress disorder: A meta-analysis. *Neurosci Biobehav Rs, 72*, 68–86. abstract.
Malchiodi C (2012). Art therapy in practice: Ethics, evidence, and cultural sensitivity. In C Malchiodi (Ed.), *Handbook of art therapy* (2nd edition, pp. 42–51). New York: Guilford.
Malchiodi C (ed.) (2015). *Creative interventions with traumatized children*. New York: Guilford.
Malik S, Wells A, & Wittkowski A (2015). Emotion regulation as a mediator in the relationship between attachment and depressive symptomatology: A systematic review. *J Affect Disorders, 172*, 428–444.
Maloney J, Lawlor M, Schonert-Reichl K, & Whitehead J (2016). A Mindfulness-Based Social and Emotional Learning curriculum for school-aged children: The MindUP Program. In K Schonert-Reichl, R Roeser (Eds), *Handbook of mindfulness in education* (pp. 313–333). New York: Springer.
Mandelli L, Petrelli C, & Serretti A (2015). The role of specific early trauma in adult depression: A meta-analysis of published literature. Childhood trauma and adult depression. *Eur Psychiat, 30*, 665–680.
Manders W, Dekovic M, Asscher J, van der Laan, P, & Prins P (2013). Psychopathy as predictor and moderator of Multisystemic Therapy outcomes among adolescents treated for antisocial behavior. *J Abnorm Child Psychol, 41*, 1121–1132.
Mann M (2010). Shame veiled and unveiled: The shame affect and its re-emergence in the clinical setting. *Am J Psychoanal, 70*, 270–281.
Mann T, Hund A, Hesson-McInnis M, & Roman Z (2017). Executive functioning predicts academic and social-emotional aspects of school readiness. *Mind Brain Educ, 11*(1), 21–31.
Manso J, Garcia-Baamonde M, & Alonso M (2011). Design of a language stimulation program for children suffering abuse. *Childr & Youth Services Rev, 33*, 1325–1331.
Manuel J, & Moyers T (2016). Review: The role of ambivalence in behavior change. *Addiction, 111*, 1908–1913.
Marazziti D, Dell'Osso B, Dell'Osso M, Consoli G, & Del Debbio A (2007). Romantic attachment in patients with mood and anxiety disorders. *CNS Spectrums, 12*, 751–756.
Markese S (2011). Dyadic trauma in infancy and early childhood: Review of the Literature. *JICAP, 10*, 341–378.
Marks R (2018). Sleep disturbances, stress, obesity and osteoarthritis. *EC Orthopaedics, 9*(6), 356–367.
Marshall A (2016). Developmental timing of trauma exposure relative to puberty and the nature of psychopathology among adolescent girls. *J Am Acad Child Adolesc Psychia, 55*(1), 25–32.
Marshall P, & Meltzoff A (2014). Neural mirroring mechanisms and imitation in human infants. *Phil Trans R Soc Lond B Biol Sci, 369*(1644), 20130620.
Marshall P, Reeb B, Fox N, Nelson C, & Zeanah C (2008). Effects of early intervention on EEG power and coherence in previously institutionalized children in Romania. *Dev Psychopathol, 20*, 861–880.
Marshall A. (2016). Developmental timing of trauma exposure relative to puberty and the nature of psychopathology among adolescent girls. *J Am Acad Chld Psy, 55*(1), 25–32.
Martin A, Razza R, & Brooks-Gunn J (2013). Sustained attention at age 5 predicts attention-related problems at age 9. *Int J Behav Dev, 36*(6), 413–419.
Martin C, Cromer L, DePrince A, & Freyd J (2013). The role of cumulative trauma, betrayal, and appraisals in understanding trauma symptomatology. *Psychol Trauma-US, 52*(1), 110–118.
Martin J, Hiscock H, Hardy P, Davey B, & Wake M (2007). Adverse associations of infant and child sleep problems and parent health: an Australian population study. *Pediatrics,119*, 947–955.
Martin R, Puhlik-Doris P, Larsen G, Gray J, & Weir K (2003). Individual differences in uses of humor and their relation to psychological well-being: Development of the Humor Style Questionnaire. *J Res Pers, 37*, 48–75.
Martin TL, & Doka KJ (2000). *Men don't cry … women do: Transcending gender stereotypes of grief.* Philadelphia: Brunner-Mazel.
Martinelli A, Ackermann K, Bernhard A, Freitag C, & Schwenk C (2018). Hostile attribution bias and aggression in children and adolescents: A systematic literature review on the influence of aggression subtype and gender. *Aggress Violent Beh, 39*, 25–32.

Marusak H, Martin K, Etkin A, & Thomason M (2015). Childhood trauma exposure disrupts the automatic regulation of emotional processing. *Neuropsychopharmacology, 40*, 1250–1258.

Marvin RS (1977). An ethological-cognitive model for the attenuation of mother–child attachment behavior. In T Alloway, L Krames, P Pliner (Eds), *Advances in the study of communication and affect: Vol. 3. Attachment behaviors* (pp. 25–60). New York: Plenum.

Masgutova S (2016). Posttrauma recovery in children of Newtown, CT using MNRI Reflex Integration. *Trauma Stress Disor Treat, 5*:5. doi: 10.4172/2324-8947.1000163.

Mash E, & Dozois D (2003). Child psychopathology: A developmental systems perspective. In E Mash, R Barkley (Eds), *Child psychopathology* (2nd ed., pp. 3–71). New York: Guilford.

Masten A, & Cicchetti D (2010). Developmental cascades. *Dev Psychopathol, 22*, 491–495.

Masten A, & Narayan A (2012). Child development in the context of disaster, war, and terrorism: Pathways of risk and resilience. *Annu Rev Psychol, 63*, 227–267.

Masten A, & Osofsky J (2010). Disasters and their impact on child development: Introduction to the special section. *Child Dev, 81*(4), 1029–1039.

Masten A, & Powell J (2003). A resilience framework for research, policy and practice. In SS Luthar (ed.), *Resilience and vulnerability: Adaptation in the context of childhood adversities* (pp. 1–25). New York: Cambridge University Press.

Masten C, Guyer A, Hodgdon H, McClure E, Charney D, Ernst M et al. (2008). Recognition of facial emotions among maltreated children with high rates of posttraumatic stress disorder. *Child Abuse Neglect, 32*, 139–153.

Matheson H, Moore C & Akhatar N (2013). The development of social learning in interactive and observational contexts. *J Exp Child Psychol, 114*, 161–172.

Maxwell S, Zepeda A, & Rzotkiewicz A (2018). Peers, social control, or guilt? Self-conscious emotions as explanation for antisocial behavior. *Deviant Behav, 39*(3), 322–331.

Mayseless O (2005). Ontogeny of attachment in middle childhood: Conceptualization of normative changes. In K Kerns, R Richardson (Eds), *Attachment in middle childhood* (pp. 1–23). New York: Guildford.

Medina J, Vujanovic A, Smits J, Irons J, Zvolensky M, & Bonn-Miller M (2011). Exercise and coping-oriented alcohol use among a trauma-exposed sample. *Addict Behav 36*, 274–277.

Medina L, Garcia C, Urbina A, Manjarrez J, & Moyaho A (2013). Female vibration discourages male courtship behaviour in the Amarillo fish (*Girardinichthys multiradiatus*). *Behav Processes, 100*, 163–168. abstract.

Mehrani M, & Peterson C (2016). Interviewing preschoolers: Response biases to yes–no questions. *Appl Cognit Psychol, 31*(1), 91–98.

Mehta B, & Bhandari B (2016). The mirror neuron system: Basic concepts. *International Physiology, 4*(2), 77–80.

Meiser-Stedman R, Dalgleish T, Glucksman E, Yule W, & Smith P (2009). Maladaptive cognitive appraisals mediate the evolution of posttraumatic stress reactions: a 6-month follow-up of child and adolescent assault and motor vehicle accident survivors. *J Abnorm Psychol, 118*, 778–787.

Melhem N, Day N, Shear M, Day R, Reynolds C, & Brent D (2004). Traumatic grief among adolescents exposed to a peer's suicide. *Am J Psychiat, 161*, 1411–1416.

Melhem N, Keilp J, Porta G, Oquendo M, Burke A, Stanley B, Cooper T, Mann J, Brent D (2016). Blunted HPA axis activity in suicide attempters compared to those at high risk for suicidal behavior. *Neuropsychopharmacology, 41*, 1447–1456.

Melhem N, Moritz G, Walker M, Shear M, & Brent D (2007). Phenomenology and correlates of complicated grief in children and adolescents. *JAACAP, 46*(4), 493–499.

Melhem N, Walker M, Moritz G, & Brent D (2008). Antecedents and sequelae of sudden parental death in offspring and surviving caregivers. *Arch Pediat Adol Med, 162*, 403–410.

Mello C & Nader K (2012). Teaching Coping and Social Skills to Elementary School Children. In K Nader (Ed.), *School rampage shootings and other youth disturbances: Early preventive interventions* (pp. 103–126). New York: Routledge.

Meltzoff A (1995). What infant memory tells us about infantile amnesia: Long-term recall and deferred imitation. *J Exper Child Psychology, 59*, 497–515.

Meltzoff A, & Decety J (2003). What imitation tells us about social cognition: a rapprochement between developmental psychology and cognitive neuroscience. *Phil Trans R Soc Lond B, 358*, 491–500.

Meltzoff A & Moore M (1997). Explaining facial imitation: A theoretical model. *Early Dev Parenting, 6*, 179–192.

Meltzoff A, & Moore M (1995). Imitation, memory, and the representation of persons. *Infant Behav Dev, 17*, 83–99.

Meltzoff A, & Moore M (1977). Imitation of facial and manual gestures by human neonates. *Science, 198*, 75–78.

Mendelsohn A, Cates C, Weisleder A, Johnson S, Seery A, Canfield C et al. (2018). Reading aloud, play, and social-emotional development. *Pediatrics, 141*(5), May 2018:e20173393.

Merritt C, & Tharp I (2013). Personality, self-efficacy and risk-taking in parkour (free-running). *Psychol Sport Exerc, 14*, 608–611.

Merritt D, & Klein S (2015). Do early care and education services improve language-development for maltreated children? Evidence from a national child welfare sample. *Child Abuse Neglect, 39*, 185–196.

Mersky H (1992). Manufacture of personalities. *British J Psychiatry, 160*, 327–340.

Merz E, Landry S, Johnson U, Williams J, & Jung K (2015). Effects of a responsiveness–focused intervention in family child carehomes on children's executive function. *Early Child Res Q 34*, 128–139.

Merz E, Landry S, Zucker T, Barnes M, Assel M, Taylor H et al. (2016). Parenting predictors of delay inhibition in socioeconomically disadvantaged preschoolers. *Inf Child Dev, 25*(5), 371–390.

Metz M, Majdandzic M, & Bogels S (2016). Concurrent and predictive associations between infants' and toddlers' fearful temperament, coparenting, and parental anxiety disorders. *J Clin Child Adolesc, 47*(4), 569–580. abstract.

Meuwissen A, & Carlson S (2015). Fathers matter: The role of father parenting in preschoolers' executive function development. *J Exp Child Psychol, 140*, 1–15.

Meuwissen A, & Englund M (2016). Executive function in at-risk children: Importance of father-figure support and mother parenting. *Journal of Applied Dev Psychol, 44*, 72–80.

Meyer M, Bekkering H, Paulus M, & Hunnius S (2010). Joint action coordination in 26- and 3-year-old children. *Fontiers in Human Neurosci, 4*, 1–7. (article 220)

Meyer M, van der Wel R, & Hunnius S (2016). Planning my actions to accommodate yours: Joint action development during early childhood. *Philos T R Soc B, 371* (1693), 20150371.

Meyer M, Williams K, & Eisenberger N (2015). Why social pain can live on: Different neural mechanisms are associated with reliving social and physical pain. *PLoS ONE 10*(6), e0128294.

Mezulis A, Abramson L, Hyde J, & Hankin B (2004). Is there a universal positivity bias in attributions?: A meta-analytic review of individual, developmental, and cultural differences in the self-serving attributional bias. *Psycholog Bulletin, 130*(5), 711–747.

Mezulis A, Hyde J, & Abramson L (2006). The developmental origins of cognitive vulnerability to depression: Temperament, parenting, and negative life events in childhood as contributors to negative cognitive style. *Dev Psychol, 42*(6), 1012–1025.

Miconi D, Moscardino U, Ronconi L, & Altoe G (2017). Perceived parenting, self-esteem, and depressive symptoms in immigrant and non-immigrant adolescents in Italy: A multigroup path analysis. *J Child Fam Stud, 26*, 345–356.

Middlebrooks J, & Audage N (2008). *The effects of childhood stress on health across the lifespan.* Atlanta, GA: CDC and Prevention, National Center for Injury Prevention and Control.

Miendlarzewska E, & Trost W (2014). How musical training affects cognitive development: Rhythm, reward and other modulating variables. *Front Neurosci*, 7(279). doi: 10.3389/fnins.2013.00279.

Mikolajewski A, Scheeringa M, & Weems C (2017). Evaluating Diagnostic and Statistical Manual of Mental Disorders, Fifth Edition Posttraumatic Stress Disorder diagnostic criteria in older children and adolescents, *J Chld Adolesc Psychopharmacol*, 27(4), 374–382.

Mikulincer M, & Shaver P (2009). An attachment and behavioral systems perspective on social support. *J Soc Pers Relat, 26*(1), 7–19.

Mikulincer M, & Shaver P (2008). Adult attachment and affect regulation. In J Cassidy, P Shaver (Eds), *Handbook of attachment: Theory, research, and clinical applications* (2nd ed., pp. 503–531). New York: Guilford.

Mikulincer M, & Shaver P (2007). *Attachment in adulthood: Structure, dynamics, and change.* New York: Guilford.

Mikulincer M, Shaver P, & Pereg D (2003). Attachment theory and affect regulation: The dynamics, development, and cognitive consequences of attachment-related strategies. *Motiv Emotion*, 27(2), 77–102.

Miles C (1893). A study of individual psychology. *Am J Psychol, 6*, 534–558.

Miller D, Vachon D, & Aalsma M (2012). Negative affect and emotion dysregulation: Conditional relations with violence and risky sexual behavior in a sample of justice-involved adolescents. *Crim Justice Behav, 39*(10), 1316–1327. abstract.

Miller P, & Eisenberg N (1998). The relation of empathy to aggressive and externalizing/antisocial behavior. *Psychol Bull, 103*, 324–344.

Miller S, Miller C, Bloom J, Hynd G, & Craggs J (2006). Right hemisphere brain morphology, Attention-Deficit Hyperactivity Disorder (ADHD) subtype, and social comprehension. *J Child Neurol, 21*(2), 139–144.

Miller W, & Rollnick S (2002). *Motivational Interviewing: Preparing people for change.* New York: Guilford.

Mills K, Goddings A, Clasen L, Giedd J, & Blakemore S (2014). The developmental mismatch in structural brain maturation during adolescence. *Dev Neurosci 36*, 147–160.

Mills R (2003). Possible antecedents and developmental implications of shame in young girls. *Inf Child Dev, 12*, 329–349.

Milrod B, Markowitz J, Gerber A, Cyranowski J, Altemus M et al. (2014). Childhood separation anxiety and the pathogenesis and treatment of adult anxiety. *Am J Psychiatry, 171*, 34–43.

Mindell J, & Lee C (2015). Sleep, mood, and development in infants. *Infant Behav Dev, 41*, 102–107.

Mink D, Henning A & Aschersleben G (2014). Infant shy temperament predicts preschoolers Theory of Mind. *Infant Behav Dev, 37*, 66–75. abstract.

Mireault G, Crockenberg S, Sparrow J, Cousineau K, Pettinato C, & Woodard K (2015). Laughing matters: Infant humor in the context of parental affect. *J Exp Child Psychol, 136*, 30–41.

Mireault G, Crockenberg S, Sparrow J, Cousineau K, Pettinato C, Woodard K, & Malzac K (2014). Social looking, social referencing and humor perception in 6- and-12-month-old infants. *Infant Behav Dev, 37*, 536–545.

Mireault G, Sparrow J, Poutre M, Perdue B, & Macke L (2012). Infant humor perception from 3- to 6-months and attachment at one year. *Infant Behav Dev, 35*, 797–802. Abstract.

Mischel W, Ayduk O, Berman M, Casey B, Gotlib I, Jonides J et al. (2011). Willpower over the life span: decomposing self-regulation. *Soc Cogn Affect Neur, 6*(2), 252–256.

Mithyantha R, Kneen R, McCann E, & Gladstone M (2017). Current evidence-based recommendations on investigating children with global developmental delay. *Arch Dis Child, 102*, 1071–1076.

Moffitt T, Arseneault L, Belsky D, Dickson N, Hancox R, Harrington H et al. (2011). A gradient of childhood self-control predicts health, wealth, and public safety. *P Natl A Sci USA, 108*, 2693–2698.

Mohr C, & Messina S (2015). Brain dysfunctions, psychopathologies, and body image distortions. *Eur Psychol, 20*(1), 12–81.

Moll H, & Meltzoff A (2011). How does it look? Level 2 perspective-taking at 36 months of age. *Child Dev, 82*, 661–673.

Monaco N, & Gaier E (1987). Developmental level and children's responses to the explosion of the Space Shuttle Challenger. *Early Child Res Q, 2*, 83–95.

Monette S, Bigras M, & Lafrenière M-A (2015). Structure of executive functions in typically developing kindergarteners. *J Exp Child Psychol, 140*, 120–139.

Montgomery E (2011). Trauma, exile and mental health in young refugees. *Acta Psychiatr Scand, 124*(Suppl. 440), 1–46. abstract.

Montirosso R, & Provenzi L (2015). Implications of epigenetics and stress regulation on research and developmental care of preterm infants. *JOGNN, 44*(2), 174–182.

Moore S, & Zoellner L (2007). Overgeneral autobiographical memory and traumatic events: An evaluative review. *Psychol Bull, 133*(3), 419–437.

Moore-Mallinos J (2005). *Do you have a secret? (Let's talk about it!)*. Hauppauge, NY: Barrons Educational Series.

Morales M, Mundy P, Crowson M, Neal R, & Delgado C (2005). Individual differences in infant attention skills, joint attention, and emotion regulation behavior, *Int J Behav Dev, 29*, 259–263.

Morales S, Beekman C, Blandon A, Stifter C, & Buss K (2015). Longitudinal associations between temperament and socioemotional outcomes in young children: The moderating role of RSA and gender. *Dev Psychobiol, 57*, 105–119.

Moran O, Almada P, & McHugh L (2018). An investigation into the relationship between the three selves (Self-as-Content, Self-as-Process and Self-as-Context) and mental health in adolescents. *J Contextual Behav Sci, 7*, 55–62.

Moran O, Almada P, & McHugh L (2018). An investigation into the relationship between the three selves (Self-as-Content, Self-as-Process and Self-as-Context) and mental health in adolescents. *J Contextual Behav Sci, 7*, 55-62.

Morgan A, & Jorm A (2008). Self-help interventions for depressive disorders and for depressive symptoms: a systematic review. *Ann Gen Psychiatry, 7*, 13. doi: 10.1186/1744-859X-7-13.

Morris A, Gabert-Quillen C, Friebert S, Carst N, & Delahanty D (2016). The indirect effect of positive parenting on the relationship between parent and sibling bereavement outcomes after the death of a child. *J Pain Symptom Manag, 51*(1), 60–70.

Morris G, Baker-Ward L, & Bauer P (2010). What remains of that day: The survival of children's autobiographical memories across time. *Appl Cognitive Psych, 24*, 527–544.

Morris T, Hudson J, & Dodd H (2014). Risk-taking and inhibitory control in behaviourally inhibited and disinhibited preschool children. *Pers Indiv Differ, 71*, 113–117.

Morris T, & Oosterfoff B (2016). Observed mother and father rejection and control: Association with child social anxiety, general anxiety, and depression. *J Child Fam Stud, 25*(9), 2904–2914.

Morrison A, & Heimberg R (2013). Attentional control mediates the effect of social anxiety on positive affect. *J Anxiety Disord, 27*, 56–67.

Mortola J, Marghescu D, & Siegrist-Johnstone R (2016). Thinking about breathing: Effects on respiratory sinus arrhythmia. *Resp Physiol Neurobi, 223*, 28–36.

Moser J, Durbin C, Patrick C, & Schmidt N (2015a). Combining neural and behavioral indicators in the assessment of internalizing psychopathology in children and adolescents. *J Clin Child Adolesc, 44*(2), 329–340.

Moser M, Johnson S, Dalgleish T, Lafontaine M, Wiebe S, & Tasca G (2015b). Changes in relationship-specific attachment in emotionally focused couple therapy. *J Marital Fam Ther, 42*(2) 231–245. abstract.

Moses J, & Villodas M (2017). The potential protective role of peer relationships on school engagement in at-risk adolescents. *J Youth Adolescence, 46*, 2255–2272.

Moss E, & Lecompte V (2015). Attachment and socioemotional problems in middle childhood. In special issue: G Bosmans, K Kerns (Eds), Attachment in middle childhood: Theoretical advances and new directions in an emerging field. *New Dir Child Adoles, 148*, 63–76.

Moss E, Pascuzzo K, & Simard V (2012). Treating insecure and disorganized attachments in school-aged children. In K Nader (ed.), *School rampage shootings and other youth disturbances: Early preventive interventions* (pp. 127–157). New York: Taylor & Francis.

Moss E, Rousseau D, Parent S, St-Laurent D, & Saintonge J (1998). Correlates of attachment at school age: Maternal reported stress, mother–child interaction, and behaviour problems. *Child Dev, 69*, 1390–1404.

Moul C, Dobson-Stone C, Brennan J, Hawes D, Dadds M (2013). An exploration of the serotonin system in antisocial boys with high levels of callous-unemotional traits. *PLoS ONE, 8*(2), e56619. doi: 10.1371/journal.pone.0056619. abstract.

Moutsiana C, Johnstone T, Murray L, Fearon P, Cooper P, Pliatsikas C et al. (2015). Insecure attachment during infancy predicts greater amygdala volumes in early adulthood. *J Child Psychol Psyc, 56*, 540–548.

Mueller A, Brocke B, Fries E, Lesch K, & Kirschbaum C (2010). The role of the serotonin transporter polymorphism for the endocrine, stress response in newborns. *Psychoneuroendocrino, 35*, 289–296.

Mulder T, Kuiper K, van der Put C, Stams G, & Assink M (2018). Risk factors for child neglect: A meta-analytic review. *Child Abuse Neglect*, 77, 198–210.

Müller M, Forstmeier S, Wagner B, & Maercker A (2011). Traditional versus modern values and interpersonal factors predicting stress response syndromes in a Swiss elderly population. *Psychol Health Med, 16*, 631–640.

Muller N, & Midgley N (2015). Approaches to assessment in time-limited Mentalization-Based Therapy for Children (MBT-C). *Front Psychol, 6*, 1063. doi: 10.3389/fpsyg.2015.01063.

Muller R, Vascotto A, Konanur S, & Rosenkranz S (2013). Emotion regulation and psychopathology in a sample of maltreated children. *J Child Adolesc Trauma, 6*, 25–40. abstract.

Műllerová J, Hensen M, Contractor A, Elhai J, & Armour C (2016). Dissociative features in Posttraumatic Stress Disorder: A latent profile analysis. *Psychol Trauma-US, 8*(5), 601–608.

Munafo M (2012). The serotonin transporter gene and depression. *Depress Anx, 29*, 915–917.

Munafo M, Brown S, & Hariri A (2008). Serotonin transporter (5-HTTLPR) genotype and amygdala activation: A meta-analysis. *Biol Psychiat, 63*, 852–857.

Munafo M, Clark T, & Flint J (2004). Are there sex differences in the association between the 5HTT gene and neuroticism? A meta-analysis. *Personal Individ Diff, 37*, 621–626. abstract.

Munafo M, Freimer N, Ng W, Ophoff R, Veijola S, Miettunen J et al. (2009). 5-HTTLPR genotype and anxiety-related personality traits: a meta-analysis and new data. *Am J Med Genet, 150B*(2), 271–281.

Mundorf E, & Paivio S (2011). Narrative quality and disturbance pre- and post-Emotion-Focused Therapy for child abuse trauma. *J Traum Stress, 24*(6), 643–650.

Mundy P, Gwaltney M, & Henderson H (2010). Self-referenced processing, neurodevelopment and joint attention in autism. *Autism, 14*(5), 408–429.

Muris P, Hendriks E, & Bot S (2016a). Children of few words: Relations among selective mutism, behavioral inhibition, and (social) anxiety symptoms in 3- to 6-Year-Olds. *Child Psychiat Hum D, 47*, 94–101.

Muris P, Meesters C, Heijmans J, van Hulten S, Kaanen L, Oerlemans B et al. (2016b). Lack of guilt, guilt, and shame: a multi‑informant study on the relations between self‑conscious emotions and psychopathology in clinically referred children and adolescents. *Eur Child Adolesc Psychiatry, 25*, 383–396.

Muris P, Meesters C, & van Asseldonk M (2018). Shame on Me! Self-monscious emotions and Big Five personality traits and Their Relations to anxiety disorders symptoms in young, nonclinical adolescents. *Child Psychiat Hum D*, 49, 268–278.

Murphy B, & Perez M (2018, Feb. 23). Florida school shooting: sheriff got 18 calls about Nikolas Cruz's violence, threats, guns. usatoday.com/story/news/nation-now/2018/02/23/florida-school-shooting-sheriff-got-18-calls-cruzs-violence-threats-guns/366165002.

Murphy B, Shepard S, Eisenberg N, & Fabes R (2004). Concurrent and across time prediction of young adolescents' social functioning: The role of emotionality and regulation. *Soc Dev, 13*(1), 56–86.

Murphy D, Daly E, Schmitz N, Toal F, Murphy K, Curran S, et al. (2006). Cortical serotonin 5-HT2A receptor binding and social communication in adults with Asperger's syndrome: an in vivo SPECT study. *Am J Psychiatry, 163*, 934–936.

Murphy E (2013). *The developing child.* Gainsville, FL: CAPT, Inc.

Murphy E (2008). *The chemistry of personality: A guide to teacher–student interaction in the classroom.* Gainsville, FL: CAPT, Inc.

Murphy S, Elklit A, Dokkedahl S, & Shevlin M (2016). Testing the validity of the proposed ICD-11 PTSD and complex PTSD criteria using a sample from Northern Uganda. *Europ J Psychotraumatol*, 7(1), 32678 dx.doi.org/10.3402/ejpt.v7.32678.

Murray C, & Son L (1998). The effect of multiple victimization on children's cognition: Variations in response. *J Aggress Maltreat T*, *2*(1), 131–146.

Murray J, Theakston A, & Wells A (2015). Can the attention training technique turn one marshmallow into two? Improving children's ability to delay gratification. *Behav Res Therapy*, 77, 34–39.

Murray L, Cohen J, & Mannarino A (2013). Trauma-Focused Cognitive Behavioral Therapy for youth who experience continuous traumatic exposure. *Peace Confl*, *19*(2), 180–195.

Myers L (2006, December, 7). Were the levees bombed in New Orleans? *NBC Nightly News*. Downloaded 1-30-16 from www.nbcnews.com/id/10370145/na/nvxnightlynewswith.

Nader K (Ed.) (2016). *Assessment of trauma in youths: Understanding issues of age, complexity, and associated variables*. New York: Routledge.

Nader K (2015). Differential Diagnosis in the assessment of children and adolescents after crises and traumatic events. In NB Webb (ed.), *Play Therapy with Children in Crisis: Individual, group, and family treatment* (4th ed., pp. 22–49). New York: Guilford.

Nader K (2012a). Early interventions. In C Figley (ed.). *Encyclopedia of Trauma* (pp. 219–223). New York: Sage.

Nader K (2012b). Grief, complicated. In C Figley (ed.). *Encyclopedia of Trauma* (pp. 289–293). New York: Sage.

Nader K (ed.) (2012c). *School rampage shootings and other youth disturbances: Early preventive interventions*. New York: Routledge.

Nader K (2010). Helping traumatized children in school. © Nader & Gift from Within. Available from www.sourcemaine.com.

Nader K (2008). *Understanding and assessing trauma in children and adolescents: Measures, methods, and youth in context*. New York: Routledge.

Nader K (2006). Childhood trauma: The deeper wound. In JP Wilson (Eds.*), The posttraumatic self: Restoring meaning and wholeness to personality* (pp. 117–156). New York: Routledge.

Nader K (2004). Treating traumatized children and adolescents: Treatment issues, modalities, timing, and methods. In NB Webb (Ed.), *Mass trauma and violence: Helping families and children cope*. New York: Guilford.

Nader K (2002). Treating Children after Violence in Schools and Communities. In NB Webb (ed.), *Helping bereaved children* (2nd ed., pp. 214–244). New York: Guilford.

Nader K (2001). Guilt following Traumatic Events. Available from www.giftfromwithin.org/.../Guilt-Following-Traumatic-Events.html.

Nader K (1999/2000). *Psychological first aid for trauma, grief and traumatic grief* (3rd ed). Austin, TX: Two Suns.

Nader K (1997). Treating traumatic grief in systems. In C Figley, B Bride, N Mazza (Eds), *Death and trauma: The traumatology of surviving* (pp. 159–192). London: Taylor & Francis.

Nader K (1994). Countertransference in treating trauma and victimization in childhood. In J Wilson & J Lindy (Eds), *Countertransference in the treatment of posttraumatic stress disorder* (pp. 179–205). New York: Guilford.

Nader K, Dubrow N, & Stamm B. (Eds) (1999). *Honoring differences: Cultural issues in the treatment of trauma and loss*. Philadelphia, PA: Taylor and Francis.

Nader K, & Fletcher K (2014). Childhood Posttraumatic Stress Disorder. In E Mash, R Barkley (Eds), *Child Psychopathology* (3rd ed., pp. 476–528). New York: Guilford.

Nader K, & Layne C (2009). Maladaptive grieving in children and adolescents: Discovering developmentally linked differences in the manifestation of grief. *Stress Points*, *23*, 12–15.

Nader K, & Mello C (2001). Interactive trauma/grief focused therapy. In P Lehmann & N Coady (Eds), *Theoretical perspectives for direct social work practice: A generalist-eclectic approach* (pp. 382–401). New York: Springer.

Nader K, & Nader W (2012). Youth at risk: Targeted shootings, other school violence, and suicides. In K Nader (ed.) *School rampage shootings and other youth disturbances: Early preventive interventions* (pp. 33–70). New York: Routledge.

Nader K, & Pollack W (2012). Early interventions: Preventing aggression and enhancing connection among youth and adults. In K Nader (ed.). *School rampage shootings and other youth disturbances: Early preventive interventions* (pp. 245–264). New York: Routledge.

Nader K, & Pynoos R (1993). School disaster: Planning and initial interventions. *J Soc Behav Pers*, *8*(5), 299–320.

Nader K, & Pynoos R (1991). Play and Drawing as tools for interviewing traumatized children. In C Schaefer, K Gitlin, A Sandgrund (Eds), *Play, Diagnosis and Assessment* (pp. 375–389). New York: John Wiley.

Nader K, Pynoos R, Fairbanks L, & Frederick C (1990). Children's PTSD reactions one year after a sniper attack at their school. *Am J Psychiat*, 147, 1526–1530.

Nader K, & Salloum A (2011). Complicated grief reactions in children and adolescents. *J Child Adolesc Trauma, 4*, 233–257.

Nader K, & Weems C (2011). Understanding and assessing cortisol levels in children and adolescents. *J Child Adolesc Trauma, 4*, 318–338.

Naramore R, Bright M, Epps N, & Hardt N (2017). Youth arrested for trading sex have the highest rates of childhood adversity: A statewide study of juvenile offenders. *Sex Abuse-J Res Tr, 29*(4), 396–410.

Neff, K (2003). The development and validation of a scale to measure self compassion. *Self Identity, 2*, 223–250.

Neimeyer R (ed.) (2001). *Meaning reconstruction and the experience of loss*. Washington, DC: American Psychological Association.

Neimeyer R, & Burke L (2017). Spiritual Distress and Depression in Bereavement: A Meaning-Oriented Contribution. *J Rational-Emotive & Cog-Behav Ther, 35*(1), 38–59.

Neimeyer R, Herrero O, & Botella L (2006). Chaos to coherence: Psychotherapeutic integration of traumatic loss. *J Constr Psychol, 19*, 127–146.

Nelson C, Furtado E, Fox N, & Zeanah C (2009). The deprived human brain. *Am Sci, 97*, 222–229.

Nelson C, Thomas K, & de Haan M (2008). Neural bases of Cognitive Dev. In W Damon, R Lerner (Eds), *Child and adolescent development: An advanced course (pp*. 19–53). New York: Wiley.

Nelson H, Nygren P, Walker M, Panoscha R (2006). Screening for speech and language delay in preschool children: systematic evidence review for the US Preventive Services Task Force. *Pediatrics, 117*(2), e298–319. www.pediatrics.org/cgi/content/full/117/2/e298.

Nelson T, Nelson J, Kidwell K, James T, & Espy K (2015). Preschool sleep problems and differential associations with specific aspects of executive control in early elementary school. *Dev Neuropsychol, 40*(3), 167–180.

Neuner F, Catani C, Ruf M, Schauer E, Schauer M, & Elbert T (2008). Narrative Exposure Therapy for the treatment of traumatized children and adolescents (KidNET): From neurocognitive theory to field intervention. *Child Adol Psych Cl, 17*(3), 641–664.

Neuner F, Pfeiffer A, Schauer-Kaiser E, Odenwald M, Elbert T, & Ertl V (2012). Haunted by ghosts: Prevalence, predictors and outcomes of spirit possession experiences among former child soldiers and war-affected civilians in Northern Uganda. *Soc Sci Med, 75*(3), 548–554.

Newman L, Judd F, Olsson C, Castle D, Bousman C, Sheehan C et al. (2016). Early origins of mental disorder – risk factors in the perinatal and infant period. *BMC Psychiatry, 16*:270. doi: 10.1186/s12888-016-0982-7.

Newman L, & Stevenson C (2008). Issues in Infant–Parent Psychotherapy for mothers with Borderline Personality Disorder. *Clin Child Psychol P, 13*(4), 505–514.

Newton-Howes G, Horwood J, & Mulder R (2015). Personality characteristics in childhood and outcomes in adulthood: Findings from a 30 year longitudinal study. *Aust NZ J Psychiat, 49*(4) 377–386.

Niarchou M, Zammit S, Escott-Price V, Owen M, van den Bree M (2014). Exploring the indirect effects of catechol-Omethyltransferase (COMT) genotype on psychotic experiences through cognitive function and anxiety disorders in a large birth cohort of children. *Am J Med Genet Part B, 165B*, 410–420.

NICHD Early Child Care Research Network (2002). Early child care and children's development prior to school entry: results from the NICHD Study of Early Child Care. *Am Educ Res J, 39*, 133–164.

Nichols K, Fox N, & Mundy P (2005). Joint attention, self-recognition and neurocognitive functioning, *Infancy*, 7, 35–51.

Nicholson A, Sapru I, Densmore M, Frewen P, Neufeld R, Theberg J et al. (2016). Unique insula subregion resting-state functional connectivity with amygdala complexes in posttraumatic stress disorder and its dissociative subtype. *Psychiat Res: Neuroimaging, 250*, 61–72.

Nicholson N, Soane E, Fenton-O'Creevy M, & Willman P (2005). Personality and domain-specific risk-taking. *J Risk Res, 8*(2), 157–176.

Niec L, Barnett M, Prewett M, & Shanley J (2016). Group Parent–child Interaction Therapy: A randomized control trial for the treatment of conduct problems in young children. *J Consult Clin Psychol, 84*(8), 682–698.

Nielsen M, Slade L, Levy J, & Holmes A (2015). Inclined to see it your way: Do altercentric intrusion effects in visual perspective-taking reflect an intrinsically social process? *J Exp Psychol, 68*(10), 1931–1951.

Nigro G, & Wolpow S (2004). Interviewing young children with props: Prior experience matters. *Appl Cognitive Psych, 18*, 549–565.

Nikitopoulos J, Zohsel K, Blomeyer D, Buchmann A, Schmid B, Jennen-Steinmetz C et al. (2014). Are infants differentially sensitive to parenting? Early maternal care, DRD4 genotype and externalizing behavior during adolescence. *J Psychiatric Research, 59*, 53–59.

Niles A, Haltom K, Mulvenna C, Lieberman M, & Stanton A (2014). Randomized controlled trial of expressive writing for psychological and physical health: The moderating role of emotional expressivity. *Anxiety Stress Copin, 27*(1), 1–17. abstract. doi:10.1080/10615806.2013.802308.

Nishi D, Matsuoka Y, & Kim Y (2010). Posttraumatic growth, posttraumatic stress disorder and resilience of motor vehicle accident survivors. *BioPsychoSoc Med*, *4*(1), doi: 10.1186/1751-0759-4-7.

Noah, T (2017). *Born a crime: Stories from a South African childhood*. London: John Murray.

Nomura Y, & Chemtob C (2009). Effect of maternal psychopathology on behavioral problems in preschool children exposed to terrorism: Use of generalized estimating iquations to Integrate multiple informant reports. *Arch Pediatr Adolesc Med*, *163*(6), 531–539.

Norbury A, Manohar S, Rogers R, & Husain M (2013). Dopamine modulates risk-taking as a function of baseline sensation seeking trait. *J Neurosci*, *33*, 12982–12986.

Norris A, Torres-Thomas S, & Williams E (2014). Adapting cognitive interviewing for early adolescent Hispanic girls and sensitive topics. *Hispan Health Care Internat*, *12*(3), 111–119.

Northoff G, Heinzel A, de Greck M, Bermpohl F, Dobrowolny H, & Panksepp J (2006). Self-referential processing in our brain: A meta-analysis of imaging studies on the self. *NeuroImage*, *31*, 440–457.

Nutley SB, & Söderqvist S (2017). How Is Working Memory Training Likely to Influence Academic Performance? Current Evidence and Methodological Considerations. *Front Psychol*, *8*(69), 1–12.

Nuttall A, Valentino K, Comas M, McNeill A, & Stey P (2014). Autobiographical memory specificity among preschool-aged children. *Dev Psychol*, *50*(7), 1963–1972.

Nyman E, Miettunen J, Freimer N, Joukamaa M, Jaki P et al. (2011). Impact of temperament on Depress Anxiety symptoms and depressive disorder in a population-based birth cohort. *J Affect Disorders*, *131*, 393–397.

Nystrom P (2008). The infant mirror neuron system studied with high density EEG. *Soc Neurosci*, *3*(34), 334–347.

Nystrom P, Ljunghammar T, Rosander K, & von Hofsten C (2011). Using mu rhythm desynchronization to measure mirror neuron activity in infants. *Developmental Sci*, *14*, 2, 327–335. abstract.

Oates D, & Ray W (2008). Dissociative tendencies and facilitated emotional processing. *Emotion*, *8*(5), 653–661.

Obeid N, Norris M, Buchholz A, Henderson K, Goldfield G, Bedford S, & Flament M (2018). Socio-emotional Predictors of Body Esteem in Adolescent Males. *Psychol Men Masculin*, *19*(3), 439–445.

Obradovic J, Portilla X, & Ballard P (2016). Biological sensitivity to family income: Differential effects on early executive functioning. *Child Dev*, *87*(2), 374–384.

Ochberg F (2002). A primer on interviewing victims. In MB Williams, J Sommer (Eds), *Simple and complex posttraumatic stress disorder* (pp. 351–360). New York: Haworth Press.

O'Connor D, Green J, Ferguson E, O'Carroll R, O'Connor R (2018). Effects of childhood trauma on cortisol levels in suicide attempters and ideators. *Psychoneuroendocrino*, *88*, 9–16. abstract.

O'Connor E, Cappella E, McCormick M, & McClowry S (2014a). An examination of the efficacy of INSIGHTS in enhancing the academic and behavioral development of children in early grades. *J Educ Psychol*, *106*(4), 1156–1169.

O'Connor E, Cappella E, McCormick M, & McClowry S (2014b). Enhancing the academic development of shy children: A test of the efficacy of INSIGHTS. *School Psychol Rev*, *43*(3), 239–259. abstract.

O'Connor T, Ben-Shlomo Y, Heron J, Golding J, Adams D, Glover V (2005). Pre-natal anxiety predicts individual differences in cortisol in preadolescent children. *Biol Psychiatry*, *58*, 211–217.

O'Connor T, Marvin R, Rutter M, Olrick J, Bretner P (2003). English and Romanian Adoptees (ERA) Study Team. Child-parent attachment following early institutional deprivation. *Dev Psychopathol*, *15*, 19–38.

O'Donnel K, Dorsey S, Gong W, Ostermann J, Whetten R, Cohen J et al. (2014). Treating maladaptive grief and posttraumatic stress symptoms in orphaned children in Tanzania: Trauma-Focused Cognitive Behavioral Therapy. *J Traum Stress*, *27*, 664–671.

Ogden P, Minton K, & Pain C (2006). *Trauma and the body: A sensorimotor approach to psychotherapy*. New York: WW Norton.

Ogle C, Block S, Harris L, Goodman G, Pineda A, Timmer S et al. (2013). Autobiographical memory specificity in child sexual abuse victims. *Dev Psychopathol*, *25*, 321–332.

Okanda M, Moriguchi Y, & Itakura S (2010). Language and cognitive shifting: Evidence from young monolingual and bilingual children. *Psychol Rep*, *107*(1), 68–78.

Olafson E, Boat B, Putnam K, Thieken L, Marrow M, & Putnam F (2016). Implementing trauma and grief component therapy for adolescents and think trauma for traumatized youth in secure juvenile justice settings. *J Interpers Violence*, *33*(16), 2537–2557.

Olds D, Sadler L, & Kitzman H (2007). Programs for parents of infants and toddlers: Recent evidence from randomized trials. *J Child Psychol Psyc*, *48*, 355–391.

Olino T, Klein D, Dyson M, Rose S, & Durbin C (2010). Temperamental emotionality in preschool-aged children and Depressive Disorders in parents: Associations in a large community sample. *J Abnorm Psychol*, *9(3)*, 468–478.

Olvera R, Semrud-Clikeman M, Pliszka S, & O'Donnell L (2005). Neuropsychological deficits in adolescents with conduct disorder and comorbid bipolar disorder: a pilot study. *Bipolar Disord*, *7*, 57–67.

Ometto M, de Oliveira P, Miliono A, dos Santos B, Scivoletto S, Busatto G et al. (2016). Social skills and psychopathic traits in maltreated adolescents. *Eur Child Adolesc Psychiatry*, *25*, 397–405.

Oniszczenko W, & Dragan W (2012). Association between temperament in terms of the Regulative Theory of Temperament and DRD4 and DAT1 gene polymorphisms. *Compr Psychiat*, *53*, 789–796.

Oosterhoff B, Kaplow J, & Layne C (in press). Links between bereavement due to sudden death and academic functioning: Results from a nationally representative sample of adolescents. *School Psychol Quart.*

Ordway M, Sadler L, Holland M, Slade A, Close N, & Mayes L (2018). A home visiting parenting program and child obesity: A randomized trial. *Pediatrics*, *41*(2), e20171076.

Ordway M, Sadler L, Slade A, Dixon J, Close N, & Mayes L (2014). Lasting effects of an interdisciplinary home visiting program on child behavior: Preliminary follow-up results of a randomized trial. *J Pediatr Nurs*, *29*(1), 3–13.

Ordway M, Webb D, Sadler L, & Slade A (2015). Parental reflective functioning: An approach to enhancing parent–child relationships in pediatric primary care. *J Pediatr Health Car*, *29*(4), 325–334.

Ørner R (2007). Guest editorial. Implementing NICE guidance for posttraumatic stress disorder in primary care: A new set of criteria for quality assessment. *Qual Prim Care*, *15*(5). 261–4.

Oshri A, Duprey E, Kogan S, Carlson M, & Liu S (in press). Growth patterns of future orientation among maltreated youth: A prospective examination of the emergence of resilience. *Dev Psychol.*

Oshri A, Sutton T, Warner J, & Miller J (2015). Child maltreatment types and risk behaviors: Associations with attachment style and emotion regulation dimensions. *Pers Indiv Differ73*, 127–133.

Osofsky H, Hansel T, Osofsky J, & Speier A (2015a). Factors contributing to mental and physical health care in a disaster-prone environment. *Behav Med*, *41*(3), 131–137.

Osofsky H, Osofsky J, Kronenberg M, Brennan A, & Hansel T (2009). Posttraumatic Stress Symptoms in Children After Hurricane Katrina: Predicting the Need for Mental Health Services. *Am J Orthopsychiat*, *79*(2), 212–220.

Osofsky J (2018). Commentary: Understanding the impact of domestic violence on children, recognizing strengths, and promoting resilience: reflections on Harold and Sellers (2018). *J Child Psychol Psyc*, *59*(4), 403–404.

Osofsky J (2011). Vicarious traumatization and the need for self-care in working with traumatized young children. In J Osofsky (Ed.), *Clinical work with traumatized young children* (pp. 336–348). New York: Guilford.

Osofsky J (2009). Perspectives on helping traumatized infants, young children and their families. *Inf Mental Hlth J*, *30*(6), 673–677.

Osofsky J, & Lieberman A (2011). A call for integrating a mental health perspective into systems of care for abused and neglected Infants and young children. *Am Psychol*, *66*(2), 120–128.

Osofsky J, Kronenberg M, Bocknek E, & Hansel T (2015b). Longitudinal impact of attachment-related risk and exposure to trauma among young children after Hurricane Katrina. *Child Youth Care For*, *44*, 493–510.

Osofsky J, Osofsky H, Weems C, King L, & Hansel T (2015c). Trajectories of posttraumatic stress disorder symptoms among youth exposed to both natural and technological disasters, *J Child Psychol Psyc*, *56*(12), 1347–1355.

Oswald L, Zandi P, Nestadt G, Potash J, Kalaydjian A, & Wand G (2006). Relationship between cortisol responses to stress and personality. *Neuropsychopharmacology*, *31*, 1583–1591.

Otawa T, York T, Gardner C, Kendler K, & Hettema J (2014). The impact of childhood parental loss on risk for mood, anxiety and substance use disorders in a population-based sample of male twins. *Psychiat Res*, *220*(1–2), 404–409.

O'Toole C, Furlong M, McGilloway S, & Bjorndal A (2017). Preschool and school-based mindfulness programmes for improving mental health and cognitive functioning in young people aged 3 to 18 years. *Cochrane Db Syst Rev*, Issue 1. Art. No.: CD012518.

Otte R, Donkers F, Braeken M, & Van den Bergh B (2015). Multimodal processing of emotional information in 9-month-old infants II: Pre-natal exposure to maternal anxiety. *Brain Cognition*, *95*, 107–117.

Overbeek G, Vollebergh W, de Graaf R, Scholte R, de Kemp R, & Engels R (2006). Longitudinal associations of marital quality and marital dissolution with the incidence of DSM-III-R disorders. *J Fam Psychol*, *20*, 284–291.

Overbeek M, De Schipper J, Willemen A, Lamers-Winkelman F, & Schuengel C (2015). Mediators and treatment factors in intervention for children exposed to inter-parental violence. *J Clin Child Adolesc*, 46(3), 411–427. abstract.

Overgaard K, Aase H, Torgersen S, Reichborn-Kjennerud T, Oerbeck B et al. (2014). Continuity in features of anxiety and attention deficit/hyperactivity disorder in young preschool children. *Eur Child Adolesc Psychiatry*, *23*, 743–752.

Overgaard K, Aase H, Torgersen S, & Zeiner P (2012). Cooccurrence of ADHD and anxiety in preschool children. *J Atten Disord, 20*(7), 573–580.

Owen J, Quirk K, & Manthos M (2012). I get no respect: The relationship between betrayal trauma and romantic relationship functioning. *J Trauma & Dissoc, 13*, 175–189.

Oxford M, Harachi T, Catalano R, & Abbott R (2000). Preadolescent predictors of stubstance initiation: A test of both the direct and mediated effect of family social control factors on deviant peer associations and substance initiation. *Am J Drug Alcohol Ab, 27*(4), 599–616.

Özdemir F, & Tüfekci F (2014). The effect of individualised developmental care practices on the growth and hospitalisation duration of premature infants: the effect of mother's scent and flexion position. *J Clin Nurs, 23*, 3036–3044.

Paavonen E, Porkka-Heiskanen T, Lahikainen A (2009a). Sleep quality, duration and behavioral symptoms among 5–6-year-old children. *Eur Child Adolesc Psychiatry, 18*(12), 747–754.

Paavonen E, Räikkönen K, Lahti J, Komsi N, Heinonen K, Pesonen A et al. (2009b). Short sleep duration and behavioral symptoms of attention-deficit/hyperactivity disorder in healthy 7- to 8-year-old children. *Pediatrics, 123*(5), e857–864.

Pade H, Taube D, Aalborg A, & Reiser P (2006). An immediate and long-term study of a temperament and parent–child interaction therapy based community program for preschoolers with behavior problems. *Child Fam Behav Ther, 28*(3), 1–28.

Page R, Yanagishita J, Suwanteerangkul J, Zarco E, Mei-Lee C, & Miao N-F (2006). Hopelessness and loneliness among suicide attempters in school-based samples of Taiwanese, Philippine and Thai Adolescents. *School Psychol Int, 27*(5), 583–598.

Paivio S, Jarry J, Chagigiorgis H, Hall I, & Ralston M (2010). Efficacy of two versions of emotion-focused therapy for resolving child abuse trauma. *Psychother Res, 20*, 353–366.

Paivio S & McCulloch C (2004). Alexithymia as a mediator between childhood trauma and self-injurious behaviors. *Child Abuse Neglect 28*, 339–354.

Paksarian D, Eaton W, Mortensen P, Merikangas K, & Pederson C (2015). A population-based study of the risk of schizophrenia and bipolar disorder associated with parent–child separation during development. *Psychol Medi, 45*, 2825–2837.

Palmason H, Moser D, Sigmund J, Vogler C, Hanig S, Schneider A et al. (2010). Attention-deficit/hyperactivity disorder phenotype is influenced by a functional catechol-O-methyltransferase variant. *J Neural Transm, 117*(2), 259–267.

Panesi S, & Morra S (2016). Drawing a dog: The role of working memory and executive function. *J Exp Child Psychol, 152*, 1–11.

Panksepp J (2007). Can PLAY diminish ADHD and facilitate the construction of the social brain? *J Can Acad Child Adolesc Psychiatry, 16*(2), 57–66.

Panksepp J (1998). *Affective neuroscience: The foundations of human and animal emotions.* Oxford: Oxford University Press.

Papa A, & Bonanno G (2008). Smiling in the face of adversity: The interpersonal and intrapersonal functions of smiling. *Emotion, 8*(1), 1–12.

Papageorgiou K, & Ronald A (2013). "He who sees things grow from the beginning will have the finest view of them": A systematic review of genetic studies on psychological traits in infancy. *Neurosci Biobehav Rs, 37*, 1500–1517.

Pappa I, Mileva-Seitz V, Bakermans-Kranenburg M, Tiemeier H, & van IJzendoorn M (2015). The magnificent seven: A quantitative review of dopamine receptor d4 and its association with child behavior. *Neurosci Biobehav Rs, 57*, 175–186.

Parisette-Sparks A, Bufferd S, & Klein D (2015). Parental predictors of children's shame and guilt at age 6 in a multimethod, longitudinal study. *J Clin Child Adoles, 46*(5), 721–731.

Park M, Chang E, & You S (2015). Protective role of coping flexibility in PTSD and depressive symptoms following trauma. *Pers Indiv Differ, 82*, 102–106.

Parker C, Doctor R, Selvam R (2008). Somatic therapy treatment effects with tsunami survivors. *Traumatology*, 14(3), 103–109.

Parlar M, Frewen P, Oremus C, Lanius R, & McKinnon M (2016). Dissociative symptoms are associated with reduced neuropsychological performance in patients with recurrent depression and a history of trauma exposure. *Europ J Psychotraumato.* 7(1), doi: 10.3402/ejpt.v7.29061.

Parrish C, & Radomsky A (2010). Why do people seek reassurance and check repeatedly? An investigation of factors involved in compulsive behavior in OCD and depression. *J Anxiety Disord, 24*, 211–222. abstract.

Pascual-Leone A, Amedi A, Fregni F, & Merabet L (2005). The plastic human brain cortex. *Annu Rev Neurosci, 28*, 377–401.

Pasupathi M, & Wainryb C (2010). On telling the whole story: Facts and interpretations in autobiographical memory narratives from childhood through midadolescence. *Dev Psychol, 46*(3), 735–746.

Patel R, Spreng R, Shin L, & Girard T (2012). Neurocircuitry models of posttraumatic stress disorder and beyond: a meta-analysis of functional neuroimaging studies. *Neurosci Biobehav Rev, 36*, 2130–2142.

Pat-Horenczyk R, Kenan A, Achituv M, & Bachar E (2014). Protective factors based model for screening for posttraumatic distress in adolescents. *Child Youth Care For, 43*, 339–351.

Pat-Horenczyk R, Peled O, Daie A, Abramovitz R, Brom D, & Chemtob C (2007). Adolescent exposure to recurrent terrorism in Israel: Posttraumatic distress and functional impairment. *Am J Orthopsychiat*, 77(1), 76–85.

Pattwell S, Lee F, & Casey B (2013). Fear learning and memory across adolescent development. *Hormones Behav, 64*, 380–389.

Payne P, Levine P, & Crane-Godreau M (2015). Somatic experiencing: using interoception and proprioception as core elements of trauma therapy. *Front Psychol*, 6(93), doi: 10.3389/fpsyg.2015.00093.

Pearlman L, Wortman C, Feuer C, Farber C, & Rando T (2014). *Treating traumatic bereavement: A practitioner's guide.* New York: Guilford.

Pearlman M, Schwalbe K, & Cloitre M (2010). *Grief in childhood: Fundamentals of treatment in clinical practice.* Washington, DC: APA.

Pears K, Fisher P, Bruce J, Kim H, & Yoerger K (2010). Early elementary school adjustment of maltreated children in foster care: The roles of inhibitory control and caregiver. *Child Dev, 81*(5), 1550–1564.

Pechtel P, Lyons-Ruth K, Anderson C, & Teicher M (2014). Sensitive periods of amygdala development: The role of maltreatment in preadolescence. *NeuroImage, 97*, 236–244.

Pedro-Carroll JL (2005). Fostering children's resilience in the aftermath of divorce: The role of evidence-based programs for children. *Fam Court Rev, 43*(1), 52–64.

Peeters M, Cillessen A, & Scholte R (2010). Clueless or Powerful? Identifying Subtypes of Bullies in Adolescence. *J Youth Adolescence, 39*, 1041–1052.

Peh C, Shahwan S, Fauziana R, Mahesh M, Sambasivam R, Zhang Y et al. (2017). Emotion dysregulation as a mechanism linking child maltreatment exposure and self-harm behaviors in adolescents. *Child Abuse Neglect 67*, 383–390. abstract.

Pelaez M, Field T, Pickens J, & Hart S (2008). Disengaged and authoritarian parenting behavior of depressed mothers with their toddlers. *Infant Behav Dev, 31*, 145–148.

Pellegrini A (2009). *The role of play in human development.* New York: Oxford University Press.

Pellegrini A (2001). Practitioner review: The role of direct observation in the assessment of young children. *J Child Psychol Psyc, 42*(7), 861–869.

Pellegrini A, Dupuis D, & Smith P (2007). Play in evolution and development. *Dev Rev, 27*, 261–276.

Pellegrini A, & Goldsmith S (2003). "Settling in": A short-term longitudinal study of ways in which new children come to play with classmates. *Emot Behav Diffic, 8*, 140–151.

Pellegrini A, & Smith P (Eds) (2005). *The nature of play: Great apes and humans.* New York: Guilford.

Pellegrini A, & Smith P (1998). Physical activity play: The nature and function of a neglected aspect of play. *Child Dev, 69*(3), 577–598.

Peltola M, Forssman L, Puura K, van IJzendoorn M, & Lappan J (2015). Attention to faces expressing negative emotion at 7 months predicts attachment security at 14 months. *Child Dev*, doi: 10.1111/cdev.12380.

Peltonen K, Kangaslampi S, Qouta S, & Punamäki R (2017). Trauma and autobiographical memory: contents and determinants of earliest memories among war-affected Palestinian children. *Memory, 25*(10), 1347–1357.

Peltz J, Rogge R, Rogosch F, Cicchetti D, & Toth S (2015). The benefits of Child–Parent Psychotherapy to marital satisfaction. *Fam Syst Health, 33(*4), 372–382.

Penberthy JK (2012). Mindfulness based interventions for addictions: What is next? *J Addict Res Ther, 3*(5), e116. doi.org/10.4172/2155-6105.1000e116.

Peng P, & Miller A (2016). Does attention training work? A selective meta-analysis to explore the effects of attention training and moderators. *Learn Individ Differ, 45*, 77–87.

Peng X, Lin P, Wu X, Gong R, Yang R, & Wang A (2017). Insular subdivisions functional connectivity dysfunction within major depressive disorder. *J Affect Disorders, 227*, 280–288.

Penley J, Tomaka J, & Wieve J (2002). The association of coping to physical and psychological health outcomes: a meta-analytic review. *J Behav Med, 25*, 551–603.

Pérez H, Ikram M, Direk N, Prigerson H, Freak-Poli R, Verhaaren B et al. (2014). Cognition, structural brain changes and complicated grief: A population-based study. *Psychol Med, 45*(7), 1389–1399.

Pérez L, Abrams M, López-Martinez A, & Asmundson G (2012). Trauma exposure and health: The role of depressive and hyperarousal symptoms. *J Traum Stress, 25*, 641–648.

Perlman W, Webster M, Herman M, Kleinman J, & Weickert C (2007). Age-related differences in glucocorticoid receptor mRNA levels in the human brain. *Neurobiol Aging, 28*, 447–458.

Perroud N, Jaussent I, Guillaume S, Bellivier F, Baud P, Jollant F et al. (2010). COMT but not serotonin-related genes modulates the influence of childhood abuse on anger traits. *Genes Brain Behav, 9*, 193–202.

Perry B (2009). Examining child maltreatment through a neurodevelopmental lens: Clinical applications of the neurosequential model of therapeutics. *J Loss & Trauma, 14*(4), 240–255.

Perry B (2006). Applying principles of neurodevelopment to clinical work with maltreated and traumatized children. In NB Webb (ed.), *Working with traumatized youth in child welfare* (pp. 27–52). New York: Guilford.

Perry B, Pollard R, Blakely T, Baker W, & Vigilante D (1995). Childhood trauma, the neurobiology of adaptation and "use-dependent" development of the brain: How "states" become "traits." *Inf Mental Hlth J, 16*(4), 271–291.

Pesce C, Masci I, Marchetti R, Vazou S, Saakslahtl A, & Tomporowski P (2016). Deliberate play and preparation jointly benefit motor and cognitive development: Mediated and moderated effects. *Front Psychol*, 7:349. doi: 10.3389/fpsyg.2016.00349.

Peterson C, Dowden C, & Tobin J (1999). Interviewing preschoolers: Comparisons of yes/no and wh-+questions. *Law Human Behav, 23*, 539–556.

Peterson C, & McCabe A (1991). Linking children's connective use and narrative macrostructure. In A McCabe, C Peterson (Eds), *Developing narrative structure* (pp. 29–53). Hillsdale, NJ: Lawrence Erlbaum.

Peterson C, Morris G, Baker-Ward L, & Flynn S (2014). Predicting which childhood memories persist: Contributions of memory characteristics. *Dev Psychol, 50*(2), 439–448.

Peterson C, & Rideout R (1998). Memory for medical emergencies experienced by one and two year olds. *Dev Psychol, 34*, 1059–1072.

Peterson J, Bellows A, & Peterson S (2015). Promoting connection: Perspective-taking improves relationship closeness and perceived regard in participants with low implicit self-esteem. *J Exp Soc Psychol, 56*, 160–164.

Pfeffer C, Altemus M, Heo M, & Jiang H (2007). Salivary cortisol and psychopathology in children bereaved by the September 11, 2001, terror attacks. *Biol Psychiat, 61*, 957–965.

Pfefferbaum B, Stuber J, Galea S, & Fairbrother G (2006). Panic reactions to terrorist attacks and probable posttrauamtic stress disorder in adolescents. *J Traum Stress, 19*, 217–228.

Pfefferbaum B, Weems C, Scott B, Nitiema P, Noffsinger M, Pfefferbaum R, Varma V, & Chakraburtty A (2013). Research methods in child disaster studies: A review of studies generated by the September 11, 2001, terrorist attacks; the 2004 Indian Ocean tsunami; and Hurricane Katrina. *Child Youth Care For, 42*, 285–337.

Pfeiffer E, Sachser C, de Haan A, Tutus D, & Goldbeck L (2017). Dysfunctional posttraumatic cognitions as a mediator of symptom reduction in Trauma-Focused Cognitive Behavioral Therapy with children and adolescents: Results of a randomized controlled trial. *Behav Res Ther, 97*, 178–182.

Phares V, Rojas A, Thurston I, & Hankinson J (2010). Including fathers in clinical interventions for children and adolescents. In ME Lamb (Ed.), *The role of the father in child development* (5th ed., pp. 459–485). Hoboken, NJ: Wiley.

Piaget J (1962). *Play, dreams and imitation*. New York: Norton.

Piaget J (1952). *The origins of intelligence in children*. New York: International Universities Press.

Piaget J & Inhelder B (1969). *Psychology of the Child*. New York: Basic Books.

Pickles A, Durkin K, Mok P, Toseeb U, & Conti-Ramsden G (2016). Conduct problems co-occur with hyperactivity in children with language impairment: A longitudinal study from childhood to adolescence. *Autism Devel Lang Impair, 1*, 1–11. doi: 10.1177/2396941516645251.

Pillow B (1995). Two trends in the development of perspective-taking: an elaboration of the passive-active hypothesis. *Int J Behav Dev, 18*(4), 649–676.

Pincus D, Eyberg S, & Choate M (2005). Adapting parent–child interaction therapy for children with separation anxiety disorder. *Educ Treat Children, 28*, 163–181.

Pincus D, Santucci L, Ehrenreich J, Eyberg S (2008). The implementation of Modified Parent–child Interaction Therapy for youth with Separation Anxiety Disorder. *Cogn Behav Pract, 15*, 118–125.

Piotrowski J, Lapierre M, & Linebarger D (2013). Investigating correlates of self-regulation in early childhood with a representative sample of English-speaking American families. *J Child Fam Stud, 22*, 423–436.

Pirutinsky S (2014). Does Religiousness increase self-control and reduce criminal behavior? A longitudinal analysis of adolescent offenders. *Crim Justice & Behav, 41*(11), 1290–1307.

Pitman R, Bolshakov V, Brunet A, & Nader K (2010). Developing memory reconsolidation blockers as novel PTSD treatments. Prepared for US army. Downloaded 1-26-18, www.researchgate.net/publication/235074123.

Pizzagalli D (2014). Depression, stress, and anhedonia: toward a synthesis and integrated model. *Annu Rev Clin Psychol., 10*, 393–423.

Platinga L, Bremner J, Miller A, Jones D, Veledar E, Goldberg J, & Vaccarine V (2013). Association between Posttraumatic Stress Disorder and Inflammation: A Twin Study. *Brain Behav Immun, 30*, 125–132.

Pluess M, Belsky J, Way B, & Taylor S (2010). 5-HTTLPR moderates effects of current life events on neuroticism: Differential susceptibility to environmental influences. *Prog Nuero-Psychoph, 34*, 1070–1074.

Pluess M, Velders F, Belsky J, van IJzendoorn M, Bakermans-Kranenburg M, Jaddoe V et al. (2011). Serotonin transporter polymorphism moderates effects of pre-natal maternal anxiety on infant negative emotionality. *Biol Psychiat, 69*, 520–525.

Poehlmann-Tynan J, Vigna A, Weymouth L, Gerstein E, Burnson C, Zabransky M et al. (2016). A pilot study of contemplative practices with economically disadvantaged preschoolers: Children's empathic and self-regulatory behaviors. *Mindfulness*, 7, 46–58.

Polan H, & Hofer M (2018). Psychobiological Origins of Infant Attachment and Its Role in Development. In J Cassidy, P Shaver (Eds), *Handbook of attachment* (3rd ed., pp. 117–132). New York: Guilford.

Polcari A, Rabi K, Bolger E, & Teicher M (2014). Parental verbal affection and verbal aggression in childhood differentially influence psychiatric symptoms and well-being in young adulthood. *Child Abuse Neglect 38*, 91–102.

Pole N, Best S, Metzler T, & Marmar C (2005). Why are Hispanics at greater risk for PTSD? *Cult Divers Ethn Min, 11*(2), 144–161.

Pollak S (2008). Mechanisms linking early experience and the emergence of emotions. *Current Direc in Psychol Sci, 17*(6), 370–375.

Pollak S, Cicchetti D, Hornung K, & Reed A (2000). Recognizing emotion in faces: Developmental effects of child abuse and neglect. *Dev Psychol, 36*(5), 679–688.

Pollack W (2001). The importance of family: Preventing violence through family connection. *The Brown University CABL, 17*(12), 1, 3–4.

Pollack W (1982). "I"ness and "we"ness: Parallel lines of development. Unpublished doctoral dissertation. Boston University.

Pontari B, & Schlenker B (2000). The influence of cognitive load on self-presentation: Can cognitive busyness help as well as harm social performance? *J Pers Soc Psychol, 78*(6), 1092–1108.

Porges SW (2009). The polyvagal theory. *Clev Clin J Med, 76*(Suppl. 2), S86–S90.

Pos A, & Greenberg L (2012). Organizing awareness and increasing emotion regulation: Revising chair work in Emotion-Focused Therapy for borderline personality disorder. *J Pers Disorders, 26*(1), 84–107.

Posner K, Melvin G, Murray D, Gugga S, Fisher P, Skrobala A et al. (2007). Clinical presentation of Attention-Deficit/Hyperactivity Disorder in preschool children: The preschoolers with Attention-Deficit/Hyperactivity Treatment Study (PATS). *J Child Adol Psychop, 17*(5), 547–562.

Posner M, & Rothbart M (2007a). Research on attention networks as a model for the integration of Psychol Sci, *Annu Rev Psychol, 58*, 1–23.

Posner M, & Rothbart M (2007b). *Educating the Human Brain*. Washington DC: American Psychological Association.

Posner M, Rothbart M, Sheese B, & Voelker P (2014). Developing attention: Behavioral and brain mechanisms. *Adv Neurosci*, doi: 10.1155/2014/405094.

Posner M, Rothbart M, & Voelker P (2016). Developing brain networks of attention. *Curr Opin Pediatr, 28*(6), 720–724.

Potasz C, Vilela de Varela M, de Carvalho L, Prado L, & Prado G (2013). Effect of play activities on hospitalized children's stress: a randomized clinical trial. *Scand J Occup Ther, 20*, 71–79.

Powers K, Somerville L, Kelley W, & Heatherton T (2016). Striatal associative learning signals are tuned to in-groups. *J Cognitive Neurosci, 28*(9), 1243–1254.

Powers K, Worsham A, Freeman J, Wheatley T, & Heatherton T (2014). Social connection modulates perceptions of animacy. *Psychol Sci, 25(10), 1943–1948.*

Premack D, & Woodruff G (1978). Does the chimpanzee have a theory of mind? *Behav Brain Sci, 1*(4), 515–526.

Price J, & Lento J (2001). The nature of child and adolescent vulnerability. In R Ingram, J Price (Eds), *Vulnerability to Psychopathology: Risk Across the Lifespan* (pp. 20–38). New York: Guilford.

Price M, Spinazzola J, Musicaro R, Turner J, Suvak M et al. (2017). Effectiveness of an extended Yoga treatment for women with chronic Posttraumatic Stress Disorder. *J Altern Complement Med, 23*(4), 300–309.

Prigerson H, Bierhals A, Kasl S, Reynolds C, Shear M, Day N et al. (1997). Traumatic grief as a risk factor for mental and physical morbidity. *Am J Psychiat, 154*, 616–623.

Prigerson H, Horowitz M, Jacobs S, Parkes C, Aslan M, Goodkin K et al. (2009). Prolonged Grief Disorder: Psychometric validation of criteria proposed for DSM-V and ICD-11. *PLoS Medicine, 6*(8), e1000121.

Prigerson H, Shear M, Jacobs S, Reynolds C, Maciejewski P, Davidson J et al. (1999). Consensus criteria for traumatic grief. *Brit J Psychiat, 174*, 67–73.

Propper C, Moore G, Mills-Koonce W, Calkins S, Halpern C, Hill-Soderlund et al. (2008). Gene–Environment contributions to the development of infant vagal reactivity: The Interaction of dopamine and maternal sensitivity. *Child Dev, 79*(5), 1377–1394.

Proyer R, Gander F, Wellenzohn S, & Ruch W (2014). Positive psychology interventions in people aged 50–79 years: long-term effects of placebo-controlled online interventions on well-being and depression. *Aging Ment Health, 18*(8), 997–100.

Pryce C, Ruedi-Bettschen D, Dettling A, Weston A, Russig H, Ferger B et al. (2005). Long-term effects of early life environmental manipulations in rodents and primates: potential animal models in depression research. *Neurosci Biobehav Rev*, *29*(4–5), 649–674.

Psouni E, & Apetroaia A (2014). Measuring scripted attachment-related knowledge in middle childhood: the Secure Base Script Test. *Attach Hum Dev*, *16*(1), 22–41.

Psychogiou L, Nath S, Kallitsoglou A, Dimatis K, Parry E, Russell A et al. (2018). Children's emotion understanding in relation to attachment to mother and father. *Brit J Dev Psychol*, doi: 10.1111/bjdp.12239.

Puetz V, Parker D, Kohn N, Dahmen B, Verma R, & Konrad K (2017). Altered brain network integrity after childhood maltreatment: A structural connectomic DTI-study. *Hum Brain Mapp*, *38*, 855–868.

Puff J, & Renk K (2015). Preschool PTSD Treatment (PPT) for a young child exposed to trauma in the Middle East. *Clin Case Stud*, *14*(5) 388–404.

Pugin F, Metz A, Stauffer M, Wolf M, Jenni O, & Huber R (2015). Working memory training shows immediate and long-term effects on cognitive performance in children and adolescents. *F1000Research*, 3:82. doi: 10.12688/f1000research.3665.3.

Punamäki R, Qouta S, & El-Sarraj E (2001). Resiliency factors predicting psychological adjustment after political violence among Palestinian children. *Int J Behav Dev*, *25*(3), 256–267.

Purdie V, & Downey G (2000). Rejection sensitivity and adolescent girls' vulnerability to relationship-centered difficulties. *Child Maltreatment*, *5*(4), 338–349.

Putnam F (1997). *Dissociation in children and adolescents: A developmental perspective*. New York: Guilford.

Putnam F, Helmers K, Horowitz L, & Trickett P (1995). Hypnotizability and dissociativity in sexually abused girls. *Child Abuse Neglect*, *19*(5), 645–655.

Putnam S, Ellis L, & Rothbart M (2001). The structure of temperament from infancy through adolescence. In A Eliasz, A Angleitner (Eds), *Advances in research on temperament* (pp. 165–182). Lengerich, Germany: Pabst Science.

Putnam S, Gartstein M, & Rothbart M (2006). Measurement of fine-grained aspects of toddler temperament: The Early Childhood Behavior Questionnaire. *Infant Behav Dev*, *29*, 386–401.

Püttker K, Thomsen T, & Bockmann A (2015). Sekundäre Traumatisierung bei Traumatherapeutinnen [Secondary trauma in trauma therapists: Empathy as a risk factor and accommodative coping as a protective factor]. *Zeitschrift für Klinische Psychologie und Psychotherapie*, *44*(4), 254–265.

Pynoos R, & Eth S (1986). Witness to violence: The child interview. *J Amer Acad Child Ps*, *25*(3), 306–319.

Pynoos R, & Eth S (1985). Children traumatized by witnessing acts of personal violence. In S Eth, R Pynoos (ed.), *Posttraumatic stress in children*. Washington, DC: American Psychiatric Association Press.

Pynoos R, Frederick C, Nader K, Arroyo W, Eth S, Nunez W, Steinberg A, & Fairbanks L (1987). Life threat and posttraumatic stress in school age children. *Arch Gen Psychiat*, *44*, 1057–1063.

Pynoos R, & Nader K (1988). Psychological first aid and treatment approach for children exposed to community violence: Research implications. *J Traum Stress*, *1*(4), 445–473.

Qu Y, Galvan A, Fuligni A, Lieberman M, & Telzer E (2015). Longitudinal changes in prefrontal cortex activation underlie declines in adolescent risk-taking. *J Neurosci*, *35*, 11308–11314.

Quach D, Jastrowski Mano K, & Alexander K (2015). A randomized controlled trial examining the effect of mindfulness meditation on working memory capacity in adolescents. *J Adolescent Health*, *58*(5), 489–496.

Qouta S, Peltonen K, Diab S, Suvi A, Palosaari E, & Punamäki R-L (2016). Psychosocial intervention and dreaming among war-affected Palestinian children. *Dreaming*, *26*(2), 95–118.

Qouta S, Punamäki R-L, & El-Sarraj E (2008). Child development and family mental health in war and military violence: The Palestinian experience. *Int J Behav Dev*, *32*(4), 310–321.

Qiu A, Tuan T, Ong M, Li Y, Chen H, Rifkin-Graboi A et al. (2015). COMT haplotypes modulate associations of antenatal maternal anxiety and neonatal cortical morphology. *Am J Psychiatry*, *172*, 163–172. abstract.

Rabinak C, Angstadt M, Welsh R, Kenndy A, Lyubkin M, Martis B, & Phan K (2011). Altered amygdala resting-state functional connectivity in post-traumatic stress disorder. *Front Psychiatry*, *2*, 62, http://dx.doi.org/10.3389/fpsyt.2011.00062.

Rabinowitz J, Drabick D, Reynolds M, Clark D, & Olino T (2016). Child Temperamental flexibility moderates the relation between positive parenting and adolescent adjustment. *J Appl Dev Psychol*, *43*, 43–53.

Raby K, Steele R, Carlson E, & Sroufe L (2015). Continuities and changes in infant attachment patterns across two generations. *Attach Hum Dev*, *17*(4), 414–428.

Raffington L, Prindle J, Keresztes A, & Shing Y (2018). Blunted cortisol stress reactvity in low-income children relates to lower memory function. *Psychoneuroendocrino*, *90*, 110–121. abstract.

Raleigh H, Brien L, & Eisen A (2002). Parent training treatment manual for separation anxious children. Unpublished manuscript. Farleigh Dickinson University, Teaneck, NJ.

Ramey C, McGinness G, Cross L, Collier A, & Barrie-Blackley S (1982). The Abecedarian approach to social competence: Cognitive and linguistic intervention for disadvantaged preschoolers. In K Borman (ed.), *The social life of children in a changing society* (pp. 14–174). Hillsdale, NJ: Erlbaum.

Ramsauer B, Lotzin A, Mühlhan C, Romer G, Nolte T, Fonagy P et al. (2014). A randomized controlled trial comparing Circle of Security intervention and treatment as usual as interventions to increase attachment security in infants of mentally ill mothers: study protocol. *BMC Psychiatry 14*, 24–35.

Rankin Williams L, Degnan K, Perez-Edgar K, Henderson H, Rubin K, Pine D et al. (2009). Impact of behavioral inhibition and parenting style on internalizing and externalizing problems from early childhood through adolescence. *J Abnorm Child Psychol, 37*, 1063–1075.

Rashwan M, Gregg D, Somers C, Hoffman A, Yoon J, & Barnett D (2017). Adolescent attachment in multiple contexts: Associations with emotional and behavioral functioning in the United States Midwest. *Soc Dev Issues 39*(1), 54–67.

Ratnamohan L, & Kozlowska K (2017). When things get complicated: At-risk attachment in children and adolescents with chronic pain. *Clin Child Psychol P, 22*(4) 588–602. abstract.

Ravary A, & Baldwin M (2018). Self-esteem vulnerabilities are associated with cued attentional biases toward rejection. *Pers Indiv Differ, 126*, 44–51.

Rayson H, Bonaiuto J, Ferrari P, & Murray L (2016). Mu desynchronization during observation and execution of facial expressions in 30-month-old children. *Developm Cogni Neurosci, 19*, 279–287.

Razza R, Bergen-Cico D, & Raymond K (2013). Enhancing preschoolers' self-regulation via Mindful Yoga. *J Child Fam Stud, 24*(2), 372–385.

Ready C, Hayes A, Yasinski C, Webb C, Gallop R, Deblinger E et al. (2015). Overgeneralized beliefs, accommodation, and treatment outcome in youth receiving Trauma-Focused Cognitive Behavioral Therapy for childhood trauma. *Behav Ther, 46*(5), 671–688.

Reese E, Haden C, & Fivush R (1993). Mother–child conversations about the past: Relationships of style and memory over time. *Cognitive Dev, 8*, 403–430.

Reid K, Littlefield L, & Hammond S (2008). Early intervention for preschoolers with behaviour problems: Preliminary findings for the Exploring Together Preschool Program. Australian e-*Journal for the Advancement of Mental Health*, 7(1), 15–29.

Reilly S, Wake M, Bavin E, Prior M, Williams J, Bretherton L et al. (2007). Predicting language at 2 years of age: A Prospective community study. *Pediatrics,120*, e1441-e1449.

Reilly S, Wake M, Ukoumunne O, Bavin E, Prior M, Cini E et al. (2010). Predicting language outcomes at 4 years of age: Findings from early language in Victoria Study. *Pediatrics, 126*(6), e1530-e1537.

Rekart K, Mineka S, Zinbarg R, & Griffícth J (2007). Perceived family environment and symptoms of emotional disorders: The role of perceived control, attributional style, and attachment. *Cognitive Ther Res, 31*(4), 419–436.

Resick P, Bovin M, Calloway A, Dick A, King M, Mitchell K (2012a). A critical evaluation of the complex PTSD literature: Implications for DSM-5. *J Traum Stress, 25*, 241–251. abstract.

Resick P, Suvak M, Johnides B, Mitchell K, & Iverson K (2012b). The impact of dissociation on PTSD treatment with cognitive processing therapy. *Depress Anxiety, 29*(8), 718730.

Restak R (2013). Laughter and the brain. *Am Scholar*, 18–27.

Rettew D, Althoff R, Dumenci L, Ayer L, & Hudziak J (2008). Latent profiles of temperament and their relations to psychopathology and wellness. *J Am Acad Child Psy, 47*(3), 273–281.

Rettew, D, Copeland W, Stanger C, & Hudziak J (2004). Associations between temperament and DSM-IV externalizing disorders in children and adolescents. *J Dev Behav Pediatr, 25*, 383–391.

Reynolds G, Bahrick L, Lickliter R, & Guy M (2014). Neural correlates of intersensory processing in 5-month-old infants. *Dev Psychobiol, 56*(3), 355–372.

Reynolds G, & Richards J (2008). Attention and early brain development. *Encyclopedia of Early Childhood Development*, downloaded 6-14-17, www.child-encyclopedia.com/brain/according-experts/stress-and-early-brain-development.

Rhodes A (2015). Claiming peaceful embodiment through yoga in the aftermath of trauma. *Complement Ther Clin, 21*, 247–256.

Ribaudo J (2016). Restoring safety: An attachment-based approach to clinical work with a traumatized toddler. *Inf Mental Hlth J, 37*(1), 80–92.

Ritter J, Bruck C, Jacob H, Wildgruber D, & Kreifelts B (2015). Laughter perception in social anxiety. *J Psychiatr Res, 60*, 178–184.

Rizzolatti G, & Craighero L (2004). The mirror-neuron system. *Ann Rev Neurosci 27*, 169–192.

Rizzolatti G, Craighero L, & Fadiga L (2002). The mirror system in humans. In M Stamenov, V Gallese (Eds) *Mirror neurons and the evolution of brain and language* (pp. 38–59). Philadelphia, PA: John Benjamins Publishing.

Roazzi A, Attili G, Di Pentima L, & Toni A (2016). Locus of control in maltreated children: the impact of attachment and cumulative trauma. *Curr Psychol, 29*(8). doi: 10.1186/s41155-016-0025-9.

Robarts J (2006). Music therapy with sexually abused children. *Clin Child Psychol P, 11*(2), 249–269.

Roberts Y, English D, Thompson R, & White C (2018). The impact of childhood stressful life events on health and behavior in at-risk youth. *Child Youth Serv Rev, 85*, 117–126.

Robertson D, Biaggioni I, Burnstock G, Low P, & Paton J (2012). *Primer on the autonomic nervous system* (3rd ed.). New York: Elsevier.

Robinson L, Boris N, Heller S, Rice J, Zeanah C, Clark C et al. (2012). The good enough home? Home environment and outcomes of young maltreated children. *Child Youth Care For, 41*, 73–88.

Rochat P (2011). The self as phenotype. *Conscious Cogn, 20*, 109–119.

Rochat P (2003). Five levels of self-awareness as they unfold early in life. *Conscious Cogn 12*, 717–731.

Rocheleau C, Webster G, Bryan A, & Frazier J (2004). Moderators of the relationship between exercise and mood changes: Gender, exertion level, and workout duration. *Psychol Health, 19*(4), 491–506. abstract.

Rodrigues S, LeDoux J, & Sapolsky R (2009). The influence of stress hormones on fear circuitry. *Annu Rev Neurosci, 32*, 289–313.

Roediger H, Zaromb F, & Goode M (2008). A Typology of Memory Terms. In R Menzel (ed.), *Learning Theory and Behavior* (Vol. 1, pp. 11–24) of J Byrne (ed.) *Learning and memory: A comprehensive reference* (4 vols). Oxford: Elsevier.

Rogers CR (1980). *A way of being*. Boston, MA: Houghton Mifflin.

Rogers J, Raveendran M, Fawcett G, Fox A, Shelton S, Oler J et al. (2013). CRHR1 genotypes, neural circuits and the diathesis for anxiety and depression. *Mol Psychiatry, 18*(6), 700–707.

Roisman G, & Fraley R (2008). A behavior–genetic study of parenting quality, infant attachment security, and their covariation in a nationally representative sample. *Dev Psychol, 44*, 831–839.

Roley-Roberts M, Hill R, Layne C, Goldenthal H, & Kaplow J (in press). Cause of caregiver death and surviving caregiver coping style predict thwarted belongingness in bereaved youth. *Arch Suicide Res*, https://doi.org/10.1080/13811118.2018.1470949.

Rollins L, & Riggins T (2016). Cohort-sequential study of conflict inhibition during middle childhood. *Int J Behav Dev, 41*(6), 663–669.

Rollo D, & Buttiglieri F (2009). Mother and Infant talk about mental states: Systemic emergence of psychological lexicon and theory of mind understanding. In G Minati, M Abram, E Pessa (Eds), *Processes of emergence of systems and systemic properties* (pp. 777–786). Singapore: World Scientific Publishing Co Pte Ltd.

Rollo D, & Sulla F (2016). Maternal talk in cognitive development: Relations between psychological lexicon, semantic development, empathy, and temperament. *Front Psychol*, 7, 394. doi: 10.3389/fpsyg.2016.00394.

Romano E, Babchishin L, Marquis R, & Frechette S (2015). Childhood maltreatment and educational outcomes. *Trauma Violence Abus, 16*(4) 418–437. abstract.

Romeo R (2003). Puberty: a period of both organizational and activational effects of steroid hormones on neurobehavioral development. *J Neuroendocrinol, 15*, 1185–1192.

Romeo R, & McEwen B (2006). Stress and the adolescent brain. *Ann NY Acad Sci, 1094*(1), 202–214.

Roos S, Hodges E, & Salmivalli C (2014). Do guilt- and shame-proneness differentially predict prosocial, aggressive, and withdrawn behaviors during early adolescence? *Dev Psychol, 50*(3), 941–946.

Rose S, Feldman J, & Jankowski J (2012a). Implications of infant cognition for executive functions at age 11. *Psychol Sci, 23*(11), 1345–1355.

Rose S, Feldman J, Jankowski J, & Rossem R (2012b). Information processing from infancy to 11 years: Continuities and prediction of IQ. *Intelligence 40*, 445–457.

Roskam I, Stievenart M, Meunier J-C, & Noel M-P (2014). The development of children's inhibition: Does parenting matter? *J Exp Child Psychol, 122*, 166–182.

Rosner R, Kruse J, & Hagl M (2010). A meta-analysis of interventions for bereaved children and adolescents. *Death Stud, 34*(2), 99–136.

Ross E, & Kearney C (2017). Posttraumatic symptoms among maltreated youth using classification and regression tree analysis. *Child Abuse Neglect 69*, 177–187.

Rossi E (1993). *The psychobiology of mind-body healing: New concepts of therapeutic hypnosis* (Rev ed.). New York: W W Norton.

Rossouw T (2015). The use of Mentalization-Based Treatment for Adolescents (MBT-A) with a young woman with mixed Personality Disorder and tendencies to self-harm. *J Clin Psychol, In Session, 71*, 178–187.

Rossouw T, & Fonagy P (2012). Mentalization-based treatment for self-harm in adolescents: A randomized controlled trial. *J Amer Acad Child & Adolesc Psychia*, 51(12), 1304–1313.

Rostilla M, Berg L, Arat A, Vinnerljung B, & Hjern A (2016). Parental death in childhood and self-inflicted injuries in young adults-a national cohort study from Sweden. *Eur Child Adolesc Psychiatry, 25*, 1103–1111.

Rotenberg K, Addis N, Betts L, Corrigan A, Fox C, Hobson Z et al. (2010). The relation between trust beliefs and loneliness during early childhood, middle childhood, and adulthood. *Pers Soc Psychol B, 36*(8) 1086–1100.

Rotge J-Y, Lemogne C, Hinfray S, Huguet P, Grynszpan O, Tartour E et al. (2015). A meta-analysis of the anterior cingulate contribution to social pain. *SCAN, 10*,19–27.

Rothbart M (2011). *Becoming who we are*. New York: Guilford.

Rothbart M, Ahadi S, & Hershey K (1994). Temperament and social behavior in childhood. *Merrill-Palmer Q, 40*, 21–39.

Rothbart M, Ahadi S, Hershey K, & Fisher P (2001a). Investigations of temperament at three to seven years: The Children's Behavior Questionnaire. *Child Dev, 72*, 1394–1408.

Rothbart M, & Bates J (2008). Temperament. In W Damon, R Lerner (Eds) *Child and adolescent development: An advanced course* (pp. 54–92). New York: Wiley.

Rothbart M, & Bates J (2006). Temperament. In N Eisenberg, W Damon, R Lerner (Eds), *Handbook of child psychology: Vol. 3: Social, emotional, and personality development* (6th ed., pp. 99–166). Hoboken, NJ: Wiley.

Rothbart M, Chew K, & Gartstein M (2001b). Assessment of temperament in early development. In L Singer, P Zeskind (Eds), *Biobehavioral assessment of the infant* (pp. 190–208). New York: Guilford Press.

Rothbart M, Derryberry D, & Posner M (1994). A psychobiological approach to the development of temperament. In J Bates, T Wachs (Eds), *Temperament: Individual differences at the interface of biology and behavior* (pp. 83–116). Washington, DC: APA.

Rothbart M, & Rueda M (2005). The development of effortful control. In U Mayr, E Awh, S Keele (Eds), *Developing individuality in the human brain: A festschrift honoring Michael Posner* (pp. 167–188). Washington, DC: APA.

Rothschild B (2006). *Help for the helper: The psychophysiology of compassion fatigue and vicarious trauma*. New York: Norton.

Roussos A, Goenjian A, Steinberg A, Sotiropoulou C, Kakaki M, Kabakos C et al. (2005). Posttraumatic stress and depressive reactions among children and adolescents after the 1999 earthquake in Ano Liosia, Greece. *Am J Psychiatry, 162*, 530–537.

Roy A, Xian-Zhang H, Janal M, & Goldman D (2007). Interaction between childhood trauma and serotonin transporter gene variation in suicide. *Neuropsychopharmacology, 32*, 2046–2052.

Roy A, Fudge J, Kelly C, Perry J, Daniele T, Carlisi C et al. (2013). Intrinsic functional connectivity of amygdala-based networks in adolescent generalized anxiety disorder. *J Am Acad Child Psy, 52*, 290–299.

Roy A, Gorodetsky E, Yuan Q, Goldman D, & Enoch M (2010). The interaction of FKBP5, a stress related gene, with childhood trauma increases the risk for attempting suicide *Neuropsychopharmacology, 35*, 1674–1683.

Roy A, Xian-Zhang H, Janal M, & Goldman D (2007). Interaction between childhood trauma and serotonin transporter gene variation in suicide. *Neuropsychopharmacology, 32*, 2046–2052.

Rubia K (2013). Functional brain imaging across development. *Eur Child Adolesc Psychiatry 22*, 719–731.

Rubin K, Bukowski W, Parker J & Bowker J (2008). Peer interactions, relationships, and groups. In W Damon, N Eisenberg (Eds), *Handbook of child psychology, Volume 3. Social, emotional, and personality development* (5th ed., pp. 141–180). New York: Wiley.

Rubin K, & Burgess K (2001). Social withdrawal and anxiety. In M Vasey, MR Dadds (Eds), *The developmental psychopathology of anxiety* (pp. 407–434). New York: Oxford University Press.

Rubin K, Cheah C, & Fox N (2001). Emotion regulation, parenting, and display of social reticence in preschoolers. *Early Educ Dev, 1*, 97–115.

Rucevic S, & Ajdukovic M (2016). Problem behaviors, childhood victimization, and attachment quality in Croatian sample of community and referred psychopathic-like adolescents. *Crim Justice Behav, 43*(5), 564–582.

Rueda M, Posner M, Rothbart M (2005). The development of executive attention: contributions to the emergence of self-regulation. *Dev Neuropsychol, 28*(2), 573–594.

Ruf M, & Schauer M (2012). Facing childhood trauma: Narrative Exposure Therapy within a cascade model of care. In J Murray (ed.). *Exposure therapy: New developments* (pp. 229–262). Germany: Nova Science Publishers.

Ruf M, Schauer M, Neuner F, Catani C, Schauer E, & Elbert T (2010). Narrative Exposure Therapy for 7- to 16-year-olds: A randomized controlled trial with traumatized refugee children. *J Traum Stress, 23*(4), 437–445.

Rusby J, Westling E, Crowley R, & Light J (2014). Psychosocial correlates of physical and sedentary activities of early adolescent youth. *Health Educ Behav, 41*(1) 42–51. Abstract.

Russell E, & Fosha D (2008). Transformational affects and core state in AEDP: The emergence and consolidation of joy, hope, gratitude, and confidence in (the Solid Goodness of) the Self. *J Psychother Integra, 18*(2), 167–190.

Rutter M (2003). Commentary: Causal processes leading to antisocial behavior. *Dev Psychol, 39*(2), 372–378.

Rutter M, Colvert E, Kreppner J, Beckett C, Castle J, Groothues C et al. (2007). Early adolescent outcomes for institutionally-deprived and non-deprived adoptees. I: disinhibited attachment. *J Child Psychol Psyc, 48*(1), 17–30.

Rutter M, Kreppner J, & Sonuga-Barke E (2009). Emanuel Miller Lecture: Attachment insecurity, disinhibited attachment, and attachment disorders: Where do research findings leave the concepts? *J Child Psychol Psyc, 50*(5), 529–543.

Ruttle P, Serbin L, Stack D, Schwartzman A, & Shirtcliff E (2011). Adrenocortical attunement in mother–child dyads: Importance of situational and behavioral characteristics. *Biol Psychol, 88*, 104–111.

Rynearson E, & Salloum A (2011). Restorative retelling: Revisiting the narrative of violent death. In R Neimeyer, D Harris, H Winokuer & G Thornton (Eds), *Grief and bereavement in contemporary society: Bridging research and practice* (pp. 177–188). New York: Routledge.

Sadeh A, Flint-Ofir E, Tirosh T, & Tikotzky L (2007). Infant sleep and parental sleeprelated cognitions. *J Fam Psychol, 21*, 74–87.

Sadeh A, Tikotzky L, & Scher A (2010). Parenting and infant sleep. *Sleep Med Rev, 14*, 89–96.

Sadler L, Slade A, Close N, Webb D, Simpson T, Fennie K, & Mayes L (2013). Minding the Baby®: Enhancing reflectiveness to improve early health and relationship outcomes in an interdisciplinary home visiting program. *Inf Mental Hlth J, 34*, 391–405.

Sadler L, Slade A, & Mayes L (2007). *Minding the baby®: Program overview and summary of initial findings*. New Haven, CT: Yale Child Study Center, Yale School of Nursing, and Fair Haven Community Health Center.

Sadler L, Slade A, & Mayes L (2006). Minding the baby®: a mentalization-based parenting program. In J Allen, P Fonagy (Eds), *Handbook of mentalization-based treatment*. Chichester, UK: Wiley.

Sadowski H, Trowell J, Kolvin I, Weeramanthri T, Berelowitz M, & Gilbert L (2003). Sexually abused girls: patterns of psychopathology and exploration of risk factors. *Eur Child Adoles Psy, 12*, 221–230.

Saile R, Ertl V, Neuner F, & Catani C (2015). Children of the postwar years: A two-generational multilevel risk assessment of child psychopathology in northern Uganda. *Dev Psychopathol*, 28(2), 607–620.

St. George J, & Freeman E (2017). Measurement of father–child rough-and-tumble play and its relations to child behavior. *Inf Mental Hlth J, 38*(6), 709–725.

St Petersburg–USA Orphanage Research Team. (2008). The effects of early social-emotional and relationship experience on the development of young orphanage children. *Monogr Soc Res Child, 73*(3), vii–295.

Salley B, Panneton R, & Colombo J (2013). Separable attentional predictors of language outcome. *Infancy, 18*(4), 462–489.

Salloum A (2015). *Grief and trauma in children: An evidence-based treatment manual*. New York: Routledge.

Salloum A (2008). Group therapy for children experiencing grief and trauma due to homicide and violence: a pilot study. *Res Social Work Prac, 18*(3), 198–211.

Salloum A (2006). Project LAST (loss and survival team) elementary age grief and trauma intervention manual. Unpublished treatment manual, Children's Bureau of New Orleans.

Salloum A, Garside L, Irwin C, Anderson A, & Francois A (2009). Grief and Trauma Group Therapy for children after Hurricane Katrina. *Soc Work Groups, 32*(1), 64–79.

Salloum A, & Overstreet S (2012). Grief and trauma intervention for children after disaster: Exploring coping skills versus trauma narration. *Behav Res Ther, 50*, 169–179.

Salloum A, & Overstreet S (2008). Evaluation of individual and group grief and trauma interventions for children post-disaster. *J Clin Child Adolesc, 37*(3), 495–507.

Salloum A, Wang W, Robst J, Murphy T, Scheeringa M, Cohen J, & Storch E (2016). Stepped care versus standard trauma-focused cognitive behavioral therapy for young children. *J Child Psychol Psyc, 57*(5), 614–622.

Salmivalli C, & Nieminen E (2002). Proactive and reactive aggression among school bullies, victims and bully-victims. *Aggressive Behav, 28*, 30–44.

Salmon K, O'Kearney R, Reese E, & Fortune C (2016). The role of language skill in child psychopathology: Implications for intervention in the early years. *Clin Child Fam Psychol Rev, 19*, 352–367.

Salmon P, Lush E, Jablonski M, & Sephton S (2009). Yoga and mindfulness: Clinical aspects of an ancient mind/body practice. *Cogn Behav Pract, 16*, 59–72.

Salomonsson B (2016). Infantile defences in parent–infant psychotherapy: The example of gaze avoidance. *Int J Psychoanal, 97*, 65–88.

Salomonsson B (2013). Transferences in parent–infant psychoanalytic treatments. *Int J Psychoanal, 94*(4), 767–792.

Saltzman W, Layne C, Pynoos R, Olafson E, Kaplow J, & Boat B (2018). *Trauma and grief component therapy for adolescents: A modular approach to treating traumatized and bereaved youth*. Cambridge University Press.

Samson D, Apperly I, Braithwaite J, Andrews B, & Scott S (2010). Seeing it their way: Evidence for rapid and involuntary computation of what other people see. *J Exp Psychol Hum, 36*(5), 1255–1266.

Sanger K, & Dorjee D (2016). Mindfulness training with adolescents enhances metacognition and the inhibition of irrelevant stimuli: Evidence from event-related brain potentials. *Trends Neurosci Educ, 5*, 1–11.

Sandler I, Ayers T, Tein J-Y, Wolchik S, Millsap R, Khoo S et al. (2010a). Six-year follow-up of a preventive intervention for parentally-bereaved youth: A randomized controlled trial. *Arch Pediat Adol Med, 164*, 907–914.

Sandler I, Ayers T, Wolchik S, Tein J, Kwok O, Haine R et al. (2003). The family bereavement program: Efficacy evaluation of a theory-based prevention program for parentally bereaved children and adolescents. *J Consult Clin Psych, 71,* 587–600.

Sandler I, Gunn H, Mazza G, Tein J-Y, Wolchik S, Kim H et al. (in press). Three perspectives on mental health problems of young adults and their parents at a 15-year follow-up of the Family Bereavement Program. *J Consult Psychol,*/dx.doi.org/10.1037/ccp0000327.

Sandler I, Ma Y, Tein J-Y, Ayers T, Wolchik S, Kennedy C, & Millsap R (2010b). Long-term effects of the Family Bereavement Program on multiple indicators of grief in parentally bereaved children and adolescents. *J Consult Clin Psych, 78,* 131–144. abstract.

Sandler I, Tein J-Y, Cham H, Wolchik S, & Ayers T (2016a). Long-term effects of the Family Bereavement Program on spousally bereaved parents: Grief, mental health problems, alcohol problems, and coping efficacy. *Dev Psychopathol, 28,* 801–818.

Sandler I, Tein J-Y, Wolchik S, & Ayers T (2016b). The effects of the Family Bereavement Program to reduce suicide ideation and/or attempts of parentally bereaved children six and fifteen years later. *Suicide Life-Threat, 46*(1), S32-S38. abstract.

Sandler I, Wolchik S, Ayers T, Tein J-Y, Coxe S, & Chow A (2008). Linking theory and intervention to promote resilience in parentally bereaved children. In Stroebe M (ed.) *Handbook of bereavement research and practice: advances in theory and intervention* (pp. 531–550). Washington, DC: APA.

Sansone R, & Sansone L (2006). Borderline Personality Disorder and body image. In M Kindes (ed.). *Body Image: New Research* (pp. 131–144). New York: Nova Biomedical Books.

Santarnecchi E, Galli G, Polizzotto N, Rossi A, & Rossi S (2014). Efficiency of weak brain connections support general cognitive functioning. *Hum Brain Mapp, 35,* 4566–4582.

Sapolsky RM (2007). Stress, Stress-Related Disease, and Emotional Regulation. In J Gross (ed.), *Handbook of emotion regulation* (pp. 606–615). New York: Guilford.

Sapolsky RM (2000). Glucocorticoids and hippocampal atrophy in neuropsychiatric disorders. *Arch Gen Psychiat, 57,* 925–935.

Sapolsky RM (1998). *Biology and human behavior: The neurological origins of individuality* [Videotape series]. Chantilly, VA: The Teaching Company.

Satpute A, & Lieberman M (2006). Integrating automatic and controlled processes into neurocognitive models of social cognition. *Brain Res, 1079*(1), 86–97.

Savitz J, van der Merwe L, Newman T, Solms M, Stein D, & Ramesar R (2007). The relationship between childhood abuse and dissociation. Is it influenced by catechol-Omethyltransferase (COMT) activity? *Internat J Neuropsychopharmacol, 11,* 149–161.

Scaramella L, Sohr-Preston S, Callahan K, & Mirabile S (2008). A test of the family stress model on toddler-aged children's adjustment among Hurricane Katrina impacted and nonimpacted low-income families. *J Clin Child Adolesc Psychol, 37,* 530–541.

Schaefer CE (1990). Night waking and temperament in early childhood. *Psychol Rep, 67*(1), 192–194.

Schaefer CE (2003). *Play therapy with adults.* New York: Wiley.

Schafer M, & Ferraro K (2013). Childhood misfortune and adult health: Enduring and cascadic effects on somatic and psychological symptoms? *Journal of Aging and Health, 25*(1), 3–28.

Schappin R, Wijnroks L, Venema M, & Jongmans M (2018). Exploring predictors of change in behavioral problems over a 1-year period in preterm born preschoolers. *Infant Behav Dev 50,* 98–106. abstract.

Scheeringa M (2016). *Treating PTSD in preschoolers: A clinical guide.* New York: Guilford.

Scheeringa M (2011). PTSD in children younger than age of 13: Toward developmentally sensitive assessment and management. *J Child Adolesc Trauma, 4,* 181–197.

Scheeringa M, Amaya-Jackson L, & Cohen J (2010). *Preschool PTSD treatment.* Unpublished manuscript, Department of Psychiatry and Neurology, Tulane University Health Sciences Center, New Orleans, LA.

Scheeringa M, & Gaensbauer T (2000). Posttraumatic stress disorder. In C Zeanah (ed.), *Handbook of infant mental health* (2nd ed., pp. 369–381). New York: Guilford.

Scheeringa M, Lilly M, Staiger A, Heller M, Jones E, & Weems C (2017). Do children and adolescents have different types of trauma narratives and does it matter? Reliability and face validation for a narrative taxonomy. *J Traum Stress, 30*(3), 323–327.

Scheeringa M, Myers L, Putnam F, & Zeanah C (2012). Diagnosing PTSD in early childhood: An empirical assessment of four approaches. *J Traum Stress, 25,* 359–367.

Scheeringa M, Myers L, Putnam F, & Zeanah C (2015). Maternal factors as moderators or mediators of PTSD symptoms in very young children: A two-year prospective study. *J Fam Viol, 30,* 633–642.

Scheeringa M, Peebles C, Cook C, & Zeanah C (2001). Toward establishing procedural, criterion, and discriminant validity for PTSD in early childhood. *J Am Acad Chld Psy, 40*(1), 52–60.

Scheeringa M, & Weems C (2014). Randomized placebo-controlled D-Cycloserine with Cognitive Behavior Therapy for pediatric Posttraumatic Stress. *J Child Adol Psychop, 24*(2), 69–77.

Scheeringa M, Weems C, Cohen J, Amya-Jackson L, & Guthrie D (2011). Trauma-focused cognitive behavioral therapy for posttraumatic stress disorder in three through six year-old children: a randomized clinical trial. *J Child Psychol Psyc, 52*(8), 853–860.
Scheeringa M, & Zeanah C (2001). A relational perspective on PTSD in early childhood. *J Traum Stress 14*, 799–815.
Scheeringa M, Zeanah C, & Cohen J (2011). PTSD in children and adolescents: Toward an empirically based algorithm. *Depress Anxiety, 28*, 770–782.
Scheeringa M, Zeanah C, Myers L, & Putnam F (2005). Predictive validity in a prospective follow-up of PTSD in preschool children. *J Am Acad Chld Psy, 44*, 899–906.
Scheffers M, Busschbach J, Bosscher R, Wiersma D, Aerts L, & Schoevers R (2017). Body image in patients with mental disorders: Characteristics, associations with diagnosis and treatment outcome. *Compr Psychiat 74*, 53–60.
Schel M, & Crone E (2013). Development of response-inhibition in the context of relevant versus irrelevant emotions. *Front Psychol*, 4:383. doi: 10.3389/fpsyg.2013.00383.
Sher-Censor E, Shulman C, & Cohen E (2018). Associations among mothers' representations of their relationship with their toddlers, maternal parenting stress, and toddlers' internalizing and externalizing behaviors. *Infant Behav Dev, 50*, 132–139.
Schimmenti A, & Bifulco A (2015). Toward a better understanding of the relationship between childhood trauma and psychiatric disorders: Measurement and impact on Addict Behav. *Addict Behav, 64*, 314–320.
Schippell P, Vasey M, Cravens-Brown L, & Bretveld R (2003). Suppressed attention to rejection, ridicule, and failure cues: A unique correlate of reactive but not proactive aggression in youth. *J Clin Child Adolesc, 32*(1), 40–55.
Schneider R, Arch J, Landy L, & Hankin B (2016). The longitudinal effect of emotion regulation strategies on anxiety levels in children and adolescents. *J Clin Child Adolesc* 1–14, doi: 10.1080/15374416.2016.1157757.
Schnyder U, Bryant R, Ehlers A, Foa E, Hasa A, Mwiti G et al. (2016). Culture-sensitive psychotraumatology. *Eur J Psychotraumato*, 7, 31179 dx.doi.org/10.3402/ejpt.v7.31179.
Schoenfeld B, & Contreras B (2016). Attentional focus for maximizing muscle development: The mind-muscle connection. *Strength Cond J, 38*(1), 27–29.
Schoenfelder E, Sandler I, Millsap R, Wolchik S, Berkel C, & Ayers T (2013). Caregiver responsiveness to the Family Bereavement Program: What predicts responsiveness? *Prev Sci, 14*, 545–556.
Schofield C, Coles M, & Gibb B (2009). Retrospective reports of behavioral inhibition and young adults' current symptoms of social anxiety, depression, and anxious arousal. *J Anxiety Disord, 23*, 884–890.
Schonert-Reichl K (2012). Promoting Empathy in School-Aged Children: Current State of the Field and Implications for Research and Practice. In K Nader (ed.) *School rampage shootings and other youth disturbances: Early preventive interventions* (pp. 159–203). New York: Routledge.
Schonert-Reichl K, Oberle E, Lawlor M, Abbott D, Thomson K, Oberlander T, Diamond A (2015). Enhancing cognitive and social-emotional development through a simple-to-administer mindfulness-based school program for elementary school children: A randomized controlled trial. *Dev Psychol, 51*(1), 52–66.
Schonert-Reichl K, & Roeser R (2016). Mindfulness in education: Introduction and overview of the handbook. In K Schonert-Reichl & R Roeser (Eds), *Handbook of mindfulness in education, mindfulness in behavioral health* (pp. 3–15). New York: Springer-Verlag.
Schonert-Reichl K, & Stewart Lawlor M (2010). The effects of a mindfulness-based education program on pre- and early adolescents' wellbeing and social and emotional competence. *Mindfulness, 1*, 137–151.
Schore A (2003). Early relational trauma, disorganized attachment, and the development of a predisposition to violence. In M Solomon, D Siegel (Eds), *Healing trauma* (pp. 107–167). New York: Norton.
Schore A (2001). The effects of early relational trauma on right brain development, affect regulation, and infant mental health. *Inf Mental Hlth J, 22*, 201–269.
Schore A (1996). The experience-dependent maturation of a regulatory system in the orbitofrontal cortex and the origin of developmental psychopathology: Social-environmental risk factors. *Pediatrics, 79*, 343–350.
Schott W, Crookston B, Lundeen E, Stein A, & Behrman J (2013). Periods of child growth up to age 8 years in Ethiopia, India, Peru and Vietnam: Key distal household and community factors. *Soc Sci Med, 97*, 278–287.
Schubeler D (2015). Function and information content of DNA methylation. *Nature, 517*, 321–326.
Schuch F, Vasconcelos-Moreno M, Borowsky C, Zimmerman A, Rocha N, & Fleck M (2015). Exercise and severe major depression: Effect on symptom severity and quality of life at discharge in an inpatient cohort. *J Psychiatric Res 61*, 25–32. abstract.
Schuettler D, & Boals A (2011). The path to Posttraumatic Growth versus Posttraumatic Stress Disorder: Contributions of event centrality and coping. *J Loss Trauma, 16*, 180–194.
Sciaraffa M, Zeanah P, & Zeanah C (2018). Understanding and promoting resilience in the context of adverse childhood experiences. *Early Childhood Educ J, 46*, 343–353.

Scott L, Stepp S, Hallquist M, Whalen D, Wright A, & Pilkonis P (2015). Daily shame and hostile irritability in adolescent girls with Borderline Personality Disorder symptoms. *Personal Disord, 6*(1), 53–63.

Scott S, Briskman J, & O'Connor T (2014). Early prevention of antisocial personality: long-term follow-up of two randomized controlled trials comparing indicated and selective approaches. *Am J Psychiat, 171*(6), 649–57.

Scott S, Lavan N, Chen S, & McGettigan C (2014). The social life of laughter. *Trends Cogn Sci, 18*(12), 618–620.

Sebastian C, Burnett S, & Blakemore S-J (2008). Development of the self-concept during adolescence. *Trends Cogn Sci, 12*(11), 441–444.

Secrist M, Dalenberg C, & Gevirtz R (2018). Contributing factors predicting nightmares in children: Trauma, anxiety, dissociation, and emotion regulation. *Psychol Trauma-US*, dx.doi.org/10.1037/tra0000387.

Séguin J, Nagin D, Assaad J, & Tremblay R (2004). Cognitive-neuropsychological function in chronic physical aggression and hyperactivity. *J Abnorm Psychol, 113*, 603–616.

Séguin J, & Zelazo P (2005). Executive function in early physical aggression. In R Tremblay, W Hartup, J Archer (Eds), *Developmental origins of aggression* (pp. 307–329). New York: Guilford.

Séguin-Lemire A, Hébert M, Cossette L, & Langevin R (2017). A longitudinal study of emotion regulation among sexually abused preschoolers. *Child Abuse Neglect*, 63, 307–316. abstract.

Sekl JR (2007). Glucocorticoids, developmental "programming" and the risk of affective dysfunction. *Prog Brain Res, 167*, 17–34.

Selby E, Anestis M, & Joiner T (2007). Daydreaming about death: Violent daydreaming as a form of emotion dysregulation in suicidality. *Behav Modif, 31*(6), 867–879.

Sellers P, & Bjorklund D (2014). The development of adaptive memory. In B Schwartz, M Howe, M Toglia, & H Otgaar (Eds), *What's adaptive about adaptive memory?* New York: Oxford University Press.

Selman RL (1971). Taking another's perspective: Role-taking development in early childhood. *Child Development, 42*, 1721–1734.

Selman RL, & Byrne D (1974). A structural developmental analysis of levels of role taking in middle childhood. *Child Dev, 45*, 803–806.

Seltzer L, Ziegler T, & Pollak S (2010). Social vocalizations can release oxytocin in humans. *Proc R Soc B: Biological Sciences, 277*, 2661–2666.

Semple R, Lee J, Rosa D, & Miller L (2010). A randomised trial of mindfulness-based cognitive therapy for children: Promoting mindful attention to enhance social-emotional resiliency in children. *J Child Fam Stud, 19*, 218–229.

Semrud-Clikeman M, & Glass K (2010). The Relation of humor and child development: Social, adaptive, and emotional aspects. *J Child Neurol, 25*, 1248–1260.

Shaffer P, Vogel D, & Wei M (2006). Mediating roles of anticipated risks, anticipated benefits, and attitudes on the decision to seek professional help: An attachment perspective. *J Couns Psychol, 53*(4), 442–452.

Shakespeare-Finch J, Gow K, Smith S (2005). Personality, coping and posttraumatic growth in emergency ambulance personnel. *Traumatology, 11*, 325–334.

Shamir-Essakow G, Ungerer J, & Rapee R (2005). Attachment, behavioral inhibition, and anxiety in preschool children. *J Abnorm Child Psych, 33*(2), 31–143.

Sharma B, Lee T, & Nam E (2017). Loneliness, insomnia and suicidal behavior among school-going adolescents in western Pacific Island countries: Role of violence and injury. *Int J Environ Res Public Health, 14*(7), 791. doi: 10.3390/ijerph14070791. abstract.

Sharp C, & Fonagy P (2015). Practitioner Review: Borderline personality disorder in adolescence: recent conceptualization, intervention, and implications for clinical practice. *J Child Psychol Psyc, 56*(12) 1266–1288.

Sharp C, Ha, C, Carbone C, Kim S, Perry K, Williams L et al. (2013). Hyper-mentalizing in adolescent inpatients: Treatment effects and association with Borderline traits. *J Pers Disorders, 27*(1), 3–18.

Shaver P, Mikulincer M, Gross J, Stern J, & Cassidy J (2018). A lifespan perspective on attachment and care for others: Empathy, altruism, and prosocial behavior. In J Cassidy, P Shaver (Eds), *Handbook of attachment* (3rd ed., pp. 881–916). New York: Guilford.

Shaw D, & Gross H (2008). What we have learned about early childhood and the development of delinquency. In A Liberman (ed.), *The long view of crime: A synthesis of longitudinal research* (pp. 79–127). New York: Springer.

Shear M, Dennard S, Crawford M, Cruz M, Gorscak B, & Oliver L (2006). Developing a two-session intervention for church-based bereavement support. Paper presented at the International Society for Traumatic Stress Studies Conference, Hollywood, CA.

Shear M, Simon N, Wall M, Zisook S, Neimeyer R, Duan N et al. (2011). Complicated grief and related bereavement issues for DSM-5. *Depress Anxiety, 28*(2), 103–117.

Sheese B, Voelker P, Rothbart M, & Posner M (2007). Parenting quality interacts with genetic variation in dopamine receptor D4 to influence temperament in early childhood. *Dev Psychopathol, 19*, 1039–1046.

Sheikh M, Abelson B, & Olsen J (2016). Differential recall bias, intermediate confounding, and mediation analysis in life course epidemiology: An analytic framework with empirical example. *Front Psychol*, 7, 1828. doi: 10.3389/fpsyg.2016.01828.

Sheinkopf S, Mundy P, Claussen A, & Willoughby J (2004). Infant joint attention skill and preschool behavioral outcomes in at-risk children, *Dev Psychopathol, 16*, 273–293.

Shen Y-P, & Armstrong S (2008). Impact of group sand-tray therapy on the self-esteem of young adolescent girls. *JSGW, 33*, 118–137.

Sheppard K, & Cheatham C (2017). Executive functions and the v-6-to-v-3 fatty acid ratio: a cross-sectional study. *Am J Clin Nutr, 105*, 32–41.

Shevlin M, Dorahy M, & Adamson G (2007). Trauma and psychosis: An analysis of the National Comorbidity Survey. *Am J Psychiat, 164*(1), 166–169.

Shi X, Zhou Y, Geng F, Li Y, Zhou J, Lei B et al. (2018). Posttraumatic stress disorder symptoms in parents and adolescents after the Wenchuan earthquake: A longitudinal actor-partner interdependence model. *J Affect Disorders, 226*, 301–306.

Shibata M, Terasawa Y, & Umeda S (2014). Integration of cognitive and affective networks in humor comprehension. *Neuropsychologia, 65*, 137–145.

Shiner R, & Caspi A (2008). Personality development. In W Damon, R Lerner (Eds), *Child and adolescent development: An advanced course* (pp. 182–215). New York: Wiley.

Shoemaker WJ (2012). The social brain network and human moral behavior. *Zygon, 47*(4), 806–820.

Shonkoff J, et al. (2012). The committee on psychosocial aspects of child and family health: The lifelong effects of early childhood adversity and toxic stress. *Pediatrics, 129*(1), e232–246.

Shonkoff J, & Phillips D (Eds) (2000). *From neurons to neighborhoods: The science of early childhood development.* Washington, DC: National Academies Press.

Shors T, Anderson L, Curlik D, & Nokia S (2012). Use it or lose it: How neurogenesis keeps the brain fit for learning. *Behav Brain Res, 227*(2), 450–458.

Shumaker D, Miller C, Ortiz C, & Deutsch R (2011). The forgotten bonds: The assessment and contemplation of sibling attachment in divorce and parental separation. *Fam Court Rev, 49*, 46–58.

Si J, Yang J, Xue L, Yang C, Luo Y, Shi H et al. (2012). Activation of NF-kB in basolateral amygdala is required for memory reconsolidation in auditory fear conditioning. *PLoS ONE*, 7(9), e43973. doi: 10.1371/journal.pone.0043973. abstract.

Sibley M, Graziano P, Kuriyan A, Coxe S, Pelham W, Rodriguez L et al. (2016). Parent–teen behavior therapy Motivational Interviewing for adolescents with ADHD. *J Consult Clin Psych, 84*(8), 699–712.

Sichari M, Wakhungu J, & Maragia S (2015). Effects of traumatized antenatal mothers on their preschool children in Mt. Elgon Region, Kenya. *J Educ Practice, 6*(31), 80–94.

Siegel DJ (2003). An interpersonal neurobiology of psychotherapy: The developing mind and the resolution of trauma. In M Solomon, D Siegel (Eds), *Healing trauma* (pp. 1–56). New York: WW Norton.

Siegel DJ (1999). *The developing mind: How relationships and the brain interact to shape who we are.* New York: Guilford Press.

Siegel DJ (1996). Cognition, memory and dissociation. *Child Adol Psych Cl, 5*(2), 509–536.

Siegel J (2013). An expanded approach to batterer intervention programs incorporating neuroscience research. *Trauma Violence Abus, 14*(4), 295–304.

Sikdar S, Beach K, Paun M, Vaezv S, Kim Y (2006). Ultrasonic interrogation of tissue vibrations in arterial and organ injuries: preliminary in vivo results. *Ultrasound Med Biol, 32*(8), 1203–14. abstract.

Silberg JL (2013). *The child survivor.* New York: Routledge.

Silberg JL (2004). The treatment of dissociation in sexually abused children from a family/attachment perspective. *Psychotherapy: Theory, Research, Practice, Training, 41*(4), 487–495.

Silberg JL (2000). Fifteen years of dissociation in maltreated children: Where do we go from here? *Child Maltreatment, 5*, 119–136.

Silberg JL (ed.) (1998a). *The dissociative child: Afterword.* Baltimore: Sidran Press. Retrieved May 24, 2005, from www.sidran.org/sidcafter.html.

Silberg JL (ed.) (1998b). *The dissociative child: Diagnosis, treatment, and management* (2nd ed). Baltimore: Sidran Press.

Silberg JL, Copeland W, Linker J, Moore A, Roberson-Nay R, & York T (2016). Psychiatric outcomes of bullying victimization: A study of discordant monozygotic twins. *Psycholog Medicine, 46*, 1875–1883.

Silverman W, Pina A, & Viswesvaran C (2008). Evidence-based psychosocial treatments for phobic and anxiety disorders in children and adolescents. *J Clinic Child Adolesc Psychol, 37*, 105–130.

Simcock G, & Hayne H (2002). Breaking the Barrier. Children fail to translate their preverbal memories into language. *Psychol Sci, 13*, 225–231.

Simeon D, Yehuda R, Cunill R, Knutelska M, Putnam F, & Smith L (2007). Factors associated with resilience in healthy adults. *Psychoneuroendocrino, 32*, 1149–1152.

Simlesa S, & Cepanec M (2015). Development of executive functions during childhood. In N Smelser, P Baltes (Eds), J Wright (Ed-in-chief), *International encyclopedia of the social & behavioral sciences* (2nd ed., pp. 489–496). Philadelphia, PA: Elsevier.

Simons L, & Conger R (2007). Linking mother–father differences in parenting to a typology of family parenting styles and adolescent outcomes. *J Fam Issues, 28*(2), 212–241.

Simpson J, & Belsky J (2018). Attachment theory within a modern evolutionary framework. In J Cassidy, P Shaver (Eds), *Handbook of attachment* (3rd ed., pp. 91–116). New York: Guilford.

Simpson J, Griskevicius V, Kuo S, Sung S, & Collins W (2012). Evolution, stress, and sensitive periods: The influence of unpredictability in early versus late childhood on sex and risky behavior. *Dev Psychol, 48*, 674–686.

Sinclair D, Purves-Tyson T, Allen K, & Weickert C (2014). Impacts of stress and sex hormones on dopamine neurotransmission in the adolescent brain. *Psychopharmacology, 231*, 1581–1599.

Singh N, Lancioni G, Winton A, & Singh J (2007). Mindful parenting decreases aggression and increases social behavior in children with developmental disabilities. *Behav Modif, 31*(6), 749–771.

Singh N, Singh A, Lancioni G, Singh J, Winton A, & Adkins A (2010). Mindfulness training for parents and their children with ADHD increases the children's compliance. *J Child Fam Stud, 19*, 157–166.

Slade A, Sadler L, Dios-Kenn C, Webb D, Currier-Ezepchick J, Mayes L (2005). Minding the Baby: A Reflective Parenting Program. *Psychoanal St Child, 60*, 74–100.

Sloan D, Marx B, Epstein E, & Lexington J (2007). Does altering the writing instructions influence outcome associated with written disclosure? *Beh Ther, 38*, 155–168.

Slone M, & Mann S (2016). Effects of war, terrorism and armed conflict on young children: A systematic review. *Child Psychiat Hum D, 47*(6), 950–965.

Smaling H, Huijbregts S, van der Heijden K, Hay D, van Goozen S, & Swaab H (2016). Pre-natal reflective functioning and development of aggression in infancy: The roles of maternal intrusiveness and sensitivity. *J Abnorm Child Psychol, 45*(2), 237–248.

Smith C, & Day K (2018). Parenting, anger, and effortful control as predictors of child externalizing behavior: The role of child sex as a moderator. *Int J Behav Dev, 42*(2), 248–256.

Smith JD, Woodhouse S, Clark C, & Skowron E (2016a). Attachment status and mother–preschooler parasympathetic response to the strange situation procedure. *Biol Psychol, 114*, 39–48.

Smith JM (2015). Breastfeeding and language outcomes: A review of the literature. *Journal of Communication Disorders, 57*, 29–40.

Smith M, Sherry S, Chen S, Saklofske D, Flett G, & Hewitt P (2016b). Perfectionism and narcissism: A meta-analytic review. *J Res Pers, 64*, 90–101.

Smyke A, Dumitrescu A, & Zeanah C (2002). Attachment disturbances in young children: I. The continuum of caretaking casualty. *J Am Acad Child Psy, 41*, 972–982.

Smyke A, Koga S, Johnson D, Fox N, Marshall P, Nelson C et al. (2007). The caregiving context in institution-reared and family-reared infants and toddlers in Romania. *J Child Psychol Psyc, 48*, 210–218.

Smyke A, Zeanah C, Fox N, & Nelson C (2009). A new model of foster care for young children: The Bucharest early intervention project. *Child Adol Psych Cl, 18*, 721–734.

Smyke A, Zeanah C, Gleason M, Drury S., Fox N, Nelson C, & Guthrie D (2012). A randomized controlled trial comparing foster care and institutional care for children with signs of reactive attachment disorder. *Am J Psychiat, 169*, 508–514.

Snook L, Paulson L, Roy D, Phillips L, & Beaulieu C (2005). Diffusion tensor imaging of neurodevelopment in children and young adults. *Neuroimage, 26*, 1164–1173.

Söderqvist S, & Bergman-Nutley S (2015). Working memory training is associated with long term attainments in math and reading. *Front Psychol, 6*, 1711. doi: 10.3389/fpsyg.2015.01711.

Söderqvist S, Nutley S, Ottersen J, Grill K, & Klingberg T (2012). Computerized training of nonverbal reasoning and working memory in children with intellectual disability. *Front Hum Neurosci, 6*, 271. doi: 10.3389/fnhum.2012.00271.

Söderstrom K, & Skårderud F (2009). Minding the Baby: Mentalization-based treatment in families with parental substance use disorder: Theoretical framework. *Nordic Psychology, 61*(3), 47–65.

Soliman F, Glatt C, Bath K, Levita L, Jones R, Pattwell S, et al. (2010). A genetic variant BDNF polymorphism alters extinction learning in both mouse and human. *Science, 327*, 863–866.

Solnit AJ (1987). A psychoanalytic view of play. *Psychoanal Stud Child, 42*, 205–219.

Solomon J, & George C (2018). The measurement of attachment security and related constructs in infancy and early childhood. In J Cassidy, P Shaver (Eds), *Handbook of attachment* (3rd ed., pp. 366–397). New York: Guilford.

Sommerfeld E (2009). The subjective experience of generosity. In M Mikulincer, P Shaver (Eds), *Prosocial motives, emotions, and behavior: The better angels of our nature* (pp. 303–323). Washington, DC: APA.

Song J, Miller A, Leung C, Lumeng J, & Rosenblum K (2018). Positive parenting moderates the association between temperament and self-regulation in low-income toddlers. *J Child Fam Stud, 27*(7), 2354–2364.

Sørensen L, Plessen K, & Lundervold A (2012). The impact of inattention and emotional-problems on cognitive control in primary school children. *J Atten Disord, 16*(7), 589–599.

Sotres-Bayon F, Cain C, & LeDoux J (2006). Brain mechanisms of fear extinction: historical perspectives on the contribution of prefrontal cortex. *Biol Psychiat, 60*, 329–336.

South S, Schafer M, & Ferraro K (2015). Genetic and environmental overlap between childhood maltreatment and adult physical health. *Twin Res Hum Genet, 18*(5), 533–544.

Southall C, & Campbell, J (2015). What does research say about social perspective-taking interventions for students with HFASD? *Except Children, 8*(2), 194–208.

Southgate V, Johnson M, Osborne T, & Csibra G (2009). Predictive motor activation during action observation in human infants. *Biol Lett-UK, 5*(6), 769–772.

Sowislo J, & Orth U (2013). Does Low Self-Esteem Predict Depress Anxiety? A meta-analysis of longitudinal studies. *Psychol Bull, 139*(1), 213–240.

Spann M, Mayes L, Kalmar J, Guiney J, Womer F, Pittman B et al. (2012). Childhood abuse and neglect and cognitive flexibility in adolescents. *Child Neuropsychol, 18*(2), 182–189.

Spear L (2000). The adolescent brain and age-related behavioral manifestations. *Neurosci Biobehav Rev, 24*, 417–463.

Spinazzola J, Habib M, Knoverek A, Arvidson J, Nisenbaum J, Wentworth R et al. (2013). The heart of the matter: Complex trauma in child welfare. In T LaLiberte, T Crudo (Eds), *CW360°:Trauma-informed child welfare practice* (pp. 8–9, 37). University of Minnesota: School of Social Work. Downloaded 8-8-18 from cascw.umn.edu/portfolio-tags/cw360.

Spinazzola J, Hodgdon H, Liang L, Ford J, Layne C, Pynoos R et al. (2014). Unseen wounds: The contribution of psychological maltreatment to child and adolescent mental health and risk outcomes. *Psychol Trauma-US, 6*(S1), S18–S28.

Spinazzola J, Rhodes A, Emerson D, Earle E, & Monroe K (2011). Application of yoga in residential treatment of traumatized youth. *J Amer Psychiat Nurses Assoc, 17*(6), 431–444.

Spinazzola J, van der Kolk B, & Ford J (in press). When nowhere is safe: Interpersonal atrauma and attachment adversity as antecedents of Posttraumatic Stress Disorder and Developmental Trauma Disorder. *J Traum Stress.*

Spinrad T, Eisenberg N, Granger D, Eggum N, Sallquist J, Haugen R et al. (2009). Individual differences in preschoolers' salivary cortisol and alpha-amylase reactivity: Relations to temperament and maladjustment. *Horm Behav, 56*, 133–139.

Spuij M, Dekovic M, & Boelen P (2015). An open trial of "Grief-Help": A Cognitive Behavioural treatment for prolonged grief in children and adolescents. *Clin Psychol Psychother, 22*, 185–192.

Spuij M, van Londen-Huiberts A, & Boelen P (2013). Cognitive behavioral therapy for prolonged grief in children: Feasibility and multiple baseline study. *Cognitive and Behav Prac, 20*, 349–361.

Sroufe L (2018). The place of attachment in development. In J Cassidy, P Shaver (Eds), *Handbook of attachment* (3rd ed., pp. 997–1011). New York: Guilford.

Sroufe L, Egeland B, Carlson E, & Collins A (2005). *The development of the person: The Minnesota study of risk and adaptation from birth to adulthood.* New York: Guilford.

Sroufe L, & Waters E (1977). Attachment as an organizational construct. *Child Dev, 48*, 1184–1199.

Stacks A, Muzik M, Wong K, Beeghly M, Huth-Bocks A, Irwin J, & Rosenblum K (2014). Maternal reflective functioning among mothers with childhood maltreatment histories: Links to sensitive parenting and infant attachment security. *Attach Hum Deve, 16*, 515–533.

Staf A, & Almqvist K (2015). How children with experiences of intimate partner violence towards the mother understand and relate to their father. *Clin Child Psychol P, 20*(1), 148–163.

Stain H, Bronnick K, Hegelstad W, Joa I, Johannessen J, Langeveld J, Mawn L, & Larsen T (2014). Impact of interpersonal trauma on the social functioning of adults with first-episode psychosis. *Schizophrenia Bull, 40*(6), 1491–1498.

Stalfa F (2010). "Posthumous disillusionment" as a type of complicated grief. *J Pastoral Care Counsel, 64*(2), 71–78.

Stamoulis C, Vanderwert R, Zeanah C, Fox N, & Nelson C (2017). Neuronal networks in the developing brain are adversely modulated by early psychosocial neglect. *J Neurophysiol, 118*(4), 2275–2288.

Stamoulis C, Vanderwert R, Zeanah C, Fox N, & Nelson C (2015). Early psychosocial neglect adversely impacts developmental trajectories of brain oscillations and their interactions. *J Cognitive Neurosci, 27*(12), 2512–2528.

Stavrianopoulos K, Faller G, & Furrow J (2014). Emotionally Focused Family Therapy: Facilitating change within a family system. *J Couple Relatsh Ther, 13*, 25–43.

Steele H & Steele M (2005). The construct of coherence as an indicator of attachment security in middle childhood: The friends and family interview. In K Kerns, R Richardson (Ed.), *Attachment in middle childhood* (pp. 137–160). New York: Guilford.

Steele M, Bate J, Nikitiades A, & Buhl-Nielsen B (2015). Attachment in adolescence and Borderline Personality. *JICAP, 14*, 16–32.

Steele W, & Raider M (2001). *Structured sensory intervention for traumatized children, adolescents and parents: Strategies to alleviate trauma.* New York: The Edwin Mellen Press.

Steenari M, Vuontela V, Paavonen E, Carlson S, Fjallberg M, & Aronen E (2003). Working memory and sleep in 6- to 13-year-old schoolchildren. *J Amer Acad Child & Adolesc Psychiatry, 42*, 85–92.

Stein D, Koenen K, Friedman M, Hill E, McLaughlin K, Petukhova, M et al. (2013). Dissociation in posttraumatic stress disorder: Evidence from the world mental health surveys. *Biol Psychiat, 73*, 302–312.

Stein D, McLaughlin K, Koenen K, Atwoli L, Friedman M, Hill E et al. (2014). DSM-5 and ICD-11 definitions of posttraumatic stress disorder: Investigating "narrow" and "broad" approaches. *Depress & Anxiety, 31*, 494–505.

Stein P, & Kendall J (2004). *Psychological trauma and the developing brain: Neurologically based interventions for troubled children.* New York: Haworth Press.

Steinberg L, Albert D, Cauffman E, Banich M, Graham S, Woolard J (2008). Age differences in sensation seeking and impulsivity as indexed by behavior and self-report: Evidence for a dual systems model. *Dev Psychol, 44*(6), 1764–1778.

Steinberg L, & Silk J (2002). Parenting adolescents. In M Bornstein (Ed.), *Handbook of parenting: Vol 1. Children and parenting* (2nd ed., pp. 103–133). Mahwah, NJ: Erlbaum.

Stempel H, Cox-Martin M, Bronsert M, Dickinson L, & Allison M (2017). Chronic school absenteeism and the role of adverse childhood experiences. *Acad Pediatr, 17*, 837–843.

Steuwe C, Daniels J, Frewen P, Densmore M, Pannasch S, Reiss J, & Lanius R (2014). Effect of direct eye contact in PTSD related to interpersonal trauma: An fMRI study of activation of an innate alarm system. *Soc Cogn Affect Neurosci, 9*(1), 88–97.

Stevens J, Ely T, Sawamura T, Guzman D, Bradley B, Ressler K, & Javanovic T (2016). Childhood maltreatment predicts reduced inhibition-related activity in the rostral anterior cingulate in PTSD, but not trauma-exposed controls. *Depress Anxiety, 33*(7), 614–622.

Stevens M, Kiehl K, Pearlson G, & Calhoun V (2007). Functional neural networks underlying response-inhibition in adolescents and adults. *Behav Brain Res, 181*(1), 12–22.

Stevens S, Sonuga-Barke E, Kreppner J, Beckett C, Castle J et al. (2008). Inattention/overactivity following early severe institutional deprivation: Presentation and associations in early adolescence. *J Abnorm Child Psychol, 36*, 385–398. abstract.

Stevenson M, & Crnic K (2013). Intrusive fathering, children's self-regulation and social skills: a mediation analysis. *J Intell Disabil Res, 57*(6), 500–512.

Sterzer P, Stadler C, Poustka F, & Kleinschmidt A (2007). A structural neural deficit in adolescents with conduct disorder and its association with lack of empathy. *Neuroimage, 37*, 335–342.

Stockdale L, Coyne S, Nelson E, & Erickson D (2015). Borderline personality disorder features, jealousy, and cyber-bullying in adolescence. *Pers Indiv Differ, 83*, 148–153.

Stoeber J, Sherry S, & Nealis L (2015). Multidimensional perfectionism and narcissism: Grandiose or vulnerable? *Pers Indiv Differ, 80*, 85–90.

Stolbach B, Minshew R, Rompala V, Dominguez R, Gazibara T, & Finke R (2013). Complex trauma exposure and symptoms in urban traumatized children: A preliminary test of proposed criteria for developmental trauma disorder. *J Traum Stress, 26*, 1–9.

Stotz S, Elbert T, Muller V, & Schauer M (2015). The relationship between trauma, shame, and guilt: findings from a community-based study of refugee minors in Germany, *Eur J Psychotraumato, 6*(1), 25863. doi: 10.3402/ejpt.v6.25863.

Strom I, Aakvaag H, Birkeland M, Felix E, & Thoresen S (2018). The mediating role of shame in the relationship between childhood bullying victimization and adult psychosocial adjustment. *Eur J Psychotraumato, 9*, 1, 1418570. doi: 10.1080/20008198.2017.1418570.

Stroud C, Sosoo E, & Wilson S (2018). Rumination, excessive reassurance seeking, and stress generation among early adolescent girls. *J Early Adolescence, 38*(2), 139–163.

Stuewig J, & McCloskey L (2005). The relation of child maltreatment to shame and guilt among adolescents: Psychological routes to depression and delinquency. *Child Maltreat, 10*, 324–336.

Stulmaker H, Lertora I, & Garza Y (2015). Facilitating empathic perspective-taking in beginning Child-Centered Play Therapists: The role of supervision. *Int J Play Ther, 24*(4), 177–189.

Sturge-Apple M, Davies P, Martin M, Cicchetti D, & Hentges R (2012). An examination of the impact of harsh parenting contexts on children's adaptation within an evolutionary framework. *Dev Psychobiol, 48*, 791–805.

Suchodoletz A, Slot P, & Shroff D (2017). Measuring executive function in Indian mothers and their 4-year-old daughters. *PsyCh Journal, 6*, 16–28.

Suddendorf T, & Butler D (2013). The nature of visual self-recognition. *Trends in Cogni Sci, 17*(3), 121–127.

Sui-Ling L, Kuo-Wei Y, Shen-Hao L, Wen-I L, & Jing-Long H (2013). Maturation of Toll-like receptor 1–4 responsiveness during early life. *Early Hum Dev, 89*, 473–478.

Sullivan P, Keller M, Paternostro J, & Friedberg R (2015). Treating emotionally dysregulated and perfectionistic youth with transdiagnostic cognitive behavioral procedures. *J Contemp Psychother, 45*(3), 151–158.

Sullivan P, & Knutson J (2000). Maltreatment and disabilities: A population-based epidemiological study. *Child Abuse Neglect, 24*(10), 1257–1273.

Sunderland M (2018). *Draw on your emotions and the emotion cards*. New York: Routledge.

Suomi SJ (1991). Early stress and adult emotional reactivity in rhesus monkeys. *Ciba F Symp, 156*, 171–189.

Suomi SJ (2005). Genetic and environmental factors influencing the expression of impulsive aggression and serotonergic functioning in rhesus monkeys. In R Tremblay, W Hartup, J Archer (Eds), *Developmental origins of aggression* (pp. 63–82). New York: Guilford.

Suor J, Sturge-Apple M, Davies P, Cicchetti D, & Manning L (2015). Tracing differential pathways of risk: Associations among family adversity, cortisol and cognitive functioning in childhood. *Child Dev, 86*(4), 1142–1158.

Sur S, & Sinha V (2009). Event-related potential: An overview. *Ind Psychiatry J, 18*(1), 70–73.

Sutherland K, & Bryant R (2007). Rumination and overgeneral autobiographical memory. *Behav Res Ther, 45*, 2407–2416.

Sutton-Smith B (2009). *The ambiguity of play*. Cambridge, MA: Harvard University Press.

Suveg C, Kendall P, Comer J, & Robin J (2006). Emotion-focused cognitive behavioral therapy for anxious youth: A multiple baseline evaluation. *J Contemp Psychother, 36*, 77–85.

Swannell S, Martin G, Page A, Hasking P, Hazell P, Taylor A, & Protani M (2012). Child maltreatment, subsequent non-suicidal self-injury and the mediating roles of dissociation, alexithymia and self-blame. *Child Abuse Neglect, 36*, 572–584. abstract.

Sylvestre A, & Merette C (2010). Language delay in severely neglected children: A cumulative or specific effect of risk factors? *Child Abuse Neglect, 34*, 414–428.

Szalai A (2004). C-reactive protein (CRP) and autoimmune disease: Facts and conjectures. *Clin Deve Immunol, 11*(3–4), 221–226.

Szentágotai-Tătar A, & Miu A (2016). Individual differences in emotion regulation, childhood trauma and proneness to shame and guilt in adolescence. *PLoS ONE 11*(11), e0167299. doi: 10.1371/journal.pone.0167299.

Szentágotai-Tătar A, Chiş A, Vulturar R, Dobrean A, Cândea D, Miu A (2015). Shame and guilt-proneness in adolescents: Gene-environment interactions. *PLoS ONE 10*(7), e0134716. doi: 10.1371/journal.pone.0134716. abstract.

Talwar S (2007). Accessing traumatic memory through art making: An art therapy trauma protocol (ATTP). *Art Psychother, 34*, 22–35.

Tamm L, & Nakonezny P (2015). Metacognitive executive function training for young children with ADHD. *Atten Defic Hyperact Disord*, 7(3), 183–190.

Tang B, Liu X, Liu Y, Xue C, & Zhang L (2014). A meta-analysis of risk factors for depression in adults and children after natural disasters. *BMC Public Health, 14*(1), 623.

Tang W, Zhao J, Lu Y, Zha Y, Liu H, Sun Y et al. (2018). Suicidality, posttraumatic stress, and depressive reactions after earthquake and maltreatment: A cross-sectional survey of a random sample of 6132 Chinese children and adolescents. *J Affect Disorders, 232*, 363–369. abstract.

Tangney J (1990). Assessing individual differences in proneness to shame and guilt: Development of the Self-conscious Affect and Attribution Inventory. *J Pers Soc Psychol, 59*, 102–111.

Tangney J, Miller R, Flicker L, & Barlow D (1996). Are shame, guilt, and embarrassment distinct emotions? *J Pers Soc Psychol, 70*(6), 1256–1269.

Tangney J, Stuewig J, & Martinez A (2014). Two faces of shame: Understanding shame and guilt in prediction of jail inmates' recidivism. *Psychol Sci, 25*(3), 799–805.

Tangney J, Wagner P, Fletcher C, & Gramzow R (1992). Shamed into anger: The relation of shame and guilt to anger and self-reported aggression. *J Pers Soc Psychol, 62*(4), 669–675.

Tanyel N (2009). Emotional regulation: Developing toddlers' social competence. *Dimensions of Early Childhood, 37*(2), 10–15.

Tarullo A, & Gunnar M (2006). Child maltreatment and the developing HPA axis. *Horm Behav, 50*, 632–639.

Taumoepeau M, & Ruffman T (2006). Mother and infant talk about mental states relates to desire language and emotion understanding. *Child Dev*, 77, 465–481.

Taylor SE (2002). *The tending instinct*. New York: Times Books.

Taylor Z, Eisenberg N, Spinrad T, Eggum N, & Sulik M (2013a). The relations of ego-resiliency and emotion socialization to the development of empathy and prosocial behavior across early childhood. *Emotion, 13*(5), 822–831.

Taylor Z, Eisenberg N, Spinrad T, & Widaman K (2013b). Longitudinal relations of intrusive parenting and effortful control to ego-resiliency during early childhood. *Child Dev, 84*(4), 1145–1151. abstract.

Taylor-Colls S, & Fearon R (2015). The effects of parental behavior on infants' neural processing of emotion expressions. *Child Dev, 86*(3), 877–888.

Tearne J, Allen K, Herbison C, Lawrence D, Whitehouse A, Sawyer M et al. (2015). The association between prenatal environment and children's mental health trajectories from 2 to 14 years. *Eur Child Adoles Psychia, 24*, 1015–1024. abstract.

Teasdale J, Segal Z, & Williams JMG (1995). How does cognitive therapy prevent depressive relapse and why should attentional control (mindfulness training) help? *Behav Res Ther, 33*, 25–39.

Tedeschi R, & Calhoun L (2004). Posttraumatic growth: Conceptual foundations and empirical evidence. *Psychol Inq, 15*, 1–18.

Tedeschi R, & Calhoun L (1996). The posttraumatic growth inventory: Measuring the positive legacy of trauma. *J Traum Stress, 9*, 455–471.

Teicher M, & Samson J (2016). Annual Research Review: Enduring neurobiological effects of childhood abuse and neglect. *J Child Psychol Psyc, 57*(3), 241–266.

Teicher M, Samson J, Polcari A, & Andersen S (2009). Length of time between onset of childhood sexual abuse and emergence of depression in a young adult sample: A retrospective clinical report. *J Clin Psychiat, 70*, 684–691.

Tein J-Y, Sandler I, Ayers T, & Wolchik S (2006). Mediation of the effects of the Family Bereavement Program on mental health problems of bereaved children and adolescents. *Prev Sci*, 7(2), 179–195.

Tener D, Lang-Franco N, & Ofir S (2012). The use of medical clowns as a psychological distress Buffer during anogenital examination of sexually abused children. *J Loss Trauma, 17*, 12–22.

Terr L (1991). Childhood traumas: An outline and overview. *Am J Psychiat, 148*, 10–20.

Terr L (1981). Forbidden games: Posttraumatic child's play. *J Am Acad Child PS, 20*, 741–760.

Terr L (1979). Children of Chowchilla: Study of psychic trauma. *Psychoanal Stud Chil, 34*, 547–623.

Tessier V, Normandin L, Ensink K, & Fonagy P (2016). Fact or fiction? A longitudinal study of play and the development of reflective functioning. *B Menninger Clin, 80*(1), 60–79.

Teves D, Videen T, Cryer P, & Powers W (2004). Activation of human medial prefrontal cortex during autonomic responses to hypoglycemia. *P Natl A Sci USA, 101*(16), 6217–6221. abstract.

Thabet A, Ibraheem A, Shivram R, Winter E, & Vostanis P (2009). Parenting support and PTSD in children of a war zone. *Internat J Soc Psychia, 55*, 226–237.

Thabet A, Tawahina A, Punamäki R, & Vostanis P (2015). Prevalence and mental health function of resilience in condition of military siege and violence in a Palestinian community sample. *J Psychiatry, 18*(3), doi.org/10.4172/psychiatry.1000274.

Thai N, Taber-Thomas B, & Perez-Edgar K (2016). Neural correlates of attention biases, behavioral inhibition, and social anxiety in children: An ERP study. *Dev Cogn Neruos-Neth, 19*, 200–210.

Thielen J-W, Hong D, Rankouhi S, Wiltfang J, Fernancez G, Norris D, & Tendolkar I (2018). The increase in medial prefrontal glutamate/glutamine concentration during memory encoding is associated with better memory performance and stronger functional connectivity in the human medial prefrontal–thalamus–hippocampus network. *Hum Brain Mapp, 39*(6), 2381–2390.

Thierry K, Vincent R, Bryant H, Kinder M, & Wise C (2018). A self-oriented mindfulness-based curriculum improves prekindergarten students' executive functions. *Mindfulness*, https://doi.org/10.1007/s12671-018-0888-1.

Thierry K, Bryant H, Nobles S, & Norris K (2016). Two-year impact of a mindfulness-based program on preschoolers' self-regulation and academic performance. *Early Educ Dev, 27*, 805–821.

Thomas J, Jamieson G, & Cohen M (2014). Low and then high frequency oscillations of distinct right cortical networks are progressively enhanced by medium and long term Satyananda Yoga meditation practice. *Front Hum Neurosci, 8*(197), 1–13. abstract. doi: 10.3389/fnhum.2014.00197.

Thomas R, DiLillo D, Walsh K, Polusny M (2011). Pathways from child sexual abuse to adult depression: The role of parental socialization of emotions and alexithymia. *Psychol Violence, 1*(2), 121–135.

Thomassin K, Shaffer A, Madden A, & Londino D (2016). Specificity of childhood maltreatment and emotion deficit in nonsuicidal self-injury in an inpatient sample of youth. *Psychiat Res, 244*, 103–108.

Thomsen T, Püttker K, & Weberling J (2017). Can empathy make therapists sick? The role of empathy and coping in secondary trauma in trauma therapists. In C Edwards (ed.), *Psychology of empathy: New research* (Chapter 5). Hauppauge, NY: Nova Science Publishers. (prepublication copy).

Thompson J, Sonuga-Barke E, Morgan A, Cornforth C, Turic D, Ferguson L et al. (2011). The catechol-O-methyltransferase (COMT) Val158Met polymorphism moderates the effect of antenatal stress on childhood behavioural problems: longitudinal evidence across multiple ages. *Devel Med & Child Neurobio, 54*, 148–154.

Thompson R, Kaczor K, Lorenz D, Bennett B, Meyers G, & Pierce M (2017). Is the use of physical discipline associated with aggressive behaviors in young children? *Acad Pediatr, 17*(1), 34–44.

Thornback K, & Muller R (2015). Relationships among emotion regulation and symptoms during trauma-focused CBT for school-aged children. *Child Abuse Neglect 50*, 182–192.

Thurman W, Johnson K, Gonzalez D, & Sales A (2018). Teacher support as a protective factor against sadness and hopelessness for adolescents experiencing parental incarceration: Findings from the 2015 Texas Alternative School Survey. *Child Youth Serv Rev, 88*, 558–566.

Thygeson M, Hooke M, Clapsaddle J, Robbins A, & Moquist K (2010). Peaceful Play Yoga: Serenity and balance for children with cancer and their parents. *J Pediatr Oncol Nurs, 27*, 276–284.

Tibu F, Humphreys K, Fox N, Nelson C, & Zeanah C (2014). Psychopathology in young children in two types of foster care following institutional rearing. *Inf Mental Hlth J, 35*(2), 123–131.

Tibu F, Sheridan M, McLaughlin K, Nelson C, Fox N, & Zeanah C (2016a). Disruptions of working memory and inhibition mediate the association between exposure to institutionalization and symptoms of attention deficit hyperactivity disorder. *Psychol Med, 46*, 529–541. abstract.

Tibu F, Sheridan M, McLaughlin K, Nelson C, Fox N, & Zeanah C (2016b). Reduced working memory mediates the link between early institutional rearing and symptoms of ADHD at 12 years. *Front Psychol, 7*, 1–9.

Tillman C, Brocki K, Sørensen L, & Lundervold A (2013). A longitudinal examination of the developmental executive function hierarchy in children with externalizing behavior problems. *J Atten Disord, 19*(6), 496–506.

Timulak L & McElvaney J (2016). Emotion-Focused Therapy for Generalized Anxiety Disorder: An overview of the model. *J Contemp Psychother, 46*, 41–52.

Tinnen L, Bills L, & Gantt L (2002). Short-term treatment of simple and complex PTSD. In MB Williams, J Sommer (Eds), *Simple and complex posttraumatic stress disorder* (pp. 99–118). New York: Haworth Maltreatment and Trauma Press.

Tirlea L, Truby H, & Haines T (2013). Investigation of the effectiveness of the "Girls on the Go!" program for building self-esteem in young women: Trial protocol. *SpringerPlus, 2*(1), 683. doi: 10.1186/2193-1801-2-683.

Tolan P, Gorman-Smith D, Henry D, Chung K, & Hunt M (2002). The relation of patterns of coping of inner-city youth to psychopathology symptoms. *J Res Adolescence, 12*, 423–449.

Tomasello M, & Carpenter M (2007). Shared intentionality. *Developmental Sci, 10*, 121–125.

Tomasello M, Carpenter M, Call J, Behne T, & Moll H (2005). In search of the uniquely human. *Behav Brain Sci, 28*, 721–727.

Tomko R, Lane S, Treloar H, Pronove L Brown W, Solhan M et al. (2015). Undifferentiated negative affect and impulsivity in Borderline Personality and Depressive Disorders: A momentary perspective. *J Abnorm Psychol, 124*(3), 740–753.

Tompsett C, Mahoney A, & Lackey J (2016). Sibling aggression among clinic-referred children and adolescents. *J Clin Child Adolesc*, doi: 10.1080/15374416.2016.1138409.

Toohey J (2012). Depression during pregnancy and postpartum. *Clinical Obstet Gynecol, 55*, 788–797.

Toth S, Maughan A, Manly J, Spagnola M, & Cicchetti D (2002). The relative efficacy of two interventions in altering maltreated preschool children's representational models: Implications for attachment theory. *Dev Psychopathol, 14*, 877–908.

Toth S, Rogosch F, Manly J, & Cicchetti D (2006). The efficacy of toddler-parent psychotherapy to reorganize attachment in the young offspring of mothers with major depressive disorder: A randomized preventive trial. *J Consult Clin Psych, 74*, 1006–1016.

Tottenham N, Shapiro M, Telzer E, & Humphreys K (2012). Amygdala response to mother, *Dev Sci, 15*(3), 307–319.

Touchette E, Petit D, Seguin J, Boivin M, Tremblay R, & Montplaisir J (2007). Associations between sleep duration patterns and behavioral/cognitive functioning at school entry. *Sleep, 30*(9), 1213–1219.

Towe-Goodman N, Willoughby M, Blair C, Gustafsson H, Mills-Koonce W, Cox M, Family Life Project Key investigators (2014). Fathers' sensitive parenting and the development of early executive functioning. *J Fam Psychol, 28*(6), 867–876. abstract.

Trepal H, Wester K, & Merchant E (2015). A cross-sectional matched sample study of nonsuicidal self-injury among young adults: support for interpersonal and intrapersonal factors, with implications for coping strategies. *Child Adoles Psychia Ment Health, 9*(1), 1–10.

Trivedi J, Tripathi A, Dhanasekaran S, & Moussaoui D (2014). Preventive psychiatry: Concept appraisal and future directions. *Int J Soc Psychiatr, 60*(4), 321–329.

Trotta A, Murray R, & Fisher H (2015). The impact of childhood adversity on the persistence of psychotic symptoms: a systematic review and meta-analysis. *Psychol Med, 45*, 2481–2498.

Trottier K, & MacDonald D (2017). Update on psychological trauma, other severe adverse experiences and eating disorders: State of the research and future research directions. *Curr Psychiatry Rep, 19*, 45. doi: 10.1007/s11920-017-0806-6.

Trujillo K, Lewis D, Yeager C, & Gidlow B (1996). Imaginary companions of school boys and boys with Dissociative Identity Disorder/Multiple Personality Disorder: A normal to pathological continuum. *Child Adol Psych Cl, 5*, 375–391.

Tsui T, Lahat A, & Schmidt L (2017). Linking temperamental shyness and social anxiety in childhood and adolescence: Moderating influences of sex and age. *Child Psychiat Hum D, 48*, 778–785.

Tu K, Marks B, & El-Sheikh M (2017). Sleep and mental health: the moderating role of perceived adolescent–parent attachment. *Sleep Health, 3*, 90–97.

Tucker C, Finkelhor D, Turner H, & Shattuck A (2013a). Association of sibling aggression with child and adolescent mental health. *Pediatrics, 132*(1), 79–84.

Tucker R, Judah M, O'Keefe V, Mills A, Lechner W, Davidson C et al. (2013b). Humor styles impact the relationship between symptoms of social anxiety and depression. *Pers Indiv Differ, 55*, 823–827.

Tull M, Jakupcak M, Paulson A, & Gratz K (2007). The role of emotional inexpressivity and experiential avoidance in the relationship between posttraumatic stress disorder symptom severity and aggressive behavior among men exposed to interpersonal violence. *Anxiety Stress Copin, 20*(4), 337–351.

Tulving E (2002). Episodic memory: From mind to brain. *Annu Rev Psychol, 53*, 1-25.

Tunbridge E, Farrell S, Harrison P, & Mackay C (2013). Catechol-O-methyltransferase (COMT) influences the connectivity of the prefrontal cortex at rest. *NeuroImage, 68*, 49–54.

Tuncgenc B, Cohen E, & Fawcett C (2015). Rock with me: The role of movement synchrony in infants' social and nonsocial choices. *Child Dev, 86*(3), 976–984.

Turner H, Finkelhor D, Hamby S, & Henly M (2017). Victimization and adversity among children experiencing war-related parental absence or deployment in a nationally representative US sample. *Child Abuse Neglect, 67*, 271–279.

Turner H, Finkelhor D, & Ormrod R (2010). Poly-victimization in a national sample of children and youth. *Am J Prev Med, 38*, 323–330.

Turner R, & Lloyd D (2004). Stress burden and the lifetime incidence of psychiatric disorder in young adults. *Arch Gen Psychiatry, 61*, 481–488.

Turunen T, Haravuori H, Punamäki R, Suomalainen L, & Marttunen M (2014). The role of attachment in recovery after a school-shooting trauma. *Eur J Psychotraumato, 5*(1), doi.org/10.3402/ejpt.v5.22728.

Twemlow S, Biggs B, Nelson T, Vernberg E, Fonagy P, & Twemlow S (2008). Effects of participation in a martial arts-based antibullying program in elementary schools. *Psychol Sch, 45*(10), 947–959.

Twemlow S, Fonagy P, Sacco F, Gies M, Evans R, & Ewbank R (2001). Creating a peaceful school learning environment: A controlled study of an elementary school intervention to reduce violence. *Am J Psychiat, 158*, 808–810.

Twemlow S, Sacco F, & Twemlow S (1999). *Creating a peaceful school learning environment: A training manual for elementary schools.* Agawam, MA: T & S Publishing Group.

Tyrka A, Price L, Gelernter J, Schepker C, Anderson G, & Carpenter L (2009). Interaction of Childhood Maltreatment with the Corticotropin-Releasing Hormone Receptor Gene: Effects on HPA Axis Reactivity. *Biol Psychiatry, 66(7)*, 1–10.

Udwin O, Boyle S, Yule W, Bolton D, & O'Ryan D (2000). Risk factors for long-term psychological effects of a disaster experienced in adolescence: Predictors of post traumatic stress disorder. *J Child Psychol Psyc, 41*, 969–979.

Uematsu A, Matsui M, Tanaka C, Takahashi T, Noguchi K, Suzuki M, & Nishijo H (2012). Developmental trajectories of amygdala and hippocampus from infancy to early adulthood in healthy individuals. *PLoS One*, 7, e46970.

Vaid J, Hull R, Heredia R, Gerkens D, & Martinez F (2003). Getting a joke: The time course of meaning activation in verbal humor. *J Pragmatics, 35*(9), 1431–1449.

Vaish A, Carpenter M, & Tomasello M (2010). Young children selectively avoid helping people with harmful intentions. *Child Dev, 81*, 1661–1669. abstract.

Vaish A, Missana M, & Tomasello M (2011). Three-year-old children intervene in third-party moral transgressions. *Brit J Dev Psychol, 29*, 124–130. abstract.

Valentino K, Bridgett D, Hayden L, & Nuttall A (2012). Abuse, depressive symptoms, executive functioning, and overgeneral memory among a psychiatric sample of children and adolescents. *J Clin Child Adolesc, 41*, 491–498.

Valentino K, Cicchetti D, Rogosch F & Toth S (2008). True and false recall and dissociation among maltreated children: The role of self-schema. *Dev Psychopathol, 20*, 213–232.

Valiente C, Eisenberg N, Fabes R, Spinrad T, & Sulik M (2014). Coping across the transition to adolescence: Evidence of interindividual consistency and mean-level change. *J Early Adolescence, 35*(7), 947–965.

Valiente C, Lemery-Chalfant K, & Reiser M (2007). Pathways to problem behaviors: Chaotic homes, parent and child effortful control, and parenting. *Soc Dev*, *16*, 249–267.

Vallotton C, & Ayoub C (2010). Use your words: The role of language in the development of toddlers' self-regulation. *Early Child Res Q*, *26*(2), 169–181.

van Daele T, Griffith J, Van den Bergh O, & Hermans D (2014). Overgeneral autobiographical memory predicts changes in depression in a community sample. *Cognition Emotion*, *28*(7), 1303–1312.

Van den Bergh B, & Mulder E (2012). Fetal sleep organization: A biological precursor of self-regulation in childhood and adolescence? *Biol Psychol*, *89*, 584–590.

van Denderen M, Keijser J, Gerisma C, Huisman M, & Boelen P (2014). Revenge and psychological adjustment after homicidal loss. *Aggressive Behav*, *40*, 504–511.

van den Bos W, van Dijk E, & Crone E (2012). Learning whom to trust in repeated social interactions: A developmental perspective. *Group Process Interg*, *15*(2), 243–256.

van der Donk M, Hiemstra-Beernink A, Tjeenk-Kalff A, van der Leij A, and Lindauer R (2016). Predictors and moderators of treatment outcome in cognitive training for children with ADHD. *J Atten Disord*, doi: 10.1177/1087054716632876.

van der Kolk B (2003). Posttraumatic stress disorder and the nature of trauma. In M Solomon, D Siegel (Eds), *Healing trauma* (pp. 168–195). New York: WW Norton.

van der Kolk B, Stone L, West J, Rhodes A, Emerson D, Suvak M, & Spinazzola J (2014). Yoga as an adjunctive treatment for Post-Traumatic Stress Disorder: A randomized controlled trial. *J Clin Psychiat*, *75*(6), e559–565.

Van der Oord S, Bogels S, & Peijnenburg D (2012). The effectiveness of mindfulness training for children with ADHD and mindful parenting for their parents. *J Child Fam Stud*, *21*, 139–147.

van Dooren W, & Inglis M (2015). Inhibitory control in mathematical thinking, learning and problem-solving: a survey. *ZDM Math Ed*, *47*, 713–721.

van Duijvenvoorde A, Huizenga H, Somerville L, Delgado M, Powers A, Weeda W et al. (2015). Neural correlates of expected risks and returns in risky choice across development. *J Neurosci*, *35*(4), 1549–1560. abstract.

van Ee E, Jongmans M, van der Aa N, & Kleber R (2016). Attachment representation and sensitivity: Moderating role of Posttraumatic Stress Disorder in a refugee sample. *Fam Process*, *56*(3), 781–792. abstract.

van Elk M, van Schie H, Hunnius S, Vesper C, & Bekkering H (2008). You'll never crawl alone: Neurophysiological evidence for experience-dependent motor resonance in infancy. *NeuroImage*, *43*(4), 808–814.

van Gestel S, Forsegren T, Claes S, Del-Favero J, van Duijn GM, Sluijs S et al. (2002). Epistatic effect of genes from the dopamine and serotonin systems on the temperament traits of novelty seeking and harm avoidance. *Mol Psychiatr*, 7, 448–450.

van Hoof M, van den Bulk B, Rombouts S, Rinne-albers M, van der Wee N, van IJzendoorn M et al. (2017). Emotional face processing in adolescents with childhood sexual abuse-related posttraumatic stress disorder, internalizing disorders and healthy controls. *Psychiat Research-Neuroim*, *264*, 52–59.

Van Horn P, Gray L, Pettinelli B, & Estassi N (2013). Child–Parent Psychotherapy with traumatized young children in kinship care: Adaptation of an evidence-based intervention. In J Osofsky (Ed.), *Clinical work with traumatized young children* (pp. 55–74). New York: Guilford.

van IJzendoorn M (1995). Adult attachment representations, parental responsiveness, and infant attachment: A meta-analysis on the predictive validity of the adult attachment interview. *Psychol Bull*, *117*, 387–403.

van IJzendoorn M, & Bakermans-Kranenburg M (2010). Invariance of adult attachment across gender, age, culture, and socioeconomic status? *J Soc Pers Relat*, *27*(2), 200–208.

van IJzendoorn M, Bard K, Bakermans-Kranenburg M, & Ivan K (2009). Enhancement of attachment and cognitive development of young nursery-reared chimpanzees in responsive versus standard care. *Dev Psychobiol*, *51*, 173–185.

van IJzendoorn M, Schuengel C, & Bakermans-Kranenburg M (1999). Disorganized attachment in early childhood: Meta-analysis of precursors, concomitants, and sequelae. *Dev Psychopathol*, *11*, 225–249.

van Marle H (2015). PTSD as a memory disorder. *Eur J Psychotraumato*, *6*(1), doi: 10.3402/ejpt.v6.27633.

van Nierop M, Lecei A, Myin-Germeys I, Collip D, Viechtbauer W, Jacobs N et al. (2018). Stress reactivity links childhood trauma exposure to an admixture of depressive, anxiety, and psychosis symptoms. *Psychiat Res*, *260*, 451–457.

van Rooij S, Geuze E, Kennis M, Rademaker A, & Vink M (2015). Neural correlates of inhibition and contextual cue processing related to treatment response in PTSD. *Neuropsychopharmacology*, *40*, 667–675.

van Rooij S, Stevens J, Ely T, Fani N, Smith A, Kerley K et al. (2016). Childhood trauma and COMT genotype interact to increase hippocampal activation in resilient individuals. *Front Psychiatry*, 7, 156. doi: 10.3389/fpsyt.2016.00156.

van Veen T, Wardenaar K, Carlier I, Spinhoven P, Penninx B, & Zitman F (2013). Are childhood and adult life adversities differentially associated with specific symptom dimensions of depression and anxiety? Testing the tripartite model. *J Affect Disord*, *146*, 238–245.

Vaughn B, & Bost K (2018). Attachment and temperament as intersecting developmental products and interacting developmental contexts throughout infancy and childhood. In J Cassidy, P Shaver (Eds), *Handbook of attachment* (3rd ed., pp. 202–222). New York: Guilford.

Vaughan Van Hecke A, Mundy P, Acra C, Block J, Delgado C, Parlade M, Neal A, Meyer J, & Pomares Y (2007). Infant joint attention, temperament, and social competence in preschool children, *Child Dev*, *78*, 53–69.

Velotti P, Elison J, & Garofalo C (2014). Shame and aggression: Different trajectories and implications. *Aggress Violent Beh*, *19*, 454–461.

Venta A, Hatkevich C, Mellick W, Vanwoerden S, & Sharp C (2017). Social cognition mediates the relation between attachment schemas and Posttraumatic Stress Disorder. *Psychol Trauma-US*, *9*(1), 88–95.

Verbeke L, De Caluwé E, & De Clercq B (2017). A five-factor model of developmental personality pathology precursors. *Personal Disord*, *8*(2), 130–139.

Veríssimo M, Santos A, Vaughn B, Torres N, Monteiro L, & Santos O (2011). Quality of attachment to father and mother and number of reciprocal friends. *Early Child Dev Care*, *181*, 27–38.

Vermetten E, & Spiegel D (2014). Trauma and dissociation: Implications for Borderline Personality Disorder. *Curr Psychiatry Rep*, *16*, 434. doi: 10.1007/s11920-013-0434-8.

Verschueren K, & Marcoen A (2005). Perceived security of attachment to mother and father: Developmental differences and relations to self-worth and peer relationships at school. In K Kerns, R Richardson (Eds), *Attachment in middle childhood* (pp. 212–230). New York: Guilford.

Viana A, Kiel E, Alfano C, Dixon L, & Palmer C (2017). The contribution of temperamental and cognitive factors to childhood anxiety disorder symptoms: A closer look at negative affect, behavioral inhibition, and anxiety sensitivity. *J Child Fam Stud*, *26*, 194–204.

Vickery C, & Dorjee D (2016). Mindfulness training in primary schools decreases negative affect and increases meta-cognition in children. *Front Psychol*, *6*, 2025. doi: 10.3389/fpsyg.2015.02025.

Villanueva L, Górriz A, Prado-Gascó V, & González R (2015). The role of emotion awareness and mood: Somatic complaints and social adjustment in late childhood. *Psychol Health Med*, *20*(4), 419–430.

Villabø M, Narayanan M, Compton S, Kendall P, & Neumer S-P (2018). Cognitive Behavioral Therapy for youth anxiety: An effectiveness evaluation in community practice. *J Consult Clin Psych*, *86*(9), 751–764.

Virji-Babul N, Rose A, Moiseeva N, & Makan N (2012). Neural correlates of action understanding in infants: Influence of motor experience. *Brain Behav*, *2*(3), 237–242.

Vivrette R, Briggs E, Lee R, Kenney K, Houston-Armstrong T, Pynoos R, & Kiser L (2018). Impaired caregiving, trauma exposure, and psychosocial functioning in a national sample of children and adolescents. *J Child Adolesc Trauma*, *11*, 187–196.

Voelker P, Sheese B, Rothbart M, & Posner M (2009). Variations in catechol-O-methyltransferase gene interact with parenting to influence attention in early development, *Neurosci*, *164*(1), 121–130.

Vreeke L, Muris P (2012). Relations between behavioral inhibition, Big Five personality factors, and Anxiety Disorder symptoms in non-clinical and clinically anxious children. *Child Psychiatry Hum Dev*, *43*(6), 884–894.

Wahlström L, Michelsen H, Schulman A, & Backheden M (2010). Childhood life events and psychological symptoms in adult survivors of the 2004 tsunami. *Nord J Psychiat*, *64*, 245–252.

Walker E, Katon W, Russo J, von Korff M, Lin E, Simon G et al. (2000). Predictors of outcome in a primary care depression trial. *J Gen Intern Med*, *15*(12), 859–867.

Walker O, Degnan K, Henderson H, & Fox N (2015). Early social fear in relation to play with an unfamiliar peer: Actor and partner effects. *Dev Psychol*, *51*(11), 1588–1596.

Walker S, Berthelsen D, & Irving K (2001). Temperament and peer acceptance in early childhood: Sex and social status differences. *Child Study J*, *31*, 177–192.

Walkup J, Albano A, Piacentini J, Birmaher B, Compton S, Sherrill J et al. (2008). Cognitive behavioral therapy, sertraline or a combination in childhood anxiety. *N E J Med*, *359*, 2573–2766.

Waller R, Baskin-Sommers A, & Hyde L (2016). Examining predictors of callous-unemotional traits trajectories across adolescence among high-risk males. *J Clin Child Adolesc*, *47*(3), 444–457.

Waller R, Hyde L, Grabell A, Alves M, & Olsen S (2015). Differential associations of early callous-unemotional, oppositional, and ADHD behaviors: Multiple domains within early-starting conduct problems? *J Child Psychol Psyc*, *56*(6), 657–666.

Wang D, Aten J, Boan D, Jean-Charles W, Griff K, Valcin V et al. (2016). Culturally adapted spiritually oriented Trauma-Focused Cognitive Behavioral Therapy for child survivors of Restavek. *Spirituality in Clinical Practice*, *3*, 224–236.

Wang W, Feng J, Ji C, Mu X, Ma Q, Fan Y et al. (2017). Increased methylation of glucocorticoid receptor gene promoter 1 F in peripheral blood of patients with generalized anxiety disorder. *J Psychiatr Res*, *91*, 18–25.

Wang Y, Nomura Y, Pat-Horenczyk R, Duppelt O, Abramovitz R, Brom D, & Chemtob C (2006). Association of direct exposure to terrorism, media exposure to terrorism, and other trauma with emotional and behavioral problems in preschool children. *Ann NY Acad Sci*, *1094*, 363–368.

Warner E, Koomar J, Lary B, & Cook A (2013). Can the body change the score? Application of sensory modulation principles in the treatment of traumatized adolescents in residential settings. *J Fam Violence, 28*(7), 729–738.

Warner E, Spinazzola J, Sestcott A, Gunn C, & Hodgdon H (2014). The body can change the score: Empirical support for somatic regulation in the treatment of traumatized adolescents. *J Child Adol Trauma,* 7(4), 237–246.

Warreyn P, Ruysschaert L, Wiersema J, & Roeyers H (2013). Infants' mu suppression during the observation of real and mimicked goal-directed actions. *Devel Sci, 16*(2), 173–185.

Wartner U, Grossman K, Fremmer-Bombik E, & Suess G (1994). Attachment patterns at age six in south Germany: Predictability from infancy and implication for preschool behaviour. *Child Dev, 65,* 1014–1027.

Wass S, Porayska-Pomsta K, & Johnson M (2012). Training attentional control in infancy. *Curr Biol, 21*(18), 1543–1547.

Waters L (2016). The relationship between child stress, child mindfulness and parent mindfulness. *Psychology,* 7, 40–51.

Waters S, Hagan M, Rivera L, & Lieberman A (2015). Improvements in the child-rearing attitudes of Latina mothers exposed to interpersonal trauma predict greater maternal sensitivity toward their 6-month-old infants. *J Traum Stress, 28,* 426–433.

Waugh W, & Brownell C (2017). "Help yourself!" What can toddlers' helping failures tell us about the development of prosocial behavior? *Infancy, 22*(5), 665–680.

Webb C, Hayes A, Grasso D, Berman, I., Laurenceau J, & Deblinger E (2014). Trauma-focused cognitive behavior therapy for youth: Effectiveness in a community setting. *Psychol Trauma-US, 6*(5), 555–562.

Webb NB (ed.) (2015). *Play therapy with children and adolescents in crisis* (4th ed.). New York: Guilford.

Webb NB (ed.) (2010). *Helping bereaved children: A handbook for practitioners* (3rd ed.). New York: Guilford.

Webb, NB (ed.) (2004). *Mass trauma, stress, and loss: Helping children and families cope.* New York: Guilford.

Webb, NB (ed.) (2002). *Helping bereaved children* (2nd ed., pp. 214–244). New York: Guilford.

Webster-Stratton C (2016). The Incredible Years® Series: A developmental approach in family-based prevention programs for children and adolescents: Theory, research and large-scale dissemination. M Van Ryzin, K Kumpfer, G Fosco, & M Greenberg (Eds) (pp. 42–67). New York: Psychology Press.

Webster-Stratton C (2008). *How to promote children's social and emotional competence.* London: Sage.

Webster-Stratton C (2001). The Incredible Years®: Parents, teachers, and children training series. *Resid Treat Child Youth, 18*(3), 31–45.

Webster-Stratton C (1987). *Parents and children: A 10-program videotape parent training series with manuals.* Eugene, OR: Castalia.

Webster-Stratton C, & Bywater T (in press). Incredible Years®: An internationally evidenced multimodal approach to enhancing child outcomes. In B Fiese (Ed-in-Chief), *APA Handbook of contemporary family psychology (Vol. 3): Family therapy and training.* Washington, DC: APA.

Webster-Stratton C, Gaspar M, & Seabras-Santos M (2012). Incredible Years® Parent, Teachers and Children's Series: Transportability to Portugal of early intervention programs for preventing conduct problems and promoting social and emotional competence. *Psychosocial Intervention, 21*(2), 157–169.

Webster-Stratton C, & Herman K (2010). Disseminating Incredible Years® Series Early Intervention Programs: Integrating and sustaining services between school and home *Psychol Sch, 47*(1), 36–54.

Webster-Stratton C, & Reid M (2010). The Incredible Years® parents, teachers and children training series: A multifaceted treatment approach for young children with conduct problems. In J Weisz, A Kazdin (Eds), *Evidence-based psychotherapies for children and adolescents* (2nd ed., pp. 194–210). New York: Guilford.

Webster-Stratton C, Reid M, & Beauchaine T (2011). Combining parent and child training for young children with ADHD. *J Clin Child Adolesc, 40*(2), 1–13.

Webster-Stratton C, Reid M, & Hammond M (2001). Preventing conduct problems, promoting social competence: A parent and teacher training partnership in Head Start. *J Clin Child Psychol, 30,* 283–302.

Webster-Stratton C, Rinaldi J, & Reid J (2011). Long-term outcomes of Incredible Years® parenting program: Predictors of adolescent adjustment. *Chld Adol Ment H-UK, 16,* 38–46.

Weems C, & Carrion V (2009). Diurnal salivary cortisol in youth: Clarifying the nature of posttraumatic stress dysregulation. *J Pediatr Psychol, 34,* 389–395.

Weems C, Pina A, Costa N, Watts S, Taylor L, & Cannon M (2007). Predisaster trait anxiety and negative affect predict posttraumatic stress in youths after Hurricane Katrina. *J Consult Clin Psych, 75*(1), 154–159.

Wegener I, Feiser F, Alfter S, Mierke J, Imbierowicz K, Kleiman A et al. (2015). Changes of explicitly and implicitly measured self-esteem in the treatment of major depression: Evidence for implicit self-esteem compensation. *Compr Psychiat, 58,* 57–67.

Weinfield N, Whaley G, & Egeland B (2004). Continuity, discontinuity, and coherence in attachment from infancy to late adolescence: Sequelae of organization and disorganization. *Attach Hum Dev, 6,* 73–97.

Weinreb M, & Groves B (2015). Child–Parent Psychotherapy after child exposure to parental violence. In Webb NB (Ed.), *Play therapy with children and adolescents in crisis* (4th ed., pp. 99–117). New York: Guilford.

Weiss N, Gratz K, & Lavender J (2015). Factor Structure and Initial validation of a multidimensional measure of difficulties in the regulation of positive emotions: The DERS-Positive. *Behav Modif, 39*(3), 431–453.

Wekerle C, Wolfe D, Dunston J, & Alldred T (2014). Child maltreatment. In E Mash, R Barkley (Eds) *Child psychopathology* (3rd ed., pp. 737–798). New York: Guilford.

Welles S, Patel F, & Chilton M (2017). Does employment-related resilience affect the relationship between childhood adversity, community violence, and depression? *J Urban Health, 94*, 233–243.

Wells A (1990). Panic Disorder in association with relaxation induced anxiety: An attentional training approach to treatment. *Behav Ther, 21*, 273–280.

Wenig M (2003). *YogaKids: Educating the whole child through yoga*. New York: Stewart, Tabori and Chang.

Werner K, & Griffin M (2012). Peritraumatic and persistent dissociation as predictors of PTSD symptoms in a female cohort. *J Traum Stress, 25*, 401–407.

Wessel J, Conner C, Aron A, & Tandon N (2013). Chronometric electrical stimulation of right inferior frontal cortex increases motor braking. *J Neurosci, 33*, 19611–19619.

Wesselhoeft R, Heiervang E, Kragh-Sorensen P, Soresen M, & Bilenberg N (2016). Major depressive disorder and subthreshold depression in prepubertal children from the Danish National Birth Cohort. *Compr Psychiat, 70*, 65–76.

Wester K, Downs H, & Trepal H (2016). Factors linked with increases in nonsuicidal self-injury: A case study. *CORE*, 7(1), 3–20.

Wester K, & Trepal H (2015). Nonsuicidal self-injury: Exploring the connection among race, ethnic identity, and ethnic belonging. *J College Student Develop, 56*(2), 127–139.

Westermeyer J, & Uecker J (1997). Predictors of hostility in a group of relocated refugees. *Cult Divers Ment Health, 3*(1), 53–60.

Wetzel N (2014). Development of control of attention from different perspectives. *Front Psychol, 5*. doi: 10.3389/fpsyg.2014.01000.

White L, Degnan K, Henderson H, Perez-Edgar K, Walker O, Schechner T et al. (2017). Developmental relations among behavioral inhibition, anxiety, and attention biases to threat and positive information. *Child Dev, 88*(1), 141–155.

White L, Klein A, von Klitzing K, Graneist A, Otto Y, Hill J, Over H, Fonagy P & Crowley M (2016). Putting ostracism into perspective: Young children tell more mentalistic stories after exclusion, but not when anxious. *Front Psychol*, 7, 1926. doi: 10.3389/fpsyg.2016.01926.

White L, Wu J, Borelli J, Rutherford H, David D, Kim-Cohen J et al. (2012b). Attachment dismissal predicts frontal slow-wave ERPs during rejection by unfamiliar peers. *Emotion, 12*(4), 690–700.

White M, Bogdan R, Fisher P, Munoz K, Williamson D, & Hariri A (2012a) FKBP5 and emotional neglect interact to predict individual differences in amygdala reactivity. *Genes Brain Behav, 11*, 869–878.

Whitlock J, Eells G, Cummings N, Purington A (2009). Nonsuicidal self-injury in college populations: mental health provider assessment of prevalence and need. *J Colleg Stud Psychother, 23*, 172–183.

Whittle S, Liu K, Bastin C, Harrison B, & Davey C (2016). Neurodevelopmental correlates of proneness to guilt and shame in adolescence and early adulthood. *Devel Cog Neurosci, 19*, 51–57.

Wieland S, & Silberg J (2013). Dissociation-focused therapy. In J Ford, C Courtois (Eds), *Treating complex traumatic stress disorders in children and adolescents*. New York: Guilford.

Williams J, & Broadbent K (1986). Autobiographical memory in suicide attempters. *J Abnorm Psychol, 95*, 144–149.

Williams J, Russell I, & Russell D (2008). Mindfulness-based cognitive therapy. *J Consulting and Clin Psychol, 76*(3), 524–529.

Williams L, Degnan K, Perez-Edgar K, Henderson H, Rubin K et al. (2009). Impact of behavioral inhibition and parenting style on internalizing and externalizing problems from early childhood through adolescence. *J Abnorm Child Psych, 37*(8), 1063–1075.

Williams M, Carson M, Zamora I, Harley E, & Lakatos P (2014). Child–Parent Psychotherapy in the context of the developmental disability and medical service systems. *Pragmatic Case Studies in Psychotherapy, 10*(Module 3, Article 3), 212–226.

Williford A, Carter L, & Pianta R (2018). Attachment and school readiness. In J Cassidy, P Shaver (Eds), *Handbook of attachment* (3rd ed., pp. 966–982). New York: Guilford.

Wimalaweera S, & Moulds M (2008). Processing memories of anger eliciting events: the effect of asking "why" from a distance. *Behav Res Ther, 46*, 402–409.

Winblad N, Changaris M, & Stein P (2018). Effect of Somatic Experiencing resiliency-based trauma treatment training on quality of life and psychological health as potential markers of resilience in treating professionals. *Front Neurosci, 12*(70), doi: 10.3389/fnins.2018.00070.

Winnicot DW (1971). *Therapeutic consultations in child psychiatry*. New York: Basic Books.

Witkin SJ (2005). Assessing developmental level when representing foster care children. *Human Rights: Journal of the Section of Individual Rights & Responsibilities, 32*(1), 8.

Wittmer D (2012). The wonder and complexity of infant and toddler peer relationships. *NAEYC, 67*(4), 16–25.

Wolf OT (2003). HPA axis and memory. *Best Pract Res Clin Endocrinol Metab, 17*, 287–299.

Wolke D, Woods S, & Samara M (2009). Who escapes or remains a victim of bullying in primary school? *Brit J Dev Psychol, 27*, 835–851.

Wolmer L, Hamiel D, Barchas J, Slone M, & Laor, N (2011a). Teacher-delivered resilience-focused intervention in schools with traumatized children following the second Lebanon war. *J Traum Stress, 24*(3), 309–316.

Wolmer L, Hamiel D, & Laor N (2011b). Preventing children's Posttraumatic Stress after disaster with teacher-based intervention: A controlled study. *J Amer Acad Child & Adoles Psychia, 50*(4), 340–349.

Wolmer L, Hamiel D, Margalit N, Versano-Eisman T, Findler Y et al. (2016). Enhancing children's resilience in schools to confront trauma: The impact on teachers. *Isr J Psychiatry Relat Sci, 53*(2), 25–32.

Wolmer L, Laor N, & Yazgan Y (2003). School reactivation programs after disaster: Could teachers serve as clinical mediators? *Child Adol Psych Cl, 12*, 363–381.

Wolmer L, Laor N, Dedeoglu C, Siev J, & Yazgan Y (2005). Teacher-mediated intervention after disaster: a controlled three-year follow-up of children's functioning. *J Child Psychol Psyc, 46*(11), 1161–1168.

Wong A, Dirghangi S, & Hart S (2018). Self-concept clarity mediates the effects of adverse childhood experiences on adult suicide behavior, depression, loneliness, perceived stress, and life distress. *Self Identity*. doi.org/10.1080/15298868.2018.1439096.

Wood A, Dawe S, & Gullo M (2013). The role of personality, family influences, and prosocial risk-taking behavior on substance use in early adolescence. *J Adolescence, 36*, 871–881. abstract.

Worden JW (2009). *Grief counseling and grief therapy: A handbook for mental health practitioners* (4th ed.). New York: Springer Publishing.

World Health Organization (WHO) (2015). ICD-11 Beta draft: Mental and behavioral disorders. Available at: http://apps.who.int/classifications/icd11/browse/l-m/en.

World Health Organization (WHO) (2014). *Preventing suicide: A global imperative*. Geneva, Switzerland: WHO.

World Health Organization (WHO) (1992/2004). *International Classification of Diseases, 10th revision (ICD–10)*. Geneva, Switzerland: WHO.

Wu C-L, Tseng L-P, An C-P, Chen H-C, Chan Y-C, Shih C-I, & Zhuo S-L (2014). Do individuals with autism lack a sense of humor? A study of humor comprehension, appreciation, and styles among high school students with autism. *Res Autism Spect Dis, 8*, 1386–1393.

Wynter K, Rowe H, Tran T, & Fisher J (2016). Factors associated with father-to-infant attachment at 6 months postpartum: A community-based study in Victoria, Australia. *J Reprod Infant Psyc, 34*(2), 185–195.

Wyss N, Kannass K, & Haden C (2013). The effects of distraction on cognitive task performance during toddlerhood. *Infancy, 18*(4), 604–628.

Xavier A, Cunha M, & Pinto-Gouveia J (2018). Daily peer hassles and non-suicidal self-injury in adolescence: Gender differences in avoidance-focused emotion regulation processes. *J Child Fam Stud, 27*, 59–68.

Xavier A, Pinto-Gouveia J, & Cunha M (2016). Non-suicidal self-injury in adolescence: The role of shame, self-criticism and fear of self-compassion. *Child Youth Care For, 45*, 571–586.

Yaman A, Mesman J, van Ijzendoorn M, & Bakermans-Kranenburg M (2010). Parenting and toddler aggression in second-generation immigrant families: The moderating role of child temperament. *J Fam Psychol, 24*, 208–211.

Yang C-C, Barros-Loscertales A, Pinazo D, Ventura-Campos N, Borchardt V, Bustamante J-C et al. (2016). State and training effects of mindfulness meditation on brain networks reflect neuronal mechanisms of its antidepressant effect. *Neural Plast*, 9504642, doi: 10.1155/2016/9504642.

Yang Y, Shields G, Guo C, & Liu Y (2018). Executive function performance in obesity and overweight individuals: A meta-analysis and review. *Neurosci Biobehav Rs, 84*, 225–244.

Yap A, Kwan Y, & Ang S (2016). A systematic review on the effects of active participation in rhythm-centered music making on different aspects of health. *Eur J Integr Med*, 9, 44–49.

Yasinski C, Hayes A, Ready C, Cummings J, Berman I, McCauley T, Webb C, & Deblinger E (2016). In-session caregiver behavior predicts symptom change in youth receiving Trauma-Focused Cognitive Behavioral Therapy (TF-CBT). *J Consult Clin Psych, 84*(12), 1066–1077.

Yates T, Egeland B, & Sroufe A (2003). Rethinking resilience: A developmental process perspective. In S Luthar (ed.), *Resilience and vulnerability: Adaptation in the context of childhood adversities* (pp. 243–266). New York: Cambridge University Press.

Yehuda R, Hoge C, McFarlane A, Vermetten E, Lanius R et al. (2015). Post-traumatic stress disorder. *Nature Reviews: Disease Primers, 1*(1), 15057. doi: 10.1038/nrdp.2015.57.

Yew S, & O'Kearney R (2013). Emotional and behavioural outcomes later in childhood and adolescence for children with specific language impairments: meta-analyses of controlled prospective studies. *J Child Psychol Psyc, 54*(5), 516–524. abstract.

Yew S, & O'Kearney R (2015). The role of early language difficulties in the trajectories of conduct problems across childhood. *J Abnorm Child Psychol, 43*, 1515–1527.

Yoon S (2017). Fostering resilient development: Protective factors underlying externalizing trajectories of maltreated children. *J Child Fam Stud, 27*(2), 443–452.

Yoshimura S, Ueda K, Suzuki S, Onoda K, Okamoto Y, & Yamawaki S (2009). Self-referential processing of negative stimuli within the ventral anterior cingulate gyrus and right amygdala. *Brain Cogn, 69*, 218–225.

You D, Youngstrom E, Feeny N, Youngstrom J, & Findling R (2015). Comparing the diagnostic accuracy of five instruments for detecting Posttraumatic Stress Disorder in youth. *J Clin Child Adolesc, 46*(4), 511–522.

You J, Deng B, Lin M-P, & Leung F (2016a). The interactive effects of impulsivity and negative emotions on adolescent nonsuicidal self-injury: A latent growth curve analysis. *Suicide Life-Threat, 46*(3), 266–283. abstract.

You J, Lin M, Xu S, & Hu W (2016b). Big Five personality traits in the occurrence and repetition of non-suicidal self-injury among adolescents: The mediating effects of depressive symptoms. *Pers Indiv Differ, 101*, 227–231.

Young A, Luyster R, Fox N, Zeanah C, & Nelson C (2017). The effects of early institutionalization on emotional face processing: Evidence for sparing via an experience-dependent mechanism. *Brit J Dev Psychol, 35*, 439–453. abstract.

Young E, & Altemus M (2004). Puberty, ovarian steroids, and stress. *Ann NY Acad Sci, 1021*, 124–133.

Young E, & Veldhuis J (2006). Disordered adrenocorticotropin secretion in women with major depression. *J Clin Endocr Metab, 91*, 1924–1928.

Young J, & Widom C (2014). Long-term effects of Child Abuse Neglect on emotion processing in adulthood. *Child Abuse Neglect, 38*, 1369–1381. abstract.

Yu L, Norton S, & McCracken L (2017). Change in "Self-as-Context" ("Perspective-taking") occurs in acceptance and commitment therapy for people with chronic pain and is associated with improved functioning. *J Pain, 18*(6), 664–672.

Yue X, & Hui A (2015). Humor styles, creative personality traits, and creative thinking in a Hong Kong sample. *Psychol Rep: Mental & Physical Health, 117*(3), 845–855.

Yue X, Liu K, Jiang F, & Hiranandani N (2014). Humor Styles, self-esteem, and subjective happiness. *Psychol Rep: Mental & Physical Health, 115*(2), 517–525.

Yule W, Bolton D, Udwin O, Boyle S, O'Ryan D, & Nurrish J (2000). The long-term psychological effects of a disaster experienced in adolescence: I. The incidence and course of PTSD. *J Child Psychol Psyc, 41*, 503–511.

Zahn-Waxler C, & Radke-Yarrow M (1982). The development of altruism: Alternative research strategies. In N Eisenberg (Ed.), *The development of prosocial behavior* (pp. 109–137). New York: Academic Press.

Zahn-Waxler C, Radke-Yarrow M, Wagner E, & Chapman M (1992). Development of concern for others. *Dev Psychol, 28*, 126–136.

Zarra-Nezhad M, Kiuru N, Aunola K, Zarra-Nezhad M, Ahonen T, Poikkeus A-M, Nurmi J-E (2014). Social withdrawal in children moderates the association between parenting styles and the children's own socioemotional development. *J Child Psychol Psyc, 55*, 1260–1269.

Zeanah C, Berlin L, & Boris N (2011a). Practitioner review: Clinical applications of attachment theory and research for infants and young children. *J Child Psychol Psyc, 52*(8), 819–833.

Zeanah C, & Boris N, & Lieberman A (2000). Attachment disorders of infancy. In A Sameroff, M Lewis, & S Miller. *Handbook of developmental psychopathology* (2nd ed., pp. 293–307). New York: Plenum Publishers.

Zeanah C, Chesher T, Boris N, Walter H, Bukstein O, Bellonci C et al. (2016). Practice parameter for the assessment and treatment of children and adolescents with Reactive Attachment Disorder and Disinhibited Social Engagement Disorder. *J Am Child Psy, 55*, 990–1003.

Zeanah C, Egger H, Smyke A, Nelson C, Fox N, Marshall P, & Guthrie D (2009). Institutional rearing and psychiatric disorders in Romanian preschool children. *The Am J Psychiat, 166*(7), 777–785.

Zeanah C, Gunnar M, McCall R, Kreppner J, & Fox N (2011b). VI. Sensitive periods. *Monogr Soc Res Child Dev, 76*(4), 147–162.

Zeanah C, Nelson C, Fox N, & Smyke A (2003). Designing research to study the effects of institutionalization on brain and behavioral development: the Bucharest early intervention project. *Dev Psychopathol, 15*(4), 885–907.

Zeanah C, Scheeringa M, Boris N, Heller S, Smyke A, Trapani J (2004). Reactive attachment disorder in maltreated toddlers. *Child Abuse Neglect, 28*, 877–888.

Zeanah C, & Smyke A (2009). Disorders of attachment. In C Zeanah (Ed.), *Handbook of infant mental health* (3rd ed., pp. 421–434). New York: Guilford.

Zeanah C, & Smyke A (2008). Attachment disorders in family and social context. *Infant Ment Health J, 29*(3), 219–233.

Zeanah C, Smyke A, Koga S, & Carlson E (2005). Attachment in institutionalized and community children in Romania. *Child Dev, 76*(5), 1015–1028.

Zeidner M, Hadar D, Matthews G, & Roberts R (2013). Personal factors related to compassion fatigue in health professionals. *Anxiety Stress Copin, 26*(6), 595–609. abstract.

Zeigler-Hill V (2011). An Implicit Theory of Self-Esteem: The consequences of perceived self-esteem for romantic desirability. *Evol Psychol, 9*(2), 147–180.

Zelazo P, & Lyons K (2011). Mindfulness training in childhood. *Hum Dev, 54*, 61–65.

Zentner, M, & Shiner R (2012). Fifty years of progress in temperament research: A synthesis of major themes, findings, and challenges and a look forward. In M Zentner & R Shiner (Eds), *Handbook of temperament* (pp. 673–700). New York: Guilford.

Zero to Three (2005). *Diagnostic classification: 0–3. Diagnostic classification of mental health and developmental disorders of infancy and early childhood.* Arlington, VA: National Center for Clinical Infant Programs.

Zevalkink J, Verheugt-Pleiter A, & Fonagy P (2012). Mentalization informed Psychoanalytic Psychotherapy. In A Bateman, P Fonagy (Eds), *Handbook of Mentalizing in Mental Health Practice* (pp. 129–158). Washington DC: APA.

Zhang S, Su F, Li J, & Chen W (2018a). The analgesic effects of maternal milk odor on newborns: A meta-analysis. *Breastfeed Med, 13*(5), 327–334. abstract.

Zhang W, Finy M, Bresin K, & Verona E (2015). Specific patterns of family aggression and adolescents' self and other-directed harm: The moderating role of personality. *J Fam Viol, 30*, 161–170.

Zhang W, Rajendran K, Ham J, Finik J, Buthmann J, Davey K et al. (2018b). Prenatal exposure to disaster-related traumatic stress and developmental trajectories of temperament in early childhood: Superstorm Sandy pregnancy study. *J Affect Disorders, 234*, 335–345.

Zhang Y, Kohnstamm G, Slotboom A, Elphick E, & Cheung P (2002). Chinese and Dutch parents' perceptions of their children's personality. *J Genet Psychol, 163*(2), 165–178.

Zhang Z, Chen T, Jin X, Yan C, Shen X, & Li S (2013). Sleep patterns, sleep problems and associations with reported sleep quality in Chinese school-aged children. *Am J Public Health Res, 1*(4), 93–100.

Zhou Q, Eisenberg N, Losoya S, et al. (2002). The relations of parental warmth and positive expressiveness to children's empathy-related responding and social functioning: a longitudinal study. *Child Dev, 73*(3), 893–915.

Zhou Q, Main A, & Wang Y (2010). The relations of temperamental effortful control and anger/frustration to Chinese children's academic achievement and social adjustment: A longitudinal study. *J Educ Psychol, 102*, 180–196.

Zhou Y, Wang Z, Qin L, Wan J, Sun Y, Su, S et al. (2012). Early altered resting-state functional connectivity predicts the severity of post-traumatic stress disorder symptoms in acutely traumatized subjects. *PLoS One, 7*, e46833.

Zimmer-Gembeck M, Nesdale D, Webb H, Khatibi M, & Downey G (2016). A longitudinal rejection sensitivity model of depression and aggression: Unique roles of anxiety, anger, blame, withdrawal and retribution. *J Abnorm Child Psychol, 44*, 1291–1307.

Zimmer-Gembeck M, & Skinner E (2015). Adolescent vulnerability and the distress of rejection: Associations of adjustment problems and gender with control, emotions, and coping. *J Adolescence, 45*, 149–159. abstract.

Zimmer-Gembeck M, Trevaskis S, Nesdale D, & Downey G (2014). Relational victimization, loneliness and depressive symptoms: Indirect associations via self and peer reports of rejection sensitivity. *J Youth Adolescence, 43*, 568–582. abstract.

Zisook S, Reynolds C, Pies R, Simon N, Lebowitz, B, Madowitz J et al. (2010). Bereavement, complicated grief, and DSM, part 1: Depression. *J Clin Psychiat, 71*, 955–956.

Zosh J, Fisher K, Golinkoff R, & Hirsh-Pasek K (2013). The ultimate block party: Bridging the science of learning and the importance of play. Honey M, Kanter D (Eds), *Design, make, play: Growing the next generation of STEM Innovators* (pp. 95–118). New York: Routledge.

Zubrick S, Taylor C, Rice M, & Slegers D (2007). Late language emergence at 24 months: An epidemiological study of prevalence, predictors, and covariates. *J Speech Lang Hear Res, 50*, 1562–1592.

Zuroff D, Sadikaj G, Kelly A, & Leybman M (2016). Conceptualizing and measuring self-criticism as both a personality trait and a personality state. *J Personality Assess, 98*(1), 14–21.

Zuromski K, Resnick H, Price M, Kilpatrick D, & Ruggiero K (in press). Suicidal ideation among adolescents following natural disaster: The role of prior interpersonal violence. *Psychol Trauma US*, http://dx.doi.org/10.1037/tra0000365.

Subject Index

Page numbers in **bold** denote tables, those in *italic* denote boxes.

References to the Appendix (online material) are annotated **A**-Section Heading, **A-1.1**; etc

Author Index

www.ingramcontent.com/pod-product-compliance
Lightning Source LLC
LaVergne TN
LVHW082345011026
849160LV00024B/1071
9781138605206